San Francisco Probate 1906 - 1942

Volume II
Surnames
Starting with
L - Z

Compiled by
Vernon A. Deubler

Register of Actions

California Genealogical Society & Library
CaliforniaAncestors.org

Library of Congress Control Number 2010926283
ISBN (vol. ɪɪ) 978-0-9785694-8-8

Published by
California Genealogical Society
California Genealogical Society and Library
2201 Broadway, Suite LL2
Oakland, California 94612-3031

Telephone: 510-663-1358   Fax: 510-662-1596
Website: *CaliforniaAncestors.org*

ACKNOWLEDGEMENTS

The California Genealogical Society acknowledges with gratitude the many people who contributed to compiling this index, including Carol Backhus, Dorothy Fowler, Gloria Hanson, Patti Melvin, Nancy Servin and in particular, the most diligent proofreader, Anita Dean, who single handedly reviewed more than two-thirds of this index.

In addition, we extend our thanks to Barbara Close, Jerry McGovern, and Cathy Paris for transforming and publishing the index as reference books.

INTRODUCTION

In the early 1980s the Superior Court in San Francisco completed the filming of the Registers of Action for probate cases dating from the 1906 Earthquake and Fire through March 1942. After learning that the intent was to destroy the original oversize volumes, the California Genealogical Society (CGS) obtained the originals. These priceless volumes became a fixture on our shelves and were indexed. The registers covered the period from April 12, 1906 to March 27, 1942, with the exception of one lost register (volume 11) covering the two-month period, January 9 to March 17, 1908. Some of the cases were not finalized until the mid 1980s.

This publication is an index to 179 volumes, each containing 500 pages. Included are 108,998 names, aliases and minors names representing over 85,500 probates and guardianship proceedings. Each case is identified as "D" - death, "M" - minor or "I" - incompetent.

Each Register of Actions captures in abbreviated fashion every transaction required to process the probate. Many of the transactions are routine administrative actions, such as the recording of an affidavit, public notification of time and place of future actions or hearings, voucher files, etc. Some probate proceedings required years to complete. Entries for wills, mailings to heirs, final settlements and distributions of assets may lead to useful genealogical information. Rarely are original wills retained in the files that are indexed, but register entries usually point to locations where these documents have been transcribed or summarized.

Many of the probates from 1906 were ongoing proceedings from before the fire and represent reopened and reconstructed files. A date of "1906" may, therefore, be misleading and refer to earlier probate proceedings no longer in existence. Other probates from before 1906 may have been re-opened when additional assets were uncovered. Those will bear the date of re-opening and not the date of the original filing.

To order a photocopy of a probate register, please use the Lookups feature on the society's website, *CaliforniaAncestors.org*. If you prefer to place your order by regular mail, use a photocopy of the form at the back of this book. Please send written request(s), and payment to:

California Genealogical Society
2201 Broadway, LL2
Oakland, CA 94612-3031

To obtain pages from the probate file, you may order research services from CGS. Superior court staff will not do research. CGS researchers can review the register, request a pull of the original file, and examine the file for items that may provide needed genealogical information. At present this requires two trips to the Superior Court in San Francisco, one to request the file be removed from storage (which normally takes three days) and the second to review the file itself. Please remit $50 (members) or $70 (non-members) when ordering these services. This covers 2 hours of research time, a $10 court fee to pull the file, and a copy of up to 5 pages from the file.

NAME	NUMBER	TYPE	YEAR
L'HEUREUX			
Charles O.	88476	D	1941
Josephine P.	74621	D	1937
LAAKSONEN			
Gus	37422	D	1923
LAAMACK			
Gustav	16378	D	1913
LABAK			
Ignaz	62363	D	1932
LABARTHE			
Justin	1178	D	1906
LABASTARDE			
Julius	50973	D	1928
Peter Julius	50973	D	1928
Pierre Jules	50973	D	1928
LABASTIDA			
Rosendo	30158	D	1920
LABATAILLE			
Jacques	24946	D	1918
Marie	18096	D	1914
Rene	66298	D	1934
LABATT			
Henry J., Mrs.	83082	D	1940
Lida B.	83082	D	1940
LABAYE			
Alice S.	47488	D	1927
LABBE			
Jeanne Clotilde	85436	D	1940
LABEL			
Babet	36271	D	1923
Isidor	55069	D	1930
Jennie	70621	D	1935
Rebecca Ina	20886	I	1916
Rebecca Ina	23015	D	1917
Rudy	56060	D	1930
Susan	72151	D	1936
LABELL			
Beryl	79380	D	1938
LABELLA			
Marie	72503	M	1936
Verdi	72503	M	1936
LABERGE			
Clifford	27523	M	1919
Gerald	39127	M	1924
Phoebe	40667	M	1924
Walter C.	10702	D	1910

NAME	NUMBER	TYPE	YEAR
LABERTOUIRE			
Maria	12830	D	1912
LABETOURE			
Mria	12830	D	1912
LABETT			
Jose	49227	D	1928
LABHARD			
Charlotte T.	52844	D	1929
LABO			
Peter	26641	D	1919
LABORDE			
Arnaud	66338	D	1934
Arnold	66338	D	1934
Etienne	62531	D	1932
Jean	60763	D	1932
John	21475	D	1916
LABORDETTE			
Edouard	3145	D	1907
Marie Philomene	17111	D	1914
Philomene M.	17111	D	1914
LABORIE			
Honorine	66973	D	1934
LABOUR			
Arthur	34776	D	1922
LABOURDETTE			
Cecile	76966	D	1937
Therese Lantie	55386	D	1930
LABOVICH			
Marie	22887	D	1917
Maurice	55037	D	1930
LABRASH			
George Edward, Jr.	78155	M	1938
LABRIOBA			
Katherine	37467	M	1923
LABRO			
Pierre	39203	D	1924
LABRUZZI			
Lorenzo	28896	D	1920
LAC(C)HINI			
Isabella	2660	D	1907
LACATON			
Christine	89298	D	1942
LACAU			
Suzanne	66078	D	1934
LACAVA			
Edward W. E.	66225	M	1934

NAME	NUMBER	TYPE	YEAR
Emma	49194	D	1928
Felix	71505	D	1936
Vivian T.	66225	M	1934
LACAW			
Joseph	35424	D	1922
LACAY			
Jean	2499	D	1906
LACAZE			
Florence	14712	M	1913
Isabelle	14712	M	1913
Jean Baptiste	6479	D	1908
Max V.	12586	D	1911
Yrma M.	81201	D	1939
LACAZETTE			
Marie A.	16475	D	1913
LACEY			
Albert Ernest	62323	D	1932
Edward	46863	D	1927
George T.	81158	M	1939
Hannah C.	2200	D	1906
Henrietta	584	D	1906
John L., Jr.	81158	M	1939
John Maurice	27702	D	1919
Mary J.	67995	D	1934
Michael	8502	D	1909
William Milton	10609	D	1910
LACHAPELLE			
Emire	7400	I	1909
Joseph J.	14124	D	1912
Marie T.	64718	M	1933
Wilfred A	64254	D	1933
William Severox	69616	D	1935
LACHENICHT			
Hugo	24316	D	1918
LACHER			
Antone	9343	D	1910
Jennie	9192	D	1910
Theresia	19500	D	1915
LACHINI			
Fred	12435	M	1911
Fred	15290	D	1913
Joseph	12435	M	1911
Louis	12435	M	1911
Margaret	12435	M	1911
LACHMAN			
Abraham	20236	D	1916
Bertha	40042	D	1924

NAME	NUMBER	TYPE	YEAR
Emma	50204	D	1928
Frank	89169	D	1942
Harry	57838	D	1931
Marea E.	77074	D	1937
Marie L.	87103	D	1941
Rudolph	49283	D	1928
Samuel	3603	D	1907
Theresa	48039	D	1927
LACHMUND			
Paul Moore	86448	D	1941
LACHTMAN			
Anna	63627	D	1933
LACKAS			
Lucy R.	55706	D	1930
LACKEMAN			
Charles E.	84610	D	1940
Magdalena	41933	D	1925
Magdalena	41933	D	1925
LACKENBACH			
Betty Brunzell	50016	D	1928
Fred I.	69685	D	1935
LACKER			
Joseph	33920	D	1922
LACKEWANDT			
Emilie B.	33943	D	1922
LACKEY			
James M.	29144	D	1920
LACKMANN			
Eugenie	12320	D	1911
Fred Henry	57261	I	1930
Fred Henry	60512	D	1931
Harry K.	86929	M	1941
LACKNER			
William	39291	D	1924
LACKWANDT			
Herman D.	85363	D	1940
LACLERGUE			
Jean Baptiste	86033	D	1941
LACOMBE			
Adrien	80276	D	1939
Armand	80276	D	1939
Carol Treat	68909	M	1935
Cecil Treat	68909	M	1935
John Albert	68860	M	1935
Jules	74738	D	1937
Nancy Treat	68909	M	1935

NAME	NUMBER	TYPE	YEAR
LACOMME			
Bernard	22515	D	1917
LACOMY			
Ernestine	4725	M	1907
Henry	4725	M	1907
LACOSTA			
Gesusa	72250	D	1936
LACOSTE			
Anna Rose	59890	M	1931
Frank	2605	D	1907
Honore	7993	D	1909
Jean	13550	D	1912
Jean Francois	13551	M	1912
Jean Pierre	44877	D	1926
Jeanne L.	82277	D	1939
John	80566	D	1939
Josephine H.	294	D	1906
Juan Francisco	13551	M	1912
Marie	18933	D	1915
Marie	53836	D	1929
Michel	27130	D	1919
LACROIX			
Eliza	4056	D	1907
LACROUTS			
Anna	45769	I	1926
Gabriel	57710	D	1931
Jean P.	1958	D	1906
LACU			
Louis	29769	M	1920
Louis	40048	D	1924
Michel	27449	D	1919
Remi	29769	M	1920
LACY			
Albert A.	56881	M	1930
Anita Marie	41822	D	1925
Anita Marie	41822	D	1925
Anne	33569	D	1922
Edward L.	78720	D	1938
Elizabeth C.	33394	D	1922
Eugene F.	80325	I	1939
Eugene F.	80444	D	1939
Helen F.	59363	I	1931
James	65142	D	1933
Joseph	67401	D	1934
Margaret	5760	I	1908
Margaret C.	29180	D	1920
Robert	83718	D	1940
Timothy M.	22917	D	1917

NAME	NUMBER	TYPE	YEAR
Walter W.	78233	D	1938
LADA			
Lillian E. M.	27524	D	1919
Marie	53315	D	1929
LADAGNOUS			
Marianne	12622	D	1911
Marie Anne	12622	D	1911
LADAR			
Annie	1891	D	1906
Max	24241	D	1918
Morris	55093	D	1930
LADARRE			
Jean	17778	D	1914
LADD			
Charles Douglass	2012	D	1906
Ellen	10433	I	1910
Frank B.	34014	D	1922
Helen B.	46036	D	1926
Howard M.	48680	D	1927
Leonard T.	77025	D	1937
Margaret H.	52774	D	1929
Mary Gertrude	72966	D	1936
Mary K.	50548	I	1928
Mary K.	72966	D	1936
William	11003	D	1911
William Day	6618	D	1908
William W.	27266	D	1919
Winfield Scott	52980	D	1929
LADELLE			
Francee	85581	D	1940
LADER			
Samuel Abraham	24385	M	1918
LADEWIG			
Herbert	44980	I	1926
LADIRA			
Auguste	40308	D	1924
LADLEY			
James Dixon	47554	D	1927
LADROADE			
Louis	36186	D	1923
LADY			
Harvey L.	15209	D	1913
LAE			
Anna	45769	I	1926
LAEMANN			
Anna	2864	D	1907

Name	Number	Type	Year
Laewi			
William	43452	D	1926
Lafabreque			
Joseph	51848	D	1929
Lafaille			
Marie Emma	8294	D	1909
Lafarge			
Jeanne	39380	D	1924
LaFata			
Anna	55748	D	1930
Antonino	60585	D	1932
Antonio	60585	D	1932
Rosolino	39446	D	1924
Lafaurie			
Anna	75843	D	1937
Etienne	64969	D	1933
Ivonne	65132	M	1933
Jeannette	65132	M	1933
Yvonne	65132	M	1933
Lafee			
Albert	42276	M	1925
Albert Paul	42526	M	1925
Albert Paul	56381	D	1930
Hazel	42276	M	1925
Hazel Rose	42526	M	1925
James	42276	M	1925
James	42526	M	1925
Marcus	42281	D	1925
Renee	42378	M	1925
Sarah	42276	M	1925
Sarah	42526	M	1925
Laferty			
Isaac D.	36289	D	1923
Lafferty			
James Francis	70354	M	1935
Winnifred	68932	I	1935
Winnifred	69498	D	1935
Laffey			
Katherine	44847	D	1926
Thomas P.	49304	D	1928
Laffon			
Marie	6864	M	1908
Laffranchini			
Antonio	55068	D	1930
Lafitte			
Geraldine Florence	75061	D	1937
Rose	66102	D	1934

Name	Number	Type	Year
Lafkas			
Peter	85029	D	1940
Laflan			
William	34826	D	1922
Laflin			
Adele	84679	D	1940
James	39686	D	1924
Matilda	83562	D	1940
Lafon			
Andrien	78146	I	1938
Catherine	76258	D	1937
Constant	88845	I	1942
Henrietta	88844	M	1942
Henriette	73514	D	1936
Laurent	66785	D	1934
Lafontaine			
Emma C., MD	88504	D	1941
LaForce			
John Horatius	83618	D	1940
LaForest			
Carrie S.	68144	D	1934
Emile	71300	D	1935
Laforgue			
Jean M.	23160	D	1917
Louise	23234	I	1917
LaForrest			
Carrie S.	68144	D	1934
LaFountain			
Richard Guy, Jr.	74265	M	1936
Lafourguette			
Emilie P.	47708	D	1927
Jacques	39102	D	1924
Lafranchi			
Angelo	31064	D	1921
Elizabeth	36919	D	1923
Ziffero	73297	D	1936
Lafrentz			
Bertha	15989	D	1913
George Theodore	82723	D	1939
Lafrenz			
Rita	83965	I	1940
Lagan			
Edward	72512	D	1936
Hugh	18048	D	1914
Hugo G.	41663	D	1925

Name	Number	Type	Year
Lagarde			
Celestine	19707	D	1915
Lucine	73029	D	1936
Lagarrigue			
Eugene	86080	D	1941
Lagauterie			
Frejus Rene Comte	9161	D	1910
Lage			
Henry Joseph	65466	I	1933
Lager			
Adolph R.	31625	D	1921
Emil B.	26080	D	1919
Julia	29440	D	1920
Lagerberg			
Charles	80446	D	1939
Lagergren			
Carl Henry	30583	D	1920
Lagier			
Maria A.	12893	D	1912
Marie Josephine	12893	D	1912
Lago			
Eleanor Myra Niebla	71434	M	1936
Lagomarisan			
Catherine	6119	D	1908
Lagomarisano			
Catherine	6119	D	1908
Lagomarsino			
Adolph R.	31625	D	1921
Andrea	84588	D	1940
Andrew	84588	D	1940
Angiolina	38753	M	1924
Anna	80051	D	1938
Armand	52731	M	1929
Arthur Terence	82132	M	1939
Carlo	15611	D	1913
Caterina	60868	D	1932
Catherine	6119	D	1908
Catherine	44198	M	1926
Charles	15611	D	1913
Eda	40566	D	1924
Ethel	44198	M	1926
Fortunato	38753	M	1924
George	69255	D	1935
Giovanni	3383	D	1907
Giovanni	29222	D	1920
Giovanni	38753	M	1924
Giuseppe	38753	M	1924

Key: D = death; M = minor; I = incompetent

NAME	NUMBER	TYPE	YEAR
James	87099	D	1941
John	29222	D	1920
Joseph	44198	M	1926
Joseph	69255	D	1935
Louis	89573	D	1942
Maria	65173	I	1933
Maria	67621	D	1934
Rose	75721	D	1937
Silvio	44546	D	1926
Stefano	61186	D	1932
Stephen	52654	D	1929
Teresa	50438	D	1928
LAGONSKI			
Theodore	4217	D	1907
LAGORIO			
Angela	54074	D	1929
Anton	55591	M	1930
Antonia	11376	D	1911
LAGOTE			
Jean Turon	18741	D	1915
LaGRANGE			
Roy W.	37904	D	1923
LAGRAVE			
Catherine	973	D	1906
Gabriel	18078	D	1914
James A.	72643	I	1936
LAGREEN			
Allan	78957	D	1938
Carl Henry	30583	D	1920
LAGRIEN			
Henry	30583	D	1920
LAGUILLO			
Louis P.	24535	M	1918
LAHADERNE			
Bernard	80619	M	1939
Peter	77595	D	1938
Pierre	77595	D	1938
LAHAILLE			
Jean	15285	D	1913
John	15285	D	1913
LAHANEY			
Joseph F.	34946	D	1922
Mary E.	14391	D	1912
LAHANIER			
E. Josephine	51827	D	1929
Eugenie	51827	D	1929

NAME	NUMBER	TYPE	YEAR
LAHARRAQUE			
Jean	23467	D	1917
LAHAYE			
Frank	29160	M	1920
Frank H.	29159	D	1920
LAHEEN			
Thomas	74539	D	1937
LAHERTY			
Margaret I.	73859	D	1936
Richard, Jr.	73960	M	1936
LAHEUGUERE			
Eliza	28427	D	1919
LAHEY			
Arthur Gilbert	47500	D	1937
Arthur Gilbert	74500	D	1937
John	48571	D	1927
Mary	33216	D	1922
Thomas	74539	D	1937
Thomas J.	71961	D	1936
LAHIFF			
Catherine	4024	D	1907
Mary E.	4897	D	1907
LAHMANN			
Theodore	38119	D	1924
LAHN			
Henry	81927	D	1939
LAHONCLES			
Felix	84181	D	1940
LaHONDES			
Felix	84181	D	1940
LAHR			
Christian	87420	D	1941
LAHTINEN			
Charles V.	72303	D	1936
LAHUSEN			
George W.	31859	M	1921
George W.	73119	D	1936
LAI			
Marie	24310	M	1918
Yee Lan	39383	D	1924
Young Wah	89779	D	1942
LAIB			
Joseph	19516	D	1915
Theresa A.	74901	D	1937
William J.	27365	D	1919

NAME	NUMBER	TYPE	YEAR
LAIDLAW			
Harold Beverly	1448	M	1906
Henri Deloss, Jr.	19857	D	1915
LAIDLEY			
Mary A.	2430	D	1906
LAIHO			
Arvo	55091	D	1930
LAILHACAR			
Jean Pierre	39901	D	1924
John P.	39901	D	1924
LAILLETT			
Eugene	6967	D	1908
LAILOA			
Gio Batta	70462	D	1935
LAIN			
Chin	79653	D	1938
LAINE			
Dionisia	30241	D	1920
Frederick	76828	M	1937
J. R., Mrs.	32939	D	1921
John	76828	M	1937
Laura E.	32939	D	1921
LeRoy Charles	49767	M	1928
Maria K.	28874	D	1920
Olga M.	73737	D	1936
LAINER			
Agnes	51651	D	1928
Richard	12124	D	1911
LAING			
Charles D.	37970	D	1923
Doris W.	63554	D	1933
Isabella	80695	D	1939
LAINO			
Francesco	45663	D	1926
LAIOLA			
Gio Batta	47653	I	1927
LAIOLO			
Antonio	61582	D	1932
LAIOSA			
Giovanni	52104	M	1929
Lucio	52104	M	1929
Maria	52104	M	1929
Niva	48011	D	1927
Rosa	52104	M	1929
LAIR			
Henrietta	15669	D	1913

NAME	NUMBER	TYPE	YEAR	NAME	NUMBER	TYPE	YEAR	NAME	NUMBER	TYPE	YEAR
LAIRAMORE				**LAKER**				**LAMANET**			
Florence A.	26731	I	1919	Joseph	33920	D	1922	Anna	50655	D	1928
Howard L.	26730	D	1919	**LAKIN**				Pierre	37274	D	1923
LAIRD				Joseph J.	71090	D	1935	**LAMAR**			
Daniel	46396	D	1927	**LAKNER**				Albert B.	48708	M	1927
Daniel	55148	D	1930	Max	53244	D	1929	Alice E.	48708	M	1927
Mary A.	1730	D	1906	**LALANDE**				Horace Edward	82553	M	1939
Russell Ernest	69618	D	1935	Alice H.	78971	D	1938	Mary Louise	75648	M	1937
William Woodward	42571	D	1925	**LALANNE**				Paul S	48708	M	1927
LAIST				Eleanor	41196	M	1925	Richard Morton	75648	M	1937
Anna	50815	D	1928	Jacques	6345	D	1908	**LAMARGUE**			
LAITA				John	33266	I	1922	Elvira	9264	M	1910
Charles J.	40322	D	1924	Lorraine	41196	M	1925	**LAMARK**			
LAJANETTE				Rose	43022	I	1925	Ray L.	72913	D	1936
A.	79776	D	1938	**LALINE**				**LAMARQUE**			
LAJANNETTE				Hannah	79672	D	1938	Elizabeth	9051	D	1910
A.	79776	D	1938	**LALL**				Elvira	9264	M	1910
LAJEUNESSE				Edward	89743	D	1942	**LAMARRE**			
Carden F.	3316	M	1907	**LALLEMENT**				Marie	2027	D	1906
Lyle W.	3316	M	1907	Alfonse	15665	D	1913	**LAMAYSOU**			
LAJEUNNETTE				**LALLY**				Rosalie	77431	D	1938
Alexander	79776	D	1938	Bartholomew C.	24388	D	1918	**LAMB**			
LAJUS				Charlotte G.	42853	D	1925	Alexander M.	17532	D	1914
Augustine	37027	D	1923	Dennis J.	6644	D	1908	Catherine	15304	D	1913
Marc	33979	D	1922	H. T.	79348	D	1938	Charles	21362	D	1916
LAKE				James P.	15141	I	1913	Charles W.	50173	D	1928
Aubrey	3188	M	1907	James P.	19825	D	1915	Clarence H.	2559	D	1906
Elizabeth	89764	I	1942	John	2017	D	1906	Frances V.	1931	D	1906
George W.	2409	D	1906	John	2299	M	1906	George Frederick	56996	D	1930
Georgia F.	47169	D	1927	John	7513	M	1909	John E.	60586	D	1932
Hattie W.	72415	D	1936	John	20829	I	1916	Mary P.	44483	D	1926
Hedwig Wittenberg	72415	D	1936	John	31166	D	1921	May	43882	D	1926
Helen L.	35552	I	1922	John	55114	D	1930	Peter	9488	D	1910
Henry	31237	D	1921	Mary	38310	M	1924	Peter	14010	D	1912
James L.	39751	I	1924	Mary F.	50978	D	1928	Philip	42475	D	1925
James R.	3188	M	1907	Michael	38310	M	1924	Preston C.	62796	D	1932
Joan	71262	M	1935	Patrick	38310	M	1924	**LAMBE**			
Myra Clark	4861	D	1907	Robert E.	46662	D	1927	Patrick	11402	D	1911
Patricia	71261	M	1935	Thomas	2299	M	1906	**LAMBERGER**			
Walter Vyse	3188	M	1907	Thomas	38310	M	1924	Friederich Georg	27559	I	1919
LAKELY				**LALOLI**				Georg F.	27559	I	1919
Bernhard	8250	D	1909	Tranquillo	88599	D	1941	**LAMBERT**			
LAKEMAN				**LALUS**				Albert Maurice	27716	D	1919
Anna	71899	D	1936	George	11160	D	1911	Anna S.	4929	D	1907
LAKEMEYER				**LAM**				Annie E.	25404	D	1918
Eugene Edwin	1742	D	1906	Chung	48619	D	1927	Catherine	8397	D	1909
								Charles William	47856	M	1927

NAME	NUMBER	TYPE	YEAR	NAME	NUMBER	TYPE	YEAR	NAME	NUMBER	TYPE	YEAR
Daniel	67700	D	1934	Joseph Noel	17561	D	1914	**LAMOREUX**			
Darcy	61691	I	1932	**LAMEIR**				Clara L.	74871	D	1937
Dewey H.	43299	I	1926	John Burt	63201	D	1932	**LAMOTT**			
Earl Benson	23288	D	1917	**LAMERDIN**				Herbert McKenzie	24647	M	1918
Eliza	46085	D	1926	August	80001	D	1938	**LAMOTTE**			
Eudora	77955	M	1938	**LAMERSALL**				Charles	46135	D	1927
George	56703	D	1930	Eunice J.	20067	D	1915	Francis Victor	12011	I	1911
George W.	57336	D	1930	**LAMEY**				Francis Victor	20966	D	1916
Gilman	87215	D	1941	Elizabeth J.	64684	D	1933	Jules	20253	D	1916
Josephine Saure	86032	D	1941	Frank	38681	D	1924	Louis C.	81454	D	1939
Lavinia E.	78190	D	1938	**LAMEYSE**				**LAMOURE**			
Malvin	25286	M	1918	Marie	68924	D	1935	Albert P.	26374	D	1919
Marie Barbara	53735	D	1929	**LAMKAN**				**LAMP**			
Martin	67954	D	1934	John	14990	D	1913	Marie C.	18432	D	1915
Matilda	73432	D	1936	**LAMKINEN**				**LAMPAS**			
Michael J.	35223	D	1922	Anna	24677	D	1918	John	23069	I	1917
Pierre	1441	D	1906	**LAMM**				**LAMPATHYARES**			
Sarah	701	D	1906	Rosalie	14531	D	1912	Eoannes	23069	I	1917
Tea	89706	D	1942	Rudolph Otto	45102	D	1926	**LAMPE**			
William Wallace	45952	D	1926	**LAMME**				Catherine	89158	D	1942
LAMBERTH				Catherine Helling	87434	D	1941	Charles	18709	D	1915
Henry N.	11045	D	1911	**LAMMERS**				Johan	11960	D	1911
LAMBERTON				Carrie M.	24504	D	1918	Johannes	65655	D	1933
Minerva Eaton	78718	D	1938	Peter Eilers	69610	I	1935	Tenezze	75172	D	1937
LAMBERTSON				**LAMMI**				Tenezzi	75172	D	1937
Emma	62138	I	1932	Eugene R.	89711	I	1942	Theresa	75172	D	1937
Harry V.	62064	D	1932	Samuel Richard	65314	D	1933	**LAMPETER**			
LAMBLA				**LAMMON**				George	89966	D	1942
Augustine	57984	D	1931	David	31417	D	1921	**LAMPHEAR**			
Jules	23795	D	1917	Josephine	46460	D	1927	Edward	12785	D	1912
LAMBLEY				Theresa M.	31418	D	1921	William T.	56994	I	1930
Constance E.	74031	I	1936	**LAMOGLIA**				William T.	64994	D	1933
Constance E.	76270	D	1937	Joseph	69701	D	1935	**LAMPINEN**			
George J.	63643	D	1933	**LAMONS**				Albert E.	81915	D	1939
LAMBROPOULOS				Ella F.	68935	D	1935	Esaias	81915	D	1939
Evangelo	41725	D	1925	**LAMONT**				**LAMPKE**			
Evangelo	41725	D	1925	Hattie Emma	16004	D	1913	Anna M.	36400	D	1923
LAMBROS				James	21354	D	1916	**LAMPPINEN**			
John	78124	D	1938	Stella M.	31774	D	1921	Esaias	81915	D	1939
LAMBRUS				**LAMONTAGNE**				**LAMPRAS**			
Michaels	76936	D	1937	Edward Clinton	11462	M	1911	Basil	42227	D	1925
LAMBURTH				**LAMONTE**				**LAMPROPOULOS**			
Loretta	74795	D	1937	Mary	42560	D	1925	Evangelo	41725	D	1925
LAME				**LAMOREAUX**				Evangelo	41725	D	1925
Genevieve	52078	D	1929	Clara L.	74871	D	1937	**LAMPROPOULOUS**			
James	17561	D	1914					John	78124	D	1938
Joseph	12972	I	1912								

NAME	NUMBER	TYPE	YEAR	NAME	NUMBER	TYPE	YEAR	NAME	NUMBER	TYPE	YEAR
LAMPROS				Ben	80106	I	1938	LANDERSTEDT			
Basil	42227	D	1925	David	83698	D	1940	Per E.	30080	I	1920
LAMPSON				Dewis	13555	D	1912	LANDGARD			
John F.	65680	M	1933	LANDE				Norman Michael	80603	I	1939
Walter A.	65680	M	1933	David	82174	D	1939	LANDGRAF			
LAN				Esther	22251	D	1917	Carl Richard	78526	D	1938
Wong Poy, Mrs.	36566	D	1923	Francis	40142	D	1924	LANDGRAFF			
LANAGAN				Maria R.	4783	D	1907	Hattie M.	6702	I	1908
Daniel W.	43367	D	1926	Marion	68759	I	1935	Joseph, Jr.	47092	M	1927
James	88614	D	1941	William J.	50774	D	1928	LANDGREEN			
Thomas	9782	D	1910	LANDECKER				William	17887	I	1914
LANAHAN				Fannie S.	76516	D	1937	LANDGREN			
William	14250	D	1912	Hugo	85946	D	1941	William	53470	D	1929
LANATA				Leopold	89139	D	1942	LANDINGER			
Irma	66979	M	1934	Sally D.	76457	D	1937	Paul	54569	D	1929
LANCASTER				Sarah	17436	D	1914	LANDINI			
Clara	29756	D	1920	Saul D.	76457	D	1937	Antonio	36601	D	1923
Cora M.	72827	D	1936	LANDELIUS				Carolina	85936	D	1940
Marie G.	41101	M	1925	Oscar F.	21909	D	1916	Felix	56269	M	1930
William H.	72769	D	1936	LANDELLS				Louis	29302	D	1920
LANCE				Gavin Bell	54169	D	1929	Luigi	72805	D	1936
Willie R.	51927	D	1929	Janet Campbell	89040	D	1942	Riccardo	41275	D	1925
LANCELOT				LANDEN				LANDIS			
Edith Lucille	37012	M	1923	Margaret Eugenia	35590	D	1922	Edward Casper	82455	D	1939
LANCI				LANDENBERGER				Jacob K.	29520	D	1920
Giuseppe	66292	D	1934	Charles F.	70608	D	1935	Louise E.	64833	I	1933
Josephine	71599	D	1936	LANDER				Philip Flint	10538	M	1910
LANCY				Charles J.	48285	D	1927	LANDMAN			
Anna	56735	D	1930	Elfrida	51453	D	1928	Julian	64236	M	1933
LAND				Elizabeth	12207	D	1911	LANDO			
Chauncey B.	6028	D	1908	Elsie	56875	D	1930	Hannah	23482	D	1917
Elizabeth	6821	D	1908	Frank C.	21185	D	1916	Meyer	64647	D	1933
Elmer W.	80424	D	1939	LANDERS				Morris	89365	D	1942
George B.	23144	D	1917	Amelia	14700	D	1913	LANDOLFI			
Harriet	484	D	1906	Amy	14700	D	1913	Amalio	78564	D	1938
Jack	74161	M	1936	David	16123	D	1913	Sofia	80779	D	1939
John B.	79454	I	1938	David W.	40851	D	1925	LANDON			
Otto	37355	D	1923	Edward R.	45428	M	1926	Bert N.	39089	I	1924
LANDA				John	39068	D	1924	Clara E.	23489	D	1917
David	85930	D	1940	John	67693	D	1934	Evelyn	22598	D	1917
Ferdinand	68078	M	1934	Katherine G.	45428	M	1926	Florence E.	83465	D	1940
Marjorie	39554	M	1924	Mary	24254	D	1918	Florence Lemon	1095	D	1906
LANDAN				Mary A.	48433	D	1927	Gardner, Jr.	24137	D	1918
Hinda	609	M	1906	Mary Ellen	25299	D	1918	Mary A.	65499	D	1933
LANDAU				Michael R.	20231	D	1916	LANDOU			
Abraham	12897	M	1912	Patrick	11851	D	1911	Rubin	11759	I	1911

NAME	NUMBER	TYPE	YEAR
LANDRAM			
William R.	83006	D	1940
LANDREAU			
Clement	13275	D	1912
LANDREVILLE			
Ernest J.	27445	D	1919
LANDRIGAN			
John	85559	D	1940
LANDRY			
Joseph	46224	I	1927
LANDSBERG			
Albert	37664	D	1923
Esther	43418	I	1926
Jack N.	77159	D	1937
Mary	47065	D	1927
LANDSBERGER			
Josette	58871	M	1931
Nathan J.	78085	D	1938
Philip	49001	D	1928
Ramon Hill	30216	D	1920
LANDSBOROUGH			
Isabella Louisa	77560	D	1938
LANDSBURG			
Edward E.	52425	D	1929
Ellen	61404	D	1932
John	20392	D	1916
LANDSCHNEIDER			
Henry	81927	D	1939
LANDTBOM			
James J.	64574	D	1933
Kate	64575	D	1933
LANDU			
Burih	11436	D	1911
LANDUCCI			
Casimero	11843	D	1911
Dora	29474	M	1920
Dorothy Ann	72137	M	1936
Fred	89467	D	1942
Guglielmo	71741	D	1936
Ida	88151	I	1941
Jessie	86459	D	1941
Lorenzo G.	26905	D	1919
Louis	29474	M	1920
LANDUCI			
Marianna	19532	D	1915

NAME	NUMBER	TYPE	YEAR
LANDWEHR			
John H.	57143	D	1930
LANDY			
Esther Newman	54563	D	1929
Jerry	25957	M	1918
Rose	54612	D	1929
LANE			
Alice	42948	D	1925
Anna G.	54553	D	1929
Arthur W.	15901	D	1913
Carlton V.	77158	D	1937
Charles A.	17368	D	1914
Charles Cameron	60931	D	1932
Charles D.	12002	D	1911
Charles Edward	40185	D	1924
Charles H.	68293	D	1934
Clarence Gordon	83533	D	1940
Dennis A.	62761	D	1932
Dionysus A.	62761	D	1932
Don Q.	34742	I	1922
Dorothy Estella	83388	D	1940
Edwin S.	51054	I	1928
Elizabeth M.	20806	D	1916
Ellen Catharine	71570	M	1936
Eugenie	89705	D	1942
Eva Josephine	72557	D	1936
Ewing G.	60016	I	1931
Felicia C.	54062	D	1929
Fralley Amos	17044	D	1914
Franklin K.	32098	D	1921
Gertrude	44275	D	1926
Harold Vernon	57176	I	1930
Jack Hilton	46014	M	1926
James A.	39823	D	1924
John	6342	D	1908
Lawrence Milton	30071	I	1920
Lizzie L.	24301	I	1918
Lizzie L.	24404	D	1918
Louis L.	85785	D	1940
Lucy C.	82187	D	1939
Lydia S.	18453	D	1915
Lydia Spencer	19741	D	1915
Marcene	55656	M	1930
Mary	24906	D	1918
Mary	60821	D	1932
Mary Frances	22957	D	1917
Paul G.	8926	D	1909
Peter F.	5739	D	1908

NAME	NUMBER	TYPE	YEAR
Spencer G.	34235	D	1922
Thomas	14879	D	1913
Thomas P.	52913	D	1929
Timothy	34880	D	1922
Virginia	76377	I	1937
Virginia	86953	D	1941
W. B.	19745	D	1915
William	9326	D	1910
William	82305	D	1939
William E.	48500	D	1927
William Herbert, Jr.	55656	M	1930
William R.	85450	D	1940
LANFAR			
Adaline Lindsay	71205	D	1935
Hallie Louise	79123	D	1938
LANG			
Adelaide	17864	D	1914
Adolph C.	30409	D	1920
Albert	6487	D	1908
Alexander E.	60660	D	1932
Anna	88322	D	1941
Arthur	60170	D	1931
Carrie	33946	D	1922
Charles H.	59430	D	1931
Elsie	53831	D	1929
Ernest	24927	D	1918
Esther	53530	D	1929
George F., Mrs.	70931	D	1935
Giles B.	38872	D	1924
Henry Adolph	35045	M	1922
Hulda Paulina	83506	D	1940
James Patrick	14926	M	1913
Jane	39506	D	1924
John	73912	D	1936
Joseph	56336	D	1930
Joseph Wilson	14926	M	1913
Louis	1105	D	1906
Lyman	62339	I	1932
Mary	61038	D	1932
Mary S.	70931	D	1935
Michael	14779	D	1913
Sallie S.	29572	D	1920
Sophie	49406	D	1928
Thomas Francis	14926	M	1913
William Henry	81683	D	1939
LANGAN			
James	3369	D	1907
Mary Harrison	88755	D	1941

Key: D = death; M = minor; I = incompetent

NAME	NUMBER	TYPE	YEAR	NAME	NUMBER	TYPE	YEAR	NAME	NUMBER	TYPE	YEAR
Owen	3234	D	1907	**LANGENDERFER**				**LANGRIDGE**			
Peter T.	39594	D	1924	Edward A.	54366	D	1929	Dolores Ethel	62579	M	1932
LANGDON				**LANGER**				William Newell	62579	M	1932
Annie	13320	D	1912	Henry John	82158	D	1939	**LANGSDORF**			
Elizabeth Caroline	31647	I	1921	John	43563	D	1926	Jacob	48719	D	1927
Katherine	27337	D	1919	Kathrina	77354	D	1937	**LANGSHAW**			
Leonard J.	48432	D	1927	Lesley Gutman	77243	D	1937	Barbara	64243	D	1933
Perry A.	50409	D	1928	**LANGERMAN**				Henry J.	62956	D	1932
LANGE				Albert L.	27370	D	1919	**LANGSTADTER**			
Agnes	35393	D	1922	**LANGERMANN**				Daniel	85086	D	1940
Benjamin	17463	D	1914	Alfred Theodore	17734	M	1914	Isaiah S.	73239	D	1936
Bernhard	17463	D	1914	Friedericka	1192	D	1906	Pauline	50783	D	1928
Carl	4452	D	1907	**LANGES**				**LANGSTAFF**			
Catherine	51635	D	1928	George	6101	D	1908	Aurilla	77494	I	1938
Emil H.	67678	D	1934	**LANGEVIN**				Eleanor S.	40111	D	1924
Emma	2889	D	1907	Edward	49445	D	1928	May	77494	I	1938
Frank F.	68059	D	1934	Jean	73464	D	1936	**LANGSTROTH**			
Franz	50483	D	1928	John	73464	D	1936	Dora Julia	26458	D	1919
Fred	87128	D	1941	**LANGFORD**				Dora Winn	26458	D	1919
Frederick	6577	D	1908	Catherine F.	49788	D	1928	Lovell, Jr.	28835	D	1920
George Daniel	85477	D	1940	Sophie Holmes	55896	D	1930	**LANGTON**			
H. N.	45421	D	1926	**LANGHORNE**				Mary	70447	D	1935
Hermann	52949	D	1929	James Potter	35876	D	1923	William M.	15157	D	1913
J. A. B.	22331	D	1917	**LANGLEY**				**LANGTRE**			
John	51354	D	1928	Hannah	19346	D	1915	Florence O.	61830	D	1932
Josepha	36042	D	1923	Jennie	64092	D	1933	**LANGTRY**			
Julius Blom	22331	D	1917	Martin	16397	D	1913	Florence N.	47632	D	1927
Leta	63447	D	1933	Mary F.	41233	D	1925	James H.	33439	I	1922
Mabel Woodword	86441	D	1941	Virginia Elizabeth	64092	D	1933	James H.	34726	D	1922
Mary C.	15982	D	1913	Walter M.	22428	D	1917	Nellie	47632	D	1927
Minna	88751	D	1941	**LANGLOIS**				**LANGWORTHY**			
Paul	24783	D	1918	Bertha B.	43752	D	1926	Louise	75320	D	1937
Sophie	65111	I	1933	Dorothy Silver	87095	D	1941	Louise	74739	I	1937
Sophie	65375	D	1933	Elizabeth	73186	D	1936	**LANIGAN**			
W. A., Mrs.	36042	D	1923	Marcelle L.	71042	D	1935	Bertha	29612	D	1920
Wilhelm	19603	D	1915	**LANGLOTZ**				Mary	19961	D	1915
William	16183	D	1913	Fredericka	14057	D	1912	Thomas	9782	D	1910
William	71565	D	1936	**LANGMUTH**				**LANING**			
LANGEIL				Emil	3267	D	1907	Warren E.	66789	D	1934
James J., Jr.	84998	D	1940	**LANGNER**				**LANKENAU**			
LANGELLA				George	59402	D	1931	Edwin	31722	M	1921
Antonio	53186	D	1929	**LANGO**				Fred	18498	D	1915
LANGENBERGER				John	89396	D	1942	Frederick J.	52146	D	1929
C. H. Frederick	35356	D	1922	Wilhelm	16183	D	1913	Grace	31722	M	1921
Ferdinand	35356	D	1922	**LANGOVICH**				Henry	6039	D	1908
Frederick	35356	D	1922	Vido	23705	D	1917	Leslie	31722	M	1921
Fredrick	35356	D	1922					Richard	31722	M	1921

NAME	NUMBER	TYPE	YEAR
LANKINEN			
Anna	24677	D	1918
LANKTREE			
Norah A.	74523	I	1937
Norah A.	81886	D	1939
LANN			
Dorothy Elinor	74091	M	1936
Emma Louise	72354	D	1936
Stanley Hall	74091	M	1936
LANNEGRAND			
Frances	47630	I	1927
Henri	48046	D	1927
LANNES			
Jean Pierre	64219	D	1933
John	1067	D	1906
LANNESSUS			
Raymond	38366	D	1924
LANNIN			
Eileen	38428	M	1924
James	38428	M	1924
Patrick Joseph	73591	D	1936
LANNING			
Warren E.	66789	D	1934
LANNON			
Elizabeth M.	89541	D	1942
Evelyn	591	D	1906
John	62069	D	1932
Thomas	8541	D	1909
LANOT			
Cyprien	16165	D	1913
LANOUE			
Mary E.	23878	D	1918
LANPHEAR			
William E.	29617	I	1920
LANPHER			
Agnes	1409	D	1906
LANSCHE			
Hattie M.	32561	D	1921
LANSENDERFER			
Joseph	53135	D	1929
LANSER			
Lawrence Andrew	67961	D	1934
LANSFIELD			
William T.	74867	D	1937
LANSING			
Alice	82302	D	1939

NAME	NUMBER	TYPE	YEAR
Emma	2572	D	1906
John J.	22722	D	1917
Mary Rebecca	23366	D	1917
LANSTRUM			
Frederick	42028	D	1925
LANTHIERE			
Evelyn	52874	M	1929
Joseph	52874	M	1929
Margaret	52874	M	1929
Mary	52874	M	1929
LANTIE			
Therese	55386	D	1930
Vincent	86585	D	1941
LANTRY			
H. E.	292	D	1906
LANUM			
Nina W.	64344	D	1933
LANZENDORF			
Herman	82578	D	1939
LAPACHET			
Bernard P.	31384	D	1921
Catherine	20301	D	1916
Emile J.	82342	D	1939
LAPAGE			
Charlotte Emily	84983	D	1940
LAPASSEIG			
Julien Loustau	30057	D	1920
LAPEL			
Susie A.	72151	D	1936
LAPEROU			
Barthelemy	23469	D	1917
LAPEYRI			
Martin	75071	D	1937
Michel	68942	D	1935
LAPFGEER			
William August	7660	D	1909
LAPIDGE			
Mary Ann	7373	D	1909
LAPIERRE			
Albina	55527	D	1930
Alphonse	9017	D	1910
J. Marsan	11064	D	1911
Malvina	55527	D	1930
LAPKOUSKI			
Konstanty	65471	D	1933

NAME	NUMBER	TYPE	YEAR
LAPLACE			
Addie M.	73803	D	1936
Francis Fernand	54173	D	1929
Marguerite	19644	D	1915
Pierre	58681	D	1931
LAPLAIN			
Lillie A.	74983	D	1937
LAPLANT			
David	81604	M	1939
LAPOINT			
Arthur J.	41353	D	1925
LAPORT			
Marie Ann	219	D	1906
LAPORTE			
Louis	10054	D	1910
LAPOUBLE			
Ernest	15350	D	1913
LAPP			
Amalia	71266	D	1935
LAPPIN			
James C.	67556	I	1934
LAPSLEY			
Robert M.	68081	D	1934
LAPTHORN			
Charles Holton	24049	I	1918
LAPUH			
Mike	69836	D	1935
LAPUHAS			
Mike	69836	D	1935
LAPZICH			
Gustav Adolf	44833	D	1926
LAPZIES			
Gustav Adolf	44833	D	1926
LAQUERRE			
William B.	56013	I	1930
LAQUILLO			
Benigno	74909	D	1937
Louis P.	24535	M	1918
LARA			
Jose	18923	D	1915
Juana	43289	D	1925
LARACCA			
Leo	83665	D	1940
LARAIA			
Egidio A.	57145	I	1930
Egidio Anthony	66784	D	1934

NAME	NUMBER	TYPE	YEAR
Maria Rocca	48992	D	1928
Rocco Mario	66106	D	1934
LARALES			
Lorita	79351	D	1938
LARAMIE			
Catherine	49648	D	1928
LARBIG			
Angelina	52661	D	1929
Nicholas	3294	D	1907
LARDNER			
John	63650	D	1933
LARGAN			
Elizabeth	9308	I	1910
James	2340	I	1906
James J.	2368	D	1906
James T.	48230	D	1927
LARGE			
Claudius	73959	D	1936
LARGENT			
Clarence	25767	M	1918
Leon	25767	M	1918
Louis	25767	M	1918
Robert L.	25714	D	1918
LARGENTE			
Pierre	33449	D	1922
LARI			
Angiolina	70319	D	1935
LARIMER			
Helen F.	34461	D	1922
LARIMORE			
Jean R.	69799	D	1935
LARKEN			
Anita A.	41413	D	1925
LARKHAUS			
Frederick W.	1695	D	1906
LARKIN			
Annie J.	8104	D	1909
Catherine	80869	D	1939
Edward J.	78354	D	1938
Elizabeth	68156	D	1934
Francis Philip	78828	D	1938
Francis Raymond	19534	I	1915
George Henry	2220	M	1906
Johanna	8300	D	1909
John J.	204	D	1906
Joseph Y., Jr.	46056	I	1926
Julia	44440	D	1926

NAME	NUMBER	TYPE	YEAR
Lawrence H.	49408	I	1928
Lizzie	27723	I	1919
Margaret Jane	37895	D	1923
Marguerite M.	44448	D	1926
Mary	13907	D	1912
Mary Rose	23714	D	1917
Peter J.	74757	D	1937
Robert Emmet	35100	D	1922
Theresa Margaret	62048	D	1932
Thomas	12734	D	1911
Thomas O.	24470	D	1918
Thomas P., Jr.	65942	M	1933
Thomas Paul	62184	D	1932
William	79959	D	1938
William Henry	18188	D	1914
William Lawrence	83024	D	1940
LARKINS			
Alberta	66755	M	1934
Alice Maud	54782	D	1930
Allan, Jr.	66755	M	1934
Harriet A. F.	56691	I	1930
Harriet Ann F.	59799	D	1931
James A.	69540	D	1935
John Kenneth	66755	M	1934
Maud	54782	D	1930
William	15758	D	1913
William Louis	66755	M	1934
LARNED			
Isabelle	22513	D	1917
LARNEY			
John H.	44915	D	1926
LAROCCA			
Accursia	25902	M	1918
Accursio	83665	D	1940
Alfonso	25902	M	1918
Antonio	25549	D	1918
Concetta	25902	M	1918
Katherine	48908	D	1928
Leo	83665	D	1940
Maria	77272	D	1937
Mary	25902	M	1918
Pietro	77535	D	1938
Salvatore	29037	D	1920
LAROCHE			
Jeanne N.	12311	D	1911
LAROMER			
Minnie G.	64532	D	1933

NAME	NUMBER	TYPE	YEAR
LAROMY			
Frank William	71239	D	1935
LAROSA			
Rosaria	54786	D	1930
Vincent	41661	D	1925
LAROSE			
Dolores Yvonne	59237	M	1931
Zenaide	43654	D	1926
LAROSSA			
Francisco	32276	D	1921
LARRABEE			
Colden B.	2761	D	1907
Elizabeth L.	30372	D	1920
John Jay	7997	D	1909
LARRAILLE			
Michael Joseph	82420	I	1939
LARRASQUET			
Clement	87688	D	1941
LARRE			
Maria	24285	D	1918
LARRECOU			
Noel	11164	D	1911
LARRIEU			
Jean	6586	D	1908
LARROCHE			
Catherine Domengine	24961	D	1918
Catherine Laragnouet	24961	D	1918
Leon Vincent	906	D	1906
Marguerite	44468	D	1926
LARROUY			
Hortense	25452	D	1918
Jean Baptiste	81638	D	1939
LARS(S)ON			
Christina	4397	I	1907
LARSEN			
Adelina	65695	D	1933
Adolph	40811	D	1925
Albert William	37385	M	1923
Alfred	13512	M	1912
Alfred P.	18844	D	1915
Alvin Charles	51066	M	1928
Alvin Lloyd	30260	M	1920
Ana Marie	75388	D	1937
Anne Katrine	57059	D	1930
Antone	54292	D	1929
August F.	87295	D	1941
Augusta	58917	D	1931

NAME	NUMBER	TYPE	YEAR	NAME	NUMBER	TYPE	YEAR	NAME	NUMBER	TYPE	YEAR
Axel F.	78927	D	1938	Maude	75483	D	1937	Eric Hugo	34546	D	1922
C. V. V. E.	52718	D	1929	Milton	16448	M	1913	Erik Gustaf	89880	D	1942
Carl	3774	D	1907	Myron Arnold	30260	M	1920	Ernest G.	47723	D	1927
Carl G.	51283	D	1928	Natalie	30986	M	1921	F.	26017	D	1918
Carl Laurits Marius	59841	D	1931	Nels Peter	3713	D	1907	Frederick	16061	D	1913
Christian	67645	I	1934	Niels C. N. T.	61966	D	1932	George Peter	62800	D	1932
Christian	74717	D	1937	Niels T.	63559	M	1933	Gustaf Adolf	80070	D	1938
Christian A. M.	64957	D	1933	Norstjana	9570	M	1910	Gustave	60457	D	1931
Christian Frederik	21723	I	1916	Oscar Thune	84126	D	1940	Hans P.	34521	D	1922
Clara Maude	75483	D	1937	Philip	16448	M	1913	Hildegard	84462	D	1940
Clara V. E.	52718	D	1929	Rachiel	55249	D	1930	Hildur Ingeborg	4324	M	1907
Clara Virginia	52718	D	1929	Ray	55249	D	1930	Johanna P.	25858	D	1918
Clyde	41883	I	1925	T., Mrs.	52718	D	1929	John	16643	D	1914
Clyde	41883	I	1925	Theodora T.	2298	M	1906	John	43199	D	1925
Daniel	27378	D	1919	Walter C.	33529	M	1922	John B.	78552	D	1938
Dorthea	9239	D	1910	William Rasmus	77932	D	1938	John Doe	81966	M	1939
Edith	61104	M	1932	**LARSON**				John Edward	47933	M	1927
Einer C. A.	76374	D	1937	Albert	80601	D	1939	John L.	46788	D	1927
Ellen Emily	51067	M	1928	Alec	62576	D	1932	Knut	16927	D	1914
Etta	61104	M	1932	Alexander Edward	88458	D	1941	Lars Erik	36560	D	1923
Eugene Michael	79871	M	1938	Algot E.	19256	D	1915	Leslie	17448	M	1914
Frederik Johan	59915	D	1931	Alice E.	40987	D	1925	Louise	58730	I	1931
George	3690	D	1907	Alice Wilhelmina	89773	D	1942	Lydia C.	25552	D	1918
H. H.	70442	I	1935	Amelia	17890	M	1914	Marion Arthur	70563	M	1935
Hans	44060	D	1926	Andrew	20453	D	1916	Marjorie Marilyn	70563	M	1935
Harold L.	35010	D	1922	Andrew	22918	D	1917	Mary	71456	D	1936
Hazel Bernice	67806	M	1934	Anna Lovisa	83955	D	1940	Mathilda	17849	I	1914
Helen Gertrude	9239	M	1910	Annette	14809	D	1913	Matilda	15444	I	1913
Henry	70442	I	1935	August	17664	D	1914	Matilda Erikson	62813	D	1932
Herman R.	41123	D	1925	Axel	23093	D	1917	Minnie	59297	D	1931
Inger C. C.	7449	D	1909	Betty	71676	D	1936	Olaf	62576	D	1932
John	4388	D	1907	Carl	48736	I	1927	Olga	17890	M	1914
John	54812	D	1930	Carl	86300	D	1941	Oscar	17890	M	1914
John B.	78552	D	1938	Carl W.	39045	D	1924	Oscar Edward	82925	D	1939
Karl Peter	22230	D	1917	Catherine	1346	D	1906	Peter Henry	49950	D	1928
Klaus Peter	59462	I	1931	Catherine	54052	D	1929	Ralph E.	76979	I	1937
Knute C.	85789	D	1940	Charles	2421	D	1906	Roy Everett Emanuel	4324	M	1907
Lars A. K.	72713	D	1936	Charles	86300	D	1941	Sam	39602	I	1924
Lars Martin	41899	D	1925	Charles H.	68707	D	1935	Skuli Einar	41961	D	1925
Lars Martin	41899	D	1925	Christina	61773	D	1932	Skuli Einar	41961	D	1925
Lars P.	59925	I	1931	Christoffer L.	32463	D	1921	Victor E.	59229	D	1931
Lauritz	13512	M	1912	Clyde E.	41170	I	1925	William C.	79533	D	1938
Lawrence M.	38410	D	1924	Clyde E.	41883	I	1925	**LARSSON**			
Louis Albert	30884	D	1920	Clyde E.	41883	I	1925	Ernest.	22768	D	1917
Ludwig E.	66912	D	1934	Conrad B.	29569	D	1920	**LARTIGUE**			
Margaret	82353	D	1939	David	34472	D	1922	Gregoire	84125	D	1940
Margaretha Agnes	44945	D	1926	Edward J.	25782	D	1918	**LaRUE**			
Maria	13089	D	1912	Elise Francisca	4324	M	1907	Burton	27239	D	1919
Marie	2738	D	1907	Emil	80968	D	1939				

NAME	NUMBER	TYPE	YEAR
Calhoun Lee	43715	D	1926
Lu Ella	55696	D	1930
LARZELERE			
Elizabeth G.	29141	D	1920
Leigh R.	52220	D	1929
Naomi	9936	D	1910
William R.	47070	D	1927
William Remson	53993	D	1929
LaSALLE			
Annie E.	44318	D	1926
Jean Louis	59105	D	1931
LaSANCE			
Christopher J.	56638	D	1930
LASAR			
Augustin A.	68591	D	1934
Emanuel	4198	D	1907
Gerald	8629	M	1909
Isaac	4663	I	1907
Isaac	7709	D	1909
Isaac	52724	D	1929
Leopold	4817	D	1907
Marcus	4450	D	1907
Nellie P.	77850	D	1938
LASCELLE			
Harvey Wendell	48447	D	1927
LASCHENCO			
Catherine P.	72969	D	1936
Daniel	73449	D	1936
Daniel, Jr.	73450	D	1936
Nicholas	50922	D	1928
LASCHENKOHL			
Frederick William	20317	D	1916
LASCLOTTES			
Marie Jeanne	3751	D	1907
LASELL			
Frederick A.	26321	D	1919
LaSELLE			
Burton I.	45776	D	1926
Joseph A.	37009	D	1923
LaSELVE			
Charles Melvin	13832	D	1912
Melvin	13832	D	1912
LASH			
Emma H.	76685	D	1937
Janet	37208	M	1923
LASHER			
Elizabeth Ann	69777	M	1935

NAME	NUMBER	TYPE	YEAR
Jean Goodrich	69777	M	1935
LASINSKY			
Harry	79619	M	1938
Nathan	79619	M	1938
Sonia	79619	M	1938
LASK			
Frances Louise	27137	D	1919
George E.	71897	D	1936
Louis	2601	D	1907
Rebecca	19856	D	1915
LASKER			
James H.	41530	D	1925
Margaret H.	38740	D	1924
LASKEY			
Newell H.	70624	I	1935
LASKY			
Beatrice	81112	I	1939
Minnie	25879	D	1918
Theresa	62481	D	1932
LASPA			
Maria	34267	D	1922
LASPLAZAS			
Francisco	21697	D	1916
LASS			
Christine F.	10962	M	1910
Frederick	16008	D	1913
Peter G.	10962	M	1910
LASSA			
Jose	31223	D	1921
LASSABATERE			
Joseph	74733	D	1937
LASSALLE			
Antoine	63257	D	1932
Bathilde	788	D	1906
Marie	89930	D	1942
Victorine	53461	M	1929
Victorine	76174	M	1937
LASSALLETTE			
Jacques	25735	D	1918
LASSEGUES			
Jeanne Marie	81519	D	1939
Pierre	79874	D	1938
LASSEN			
Camilia Pearl	18585	M	1915
Ida Mae	74920	D	1937
Julius P.	18311	D	1914

NAME	NUMBER	TYPE	YEAR
LASSERMAN			
Pauline	79290	D	1938
LASSERRE			
Jean	10324	D	1910
Jean	36831	D	1923
Jean Baptiste	32122	D	1921
Jean Pierre	32122	D	1921
LASSIG			
Paul	22098	D	1917
LASSING			
Frederick	9207	D	1910
John Frederick	9207	D	1910
LASSMAN			
Loeb	34415	D	1922
LASTEIN			
Anna	30214	D	1920
LASTRA			
Pedra	4619	D	1907
LASWELL			
Ida H.	32992	D	1921
LATAPIE			
Adelaide Ernestine	13003	D	1912
Francois	78096	D	1938
Pierre E.	28202	D	1919
LATASTE			
Charles	33520	D	1922
LATCH			
Kate	16252	I	1913
Kate	36644	D	1923
LATEANA			
Nicola	49551	D	1928
LATEY			
Gertruce	75540	D	1937
LATHAM			
Emily K.	53369	D	1929
John	40427	M	1924
Joseph	33381	D	1922
Joseph	36973	D	1923
Mary McM.	80343	I	1939
Mary McM.	80519	D	1939
William B.	10867	D	1910
LATHROP			
Alice	56254	D	1930
Ariel	7280	D	1909
Henry D.	8665	D	1909
Henry S.	64780	D	1933

NAME	NUMBER	TYPE	YEAR	NAME	NUMBER	TYPE	YEAR	NAME	NUMBER	TYPE	YEAR
Ray	50660	D	1928	**LAUB**				**LAUGHLIN**			
LATIEZE				Adolph	48629	D	1927	Alexander	50983	D	1928
Charles	53154	D	1929	Brigitta	71476	D	1936	John J.	88650	D	1941
LATON				Frank	28357	D	1919	John O.	44865	D	1926
Charles A.	43109	D	1925	Pearl	61763	D	1932	Joseph J.	23553	D	1917
Charles A.	50498	D	1928	**LAUBER**				Josephine	8848	D	1909
LATORRE				Charles A.	24133	D	1918	Lawrence N.	15390	M	1913
Antonette	65497	M	1933	Leon	22863	M	1917	Lawrence Neil	13545	M	1912
Eugenio Urgel	28989	D	1920	Leon J.	31465	D	1921	Neil	15390	M	1913
Frank	65497	M	1933	**LAUBSCHER**				Patrick	42213	D	1925
LATOUR				Elise	67060	D	1934	**LAUGHRAN**			
Edmund	8524	D	1909	Louis	66983	D	1934	Frank V.	82725	D	1939
Joseph	78285	D	1938	**LAUCILLETTI**				Helen Lois	50253	M	1928
LATREILLE				Angelo	83155	D	1940	Jane	61996	D	1932
August E.	68353	D	1934	**LAUCILLOTTI**				Thomas F.	50253	M	1928
LATROUEL				Angelo	83155	D	1940	Thomas P.	76788	D	1937
Edina Dhue	26960	D	1919	**LAUCILOTTI**				**LAUGHTON**			
LATSCHA				Angelo	83155	D	1940	James	38691	D	1924
John B.	14439	D	1912	**LAUDEN**				James	47741	D	1927
LATSES				Martin K.	35719	D	1923	**LAUGIER**			
Georgias	84118	D	1940	**LAUDERDALE**				Charles F.	12452	D	1911
LATSLEY				Rose Estelle	57472	D	1930	**LAUINGER**			
Robert M.	68081	D	1934	**LAUDMANN**				John Baptist	3175	D	1907
LATTIG				Hermine	88061	D	1941	**LAUJARDIERE**			
Frank J.	55162	D	1930	**LAUDON**				Anna Marie	6370	M	1908
LATTIN				Frank	6609	D	1908	**LAULA**			
Emma Elizabeth	37707	M	1923	John	52719	D	1929	Victor	42009	D	1925
Miles Percy	37707	M	1923	Johnanna	56499	D	1930	W.	42009	D	1925
Percy Byron	37714	D	1923	**LAUENSTEIN**				**LAULHERE**			
LATTS				Theresa	55172	D	1930	Jean	19589	D	1915
George	84118	D	1940	**LAUER**				Jean Hippolyte	12214	D	1911
LATTZ				Daisy W. R.	11850	D	1911	John H.	12214	D	1911
George	84118	D	1940	Marie	26417	D	1919	**LAUMEISTER**			
LATVANEN				**LAUERMAN**				Anna T.	2695	D	1907
Esther Martha	41911	D	1925	Albert L.	60441	D	1931	Charles S.	24734	D	1918
Esther Martha	41911	D	1925	**LAUERMANN**				Delfina	57618	D	1931
LATZ				Nicholas	20669	D	1916	**LAUN**			
Benjamin	73104	D	1936	**LAUERS**				Alma Bernhardina	88253	D	1941
Estelle	73115	D	1936	Mary E.	8564	D	1909	Edward	88226	D	1941
Philip	56978	D	1930	**LAUEZZARI**				**LAUNER**			
LATZIG				Phillipa Gladys May	45478	D	1926	Fronia L.	63752	D	1933
Robert	76416	D	1937	**LAUFF**				**LAUNTZ**			
LAU				A. N.	69439	D	1935	John Andrew	71775	D	1936
Helen	14174	M	1912	Alfred Dewey	86239	D	1941	**LAUPSA**			
Sing Tsan	59432	D	1931	Mary A.	11770	D	1911	Ola	82659	D	1939
Thomas	2316	D	1906	Mary Josephine	11770	D	1911	**LAUR**			
								Andrew	77549	D	1938

NAME	NUMBER	TYPE	YEAR
LAURENCE			
F.	65060	D	1933
Minnie R.	71053	D	1935
LAURENT			
Dominigue	8911	D	1909
Giovanni Giuliano	63522	D	1933
John	63522	D	1933
LAURENTI			
Angelo	84848	M	1940
Giuseppe	84887	D	1940
Maria	51000	D	1928
LAURENZI			
Peter, Mrs.	77160	D	1937
Virginia Margaret	77160	D	1937
LAURETI			
Toni	51555	D	1928
LAURETTA			
Antonio	51555	D	1928
LAURICELLA			
Domenico	2047	D	1906
Eva H.	68504	D	1934
Rosalia	43525	D	1926
Sarah	55431	D	1930
LAURICELLI			
Sarah	55431	D	1930
LAURIDSEN			
Mads	61339	D	1932
LAURIE			
Frank J.	52246	I	1929
LAURIKS			
Octave	31021	D	1921
LAURISTON			
Jane	56218	M	1930
Patricia Ann	56218	M	1930
Robert Pyle	56218	M	1930
LAURITANO			
Gussie	86698	D	1941
Margaret	66643	D	1934
LAURITZEN			
Thomas	80439	D	1939
LAUSCHER			
Frank	52873	I	1929
LAUSEN			
A. J., Jr.	72732	D	1936
Hans C.	10327	D	1910

NAME	NUMBER	TYPE	YEAR
LAUSTEN			
Charlotte T.	31243	D	1921
Laust Peter	52216	D	1929
Sinneck Hansen	36232	D	1923
LAUTEN			
Louis Emiel	43613	M	1926
LAUTER			
Nathan	78268	D	1938
LAUTERWASSER			
Henry William	26929	D	1919
Mary E.	21205	D	1916
Mary Elizabeth	65470	D	1933
LAUTIN			
Hermine	86826	D	1941
LAUX			
Cecelia	66339	D	1934
LAVAGNINO			
Carlo	25882	D	1918
Giovanni	61612	D	1932
Josephine	84537	D	1940
Rocco	20059	D	1915
LAVALL			
Christine	41015	D	1925
Juliette Leone	46345	M	1927
L.	53201	D	1929
LAVALLE			
Paul	16037	D	1913
LAVALLEE			
Maud	53980	D	1929
LAVANTIS			
Nick	45117	D	1926
LAVARONE			
Richard	44716	D	1926
LAVARONI			
Carlo	39440	D	1924
John	38374	D	1924
John B.	23031	D	1917
LAVELL			
Andrew C.	41487	D	1925
Louis	53201	D	1929
LAVELLE			
Bridget	24161	D	1918
James	64321	D	1933
Michael J.	1367	D	1906
Paul	16037	D	1913
Pauline	19759	M	1915

NAME	NUMBER	TYPE	YEAR
Pauline Ruth	40521	M	1924
Thomas	56518	D	1930
William A.	42385	D	1925
LAVELLO			
Paul	16037	D	1913
LAVEN			
Jane	19710	D	1915
Joseph	70220	D	1935
LAVENDER			
George	80604	D	1939
LAVENROTH			
Harry	41189	I	1925
Harry	76698	D	1937
LAVENSON			
George H.	64692	D	1933
George S.	64692	D	1933
LAVENTHAL			
Bertha	8519	D	1909
Irma	30414	D	1920
Irma	30976	M	1921
Irma	32741	M	1921
Isadore	30890	D	1920
Joseph J.	2771	D	1907
Rosalie	35793	I	1923
LAVERY			
Anoria	46161	I	1927
Caroline E.	78455	M	1938
Edward	53289	D	1929
Honora	46161	I	1927
Myrtle	73333	D	1936
LAVESSIERE			
Frank	42796	D	1925
LAVEZZO			
Paul	51169	D	1928
Pellegro P.	51169	D	1928
Severino	51169	D	1928
Teresa	54868	D	1930
LAVEZZOLA			
Antonio	19587	I	1915
Antonio	83716	D	1940
LAVEZZOLI			
Rodolfo	80493	D	1939
LAVIETTE			
Fred E.	59992	D	1931
LAVIGNE			
Jean Bulhe	61642	D	1932
John Bulhe	61642	D	1932

Key: D = death; M = minor; I = incompetent

NAME	NUMBER	TYPE	YEAR
Mathilde	25090	D	1918
LAVIGNEBULHE			
Julie	63808	M	1933
LAVIGNINO			
Rocco	20059	D	1915
LAVIN			
Bridget	33495	D	1922
Delia	33367	D	1922
Delia	52841	I	1929
Delia	54678	D	1930
Jane	19710	D	1915
John Joseph	80489	D	1939
Margaret M.	85033	D	1940
LAVINBURG			
Bertha	16783	D	1914
Samuel Lewis	4950	D	1907
LaVINE			
Amelia Bauer	43099	D	1925
James J.	44767	D	1926
LAVIOSA			
Agnes M.	81151	D	1939
Louis, Jr.	70074	I	1935
LAVITT			
Joseph	69021	D	1935
LAVOIE			
Alice	22885	M	1917
LAVORAN			
Ernest, Jr.	10497	M	1910
LAVORELL			
Eugene	28322	D	1919
LaVOY			
Violet Winifred	80597	I	1939
LAVUNCHER			
Ezier Joseph	52820	D	1929
LAW			
Ada Ward	50846	D	1928
Arden Warner	53843	M	1929
Daniel	28524	D	1919
Dean Warner	53843	M	1929
Gum Sung	70585	M	1935
Hartland	37397	M	1923
Hartland	53844	M	1929
James	81095	D	1939
Laura E.	75344	D	1937
Minna L.	85764	D	1940
Nora Fellows	80305	D	1939
Virginia	53844	M	1929

NAME	NUMBER	TYPE	YEAR
Ward	37397	M	1923
Ward	53844	M	1929
Will M.	85763	D	1940
William Mowat	30629	I	1920
LAWALL			
Charles	2949	D	1907
LAWERY			
John J.	87159	D	1941
LAWESS			
Kenneth	47584	M	1927
LAWFORD			
James Henry	25075	D	1918
LAWICK			
Jacob	33629	D	1922
LAWIETTE			
Fred E.	59992	D	1931
LAWLER			
A. P.	62886	D	1932
Anna Higgenbothan	16948	M	1914
Annie	1785	D	1906
Bridget	78195	I	1938
Charles Peter	39555	D	1924
David A.	60588	D	1932
Davis B.	25596	D	1918
Edward A.	32721	M	1921
Edward J.	6165	M	1908
Eleanor	79910	D	1938
Frank W.	40659	D	1924
Frank, Jr.	73392	M	1936
Henry John	74314	D	1937
Isabelle L.	78990	D	1938
James J.	15829	D	1913
Lou Ella	74946	D	1937
Margaret	9783	D	1910
Margaret	24933	D	1918
Margaret Emily	53580	D	1929
Maria	22051	D	1917
Mary	9783	D	1910
Michael H.	15261	D	1913
Peter	33151	D	1922
Philip James	62934	D	1932
Thomas M.	9757	D	1910
Virginia Mary	16948	M	1914
LAWLESS			
Briget	794	D	1906
Hubert E.	82850	D	1939
Hugh E.	82850	D	1939
Joseph I.	81960	D	1939

NAME	NUMBER	TYPE	YEAR
Lawrence	17	D	1906
Mary	50834	D	1928
Michael J.	17712	D	1914
Nellie	17711	M	1914
Viena	17711	M	1914
LAWLOR			
Annie B.	42666	D	1925
Bridget	26943	D	1919
Elton	28863	M	1920
George J. U.	79907	D	1938
George P.	82968	D	1939
George U.	11128	D	1911
Johanna	29381	D	1920
John C.	85191	D	1940
Mary	68822	D	1935
Mary Linehan	13648	D	1912
Nicholas	57301	I	1930
William Patrick	45483	D	1926
LAWRANCE			
Elizabeth Call	16825	D	1914
LAWRENCE			
Carl	48736	I	1927
Charles S.	50718	D	1928
Emma	41508	D	1925
Esther C.	52245	I	1929
Eva M.	49913	D	1928
Eva Purnell	49913	D	1928
Evelyn Gertrude	71666	I	1936
Frances	58080	M	1931
Frank Sam	70299	D	1935
Fred	65060	D	1933
Fred C.	62102	D	1932
George	26666	M	1919
Hamilton	58079	M	1931
Harry	79619	M	1938
Harry Gilbert	60319	D	1931
Hiram David	79997	I	1938
Isabella F.	32938	D	1921
John	74974	D	1937
John Lovell	60549	D	1931
John Lowell	60549	D	1931
Kate	58078	M	1931
Leona	79619	D	1938
Margaret	88783	D	1941
Margaret H.	55918	D	1930
Mary	58077	M	1931
Mary E.	22512	D	1917
Mary Viola	58850	D	1931

NAME	NUMBER	TYPE	YEAR	NAME	NUMBER	TYPE	YEAR	NAME	NUMBER	TYPE	YEAR
Melville	41054	D	1925	Oscar Victor	16075	I	1913	John Edward	19700	D	1915
Minnie R.	71053	D	1935	Pauline P.	17020	D	1914	Marie L.	25470	D	1918
Nathan	79619	M	1938	Robert Carr	61071	M	1932	Sarah	16833	D	1914
Newbold T., Jr.	7196	M	1909	Robert Julius	29394	D	1920	William G.	18608	D	1915
Raymond F.	18137	M	1914	Sarah Ann	829	D	1906	**LAYRAE**			
Virginia Hunt	89279	D	1942	Thomas	16302	D	1913	Albert M.	48620	D	1927
W. Erwin	63841	D	1933	**LAWTON**				**LAYSON**			
William	6843	D	1908	Agnes	79848	D	1938	Mary C.	23832	D	1918
William E.	63841	D	1933	Anna I.	71004	I	1935	Wm. H.	7486	D	1909
LAWREY				Catherine	65816	D	1933	**LAYTON**			
Andrew	22749	D	1917	Charles G.	87573	D	1941	Alice G.	16065	D	1913
LAWS				Delmore Elburton	46600	D	1927	Louise	66099	I	1934
George B.	73890	D	1936	Hattie K.	8342	D	1909	**LAZANSKY**			
Grace Rose	33083	D	1921	Martha	20125	D	1915	Earl J.	81476	D	1939
Myrtle Scott	15224	M	1913	Mary	39137	D	1924	Milton	15238	D	1913
LAWSEN				Mary Ann	23780	D	1917	Sim	63607	D	1933
Hans C.	10327	D	1910	Mary Nightingale	74602	D	1937	**LAZAR**			
LAWSER				Stephen Field	24136	D	1918	Annie	21306	D	1916
Charles Joseph	73828	D	1936	Thomas F.	77404	D	1938	Solomon	29287	D	1920
LAWSON				Zephaniah	10209	D	1910	**LAZAREFF**			
Albert W.	40884	D	1925	**LAWTONS**				Nicholas F.	84368	M	1940
Alexander	48003	D	1927	Magdalena	13244	D	1912	**LAZARI**			
Alfred B.	79784	D	1938	**LAXON**				Victor	25481	D	1918
Arnot	83650	D	1940	Caroline	26686	D	1919	**LAZARIAN**			
Bendick H. C.	19041	M	1915	**LAY**				John	47427	D	1927
Bertha	83987	D	1940	Carl	4776	M	1907	**LAZARIAU**			
Bertha Cora	33515	D	1922	Delilah M.	35928	D	1923	John	47427	D	1927
Caroline Walters	56058	D	1930	**LAYBOUM**				**LAZARTE**			
Charles H.	10612	D	1910	Fannie G.	36500	D	1923	Charles Marion	58699	D	1931
Cuthbert	67834	D	1934	**LAYBOURN**				**LAZARUS**			
Dayton E.	61071	M	1932	Fannie Guild	36500	D	1923	Fannie	37571	D	1923
Dorothy E.	61071	M	1932	**LAYDEN**				Hilda	82041	M	1939
Edwin A.	85866	I	1940	James F.	35625	D	1922	Jack	36471	D	1923
Edwin S.	70162	I	1935	Theresa	10967	D	1910	Louis	85553	D	1940
Elizabeth	76656	D	1937	**LAYKO**				Milton	86705	D	1941
Frederick M.	61071	M	1932	Amelia	79016	D	1938	**LAZCANO**			
Gilbert Gregson	55063	D	1930	**LAYMAN**				Agnes G.	41538	M	1925
Helen Burns	75039	D	1937	Emil Adolph	1237	D	1906	**LAZENBY**			
James M.	71891	D	1936	Nellie G.	80938	D	1939	John F.	81989	D	1939
John	1058	D	1906	Rebecca	19767	D	1915	R. M.	73580	D	1936
John C.	40061	D	1924	**LAYNE**				**LAZIO**			
Louis N.	78562	D	1938	Alice May	71140	D	1935	Lorenzo	32963	D	1921
Mabel	62239	I	1932	Arthur D.	85305	D	1940	**LAZOWAKI**			
Mabel F.	17140	D	1914	Frank C.	83290	D	1940	Julius Adam	79641	D	1938
Mathilde A.	10201	D	1910	Ruby L.	71842	D	1936	**LAZZARESCHI**			
Maude Jane	61071	M	1932	**LAYNG**				Turibio	60852	D	1932
Nellie	55581	D	1930	Harai R.	34165	D	1922				
Norman E.	61071	M	1932								

NAME	NUMBER	TYPE	YEAR	NAME	NUMBER	TYPE	YEAR	NAME	NUMBER	TYPE	YEAR
LAZZARI				LEAHY				LEAN			
Fortunato	11027	D	1911	Agnes Marie	80039	D	1938	John	20087	D	1915
Lorenzo	88103	D	1941	Annie E.	34142	D	1922	Robert F.	61765	I	1932
LAZZARINI				Daisy M.	66172	D	1934	Romolo	24990	M	1918
Americo	34649	D	1922	Daniel	55842	D	1930	Susie A.	85627	D	1940
Mary	60598	M	1932	Daniel F.	83386	D	1940	William P.	27101	D	1919
LAZZARO				Edward N.	42194	D	1925	LEANDER			
Gaetano	68721	D	1935	Frank Joseph	81747	M	1939	Gustaf	75363	D	1937
Tom	68721	D	1935	Frank T.	46565	D	1927	LEANDO			
LAZZERI				Hannah	57515	D	1930	Robert	71677	D	1936
Agostino	88332	I	1941	James	40994	D	1925	LEANDRI			
Antonio	39665	I	1924	James	83813	M	1940	Achille	34780	D	1922
LAZZERINI				James F.	79087	D	1938	LEAP			
Davino	67370	D	1934	Johanna	57515	D	1930	Harry	38280	D	1924
Eulalia	24667	D	1918	John	48571	D	1927	Isaac Morris	38280	D	1924
LAZZERO				John Francis	28614	D	1920	LEAR			
Cardoni	67145	D	1934	John W.	9649	D	1910	Ben E.	49091	D	1928
LE(A)SAN				Julia	4004	D	1907	LEARN			
George E.	2912	D	1907	Mary	19427	D	1915	George C.	30195	D	1920
LEA				Mary Augusta	14658	D	1912	LEARNED			
Alice E.	37953	D	1923	Mary Elizabeth	35555	D	1922	Charles Burt	33918	D	1922
Maurice D.	15045	D	1913	May E.	46741	D	1927	LEARY			
Miriam P.	84987	D	1940	Michael J.	12811	D	1912	Amelia I.	51982	D	1929
Thomas	13205	D	1912	Nellie Elizabeth	61283	D	1932	Bridget F.	53785	D	1929
LEACH				Patrick	24442	D	1918	Clara	16974	M	1914
Annette	61323	D	1932	Sarah Jane	47607	D	1927	Daniel F.	44973	D	1926
Ernest L.	71364	D	1936	Thomas	88260	D	1941	Denis	45024	D	1926
George Wanson	13788	D	1912	William H.	72617	D	1936	Edward A.	30298	D	1920
Gracia Annette	61323	D	1932	LEAK				Ellen	14080	D	1912
John	54785	D	1930	Samuel	21114	D	1916	Honorah I.	50053	D	1928
Joseph	3922	D	1907	LEAKE				James J.	57878	D	1931
Melinda T.	28442	D	1919	Bessie	68137	D	1934	John	40925	I	1925
Mira	82502	D	1939	George	296	D	1906	John	75389	D	1937
Oscar	71208	D	1935	Sam	71157	D	1935	John D.	84045	D	1940
LEAF				W. S.	71157	D	1935	Joseph L.	69864	D	1935
Albert H.	47580	D	1927	LEAL				Josephine	49059	D	1928
Rosimere L.	85231	D	1940	George	22171	M	1917	Katie E.	31432	D	1921
LEAFCRANS				Jesus G.	73526	D	1936	Margaret	29614	M	1920
Charles	66530	D	1934	John	22171	M	1917	Margaret	77178	I	1937
LEAFLAM				Joseph Azazido	60740	D	1932	Margaret A.	84046	D	1940
William	34826	D	1922	Nora	81392	I	1939	Patricia	29614	M	1920
LEAH				LEALAND				Patrick Joseph	60869	D	1932
Edith L.	88036	D	1941	John	9784	D	1910	Thomas Cox	37686	D	1923
LEAHEY				LEALE				William Henry	11017	D	1911
Margaret	1183	D	1906	Lillie	18939	D	1915	William, Mrs.	52692	D	1929
Patrick	24442	D	1918	William G.	24917	D	1918	LEAS			
				LEAMAN				Goodman C.	52053	D	1929
				Valentine	52666	D	1929				

NAME	NUMBER	TYPE	YEAR	NAME	NUMBER	TYPE	YEAR	NAME	NUMBER	TYPE	YEAR
LEASE				LEBARON				Nunzia	89183	D	1942
Charles	48745	D	1927	Andrew Johnson	80139	D	1938	LECHEVALLIER			
Isabella	48744	D	1927	Carrie	35859	D	1923	Marie	80969	D	1939
LEASEN				LEBAU				Olda	81513	D	1939
Christina	89031	D	1942	Louise	15009	D	1913	LECHNER			
LEASK				LEBEAU				Bernard A.	81744	D	1939
Robert	79164	D	1938	Helen	68789	I	1935	Charry	8872	D	1909
LEATHERS				Helen Nolan	70692	D	1935	Magda	56389	D	1930
Fred H.	87560	D	1941	LEBELLE				LECHTEN			
LEATHLEY				Leslie	22604	M	1917	A. Lorraine	19695	M	1915
William Maule	52706	D	1929	LEBENBAUM				Madeleine	19695	M	1915
LEATHURBY				Louis	50962	D	1928	LECKENBY			
Flora D.	51625	D	1928	LEBERT				A. B.	34032	D	1922
Flora Joy	51627	M	1928	Adele	42816	D	1925	LECKIE			
Flora Joy	82005	M	1939	LEBLANC				Janet E.	42287	D	1925
George Halliday	81949	D	1939	A. W.	39462	D	1924	LECLAIR			
George MacKenzie	51627	M	1928	Alexandrine	19183	D	1915	Sanford D.	66520	D	1934
George MacKenzie	82005	M	1939	Alfred	39462	D	1924	LECLAIRE			
LEAU				LEBLOND				Sarah	76721	I	1937
Francois	18509	D	1915	Eleanor V.	23269	D	1917	LECLERC			
LEAVENTHAL				LEBO				Auguste	88953	D	1942
Irma	30414	D	1920	Charles S.	26023	D	1918	LECLERCQ			
LEAVENWORTH				LEBOUTEILLIER				Emerson	37822	M	1923
John James	78924	M	1938	Helen S.	80224	D	1938	Marcelle	52829	D	1929
LEAVITT				LEBOVITZ				Mary Ruth	37822	M	1923
Albion Eastman	37010	D	1923	Coley	88976	D	1942	LECLERO			
Annie Hamlin	78782	D	1938	John Doe	88976	D	1942	Marcelle	52829	D	1929
Edgar Irving	55248	D	1930	Rose	72234	D	1936	LEDBETTER			
Flora	51204	D	1928	LEBOVSKY				William H.	35456	D	1922
John Wheeler	56457	D	1930	Isaac	59638	D	1931	LEDDEN			
Joseph Parker	18869	M	1915	LEBRECHT				Dorothea	56959	M	1930
Kate Minerva	60387	D	1931	Walter John	83466	D	1940	John A.	48313	I	1927
Margaret Rose	18869	M	1915	LEBRETON				John, Jr.	56959	M	1930
Mary Cecelia	18869	M	1915	Edward J.	9438	D	1910	Lois	56959	M	1930
Samuel Arthur	18869	M	1915	Harry S.	4352	D	1907	LEDDERHOS			
LEAVY				Julia	9551	D	1910	Albert F.	8878	M	1909
Edward Henry	37065	D	1923	Pierre	27295	D	1919	Constance M.	8878	M	1909
Ellen	68662	D	1935	LECAM				LEDDY			
Francesca S.	55223	D	1930	Angelina C.	57437	D	1930	Charles Wilfred	65196	D	1933
Franklin Maurice	29003	D	1920	Henry	57852	D	1931	Eugene A.	14650	D	1912
Jean S.	15521	D	1913	Hyacinth	57852	D	1931	George M.	23219	D	1917
Julia H.	24872	D	1918	Russell G.	16592	M	1914	Hugh	5605	D	1908
P. P. F.	24892	D	1918	Russell Glenn	35154	M	1922	Mary Frances	30569	D	1920
Patrick Francis	24892	D	1918	LECATA				Stephen	32625	D	1921
LEBALLISTER				Annunziata	89183	D	1942	Thomas	14372	D	1912
Maryetta	51619	I	1928	Luigi	85515	D	1940				

NAME	NUMBER	TYPE	YEAR	NAME	NUMBER	TYPE	YEAR	NAME	NUMBER	TYPE	YEAR
LEDERER				Chan Ah	40448	D	1924	James	43136	D	1925
Gustave	75988	D	1937	Chan Bock	40448	D	1924	James Moosey	69422	D	1935
Hans	32959	D	1921	Charles F.	31425	D	1921	James Newton	89940	M	1942
John	32959	D	1921	Charles John	78503	D	1938	James W.	50415	M	1928
LEDERHANS				Charley	26956	D	1919	Jim Let	72516	D	1936
Emma	36684	D	1923	Chin	11394	D	1911	Johanna	8972	D	1910
LEDERHAUS				Chong	71584	D	1936	John	38923	D	1924
Emma	36684	D	1923	Christine Boyd	41000	M	1925	John A.	66021	M	1934
LEDERLE				Chun	11394	D	1911	John E.	40027	I	1924
John N.	31939	D	1921	Delia	4774	D	1907	John S.	39532	D	1924
LEDERMAN				Dolores Santos	46571	D	1927	Joseph	16548	I	1913
Belle Stressburger	82375	D	1939	Dorothy	68607	M	1934	Joseph	22337	M	1917
Helene Muriel	63583	M	1933	Dorothy B.	29529	D	1920	Jung	47406	D	1927
LEDFORD				Edison	30515	M	1920	Jung Qui	63719	D	1933
Nan M.	73289	D	1936	Edward T.	34493	M	1922	Kai Ling	46783	M	1927
LEDGETT				Eliza	27751	D	1919	Kate M.	7240	D	1909
Birdie	50958	D	1928	Emily	87543	M	1941	Kwong	42160	M	1925
Charles H.	28583	D	1920	Emma M.	78282	D	1938	Kwong	84622	D	1940
Dolores	30597	M	1920	Eva	48299	D	1927	Lavinia	23906	D	1918
Dorothy	30597	M	1920	Fong Ho	63128	M	1932	Lee Goon	70682	D	1935
LEDIG				Foon	59774	D	1931	Lee Mie	40347	D	1924
Ernest	33631	D	1922	Francis Elliott	40932	I	1925	Lillian F.	37835	D	1923
LEDIN				Frank	18508	D	1915	Lily	36566	D	1923
Harry	57626	D	1931	Frank	34477	M	1922	Lincoln	40868	M	1925
LEDWIDGE				Frank Joseph	86814	D	1941	Lonnie H.	69735	D	1935
John	45793	D	1926	Gan	49882	M	1928	Louis A.	7241	D	1909
LEE				George J.	10120	M	1910	Louis Eugene	76688	D	1937
Aileen	39329	M	1924	Georgia	66021	M	1934	Lucile	86980	D	1941
Albert	43853	M	1926	Gilbert	21045	D	1916	Mabel	28560	M	1920
Alfred	77177	D	1937	Gin Wah	50413	D	1928	Malcolm J.	17940	D	1914
Alice	31924	D	1921	Gong	40347	D	1924	Margaret	13419	M	1912
Allen M.	33089	M	1921	Gooh Ho	63128	M	1932	Margaret	67692	D	1934
Allen M.	69204	M	1935	Goon Lee	70862	D	1935	Margaret Sullivan	37713	D	1923
Anna	72227	D	1936	Gunerius	21045	D	1916	Maria G.	11313	D	1911
Anthony	5907	D	1908	Hang Chung	74074	D	1936	Mary	6365	D	1908
Arthur	8776	M	1909	Harry	43853	M	1926	Mary	56428	D	1930
Barbara Jean Cowan	86960	M	1941	Helen	54972	D	1930	Mary E.	6425	D	1908
Bartholemew	4991	D	1908	Henrietta	51341	D	1928	Mary E.	48299	D	1927
Benjamin F.	17708	D	1914	Henry Richard	27996	D	1919	Mee Gin	49882	M	1928
Bent O.	2016	D	1906	Herbert A.	34493	M	1922	Michael	49134	D	1928
Bernard W.	68698	D	1935	Him	27537	D	1919	Michael	77104	D	1937
Bessie	36842	D	1923	Him	81029	D	1939	Milton A.	48388	D	1927
Bessie C.	22337	M	1917	Him Sing	45679	D	1926	Minnie E.	52280	D	1929
Bette Lou	89940	M	1942	Hong Chew	80506	D	1939	Minnie Mae	34493	M	1922
Betty Boyd	41000	M	1925	Howard C.	34493	M	1922	Montrose Lucius	84057	D	1940
Billy	78220	D	1938	Hung	42160	M	1925	Moon Wing	34477	M	1922
Chan	40448	D	1924	Irving Howard	64960	M	1933	Nancy	31407	D	1921
				Jack	39899	D	1924	Ngoot	49882	M	1928
				James	33760	D	1922	Patrick J.	73409	D	1936

NAME	NUMBER	TYPE	YEAR
Peter Olaus	45327	D	1926
Poy Fun	25472	D	1918
Que	38425	D	1924
Raymond Monroe	12346	D	1911
Raymond R.	34493	M	1922
Robert E.	34493	M	1922
Robert Maxwell	58136	M	1931
Robert S.	34986	D	1922
Robert Stevens	30349	D	1920
Rose Lucy Catherine	30706	M	1920
Roy	12879	M	1912
Sam	10578	D	1910
Samuel	55446	M	1930
Samuel James	70545	D	1935
Samuel S.	50415	M	1928
Sarah Lavinia	23906	D	1918
Sebastian	74074	D	1936
Seymour	41354	D	1925
Shee	54972	D	1930
Sing	75046	D	1937
Soo	67628	D	1934
Suey	49882	M	1928
Taft	43853	M	1926
Theresa E.	73469	D	1936
Thomas	39329	M	1924
Thomas E.	87070	D	1941
Thomas Francis	86814	D	1941
Thomas J.	12246	D	1911
Thomas S.	43447	M	1926
Tong	49882	M	1928
Victor Alvin	18607	M	1915
Victor Alvin	22710	D	1917
W. Irving	26341	D	1919
Wah	50413	D	1928
Wah June	63128	M	1932
Wah Sun	63128	M	1932
Wah Yat	63128	M	1932
Walter George	40124	M	1924
Walter T.	48959	D	1928
Wellington	85509	M	1940
William G.	69955	D	1935
William James	28555	D	1919
Willie	78220	D	1938
Wing	72430	M	1936
Wing Fai	77925	M	1938
Wing Jeung	77925	M	1938
Won	38285	D	1924
Won Ying	59774	D	1931
Wong	89619	D	1942

NAME	NUMBER	TYPE	YEAR
Yet	49882	M	1928
Yin Wah	50413	D	1928
Yow Suen	78164	D	1938
Yuan	49339	D	1928
Yue	64672	D	1933
Yuen Kwong	84622	D	1940
Yuen Loy	59538	D	1931
Yum	50351	D	1928
Yut Tye	54972	D	1930
Zelma	44780	D	1926
LEEBODY			
George William	86862	D	1941
Vivienne M.	81006	D	1939
LEECH			
Joseph F.	9695	D	1910
LEECHMAN			
John	20266	D	1916
LEEDERS			
Bertha	6907	D	1908
LEEDS			
Emma B.	41097	D	1925
Isabelle Agnes	22062	D	1917
LEEGE			
Charles F.	36924	D	1923
LEEK			
Christopher	2369	D	1906
George William	46328	D	1927
LEEMAN			
Edgar W.	42125	D	1925
Wilson F.	23653	D	1917
LEEN			
Choy	7045	M	1909
LEENMAN			
Moses	10649	D	1910
LEEOTIS			
Nadine	63440	M	1933
LEEPER			
Ernest Reasnor	68265	D	1934
Robert T.	7801	M	1909
Thomas	15684	D	1913
LEES			
Margaret E.	40236	D	1924
Ogden H.	35496	D	1922
LEESE			
Rosalie	16325	I	1913

NAME	NUMBER	TYPE	YEAR
LEESON			
Eugene	26923	D	1919
LEESONE			
Anna	50300	D	1928
LEET			
Joseph James	34620	M	1922
Loretta	34620	M	1922
LEETE			
Emma W.	75489	D	1937
LEEV			
Martin	61005	D	1932
LEFALLE			
Richard	48162	I	1927
LEFANA			
Chrispin D.	35580	D	1922
LEFEL			
R.	48162	I	1927
LEFEVRE			
Florentine Viot	10452	D	1910
Hjalmar G.	14755	D	1913
Louise M.	42106	D	1925
Marie Florentine Viot	10452	D	1910
Theodore	57631	D	1931
William	25196	D	1918
William Thomas	27872	M	1919
LEFFERT			
Henry	41557	M	1925
Herman M.	39619	D	1924
LEFFINGWELL			
Anna Frances	82060	D	1939
LEFFLER			
Eugene	35125	D	1922
LEFFMANN			
David	83188	D	1940
Sigmund T.	82442	D	1939
LEFIEF			
Frank Maxim	42283	M	1925
LEFIELL			
Alfred Edgar	88969	D	1942
LEFKOVITZ			
Harry	76883	D	1937
Isaac L.	51551	D	1928
Mary	88789	D	1941
LEFLER			
Maig Michael	40874	D	1925

NAME	NUMBER	TYPE	YEAR
LEFOR			
Augustus Loyd	19497	M	1915
Gustave	4253	M	1907
Gustave	10617	D	1910
Gustave	19497	M	1915
LEFORT			
Ethel	78679	D	1938
LEFRANCOIS			
Auguste	43554	D	1926
LEGAL			
Francois	50098	D	1928
LEGALLET			
Arthur	29219	D	1920
Georges Henry	8760	D	1909
Henri	37525	M	1923
LEGARE			
Everett Austin	38962	D	1924
LEGASPE			
Andrew James	6594	D	1908
LEGERNAS			
Ole	37955	D	1923
LEGGART			
John	59364	D	1931
LEGGE			
Harry L.	25352	D	1918
LEGGETT			
Elizabeth Widney	62006	D	1932
LEGH			
Robert P.	30255	D	1920
LEGNITTO			
Luigi	73558	D	1936
LEGOFF			
Francois	50098	D	1928
LEGONESCHE			
Henri	28233	I	1919
Herrin	30624	D	1920
LEGONESCHI			
Herrin	28233	I	1919
LEGONIDECDETRAISSAN			
Frances J. M.	27529	D	1919
LEGOSS			
Francois	50098	D	1928
LEGRAND			
Auguste	57511	D	1930
Jules	25532	M	1918
Therese	32816	D	1921

NAME	NUMBER	TYPE	YEAR
LEGRAS			
Leland Stanford	42434	D	1925
LEGRIS			
Louis H.	55805	D	1930
LEGRY			
John Horace	74745	D	1937
LEGRYS			
Anna	85341	D	1940
LEHAN			
Elizabeth	11054	D	1911
Josephine	13038	I	1912
Michael	11053	D	1911
LEHANE			
John P.	24102	D	1918
LEHANEY			
Mary E.	14391	D	1912
LEHENEY			
Mary	13316	I	1912
LEHFELDT			
Henry A.	60233	I	1931
LEHIKOINEN			
Anna	19548	D	1915
Markus	26043	D	1919
LEHMAN			
Aaron	13700	D	1912
Albert Simon	89523	I	1942
Christian T.	47770	D	1927
Dorothy	47869	M	1927
Edna	63652	I	1933
Helen A.	47765	D	1927
Louise	21957	D	1916
Lucinda	46828	D	1927
Lyman	21596	D	1916
Mathias	40698	D	1925
Nancy Caroline	22446	D	1917
LEHMANN			
Armand	48437	D	1927
Bell	66261	D	1934
Carl H.	71168	D	1935
Christian H.	23732	D	1917
Elsie	76161	D	1937
Frederike Christiana	27406	D	1919
Jennie	38372	D	1924
Marie Madeleine	77221	D	1937
Mary	76326	I	1937
Max	88675	D	1941

NAME	NUMBER	TYPE	YEAR
LEHMKER			
Frederick	86552	D	1941
LEHN			
George	7202	D	1909
LEHNER			
E. Oy R.	34783	D	1922
Elmer Herman	82269	D	1939
LEHR			
Henry	25036	D	1918
LEHRBERGER			
Jacob S.	15030	D	1913
LEHRITHER			
Elsie Delorieux	28925	D	1920
LEHRKE			
Albert W.	23688	D	1917
Alvin	20777	M	1916
Christian	11661	D	1911
Hilda	20777	M	1916
Marie	76567	D	1937
LEHRKIND			
Oscar F.	83798	D	1940
LEHTINEN			
Anna Aliza	88218	D	1941
LEHUQUET			
Thomas	53382	D	1929
LEIB			
Jane G.	40891	D	1925
Samuel	89807	D	1942
T. N.	11438	D	1911
LEIBERT			
Mary E.	1845	D	1906
LEIBING			
Louis, Mrs.	66152	D	1934
Minnie	66152	D	1934
LEIBO			
Simon	78537	D	1938
LEIBOVICI			
Minnie	51786	D	1929
LEIBOWITZ			
Anna	85368	D	1940
Morris	74559	D	1937
LEIBSON			
Alfred	77177	D	1937
LEICH			
Peter A.	26867	D	1919

NAME	NUMBER	TYPE	YEAR	NAME	NUMBER	TYPE	YEAR	NAME	NUMBER	TYPE	YEAR
LEICHNER				**LEIPSIC**				**LEITHNER**			
E.	43258	D	1925	Isaac	50818	D	1928	Henry	65050	D	1933
Katharina Elisa	43258	D	1925	Sallie	7444	D	1909	Ida L.	68402	D	1934
Modesta O.	160	D	1906	**LEIRAS**				**LEITHOFF**			
LEICHTER				Jose	49389	D	1928	Charles W.	55082	D	1930
Mary Isabel	70825	M	1935	**LEIS**				**LEITZ**			
LEIDICH				Charles Jacob	85677	D	1940	Wilhelm DeSt.Paul	52963	D	1929
Christian	27004	M	1919	**LEISCHER**				**LEJEUNE**			
Elizabeth	27004	M	1919	Philipp	43132	D	1925	Alphonse	37138	D	1923
Ernest	27004	M	1919	**LEISENRING**				**LELAND**			
Louise	25467	D	1918	Franklin S.	54880	I	1930	John	9784	D	1910
William	27004	M	1919	**LEISER**				Mary	46631	D	1927
LEIFRIED				Fred	13518	D	1912	Mary L.	75243	D	1937
Lawrence Leslie	80993	M	1939	Freda	71660	D	1936	Severt O.	86757	D	1941
LEIGH				John C.	76878	D	1937	**LELONG**			
Alice Lillie Gertrude	82330	D	1939	John L.	14160	D	1912	Charles F.	38786	D	1924
Chapman J.	30091	I	1920	Louis	23568	D	1917	**LEM**			
Ella Lees	47172	D	1927	Milton	52736	D	1929	Henry	72656	M	1936
Ella M.	47172	D	1927	Rose	56187	D	1930	Hing	76800	D	1937
Ernest A.	71213	D	1935	**LEISHMAN**				Sen	73918	D	1936
LEIGHTON				Margaret	29225	D	1920	William	72656	M	1936
Charles P.	26602	D	1919	**LEISS**				**LEMA**			
J. C.	1174	D	1906	Ernest	69892	M	1935	John	78193	D	1938
John B.	55057	D	1930	Ernst	69860	D	1935	**LEMAIRE**			
John Bickford	11147	M	1911	Gertrude	69892	M	1935	Albert, Jr.	67068	M	1934
Martin	48470	D	1927	Lawrence	69892	M	1935	**LEMAITRE**			
Sophie	48192	D	1927	**LEIST**				Auguste Fleuresse	15019	D	1913
LEIHKAM				Augusta	29678	D	1920	Jules	32497	D	1921
Carl	13772	D	1912	Charles Jasper	22246	D	1917	Marie Josephine	15020	D	1913
Carl H.	9922	M	1910	Marie Louise	16126	D	1913	**LEMAN**			
Gustl	9922	M	1910	**LEISTER**				Harold Gottlieb	18826	M	1915
LEIMBACHER				John R.	86392	D	1941	Matilda	62437	D	1932
Charles Henry	587	M	1906	**LEIT**				**LEMARCHAND**			
LEINDAN				Hannah	6484	D	1908	Margherita	85680	D	1940
John	14990	D	1913	**LEITCH**				**LEMASNEY**			
LEINDECKER				Minnie	70975	D	1935	Bertha M.	25568	D	1918
Philip	66461	D	1934	Robert L.	57058	D	1930	Laura	76929	D	1937
LEINEN				**LEITE**				**LEMASTERS**			
Agneta Catherine	33194	M	1922	Hannah	3788	I	1907	Myrtle H.	89802	D	1942
Dorthy Marie	33194	M	1922	Hannah	6484	D	1908	**LEMAY**			
Loretta Lucile	33194	M	1922	**LEITH**				Marie	60548	D	1931
LEININGER				Alexander D.	88147	D	1941	**LEMBEYE**			
Louise	77923	D	1938	David F.	50177	D	1928	Marie Laborde	25712	D	1918
LEINIO				Louisa	4744	D	1907	**LEMBI**			
Gustaf	74329	D	1937	**LEITHMER**				Annibale Joe	48731	D	1927
LEINWEBER				Lina	32596	D	1921	Cesare	59844	D	1931
Martha	26955	D	1919								

NAME	NUMBER	TYPE	YEAR	NAME	NUMBER	TYPE	YEAR	NAME	NUMBER	TYPE	YEAR
LEMBKE				Laurence Mark	83966	D	1940	**LENGEMAN**			
John	46695	D	1927	Lida	58961	D	1931	Emma	46413	D	1927
Kunigunde	69643	D	1935	**LEMOS**				**LENGENFELDER**			
LEMCKE				Annie	71973	D	1936	Fred	81928	D	1939
August	35	D	1906	Joaquim DeSousa	37216	D	1923	Johann Frederick	81928	D	1939
Otto	44829	D	1926	Joseph S.	66144	D	1934	**LENGFELD**			
Otto A.	72577	D	1936	Leon	191	D	1906	Felix	77894	D	1938
LEMEY				**LEMP**				Joseph Louis	61437	D	1932
Frank	38681	D	1924	William George	38444	D	1924	**LENIHAN**			
LEMIN				**LEMPITCKE**				James	3515	D	1907
Grace	36315	D	1923	Stanley J.	53990	I	1929	Jerry J.	45219	I	1926
LEMKAU				**LEMPKE**				**LENINGSTON**			
John	14990	D	1913	Herman D.	59471	D	1931	Harry	86804	D	1941
LEMKIN				**LEMSER**				**LENN**			
Solomon	43508	D	1926	Henry	80902	D	1939	Abe	75438	D	1937
LEMLE				**LENAHAN**				**LENNARDS**			
Leon	10013	D	1910	Joseph	13261	D	1912	Mauritz	83951	D	1940
LEMLINE				Michael	30504	D	1920	**LENNEFELT**			
Henry	44356	D	1926	Sarah	41190	D	1925	George	54747	D	1930
LEMM				**LENARD**				**LENNON**			
Charles F.	832	D	1906	Joseph	59280	D	1931	Agnes Mary	73862	M	1936
Clara Bertha	55385	D	1930	Vera	62409	M	1932	Alice	6291	M	1908
LEMMAN				**LENARDSON**				Ann	14486	D	1912
Alverdo B.	72994	D	1936	Lenore E. B.	58914	D	1931	Carmel	37548	M	1923
Blanche	72994	D	1936	Mayo E.	58913	D	1931	Charles	10490	M	1910
Mary J.	2530	D	1906	**LENARO**				Charles	79197	M	1938
LEMME				Tony	49520	D	1928	Christopher	33799	D	1922
Catherine H.	41517	I	1925	**LENCIONI**				Edith Isabelle	71770	D	1936
Emil S.	33190	D	1922	Angelo	79280	D	1938	Edward	10490	M	1910
Gertrude	38733	D	1924	Domenico	87504	D	1941	Edward P.	74150	D	1936
LEMMER				Lorenzo	80709	D	1939	Eleanor	78988	I	1938
Anne Jackman	87575	D	1941	Theresa	20854	D	1916	Ella G.	7208	D	1909
John Conrad	18082	D	1914	Vasco	43966	I	1926	Ellen	52003	D	1929
LEMMERMANN				**LENDBERG**				Francis	46551	D	1927
Herman	16512	D	1913	Betty	22321	D	1917	James	14508	D	1912
LEMMON				**LENDELOF**				Jas. E.	35526	D	1922
Harry D.	24725	D	1918	Olaf	36207	D	1923	John	6683	D	1908
LEMOGE				**LENDRUM**				John	62069	D	1932
Annie T.	70933	D	1935	William E.	22309	D	1917	John A.	40539	D	1924
LEMON				**LENDWEHR**				John A., Mrs.	22410	D	1917
Annie Teague	85201	D	1940	Caroline	4337	D	1907	John J.	3366	D	1907
Hugh F.	61147	M	1932	**LENEHAN**				Joseph	33408	I	1922
James Arthur	21461	D	1916	Hugh P.	54432	D	1929	Joseph	34748	D	1922
James H.	12342	I	1911	Mary	18961	D	1915	Leo C.	71942	D	1936
James H.	12901	D	1912	William	14250	D	1912	Margaret I.	27507	D	1919
Jeanie	10246	D	1910					Margaretta	6291	M	1908
								Marion	6291	M	1908

NAME	NUMBER	TYPE	YEAR	NAME	NUMBER	TYPE	YEAR	NAME	NUMBER	TYPE	YEAR
Mary A.	8631	D	1909	**LENZE**				Bridget	5701	I	1908
Mary A.	22410	D	1917	Conrad	20858	D	1916	Charles	41119	D	1925
Mary Ellen	52291	D	1929	Otto	68680	M	1935	Clare	89433	D	1942
Nicholas	9428	D	1910	Paulina	61657	I	1932	Comoro Carol	86006	D	1941
Rebecca	6291	M	1908	Paulina	61882	D	1932	Cynthia J.	293	D	1906
Roger	30907	D	1920	**LENZEN**				Earl Star	23521	M	1917
Sarah H.	39133	I	1924	Elmer M.	6856	M	1908	Edward Pollard	65054	D	1933
Theresa A.	79187	D	1938	Kathryn M.	6856	M	1908	Ella Glenn	79983	D	1938
Thomas Francis	88508	I	1941	Theodore W.	56240	D	1930	Ellen L.	27678	D	1919
Thomas J.	45216	D	1926	Victor F.	6856	M	1908	Emma W.	82256	D	1939
Walter J.	73935	I	1936	**LENZIE**				Ernest Matthew	23521	M	1917
William	24309	D	1918	Pauline	61882	D	1932	George	55099	D	1930
LENNOX				**LENZKE**				Grace Elta	77808	D	1938
Anna	65766	D	1933	August	23375	D	1917	Hanorah	18694	D	1915
Jane	81867	D	1939	**LEO**				Harold J.	14773	M	1913
LENNSTROM				Giovanni	63670	D	1933	Harry	25790	D	1918
Mathilda Rosina	26039	D	1919	John	63670	D	1933	James A.	54953	D	1930
LENO				Joseph Wilhelm	72872	D	1936	John	11122	D	1911
Dan	16867	D	1914	Manuel	80795	D	1939	John	11637	D	1911
LENOIR				Mary D.	39307	D	1924	John P.	12389	D	1911
Auguste	19389	D	1915	**LEOFFLER**				John P.	20157	D	1915
Charles James	41770	D	1925	Catherine	49648	D	1928	John W.	11333	D	1911
Charles James	41770	D	1925	**LEON**				John W.	50764	D	1928
Fanny	80974	D	1939	Caroline Warner	85891	D	1940	Joseph B.	80598	D	1939
Joan M.	88571	M	1941	David	25149	D	1918	Joseph F.	58895	D	1931
Marie	81708	I	1939	Edward H.	20160	D	1915	Julia A.	83389	D	1940
Marie	85257	D	1940	Fellows	20162	M	1915	Kathryn Marie	51124	D	1928
LENORMAND				Fermin	73184	D	1936	Katie	14556	D	1912
Joseph	23505	D	1917	George A.	82520	D	1939	Lester Paul	23521	M	1917
Leon	14576	I	1912	George H.	20162	M	1915	Lewis	26565	D	1919
Leon	20684	D	1916	Grace M.	20162	M	1915	Margaret	79794	D	1938
Martha Bena	75068	D	1937	Herbert A.	73920	D	1936	Margaret A.	75782	D	1937
Mary	16681	D	1914	Hulda	23917	D	1918	Martin	26895	D	1919
LENOX				Leon	89468	D	1942	Mary	20670	D	1916
John	72691	D	1936	Margaret	18677	D	1915	Mary C.	20543	D	1916
Lionel R.	47807	D	1927	Maria	45597	D	1926	Mary C.	51124	D	1928
LENT				Marvin	20162	M	1915	Mary Elizabeth	12091	I	1911
Eugene	75815	D	1937	Mary Grace	20161	D	1915	Mary J.	45489	D	1926
LENTHOLD				Sallee	57356	D	1930	Mary Lee	45268	D	1926
John	47040	D	1927	Sally	56846	I	1930	Mathilda E.	40335	D	1924
LENTZ				William	58935	M	1931	May	85529	D	1940
Frederick W.	31158	D	1921	**LEONARD**				Michael Joseph	81716	D	1939
LENZ				Agnes	66460	D	1934	Stephen	17690	D	1914
William	15181	D	1913	Alexander T.	81885	D	1939	Thomas	63009	D	1932
LENZDORF				Alfred	87498	D	1941	Walter	86791	D	1941
Mary	58271	D	1931	Annie	75782	D	1937	Walter Peter	23521	M	1917
				Bella M.	22622	D	1917	William John	23521	M	1917
				Betty T.	66295	M	1934	**LEONARDI**			
								Carlo	25367	M	1918

 Key: D = death; M = minor; I = incompetent

NAME	NUMBER	TYPE	YEAR
Fanny Florence Gorla	88460	D	1941
Giovannina Righini	52575	D	1929
Giuditta	25367	M	1918
Irene	25367	M	1918
Mariano	56894	D	1930
Mary	60949	I	1932
Vittorino	25367	M	1918
LEONARDINI			
Antone	41580	D	1925
Dominica	78690	D	1938
John Louis	78500	D	1938
Maria	67402	D	1934
Pietro	69607	D	1935
LEONARDO			
Carretto	16074	D	1913
Ceretto	13416	I	1912
LEONE			
Angelo	46172	D	1927
Charles	2107	M	1906
Donata	58360	D	1931
Frankie	2107	M	1906
LEONETTI			
Antonio	56185	D	1930
LEONG			
Albert	16064	M	1913
Chew Quong	55225	M	1930
Chin Wing	56339	M	1930
Chin Wing	59531	M	1931
Fong	81751	D	1939
Fook Kay	52933	D	1929
Gee	68041	D	1934
Geet	77015	D	1937
Henry C.	67739	D	1934
Jessie	55225	M	1930
Kow	60097	D	1931
Lilly	16064	M	1913
Robert	88873	D	1942
See Nam	60198	D	1931
She Gee	88873	D	1942
Shee	81751	D	1939
Shee Yuen	59269	D	1931
Sook Kay	52933	D	1929
Tang Yok Kin	24123	M	1918
Tom See	58195	D	1931
Tom Shee	58195	D	1931
Wah	82097	D	1939
Wing	81293	D	1939
Wong Hing	81751	D	1939

NAME	NUMBER	TYPE	YEAR
Yuen Chung	68041	D	1934
LEONHARDT			
Albert A.	62518	D	1932
Carl Elliott	54716	M	1930
Nellie C.	76081	D	1937
Vivian	54716	M	1930
LEONIE			
Annie	73909	D	1936
Jung	54579	I	1929
LEOPOLD			
Adolf	74178	D	1936
B. Adolf	74178	D	1936
George A.	21402	D	1916
Gustav	74178	D	1936
Hannah	56248	D	1930
Henry A.	59973	D	1931
Johanna	56248	D	1930
LEOPOULOS			
George	63803	D	1933
LEPETICH			
Andrew	59045	D	1931
Chris	68512	D	1934
LEPHAKIS			
John	25118	D	1918
LEPI			
Mary	80081	M	1938
LEPIC			
Charlotte Louise Clare	16300	M	1913
Ghislaine Jeanna Marie	16300	M	1913
Napoleon Charles Louis	16300	M	1913
LEPINIEC			
Emile	66666	D	1934
Jules Joicken Lamotte	20253	D	1916
LEPKEY			
Anna T.	26751	D	1919
Jane	26749	D	1919
Lewis O.	26750	D	1919
Mary J.	26749	D	1919
Theresa	26751	D	1919
LEPLIN			
James B.	60918	I	1932
LEPORI			
Ernest E.	82075	D	1939
LEPPER			
Helen Marie	21713	M	1916
John	21189	D	1916
Waldemar	13911	D	1912

NAME	NUMBER	TYPE	YEAR
LEPPLA			
Carl	24640	D	1918
LEPRA			
Charles	74272	D	1936
Maria	50873	D	1928
LEPREUX			
Rene	1195	D	1906
LEQUESNE			
Edward	43195	D	1925
LERABLE			
Josephine	7093	D	1909
LERCARI			
Chiara	80122	D	1938
Chiara	75600	I	1937
Clara	75600	I	1937
Clara	80122	D	1938
Erminia	52311	D	1929
Giacomo	85281	D	1940
LERCH			
Hermina E.	63532	D	1933
LERDA			
Edward J.	73763	I	1936
Lawrence	42216	D	1925
Lorenzo	42216	D	1925
Margherita	28928	M	1920
Rosa	28928	M	1920
LERER			
David S.	69075	I	1935
Joseph	64433	D	1933
Markus	45241	D	1926
LERHKE			
Anna	19368	D	1915
LERIALLES			
Lorita	79351	D	1938
LERICHE			
Armand Joseph	53263	D	1929
LERIGER			
Raoul P.	41313	D	1925
LERIOS			
Andrew Margarites	39563	M	1924
Fila	39564	D	1924
George Margarites	39563	M	1924
Peter Margarites	39563	M	1924
LERIOTIS			
Pantalia D.	6030	D	1908

NAME	NUMBER	TYPE	YEAR
LERMOND			
Emma Lillian	73390	D	1936
Lillian	73390	D	1936
LERNER			
Evelyn	34318	M	1922
Joseph	34318	M	1922
Samuel	33167	D	1922
LEROND			
Clorinda	18718	D	1915
Frederica	52475	D	1929
LEROY			
Ione	88975	D	1942
Marie	75279	I	1937
LERTORA			
Albert Eugene	38179	D	1924
Attilio J.	18173	D	1914
LERUM			
Harry John	70779	D	1935
LERVOOG			
Ollie	44064	D	1926
LESACK			
Edward	16461	D	1913
LESAGE			
Blanche	5592	I	1908
Charles	5591	I	1908
LESE			
Rosa	81285	D	1939
LESLIE			
Ellis	13641	M	1912
Ernest	13641	M	1912
George Adam	30096	D	1920
George Darby	28640	D	1920
H. M., Mrs.	15518	D	1913
John	79765	I	1938
John	79906	D	1938
Mollie	15518	D	1913
Mona	13641	M	1912
Thomas	12883	D	1912
William Meldrum	30795	I	1920
LESS			
Adolph	41945	M	1925
Adolph	41945	M	1925
Samuel	24564	D	1918
LESSARD			
Jennie E.	42734	D	1925
LESSER			
Aaron	71184	D	1935

NAME	NUMBER	TYPE	YEAR
Anna	54183	D	1929
Edward A.	84818	D	1940
Elziabeth	38960	D	1924
Harry	79886	D	1938
Irving	4838	M	1907
Irving	9918	M	1910
J. L.	9890	D	1910
Jacob	80016	D	1938
Jessie	85465	D	1940
Julia	4878	D	1907
Julia	18612	D	1915
Lena	49179	D	1928
Lesser	9890	D	1910
Maige	54183	D	1929
Michael	73911	D	1936
Mondae	4838	M	1907
Sol	4838	M	1907
Sol L.	9918	M	1910
LESSIONS			
Ellen	15872	D	1913
LESSMAN			
Ricka	73680	D	1936
Rieka	73680	D	1936
LESSMANN			
Elizabeth Kunigunda	23003	M	1917
Francisca Theresia	23003	M	1917
Frank Bernard	23003	M	1917
Marie Christine	23003	M	1917
LESSOW			
Margaret C.	82996	D	1939
LESTER			
Charles	17239	D	1914
Frank	29946	D	1920
Henry Charles	19783	D	1915
Henry Cornelius	46886	D	1927
Karolina	11204	D	1911
Nathan L.	82788	D	1939
Thomas J.	39014	D	1924
LESTRANGE			
Elvira M.	34650	D	1922
James G.	39798	D	1924
LESTROHAN			
Felix Pierre Martin	17766	D	1914
Paul F.	18026	M	1914
Yvonne G.	18026	M	1914
LESUEUR			
Anton P.	2124	D	1906

NAME	NUMBER	TYPE	YEAR
LESYAK			
Joseph	83185	D	1940
LESZINSKY			
Gus	24981	I	1918
LESZYNSKY			
Frances	19051	D	1915
Hannah L.	66405	D	1934
Hattie L.	66406	D	1934
Samuel L.	20631	D	1916
LET			
Lee Jim	72516	D	1936
LETCHER			
Donald Eugene	79833	M	1938
Kenneth Illtred	79833	M	1938
LETCHFIELD			
Belta	42502	D	1925
LETER			
Charles	54982	D	1930
LETERME			
A. Z.	7615	D	1909
LETHERLAND			
Daisy	76591	D	1937
LETSON			
Harry Curtis	86477	D	1941
LETTICH			
Christine Alexine	66395	D	1934
M.	38710	D	1924
LETTS			
John Hughes	84198	D	1940
LEU			
Robert C.	61110	D	1932
LEUDEMANN			
Wilhelm	84305	I	1940
LEUENBERGER			
Ida H.	74119	D	1936
Paul M.	73158	D	1936
LEUHRS			
Henry P.	66469	I	1934
LEUKEL			
Christian	66493	D	1934
LEUNG			
Choy Ling	88831	M	1942
Choy Ming	88831	M	1942
Henry C.	67739	D	1934
LEUPOLD			
Arnim B.	21768	D	1916

NAME	NUMBER	TYPE	YEAR
Johann Friedrich Wilhelm	32301	D	1921
William	32301	D	1921
LEUREY			
Louis F.	65690	D	1933
LEURS			
Charlotte A.	24544	D	1918
Jane Ellen	15946	M	1913
LEUTHOLD			
Fred	68319	D	1934
John	47040	D	1927
LEUTZA			
Lena	72136	D	1936
Peter A.	57312	D	1930
LEV			
Israel	88857	D	1942
LEVACH			
Alexander	36492	D	1923
LEVAGGI			
Bernardo	53484	D	1929
Jules	46856	D	1927
Mary	53485	D	1929
LEVARONI			
Carlo	39440	D	1924
LEVE			
Joseph F.	24839	I	1918
Joseph F.	25127	D	1918
Joseph F., Jr.	12327	D	1911
Marcus S.	65765	D	1933
LEVE'			
Barbara	73880	M	1936
LEVEE			
Emmer	41192	D	1925
LEVEILLE			
Alran Frank	82949	M	1939
Bridget Lacey	52510	D	1929
Bridget M.	52510	D	1929
Frank	82949	M	1939
Margaret	52510	D	1929
LEVEN			
Bernard	57715	M	1931
LEVENBERG			
Edward E.	46125	I	1927
Edward E.	78643	I	1938
George	67230	D	1934
Milicent	81010	D	1939

NAME	NUMBER	TYPE	YEAR
LEVENE			
Albert I.	50650	D	1928
Pauline M.	69899	D	1935
LEVENSALER			
Joseph G.	36309	D	1923
LEVENSON			
Ethel Rose	18140	D	1914
Meyer David	16012	D	1913
Samuel M.	43149	D	1925
Sophie Ethel	9613	D	1910
LEVENTIS			
Nicholaos Christon	45117	D	1926
LEVENTRES			
Nicholas	45117	D	1926
LEVENTRITT			
Alvin H.	57404	D	1930
Edgar M.	82247	D	1939
Frances	59418	D	1931
Marion	66630	D	1934
Olivia	85563	D	1940
LEVERATTO			
Gio Batta	6572	D	1908
LEVERIDGE			
Henry William	78623	D	1938
LEVERMANN			
Juliane	80255	D	1939
LEVERONE			
Agostino	48875	D	1928
Amelia	85347	D	1940
Isabelle M.	55770	D	1930
Richard	44716	D	1926
LEVERONI			
Amelia	85347	D	1940
Charles	59693	M	1931
Elesio	59693	M	1931
Emilia	57677	D	1931
John	38374	D	1924
Louis	57697	D	1931
Luigi	34116	D	1922
Nicola	14915	D	1913
Richard	44716	D	1926
Rolando	62358	D	1932
LEVERS			
Elizabeth	79781	D	1938
Frederick	38543	D	1924
LEVETAG			
Ernst	63199	D	1932

NAME	NUMBER	TYPE	YEAR
LEVEY			
Benjamin	69161	I	1935
Charles C.	47848	D	1927
Charles M.	53334	D	1929
Charles, Mrs.	75365	D	1937
David L.	55279	D	1930
Emma Hintze	62936	D	1932
Herbert A.	37327	D	1923
Isadore Coleman	35033	D	1922
Johanna B.	10491	D	1910
Kate	64146	D	1933
Lewis C.	43257	D	1925
Matilde	75365	D	1937
Norma Madeline	75400	M	1937
Wesley	12840	M	1912
LEVI			
Bertha M.	89439	D	1942
Emilia	69842	D	1935
Fannie	49480	D	1928
Frances Teresa	19328	M	1915
Herman	50217	D	1928
Isaac Charles	31550	D	1921
Jacob, Jr.	10894	D	1910
Jacob, Sr.	6025	D	1908
Joseph	69479	I	1935
Mark	54993	D	1930
Rosa	54147	D	1929
Veronica Jean	85962	M	1941
LEVICK			
Ada B.	6381	D	1908
LEVIE			
Alexander J.	52772	D	1929
Lila	10771	D	1910
LEVIN			
Abraham	3377	D	1907
Abraham	39404	D	1924
Billie Dorothy	29625	M	1920
Edward	87370	M	1941
Floyd	61467	I	1932
Frances	73999	D	1936
Fredricka	8947	D	1910
Gustaf Ernest	80207	D	1938
Herman	68634	D	1935
Ida	45009	D	1926
Isadore	20938	D	1916
Jacob	6241	D	1908
Joseph	26866	D	1919
Julius	77621	D	1938

NAME	NUMBER	TYPE	YEAR
Lewis Benjamin	29625	M	1920
Louis	76723	D	1937
Louis J.	81148	D	1939
Ludwig	81274	D	1939
Martin	76283	D	1937
Mary	13388	I	1912
Mary	71669	D	1936
Matilda B.	27553	D	1919
Maurice E.	87158	D	1941
Max	33934	D	1922
Mendel	76283	D	1937
Minnie	80190	I	1938
Minnie	80442	D	1939
Morris	60545	D	1931
Rachael	37230	D	1923
Ray	37230	D	1923
Richard Grant	85264	M	1940
Robert	23236	D	1917
Robert	76816	D	1937
Sarah	45443	D	1926
Solomon	80922	D	1939
Susman	14072	I	1912
Susman	15815	D	1913
Wilfred	28954	D	1920
LEVINE			
Aaron	3926	D	1907
Esther	4718	D	1907
Harry	83762	D	1940
Julian B.	4677	M	1907
Rebecca	88578	D	1941
LEVINEY			
Louis S.	62912	D	1932
LEVINGER			
Benjamin M.	78923	D	1938
Jonas	66658	D	1934
LEVINGSTON			
Harry	86804	D	1941
Sallie	65588	D	1933
LEVINGSTONE			
Charles	46052	D	1926
LEVINS			
David	7020	D	1909
Mary R.	36069	I	1923
Mary R.	42189	D	1925
Peter	6960	D	1908
LEVINSKY			
Lesser	1476	D	1906
Louis	1476	D	1906

NAME	NUMBER	TYPE	YEAR
Mark	12851	D	1912
Rose	49081	D	1928
LEVINSOHN			
Thomas O.	43773	D	1926
LEVINSON			
Charles	35329	D	1922
Emma	47887	D	1927
Gertrude	16824	D	1914
Harry	68459	D	1934
Solomon	41646	D	1925
Thomas O.	43773	D	1926
LEVIS			
Charles	21557	D	1916
Johanna	119	D	1906
LEVISON			
Alexander	60573	D	1931
David	52455	D	1929
Emma	51213	D	1928
Hulda	73955	D	1936
Mark	4874	D	1907
Robert J.	45208	I	1926
Sarah	84392	D	1940
LEVISTON			
George	4969	D	1908
Stella Boole	88409	D	1941
Stella M.	66242	D	1934
William	539	D	1906
LEVIT			
Jeanette	64328	D	1933
Samuel	51889	D	1929
LEVITIN			
Boni	70681	D	1935
Mary	49894	D	1928
LEVITT			
Anna	65484	D	1933
Benjamin F.	40584	D	1924
Joseph	59549	D	1931
Ruth Helene	84805	D	1940
LEVITZKY			
Rosa	38245	D	1924
LEVY			
Aaron	3631	D	1907
Aaron	30797	D	1920
Aaron B.	47985	D	1927
Abraham	14053	D	1912
Abraham Hart	23268	D	1917
Abraham S.	54262	D	1929

NAME	NUMBER	TYPE	YEAR
Adolf	24466	D	1918
Adrian	25032	D	1918
Adrien	61929	D	1932
Alexander	57709	D	1931
Alfred	55626	D	1930
Alice	5575	M	1908
Amelia	4858	D	1907
Amelia	37139	D	1923
Amelia	42025	D	1925
Amelia Bloom	66003	D	1934
Anna	23149	D	1917
Annie	54856	D	1930
Aron	3631	D	1907
Arthur William	62758	M	1932
Bella Greenberg	55555	D	1930
Belle	45283	D	1926
Belle G.	70590	D	1935
Benjamin	56472	D	1930
Benjamin	77469	D	1938
Bernice Regina	62758	M	1932
Bertha	26553	D	1919
Bertha	31826	D	1921
Bertha	83595	D	1940
Bertha	83615	D	1940
Bessie	85504	I	1940
Betta	31826	D	1921
Burton	23658	M	1917
Cap B.	77469	D	1938
Catherine	17459	D	1914
Charles L.	80740	D	1939
Charlotte L.	4248	D	1907
Charlotte L.	26879	D	1919
Clara	1613	D	1906
Cyril	17775	M	1914
Daniel	9346	D	1910
David	62156	D	1932
David	70557	D	1935
David S.	34844	D	1922
Donald Ellis	80476	M	1939
Dora	18316	D	1914
Dora	87637	D	1941
Edgar	5575	M	1908
Edgar	16503	D	1913
Edward	22270	D	1917
Edward L.	46264	D	1927
Elias Abraham	62881	D	1932
Emanuel	70747	D	1935
Emanuel A.	44383	D	1926
Emile	23346	D	1917

NAME	NUMBER	TYPE	YEAR	NAME	NUMBER	TYPE	YEAR	NAME	NUMBER	TYPE	YEAR
Emma B.	80044	D	1938	Joseph	50110	D	1928	Pauline	58238	I	1931
Emma R.	37913	D	1923	Joseph	65709	D	1933	Peppie	3518	D	1907
Enid	605	M	1906	Joseph	54230	D	1929	Phil	58915	D	1931
Esther	18408	M	1915	Joseph H.	55153	D	1930	Philip P.	77695	D	1938
Esther	49591	D	1928	Joseph M.	83433	D	1940	Rachel	15949	D	1913
Esther	57566	D	1931	Joseph William	28931	D	1920	Rae E.	76687	D	1937
Eugene W.	47891	D	1927	Julian	19327	M	1915	Ralph A.	83690	D	1940
Evaline A.	31436	D	1921	Julius	50338	D	1928	Raphael	41811	D	1925
Fannie	34167	D	1922	Leah	43792	D	1926	Raphael	41811	D	1925
Fanny	82263	I	1939	Lemman	37117	D	1923	Ray	20791	I	1916
Fernand	8418	D	1909	Lena	11677	D	1911	Rebecca	42305	D	1925
Flora	51204	D	1928	Leon	21619	D	1916	Rebecca	72797	D	1936
Florence Amelia	20999	M	1916	Leonie	49274	D	1928	Reuben	67606	D	1934
Florence E.	44602	D	1926	Louis	11783	D	1911	Rosalie	3363	D	1907
Florence Selles	30705	I	1920	Louis	15539	D	1913	Rose	87828	D	1941
Frederick H.	20411	D	1916	Louis	84846	D	1940	Rose	88885	D	1942
Harris	26166	D	1919	Louis	64701	D	1933	Rosine S.	24246	D	1918
Henrietta	82639	D	1939	Lucy	21784	D	1916	Roy	17775	M	1914
Henry	3968	D	1907	Lucy H. M.	78404	D	1938	Rueben	3074	D	1907
Henry	10953	D	1910	M.	298	D	1906	Sam, Mrs.	58238	I	1931
Henry	23976	D	1918	Mannie	35854	I	1923	Samuel	54065	D	1929
Henry	24290	D	1918	Marcus	527	D	1906	Samuel	75551	D	1937
Henry M.	6074	D	1908	Marie B.	49677	D	1928	Samuel G.	52476	D	1929
Henry Raphael	49201	D	1928	Mark Washington	45709	D	1926	Samuel W.	20446	D	1916
Herbert C.	25602	D	1918	Marks D.	4271	D	1907	Sidney	10731	M	1910
Herman	19209	D	1915	Martin	88588	D	1941	Sigmund B.	64987	D	1933
Herman	39481	D	1924	Mary	33124	D	1921	Simon	39492	D	1924
Herman M.	6074	D	1908	Mary Elizabetn	51268	M	1928	Solomon	1687	D	1906
Herman M.	26714	D	1919	Matthias	34518	D	1922	Solomon J.	6726	D	1908
Hulda	47732	D	1927	Max	34518	D	1922	Sophie A.	18701	D	1915
Hulda E.	32355	D	1921	Max	71468	D	1936	Sylvain S.	33155	D	1922
Isaac	61800	D	1932	Max H.	46438	D	1927	Theo	17775	M	1914
Isabella	74	D	1906	Max, Mrs.	37913	D	1923	Theodor M.	7781	M	1909
Isidore N.	70195	D	1935	Maxwell	58649	D	1931	Theodore Martin	81929	D	1939
Isidore W.	43583	D	1926	May	39105	D	1924	Theresa M.	77285	D	1937
Jack M.	70520	D	1935	Melville S.	31101	D	1921	Theresa Z.	66504	D	1934
Jacob	4977	D	1908	Merrill	23658	M	1917	Tillie	5575	M	1908
Jacob	12751	D	1911	Milton	19327	M	1915	Tillie	7232	I	1909
Jacob	35897	D	1923	Mindell	53024	I	1929	Tillie	20191	D	1915
Jacob	55654	D	1930	Mindell	53413	D	1929	Victorine	22203	D	1917
Jane	71422	D	1936	Morris	11344	D	1911	W. Beatriz	47416	D	1927
Jeette	20099	D	1915	Morris	24574	D	1918	Wesley	12840	M	1912
Jennie S.	73868	D	1936	Morris Bernhard	1376	D	1906	William Irwin	70239	M	1935
Jenny	23283	D	1917	Moses L.	72974	D	1936	Wolff	32917	D	1921
Jesse H.	82381	D	1939	Myer S.	21714	D	1916	Yetta	20099	D	1915
Johanna	15950	D	1913	Natalia	28450	D	1919	**LEW**			
John Joseph	6860	D	1908	Nyman	70780	D	1935	Fau Wing	83322	M	1940
Joseph	23658	M	1917	Oscar S.	12287	D	1911	Fay Wah	83322	M	1940
Joseph	37987	D	1923	Pauline	10594	D	1910	Lim	46816	D	1927

NAME	NUMBER	TYPE	YEAR	NAME	NUMBER	TYPE	YEAR	NAME	NUMBER	TYPE	YEAR
Martin	61005	D	1932	**LEWINGTON**				George A.	67161	M	1934
LEWALD				Susette	54648	D	1930	George B.	53978	D	1929
Cecilia	40836	D	1925	**LEWIS**				George Henry	78632	D	1938
Constance	64455	M	1933	Abraham	14526	D	1912	George Neathaway, Jr.	60314	M	1931
Rose	89072	D	1942	Adina	42867	D	1925	Gurdon H.	78047	D	1938
Samuel	3753	D	1907	Albert	35152	D	1922	Harriet G.	10847	D	1910
Sanford G.	64365	D	1933	Alfred	56602	D	1930	Harry	78632	D	1938
LEWANDOWSKI				Alice	17987	D	1914	Harry C.	35463	D	1922
Helene	4348	D	1907	Alice	58756	D	1931	Hattie T.	44011	D	1926
LEWARNE				Alice Louise	66799	M	1934	Helena Adriana	60313	D	1931
Hallie Louise	60007	D	1931	Alvaretta	83928	D	1940	Henrietta	36558	D	1923
Harriet Louise	60007	D	1931	Amelia J.	53595	D	1929	Hilda T.	48308	D	1927
LEWEK				Annie	35984	D	1923	Howard Earnest	69397	D	1935
Alice M.	86151	D	1941	Audrey	40374	M	1924	Isabella	44868	D	1926
Henry	78208	D	1938	Bertha	27366	D	1919	Isidor	28887	D	1920
LEWEKE				Bessie	54582	D	1929	Jack F.	72465	M	1936
Christine	13828	D	1912	Betty Jane	36477	M	1923	James Edward	32041	I	1921
LEWELLEN				Blanche	89937	D	1942	James H.	9514	D	1910
Wilson	19049	D	1915	Caroline	66862	D	1934	Jane	14150	D	1912
LEWELLYN				Caroline H.	28839	D	1920	Jennie	13972	M	1912
Mary Ann	17661	D	1914	Carroll G.	67317	D	1934	Jennie	20495	D	1916
LEWENHAUPT				Charles	30858	D	1920	John	69251	M	1935
Azalea Caroline	40827	D	1925	Charles Conrad	55469	D	1930	John B.	6544	D	1908
Jan Casimir	40898	M	1925	Charles Edward	46397	D	1927	John B.	64641	D	1933
LEWENTHAL				Charles F.	83704	D	1940	John Daniels	60314	M	1931
Hannah	3712	D	1907	Charles L.	71694	D	1936	John Morgan	41066	M	1925
Jacob W.	77304	D	1937	Charles Laurie	86242	M	1941	John T.	4418	D	1907
LEWERS				Charles Thomas	14273	D	1912	John T.	38474	D	1924
Charles P.	28838	D	1920	Clara May	89042	D	1942	Joseph R.	71019	D	1935
LEWERT				Clare	41358	M	1925	Julia M.	64973	D	1933
Frieda	53306	D	1929	Clarence E.	38846	D	1924	Kate	22507	D	1917
LEWIN				David H.	47439	D	1927	Katie E.	81179	D	1939
Alexander E.	3664	D	1907	David Oldham	1357	D	1906	Katrine D.	62635	D	1932
Anna Rosalie	21778	D	1916	Donald C.	67161	M	1934	Kenneth	47584	M	1927
Arthur	40637	D	1924	Dorothy M.	89078	D	1942	Laura	80714	D	1939
Bertha Levy	26553	D	1919	Earl C.	52968	I	1929	Leslie G.	30046	M	1920
Felice Sidonia	40646	M	1924	Edna A.	41016	I	1925	Lottie A.	29855	D	1920
Harry	43498	D	1926	Edward	80265	D	1939	Lottie E.	29855	D	1920
Helmut	43498	D	1926	Edward G.	48845	D	1927	Mable Anderson	65891	D	1933
Hugo Elias	20861	I	1916	Elizabeth	4157	D	1907	Madge M.	56263	D	1930
Hugo Elias	21992	D	1916	Ellis	43319	D	1926	Manuel E.	71143	D	1935
Jacob	52391	D	1929	Emelie L.	27556	D	1919	Manuel G., Jr.	81631	D	1939
Joseph S.	67672	D	1934	Eva L.	67997	I	1934	Marcus	27001	D	1919
Leon	39473	D	1924	Evelyn	68884	I	1935	Margaet Dorothy	66799	M	1934
Peter	89180	D	1942	Fannie E.	43315	D	1926	Marie G.	5572	D	1908
Sadie	28994	D	1920	Florence	36904	M	1923	Marie M.	60448	D	1931
Theresa	66637	D	1934	Frank	4206	D	1907	Marion	74768	D	1937
				Frank R.	63163	D	1932	Mark E.	7740	D	1909
				Freda Benny	68490	D	1934	Marks	4145	D	1907

NAME	NUMBER	TYPE	YEAR	NAME	NUMBER	TYPE	YEAR	NAME	NUMBER	TYPE	YEAR
Martha	47733	I	1927	J., Mrs.	49508	D	1928	**LIBBEY**			
Mary Ann	44363	D	1926	Joseph	5869	D	1908	Katherine	71501	D	1936
Mary E.	68884	I	1935	Rose	49508	D	1928	**LIBBING**			
Mary Evelyn	72895	D	1936	Ruza	47188	I	1927	Anna Maria	70500	D	1935
Mary H.	13794	D	1912	Ruza	49508	D	1928	**LIBBRA**			
Mary Jane	69251	M	1935	**LEWOHL**				Elmira	49647	D	1928
Mary Josephine	65084	D	1933	Antone A.	44392	D	1926	**LIBBY**			
Mary T.	31919	D	1921	**LEWOLD**				Burr A.	84268	D	1940
Meyer	9600	D	1910	Rose	89072	D	1942	Catherine	43074	D	1925
Oscar	24467	D	1918	**LEWTON**				Catherine F.	78607	D	1938
Rachel	73537	D	1936	Jennie M.	46127	D	1927	Dorville	23910	D	1918
Richard	31160	D	1921	**LEWYS**				Josephine S.	38542	D	1924
Robert	75859	D	1937	Abbie Carington	41494	D	1925	Katherine A.	35333	D	1922
Robert L.	86537	D	1941	Emlyn	48198	D	1927	Louise Elizabeth	49192	D	1928
Robert N.	64324	D	1933	**LEXOW**				Warren Thompson	19097	D	1915
Rosa	16166	D	1913	Elise	87288	D	1941	Willis	6916	D	1908
Rosalie	11576	D	1911	**LEY**				**LIBERMAN**			
Rosanna	24094	M	1918	Abraham	50429	D	1928	Joseph J.	87206	D	1941
Rose Frances	62944	D	1932	Francisco	35887	D	1923	**LIBERTY**			
Rose Poebe	60477	D	1931	**LEYDEN**				Adele	15228	D	1913
Samuel	65216	D	1933	Edna Hammel Castelberg	20054	D	1915	**LIBONATI**			
Samuel L.	8374	M	1909	**LEYDON**				Rafael	56860	D	1930
Sarah	4399	D	1907	Michael	40681	D	1925	**LICATA**			
Sarah A.	64614	D	1933	**LEYERS**				Giuseppi	8655	D	1909
Sarah Alice	600	D	1906	Anna	40284	D	1924	Luigi	85515	D	1940
Solomon	10079	D	1910	**LEYKUM**				**LICAVOLI**			
Sophia	36028	D	1923	John F.	49554	D	1928	Anna	58822	D	1931
Sydney Ries	79761	D	1938	**LEYLAND**				Giovanni	52577	D	1929
Sydney Sam	86242	M	1941	William	19438	D	1915	Natale	55645	M	1930
Theresa	64558	I	1933	**LEYVA**				**LICE**			
Theresa	73376	D	1936	Narciso	21010	D	1916	Jacques	81309	D	1939
Viola Marian	60314	M	1931	**LEZER**				**LICHENSTEIN**			
William	12969	D	1912	Charles	81304	D	1939	Abraham	769	D	1906
William	34964	D	1922	**LEZIN**				Johanna	358	D	1906
William	64902	D	1933	Jean Saint	38270	D	1924	**LICHT**			
William A.	62320	I	1932	**LEZINSKY**				Eda	66076	D	1934
William H.	81805	D	1939	George	32666	D	1921	Henry	40677	D	1925
William Kidd	2482	D	1906	**LEZOTT**				James	39945	D	1924
LEWISON				Ida	47082	D	1927	Max	74751	D	1937
Jacob Louis	61314	D	1932	**LEZOTTE**				Simon L.	74750	D	1937
LEWITT				Ida	21752	I	1916	**LICHTENBERG**			
Frederick Clinton	59131	D	1931	**LIAL**				Edward F.	30278	M	1920
Susie Emma	52265	D	1929	Manuel F.	46315	D	1927	Fannie	68239	D	1934
William B.	31687	D	1921	**LIAPIS**				Leopold	70743	D	1935
LEWKOWITZ				Anastasia D.	79810	D	1938	Malvina	15859	D	1913
George	51524	I	1928					Remy	30278	M	1920
George	55404	I	1930								
J., Mrs.	47188	I	1927								

NAME	NUMBER	TYPE	YEAR
LICHTENBERGER			
Paul Hermann	69674	D	1935
LICHTENFELD			
William	26996	D	1919
LICHTENSTEDT			
Henry	44271	D	1926
LICHTENSTEIN			
Abraham	68113	D	1934
Benjamin M.	3987	D	1907
Bessie M.	3986	D	1907
Cyril	12256	M	1911
Henrietta	84224	D	1940
Isadore H.	64697	D	1933
Leopold	48262	D	1927
Moses H.	16497	D	1913
Philip	52405	D	1929
LICHTER			
Valentine	48710	I	1927
LICHTIG			
Helen	390	M	1906
LICHTNG			
Helen	390	M	1906
LICK			
E. W., Mrs.	76182	D	1937
Eugene W.	52297	D	1929
John H.	4417	D	1907
Stella H.	76182	D	1937
LICURSI			
Francesco	66147	D	1934
LIDDELL			
Lottie A.	34568	I	1922
LIDDLE			
Edwin Elliot	16109	D	1913
Mary Isabelle	57550	D	1930
Matthew George	16934	M	1914
LIDICH			
Louisa	25467	D	1918
LIE			
Peter	45327	D	1926
LIEB			
Adam Henry	67302	D	1934
Christian F.	45062	D	1926
Earl Robert	78675	D	1938
Earl Robert, Jr.	72845	M	1936
Ellen	64673	D	1933
Elmo B.	20795	D	1916
Elmo B.	56178	D	1930

NAME	NUMBER	TYPE	YEAR
Frederick Christian	45062	D	1926
Friederick H.	65434	D	1933
Jamima Bonsall	18791	D	1915
Julia Frederica	59864	D	1931
Louisa Marie	70859	D	1935
LIEBE			
George Alfred	21740	M	1916
George V.	67010	D	1934
Henry	46588	I	1927
Henry	78830	D	1938
William	60183	D	1931
LIEBENBERG			
Johanna	11543	D	1911
LIEBER			
Leopold	27131	D	1919
LIEBERT			
Henry	4288	D	1907
Johanna	82806	D	1939
Moses	20082	D	1915
LIEBES			
Benjamin	24452	D	1918
Hannah	53611	D	1929
Helena	68079	D	1934
Herman	4986	D	1908
Herman	44157	D	1926
Isaac	29675	D	1920
Julien	21204	D	1916
Philip	34290	D	1922
Sidney	3686	D	1907
LIEBHART			
Charles A.	42251	D	1925
Clarence F.	42071	M	1925
Floyd	50860	I	1928
Floyd	63413	I	1933
LIEBLER			
Edward M.	22267	M	1917
LIEBRECHT			
Anna	85382	D	1940
Harry	42137	D	1925
Johannes Hendrikus	42137	D	1925
Otto	83215	D	1940
LIEBSCHER			
Caroline W.	72364	I	1936
Caroline W.	76991	D	1937
Edward	12781	D	1912
Frank Webster	79324	D	1938

NAME	NUMBER	TYPE	YEAR
LIEBSCHUTZ			
Regina	51010	D	1928
LIEBY			
Jules	26390	D	1919
LIECHTI			
John	89092	D	1942
LIECHTY			
Raymond W.	40845	D	1925
LIEDERMAN			
Daisy	80093	D	1938
LIEDMAN			
Hattie	76022	D	1937
LIEDTKE			
August L.	40127	D	1924
LIEJEGRIST			
Claus William	28585	I	1920
LIEN			
Bessie E.	18347	D	1915
Theodore	60649	I	1932
LIENHARD			
Jacob Adolph	53134	D	1929
LIENIZ			
Edward J.	30351	D	1920
John Edward	30351	D	1920
Sarah J.	17247	D	1914
LIEORE			
Gaston L.	80191	D	1938
John G.	81507	D	1939
LIESKE			
Frank	53198	D	1929
Julius	33768	D	1922
LIESS			
Emil	24519	D	1918
LIETZ			
Adolph	69958	D	1935
Catherina E. D.	60758	D	1932
Mary Miller	88759	D	1941
LIEVRE			
Clara	44354	D	1926
Ella	88141	D	1941
Isidore	67653	D	1934
Jules	24658	D	1918
LIEWALD			
Rudolph	77783	I	1938
Rudolph Frederick	72883	I	1936

NAME	NUMBER	TYPE	YEAR
LIFCHUTZ			
Hillel	78925	D	1938
LIFF			
Samuel	44593	D	1926
LIGGETT			
Harriet Lane	81327	D	1939
Hunter	73306	D	1936
LIGGINS			
Ella Ann	88397	M	1941
LIGHT			
Arthur J.	57198	I	1930
LIGHTSTONE			
Joseph	86690	D	1941
LIGONESCHE			
Henry	28233	I	1919
LIGOURI			
Arleen Marie	82168	M	1939
LIKELY			
Barny	52536	D	1929
LIKENS			
George Willis	80301	D	1939
James William	81994	D	1939
Matilda	54084	D	1929
LILIENFELD			
Alfred	53619	D	1929
Rose	3054	D	1907
LILIENTHAL			
Bella S.	37967	D	1923
Bertha G.	64589	D	1933
Dorothy	42601	M	1925
Ernest R.	35509	D	1922
Henry	41217	D	1925
Jean Helen	42601	M	1925
Jesse W.	27414	D	1919
Jesse W.	42601	M	1925
Mathilde	11735	D	1911
P. N., Jr.	7009	M	1909
Philip Nettre	6576	D	1908
Sophie G.	68661	D	1935
Theodore M.	7009	M	1909
LILJEQUIST			
Oscar	49907	D	1928
LILJEQVIST			
Claude W.	43716	D	1926
LILL			
Konrad	7683	D	1909

NAME	NUMBER	TYPE	YEAR
LILLEY			
Alexander S.	43806	D	1926
LILLIE			
Desmond A.	81874	M	1939
Fred P.	83744	D	1940
George J.	21648	D	1916
Gladys M.	1561	M	1906
Leonard M.	81874	M	1939
Maria	5679	D	1908
Nellie Beighle Craib	21568	D	1916
Sarah Jane	853	D	1906
LILLIG			
George	31186	D	1921
LILLINERI			
Renaldo	82655	D	1939
LILLIS			
Catherine H.	78874	D	1938
Elizabeth R.	63654	D	1933
Lucy E.	37622	D	1923
Patrick	871	D	1906
Sinon C.	22204	D	1917
Thomas	22046	D	1916
LILLIVIG			
Andrew	54888	D	1930
LILLY			
Allen Jasper	65211	D	1933
John	65382	D	1933
Mary	65418	D	1933
Robert John	65382	D	1933
LILVES			
Raymond Gordon	29151	M	1920
LIM			
Chin Sir	39969	M	1924
Gong	44349	D	1926
Hung	45809	D	1926
Lew	46816	D	1927
Wai Chow	70318	M	1935
Wai Chuck	70318	M	1935
LIMACHER			
Josephine	18840	D	1915
LIMAN			
E.	64449	D	1933
LIMBAUGH			
Eve Josephi	79150	D	1938
LIMON			
Louis	64896	D	1933
Natlaie	46380	D	1927

NAME	NUMBER	TYPE	YEAR
LIMOUSIN			
Pauline Victorine	15017	D	1913
LIN			
Hong	14240	D	1912
Tom Yuk	8324	M	1909
LINALE			
Anna	66335	D	1934
Giambattista	54719	D	1930
LINANE			
Marie Ann	62105	D	1932
LINARI			
Caterina	29878	D	1920
George	46652	D	1927
John	43320	D	1926
LINCHNER			
David I.	33552	D	1922
LINCOLN			
Charles Sherman	87137	D	1941
Emma Isabelle	76546	D	1937
George A.	38359	D	1924
George Horace	52682	D	1929
George W.	7267	D	1909
Isaac Fred	20521	D	1916
Jacqueline Rose	80471	M	1939
John Willard	7121	D	1909
Mae A.	86543	D	1941
Margaret E.	20552	D	1916
Philinda Gates	39064	D	1924
Robert Leland	80471	M	1939
LIND			
Alex	32159	D	1921
Charles	63658	D	1933
Erik	53967	D	1929
Henry	48343	D	1927
John	20187	D	1915
Oscar E.	49515	I	1928
Oscar W.	77470	D	1938
Pearl	80790	D	1939
Peter Alexander	32159	D	1921
Samuel Nelson	55452	D	1930
Stanley	89544	M	1942
LINDAUER			
Gustav C.	67719	D	1934
LINDBALD			
Frank Herman	32303	D	1921
LINDBERG			
Andrew J.	31449	D	1921

NAME	NUMBER	TYPE	YEAR
Claes Victor	65807	D	1933
Clares	33244	I	1922
Clares	65807	D	1933
Edward G.	82323	D	1939
Emil	54689	D	1930
Gustaf Anton	60048	D	1931
Gustaf Arvid	71083	D	1935
Gustaf Robert	46076	D	1926
Johanna Matilda	25710	D	1918
John	56683	D	1930
Louisa	42013	D	1925
Margaret Allen	71757	D	1936
Mary	9871	D	1910
Mary	62833	D	1932
Mary C.	49579	D	1928
Mathilde	66703	D	1934
Peter	31681	D	1921
Reuben L.	44006	D	1926
Victor	33244	I	1922
Victor	65807	D	1933
LINDBLOM			
Charles Jacob	39521	D	1924
Johan Edward	27146	D	1919
LINDBOM			
Alma	74134	D	1936
August	7194	D	1909
LINDBURG			
Harold C.	58170	D	1931
LINDE			
Fred	30965	I	1921
LINDEBERG			
Charles Ferdinand	30993	D	1921
Ferdinand	30993	D	1921
LINDECKER			
Philip	66461	D	1934
LINDEGSEN			
Gustaf	51219	D	1928
LINDELL			
John	73287	D	1936
LINDELOF			
Gustav R.	65128	D	1933
Olaf	36207	D	1923
LINDEMAN			
Fritzon	17471	D	1914
Isadore	78224	D	1938
Robert	44337	I	1926

NAME	NUMBER	TYPE	YEAR
LINDEMANN			
Carl	86939	D	1941
Friedrich	18739	D	1915
Henrich	3807	D	1907
LINDEN			
Carmel Margaret	35001	M	1922
Charles G.	19775	D	1915
Charles T.	60781	D	1932
Daniel	11961	D	1911
Edward J.	295	D	1906
Emily	23973	M	1918
Henry	46508	D	1927
Joe	64729	D	1933
Josephine Lillian	35001	M	1922
Ottilia M.	19776	D	1915
Otto Gustavus	21573	D	1916
Sarah Ann	50120	D	1928
William	23021	D	1917
LINDENBERG			
Eugene	7998	D	1909
LINDENMEYER			
John	52050	D	1929
LINDER			
Bror J.	27813	D	1919
Charles	14731	D	1913
Christian J.	43851	D	1926
Gertrude	29912	M	1920
Philip, Jr.	22402	M	1917
LINDERSMITH			
Robert E.	42641	D	1925
LINDEWURTH			
D. H.	7555	D	1909
Fred	7555	D	1909
Fred	39163	D	1924
Fritz	39163	D	1924
LINDEY			
Robert	44337	I	1926
LINDFORD			
Henry C.	44450	D	1926
LINDGREN			
Axel F.	53509	D	1929
Charles John	15478	D	1913
Charlotte	44270	D	1926
Eva E.	47268	I	1927
Fred	53509	D	1929
Janet M.	82054	D	1939
John E.	42228	D	1925

NAME	NUMBER	TYPE	YEAR
John F.	17351	M	1914
Nils J.	67988	D	1934
Peter	85511	I	1940
Victor George	58211	M	1931
LINDHEIMER			
Charles J.	77556	D	1938
LINDHOLM			
Frank J.	79616	D	1938
Gustaf	66524	D	1934
LINDHORST			
August	43523	D	1926
LINDINGER			
Kate	83790	D	1940
LINDLEY			
Cecil	52487	D	1929
Curtis Holbrook	30684	D	1920
Elizabeth Mendenhall	40978	D	1925
Frances Ethel	72413	D	1936
Isabel Negus	55622	D	1930
Sade M. G.	9377	D	1910
LINDLOF			
Gustav R.	65128	D	1933
LINDNER			
Adolph	40356	I	1924
Adolph, Jr.	55048	M	1930
Albert	8077	D	1909
Bella	25940	D	1918
David	46584	D	1927
Elizabeth	2743	D	1907
Gustave	67327	D	1934
Juanita Alverna	4054	M	1907
Julius K.	85733	D	1940
Lloyd	55048	M	1930
Mary K.	58179	TYPE	1931
Melvin	55048	M	1930
Moey K.	58179	D	1931
Rose	19591	D	1915
LINDO			
Donald	62812	D	1932
Elita, II	69137	M	1935
Juanita	67415	D	1934
LINDON			
Charles T.	60781	D	1932
LINDOW			
Carl William	37240	M	1923
Edith	46325	D	1927
William J.	36978	D	1923

NAME	NUMBER	TYPE	YEAR
William Joseph	36708	I	1923
LINDQUIST			
Agnes M.	14710	M	1913
Anders Edward	13405	D	1912
Anna	50899	M	1928
Carl A.	70939	I	1935
Carl A.	83139	D	1940
Edward William	73505	D	1936
Elis A.	43537	D	1926
Gus	7880	D	1909
Gust	14824	D	1913
John	12440	D	1911
M. G.	7880	D	1909
LINDREALL			
Marguerite	20798	D	1916
LINDROB			
Lawrence Lucas	11213	D	1911
Lucy May	11214	M	1911
Maria	7767	D	1909
Sarah McGregor	11214	M	1911
LINDROS			
Charles	76038	D	1937
Elinor	57119	D	1930
LINDSAY			
Alaris June	22018	M	1916
Alfred O.	30277	I	1920
Alfred O.	48077	D	1927
Camp F.	70809	D	1935
Elizabeth	50048	D	1928
Genieve	11643	M	1911
George M.	39719	D	1924
Helen A.	82480	I	1939
Helen Anderson	82795	D	1939
Henrietta T.	76149	D	1937
Hyentha Craig	69659	D	1935
Isabella	77181	D	1937
James C.	69434	I	1935
John E.	70810	D	1935
Margaret	61031	D	1932
Margaret B.	44276	D	1926
Mary Elizabeth	23178	D	1917
Peter	75849	D	1937
Robert A.	22881	D	1917
Robert M.	62284	D	1932
LINDSBERG			
Esther	43418	I	1926
LINDSEY			
Daisy Potter	87045	D	1941

NAME	NUMBER	TYPE	YEAR
Edith	15318	D	1913
Henry Victor	30934	D	1921
LINDSKOG			
Hilda	84202	D	1940
Olaf	37060	D	1923
LINDSTROM			
Bertha	36169	D	1923
Clara	57046	D	1930
Herman	10608	D	1910
John	6191	D	1908
John F., Jr.	9977	M	1910
LINDT			
Peter, Sr.	84133	D	1940
LINDVALL			
A. R., Mrs.	12683	D	1911
LINDWALL			
Marguerite	20798	D	1916
LINEBAUGH			
Nonie G.	60592	D	1932
LINEHAN			
Annie	80392	D	1939
Catherine	17443	D	1914
Dennis	20014	D	1915
Elizabeth	35368	D	1922
Ella	16780	D	1914
Francis C.	34773	M	1922
Frank C.	20216	D	1916
Hannah Marie	73230	D	1936
Isabella	42396	D	1925
Jeremiah	61702	D	1932
John	4172	I	1907
John	4330	D	1907
John	16935	D	1914
John B.	42294	M	1925
Marion B. Farney	86697	D	1941
Mary	18961	D	1915
Michael J.	37776	D	1923
Nellie	9953	D	1910
Owen	19113	D	1915
Owen	23336	D	1917
Simon	48421	D	1927
Thomas R.	34773	M	1922
Wilfred	31033	M	1921
William	31451	D	1921
William G.	18722	D	1915
William J.	12737	D	1911
LINEMAIER			
Mary	80364	D	1939

NAME	NUMBER	TYPE	YEAR
LINES			
Anna M.	44210	D	1926
LINESS			
J. J.	33384	D	1922
LINFORTH			
James	7300	D	1909
Mary Elizabeth	4470	D	1907
Miriam B.	42190	D	1925
LING			
Jung	33764	D	1922
Lee	87559	D	1941
Lee Kai	46783	M	1927
LINGELSER			
Marie	54958	D	1930
LINK			
Anna Katherine	16401	D	1913
Emil Leo	81098	D	1939
Leo	81098	D	1939
LINKE			
William	67424	D	1934
LINKER			
Philip Dreessen	25193	M	1918
LINKESCH			
Louis	1366	D	1906
LINKIEWICZ			
Martin	48877	D	1928
LINKINS			
Mary Jane	40237	D	1924
LINKLATER			
Mary T.	71402	D	1936
LINKLITTER			
William	70381	D	1935
LINKS			
Josephine	48394	D	1927
Martha Beatrice	61789	M	1932
Robert	61789	M	1932
LINN			
Alice	54227	D	1929
Charles H.	72521	D	1936
Gust	66471	D	1934
M. A.	7363	D	1909
Pauline	22366	D	1917
LINNARD			
Harold J.	14773	M	1913
LINNEBRINNEN			
J. B.	53227	D	1929

NAME	NUMBER	TYPE	YEAR
Jean	53227	D	1929
LINNET			
Gjertine	41443	D	1925
LINNEWEBER			
Bernard	8559	D	1909
LINNGGREN			
Gustaf Valfrid	6168	D	1908
LINNIX			
Jasper	27402	D	1919
LINOBERG			
Rosina	86015	D	1941
LINQUIST			
Alfred	84722	D	1940
Gustav	14657	I	1912
LINSEY			
Zadelle	29196	M	1920
LINSKEY			
Patrick	3151	I	1907
LINSKY			
James	16793	D	1914
LINSLEY			
Annette L.	30692	D	1920
Charles H.	47253	D	1927
LINSMIER			
Margaret	77275	D	1937
LINSTRUM			
Emil G.	29432	D	1920
LINTNER			
Charles William	9872	D	1910
Jane Elizabeth	43975	D	1926
Matilda R.	78254	D	1938
LINTON			
Harvey H.	59916	I	1931
Thomas	28042	D	1919
LINTZKE			
Charles	23375	D	1917
LINVILLE			
Henry H.	59977	I	1931
Pleasant D.	4219	D	1907
LINZ			
Lulu May	25156	D	1918
LION			
Alice Annie	82095	D	1939
Bertha	50594	D	1928
Edgar Jacob	10230	D	1910

NAME	NUMBER	TYPE	YEAR
LIONARDI			
Giovanna	52575	D	1929
LIONET			
M. P.	80199	D	1938
Michele	80199	D	1938
Michele P.	80199	D	1938
LIPARI			
Salvatore	18419	D	1915
LIPMAN			
Abraham	77016	I	1937
Abraham	78419	D	1938
Alfred	40277	D	1924
Amelia F.	10391	I	1910
Berthe	57016	D	1930
Denah Honig	15283	D	1913
Florence May Taylor	68023	I	1934
Gail	46356	M	1927
Harry	73850	D	1936
Henry	73850	D	1936
Isodor	36905	D	1923
Leopold	73235	D	1936
Lottie	44983	D	1926
Louis	27179	D	1919
Melvin Irwin	59101	M	1931
Morris H.	28344	D	1919
Oscar	41373	D	1925
LIPP			
Charles E.	31810	D	1921
LIPPARD			
Miriam	56126	M	1930
LIPPERT			
Anna	83687	D	1940
Anne Josephine	15617	M	1913
Annie E.	29611	D	1920
Edward	10484	M	1910
George	10484	M	1910
Maria	9367	D	1910
Mary	9367	D	1910
Peter	86899	I	1941
William Leo	10321	D	1910
LIPPI			
Abdon	67642	D	1934
Amedeo	43587	I	1926
Angela Jennie	68155	D	1934
Antonio	6399	D	1908
Dino	13436	M	1912
Emanuella	84869	D	1940
Linda	13436	M	1912

NAME	NUMBER	TYPE	YEAR
Palmira	51575	D	1928
Pia	13436	M	1912
LIPPINCOTT			
Charles I.	66133	D	1934
Ellen Frances	40806	D	1925
J. Bradley	86255	D	1941
LIPPITT			
Betsy	10729	D	1910
John	81379	M	1939
Zerline B.	80888	D	1939
LIPPKE			
Emma	88866	D	1942
LIPPMAN			
Alexander	11097	D	1911
Belle Greene	15244	D	1913
Hyman	21158	D	1916
Jacqueline Sara	26639	M	1919
Julian	26239	D	1919
Julian Henry	26639	M	1919
Solomon	8713	D	1909
LIPPNER			
Irving Joseph	37062	D	1923
LIPPOLD			
Edward	73612	D	1936
Karl	15343	D	1913
Rea Mae	44698	D	1926
Wanda Mae	44666	M	1926
LIPPOLT			
Charles	15343	D	1913
LIPRANDI			
Giovanni Battista	30722	D	1920
Maria Luisa	30722	D	1920
Pietro	30722	D	1920
LIPSCOMB			
Joseph M.	27249	D	1919
LIPSCOMBE			
Mary Jane	36678	I	1923
LIPSETT			
Robert	4161	D	1907
LIPSEY			
James Edward	27971	D	1919
LIPSHITZ			
Isodor	36905	D	1923
LIPSIN			
F. C.	62574	D	1932

NAME	NUMBER	TYPE	YEAR
LIPSITZ			
Rose	58002	D	1931
LISAUER			
Jacob	57429	D	1930
LISBERGER			
Carrie E.	72566	D	1936
D. S., Mrs.	72566	D	1936
Daniel S.	73656	D	1936
Sylvia Virginia	83131	M	1940
LISCHER			
Philipp	43132	D	1925
LISEN			
K. Ohounne	38172	I	1924
LISIGNOLI			
Joseph	80815	D	1939
LISONAT			
Marcel	60353	D	1931
LISS			
Beatrice Louise	82942	M	1939
Clifford	82942	M	1939
Garratt	82942	M	1939
Morris S.	84128	D	1940
LISSAK			
Adolphus F.	58663	D	1931
Adolphus H.	14935	D	1913
Louis S.	16846	D	1914
Madeline H.	6383	D	1908
Maude A.	67460	D	1934
Ormond M.	13583	D	1912
Sarah Emma	45090	D	1926
LISSAUER			
Jacob	57429	D	1930
LISSER			
Alan Chapman	49537	M	1928
Louis	28291	D	1919
Rosa	54356	D	1929
LISSNER			
Abraham Leslie	62249	D	1932
Berthold	71100	D	1935
Elsa	71077	D	1935
LIST			
R. H.	14835	D	1913
LISTA			
Charles	43835	D	1926
LISTER			
Barbara	68796	D	1935

NAME	NUMBER	TYPE	YEAR
Emerich	27546	D	1919
John M.	57451	D	1930
Mary	77110	D	1937
Mary Ellen	14749	D	1913
Michael	89647	D	1942
Thomas	73031	D	1936
LISTON			
Michael	32132	D	1921
LITCHFIELD			
Bertha	39400	I	1924
Bertha	42502	D	1925
Frank Sumner	1693	M	1906
Joan Elizabeth	56409	M	1930
Joseph M.	874	I	1906
Joseph M.	6606	D	1908
Reuben Lloyd	1693	M	1906
Sarah Elizabeth	54592	D	1929
LITROFF			
Yasha	26564	I	1919
Yasha	26995	D	1919
LITSCH			
Caroline	35407	D	1922
Frank	2958	D	1907
LITTAU			
Louis	20769	I	1916
Mathias	18669	D	1915
LITTERST			
Franziska Kramer	8081	D	1909
LITTLE			
Adelia E.	19135	D	1915
Caroline Halsted	81692	I	1939
Caroline Halsted	82320	D	1939
Claire	66813	D	1934
Edna Claire	4608	M	1907
Edria J. Fowlie	80685	D	1939
Edward Peter	62783	D	1932
Edwin Charles	49403	D	1928
Ellen Elizabeth	22033	I	1916
Ellen Elizabeth	22815	D	1917
Emilie	63631	D	1933
Emma C.	28587	D	1920
Frank A.	1890	D	1906
James Edger	34286	D	1922
John Baxter	24997	D	1918
John J.	44330	M	1926
Kate	6551	D	1908
Lucie T.	60699	D	1932
Mary A.	1341	D	1906

NAME	NUMBER	TYPE	YEAR
Mary F.	1861	D	1906
Mary T.	61135	D	1932
Matilda E.	72379	D	1936
Norma Lois	4608	M	1907
Olga A.	70392	D	1935
Oscar J.	55201	D	1930
Richard G.	87415	D	1941
Robert J.	8256	D	1909
Rose H.	667	D	1906
Stephen A.	58466	D	1931
Thomas	63475	D	1933
William	1828	D	1906
William	38901	D	1924
William H.	50537	I	1928
William Henry	52209	D	1929
William T.	13660	D	1912
LITTLEFIELD			
Alden B.	10958	D	1910
Isabel	85731	D	1940
Ivory F.	39484	D	1924
James Marshall	38914	D	1924
John W.	10914	D	1910
LITTLEFORD			
Charles	25724	D	1918
Edward T.	48650	D	1927
Helena	35817	D	1923
LITTLEHALE			
Gertrude Elliott	20124	D	1915
James M.	26098	D	1919
Mary Louise Elliott	23764	M	1917
LITTLEJOHN			
George W.	44067	D	1926
LITTLEL			
Joseph C.	54367	D	1929
LITTLEWOOD			
Albert H.	60659	D	1932
Elizabeth B.	17011	D	1914
Evelyn Alice	17122	M	1914
Ramona	56824	D	1930
LITTMAN			
Charles S.	56017	D	1930
Phillip	88459	D	1941
LITTNER			
Urban	9562	D	1910
LITTOOY			
John F.	80649	D	1939

NAME	NUMBER	TYPE	YEAR	NAME	NUMBER	TYPE	YEAR	NAME	NUMBER	TYPE	YEAR
LITVINOFF				William A.	55102	D	1930	**LOBB**			
Susan A.	23679	D	1917	**LIZARRAGA**				Harry W.	61014	D	1932
LITZIUS				Emma	25281	D	1918	**LOBE**			
August	7304	D	1909	**LIZEE**				Anatole	28927	D	1920
Joseph	9660	M	1910	Napoleon	71361	D	1936	Gussye	55565	D	1930
LIURETTE				**LJUMGBERG**				Hilda	23492	D	1917
Jean	8590	D	1909	Inga	67353	D	1934	Justine	31771	D	1921
Pierre	8668	M	1909	**LJUNGBERG**				**LOBECKER**			
LIUZZA				Inga	67353	D	1934	Charles Henry	87915	D	1941
Giuseppe	49140	D	1928	**LJUNGREN**				**LOBELLO**			
Peter	50288	D	1928	Gustalva	60101	D	1931	Dominick	46218	D	1927
LIVELY				**LLAMA**				**LOBENHOFFER**			
George M.	46246	M	1927	Manuel	79104	D	1938	John P.	86873	I	1941
George M.	46432	D	1927	**LLEWELLYN**				**LOBIANCO**			
LIVERMORE				Ann	7132	D	1909	Girolima S.	27821	D	1919
Edward	8366	D	1909	Caroline	4629	D	1907	**LOBREE**			
Helen Eells	87052	D	1941	Ellen	56775	D	1930	Aaron Allan	80610	D	1939
Horatio P.	20894	D	1916	Susanna	31312	I	1921	Aaron David	81279	D	1939
Horatio P., Mrs.	87052	D	1941	Susanna	43422	D	1926	Abraham E.	50807	D	1928
Marie Emily	8296	D	1909	William	43794	D	1926	Adeline	60679	D	1932
Myrtle Marie	8709	M	1909	**LLEWELYN**				Allan A.	80610	D	1939
Violet Emily	8709	M	1909	John V.	55994	I	1930	Annie	30846	D	1920
William Francis	41570	D	1925	**LLOYD**				Carrie	65733	D	1933
LIVESEY				Bruce D.	54664	D	1930	Isaac	15774	D	1913
Richard Palmer	13236	D	1912	Christina Lettina	15846	D	1913	Lena	83752	I	1940
LIVINGSTON				Edwin E.	29050	D	1920	Lizzie	62489	D	1932
Anna M.	9841	D	1910	Frank H.	59675	D	1931	**LOBSIEN**			
Annie E.	64458	D	1933	Harry L.	80755	D	1939	Julian Sears	74828	M	1937
Clarence Hubert	52908	D	1929	John	10348	D	1910	**LOCHBAUM**			
Cora D.	81896	D	1939	John	88221	D	1941	Emma W.	17139	D	1914
DeWitt M.	17337	D	1914	Leonia L.	40015	D	1924	Jeanette	44914	D	1926
Emma	24065	D	1918	Lorette Boyd	87277	D	1941	**LOCHEAD**			
Ethel Florence	34822	M	1922	Mary Curtin	56970	D	1930	James K.	59142	M	1931
Gladys	34822	M	1922	Meredith J.	79639	D	1938	**LOCHER**			
Isaac	25186	D	1918	Pearl	35621	D	1922	Marie	29401	D	1920
James Prince	44737	D	1926	Reuben H.	7441	D	1909	**LOCICERO**			
James Prince, Jr.	45336	M	1926	Wilbur F.	24539	D	1918	Stefano	33077	D	1921
Janice Edith	34822	M	1922	William T.	63165	D	1932	**LOCK**			
Louis A.	86478	D	1941	William V.	20414	D	1916	William	41865	D	1925
Philip Hyman	34782	D	1922	**LOACH**				William	41865	D	1925
Raymond B.	34822	M	1922	John	48411	D	1927	**LOCKE**			
Rose F.	85111	D	1940	**LOAIZA**				Annie M.	78516	D	1938
Rose Madeline	34822	M	1922	Carmen	8838	M	1909	Fanny	7707	D	1909
Samuel	78824	D	1938	Dolores	43824	D	1926	George	65773	I	1933
LIVINGSTONE				**LOANE**				James B.	74132	D	1936
Anna Bella	48793	D	1927	Abraham	28751	D	1920	Lucile	8279	M	1909
Frederic A.	40388	D	1924	John M.	13990	D	1912	Nathan S.	57259	D	1930

Key: D = death; M = minor; I = incompetent

NAME	NUMBER	TYPE	YEAR	NAME	NUMBER	TYPE	YEAR	NAME	NUMBER	TYPE	YEAR
Raymond Traylor	8279	M	1909	Sigmund	37050	D	1923	Henriette	11936	D	1911
Sabrina	31416	D	1921	Solomon	6137	D	1908	Joseph M.	12762	D	1911
LOCKERD				Theresa	85115	D	1940	Marjorie Helene	25271	M	1918
Rose	88068	D	1941	Virginia F.	61994	M	1932	William G.	56842	D	1930
LOCKETT				LOEBBING				LOEWENBERG			
Will	19890	D	1915	Francisca	9203	D	1910	Fred	74652	D	1937
LOCKHART				Mary A.	51208	D	1928	Rosa	9704	D	1910
William	46956	D	1927	LOEBE				LOEWENBERGER			
LOCKHEAD				Emma	23293	I	1917	David	86528	D	1941
John H.	23275	D	1917	LOEBER				LOEWENTHAL			
LOCKIE				Florence Marie	7392	M	1909	Apolonia	58591	D	1931
William Wallace	73291	D	1936	LOEBL				Goodman	19218	D	1915
LOCKS				Emma	23293	I	1917	Myrtile	48452	I	1927
Joseph Samuel	32112	D	1921	Emma	24109	D	1918	Rachel	42647	D	1925
LOCKWOOD				LOEFFLER				LOEWY			
Bessie	41301	D	1925	Charles	50379	D	1928	Conrad	88585	D	1941
Dorothy	43212	M	1925	Frederick E.	45474	D	1926	Rosa	48643	D	1927
Edwina	43212	M	1925	George William	22308	D	1917	Walter	61102	D	1932
Susie F.	22704	D	1917	Joseph Francis	39245	D	1924	Wm.	25000	D	1918
LOCKYER				Leonhard	44216	D	1926	LOFARO			
Rae	85527	D	1940	LOEHER				Teresa	26704	D	1919
LODDEN				Marno M.	73437	D	1936	Teresa	26705	M	1919
Elizabeth	63706	D	1933	LOEMARIA				LOFFLER			
LODERHOSE				Compte Charles du Parc	88319	D	1941	Wilhelm F.	59267	D	1931
Emma	81153	I	1939	LOESCH				LOFGREN			
LODOVICA				Arthur	14782	M	1913	Alvin N.	81946	D	1939
Catterchio	79842	D	1938	Charles	25059	D	1918	Charles	26654	D	1919
LODS				Donald C.	85396	M	1940	Charles	26667	M	1919
Mathilde C.	53646	D	1929	Ernest	7975	M	1909	LOFRANO			
LODUCA				LOESER				Carmelo	77418	D	1938
Filomena	25971	D	1918	Julius	19462	D	1915	LOFSTAD			
Florence	25971	D	1918	Robert M.	34365	D	1922	John N.	17679	D	1914
LOEB				LOESHAUER				Oscar E.	50176	D	1928
Albert I.	69582	D	1935	Magdalena	56511	D	1930	LOFT			
Aron	51196	D	1928	LOESSER				Otto J.	10708	D	1910
Benjamin K.	87426	D	1941	Auguste W. H.	30874	D	1920	LOFTIS			
Gerald M.	6310	M	1908	Elvira	17242	D	1914	John	26946	D	1919
Gloria Rodrizuez	62261	D	1932	Theodor	31593	D	1921	Mary	1338	D	1906
Gustave	58191	D	1931	LOETHER				LOFTUS			
Jacob	8961	D	1910	Paul	73814	D	1936	Catherine	51822	D	1929
Jacob	55615	D	1930	LOETZ				Edward J.	72963	D	1936
Jeanette Barbara	70377	M	1935	Edward	1231	D	1906	George Thomas	89653	D	1942
Madeline	19221	M	1915	LOEVY				John	299	D	1906
Myrtle M.	61994	M	1932	Julius	21250	D	1916	Mary	1338	D	1906
Otto	25545	D	1918	LOEWE				Mary C.	65683	D	1933
Selina P.	25751	D	1918	Anna Marie	81204	D	1939	Michael	21436	D	1916
Sidney S.	6310	M	1908					Michael A.	10734	D	1910

Key: D = death; M = minor; I = incompetent

NAME	NUMBER	TYPE	YEAR
Patrick H.	47407	D	1927
Sarah	21188	D	1916
Thelma G.	84611	I	1940
William A.	69118	D	1935
LOGAN			
Alice H.	46677	D	1927
Anton, Jr.	33402	D	1922
Benjamin Boone	76914	D	1937
Cleo Pearl	67759	D	1934
Edward	37147	D	1923
Edward Clinton	28979	D	1920
Elizabeth	67389	D	1934
Ellen	74837	D	1937
Flavel L.	53656	D	1929
Frederica Furley	46853	D	1927
George T.	38199	I	1924
Hilda N.	24652	M	1918
Horace Virgil R.	2224	M	1906
Horace Virgil Rosekrans	8730	D	1909
Hugh	21996	D	1916
J. W.	4093	D	1907
J. W.	5888	D	1908
James Columbus	42170	D	1925
John A.	5887	D	1908
John R.	10703	D	1910
John Robert	55318	D	1930
Joseph M.	71699	D	1936
Julia M.	24685	D	1918
Kate	6177	D	1908
Margaret	1811	D	1906
Martha Elizabeth	36896	D	1923
Mary	61037	D	1932
Mary Ann	20624	D	1916
Milburn Hill	164	D	1906
Robert L.	67647	M	1934
Robert Lee	54702	M	1930
Roscoe Lee	43917	D	1926
Samuel James	15590	M	1913
Sarah A.	25972	D	1918
Stephen	9557	D	1910
Thomas Francis	29533	D	1920
Unity Jane	34895	D	1922
William	65026	D	1933
William John	49865	D	1928
LOGAR			
Anton	61991	D	1932
Bertha	59839	D	1931

NAME	NUMBER	TYPE	YEAR
LOGEMANN			
Henry William	84950	D	1940
LOGGIE			
Ida M.	2642	D	1907
James J.	2205	D	1906
LOGHRY			
Robert	49259	D	1928
LOGIE			
James Edgar (missing)	87860	D	1941
Mary Lauraie	41554	D	1925
Mary Lawder Mitchell	41554	D	1925
Thomas P.	38356	D	1924
William	47949	D	1927
LOGUE			
Arnold	15765	D	1913
Edward	25628	D	1918
Frank	15765	D	1913
John	15765	D	1913
Sherman L.	49497	D	1928
LOGWOOD			
Edwin I.	29852	D	1920
Edwin Isaiah, Jr.	29345	M	1920
Josephine	29345	M	1920
LOH			
Hannah	68564	D	1934
LOHENSTEIN			
Dena	46147	I	1927
LOHKE			
Andrew	57072	D	1930
LOHMAN			
Emma	62411	D	1932
John	25839	D	1918
LOHMANN			
Edward F.	24059	I	1918
John Doe	7138	D	1909
Margrete C. G.	8345	D	1909
LOHMEYER			
Charles Rothart	36212	M	1923
LOHMUELLER			
August	24004	D	1918
LOHMULLER			
August	24004	D	1918
LOHSE			
Jessie Charlotte	8851	D	1909
Marion A.	83026	D	1940
May Agnes	2020	D	1906

NAME	NUMBER	TYPE	YEAR
Thomas	70227	I	1935
LOHSEN			
Julia	19736	D	1915
LOINSEN			
Henry	78809	D	1938
LOISELLE			
Philomene	583	D	1906
LOIZZO			
Frank	33512	D	1922
LOLICH			
Anton	48407	D	1927
LOLLER			
William H.	59212	D	1931
LOLSHAUER			
Magdalena	56511	D	1930
LOMAN			
Jan Christiaan	17632	D	1914
LOMAR			
Hans Edmund	19979	M	1915
LOMAX			
Edward Lloyd	20387	D	1916
LOMBA			
Joseph P.	71959	I	1936
LOMBARD			
C. M.	7434	D	1909
Claude	51224	D	1928
Hannah	12064	D	1911
LOMBARDA			
Francesco	4723	D	1907
LOMBARDI			
Andrea	26503	D	1919
Augusto	65905	D	1933
Aurelio	77944	D	1938
Bernardino	80287	D	1939
Egisto	87798	D	1941
Eleanora	41171	D	1925
Felice	21171	M	1916
Ferdinand	50809	D	1928
Guido	89684	D	1942
Josephine	71198	D	1935
Louis Robert	87973	M	1941
Salvatore	82469	D	1939
Silvio	82469	D	1939
Vito	48325	D	1927
William H.	27874	D	1919

NAME	NUMBER	TYPE	YEAR	NAME	NUMBER	TYPE	YEAR	NAME	NUMBER	TYPE	YEAR
LOMBARDINI				Elvira	28388	D	1919	Walter Stephen	67056	M	1934
Antonio	60920	D	1932	Flora Jane	68800	D	1935	William	48069	D	1927
LOMBARDO				Florence Elise	70353	I	1935	William J.	62637	D	1932
Giuseppe	27354	D	1919	Florence T.	39434	D	1924	LONGA			
Joseph	24283	D	1918	Francis John	47896	M	1927	Pedro Jose	77882	D	1938
Philip	71369	D	1936	Frank E.	62244	I	1932	LONGABAUGH			
LOMBROS				Franklin	83888	M	1940	Elwood P.	55764	D	1930
John	78124	D	1938	George S.	23450	D	1917	LONGACHER			
LOMELINO				George W.	33261	D	1922	John	37792	D	1923
Augustinho DeCamera	32235	D	1921	Grace	60018	I	1931	LONGAR			
LOMETTI				Gregory D.	54165	D	1929	Helen	86780	D	1941
Joseph	1048	D	1906	Herbert C.	58523	D	1931	LONGERGAN			
Rosina	24126	D	1918	Isaac N.	39785	D	1924	Lena	22178	D	1917
LOMOGLIA				Isabell	75174	I	1937	LONGFELD			
Joseph	69701	D	1935	J. R.	23700	D	1917	Abraham L.	19506	D	1915
LOMOGLIO				James E.	71471	D	1936	LONGLAND			
Joseph	69701	D	1935	James Edward	56633	D	1930	Ernest Louis	75499	I	1937
LON				James J.	71632	D	1936	LONGMORE			
Chung Sow	17593	D	1914	James Madison, Mrs.	57870	D	1931	Lily R.	82954	D	1939
Wong Hong	42244	D	1925	James O.	17049	D	1914	LONGO			
LONDON				John	25908	D	1918	Catherine	85622	D	1940
Henry	69285	D	1935	John E.	11748	D	1911	Mary F.	18778	M	1915
Rosa	7621	D	1909	John H.	59386	D	1931	Rose	72082	I	1936
Theresa	13030	D	1912	John Holmes	1910	D	1906	LONGTIN			
William J.	31476	D	1921	John P.	56852	D	1930	Aimee Ida	71126	D	1935
LONDONER				John W.	1620	D	1906	Helene	70757	M	1935
Eva	39325	D	1924	John Yervant	67056	M	1934	LONGTON			
LONERGAN				Josephine J.	83854	D	1940	Charles E.	61923	D	1932
George	3605	M	1907	Kittie Jane	81523	D	1939	Jessie Foreman	73965	D	1936
James	86646	D	1941	Lucius L.	37495	D	1923	LONGWELL			
Mary H.	68557	D	1934	Luke	79504	D	1938	Juliet Taylor	47772	D	1927
LONEY				Magdalene	57870	D	1931	Pearl V.	64627	D	1933
Philip	33590	D	1922	Mar	37472	M	1923	LONGWILL			
LONG				Mar Moon	37472	M	1923	John	965	D	1906
Albert Victor	56491	D	1930	Margaret	44167	I	1926	LONNECLAVERE			
Anna	6248	D	1908	Mary	14229	D	1912	Antoine	44836	D	1926
Arthur	33087	D	1921	Mary E.	11098	D	1911	LONROTH			
Cecil Glenn	15716	M	1913	Mary T.	44193	D	1926	Frederick	34536	D	1922
Charles	41236	D	1925	Mildred S.	23633	M	1917	LONSETH			
Charles M.	38939	D	1924	Minnie E.	87671	D	1941	Louis	13029	D	1912
Charles Maurice, Jr.	47896	M	1927	Nellie	8795	D	1909	LOO			
Charles Warren	76850	M	1937	Nellie	43558	D	1926	Chong	66281	D	1934
Claude	43776	D	1926	Nette S.	23633	M	1917	Ernest M.	39094	M	1924
Daniel W.	52889	D	1929	Patrick	8800	D	1909	H. K.	33088	D	1921
David	10141	D	1910	Phyllis	54891	M	1930	Louie	76184	D	1937
Eleanor	57286	M	1930	Robert Samuel	16159	D	1913	Louis	48966	D	1928
Elise	70353	I	1935	Sarah Ella	83267	D	1940				
				Sarah F.	27360	D	1919				
				Thomas	29353	D	1920				

- 42 -

Key: D = death; M = minor; I = incompetent

NAME	NUMBER	TYPE	YEAR
Lowie	76184	D	1937
Marie	61474	D	1932
Rosalie Francois	33188	D	1922
LOOBEY			
Lillian	87408	I	1941
LOOF			
Irene	31142	M	1921
LOOMIS			
Edmond Charles	32402	M	1921
Edwin H.	33036	D	1921
Frank	19555	D	1915
Hannah Ann	7970	I	1909
Mary E.	27058	D	1919
LOON			
John	3119	M	1907
LOONEY			
Elizabeth	18887	D	1915
Grace C.	36358	M	1923
James J.	17226	D	1914
John J.	21666	D	1916
Matthew Sylvester	11768	D	1911
Patrick	14719	D	1913
LOORYA			
Helena	63452	D	1933
LOORZ			
Herman	47813	D	1927
William Henry Herman	47813	D	1927
LOOSEN			
George H.	47951	I	1927
George H.	81465	I	1939
LOPACKI			
Otton	72214	D	1936
LOPES			
Jacintho I.	78956	D	1938
LOPEZ			
Allan	71968	M	1936
Antonia	80394	D	1939
Elisa	38388	M	1924
Eustaguio	83029	D	1940
Francisco	59136	D	1931
Francisco Garcia	80986	D	1939
Herman	59932	M	1931
Jesus P.	82798	D	1939
Jose	40534	D	1924
Josefa	14210	D	1912
Manuel	54473	D	1929
Porfiria	9636	D	1910

NAME	NUMBER	TYPE	YEAR
Raymond	64037	I	1933
Robert P.	73653	D	1936
Rosaria	38388	M	1924
Thomas	65471	D	1933
Valentin	35944	D	1923
LOPLACE			
Lucile	57895	I	1931
LOPRESTI			
Giuseppe	78702	D	1938
Nofrio	14004	D	1912
LOQUE			
Bridget	20535	D	1916
John	14113	D	1912
LOQUET			
Desire	53169	D	1929
LORA			
John	20528	D	1916
LORACCA			
Antonio	25549	D	1918
LORAN			
Dennis	65556	D	1933
LORBEER			
Betty Maud	70340	M	1935
LORBER			
John	45444	D	1926
LORCH			
Minnie T.	76925	D	1937
LORD			
Charles Edwin	35409	D	1922
Eliza Lucy	6877	D	1908
Eugene Joseph	38537	M	1924
Hazel	52740	D	1929
Helen	42716	M	1925
Helen D.	10568	D	1910
James	44156	D	1926
Theodore A.	17721	D	1914
Thomas	8721	D	1909
Thomas H.	30459	D	1920
William	72987	D	1936
William	73534	D	1936
William Henry	35647	D	1923
William Henry	38537	M	1924
LORDEN			
Dennis	60631	D	1932
Hannah	33948	D	1922
Jeremiah	18115	D	1914

NAME	NUMBER	TYPE	YEAR
LORDON			
Catherine	52967	D	1929
LORDS			
Vernie F.	59840	D	1931
LOREK			
Frank J.	87751	D	1941
LOREN			
John	63645	M	1933
LORENGINI			
Emilio	79248	D	1938
LORENSEN			
Christine	24552	I	1918
LORENTZ			
Herbert	80228	D	1938
John Henry	3128	D	1907
Robert	40255	D	1924
LORENZ			
Bertha	32195	D	1921
Bonaventura E.	30538	D	1920
Emilie Louise	52335	D	1929
Franziska	37071	D	1923
George	60804	D	1932
Moses	15527	D	1913
Rudolph	17609	D	1914
Wm.	9785	D	1910
LORENZEN			
Albert Christian	76467	D	1937
Charles John	89747	D	1942
Gordon James Walter	55288	M	1930
Henry J. H.	47325	D	1927
William T.	48885	D	1928
LORENZETTI			
George	83364	D	1940
Lena	66476	D	1934
LORENZI			
Antonio	75445	D	1937
Italo	43694	D	1926
Leslie	37780	D	1923
Luigi	66241	D	1934
Victor	82450	I	1939
LORENZINI			
Fiorendo	68847	D	1935
Joseph	73692	D	1936
Vincent	80741	D	1939
LORENZO			
Antonio Yanez	43964	D	1926
Mathilda F.	52899	D	1929

NAME	NUMBER	TYPE	YEAR
Mathilda Ode	52899	D	1929
Preve	25544	D	1918
LORETTO			
James A.	59307	D	1931
LORETZ			
Fred	43398	M	1926
Kaspar	13817	D	1912
Margaretha	14185	I	1912
Margaretha	43239	D	1925
Marie	43398	M	1926
LORIGAN			
Bartholomew F.	566	D	1906
Mary Virginia	78442	M	1938
LORING			
Buelah	1868	M	1906
Charles W.	16549	D	1913
Ernest B.	88622	D	1941
Ethel H.	70824	D	1935
Ruth	1868	M	1906
Sophie L.	10922	D	1910
LORION			
Angeline	80843	D	1939
LORKE			
Joseph	46100	D	1926
LORNSTEN			
Ingebar	2303	D	1906
LOROMER			
J. Gordon	32697	I	1921
Minnie G.	64532	D	1933
LORQUIN			
Ernest F.	9105	D	1910
LORRAINE			
Alfred G.	32437	D	1921
Frank	46288	D	1927
Marckenia Hilderbrand	84273	I	1940
LORRISON			
John	41222	D	1925
LORWAM			
Michael	20143	D	1915
LORYEA			
Esther	72824	D	1936
LOSCH			
Walter	20736	M	1916
LOSCHIAVO			
Joseph	66763	D	1934

NAME	NUMBER	TYPE	YEAR
LOSCUTOFF			
Emma	80615	I	1939
John	47073	D	1927
LOSER			
Christie C.	86540	D	1941
LOSEY			
Isaac H.	43819	D	1926
LOSH			
Madge	22260	D	1917
LOSKUTOFF			
Jacob	6435	D	1908
Semen M.	8587	D	1909
LOSS			
Emma	83811	D	1940
LOSSMAN			
Augusta	71113	D	1935
Loeb	34415	D	1922
LOT			
Joe	87513	I	1941
LOTH			
Anna	81143	D	1939
Frank	78909	D	1938
M., Mrs.	81143	D	1939
LOTHERS			
Mina T.	83726	D	1940
Robert D.	83727	M	1940
LOTHHAMMER			
Mabel	45492	D	1926
LOTHROP			
Charles E.	16256	D	1913
Vinnetta I.	30829	D	1920
LOTS			
Joe	87513	I	1941
LOTT			
Mary Cynthia Gesford	52696	I	1929
Mary Gesford	83540	D	1940
LOTTS			
George	84118	D	1940
LOTZ			
Edward	1231	D	1906
Paul	16211	D	1913
LOTZE			
Wilhelm	31491	D	1921
William	31491	D	1921
LOTZIN			
Louise	65422	D	1933

NAME	NUMBER	TYPE	YEAR
LOU			
Ow Gar	87076	M	1941
LOUD			
Emily S.	33423	D	1922
Eugene Francis	6975	D	1908
LOUDERBACK			
Amelia	87533	D	1941
Elizabeth S.	50710	D	1928
Harold	88757	D	1941
Sarah V.	75043	D	1937
LOUDON			
David S.	42203	M	1925
Elizabeth M.	42203	M	1925
Louis	38489	D	1924
Louise	31531	D	1921
Winifred	53402	D	1929
LOUDSEN			
Dorothy K.	87655	D	1941
LOUDUBACK			
Harriett	84689	D	1940
LOUGEE			
Barry H.	1820	D	1906
Walter S.	1819	D	1906
LOUGEON			
Victoria	13668	D	1912
LOUGH			
Laura I.	49576	M	1928
LOUGHBOROUGH			
Marianna Z.	18848	D	1915
LOUGHERY			
John F.	2237	D	1906
LOUGHLIN			
John	41720	D	1925
John	41720	D	1925
Thomas Alexander	50928	D	1928
LOUGHMAN			
Ellen	87919	D	1941
Nellie	87919	D	1941
LOUGHMANE			
James	8813	D	1909
LOUGHNANE			
Mary Ann	27909	D	1919
LOUGHRAN			
Edward L.	11698	D	1911
Elizabeth	11816	D	1911
Ellen	72482	D	1936

NAME	NUMBER	TYPE	YEAR
Eva	11841	I	1911
Frank V.	82725	D	1939
Harry B.	54602	D	1929
Irene Jane	58438	M	1931
Jane	61996	D	1932
Leo E.	11698	D	1911
Lizzie	7619	I	1909
Margaret Y.	4229	D	1907
Mary	79717	D	1938
Thomas	58432	D	1931
Thomas P.	76788	D	1937
LOUHARD			
C. R.	87196	D	1941
LOUHART			
Benoit	87196	D	1941
LOUIE			
Hok Lum	85775	D	1940
Ida Francis	42845	M	1925
Loo	76184	D	1937
Tong Fong	58385	D	1931
Yee Hung	62231	D	1932
Yee Poo	83832	D	1940
Yen	42845	M	1925
Yuen	52059	D	1929
LOUIS			
Charles	13275	D	1912
Charles	30858	D	1920
Peter D.	65860	D	1933
Theodore J.	80455	D	1939
LOUISSON			
Edward B.	27843	D	1919
Samuel	37716	D	1923
LOUKAS			
Harry S.	87786	D	1941
LOULOUDIS			
Theodore J.	80455	D	1939
LOUPE			
Amelia	44230	D	1926
LOUPY			
Jen	85326	I	1940
John	85326	I	1940
Lucy	45480	D	1926
Marianne	37131	D	1923
Therese	55821	D	1930
LOURDEAUX			
Emile	11871	D	1911

NAME	NUMBER	TYPE	YEAR
LOURENCO			
Diogo Jose	68896	D	1935
LOURENS			
Sophia Margaretha	45672	D	1926
LOURETTI			
Antonio	51555	D	1928
LOURLTI			
Antonio	51555	D	1928
LOURY			
Bryant Philip	40658	M	1924
LOUSKI			
Walter	4883	M	1907
LOUSPLAS			
Reine	80349	D	1939
Rene	80349	D	1939
LOUSTALET			
Anna	37528	D	1923
Auriele	83047	D	1940
Jean Pierre	65924	D	1933
John P.	65924	D	1933
LOUSTALOT			
Aurelie	83047	D	1940
Jean Pierre	41130	D	1925
Zacharie	46319	D	1927
LOUSTAN			
Jean Pierre	48115	D	1927
LOUSTAU			
Jean Pierre	48115	D	1927
LOUSTAUNAU			
Eloi P.	3207	D	1907
Jean Pierre	65573	D	1933
LOUSTAUNOU			
Jean Charles	12589	D	1911
LOUTHAN			
William E.	8249	D	1909
LOUX			
Alphonse	18098	D	1914
LOVASCO			
Ciro	36395	D	1923
LOVDAL			
Fredricka	56792	D	1930
Olaf Anthony	15679	D	1913
LOVE			
Alfred Travis	51761	D	1929
Edward H.	26665	D	1919
Elizabeth Murray	51063	D	1928

NAME	NUMBER	TYPE	YEAR
Ida Louise Henderson	47601	D	1927
James Alexander	68739	D	1935
Josephine S.	16731	D	1914
Richard	17083	D	1914
Samuel H.	57089	D	1930
Thomas	42701	D	1925
LOVEGROVE			
Stella C.	50402	D	1928
LOVEJOY			
Charlotte M	29699	D	1920
George Palmer	84267	D	1940
LOVELAND			
Etta F.	13599	D	1912
Mae W.	82249	D	1939
LOVELESS			
Leonora	70451	M	1935
Susan E.	48917	D	1928
LOVELL			
Elizabeth P.	87728	D	1941
Mansfield	64534	D	1933
Minerva M. H.	56210	D	1930
LOVERICH			
Sadie	32344	D	1921
Samuel	46162	D	1927
LOVERIDGE			
Clarence H.	20445	M	1916
Earl W.	41029	I	1925
Ruth E.	20445	M	1916
LOVETT			
B. F.	15276	D	1913
Charles G.	4805	M	1907
Charles H.	4806	D	1907
James D.	68559	D	1934
John J.	43837	D	1926
John M.	73017	D	1936
Maria	37921	D	1923
Mary B.	16400	D	1913
Mary Isabelle	73335	I	1936
Maude	4805	M	1907
Samuel M.	44586	D	1926
LOVIBOND			
Thora	87748	D	1941
LOVITZ			
Herbert	55996	I	1930
LOVLIN			
Carl	76565	D	1937

Key: D = death; M = minor; I = incompetent

NAME	NUMBER	TYPE	YEAR	NAME	NUMBER	TYPE	YEAR	NAME	NUMBER	TYPE	YEAR
LOVOTTI				Laura E.	75344	D	1937	Mary F.	31394	D	1921
Angela	65958	D	1933	Martha Lena	25764	D	1918	Minnie	68074	D	1934
Pasquale	44227	D	1926	Pearl Willig McNabb	77306	D	1937	William R.	81374	D	1939
LOVRIN				Ping S.	55112	D	1930	**LOWIE**			
John	53319	D	1929	Rose	49653	D	1928	Loo	76184	D	1937
LOVRO				Saidee K.	73384	D	1936	**LOWIS**			
Christ	14191	M	1912	Susan	15316	D	1913	Ada Marjorie	50032	M	1928
LOW				Thomas Burnside	62316	D	1932	George	50032	M	1928
Charles	18638	D	1915	William D.	57328	D	1930	Peter D.	65860	D	1933
Chew F.	72665	D	1936	William E.	30498	D	1920	Robert	50032	M	1928
David	32220	M	1921	**LOWELL**				**LOWLOWDIS**			
David, Mrs.	89963	D	1942	Abner I.	7708	D	1909	Theodore	80455	D	1939
Emily F.	89963	D	1942	Alice	89022	D	1942	**LOWMAN**			
Frank	49699	M	1928	Arthur C.	53629	D	1929	Charles S.	19649	D	1915
Gam Sing	59303	D	1931	Samuel J.	15597	D	1913	Louisa Harden	31170	D	1921
John	39887	D	1924	**LOWENBERG**				**LOWNDES**			
Kum Far	32400	D	1921	Bettie	40690	D	1925	Edward R., Jr.	48380	I	1927
Mary Joey	8919	D	1909	Edmund	15561	D	1913	Frances Hoff	3337	D	1907
Men You	69230	D	1935	Emil	35882	D	1923	Francis Lloyd	40780	D	1925
Richard	17214	M	1914	George	50258	D	1928	**LOWNETHAL**			
Richard	20690	D	1916	I., Mrs.	40690	D	1925	Jacob Leon	4668	D	1907
Stephen Collins	19753	D	1915	Isidor	26514	D	1919	**LOWNEY**			
William R.	912	D	1906	Joseph	35940	D	1923	Alice E.	30101	D	1920
LOWANS				Robert	16547	D	1913	Daniel D.	40288	D	1924
Elizabeth Sophia	13107	M	1912	Virginia	7948	I	1909	Dennis J.	9679	D	1910
LOWART				**LOWENGRUND**				George F.	12446	D	1911
Donald	80775	M	1939	Jane	88130	D	1941	M. E.	31161	D	1921
Earl	80775	M	1939	Leopold	83667	D	1940	Paul F.	21182	M	1916
LOWDEN				**LOWENSTEIN**				Raymond E.	21182	M	1916
Mary Ann	53768	D	1929	Benard	45664	D	1926	Timothy J.	9110	I	1910
LOWE				Herman	52930	D	1929	Timothy J.	31833	D	1921
Andrew F.	64123	M	1933	Leah	81655	D	1939	**LOWNHOLM**			
Belle	77306	D	1937	Lena	8226	D	1909	John C.	47742	D	1927
Benard	45664	D	1926	Maurice F.	36398	D	1923	**LOWREY**			
Blanche	77306	D	1937	Nathan	83700	D	1940	Helen Frances	88145	D	1941
Catherine	20416	M	1916	Rose	73839	D	1936	John Joseph	86471	D	1941
Catherine W.	44550	D	1926	William	1250	D	1906	Peter	17853	D	1914
Chen Fat	64123	M	1933	Wolf	1250	D	1906	**LOWRIE**			
Clarence W.	21070	D	1916	**LOWENTHAL**				Charles Donald	50935	M	1928
Ella L.	89348	D	1942	Herman	53570	D	1929	James Walter	59138	D	1931
Helen M.	39118	D	1924	Jennie	17516	D	1914	John Morrison	44952	D	1926
Herbert A.	83411	I	1940	Morris S.	29779	D	1920	Laura L.	78344	D	1938
Herman	53570	D	1929	Rosalie	35793	I	1923	Robert K.	89431	M	1942
How Wy	80253	D	1939	**LOWERY**				William H.	14733	D	1913
Howard G.	51102	M	1928	Conrad	88585	D	1941	**LOWRY**			
Howard Galland	79079	I	1938	David C.	68073	D	1934	Bridget A.	47525	D	1927
Ida M.	41286	D	1925	Jess L.	71485	M	1936	Edward B.	51272	I	1928
John Harold	60112	D	1931	John A.	16079	D	1913				

NAME	NUMBER	TYPE	YEAR
Edward S.	46209	D	1927
Enoch H.	67269	D	1934
Jack Worthington	6095	M	1908
John	15046	D	1913
Margaret	25531	D	1918
Margaret Elizabeth	86842	D	1941
Ned	51272	I	1928
Patrick J.	25530	D	1918
Phinelia Marion	23699	D	1917
William Glendenning	20895	D	1916
LOXEY			
R. H.	43819	D	1926
LOY			
Allan	6261	M	1908
Henry	6261	M	1908
Lee	34476	D	1922
Lee Lun	4561	D	1907
Lee Yuen	59538	D	1931
Mary Josephine	6205	D	1908
Mary Louise	6261	M	1908
LOYALL			
Camilla F.	23996	D	1918
LOZANO			
C. A.	10541	D	1910
Luisa	69361	D	1935
LOZIER			
Alice A.	89370	D	1942
LUBA			
Babette	76939	D	1937
LUBARKSY			
Samuel	27695	D	1919
LUBATTI			
Elvera	15429	D	1913
Giovanni	75336	D	1937
Stella	30358	M	1920
LUBBACK			
Harry B.	51122	D	1928
LUBBE			
Minnie W.	37804	D	1923
LUBBEN			
Henry	15809	D	1913
LUBBERT			
Margaret	2143	D	1906
LUBECK			
Gustaf Hjalmar	46765	D	1927
Hjalmar	46765	D	1927
Victor	44322	D	1926

NAME	NUMBER	TYPE	YEAR
LUBERACKI			
Simon	41295	D	1925
LUBIMIR			
Juliana	33168	D	1922
Theresa	68811	D	1935
LUBIN			
Miriam	62397	M	1932
Samuel	75968	D	1937
Simon C.	27068	D	1919
LUBINSKI			
Leroy D.	75626	M	1937
LUBKE			
Nicolaus	1551	D	1906
LUBLINER			
Morris	17553	D	1914
LUBLINSKY			
Aaron	35336	D	1922
LUBOCK			
Hattie	4242	D	1907
LUBOSCH			
George	41260	D	1925
LUBY			
Pauline	10563	M	1910
LUCARELLI			
Frank	69709	D	1935
LUCAS			
Emilie C.	57233	D	1930
Emma A.	25174	D	1918
F. J., Mrs.	57905	D	1931
Georgia E.	53527	D	1929
Kent W.	73579	I	1936
Leroy P.	48639	D	1927
Lottie E.	56331	D	1930
Lunethe E.	13595	D	1912
Margaret E.	48699	D	1927
Margaret Lucy Anna	64878	D	1933
Matthys	60587	D	1932
Nellie	57905	D	1931
Paul	14258	I	1912
Paul	20366	D	1916
Paula	36070	M	1923
Raymond John	47312	D	1927
Walter Elmer	88233	D	1941
Walter Monroe	51075	D	1928
LUCCHESI			
Alondino	56835	D	1930
Angelo	79914	D	1938

NAME	NUMBER	TYPE	YEAR
Egidio	79260	D	1938
Emrichetta	78336	D	1938
Enrico J.	89415	D	1942
Harry	89415	D	1942
Leonello	87814	D	1941
Lorenzo	55451	I	1930
Rosa	42514	D	1925
Tullio	53582	D	1929
LUCCHETTI			
Antonietta	28653	D	1920
Francesco	32510	D	1921
Gianbattista	35713	D	1923
John	57088	I	1930
John B.	35713	D	1923
Julia	37189	I	1923
LUCCI			
Concezio	32915	I	1921
Concezio	33022	D	1921
LUCE			
Clara U.	73648	D	1936
Clarissa U.	73648	D	1936
Emilio	86436	D	1941
Frank M. L.	29186	D	1920
G. W., Mrs.	73648	D	1936
George C.	14200	D	1912
George W.	44930	D	1926
Gertrude	86435	D	1941
Mabel C.	74846	D	1937
Maria	68349	D	1934
Roy R.	75272	I	1937
LUCERO			
Francisco S.	58447	I	1931
LUCEY			
Cecilia Nadine	60621	M	1932
Charles T.	79564	D	1938
Cornelius	48928	D	1928
Dennis	59233	D	1931
Jeremiah Hughs	37054	D	1923
John	78877	D	1938
Joseph P.	24108	D	1918
Mary Catherine	79892	D	1938
Nora	60806	D	1932
LUCH			
Mary	87665	D	1941
LUCHESI			
Alondino	56836	D	1930
Clara	84444	D	1940
Pietro	82845	D	1939

NAME	NUMBER	TYPE	YEAR	NAME	NUMBER	TYPE	YEAR	NAME	NUMBER	TYPE	YEAR
LUCHESSA				**LUCKEY**				**LUDERS**			
Elizabeth R.	84768	D	1940	Clarence L.	69488	D	1935	Gustav	77937	D	1938
LUCHETTI				Prudence M.	27574	D	1919	John	77451	D	1938
Benita	27267	M	1919	**LUCKHARDT**				**LUDEWIG**			
Sue	89428	I	1942	Dorothea L.	32313	M	1921	Robert	59865	D	1931
LUCHINI				Marcella C.	32313	M	1921	**LUDINGTON**			
Francesco	62222	D	1932	Maybelle Frances	32312	D	1921	Rebecca L.	17312	D	1914
LUCHS				Wilhelm	5597	D	1908	**LUDKE**			
Alice K.	60953	D	1932	**LUCKS**				Anne Kennedy	1862	D	1906
Margaret G.	69803	M	1935	Henry	89011	D	1942	William S.	34635	D	1922
LUCHSINGER				**LUCKSHARDT**				**LUDLAM**			
George H.	17391	D	1914	Maybelle	32312	D	1921	Clarence E.	954	M	1906
John Jacob	51427	D	1928	**LUCO**				Edward H.	954	M	1906
LUCIA				Juan M.	15340	D	1913	**LUDLOW**			
Giuseppe	68212	D	1934	**LUCY**				Anna	17533	I	1914
Luigi	20238	D	1916	Benjamin Carleton	77711	D	1938	James T.	52187	D	1929
Pasquale	47370	D	1927	Charles Thomas	6871	M	1908	**LUDLUM**			
Peter	42399	M	1925	Ellen M.	5646	D	1908	Margaret M.	14491	D	1912
Sam	42399	M	1925	George D.	65756	D	1933	**LUDVIGSEN**			
Vincenzo	61824	D	1932	James W.	18943	D	1915	N. P.	32947	D	1921
LUCIANI				Mary F.	18946	D	1915	Sine, Mrs.	32947	D	1921
Vincenzo	21546	D	1916	Robert V.	44617	D	1926	**LUDVIGSON**			
Zaira	50094	I	1928	Thomas William	54617	I	1929	Lars	75056	D	1937
LUCIANO				**LUDDECKE**				**LUDWIG**			
Faustina	54187	D	1929	George F. W.	75276	D	1937	Adam	47528	D	1927
Santiago	52518	D	1929	Julius	61076	I	1932	Frank	81697	D	1939
LUCICH				Julius	63771	D	1933	Hugo Carl Paul	86931	D	1941
Beatrice Frances	54773	M	1930	**LUDDEKE**				John C.	40675	D	1924
Mike F.	86434	D	1941	Mary J.	24532	D	1918	John C.	88024	D	1941
Theodore	22897	D	1917	**LUDEKE**				John P.	48859	D	1927
LUCID				August	22737	D	1917	Louise	31280	D	1921
Maurice	15999	D	1913	Elsa	84366	D	1940	Max	33514	D	1922
LUCIO				George F.	75276	D	1937	**LUDWIGSEN**			
Giuseppe	68212	D	1934	George S.	24992	M	1918	Lars	75056	D	1937
LUCK				Mary Jane	24532	D	1918	**LUEBBERT**			
Frank C.	26860	M	1919	**LUDEMAMI**				George	19740	M	1915
Mary	87665	D	1941	Henry	59042	D	1931	William F.	19354	D	1915
LUCKE				**LUDEMAN**				William W.	19354	D	1915
Albert	85741	D	1940	August G.	81679	D	1939	**LUECKE**			
Minna Agnes	68803	D	1935	Frederick D.	55177	D	1930	Albert	85741	D	1940
LUCKENBACH				Marie	37854	D	1923	Elise Wilhelmina	3117	D	1907
Margaret	76998	D	1937	**LUDEMANN**				Mary	88685	D	1941
LUCKETT				Carl Johann Jonas	64682	D	1933	**LUEDER**			
Katherine Alice	60687	D	1932	Frederick	14348	D	1912	Mary	85892	I	1940
Oliver	61107	D	1932	J. F. C.	14348	D	1912	**LUEDERS**			
				Mary H.	11687	D	1911	Bertha	6907	D	1908
				Mary H.	12821	D	1912				

NAME	NUMBER	TYPE	YEAR	NAME	NUMBER	TYPE	YEAR	NAME	NUMBER	TYPE	YEAR
Edward Hans	9456	M	1910	Louis	40854	D	1925	LUMSDEN			
Ida	6976	D	1908	Mile	47311	M	1927	Isabelle	85976	D	1941
LUEHRS				Stepan	47311	M	1927	LUN			
Henry P.	20924	I	1916	LUKAT				Ng	79244	D	1938
LUERMANN				Elizabeth	87453	D	1941	Wong Ming	79999	D	1938
Fritz	23406	D	1917	Gustav Emil	83057	D	1940	LUNA			
LUESCHE				LUKE				Frank Della	45372	D	1926
Frank H.	82325	D	1939	Annie	68115	D	1934	John	14142	D	1912
LUETTICH				Charles Morris	67879	D	1934	Juan	14142	D	1912
Rosa	14084	D	1912	Hazel Amanda	86797	D	1941	LUNAN			
LUFT				LUKENS				Charlotte	80586	D	1939
George	25566	D	1918	Emma Mullan	18794	D	1915	Margaret	46018	D	1926
LUGEA				Emma V.	18794	D	1915	LUNARDINI			
Miguel P.	36763	D	1923	George Russell	13608	D	1912	Domenica	78690	D	1938
LUGGEN				LUKES				LUNBLADE			
Edmund A.	62572	D	1932	Annie F.	81988	D	1939	Catherine	7014	D	1909
Ernest	63866	D	1933	LUKETICH				LUND			
LUGLIANI				Elias	3726	D	1907	Adelia	69748	M	1935
Enrico	68438	I	1934	LUKIANOFF				Andrew C.	84340	D	1940
LUGODIN				Finagen	45333	D	1926	Anita B.	59942	D	1931
Jane Mary	4657	D	1907	LUKIANOWICZ				Anna Maria	40201	D	1924
LUHMAN				Justyna	51281	D	1928	Caroline	33528	D	1922
Gertrude I.	26833	M	1919	LUKICH				Charles R.	6080	D	1908
Robert H.	74963	D	1937	John	19923	M	1915	Hanna Regina	60277	D	1931
LUHN				Mary	19923	M	1915	Hans C.	52549	D	1929
Addie	12902	D	1912	Mary	68159	I	1934	Harry	23499	D	1917
Otto	10973	D	1910	LUKIDNOV				Henry	26634	D	1919
LUHRING				Finogen	45333	D	1926	Henry, Jr.	43124	D	1925
Sophie	70189	D	1935	LULL				Jens H.	11109	D	1911
LUHRS				Norman C.	26413	D	1919	Joel	47210	D	1927
Anna E. Gimbel	11667	D	1911	LUM				Josephine B.	82189	D	1939
LUIGI				Bettina	53380	M	1929	Knud Henry	26634	D	1919
Bianchi	35634	I	1923	Chew Mai	20865	D	1916	Lena Matilda	89592	D	1942
Bianchi	37170	D	1923	Louie Hok	85775	D	1940	Mads F.	10545	D	1910
LUIK				Shee	73804	D	1936	Maria E.	18403	D	1915
Minnie	17297	D	1914	Stewart Milton	41638	M	1925	Marie	24201	D	1918
LUJAK				Wing	38666	D	1924	Marie Dorthea	31599	D	1921
Luke	9710	D	1910	Young	54100	D	1929	Mildred	57337	D	1930
LUKA				LUMAZETT				Minnie	55573	D	1930
Lukac	40854	D	1925	Charles H.	55828	D	1930	Nanny Marie	24201	D	1918
LUKAC				LUMELLO				Norman L.	59941	D	1931
Louis	40854	D	1925	Mario Oreste	63332	D	1933	Sam	46778	D	1927
LUKARELLY				LUMLEY				LUNDAHL			
Frank	69709	D	1935	Abbie	58168	D	1931	Christine Elizabeth	51144	D	1928
LUKAS				George	42800	D	1925	LUNDBERG			
Ivan	47311	M	1927	Mary J.	83954	D	1940	Amanda	37226	D	1923
								August	18917	D	1915

NAME	NUMBER	TYPE	YEAR
Edward	69590	D	1935
Gunvald H.	26175	D	1919
Gustav	47582	D	1927
Harold	15185	D	1913
John August	18917	D	1915
Mandis	37226	D	1923
Paul	82412	D	1939
Sigfrid J.	52919	D	1929
LUNDBLAD			
Frieda	36461	D	1923
Nils	20610	D	1916
LUNDBLADE			
Catherine	7014	D	1909
LUNDBORG			
Bjorn Urbanas	14449	D	1912
Irving	64227	D	1933
Konrsd M.	61875	D	1932
LUNDBURG			
Hannah	72990	D	1936
Virginia Rose	60749	D	1932
LUNDEBORG			
John G.	38880	D	1924
LUNDEN			
Adolph Henry	62255	M	1932
Charles	70104	D	1935
John W.	15541	D	1913
Martha	49983	M	1928
LUNDGREN			
Agnes T.	19870	D	1915
LUNDH			
Harry	23499	D	1917
LUNDIN			
Anna F.	79163	D	1938
Gus	10016	D	1910
Mary J.	39872	D	1924
LUNDQUIST			
Albert	89136	D	1942
Ann	50754	M	1928
Augusta W.	68387	D	1934
Edward	2525	D	1906
Hrederick	2875	D	1907
John O.	10131	D	1910
Robert	85453	M	1940
LUNDSCHNEIDER			
Henry	81927	D	1939
LUNDSTROM			
Ivar	22188	D	1917

NAME	NUMBER	TYPE	YEAR
Katie A.	66093	D	1934
Knut S.	64839	D	1933
LUNDY			
Isaac	86716	D	1941
Kate E.	50241	D	1928
Malcolm David	67913	D	1934
Thomas E.	54319	D	1929
LUNEBURG			
Annie VonHadeln	51876	D	1929
LUNG			
Esther Ng Chung	25885	D	1918
Tom	13234	D	1912
LUNGHARD			
Johanna J.	69514	D	1935
LUNN			
Julia D.	62681	D	1932
Mary B.	9104	D	1910
LUNNEY			
Hugh J.	46811	D	1927
LUNNUY			
Elizabeth	70182	D	1935
LUNNY			
Ann R.	59115	D	1931
Elizabeth Greggains	30771	D	1920
LUNSDUN			
William	40783	D	1925
William	40783	D	1925
LUNSMAN			
Geraldine D.	34684	D	1922
LUNSMANN			
August Frederich Herman	20601	M	1916
August W.	18797	D	1915
Henrietta Doris Amalia	20601	M	1916
John Henry	74778	D	1937
Wilhelmina Alvina	20601	M	1916
William Henry	76992	D	1937
LUNSTEDT			
Alma F.	82252	D	1939
Edward	46251	D	1927
Mary Agnese	88511	D	1941
Theodore	76058	D	1937
LUNT			
George Crombie	28229	D	1919
George William	42082	D	1925
Jennie Chace	25941	D	1918
Robert Ernest	48219	D	1927
Stephen P.	27733	D	1919

NAME	NUMBER	TYPE	YEAR
Stephen P.	71394	D	1936
LUOMA			
Susie	41335	I	1925
LUONT			
Josephine	82189	D	1939
LUOTO			
Axel	60131	D	1931
LUPARIA			
Giuseppe	71122	D	1935
LUPESCU			
Samuel	80866	D	1939
LUPESEN			
Samuel	80866	D	1939
LUPI			
Domenico	49460	D	1928
LUPKE			
Carl William	55632	D	1930
Wilhelm	55632	D	1930
William	55319	I	1930
William	55632	D	1930
LUPO			
Vincenzo	82660	D	1939
LUPPINO			
Jasper	12995	D	1912
LURENS			
John	40740	D	1925
LURIE			
Robert Alfred	75870	M	1937
Shewell	89354	D	1942
LURMANN			
Anna M.	12101	D	1911
Charles T.	23406	D	1917
Fredrick W.	31292	D	1921
LUSBERG			
John M.	41934	D	1925
John M.	41934	D	1925
LUSE			
Henry H.	29330	D	1920
LUSERO			
Trinidad	22488	M	1917
LUSK			
Alvin	81407	D	1939
Charles B.	71820	D	1936
H., Mrs.	30882	D	1920
Martha A.	2903	D	1907
Wilhemina	30882	D	1920

NAME	NUMBER	TYPE	YEAR	NAME	NUMBER	TYPE	YEAR	NAME	NUMBER	TYPE	YEAR
LUSKY				LUTTRINGER				Margaret	40880	D	1925
Sergio	3468	D	1907	Charles	45123	D	1926	Peter	30682	D	1920
LUSTENBERGER				Enid	51274	D	1928	Rebecca	74568	D	1937
Felix Joseph	33310	D	1922	Jean Louis	75498	D	1937	Timothy A.	21403	I	1916
LUSTIG				Richmond J.	24440	D	1918	LYFORD			
Armin	8528	I	1909	LUTZ				Wilson	32877	D	1921
Irene Ackerman	68552	D	1934	Carl	64385	D	1933	LYLE			
Joseph	49545	D	1928	Dora	37892	I	1923	George Blake	83652	D	1940
William	30301	D	1920	Dora	46196	D	1927	Sarah Kelly	77326	D	1937
LUTFY				Ignaz August	46821	D	1927	Sarah M.	77326	D	1937
Sophie	40462	M	1924	John C.	48765	D	1927	LYMAN			
LUTGE				Mary	47323	D	1927	Catherine F.	71477	D	1936
Emma L.	35926	D	1923	Robert M.	63278	D	1933	Dean Briggs	1939	D	1906
Louis	40689	D	1925	William E.	14377	D	1912	Dennis N.	81508	D	1939
Richard	62054	D	1932	LUTZEN				Edith	61751	I	1932
Theodore	12284	D	1911	Gustav	65723	D	1933	Harry Gibbs	78067	D	1938
LUTHER				LUVISI				Marjory Winefred	35145	M	1922
Anita Marie	35963	I	1923	Virginia	48324	D	1927	Mary A.	31337	D	1921
Arthur	71966	D	1936	LUVRE				Mattie Thompson	43041	D	1925
Duane	46463	M	1927	Jules	24658	D	1918	William	35145	M	1922
John A.	53376	D	1929	LUX				LYMON			
John B.	9498	D	1910	Abraham L.	46046	D	1926	Elizabeth Jane	7386	D	1909
Minon W.	43938	D	1926	Alpha Blanche	36018	M	1923	LYMP			
LUTHI				Frederick	3583	D	1907	Amelia	12961	D	1912
Samuel	28407	D	1919	Frederick W.	42634	D	1925	LYNAM			
Theodor	66455	D	1934	George Herbert	73126	D	1936	Dennis	81508	D	1939
LUTHKE				Henry	89011	D	1942	Elbridge V.	31847	D	1921
Wilhelmina	54067	D	1929	Miranda W.	2098	D	1906	Mildred T.	77883	D	1938
LUTIC				LUXEMBERG				LYNCH			
Ivo	86521	I	1941	Anna	12021	M	1911	Agnes	22713	M	1917
LUTICH				Milton	12021	M	1911	Alexander	52302	D	1929
John	85367	D	1940	Moritz	8392	D	1909	Alice E.	41505	D	1925
LUTJENS				LUZUKI				Anna V.	63226	D	1932
Adelheit	56102	D	1930	Makakishi	29282	D	1920	Annie	36470	D	1923
Pauline Carrie	56407	D	1930	LYCETT				Annie	87334	D	1941
LUTTERMANN				Mary Frances	75383	D	1937	Annie	68704	D	1935
Louis	9963	D	1910	LYCETTE				Annie M.	58687	I	1931
LUTTICKEN				Mary	39655	D	1924	Annie M.	62396	I	1932
Ida	64075	D	1933	Patrick	2046	D	1906	Arthur J.	55209	I	1930
Karl F.	79966	D	1938	LYDEN				Bridget	17838	D	1914
LUTTRELL				Martin H.	38982	D	1924	Bridget	34923	D	1922
Catherine	77204	M	1937	LYDERSON				Bridget	40979	D	1925
Donald	77204	M	1937	Peder	76344	D	1937	Catherine	14350	D	1912
Eugene	77204	M	1937	LYDON				Catherine	34852	M	1922
Peter Harrison	68614	D	1934	Bridget Agatha	57304	D	1930	Catherine	59075	D	1931
				James	78636	D	1938	Catherine	36824	M	1923
				James J.	14454	D	1912	Catherine H.	50587	D	1928
								Charles F.	47341	D	1927

NAME	NUMBER	TYPE	YEAR	NAME	NUMBER	TYPE	YEAR	NAME	NUMBER	TYPE	YEAR
Charles M.	26925	D	1919	John	17350	D	1914	Mike	37351	D	1923
Charles V.	49115	D	1928	John	41643	D	1925	Nellie	80165	D	1938
Charles William	80773	D	1939	John	82717	M	1939	Nora	62724	D	1932
Chester T.	43529	D	1926	John	52271	M	1929	Nora Grady	60732	D	1932
Clara	43761	D	1926	John Aloysius	78046	D	1938	Pat	18182	D	1914
Cornelius	10000	D	1910	John Conant	88636	D	1941	Patrick	297	D	1906
Cornelius	16272	D	1913	John Edward	36824	M	1923	Patrick	16179	D	1913
Cornelius	79065	D	1938	John H.	15760	D	1913	Patrick	45940	D	1926
Dale Dennis	81966	M	1939	John H.	36503	D	1923	Patrick	62583	D	1932
Daniel Joseph	57332	D	1930	John J.	71631	D	1936	Patrick R.	48597	D	1927
Delia Q.	19450	D	1915	John Louis	45246	D	1926	Peter J.	35832	D	1923
Denis	72045	D	1936	John P.	80911	D	1939	Philip T.	74987	D	1937
Dennis	71559	I	1936	Joseph	58241	D	1931	Richard A.	27134	I	1919
Dorothy	9311	M	1910	Joseph C.	63614	D	1933	Robert	9311	M	1910
Edgar Vincent	19698	M	1915	Joseph H.	83895	I	1940	Robert Newton	59051	D	1931
Edward	23834	D	1918	Joseph H.	85793	D	1940	Rose	14751	D	1913
Edward	44904	D	1926	Josephine H.	22484	I	1917	Roseanna	87739	D	1941
Edward	65605	D	1933	Juanita	51455	D	1928	Teresa	21478	M	1916
Edward J.	74599	D	1937	Julia	7884	D	1909	Thomas	6659	D	1908
Eliza	43130	D	1925	Kathryn	54845	D	1930	Thomas	10766	D	1910
Elizabeth	43130	D	1925	Kathryn	88745	M	1941	Thomas	34925	D	1922
Elizabeth	46398	D	1927	Leo E.	60730	I	1932	Thomas B.	38556	D	1924
Elizabeth S.	49372	D	1928	Lula J.	71561	D	1936	Thomas Connor	17246	M	1914
Ellen	6759	D	1908	Lulu	71561	D	1936	Thomas J.	4252	D	1907
Erwine	45339	D	1926	Mabel	22713	M	1917	Thomas P.	49395	D	1928
Ethel Catherine	23332	D	1917	Margaret	422	D	1906	Walter	22713	M	1917
Eugene	9311	M	1910	Margaret	29286	I	1920	William	11168	D	1911
Eugene H.	48070	D	1927	Margaret	34690	D	1922	William	75409	D	1937
Eva Margaret Flynn	82461	D	1939	Margaret Mary	46143	D	1927	William Francis	79743	D	1938
Fenimore Bennett	89986	D	1942	Mary	2342	D	1906	William J.	30271	I	1920
Frank	15305	D	1913	Mary	7178	D	1909	William J.	75151	I	1937
Fred Hall	85030	D	1940	Mary	13914	D	1912	William J.	77344	D	1937
Hattie Josephine	22484	I	1917	Mary	19002	D	1915	**LYNDE**			
Henry H.	35702	D	1923	Mary	34924	D	1922	Emily May	529	D	1906
Humphrey W.	58863	D	1931	Mary	76153	D	1937	**LYNDHURST**			
James	7180	D	1909	Mary	86527	D	1941	Estelle Ada	47611	D	1927
James	32064	D	1921	Mary	39694	I	1924	**LYNDON**			
James	41819	D	1925	Mary B.	36824	M	1923	Marian	30032	D	1920
James	41819	D	1925	Mary C.	15854	D	1913	**LYNESS**			
James	48955	D	1928	Mary Ellen	21478	M	1916	James J.	33384	D	1922
James	74998	D	1937	Mary J.	84936	I	1940	Margaret	25087	D	1918
James M.	35695	D	1923	Maurice	31499	D	1921	**LYNETT**			
James P.	37828	D	1923	Michael	21478	M	1916	Ellen	6010	D	1908
Jennie	68873	D	1935	Michael C.	18877	D	1915	Frederick Martin	23266	D	1917
Jeremiah	22907	D	1917	Michael I.	86491	D	1941	**LYNG**			
Jeremiah	38479	D	1924	Michael J.	34962	D	1922	Rasmus	83242	D	1940
Jermiah	86755	D	1941	Michael J.	89002	D	1942	**LYNN**			
John	892	D	1906	Michael James	46382	D	1927	Agnes C.	57937	I	1931
John	10044	M	1910	Michael M.	31998	D	1921				

NAME	NUMBER	TYPE	YEAR
Bini	45030	D	1926
Ellen Mary	71877	D	1936
Hannah Eliza	72940	D	1936
Hoffman N.	30261	D	1920
James	3660	D	1907
William P.	40060	I	1924
LYNOTT			
Ellen	6010	D	1908
Katie	19650	D	1915
Mary Josephine	61841	D	1932
Patrick Francis	61842	D	1932
Walter J.	63727	D	1933
LYON			
Alice	50123	D	1928
Anna C.	39253	D	1924
Eleanor H.	68317	D	1934
Ella E.	83629	D	1940
Emma C.	28959	D	1920
Frank	51949	D	1929
Harvey W.	89067	D	1942
Henry	61153	D	1932
John	53938	D	1929
Louis Ferdinand Lazare	79609	D	1938
Mary	88031	D	1941
Mary Bell	59465	D	1931
Walter Seth	80513	D	1939
William Frazer	57174	I	1930
William L.	45678	D	1926
LYON(S)			
Helen Elizabeth	2523	D	1906
LYONS			
Alice	82291	I	1939
Anna Knnney	16111	D	1913
Annie	57346	D	1930
Annie	70626	D	1935
Bridget	10515	D	1910
Bridget	10587	I	1910
Catherine	6819	D	1908
Catherine	80592	D	1939
Charles A.	26629	D	1919
Cornelius J.	35159	M	1922
Daniel	70105	D	1935
Della	59907	D	1931
Edward	8180	D	1909
Edward, Jr.	25581	D	1918
Eliza	12481	D	1911
Ellen	83651	D	1940
Emilie	51332	D	1928

NAME	NUMBER	TYPE	YEAR
Frank Howard Frank	19555	D	1915
Hannah	27209	I	1919
Henry A.	41535	D	1925
Honora	84921	D	1940
Hugues J.	65140	D	1933
Jame	40773	D	1925
James	9111	D	1910
James F.	11631	D	1911
John	14116	D	1912
John	17671	D	1914
John	53938	D	1929
John	87902	I	1941
John	88450	D	1941
John Francis	68124	D	1934
John J.	3424	D	1907
John J.	38491	D	1924
John J.	63172	D	1932
John Joseph	78723	D	1938
John M.	70170	D	1935
Joseph	16690	D	1914
Julia	51382	I	1928
Julia	55634	D	1930
Kate	81348	D	1939
Leah	23177	D	1917
Louis	86834	D	1941
Maria	32972	D	1921
Mary	4595	D	1907
Mary	27719	D	1919
Mary	40080	D	1924
Mary	66539	D	1934
Mary Anastia	60312	D	1931
May A.	52999	D	1929
Monica M.	53900	D	1929
Nellie	69911	D	1935
Nora	86415	D	1941
Nora	81273	I	1939
Patrick	30479	D	1920
Patrick	33698	D	1922
Robert Emmett	30905	D	1920
Rose A.	40552	I	1924
Rose A.	56137	D	1930
Ruby	68899	D	1935
Sarah Alice	10972	D	1910
Thomas L.	26233	D	1919
Timothy F.	16772	D	1914
Timothy J.	20871	D	1916
William Henry	11096	D	1911
Winifred	741	D	1906
Winifred I.	869	I	1906

NAME	NUMBER	TYPE	YEAR
LYSETT			
Honora M.	16800	D	1914
John Patrick	2268	D	1906
LYSLE			
Edith MacDonald	49758	D	1928
Helen M.	33888	D	1922
LYTGENS			
Julius W.	33374	D	1922
LYTLE			
Amanda J. Snook	15697	D	1913
Thomas	7715	D	1909
LYTTLE			
Stanley F.	89369	D	1942
LYTTON			
Guy P.	64890	D	1933
LYTTONS			
Edward	25581	D	1918
M'GOVERN			
Chauncey	67108	D	1934
Felix Daniel Chauncey	67108	D	1934
MAACK			
Ernest	27580	D	1919
Henry J.	32597	D	1921
Marie Katherine	28094	D	1919
MAAHS			
Clara	77770	D	1938
MAARTINSEN			
Martin	53362	D	1929
MAAS			
Ambrosius	14055	D	1912
Annie	73866	D	1936
Bernhard	46872	D	1927
Jack	72993	D	1936
Joseph	65523	D	1933
Matthias	5653	D	1908
Morris I.	33582	D	1922
Oscar J.	72993	D	1936
Oscar M.	72993	D	1936
Philip H.	10410	D	1910
Philip J.	74761	D	1937
MAASS			
Alma M.	28993	D	1920
Alvin G.	12915	D	1912
Claus H.	7531	D	1909
Harry	37612	D	1923
Heinrich	37612	D	1923
Henry	37612	D	1923

NAME	NUMBER	TYPE	YEAR
Henry L.	14702	D	1913
John Frederick	37650	D	1923
Jost Henry	37612	D	1923
Louis	37573	I	1923
Louis	84959	D	1940
MAASSEN			
Edith	44226	D	1926
Emil	35711	D	1923
MAASZ			
Claus H.	7531	D	1909
MAATTA			
Howard	48227	M	1927
MABBS			
William George	57302	M	1930
MABER			
Hannah	87127	D	1941
MABREY			
Martha A.	52581	D	1929
MABRY			
Allen Douglas	64788	I	1933
Leon	82206	I	1939
MAC AVIAN			
Robert J.	68241	D	1934
MAC AVIN			
Robert J.	68241	D	1934
MACABEE			
John Edgar	63137	D	1932
MACADAM			
Katherine Madalena	4369	D	1907
MACAPAGAL			
Alexander	63243	I	1932
MACARTHUR			
Helen Augusta	48641	D	1927
Leonie Alice Maginnis	63203	D	1932
MACAULAY			
Bernard V.	75661	D	1937
MACAULEY			
Annie	30714	D	1920
Henry deBaurnonbille	33356	D	1922
James H.	7569	D	1909
Jane	7081	D	1909
Katherine E.	22871	D	1917
Maria R.	88037	D	1941
Thomas J.	16802	D	1914
Walter H.	22116	D	1917

NAME	NUMBER	TYPE	YEAR
MACAULIFFE			
Harry	57647	D	1931
MACBETH			
Hugh	19659	D	1915
MACBRIDE			
Margaret Elise	70019	M	1935
Margaret Elise	70019	M	1935
MACCAFFREY			
James	84939	D	1940
MACCAGNO			
Joseph	41575	D	1925
MACCARINI			
Pellegrino	41574	D	1925
MACCHIAVELLO			
Gaetano	56495	D	1930
MACCLEVERTY			
Mary C.	60290	D	1931
MACCLYMONT			
Catherine E.	24173	M	1918
William E.	24198	D	1918
MACCORD			
Louise	66866	D	1934
MACCORMACK			
Alexander	46037	D	1926
Lucy Ann	81651	I	1939
MACCRELLISH			
Frederick	92	D	1906
MACDERMOTT			
Daniel	36394	I	1923
Thomas	42987	D	1925
MACDONALD			
Alan	70058	D	1935
Alice S.	51353	D	1928
America Moore	81718	D	1939
Annie	75143	D	1937
Anthony	21649	D	1916
Burns, III	78388	M	1938
Burns, Jr.	21833	M	1916
Carmelita J.	26555	M	1919
Catherine Flora	45786	D	1926
Charles	30314	D	1920
Charles A.	31241	M	1921
Colin	8572	D	1909
Donald	72532	D	1936
Donald Kenneth	32263	M	1921
Duncan Roderick	17113	I	1914
Duncan Roderick	18576	D	1915

NAME	NUMBER	TYPE	YEAR
Elizabeth	71594	D	1936
Elodie B.	4525	D	1907
Elodie C.	26555	M	1919
Emma	42247	D	1925
Flora	21833	M	1916
Francis J.	26555	M	1919
George Childs	65496	D	1933
Hedley V.	26918	D	1919
Helen Crutchett	63323	D	1933
Isaiah	35810	D	1923
James C.	7906	M	1909
Jessie M.	31241	M	1921
John A.	39342	D	1924
John E.	18405	D	1915
John L.	69598	D	1935
John Munroe	32255	D	1921
John S.	46625	D	1927
John W.	23724	D	1917
Jonathan Titus	67358	D	1934
Joseph A.	33494	D	1922
Joseph D.	18126	D	1914
Kenneth	85713	D	1940
M. G.	50743	D	1928
Malcolm Lloyd	13154	D	1912
Margaret	20198	D	1915
Margaret	33479	I	1922
Margaret	53292	D	1929
Maria	20645	D	1916
Marion Francis	58845	I	1931
Mary F.	36191	D	1923
Mary I.	86532	D	1941
Mary J.	7906	M	1909
Mary J.	12907	D	1912
Mary Jane	79550	D	1938
Mary Kate	31071	D	1921
Mary L.	11018	I	1911
Minnie	50743	D	1928
Nancy Blair	78389	M	1938
Norman R.	26555	M	1919
Orlando James Winfield	21325	D	1916
Ramon B.	26555	M	1919
Sinclair	50321	M	1928
Uba B.	84747	D	1940
Walter S.	75692	D	1937
William	20144	D	1915
William A.	26555	M	1919
MACDONELL			
Ellen E.	79805	D	1938

NAME	NUMBER	TYPE	YEAR
MacDonnell			
Alexander	62250	D	1932
Alexander Edward	75693	M	1937
Edna Frances	75693	M	1937
Leonard Robert	75693	M	1937
Macdonough			
Joseph	1518	D	1906
William O'B.	16405	D	1913
MacDougall			
Amelia M.	83876	D	1940
Richard W.	66477	M	1934
Robert Donald	66477	M	1934
William C.	66477	M	1934
Mace			
Frank A.	43707	D	1926
Jeanne Camgros	44089	D	1926
John L.	16118	M	1913
Sarah D.	60870	D	1932
MacEachern			
Daniel J.	71156	D	1935
Macellari			
Maria	69043	D	1935
Macenzo			
Eugenio	58491	D	1931
MacFarland			
Kathleen	32489	I	1921
MacFarlane			
Catherine Garfield	39580	M	1924
Julie	76048	D	1937
Kala	39740	M	1924
Ku	39740	M	1924
Muriel	39740	M	1924
Peter Clark	39459	D	1924
Walter	39740	M	1924
Willet James	39580	M	1924
MacGaffee			
J. E.	60843	D	1932
Jack	60843	D	1932
MacGavin			
Dorothy	23259	M	1917
Helen	23259	M	1917
MacGruer			
George Smith	77347	D	1937
MacGuire			
James K. C.	67632	D	1934
Mach			
Charles	57052	I	1930

NAME	NUMBER	TYPE	YEAR
Machada			
Joseph	84807	I	1940
Machado			
Frances	45227	D	1926
Joseph	41265	I	1925
Machellan			
John	42824	D	1925
Machello			
John	58000	D	1931
Machi			
Nunzia	69460	D	1935
Machol			
Louis	88792	D	1941
Maciejewski			
Michael G.	86660	D	1941
Maciel			
Antonio E.	11498	D	1911
John E.	54376	D	1929
MacInnis			
Frank P.	47538	D	1927
MacIntosh			
Rebecca B.	20345	D	1916
MacIntrye			
John Lawrence	72456	D	1936
MacIver			
Christina	58359	D	1931
Mack			
Adeline Duval	31154	D	1921
Albert	8576	M	1909
Albert Christian	7134	D	1909
Augusta	72535	D	1936
Auguste Neumann	72535	D	1936
Aurora	3859	D	1907
Bertha	27953	D	1919
Bertha	30908	M	1920
Bridget	4193	D	1907
Charles	57052	I	1930
Charlotte	69051	D	1935
Christian	2030	D	1906
Clara	8241	D	1909
Daniel	11763	D	1911
Eliza D.	329	D	1906
Elizabeth	39019	D	1924
Emil	31049	I	1921
Emile	30908	M	1920
Frank P.	54490	M	1929
Frederick Edward	24945	D	1918

NAME	NUMBER	TYPE	YEAR
George W.	34905	D	1922
Harry	64261	D	1933
James K.	33803	D	1922
Jeremiah	3832	D	1907
John	50886	D	1928
Julius J.	49637	D	1928
Lena	30908	M	1920
Lois Elaine	53752	D	1929
Louisa	30908	M	1920
Margaret	1521	I	1906
Margaret Marie	21799	M	1916
Mary	20737	I	1916
Mary	62436	I	1932
Mary	64837	D	1933
Mary J.	83327	D	1940
Patrick	65029	D	1933
Patsy	65029	D	1933
Rory	3859	D	1907
Rosa	30908	M	1920
Sadie H.	84776	D	1940
Samuel G.	73314	D	1936
William	303	D	1906
William H.	1512	D	1906
Mackall			
Adele J.	84829	D	1940
Benjamin Franklin	58716	D	1931
Mackay			
Donald Stuart	17951	M	1914
Elizabeth	634	D	1906
Fred H.	10427	D	1910
Helena Stuart	17951	M	1914
Henrietta O.	69486	D	1935
Hrry Kephart	51004	D	1928
Joan Dewey	81755	M	1939
John Gray	35764	D	1923
John S.	28795	D	1920
Rebecca	4773	D	1907
Thomas	2199	D	1906
Walter	86654	M	1941
William	26999	D	1919
William A.	5678	D	1908
Mackel			
Ann	420	D	1906
Macken			
Elizabeth	15416	D	1913
Mackenreuder			
Joseph	2739	M	1907

Name	Number	Type	Year	Name	Number	Type	Year	Name	Number	Type	Year
MacKenzie				**MacKinnon**				**MacLennan**			
Addison Scobie	68264	D	1934	Christina	53407	I	1929	Gladys	77250	D	1937
Agnes	32550	D	1921	John L.	87914	D	1941	J. H.	9645	D	1910
Angus	3643	D	1907	Marguerite	20101	D	1915	James A.	61788	D	1932
Angus	27905	D	1919	Mary Ellen	77639	D	1938	Mary	68990	D	1935
Donald	62810	D	1932	**MacKintosh**				**MacLeod**			
Donald	83172	D	1940	Aird Crawford	80153	D	1938	John	72112	D	1936
Emma Jeanette	61053	D	1932	Cora	80031	D	1938	Neil James	14890	D	1913
Francis Joseph	83033	D	1940	Corienne Willis	80154	M	1938	Robert F.	44685	D	1926
James Allan	70399	D	1935	Elizabeth	63302	D	1933	William J.	36557	D	1923
Jean	76857	I	1937	Florence Margaret	68061	D	1934	**MacLymont**			
Jennie Dorsey	66372	D	1934	Stella E.	62424	D	1932	Aileen O.	10690	M	1910
John H.	63238	D	1932	William	36970	D	1923	Victor H. M.	19314	D	1915
Josephine A.	36463	I	1923	William Crawford	69217	D	1935	**MacMahon**			
Josephine A.	37736	D	1923	**MacKley**				Edith Marian	64268	D	1933
Kenneth	24281	D	1918	Arden Floyd	76401	D	1937	**MacManus**			
Malcolm Allen	53593	D	1929	**MacKlin**				Harriet E.	30540	D	1920
Mary Isabella	76756	D	1937	John	72547	D	1936	**MacMillan**			
Melville	69342	D	1935	**MacKordes**				Aeneas	39393	D	1924
Murdo	87437	D	1941	Mary	16943	I	1914	Elisabeth Campbell	11824	D	1911
William J.	63248	D	1932	**MacKrille**				P. F.	27513	D	1919
MacKey				William R.	38219	D	1924	**MacMonagle**			
Daniel	20716	D	1916	**MacKrodt**				Beverly	13806	D	1912
Edmund	10285	D	1910	Lina	50121	D	1928	**MacMullen**			
Edward A.	30324	D	1920	**MacKroth**				Elizabeth Ellen	75963	D	1937
Harry G.	83809	D	1940	Otto H.	32641	D	1921	John H.	15294	D	1913
James	8289	D	1909	**MacKy**				**MacMurchy**			
Julette	35004	D	1922	Fred	62041	D	1932	Oliver	86737	D	1941
Louise	40144	D	1924	**MacLachlan**				Thomas	43206	I	1925
Marie Ellenora	15843	M	1913	Ellen J.	75720	D	1937	**MacMurtry**			
Rose M.	42534	D	1925	**MacLaren**				W. C.	51554	D	1928
MacKie				Elsie Buck	88990	D	1942	**MacNeill**			
Andrew	60362	D	1931	J. G., Mrs.	88990	D	1942	Andrew P.	54819	D	1930
Evelyn	41230	D	1925	Jack	86324	D	1941	Annie E.	77513	D	1938
Helen DeLano	70974	D	1935	**MacLaughlin**				Douglas Gerald Alexander	78481	D	1938
Helen H.	70974	D	1935	Albert P.	83549	D	1940	**MacNevin**			
James	31068	D	1921	Mary D.	31455	D	1921	George Michael, III	48596	M	1927
James Bernard	72843	M	1936	**MacLean**				Margaret B.	67175	D	1934
Mary	27954	D	1919	D. Victor	71274	D	1935	**MacNutt**			
Mary E.	63761	D	1933	John	14603	D	1912	Archibald H.	39337	D	1924
Mary Elizabeth	43233	D	1925	L. L.	10926	D	1910	**Macomb**			
Richard	76699	I	1937	Norman A.	81643	D	1939	Catherine Sisk	67408	D	1934
Richard Thomas	52142	I	1929	Robert Donald	43880	I	1926	**Macomber**			
Robert W.	32614	D	1921	**MacLellan**				Henry J.	50491	D	1928
Thomas	41178	M	1925	John	42824	D	1925	Mary F.	31606	D	1921
MacKin								Sarah J.	32048	D	1921
Francis J.	17141	D	1914								
John Marion	71878	D	1936								

Key: D = death; M = minor; I = incompetent

NAME	NUMBER	TYPE	YEAR
MACONDRAY			
Frederick	20955	M	1916
Martha L.	66993	D	1934
MACONDRY			
Frederick William	25723	D	1918
William A.	25722	D	1918
MACOWSKY			
Jacob	62033	D	1932
MACPHAIL			
Anna N.	53066	D	1929
MACPHERSON			
Charles Henry	60889	I	1932
Clarence M.	48392	D	1927
Duncan	49908	D	1928
Harry H.	28093	D	1919
Lucille	89140	I	1942
William John	79640	D	1938
MACQUARRIE			
Theresa Barry	73202	D	1936
MACRAE			
Annie D.	69575	D	1935
MACRANDRIAS			
Elias	17747	I	1914
Elias	30176	D	1920
George	83461	D	1940
MACSEAMEN			
Henry	5716	D	1908
MACSWIFT			
Henry	53706	D	1929
MACUMBER			
Annie	7024	D	1909
Stephen	7950	I	1909
MACVEAN			
Duncan Malcolm	68405	I	1934
Duncan Malcolm	78139	D	1938
Jessie B.	42497	D	1925
MACVINE			
Josephine A.	52081	D	1929
MACY			
John	52511	D	1929
Lillian Alice	89264	D	1942
Stanley	32868	M	1921
MADARA			
Elwood M.	74241	D	1936
Hattie	71685	D	1936

NAME	NUMBER	TYPE	YEAR
MADARIS			
Morris	44960	D	1926
MADDACK			
Leonard James	78361	D	1938
MADDEN			
Albert Joseph	79370	I	1938
Archibald C.	57047	D	1930
Bernice	13760	M	1912
Bridget	11566	D	1911
Bridget	21180	D	1916
Catherine	9374	I	1910
Charles A.	72891	I	1936
Charlotte P.	1410	D	1906
Daniel	45438	I	1926
Denis	84551	D	1940
Edith	22185	D	1917
Edith G.	37964	D	1923
Edmond W.	41161	D	1925
Eleanor M.	1173	D	1906
Eleanor M.	66082	D	1934
Ellen	10122	D	1910
Ellen M.	12652	D	1911
Francis J.	39767	I	1924
Hanna	28101	D	1919
James	7587	D	1909
Janet C.	38350	D	1924
Jerome	12965	D	1912
Johanna	28101	D	1919
John	29851	D	1920
John C.	74598	D	1937
John E.	40321	I	1924
Joseph B.	30213	D	1920
Josephine	13760	M	1912
Josephine I.	58552	I	1931
Kate	15043	D	1913
Katherine Jane	85812	D	1940
Maria	60996	D	1932
Mary	24788	D	1918
Mary A.	64451	D	1933
Michael	16350	D	1913
Michael	37033	D	1923
Michael J.	67898	D	1934
Minnie G.	83099	D	1940
Patrick	9300	D	1910
Peter	20604	D	1916
Robert Willis	65665	D	1933
Rose	49100	D	1928
Theresa	37261	M	1923

NAME	NUMBER	TYPE	YEAR
Thomas	9364	D	1910
Thomas	16563	D	1914
Thomas	71661	D	1936
Thomas David	14793	M	1913
William M.	52808	D	1929
William Merritt, Jr.	37963	D	1923
MADDERN			
Charlotte E.	79421	D	1938
MADDIGAN			
Kate	13374	I	1912
Katherine	16787	D	1914
MADDOCK			
Michael A.	54682	D	1930
MADDOCKS			
Bradley B.	12401	D	1911
Howard C.	4694	D	1907
Howard C.	12402	D	1911
Howard W.	12402	D	1911
John	61622	D	1932
MADDOX			
Knox	77585	D	1938
Shirley C.	54743	D	1930
Virginia Knox	71290	D	1935
MADDUX			
Edith Walker	66728	D	1934
MADEN			
Emile	82150	D	1939
MADER			
Jacob H.	21268	D	1916
MADERA			
Hattie	71685	D	1936
MADERIOS			
Maud	49531	D	1928
MADERO			
Hattie	66801	D	1934
Peter	40397	D	1924
MADICH			
John	22277	D	1917
MADIERIOS			
Maud	49531	D	1928
MADIGAN			
Annie	14455	I	1912
David W.	37885	I	1923
David W.	44897	D	1926
Edward Joseph	46539	D	1927
John Edward	36323	D	1923
Lloyd Thomas	84631	D	1940

NAME	NUMBER	TYPE	YEAR
Sarah J.	17247	D	1914
Thomas L.	84631	D	1940
MADISON			
Anna	32060	D	1921
Christ	31397	I	1921
Christine C.	58790	D	1931
Edward F.	46265	I	1927
Elizabeth	6357	D	1908
Elizabeth	74902	I	1937
Harold G.	85151	D	1940
James	47609	D	1927
Marcellus S.	59851	D	1931
Marie H.	57864	D	1931
Marilyn Eyre	87945	M	1941
Mary	63001	I	1932
Mary Elizabeth	81942	M	1939
Walter A.	77847	D	1938
MADRID			
Benjamin	86228	D	1941
Ignacio	71185	D	1935
MADRIGAL			
Manuel S.	42878	D	1925
MADSEN			
Catherine J.	58174	D	1931
Elise Christine	17629	D	1914
Florence May	47681	D	1927
Hans	53555	D	1929
Henry L.	83261	D	1940
Olaf Jay	56454	D	1930
MADSON			
Merlin Malcolm	82106	D	1939
MADSTEN			
Andreas	6235	D	1908
MADUSKA			
William	40228	D	1924
MAEDE			
Maurice	66610	M	1934
MAESO			
Anselmo	39786	D	1924
MAESSNER			
Gottlieb	78317	D	1938
MAESTRETTI			
Adeline	22589	M	1917
Albert	8122	D	1909
John	16747	M	1914
MAESTRI			
Filomena	77757	D	1938

NAME	NUMBER	TYPE	YEAR
Giovanni	83280	D	1940
MAFFEE			
Clement	80948	D	1939
MAFFEI			
Giuseppe	16383	I	1913
Italio	47118	M	1927
Joseph	30259	M	1920
Lougi	47118	M	1927
Pauline	30259	M	1920
Pauline	40425	M	1924
Rosa	56505	D	1930
Santina	40510	D	1924
MAFROIANOS			
Dimidrios	40397	D	1924
MAGANARIS			
Theodora	75114	I	1937
MAGARRELL			
Thomas M.	63647	D	1933
William M.	64216	D	1933
MAGAT			
Benigno	60192	D	1931
MAGAURAN			
Michael	51750	D	1929
MAGEE			
Edward Joseph	73063	I	1936
Edward Joseph	73200	D	1936
Elizabeth	29218	M	1920
Helen Curtis	15339	D	1913
John	40889	D	1925
Kate	41486	D	1925
Margaret C.	29346	D	1920
Margaret Elizabeth	29218	M	1920
Martha	56528	D	1930
Mary	60116	D	1931
Mary Elizabeth House	67883	D	1934
Mary Frances	21227	D	1916
Mary I.	15103	D	1913
Rose	62642	D	1932
Thomas	29347	D	1920
Thomas, Jr.	17375	D	1914
W. H.	10282	D	1910
Walter	63699	D	1933
MAGENDIE			
Adele	18485	M	1915
Charles M.	16543	D	1913
Elizabeth	82544	D	1939
John B.	5782	D	1908

NAME	NUMBER	TYPE	YEAR
P.	67508	D	1934
Pierre	67508	D	1934
MAGER			
Fredrick	11905	D	1911
Hans A.	84952	D	1940
Severin	45818	D	1926
MAGEV			
Wilhelmine Wagener	38251	D	1924
MAGG			
Sarah	6188	D	1908
MAGGART			
Eleanor M.	20001	D	1915
Harold F.	20068	M	1915
Roy E.	20068	M	1915
MAGGI			
Benedetta	53972	D	1929
Emanuele	65213	D	1933
Umberto	66025	D	1934
MAGGINI			
Albert A.	51802	D	1929
Albert A., Jr.	52011	M	1929
Alfred F.	52011	M	1929
Charles	9575	D	1910
Erminia	46415	D	1927
James C.	52011	M	1929
MAGGIO			
Fortunato	38023	D	1923
Helena	38024	D	1923
MAGGIORA			
Biagio Della	82557	D	1939
Daniele Della	36646	D	1923
Ottavio	35282	D	1922
Peter Della	55081	D	1930
MAGGIORE			
Jack	61167	D	1932
Peter D.	68376	D	1934
Quito Della	61167	D	1932
MAGGIORI			
Jack	61167	D	1932
Quito Della	61167	D	1932
MAGGIORINI			
Paul	61366	D	1932
MAGHAKIAN			
Edward Arthur	82241	M	1939
MAGIALLI			
Luigi	25861	D	1918

Key: D = death; M = minor; I = incompetent

NAME	NUMBER	TYPE	YEAR
MAGINI			
Giovanni	40701	D	1925
MAGINIS			
Alan Preston	54969	M	1930
Alice Patricia	54968	M	1930
John J.	24414	D	1918
MAGINNIS			
Charles	7098	M	1909
Charles Leonard	41154	M	1925
Leo	7098	M	1909
Leo A.	76986	D	1937
Leonie A.	63203	D	1932
Martin	7098	M	1909
MAGINNISS			
Michael	24998	D	1918
Thomas H.	67842	D	1934
MAGINUIS			
Andrew	81902	M	1939
MAGISTRA			
Carlo	72701	D	1936
Charles A.	72701	D	1936
Mary	69533	D	1935
MAGLARAS			
Peter A.	48270	D	1927
MAGLIANO			
Carlo	84884	D	1940
MAGLOWN			
William J.	15634	D	1913
MAGNAN			
Marcel	46824	D	1927
MAGNANI			
Deodato	13335	D	1912
Lorenzo	84804	D	1940
Louis	31489	I	1921
Mariani	11460	D	1911
Peter P.	50250	D	1928
Zeffiro	37582	D	1923
MAGNAU			
Marcel	46824	D	1927
MAGNE			
Henri	37160	D	1923
Leontine	43780	D	1926
MAGNED			
Babetta	14317	D	1912
MAGNER			
Barbetta	14317	D	1912

NAME	NUMBER	TYPE	YEAR
Celia	85557	D	1940
Emanuel	70368	D	1935
Emil	13490	D	1912
Emil	85557	D	1940
Helene Marie	81570	M	1939
Jennie	15268	M	1913
Joe	42394	I	1925
John B.	7597	D	1909
Joseph	35274	D	1922
Joseph	42874	I	1925
Joseph	43922	D	1926
Mary	34984	D	1922
Max	57339	D	1930
Michael R.	86678	D	1941
Nathaniel A.	44940	D	1926
Sarah	74605	D	1937
Saul	41269	D	1925
Toby, Jr.	81570	M	1939
Winifred	68769	D	1935
MAGNES			
Emma	79782	D	1938
Leontine	56833	D	1930
Samuel D.	28956	D	1920
MAGNI			
Alberto	48364	D	1927
MAGNIER			
Nellie	38336	D	1924
MAGNIN			
Isaac	2888	D	1907
Victor	11518	D	1911
MAGNUS			
Eugene E.	45068	D	1926
Henry Christian	89877	D	1942
Max	22714	D	1917
MAGNUSEN			
Gustaf W.	51594	D	1928
Lucie A.	43121	D	1925
MAGNUSON			
Andrew	88659	I	1941
Charles A.	1626	D	1906
Charles A.	35226	D	1922
David	79538	M	1938
F. Elliot	79106	D	1938
Fred	79106	D	1938
Fritiof	79106	D	1938
Gust	51594	D	1928
MAGNUSSON			
Gustaf W.	51594	D	1928

NAME	NUMBER	TYPE	YEAR
MAGOONIS			
George	3763	D	1907
MAGORTY			
Hugh	4634	D	1907
Walter	14105	D	1912
MAGRANE			
Florence L.	74092	D	1936
John A.	45235	D	1926
MAGUIRE			
Aloysuis J.	17137	M	1914
Anna E.	86173	D	1941
Annie	44178	D	1926
Augustus B.	38354	D	1924
Christopher C.	39889	M	1924
Daniel Michael	89521	M	1942
Edward H., Mrs.	88356	D	1941
Elizabeth	21077	D	1916
Elizabeth	84643	D	1940
Ellen	5762	D	1908
Ellen	58860	D	1931
Etta J.	19731	D	1915
Frank	1	I	1906
Frank P.	55484	D	1930
George	19525	D	1915
Ida	51087	D	1928
James	16847	M	1914
James	64597	I	1933
James	70311	I	1935
James F.	16238	D	1913
James R.	35914	M	1923
James W.	50158	D	1928
John	36943	D	1923
John T.	44182	M	1926
Joseph A.	17137	M	1914
Joseph A.	53468	D	1929
Joseph J.	53468	D	1929
Katherine T.	68242	D	1934
Magdalene	17137	M	1914
Margaret Agnes	41434	D	1925
Marguerite	88356	D	1941
Marie H.	17137	M	1914
Mary	14622	D	1912
Mary	83068	D	1940
Mary Ann	80376	D	1939
Michael	64533	D	1933
Patrick J.	15126	D	1913
Phyllis	16847	M	1914
Robert C.	44183	M	1926

Key: D = death; M = minor; I = incompetent

NAME	NUMBER	TYPE	YEAR	NAME	NUMBER	TYPE	YEAR	NAME	NUMBER	TYPE	YEAR
Rose Mary	17137	M	1914	Philip	755	D	1906	Andrew D. O., Mrs.	28794	D	1920
Samuel Joseph	11814	D	1911	Rita M.	81220	M	1939	Angel	44051	D	1926
Stephen John	36261	D	1923	Rosalia A.	69355	D	1935	Annie	28794	D	1920
Susan	81575	I	1939	Thomas	80064	D	1938	Annie	28794	D	1920
Susan	82909	D	1939	Thomas F.	17210	D	1914	Annie Roche	5563	D	1908
Thomas Francis	58226	D	1931	Thomas F.	40504	D	1924	Austin	11602	M	1911
William	6395	D	1908	Thomas F.	66676	D	1934	Barholomew	55892	D	1930
William F.	35585	M	1922	William P.	11569	D	1911	Bridget	41659	D	1925
MAGUOY				**MAHERIN**				Bridget A.	30988	I	1921
John	24513	I	1918	John	20876	D	1916	Bridget Adelaide	46836	D	1927
MAHALICK				**MAHILLON**				Catharine	17808	D	1914
Jacob	57211	I	1930	August	53564	D	1929	Catherine	65388	D	1933
MAHAN				**MAHLE**				Charles E.	85005	D	1940
Harold	22851	M	1917	William G.	33740	D	1922	Charles Lester	79579	D	1938
Harry J.	14678	D	1913	**MAHLENBREY**				Cornelius	780	D	1906
Henry H.	10103	D	1910	Euphrosine	64473	D	1933	Cornelius	17930	D	1914
Henry J.	14678	D	1913	Rosa	64473	D	1933	Daniel	9059	D	1910
MAHANNY				**MAHLER**				Daniel	49163	D	1928
Gertrude	34622	D	1922	Carl	61974	D	1932	Daniel Edward	45092	D	1926
MAHAR				Harry	61974	D	1932	David	8652	D	1909
Alexander Taylor	4550	M	1907	Henry J., Jr.	64790	D	1933	David J., Jr.	6183	M	1908
Marcelle	52829	D	1929	Hermann H.	28805	D	1920	Delia	43878	D	1926
MAHAU				**MAHLSTEDT**				Delia Bolen Ryan	50658	D	1928
Marie Stephanie	77099	D	1937	William H.	43160	D	1925	Dennis	88739	D	1941
MAHER				**MAHN**				Dennis J.	14194	D	1912
Catherine	29359	D	1920	Annie	68109	D	1934	Edward J.	23525	D	1917
Edward	13031	D	1912	Herman	7006	D	1909	Elizabeth	69316	D	1935
Edward J.	83571	D	1940	**MAHNCKEN**				Ellen	19027	D	1915
Elizabeth	69024	D	1935	J. H.	16882	D	1914	Ellen	27275	D	1919
Francis J.	81220	M	1939	**MAHNKE**				Ellen	81101	I	1939
Hannah	41062	D	1925	John	83022	D	1940	Ellen	81119	D	1939
Harold	69044	I	1935	**MAHNKEN**				Emma I.	48794	D	1927
James C.	40921	D	1925	John Diedrich	45593	D	1926	Eva	33526	D	1922
John	83742	D	1940	**MAHNLIK**				Florence	50482	D	1928
Julia G.	66675	D	1934	George	4815	D	1907	Fred A.	46261	I	1927
Lottie A.	74208	D	1936	**MAHON**				Frederick Abbott	40711	I	1925
Louise	84612	D	1940	Anne	83081	D	1940	James F.	71912	M	1936
Margaret Elizabeth	70192	D	1935	Elizabeth Jane	61885	M	1932	Jeremiah	10688	D	1910
Margaret J.	14578	D	1912	Frank	15293	D	1913	Jeremiah W.	22459	D	1917
Marie	40525	D	1924	Helena	7613	D	1909	Joanna J.	31962	D	1921
Martin A.	31679	D	1921	John	855	D	1906	Johanna	4076	I	1907
Mary E.	85768	D	1940	Kate	18880	D	1915	Johanna	56056	D	1930
Mary N.	74927	I	1937	Michael J.	1698	D	1906	John D.	78888	D	1938
Mary Ruth	52928	D	1929	**MAHONEY**				John Daniel	47127	D	1927
Matthew	74914	D	1937	Alice	6183	M	1908	John H.	61805	D	1932
Michael	37954	M	1923	Ambrose	14504	M	1912	John J.	54256	D	1929
Minnie P.	45859	D	1926	Andrew D. O.	31358	D	1921	Julia	54893	D	1930
Peter M.	19623	D	1915					Julia	81789	D	1939
								Justin	11602	M	1911

NAME	NUMBER	TYPE	YEAR	NAME	NUMBER	TYPE	YEAR	NAME	NUMBER	TYPE	YEAR
Katie	66154	D	1934	Rose A.	67100	D	1934	Louise M.	52036	D	1929
Letitia Grace	67182	D	1934	Thomas	13665	D	1912	**MAILLOUX**			
Lizzie	37980	D	1923	Timothy L.	49569	D	1928	Marie Louise	40493	D	1924
Louise H.	41342	D	1925	William	60497	D	1931	**MAILOUGH**			
Lucy M.	51163	I	1928	**MAHOOD**				Agnes	6953	M	1908
Mabel O.	49141	D	1928	Beverly Josephine	37620	M	1923	**MAIN**			
Margaret	60475	D	1931	Joseph J.	68280	D	1934	Charles	1527	D	1906
Margaret E.	70979	D	1935	Raymond Foster	37620	M	1923	Charles	89385	D	1942
Margaret O.	60858	D	1932	**MAHORIC**				Crete	87030	I	1941
Mary	13521	M	1912	Joseph	66416	D	1934	Medora T.	13606	D	1912
Mary	32865	D	1921	**MAHR**				Ross B.	75406	D	1937
Mary	47425	D	1927	Christ	20112	D	1915	Sophie Edith	40055	D	1924
Mary	75376	D	1937	**MAHRAN**				**MAINA**			
Mary A.	2009	D	1906	Hannah	39097	D	1924	Carmela Scicluna	63342	D	1933
Mary Anne	37635	I	1923	James Thomas	58043	D	1931	**MAINERI**			
Mary B.	68413	D	1934	Mary A.	63006	D	1932	John	78288	M	1938
Mary J.	57579	D	1931	**MAHU**				Nick	79143	D	1938
Michael	53238	D	1929	Marie	77099	D	1937	Ronald John	78288	M	1938
Mira M.	10540	D	1910	**MAHUCKEN**				**MAINHART**			
Patricia	71557	D	1936	Henriette	80776	D	1939	Beatrice Vincent	65146	I	1933
Patrick A.	44640	D	1926	**MAI**				**MAINICH**			
Raymond M.	11602	M	1911	Angelo	58075	D	1931	Leanore Rameth	84757	D	1940
Sylvester Clyde	11602	M	1911	**MAIA**				Norah Rameth	84757	D	1940
Teresa	6183	M	1908	Jose DeFrias	14396	D	1912	**MAININI**			
Thomas	15189	M	1913	**MAIER**				Paul	42852	I	1925
Thomas	15464	D	1913	August	37935	D	1923	**MAINO**			
Thomas	29113	D	1920	Carl	83619	D	1940	Minnie Dominica	89124	D	1942
Thomas	51186	D	1928	Charles	6043	D	1908	Thomas	84416	D	1940
Thomas F.	11602	M	1911	George	37808	D	1923	**MAINZER**			
Thomas F.	68743	D	1935	Martin	72416	D	1936	Bernard	44320	D	1926
Thomas G.	9470	D	1910	Paul	86160	M	1941	Nelsie	49483	D	1928
Thomas L.	15800	D	1913	Thomas	15959	D	1913	**MAIO**			
Thomas W.	68	D	1906	**MAIKAL**				John Simoes	22874	D	1917
Timothy Ambrose	26837	D	1919	Dora	4756	D	1907	**MAIONCHI**			
Timothy L.	49569	D	1928	**MAIL**				Francesco	75863	D	1937
Wensinger F.	6183	M	1908	Jack	72175	D	1936	**MAISCH**			
William	5713	D	1908	Joseph Frank	72175	D	1936	Carl	51240	I	1928
William	60497	D	1931	**MAILHEBUAU**				Carl	58051	D	1931
William J.	13093	D	1912	Camille	40564	D	1924	Ernest	47141	D	1927
William James	54277	D	1929	**MAILHOIT**				John	10627	D	1910
MAHONY				Effie	63948	D	1933	John Edward	83246	D	1940
Andrew F.	65728	D	1933	F. E.	63948	D	1933	**MAISEL**			
Emma E.	64648	D	1933	**MAILLET**				Andrew	73311	D	1936
Francis I.	56175	D	1930	Adrien	75546	D	1937	**MAISON**			
Jeremiah	23718	D	1917	**MAILLIARD**				Nathaly E.	10823	D	1910
John J.	24083	D	1918	John Ward	71431	D	1936	William G.	26554	M	1919
John J.	76510	D	1937								
Joseph J.	76511	D	1937								
Mary M.	52981	D	1929								

NAME	NUMBER	TYPE	YEAR
MAISS			
Bernice L.	75396	M	1937
MAISSNER			
Helena P.	73205	D	1936
MAITLAND			
Louise K.	72809	D	1936
MAITOZA			
Joseph Garcia, Jr.	49892	D	1928
MAJERENOWSKI			
Felix	69650	D	1935
MAJOR			
Arthur	43767	D	1926
Stella J.	67933	D	1934
MAJOROSSY			
Kasimer G.	39913	D	1924
MAJORS			
Grant W.	61368	I	1932
MAJOULET			
Julien	31557	D	1921
MAKELA			
Gustav W.	22729	D	1917
MAKER			
Mary Loretta	64793	D	1933
MAKESTAZIO			
Stephen	11103	D	1911
MAKOWSKY			
Peter	2356	D	1906
MAKREL			
John Reilly	12269	M	1911
MAKRIS			
Odes M.	72821	D	1936
Odyseus	72821	D	1936
MALAIN			
Joe	25309	D	1918
MALAIS			
Anna	32737	D	1921
MALAN			
Louis	85156	D	1940
MALASPINA			
Charles	35155	M	1922
Elenor	35155	M	1922
Guiseppe	32001	D	1921
Louis	35155	M	1922
MALATESTA			
Arlotta	60483	D	1931
August	78055	D	1938

NAME	NUMBER	TYPE	YEAR
Emilio	38373	D	1924
Giovanni	11069	D	1911
Luigi	11012	D	1911
Margaret L.	65091	D	1933
Victor Emanuel	56395	D	1930
William	52494	M	1929
MALAYS			
Joseph	25309	D	1918
MALCOLM			
Eleanor V.	27828	D	1919
Emilie E.	60483	D	1931
George Easson Stewart	14997	D	1913
George MacEwen	62199	D	1932
MALCOLMSON			
James Henry	50090	D	1928
MALDE			
Edward	89168	D	1942
Lottie	37482	D	1923
Matilda E. Klipstein	51459	D	1928
MALECH			
Heman F.	6475	D	1908
Lillie	58408	I	1931
Lillie	64170	D	1933
MALENSEK			
John	56594	D	1930
MALERBA			
Giuseppe	25923	D	1918
Vincenzo	27418	M	1919
MALERBI			
Alexander	30854	D	1920
Carlo	72331	D	1936
MALERVA			
Giuseppe	25923	D	1918
MALEY			
Elizabeth	41543	D	1925
John	79063	M	1938
Rose	71192	D	1935
MALFAIT			
Peter	86157	D	1941
MALFANTI			
Joseph	45255	D	1926
Julia	72366	D	1936
MALFATTI			
Geremia	86943	D	1941
Serafino	46179	D	1927
MALFOTTI			
Terafino	46179	D	1927

NAME	NUMBER	TYPE	YEAR
MALGUTH			
Carl	26528	D	1919
MALICK			
Annie	64654	M	1933
Warren	44238	M	1926
MALIN			
John Fowler	76126	D	1937
Margaret	6849	D	1908
MALING			
Dorothy	18427	M	1915
Edwin Clark	18427	M	1915
Mary	18427	M	1915
MALINN			
Ann	8687	D	1909
MALISESKI			
Alexander	34150	D	1922
MALITZ			
Lillian C.	86979	D	1941
MALIZIA			
Margaret	83927	D	1940
MALLA			
Charles	19433	D	1915
MALLACK			
Hattie	80304	D	1939
MALLAK			
Hattie	80304	D	1939
MALLAMO			
Antonio	42793	D	1925
MALLECK			
Hattie	80304	D	1939
Nicholas	78265	D	1938
MALLEN			
C. N., Mrs.	53017	D	1929
Howard Christopher	63916	D	1933
Laura Alice	53017	D	1929
Ruth E.	62984	D	1932
MALLET			
Ida Adelia Marsh	28238	D	1919
Joseph	34009	D	1922
MALLETT			
Hulda F.	58933	D	1931
William Humphery	46296	D	1927
MALLEY			
Christopher	23769	D	1917
Mary	62394	D	1932
Patrick F.	54565	D	1929

NAME	NUMBER	TYPE	YEAR
MALLICK			
Hattie	80304	D	1939
MALLOMA			
Antone	69723	D	1935
Mariani	69722	D	1935
MALLON			
Bridget	13515	D	1912
Charles E.	34754	D	1922
Edith M.	55893	I	1930
Elizabeth	835	I	1906
Felice	41825	D	1925
Felice	41825	D	1925
Isaac J.	55443	D	1930
John A.	8474	D	1909
Joseph	13874	D	1912
Joseph B.	7891	D	1909
Margaret	43973	D	1926
Maria	20645	D	1916
Marion	55893	I	1930
Michael J.	4327	D	1907
Thomas	52638	D	1929
MALLORY			
John Welch	72486	D	1936
John Welch, Jr.	72489	M	1936
Robert Maxwell	72489	M	1936
MALLOUGH			
Andrew J.	6513	D	1908
MALLOY			
Annie	28980	M	1920
Charles J.	48191	D	1927
Dennis P.	46408	I	1927
Dorothy M.	48104	M	1927
John	28980	M	1920
Kate	8033	D	1909
Mary	3610	I	1907
Mary J.	46322	D	1927
Mathew	48123	I	1927
Patrick	42739	D	1925
MALLOYE			
Frank M.	59019	D	1931
May C.	81710	D	1939
MALLPELLI			
Giovanni	61823	D	1932
MALM			
Axel	63754	D	1933
Charles A.	38041	D	1924
John A.	63754	D	1933

NAME	NUMBER	TYPE	YEAR
Margaret Agnes	76815	D	1937
Mary Helena	66948	D	1934
Matilda	63604	D	1933
Sophia Christina	3275	D	1907
MALMAN			
Betty	54129	D	1929
MALMBERG			
Axel A.	33148	D	1922
MALMGREEN			
John	63900	D	1933
MALMQUIST			
Anna A.	45448	D	1926
MALMSTROM			
Hulda	32840	D	1921
MALNCELLI			
Josephine	67169	D	1934
MALO			
Louis	48066	D	1927
MALOFF			
Peter	73578	D	1936
Samuel	43364	M	1926
MALONE			
Anita Fallon	61719	D	1932
Annie	61719	D	1932
Bridget	4111	D	1907
Clarence Earl	68995	D	1935
Daniel	34172	D	1922
Frank	51719	D	1928
Henry	8607	D	1909
Irismae Ware	77845	D	1938
Jacqueline	62662	M	1932
Jane H.	19469	D	1915
Joseph S.	23206	D	1917
Margaret	86282	D	1941
Marion S.	19574	D	1915
Mary	24788	D	1918
Mary A.	10019	D	1910
Mary Doolan	18537	D	1915
P. J.	12913	D	1912
Peter	20974	D	1916
Richard Cudahy	45281	D	1926
Thomas Edward	61629	D	1932
William F.	7870	D	1909
William Richard	77722	D	1938
MALONEY			
Agnes	47595	M	1927
Anna H.	89103	I	1942

NAME	NUMBER	TYPE	YEAR
Bernard F.	53877	I	1929
Bernard F.	89530	D	1942
Bridget	17014	D	1914
Christine	47595	M	1927
Eileen	59059	M	1931
Hannah	63493	D	1933
James	57001	D	1930
James	59060	M	1931
John	48698	D	1927
John	65490	D	1933
John Edward	76404	D	1937
John H.	47779	D	1927
Joseph P.	48132	D	1927
Julia	48697	D	1927
Julie	47595	M	1927
Kittie	9992	D	1910
Lillian	70060	D	1935
M. J.	78196	D	1938
Martin	50103	D	1928
Mary	6607	D	1908
Mary	60138	D	1931
Mary A.	63218	I	1932
Mary A.	76661	D	1937
Mary L.	1342	D	1906
Michael	15079	D	1913
Nora	81219	D	1939
Patrick	70130	D	1935
Patrick H.	1143	D	1906
Peter	7421	D	1909
Phillip	19057	D	1915
Robert Emmett	59060	M	1931
Robert P.	38415	D	1924
Sarah	72095	D	1936
Thomas	56890	D	1930
Thomas J.	59231	D	1931
William	59059	M	1931
William J.	38151	I	1924
Winifred	11778	D	1911
Winifred Ellen	82331	D	1939
MALOOF			
William H.	39943	I	1924
William H.	49005	D	1928
MALOTT			
H. O., Mrs.	61589	D	1932
Howard Oliver	61588	D	1932
Ida	61589	D	1932
Watson H.	30395	D	1920

NAME	NUMBER	TYPE	YEAR	NAME	NUMBER	TYPE	YEAR	NAME	NUMBER	TYPE	YEAR
MALOUF				**MAMMINI**				Lancelot	64297	D	1933
Aneesa J.	63280	D	1933	Federico	83674	D	1940	**MANCIET**			
Nackard	62996	D	1932	**MAMRAK**				Paul	86906	D	1941
William	49005	D	1928	John	69930	D	1935	**MANCINI**			
MALOUGH				**MAMUSCIA**				Angelo	59226	D	1931
Agnes	6953	M	1908	Francesco	57991	D	1931	Gaetano	59343	D	1931
Emma	9534	M	1910	**MANADD**				Rinaldo	54040	D	1929
Joseph D.	82379	D	1939	Winifred	77546	D	1938	Ulissa	73096	D	1936
MALOY				**MANAHAN**				Ulisse	73096	D	1936
Arthur J.	65221	I	1933	Lillian Edna	10492	M	1910	Ulissi	73096	D	1936
Kate	8033	D	1909	**MANARA**				**MANCUSO**			
MALPAS				Joe	72302	D	1936	Antonio	26614	I	1919
Ida May Lathrop	59112	D	1931	**MANARD**				Giacomo	75011	D	1937
MALPELI				Louis	89250	I	1942	Pedro	22196	D	1917
Giovanni	61823	D	1932	Winifred	77546	D	1938	**MANDADA**			
MALSBARY				**MANASON**				Thomas	60493	D	1931
Emma Rebecca	64052	D	1933	Francesca	22667	M	1917	**MANDAIN**			
MALSBURG				**MANASSE**				Harry G.	59347	D	1931
John R.	88705	D	1941	Jacob	29054	D	1920	**MANDARINO**			
MALTBY				Jennie	66975	D	1934	Eleanor	55027	M	1930
Charles M.	910	D	1906	Lillie	29053	D	1920	Evelyn	55028	M	1930
H. E.	39633	D	1924	Martin	61075	D	1932	**MANDEK**			
Sarah	44800	D	1926	Nathan	73609	D	1936	Anna	26586	D	1919
Sarah	56443	D	1930	Ned	73609	D	1936	**MANDEL**			
MALTOS				**MANATON**				Arthur	45253	M	1926
Rachael	40212	D	1924	William H.	71777	D	1936	Carrie	65276	D	1933
MALTRY				**MANAUT**				Ruth	45253	M	1926
Laura	43286	D	1925	Marcel	26340	D	1919	**MANDELBERGER**			
MALUCELLI				**MANCEBO**				Frank	32472	D	1921
Giuseppina	67169	D	1934	Annie M.	59996	D	1931	**MANDELIN**			
MALUCILLI				John S.	84013	D	1940	Olga	73737	D	1936
Giuseppina	67169	D	1934	**MANCELL**				**MANDELKERN**			
MALVILLE				William	24501	D	1918	Joseph	81419	D	1939
N. B.	19723	D	1915	**MANCELY**				**MANDELSLOH**			
MALYNN				Anna P.	82360	D	1939	Nettie Ezell	48408	D	1927
Ann	8687	D	1909	Nat C., Mrs.	82360	D	1939	**MANDERLIN**			
MALZKUHN				**MANCHA**				Arthur	65700	D	1933
Herman	33831	D	1922	Henry H.	47754	I	1927	George Arthur	65700	D	1933
Wilhelmina	34478	D	1922	Howard H.	60525	D	1931	**MANDERS**			
MAMADO				**MANCHESTER**				Henry	7771	D	1909
Albert	36127	I	1923	Abby A.	8643	D	1909	Wilhelmina	8029	I	1909
MAMLER				Ira Lancelot	64297	D	1933	**MANDEVELLE**			
Nathan	67338	D	1934	Isaac	514	D	1906	H. C.	81980	D	1939
MAMMEN				John	3592	D	1907	Harry LeRoy	81980	D	1939
Ivar Jens	88526	D	1941	Joseph I.	1144	M	1906	**MANDICH**			
				Joseph I.	8398	M	1909	B.	32582	D	1921

NAME	NUMBER	TYPE	YEAR
Chris	8369	D	1909
Milos	22933	D	1917
MANDLBERGER			
Frank	32472	D	1921
MANDLER			
Fred L.	73006	D	1936
MANDONNET			
Edward	85531	D	1940
MANEELY			
Anna P.	82360	D	1939
Nat C.	64305	D	1933
Nat C., Mrs.	82360	D	1939
MANEIRO			
Santiago	86607	I	1941
Santiago	87171	D	1941
MANELICH			
Margaret M.	50235	D	1928
MANETAS			
Leonidas George	12910	D	1912
MANEY			
Anna	54983	D	1930
John	65431	D	1933
MANFELDT			
Charles Andrew Reinhold	53072	D	1929
MANFRE			
Charles	33371	M	1922
Richard	78129	M	1938
MANFREDI			
Arturo	25012	I	1918
Arturo	87778	D	1941
Emilio	4712	D	1907
Eugene	87182	D	1941
MANG			
Sophie R.	59885	D	1931
MANGAN			
Arthur James	84914	D	1940
Delia	6275	I	1908
Elizabeth	2310	D	1906
John Lee	13431	D	1912
Norah G.	23814	D	1918
Thomas	31934	D	1921
MANGANO			
Jack	25962	M	1918
MANGAPANI			
Angelo	60284	D	1931

NAME	NUMBER	TYPE	YEAR
MANGELS			
Anna C.	15687	D	1913
Claus	6778	D	1908
Claus	85848	D	1940
Emma L. S.	7655	D	1909
George	28604	D	1920
Hans M. C.	21835	D	1916
John Henry	7653	D	1909
Wilhelmina	86476	D	1941
MANGELSDORF			
Willy	83302	D	1940
MANGEON			
Charles	75313	I	1937
Charles	76247	D	1937
MANGIANTE			
Frederico	78473	D	1938
MANGINI			
Agostino	43751	D	1926
Agostino	86337	D	1941
Amelia	5630	D	1908
Andrea	73979	D	1936
Antonio	73857	M	1936
Giovanni B.	8915	D	1909
Irene	7617	M	1909
Luigi	9004	M	1910
Luigi	73857	M	1936
Marco	21976	D	1916
Maria	73857	M	1936
Mary	9004	M	1910
Nicoletta	40721	D	1925
MANGJES			
August	45909	D	1926
MANGJUS			
August Y.	45909	D	1926
MANGNUSON			
Albertina C.	20218	I	1916
MANGOLD			
Michael	37879	D	1923
MANGRUM			
Arthur Sherman	56593	D	1930
MANHEIM			
Caroline F.	64411	D	1933
Fred M.	43095	D	1925
Henriette K.	85421	D	1940
Henry S.	39628	D	1924
Lillian Maude	62277	D	1932

NAME	NUMBER	TYPE	YEAR
MANION			
Agnes R.	73415	D	1936
Mary	19457	D	1915
MANIS			
George	25579	D	1918
Julia Perdrizat	77742	D	1938
MANISCALCO			
Accursio	61335	D	1932
Giuseppe	21315	D	1916
MANISS			
Jacob	66217	I	1934
MANLEY			
Ellen F.	79802	D	1938
George A.	32092	D	1921
Robert Wilford	74038	I	1936
William R.	68282	D	1934
MANLY			
Clarence J.	76447	D	1937
Sarah Jane	68391	D	1934
MANN			
Abby A.	8809	D	1909
Alphonse	16575	I	1914
Angela M.	84490	D	1940
Azro L.	11304	D	1911
Charles S.	67359	D	1934
Elizabeth Washington	11889	M	1911
Ella O.	24699	D	1918
Emil	24861	D	1918
F. H.	75513	D	1937
Harry	75513	D	1937
Henry	44655	D	1926
Henry Rice	19946	D	1915
Horace, Jr.	68791	M	1935
Ida May	53492	D	1929
Ida Overend	18708	D	1915
J. F.	82218	I	1939
James P.	22540	D	1917
John	5839	D	1908
Joseph	59436	D	1931
Leo	25398	D	1918
Martha	26474	D	1919
Mary	57632	D	1931
Mary	56557	I	1930
Mary Ann	28999	D	1920
Mary E.	23591	D	1917
Maude L.	47654	D	1927
Moses	73780	D	1936
Philip E.	53067	D	1929

NAME	NUMBER	TYPE	YEAR	NAME	NUMBER	TYPE	YEAR	NAME	NUMBER	TYPE	YEAR
Philip Eugene	56074	D	1930	John W.	8108	D	1909	Michael J.	74509	D	1937
Robert	49870	D	1928	John W.	48795	D	1927	Peter	39264	M	1924
Russell C.	31398	D	1921	Joseph I.	29888	D	1920	Thomas	20516	D	1916
Samuel	87742	D	1941	Kate	4741	D	1907	Thomas J.	35704	D	1923
Sarah	81111	D	1939	Lucy	77226	I	1937	Thomas J.	39264	M	1924
Seth	69351	D	1935	Lydia	56340	D	1930	**MANNO**			
Sidney	58627	D	1931	Margaret	8301	D	1909	Mary	79491	D	1938
Walter M.	82980	D	1939	Margaret	34524	D	1922	**MANNON**			
William J.	888	I	1906	Margaret	45388	D	1926	Annie Mabel	80684	D	1939
MANNEL				Margraret Mary	51768	M	1929	Caroline	80456	D	1939
Elise	58611	D	1931	Mary	56557	I	1930	**MANNONI**			
F. R., Mrs.	58611	D	1931	Mary Ann	14901	D	1913	Albert, Jr.	70671	M	1935
MANNELLI				Mary Helen	7359	M	1909	Ange Toussain	21661	D	1916
Caesar J.	72423	D	1936	Maude B.	83464	D	1940	Antoine	21152	D	1916
MANNER				Maxine	81893	D	1939	Jean Baptiste	32521	D	1921
Alfred	15581	M	1913	Melvin	10154	M	1910	Paul	70671	M	1935
MANNERBERG				Michael	49676	D	1928	**MANNS**			
Amanda	13464	D	1912	Mollie	79095	D	1938	Doris Stella	52778	M	1929
MANNIE				Peter J.	86083	D	1941	Ellen	48760	D	1927
Emmett M.	6747	D	1908	Regina Dorothy	87079	D	1941	**MANNY**			
MANNIGAN				Richard	21969	D	1916	Melanie	15822	D	1913
Charles F.	64341	D	1933	Robert	74321	D	1937	**MANO**			
MANNIK				Roland Theodore	74321	D	1937	Joseph	70255	D	1935
Chris	74121	D	1936	Rose C.	89046	D	1942	**MANOGUE**			
MANNINA				Samuel E.	87177	M	1941	Albert J.	58106	I	1931
Domenico	1774	D	1906	Thomas	6142	D	1908	Bridget	24523	D	1918
Mary	8882	D	1909	Thomas	8134	D	1909	**MANON**			
MANNING				Thomas R.	81161	D	1939	James	7702	D	1909
Anna M.	49400	D	1928	William	17988	D	1914	**MANOS**			
Arthur H.	61399	D	1932	William W.	79709	D	1938	Peter	76356	D	1937
Catherine	72041	D	1936	**MANNION**				**MANOUGIAN**			
Charles	35565	D	1922	Bridget A.	66534	D	1934	Sam	80322	D	1939
Clara	10154	M	1910	Charles	41660	D	1925	**MANOUK**			
Clarence W.	14206	D	1912	Enriqueta T. V.	52643	D	1929	Herbert L.	53018	D	1929
Dolores Rose	71399	D	1936	Ferdinand Ralph	52669	M	1929	**MANOZA**			
Floyd Julious	70864	D	1935	George Henry	51858	D	1929	Angelo	61829	I	1932
Frank B.	75398	D	1937	Helen M.	24785	D	1918	**MANS**			
Franklin W.	85855	D	1940	Mary	19457	D	1915	Daniel S.	35749	D	1923
Guy Edmund	67889	D	1934	Patrick J.	15717	I	1913	**MANSE**			
Helen Elizabeth	2906	D	1907	**MANNIX**				Peter	84838	D	1940
Henry J.	1368	D	1906	Catherine J.	39264	M	1924	**MANSER**			
James L. H.	1657	D	1906	Frank P.	18050	D	1914	Peter	84838	D	1940
James William	47458	D	1927	George I.	64409	D	1933	**MANSFELDT**			
Jeremiah	74720	D	1937	Julia	26607	D	1919	Elsie Miriam	15483	D	1913
John	14306	D	1912	Julia	75593	D	1937	Eva	74362	I	1937
John	33559	D	1922	Julia	52437	D	1929	Oscar	48532	D	1927
John Joseph	88829	D	1942	Justine	39264	M	1924				
				Margaret	431	D	1906				
				Margaret M.	61859	D	1932				

NAME	NUMBER	TYPE	YEAR	NAME	NUMBER	TYPE	YEAR	NAME	NUMBER	TYPE	YEAR
MANSFIELD				MANY				Long	37472	M	1923
Charles	53072	D	1929	Elizabeth	35837	D	1923	Moon long	37472	M	1923
Eleanor	43472	D	1926	MANZ				Quock Choy	37472	M	1923
Ellen	7318	D	1909	Carl Frederick	45945	D	1926	MARA			
George C.	76764	D	1937	Frederick	45945	D	1926	Bridget	68682	I	1935
Hetta P.	6206	D	1908	MANZANO				Marie Leontine	32714	D	1921
Robert	63838	D	1933	Maria	40068	D	1924	Mary	77566	D	1938
Sydney	17253	D	1914	MANZELLA				MARABOTTI			
Walter Damon	45627	D	1926	Angelina	71574	M	1936	Dante	33226	D	1922
MANSON				Bertha Maria	71574	M	1936	MARACCHIN			
F. L.	42053	D	1925	Giuseppe	41330	D	1925	Carolina Landini	85936	D	1940
James	7689	D	1909	John	71574	M	1936	MARAGOS			
Josef	27657	D	1919	Maria	68771	D	1935	Dimitrios	54210	D	1929
Marion	7688	D	1909	Paul	62371	D	1932	James D.	54210	D	1929
Nathaniel J.	19048	D	1915	Rosalie	85884	M	1940	MARAIS			
Samuella L.	16011	D	1913	Rosario	60701	D	1932	Charles L. P.	16771	D	1914
William A.	62272	I	1932	MANZINI				Charlotte Elizabeth	11712	D	1911
MANSSON				Louis	70006	D	1935	Charlotte Elizabeth	11713	D	1911
Per	23097	D	1917	Louis	70006	D	1935	MARANETTO			
MANTEL				MANZO				Maria Teresa	40176	D	1924
Henry Richard	84503	D	1940	Domenico	70094	D	1935	Teresa	40176	D	1924
MANTJAFLARIS				MANZONI				MARANI			
George Theadore	31470	D	1921	Antonio	32037	I	1921	Anton	69411	D	1935
MANTON				MANZY				Caesar	68893	M	1935
Annie G.	18865	D	1915	Rose F.	35465	M	1922	Cesare James	68365	D	1934
Edward G.	21692	D	1916	MAPEL				Toscana	35614	D	1922
Frank W.	19761	D	1915	Agnes	89392	D	1942	MARANO			
James F.	18866	D	1915	MAPES				Francisco	35862	D	1923
MANTOR				Ruby	36474	D	1923	Frank	35862	D	1923
George A.	43992	D	1926	Warren W.	38927	D	1924	Mary	13571	D	1912
MANTZ				MAPLES				MARANTS			
Albert	37757	D	1923	Edward Thompson	72748	D	1936	Angelina	59794	D	1931
Betty Jane	77801	M	1938	MAPPA				MARASCHI			
MANUCK				John	57785	D	1931	Anthony	3273	D	1907
Benjamin	69597	D	1935	MAPPIN				MARBACH			
MANUEL				Walter W.	38027	D	1923	Joseph	17206	I	1914
Harvey S.	82515	D	1939	MAQUIRE				Joseph	17213	D	1914
Helen L.	607	M	1906	Frank	25630	D	1918	MARBLE			
Isidore	25950	D	1918	MAQULEWSKY				Harry Briggs	28596	D	1920
Tan Liu	80795	D	1939	Jacob	17250	D	1914	MARBLESTONE			
MANUELL				MAQUOY				Hattie	75261	D	1937
William H.	40100	D	1924	John	24513	I	1918	MARC			
MANUSCIA				MAR				Pierre J.	53868	D	1929
Francesco	57991	D	1931	Choy	37472	M	1923	MARCAUX			
MANWARING				Hannah	8566	M	1909	Joseph E.	66238	D	1934
Halsey E.	64731	D	1933	Josie	8566	M	1909				
Yvonne	37739	D	1923								

                   Key: D = death; M = minor; I = incompetent

NAME	NUMBER	TYPE	YEAR	NAME	NUMBER	TYPE	YEAR	NAME	NUMBER	TYPE	YEAR
MARCEBOUT				MARCHI				MARCUS			
Lucie, Mrs.	57729	D	1931	Agatha	53163	I	1929	Adolph	42424	D	1925
MARCELINO				Celestine	2545	D	1906	Carl Henry	23528	M	1917
Adonis	38685	D	1924	Giuseppe	6179	D	1908	Donald Clarence	89580	M	1942
MARCELLI				John	65456	D	1933	Elizabeth Hugo	21420	D	1916
Gaetano	56801	D	1930	Maria	65463	D	1933	Elizabeth Hugo	60999	D	1932
MARCELLIN				Olinto	54915	D	1930	Fannie	54388	I	1929
Joseph A.	79133	D	1938	Sebastiano	23999	I	1918	Gustav	43401	D	1926
MARCELLINI				Ugo	27894	M	1919	Henry C.	79487	D	1938
Domenica	58321	D	1931	MARCHINGTON				Ida	58055	D	1931
MARCELLINO				Alice Rowland	72697	D	1936	Ida Claire	23528	M	1917
Salvatore	19913	D	1915	MARCHINTON				James	53847	I	1929
MARCELLUS				Ethel C.	25003	M	1918	Jean	56380	I	1930
Clara Dolores	25221	M	1918	Evelyn J.	25003	M	1918	Louis	14794	D	1913
Phyliss Marie	25221	M	1918	Gertrude E.	25003	M	1918	Madison Joseph	89580	M	1942
MARCH				William J.	25003	M	1918	Marilyn Alice	89580	M	1942
Dean	36221	M	1923	MARCIANO				Marion Pomeroy	85207	M	1940
Minette	49195	D	1928	Antonio	945	D	1906	Ottmar	73282	I	1936
Muriel	36221	M	1923	Antonio	28252	D	1919	Ottmar	73719	D	1936
Paul	36221	M	1923	MARCILLAC				Ottoman	73282	I	1936
Ruth	36221	M	1923	Sylvie	74653	D	1937	Patricia Anne	85207	M	1940
William	36221	M	1923	MARCINKOWSKI				Ruth	53339	M	1929
MARCHAL				Joseph	18852	D	1915	Siegfried	37720	D	1923
Louis	15485	D	1913	MARCK				Virginia	88415	D	1941
Marguerite	17872	D	1914	Peter J.	36841	D	1923	MARCUSE			
MARCHAND				MARCKLEY				Amelia	57990	D	1931
Claude	60520	M	1931	Benjamin F.	23711	D	1917	Delfina	62262	D	1932
Elise	11084	D	1911	MARCO				Felix	41683	D	1925
Marguerite	47982	D	1927	Chiesa	22766	D	1917	Maude E.	27708	D	1919
Marie	58054	D	1931	Claude	68894	D	1935	MARDEN			
MARCHANT				MARCOLLO				Edward Lloyd	11835	M	1911
Rodney Hugh	9513	D	1910	Leon	10188	M	1910	Eldrid Eugene	11835	M	1911
MARCHEBAUT				Lepoldina	31083	D	1921	Elijah	37296	D	1923
L.	57729	D	1931	MARCONNIER				Horace	22349	D	1917
MARCHEBOUT				Byrne	88158	D	1941	Johanna	24781	D	1918
Henri Adolphe	44570	D	1926	MARCOTTE				Josephine E.	8811	D	1909
Lucie	57729	D	1931	Harry	30896	D	1920	Myrtle Edwina	11835	M	1911
Victor	19205	D	1915	MARCOU				Robert A.	3578	D	1907
MARCHELOS				Vasilios	16755	D	1914	MARDIN			
Panagiotis	37735	D	1923	MARCOUX				Mildred Marie	14132	M	1912
Peter	37735	D	1923	Joseph E., Jr.	68298	M	1934	MARDIS			
MARCHESI				MARCOVICH				Benjamin Alden	85218	D	1940
Samuele	33450	D	1922	Kate	76489	D	1937	MARDORF			
MARCHETTI				MARCUCCI				Martin L.	78915	D	1938
Olinto	30891	D	1920	Julia L.	12204	I	1911	MAREK			
Paul	53778	D	1929	Julia L.	14643	D	1912	Henry V.	72500	D	1936
								Tiney	72500	D	1936

NAME	NUMBER	TYPE	YEAR
MARELICH			
Margaret M.	50235	D	1928
MARENCIK			
John B.	22558	D	1917
MARENCO			
Joseph	74147	D	1936
Umberto	74213	M	1936
William	74213	M	1936
MARENGO			
Gaspero	31885	D	1921
Joseph	74147	D	1936
Manuel	77789	D	1938
Mary Jane	20492	D	1916
MARESCA			
Sophie	52806	D	1929
MARESCAUX			
Alice Warren	21343	D	1916
MARETTI			
Theresa	87744	D	1941
MARG			
Herman	30556	D	1920
William	77257	D	1937
MARGABAT			
Thomas	86994	M	1941
MARGAN			
David B.	42822	M	1925
William S.	42822	M	1925
MARGARITES			
Fila P.	39564	D	1924
MARGARONI			
Eugenia Jackson	88638	D	1941
Remo	74881	D	1937
MARGETSON			
Frederick George James	16873	D	1914
MARGEY			
Alice	2360	D	1906
Katherine	23365	I	1917
Mary	69187	D	1935
Roger	68685	D	1935
MARGGRAF			
Leopold	13151	D	1912
MARGIOTTA			
Arcangelo	81357	D	1939
MARGO			
James A.	12773	D	1911
Mary	44600	D	1926

NAME	NUMBER	TYPE	YEAR
MARGUCCI			
Mary	85147	D	1940
MARGUIRE			
Louis	56003	D	1930
MARGUIS			
Antonio	47302	D	1927
MARHAM			
Ann M.	7013	M	1909
John William	7013	M	1909
Julia M.	7013	M	1909
Sarah E.	7013	M	1909
MARHOFFER			
Frederick William	80142	D	1938
Joseph R.	81628	D	1939
MARI			
Ernesto	45524	D	1926
Francesco	51592	D	1928
James	88827	D	1942
MARIA			
Isabel	42408	I	1925
John	76072	D	1937
MARIAM			
Paul	27237	D	1919
MARIANI			
Angelo	26521	D	1919
Esther	80800	D	1939
Hilda	59558	D	1931
Katherine	35852	M	1923
Laura E.	35852	M	1923
Lillian B.	81217	D	1939
Marco	50382	D	1928
Margaret Louise	35852	M	1923
Maria	80108	D	1938
Natale	21327	D	1916
Natalina	36327	D	1923
Romeo	88134	D	1941
Stephen G.	48527	D	1927
Victoria	79602	D	1938
MARIANNO			
John Gerald	43010	M	1925
MARICH			
Meo	44815	D	1926
MARIENI			
Giovani	26050	D	1919
MARIER			
Clementine	17784	D	1914

NAME	NUMBER	TYPE	YEAR
MARIES			
Leo B.	12179	D	1911
MARIN			
Edgar George	86178	D	1941
Max	14236	D	1912
Pauline	45699	D	1926
MARINAI			
Celestino	63715	D	1933
MARINCIK			
Andrew	24605	M	1918
Annie	24392	D	1918
John B.	22558	D	1917
MARINE			
Caesar Anthony	61043	D	1932
MARINELLI			
Antonete	32277	D	1921
Antonia	60492	D	1931
Antonio	68858	D	1935
Paul	32050	M	1921
Teresa	32050	M	1921
MARINELLO			
Francesco	39179	D	1924
MARINER			
Frederic	58372	D	1931
James	16539	D	1913
MARINI			
Caesar	61043	D	1932
MARINO			
Angelo	74508	D	1937
B., Mrs.	47920	D	1927
Domenico	30156	M	1920
Fred	20603	D	1916
Giacomo	54656	D	1930
Joseph	66579	D	1934
Josephine	47920	D	1927
Minnie Mable	60205	D	1931
Rocco	15973	M	1913
MARINOS			
Dionisios	79615	D	1938
MARINOVICH			
Anton	40488	D	1924
Nicholas	83180	D	1940
Ruza	44050	D	1926
Vlaho	63943	D	1933
MARIO			
Manuel	15783	D	1913

NAME	NUMBER	TYPE	YEAR
MARION			
Bessie A.	79058	D	1938
Catherine	64386	D	1933
Glenn Morton	68299	M	1934
Henry Morton	68543	D	1934
Manuel Mena	15783	D	1913
Philomene	41847	D	1925
Philomene	41847	D	1925
Ruth	68299	M	1934
Samuel N.	59659	D	1931
MARIONE			
Francesco	35610	D	1922
MARIONI			
Amelia C.	13337	I	1912
Amelia C.	30945	D	1921
MARIOTTI			
Daniele	73863	D	1936
Lucia Martini	38668	I	1924
MARIPUU			
Johannes	36811	D	1923
John	36811	D	1923
MARIS			
Ann Sheard	73091	M	1936
Elizabeth Louise	73091	M	1936
MARISCH			
Rose	18535	D	1915
MARITZEN			
Elizabeth A.	82813	M	1939
Forence H.	74151	D	1936
June	82813	M	1939
MARK			
Cecil W.	89507	D	1942
Paul	43015	M	1925
Peter	72614	D	1936
Tau	63091	D	1932
Thos. M.	36059	D	1923
MARKARITES			
Fila P.	39564	D	1924
MARKART			
Joseph	83080	D	1940
MARKEL			
James B.	17869	D	1914
MARKETOS			
Gerasimos	79231	D	1938
J.	79231	D	1938
MARKEY			
Frank Brendon	47689	D	1927

NAME	NUMBER	TYPE	YEAR
Mary	88338	D	1941
MARKGRAF			
Mary J.	75956	D	1937
MARKHAM			
Frances Daverkosen	35306	D	1922
Frank I.	58416	D	1931
John H.	84343	I	1940
John J. F.	86001	D	1941
Mary E.	77325	D	1937
Monroe H.	15325	D	1913
MARKHEIM			
Murray	89547	D	1942
MARKIEWITZ			
Abraham	59485	I	1931
MARKIS			
Charles Pathfinder	76228	D	1937
MARKLE			
Carrie	62828	M	1932
Sannie	62828	M	1932
Wallace	55620	D	1930
MARKLES			
Isadore	59862	I	1931
MARKLEY			
James E.	52742	D	1929
MARKO			
Josef	19510	D	1915
MARKOFSKY			
Abraham	54083	D	1929
MARKOS			
William	16755	D	1914
MARKOVICH			
Maria	82588	D	1939
Mary M. B.	20555	D	1916
Stephen	38420	D	1924
MARKOVICI			
Clara	37546	M	1923
Rose	37546	M	1923
MARKOVITS			
Esther	29107	I	1920
Howard Morton	29108	M	1920
Jack	29064	D	1920
Jacob	29064	D	1920
MARKOVSKY			
Abraham	54083	D	1929
MARKOWITZ			
Abraham	77686	D	1938

NAME	NUMBER	TYPE	YEAR
Marian	64637	D	1933
Max	63722	D	1933
Peter Harold	85925	D	1940
MARKS			
Adela	40182	D	1924
Adelaide	13710	D	1912
Adelaide M.	15187	D	1913
Adolph	24606	D	1918
Albert	23043	D	1917
Albert L.	57794	D	1931
Annabelle	23217	M	1917
Annie	28484	D	1919
Bertha	8103	D	1909
Bertha	58928	D	1931
Celia	19758	D	1915
Charles	17233	M	1914
Charles Ferdinand	19441	M	1915
Edward Benjamin	19441	M	1915
Elaine	33444	M	1922
Eli	14277	D	1912
Elizabeth	18458	D	1915
Elizabeth Grace	80409	D	1939
Esme A.	72831	D	1936
Estelle A.	36118	D	1923
Esther	24378	D	1918
Esther	55639	D	1930
Frank	13240	D	1912
Gustavus H.	88805	D	1941
Hannah	13843	I	1912
Harris	35754	D	1923
Harry A.	86066	I	1941
Inez Bowen	33575	D	1922
Isaac	59017	D	1931
Isaac L.	51508	D	1928
Jacob	7406	D	1909
Jean Frances	64794	M	1933
Jesse E.	34002	D	1922
Johanna	33444	M	1922
Johanna	36166	D	1923
John A.	62919	D	1932
John L.	54170	D	1929
Joseph	21658	D	1916
Joseph, Mrs.	82533	D	1939
Josephine A.	83427	D	1940
Julia	25397	D	1918
Julia	36424	D	1923
Julia	40805	D	1925
Katie Eugenia	32691	D	1921
Larry H.	83448	D	1940

Key: *D = death; M = minor; I = incompetent*

NAME	NUMBER	TYPE	YEAR
Lazare Henry	83448	D	1940
Louis	17651	D	1914
Martin E.	81015	D	1939
Maxim H.	60603	D	1932
Maximillian	76367	D	1937
Mores	13546	D	1912
Morris	13546	D	1912
Morris	36110	D	1923
Nellie A.	81958	D	1939
Rachael Julia	82533	D	1939
Ramona	83426	D	1940
Rebecca Ina	25211	D	1918
Robert	1917	D	1906
Rose	41385	D	1925
Sarah	31801	D	1921
Sarah	39688	D	1924
Simon	8373	I	1909
Simon	9160	D	1910
Solomon	9688	D	1910
Thomas H.	20362	D	1916
William	40875	D	1925
MARKSAMEN			
Henry	5716	D	1908
MARKSON			
Mary S.	86216	D	1941
MARKSTROM			
William	61781	I	1932
William	62115	D	1932
MARKT			
Dorothy	19335	M	1915
Eldon W.	61023	D	1932
Emil R.	19335	M	1915
Emma	19335	M	1915
Ferdinand	19335	M	1915
Henry M.	19335	M	1915
Marjorie Lavern	61024	M	1932
MARKUM			
Luise M.	62772	D	1932
MARKUS			
Emilie	20252	D	1916
Fannie	54388	I	1929
Josef	29034	D	1920
MARKWITH			
Vivienne M.	81006	D	1939
MARLEY			
George	72329	D	1936
John C.	43052	D	1925

NAME	NUMBER	TYPE	YEAR
MARLIN			
Alonzo	57547	D	1930
George Washington	18012	D	1914
MARLIS			
Nick	79432	D	1938
MARLO			
Rose	43625	I	1926
MARLOW			
David K.	27383	D	1919
Ellen	68881	D	1935
Frances	15706	D	1913
Francis	15326	D	1913
Frank	15706	D	1913
James	15326	D	1913
John Robert	38682	D	1924
Louis H.	14771	D	1913
Mary Ann	23582	D	1917
William	5699	D	1908
William J.	61011	D	1932
MARLOWE			
William	60940	M	1932
MARMION			
James	27729	D	1919
Steven	63992	D	1933
MARNELL			
Adeline	22990	D	1917
Margaret	9990	D	1910
Margurate Adeline	22990	D	1917
William J.	73068	D	1936
MARNTSOS			
John	39385	D	1924
MAROHNIC			
Gasper	43947	D	1926
MARONICH			
Gasper	43947	D	1926
MAROTTI			
Richard	89138	D	1942
MAROVICH			
Lazarus W.	25975	D	1918
Philip	28709	D	1920
MARPLES			
Francis Wilkson	51325	D	1928
MARQUARD			
Ethel A.	42919	D	1925
Louise	47969	D	1927
Rudolph	80236	D	1938

NAME	NUMBER	TYPE	YEAR
MARQUART			
John H.	12306	D	1911
Lyda J.	84925	D	1940
Paul	53106	D	1929
MARQUE			
Catherine	76275	D	1937
MARQUETTE			
Jean	33617	D	1922
MARQUIE			
Louis	56003	D	1930
MARQUISE			
Emma	89151	D	1942
MARR			
Eleanor	76225	I	1937
Hazel S.	41232	D	1925
MARRA			
Salvatore	77606	D	1938
Sam	77606	D	1938
MARRACCINI			
Louis	77152	D	1937
MARRACO			
Andrea	78772	I	1938
Andrea	82296	D	1939
Andressa	82296	D	1939
Anereassa	78772	I	1938
MARRE			
Eugenie	52286	D	1929
MARREN			
John	43693	D	1926
MARRIOTT			
Frederick	40814	D	1925
Fredericka	75634	D	1937
MARRON			
Anna R.	34390	I	1922
Anna Rebecca	36307	D	1923
Catherine	24221	D	1918
James Thomas	58043	D	1931
Mary	18079	D	1914
Mary	22865	D	1917
Mary	71982	D	1936
Michael A.	15814	D	1913
Patrick	22239	D	1917
Thomas F.	4001	D	1907
MARS			
Catherine	26262	D	1919
Catherine A.	26364	D	1919
Julia A.	43248	D	1925

NAME	NUMBER	TYPE	YEAR	NAME	NUMBER	TYPE	YEAR	NAME	NUMBER	TYPE	YEAR
Samuel	43705	D	1926	Ralph	67346	I	1934	Kent P.	65492	D	1933
MARSALA				Richard T.	31393	D	1921	Lindsey P.	42835	D	1925
Luigi	53019	D	1929	Rosalie D.	12203	M	1911	Lorraine	7017	M	1909
Nicola	2694	D	1907	Ruth Elizabeth	27206	M	1919	Louis	18808	D	1915
MARSANO				Willard N.	50495	M	1928	Manning	74032	D	1936
Kiara	38248	D	1924	William E.	8601	D	1909	Margaret	1997	M	1906
MARSCHALL				**MARSHALL**				Mary	7193	D	1909
Bernice	27918	M	1919	Agnes	65392	D	1933	Matthew P.	38606	D	1924
MARSCHUTZ				Alison Reid	50936	D	1928	Minnora S.	8850	D	1909
Clementine A.	65412	D	1933	Allan John	7017	M	1909	Nellie	5690	D	1908
MARSDEN				Andrew S.	58921	I	1931	Pauline Emilie	7015	D	1909
Elizabeth	85452	D	1940	Ann	62367	D	1932	Percy	70320	D	1935
Henry	5891	D	1908	Anna	52254	D	1929	Rebecca	80672	D	1939
MARSE				Benjamin	19526	D	1915	Richard	89669	D	1942
James	65523	D	1933	Cary A.	75182	I	1937	Rose	15785	D	1913
MARSH				Catherine	63983	D	1933	Stephen Henry	77724	D	1938
Alice Louise	60937	I	1932	Charles Arthur	87541	M	1941	Thomas A.	29536	D	1920
Alice Louise	54419	I	1929	Charles James	41070	D	1925	Thomas A.	30828	M	1920
Calanthe E.	20933	D	1916	Charles S.	40033	D	1924	William	26084	D	1919
Charles	49066	D	1928	Clyde Marion	7017	M	1909	William	35453	D	1922
Clara B.	40752	D	1925	Dolina	55396	D	1930	William C.	43911	I	1926
David W.	39928	D	1924	Dora	59014	D	1931	**MARSHUTZ**			
Elmer Dice	62943	I	1932	Eleanor S.	5690	D	1908	Clementine A.	63982	I	1933
Everett I.	12203	M	1911	Ella Rita	86776	D	1941	Leon Charles	32253	D	1921
Francis Elmer	22457	M	1917	Emilie B.	3654	D	1907	**MARSICANO**			
Frederick Delano	78343	D	1938	Eugene Lee	59068	M	1931	Patrizio	13569	D	1912
George	12203	M	1911	Frances B.	82475	D	1939	Thomas	5966	D	1908
George Henry	31710	D	1921	Frank	16614	D	1914	**MARSILI**			
George W.	24142	D	1918	Frank Sterling	7017	M	1909	Joseph Francis	61012	D	1932
Goldie D.	50493	I	1928	Frederick	59047	D	1931	**MARSON**			
Harold	72841	M	1936	George E.	29986	D	1920	Anne	33910	D	1922
Henry	29968	D	1920	George W.	54408	D	1929	O. T.	13360	D	1912
Herbert W.	24265	I	1918	Gordon Earl	29986	D	1920	**MARSTEN**			
Herbert W.	26191	D	1919	Henry P.	30828	M	1920	Alf.	58467	D	1931
Irene	12203	M	1911	Hoyle	78583	D	1938	Alfred L.	74977	D	1937
J. Everett	50850	D	1928	Irving	9471	D	1910	Alice Elizabeth	58499	M	1931
John	12203	M	1911	James Alexander	30828	M	1920	**MARSTON**			
John Alfred	23396	D	1917	James G.	65200	D	1933	Alonzo C.	18481	I	1915
Leroy, Jr.	72841	M	1936	James Henry	8133	D	1909	Frank Wheeler	67526	D	1934
Louis	50164	D	1928	John	14659	D	1912	J. H.	28023	D	1919
Lucile B.	58255	D	1931	John B.	62713	D	1932	John	57160	I	1930
Lucy E.	55297	D	1930	John B., Mrs.	63983	D	1933	Lula Modie Fuller	74772	D	1937
Manuel Joseph	68214	D	1934	John F.	45088	D	1926	Mary A.	38929	D	1924
Maria Nicasia	68474	I	1934	John H.	78781	D	1938	Minerva Arcadia	83128	I	1940
Maria Nicasia	78021	D	1938	John, Jr.	52033	I	1929	Susan Adelaide	88352	D	1941
Matthew E.	50494	M	1928	John, Jr.	62639	D	1932	W. H.	39216	D	1924
Merle Alfred	68902	D	1935	Juana	1309	I	1906	**MARTA**			
Merrill A.	12203	M	1911	Juana B.	13853	D	1912	Peter	85990	D	1941
				Kenneth	7017	M	1909				

NAME	NUMBER	TYPE	YEAR	NAME	NUMBER	TYPE	YEAR	NAME	NUMBER	TYPE	YEAR
MARTEL				Nellie G.	17386	M	1914	Charles	89692	D	1942
Adele Francis	65507	D	1933	**MARTIGNONE**				Charles Beuers	53251	D	1929
Jane	39112	D	1924	Angelo	83661	D	1940	Charles D.	80170	D	1938
MARTELL				Teresa	83662	D	1940	Charles F.	6463	D	1908
Delia B.	27470	D	1919	**MARTIGNONI**				Charles Robert	57828	D	1931
Edward J.	25247	D	1918	Angelo	83661	D	1940	Charles T.	37040	D	1923
Frances	6198	D	1908	Teresa	83662	D	1940	Christopher	19876	D	1915
Frank H.	73854	D	1936	**MARTILLA**				Claire J.	43253	D	1925
Harry Gaylord	64608	D	1933	Hjalmar	47569	D	1927	Coleman	34802	D	1922
Ida	30291	M	1920	**MARTIN**				Cora J.	55264	D	1930
Rose Maria	85671	D	1940	Abbie	44549	D	1926	Cornelius L.	7649	D	1909
MARTEN				Abbie	60697	D	1932	Curtis A.	71066	D	1935
Carena F.	68655	D	1935	Addie L.	14480	D	1912	Edward	5702	D	1908
Maria Fina	35532	I	1922	Albert J.	80072	D	1938	Edward	88009	D	1941
MARTENS				Albert P.	57172	I	1930	Edward E.	67831	D	1934
Adolph	51903	I	1929	Alexander	24152	D	1918	Edward Francis	67736	M	1934
Adolph	56138	D	1930	Alexander Moor	10238	D	1910	Edward J.	67695	D	1934
Cacilie	27928	D	1919	Alfonzo	73875	D	1936	Edward Miles	65391	D	1933
Caroline	53744	D	1929	Alice E.	9231	D	1910	Eleanor	50434	D	1928
Dora	12100	D	1911	Alice Evelyn	6020	I	1908	Elizabeth	3032	D	1907
Edward William	46820	M	1927	Alice Jane	76047	D	1937	Elizabeth	12755	D	1911
Ferdinand H.	16605	D	1914	Alphonsine Rouillon	61121	D	1932	Elizabeth Ann	51178	D	1928
Fritz	46628	D	1927	Amelia V.	7699	D	1909	Ellen Sumner	64851	D	1933
Herman	82887	D	1939	Amy	35303	D	1922	Ellen Teresa	79020	D	1938
John	85198	D	1940	Andrew Wasson	50384	D	1928	Elsie Delorieux	28925	D	1920
Minna	81326	D	1939	Angus McDonald	23131	I	1917	Elysee Henri	45834	D	1926
Paul Wilhelm	12508	D	1911	Angus McDonald	48694	I	1927	Emma Ruth	28657	D	1920
MARTENSEN				Angus McDonald	62870	D	1932	Emmogene	12728	M	1911
Augusta	84663	D	1940	Anita G.	88487	D	1941	Ethel	57500	D	1930
MARTENSON				Anna Marie	67587	D	1934	Etta M.	57751	D	1931
Marie	55759	D	1930	Anna Ropes	33315	D	1922	Eudora Louise	13202	D	1912
MARTEY				Barbara	49214	M	1928	Evelyn D.	61238	D	1932
Frank	61167	D	1932	Bridget	2997	D	1907	Frances	28493	I	1919
MARTHINSEN				Bridget	32090	D	1921	Frances	77992	I	1938
Grace	85997	D	1941	Bruce	7700	M	1909	Frances Adele	58008	D	1931
MARTHINUSEN				Caroline C.	11731	I	1911	Frances Veronica	20249	D	1916
Gracieuse	85997	D	1941	Caroline C.	74456	D	1937	Francois	21919	D	1916
MARTICH				Caroline M.	74081	D	1936	Frank	45330	D	1926
Matt	79017	D	1938	Carrie	54119	I	1929	Frank J.	82333	D	1939
MARTIE				Carrie C.	44843	D	1926	Frank L.	29590	D	1920
Frank	61167	D	1932	Carrie Margarette	74081	D	1936	Frederick Richard	59003	I	1931
Fred	61167	D	1932	Catherine	1591	D	1906	Fruto	89527	D	1942
Fred	61167	D	1932	Catherine G.	4199	D	1907	George	8404	I	1909
MARTIEN				Cecilia Frances	62655	D	1932	George	8706	D	1909
Albert L.	17517	D	1914	Charles	34087	M	1922	George	23943	D	1918
Henry	61225	D	1932	Charles	39915	I	1924	George	80369	D	1939
Leola R.	17386	M	1914	Charles	44961	D	1926	George Adams	62709	D	1932
				Charles	63087	D	1932	George E.	71063	I	1935
								George J.	80707	D	1939

NAME	NUMBER	TYPE	YEAR	NAME	NUMBER	TYPE	YEAR	NAME	NUMBER	TYPE	YEAR
George J.	86517	D	1941	Libby	12755	D	1911	Robert E. E.	60971	D	1932
H. C.	30989	D	1921	Lillian O.	43009	D	1925	Robert S.	83677	D	1940
Hallie Bost	89378	D	1942	Lillian W.	60719	D	1932	Rose M.	75655	D	1937
Henry J.	45801	D	1926	Lilly Oelrichs	60286	D	1931	Samuel	32237	D	1921
Herman S.	73962	D	1936	M. H.	57268	D	1930	Samuel Robert	83677	D	1940
J. Mrs.	48821	D	1927	Magnus	18912	D	1915	Sarah M. Johnson	17797	D	1914
James	69392	D	1935	Margaret	27121	I	1919	Sophia	12106	D	1911
James	76630	D	1937	Margaret A.	13384	D	1912	Sophie	56591	D	1930
James Elmer	88161	D	1941	Marie	42103	M	1925	Susie	41335	I	1925
James G.	42713	D	1925	Martin	34108	D	1922	Terence P.	81648	D	1939
James G.	43316	D	1926	Martin	57268	D	1930	Thomas C.	58483	D	1931
James H.	64773	D	1933	Mary	12065	D	1911	Thomas C.	74160	D	1936
James Ross	2413	D	1906	Mary	25471	D	1918	Thomas J.	68571	D	1934
James Turner	55387	D	1930	Mary	35532	I	1922	Vicente F.	67923	D	1934
Jane Leach	53614	D	1929	Mary	80967	D	1939	Violet Mallory	65384	D	1933
Janet	38165	D	1934	Mary	48821	D	1927	Virginia H.	73771	D	1936
Jean	3989	D	1907	Mary A.	6771	D	1908	Walter J.	50012	D	1928
Jean M.	54069	D	1929	Mary A.	19701	D	1915	Wilhelmina	38696	D	1924
Jeanette Pearl	36066	M	1923	Mary Amelia	40192	D	1924	William	3856	D	1907
Jeffreys	1320	M	1906	Mary Ann	18131	D	1914	William	29471	D	1920
Jennie	73771	D	1936	Mary Ann	21489	D	1916	William	38907	M	1924
Jennie A.	83664	D	1940	Mary Ann	31895	D	1921	William	48481	D	1927
Jennie E.	22209	D	1917	Mary Anna	43397	D	1926	William	79167	D	1938
Johanna	41073	D	1925	Mary B.	27082	D	1919	William Henry	68015	D	1934
John	8753	D	1909	Mary Evelina	45943	I	1926	William J.	20313	D	1916
John	27436	I	1919	Mary J.	8750	D	1909	William J.	86135	I	1941
John	34087	M	1922	Melena D.	40007	D	1924	William Lawson	50028	D	1928
John	43920	D	1926	Michael	14856	D	1913	William Leland	59392	M	1931
John	44662	D	1926	Michael	23600	D	1917	**MARTINA**			
John	50095	D	1928	Michael	39198	D	1924	Julia A.	79223	D	1938
John B.	16196	D	1913	Michael J.	64352	I	1933	Mario J.	31587	D	1921
John B.	80194	D	1938	Michael J.	82334	D	1939	Scolastica	53388	D	1929
John Bell	70101	D	1935	Michael Leo	23861	D	1918	**MARTINDALE**			
John F.	80525	D	1939	Minnie G.	589	D	1906	Mary G. Pope	16884	D	1914
John Francis	75421	D	1937	Miriam	32451	D	1921	**MARTINE**			
John J.	17186	D	1914	Nellie V.	35811	D	1923	Wilhelmina	89486	D	1942
John J.	26981	D	1919	Oliver B.	40315	D	1924	**MARTINEAUT**			
John Joseph	36203	D	1923	Ollie	73875	D	1936	Eugene D.	20281	D	1916
John Theodor	71870	D	1936	Oscar A.	40829	D	1925	**MARTINELLI**			
John Wilson	59392	M	1931	Patrick	14955	D	1913	A.	30713	D	1920
Joseph	31948	D	1921	Patrick	22725	D	1917	Adolf	1835	D	1906
Joseph E.	12174	D	1911	Peter	68784	D	1935	Carlo	26457	D	1919
Joseph Thomas	75810	D	1937	Peter D.	18297	I	1914	Constantino	47911	D	1927
Joseph, Jr.	49214	M	1928	Peter D.	18919	D	1915	Creoza	53717	D	1929
Julia	59056	D	1931	Peter G.	2985	D	1907	Creza	53717	D	1929
Julia Marie Lowell	51044	D	1928	Raymond J.	57687	D	1931	Emile	31958	M	1921
Julius E.	42167	D	1925	Reginald	20664	M	1916	Francisco	22499	D	1917
Kent M.	54552	M	1929	Reinhold Nicholas	38222	M	1924	Frediano	22400	D	1917
Laurettta Gean	54552	M	1929	Robert Asa	68390	D	1934				

NAME	NUMBER	TYPE	YEAR
Joe	47911	D	1927
Naraso	11625	D	1911
Palmira	11617	D	1911
MARTINES			
Anita	27671	M	1919
Ernest	27671	M	1919
Fidel	27762	D	1919
Floripe	27671	M	1919
MARTINET			
Alexander J. O.	57479	D	1930
Marie Olga	69801	D	1935
MARTINEZ			
Alheraldine	43350	D	1926
Alma	43350	D	1926
Altheraldine	43350	D	1926
Bessie	6437	M	1908
Concepcion	40638	D	1924
Federico	78304	D	1938
Francisco Arribas	51023	D	1928
Frank	31983	D	1921
Frank	42850	D	1925
Frank	45312	D	1926
Graciana	88313	D	1941
Ida J.	23204	D	1917
James	39891	I	1924
John	40750	M	1925
Juan B.	61915	D	1932
Libertario	40750	M	1925
Libertario	47761	M	1927
Lola B.	21891	I	1916
Lolita B.	21936	D	1916
Margarita	15720	D	1913
Maria	82083	D	1939
Nicholas S.	87563	D	1941
Pauline Clift	61930	D	1932
Petra	40750	M	1925
Petra	45697	M	1926
Ramon	30718	D	1920
Tiburcio	40750	M	1925
Tiburcio	47761	M	1927
Zacarias	40750	M	1925
Zacarias	41156	D	1925
Zacarias	47761	M	1927
MARTINI			
Frank J.	87781	D	1941
Fred A.	26605	D	1919
Joseph	68744	D	1935
Pasquina	67147	D	1934

NAME	NUMBER	TYPE	YEAR
Pietro	74470	D	1937
Raffaello	39323	D	1924
MARTINICH			
George	26994	D	1919
MARTINKO			
Maria F.	80868	D	1939
MARTINO			
Nello Da Sam	27595	D	1919
MARTINOFF			
Robert William	7541	D	1909
MARTINOVICH			
Nicholas	43162	D	1925
Saverio	10304	D	1910
MARTINS			
John Jacob	36218	D	1923
MARTINSON			
Constance	10211	M	1910
Joseph F.	68392	D	1934
Leonide	10211	M	1910
MARTINUCCI			
Ardelia	58950	M	1931
MARTINWZ			
Roque	87994	D	1941
MARTLIN			
William B.	21156	D	1916
MARTORANA			
Charles, Jr.	68199	M	1934
MARTORELLA			
Angelo	83751	D	1940
Caterina	7206	D	1909
MARTRADOMENICO			
Vito	72901	D	1936
MARTUCCI			
Michele	23136	D	1917
MARTY			
Charles M.	1108	M	1906
Elsie	76429	D	1937
Ernest	81358	D	1939
Eugene J.	14953	M	1913
Eugenie	13493	D	1912
Frank	61167	D	1932
Fred	61167	D	1932
Germain	83146	D	1940
Jules	32004	D	1921
Prosper L.	14953	M	1913

NAME	NUMBER	TYPE	YEAR
MARTZ			
Lewis N.	59305	D	1931
MARTZOLF			
Charles D.	42768	D	1925
MARUM			
Thomas C.	23916	D	1918
MARVIN			
Clifford H.	79114	D	1938
Eugene Grant	44266	D	1926
Frank William	29324	D	1920
Harry LeFevre	30274	D	1920
Lillian Field	74747	D	1937
Sarah A.	87121	D	1941
MARWEDEL			
Charles Ferdinand	12499	D	1911
MARX			
Belle	86035	D	1941
Daniel	42230	D	1925
Edna Marie	26791	D	1919
Henri	49337	D	1928
Jacob	13153	D	1912
John	18003	D	1914
Joseph	63155	D	1932
Jules	57938	M	1931
Lawrence	50745	D	1928
Lena	64200	D	1933
Lucien	57939	M	1931
Melville M.	29319	D	1920
Rebecca	8663	D	1909
Rene, Jr.	57940	M	1931
Stanley Johnson	42755	M	1925
William C.	82497	D	1939
MARXEN			
Elizabeth	52599	D	1929
MARYANSKI			
Karol S.	40660	D	1924
MARYE			
George T., Jr	65271	D	1933
Helen	3084	D	1907
MARZ			
Charlotte	77614	D	1938
MARZALF			
Elmer	81420	M	1939
MARZILLIUS			
John	63816	D	1933
MARZOBO			
Eugenia	32005	I	1921

NAME	NUMBER	TYPE	YEAR
MARZOLA			
Eugenia	32005	I	1921
Eugenia	35054	D	1922
Silvio	49678	D	1928
MARZOLF			
Elmer	81420	M	1939
John Emil	58907	D	1931
Mary	45671	D	1926
MARZOLINO			
Antonio	38685	D	1924
MARZOLO			
Eugenia	35054	D	1922
Silvia	35127	I	1922
Silvio	49678	D	1928
MARZYCK			
Teresa	11886	D	1911
MAS			
Tom	75197	D	1937
MASAREA			
Luigi	3269	D	1907
MASARIE			
F.	1283	I	1906
Fedele	45078	D	1926
Guistina	52576	D	1929
Luigi	3269	D	1907
MASCARICH			
George	2489	M	1906
MASCHIO			
Amedeo	58517	D	1931
Catherine	65376	D	1933
Colombo	47154	D	1927
Louise	62940	D	1932
Luigia	62940	D	1932
MASCHKE			
Alwine	24883	D	1918
MASELOS			
Cosmos	54551	D	1929
MASETTI			
Adolph	48457	D	1927
MASH			
Laura	39218	D	1924
Samuel Lawrence	53314	D	1929
MASHTAKOFF			
John	58358	D	1931
MASI			
Jane M.	22096	D	1917

NAME	NUMBER	TYPE	YEAR
MASICH			
Antone	72283	D	1936
MASINI			
Santi	77055	D	1937
MASKEY			
Frank	23191	D	1917
MASKOW			
Frances	32637	M	1921
Frank	32638	D	1921
Harry	38967	D	1924
Otto M.	28298	D	1919
MASNAGHETTI			
Francesco	18696	D	1915
MASOERO			
Adelaide M.	38908	D	1924
MASON			
Annie	19074	D	1915
Annie	72272	D	1936
Christiana Langdon	26674	M	1919
Daniel	41710	D	1925
Daniel Walker	74387	D	1937
E. A.	46683	D	1927
Edward W.	68226	D	1934
Effie Mabel	45805	D	1926
Eli	46683	D	1927
Eliza J.	46156	D	1927
Emerson S.	84183	I	1940
Emilie M.	45252	D	1926
Estelle M.	41361	D	1925
Florence Harding	85466	D	1940
Florence McLaine	13403	M	1912
Foster H.	11273	D	1911
Frank E., Mrs.	83633	D	1940
Frederick E.	42262	D	1925
George E.	80976	I	1939
George E.	89967	D	1942
George H.	50153	D	1928
George J.	30153	D	1920
Harold	41793	M	1925
Harold	41793	M	1925
Inez Maud	72125	D	1936
James	5933	D	1908
James	45465	D	1926
Jay	52614	D	1929
John	82756	D	1939
John E.	1362	D	1906
John Harding	69080	D	1935
Louise	6283	D	1908

NAME	NUMBER	TYPE	YEAR
Lucy A.	70690	D	1935
Lucy Tolley	70690	D	1935
Marie	89925	M	1942
Marion E.	43390	M	1926
Marion E.	87967	I	1941
Mary E.	60320	D	1931
Mary G.	83633	D	1940
N. H. A.	3276	D	1907
Nellie	80536	I	1939
Nellie O.	79489	D	1938
Paul Williams	30789	D	1920
William	69263	D	1935
William F.	35477	D	1922
MASONI			
Alice	61742	M	1932
Felice	61742	M	1932
Felix	61742	M	1932
MASS			
Albertine E.	4534	D	1907
James C.	53327	D	1929
Joseph Mora, V	50872	M	1928
MASSA			
Agostina	34459	I	1922
Lorenzo	35310	D	1922
Scabatta	28310	D	1919
MASSABO			
Maurizio	30783	D	1920
MASSAGLI			
Alfred	45449	M	1926
Americo	45449	M	1926
Eda	45449	M	1926
Enrico	48888	M	1928
Giovanni	42461	D	1925
Raffaello	47387	D	1927
Renato	45449	M	1926
MASSAGLIA			
Oreste	79045	I	1938
MASSALE			
Adelaide Teresa	87443	D	1941
Adelina	87443	D	1941
MASSANO			
Giovanni	47163	D	1927
John	47163	D	1927
MASSARA			
Giovanni	71795	D	1936
MASSE			
Joseph Henry	56944	D	1930

NAME	NUMBER	TYPE	YEAR
MASSEI			
Elizabeth C.	26800	D	1919
Nicola	24759	D	1918
MASSERA			
Antonio	26786	D	1919
MASSET			
Auguste	309	D	1906
MASSEY			
Atkins J.	18159	D	1914
Florence Cecilia	18032	M	1914
Frances	18275	D	1914
Henry H.	4759	D	1907
Mary C.	18068	D	1914
MASSIE			
H. C.	10171	D	1910
Maria K.	38406	D	1924
MASSIGOGE			
Jean	45951	D	1926
John	45951	D	1926
MASSIMINO			
Gerlando	73555	D	1936
Gilardo	73555	D	1936
MASSINI			
Santi	77055	D	1937
MASSOERO			
Cesare	77443	D	1938
MASSOL			
Angelia F.	80561	D	1939
MASSOLE			
Adelaide Teresa	87443	D	1941
Adelina	84302	I	1940
Adelina	87443	D	1941
George	82522	D	1939
Italo George	82522	D	1939
Pietro Ricardo	82523	D	1939
Richard Peter	82523	D	1939
MASSOLETTI			
Angela	66770	D	1934
Blanche	6185	M	1908
Charles Redfield	68097	D	1934
Giacomo	54708	D	1930
Rose	66322	D	1934
MASSON			
Anna R.	34390	I	1922
Francis P.	18706	D	1915
Katherine	65053	D	1933
Marguerite	74785	D	1937

NAME	NUMBER	TYPE	YEAR
Phillip Joseph	35044	M	1922
Thomas	50319	D	1928
MASSONABE			
Anna	36361	D	1923
MASSONI			
Achille	387	D	1906
MASSUCCO			
Aurelio	21877	D	1916
MAST			
C. L.	14270	D	1912
MASTANZA			
Chris	34012	D	1922
Risto	34012	D	1922
MASTEN			
Benjamin B., Mrs.	80244	D	1939
Delle Littlepage Raynor	80244	D	1939
Joseph Manuel	83350	D	1940
MASTERNICH			
Martin	31900	D	1921
MASTERS			
George Schuyler	10900	D	1910
Harrison J.	83514	D	1940
Hayward B.	21662	D	1916
Henry	17811	D	1914
India	2622	D	1907
William George	70443	D	1935
William Henry	42910	D	1925
MASTERSON			
Catherine M.	51177	D	1928
Charles R.	72642	D	1936
Ella	67454	D	1934
Ella C.	87246	D	1941
Ellen	67454	D	1934
George H.	302	D	1906
Jennie	60909	D	1932
Laurence	14393	D	1912
Lucy	61590	D	1932
Patrick J.	66766	D	1934
Teresa	87329	I	1941
William	183	D	1906
MASTICK			
Mary L.	1562	I	1906
MASTON			
Mary Jane	55217	D	1930
MASTRADOMENICO			
Vito	72901	D	1936

NAME	NUMBER	TYPE	YEAR
MASTRANGELO			
Nicholas	75259	I	1937
MASTRODOMENICO			
Gaetano	31447	I	1921
Gustave	31447	I	1921
MASTROEOLO			
Joe	77609	D	1938
MASURY			
Lucette	3444	M	1907
MATCHIM			
John Frederick	32663	I	1921
MATCHIN			
John Frederick	61284	D	1932
MATEOVICH			
N. M.	12860	D	1912
MATERNE			
Edward	76205	I	1937
MATES			
George A.	55753	I	1930
MATHAIS			
Charles Gifford	6718	M	1908
MATHAUSER			
John Barton	79245	D	1938
Joseph	67172	I	1934
MATHEI			
Mary	29354	D	1920
Philipp	18520	D	1915
MATHEN			
Pablo	38430	D	1924
MATHER			
Squier R.	6497	D	1908
MATHERON			
Joseph	40516	D	1924
Neomie	25214	D	1918
Valentin	24584	D	1918
MATHERS			
Amalia	85217	D	1940
William Henry	74789	D	1937
MATHES			
Jake	39493	D	1924
Lena	71104	D	1935
MATHESON			
Jessie H.	36958	D	1923
John	55407	D	1930
John	65691	D	1933
John Harry	58692	I	1931

NAME	NUMBER	TYPE	YEAR	NAME	NUMBER	TYPE	YEAR	NAME	NUMBER	TYPE	YEAR
Quentin Robert	61768	D	1932	Rose	60633	I	1932	Elizabeth Louisa (L. B.)	4042	D	1907
Sarah E.	27566	I	1919	**MATHIEU**				Floyd S.	54089	D	1929
MATHEU				Albert	48819	M	1927	Floyd Simpson	33234	D	1922
Carmen	68949	I	1935	Caroline	31175	D	1921	Frances	38229	D	1924
Pablo	38430	D	1924	Martin	24400	D	1918	Ida Margaret	13802	M	1912
MATHEW				**MATHIEW**				John	32272	D	1921
Frank Theobald	82210	D	1939	Martin	24400	D	1918	John	33813	D	1922
MATHEWS				**MATHINDAKIS**				Lillie B.	56099	D	1930
Agnes C.	60058	I	1931	George	63229	D	1932	Lily	33125	M	1921
Anna Wainwright	53671	D	1929	**MATHIS**				Ludvig	34631	D	1922
Annie	52456	D	1929	Jacob L.	57212	D	1930	Martin	59764	D	1931
Bernard Joseph	61423	D	1932	**MATHISEN**				Mathias	60797	D	1932
Bruno Anton	58704	D	1931	David	71023	D	1935	Selma	23794	D	1917
Catherine C.	12336	D	1911	Marilyn Roberta	58734	M	1931	William	23436	D	1917
Charles C.	63328	D	1933	Peter	20728	D	1916	**MATTA**			
Dale	40233	D	1924	Walter Francis	56920	M	1930	Alfred V.	66903	I	1934
Frances Teresa	29704	M	1920	**MATHISON**				Maria Emilia da Silveira	2285	D	1906
George S.	47256	D	1927	Catherine	51082	M	1928	**MATTEI**			
James F.	1030	D	1906	Dorothy	51082	M	1928	C. G.	44288	D	1926
Joseph J.	6225	D	1908	Peter	20728	D	1916	Leo	75090	D	1937
Louise	64374	D	1933	**MATHOUSER**				**MATTEOLI**			
Martha (Mattie)	4487	M	1907	John Barton	79245	D	1938	Remo	39783	M	1924
Mary Agnes	29704	M	1920	**MATHSON**				**MATTESON**			
Theresa C.	75675	D	1937	Ernest Martin	60445	D	1931	Christian	36124	D	1923
Victor Edward	46511	D	1927	**MATLI**				Erastus Potter	59227	D	1931
MATHEWSON				Melania	28637	D	1920	Sylvia	83702	I	1940
Emeline A.	64397	D	1933	**MATLOCK**				**MATTEUCCI**			
Eva	71673	D	1936	Claude C.	80447	D	1939	Enrico	10535	M	1910
May C.	15594	D	1913	**MATLY**				Evelina	10535	M	1910
Nellie	44504	D	1926	Julia	49626	D	1928	Teresa	11756	D	1911
Robert	14854	D	1913	**MATOS**				Vincenzo	10535	M	1910
Thomas D.	22996	D	1917	Anthony R.	27381	D	1919	**MATTHAI**			
MATHEZ				Anton	19596	D	1915	John C. H.	15787	D	1913
Fritz H.	37120	D	1923	**MATRAIA**				Mary E.	23797	D	1917
MATHIAS				Emma	307	D	1906	Rose	23051	D	1917
Gonzales F.	39782	I	1924	**MATRAMAN**				**MATTHAUSER**			
Nicholas	84941	D	1940	Jean	55545	D	1930	John Barton	79245	D	1938
Robert F. L.	6814	D	1908	**MATRE**				**MATTHEAD**			
Walter	56446	D	1930	John	38709	D	1924	Charles	19028	D	1915
MATHIEN				**MATSCHEK**				**MATTHESEN**			
Albert	48819	M	1927	Ferdinand Landerlin	44763	D	1926	Anders	52353	D	1929
Caroline	31175	D	1921	**MATSEN**				Andrew	52353	D	1929
MATHIESEN				Andrew	6235	D	1908	**MATTHESON**			
Johan G.	32632	D	1921	**MATSON**				Annie Louise	79921	D	1938
John	32632	D	1921	Bernice Marie	13801	M	1912	**MATTHEW**			
MATHIESON				Carl Rudolf	27485	M	1919	Jean Elizabeth	67478	M	1934
Jack G.	15562	D	1913					Martha	65410	D	1933

- 78 -

Key: D = death; M = minor; I = incompetent

NAME	NUMBER	TYPE	YEAR	NAME	NUMBER	TYPE	YEAR	NAME	NUMBER	TYPE	YEAR
Minnie C.	58299	D	1931	**MATTICE**				**MATTTOON**			
Morris S.	51830	D	1929	Leroy John	59024	I	1931	Nellie F.	74547	D	1937
MATTHEWS				**MATTICEVICH**				**MATULICH**			
Annie	83856	D	1940	Nicholas	4846	D	1907	Alessandro	12039	D	1911
Charles L.	47938	D	1927	**MATTIER**				Ann J.	83444	M	1940
Emanuel	4779	D	1907	Louis C.	48326	D	1927	Domenica	50284	D	1928
Frank	61282	D	1932	**MATTINGLY**				Frank G.	83445	D	1940
Hannah	73005	D	1936	Antoinette M.	29655	M	1920	George	75707	D	1937
Isabella	80380	D	1939	Richard C.	17095	D	1914	Matt J.	87489	D	1941
James	61687	I	1932	Sarah Marie	29655	M	1920	Matthew J.	45604	I	1926
John	1131	D	1906	Sarah T.	24970	I	1918	**MATUSSECK**			
Julius Elmer	44981	I	1926	Sarah T.	29585	D	1920	Max	60352	D	1931
Lemuel Tompkins	78323	D	1938	Victoria E.	20384	M	1916	**MATZELLE**			
M. H.	18219	D	1914	**MATTISIN**				Louisa	73468	D	1936
M. S.	18219	D	1914	A. Vyacheflavov	78400	D	1938	**MATZEN**			
M. S.	51830	D	1929	**MATTISON**				Augusta C.	69739	D	1935
Margaret Jeannette	86240	D	1941	Theresa J.	32920	D	1921	Christina	45051	D	1926
Mary	10890	D	1910	**MATTMAN**				**MATZENBACH**			
Mary	42650	D	1925	Elizabeth	88251	D	1941	Emma W.	89552	D	1942
Marzell M.	14611	D	1912	Elizabeth	84333	I	1940	**MATZKEWITZ**			
Michael Malott	32735	D	1921	**MATTMANN**				Santos	30108	D	1920
Patrick	14522	D	1912	Carl F.	69824	M	1935	**MAU**			
Robert Lowman	2308	M	1906	**MATTOCK**				John Carl August	8647	D	1909
Rosalie Lloyd	2308	M	1906	Charles Wilfrid	59679	D	1931	John W.	43942	D	1926
Saul	55599	D	1930	**MATTONA**				Marguerite Dorothy	89261	D	1942
Thomas	5874	D	1908	Alfonso	54281	D	1929	Ottilia	5676	D	1908
MATTHEY				**MATTOON**				**MAUBEC**			
Louise M.	67690	I	1934	Frances Vina	14760	D	1913	Vue H.	2027	D	1906
Louise M.	81263	D	1939	**MATTOS**				**MAUBERRET**			
Robert H.	48733	D	1927	Manual Antonio	27210	D	1919	Adolph Louis	76127	D	1937
MATTHEYS				Mario Pereira	41011	D	1925	Seraphine Pauline	74401	D	1937
Pierre	51298	D	1928	**MATTSON**				**MAUCHER**			
MATTHHORST				Albert	37476	I	1923	John	47326	D	1927
Anita E.	13783	M	1912	Anna	46583	D	1927	**MAUER**			
MATTHIAS				Edna	20347	M	1916	A. M., Mrs.	35278	I	1922
Clara P.	54638	D	1930	Elise	20347	M	1916	Bertha Cecilia	75515	D	1937
Henry	17781	I	1914	Esther	20347	M	1916	**MAUNAS**			
MATTHIES				George	20347	M	1916	Andre	29049	D	1920
Henry C.	73141	D	1936	Jack	41375	D	1925	Pierre Andre	29049	D	1920
Lena	10439	D	1910	Johan	32272	D	1921	**MAUNDER**			
Thresa	57063	D	1930	John	310	D	1906	Mary Ann	45026	D	1926
MATTHIESEN				Martin	60848	I	1932	Matthew C.	61874	D	1932
Herman	66226	D	1934	Martin Werner	32974	D	1921	**MAUNDRELL**			
John	14498	D	1912	Mathias Ivar	52704	D	1929	Harry	40122	I	1924
Margaretha	25203	D	1918	Rowena Mary	87610	D	1941	Harry	41693	D	1925
MATTHIS				**MATTSSON**				Mary D.	41838	D	1925
Mary A.	74063	D	1936	Anna	13945	D	1912				

NAME	NUMBER	TYPE	YEAR
Mary D.	41838	D	1925
MAUPIN			
George G.	18367	D	1915
MAURER			
Anna	17631	I	1914
Charles J.	24893	D	1918
Clemens	54961	D	1930
Elizabeth Frances	24894	I	1918
Frank	87803	D	1941
Frederick August	55402	D	1930
George	7478	D	1909
Louisa	72080	D	1936
Marianna	70841	D	1935
W. Edward	70024	I	1935
MAURINO			
Frank	37089	D	1923
MAURIZIO			
Sebastian	26000	D	1918
MAURS			
Louis	68532	D	1934
MAUS			
John	79952	D	1938
MAUSER			
Albert	15553	D	1913
Donald	55865	M	1930
Henry	51064	D	1928
Rose	54280	D	1929
MAUSERT			
Otto F.	77391	D	1937
MAUSSANG			
Pascal P.	28121	D	1919
MAUSSHARDT			
August	81696	D	1939
Christina	50481	D	1928
MAUTER			
Louis	27652	D	1919
MAUTINO			
Marietta	70214	D	1935
MAUTONE			
Felice	43082	D	1925
MAUVAIS			
Carol Mae	77101	M	1937
MAUZY			
H. B.	35699	D	1923
Hannah	35699	D	1923

NAME	NUMBER	TYPE	YEAR
MAVERS			
William G.	62864	D	1932
MAVIUS			
Carlotta Georgina	64604	D	1933
MAWHINNEY			
Arthur	18500	D	1915
MAWSON			
Alice	70878	D	1935
MAX			
Aaron	16456	D	1913
George H.	68954	I	1935
Rachel	34753	D	1922
Rosalia	67129	D	1934
MAXSON			
Harold Frark	73746	M	1936
Herbert Gardner	73435	D	1936
Jean Patricia	73745	M	1936
Louis W.	24106	D	1918
MAXWELL			
Agnes R.	50552	D	1928
Alice Evelyn	19804	M	1915
Alice F.	13461	D	1912
Antone	42004	D	1925
Charles	7039	D	1909
Claudia Maxine	58942	M	1931
Dolores E.	71448	M	1936
Elena D.	64164	D	1933
Elinor	74278	D	1936
Elizabeth M.	86605	D	1941
Eva	17558	D	1914
Franklin	17094	D	1914
George R.	38686	M	1924
George R. E.	5750	I	1908
Irvin Lee	70655	M	1935
J. R., Mrs.	46490	D	1927
Jerome M.	66885	D	1934
John W. C.	43793	D	1926
Joseph M.	67379	D	1934
Maria	22476	D	1917
Minnie	46490	D	1927
Pearl	72551	D	1936
Perry Higgins	64017	D	1933
Thomas Joseph	67221	D	1934
Virginia O.	38686	M	1924
William J., Jr.	71448	M	1936
William Grey	19112	D	1915
MAY			
Adeline F.	19760	D	1915

NAME	NUMBER	TYPE	YEAR
Alfred	47052	D	1927
Angelo M.	72618	D	1936
Aron	34280	D	1922
Bessie J.	42962	D	1925
Cecilia C.	38653	D	1924
E. F.	55899	D	1930
Edward	7656	D	1909
Elizabeth L.	2981	D	1907
Elsie DeRemer	79789	D	1938
Frank	923	I	1906
Frank	85413	D	1940
Friederich	34263	D	1922
Gustave	59900	D	1931
Harriet E.	7407	D	1909
Harry	80760	D	1939
Henriette F.	40714	D	1925
Herbert Frances	51957	D	1929
Hilda M.	87464	D	1941
Isabella C.	46990	D	1927
Jacob H.	28293	D	1919
James	2325	D	1906
Jeannette	16044	D	1913
Jin Mun	73738	D	1936
John	22874	D	1917
John F.	81341	D	1939
Joseph	7976	D	1909
Julia F.	22435	D	1917
Ke Choo	73738	D	1936
Laura B.	81065	D	1939
Louis	8547	M	1909
Louis	23249	D	1917
Margaret	73535	D	1936
Margaret C.	63969	D	1933
Matilda	85810	D	1940
Mayer	15591	D	1913
Robert	50151	M	1928
Robert B.	18801	D	1915
Rofena C.	61831	D	1932
William	17437	D	1914
William	78784	D	1938
William Boardman	15165	D	1913
Yee	60892	D	1932
Yee Quan	60892	D	1932
MAYBACH			
Curtis Caldwell	21858	M	1916
Frieda Helen	21858	M	1916
MAYBELL			
Claude	4312	D	1907

NAME	NUMBER	TYPE	YEAR	NAME	NUMBER	TYPE	YEAR	NAME	NUMBER	TYPE	YEAR
MAYBERRY				John Louis	12618	D	1911	Paul H.	41085	I	1925
Earl W.	30957	D	1921	Josephine L.	22991	D	1917	**MAYFIELD**			
William	3203	D	1907	Jules	2117	D	1906	Mary	62440	I	1932
MAYBLUM				Leland	17728	M	1914	Mary	65864	D	1933
Jacob J.	46289	D	1927	Lena	50654	D	1928	Max	65940	D	1933
Louis	74586	D	1937	Lena	53409	D	1929	**MAYHEW**			
Louis	87391	D	1941	Lenora	76333	I	1937	Frank E.	78099	D	1938
MAYBURY				Leonora	81577	D	1939	**MAYLE**			
Richard	1812	D	1906	Louis C.	4959	M	1907	Ella	4411	D	1907
MAYDAHL				Margaretha	16241	D	1913	**MAYLER**			
Hanna	68450	D	1934	Maurice E.	3575	D	1907	Harry	61974	D	1932
MAYDER				Max	62063	D	1932	**MAYLING**			
Elsie A.	6806	D	1908	Max	82759	D	1939	John C.	82785	D	1939
Lorine Ruth	6749	M	1908	Morris	14861	D	1913	**MAYMAN**			
MAYE				Paula	67332	D	1934	James B.	68034	D	1934
Lotta	64604	D	1933	Raymond	17728	M	1914	**MAYN**			
MAYER				Richard	70331	D	1935	William Henry	48878	D	1928
Abraham	17494	D	1914	Roberta	4959	M	1907	**MAYNARD**			
Albert H.	75212	D	1937	Rosebud	79042	M	1938	Abbott T.	49375	D	1928
Allen L.	81769	D	1939	Sam Albert	82538	D	1939	Adeline	12945	D	1912
Anna	36163	D	1923	Samuel D.	34843	D	1922	Alma E.	82220	D	1939
Arnold	79042	M	1938	Sarah B.	63107	D	1932	Caroline L.	16230	D	1913
August	65135	D	1933	Sophia	68869	D	1935	Eva P.	32032	D	1921
August Walter	62976	D	1932	Susie	18668	D	1915	George H.	27448	D	1919
Barbara Anne	11953	M	1911	Theodore	41113	D	1925	Gustave Charles	50192	D	1928
Carmen	17728	M	1914	Theresa A.	63544	D	1933	Harry H.	64842	D	1933
Carmen	17997	D	1914	Tillie	14903	D	1913	Maria	6527	D	1908
Catherine L.	51016	D	1928	Walter	84901	D	1940	Marjory	67689	M	1934
Charles	15500	D	1913	Wanda	50225	D	1928	Mary A.	8457	D	1909
Charles	36879	D	1923	Wendelin	1707	D	1906	Nova Z.	53945	D	1929
Charles, Jr.	25209	D	1918	**MAYERLE**				Robert Glenn	67689	M	1934
Christian Gottlob	43224	D	1925	George	54593	D	1929	**MAYNE**			
Elisabeth	69788	D	1935	Peter	38123	D	1924	Alfred Ernest	69448	D	1935
Ethel Laura	4477	M	1907	**MAYERS**				Elizabeth Robinson	63508	D	1933
Eva	41640	D	1925	Alfred	6038	D	1908	**MAYNTZER**			
Ferdinand	69542	D	1935	Alfred M.	10009	D	1910	Walter	3604	D	1907
Frank A.	81680	D	1939	Annie R.	54601	D	1929	**MAYO**			
Hannah	29438	D	1920	August	55523	D	1930	Alfred McDevitt	8341	D	1909
Henry	556	D	1906	Carrie	79125	D	1938	Arthur Randolph	52790	D	1929
Henry	3136	D	1907	Edgar John	26440	D	1919	Edward P.	34832	I	1922
Henry	27948	M	1919	Felix	69650	D	1935	Elgin	70371	D	1935
Henry J.	45390	D	1926	Robert William	58519	D	1931	George	86648	D	1941
Henry L.	79294	D	1938	Sophie	68240	D	1934	Guillermo	86648	D	1941
Heyman	3136	D	1907	Thomas J.	12049	D	1911	Katharine H. W.	64506	D	1933
J. R.	70331	D	1935	**MAYERSON**				Larry G.	12138	M	1911
James W.	50635	D	1928	Sadie	60513	D	1931	Mary Elizabeth	62237	D	1932
Johanna S.	13966	D	1912	**MAYES**				William	86883	D	1941
John G.	13560	D	1912	Emmet	49519	D	1928				

NAME	NUMBER	TYPE	YEAR	NAME	NUMBER	TYPE	YEAR	NAME	NUMBER	TYPE	YEAR
MAYOLO				**MAZUIR**				**MCADAM**			
Jose Antonio	83723	D	1940	Alexander Jean	49994	D	1928	Alexander J.	23639	D	1917
MAYRHOFER				**MAZZA**				Hugh	49175	D	1928
Antonia	8052	D	1909	Antonia	29217	D	1920	Jane	48430	D	1927
Leonhart	9270	D	1910	Beulah E.	75542	I	1937	Marion A.	83026	D	1940
Nickolis	64280	D	1933	Constantino	46101	D	1926	**MCADAMS**			
Rudolph A.	23318	D	1917	Costantino	46101	D	1926	Annie T.	73818	D	1936
Virginia	28367	M	1919	Emilie	1904	D	1906	Della	50598	D	1928
Walker	25519	D	1918	Rosa	35716	D	1923	Elizabeth	39570	D	1924
Walter N.	22292	M	1917	Salvatore	51420	D	1928	Flossie	5524	M	1908
MAYRISCH				**MAZZACATO**				John James	5950	D	1908
Annie	56866	D	1930	Edward	89812	D	1942	Lizzie	36305	D	1923
Ellen A.	64083	D	1933	**MAZZAFERRO**				**MCADOO**			
Frederick A.	84090	D	1940	Battista	61528	D	1932	Barbara	77287	M	1937
MAYS				**MAZZALI**				James A.	12536	D	1911
Mary S.	28141	D	1919	Vincent	20582	D	1916	**MCAFEE**			
Roberta Vera	35022	M	1922	**MAZZELLA**				Clark William	506	D	1906
MAYSENHOLDER				Francesco	47083	D	1927	Edwin	30659	D	1920
Emilie	44413	D	1926	**MAZZERA**				Lloyd T.	89710	D	1942
MAYSONNANE				Giuseppe	77228	D	1937	Robert A.	76720	D	1937
Marie	87257	D	1941	**MAZZINI**				**MCALEER**			
MAYSONNAVE				Achilles J.	47594	D	1927	John	71173	D	1935
Philipe	14619	D	1912	Annie	36078	I	1923	**MCALESTER**			
Pierre	51531	D	1928	Annie	47456	I	1927	William F.	26575	D	1919
Pierre	87978	D	1941	Carmen Mary	43430	M	1926	**MCALISTER**			
MAYSOUNAVE				Edward Francis	22839	D	1917	Hanora	18263	D	1914
Ph.	14619	D	1912	Margaret Louise	21683	M	1916	Hanorah	18208	I	1914
MAYVILLE				**MAZZONI**				Isabel H.	14359	D	1912
Francis	12955	D	1912	Achilee	387	D	1906	Nellie Victoria Caroline	32744	D	1921
MAZEAN				**MAZZUCATE**				**MCALLEN**			
Joseph John	86068	D	1941	Ezio	89812	D	1942	Dennis	14961	D	1913
MAZEAU				**MAZZUCATO**				**MCALLISTER**			
Joseph John	86068	D	1941	Ezio	89812	D	1942	Alexander J.	58107	D	1931
Margaret Julia	19528	D	1915	**MAZZUCCHI**				Amelia H.	18335	D	1914
MAZELLA				Eugen	65198	D	1933	Frances	80657	I	1939
Rose	48033	D	1927	Felice	44290	D	1926	James U.	58231	I	1931
MAZENAUER				Giuseppe	24411	D	1918	Mary	5980	D	1908
Anita	67046	D	1934	**MAZZUCCI**				Mary Louise	53014	D	1929
Anita M.	68012	M	1934	Carlo	61860	I	1932	W. F. M.	24374	D	1918
MAZETTI				**MAZZUCHI**				Walter Franklin	41321	D	1925
P.	36719	D	1923	Felice	44290	D	1926	William	76818	D	1937
P.	36719	D	1923	**MAZZUEATO**				William Morse	61152	D	1932
MAZONE				Maria	43490	D	1926	**MCALONE**			
Albert	37305	D	1923	**MCABEE**				Melvin L.	25746	D	1918
MAZOUE				John Baptist	18813	D	1915	**MCALPIN**			
Dominick	22698	D	1917					Alan A.	2189	D	1906
								Annie	46192	I	1927

NAME	NUMBER	TYPE	YEAR
Jennie	46191	D	1927
Margaret	11739	I	1911
Margaret	12114	D	1911
MCALPINE			
Annie	46192	I	1927
Jennie	46191	D	1927
MCANDREWS			
Anthony	16449	D	1913
Bridgit	52402	D	1929
Florence	60872	I	1932
J. C.	22940	D	1917
Patrick	57919	I	1931
MCANENY			
Sarah	10560	D	1910
MCANULTY			
Paul	19432	D	1915
MCAOY			
Catherine Annie	31046	D	1921
MCARAN			
Patrick	67654	D	1934
Patrick	76144	D	1937
MCARAVY			
Ellen Jane	25981	D	1918
MCARDLE			
Agnes	6122	D	1908
Arthur Gordon	17024	D	1914
Barbara Mary	81953	M	1939
Bernard	40424	D	1924
Bernard S.	26950	D	1919
Blanche	81953	M	1939
Catherine	29328	D	1920
Frank Dominic	86556	D	1941
James F.	23280	D	1917
Kathryn	37266	D	1923
Louis B.	47109	D	1927
Owen	60191	D	1931
Rose	71146	D	1935
MCARTHUR			
Anna J.	13652	D	1912
Edward Hinkley	67681	D	1934
George	11558	D	1911
Greely	7651	D	1909
Henry	84721	D	1940
Jemima A.	19010	D	1915
L., Mrs.	35751	D	1923
Malitta J.	35751	D	1923
Mildred Upton	12833	M	1912

NAME	NUMBER	TYPE	YEAR
William P.	4740	D	1907
MCARTOR			
Gene	46789	D	1927
MCASEY			
Delia	29725	D	1920
June	71062	M	1935
Lillie	38221	D	1924
Marshall	71062	M	1935
MCASKILL			
Donald J.	29236	D	1920
Ellen	47156	D	1927
MCATEE			
Elouise Agnes	27435	M	1919
Frances Linwood	36838	M	1923
John	15772	D	1913
John Elder	36838	M	1923
Levonna Louese	36839	M	1923
Sylvester J., Jr.	36838	M	1923
MCAULAY			
Emma E.	22591	D	1917
MCAULEY			
Edna	57435	D	1930
Frances J.	48058	D	1927
Henry	10066	D	1910
James Joseph	26849	D	1919
Mary	4732	D	1907
MCAULIFFE			
Bridget	81258	D	1939
Catherine	75129	D	1937
Cornelius	1645	D	1906
Cornelius	74858	D	1937
Daniel M.	41082	D	1925
Dennis F.	49750	D	1928
Dennis J.	77820	D	1938
Edgar A.	60322	I	1931
Eugene	21293	D	1916
Eugene	34918	D	1922
Eugene Timothy	9925	D	1910
George P.	41547	D	1925
Grissella	40025	D	1924
James	81614	D	1939
Jeremiah M.	3832	D	1907
Joseph A.	87085	D	1941
Joseph P.	83392	D	1940
Margaret	11127	D	1911
Mary	58347	D	1931
Mary E.	61146	D	1932

NAME	NUMBER	TYPE	YEAR
MCAVOY			
Catherine Annie	34378	D	1922
Edward	34663	D	1922
Frank	35060	D	1922
Goldwin	57283	D	1930
Hugh B.	4825	D	1907
James Patrick	35956	I	1923
Kate	54515	D	1929
Margaret A.	14153	D	1912
Mary	1206	D	1906
Michael	8989	D	1910
Virgil	74769	D	1937
MCBAIN			
Andrew	44469	D	1926
MCBARRON			
Sarah	61895	D	1932
MCBEAN			
Agnes Perkins	80454	D	1939
Esther	14221	D	1912
Jane V.	54393	I	1929
Mary S.	68494	I	1934
Peter McG.	35122	D	1922
Richard F.	51350	D	1928
MCBENNETT			
Bridget	77151	D	1937
MCBETH			
Kate C.	21079	D	1916
MCBIRNEY			
H., Mrs.	38004	D	1923
Mary Elizabeth	38004	D	1923
Samuel	46228	D	1927
MCBOURNIE			
Ethel Pearl	3607	M	1907
MCBRAYER			
Jessie	16442	M	1913
MCBREARTY			
John A.	64045	D	1933
Michael J.	86529	D	1941
MCBRIDE			
Annie	35547	D	1922
C. C.	68801	D	1935
Cahterine Z.	72589	D	1936
Charles	84835	M	1940
Clara E.	88560	D	1941
Edward	23020	D	1917
Eliza	46805	D	1927
Fred Bradley	19662	M	1915

NAME	NUMBER	TYPE	YEAR	NAME	NUMBER	TYPE	YEAR	NAME	NUMBER	TYPE	YEAR
John	45331	D	1926	Nicholas	43748	D	1926	Llewellyn	27008	D	1919
John	72709	D	1936	Owen	3582	D	1907	Margaret	49309	D	1928
Kittie L.	12537	D	1911	Patricia Joyce	61951	M	1932	Margaret	73416	D	1936
Loma C.	15211	D	1913	Patrick F.	46221	D	1927	Martha Louise	31500	D	1921
Lucile	75382	D	1937	Patrick J.	52716	D	1929	Philip	20831	D	1916
Margaret M.	48250	D	1927	Richard Hart	88483	M	1941	Richard	31517	D	1921
Mary	11701	D	1911	Terrance	1816	D	1906	Thomas Raymond	37037	D	1923
Mary Elizabeth	324	D	1906	Thomas Francis	23970	D	1918	Thomas, Jr.	14032	M	1912
Michael	38899	D	1924	Walter J.	89429	D	1942	William	10147	D	1910
Patricia	84835	M	1940	William B.	52690	M	1929	William	25368	D	1918
Patrick	247	D	1906	William F.	45137	M	1926	**McCallan**			
Rose Marie	38583	M	1924	**McCafferty**				John	64947	D	1933
Thomas	11517	D	1911	Anne J.	83347	D	1940	**McCallister**			
Thomas Edward	11618	M	1911	Hugh	46159	D	1927	A. C.	44947	D	1926
Winifred Lucile	75382	D	1937	James	8240	D	1909	Frances May	27027	D	1919
McBrien				Michael Hugh	49547	D	1928	Frank M.	27027	D	1919
Hazel	63490	D	1933	**McCaffery**				**McCallum**			
McBryde				Bridget	13299	D	1912	Andrew T. G.	78133	D	1938
Elizabeth Amelia	45047	D	1926	Emily Louise	62922	D	1932	Bridget	35347	D	1922
Mollie Beatrice	14633	M	1912	Francis	63018	D	1932	Elizabeth Ann	34560	D	1922
McBurley				Francis Logan	73255	M	1936	James A.	35348	D	1922
Frank	9775	D	1910	Hugh	65139	D	1933	John	38787	D	1924
McCabe				Hugh D.	38070	D	1924	Minnie E.	82971	D	1939
Amarilla A.	2408	I	1906	Irene	25475	D	1918	Neil	699	D	1906
Annie	23110	I	1917	James Henry	18588	D	1915	**McCamish**			
Annie	23405	D	1917	Julia	28509	D	1919	John	79457	M	1938
Barney	60040	D	1931	Patrick	49022	D	1928	**McCandless**			
Catherine	89834	D	1942	Rosanna	14534	D	1912	John A.	55271	D	1930
Charles	70575	D	1935	Walter Alton	73255	M	1936	**McCann**			
Elizabeth A.	69512	D	1935	**McCaffrey**				Aileen	3266	M	1907
Ellen	7316	D	1909	Hugh D.	38070	D	1924	Albert	58279	M	1931
Ellen	21492	D	1916	James	84939	D	1940	Annie P.	71603	D	1936
Horace Livermore	79750	D	1938	Julia	28509	D	1919	Bridget	453	D	1906
James	19994	D	1915	Lloyd	74548	D	1937	Catherine	13216	D	1912
James	87280	D	1941	Mary E.	69471	D	1935	Catherine	59129	I	1931
James H.	62619	D	1932	**McCahen**				Charles F.	14199	M	1912
John	25222	D	1918	Isidore	33956	D	1922	Charles Thomas, Sr.	14667	D	1913
John	35561	D	1922	**McCahon**				Claire Sherman	31735	D	1921
John	68555	D	1934	George	40633	D	1924	Clara J.	800	D	1906
John C., Jr.	52691	M	1929	Mary J.	47808	D	1927	Cornelius	23605	D	1917
Joseph	71657	D	1936	**McCain**				David	3266	M	1907
Margaret	10296	D	1910	Lissette	5635	D	1908	Ellen	24194	D	1918
Margaret Selina	86970	D	1941	**McCall**				Ellen L.	1161	D	1906
Marie	76440	M	1937	Alexander	27368	D	1919	Eugene J.	14199	M	1912
Mary	23313	D	1917	Edward	32773	M	1921	Francis P.	39982	D	1924
Matthew	38869	D	1924	Elizabeth Ann	30070	D	1920	Frank G.	87240	D	1941
Michael Joseph	71527	I	1936	Elvin C.	75083	D	1937	Grace F.	14199	M	1912
Michael Joseph	71657	D	1936	Henry A., Jr.	21024	D	1916	Hannah	14525	D	1912

NAME	NUMBER	TYPE	YEAR	NAME	NUMBER	TYPE	YEAR	NAME	NUMBER	TYPE	YEAR
Helen G.	14199	M	1912	Claire F.	80011	M	1938	Cornelius	126	D	1906
James	9049	D	1910	**McCarroll**				Cornelius	9930	D	1910
James	34871	D	1922	Alice Gertrude	48741	M	1927	Daniel	62471	D	1932
James Fitzpatrick	73123	M	1936	Bernard	40424	D	1924	Daniel	70108	D	1935
James Joseph	51182	D	1928	George Joseph	48741	M	1927	Daniel Florence	78002	D	1938
Jane Potter	32707	D	1921	George P.	23312	I	1917	Daniel J.	67575	D	1934
Joan Player	77261	M	1937	**McCarron**				Daniel W.	42215	D	1925
John	9552	D	1910	Mary Ann	23180	I	1917	Delia	32768	D	1921
John J.	10270	D	1910	Michael	32441	D	1921	Denis E.	12365	D	1911
John Joseph	85684	D	1940	**McCarry**				Dennis	3285	D	1907
John W.	48615	M	1927	Mary	15196	D	1913	Dennis	45279	D	1926
John W.	49577	M	1928	**McCarte**				Dennis	47657	D	1927
John Walter	32708	M	1921	Henrietta	50724	D	1928	Dennis J.	82312	D	1939
John William	45510	D	1926	James	318	D	1906	Dennis Joseph	8714	D	1909
Leslie	3266	M	1907	**McCarter**				Dennis, Jr.	4065	I	1907
Loretta V.	8086	M	1909	Lula	42271	I	1925	Dennis, Jr.	7608	D	1909
Lucy Jessie	86117	D	1941	**McCarthy**				Edna M.	27050	M	1919
Margaret	26145	M	1919	Agnes	79922	I	1938	Elizabeth	2253	M	1906
Mary B.	26128	D	1919	Agnes Joyce	80504	D	1939	Elizabeth	41359	D	1925
Mary Jane	35768	D	1923	Albert A.	54909	I	1930	Elizabeth Frances	12364	D	1911
Mary L.	63673	D	1933	Andrew G.	50864	D	1928	Ella Louise	82261	D	1939
Mary M.	26144	D	1919	Anne	6129	I	1908	Ellen	5765	D	1908
Michael	452	D	1906	Annie	5539	D	1908	Ellen	11882	D	1911
Michael	2323	D	1906	Annie	76042	D	1937	Ellen	22124	D	1917
Millie	47692	I	1927	Bartholomew	26987	D	1919	Ellen	29250	D	1920
Nellie	68935	D	1935	Bartholomew	42889	D	1925	Ellen	31510	D	1921
Peter	3551	D	1907	Bernard	55001	D	1930	Ellen	89610	D	1942
Peter	6466	D	1908	Bridget	565	D	1906	Ellen	80411	D	1939
Philip D.	14199	M	1912	Bridget	77702	D	1938	Eugene	8075	D	1909
Sara Chambaud	66130	D	1934	Bridget	51364	D	1928	Eugene H.	62711	D	1932
Susan Irene	15586	M	1913	Caroline	9867	D	1910	Florence	9395	D	1910
Thomas J.	73381	D	1936	Carrie B.	41228	D	1925	Florence	67180	I	1934
Thomas Joseph	61336	D	1932	Catharine C.	38063	D	1924	Frances Marie	73668	M	1936
William	10998	D	1911	Catherine	62	D	1906	Francis C.	62454	D	1932
William D.	49521	D	1928	Catherine	17604	D	1914	Francis Joseph	305	D	1906
William David	77261	M	1937	Catherine	55003	D	1930	Francis Leslie	31214	M	1921
McCants				Catherine	67131	D	1934	Frank Z.	83409	D	1940
Eleanor Virginia	46572	D	1927	Catherine E.	46170	D	1927	Genevieve	16057	I	1913
Melnotte	50814	D	1928	Catherine E.	68897	D	1935	George Francis	46190	D	1927
McCardell				Cathern	7162	I	1909	George Grant	62458	D	1932
Maria	4750	D	1907	Cathern	7529	D	1909	George John	73600	D	1936
McCarren				Charles	9759	D	1910	George W.	27191	D	1919
Mary	29007	D	1920	Charles	51806	D	1929	George Washington	55959	D	1930
McCarreu				Charles	64662	M	1933	Gertrude A.	72604	I	1936
Alexander J.	45192	D	1926	Charles Edward	63258	D	1932	Hannah	22530	D	1917
McCarrick				Charles J.	83269	D	1940	Hannora A.	17630	D	1914
Anna	78176	D	1938	Charles M.	85121	D	1940	Harold B.	20750	I	1916
Anna E.	70803	D	1935	Charlotte Hannah	31682	D	1921	Harold E.	27050	M	1919
								Harriet	33843	D	1922

Key: D = death; M = minor; I = incompetent

Name	Number	Type	Year	Name	Number	Type	Year	Name	Number	Type	Year
Harry	52781	D	1929	John W.	44917	D	1926	Nicholas	89727	D	1942
Helen	22124	D	1917	John W.	47746	D	1927	P. H.	64908	D	1933
Helen	58535	M	1931	Joseph	42068	D	1925	Patrick	8066	D	1909
Helen Josephine	30035	D	1920	Julia	2651	D	1907	Patrick	16535	D	1913
Helena	38849	D	1924	Julia	22269	D	1917	Patrick	72472	D	1936
Henry	52781	D	1929	Julia Berggren	80960	D	1939	Patrick	40688	D	1925
Honora Patricia Bernice	42295	M	1925	Julia Christina	80960	D	1939	Patrick F.	66053	D	1934
Honoria	69201	D	1935	Justin	18265	D	1914	Peter	1570	D	1906
J. Roger	55424	D	1930	Justin J.	78680	D	1938	Peter	73517	D	1936
James	1900	D	1906	Justin V.	27050	M	1919	Richard Aloysius	85432	D	1940
James	2253	M	1906	Kate	4880	D	1907	Robert	29479	I	1920
James	32043	D	1921	Kate	13033	D	1912	Robert B.	85009	M	1940
James	62116	D	1932	Katerine	2253	M	1906	Roger	55424	D	1930
James B.	18185	D	1914	Katherine	36724	D	1923	Sarah C.	73714	D	1936
James F.	86773	D	1941	Katherine	88710	D	1941	Sophia	68470	D	1934
James F.	87294	D	1941	Loretta V.	3379	M	1907	Susan H.	27437	D	1919
James J.	57848	I	1931	Mabel	4233	M	1907	Sylvester	58624	M	1931
James J.	69390	D	1935	Margaret	2479	D	1906	Thomas	3263	M	1907
James J.	74490	D	1937	Margaret	17665	D	1914	Thomas	4906	D	1907
James P.	45854	D	1926	Margaret	42184	D	1925	Thomas	47502	D	1927
James T.	25246	D	1918	Margaret	47333	D	1927	Thomas	68016	D	1934
Jane M.	87445	D	1941	Margaret E.	20083	D	1915	Thomas H.	27037	I	1919
Jeanette	53420	M	1929	Margret E.	3218	I	1907	Thomas H.	56206	D	1930
Jeremiah	3263	M	1907	Marie B.	70330	I	1935	Thomas M. J.	10292	D	1910
Jeremiah	9758	D	1910	Mary	2730	D	1907	Timothy	7762	D	1909
Jeremiah	22316	D	1917	Mary	17665	D	1914	Timothy	12088	D	1911
Jeremiah	40834	D	1925	Mary	30894	D	1920	Timothy D.	48997	D	1928
Jeremiah D.	68229	D	1934	Mary	43979	D	1926	Timothy F.	25358	D	1918
Jermiah	44872	D	1926	Mary	56971	D	1930	Timothy V.	74443	D	1937
Joanna	5566	D	1908	Mary	34556	D	1922	Vivian	4233	M	1907
Joanna T.	2361	D	1906	Mary Agnes	65814	D	1933	Walter	4233	M	1907
John	1317	D	1906	Mary Ann	2943	D	1907	William D.	87113	D	1941
John	15110	D	1913	Mary D.	87796	D	1941	William G.	69383	D	1935
John	15376	D	1913	Mary E.	44109	D	1926	William George	27283	M	1919
John	20033	D	1915	Mary E.	78746	D	1938	William J.	30670	D	1920
John	32002	D	1921	Mary Ellen	47782	D	1927	William Simpson	38515	D	1924
John	65647	D	1933	Mary Theresa	51701	D	1928	**McCartney**			
John Dennis	48872	M	1928	Michael	18205	D	1914	Catherine	17579	D	1914
John Eugene	74522	D	1937	Michael	28179	D	1919	Ellen	83235	D	1940
John F.	48383	D	1927	Michael	45629	D	1926	Leonora S.	19114	D	1915
John F.	81250	D	1939	Michael	76389	I	1937	Samuel	6299	D	1908
John J.	42295	M	1925	Michael	81375	D	1939	**McCarton**			
John J.	57613	D	1931	Michael	58977	D	1931	John	45743	D	1926
John J.	58038	I	1931	Michael P.	82427	D	1939	**McCarty**			
John J.	62110	D	1932	Minnie	39028	I	1924	A. D., Mrs.	73418	D	1936
John J.	82089	D	1939	Minnie	56971	D	1930	Alexander Donald	82307	D	1939
John J.	86587	D	1941	Nancy	6129	I	1908	Andrew C.	24716	D	1918
John P.	37485	D	1923	Nellie	4303	D	1907	Andrew J.	77563	D	1938
John Richard	68237	D	1934	Nellie	38951	D	1924				

Key: D = death; M = minor; I = incompetent

NAME	NUMBER	TYPE	YEAR
Ann Lipscombe	48243	D	1927
Annie M. E.	66389	D	1934
Bridget	12752	D	1911
Carmelita G.	12439	M	1911
Edward J.	64264	D	1933
Francis Joseph	1689	D	1906
George T.	25631	D	1918
George Thomas	25422	D	1918
Gertrude	19811	D	1915
Helen Walker	73418	D	1936
James	28939	D	1920
James J.	51745	D	1929
Jennie Flack	77229	D	1937
John	57130	I	1930
John	59681	D	1931
John W.	22348	I	1917
John W.	22855	D	1917
Louis Philippe	5771	D	1908
Lucile Ruth	29223	D	1920
Lucille	25433	M	1918
Luke	2274	D	1906
Mary	80721	D	1939
Matthew W.	68892	D	1935
Nellie	4593	D	1907
Thomas	4956	D	1907
Thomas L.	37666	D	1923
William E.	5504	D	1908

McCaskey

NAME	NUMBER	TYPE	YEAR
Benjamin Franklin	73605	D	1936

McCaslin

NAME	NUMBER	TYPE	YEAR
Andrew	6308	D	1908
Charlotte A.	6251	D	1908
Gertrude	70985	D	1935

McCaughey

NAME	NUMBER	TYPE	YEAR
Catherine	89572	I	1942
James	54657	D	1930
Mabelle Augusta	61881	D	1932

McCaul

NAME	NUMBER	TYPE	YEAR
Ellen Jane	39199	D	1924

McCauley

NAME	NUMBER	TYPE	YEAR
Albert Arthur	46701	D	1927
Barbara Ellen	48990	M	1928
Daisy M.	87308	D	1941
Dale Lang	49484	M	1928
Edward Joseph	65669	D	1933
Henry	10066	D	1910
Hugh	81488	D	1939
James	19190	I	1915

NAME	NUMBER	TYPE	YEAR
James Stewart	85186	D	1940
Jane	17075	D	1914
Jean Ann	48990	M	1928
John	13014	D	1912
John E.	51623	D	1928
Laura	39702	D	1924
Mary	4732	D	1907
Mary A.	47151	D	1927
Samuel P.	89859	D	1942
William	26261	D	1919

McCaull

NAME	NUMBER	TYPE	YEAR
Ida	70283	I	1935
Ida	71147	D	1935

McCaullie

NAME	NUMBER	TYPE	YEAR
Ethel L.	33938	D	1922

McCausland

NAME	NUMBER	TYPE	YEAR
Edward	52469	D	1929

McCaw

NAME	NUMBER	TYPE	YEAR
Susanna H.	87027	D	1941
William N.	24614	I	1918
William N.	74127	D	1936

McCay

NAME	NUMBER	TYPE	YEAR
Sarah Webber	74024	D	1936

McCherry

NAME	NUMBER	TYPE	YEAR
Barney	43383	D	1926

McChesney

NAME	NUMBER	TYPE	YEAR
Agnes	38483	D	1924
Alexander	46109	D	1926
Horace B.	67162	I	1934
Sarah Jewett	44770	D	1926

McClain

NAME	NUMBER	TYPE	YEAR
Charles	32673	D	1921
James D.	3194	I	1907
Margaret	65530	D	1933
Mary E.	62017	D	1932
Sarah	35320	D	1922
William Thomas	78943	D	1938

McClair

NAME	NUMBER	TYPE	YEAR
Edward Dean	70777	D	1935

McClaire

NAME	NUMBER	TYPE	YEAR
James H.	65081	D	1933

McClanahan

NAME	NUMBER	TYPE	YEAR
Mary O.	52108	D	1929

McClaskey

NAME	NUMBER	TYPE	YEAR
Kate	63245	D	1932

McClatchy

NAME	NUMBER	TYPE	YEAR
Adaline H.	79904	D	1938

NAME	NUMBER	TYPE	YEAR
Charlotte M.	21830	D	1916
Mary Agnes	52670	M	1929
Valentine Stuart	78621	D	1938

McClean

NAME	NUMBER	TYPE	YEAR
Harold	29085	M	1920
Robert Hugh	29085	M	1920

McCleary

NAME	NUMBER	TYPE	YEAR
Elizabeth	73090	D	1936
Elizabeth	82593	D	1939

McCleery

NAME	NUMBER	TYPE	YEAR
J. L.	20778	D	1916

McClellan

NAME	NUMBER	TYPE	YEAR
George B.	26329	D	1919
James L.	61826	I	1932
James L.	69651	D	1935
Jessie Lee	77665	M	1938
John	33099	D	1921
John	35038	D	1922
Mary Elizabeth	59311	D	1931
Mary Jane	83952	D	1940
Nellie R.	71307	D	1935
William Patrick	54287	D	1929
William S.	9116	D	1910
William Walton	86775	D	1941

McClelland

NAME	NUMBER	TYPE	YEAR
Henry R.	37919	I	1923
Marie	36308	I	1923
Mary Martha	35502	D	1922
William George	47094	D	1927

McClements

NAME	NUMBER	TYPE	YEAR
John	73227	D	1936

McClenahan

NAME	NUMBER	TYPE	YEAR
Walter	45385	D	1926

McCleod

NAME	NUMBER	TYPE	YEAR
Ruth	75798	I	1937

McClintock

NAME	NUMBER	TYPE	YEAR
Bertha	37927	D	1923
Caroline	42608	D	1925
Eugenie I.	70418	I	1935
Everett M.	83167	D	1940
Harry Holliday	84241	D	1940
John	79625	D	1938

McClory

NAME	NUMBER	TYPE	YEAR
Alice	4433	M	1907
John Francis	4433	M	1907
Rose	4433	M	1907

NAME	NUMBER	TYPE	YEAR	NAME	NUMBER	TYPE	YEAR	NAME	NUMBER	TYPE	YEAR
McCLOSKEY				**McCLUSKEY**				**McCONCHIE**			
Catherine	21273	D	1916	Annie Louise	84284	D	1940	Mary Curtin	56970	D	1930
Ella V.	13361	D	1912	Elizabeth	2514	D	1906	**McCONE**			
Ellen W.	55206	D	1930	Francis J.	9177	M	1910	Alicia	24612	D	1918
James B.	17457	D	1914	**McCLYMANT**				Ellen M.	67511	D	1934
James M.	34973	D	1922	John M.	70562	D	1935	**McCONIGLE**			
James Renwick	4316	D	1907	**McCOLGAN**				Margaret	6705	D	1908
John	7983	D	1909	Daniel A.	31875	D	1921	William	18620	I	1915
Joseph J.	31424	D	1921	Dorothy	70740	M	1935	**McCONIHE**			
Lizzie	3104	D	1907	Edgar J.	62328	D	1932	Mary	17488	D	1914
Margaret	47228	D	1927	George W.	46175	D	1927	**McCONKEY**			
Mary E.	62034	D	1932	James	51015	D	1928	Thomas G.	12740	I	1911
Michael	12132	D	1911	Margaret J.	26940	D	1919	Thomas G.	13146	D	1912
Rosina A.	19094	D	1915	Patrick	28435	D	1919	**McCONNELL**			
Thomas L.	14685	D	1913	**McCOLGIN**				Andres	3848	D	1907
McCLOSKY				Abbie W.	42047	D	1925	Edward Giles	42917	D	1925
Margaret	83846	D	1940	**McCOLLAM**				James Alexander	30640	D	1920
Rosina	18363	I	1915	Christy A.	68601	D	1934	John	6017	I	1908
McCLOUD				Sarah	62151	I	1932	Reason Ellis	36273	D	1923
Alexander	6514	D	1908	**McCOLLISTER**				**McCONNON**			
Annie	23950	D	1918	Mary Eloise	26872	D	1919	Michael J.	41885	D	1925
Elizabeth Leger	53439	D	1929	William Morse	60279	I	1931	Michael J.	41885	D	1925
James L.	27254	D	1919	**McCOLLOUGH**				**McCONOCHIE**			
John G.	49514	D	1928	Mabelle Margaret	69991	D	1935	Bessie	31124	D	1921
Smith M.	44757	D	1926	**McCOLLUM**				**McCONOLOGUE**			
McCLUER				Bridget	35347	D	1922	James	41277	D	1925
Frank	17381	D	1914	Charles	8764	D	1909	Mary E.	38642	D	1924
McCLURE				James A.	35348	D	1922	William Edward	82564	D	1939
Agnes Herold	79848	D	1938	**McCOMB**				**McCONSTILLE**			
Charles W.	84569	D	1940	Edmund	51383	D	1928	Bridget	89172	I	1942
Cora Lambert	49624	D	1928	Josephine S.	61633	D	1932	**McCONVILLE**			
Denny Hanks	83356	D	1940	Zillah Fox	69052	D	1935	John Thomas	28041	D	1919
Earl J.	30839	D	1920	**McCOMBE**				**McCOOEY**			
Elizabeth E.	42692	D	1925	Alvira G.	19640	D	1915	Margaret	59575	D	1931
Emilia	48940	M	1928	**McCOMBER**				**McCOOK**			
Gabrielle Rose	17412	M	1914	Frank H.	36473	D	1923	Elizabeth Jane	66428	M	1934
George	31941	D	1921	**McCOMMONS**				James	37562	D	1923
Hannah	38776	D	1924	Willis A.	39076	D	1924	James J.	65562	D	1933
Lusina	21137	D	1916	**McCONACHIE**				**McCOOL**			
Michael	64776	D	1933	Alexander	37328	D	1923	Elmer F.	71646	D	1936
Patricia	48940	M	1928	**McCONAGHY**				Harriet Adeline	44866	D	1926
Peter	51518	M	1928	Samuel J.	23994	D	1918	James	39287	I	1924
Peter L.	68485	I	1934	Silas	81784	D	1939	James	42265	D	1925
Peter L.	79050	D	1938	**McCONALOGUE**				**McCORD**			
Peter L., Mrs.	21137	D	1916	John	48585	D	1927	George	31392	D	1921
Richard	48940	M	1928	William Vincent	73752	D	1936	Jennie	11773	D	1911
Thomas	51518	M	1928								
William S.	72083	D	1936								

NAME	NUMBER	TYPE	YEAR	NAME	NUMBER	TYPE	YEAR	NAME	NUMBER	TYPE	YEAR
Martha R.	59443	D	1931	James E.	66516	D	1934	**McCorrison**			
Virginia	11773	D	1911	James H.	72385	D	1936	Mary F.	20275	D	1916
William	29999	D	1920	Jennie E.	38380	D	1924	**McCosker**			
McCorkell				John	3020	D	1907	David M.	1691	D	1906
Catherine	17061	D	1914	John	3517	D	1907	**McCottrey**			
McCormack				John	31231	D	1921	Mary	57827	D	1931
Alex D.	46037	D	1926	John	50909	D	1928	Teresa H.	80249	D	1939
Edward J.	33824	M	1922	John	60426	D	1931	**McCourt**			
Emma N.	19844	D	1915	John	69257	D	1935	Alice	2388	D	1906
Helen A.	22806	D	1917	John A.	2403	D	1906	Peter	44080	D	1926
Isadore Blake	15981	D	1913	John J.	65519	I	1933	Roseanna	33040	D	1921
James J.	34694	D	1922	John S.	65185	D	1933	**McCourtney**			
Richard Francis	78062	M	1938	John T.	33560	D	1922	Charles Hamilton	41341	D	1925
Robert H.	35144	D	1922	John T.	45858	D	1926	Jane T.	77690	D	1938
Sarah	66743	D	1934	Joseph B.	12349	M	1911	**McCowen**			
William	7552	D	1909	Kate	12275	D	1911	James P.	76684	D	1937
McCormick				Leonora	6152	D	1908	**McCoy**			
Agnes	6608	D	1908	Margaret	13432	D	1912	Alexander	27506	D	1919
Albert F.	87600	I	1941	Margaret J.	21577	D	1916	Charles L.	31540	D	1921
Albert F.	87724	D	1941	Marguerite R.	87129	D	1941	Daniel	11329	D	1911
Annie	54452	D	1929	Maria	10398	D	1910	David James	72513	D	1936
Benjamin	87062	D	1941	Marshall U.	80435	D	1939	Frank	24589	M	1918
Catherine H.	68958	D	1935	Mary	15663	D	1913	Frank Edwin	79652	I	1938
Catherine J.	80853	D	1939	Mary	20274	D	1916	Jane Berkeley	42617	D	1925
Cecelia	9	D	1906	Mary	36243	D	1923	Johanna	66466	D	1934
Charles	43866	D	1926	Mary A.	32812	D	1921	Kate C.	72290	D	1936
Charles A.	27388	D	1919	Mary Ann	27225	D	1919	Margaret	87029	D	1941
Charles E.	27388	D	1919	Minnie	78308	I	1938	Matthew	20976	D	1916
Claire Ardys	23955	I	1918	Nicholas C.	58196	D	1931	Michael	48279	D	1927
Edith E.	7990	D	1909	Patrick	12147	D	1911	Morris	36241	M	1923
Edward J.	9466	D	1910	Peter J.	65980	D	1933	Sarah Webber	74023	D	1936
Ellen E.	35686	D	1923	Ruth	12456	M	1911	Stacia Alice	40297	M	1924
Ernest O.	38104	D	1924	Ruth	75798	I	1937	Stacia C.	72184	D	1936
Eugene	15876	I	1913	Sarah J.	25350	D	1918	Thomas	7927	D	1909
Eugene J.	17001	D	1914	Thomas	26298	D	1919	Wade	36241	M	1923
Florence C.	87552	D	1941	Thomas E.	65207	M	1933	Wade H.	50399	D	1928
Frances Jennings	53499	D	1929	Virginia	38380	D	1924	**McCracken**			
Francis J.	59674	D	1931	W. S.	1041	D	1906	Adele Margurite	43441	D	1926
Frank L.	83446	D	1940	William	1942	D	1906	Allwyn	51448	M	1928
George	38712	D	1924	William B.	76558	D	1937	Alroyn	51448	M	1928
George	38716	D	1924	William H.	56556	D	1930	Arthur	5633	D	1908
George F.	64602	D	1933	William Henry	17273	D	1914	Ellen F.	12835	D	1912
George J.	21231	D	1916	William W.	83912	D	1940	Etta	31008	D	1921
Gerald	12456	M	1911	**McCormik**				John H.	8532	D	1909
Horatio A.	43370	D	1926	Genevieve F.	4398	M	1907	Margaret I.	18742	D	1915
Isabel M.	32327	D	1921	**McCornock**				Mary E.	29399	D	1920
Isabel Tucker	32327	D	1921	Laura B.	87326	D	1941	Sarah E.	70406	D	1935
James	24446	D	1918								

NAME	NUMBER	TYPE	YEAR
MCCRAE			
Robert	43658	D	1926
MCCRARY			
Daisy L.	35314	D	1922
MCCRAY			
Oscar	64018	D	1933
MCCREA			
Agnes Irene	83106	D	1940
George	40231	D	1924
John	63050	D	1932
Mary E.	82441	D	1939
MCCREADIE			
Janis	40138	M	1924
MCCREADY			
Charlotte Ann	3260	D	1907
Daniel J.	24700	D	1918
Georgina E.	79575	D	1938
MCCREAGH			
Mary	63579	I	1933
Mary	64088	D	1933
MCCREARY			
Charles	59463	I	1931
Marie	36308	I	1923
MCCREEDY			
Sarah J.	62410	D	1932
MCCREERY			
Agnes E.	61820	D	1932
Andrew	41949	M	1925
Andrew	41949	M	1925
Andrew B.	15221	D	1913
Isabelle	27318	D	1919
John Buchanan	58712	D	1931
Lawrence	21065	D	1916
Walter Adolph	13946	I	1912
Walter E.	40210	D	1924
William J.	41949	M	1925
William J.	41949	M	1925
MCCRICKARD			
James P.	85541	D	1940
MCCRINDLE			
William	28044	D	1919
MCCRINK			
Hugh	32794	D	1921
MCCRONE			
Day S.	85615	D	1940
Josephine	51644	D	1928

NAME	NUMBER	TYPE	YEAR
MCCROSKEY			
Anna E.	76918	D	1937
Orrell E.	86087	D	1941
MCCRUM			
Helen M.	44091	D	1926
MCCRYSTLE			
Margaret L.	86707	D	1941
Mary Ann	27565	D	1919
MCCUARY			
Hazel	79229	I	1938
MCCUBREY			
Lowell B.	23388	D	1917
MCCUE			
James	27345	D	1919
James J.	11856	D	1911
John B.	48816	D	1927
Raymond	60113	I	1931
Thomas	15078	D	1913
MCCULLAH			
Nora	38287	D	1924
MCCULLOCH			
Allan	39985	D	1924
David	33857	D	1922
John C.	89327	D	1942
Mary	35784	D	1923
May Jean	56904	D	1930
Samuel	29463	D	1920
MCCULLOUGH			
Alfred Robert	44484	D	1926
Alice	21230	D	1916
Arthur R.	39241	M	1924
Catherine A.	46722	D	1927
Clara Eleanora	89245	D	1942
Dorothy	25360	M	1918
Eleonore	47459	D	1927
Elizabeth	87409	D	1941
Frances	25434	D	1918
Irene Margaret	49927	D	1928
Jack	39241	M	1924
Jack Arlington	47547	M	1927
James	89818	D	1942
John G.	20850	D	1916
John P.	56427	D	1930
Katherine M.	39240	D	1924
Margaret	23739	D	1917
Martha	31232	D	1921
Michael	7183	D	1909

NAME	NUMBER	TYPE	YEAR
Oscar V.	50634	D	1928
Peter Patrick	81110	D	1939
Thomas	76266	D	1937
Thomas Joseph	41550	D	1925
MCCULLUM			
Bridget	35347	D	1922
James A.	35348	D	1922
MCCULLY			
Anastasia	4387	D	1907
MCCUMMINGS			
Isaac	41404	D	1925
MCCUNE			
Alexander C.	17805	D	1914
Roy Henry	34411	D	1922
MCCUNN			
John	11092	D	1911
MCCURDY			
Edward A.	6645	D	1908
Emilie Gordon	89766	D	1942
Gladys	1128	M	1906
Gladys M.	9973	D	1910
Sarah A.	87807	D	1941
MCCURRY			
James	8280	D	1909
James M.	1856	I	1906
MCCUSKER			
Anne M.	80696	D	1939
Joseph	21612	D	1916
Owen	75137	D	1937
Thomas	12426	D	1911
MCCUTCHAN			
Nettie R. L.	66004	D	1934
Nettie Waverly	66004	D	1934
Waverly Nettie	66004	D	1934
MCCUTCHEN			
Carl Clifford	68632	M	1934
Mary Elizabeth	7420	D	1909
MCCUTCHEON			
Sadie J.	42637	D	1925
William Henry	47897	D	1927
MCDADE			
John J.	76910	I	1937
John J.	77020	D	1937
Margaret	85251	D	1940
MCDANIEL			
Albert	43135	D	1925
C. Edna	34173	D	1922

NAME	NUMBER	TYPE	YEAR	NAME	NUMBER	TYPE	YEAR	NAME	NUMBER	TYPE	YEAR
Douglas	5570	D	1908	Thomas	60715	D	1932	Angus J.	84920	I	1940
Genevieve Edna	36771	M	1923	Thomas Joseph	45759	D	1926	Anne Marie	85167	M	1940
Willard	44560	D	1926	Thomas Joseph	73662	D	1936	Annie	25314	D	1918
William Henry	36771	M	1923	Thomas Robert	62651	M	1932	Annie	40110	D	1924
William Henry	36898	D	1923	Thos.	42987	D	1925	Annie	39232	D	1924
McDaniels				Wilkes	31113	D	1921	Annie E.	40949	D	1925
Douglas	5570	D	1908	William	19562	M	1915	Annie Elizabeth	59466	D	1931
John H.	70344	D	1935	Winnie (nee Meehan)	14022	D	1912	Archie	68901	D	1935
McDearmon				**McDevitt**				Bernard	61332	D	1932
Chesley	48353	D	1927	Alfred Mayo	8341	D	1909	Bernard F.	11719	I	1911
McDermid				Andrew	21358	D	1916	Bernard F.	16389	D	1913
Hamsie W.	61726	D	1932	Bernard	33773	I	1922	Bridget	52352	I	1929
Hansie W.	61726	D	1932	Catherine	4864	D	1907	Bridget	52959	D	1929
McDermitt				Charles	25599	D	1918	Carrie Frances	33132	D	1922
W.	31113	D	1921	Frances	52463	D	1929	Catherine	22125	D	1917
McDermott				James A.	76406	D	1937	Charles E.	63919	I	1933
Alice	71881	D	1936	James E.	48105	D	1927	Charles Henry	64716	D	1933
Annie H.	86076	D	1941	Joseph F.	83916	D	1940	Charles Malcolm	75905	D	1937
Bridget	21745	D	1916	Joseph Francis	48902	D	1928	Charles Robert	63809	M	1933
Bridget	75820	D	1937	Joseph Francis	83909	M	1940	Christina	2466	M	1906
Celia E.	70389	D	1935	Joseph T.	74834	D	1937	Clara Barbara	88043	D	1941
Delia	15097	I	1913	Mary	64369	I	1933	Delia	29426	D	1920
Delia	18982	D	1915	Mary F.	30542	D	1920	Donald	30784	D	1920
Elizabeth	17382	D	1914	Nellie	58884	D	1931	Duncan D.	55618	D	1930
Frank J.	46742	D	1927	Rubena L.	45293	D	1926	Edward	16152	D	1913
Grace	16876	I	1914	Ruth	83909	M	1940	Edward James	51586	D	1928
James	144	D	1906	Vincent P.	48103	D	1927	Elizabeth	2466	M	1906
James	48727	D	1927	William M.	16997	D	1914	Elizabeth	12378	D	1911
James W.	3691	D	1907	**McDivitt**				Ellen M.	50022	D	1928
John	54411	D	1929	Jesse M.	57763	D	1931	Emilie Marie Christine	16310	D	1913
John H.	64160	D	1933	Louise	61632	D	1932	Emma	19482	D	1915
John W.	16742	D	1914	**McDonagh**				Ernest	87207	D	1941
John W.	47251	D	1927	Lawrence	9762	D	1910	Florence	10380	M	1910
John W.	61296	D	1932	**McDonald**				Frank	5917	M	1908
Katie A.	69766	D	1935	Ada	39948	D	1924	Frank V.	2159	D	1906
Leila France	85649	D	1940	Agnes Elizabeth	23299	D	1917	Frederick	2466	M	1906
Malvine O. H., Mrs.	71881	D	1936	Albert R.	4010	D	1907	George	49466	D	1928
Martin	771	D	1906	Alexander	596	D	1906	George	49621	D	1928
Martin	33421	D	1922	Alexander	12484	D	1911	George C.	28519	D	1919
Mary	52512	D	1929	Alexander	28666	D	1920	George H.	79014	D	1938
Mary A.	82262	D	1939	Alexander	76141	D	1937	Gertrude	15557	D	1913
Mary Logan	61037	D	1932	Alexander D.	66495	D	1934	Gertrude	62081	I	1932
Michael	44701	D	1926	Alice	28408	D	1919	Hannah	20923	D	1916
Michael J.	80017	D	1938	Alice Booth	61683	D	1932	Harriet Bamford	80473	D	1939
Patrick	1089	D	1906	America Moore	81718	D	1939	Henry	40629	I	1924
Ralph	85550	D	1940	Andrew	20457	D	1916	Hugh	2466	M	1906
Sarah	1025	D	1906	Aneas	87207	D	1941	Hugh	19162	D	1915
Thomas	9827	D	1910	Angus F.	18027	D	1914	James	31399	D	1921
								James	65114	D	1933

NAME	NUMBER	TYPE	YEAR	NAME	NUMBER	TYPE	YEAR	NAME	NUMBER	TYPE	YEAR
James F.	40268	D	1924	Mary Jane	79550	D	1938	Mary M.	12297	D	1911
James M.	3875	D	1907	Mary Margaret	25269	D	1918	May Agnes	16805	D	1914
Jasper	16291	D	1913	May T.	59426	D	1931	Mollie T.	58492	D	1931
Jennie	59314	D	1931	Merle Viola	58344	D	1931	Nora	56113	I	1930
Joanna	7247	D	1909	Michael	6111	D	1908	P. H.	21356	D	1916
John	53373	D	1929	Michael	10559	D	1910	Patrick	4278	D	1907
John	70674	D	1935	Nora	65716	D	1933	Raymond F.	7272	M	1909
John	46682	D	1927	Nora A.	42022	D	1925	Thomas A.	7272	M	1909
John A.	88175	D	1941	Patrick	2476	D	1906	Thomas F.	7271	D	1909
John B.	16501	D	1913	Patrick	55851	D	1930	Thomas Henry	37198	D	1923
John D.	27572	M	1919	Patrick A.	35518	D	1922	William H.	56361	D	1930
John Francis	57224	D	1930	Peter A.	68725	D	1935	William P.	7272	M	1909
John J.	36407	D	1923	R. H., Jr.	16102	D	1913	**McDonogh**			
John T.	47359	I	1927	Robert	2466	M	1906	Festus	9479	D	1910
John W.	23724	D	1917	Roderick	3426	D	1907	Lawrence	9762	D	1910
Jonathan Titus	67358	D	1934	Thomas F.	80353	D	1939	**McDonough**			
Joseph A.	33494	D	1922	Viva Elizabeth	30751	D	1920	Bridget	9076	D	1910
Joseph F.	20165	D	1915	Wilhelmina O.	35985	D	1923	Bridget M.	15348	D	1913
Joseph H.	66823	D	1934	William	26013	D	1918	Celia	22404	D	1917
Josephine Marie	37171	M	1923	William	30497	D	1920	Christopher	39319	D	1924
Julia	84777	D	1940	William Claude	85951	D	1941	Edna M.	85914	D	1940
Kate	38590	D	1924	William F.	13083	D	1912	Elisabeth Priddy	69882	M	1935
Katherine	31686	D	1921	William J.	43196	D	1925	Festus	9167	D	1910
Katherine	86624	D	1941	William Ronald	52826	D	1929	Gloria	67337	M	1934
Kenneth	85713	D	1940	**McDonnell**				Hugh	58369	D	1931
Lawrence J.	9786	D	1910	Agnes	24393	D	1918	J. N.	18304	D	1914
Lisette	464	D	1906	Alexander	425	D	1906	John	11222	D	1911
Magdalena	48332	D	1927	Alexander	4454	I	1907	John	56870	D	1930
Mamie	14555	D	1912	Bridget	23684	I	1917	Martin	41506	D	1925
Marcella Ruth	29075	M	1920	Bridget	33317	D	1922	Mary	873	D	1906
Margaret	9238	D	1910	Catherine	16657	D	1914	Mary	43875	D	1926
Margaret	13686	D	1912	Catherine	22125	D	1917	Patrick	15547	I	1913
Margaret	41861	D	1925	Charles J.	54463	D	1929	Patrick	20675	D	1916
Margaret	41861	D	1925	Edward G.	34533	D	1922	Patrick	29313	D	1920
Margaret	47089	D	1927	Ellen	46373	D	1927	Thomas	31430	D	1921
Marion Jasper	16291	D	1913	James	34532	D	1922	William Clinton	7962	M	1909
Mary	8907	M	1909	James	48720	D	1927	William E.	78515	D	1938
Mary	43290	D	1925	John	22385	D	1917	**McDonovan**			
Mary Agnes	14785	I	1913	John	72939	D	1936	Mary	67810	D	1934
Mary Agnes	19330	D	1915	John F.	19292	D	1915	**McDougal**			
Mary Ann	165	D	1906	John J.	65351	D	1933	Alice Hynes	55636	D	1930
Mary Ann	38806	D	1924	Josephine Ailene	14956	M	1913	**McDougald**			
Mary D.	83585	D	1940	Julia	22142	I	1917	Donald A.	44949	D	1926
Mary E.	69775	D	1935	Lawrence	3070	D	1907	**McDougall**			
Mary E.	83892	D	1940	Lawrence	52349	D	1929	Alice	80443	D	1939
Mary Ellen	76562	D	1937	Mary	920	D	1906	B. D., Mrs.	80443	D	1939
Mary Ellida	87990	D	1941	Mary A.	77215	D	1937	Duncan	39524	D	1924
Mary J. L.	70413	D	1935	Mary Agnes	73782	M	1936	Hugh R.	54595	D	1929
Mary Jane	44199	I	1926	Mary C.	26672	D	1919				

NAME	NUMBER	TYPE	YEAR
Jane Morrow	83837	D	1940
John Wallace	23678	D	1917
Linda	32270	D	1921
Lottie	66977	D	1934
Louisa	66430	D	1934
Mary Alice	80443	D	1939
Samuel A.	82140	D	1939
McDougold			
John E.	54750	D	1930
McDowall			
John R.	71418	D	1936
Marcus	2923	D	1907
McDowell			
Alexander	89642	D	1942
Alice	2388	D	1906
Arthur Roscoe	78569	D	1938
Edgar	27442	D	1919
Elizabeth	38959	D	1924
Floyd Lyle	51743	D	1929
Frederick L.	54222	D	1929
George S., Jr.	31462	M	1921
Leonora	55197	M	1930
Lizzie	55197	M	1930
Margaret	55197	M	1930
Martin	81432	D	1939
Mary R.	58328	D	1931
Susan I.	61164	D	1932
William John	39542	M	1924
McDyer			
Charles	17373	D	1914
McEachern			
Adelaide C.	29814	D	1920
Daniel	68184	D	1934
Donald A.	68184	D	1934
McEachran			
Eliza A.	12763	D	1911
McEldowney			
James	33845	D	1922
John	46694	D	1927
Mary	36810	D	1923
McEleaney			
John A.	24537	D	1918
McElhaney			
Homer C.	57267	D	1930
McElherron			
Elizabeth Eyler	26367	M	1919

NAME	NUMBER	TYPE	YEAR
McElligott			
Sarah Jane	50111	D	1928
Thomas	62744	D	1932
McEllin			
Dennis	14961	D	1913
McElroy			
Ann Jane	1403	D	1906
Bernard Francis	65704	D	1933
Catherine	48929	D	1928
Elizabeth Mary	48929	D	1928
Ellen M.	40969	D	1925
Ellen Maria	17547	I	1914
Fred	63296	I	1933
Harry L.	57529	D	1930
Hugh	11611	D	1911
James R.	84055	D	1940
John	3372	D	1907
John Joseph	63423	D	1933
John O.	22860	D	1917
Louise	23809	D	1917
Mary	10975	D	1910
Mary	31031	I	1921
Mary	34324	D	1922
Owen J.	62299	D	1932
Peter James	48930	D	1928
Robert	8802	D	1909
Robert J.	3719	D	1907
Thomas F.	26610	D	1919
vivian I.	50639	M	1928
William J.	86426	D	1941
McElvaine			
Ray	41634	D	1925
McElwain			
George B.	18673	M	1915
Patrick	77611	D	1938
Sarah	84549	D	1940
Sarah	38300	D	1924
McElwee			
Mary Abijah	21172	D	1916
McEnerney			
C. L.	45032	I	1926
Genevieve	87302	D	1941
John P.	72163	D	1936
Margaret	22460	D	1917
McEnery			
Emily Catherine	89285	D	1942
Henrietta M. McL.	4090	D	1907

NAME	NUMBER	TYPE	YEAR
McEnhill			
John	12797	D	1912
McEnroe			
Philip	1467	D	1906
Thomas F.	30344	D	1920
McEntee			
James Boyland	18994	D	1915
James J.	73507	D	1936
Joseph F.	41795	D	1925
Joseph F.	41795	D	1925
Margarita Concepcion	51201	D	1928
Mary	57985	D	1931
Terry	30545	D	1920
Walter F.	635	D	1906
McEnteer			
Frank P.	40072	D	1924
McErlane			
Chester H.	44927	D	1926
McErlean			
Michael A.	20185	D	1915
McEvoy			
Elizabeth F.	84414	D	1940
James	85555	D	1940
James F.	36844	D	1923
James J.	4967	I	1908
Margaret	13749	I	1912
Margaret A.	14153	D	1912
Mary E.	3636	D	1907
Michael A.	80925	D	1939
Patrick	44954	D	1926
McEwan			
Margaret	15587	D	1913
McEwen			
Alan	74384	D	1937
Annie G.	54875	D	1930
Arthur Irwin	66349	M	1934
Daniel	37684	D	1923
Elizabeth Michelson	11386	D	1911
Ella D.	28594	D	1920
Evangeline A.	19592	M	1915
Frances D.	19592	M	1915
Frank W.	16508	D	1913
Helen E.	19592	M	1915
James	30150	D	1920
John Antonio	19645	D	1915
Mary Boyd	71792	D	1936
Myrtle Jane	66349	M	1934

NAME	NUMBER	TYPE	YEAR	NAME	NUMBER	TYPE	YEAR	NAME	NUMBER	TYPE	YEAR
Nora A.	53320	D	1929	Robert D.	53799	D	1929	MCGARRICK			
William H.	40167	D	1924	Robert Floyd	53902	M	1929	J.	39708	D	1924
MCFADDEN				Robert L.	63220	D	1932	MCGARRITY			
Charles	29959	D	1920	Sarah	8624	D	1909	Donald Dennie	45998	D	1926
Elizabeth	16084	D	1913	Susie B.	32042	D	1921	Margaret	322	D	1906
Elizabeth	55372	D	1930	Teresa C.	28422	D	1919	MCGARRY			
Emma	35444	D	1922	Thomas F.	22506	D	1917	Dolores Catherine	84377	M	1940
Florence	62939	M	1932	Wallace	76668	I	1937	John	82716	D	1939
Francis John	59926	I	1931	William J.	39658	M	1924	MCGARVEY			
John	80882	D	1939	MCFARLANE				Thomas D.	35268	D	1922
Mary I.	43881	D	1926	Alexander W.	46375	D	1927	MCGARVIN			
Michael	33172	D	1922	Cunningham J.	50135	D	1928	Frank P.	71280	D	1935
Patrick	43090	D	1925	John	69741	D	1935	MCGAUGHEY			
Sarah	47990	D	1927	John Daniel	45234	D	1926	Patrick	58296	D	1931
Tana	41766	D	1925	Joseph I.	70583	I	1935	MCGAULEY			
Tana	41766	D	1925	Josephine M.	78873	D	1938	Eustace F.	31757	D	1921
MCFADYEN				Lorraine Frances	47698	D	1927	Eustace F.	33436	D	1922
Archibald	28432	D	1919	Maggie Matheson	48102	D	1927	MCGAVIN			
MCFALL				Mary	52608	D	1929	Walter J. S.	49499	D	1928
Daniel J.	41613	D	1925	MCFAUL				William	61309	D	1932
MCFARLAN				Elizabeth	46519	D	1927	MCGEARY			
Addie L.	20656	D	1916	Lanson R.	27391	D	1919	Hannah	9547	D	1910
Fredric K.	69812	D	1935	Wilmot P.	48627	D	1927	John	3742	D	1907
Michael	14653	D	1912	MCFEE				Katharine	73672	D	1936
MCFARLAND				Benjamin	5910	D	1908	MCGEE			
Ada	36884	D	1923	Joseph Roger	54624	D	1929	Alfred	7311	M	1909
Adele I.	87455	D	1941	MCFEELY				Catherine	8246	D	1909
Alexander W.	46375	D	1927	Charles	30445	D	1920	Catherine	49417	D	1928
Alvin	67871	D	1934	MCFIE				Charles	7311	M	1909
Andrew G., Jr.	39658	M	1924	Daniel	46635	D	1927	Edward J.	41864	D	1925
C. D.	85523	D	1940	MCGAFFIGAN				Edward J.	41864	D	1925
Emmett Ellsworth	89100	D	1942	Bridget	89833	D	1942	Ethel	38984	M	1924
Frank Guy	72564	D	1936	Patrick	78609	D	1938	Frances E.	30950	D	1921
Harry	76212	I	1937	MCGAHEY				George H.	84482	I	1940
Helen Frances	57040	D	1930	Patrick	86465	D	1941	James	14056	D	1912
Isabella Wallace	51239	D	1928	Robert	40162	D	1924	James	61097	D	1932
James R.	88534	D	1941	MCGAIN				James E.	28636	D	1920
Jennie H.	51926	D	1929	W. M.	47328	D	1927	James M.	16541	M	1913
Lorraine Frances	47698	D	1927	William	47328	D	1927	Jennie A.	70242	D	1935
Mabel	81058	I	1939	MCGANN				Jerome	16541	M	1913
Mabel	84521	I	1940	Frank P.	67059	D	1934	John	35275	D	1922
Maggie	13525	D	1912	James	36460	I	1923	John C.	28142	D	1919
Maggie Matheson	48102	D	1927	James	62509	D	1932	John N.	70984	I	1935
Mary Celia	41122	D	1925	Joseph	36460	I	1923	John N.	74894	D	1937
Michael	14653	D	1912	MCGANNEY				John P.	66949	D	1934
Octavia	3682	D	1907	Daniel C.	75184	D	1937	Lillie	7311	M	1909
Oliver C.	43786	D	1926					Mary	9654	D	1910
Ollie M.	15719	D	1913								

NAME	NUMBER	TYPE	YEAR	NAME	NUMBER	TYPE	YEAR	NAME	NUMBER	TYPE	YEAR
May	7311	M	1909	Ella	37112	D	1923	John H.	39376	D	1924
Ola	64326	D	1933	Ida A.	2354	D	1906	Margaret E.	11195	D	1911
Patrick	58550	D	1931	Jennie	29608	D	1920	Partick J.	37551	D	1923
Peter	50744	D	1928	Lincoln A.	24518	M	1918	**McGinnis**			
Rose	62642	D	1932	Mary Jane	29608	D	1920	Bridget	49695	D	1928
Sarah M.	53102	D	1929	William	64819	D	1933	Edward	84883	D	1940
Thomas	15777	D	1913	**McGillan**				Elinor M.	20733	D	1916
Vivian	22637	M	1917	Aletta B.	79666	D	1938	Genevieve	56342	M	1930
Walter	7311	M	1909	**McGillian**				Jane V.	7522	I	1909
William	7311	M	1909	Rodger	13134	D	1912	Jane V.	22956	D	1917
William H.	70178	D	1935	**McGillicuddy**				Robert John	22071	D	1917
McGeehan				Edward	49756	M	1928	Rosa	60837	D	1932
Charles	78806	D	1938	Eleanor	49756	M	1928	Thomas	36360	D	1923
McGeeney				Eugene	49756	M	1928	William H.	62935	D	1932
Frank A.	85625	D	1940	Hannah	39924	D	1924	William J.	3214	D	1907
McGeever				Jeremiah	41831	D	1925	**McGinnity**			
Michael	79797	D	1938	Jeremiah	41831	D	1925	Margaret	4045	D	1907
McGenity				John	89609	D	1942	**McGinty**			
Edward	39938	D	1924	Nora	88694	D	1941	James P.	34791	D	1922
Mary	72897	D	1936	Owen	1316	D	1906	Jeannette M.	19151	M	1915
McGeoch				**McGillin**				Margaret Mabel	19151	M	1915
John	47446	D	1927	Jennie	665	D	1906	Peter	58394	D	1931
McGeorge				**McGillis**				**McGirr**			
Mary J.	79410	D	1938	Mary Margaret	22148	D	1917	John T.	84859	D	1940
McGeough				**McGillivray**				**McGivern**			
Ellen	2481	D	1906	Donald	38185	D	1924	Edward J.	13739	D	1912
James	16823	D	1914	George	53757	D	1929	John	51966	D	1929
Patrick	56934	D	1930	Harriet	53758	D	1929	John Hugh	72560	D	1936
Rose T.	45924	D	1926	Roderick	29559	D	1920	Teresa	26234	D	1919
Thomas	10503	D	1910	**McGilvery**				**McGivney**			
McGerry				Ann L.	12301	D	1911	James Edward	19413	L	1915
Ellen M.	21753	M	1916	Daniel	72677	D	1936	Margaret	18543	I	1915
William B.	21623	D	1916	Emma May Folsom	76409	D	1937	Margaret	24199	D	1918
McGettigan				Mabel Estelle	11251	M	1911	**McGlade**			
Charles D.	57840	D	1931	Richard	68961	D	1935	Catherine J.	52350	D	1929
Edward T.	84657	D	1940	Thomas	55464	D	1930	John Joseph	88859	D	1942
Noel	10539	M	1910	**McGinley**				**McGlashan**			
McGhee				Jane	21282	D	1916	Earl L.	28424	D	1919
Ann Frances	59440	D	1931	**McGinn**				Henrietta Elizabeth	28456	M	1919
James	61097	D	1932	Ellen	2592	D	1907	Robert Charles	28456	M	1919
John T.	69304	D	1935	Hannah	27511	D	1919	**McGlaughlin**			
McGibbon				Joseph S.	3585	D	1907	Anne	2446	D	1906
Isabella	38226	D	1924	Mary A.	52150	D	1929	**McGlennan**			
McGiffin				**McGinness**				Catherine M.	58711	D	1931
Margaret	32017	D	1921	Bridget	49695	D	1928	**McGlennon**			
McGill				**McGinney**				Agnes Mary	45349	D	1926
Charles A.	39276	D	1924	Frank T.	13194	D	1912	Elizabeth	6758	D	1908

Name	Number	Type	Year	Name	Number	Type	Year	Name	Number	Type	Year
John Leo	11397	M	1911	**McGonigle**				Dolly	76462	D	1937
Richard J.	11397	M	1911	Dennis F.	3354	D	1907	Evelyn A.	58936	D	1931
McGlew				Jennie	82955	I	1939	Frank T.	59640	I	1931
Anastasia	7696	D	1909	**McGorey**				George	47372	M	1927
McGlinchey				Susan	86708	D	1941	Hannah	43076	D	1925
Mary K.	7018	M	1909	**McGorlick**				Helen Marie	18885	M	1915
McGlinn				James	35537	D	1922	Horace M.	79383	D	1938
John	10810	D	1910	**McGough**				James	82704	D	1939
McGlone				Patrick	73502	D	1936	John	5757	D	1908
John William	65516	D	1933	Thomas	29192	I	1920	John F.	70995	D	1935
Mary C.	88788	D	1941	Vernon	32989	D	1921	John J.	16258	D	1913
McGlynn				**McGourty**				Leslie R.	61793	D	1932
Addie Estelle	51804	D	1929	Francis	41706	D	1925	Margaret	18477	D	1915
Anna	57568	D	1931	**McGovern**				Margaret H.	24300	I	1918
Chester	51578	D	1928	Annie F.	41620	M	1925	Mary	8272	D	1909
Francis J.	34169	D	1922	Barbara Elizabeth	78063	M	1938	Mary	26204	D	1919
Frank	65859	D	1933	C. J.	45628	D	1926	Mary	26647	D	1919
Harold	12042	M	1911	Christine Margaret	41620	M	1925	Mary A.	12613	D	1911
Harold	33849	D	1922	Elizabeth	12818	D	1912	Mary E.	43453	D	1926
John	13371	M	1912	Ellen	20401	D	1916	Mary F.	66670	D	1934
John F.	33231	D	1922	Ellen Mary	49028	D	1928	Mary, Jr.	47371	M	1927
Leslie	12042	M	1911	Emma F.	15875	D	1913	Mathew	6643	D	1908
Margaret	13371	M	1912	Francis P.	48495	D	1927	Matthew Bernard, Jr.	39176	M	1924
Margaret	67499	D	1934	Frank	21124	D	1916	Peter	10537	D	1910
Mary E.	43421	D	1926	Genevieve R.	41829	D	1925	Peter	15425	D	1913
Patrick J.	35748	D	1923	Genevieve R.	41829	D	1925	Philip E.	49127	D	1928
Thomas	14082	I	1912	George P.	77772	D	1938	Rachel Cleveland	39175	D	1924
Uceba M.	80856	D	1939	Honora	26014	I	1918	Richard C.	51405	D	1928
McGogy				Isabella	78647	D	1938	Robert Cleveland	68588	D	1934
James Frank	84738	D	1940	James	86610	D	1941	Sybil Alice	18885	M	1915
McGoldrich				James E.	32031	D	1921	Thaddeus H.	35717	D	1923
Suaan	58005	D	1931	John	62924	D	1932	Thomas	20749	D	1916
McGoldrick				John	86761	D	1941	Thomas A.	26444	D	1919
Anna Catherine	13176	M	1912	Katherine E	57013	D	1930	Thomas James	56366	D	1930
Catherine E.	11076	M	1911	Lionie Eugenie	50988	D	1928	Tim	35717	D	1923
Charles F.	11076	M	1911	Margaret	17848	D	1914	Walker G.	18885	M	1915
Elizabeth M.	11076	M	1911	Mary	41620	M	1925	Walter Cleveland	68588	D	1934
Esther M.	3320	D	1907	Mary	63432	D	1933	Winifred	13645	D	1912
John J.	11076	M	1911	Michael	78065	D	1938	**McGower**			
Thomas P.	11076	M	1911	Michael	51749	D	1929	John	63746	D	1933
McGolgan				Michael J.	73267	D	1936	**McGown**			
Cornelius	51242	D	1928	Patrick W.	48746	D	1927	Dudley Brooke	80909	D	1939
McGonagle				Peter J.	33763	D	1922	**McGrade**			
Harriet	30356	I	1920	Robert M.	78064	M	1938	Maria	11583	D	1911
McGonigal				Theresa	36889	D	1923	**McGrady**			
C. D.	56271	D	1930	William R.	50662	D	1928	James	62194	D	1932
				McGowan				Thomas	4722	D	1907
				Charon June	89788	M	1942				

NAME	NUMBER	TYPE	YEAR
MCGRAIL			
Thomas	20606	D	1916
MCGRAIT			
Catherine	32595	D	1921
MCGRANAGHAN			
Alice	35606	D	1922
Hugh	10725	D	1910
Joseph	55850	D	1930
MCGRATH			
Anita E.	41355	D	1925
Annie	43972	D	1926
Bridget Delia	80990	D	1939
Bryant	50682	I	1928
Catharine	16154	D	1913
Daniel	11179	D	1911
Delia	80492	D	1939
Edmond	19288	D	1915
Edmund Marshall	46214	D	1927
Elizabeth	51498	I	1928
Elizabeth	88889	I	1942
Ellen	53463	D	1929
Ellen	69418	D	1935
Fannie	21064	D	1916
Frances Theresa	29856	D	1920
George F.	50292	D	1928
George Raymond	68233	I	1934
Honora J.	50362	D	1928
J. J.	12778	D	1912
James	10590	D	1910
James J.	11150	D	1911
James J.	32671	D	1921
James Matthew	20944	D	1916
Johanna	25774	D	1918
John	24551	D	1918
John	48147	D	1927
John	50997	D	1928
John	59036	D	1931
John E.	16637	D	1914
John J.	76738	D	1937
Joseph Patrick	67125	D	1934
Kate	17293	D	1914
Kate	30933	D	1921
Kate C.	26983	D	1919
Kate M.	26983	D	1919
Margaret	10664	D	1910
Margaret Ellen	47342	D	1927
Mary	10664	D	1910
Mary Catherine	7984	D	1909

NAME	NUMBER	TYPE	YEAR
Mary Margaret	63696	D	1933
Michael J.	50871	D	1928
Nellie	83098	D	1940
P. H.	32147	D	1921
Patreick	32147	D	1921
Patrick	5938	D	1908
Patrick	58594	D	1931
Patrick F.	22623	D	1917
Roseinia	88797	I	1941
Thomas	11538	D	1911
Thomas	56961	D	1930
Thomas Francis	38250	D	1924
William	17648	D	1914
William	81794	D	1939
William A.	80658	M	1939
William Davit	51510	D	1928
MCGRAW			
Elisabeth	48743	D	1927
Mary E.	64456	D	1933
Robert E.	55640	M	1930
MCGRAYAN			
Maud Alice	73160	D	1936
MCGREAL			
Patrick J.	51948	D	1929
MCGREEVY			
Annie	56065	D	1930
Annie Elizabeth	55159	D	1930
Annie L.	33567	I	1922
Bridget A.	8686	D	1909
Charles H.	22982	D	1917
Corabell	37073	D	1923
John F.	5779	M	1908
Lizzie	5779	M	1908
Margaret	5779	M	1908
Rosanna	7769	D	1909
MCGREGOR			
Archibald Henderson	20760	D	1916
Archie	74357	I	1937
Archie	79396	I	1938
Archie C.	70789	I	1935
Dorothy May	79254	D	1938
Eliza H.	60215	D	1931
Flora	81055	D	1939
Janet Ann	78799	M	1938
Jessie	21284	D	1916
John A.	89790	D	1942
Laura	49704	D	1928
William	10316	D	1910

NAME	NUMBER	TYPE	YEAR
William	24486	D	1918
MCGREW			
Anna	36533	D	1923
Inga	75585	D	1937
Milford H.	55441	D	1930
MCGROREY			
Edward W.	86398	D	1941
Thomas	31505	D	1921
MCGROUGH			
Patrick	56934	D	1930
MCGROUTHER			
Martha Elizabeth	55752	D	1930
Robert	46132	D	1927
MCGRUDER			
Catherine	2793	D	1907
Charles H.	86642	D	1941
Fannie M.	82070	D	1939
MCGRUER			
George Smith	77347	D	1937
MCGUAN			
Eliza J.	69884	D	1935
MCGUARRIE			
Mary E.	14214	I	1912
MCGUERN			
Nora E.	19821	M	1915
MCGUFFICK			
Elizabeth	49016	D	1928
Leah J.	57772	D	1931
MCGUIGAN			
Catharine E.	68394	D	1934
Daniel	6056	D	1908
Delia	8318	D	1909
Edward	63455	D	1933
John	39412	D	1924
MCGUINESS			
Cora L.	71191	D	1935
John	83898	D	1940
MCGUINN			
Charles	45661	D	1926
Francis	45661	D	1926
Madeline May	45661	D	1926
Martin Joseph	45661	D	1926
William James	45661	D	1926
MCGUINNIS			
Genevieve	56342	M	1930

NAME	NUMBER	TYPE	YEAR
McGuire			
AdaBelle Morgan	72867	D	1936
Adeline	48560	D	1927
Alice G.	2554	D	1906
Anna	87557	D	1941
Arnie Elbs	51971	D	1929
Arnie M.	51971	D	1929
Catherine	13955	D	1912
Catherine F.	63347	M	1933
Charles J.	63862	D	1933
Edward Campbell	84669	D	1940
Ella F.	33587	D	1922
Ernest L.	51244	D	1928
Ernest L.	82314	D	1939
Francis James	18518	D	1915
Frank	38661	D	1924
Frank	77966	D	1938
Henry	68273	D	1934
J. M.	86867	D	1941
James	23187	D	1917
James	56213	I	1930
John	45023	D	1926
John	57654	D	1931
John J.	82429	D	1939
John P.	3783	D	1907
Joseph	27790	D	1919
Julia	34519	D	1922
Mary	11805	D	1911
Mary A.	66976	I	1934
Mary A.	68786	D	1935
Maud J.	64209	D	1933
May B.	30161	D	1920
Nellie	80600	D	1939
Patrick Henry	68273	D	1934
Peter	9760	D	1910
Philip P.	68506	D	1934
Rena	68625	D	1934
Sophia	58892	D	1931
Sophia	59113	D	1931
Thomas Francis	62997	D	1932
William	9970	D	1910
McGuirk			
Benedict	21547	I	1916
Benedict King	61844	D	1932
Catherine	11289	D	1911
Thomas	11217	D	1911
McGurk			
Michael	10960	D	1910

NAME	NUMBER	TYPE	YEAR
Steven	38212	D	1924
McGurn			
John	63180	D	1932
McGurren			
Henry F.	86940	D	1941
McGurty			
Francis	41706	D	1925
McHale			
Mary	33783	D	1922
Mary	47526	D	1927
McHardy			
Norman Farquhar	50347	I	1928
McHarris			
Mark	66315	I	1934
McHenry			
Charles	6801	D	1908
Julia	28073	D	1919
Michael J.	1063	D	1906
Peter	51127	I	1928
Peter J.	60056	D	1931
Peter N.	63007	D	1932
Rolph	81329	D	1939
William Henry	42877	I	1925
McHeur			
Jessie	22652	D	1917
McHugh			
Annie	45879	D	1926
Annie Josephine	50810	M	1928
Annie M.	64460	D	1933
Catherine	31348	D	1921
Charles	14399	M	1912
Charles	50463	D	1928
Charles	75526	I	1937
Charles Joseph	50810	M	1928
Dode	65572	D	1933
Dorothy	14399	M	1912
Felix	71326	D	1936
Felix J.	89827	D	1942
Frank	29434	D	1920
George Emmett	83778	D	1940
Hugh V.	20332	I	1916
James	27345	D	1919
James H.	58059	D	1931
James J.	85157	D	1940
John B.	48816	D	1927
John Bernard	50810	M	1928
John Joseph	39625	D	1924

NAME	NUMBER	TYPE	YEAR
Joseph J.	37126	I	1923
Josephine	65572	D	1933
Katherine	46553	D	1927
Katherine	82743	D	1939
Llewellyn D.	32249	D	1921
Mary Elizabeth	50810	M	1928
Mary Virginia	19797	D	1915
Michael	64461	D	1933
Owen	66527	D	1934
Owen I.	86625	D	1941
Patrick	4419	D	1907
Patrick	9044	D	1910
Peter J.	68209	D	1934
Peter, Sr.	68209	D	1934
Thomas	47240	D	1927
McIlvain			
Andrew Jackson	66023	D	1934
George Turner	33702	D	1922
McIlwrath			
Robert	49857	I	1928
McInerney			
Annie J.	53257	D	1929
Edward J.	51291	M	1928
Elizabeth A.	76116	D	1937
Gertruce Catherine Marie	41690	M	1925
Lawrence E.	51291	M	1928
Margaret V.	51400	D	1928
Patrick	22586	D	1917
Thomas	3930	D	1907
Thomas Mortimer	41690	M	1925
William	24288	D	1918
McInerny			
Ellen	33649	D	1922
John F.	25498	D	1918
Kate J.	89792	D	1942
Lawrence J.	57148	I	1930
Rose	4016	I	1907
Teresa Josephine	72014	D	1936
McInnes			
A. M.	5826	D	1908
Hugh	76238	I	1937
John M.	48636	D	1927
John P.	20056	D	1915
Lillian M	65038	D	1933
Lillian Skinner	65038	D	1933
Margaret	5593	D	1908
Mary A.	5768	I	1908
Michael A.	10584	D	1910

NAME	NUMBER	TYPE	YEAR	NAME	NUMBER	TYPE	YEAR	NAME	NUMBER	TYPE	YEAR
MCINNIS				**MCIVER**				George W.	62664	D	1932
Catherine Elizabeth	12400	D	1911	Donald	78161	D	1938	Geraldine	75959	M	1937
Mary	84134	D	1940	John A.	35673	D	1923	John B.	19440	D	1915
MCINTIRE				**MCIVOR**				Kenneth Albert	88651	M	1941
Bartolo	41592	D	1925	William N.	25407	D	1918	Mary A. M.	19439	D	1915
MCINTOCH				**MCKAGE**				R. J.	8967	D	1910
Julia	82510	D	1939	Hanora	1957	D	1906	Thelma	75959	M	1937
MCINTOSH				**MCKAHARAY**				**MCKEANY**			
Ada	49814	D	1928	John	84184	D	1940	Julia	58968	D	1931
Catherine	13531	D	1912	**MCKAY**				**MCKEARNY**			
Donald	4138	I	1907	Alexander	36712	I	1923	Andrew	39660	D	1924
Hortense G.	55727	D	1930	Alexander	37159	D	1923	**MCKEE**			
Kenneth Goad	50419	D	1928	Alexander	74156	I	1936	Albert C.	82671	I	1939
L. Anna	83739	D	1940	Angus	21990	D	1916	Annie	14265	D	1912
Lachlan	44892	D	1926	Ann	75638	D	1937	Charles Augustine	6518	M	1908
Lydia Annette	83739	D	1940	C. A.	46433	D	1927	Daisy L.	89159	D	1942
Margaret	28389	D	1919	Clarice	82833	D	1939	David	2974	D	1907
Raymond Pierce	49548	D	1928	Cornelius	46433	D	1927	Donald	58323	D	1931
MCINTRYE				David M.	76455	D	1937	Eleanor	54300	D	1929
John Lawrence	72456	D	1936	Donald B.	77804	M	1938	Eva E.	27453	D	1919
MCINTYRE				Edith Margaret	39283	D	1924	George	50917	D	1928
Alexander	79792	D	1938	Eugenie Hill	46942	D	1927	Gertrude Elizabeth	6518	M	1908
Anna E.	38480	D	1924	Gladys	2153	D	1906	Helen Louise	66671	D	1934
Annie J.	76867	D	1937	Hattie A.	45291	D	1926	Rosy	10245	D	1910
Anthony	29072	D	1920	Jane A.	76585	D	1937	Samuel	17157	D	1914
Charles S.	50342	D	1928	Jennie E.	56212	D	1930	Thomas W.	79499	D	1938
Christina C.	64943	D	1933	Joan Dewey	81755	M	1939	W. T.	1763	D	1906
Flora Lillie	30867	D	1920	John	47759	I	1927	**MCKEEGAN**			
Francis Peter	30575	D	1920	John	48257	D	1927	Sarah Katherine	66764	D	1934
J. B.	36872	D	1923	john H.	57800	D	1931	**MCKEERNAN**			
James B.	474	D	1906	John M.	48442	D	1927	Mary	934	D	1906
James William	28139	D	1919	John N.	21927	D	1916	**MCKEEVER**			
John	13455	D	1912	Kenneth	77804	M	1938	Mary C.	79081	D	1938
Josephine L.	19862	D	1915	Lillian	34397	D	1922	Michael	79797	D	1938
Lillian E.	63703	D	1933	Malcolm Leslie	74192	D	1936	**MCKELL**			
Martha M.	74581	D	1937	Margaret	22793	D	1917	William Scott	80042	D	1938
Mary	52316	D	1929	Margaret	58131	M	1931	**MCKELLAR**			
Peter	19465	D	1915	Patrick Joseph	59609	D	1931	John	124	D	1906
Robert E.	36688	D	1923	Sophie	42180	D	1925	Thomas	68569	D	1934
Robert Elmer	39722	M	1924	Stuart R.	76586	D	1937	**MCKELLER**			
Robert James	63837	D	1933	Thomas D.	8421	D	1909	John	50738	D	1928
Wm. H.	327	D	1906	William	20486	D	1916	**MCKELLIP**			
MCISAAC				**MCKEAGUE**				Joann C.	73617	I	1936
Daniel	81125	D	1939	Hanora	1957	D	1906	**MCKELVEY**			
Dorothy Jean	80832	M	1939	**MCKEAN**				Angelina	40369	D	1924
John R.	10020	I	1910	Arlene Joyce	88651	M	1941	Elnora	32361	D	1921
Mary Evelyn	80832	M	1939	David A.	55024	D	1930	Florence	39732	M	1924
				Floyd Kenneth	87142	D	1941				

NAME	NUMBER	TYPE	YEAR	NAME	NUMBER	TYPE	YEAR	NAME	NUMBER	TYPE	YEAR
Patrick	20228	D	1916	Owen	4103	D	1907	Kenneth A.	36049	D	1923
McKendrick				Owen M.	2066	D	1906	Kenneth E.	29954	D	1920
Mary Ann	29637	D	1920	Patricia	55600	M	1930	Kenneth H.	83612	D	1940
Walter	45519	D	1926	Patrick J.	16996	D	1914	Kenneth R.	36049	D	1923
McKenna				Peter	29343	D	1920	Mae	51517	D	1928
Alice	48207	M	1927	Rosa	4016	I	1907	Malcolm	88232	D	1941
Ann	6655	D	1908	Thomas	46889	D	1927	Margaret	46979	M	1927
Audrey	51176	M	1928	Thomas P.	55499	D	1930	Margaret A.	38203	I	1924
Benjamin Henry	60117	D	1931	Walter F.	12939	M	1912	Margaret Ann	44135	D	1926
Bernard	19434	D	1915	Walter F.	23391	D	1917	Mary	326	D	1906
Bernard	34710	D	1922	William	73969	M	1936	Maud	67924	D	1934
Bernard	62368	D	1932	William Henry	42877	I	1925	Neita Marjorie	89091	M	1942
Cassy	30772	M	1920	William Henry	61286	D	1932	Sinclair	31987	D	1921
Catherine	7452	D	1909	**McKenney**				William	6925	D	1908
Catherine	30772	M	1920	Donald M.	35437	M	1922	William	40803	D	1925
Catherine	37461	D	1923	Herbert E.	35437	M	1922	William	56399	D	1930
Catherine A.	43848	D	1926	John P.	76407	I	1937	Winifred A.	22536	D	1917
Daniel	17956	D	1914	Marion L.	35437	M	1922	**McKeon**			
Dorris E.	12367	M	1911	Rose	54327	D	1929	Anna Loretta	14362	M	1912
Edward	55141	D	1930	William	62192	D	1932	Annie	44592	D	1926
Elizabeth Belle	46983	D	1927	William Henery	42877	I	1925	Carrie	17760	M	1914
Ella	62077	D	1932	William Henry	61286	D	1932	Charles	38371	D	1924
Fannie	84790	D	1940	**McKennon**				Edward J.	23674	D	1917
George	65206	D	1933	Mary L.	68560	D	1934	Elizabeth	23442	D	1917
Harry E.	12367	M	1911	**McKenny**				Eugene	29560	D	1920
Henry	58549	D	1931	William Henry	61286	D	1932	Frank P.	88482	D	1941
James	46859	I	1927	**McKenry**				Isabella	32146	D	1921
James	51001	D	1928	William Henry	42877	I	1925	James	14581	D	1912
James	60293	D	1931	**McKensie**				John	2840	D	1907
James Edgar	12939	M	1912	James	3235	D	1907	John B.	19440	D	1915
James Edgar	23392	D	1917	**McKenty**				Leonora	86723	D	1941
James Francis	11932	D	1911	Emanuelita	49881	D	1928	Lulu McKee	73564	D	1936
James Patrick	12623	D	1911	**McKenzie**				Margaret	70703	D	1935
John	16223	D	1913	Agnes	32550	D	1921	Mary A. M.	19439	D	1915
John	22453	D	1917	Angus	3643	D	1907	Patrick	14598	I	1912
John	41447	D	1925	Colin Mortimore	23483	D	1917	Patrick	22587	D	1917
John Edwin	42353	I	1925	Dan	36206	D	1923	Patrick J.	18597	D	1915
Louise M.	81366	D	1939	Donald B.	53687	D	1929	Rose	30011	D	1920
Martin W.	12367	M	1911	George Claire	89091	M	1942	Sarah E.	30010	D	1920
Mary	78514	D	1938	Harry A.	78591	D	1938	Thomas	28617	D	1920
Mary C.	25195	I	1918	Hector D.	33373	D	1922	William	27782	D	1919
Mary C.	26097	D	1919	James	1978	D	1906	**McKeone**			
Matthew T.	50162	D	1928	James Joseph	19204	D	1915	Fannie Ann	3069	D	1907
Michael	65648	D	1933	Janette	70959	D	1935	**McKeown**			
Michael J.	89482	D	1942	John	72159	I	1936	Barbara Lee	62421	M	1932
Mildred A.	12367	M	1911	John W.	55834	D	1930	Catherine	16467	D	1913
Murray	74686	M	1937	Joseph	87153	I	1941	Joseph P.	18314	D	1914
Newton	74686	M	1937	Julia	42951	D	1925	Maud	86954	D	1941
Norine	48207	M	1927								

Key: D = death; M = minor; I = incompetent

NAME	NUMBER	TYPE	YEAR
Thomas	48999	D	1928
Winifred	53848	D	1929
Winifred M.	83376	D	1940
McKERICHER			
Edwin D.	78646	D	1938
McKERNAN			
Hugh B.	22666	D	1917
McKERRON			
Catherine	4687	D	1907
Helen	81254	D	1939
John A.	64766	D	1933
McKEVITT			
Hazel	87479	D	1941
McKEWEN			
John M.	2822	D	1907
Mary A.	28146	D	1919
McKEY			
Mercedes	89725	M	1942
Robert	89725	M	1942
McKIBBEN			
James	7956	D	1909
Mary	22876	D	1917
McKIBBIN			
Charles	19319	D	1915
McKIBBINS			
Frank	13183	D	1912
McKILLOP			
Frederick	70315	M	1935
Infanta	70288	D	1935
Isabella	23218	D	1917
James	70315	M	1935
William	70315	M	1935
McKILLYS			
Annie J.	10917	D	1910
McKIMMIE			
Donald	49720	M	1928
Paul	49720	M	1928
William, Jr.	49720	M	1928
McKIMMINS			
George	78887	D	1938
McKINLAY			
Helen May	84811	D	1940
McKINLEY			
Amanda J.	65964	D	1933
B. F., Mrs.	59994	D	1931
Caroline Emily	62631	M	1932

NAME	NUMBER	TYPE	YEAR
Carrie A.	37237	D	1923
Eunice	26715	M	1919
Lovina Jane	34222	I	1922
Mary A.	59994	D	1931
Walker	26715	M	1919
Walker L.	26713	D	1919
McKINNEY			
Della	47870	I	1927
E. C.	86131	D	1941
Edward	66780	D	1934
Edward	43242	D	1925
Frank	78266	D	1938
George	59918	D	1931
Henry	64406	D	1933
James	77823	D	1938
Jessie T.	58843	D	1931
Luther William	69704	D	1935
Mary C.	25195	I	1918
Mary C.	26097	D	1919
McKINNON			
Adela M.	43703	D	1926
Albert A.	40289	D	1924
Aungus	21635	D	1916
Christine	81025	D	1939
Claudine	45290	M	1926
Daniel A.	41419	D	1925
Donald	45290	M	1926
Ellen	45290	M	1926
Flora	78152	D	1938
Francis Eugene	2664	M	1907
Helen	45290	M	1926
John	26085	D	1919
John L.	33482	D	1922
Jovita B.	26062	D	1919
Marion	45290	M	1926
Norman	40041	D	1924
Thomas, Jr.	45548	M	1926
McKINSEY			
Robert Benton	34752	M	1922
Thomas Warren	34752	M	1922
McKINSTRY			
Laura L.	68051	D	1934
McKINTY			
Jackson	59	D	1906
McKIRAHAN			
Merlin Evart	78440	D	1938
McKITTRICK			
John	16379	D	1913

NAME	NUMBER	TYPE	YEAR
John F.	72727	D	1936
Katherine M.	20309	I	1916
McKLEM			
Kathleen May	72004	M	1936
McKNEW			
Henry L.	67661	D	1934
Jane	31183	D	1921
McKNIGHT			
Edward	28019	D	1919
J. W.	51460	D	1928
James	80285	D	1939
Louise Jane	52315	M	1929
R. D.	62745	D	1932
McKOWEN			
William R.	12416	D	1911
McKOWN			
Florence	60872	I	1932
Mary Ella	24232	D	1918
McKREE			
Charles G.	45029	M	1926
John N.	45041	D	1926
McKURTH			
Gladys Barbara	77415	M	1938
McLACHLAN			
Alexander	62118	D	1932
John	52325	D	1929
McLAFFERTY			
James	9184	D	1910
McLAGAN			
James L.	14360	D	1912
McLAIN			
B. H.	39227	D	1924
James L. F.	33249	I	1922
John F.	37431	D	1923
William O.	46440	D	1927
McLAINE			
Sarah C.	57450	D	1930
McLAMB			
Florence Marie	65912	D	1933
Marie Louise	65913	M	1933
McLANE			
Addie	37167	D	1923
Allan	323	D	1906
Catherine	4737	D	1907
Charles A.	80028	D	1938
Charles E.	58745	D	1931
Charles Lee	51767	M	1929

NAME	NUMBER	TYPE	YEAR	NAME	NUMBER	TYPE	YEAR	NAME	NUMBER	TYPE	YEAR
Ellen	32135	D	1921	Denis	58145	D	1931	Margaret	76179	I	1937
Frank J.	63355	D	1933	Dorothy M.	54528	M	1929	Margaret A.	6787	D	1908
Gladys I.	51767	M	1929	Edward	325	D	1906	Margaret M.	4508	D	1907
Harold	65935	I	1933	Edward	4598	M	1907	Marion	53741	M	1929
Hugh	34323	D	1922	Edward	29022	D	1920	Martin	81879	D	1939
John A.	24537	D	1918	Edward	53741	M	1929	Mary	5511	D	1908
William W.	51767	M	1929	Edward Hoyt	70695	M	1935	Mary	14695	D	1913
McLaren				Elizabeth	16858	D	1914	Mary A.	50578	D	1928
Albert	6600	M	1908	Ellen T.	63830	D	1933	Mary Atha	21252	D	1916
George A.	6601	D	1908	Emily A.	54403	D	1929	Mary D.	31455	D	1921
Harry Angell	10008	D	1910	Esther	4598	M	1907	Mary Jane	47566	D	1927
Jane	45795	D	1926	Esther E.	82633	D	1939	Mary R.	1791	D	1906
Linie Loyall	86369	D	1941	F. J., Mrs.	26650	D	1919	Michael	197	D	1906
William Starr	80262	D	1939	Francis A.	66187	D	1934	Michael	3731	D	1907
McLarty				Frank E.	6946	D	1908	Michael	7492	D	1909
Jennie	11202	D	1911	George	4598	M	1907	Michael J.	74065	D	1936
William	80943	D	1939	George	28323	D	1919	Michael James	71025	D	1935
McLauchlan				Gladys	60802	M	1932	Olivia Hoyt	71010	D	1935
Mark A.	88228	D	1941	Gwendolin	60802	M	1932	Patrick	1705	D	1906
McLaughlin				Harry Joseph	33971	I	1922	Patrick	19816	D	1915
Ada	7037	D	1909	Hazel	4598	M	1907	Patrick Joseph	76783	D	1937
Agnes	64373	I	1933	Helen Jane	26650	D	1919	Robert	19653	I	1915
Agnes M.	71675	D	1936	Hugh	4598	M	1907	Robert	51770	D	1929
Alexander	50983	D	1928	Isabel Lois	4940	M	1907	Rose	54430	M	1929
Alexander Douglas	84727	D	1940	James	22300	D	1917	Sarah J.	62111	D	1932
Alfred	6133	D	1908	James	58058	D	1931	Steven J.	26467	D	1919
Alice	67958	D	1934	James	72411	D	1936	Thomas F.	69923	D	1935
Alice	53741	M	1929	James	87619	D	1941	Thomas Henry	42832	D	1925
Anna	11435	M	1911	James Edward	16340	D	1913	W. H.	49824	D	1928
Anna J.	19501	D	1915	James H.	20529	D	1916	Walter	4598	M	1907
Annie	25679	D	1918	James P.	68616	D	1934	Wilhelmina R.	66384	D	1934
Annie	48267	D	1927	Jean	12766	M	1911	William	10213	D	1910
Armour	13895	D	1912	John	18430	D	1915	William	23965	D	1918
Armour	28237	D	1919	John	19247	D	1915	**McLaughtin**			
Armour M., Jr.	13930	M	1912	John	27943	I	1919	John	35675	D	1923
Arthur	4598	M	1907	John	67573	I	1934	**McLaurin**			
Audrey May	43930	D	1926	John	74897	D	1937	Harry D.	3416	D	1907
Barney	79731	I	1938	John H.	32904	D	1921	**McLea**			
Barney	82852	D	1939	John L.	14086	I	1912	Annie D.	3784	D	1907
Bernard	46443	D	1927	John L.	14122	D	1912	Donald	74986	D	1937
Catherine	11163	D	1911	John R.	4598	M	1907	Jennie C.	48530	D	1927
Charles	27927	D	1919	John W.	41615	D	1925	**McLean**			
Charlotte Grace	19502	D	1915	Joseph F.	43747	I	1926	A. D.	14574	D	1912
Charlotte I.	61033	D	1932	Joseph F.	70326	D	1935	Alexander	41110	D	1925
Charlotte S.	55260	I	1930	Joseph H.	27467	D	1919	Alfred A.	57855	D	1931
Cyrus	4598	M	1907	Judge	76362	M	1937	Algier	16007	M	1913
Daniel W.	89970	D	1942	Lorraine	20691	M	1916	Angus John	38732	D	1924
David	5855	D	1908	Margarat	533	D	1906	C.	35321	D	1922
				Margaret	39364	D	1924				

NAME	NUMBER	TYPE	YEAR	NAME	NUMBER	TYPE	YEAR	NAME	NUMBER	TYPE	YEAR
Caroline A.	15520	I	1913	**McLENNAN**				**McLOUGHLIN**			
Carrie Bliss	4611	D	1907	Alexander	63214	D	1932	Emma Theresa	65385	I	1933
Cora H.	49663	D	1928	Bruce	67886	D	1934	Francis Joseph	87263	D	1941
Cornelia	72581	D	1936	David M. T.	46442	D	1927	George J.	63729	D	1933
Dorothy B.	62822	D	1932	Hattie	51922	D	1929	John	19247	D	1915
Edith	23237	M	1917	John	16914	D	1914	Patrick	19816	D	1915
Edith E.	48249	D	1927	Mary	68990	D	1935	William John	51315	D	1928
Edward Earl	68400	M	1934	**McLEOD**				**McLURE**			
Edward T.	14429	I	1912	Alice	49978	D	1928	John	6040	D	1908
Elizabeth F.	64509	D	1933	Angus	47749	D	1927	**McMACKEN**			
George	40231	D	1924	Benjamin F.	49979	D	1928	May Theresia	16072	M	1913
Hector	32973	D	1921	George	379	D	1906	**McMAHAN**			
Ileen S.	72932	D	1936	George William	76572	D	1937	California V.	16778	D	1914
James	33603	D	1922	Gwendolene	19141	M	1915	Calvin C.	42570	D	1925
James	45105	D	1926	Hattie Francis	70341	D	1935	James	49837	D	1928
John	28914	D	1920	Janet	71196	D	1935	Joel	66045	D	1934
John C.	58478	D	1931	John	29679	I	1920	Lavenia Ellen	9494	D	1910
John C.	74982	D	1937	John N.	5748	D	1908	Matthew B.	19518	D	1915
John R.	85435	D	1940	Lulu	47817	D	1927	Sarah	49836	D	1928
Josephine	4370	D	1907	Malcolm R.	49744	D	1928	**McMAHON**			
Kenneth McKenzie	79897	D	1938	Margaret E.	34900	I	1922	Abraham Joseph	29200	D	1920
Malcom	32169	D	1921	Margaret E.	71488	D	1936	Andrew C.	32955	D	1921
Margaret Burns	8556	D	1909	Murdo	88928	D	1942	Annie	18972	D	1915
Marguerite C.	61754	D	1932	Neil James	14890	D	1913	Bernard	28660	D	1920
Marian E.	75303	D	1937	Robert	65676	D	1933	Bessie	13781	I	1912
Martha J.	14428	I	1912	Thomas R.	9319	D	1910	Bridger	30968	D	1921
May Josephine	77769	D	1938	Viola D.	77798	D	1938	Dennis	3858	D	1907
Motia T.	68348	D	1934	William R.	52159	D	1929	Dennis	21047	I	1916
Murdock M.	56899	I	1930	**McLERAN**				Edgar Jeffries	77170	D	1937
Murdock M.	57293	D	1930	Charles Alexander	82417	D	1939	Edwin T.	80828	I	1939
Myra	28698	D	1920	Madeline E.	59590	D	1931	Elizabeth	1491	D	1906
Norman H.	56131	D	1930	Mary	44773	D	1926	Elizabeth R.	13704	D	1912
Peter	10289	D	1910	Molly	44773	D	1926	Francis C.	8504	I	1909
Rainey M.	8557	D	1909	Ralph	50772	D	1928	Frank	25880	D	1918
Richard	10100	M	1910	**McLERIE**				George Lewis	85708	D	1940
Robert J.	23184	D	1917	Charles R.	55847	D	1930	George T.	10516	D	1910
Ronald Albert	73871	D	1936	Henrietta	52645	D	1929	Helen	11899	M	1911
Sarah	18385	D	1915	Henry J.	3805	D	1907	Henry	37785	D	1923
Simon	89897	D	1942	John Alexander	75597	D	1937	Hope	88305	M	1941
Thos. G.	54858	D	1930	**McLINDEN**				Hugh	6788	D	1908
Walter Scott	77335	D	1937	Daniel	35952	D	1923	Hugh Francis	86972	D	1941
William	10100	M	1910	James	23190	D	1917	Isaac	21685	D	1916
William	62288	D	1932	**McLOGAN**				James	28086	D	1919
William Melville	62823	D	1932	James L.	14360	D	1912	James	62480	D	1932
McLELLAN				**McLOONE**				James A.	63011	D	1932
John	70890	D	1935	Frank W.	29620	D	1920	Jane	3451	D	1907
Margaret	76073	D	1937	John	33550	D	1922	John	6723	D	1908
Robert Alden	82431	D	1939					John	10898	D	1910

Key: D = death; M = minor; I = incompetent

NAME	NUMBER	TYPE	YEAR
John	53658	D	1929
Kate	10022	D	1910
Kate	18880	I	1915
Katie	48869	D	1928
Letitia	14741	D	1913
Mabel	31631	D	1921
Margaret	4447	D	1907
Margaret I.	77921	D	1938
Martin	54619	D	1929
Mary	11899	M	1911
Mary	70071	D	1935
Mary Alice	48076	D	1927
Mary Ann	63339	I	1933
Mary Ann	64762	D	1933
Mary E.	89302	D	1942
Mary Rose	17159	D	1914
Michael	7676	D	1909
Michael J.	57415	D	1930
Patrick	3432	D	1907
Patrick J.	17262	D	1914
Philip P.	40848	D	1925
Rose	17159	D	1914
Sheamus	63011	D	1932
Thomas	16337	D	1913
Thomas J.	3542	D	1907
Thomas Morgan	867	D	1906
William	4367	D	1907
William	44807	D	1926
McMains			
Adelaide F.	51372	D	1928
McManamly			
William	76488	D	1937
McManass			
Susie M.	74361	D	1937
McMann			
Anna	18249	D	1914
William	1304	D	1906
McMannon			
Ella	32466	M	1921
Evelyn	32466	M	1921
Florence	32466	M	1921
Frank	32466	M	1921
Frank	32856	D	1921
McManoman			
Bridget	4193	D	1907
McManus			
Anne R.	74929	D	1937
Bernard	54625	D	1929

NAME	NUMBER	TYPE	YEAR
Catherine A.	48526	D	1927
Desmond D.	57443	M	1930
Ella	61414	I	1932
Ellen	41937	D	1925
Ellen	41937	D	1925
Evelyn Teresa	61696	D	1932
Floretta C.	89391	D	1942
Helen	41937	D	1925
Helen	41937	D	1925
Herbert L.	1639	D	1906
Hester Elizabeth	3973	D	1907
Hester Elizabeth Cutter	19513	D	1915
Hugh W.	46522	M	1927
James	11046	D	1911
James Francis	55991	M	1930
James Joseph	70427	D	1935
Jane	12226	D	1911
John	19884	D	1915
Loretta	89391	D	1942
Mary C.	57443	M	1930
Mathew H.	73983	D	1936
Patrick	25978	D	1918
Patrick	77408	D	1938
Philip J.	8297	D	1909
McMaster			
D. J.	23380	D	1917
Rachel Ellen	31793	I	1921
Rachel Ellen	70049	D	1935
Sarah	72391	D	1936
McMaugh			
Robert	12489	D	1911
McMenamie			
James	37378	D	1923
McMenamin			
Hugh	50951	D	1928
James	78271	D	1938
Sarah	68307	D	1934
McMenemy			
James	78271	D	1938
McMenomey			
Anna	17633	D	1914
Charles Francis Henry	17658	M	1914
Ruth Gertrude	17658	M	1914
McMenomin			
James	78271	D	1938
McMenomy			
Arthur James	15073	M	1913
Edward Michael	15073	M	1913

NAME	NUMBER	TYPE	YEAR
Katherine	9223	D	1910
Margaret	6942	D	1908
Michael Joseph	14078	D	1912
McMichael			
Archie	42198	M	1925
Archy	40300	D	1924
Daniel Webster	85586	D	1940
Harry R.	55247	D	1930
James	6072	D	1908
Joseph B.	42198	M	1925
Robert M.	14545	D	1912
McMillan			
Anabella	3	D	1906
Anthony Lane	35758	D	1923
Daniel	30827	D	1920
Ella	81085	D	1939
Ellen	89038	I	1942
Flora Ann	42753	D	1925
Genevieve	35007	D	1922
George T.	7982	M	1909
James	72373	D	1936
John	4666	D	1907
John Duncan	19616	D	1915
John Harry	35008	M	1922
Laura Cyr	42818	M	1925
Paul F.	14013	D	1912
Raymond H.	49063	M	1928
Robert	64492	D	1933
Ronald George	43646	D	1926
Rosetta	62484	D	1932
Sarah	25816	D	1918
Verna Marie	68755	M	1935
McMillen			
Ella J.	27979	D	1919
Roy	88753	D	1941
William Roy	88754	M	1941
McMillin			
James Fred	45956	I	1926
James Fred	46113	I	1926
McMinn			
Clyde A.	59247	D	1931
Robert Lee	84010	D	1940
McMorry			
William H.	58411	D	1931
McMullan			
Charles	21269	D	1916
Rose	88068	D	1941

NAME	NUMBER	TYPE	YEAR
MCMULLEN			
Anne	59182	D	1931
Annie	35795	I	1923
George C.	35568	D	1922
Lewis G.	5559	D	1908
MCMULLIN			
Harry F.	28258	D	1919
Roma G.	6647	M	1908
Virginia	60733	D	1932
William J.	6647	M	1908
MCMUNN			
Ellen Mary	45569	D	1926
James	45570	D	1926
MCMURDO			
Genevieve Imilian	16482	M	1913
George Henry	16482	M	1913
Vincent Paul	16482	M	1913
MCMURRAY			
Bridget	6481	D	1908
Edith	81556	D	1939
Ellen	13013	D	1912
James B.	20389	D	1916
James D.	11757	D	1911
John P.	7528	D	1909
Louisa F.	29528	D	1920
Louise J.	29528	D	1920
Margaret Harriet	21755	M	1916
Raymond W.	39267	D	1924
Stephen George	23908	D	1918
William T.	51305	D	1928
MCMURRY			
William T.	51305	D	1928
MCMURTEY			
Walter C.	51554	D	1928
MCMURTRIE			
Samuel	18093	D	1914
Thomas	10853	D	1910
Thomas	85567	D	1940
MCMURTRY			
Annie	8055	D	1909
Irene M.	57374	D	1930
L. B.	35789	D	1923
Walter C.	51554	D	1928
MCMURTY			
Irene M.	57374	D	1930
MCNAB			
Christine	45461	D	1926

NAME	NUMBER	TYPE	YEAR
Gavin	48881	D	1928
James	20678	D	1916
Lulu Elsie	86416	D	1941
Mary	52677	D	1929
MCNABB			
Belle	77306	D	1937
Blanche	77306	D	1937
Pearl Willig	77306	D	1937
Teresa	65598	D	1933
MCNABOE			
Thomas	60486	D	1931
MCNAIR			
William Wilson	60818	D	1932
MCNALLY			
Adella	82948	D	1939
Bridger	57886	D	1931
Bridget	57886	D	1931
Bridget Gertrude	46008	D	1926
Catherine	13179	D	1912
Catherine Theresa	7274	M	1909
Elizabeth	42482	D	1925
Eva F. Palmer	27088	D	1919
Frank J.	82947	D	1939
Frank L.	77866	D	1938
James	48628	D	1927
James A.	17169	D	1914
James J.	53841	D	1929
John	7787	D	1909
John Edward	7501	D	1909
John H.	53705	D	1929
Mary A.	13626	D	1912
Mary Agnes	7274	M	1909
Michael Joseph	7274	M	1909
Minnie	13626	D	1912
Patrick J.	55034	D	1930
Rose	82752	D	1939
Vincent P.	76222	M	1937
William	7274	M	1909
William F.	46349	D	1927
MCNAMARA			
Agnes	58608	D	1931
Alice	84506	D	1940
Andrew	25887	D	1918
Ann	54014	I	1929
Ann	80590	D	1939
Bertha	70640	D	1935
Bridget	7021	D	1909
Delia	7021	D	1909

NAME	NUMBER	TYPE	YEAR
Florence	56555	D	1930
George	14631	I	1912
Herbert V.	83518	D	1940
J. B.	53486	D	1929
James A.	18279	D	1914
James J.	63036	D	1932
Jennie	43850	D	1926
Joseph	24325	D	1918
Margaret	56629	D	1930
Mary	79577	D	1938
Matthew	12529	D	1911
Matthew	87662	D	1941
Michael Francis	75839	D	1937
Patrick	20072	D	1915
Patrick	88117	D	1941
Patrick	79328	D	1938
Patrick J.	51255	D	1928
Patrick J.	51434	D	1928
Peter	57652	D	1931
Roady	52230	I	1929
Rose	13500	I	1912
Terence	12621	D	1911
Thomas	34334	D	1922
Thomas J.	75481	D	1937
William	20761	D	1916
William	85666	D	1940
William Joseph	37270	D	1923
MCNAMEE			
Mary	84367	D	1940
Patrick	82715	D	1939
Sarah	38385	D	1924
MCNAUGHT			
Duncan	30528	D	1920
Mary Catharine	26880	D	1919
Thomas	53903	D	1929
William	62025	D	1932
MCNAUGHTON			
Annetta	42430	D	1925
Belle	59750	D	1931
John A.	55617	D	1930
MCNEALY			
Gail Jones	88109	M	1941
Willard	55123	M	1930
MCNEE			
Alexander	19324	D	1915
Eldon R.	64818	D	1933
John H.	19325	D	1915
Robert Eldon	64940	M	1933

NAME	NUMBER	TYPE	YEAR	NAME	NUMBER	TYPE	YEAR	NAME	NUMBER	TYPE	YEAR
McNeil				**McNulty**				**McPartlen**			
Annie	20849	D	1916	Aaron W.	68931	D	1935	Hugh	81941	D	1939
Elizabeth	44134	D	1926	Anne	56302	D	1930	**McPhail**			
Guy L., Jr.	68938	M	1935	Daniel A.	28646	D	1920	Anna N.	53066	D	1929
Halmer E.	40544	D	1924	Edward C. D.	75009	D	1937	Arna Frances	71866	D	1936
Mary	18800	D	1915	Emma H.	25268	I	1918	Susie	42443	D	1925
Mary A.	14326	D	1912	Frances Sophia	11729	D	1911	**McPhederain**			
Stephen C.	72504	D	1936	George	54406	D	1929	Elizabeth	77353	D	1937
Suezanne A.	68938	M	1935	George H.	20103	D	1915	**McPhederan**			
Wilton James	70553	D	1935	Gertrude I.	20102	M	1915	Elizabeth	77353	D	1937
McNeill				Gertrude I.	34426	I	1922	**McPhee**			
Allan A.	39138	I	1924	Gertrude I.	36102	D	1923	Annie R.	10176	D	1910
Allan A.	39265	D	1924	J. T.	34504	D	1922	Bonita Jean	69239	M	1935
Arthur	32144	D	1921	James	63310	D	1933	Charles A.	6242	D	1908
Edith Daragh	77017	M	1937	Jane	21282	D	1916	Ellen	26829	D	1919
Edwin	328	D	1906	Joseph	71470	D	1936	Ellen C.	61646	D	1932
Ida May	72825	D	1936	Margie	81493	D	1939	Francis	26873	M	1919
James J.	74531	D	1937	Oliver	59498	D	1931	Irene Janet	69239	M	1935
McNeilly				Owen E.	76291	D	1937	James A.	15454	D	1913
Evaline	32828	D	1921	Raymond W.	62759	D	1932	Mary A.	26883	D	1919
McNelis				Robert C.	32515	D	1921	Penelope Louise	47776	D	1927
Sarah	66938	D	1934	Sarah	64554	D	1933	**McPherson**			
McNerny				Thomas	23859	D	1918	Archibald	20278	D	1916
Ellen	33649	D	1922	Thomas Francis	85173	D	1940	Charles Mervyn	71142	D	1935
McNess				William H.	39562	D	1924	Elizabeth	4297	D	1907
Bina T.	77237	D	1937	**McNutt**				Ernest F.	52426	D	1929
James Joseph	68946	D	1935	Aileen	11242	M	1911	Helen	79769	D	1938
McNevin				Aileen	56035	D	1930	John	58244	D	1931
Peter Collins	55800	D	1930	Annie	6180	D	1908	John A.	15022	D	1913
William J.	76137	D	1937	Linda	58543	M	1931	Lucy Maynard	49088	D	1928
McNicall				Marie Louise	58544	M	1931	Margaret Helen	79769	D	1938
Juliet I.	43898	D	1926	Mary D.	88818	D	1942	William	66622	D	1934
McNichol				Mary Louise	32720	D	1921	William Henry	48808	D	1927
Mary Isabelle	87118	D	1941	Maud M.	11233	D	1911	William, Jr.	20594	D	1916
Sarah	17278	D	1914	Robert	81969	D	1939	**McPhie**			
McNicholas				William F.	41205	D	1925	John J.	17174	D	1914
Mary P.	87586	D	1941	William Fletcher. Jr.	45260	D	1926	**McPhillips**			
McNicholl				**McOmie**				Annie	87731	D	1941
Henry	17097	D	1914	Margaret	67381	D	1934	Edward	1404	D	1906
McNicoll				**McPadden**				Edward E.	24185	D	1918
Andrew Jackson	59660	D	1931	Beesy	18013	D	1914	John	4844	D	1907
Frances	59742	D	1931	**McPartlan**				John	48357	I	1927
John R.	73795	D	1936	Hugh	81941	D	1939	John	61473	D	1932
McNiel				**McPartland**				**McPike**			
James A.	88931	D	1942	Alexander John	38277	D	1924	A. J., Mrs.	59224	D	1931
McNish				Hugh	81941	D	1939	Andrew J., Jr.	44229	D	1926
Gordon	47743	D	1927	Margaret	57754	D	1931	Henry Halliday	84812	D	1940
				Percy D.	64051	D	1933				

NAME	NUMBER	TYPE	YEAR	NAME	NUMBER	TYPE	YEAR	NAME	NUMBER	TYPE	YEAR
Minerva	59224	D	1931	**McQuillin**				T. B.	17928	D	1914
McQuade				Charles S.	76547	D	1937	**McSherry**			
Catherine	57683	D	1931	**McQuirk**				Bernard	43383	D	1926
Catherine B.	83666	I	1940	James	5756	D	1908	Howard L.	69022	D	1935
Francis	18725	D	1915	**McRae**				James	70461	D	1935
George A.	80076	D	1938	Oscar	64018	D	1933	Joseph M, Jr.	76899	M	1937
Henry	18568	D	1915	William Coleridge	48182	D	1927	Kathleen Ann	76899	M	1937
McQuaid				**McRath**				Margaret	12345	I	1911
Carrie	71903	D	1936	Alexander	63664	D	1933	Margarete	30909	D	1920
Daniel J.	58437	D	1931	**McRobbie**				Mary	15543	D	1913
Frank	18725	D	1915	Mildred Loraine	47304	M	1927	Phillip	18523	D	1915
Harry	18568	D	1915	**McRoberts**				**McSorley**			
Mary	79475	D	1938	Martha Louise Marie	77741	D	1938	John	3086	D	1907
Mary	76021	D	1937	**McRowe**				Michael	25213	D	1918
Mary Belle	14008	D	1912	James Paschal	55781	D	1930	**McStocker**			
Owen	72526	D	1936	**McServe**				Frank B.	52161	D	1929
Thomas F.	79474	D	1938	John S.	8584	D	1909	**McSweeney**			
McQuaide				**McShane**				Adelaide Foote	87666	D	1941
Annie B.	88092	D	1941	Alta Lucile	52489	M	1929	Denis	57610	D	1931
Arthur T.	80237	D	1939	Bernard	28857	M	1920	Ellen	5732	D	1908
Emma L.	28176	D	1919	Cecilia Olivia	86249	D	1941	Francis Daniel	82774	M	1939
James P.	39576	D	1924	Charles	28857	M	1920	Garrett	70430	D	1935
Joseph P.	38997	D	1924	Edward	28857	M	1920	H.	25088	D	1918
June	65345	M	1933	Eva	65973	D	1933	Jeremiah	52138	D	1929
Margaret	22179	D	1917	George C.	57290	D	1930	Julia	10191	D	1910
Owen J.	2384	D	1906	James J.	2067	D	1906	Julia	32134	M	1921
Stephen	28684	D	1920	John J.	39624	D	1924	Katherine	70601	D	1935
McQuarrie				John T.	39624	D	1924	Margaret	30502	D	1920
Mary	16869	D	1914	Mary	76060	I	1937	Mary	70138	D	1935
Mary E.	14214	I	1912	Mary	85085	D	1940	Mary	75666	D	1937
Murdoch A.	18649	D	1915	Michael	26170	D	1919	**McSweeny**			
McQueen				Michael	28857	M	1920	Elizabeth	52298	D	1929
Alfred W.	17854	D	1914	Owen	31094	D	1921	**McSwegan**			
David W.	28124	D	1919	Virginia Margaret	87469	D	1941	Elizabeth	68672	D	1935
Jane	17504	I	1914	William John	52490	D	1929	Philip	7939	D	1909
Jane	21551	D	1916	**McSharry**				**McSwiney**			
Norman Hobdy	51033	M	1928	Charles Thomas	32690	D	1921	Mary A.	10707	D	1910
McQuigg				Edward S.	68584	I	1934	Mary Agatha	9807	I	1910
Frances F.	19358	D	1915	Edward S.	86011	D	1941	Mary G.	24373	D	1918
McQuilken				John J.	73583	D	1936	Mary J.	24373	D	1918
Patrick	19317	D	1915	**McShea**				**McSwyny**			
Peter	19317	D	1915	George W.	11423	D	1911	Barbara Josephine	54377	M	1929
McQuilkin				Margaret	686	D	1906	Josephine	67696	D	1934
Peter	19317	D	1915	**McSheehy**				**McTaggart**			
McQuillan				Catherine	166	D	1906	Annie	26171	D	1919
Edward	70296	I	1935	Elizabeth V.	63101	D	1932	**McTague**			
				Mary	20274	D	1916	George	63814	D	1933

NAME	NUMBER	TYPE	YEAR	NAME	NUMBER	TYPE	YEAR	NAME	NUMBER	TYPE	YEAR
Thomas	36709	D	1923	McVEY				MEACHAM			
McTAINAHAN				Catherine	1220	M	1906	Isabelle W.	86048	D	1941
Georgia	33440	D	1922	Catherine F.	61155	D	1932	Sophrina	29659	I	1920
McTAMNEY				Charles Patrick	1220	M	1906	MEACHMAN			
Joseph P.	65991	D	1933	Charles Patrick	24331	D	1918	Sophronia E.	29808	D	1920
Mary Anna	56708	D	1930	George	46555	I	1927	MEAD			
McTARNAHAN				Hugh	48007	D	1927	Blanche Durant	24772	M	1918
Georgia	33440	D	1922	James	19339	D	1915	Charles Henry, Jr.	3168	D	1907
McTAVISH				John	19339	D	1915	Clara B.	51674	D	1928
Frank	73638	I	1936	John	43549	D	1926	Clara Friels	51674	D	1928
McTEAGUE				John Francis	62142	D	1932	Ellen Jayne	49523	M	1928
Peter	86406	I	1941	Katherine F.	58782	I	1931	Frederick H.	57458	D	1930
Peter	81606	I	1939	Maria	37279	D	1923	Ida M.	87160	D	1941
McTERNEY				Mary	61992	D	1932	Julia L.	81567	D	1939
Harry C.	81714	D	1939	Nellie	45106	D	1926	Lillian E.	75106	D	1937
Henry C.	81714	D	1939	Patrick H.	1752	D	1906	Louis D.	21213	I	1916
McTIERNAN				Ulrica K. E.	69827	D	1935	Louis D.	24771	D	1918
Charles	4920	D	1907	McVICKAR				Selden H.	76499	D	1937
James	88004	D	1941	Catharine	1273	D	1906	Tomacina L.	32199	I	1921
McTIGUE				John	1331	D	1906	William C.	17085	D	1914
Fannie	17407	D	1914	McVICKER				William H.	64843	D	1933
Frances C.	61707	D	1932	Alexander	14936	D	1913	MEADE			
Frances C.	62377	D	1932	Annie E.	11354	I	1911	Edward F.	58193	D	1931
McTIQUE				McWETHY				John J.	77768	D	1938
Richard A.	17513	D	1914	William E.	18634	D	1915	Nellie	48047	D	1927
McVANN				McWHINNEY				Patrick H.	4925	D	1907
J. E.	42293	D	1925	Emma C.	66781	D	1934	Patrick J.	67206	D	1934
McVANNER				McWHIRTER				MEADER			
James	64982	D	1933	Charles O.	46785	D	1927	Alexander James	71218	D	1935
McVARY				David	682	D	1906	Ann R.	3579	D	1907
Owen	68300	D	1934	Isabella	18827	D	1915	Hames C.	58151	D	1931
McVAY				McWHORTER				Joseph E.	30711	D	1920
David Harley	87791	M	1941	Francis Eulah	27441	M	1919	Zelie Duclos	25365	D	1918
McVEIGH				McWILLIAMS				Zelie Marquerite	25365	D	1918
Emilia	50242	D	1928	Anna E.	36640	D	1923	MEADIRS			
McVENN				John	23649	D	1917	Morris	44960	D	1926
Gertrude E.	33804	D	1922	John A.	63655	D	1933	MEADOR			
McVERAY				Juliie A.	53184	D	1929	John E.	28675	D	1920
Elizabeth	70009	D	1935	Katherine F.	66151	D	1934	MEADOWCROFT			
Elizabeth	70009	D	1935	Laura H.	11339	I	1911	Barbara	30888	D	1920
McVERRY				Michael	3693	D	1907	MEADOWS			
Agnes	79447	D	1938	McWILLIE				Addie L.	20656	D	1916
Joseph G.	54095	D	1929	George	21959	D	1916	Norman	60239	D	1931
Mary A.	73003	D	1936	McWITHEY				MEADS			
Thomas	13522	D	1912	Roy	69456	D	1935	Annie A.	7211	D	1909
				MEABURN				Manuel Sear	44026	D	1926
				Auguste	29850	D	1920				

NAME	NUMBER	TYPE	YEAR	NAME	NUMBER	TYPE	YEAR	NAME	NUMBER	TYPE	YEAR
MEAGER				MEANS				MECKLENBURG			
William	10663	D	1910	Samuel B.	68731	D	1935	Emma	35458	D	1922
MEAGHER				MEANWELL				MECREDY			
Alyce G.	73410	D	1936	Charles	22265	D	1917	Wiliam J.	30003	D	1920
Bridget E.	32029	D	1921	MEANY				MEDARD			
Daniel	12176	D	1911	George R.	39581	M	1924	Alphonse B.	55676	D	1930
Elizabeth M.	27848	D	1919	James	79219	D	1938	Celine	31233	D	1921
Ellen	51989	D	1929	Pete, Mrs.	89878	D	1942	George A.	31509	D	1921
Ida Helen	69231	D	1935	Stephen J.	33874	D	1922	MEDAU			
Ida May	69231	D	1935	Stephen J.	35080	D	1922	Emil C.	14750	D	1913
James F.	57974	D	1931	MEARA				John Edward	39153	M	1924
Jeremiah	2910	D	1907	Mary	77566	D	1938	May	65108	D	1933
John	1896	D	1906	MEARNS				Sumner	39153	M	1924
Joseph Francis	27726	D	1919	Frank	78641	D	1938	MEDD			
Marguerite Josephine	10033	M	1910	George S.	9022	D	1910	John Edward	83535	D	1940
Mary	74927	I	1937	James	40271	D	1924	MEDEIROSA			
Mary A.	20834	D	1916	MEARS				Antone	58684	D	1931
Mary Rose	10033	M	1910	Elizabeth	20868	D	1916	MEDEUS			
Thomas	61091	D	1932	Elizabeth	32022	M	1921	John	16875	D	1914
William J.	14701	D	1913	Georgiana	32022	M	1921	MEDICE			
William Joseph	11511	D	1911	Josephine	32022	M	1921	Lillie	18984	D	1915
MEAGLES				Mamie	74237	I	1936	MEDICH			
Edward John, Jr.	81634	D	1939	Winifred	63802	I	1933	Joe	21290	D	1916
Elizabeth	4654	D	1907	MEATH				MEDICI			
George W.	11433	D	1911	Peter J.	67121	D	1934	Graziano	25674	D	1918
Rachel Munday	76366	D	1937	MEBACH				Rosario	27770	M	1919
MEAHIN				Julia C.	85944	D	1940	MEDINA			
Neal	13413	D	1912	MEBIUS				Arthur H.	46771	I	1927
MEAKIN				Eliza	31943	D	1921	Camilo	57239	D	1930
Ellen	11545	D	1911	Freidrich	77263	D	1937	Crispin	77227	D	1937
Naomi Brunker	73798	D	1936	M. Frederic	77263	D	1937	Dionicio	76483	D	1937
MEAKINS				MECCHI				Margarita	42693	D	1925
Jean T.	77587	D	1938	Angelo	84602	M	1940	V. D.	40691	D	1925
MEALEY				Carlo	68094	D	1934	Vidal	40691	D	1925
Adelaide Savage	13250	D	1912	Dario	34138	D	1922	William H.	20912	D	1916
Annie	10325	D	1910	Francisco	39770	D	1924	MEDING			
MEALS				Milton M.	29538	M	1920	Gloria Beulah	63242	M	1932
Lea B.	72437	D	1936	Raymond H.	25514	D	1918	MEDINGER			
Lucinda	10496	D	1910	Raymond J.	29538	M	1920	Minnie	42349	I	1925
MEALY				MECHAN				MEDLER			
Joseph J.	41463	I	1925	Mary	56105	D	1930	Clarence W.	51410	D	1928
Mary	27000	D	1919	MECHERIN				MEDLEY			
MEANEY				Patrick W.	81298	D	1939	Alfred F.	42887	D	1925
Caroline L.	156	D	1906	MECKLENBERG				Martha J.	60903	D	1932
Chester L.	3965	M	1907	Emma	35458	D	1922	MEDLOCK			
Elise A.	3965	M	1907	Natalie Herzogin Zu	60286	D	1931	James Franklin	1297	M	1906
Lewis J.	14978	D	1913								

NAME	NUMBER	TYPE	YEAR	NAME	NUMBER	TYPE	YEAR	NAME	NUMBER	TYPE	YEAR
James Franklin	1406	D	1906	Patrick	37184	D	1923	**MEFFERT**			
Nellie Agnes	1297	M	1906	Patrick	83346	D	1940	Stuart V.	38945	D	1924
MEDO				Patrick J.	11947	D	1911	**MEFRET**			
Frank A.	35966	D	1923	Raymond	9182	M	1910	Xavier	9363	D	1910
MEDOVICH				Winnie	14022	D	1912	**MEGNA**			
Milo Marko	58289	D	1931	**MEEHEN**				Maria	20567	D	1916
MEDUS				Patrick	83346	D	1940	**MEHAGEN**			
Mary Perre	58601	D	1931	**MEEK**				Hannah	1863	D	1906
MEDVE				Bazel E.	19008	D	1915	**MEHEDINTEANU**			
Emma	34423	M	1922	Edward Hurst	31027	D	1921	Constantin I.	28242	D	1919
MEDVEDEFF				Emma	67644	D	1934	**MEHEGAN**			
John	44076	D	1926	Louis Calvin	73159	D	1936	Alice	75213	D	1937
MEE				Thomas Herbert	66275	D	1934	Annie E.	17107	D	1914
Ann	69431	D	1935	**MEEKER**				George	12906	D	1912
James	1109	D	1906	Dorleska Leone	61748	M	1932	Marie	25250	M	1918
John T.	86247	D	1941	James Denman	1985	D	1906	Patrick J.	25998	D	1918
Jow	88840	D	1942	Lewis E.	29530	D	1920	William W.	62157	D	1932
Nadge M.	78757	D	1938	Milo M.	78726	D	1938	**MEHERIN**			
Patrick	12370	D	1911	Ralph Waldo	41252	D	1925	Eleanor F.	38552	D	1924
MEECHAM				Victorine Maria	3976	D	1907	Genevieve A.	78114	D	1938
Albert E.	77553	D	1938	**MEEKS**				John	20876	D	1916
Andrew	80690	D	1939	Everett	4121	M	1907	Mark M.	71867	D	1936
Celia	79405	D	1938	Mary J. B.	14817	D	1913	**MEHES**			
Esther	14886	M	1913	Rowena Fischer	5823	M	1908	Anna S.	15380	D	1913
MEEDAN				**MEELEY**				**MEHIR**			
Bernice Evelyn	76801	M	1937	Mary	27000	D	1919	Peter G.	72494	D	1936
MEEGAN				**MEENAN**				**MEHL**			
Mary	53096	D	1929	Harry Edward	71667	D	1936	Emma E.	49782	D	1928
MEEHAN				Hugh	23220	D	1917	**MEHLE**			
Anita	9182	M	1910	Julia E.	17281	D	1914	Richard	21378	D	1916
Annie	43619	D	1926	Margaret	63299	D	1933	**MEHLHOP**			
Elizabeth	30678	D	1920	**MEENE**				Dietrich	83154	D	1940
George H.	3282	D	1907	Adelheid	72433	D	1936	**MEHRKENS**			
Harold I.	48412	M	1927	Henry	72432	D	1936	P., Mrs.	64277	D	1933
Henrietta	16125	D	1913	**MEENIKE**				Wilhelmina A.	64277	D	1933
James G.	60805	D	1932	John F. W.	77048	D	1937	**MEHRTEN**			
John Francis	48412	M	1927	**MEERTIEF**				J. A.	308	D	1906
Laurence J.	68152	D	1934	Abraham	65044	D	1933	**MEHRTENS**			
Leonard J.	53716	D	1929	Rosa Walter	38770	D	1924	Henry George	63878	D	1933
Margaret	18906	D	1915	**MEESE**				Herman	382	D	1906
Margaret	41310	I	1925	Thomas Palmer	82297	D	1939	Isabella	65068	D	1933
Margaret	65373	D	1933	**MEEUE**				Jacob	61917	D	1932
Margaret G.	52812	D	1929	Adelheid	72433	D	1936	**MEHRTINS**			
Mary	17634	D	1914	Henry	72432	D	1936	Dorothy	75985	D	1937
Mary	17949	D	1914	**MEEVE**				**MEHS**			
Mary	74980	D	1937	Adelheid	72433	D	1936	Hugo	10363	D	1910
Nellie Frances	23261	D	1917	Henry	72432	D	1936				

NAME	NUMBER	TYPE	YEAR	NAME	NUMBER	TYPE	YEAR	NAME	NUMBER	TYPE	YEAR
MEI				**MEIKODICES**				Wilhelm	23496	D	1917
Eleanor	29169	M	1920	George	63229	D	1932	William	23496	D	1917
Pellegrino	29169	M	1920	**MEILANDT**				**MEINZER**			
MEIBORG				John	44543	D	1926	Charles	60366	D	1931
Carl	79299	D	1938	**MEILER**				**MEIRAN**			
MEICHAELS				John	17236	D	1914	Harry	64764	D	1933
Lizzie	20350	D	1916	**MEINBERG**				**MEIRDIERCKS**			
MEIENBERG				Maurus	3966	D	1907	George	62751	D	1932
Alois Josef	21053	D	1916	William	8514	D	1909	**MEIRHOFF**			
Regina	34585	D	1922	**MEINBERGER**				Augusta	36689	D	1923
MEIER				Valentine, Jr.	84523	D	1940	**MEISEL**			
Anna	43084	D	1925	**MEINECKE**				Edith	63956	M	1933
Charlotte Chrichton	56563	D	1930	Angelita	11923	D	1911	Henry C.	60561	D	1931
Frank	65417	D	1933	Ines C.	32696	D	1921	Herman A.	18888	D	1915
Frederick Frank	11996	D	1911	William	47790	D	1927	Sophia	19179	D	1915
Friederike	70287	D	1935	**MEINERE**				**MEISNER**			
George Martin	19073	D	1915	Rudolph	57528	D	1930	Ethel	24730	M	1918
Helen	39680	M	1924	**MEINERT**				Helen	24730	M	1918
John W.	87107	D	1941	Augusta	73739	D	1936	**MEISS**			
Joseph	87097	D	1941	Hermann	6024	D	1908	Minnie E.	10024	M	1910
Louise C.	16804	D	1914	John T.	44037	D	1926	**MEISSEL**			
Louise Friederike Amalia	70287	D	1935	Teresa	75918	D	1937	Daniel Frederick	18423	D	1915
Mary	51214	D	1928	Terese	56064	D	1930	**MEISSNER**			
Minnie	56498	I	1930	**MEINHARDT**				Carl G.	50829	D	1928
Minnie	65575	D	1933	Charlotte	85321	D	1940	Caroline	27968	D	1919
William D.	66598	D	1934	Nora Lyons	47247	D	1927	Emma C.	11019	D	1911
William G.	13496	D	1912	**MEINHART**				Ethel	24730	M	1918
MEIERDIERCKS				Fannie L.	52891	D	1929	Fridrika	49161	I	1928
Ruth	77528	D	1938	**MEINHOLD**				Helen	24730	M	1918
MEIERDIERKS				Fred, Jr.	23109	M	1917	Otto R.	10387	D	1910
Annie	52906	I	1929	William	23109	M	1917	**MEISTER**			
George W., Jr.	46391	M	1927	**MEINIKE**				Hermann A.	16216	D	1913
John	58637	I	1931	John William	77048	D	1937	**MEISTERS**			
John	60179	D	1931	**MEININGER**				Gerhard	18953	D	1915
Meta E.	45656	D	1926	Louis	2734	D	1907	Paul	20532	M	1916
William Augustus	62104	D	1932	Minna	44331	D	1926	Powell	20532	M	1916
MEIGHAN				Simon L.	47893	D	1927	**MEITZNER**			
Katherine	10368	D	1910	**MEINKE**				Friedericke	61527	D	1932
Margaret	23075	D	1917	Elfrieda	85456	D	1940	**MEIXNER**			
MEIGS				John	901	D	1906	Margaret	81962	I	1939
Delia Wolf	68888	D	1935	**MEINKING**				**MEIZEL**			
F. M.	37560	D	1923	Christoph H.	17056	D	1914	Joseph	60119	D	1931
John J., Mrs.	68888	D	1935	**MEINOLD**				**MEJIA**			
Martha E.	44684	D	1926	Anton	33795	D	1922	Encarnacion	22544	D	1917
Titus B.	15938	D	1913	**MEINS**				Gertrude	71800	D	1936
MEIKEL				Johanna	48700	D	1927				
Dora	4756	D	1907								

NAME	NUMBER	TYPE	YEAR	NAME	NUMBER	TYPE	YEAR	NAME	NUMBER	TYPE	YEAR
MEL				**MELLOC**				**MELZ**			
Clara F.	80913	D	1939	Nonie E.	76263	D	1937	Fred	27170	D	1919
MELANEPHY				**MELLON**				**MEMMOTT**			
John	39774	D	1924	Annie M.	36333	D	1923	Ellen H.	80311	D	1939
MELANI				**MELLONI**				**MENA**			
Elmo B.	46972	M	1927	Giacomo	89954	D	1942	Frank	15226	D	1913
MELANITES				**MELLOR**				Manuel	15783	D	1913
George	26326	D	1919	Benjamin Joseph	72909	I	1936	Marion Manuel	15783	D	1913
MELANO				Benjamin Joseph, Jr.	77241	M	1937	**MENAGER**			
Giacomo	50741	D	1928	William	57684	D	1931	Henriette Luce LaProvost	67740	D	1934
MELBORN				**MELLOY**				**MENARA**			
Charles E.	38897	D	1924	Francis	13952	D	1912	Giuseppe	72302	D	1936
Emil	38897	D	1924	Mary	864	D	1906	**MENARD**			
MELCHER				**MELLS**				Charles E.	86299	D	1941
Freda	49447	D	1928	Joseph	929	D	1906	**MENASSES**			
Iris	18703	M	1915	**MELLUISH**				Kate	49097	D	1928
MELECHIONNE				Louisa A.	49803	D	1928	Mortitz	47206	D	1927
Rosa	27489	D	1919	**MELLYNN**				**MENCARINI**			
MELENDY				Katherine L	42177	D	1925	Alfred	21566	D	1916
Harry A.	73144	I	1936	**MELMON**				**MENCHEN**			
MELEY				Bessie	79941	D	1938	Oscar	3399	D	1907
Frank	44598	D	1926	**MELROSE**				**MENCHETTI**			
MELIA				Allan	89499	D	1942	Carlotta	58178	D	1931
Bessie D.	78259	D	1938	Margaret M.	29339	M	1920	Daniele	57549	D	1930
Bessie Elizabeth	78259	D	1938	Mildred M.	29339	M	1920	**MENCORINI**			
Michael J.	29020	D	1920	Nell	78530	D	1938	Alfred	21566	D	1916
MELIUS				Ruth E.	29339	M	1920	**MENDEL**			
Frank	89816	I	1942	**MELSKOV**				Dora	23403	D	1917
MELKONIAN				Oscar	32965	D	1921	Flora	48397	D	1927
Mugardich	43527	D	1926	**MELSON**				Mendel P.	22862	D	1917
MELL				Henry J.	89640	D	1942	**MENDELL**			
Anthony W.	68889	D	1935	**MELSTED**				Ellen Adair	39242	D	1924
MELLA				Anne	38276	D	1924	George H.	10444	D	1910
Bessie D.	78259	D	1938	**MELTON**				George Henry, Jr.	65322	D	1933
MELLAR				Stella Porter	83370	D	1940	**MENDELSEN**			
Benjamin J.	86342	I	1941	**MELTZER**				Lena	80121	D	1938
MELLER				Otto	47520	D	1927	**MENDELSOHN**			
Josef	62303	D	1932	**MELVILLE**				Aaron	13897	I	1912
Sarah	78015	D	1938	Dorothy	20179	M	1915	Felix	54405	D	1929
MELLETZ				Edward	72328	D	1936	Hattie Henrietta	55531	D	1930
Julia A.	32460	D	1921	Emelie	61600	I	1932	Max	82486	D	1939
MELLISS				Emelie	61958	D	1932	Rosa	14870	D	1913
Frances Pauline Bolton	15575	D	1913	**MELVIN**				**MENDELSON**			
MELLO				Charles F.	79031	D	1938	Annie	62040	D	1932
Anna	42506	D	1925	Henry A.	29552	D	1920	Bertha	27154	D	1919
Anthony E.	31481	D	1921	Rose Fahey	79030	D	1938	Charlotte	27155	M	1919

NAME	NUMBER	TYPE	YEAR	NAME	NUMBER	TYPE	YEAR	NAME	NUMBER	TYPE	YEAR
Clara	54806	D	1930	**MENDOZA**				Garabed	38714	I	1924
Clorine	27155	M	1919	Anna	49341	D	1928	**MENKE**			
Dorothy Z.	26813	M	1919	Anna C.	48711	I	1927	Allette J.	51590	D	1928
Esther	26469	D	1919	Benjamin	70710	D	1935	August	15963	D	1913
Hazel	10701	M	1910	Emilia	50242	D	1928	George	68660	D	1935
Julius	1747	D	1906	Gloria	81054	M	1939	Henrietta	88499	D	1941
Leon	82408	D	1939	Minnie	81054	M	1939	Tina	80034	D	1938
Louis	26373	D	1919	Porfidio	77782	D	1938	**MENNE**			
Philip R.	26813	M	1919	Thomas	81054	M	1939	Elizabeth M.	2234	D	1906
Stella	10701	M	1910	Vincent	70710	D	1935	Frieda F.	83763	D	1940
Walter	26211	D	1919	**MENEIN**				Jean Davidson	56083	D	1930
Walter J.	26813	M	1919	Marie	61638	D	1932	Lorenz	30614	D	1920
MENDELSSOHN				**MENERICH**				**MENNEMAN**			
Joseph	29306	D	1920	Frank	27882	D	1919	Hilda	28891	M	1920
MENDENHALL				**MENESINI**				**MENNIE**			
Annette	85988	I	1941	Carolina	76110	D	1937	A., Mrs.	48064	D	1927
Irene	75880	D	1937	Emilio	7171	D	1909	Alexander	63743	D	1933
Jesse V.	75275	D	1937	Guido	39989	D	1924	Nettie	48064	D	1927
Joseph L.	62075	I	1932	**MENET**				William Wallace	72630	D	1936
MENDES				Kinan	13973	D	1912	**MENNIG**			
Joao D'Abreu	26856	D	1919	**MENETREY**				William H.	66059	D	1934
Manuel F.	27814	D	1919	Charles L.	66898	D	1934	**MENNING**			
MENDESSOLLE				Christine	23822	D	1918	Maxine	81893	D	1939
Rachel	51993	D	1929	**MENGEL**				**MENNUCCI**			
Rebecca	51993	D	1929	John	1045	I	1906	Eustachio	80345	D	1939
MENDEZ				John	8799	D	1909	**MENOTTI**			
Anthony	73608	M	1936	**MENGELOPOULOS**				Napoleon	61055	D	1932
Grace	76548	M	1937	Nicholas	79011	D	1938	**MENOWN**			
Jose	63092	D	1932	**MENGES**				James	25353	D	1918
Manuel F.	27814	D	1919	Henry H.	70595	D	1935	**MENSER**			
MENDIARA				Margaret	70596	D	1935	William L.	24754	D	1918
Jose	56777	D	1930	**MENGLER**				**MENTA**			
MENDIETA				August H.	65353	D	1933	Wilhem	62235	D	1932
William	53648	D	1929	**MENHENNET**				**MENTLICK**			
MENDIGUREN				Herbert	29580	D	1920	Johan	28610	D	1920
Policarpo	87198	D	1941	**MENICHETTI**				**MENTON**			
MENDONCA				Ettore	56666	D	1930	William H.	27895	I	1919
Anna	49341	D	1928	**MENICUCCI**				**MENTZ**			
MENDONSA				Francesca	60982	M	1932	Charles H.	30227	D	1920
Anna C.	48711	I	1927	Joseph	77050	D	1937	**MENTZEL**			
Anna C.	49341	D	1928	Lillian	60982	M	1932	Clara	37510	D	1923
Manuel Paul	62603	D	1932	**MENIHAN**				Klara	37510	D	1923
MENDOSA				Margaret	47113	D	1927	**MENTZER**			
Beatrice	46831	D	1927	Patrick	15282	D	1913	Ella	56172	D	1930
MENDOUSA				**MENJIGIAN**				Harry	88570	D	1941
Manuel Paul	62603	D	1932	Charles	38714	I	1924				

NAME	NUMBER	TYPE	YEAR	NAME	NUMBER	TYPE	YEAR	NAME	NUMBER	TYPE	YEAR
MENUTIS				William	38882	D	1924	Martin V.	55743	D	1930
Frieda	63010	D	1932	MERGEN				MERLINI			
MENZEL				Christine M.	66648	D	1934	Giuseppe	44933	I	1926
Alexander	24905	D	1918	Matthew Bernard	65982	D	1933	MERLO			
Daisy	13878	D	1912	MERGENS				Andrew	59018	D	1931
William	43403	D	1926	Matthew	9241	D	1910	Carlo	22632	D	1917
William	57352	D	1930	Sarah A.	15431	D	1913	Davide	73399	D	1936
MENZIE				MERGOTTI				Louis	48066	D	1927
Robert D.	42336	D	1925	Santino	24429	D	1918	Luigi	48066	D	1927
MENZIES				MERGUIRE				Margherita	79677	D	1938
Charles F.	79844	I	1938	Elizabeth A.	27822	D	1919	Rose	43625	I	1926
Stewart	46626	D	1927	MERIGAN				MERLOTTI			
W. P. C.	76288	I	1937	Michael	17455	D	1914	Luigi	33786	D	1922
MENZIGIAN				MERILL				Maria	84025	D	1940
Charles	38714	I	1924	Eula	89879	D	1942	Mario	33169	D	1922
MENZINSKY				MERILLION				MERLOW			
Mary	82738	D	1939	Charles M.	61393	I	1932	Johanna	76248	D	1937
MEOCHI				Ralph P.	51014	D	1928	MERMET			
Anna	30463	D	1920	MERINCIK				Louis	23389	D	1917
MEON				Annie	24392	D	1918	MERMON			
Fredericke	50879	D	1928	MERION				Albert	68576	D	1934
MERALLS				Catherine	64386	D	1933	MERNIN			
Lizzie A.	6898	D	1908	MERITHEW				Gertrude C.	82517	D	1939
MERAZA				Harriet	7564	D	1909	MERO			
Angelina	89712	D	1942	Hattie D.	18691	D	1915	Florissa	33085	D	1921
MERCADIER				MERKEL				Nina	89583	D	1942
Gustave	7968	D	1909	Marie L.	78962	D	1938	MEROLA			
MERCADO				MERKELBACH				Rose	88028	D	1941
Heliodoro	84065	M	1940	William	31823	D	1921	MERONI			
Leo	84065	M	1940	MERKELSEN				Angelo	54918	D	1930
MERCER				Carl	79140	D	1938	MEROUX			
Anna E. Steinkamp	54721	M	1930	MERKER				Ruby R.	18529	D	1915
Edwin	72803	D	1936	Anna Francis	12707	D	1911	MEROZ			
Henry W.	35869	D	1923	MERKI				Louis	41203	D	1925
Martha J.	45817	D	1926	Louise Emilie	65023	D	1933	MERRALLS			
MERCHANT				MERKLE				William A.	17850	D	1914
Anna	52279	D	1929	Charles A.	77700	D	1938	MERRELL			
MEREDITH				Michael	20694	D	1916	Charles G.	69244	D	1935
Alfred	36711	D	1923	MERKLEY				Harriett	68913	D	1935
Eilce	2680	M	1907	Dorothy Estella	83388	D	1940	Harry D.	69220	D	1935
J. M.	48496	D	1927	MERLE				Hattie P.	68913	D	1935
Lewis E.	137	D	1906	Catherine V.	42303	D	1925	Wilson R.	57622	D	1931
Mary Jane	417	D	1906	Henri Eugene	84169	D	1940	MERRIAM			
Milton	2680	M	1907	Leopold V.	41887	D	1925	Belle	70860	D	1935
Myrle Martin	54369	D	1929	Leopold V.	41887	D	1925	MERRICK			
Sherwood E.	70611	I	1935	Marguerite H.	821	D	1906	James Clarence	59200	D	1931

NAME	NUMBER	TYPE	YEAR	NAME	NUMBER	TYPE	YEAR	NAME	NUMBER	TYPE	YEAR
Lucille	79998	I	1938	J. C.	24483	D	1918	Helen H.	85909	D	1940
Lucille	85714	D	1940	Jack	24483	D	1918	**MERX**			
Maud M.	64141	D	1933	Leonia	50034	D	1928	Emil O. H.	9061	D	1910
Robert W.	64184	D	1933	William E.	53771	D	1929	**MERZ**			
MERRIFIELD				**MERRIWEATHER**				Adolf	77334	D	1937
Adelia	89559	D	1942	Charlotte	26027	D	1918	Antonia	83255	D	1940
Sarah E.	24103	D	1918	**MERRY**				Antonio	83255	D	1940
MERRILL				Edwin F.	73689	D	1936	Clara Anna	45066	D	1926
Alice M.	8613	M	1909	William Lawrence	13073	D	1912	Hannah	80383	D	1939
Bridget	14207	D	1912	**MERRYFIELD**				Ida	28006	D	1919
Charles	10018	D	1910	Elena	18452	D	1915	John	23267	D	1917
Edward L.	10807	D	1910	**MERSEREAU**				Lena	30030	D	1920
Elizabeth	2879	I	1907	Frederick Esdras	81066	D	1939	Marie	10677	D	1910
Emma Marian	88241	I	1941	Ross	37513	D	1923	**MERZBACH**			
Eula	89879	D	1942	**MERSFELDER**				Felix H.	20508	D	1916
Frank	2933	M	1907	Charles	28017	D	1919	Silvius H.	2913	D	1907
Frank	2934	D	1907	**MERSING**				Stella	71406	D	1936
Frank C.	15970	D	1913	George J.	25946	D	1918	**MERZLIAK**			
Frank Henry	3062	D	1907	**MERSKI**				James	11504	D	1911
George C.	25137	D	1918	Irvin Lee	70655	M	1935	**MESA**			
George P.	8613	M	1909	**MERSLICH**				Emma	58587	D	1931
George W.	1673	D	1906	Ann	26411	D	1919	**MESAITICH**			
Hugh Anthony	88852	M	1942	**MERTENS**				John	74442	D	1937
Jacqueline	88721	M	1941	Adelheid	44127	D	1926	**MESCAL**			
James W.	14038	D	1912	Alida	44127	D	1926	Mary	63042	D	1932
John S.	7479	D	1909	Ferdinand	22706	D	1917	**MESCHKE**			
Margaret	65772	D	1933	**MERTES**				Charles	47944	D	1927
Mary Elizabeth	43502	D	1926	Peter F.	81425	D	1939	Otto R.	17395	D	1914
Oliver S.	71808	D	1936	**MERTON**				**MESENBURG**			
Raymond	2933	M	1907	Josephine G.	51346	D	1928	Augusta	69222	D	1935
Rose M.	8613	M	1909	Lewis B.	24750	D	1918	**MESEREAU**			
Salome	15605	D	1913	**MERTZ**				Naomi	45605	D	1926
MERRIMAN				Charlotte	77614	D	1938	**MESERVE**			
Edward	46846	D	1927	John J.	48980	D	1928	Clara E.	7110	D	1909
Ellen	66500	D	1934	**MERVER**				John S.	8584	D	1909
Eward	46846	D	1927	Anton	44162	D	1926	**MESETH**			
Francis	18080	I	1914	**MERVIN**				Emil S.	47671	D	1927
Francis	18812	D	1915	Helen Martha	51689	D	1928	Lillian A.	43813	I	1926
Helene	66500	D	1934	**MERVY**				Lillian O.	49737	I	1928
Rose Anne	23010	D	1917	Emil Claud	69094	D	1935	Samuel	47671	D	1927
MERRITT				Emile Didier	26283	M	1919	**MESIC**			
Barbara	27765	M	1919	Emile Didier	42686	M	1925	John	30310	I	1920
Carl	21277	D	1916	Hattie Mae	81469	D	1939	**MESICK**			
Catherine	76187	D	1937	Medora Vaux	39547	D	1924	Mary A.	6189	D	1908
Emma L.	79688	D	1938	**MERWIN**				Richard S.	9267	D	1910
George W.	49583	D	1928	Daniel Shelby	85910	D	1940				
Gertrude Johnson	88648	D	1941								
Grace	86039	D	1941								

Key: D = death; M = minor; I = incompetent

NAME	NUMBER	TYPE	YEAR	NAME	NUMBER	TYPE	YEAR	NAME	NUMBER	TYPE	YEAR
MESMER				**METCALF**				**METYER**			
A. J.	42691	D	1925	Ardelia S.	18109	D	1914	Albert	944	D	1906
MESQUITA				Edward	30493	D	1920	**METZ**			
Dorothy	41259	I	1925	Francis	17374	D	1914	Frank, Jr.	24720	D	1918
MESSARA				Fred Clark	75305	D	1937	Louis	43443	D	1926
Antonio	26786	D	1919	George Earnest	63671	D	1933	**METZENER**			
MESSER				James J.	67274	D	1934	Katharina	24305	D	1918
Conrad	18454	D	1915	Joseph	19083	I	1915	**METZEROTT**			
Ella Bodwell	19666	D	1915	Margaret C.	82918	D	1939	G.	47067	D	1927
Nathaniel T.	3322	D	1907	Mary	18894	I	1915	W. C.	47067	D	1927
Nathaniel Thayer, Jr.	45256	M	1926	Michael	18896	I	1915	William G.	47067	D	1927
MESSERSMITH				Michael	22443	D	1917	**METZGER**			
Maria L.	58277	D	1931	Teresa	18895	I	1915	Agnes	6122	D	1908
MESSERVE				William Edmund	61866	D	1932	Frederick	10613	M	1910
Abraham	3866	D	1907	**METCALFE**				Henry	48175	D	1927
MESSICK				Eva	75416	D	1937	Katharine	68086	D	1934
Andrain	45369	M	1926	John	15257	D	1913	Louis	43377	D	1926
Dee J.	45369	M	1926	Richard G.	65439	D	1933	Morris	4368	D	1907
Mary A.	6189	D	1908	**METHENY**				Rebecca	17718	D	1914
MESSINA				Frank	82380	D	1939	Samuel	17719	M	1914
Antonio	60115	D	1931	**METHNER**				William	10613	M	1910
Frances	71228	D	1935	George	86909	D	1941	**METZLER**			
Paul	76014	D	1937	**METIUS**				Gertrude	11158	D	1911
MESSINEO				Carl A.	38260	D	1924	**METZNER**			
Carmel	42263	M	1925	**METIVIER**				Annie A.	78121	D	1938
MESSINGER				Leonide	9585	D	1910	Catherine	24718	D	1918
Walter	48088	D	1927	**METRAL**				Charles F.	59010	D	1931
MESSNER				Alesandre	18816	D	1915	Jacob C.	53676	D	1929
Alfred J.	40602	D	1924	**METSON**				John	34341	D	1922
George	33456	D	1922	Elizabeth	29689	D	1920	Josephine A.	41698	D	1925
MESTON				J. K., Mrs.	29689	D	1920	**MEUCCI**			
Robert	27151	D	1919	Josephine K.	11827	D	1911	Modesto	48933	D	1928
MESTRE				**METTE**				**MEUSDORFFER**			
Alfred	46800	I	1927	Sybil D.	39879	I	1924	Emilie R.	77421	D	1938
Alfred Charles Gerald	69097	D	1935	**METTEN**				**MEUSER**			
Alfred G.	69097	D	1935	Emma	18817	D	1915	Alice L.	50823	D	1928
MESZAROS				**METTENET**				Laura	66642	D	1934
Alexander	63741	D	1933	Lucien	50941	I	1928	William L.	24754	D	1918
Juliana	27072	D	1919	**METTHEZ**				**MEUSSDORFELT**			
METASTAZIO				Gustave	24312	D	1918	Johanna L.	7471	D	1909
Emilio	2812	D	1907	**METTLER**				**MEUSSDORFFER**			
Rosie	908	D	1906	Albert	39039	D	1924	Anna Caroline	47449	D	1927
Stephen	11103	D	1911	**METTMANN**				Anna J.	44762	D	1926
METCAFFE				Francis H.	40051	I	1924	Anna L.	8747	I	1909
Michael	22443	D	1917	Francis H.	42848	D	1925	Betty Caroline	55773	M	1930
				Wilhelmina E.	67352	D	1934	Charles G.	14345	D	1912
								Fred W.	53464	D	1929

NAME	NUMBER	TYPE	YEAR	NAME	NUMBER	TYPE	YEAR	NAME	NUMBER	TYPE	YEAR
George W.	32067	D	1921	Bernhard	12127	D	1911	Friedrich	77721	D	1938
John Charles	36592	D	1923	Betsy	39020	D	1924	Fritz	25071	D	1918
MEXBAUER				Caroline L.	72100	M	1936	Fritz	37111	D	1923
Anna	54898	D	1930	Carrie A.	60856	D	1932	Genevieve	12919	D	1912
MEXIA				Catheine	74355	D	1937	Genevieve	49040	D	1928
J. Romulo	3649	D	1907	Catherina S.	17121	D	1914	George	45839	D	1926
Ynes E. J.	78983	D	1938	Cauffman H.	311	D	1906	George Henry Christian	51747	D	1929
MEYBERG				Charles	22202	D	1917	Georgia Marie	27016	M	1919
Leo J.	48059	D	1927	Charles	48725	M	1927	Gerda	86937	M	1941
MEYENBORG				Charles F.	65051	D	1933	Gerhard	9358	D	1910
August Arnold Molitze	14698	D	1913	Christian B. G.	27778	D	1919	Gesiene	70733	D	1935
MEYER				Christopher	88320	D	1941	Gloria	48725	M	1927
Abraham	52052	D	1929	Clara G.	49082	D	1928	Gustave A.	37544	D	1923
Adelaide K.	24707	M	1918	Clara Julina	23824	D	1918	H. L. E.	15681	D	1913
Adelheid	24604	D	1918	Clara Pearl	64111	D	1933	Harriet	46182	D	1927
Adolph	29398	D	1920	Cord	83443	D	1940	Harriet E.	85352	D	1940
Agnes	32949	D	1921	Daniel	12210	D	1911	Harry	15419	M	1913
Albert	6851	D	1908	Degener	75904	D	1937	Harry S.	52217	D	1929
Albert	8388	D	1909	Diedrich	8488	D	1909	Harry W.	41493	I	1925
Albert	11382	D	1911	Diedrich	30132	D	1920	Harry W.	66036	D	1934
Albert	58377	D	1931	Dorothea	48725	M	1927	Heinrich C. E.	18112	D	1914
Albert	40696	D	1925	Duderich	13746	D	1912	Helen	22207	D	1917
Albert G.	77594	D	1938	Edna E.	74691	D	1937	Henry	21603	D	1916
Aldean A.	45515	D	1926	Eduard	75958	D	1937	Henry	32896	D	1921
Aleck M.	57625	D	1931	Edwin L.	69319	D	1935	Henry	46092	D	1926
Alfred	49845	D	1928	Eldred L.	3208	M	1907	Henry	55804	D	1930
Aline S.	72101	M	1936	Elise	36826	D	1923	Henry G.	19763	I	1915
Andrew H.	30922	D	1921	Emanuel	12121	D	1911	Henry G.	33306	I	1922
Anna	48822	D	1927	Emil	52594	D	1929	Henry G.	33428	D	1922
Anna	77660	I	1938	Emilie	6850	D	1908	Henry H. L.	50750	D	1928
Anna	85341	D	1940	Erick F.	43954	D	1926	Henry J.	24707	M	1918
Anna G.	83561	D	1940	Erna Semmel	88194	D	1941	Herman	66037	D	1934
anna Maria	54183	D	1929	Ernest	76436	D	1937	Herman M. D.	268	D	1906
Annie	24604	D	1918	Ernest August	52647	D	1929	Herman N.	21956	D	1916
Annie M. J.	14790	D	1913	Ernest F.	72429	D	1936	Hermann Friedrich	75801	D	1937
Anton	85604	D	1940	Esther	9630	M	1910	Hinrich Jacob	5525	D	1908
Aron	17969	D	1914	Fanny	27403	D	1919	Hugo	127	D	1906
August	47007	D	1927	Ferdinand	26536	D	1919	Hulda	17354	D	1914
August	71950	D	1936	Flora	7730	D	1909	Ida	52743	D	1929
August	62309	D	1932	Florence I.	52530	D	1929	Ida	75904	D	1937
August W.	43378	D	1926	Fred	25339	D	1918	Isabelle	89863	D	1942
Augusta	48600	D	1927	Fred	37111	D	1923	Isadore	79510	D	1938
Auguste	51550	D	1928	Fred William	31201	D	1921	J. H. W. F.	3126	D	1907
Augustine Elisa	73951	D	1936	Freda M.	37812	D	1923	Jacob	36617	D	1923
Barthold	86443	D	1941	Frederick	41078	D	1925	Jennie C. D.	43645	D	1926
Basil	33286	M	1922	Frederick Adolph	31899	M	1921	Jerome	21732	D	1916
Benno	26311	D	1919	Frederick Conrad George	63281	D	1933	Jessie H.	34577	D	1922
Bernadina Frenzel	25162	D	1918	Frederick H.	85790	D	1940	Johan Fredrick Winther	28220	D	1919
				Fredrick	28220	D	1919	Johan J. F.	41078	D	1925

NAME	NUMBER	TYPE	YEAR	NAME	NUMBER	TYPE	YEAR	NAME	NUMBER	TYPE	YEAR
John	12129	D	1911	Robert Lee	32892	I	1921	Harry	88807	D	1941
John	78175	D	1938	Runhardt Lossius	29060	D	1920	Henry John	40627	D	1924
John Henry	74718	D	1937	Samuel	19978	D	1915	Henry W.	21615	D	1916
John Herman	66037	D	1934	Samuel	40900	D	1925	Herman	48345	D	1927
Joseph J.	43203	D	1925	Sara	84040	D	1940	Herman Charles	67716	D	1934
Julia	4266	M	1907	Sarah	20269	D	1916	Honora	44240	I	1926
Julius	18198	D	1914	Sarah A.	53788	D	1929	Honora	54510	D	1929
Julius	23303	D	1917	Sarah T.	25348	D	1918	J.	6595	D	1908
Katherine	58011	D	1931	Selda	87707	D	1941	Jacob	71480	D	1936
L. C.	25157	D	1918	Selly	12588	D	1911	John	39083	I	1924
Lea	6034	I	1908	Sol F.	88344	D	1941	John	56243	D	1930
Leah	10343	D	1910	Sophie	41586	D	1925	Joseph	43203	D	1925
Lena F.	25162	D	1918	Stella	87941	D	1941	Julius	41416	D	1925
Lena M.	88364	D	1941	Theophile	12714	I	1911	Lillian Kallstrom	89855	D	1942
Leonard Frederick	18928	M	1915	Thomas	72019	D	1936	Malcolm P.	37549	I	1923
Leopold C.	956	D	1906	Thomas H.	38766	M	1924	Malcolm P.	64443	D	1933
Louis	40818	D	1925	Tillie	51547	D	1928	Marie M.	60448	D	1931
Louis	50113	D	1928	Wanda F.	25672	D	1918	Mary	64907	I	1933
Louis Adolph Anton	84445	D	1940	William	45754	D	1926	Mary	86236	D	1941
Louise	14369	D	1912	William	47983	D	1927	Mary Florence	74184	D	1936
Louise G.	89538	D	1942	William	52675	D	1929	May	78406	I	1938
Lucretia	38840	I	1924	William D.	9954	D	1910	Mollie Manning	79095	D	1938
Marcus C.	19124	D	1915	William F.	38628	D	1924	Pearl	32231	D	1921
Marie	22305	D	1917	William Frederick	1135	M	1906	Recha	47995	D	1927
Marie	77116	D	1937	William W.	41979	M	1925	Roma Lenore	44203	M	1926
Marie F.	84607	D	1940	William W.	41979	M	1925	Sarah Nancy	82008	D	1939
Marie Katharine	50728	D	1928	**MEYERFELD**				Victoria	45794	D	1926
Marjorie Katherine	30911	M	1920	Morris, Jr.	69981	D	1935	W.	24115	D	1918
Marjorie Leila	55530	M	1930	Moses	9978	D	1910	William	35383	D	1922
Martin	82000	D	1939	Sarah	72057	D	1936	William	36417	D	1923
Martin A.	37013	D	1923	**MEYERHOF**				William	52675	D	1929
Martin Adolph	31899	M	1921	Paul Max	85458	D	1940	William	72246	D	1936
Mary Elizabeth	89625	D	1942	**MEYERS**				William	88303	D	1941
Mary J.	51507	D	1928	Arthur Harry	84464	D	1940	William F.	52351	D	1929
Mary Pauline	87947	M	1941	Benjamin B.	76093	D	1937	William Stephen	78141	D	1938
Mathilda S.	7551	D	1909	Catherine	22736	D	1917	William Stephen, Jr.	78615	M	1938
Matilda M.	89166	D	1942	Catherine	27348	D	1919	**MEYERSON**			
Matthias Deidrich	23327	D	1917	Celestine	46309	D	1927	Millie	55928	D	1930
Mildred A.	81042	D	1939	Clara Smith	49082	D	1928	**MEYERSTEIN**			
Minnie	80100	D	1938	Dennis	64050	D	1933	Caesar Victor	33731	D	1922
Norbert	49170	D	1928	Elizabeth	11086	D	1911	Clara LaRue	22425	M	1917
Otto C. W.	77031	D	1937	Esther	20034	D	1915	Jane I.	60966	D	1932
Pauline	34339	D	1922	Eugene W.	35705	D	1923	Joseph	21972	D	1916
Philip C.	4422	D	1907	Florence	74184	D	1936	Lewis	2513	D	1906
Philip C., Jr.	6646	M	1908	Frances Y.	44202	D	1926	Sarah	76896	D	1937
Rachel	56278	D	1930	Frederick V.	19047	D	1915	**MEYLICH**			
Raymond	38334	I	1924	Harry	32131	D	1921	Helene	68561	D	1934
Reinhardt	29060	D	1920	Harry	32340	D	1921				
Robert Lee	3073	I	1907								

NAME	NUMBER	TYPE	YEAR
MEYLOU			
Jean	17810	D	1914
MEYN			
Charles	12232	M	1911
Edith C.	73768	D	1936
Harry P.	18227	D	1914
Ida	12232	M	1911
Sadie	12232	M	1911
William Matthias	11943	D	1911
MEYRAN			
Catherine Josephine	32088	D	1921
MEYSE			
Henrietta	33600	D	1922
Maurice	33865	D	1922
MEZA			
Ralph	38010	D	1923
MEZES			
Juliet Johnson	2690	D	1907
MEZQUIDA			
Mateo M.	49481	D	1928
MEZZUCCO			
Felice	16777	D	1914
MEZZUCO			
Felice	16777	D	1914
MHYRE			
Hilda	12140	M	1911
Irene	12140	M	1911
Selma	12140	M	1911
MI			
Mark	16792	D	1914
MIALACQ			
Louis	25793	D	1918
MIALOCQ			
Alfred	34509	M	1922
Andre	80700	D	1939
Jean	23022	D	1917
Urbain	34509	M	1922
MIBACH			
Joseph H.	74158	D	1936
Mathias	12776	D	1911
MICALIZZI			
Francesco	47786	D	1927
MICELI			
Florine Angelina	72871	M	1936
MICHAEL			
Bertha	43374	D	1926

NAME	NUMBER	TYPE	YEAR
Dave	68863	D	1935
David	17943	D	1914
Dora G.	4756	D	1907
Elizabeth	43374	D	1926
Elizabeth	51609	D	1928
Jacob W.	28205	D	1919
James	42619	D	1925
James	67051	M	1934
Janet	67051	M	1934
Joseph	13418	D	1912
M. F.	57993	D	1931
Maria	20410	D	1916
Marie	78975	D	1938
Marie Loomis	78975	D	1938
Peter	34922	D	1922
Philip	34151	D	1922
Rebecca	10697	I	1910
Robert	1197	M	1906
Sarah	7944	D	1909
Solomon	60637	D	1932
MICHAELIAN			
John	47365	D	1927
MICHAELIS			
Albert Frederick	47217	D	1927
Helena	25984	D	1918
MICHAELS			
Benjamin	20906	D	1916
Edward	51717	D	1928
Gustave	50898	M	1928
Lizzie	20350	D	1916
Louis J.	66185	D	1934
Louis L.	55901	D	1930
Maurice	23226	D	1917
Morris	23226	D	1917
Pauline	48843	D	1927
Ralph A.	61684	D	1932
Sarah	79992	D	1938
Solomon	60637	D	1932
MICHAELSON			
Albert Frederick	79628	D	1938
Ella R.	7317	D	1909
MICHALEK			
Margaret Henrietta	50149	D	1928
MICHALITSCHKE			
Anton	19971	D	1915
Curt	30702	M	1920
Joseph	27211	D	1919
Walter	30702	M	1920

NAME	NUMBER	TYPE	YEAR
MICHALIZZI			
Frank	47786	D	1927
MICHAU			
Louis	7685	D	1909
Marguarite	37463	D	1923
MICHAUD			
Emma	21303	D	1916
Julie	54010	I	1929
Louis	7685	D	1909
MICHAUX			
John Randolph	12831	D	1912
MICHEELSEN			
Fritz	32372	D	1921
MICHEIM			
Karl	28920	D	1920
MICHEL			
Adele	5963	M	1908
Albert F.	1122	M	1906
August	1121	M	1906
Camilla	5963	M	1908
Camilla	83741	D	1940
Charles	27602	D	1919
Conrad	21664	D	1916
Florence B.	78885	D	1938
Frances	84228	D	1940
Hennie	5963	M	1908
John B.	42149	D	1925
Josaphine	5963	M	1908
Josephine	81645	D	1939
Louis D.	68072	D	1934
Margaretha	32636	D	1921
Peter	34922	D	1922
MICHELANGELO			
Puma	72031	D	1936
MICHELENA			
Fernando	31345	D	1921
MICHELETTI			
Albert J.	54536	D	1929
Amerigo	16304	D	1913
Biagio	78318	D	1938
Bridget B.	6533	D	1908
Clara	71499	I	1936
Enrico	35017	D	1922
Liberata	32669	D	1921
Maria	68864	D	1935
Mariuccia	68864	D	1935
Pietro	6995	D	1908

Key: D = death; M = minor; I = incompetent

NAME	NUMBER	TYPE	YEAR
Pietro	15864	D	1913
Umberto J.	54536	D	1929
MICHELFELDER			
W. H.	52256	D	1929
MICHELI			
Cecilia	6884	M	1908
Emilio	67236	D	1934
Joe	6884	M	1908
Mary De	89498	D	1942
Peter	6884	M	1908
Theresa L.	60737	D	1932
MICHELL			
Annie	20284	D	1916
MICHELLETTI			
Michele	47619	D	1927
MICHELOTTI			
Guiseppe	35783	D	1923
MICHELS			
Augusta	77119	D	1937
Carrie	79234	D	1938
Leopold	30825	D	1920
MICHELSEN			
Grace	44883	D	1926
Mary	31995	I	1921
Olive C.	49168	D	1928
Oswald Julius Brunu	45155	D	1926
William	17882	D	1914
MICHELSON			
Abraham	34810	D	1922
Elizabeth	79489	D	1938
Helen A.	25319	M	1918
John J.	39787	D	1924
John J. H.	22905	D	1917
Josephine	63464	D	1933
Julie A.	63438	D	1933
Lloyd H.	25319	M	1918
Martha A.	85749	D	1940
Pauline	51787	D	1929
William Cole	67948	M	1934
William F.	35643	D	1923
MICHELSSEN			
Edward Sophus	79563	D	1938
MICHESEN			
Benjamin P.	80087	D	1938
MICHLER			
Eleanor E.	62247	D	1932
Eleonore E.	62247	D	1932

NAME	NUMBER	TYPE	YEAR
MICIONE			
Pasquale D.	78011	I	1938
Pasquale D.	78995	D	1938
MICKE			
Joseph B.	24576	D	1918
MICKELSEN			
Irma	66979	M	1934
Sigurd	41689	I	1925
Sigurd	44824	I	1926
MICKELSON			
Magnus Strand	60378	D	1931
Petronella	15436	D	1913
Sigurd	64869	D	1933
MICKELWAIT			
Gladys Butler	50675	D	1928
MICKEY			
Joseph B.	24576	D	1918
Roy Joseph	89873	D	1942
MICKLE			
Kathryn Clark	87244	D	1941
MICKLEY			
Meta Katharina	24413	D	1918
MICOMO			
Umberto	49053	D	1928
MICONA			
Umberto	49053	D	1928
MICONO			
Umberto	49053	D	1928
MICROS			
Vasilios Const.	11758	D	1911
MIDDAUGH			
Charlotte E.	79421	D	1938
MIDDLEKAUFF			
Frank E.	64484	D	1933
MIDDLEMAS			
Stuart	45199	D	1926
MIDDLEMISS			
Anna M.	56091	D	1930
Annette	54444	M	1929
Annette	56091	D	1930
Cliff, Mrs.	56091	D	1930
Clifford Barnett	59393	I	1931
MIDDLETON			
Annie C	28712	D	1920
Frank L.	40860	D	1925
George Westley	75022	D	1937

NAME	NUMBER	TYPE	YEAR
Geroge W., III	57440	M	1930
Harriet Baldwin	55624	D	1930
James R.	52861	D	1929
Joseph H.	6878	D	1908
Maude Emma	52449	I	1929
Sarah M.	14843	D	1913
MIDTBO			
Ernest	82093	D	1939
MIEBACH			
Walter Carl	62482	M	1932
MIELENZ			
Edward Rudolph	62708	D	1932
MIELICH			
De Los Chester	89636	M	1942
MIELKE			
Charles	71084	D	1935
MIER			
Frederick Siegfred	36310	D	1923
Grace	40676	M	1924
Ralph N.	84108	D	1940
Sarah	33706	D	1922
Siegfred	36310	D	1923
MIERS			
Florence E.	13556	I	1912
Florence E.	16066	D	1913
MIERSON			
Bernard	85776	D	1940
Carol Jane	85582	M	1940
Max	78123	D	1938
Sally Anne	85582	M	1940
Soloman Henry	73253	D	1936
MIESNER			
John	54494	D	1929
MIETZSCH			
Ernest	23719	I	1917
Ernst	25194	D	1918
MIFSUD			
Cristina	89936	D	1942
Frank	76415	D	1937
MIGGINS			
Thomas	20550	D	1916
MIGHELL			
William E.	23308	D	1917
MIGHELS			
Ella S. Simmins	68638	D	1935
Ella Sterling	68638	D	1935

NAME	NUMBER	TYPE	YEAR
MIGLIAOACCA			
Joseph A.	76642	D	1937
MIGLIAVACCA			
Alice I.	70490	D	1935
Evelyn Louise	70507	D	1935
Joseph A.	76642	D	1937
MIGLIO			
John B.	52761	D	1929
MIGNACCO			
Attillio	38472	D	1924
Ernest	73799	D	1936
Marco	47558	D	1927
MIGNAULT			
Octave	76181	D	1937
Walter	79537	M	1938
Yvonne Alice	70767	D	1935
MIGNDA			
Henry John	73067	D	1936
MIGUELAJANREGUY			
Miguel	677	I	1906
MIGUELAJAUREGUY			
Maria	2678	D	1907
MIGUELIS			
Javier Perez	27741	D	1919
MIGUET			
Francois	8118	D	1909
MIHAILOVITS			
Charles	54669	D	1930
MIHALEK			
Anna	71722	D	1936
George	78497	M	1938
Matus	67911	D	1934
Mike	67911	D	1934
MIHAN			
Frank	15194	D	1913
Kate M.	50078	D	1928
Patrick F.	63576	D	1933
MIHOCEVICH			
Duro	49388	D	1928
George	49388	D	1928
Guro	49388	D	1928
MIHR			
Pauline	46215	D	1927
MIJUAN			
Wong	61785	D	1932

NAME	NUMBER	TYPE	YEAR
MIKAMI			
Sakae	51831	D	1929
MIKEALIAN			
Kukor	46548	D	1927
MIKESELL			
Charles E.	74791	D	1937
MIKKELSEN			
Christen Peter	79962	D	1938
Ida Alexandria	76091	D	1937
Theo. M.	32261	D	1921
MIKKLESON			
Robert	19177	D	1915
MIKLAU			
Anton	79583	D	1938
MIKOL			
Martin	33318	D	1922
MIKOLAJCZYK			
Martin	33318	D	1922
MIKOLAPTIS			
Jan	11836	D	1911
MILAN			
Catherine	29247	D	1920
Fruto Estonactoc	89527	D	1942
MILANESIO			
Angiolena	72425	D	1936
Virgilio	44084	D	1926
MILANI			
Angelina	83496	D	1940
Antionetta	44008	D	1926
Domenico	54697	D	1930
Fioravante	2512	D	1906
Giuseppe	13574	D	1912
Giuseppe	83497	D	1940
Rinaldo	50586	D	1928
Rita	63663	D	1933
MILATOVICH			
Antonio	27959	D	1919
Joseph	13885	D	1912
MILBURN			
Ernest W.	73544	D	1936
Ethelbert	28318	D	1919
MILCOVICH			
John	23227	D	1917
MILES			
Bernard	6404	D	1908
Charles H.	57571	D	1931

NAME	NUMBER	TYPE	YEAR
Emma N.	84575	D	1940
Evan	5918	D	1908
George Herbert	32330	D	1921
James	54344	D	1929
Joseph T.	6725	D	1908
Julia	20766	I	1916
Julia	20903	D	1916
Katherine S.	42386	D	1925
Lillian H.	58252	D	1931
Louis	18379	D	1915
Margaret A.	60628	D	1932
Marie Louise	22461	D	1917
Martha Alice	5964	I	1908
Martha Alice	67018	D	1934
Rebecca O.	13305	D	1912
Sara Ann	13429	D	1912
Susan Clementine	59313	D	1931
Thomas E.	48664	D	1927
William	4872	D	1907
MILETICH			
Steve	85384	D	1940
Styepo	85384	D	1940
MILETIN			
Stephan	46269	D	1927
MILEY			
Annette D.	11199	I	1911
Annette Dorothea	73786	I	1936
Annette Dorothea	74728	D	1937
Mathilde Ursula	752	D	1906
MILHAU			
Alix	27505	D	1919
MILHOLLAND			
James C.	78913	D	1938
MILHOLOVICH			
Vincent	72103	D	1936
MILIANESIO			
Angelina	72425	D	1936
MILIAS			
Mary	83351	D	1940
MILICH			
Nick	71176	D	1935
MILINOVICH			
Mitar	29721	D	1920
MILISICH			
Stephen	65870	D	1933
MILKOP			
Minna	67461	D	1934

NAME	NUMBER	TYPE	YEAR	NAME	NUMBER	TYPE	YEAR	NAME	NUMBER	TYPE	YEAR
MILLAN				Annie C.	558	D	1906	Elise Josephine	50050	M	1928
David C.	36778	D	1923	Annie May	67189	D	1934	Eliza G.	9857	D	1910
Maria DelCarmen	33947	M	1922	Arline Patricia	71442	M	1936	Elizabeth Barton	85696	D	1940
MILLANE				August	37059	D	1923	Elizabeth Elsie	30439	M	1920
Henry T.	63626	D	1933	Augusta	65699	D	1933	Elizabeth J.	37430	D	1923
MILLAR				B. F.	49002	D	1928	Elizabeth L.	24580	D	1918
Clayton B.	85199	D	1940	Barbara D.	12254	M	1911	Ellis M.	65291	D	1933
David	24012	D	1918	Barbara Jean	67510	M	1934	Elma	72372	D	1936
Hugh Blyth	18867	D	1915	Bernard	6903	D	1908	Emil	13887	I	1912
James B. F.	40383	D	1924	Bertha Rohrs	20432	D	1916	Emil H.	75287	D	1937
Mary A.	53859	D	1929	Bettijean Dolores	71442	M	1936	Emily	81311	D	1939
Robert F.	77338	D	1937	Bridget Elizabeth	43438	D	1926	Emma	70076	D	1935
Thomas	39429	D	1924	Carl	10912	D	1910	Emma C.	66271	D	1934
MILLARD				Caroline	50073	I	1928	Emma Floyd	19880	M	1915
Caroline A.	37962	D	1923	Catharina	24608	D	1918	Emma G.	73740	D	1936
Charlotte Jane	26722	D	1919	Catherine	66332	D	1934	Ernst	45315	D	1926
Edward Brewer	62451	D	1932	Charles	18921	D	1915	Ethel	12704	M	1911
Jack	82487	D	1939	Charles	23636	D	1917	Etta Butler	62160	D	1932
Jean	20320	I	1916	Charles A.	48128	D	1927	Eunice C.	2164	M	1906
John	20320	I	1916	Charles B.	78024	D	1938	Ewald Frederick	25898	D	1918
Joseph Henry	43177	D	1925	Charles E.	39753	I	1924	Ewald Frederick	27398	D	1919
MILLBERRY				Charles F.	31580	D	1921	Ferdinand	44739	D	1926
Guy S., Mrs.	67216	D	1934	Charles G.	6244	D	1908	Flora McDonald	78293	D	1938
Helen E.	67216	D	1934	Charles Henry	67845	M	1934	Framcis M.	30929	D	1921
MILLEGAN				Charles Horatio	55859	D	1930	Frances	12704	M	1911
Charles W.	65744	D	1933	Charles L.	30807	D	1920	Francis W.	62895	D	1932
MILLER				Charlotte L.	82820	D	1939	Frank	34356	D	1922
Aaron	79587	D	1938	Christ	38147	D	1924	Frank A.	58831	D	1931
Adelaide	41953	D	1925	Christina	15578	M	1913	Frank H.	29901	D	1920
Adelaide	41953	D	1925	Christopher C.	89830	D	1942	Frank T.	5651	D	1908
Adele J.	76916	D	1937	Clara	79161	I	1938	Frederick C. H.	44287	D	1926
Adeline H.	49919	D	1928	Cleo G. J.	30024	D	1920	Frederick H. C.	70909	D	1935
Adolph	62432	D	1932	Clyde H.	63996	D	1933	Frederick P.	70751	D	1935
Agnes L.	42067	D	1925	Clyde M.	68968	D	1935	George	2450	D	1906
Alexander Charles	57448	D	1930	Cyrus Gray	37286	M	1923	George	41855	I	1925
Alexander J.	12938	D	1912	Daniel	88050	D	1941	George	41855	I	1925
Alice	49256	I	1928	David	71769	D	1936	George	76019	D	1937
Alice E.	61761	D	1932	Delia	77219	D	1937	George A.	36385	D	1923
Alice Teresa	17007	D	1914	Dolores	71718	M	1936	George A.	56608	D	1930
Alma	28414	D	1919	Donald	84976	M	1940	George B.	12040	M	1911
Alva Scott	41149	D	1925	Dwight L.	38339	I	1924	George E.	60860	D	1932
Andrew	47035	I	1927	Ed	37817	D	1923	George F.	78616	D	1938
Andrew	47071	D	1927	Edward J.	50000	D	1928	George F. A.	32937	D	1921
Anita	72105	D	1936	Edward Peter	11499	D	1911	George T.	42814	D	1925
Ann	83801	D	1940	Eilert	69405	D	1935	George W.	49718	D	1928
Anna	62904	D	1932	Eilert	68950	I	1935	George W.	73470	D	1936
Anna E.	12704	M	1911	Eleanor	6128	M	1908	Georgia Shaw	63764	D	1933
Annie	11682	D	1911	Eleanor C.	34146	I	1922	Gerard J.	40497	I	1924
				Elise Josephine	48022	M	1927	Grace Jones	80691	D	1939

Name	Number	Type	Year	Name	Number	Type	Year	Name	Number	Type	Year
Grant	55890	I	1930	Jean E.	68936	D	1935	Lottie J.	65932	D	1933
Hans Peter	43564	D	1926	Jeanette	63944	D	1933	Lou	66722	D	1934
Harold A.	82706	D	1939	Jefferson	30503	D	1920	Louis	12268	D	1911
Harriet	8072	D	1909	Jesse Harrison	74416	D	1937	Louis	75179	D	1937
Harriet J.	83699	D	1940	Jessie J.	18220	D	1914	Louis	34860	D	1922
Harrison G.	46072	D	1926	Jessie Mae	49169	D	1928	Louis H. P.	87761	D	1941
Harry	10854	D	1910	Johanna	29639	D	1920	Lucille	52029	M	1929
Harry A.	58648	M	1931	Johanna	41800	D	1925	Lydia	49801	D	1928
Harry H.	37581	D	1923	Johanna	41800	D	1925	Mabel	48448	M	1927
Harry W.	82684	D	1939	John	13155	D	1912	Madeline Bohrmann	72501	D	1936
Harvey A.	64565	D	1933	John	20320	I	1916	Madeline M.	49321	M	1928
Helen	48448	M	1927	John	23176	M	1917	Madge I.	71717	I	1936
Helen Catherine	67509	M	1934	John	33608	D	1922	Margaret	46947	D	1927
Helen Duncan	32577	D	1921	John	40651	D	1924	Margaret Grismer	16885	M	1914
Helen L.	29938	M	1920	John	45408	D	1926	Margaret H.	82718	D	1939
Helen Wright	37188	D	1923	John	68724	D	1935	Margaret Rose	66765	D	1934
Henrietta	47954	D	1927	John	70157	D	1935	Margrethe	64196	D	1933
Henrietta	49247	D	1928	John	70775	D	1935	Maria	70361	I	1935
Henrietta	45142	I	1926	John	89724	I	1942	Marie	41218	D	1925
Henry	21686	D	1916	John	89990	D	1942	Marie Bernadette	18492	M	1915
Henry	21695	D	1916	John A.	41790	D	1925	Marie Rose	82479	D	1939
Henry	36423	D	1923	John A.	41790	D	1925	Marion M.	78167	D	1938
Henry	75594	D	1937	John C.	38867	D	1924	Marion Manona	78167	D	1938
Henry	46840	I	1927	John David	2259	D	1906	Marion P.	78800	D	1938
Henry J.	73417	D	1936	John G.	79382	D	1938	Marion Sanders	78167	D	1938
Herman	51855	D	1929	John H.	65042	D	1933	Mark A.	56226	D	1930
Herman	53728	D	1929	John Henry	62989	D	1932	Martha	36152	D	1923
Herny W.	64986	D	1933	John Henry	70495	D	1935	Martin	51844	D	1929
Howard Leslie	79329	D	1938	John M.	43394	I	1926	Martin M.	89780	D	1942
Isaac	41781	D	1925	John Matthew	55983	D	1930	Mary	34114	D	1922
Isaac	41781	D	1925	John W.	23937	D	1918	Mary	54738	I	1930
Isabella L.	27683	D	1919	John Wallace	20709	D	1916	Mary	88759	D	1941
Isabelle A.	45546	D	1926	Joseph	38308	D	1924	Mary	68884	I	1935
J.	85603	D	1940	Joseph C.	25794	D	1918	Mary A.	15167	D	1913
J. A.	47910	D	1927	Joseph C.	31501	D	1921	Mary A.	22657	D	1917
J. Giles	83886	D	1940	Joseph Henry	71716	D	1936	Mary B.	68413	D	1934
J. J.	38540	I	1924	Joseph Henry	71718	M	1936	Mary E.	50918	D	1928
J. S.	38682	D	1924	Josephine Gertrude	73278	D	1936	Mary E.	59804	D	1931
Jack	39596	D	1924	June	73967	M	1936	Mary Ellen	16464	I	1913
Jack	78986	D	1938	Kate C.	4871	D	1907	Mary H.	35030	I	1922
Jacob F.	63491	D	1933	Katharine Henderson	36928	M	1923	Mary Margaret	72914	M	1936
Jacob J.	63491	D	1933	Kathleen C.	46404	D	1927	Mary T.	35129	D	1922
James C.	43709	D	1926	Kathryn Batkin	74959	D	1937	Mathilde Henriette	60576	D	1931
James C.	89515	D	1942	Katie	4731	D	1907	Max	63870	D	1933
James G.	72711	D	1936	Kendrick Wright	37285	M	1923	Maybelle	29938	M	1920
James H.	65715	D	1933	Laurie M.	37497	D	1923	Michael	19157	D	1915
James L.	53305	D	1929	Lena	46352	D	1927	Minnie	78857	D	1938
Jane	70717	D	1935	Lillian	64262	I	1933	Minnie Agnes	69829	D	1935
Jasper C.	11350	I	1911	Lillie Scott	70910	D	1935	Morris	84817	M	1940

NAME	NUMBER	TYPE	YEAR
Nancy	30233	D	1920
Nelse	61779	D	1932
Olivia	81314	D	1939
Ophelia	60299	D	1931
Orlando W.	72937	D	1936
Orr Lee	19880	M	1915
Oscar Phineas, Jr.	80359	D	1939
Osro C.	73584	D	1936
Otto K.	71544	I	1936
Otto K.	72207	D	1936
Paul	84817	M	1940
Pauline	16386	D	1913
Peter	46144	D	1927
Peter	63183	D	1932
Randolph C.	20696	D	1916
Raymond D.	58545	I	1931
Renata	21201	D	1916
Richard	66915	D	1934
Richard	41010	I	1925
Robert	10448	D	1910
Robert	20046	D	1915
Robert	83819	D	1940
Robert E.	76411	D	1937
Robert F.	10422	D	1910
Robert H., Jr.	38971	M	1924
Robert M.	49638	D	1928
Robert, Jr.	84976	M	1940
Ruth R.	34425	D	1922
Samuel	31390	D	1921
Sara Helen	66084	D	1934
Sarah	36254	D	1923
Sarah A.	82499	D	1939
Sarah E.	52627	D	1929
Sarah W.	2667	D	1907
Sigurd T.	81596	D	1939
Sigwald	29592	D	1920
Sophia Lillian	67085	D	1934
Sophie	59350	D	1931
Sophie	69135	D	1935
Stephen W.	40091	D	1924
Susan B.	2792	D	1907
Susanna F.	32894	D	1921
Susie	79648	D	1938
Susie G.	83335	D	1940
Teresa F.	59120	D	1931
Teresa S.	72123	D	1936
Thelma	8774	M	1909
Theodore J.	58648	M	1931
Thomas	27419	D	1919
Thomas	47734	D	1927
Virginia	73968	M	1936
W. A. L.	12268	D	1911
Walter	89123	D	1942
William	8095	D	1909
William	10678	D	1910
William	24749	D	1918
William	34812	D	1922
William	38627	D	1924
William	41441	D	1925
William A.	35239	D	1922
William Caldwell	40896	D	1925
William E.	67199	D	1934
William F.	29681	D	1920
William G.	59729	D	1931
William H.	35350	D	1922
William H.	57696	D	1931
William Hamilton	84989	D	1940
William J.	45633	D	1926
William Otis	64670	D	1933
William P.	55898	D	1930
William P., Jr.	55926	D	1930
William Penn	69757	D	1935
William S.	58127	D	1931
Willis Earl	44234	D	1926
Winifred	65144	I	1933
Winifred	65295	D	1933
MILLERICK			
Philip J.	27423	D	1919
MILLETTO			
Jose	85448	D	1940
MILLHOUSE			
Marie Louise	22157	M	1917
MILLIGAN			
Albert J.	83062	D	1940
Marie T.	66895	I	1934
Marie Turnbull	74939	D	1937
Robert	4098	D	1907
Robert	88292	D	1941
Robert E.	84699	D	1940
MILLIKEN			
Alice	35244	D	1922
Charles T.	67138	D	1934
Frankie May	72285	D	1936
Horace F.	54710	D	1930
Rebekah A.	24996	D	1918
MILLIKIN			
Daisy	47735	D	1927
Linda	47735	D	1927
MILLINGTON			
Jane Paddock	37097	D	1923
Mary Ann H.	52262	D	1929
MILLISACK			
Jerry	55130	D	1930
Parker B.	55130	D	1930
MILLMEISTER			
Agnes	2138	D	1906
MILLOGLAV			
Edward C.	26020	D	1918
MILLON			
Auguste	39292	D	1924
Virginie	66722	D	1934
MILLS			
Alice J.	38236	I	1924
Alice J.	40640	D	1924
Ardella	9077	D	1910
Beatrice	48194	D	1927
Bessie	62029	D	1932
Carolin Edna	77281	D	1937
Charles Albert	40895	D	1925
Charles G.	35473	D	1922
Charles J.	57926	D	1931
Charles Woodruff	58379	D	1931
Darius Ogden	9046	D	1910
E. H.	59671	D	1931
Edmund S.	89536	M	1942
Edward	37994	D	1923
Evan C.	77249	D	1937
Eveleen Blosssom	32353	I	1921
Frank H.	12869	D	1912
Harry G.	84644	I	1940
Hellen M.	52993	D	1929
Ida E.	80069	D	1938
Isabella F.	60710	D	1932
James	8344	D	1909
Jerry	55130	D	1930
Joseph	11670	D	1911
Laura Malvina	68956	D	1935
Lawrence A.	74028	D	1936
Lorenzo D.	79993	I	1938
Margaret	47395	D	1927
Maria Elizabeth	51130	D	1928
Mary	79363	D	1938
Mary E.	49286	D	1928
Mary Eugenie	43180	I	1925
Minnie D.	21056	D	1916

Key: D = death; M = minor; I = incompetent

NAME	NUMBER	TYPE	YEAR
Norman T.	38069	D	1924
Ross H.	69983	D	1935
S. B.	29405	D	1920
William K.	3765	D	1907
William Lucas Bisset	74438	D	1937
MILLSAP			
Bertha S.	87477	D	1941
MILLSPAUGH			
Jean M.	77255	M	1937
MILLWARD			
Charles	26389	D	1919
John	46154	D	1927
MILLY			
Charles	23677	D	1917
Dorothy	61630	M	1932
Emil F.	71806	D	1936
Jerome	9171	I	1910
Jerome	11145	D	1911
Jerome	61630	M	1932
Louisa	69977	D	1935
MILLZNER			
Henry S.	12016	D	1911
Sarah	9100	D	1910
MILNE			
John Farguhar	26067	D	1919
MILONAS			
Haralmbos	10854	D	1910
John K., Jr.	82957	M	1939
Timothy	82957	M	1939
MILOSEVICH			
George	58924	M	1931
Nikolos	76694	D	1937
Novica	76694	D	1937
MILOSKY			
Emma	82359	D	1939
MILOSLAVICH			
Peter	88172	D	1941
MILROY			
Emma L.	19750	D	1915
MILTENBERGER			
Louisa A.	27262	D	1919
MILTER			
John Dairo	2259	D	1906
MILTON			
Alexander M.	76749	D	1937
Elizabeth	33018	D	1921
Frank B.	36367	D	1923

NAME	NUMBER	TYPE	YEAR
Harriet S.	84067	D	1940
Hope Mona	46475	D	1927
Joseph W.	56722	D	1930
MILUCKY			
Anna	62091	D	1932
Paul	46639	D	1927
MINA			
Frank	15226	D	1913
Mary L.	81028	D	1939
MINAHAN			
Mary Agnes	52617	D	1929
William	86611	D	1941
MINAKER			
Andrew J.	74455	D	1937
Arthur W.	15396	D	1913
William Edwin	88984	D	1942
MINAMI			
Frank Charles	31276	D	1921
Mohe	31276	D	1921
MINARDI			
Guiseppina	88886	D	1942
MINAUFF			
Willie	65094	D	1933
MINCHAN			
Anne	78025	D	1938
MINCHIN			
Abraham C.	19158	D	1915
Ida	61319	D	1932
MINDERMAN			
Adeline	76964	D	1937
Henry	34993	D	1922
MINDHAM			
Jane	462	I	1906
MINEAR			
Cleora H.	80912	I	1939
MINECK			
Mary	47745	M	1927
Paul	47745	M	1927
MINEDEW			
Stella F.	87602	D	1941
MINEHAN			
Anne	78025	D	1938
James	33057	D	1921
Jenny	67414	D	1934
Joseph F.	63952	D	1933
Mary A.	44000	D	1926

NAME	NUMBER	TYPE	YEAR
Raymond	86553	D	1941
Thomas	14840	D	1913
MINELLI			
Ines	20799	M	1916
Tosca	20799	M	1916
Zanobi	19420	D	1915
MINER			
Frank W.	53284	D	1929
George H.	3618	M	1907
Helen M.	73694	D	1936
James D.	66081	D	1934
Jane D.	32755	I	1921
John Ledley	33532	M	1922
John R.	3618	M	1907
Kingsley J.	76278	I	1937
Margaret Beatrice	66248	D	1934
Marie S.	34680	I	1922
Mary A.	37093	D	1923
Mary T.	87398	D	1941
Oren Franklin	35692	D	1923
Ralph Wardlaw	70801	D	1935
Rosie	73570	I	1936
Russell C.	44231	I	1926
Thomas E.	71212	D	1935
MINERE			
Rudolph	57528	D	1930
MINES			
Flaiel S.	2425	D	1906
MINESINGER			
Estelle	8334	D	1909
MINETTA			
John	56631	D	1930
MINETTI			
Frederico Perelli	29429	D	1920
MING			
On	79846	D	1938
Quan	69508	D	1935
MINGST			
August P. H.	78107	D	1938
Christian Heinrich	80274	D	1939
Eleanore June	79555	M	1938
Herman	81237	M	1939
Irene I.	77297	I	1937
Irene Ida	77366	D	1937
Johana	73878	D	1936
Ruth	81237	M	1939
William H.	72161	D	1936

Key: D = death; M = minor; I = incompetent

NAME	NUMBER	TYPE	YEAR
MINI			
Catherine	45220	I	1926
MINIER			
Marie Josephine	60752	I	1932
MINIFIE			
Alicia	88069	D	1941
C. G., Mrs.	88069	D	1941
Charles Granville	39186	D	1924
MINIHAN			
Daniel J.	79298	D	1938
Margaret	71285	D	1935
MINJAULAT			
John Peters	82356	D	1939
MINK			
Josefina	54347	D	1929
Josephine	12113	I	1911
MINKIEWITZ			
Thomas R.	53495	D	1929
MINKOVSKY			
Haskel	26327	D	1919
MINNE			
Peter	61017	D	1932
Pierre	61017	D	1932
MINNICK			
John	74228	D	1936
MINO			
G.	21736	D	1916
John	21736	D	1916
MINOR			
Alma V.	49018	D	1928
Candace A.	29578	D	1920
Charles	46678	D	1927
Elizabeth Isabel	83869	D	1940
Frank Max	87259	D	1941
Jack	33532	M	1922
John E.	71609	D	1936
MINORE			
Rosaria	51207	D	1928
MINOTT			
Anna H.	21791	D	1916
MINT			
Tung	22165	D	1917
MINTO			
Mary V.	26843	D	1919
William	42762	M	1925

NAME	NUMBER	TYPE	YEAR
MINTURN			
Charles	24273	D	1918
Jonas	6239	D	1908
MINTZ			
Louis	67292	D	1934
MINTZER			
Eugenia E.	11353	D	1911
William	12506	D	1911
William	12507	M	1911
MINVIELLE	.		
Alice M.	49620	M	1928
Ruth R.	49620	M	1928
MINVILLE			
Alice M.	49620	M	1928
MINZENMAYER			
Sarah	56450	D	1930
Tillie	65646	D	1933
MIQEL			
Louis	22195	D	1917
MIQHELL			
William E.	23308	D	1917
MIQUELAJAUREGUY			
Miguel	1932	D	1906
MIRABELLA			
Francesca	81773	D	1939
MIRABITO			
Anna	78100	M	1938
Benjamin	73036	D	1936
Edmond	78100	M	1938
MIRAGLI			
Mary	36466	D	1923
MIRAGLIA			
Filippo	66113	D	1934
Francesco	71233	D	1935
Maria	36466	D	1923
Rosina	66112	D	1934
Theresa	82999	D	1940
MIRAMONTES			
Christopher	80654	I	1939
Christopher	80880	D	1939
MIRANDA			
Louisa	73575	D	1936
Luisa	73575	D	1936
Mary	31631	D	1921
MIRANDE			
Martin	81972	D	1939

NAME	NUMBER	TYPE	YEAR
MIRANTE			
Levia	77324	D	1937
MIRASSOU			
Angelique	60272	D	1931
Anna	55355	D	1930
Elizabeth	38021	D	1923
Isabelle	38021	D	1923
Jean Pierre	59127	D	1931
Marc	60273	D	1931
Vincent	38261	I	1924
Vincent	42605	D	1925
MIREJOVSKY			
Blanche	28826	D	1920
H., Mrs.	28826	D	1920
MIRES			
Edward	26198	D	1919
Lydia E.	27912	D	1919
Susan J.	70393	D	1935
MIRFIELD			
Charles A.	67119	D	1934
MIRFIN			
Arthur A.	75077	D	1937
MIRK			
Alta Mable	81206	D	1939
MIRNOFF			
Sophie	88913	D	1942
MIRRASOUL			
Virginie	55199	D	1930
MIRRROFF			
Michael	79908	D	1938
MIRSKY			
Bernard	88269	D	1941
MIRZOIAN			
Hamazasp	55831	D	1930
Hamo	55831	D	1930
MISCH			
Mayer	14089	D	1912
Meyer	14089	D	1912
Rosa	20618	D	1916
MISEROTTI			
Vittorio	50359	D	1928
MISH			
Jennie	17216	D	1914
Julius	44614	D	1926
Sarah	20233	D	1916
Solomon Charles	26805	D	1919

NAME	NUMBER	TYPE	YEAR	NAME	NUMBER	TYPE	YEAR	NAME	NUMBER	TYPE	YEAR
Sylvan	68043	D	1934	James Fred	75050	D	1937	Harry J.	33758	D	1922
Wanda	50722	I	1928	**MITCHELL**				Henry	25915	I	1918
MISHKIN				Agnes	50355	D	1928	Henry A.	25204	D	1918
Mary	69032	D	1935	Albert J.	42048	D	1925	Henry F.	76808	D	1937
MISHKIND				Alexander	21575	D	1916	Henry Fred	70308	D	1935
Annie	48751	D	1927	Alfred	17794	I	1914	Henry Thomas	56932	D	1930
MISION				Alfred	17888	D	1914	Herbert S.	8908	M	1909
Lucas	44096	I	1926	Annie	20284	D	1916	James	50260	D	1928
Lucas	62300	D	1932	Bartholomew	22516	D	1917	James Edward	28158	D	1919
MISIPPO				Bridget	4822	D	1907	James J.	9441	D	1910
Angelina	31350	D	1921	Bridget	24482	D	1918	James McL.	77295	D	1937
MISKEL				Capitola	52832	D	1929	James McL., Jr.	77412	M	1938
Harold J.	29747	D	1920	Catherine	7233	D	1909	Jeanie	69909	D	1935
James	53849	D	1929	Charles	7911	D	1909	John	5783	D	1908
Jane	53100	D	1929	Charles	15068	D	1913	John	34417	D	1922
Laurence A.	54855	D	1930	Charles	46354	D	1927	John	62973	M	1932
Mary E.	78074	D	1938	Charles	83998	D	1940	John A.	55612	D	1930
William F.	43803	D	1926	Charles McN.	77034	D	1937	John Barnett	75349	D	1937
MISKOWSKI				Charlotte E.	56219	D	1930	John Francis	21383	M	1916
Joseph	41470	I	1925	Charlotte M.	56219	D	1930	John H.	42462	D	1925
MISKULIN				Clara	21383	M	1916	John Joseph	75480	D	1937
George	60589	I	1932	Clarence A.	47976	M	1927	John M.	64417	D	1933
MISLADEN				David G.	63588	D	1933	John R.	8908	M	1909
Peter	50989	D	1928	Dennis F.	30903	D	1920	John Renton	71693	D	1936
MISNER				Dorothy	62973	M	1932	Joseph	23431	D	1917
Anna	36804	D	1923	Dorothy	68341	M	1934	Joseph Albert	49609	M	1928
Elemuel H.	45202	D	1926	Dwight	2075	M	1906	Joseph H.	77570	D	1938
Henry Elemuel	45202	D	1926	Edith Austin	86120	D	1941	Kate	1255	D	1906
MISPLACIDO				Edward J.	69602	D	1935	Kingsley C.	59381	D	1931
Cristuto	75207	D	1937	Eleanor B.	43795	D	1926	Lee	21349	I	1916
MISRACH				Eleanor S.	19005	D	1915	Lela	41985	D	1925
Sarah	27412	D	1919	Elizabeth Patterson	23707	D	1917	Lela	41985	D	1925
MISTELE				Ellen	54248	D	1929	Lillian M.	76796	D	1937
Ernest	79024	D	1938	Emma V.	70539	D	1935	Lucille Eleanor	49609	M	1928
MISURACA				Ernest William	82638	M	1939	Lucille G.	49691	D	1928
Pietra	58155	D	1931	Eva	84228	D	1940	Lydia G.	48993	D	1928
MITAU				Florence E.	32780	D	1921	Margaret	9158	D	1910
Fannie S.	57405	D	1930	Florence S.	8908	M	1909	Margaret	18414	D	1915
Marin Sachs	17824	M	1914	Forrest E.	64415	D	1933	Margaret	59489	D	1931
Morris	80381	D	1939	Frances Lucille	49691	D	1928	Margaret	73776	D	1936
MITCH				Frank	69875	D	1935	Margaret Judge	24473	D	1918
Frank	56923	I	1930	George	16544	D	1913	Marion L.	31344	D	1921
MITCHEEL				George Eldridge	58361	D	1931	Martha	68537	M	1934
Patrick	259	D	1906	George M.	72148	D	1936	Mary	1784	D	1906
MITCHEL				George R.	8729	D	1909	Mary	9157	D	1910
Charles	85805	D	1940	Geroge F.	41566	D	1925	Mary	16010	D	1913
				Grace Pitkin	62731	D	1932	Mary Boden	45891	D	1926
				Harold J.	59584	D	1931	Mary F.	49968	D	1928
				Harry	59076	D	1931	Mary P.	32416	D	1921

NAME	NUMBER	TYPE	YEAR
Micael Aron	14811	D	1913
Michael	13041	D	1912
Muriel	6011	M	1908
Nancy Alice	66608	I	1934
Nellie E.	15516	D	1913
Nicolas J.	55015	D	1930
Oliver	59498	D	1931
Patrick	12455	D	1911
Pearl	72551	D	1936
Robert	192	D	1906
Robert C.	42928	D	1925
Robley Jay	52410	I	1929
Roland C.	83394	D	1940
Roscoe Lee	80240	I	1939
Samuel	3738	M	1907
Samuel	70309	D	1935
Samuel E.	21029	D	1916
Samuel J.	29666	D	1920
Sarah Matilda	60581	D	1932
Solomon	14540	D	1912
Stanislaus C.	47943	D	1927
Theodore J.	50621	D	1928
Thomas	27384	D	1919
Thomas	78880	D	1938
Thomas F.	59360	D	1931
Thomas H.	46911	D	1927
Thomas L.	8908	M	1909
William	6084	D	1908
William	8660	D	1909
William	58258	D	1931
William E.	38865	I	1924
William Edward	31099	I	1921
William F.	61907	D	1932
William H.	84560	D	1940
William Herbert	88684	D	1941
William J.	83970	D	1940
MITCHEM			
Ella Holmes	66269	D	1934
MITCHINSON			
John	46500	D	1927
MITHCELL			
William	1573	D	1906
MITHCHELL			
Thomas F.	1615	D	1906
MITLER			
Elizabeth Elsie	30710	M	1920
Margaret M. G.	89505	D	1942

NAME	NUMBER	TYPE	YEAR
MITLING			
Edward	86634	M	1941
Ernestine Bondistel	86634	M	1941
MITRAKOS			
George Peter	89268	D	1942
MITTELMAN			
Edith	77169	M	1937
Joseph	77169	M	1937
Miriam	77169	M	1937
MITTEMPERGHER			
Adelaide	83505	D	1940
MITTENBERGER			
Louise	27262	D	1919
MITTINI			
Giuseppe	6955	M	1908
Giuseppe	26077	D	1919
MITTLEMAN			
Arthur	46119	I	1926
MIX			
Annie McC.	23208	D	1917
Buck	85450	D	1940
Frances	12932	M	1912
Franz	10931	D	1910
Lottie B.	22688	D	1917
Pauline	12932	M	1912
Theresa	12932	M	1912
William Robert	85450	D	1940
MIYAKE			
Chujiro	46603	D	1927
MIYASAKI			
Yonokichi	23971	D	1918
MIZE			
Carrie Dunkeson	54675	D	1930
Robert	56536	M	1930
MIZEL			
Rebekah	54823	D	1930
MIZNER			
Edgar A.	26105	D	1919
Ella Watson	18969	D	1915
Lansing	30211	D	1920
William G.	48493	D	1927
MIZONO			
Akira	72316	M	1936
MIZRAHI			
Sarah	78329	D	1938

NAME	NUMBER	TYPE	YEAR
MJELLE			
Hans Christoffersen	36951	D	1923
MLADINICH			
Louis	51199	D	1928
MLAIN			
Joseph	25309	D	1918
MLAYS			
Joseph	25309	D	1918
Zarify	32737	D	1921
MOALE			
Edward	16128	D	1913
MOAN			
Catherine	14157	D	1912
Edward	14155	D	1912
MOBERG			
Walter	60114	D	1931
MOCABEE			
John Edgar	63137	D	1932
John W.	88341	D	1941
MOCK			
Chew	41067	D	1925
Mary J.	83327	D	1940
William Felix	81266	D	1939
MOCKEL			
Elizabeth	22019	D	1916
Katharina	22019	D	1916
MOCKER			
Andrew	69151	D	1935
DeForrest Edwin	18386	M	1915
Marietta Ruth	18386	M	1915
MOCKFORD			
William	32013	D	1921
MOCKLAR			
Teresa	10967	D	1910
William	12122	D	1911
MOCKLER			
Charles E.	39621	D	1924
John	5747	D	1908
John, Jr.	8333	I	1909
Thomas	72475	D	1936
William	72476	D	1936
MODENA			
Guiseppe	85035	D	1940
Vincent	46195	D	1927
MODESTO			
Muciadri	48933	D	1928

NAME	NUMBER	TYPE	YEAR	NAME	NUMBER	TYPE	YEAR	NAME	NUMBER	TYPE	YEAR
MODIC				**MOESER**				**MOGENTALE**			
John	22277	D	1917	Gussie	30794	D	1920	Nellie	65522	D	1933
MODICH				**MOESSNER**				**MOGGIO**			
John	22277	D	1917	Gottlieb	78317	D	1938	Victorina	59955	D	1931
MODLIN				**MOESTA**				**MOGIAN**			
Irene Eleanor	52732	M	1929	John Doe	7137	D	1909	Harry	59374	M	1931
MODRY				**MOFFAT**				**MOGLIA**			
Louise Rae	86312	D	1941	Agnes Anne	44776	D	1926	Carolina	67619	I	1934
Southard M.	85545	D	1940	James Campbell	11564	D	1911	Felice	67538	D	1934
MOE				John R.	2626	D	1907	Felix	67539	D	1934
Annie L.	80176	D	1938	Robert	15834	D	1913	Giovanni	58559	D	1931
Harry	9299	D	1910	Robert	49416	D	1928	**MOHAUPT**			
Ole J.	83877	D	1940	Sarah Halket	55965	D	1930	Armand	88801	D	1941
MOECKEL				**MOFFATT**				Charles A.	31361	D	1921
Ernest	69203	D	1935	George H.	72852	D	1936	**MOHL**			
MOEGLING				Leon E.	20286	M	1916	Adam	41527	D	1925
Babetta	30123	D	1920	Lizzie Wray	45321	D	1926	**MOHLE**			
MOEHLENBROCK				**MOFFET**				William G.	33740	D	1922
Henry F.	66657	D	1934	Matilda	33434	D	1922	**MOHLER**			
MOEHRLE				Samuel	44334	D	1926	Ingebor L.	54396	D	1929
Charles Edward	71291	D	1935	**MOFFETT**				**MOHNS**			
Louisa	17974	D	1914	William E.	57177	I	1930	Anna	35279	D	1922
MOELK				**MOFFIT**				**MOHOLY**			
Henry Peter	20913	D	1916	Agnes	44776	D	1926	John	8467	D	1909
MOELLER				**MOFFITT**				Mary	2238	D	1906
Christine	57294	D	1930	Augusta L.	52008	D	1929	**MOHORIC**			
Elizabeth Brady	32897	D	1921	Florence Jane	79623	D	1938	Joseph	66416	D	1934
Emma	19009	M	1915	Francis James	52214	M	1929	**MOHR**			
Gustav E. F.	16665	D	1914	John Ward	62549	D	1932	Adolph	5671	D	1908
John	22	D	1906	Mary Virginia	37185	D	1923	Adolph	9632	M	1910
Sophia	19009	M	1915	Murray M.	72304	D	1936	Anna Catherina	30791	D	1920
MOEN				Sheila Louise	52214	M	1929	Anna Louise	11492	D	1911
Thorstein Jorgensen	66769	D	1934	**MOGAN**				Billie Elise	49728	M	1928
MOENCH				Austin J.	40195	D	1924	Edmund F. S.	12249	M	1911
William	48291	D	1927	Constance Marie	50956	M	1928	Elsie	9632	M	1910
MOENNING				Edna Mae	43356	M	1926	George L.	70675	D	1935
Lina	13421	D	1912	Frank J.	44307	D	1926	H. H.	53444	D	1929
MOERBEEK				John	8070	D	1909	Henry	1679	D	1906
Johannes Josephus	68987	D	1935	John	43356	M	1926	Herman	44878	D	1926
John	68987	D	1935	Joseph F.	11172	D	1911	Herman Albert	68010	D	1934
MOESCH				Margaret	29171	D	1920	Howard E., Jr.	56927	M	1930
Frank	28906	I	1920	Margaret	39637	D	1924	Ida	9632	M	1910
George	12467	D	1911	Sarah	45186	D	1926	Jacob Friedrich	73619	D	1936
George John William	64948	I	1933	**MOGAU**				John	9632	M	1910
Johanna	46789	D	1927	Sarah	45186	D	1926	John	21985	D	1916
				MOGENSEN				John A.	19387	D	1915
				Martin C.	9464	D	1910	Jsoeph M.	81174	D	1939

NAME	NUMBER	TYPE	YEAR
Lorraine Adle	56926	M	1930
Louis B.	13534	M	1912
Marilyn	56927	M	1930
Marx	9632	M	1910
Marx Julius Rudolph	49883	D	1928
Mathilda	72068	D	1936
Matthaus	31381	D	1921
Michael	22436	D	1917
Rosalia	43948	D	1926
Rudolph	49883	D	1928
Rudolph Allen	56926	M	1930
Selby	82362	D	1939
Warren George	56926	M	1930
Wilhelmine	85449	D	1940
William	9632	M	1910
MOHRDICK			
Martin Henry	43557	D	1926
MOHRHARDT			
Basilia	36465	D	1923
Ecward F.	47171	D	1927
Edward F.	25662	M	1918
Mary F.	1389	D	1906
MOHRIG			
Edna	25401	M	1918
Edwin	24628	D	1918
Edwin C.	25511	D	1918
Ethel	25510	D	1918
MOHRMAN			
Charlotte	60610	D	1932
MOHRMANN			
Frederick	11527	D	1911
Matthias	15847	D	1913
William F.	24493	I	1918
MOHS			
O. Kemper	81533	D	1939
Oscar K.	81534	D	1939
MOHUN			
Charles C., Jr.	9526	M	1910
MOIR			
Allan Macrae	13847	D	1912
Henry Patterson	55437	D	1930
MOISANT			
John B.	11454	D	1911
Juan B.	11454	D	1911
Mary A.	46679	D	1927
Stanle	11453	M	1911

NAME	NUMBER	TYPE	YEAR
MOISE			
Elsie Harriett	12540	M	1911
Eva	53832	D	1929
Hettie	65336	D	1933
Kate F. L.	12425	D	1911
Laura Mason	45299	D	1926
Leon L.	60536	D	1931
Lionel H.	89548	D	1942
MOISEENKO			
Peter	24618	D	1918
MOISIO			
Pasqualina	87599	I	1941
Realdo	81410	D	1939
MOITOZA			
Anthony	61267	D	1932
MOLACZYK			
Isaac	65719	D	1933
MOLCH			
Peter	42520	I	1925
MOLDENHAUER			
Henry	21338	D	1916
Louise W.	73434	D	1936
MOLDRUP			
Beatrice Louise	3448	M	1907
Eleanor Belle	4084	D	1907
Loris Wesley	3448	M	1907
MOLE			
Josiah	29431	D	1920
MOLEMA			
Ellena	15047	D	1913
MOLENDA			
Charles J.	44583	D	1926
MOLER			
Floyd C.	43531	M	1926
MOLERA			
Andrew J.	59935	D	1931
Eusebius J.	61258	D	1932
Francisca Guadalupe	25102	D	1918
MOLFINI			
Albert Andrew	84996	D	1940
Alberto Andrea	84996	D	1940
MOLFINO			
Paolo	40810	D	1925
MOLIERE			
Harry L.	38928	D	1924

NAME	NUMBER	TYPE	YEAR
MOLINA			
John	21026	M	1916
Maria	74250	D	1936
MOLINARI			
A. Gaynor	59615	D	1931
Bianca	21632	D	1916
Bianchina	21632	D	1916
Carlo	55049	D	1930
Charles	55049	D	1930
Frank A.	64171	D	1933
Gaynor Anthony	59615	D	1931
Giacomo	7281	D	1909
Giovanni	54242	D	1929
Giovanni B.	67442	D	1934
James W.	15839	D	1913
Marie	59479	I	1931
Martha Shrader	59473	D	1931
Paul	65838	D	1933
Pietro	7858	D	1909
Pompeo	43186	D	1925
Rose	81086	D	1939
Theresa A.	79401	D	1938
MOLINARY			
Florence	48220	D	1927
MOLINE			
George	28078	D	1919
MOLINEAUX			
Emily E.	27339	D	1919
Henry	11495	D	1911
MOLINENGO			
Giuseppe	23835	D	1918
MOLINO			
Marie	83901	D	1940
Philip	47722	D	1927
MOLITER			
Peter	37746	D	1923
MOLITOR			
Fred	56580	I	1930
Fred	56985	D	1930
MOLL			
Emma Louise	64618	D	1933
MOLLATH			
August	27802	M	1919
Leopold	27802	M	1919
MOLLAY			
Susan	63315	D	1933

NAME	NUMBER	TYPE	YEAR
MOLLE			
Joseph	60720	I	1932
MOLLEDA			
Frank H.	53075	D	1929
Laura	78659	D	1938
MOLLENKOPF			
Constancia	13097	D	1912
MOLLER			
Angeline B.	3249	M	1907
Bill	16198	D	1913
Blanch A.	3249	M	1907
Blanche A.	8479	M	1909
Cecilia O.	79271	D	1938
Christian	38147	D	1924
Claus	40616	D	1924
Clifford R.	8479	M	1909
Edward H.	19941	I	1915
Elsa	80686	I	1939
Emma	24855	I	1918
Emma	39457	D	1924
James	37479	I	1923
Jens	37479	I	1923
Jens N.	40631	D	1924
Johann Hinrich	62989	D	1932
John D.	9070	D	1910
Louis	41350	D	1925
Onward R.	8479	M	1909
Richard W.	60787	D	1932
Theodor G.	85608	D	1940
Zelma L.	57630	M	1931
MOLLET			
Thomas G.	42582	D	1925
MOLLEY			
Catherine E.	70970	D	1935
MOLLISON			
Allan	68238	D	1934
H. L., Mrs.	1360	D	1906
MOLLOY			
Alice Beebe	73941	D	1936
Annie	28980	M	1920
Annie	48969	D	1928
Annie Mary	28602	M	1920
Bessie A.	38085	D	1924
Catherine M.	694	I	1906
Catherine M.	7988	D	1909
Cecilia Little	77387	D	1937
Cecilia V.	77387	D	1937
Christie	28602	M	1920

NAME	NUMBER	TYPE	YEAR
Delia	28602	M	1920
Ellie	28602	M	1920
Francis	78686	D	1938
John	28590	D	1920
John	28602	M	1920
John	28980	M	1920
Josephine Theresa	84371	D	1940
Mary	17560	D	1914
Mary	20959	D	1916
Mary	28602	M	1920
Mary Anne	77736	D	1938
Michael	1943	D	1906
Michael	28602	M	1920
Patrick	28602	M	1920
Patrick	42739	D	1925
Peter	18251	D	1914
Peter	28602	M	1920
Thomas	8291	D	1909
Thomas	28602	M	1920
MOLMARK			
Preben A.	76632	D	1937
MOLOFF			
Samuel	43364	M	1926
MOLONEY			
James	24380	D	1918
Mary	42702	D	1925
Patrick	11575	D	1911
MOLONY			
Edward James	86513	D	1941
James J.	46515	D	1927
James L.	54290	D	1929
Martin	79093	D	1938
MOLOUGH			
Joseph D.	82379	D	1939
MOLSCH			
Johanna	46789	D	1927
MOLSER			
Gussie	30794	D	1920
MOLTEDO			
Giulio	21801	D	1916
MOLTEN			
Frank J.	59782	D	1931
MOLTENI			
Erminia	38459	D	1924
MOLTUED			
Harold Th.	83243	D	1940

NAME	NUMBER	TYPE	YEAR
MOLTZEN			
August F.	24437	D	1918
MOMADIAN			
Sam	33682	D	1922
Solomon	33682	D	1922
MOMBACH			
Annie	45135	D	1926
Elizabeth	22857	D	1917
Maria	26345	D	1919
Mary	26345	D	1919
MOMJIAN			
G.	73237	D	1936
Kerikor	73237	D	1936
Kerkor	73237	D	1936
MOMONT			
John	17528	D	1914
MOMSEN			
Wilhelmine	20095	D	1915
MON			
Louise Dolores	56569	D	1930
Max	20775	D	1916
Ng Yee	16652	D	1914
On	79846	D	1938
Won Dow	38285	D	1924
MONA			
Mary	16487	D	1913
Victor Joseph	64891	D	1933
MONACO			
Feliciana	11832	D	1911
John D.	8533	D	1909
Liberata	26887	D	1919
Louis P.	83192	D	1940
MONAGHAN			
Anney	30716	D	1920
Ascella	8347	M	1909
Bridget	9234	D	1910
Daniel	7341	D	1909
Edward M.	9626	D	1910
Evelyn Ann	72864	M	1936
Joseph C.	89142	D	1942
Mae Loretta	20992	D	1916
Nora	50140	I	1928
Nora	52153	D	1929
Patrick	12087	D	1911
Thomas F.	23708	D	1917
William	12390	D	1911

NAME	NUMBER	TYPE	YEAR
MONAHAN			
Andrew J.	86042	I	1941
Catharine	15505	D	1913
Elizabeth Bernice	57464	M	1930
Elizabeth Bernice	85685	D	1940
Frances Anna	57465	M	1930
Frank J.	61776	D	1932
Frank L.	74530	D	1937
Hannah Dailey	39967	D	1924
Henry	12595	D	1911
John	22743	D	1917
Joseph D.	45314	D	1926
Katerine McLaughlin	63759	D	1933
Michael J.	71786	D	1936
Thomas	24453	I	1918
Thomas F.	59707	D	1931
Timothy	36581	I	1923
W. A. W.	34930	D	1922
William P.	57464	D	1930
MONASCH			
Esther	62778	D	1932
Samuel	31422	D	1921
MONCH			
George J.	21176	D	1916
MONCHANT			
Emily	23324	D	1917
MONCHARSH			
Samuel M.	44955	D	1926
MONCHAUT			
Emily	23324	D	1917
MONCKS			
Margaret B.	84086	D	1940
MONCKTON			
Lucie Yerby	72698	D	1936
MONCLA			
Blanche Laure	59969	D	1931
Laure Blanche	59969	D	1931
MONCRIEFF			
Agnes	74079	D	1936
MONCURE			
Richard A.	37202	D	1923
MONDADA			
Thomas	60493	D	1931
MONDANI			
Gelsomina	40914	M	1925
Gelsomina	47477	M	1927
Mary	40914	M	1925

NAME	NUMBER	TYPE	YEAR
Mary	47477	M	1927
Peter	40914	M	1925
Peter	47477	M	1927
Rose	40914	M	1925
Rose	47477	M	1927
MONDEK			
Joseph Anthony	24648	M	1918
Veronica Catherine	24648	M	1918
MONDELET			
Francois	4622	D	1907
MONDELLO			
Filippo	51086	D	1928
MONDELOT			
Francois	4622	D	1907
MONDET			
Jules	54233	D	1929
Julious	54233	D	1929
MONDOT			
Celestin	53057	D	1929
Emile	74938	D	1937
MONE			
Warren Reginald	70976	M	1935
MONEGHAN			
Anney	30716	D	1920
MONELL			
F. Coates	79052	D	1938
Frederick C.	79052	D	1938
Hilda B.	88921	D	1942
MONESTIER			
Charles	41036	M	1925
Ellen	41140	D	1925
Louise	37282	D	1923
MONET			
Catherine Clementine	5576	M	1908
Charles	1114	D	1906
Clementine	80491	D	1939
Emma	22744	D	1917
John Baptiste	5576	M	1908
John Baptiste Marius	27488	D	1919
Mary Ethel	5576	M	1908
Theresa Loretta	5576	M	1908
MONEY			
George	75590	D	1937
MONG			
Chin Suey	39037	D	1924
Leen Foong	35169	M	1922
Leen Oi	35169	M	1922

NAME	NUMBER	TYPE	YEAR
MONGA			
Joseph	19949	M	1915
Matilda	19949	M	1915
MONGE			
Antonietta	51951	D	1929
Bonifacio	37834	I	1923
Joseph	31004	D	1921
MONGI			
Albert	52201	M	1929
Katherine	52406	M	1929
MONGIE			
Albert	32281	M	1921
Catherine	32281	M	1921
Giuseppe	31004	D	1921
MONGLEEN			
Foong	35169	M	1922
Ho	35169	M	1922
Leen Ho	35169	M	1922
Oi	35169	M	1922
MONGOLIAS			
Vasilios	16198	D	1913
MONI			
Armida	78655	D	1938
Attilio	28200	D	1919
Jacob	7027	D	1909
MONICA			
Sister	14002	D	1912
MONIGHETTI			
Joseph O.	33158	D	1922
MONK			
Alma Loraine Marie	3864	M	1907
John	58539	D	1931
M. J. (nee Strueder)	3706	D	1907
Mary	3706	D	1907
Mary E.	3706	D	1907
William D.	31336	I	1921
MONKMAN			
Louisa A.	4695	D	1907
MONKS			
Annie M.	56992	D	1930
MONNICH			
Sophie	65266	D	1933
MONNIER			
Anna	35628	D	1922
Anne	40299	D	1924
George	75	D	1906
Juanita	36910	M	1923

Key: D = death; M = minor; I = incompetent

NAME	NUMBER	TYPE	YEAR	NAME	NUMBER	TYPE	YEAR	NAME	NUMBER	TYPE	YEAR
Madeleine M.	16666	D	1914	**MONSEIGNEUR**				Mary	40914	M	1925
Madeline	36910	M	1923	Bertha	82864	D	1939	Peter	40914	M	1925
Peter	15918	D	1913	**MONSEN**				Rose	40914	M	1925
Violet	36910	M	1923	Andrew	89148	D	1942	**MONTARINO**			
MONNISH				Louis	56070	D	1930	Modesto	34204	D	1922
W. A.	8976	D	1910	Ole	19037	D	1915	**MONTAUBAN**			
MONOMACHOFF				**MONSON**				Etienne	19407	D	1915
Vladimir	42051	M	1925	Burdett H.	2092	D	1906	**MONTCHARMONT**			
MONOZON				Christina	61057	D	1932	Wilhelmina	89478	D	1942
Louis	70491	D	1935	Ella	2998	D	1907	**MONTE**			
MONRAD				George S.	26765	D	1919	Chris	15405	D	1913
Henry Godfried	51275	D	1928	Oscar	86152	D	1941	Cipriano D.	2623	D	1907
Mary L.	44505	D	1926	**MONSSON**				Manuel	76674	M	1937
MONRAZ				Johanna	35890	D	1923	Manuel	57582	D	1931
Mike	44832	I	1926	Per	23097	D	1917	Nellie S.	70828	I	1935
MONREJAU				**MONSUS**				Nellie S.	75756	D	1937
Joseph Pouly	14435	D	1912	Rebecca	38746	D	1924	Pete S.	75014	D	1937
MONREJEAU				**MONTAGUE**				**MONTEAGLE**			
Joseph Pouly	14435	D	1912	Charles	27625	M	1919	Jeanne Havens	56671	M	1930
MONREPOS				Delia	51339	D	1928	Louis F.	84733	D	1940
Raphael	68830	D	1935	Edward	27625	M	1919	Lydia Paige	53594	D	1929
MONROE				Edward F.	25580	D	1918	Patricia Havens	56671	M	1930
Charles A.	69246	D	1935	Elizabeth Mary	5579	D	1908	**MONTEDONICO**			
Charles T.	70467	D	1935	Fred	27625	M	1919	Antonio	15453	D	1913
Emma	71309	D	1935	Harry	27625	M	1919	**MONTELIUS**			
Florence M.	14568	D	1912	John	27625	M	1919	Hulda Mary	84487	D	1940
Frank E.	44771	D	1926	John I.	60597	I	1932	**MONTELL**			
Harry	28538	D	1919	Royal E.	35048	I	1922	Adam	89162	D	1942
Henry E.	85800	D	1940	Ruth	27625	M	1919	E. H.	21357	D	1916
Jack Lewis	70470	M	1935	Wilfred W.	30382	D	1920	Francisca Gamero	59390	D	1931
Josephine M.	70468	D	1935	**MONTAIGUT**				H. H., Mrs.	85235	D	1940
Mark	49492	D	1928	Helene	85417	I	1940	Henry H.	19549	D	1915
Mary Ann	22653	D	1917	**MONTALBETTI**				John Henry Montague	80254	D	1939
Mary Ann	31157	D	1921	Linda	24727	M	1918	Susan C.	85235	D	1940
Robert Lee	75464	D	1937	**MONTALDO**				**MONTERO**			
Robert R., Mrs.	71309	D	1935	Arthur S.	68844	D	1935	Anastacia	36036	D	1923
Thomas Holt	41736	M	1925	Attilis S.	68844	D	1935	**MONTES**			
Thomas Holt	41736	M	1925	**MONTALVA**				Eleno	54647	D	1930
Warren L.	84007	D	1940	Edith	52337	M	1929	Robert	36538	D	1923
William C.	16313	D	1913	Frederick	52337	M	1929	**MONTEVERDE**			
MONSA				Ida	51087	D	1928	Harry	45621	M	1926
Angelo	61829	I	1932	Victor	52337	M	1929	Julia	47205	D	1927
MONSARRAT				Virginia	52337	M	1929	Manuel	4810	D	1907
May Carr	58169	D	1931	**MONTANER**				Mario	45621	M	1926
MONSEES				Jose Maria	46071	D	1926	Mary	31024	D	1921
Louis	42075	D	1925	**MONTANI**				Mary	45621	M	1926
				Gelsomina	40914	M	1925	Mary	78997	D	1938

NAME	NUMBER	TYPE	YEAR
Robert	45621	M	1926
Romona	4809	D	1907
MONTEZ			
Domingo	9787	D	1910
MONTGOMERY			
Aubrey Winnifred	59397	D	1931
Cary Ress	20184	D	1915
Douglass W.	89012	D	1942
Elizabeth S.	6931	M	1908
Ellen Sargent	5802	D	1908
Esther Alvira	64312	D	1933
Florence	8575	M	1909
Frances A.	47587	D	1927
Genevieve A.	83785	D	1940
George	2775	D	1907
George	43142	D	1925
George	42181	I	1925
Grey	19968	D	1915
John	11335	D	1911
Joseph Charles	18510	D	1915
Lawrence A.	66119	D	1934
Mary A.	19968	D	1915
Mary F.	79683	D	1938
Minnie	8575	M	1909
Pius Leo	52836	D	1929
Pius S.	52836	D	1929
Ruth	41079	D	1925
Samuel R.	41412	D	1925
Truth N.	73950	I	1936
William S.	6931	M	1908
MONTICONE			
Joseph	57386	D	1930
MONTIEL			
Gertrude A.	56039	D	1930
MONTINI			
Arnoldo	54040	D	1929
MONTLUZEN			
Jos. A. de	6444	D	1908
MONTOBBIO			
Margherita	70968	D	1935
MONTOMCY			
Leontine	14370	D	1912
MONTROSE			
Ellery D.	57031	D	1930
MONTURCY			
Leontine	14370	D	1912

NAME	NUMBER	TYPE	YEAR
MONZONI			
Antonio	32491	D	1921
MONZZA			
Angelo	61829	I	1932
MOOCK			
Mary Elizabeth	21223	D	1916
MOODY			
Ada B.	40828	D	1925
Charles E.	37634	D	1923
Frederick S.	73511	D	1936
George W.	13644	M	1912
Ida J.	64053	D	1933
Robert R.	81555	D	1939
Wave Walter	37338	D	1923
William C.	34389	D	1922
MOON			
Albert Tilton	13975	M	1912
Anna Ehleiter	87102	D	1941
Dorothy	6167	M	1908
Edward Laurence	73993	D	1936
Frederick	88645	I	1941
Julia L.	78547	D	1938
Laura	6167	M	1908
Orean Alonzo	52310	D	1929
William John	66762	D	1934
MOONEY			
Alice	8245	D	1909
Ann	7710	D	1909
Annie	6508	D	1908
Carrie M.	68836	I	1935
Carrie May	70046	D	1935
Cathrine	24132	D	1918
Cornelius	16729	D	1914
Daniel Wallace	63913	D	1933
Elizabeth Josephine	57701	I	1931
Elizabeth Josephine	57818	D	1931
Ellen A.	65371	D	1933
Hugh P.	58200	D	1931
James	85809	D	1940
John	29361	D	1920
John	75776	D	1937
Karl Templeton	25111	M	1918
Lucy	2424	D	1906
Mary	29297	D	1920
Mary	67975	D	1934
Mary Ann	35587	D	1922
Michael	8244	D	1909
Norman J.	42060	I	1925

NAME	NUMBER	TYPE	YEAR
Petra W.	3265	I	1907
Richard	15296	I	1913
Richard	25779	D	1918
Squire V.	25110	D	1918
Thomas J.	89398	D	1942
William	7542	M	1909
William	66693	D	1934
MOOR			
Edward Norton	74395	D	1937
MOORCROFT			
William McKibben	13263	D	1912
MOORE			
A.	87207	D	1941
Adele	25990	I	1918
Albert H.	30959	M	1921
Albert H.	45249	D	1926
Alexander Freeman	63794	D	1933
Alivina	46419	D	1927
Anna	35510	D	1922
Annie T.	83253	I	1940
Annie T.	84164	D	1940
Antone	56209	D	1930
Arthur	77498	D	1938
Belle J.	66035	D	1934
Benjamin Frank	80107	D	1938
Caldwell	4516	M	1907
Catharine	22310	D	1917
Catherine	25991	M	1918
Catherine	53152	D	1929
Cesare	1762	D	1906
Charles Cadwell	61568	D	1932
Charles Edward, III	89489	M	1942
Charles F.	47828	I	1927
Charles H.	8426	D	1909
Charles H.	82069	D	1939
Charles S.	29342	D	1920
Clarence C.	34554	I	1922
Cora Fenwick	77174	D	1937
Cora Jean	57975	M	1931
Cora Wilbur	52384	D	1929
Daniel H.	304	D	1906
Daniel Kermit	73907	D	1936
Deniver, Jr.	66956	M	1934
Edward	6364	D	1908
Elijah L.	52189	D	1929
Eliza L.	1311	D	1906
Elizabeth	34218	D	1922
Elizabeth C.	8356	D	1909

Name	Number	Type	Year	Name	Number	Type	Year	Name	Number	Type	Year
Elizabeth Eugenie	89489	M	1942	John C.	60051	D	1931	Richard Elliott	85773	M	1940
Elizabeth Hogue	84802	D	1940	John L.	87700	D	1941	Robert Bruce	17332	D	1914
Ellen	30147	D	1920	John R.	41132	D	1925	Roger L.	47363	D	1927
Elva Amanda	76129	D	1937	John W.	76430	D	1937	Rosetta	71460	D	1936
Emma Gustel	22900	M	1917	John Whittier	89489	M	1942	Roy D.	65865	D	1933
Emma S.	43184	D	1925	Johnanna Genvieve	46789	D	1927	Ruth Cecelia	22900	M	1917
Ethel Cecil	18043	M	1914	Joseph E.	46401	D	1927	Sadie J.	41237	D	1925
Ethel Cecil	26414	D	1919	Julia	23278	D	1917	Samuel J.	88000	D	1941
Eugene C.	80667	D	1939	Katherine T.	64004	D	1933	Sarah Alice	76568	D	1937
Eulalie	87343	D	1941	Kermit	73907	D	1936	Sarah L.	30240	D	1920
Florence Cornwall	16958	D	1914	Lewis A.	33412	D	1922	Shelley	74345	D	1937
Framl G.	1981	D	1906	Lewis W.	995	D	1906	Shirley	74345	D	1937
Frana E.	86308	D	1941	Lola Jessie	24617	D	1918	Sophia	8496	D	1909
Frank	51714	D	1928	Louisa	34102	D	1922	Stanley Williams	36083	I	1923
Fred E.	26911	D	1919	Louise Mackey	40144	D	1924	Stanley Williams	78678	D	1938
Fred Everett	53791	D	1929	Luke	56008	D	1930	Stephen	16812	D	1914
Frederic Houghton	58205	D	1931	Maggie	44480	D	1926	Stephen B.	16812	D	1914
Frederick Charles	75855	D	1937	Manuel F.	2219	D	1906	Susan A.	6892	D	1908
Gene	46789	D	1927	Margaret	8120	D	1909	Susannah A.	6892	D	1908
George E.	73220	D	1936	Margaret Arabelle	66792	D	1934	Sylvester	16106	D	1913
George J.	27106	D	1919	Margaret Hendry	83275	D	1940	T. W., Mrs.	61122	D	1932
George John	49541	D	1928	Marie	25991	M	1918	Thomas	25991	M	1918
George R.	43028	D	1925	Martha Norrick	85075	I	1940	Thomas	28705	D	1920
George T.	75700	D	1937	Mary	23030	D	1917	Thomas	41783	D	1925
Glenness H.	70415	I	1935	Mary	73518	D	1936	Thomas	41783	D	1925
H. R.	14259	D	1912	Mary	77600	D	1938	Thomas	44939	D	1926
Hannah	3908	D	1907	Mary	54104	D	1929	Thomas C.	61094	D	1932
Hannah	15263	D	1913	Mary Agnes	64740	D	1933	Thomas H.	57187	I	1930
Harry Marilao	22900	M	1917	Mary Anne	89489	M	1942	Thomas W.	3990	I	1907
Harry Thornton	76741	D	1937	Mary E.	33820	D	1922	Walter	86227	D	1941
Helena Neva	59448	D	1931	Mary Elizabeth	9147	D	1910	Walter J.	54192	D	1929
Henry	35156	D	1922	Mary Jane	78144	D	1938	Walter M.	34171	I	1922
Herbert T.	11946	D	1911	Mary Teresa Hope	61122	D	1932	Wesley Chadbourne	32034	D	1921
Hetty A.	42029	D	1925	Matilda	73161	I	1936	William	34599	D	1922
Hilliard	89663	D	1942	Matilda E.	73784	I	1936	William Frederick	75865	D	1937
Howard H.	43264	D	1925	Maurice	64971	D	1933	William H.	29870	D	1920
Isaac William	59057	I	1931	Minnie Elizabeth	81739	D	1939	William S.	44982	D	1926
Isidor C.	3496	D	1907	Nancy	13504	D	1912	Woodruff Mason	19250	D	1915
James	59080	D	1931	Narissa	68483	D	1934	**MOORECROFT**			
James J.	10055	D	1910	Nathaniel	6247	D	1908	Frederick	14694	D	1913
James W.	53085	I	1929	Neil A.	57950	I	1931	**MOOREHEAD**			
Jane Swan	73734	I	1936	Nellie	64661	D	1933	Rose	37729	I	1923
Jennie	2	D	1906	Owen	78111	D	1938	**MOOREHOUSE**			
John	19227	D	1915	Patrick	34605	D	1922	Audrey	69942	M	1935
John	34448	I	1922	Percy Ronald	70033	D	1935	Bert	69942	M	1935
John	35604	I	1922	Philip	69150	D	1935	Charles	20186	D	1915
John	48880	D	1928	Pierre C.	35785	I	1923	Charles	69942	M	1935
John	53630	D	1929	Pierre C.	36340	D	1923	June	69942	M	1935
John C.	59438	I	1931	Raymond	25961	I	1918				

Key: D = death; M = minor; I = incompetent

NAME	NUMBER	TYPE	YEAR	NAME	NUMBER	TYPE	YEAR	NAME	NUMBER	TYPE	YEAR
Louise	69942	M	1935	MORALES				James, Jr.	32608	I	1921
MOORHOUSE				Diego	49036	D	1928	John	11867	D	1911
H. D.	73932	D	1936	Jose	55073	D	1930	John	17693	D	1914
Herbert	73932	D	1936	MORAN				John	23394	D	1917
MOORMAN				Albert	30620	M	1920	John	53939	D	1929
Charles	6580	M	1908	Alice	63286	D	1933	John J.	14572	D	1912
Grace	6580	M	1908	Annie	2945	D	1907	Kate	41632	D	1925
Helen	6580	M	1908	Annie	19261	D	1915	Louis J., Mrs.	71679	D	1936
Louise J. Mayo	55921	D	1930	Annie	46768	D	1927	M. A.	47838	D	1927
Ruth	6580	M	1908	Annie E.	38992	I	1924	Margaret	29913	I	1920
William C.	56034	I	1930	Annie E.	39178	D	1924	Margaret	33103	D	1921
William C.	62672	I	1932	Bernard J.	41914	D	1925	Marguerite	33331	D	1922
MOORS				Bernard J.	41914	D	1925	Marsh	47838	D	1927
Anna J.	50478	D	1928	Bernard J.	47150	D	1927	Martin	53839	D	1929
Harry Jay	45036	D	1926	Bridget	16853	D	1914	Martin	58063	I	1931
MOOSE				Celia	67989	D	1934	Martin	89377	D	1942
Emma List	87854	D	1941	Charles	56634	D	1930	Mary	9818	D	1910
Gustave	86836	D	1941	Christine M. J.	14561	D	1912	Mary Bernice Moore	86636	D	1941
Hettie S.	66203	D	1934	Christopher J.	57385	D	1930	Mary R.	74765	D	1937
MOOSER				Daniel C.	29817	D	1920	May	86839	D	1941
Celina	27735	D	1919	Daniel M.	51486	D	1928	Michael	40428	D	1924
Louise	32664	D	1921	David	61355	D	1932	Michael	43742	I	1926
MOOSIE				Edmund P.	57601	D	1931	Nord	22660	D	1917
John	2956	D	1907	Edward	35485	D	1922	Oliver P.	61533	D	1932
Michael	2957	M	1907	Edward	42687	D	1925	Owen	14415	D	1912
Michael J.	89472	D	1942	Edward F.	46336	D	1927	Patrick	26184	D	1919
MOOSLIN				Eliza	26675	D	1919	Patrick L.	83270	D	1940
Michael	71076	D	1935	Elizabeth	8189	D	1909	Peter	1264	D	1906
MOOTE				Elizabeth	44786	I	1926	Prudenence W.	53695	D	1929
Annie H.	6730	D	1908	Elizabeth	47693	D	1927	Prudent W.	53695	D	1929
MOQULEWSKY				Elmer M.	48466	I	1927	Staunton Bryan	85501	D	1940
Jacob	17250	D	1914	Estelle Patricia	73835	M	1936	Susan M.	74361	L	1937
MORA				Eugene F.	14620	D	1912	Thomas	18411	D	1915
Francis	10817	D	1910	Frances	28226	D	1919	Thomas	21716	D	1916
Giovanni	59342	D	1931	Francis	54094	D	1929	Thomas	32332	D	1921
MORABITO				Frank	30620	M	1920	Thomas	58992	D	1931
Grazia	25909	D	1918	Frank M.	18830	I	1915	Thomas A.	17244	D	1914
MORAGGI				Frank M.	22161	D	1917	Thomas J.	21509	D	1916
Carlo	63586	D	1933	Freida E.	70572	D	1935	Thomas P.	28306	D	1919
MORAGHAN				Harry	30620	M	1920	Victoria	10929	D	1910
John O.	7887	D	1909	Honora	22660	D	1917	Vincent	30620	M	1920
MORAHAN				Irving L.	63374	D	1933	William	63745	D	1933
Ethel Mary	24336	M	1918	Isabella F.	71679	D	1936	William Martin	25217	D	1918
MORAIS				James	11660	D	1911	William R.	35429	D	1922
Marguerite	83212	D	1940	James	40276	D	1924	MORAND			
				James F.	10297	D	1910	Auguste	85240	D	1940
				James M.	1718	D	1906	Clotilde	78863	D	1938
				James P.	73231	I	1936	MORANDO			
				James P.	76318	D	1937	Fernando	41027	I	1925

NAME	NUMBER	TYPE	YEAR
Louis	41027	I	1925
Mary	44148	D	1926
Theresa G.	52578	D	1929
MORANO			
Proceso	75458	I	1937
MORASCH			
Peter	47980	D	1927
MORAWETZ			
Joseph	58476	D	1931
MORAWSKI			
Adolph	38146	D	1924
Stanley	26803	M	1919
MORAZ			
Alex	65671	D	1933
Mike	44832	I	1926
MORBIO			
Alberta	22674	M	1917
MORBY			
Seth	41779	D	1925
Seth	41779	D	1925
MORCEL			
Georges	19248	D	1915
Roger	21929	M	1916
MORCHIO			
Harriet B.	70048	D	1935
MORCK			
David	51320	D	1928
Peter J.	36841	D	1923
MORCONI			
Michele	65237	D	1933
MORD			
John A., Jr.	36534	M	1923
MORDASINI			
Mary	70523	D	1935
MORDAUNT			
Isabel	63236	D	1932
Josefina	60529	I	1931
Margaret	3538	D	1907
MORDEN			
Alma	69913	D	1935
MORDICA			
Windsor Raymond	41656	M	1925
MORDIN			
John	32838	D	1921
MORDINOIO			
Giovanni	34571	D	1922

NAME	NUMBER	TYPE	YEAR
MORDONA			
John	34571	D	1922
MORDT			
Elise	61428	D	1932
MORE			
Alexander Martin	80602	D	1939
Bethyl Shirley	33860	M	1922
Elizabeth Love	33585	D	1922
Frank	79196	D	1938
Lois Frances	33860	M	1922
MOREAU			
Charles L.	86102	D	1941
Constance	306	D	1906
Frank	48093	D	1927
George	8902	D	1909
Jean Evelyn	55891	M	1930
Joseph	7734	D	1909
Louise M.	62891	D	1932
Marie Louise	62891	D	1932
Mary	9002	D	1910
MOREHEAD			
Nellie Nonie	60592	D	1932
MOREHOUSE			
Charles	60789	I	1932
Charles A.	87213	D	1941
Elizabeth M.	34084	D	1922
Frank B.	21330	M	1916
Henry S.	75894	D	1937
Louis C.	67698	I	1934
Marion B.	21330	M	1916
Morono	8679	M	1909
Rebecca	2515	D	1906
Seward	75894	D	1937
MOREL			
Frank	74097	D	1936
Rose	41904	D	1925
Rose	41904	D	1925
MORELAND			
James A.	18113	D	1914
MORELLE			
Frank	52496	D	1929
MORELLI			
Frank	52496	D	1929
Lawrence Alfred	31167	D	1921
Louis	43986	D	1926
Roger	27594	D	1919

NAME	NUMBER	TYPE	YEAR
MORELLO			
Domenico	60176	D	1931
MOREN			
Anna C.	83193	D	1940
George Gottfrid	85102	D	1940
MORENA			
Saveria	79605	D	1938
MOREND			
Oscar H.	62592	D	1932
MORENIER			
Joseph	43713	D	1926
MORENO			
Carmen	83570	D	1940
Edward	45276	D	1926
Edward H.	43836	I	1926
Feliciano	63326	D	1933
Felix	6932	M	1908
Frank	86208	M	1941
Maurice	80746	D	1939
Nicholas	49585	D	1928
Pachita	4434	M	1907
Peter	22149	D	1917
Rafael	62798	D	1932
MORESCO			
Giovanni	68211	I	1934
MORESI			
Adelina	37928	D	1923
S.	22306	D	1917
MORETON			
Bertha	69692	D	1935
MORETTI			
Attilio	18842	D	1915
Francesco	60713	D	1932
Helen	20853	M	1916
Romeo	20853	M	1916
MOREY			
Charles E.	6707	D	1908
Elbert Murray	56802	D	1930
Lyell B.	13190	M	1912
MORFFEW			
Margaret J.	28335	D	1919
MORFORD			
Virginia Frances	56140	M	1930
MORGAN			
A. E.	60346	I	1931
AdaBelle	72867	D	1936
Alfred S.	85621	D	1940

Key: D = death; M = minor; I = incompetent

NAME	NUMBER	TYPE	YEAR	NAME	NUMBER	TYPE	YEAR	NAME	NUMBER	TYPE	YEAR
Alice	72165	D	1936	John P.	58784	D	1931	**MORGENSTERN**			
Alice J.	78701	D	1938	John S. D.	65503	D	1933	Alfred William	34063	D	1922
Alicia Marshall	71846	D	1936	John S., Sr.	36900	D	1923	Mayer	13964	D	1912
Allie	64936	D	1933	John William	80183	M	1938	Samuel	496	D	1906
Amelia Garratt	7130	D	1909	Joseph B.	53891	D	1929	**MORGENTHAL**			
Arnie B.	71115	D	1935	Joseph P.	53891	D	1929	Anton	9323	D	1910
Arnold L.	67411	D	1934	Josephine	72506	D	1936	**MORGENTHAU**			
Barbara	80183	M	1938	June	80183	M	1938	Leopold	1007	D	1906
Betty	71664	D	1936	Laura E.	77080	D	1937	**MORHOFF**			
Burrows W.	3580	M	1907	Lee	32020	D	1921	Elenora	22213	M	1917
Catherine E.	42730	D	1925	Lucy	52087	D	1929	Geraldine	59167	D	1931
Charles Augustus	14541	D	1912	Lucy	86112	D	1941	Nora	19557	D	1915
Charles R.	72964	D	1936	Margaret	18095	D	1914	William C.	62217	I	1932
Claire	89679	I	1942	Margaret	18811	D	1915	**MORI**			
Clara E.	40205	D	1924	Margaret	60980	D	1932	Edith	54013	D	1929
Clara E.	72237	D	1936	Mary	60980	D	1932	Giovanni	59342	D	1931
David B.	42822	M	1925	Mary	81967	D	1939	Jack	53974	D	1929
David Morris	41363	D	1925	Max	75560	D	1937	Leopold	47531	D	1927
Doris Kern	67797	M	1934	Maymie	17954	D	1914	Leopoldo	52458	D	1929
Dorothy	9090	D	1910	Michael	25414	D	1918	Pietro	32683	D	1921
Edna Charlotte	67798	M	1934	Mildred	11176	M	1911	Rhea	58237	M	1931
Eleanor A. W.	55174	D	1930	Richard Sumner	10467	D	1910	Rhea M.	57627	D	1931
Elizabeth	42971	D	1925	Robert N.	69945	D	1935	**MORIANE**			
Elizabeth Wainwright	53275	D	1929	Rose E.	16749	D	1914	Louisa	35620	D	1922
Ella A. W.	55174	D	1930	Samual George	83015	D	1940	**MORIARITY**			
Ella W.	9850	D	1910	Samuel W.	86474	D	1941	John P.	84403	D	1940
Elmer Clarence	53568	I	1929	Sophia E.	9914	D	1910	**MORIARTY**			
Emma L.	71277	D	1935	Susan D.	33355	D	1922	Agnes Loretta	27759	D	1919
Everard Milton	26734	D	1919	Thomas G.	3471	D	1907	Anna	60942	D	1932
Francis Edward, Jr.	80183	M	1938	Tom	81268	D	1939	Catherine A.	48575	D	1927
Frank J.	44307	D	1926	Vaughan	36716	D	1923	Charles W.	83959	D	1940
Frederic	62646	D	1932	W. I.	10385	D	1910	Daniel J.	44964	D	1926
Frederick C.	39869	D	1924	Walter O., Jr.	38629	M	1924	Daniel W.	89798	I	1942
George	36780	D	1923	William	2866	D	1907	Ellen	45201	I	1926
George Arthur	40263	D	1924	William	50628	D	1928	Ellen	72075	D	1936
George R.	41773	D	1925	William A.	17983	D	1914	Eugene	4523	D	1907
George R.	41773	D	1925	William H.	18594	D	1915	James	48306	D	1927
Harry	87293	D	1941	William M.	19652	D	1915	John	4270	D	1907
Harry A.	74642	I	1937	William P.	4546	D	1907	John	49988	D	1928
Helen	3286	M	1907	William S.	42822	M	1925	John Joseph	61216	D	1932
Helene	83760	D	1940	Wilma	80183	M	1938	John P.	55583	D	1930
Hiram H.	44045	D	1926	**MORGANS**				Margaret	16051	D	1913
Horace W.	34682	D	1922	Morgan	3385	D	1907	Marilyn Jean	82984	M	1939
Horace W.	77254	D	1937	**MORGANSTERN**				Mary	11689	D	1911
James A.	89522	D	1942	Irwin H.	31964	M	1921	Sarah E. McQuaide	25388	D	1918
James L.	63938	D	1933	**MORGENSEN**				Seamus	47480	D	1927
John	29270	D	1920	J. Julius	20879	D	1916				
John	50704	D	1928								
John A.	74642	I	1937								

NAME	NUMBER	TYPE	YEAR	NAME	NUMBER	TYPE	YEAR	NAME	NUMBER	TYPE	YEAR
MORICONI				James F.	20487	D	1916	Ida M.	43690	I	1926
Goffredo	24028	D	1918	James T.	20487	D	1916	Margaret A.	55722	D	1930
Poalino	29970	D	1920	Martin	9080	D	1910	Rhinette	71852	I	1936
MORIEN				Mary	27931	D	1919	Rhinette	75862	D	1937
Victorine	38831	I	1924	Rose	84121	D	1940	**MORRICE**			
Victorine	39507	D	1924	Sarah M.	49833	D	1928	Catherine	64668	D	1933
MORILLA				**MORLOCK**				**MORRILL**			
Francisca	73329	D	1936	Adele	55873	M	1930	Arthur L.	34676	D	1922
Toribio	59144	I	1931	Catherine A.	72764	D	1936	Bryan	75314	D	1937
Toribio	82194	D	1939	Charles G.	49611	D	1928	Emma B.	53361	D	1929
MORILLO				Fred H., Mrs.	72764	D	1936	Frederick L.	8093	I	1909
Earl	33287	M	1922	Marie Ruth	55324	M	1930	Mary Agnes	64686	D	1933
MORIN				Minnie T.	12004	D	1911	Pauline B.	24027	D	1918
Adrian Lewis	47261	D	1927	Naomi	55873	M	1930	**MORRIN**			
MORINE				**MORMINO**				Anna	31282	M	1921
Daniel G.	23321	D	1917	Pietro	46505	D	1927	Gertrude	31282	M	1921
MORINI				**MORNEAU**				Irene	21411	D	1916
Giuseppe	4522	M	1907	Emilie	78451	D	1938	Peter J.	29950	I	1920
Leonarda Maria	75330	D	1937	**MORNING**				Peter J.	30675	D	1920
MORINO				Daniel W.	77481	D	1938	**MORRIS**			
Maurice	80746	D	1939	**MORO**				Abraham	2263	D	1906
MORISUYE				Francisco Rodriquez	27514	D	1919	Abraham	3344	D	1907
Joe	44472	M	1926	**MORON**				Abraham	41103	D	1925
MORITA				John J.	21804	D	1916	Adelaide A.	53416	D	1929
Fumiko	79838	M	1938	**MORONEY**				Adelaide F.	26026	D	1918
Kiyoko	79838	M	1938	Ellen	11782	D	1911	Alice Lydia	50179	D	1928
Shijeru	79838	M	1938	J. Frank	26806	D	1919	Alvin	29714	M	1920
MORITZ				John	42653	D	1925	Amelia	20215	D	1916
Friederick	5614	D	1908	Lee D.	33766	D	1922	Amos	25263	D	1918
Joseph	52467	D	1929	Peter J.	62617	D	1932	Anita	28031	M	1919
Metha	3012	D	1907	**MORONG**				Anna Josephine	74478	D	1937
MORIZIO				Myra E.	7895	D	1909	Anna M.	69332	D	1935
Annie	20755	D	1916	**MOROSALI**				Anna May	73667	D	1936
Sebastian	16269	D	1913	Carlo	36184	D	1923	Annie	4814	I	1907
Sebastian	26000	D	1918	**MOROSI**				Annie	4893	D	1907
MORK				Cora	17092	M	1914	Arthur S.	54821	D	1930
Andrew	41096	D	1925	**MOROSOLI**				Arthur Sydney	83968	I	1940
Carl P.	63707	D	1933	Carlo	36184	D	1923	Avis Maud	76569	D	1937
MORKEN				**MOROZ**				Barbara H. S.	41014	D	1925
Clara W.	64376	D	1933	Alexander	65671	D	1933	Berneice	28031	M	1919
MORLEY				Stephen L.	47178	D	1927	Bertha Green	82197	D	1939
Anna	38249	I	1924	**MORPHY**				Betty Jane	69408	M	1935
Catherine	66962	D	1934	Minnie A.	59906	D	1931	Brougham F.	51727	M	1928
Dora	34687	D	1922	**MORRELL**				C. R.	46667	D	1927
Frederick H.	32273	D	1921	A. J.	2576	D	1906	Cecilia B.	66718	D	1934
George	46672	I	1927	Charles H.	9474	D	1910	Charles	67879	D	1934
				Henrietta	2577	D	1906	Charles	63943	D	1933
								Charles C.	15247	D	1913

NAME	NUMBER	TYPE	YEAR	NAME	NUMBER	TYPE	YEAR	NAME	NUMBER	TYPE	YEAR
Charles S.	88555	I	1941	John T.	85203	D	1940	Theodore	14212	D	1912
Chester	46667	D	1927	John W.	79551	I	1938	Theresa Gertrude	76236	D	1937
Constantine	41206	D	1925	John W.	79629	D	1938	Thomas	9761	D	1910
Cora	46839	D	1927	Joseph	53981	D	1929	Vincent V.	56122	M	1930
Coral E.	59886	D	1931	Josephine	89179	I	1942	Ward	82622	D	1939
David	1344	D	1906	Julia	1733	M	1906	Willard B.	63291	D	1933
Edward	35528	D	1922	Justus T.	5573	D	1908	William	58742	D	1931
Edward Hart	26336	D	1919	Katherine A.	69638	D	1935	William G.	53417	D	1929
Edward W.	1609	D	1906	Katherine J.	69638	D	1935	William Truxtun	78102	D	1938
Eileen	28031	M	1919	Katherine M.	20173	D	1915	Wyndham Augustus	69713	D	1935
Elizabeth	82281	D	1939	Leon E.	83179	D	1940	**MORRISEY**			
Elizabeth	45922	D	1926	Lessie W.	69196	I	1935	Alexander	20004	D	1915
Ellanor	20452	D	1916	Louisa	64719	D	1933	Charles	52798	M	1929
Fannie S.	57501	D	1930	Louise P.	78281	D	1938	David	33171	D	1922
Fanny	4526	D	1907	Lucile E.	63616	I	1933	Henry H.	52798	M	1929
Flora Alice	80047	D	1938	Marcus K.	17067	D	1914	James	52798	M	1929
Florence	28031	M	1919	Margaret	696	D	1906	James Francis	25198	D	1918
Florence M.	56122	M	1930	Margaret	16052	D	1913	John E.	52798	M	1929
Francis Thomas	66170	D	1934	Margaret	78596	D	1938	Lillie A.	55924	D	1930
Frank	5754	D	1908	Margaret E.	88131	D	1941	Nicholas	68852	D	1935
Frank	9851	D	1910	Mary	13683	D	1912	Thomas	68287	D	1934
Fred J.	51727	M	1928	Mary	16478	D	1913	**MORRISON**			
Frederick	48561	D	1927	Mary A.	51647	D	1928	A. A.	63865	D	1933
George W.	14062	D	1912	Mary Agnes	56122	M	1930	Agnes	58423	D	1931
Gus	41206	D	1925	Mary E.	52428	D	1929	Agnes I.	89565	D	1942
Hannah	1345	D	1906	Mary E.	56570	D	1930	Alexander	20004	D	1915
Hannah	1732	I	1906	Mary E.	83528	D	1940	Alexander F.	33090	D	1921
Harold Clarence	26318	M	1919	Mary W.	33043	D	1921	Alice	3028	D	1907
Harrie Chester	56358	D	1930	Mathilde E.	51726	D	1928	Alice	20571	M	1916
Henry	1083	D	1906	May L.	32717	D	1921	Anna	63865	D	1933
Henry	47332	D	1927	Michael Edward	70515	D	1935	Arlina S.	57279	I	1930
Henry	52976	D	1929	Michael J.	44818	D	1926	Charles	33981	D	1922
Herman	78761	D	1938	Milton E.	69407	D	1935	Charles J.	57281	D	1930
Irving A.	21376	D	1916	Minnie	57736	D	1931	Elizabeth G.	12471	D	1911
Irving Aaron	1257	M	1906	Muriel	65432	M	1933	Ella	66656	D	1934
J. H.	22022	I	1916	Nicholas	80184	D	1938	Estelle	8999	M	1910
Jack Clifford	82763	M	1939	Norman K.	61276	D	1932	Eugenia L.	51161	D	1928
Jack W.	69408	M	1935	Oscar Raymond	81026	D	1939	Euphemia S.	33982	D	1922
James	33410	D	1922	Pauline	80101	D	1938	Frank C.	42631	D	1925
James	53197	D	1929	Richard Warner	39004	M	1924	George Edward	25181	M	1918
James L.	31726	D	1921	Robert Hendy	83408	D	1940	George L.	20571	M	1916
James L.	54314	I	1929	Rosa	26352	D	1919	George W.	1556	D	1906
James L.	55184	D	1930	Rose	55272	D	1930	Georgie	29251	D	1920
James William	1733	M	1906	Samuel S.	80975	D	1939	Harry A.	81974	M	1939
Jefferson D.	59912	D	1931	Sarah	11623	D	1911	Harry F., Jr.	81974	M	1939
John	39385	D	1924	Sarah	46465	D	1927	Helen	72375	I	1936
John	73549	D	1936	Sidney Hooper	61320	D	1932	Isabella	81500	D	1939
John James	42109	D	1925	Simon	13854	D	1912	James	83924	I	1940
John M.	56117	D	1930	Stanley Harold	42840	M	1925	James C.	31612	D	1921

Key: D = death; M = minor; I = incompetent

NAME	NUMBER	TYPE	YEAR
Janet	17154	D	1914
Jean L.	18232	D	1914
John M.	33684	D	1922
Lauchlin	35423	D	1922
Lew	15558	D	1913
Lewis	3404	D	1907
Lillian Maxine	25181	M	1918
Magdalena	44871	D	1926
Margaret M.	58423	D	1931
Mattie	18886	D	1915
May T.	82413	D	1939
Michael	14154	D	1912
Perry	17335	D	1914
Sarah	17836	D	1914
William D.	89785	D	1942
William George	40935	D	1925
William John	27833	D	1919
MORRISSETTE			
Frances Mary	82525	M	1939
MORRISSEY			
Amanda W.	69967	D	1935
Ann	33463	M	1922
Bartholomew S.	555	I	1906
Catherine M.	66705	D	1934
Elizabeth	13026	D	1912
James Henry	50971	D	1928
Johanna	39087	D	1924
John Joseph	16025	D	1913
John William	58534	D	1931
Joseph G.	33463	M	1922
Joseph G.	34917	D	1922
Lillie A.	55924	D	1930
Malvina	69990	D	1935
Mary	35898	D	1923
William H.	4482	D	1907
Winifred	1204	D	1906
MORRITSEN			
O.	28292	D	1919
MORRO			
Battista	59668	D	1931
MORROSCO			
Frank W. G.	13744	D	1912
MORROW			
Elizabeth A.	66068	M	1934
Eugene Dale	89145	I	1942
Grant	27832	M	1919
Helen E.	66068	M	1934
Howard	88326	D	1941

NAME	NUMBER	TYPE	YEAR
Howard L.	79539	D	1938
James A.	9091	D	1910
Kate Rowley	75739	I	1937
Lydia Houghton	50857	D	1928
Mary J.	3912	D	1907
Maryle	57390	M	1930
Noel Philip	55980	D	1930
Robert	27832	M	1919
Robert F.	24663	D	1918
Robert Head	74391	D	1937
Robert M.	66068	M	1934
Samuel A.	72961	D	1936
Theresa Carpaneto	89267	D	1942
Thomas	75322	I	1937
Thomas G.	75234	I	1937
Thomas J.	80816	D	1939
Vernon M.	48870	D	1928
W. C., Mrs.	50857	D	1928
Weldon	27832	M	1919
William	37673	I	1923
William	37977	I	1923
William W.	53569	D	1929
MORRRIS			
Catherine	2970	D	1907
MORSE			
Anthony Wayne	81776	D	1939
Caroline Frances	4541	D	1907
Charles C.	1180	D	1906
Charles C.	24559	D	1918
Charles Percy	86968	D	1941
Charles S.	24559	D	1918
Cora A.	1326	D	1906
Cora Belle	72449	D	1936
Cora Idella	72449	D	1936
Douglass H.	22774	D	1917
Edna	54752	M	1930
Edward	62374	D	1932
Edward A.	842	D	1906
Franklin B.	53908	D	1929
George Edward	421	D	1906
George L.	6393	D	1908
George Winfield	80670	D	1939
Isaac Harrison	42622	D	1925
Jacob	65523	D	1933
James	38664	D	1924
James Edward	71812	D	1936
Jessie Patten	75908	D	1937
Johanna	72807	D	1936
John Jacob	31190	D	1921

NAME	NUMBER	TYPE	YEAR
Joseph	34348	D	1922
Margaret Mary	51735	D	1929
Margery Stevens	75907	D	1937
Marjorie McKinley	11484	M	1911
Mary E.	42921	D	1925
Myrtle	54752	M	1930
MORSER			
Edward John	81150	D	1939
Mignon Margaret	80553	D	1939
MORTARINO			
Modesto	34204	D	1922
MORTEDE			
Michele	64431	D	1933
Mike	64431	D	1933
MORTENSEN			
Alfred William	14050	D	1912
Conrad	55795	D	1930
George	81301	D	1939
Jorgen	81301	D	1939
Katherine Rice Lewis	22507	D	1917
Martin P.	72834	D	1936
Minnie L.	72835	I	1936
Minnie L.	73323	D	1936
Niels	9609	D	1910
Patricia Dolores	55699	M	1930
Peter D.	84775	D	1940
Thelma Miram	55699	M	1930
MORTENSON			
Charles G.	57399	D	1930
Ida Florence	79811	D	1938
Ida Lenoir	79811	D	1938
MORTIGIA			
Mathias M.	44709	D	1926
Matias, Jr.	48209	D	1927
Porfiria L.	9636	D	1910
MORTIGLIENGO			
Frank	23452	D	1917
MORTIMER			
Harry W.	7497	D	1909
Henry W.	7497	D	1909
MORTOLA			
Herbert	78286	D	1938
Prosper	56363	D	1930
Prospero	77208	D	1937
MORTON			
Carrie L.	63840	I	1933
Carrie L.	84710	D	1940

NAME	NUMBER	TYPE	YEAR	NAME	NUMBER	TYPE	YEAR	NAME	NUMBER	TYPE	YEAR
Charles	29097	D	1920	Joseph	48484	D	1927	Sarah Naomi	43758	D	1926
Clara A.	48019	D	1927	**MOSCHEN**				**MOSELY**			
Cora Wallace	58557	D	1931	Maria	79158	D	1938	Jack	25507	D	1918
Earle Hamilton	67808	D	1934	**MOSCHIN**				**MOSEMAN**			
Eleanor M. H.	65539	D	1933	Maria	79158	D	1938	John H.	69550	D	1935
Ella J.	26332	D	1919	**MOSCHINI**				**MOSER**			
Ellen	65801	D	1933	Gabriello	72301	D	1936	Anton	48488	D	1927
Ellen Elizabeth	10412	I	1910	Maria	29478	D	1920	Bartolomeo	9605	D	1910
Erik B.	54826	D	1930	Maria	79158	D	1938	Blanche	14613	D	1912
Frank	61225	D	1932	Rinald	84106	D	1940	Gregory F.	71909	D	1936
George	19838	M	1915	**MOSCONE**				Herman	58635	D	1931
George F.	13859	M	1912	Felice	34144	D	1922	Johanna C.	82421	D	1939
George W.	50698	M	1928	Filippo	60604	D	1932	Joseph	22066	D	1917
Henry David	22679	D	1917	Giuseppe	38877	I	1924	Peter	13465	D	1912
Henry F.	13859	M	1912	Giuseppe	40724	D	1925	**MOSES**			
Howard E.	80834	D	1939	Liugi	28735	D	1920	Charles Smith	60859	D	1932
Isabel Wilson	13503	D	1912	Louis	28735	D	1920	David M.	35939	I	1923
Isabella	36438	D	1923	Michael	65237	D	1933	Emma R.	46945	D	1927
James	24023	D	1918	**MOSCONI**				Fannie	54925	D	1930
James Hamilton	9932	D	1910	Alessio	80221	D	1938	Frank M.	54422	D	1929
James Proctor	51456	D	1928	Alfonso	80221	D	1938	John H.	5981	D	1908
Jennie Agnes	74078	D	1936	Emilia	26031	M	1918	Joseph	10550	D	1910
John C.	13814	M	1912	Evelyn Grace	65260	M	1933	Marguerite	149	M	1906
Joseph	41474	D	1925	Giuseppe	38877	I	1924	Montague T.	47958	D	1927
Joseph P.	13859	M	1912	Giuseppe	40724	D	1925	Rebecca	79171	D	1938
Josephine	75491	D	1937	Harold	26031	M	1918	Rebecca Farr	69789	D	1935
Laurence Bunker	72076	D	1936	Harry	38009	D	1923	Samuel	46338	D	1927
Lucy J.	68296	D	1934	Leonora	26031	M	1918	Sophia	47101	D	1927
Mabel	88891	D	1942	Lois	40109	M	1924	Wm. S.	14717	D	1913
Margaret	49325	D	1928	Margaret	25042	D	1918	Yetta	26889	D	1919
Mary	57444	D	1930	Michael	65237	D	1933	**MOSESI**			
Patrick C.	13769	D	1912	Peter	26031	M	1918	Gualtiero Walter	74297	D	1937
Paul Caylor	66196	M	1934	Santino	25905	D	1918	Walter	74297	D	1937
Ruth	51465	D	1928	**MOSCONIA**				**MOSHEIM**			
Thomas	3459	D	1907	Peter	26031	M	1918	Adolf	67273	D	1934
MOSBACHER				**MOSCOVITZ**				**MOSHER**			
Jennie	70621	D	1935	Annie	23590	M	1917	Abby Adell	56982	D	1930
Sophia	16299	D	1913	Bessie	23590	M	1917	Alvin H.	67043	D	1934
MOSBARDA				Leon	23590	M	1917	Fred	25480	D	1918
Ernest	48376	D	1927	Oscar	23590	M	1917	Horace G.	43590	D	1926
MOSBY				Pearl	23590	M	1917	Susabel	4124	M	1907
Ardrene R.	73597	M	1936	Sarah	23590	M	1917	William B.	36431	D	1923
Elenora	37941	I	1923	**MOSE**				**MOSHNICKOFF**			
Thomas T.	30063	D	1920	Fortunato	52333	D	1929	Jaaho	41375	D	1925
MOSCA				**MOSEBACH**				**MOSIAS**			
F. C.	76557	D	1937	Henry	43757	D	1926	Gertrude	38915	M	1924
Felix	76557	D	1937	Naomi	43758	D	1926				
Giuseppe	49659	D	1928								

NAME	NUMBER	TYPE	YEAR
MOSIER			
Josephine	78578	D	1938
Peter	13465	D	1912
MOSKIVITZ			
Hyman	66029	D	1934
MOSKOVITZ			
Joseph	67926	D	1934
MOSKOW			
Frank	32638	D	1921
MOSKOWITE			
Anna	79923	D	1938
Arthur H.	47503	D	1927
MOSKOWITZ			
Arthur H.	47503	D	1927
I.	26808	D	1919
Murray	49885	D	1928
MOSLEY			
Charles J.	3971	D	1907
Francis A.	50	D	1906
George Bateman	51296	D	1928
MOSS			
Alfred T.	1276	I	1906
Anna	49493	D	1928
Benjamin F.	83303	D	1940
Blanche Marie	53120	D	1929
Daisy S.	44582	D	1926
Delia F.	19980	D	1915
Dorothy Hermine	47380	M	1927
George	30359	D	1920
George A.	16228	D	1913
Gertrude	12607	D	1911
Harry	88950	D	1942
J. Mora	31888	D	1921
Jacob	65306	D	1933
Jacob	69916	D	1935
James C.	53327	D	1929
Leopold	16226	D	1913
Mabel	84515	D	1940
Margaret F.	42427	D	1925
Margaret Frances	50813	D	1928
Margaret Mary	51735	D	1929
Mary	71920	D	1936
Mary	71994	M	1936
Mary, Jr.	69948	M	1935
Phillis	31946	M	1921
MOSSAWIR			
Salim I.	88349	D	1941

NAME	NUMBER	TYPE	YEAR
MOSSFORD			
Moses	2904	D	1907
MOSSI			
John E.	60094	I	1931
MOSSLER			
Caroline	46878	D	1927
Fred	79799	D	1938
MOSSMAN			
Minnie	56165	D	1930
MOSSMAYER			
A. L.	53179	D	1929
MOSSO			
Carlo	77186	D	1937
MOSTAHINICH			
Edith K.	82313	D	1939
MOSTARDA			
Ernesto	48376	D	1927
MOSTOVOY			
Geraldine Ann	55265	M	1930
MOSUNIC			
Rose C.	49526	D	1928
MOTE			
Elmer E.	23562	D	1917
MOTETTA			
Antonio	23479	D	1917
Edvige	27771	M	1919
Giacomo	27771	M	1919
Romeo	27771	M	1919
Zefferino	27771	M	1919
MOTONARI			
Frank	79976	D	1938
Hiroo	79976	D	1938
MOTRONI			
Agostino	1236	D	1906
Beatrice	38822	M	1924
Giuseppe	25639	D	1918
Herbert	38822	M	1924
Herbert J.	25800	D	1918
Lorenza	24155	D	1918
MOTSKIER			
Fred	56884	D	1930
MOTT			
Amelia Huntington	1208	D	1906
Amelia M.	1208	D	1906
Barbara Jean	66547	M	1934
Charles W.	60663	D	1932

NAME	NUMBER	TYPE	YEAR
Ernest J.	42591	D	1925
Frederick	59412	D	1931
Honora	18931	D	1915
Jessie	59957	D	1931
Rhoda E.	23432	M	1917
T. Egbert	16003	D	1913
Warren	66547	M	1934
MOTTE			
Joseph	39964	D	1924
Theophile	59683	D	1931
MOTTROM			
John	67133	D	1934
Matilda	40869	D	1925
MOTZER			
Conrad	24087	D	1918
MOUGE			
Fredericka	62909	D	1932
MOUGHTON			
Alfred	55993	D	1930
MOUILLESEAUX			
Elise	80082	D	1938
MOULDER			
Bayard	45700	M	1926
Brayton	45700	M	1926
Helen	45700	M	1926
Jackson	45700	M	1926
Johnson	45700	M	1926
Kenneth	45700	M	1926
Louis Emanuel	45700	M	1926
Louisa J.	44205	D	1926
Louise	45700	M	1926
Louise B.	44205	D	1926
Robert	45700	M	1926
MOULIN			
Albert	33256	D	1922
MOULLIN			
Bertha Julia	78683	D	1938
MOULTHROP			
Charles W.	30746	D	1920
MOULTON			
Adaline W.	31404	D	1921
Anne S.	35848	D	1923
Eleonora Rose	58579	D	1931
Gordon A.	39452	I	1924
Gordon A.	79699	D	1938
John Edward	28443	D	1919
Mabel	7813	D	1909

NAME	NUMBER	TYPE	YEAR	NAME	NUMBER	TYPE	YEAR	NAME	NUMBER	TYPE	YEAR
Rosina	58579	D	1931	Lyman I.	52863	D	1929	Elizabeth	84760	I	1940
Thelma	6587	M	1908	**MOXEY**				Elizabeth	85441	D	1940
MOUNIC				Oliver Newton	68581	D	1934	Ellen	9953	D	1910
Alice	2471	M	1906	**MOXLEY**				Hanorah	13988	D	1912
MOUNICOU				Elizabeth W. H.	860	D	1906	J., Mrs.	13988	D	1912
Pierre	25661	D	1918	Gage H.	78	I	1906	John	5680	D	1908
MOUNT				**MOY**				John	27464	D	1919
Lavonia Louisa	16790	D	1914	Jung Qui	63719	D	1933	Mary A.	5596	M	1908
MOUNTAIN				Lee Jung Qui	63719	D	1933	Nora T.	82583	D	1939
Edward	62273	D	1932	Qui	63719	D	1933	Patrick T.	33749	D	1922
MOUNTFORD				Yoong	51099	D	1928	Timothy	36581	I	1923
Florence Margaret	15903	M	1913	**MOYCE**				Timothy J.	17681	D	1914
MOURET				Harry Cedric	83468	D	1940	Timothy P.	72058	D	1936
Marie Jeanne	2751	D	1907	Mary F.	83459	D	1940	**MOYSE**			
MOURITZEN				**MOYE**				Henriette	33600	D	1922
Johannes	35322	D	1922	Catherine Francis	26299	D	1919	Maurice	33865	D	1922
MOURN				Mary	32997	M	1921	Russell Albert	83872	D	1940
Margaret	53948	D	1929	Mary H.	50577	M	1928	**MOZEAN**			
Sophie	7315	D	1909	Mary Hanora	26300	M	1919	Joseph John	86068	D	1941
William	69915	D	1935	Milton	26300	M	1919	**MOZEAU**			
MOUSER				Milton	32997	M	1921	Joseph John	86068	D	1941
Silas Mercer	9314	D	1910	Milton J.	50577	M	1928	**MOZEK**			
MOUSNIER				**MOYER**				Hugo G.	82508	D	1939
Elise Therese	74408	D	1937	G. F.	19953	D	1915	Hugo S.	82508	D	1939
MOUTRY				Henry J.	5525	D	1908	**MPELESIA**			
Mary A.	74135	I	1936	John	48013	D	1927	Nickolaos	62251	D	1932
Mary Aloise	83932	D	1940	Lillian	40788	D	1925	**MRAKULOCK**			
MOVAN				Mary	87727	D	1941	Rade	32225	I	1921
Margaret	29913	I	1920	**MOYERUS**				**MUAH**			
MOVERT				Pierre	17541	D	1914	Amalia Sophia	54392	D	1929
Anton	113	D	1906	**MOYLAN**				**MUAT**			
MOWAT				Dennis	13386	D	1912	Amalia Sophia	54392	D	1929
Donald	31036	D	1921	**MOYLE**				**MUCHA**			
Elizabeth W.	63305	D	1933	Marylin	57707	M	1931	Hattie	81498	D	1939
Robert	63513	M	1933	William John	37709	D	1923	**MUCHER**			
MOWATT				**MOYLES**				Walter P.	57673	D	1931
D. M.	45717	D	1926	Andrew	21389	M	1916	**MUCHNA**			
MOWBRAY				Andrew J.	12845	D	1912	Lisa lotte	66227	M	1934
Jack Bamber	86850	M	1941	Bridget	11533	D	1911	**MUCHO**			
James Alexander, Jr.	16879	D	1914	James	21389	M	1916	Katie	58149	D	1931
Melton V.	71633	D	1936	Virginia	21389	M	1916	**MUCHOW**			
MOWERT				**MOYNAHAN**				Carl	88468	I	1941
Anton	113	D	1906	Cornelius	83796	D	1940	Katie	58149	D	1931
MOWRY				**MOYNIHAN**				**MUDDE**			
Laura A.	4556	D	1907	Cornelius	83796	D	1940	Luke	45607	D	1926
Lucy Malvina	27346	D	1919	Denis	52105	D	1929				
				Dennis	52792	D	1929				

Key: D = death; M = minor; I = incompetent

NAME	NUMBER	TYPE	YEAR
MUDGE			
Robert Gordon	28330	D	1919
MUDGETT			
James G.	41365	D	1925
MUDRICH			
Charles	79313	M	1938
MUEGGE			
Bertha	20338	D	1916
Elizabeth	88602	D	1941
Gladys D.	22452	M	1917
Herbert H.	22452	M	1917
MUEHE			
Lillian	70036	D	1935
MUELHAUPT			
Frank	11829	D	1911
MUELLER			
Amanda P.	12746	D	1911
Anna	52678	D	1929
Cornelius	44196	D	1926
Eilert	68950	I	1935
Emil O.	21965	D	1916
Fannie W.	60358	D	1931
Florentine	21866	D	1916
Francis C.	39712	M	1924
George	43261	D	1925
George	59570	D	1931
George Friedrich Paul	42485	D	1925
George L.	53379	D	1929
George T. O.	21581	D	1916
Henry	70593	D	1935
Herman	69806	D	1935
Jacob	57552	D	1930
Johan	28724	D	1920
John	50575	D	1928
John	79431	D	1938
Lawrence George	49866	M	1928
Marie Lena	3351	D	1907
Mary A.	9150	D	1910
Minnie	78857	D	1938
Peter	52155	D	1929
Richard	45101	D	1926
Robert F.	10422	D	1910
Robert Stanley	49866	M	1928
Stephanus A.	49918	D	1928
Viola	72975	D	1936
MUENCH			
Hermann G.	51205	D	1928

NAME	NUMBER	TYPE	YEAR
MUENZ			
John W.	15393	M	1913
MUES			
Carsten Diedrich	20235	D	1916
MUESSIGGANG			
Theresia	43635	D	1926
MUFFLER			
William	54791	D	1930
MUFFLY			
John D.	58560	D	1931
MUGAINI			
Angela	89872	D	1942
MUGAN			
Catherine	12182	D	1911
Elizaberh M.	79128	D	1938
John C.	8030	D	1909
Susan C.	89324	D	1942
William G., Mrs.	79128	D	1938
William Gordon	73154	D	1936
MUGELE			
Anna	53016	D	1929
Fred G.	77473	D	1938
George	68033	D	1934
Gottlieb Frederick	57215	D	1930
MUGFORD			
Raymond	85185	I	1940
Raymond	85846	D	1940
MUGGE			
Charles H.	16413	D	1913
George	4973	M	1908
George D.	57158	I	1930
Henrietta	4973	M	1908
Louis	4973	M	1908
MUGGLEY			
H. H.	65953	D	1933
Herny	65953	D	1933
MUGNAINI			
Angelina Margherite	89872	D	1942
MUHEIM			
Karl	28920	D	1920
William	20038	D	1915
MUHEKER			
Doris Elizabeth	47513	M	1927
Henry Abert	47513	M	1927
MUHL			
Adolph J.	14831	D	1913

NAME	NUMBER	TYPE	YEAR
Mary	18538	D	1915
William J. G.	43113	D	1925
MUHLBERGER			
Antone	61111	D	1932
MUHLENDOFF			
Harry	61010	D	1932
MUHLENFELD			
Mary A.	33383	D	1922
Nellie F.	88181	D	1941
MUHLKER			
August Albert	44405	D	1926
MUHLMAN			
Albert	49693	D	1928
MUHLMANN			
Karl Albert	49693	D	1928
MUHR			
Marie	83962	I	1940
MUHS			
Henry A. A.	48801	D	1927
MUIR			
Adam J.	32465	D	1921
Agnes	51983	D	1929
John McArthur	59810	D	1931
Marie C.	85756	D	1940
Mary	9411	I	1910
Mary	16901	D	1914
Maude L.	34586	I	1922
Robert Ballantine	81873	D	1939
MUIRHEAD			
Louisa M.	11721	D	1911
Margaret E.	22347	D	1917
Thomas	41848	D	1925
Thomas	41848	D	1925
MUKAYAMA			
Kenji	68802	D	1935
MULARGIA			
Antonio	22479	D	1917
MULCAHY			
Bridget	44774	D	1926
Bridget	63298	D	1933
Clara	19773	D	1915
David	57995	D	1931
Ellen	48393	D	1927
Eva Marie	78110	D	1938
Gertrude M.	64444	M	1933
John	74014	D	1936
Mary E.	82642	D	1939

Key: D = death; M = minor; I = incompetent

NAME	NUMBER	TYPE	YEAR	NAME	NUMBER	TYPE	YEAR	NAME	NUMBER	TYPE	YEAR
Maurice	20518	D	1916	**MULHOLLAND**				**MULLEDY**			
Mellie	48393	D	1927	Alice E.	83917	D	1940	Daniel	55321	D	1930
Michael A.	57469	D	1930	Fred E.	11918	D	1911	**MULLEE**			
Nellie	48393	D	1927	George P.	60528	D	1931	Ann	33243	D	1922
Nora Hegarty	88472	D	1941	Nancy	13504	D	1912	Delia M.	19062	D	1915
Thomas	26711	D	1919	Owen	13619	D	1912	Frances	7141	D	1909
Thomas	65738	D	1933	Sarah A.	20208	D	1916	Thomas F.	67731	D	1934
Thomas F.	83209	D	1940	**MULICK**				**MULLEN**			
MULCARE				Ignacy A.	69573	D	1935	Anna Marie	84701	I	1940
James	67022	D	1934	J.	69573	D	1935	Bessie Parks	70356	D	1935
Patrick	39698	D	1924	**MULL**				Catherine	7344	D	1909
MULCHAY				O. S.	82134	D	1939	Catherine	64545	I	1933
James H.	78974	D	1938	**MULLADY**				Catherine	40622	D	1924
MULCREVY				Daniel	55321	D	1930	Edna Mary	85914	D	1940
Harry I.	72046	D	1936	**MULLALLY**				Ellen	79600	D	1938
James P.	10322	D	1910	John E.	12927	D	1912	Francis	45714	D	1926
MULCRONE				Patrick	70536	D	1935	James J.	73077	D	1936
Alice	56015	D	1930	**MULLALY**				James Joseph	85905	D	1940
MULDOWNEY				Ellen	1275	D	1906	James W.	59435	D	1931
Mary M.	42594	D	1925	**MULLAN**				James W.	59761	D	1931
MULE				Catherine	40622	D	1924	Joanna	60731	D	1932
Celestine	57860	D	1931	James	26964	D	1919	John	35313	D	1922
MULE'				James J.	77822	D	1938	John B.	15933	D	1913
Michael	74240	D	1936	**MULLANE**				John Edward	47104	D	1927
MULERTZ				Anna	36960	D	1923	John H.	8593	D	1909
Catharine D.	37587	D	1923	Clement	14289	M	1912	John H.	15933	D	1913
MULFORD				Edward	14289	M	1912	John S.	61694	D	1932
Edwin Stanton	78346	D	1938	Edward A.	56318	D	1930	Louis	55683	D	1930
Ira S.	61890	D	1932	Ellen	48815	D	1927	Margaret	27377	D	1919
MULGREW				Margaret	20612	D	1916	Margaret A.	68075	D	1934
Frank L.	47571	D	1927	Patricia M.	67300	M	1934	Mary	3417	D	1907
MULHALL				Philip J.	89322	D	1942	Mary Florence	74576	D	1937
Joseph	19200	D	1915	**MULLANEY**				Mary Martha	89899	D	1942
Thomas E.	57971	D	1931	Anna	22524	D	1917	Mary T.	81767	D	1939
MULHAUPT				Eugene A.	80808	D	1939	Norma	14097	M	1912
Francis Anton	5960	D	1908	Louise B.	14762	D	1913	Patrick	84330	D	1940
MULHEARN				**MULLANY**				Patrick	61853	D	1932
Margaret	33504	D	1922	Catherine	16641	D	1914	Robert James	87636	M	1941
MULHERAN				Ellen	2777	D	1907	Shirley	88086	M	1941
Ellen	3873	D	1907	James	72854	D	1936	Thomas P.	69729	D	1935
MULHERN				James	44566	D	1926	William	53524	D	1929
John	41007	D	1925	Michael	57056	D	1930	William M.	44810	I	1926
Mary A.	25094	D	1918	Thomas	43270	D	1925	**MULLENDER**			
MULHERNE				**MULLARKY**				Belleshe J.	17064	M	1914
Ellen	3873	D	1907	Mary A.	25854	D	1918	Lizzie Marie	19291	D	1915
				MULLAY				Thomas	59628	D	1931
				Gertrude Ellinor	89259	D	1942	William J.	15671	D	1913

NAME	NUMBER	TYPE	YEAR	NAME	NUMBER	TYPE	YEAR	NAME	NUMBER	TYPE	YEAR
MULLENS				Heinrich Julius	691	D	1906	Philomena	78747	D	1938
Michael Henry	74884	D	1937	Henriette Maude	89471	D	1942	Reinhold	43618	D	1926
MULLER				Henry	16162	D	1913	Richard	45101	D	1926
Adele	79927	D	1938	Henry	21695	D	1916	Rudolph	17240	D	1914
Adelheit	13862	D	1912	Henry	56734	D	1930	Sophie	34225	D	1922
Adolf	49073	D	1928	Herman	13614	D	1912	Sylvester E.	59860	D	1931
Adolf	84096	D	1940	Herman Wilhelm	18280	D	1914	Walter A., Jr.	35567	D	1922
Adolph W.	20634	D	1916	Hermann	52592	D	1929	Walter F.	35608	D	1922
Agnes	3741	D	1907	Hildegard	2209	D	1906	William F.	2609	D	1907
Aleck	87836	D	1941	J. W.	47057	D	1927	**MULLERING**			
Alice	48242	M	1927	James	43136	D	1925	Mary Elizabeth	29563	D	1920
Anna	52678	D	1929	James A.	41855	I	1925	**MULLERRING**			
Anton	46381	D	1927	James A.	41855	I	1925	August	24968	D	1918
August	16213	D	1913	Johann	17741	D	1914	**MULLERY**			
August Herrmann	48124	D	1927	John	17741	D	1914	Michael J.	15825	I	1913
Bertha	60468	D	1931	John Arnold	44959	I	1926	**MULLHEARON**			
Carmelita	2211	M	1906	John H.	29534	D	1920	E.	3873	D	1907
Carrie B.	30253	D	1920	John H.	56664	D	1930	**MULLIGAN**			
Charles	16599	D	1914	John P.	33324	D	1922	Anna	4547	M	1907
Charles Frederick	65609	D	1933	Karl	27312	D	1919	Bridget	21962	D	1916
Charles L.	37781	D	1923	Karl	37803	D	1923	Catherine	80879	I	1939
Christian	24013	D	1918	Karl Otto	75910	D	1937	Catherine F.	82193	D	1939
Christiana	51052	D	1928	Katherine	57646	D	1931	Dan E.	68816	D	1935
Christina	15578	M	1913	Laura S.	49900	D	1928	Ellen	2592	D	1907
Christine Wilhelmine	31839	D	1921	Lettie L.	65541	D	1933	Ellen	11004	D	1911
Claudine Cotton	84860	D	1940	Lillian	64262	I	1933	James F.	2636	D	1907
Claudine G.	84860	D	1940	Louisa	26279	I	1919	James K.	38278	D	1924
Cora G.	53537	D	1929	Louisa	45364	D	1926	John C.	46545	D	1927
Cordella R.	55330	D	1930	Louise Maria	52375	D	1929	Joseph Albert	77333	D	1937
Cornelius	44196	D	1926	Lucille	48242	M	1927	Laurence	35957	D	1923
Dietrich	28879	D	1920	Margaret	10039	D	1910	Lawrence	34464	I	1922
Dora L.	63644	D	1933	Margaretha	10039	D	1910	Margaret Gertrude	4547	M	1907
Doris C.	63644	D	1933	Margaretha	21157	D	1916	Patrick E.	51671	D	1928
Edward A.	27288	D	1919	Margrethe	64196	D	1933	Peter	39110	D	1924
Eleonora	16483	D	1913	Marian	79676	D	1938	Peter	58342	D	1931
Elise	66967	D	1934	Marie Lena	19295	D	1915	William	79433	D	1938
Elizabeth M.	4671	D	1907	Martin	51844	D	1929	**MULLIN**			
Ellen St.Laurence	24822	D	1918	Mary A.	9150	D	1910	Alice L.	76384	D	1937
Ernst G.	45315	D	1926	Mary Louise	52375	D	1929	Bridget	10932	D	1910
Ethel	48242	M	1927	Melvin E.	29466	M	1920	Catherine	40622	D	1924
Frank F.	38377	D	1924	Meyer	64899	D	1933	Frank D.	57803	D	1931
Frederick W.	13615	D	1912	Nathalie	5693	D	1908	George Adams	63106	D	1932
Friedericke R.	1469	D	1906	Opal	58240	D	1931	James F.	50386	I	1928
George	70564	I	1935	Otto	75910	D	1937	John	53661	D	1929
Gerhard Peter	4339	M	1907	Peter	54081	D	1929	John Joseph	2925	M	1907
Grace C.	29466	M	1920	Peter Joseph	27294	D	1919	John Joseph	35880	D	1923
Hans J.	2351	D	1906	Philip C.	46776	D	1927	Leslie Edward	2925	M	1907
Harry Henry	61010	D	1932	Philipp	15801	D	1913	Lillie	73232	D	1936
Heinrich	55268	D	1930	Philomena	17173	I	1914				

NAME	NUMBER	TYPE	YEAR
Louise Elizabeth	29504	D	1920
Mardis Adele	81389	M	1939
Margaret	26630	I	1919
Mary J.	81767	D	1939
Mary T.	81767	D	1939
Raymond James	2925	M	1907
Ward Joseph	2925	M	1907
William Michael	61838	D	1932
MULLINS			
Catherine	46855	D	1927
Charles Frederick	44796	D	1926
Daniel T.	72601	D	1936
Dora Bertha	44243	D	1926
Edward	84060	M	1940
George P.	79686	I	1938
Jacqueline	86207	M	1941
James F.	63029	D	1932
Jane	75326	D	1937
Mary	68963	I	1935
Mary	69546	D	1935
Mary J.	56599	D	1930
Michael Henry	74884	D	1937
Nora	40505	D	1924
Robert Francis	16352	M	1913
Thomas Joseph	43946	D	1926
William F.	71637	D	1936
MULLOOLY			
Michael	54116	D	1929
Mike	51343	D	1928
MULLOY			
Eleanora Lewellyn	88961	M	1942
Ella F.	9931	D	1910
Kate	6338	D	1908
Kate	8033	D	1909
Michael	51343	D	1928
MULQUEENEY			
Thomas	26129	D	1919
MULRANEY			
Annie J.	87429	I	1941
MULREANY			
Elizabeth	17877	D	1914
Rita	83304	M	1940
MULRENIN			
Edward F.	29374	D	1920
MULROY			
Frederick	31898	D	1921
Honora Isabelle	61513	D	1932
Richard	37124	D	1923

NAME	NUMBER	TYPE	YEAR
MULTNER			
Ardis	10200	M	1910
MULVANEY			
Nicholas	26798	I	1919
Nicholas	37287	D	1923
MULVANY			
John	30392	D	1920
Meta Margarete	66653	D	1934
MULVEY			
Clara F.	39122	D	1924
Frank	30456	D	1920
Harriett	4413	D	1907
James D.	71926	D	1936
Mary Hester	74203	D	1936
Thomas	42749	D	1925
MULVIHILL			
Daniel	46970	M	1927
Daniel F.	52990	D	1929
Frank	46970	M	1927
Harry	46970	M	1927
Joseph	58854	D	1931
Julia E.	86886	D	1941
Margaret	46919	D	1927
Michael	49503	D	1928
Michael	71953	I	1936
Pierce B.	67568	D	1934
MULVILLE			
Elizabeth	75567	D	1937
Margaret Frances	86846	D	1941
MUMAUGH			
John S.	58398	D	1931
MUMBY			
James Olpha	80555	D	1939
MUMFORD			
John Henry	13611	M	1912
MUN			
May Jin	73738	D	1936
MUNAKATA			
M.	2146	D	1906
MUNAY			
Robert Henderson	37064	M	1923
MUNCEY			
James I.	51997	D	1929
MUNCH			
Catterina	37052	D	1923

NAME	NUMBER	TYPE	YEAR
MUNCK			
Charles Emil	39501	D	1924
Sarah Elisabeth	35803	D	1923
MUNDAY			
Frank	31288	D	1921
MUNDEGL			
Kate	19138	D	1915
MUNDELIUS			
Mary	11461	I	1911
MUNDHENK			
Marie Michael	78975	D	1938
MUNDINGER			
Sophie A.	42410	D	1925
Sophie Barbara	42410	D	1925
MUNDT			
Fred	23836	D	1918
MUNDWYLER			
Frederick	26104	D	1919
John Jacob	19558	D	1915
MUNDY			
Frank	87895	I	1941
George B.	60027	I	1931
James H.	13830	D	1912
Minnie Maddux	23112	D	1917
MUNEZ			
G.	33345	I	1922
MUNFREY			
Sarah	18674	D	1915
William	18675	D	1915
MUNGER			
Edward Merrick	7199	M	1909
Merrick Edward	7199	M	1909
MUNIER			
Joseph	54085	M	1929
Joseph N.	16689	D	1914
Marie L.	52747	D	1929
MUNIZ			
Stanley	31684	D	1921
MUNK			
Gustav Eugen	62028	D	1932
Gustav H.	62555	D	1932
Katie	4731	D	1907
William C.	72017	I	1936
MUNKHOUSE			
Alfred Frederich	58331	D	1931

Key: D = death; M = minor; I = incompetent

NAME	NUMBER	TYPE	YEAR
MUNN			
Charles E.	59294	D	1931
Lois Whitney	32244	M	1921
Mildred	28829	D	1920
MUNOZ			
Fernando	36556	I	1923
Geronimo	33345	I	1922
Jose Benjamin	58744	D	1931
MUNRO			
Emma	71309	D	1935
Horace N.	79878	D	1938
John	19398	D	1915
Margaret	19309	D	1915
Robert Lee	75464	D	1937
Robert R.	11345	D	1911
Robert R., Mrs.	71309	D	1935
MUNROE			
Charles A.	69246	D	1935
Louis F.	33182	D	1922
Margaret	11890	D	1911
Margaret	82996	D	1939
MUNSIL			
John Edward	52026	D	1929
MUNSON			
Abitha M.	52522	D	1929
Alice	75752	M	1937
Alice Ann	44850	M	1926
Betty	75752	M	1937
Catharine	11537	D	1911
Edgar C.	52369	D	1929
Ella	73165	D	1936
Gene Deer	68684	M	1935
Herrick C.	73512	I	1936
Hubert A.	41702	D	1925
Janet	82163	M	1939
Margaret	8350	D	1909
Mary	75752	M	1937
Niels	75637	D	1937
Robert	75752	M	1937
MUNSTER			
Henry	47017	D	1927
Herman	75867	D	1937
John H.	68053	D	1934
MUNT			
Katherine	23101	D	1917
MUNTER			
Leo	70099	D	1935

NAME	NUMBER	TYPE	YEAR
MUNTERDE			
Francisco	17167	D	1914
MUNTIGE			
Joseph	27246	D	1919
MUNTIGL			
Joseph	27246	D	1919
Kate	19138	D	1915
MUNZ			
Gottfried	65025	D	1933
Grattfried	65025	D	1933
MUNZENMAIER			
Anna Maria Wolber	18214	D	1914
MUNZER			
Samuel	20045	D	1915
MURAI			
Miyeko	63465	M	1933
MURAMATS			
Serabaro	56702	D	1930
MURASE			
Tane	11442	M	1911
MURASKI			
Lena	58157	D	1931
MURASKY			
Frank J.	72051	D	1936
Frederick A, Jr.	49292	M	1928
Leo A.	72723	D	1936
Mary G.	69476	D	1935
Norma Dearborn	78793	D	1938
Stanley James	79170	M	1938
William	33895	D	1922
MURAT			
Erwin J., Jr.	74890	M	1937
MURATORE			
Pietro	42224	D	1925
Romana	43661	M	1926
Secondina	43661	M	1926
MURAY			
Roy W.	49027	D	1928
MURBAR			
William Martin	65129	D	1933
MURBER			
William Martin	65129	D	1933
MURCH			
Ruel Hubert	66065	D	1934
MURCHIO			
Paolina	20683	D	1916

NAME	NUMBER	TYPE	YEAR
MURCHISON			
Peter Simon	29792	D	1920
MURDOCH			
Louisa J.	26603	D	1919
MURDOCK			
Eleanor	7810	D	1909
George W.	71043	D	1935
Isaiah	20500	D	1916
Nannie W.	3449	D	1907
Robert B.	28008	D	1919
Samuel	23720	I	1917
William E.	17341	D	1914
Winifred	53402	D	1929
MURIALE			
Nicola	57538	D	1930
MURIFF			
Jerome Joseph	44022	D	1926
MURISET			
Jessie	83292	D	1940
MURISON			
Elizabeth Livingston	69077	D	1935
John Randolph	4885	M	1907
MURK			
Aleida H.	48139	D	1927
George Alex	14665	D	1913
MURKEN			
Adeline	14335	M	1912
Henry	14335	M	1912
Mathilde	14335	M	1912
MURLEY			
Raymond James	2375	M	1906
MURNANE			
Anne G.	63994	D	1933
Mary	17659	D	1914
MURNIK			
Louis	20909	D	1916
MURPHISON			
Vera	17905	D	1914
MURPHY			
Adam H.	3394	D	1907
Agnes	28180	D	1919
Alfred J.	30313	D	1920
Alice	71047	D	1935
Alyce Sullivan	89099	D	1942
Anna	26475	D	1919
Anna	39018	D	1924
Anna	77426	D	1938

NAME	NUMBER	TYPE	YEAR	NAME	NUMBER	TYPE	YEAR	NAME	NUMBER	TYPE	YEAR
Anna A.	38134	D	1924	Daniel	72861	D	1936	Frank	42522	I	1925
Annette	46893	D	1927	Daniel C.	65339	D	1933	Frank A.	62515	D	1932
Annie	7624	M	1909	Daniel C.	84824	D	1940	Frank J.	36231	D	1923
Annie	88015	I	1941	Daniel Driscoll	23987	D	1918	Frank M.	28541	D	1919
Annie	34129	D	1922	Daniel F.	60472	D	1931	Fred	42389	D	1925
Annie C.	37565	D	1923	Daniel J.	27132	D	1919	George	11317	M	1911
Annie F.	45814	D	1926	Daniel T.	28598	D	1920	George A.	52409	D	1929
Annie J.	33580	D	1922	Daniel T.	88434	D	1941	George H.	51258	D	1928
Annie Josephine	24394	D	1918	David C. B.	59753	D	1931	George Leo	65236	D	1933
Annie Maria	77840	D	1938	David J.	47679	D	1927	George R.	72515	D	1936
Annie T.	45814	D	1926	Delia	33687	D	1922	George Robert	62917	M	1932
Anthony	12711	D	1911	Denies G.	49796	I	1928	George Thomas	73837	D	1936
Anthony L.	18719	D	1915	Denies G.	70449	D	1935	George W.	71200	D	1935
Archibald	6341	D	1908	Denis B.	3425	D	1907	Grace	3588	M	1907
Barbara Ann	50891	M	1928	Dennis	16701	D	1914	Hamlin H.	5548	D	1908
Blanche Broderick	37627	D	1923	Dennis	34453	D	1922	Hannah	3374	D	1907
Bridget	3791	D	1907	Dennis	36969	I	1923	Hannah	13992	D	1912
Bridget	10554	D	1910	Dennis	67012	D	1934	Hannah	59433	D	1931
Bridget	18326	D	1914	Dennis B.	8931	D	1909	Hannah B.	74166	D	1936
Bridget	41750	D	1925	Dennis J.	41471	I	1925	Hanorah	17621	D	1914
Bridget	41750	D	1925	Dennis J.	69373	I	1935	Harold T.	34314	I	1922
Bridget Rider	24162	D	1918	Edmond J.	12749	D	1911	Harriet W.	88963	D	1942
C., Mrs.	76077	D	1937	Edward	25159	D	1918	Helen D.	20142	M	1915
Caroline	22264	D	1917	Edward	67914	M	1934	Helena	77140	D	1937
Caroline	88538	D	1941	Edward F.	34645	D	1922	Henry	27737	D	1919
Catherine	10859	D	1910	Edward Francis	80806	D	1939	Henry	72629	D	1936
Catherine	17182	D	1914	Edward Joseph	34191	D	1922	Ida V.	88901	D	1942
Catherine	32011	M	1921	Edward William	87267	D	1941	Irene Mary	71879	D	1936
Catherine	82216	D	1939	Eleanor	61462	M	1932	James	2240	D	1906
Catherine F.	66246	D	1934	Eliza	9296	D	1910	James	3544	D	1907
Catherine Patricia	69105	D	1935	Elizabeth M. T.	88424	D	1941	James	8220	D	1909
Cecil M.	66443	D	1934	Ellen	1590	D	1906	James	11458	D	1911
Cecilia M.	66443	D	1934	Ellen	7750	D	1909	James	15832	D	1913
Charles	20837	D	1916	Ellen	22611	D	1917	James	18653	D	1915
Charles	63350	D	1933	Ellen	30441	D	1920	James A.	9074	D	1910
Charles Henry	69061	D	1935	Ellen	51095	D	1928	James D.	34183	D	1922
Charles J.	67150	D	1934	Ellen	80083	D	1938	James J.	72751	D	1936
Charles K.	39726	M	1924	Ellen	56387	D	1930	James J.	85816	D	1940
Charles Morris	85282	I	1940	Emma	8534	D	1909	James K.	32010	D	1921
Charles Morris	85655	D	1940	Eva M.	72649	D	1936	James T.	41155	D	1925
Charles S.	9142	M	1910	Flora J.	8089	D	1909	Jeannette Agnes	42419	D	1925
Charles S.	29392	D	1920	Frances	72436	D	1936	Jennie	38952	D	1924
Con C.	85957	D	1941	Frances Enright	31548	D	1921	Jeremiah	57814	D	1931
Cornelius	44296	D	1926	Frances Gertrude	12296	M	1911	Jeremiah	57867	D	1931
Cornelius E.	39442	I	1924	Francis	8440	M	1909	Jeremiah J.	29269	D	1920
Cornelius J.	7885	D	1909	Francis A.	66223	D	1934	Jeremiah M.	23362	D	1917
Daniel	19351	D	1915	Francis John	33924	D	1922	Johanna	7790	D	1909
Daniel	29765	D	1920	Frank	12861	D	1912	Johanna	18950	D	1915
Daniel	59494	D	1931	Frank	38217	D	1924	Johanna	34134	D	1922

Key: D = death; M = minor; I = incompetent

NAME	NUMBER	TYPE	YEAR	NAME	NUMBER	TYPE	YEAR	NAME	NUMBER	TYPE	YEAR
John	301	D	1906	Margaret	9128	D	1910	Mary F.	8090	D	1909
John	1181	D	1906	Margaret	11241	D	1911	Mary Frances	65793	D	1933
John	7107	D	1909	Margaret	23873	D	1918	Mary J.	2201	D	1906
John	8545	D	1909	Margaret	32011	M	1921	Mary J.	41595	D	1925
John	9819	D	1910	Margaret	46418	D	1927	Mary Jane	49251	D	1928
John	17183	D	1914	Margaret	37672	D	1923	Mary Pope	37241	D	1923
John	18581	D	1915	Margaret A.	18973	D	1915	Mary Turnbull	70948	D	1935
John	20142	M	1915	Margaret Ann	16725	D	1914	Matthew	32232	D	1921
John	34338	D	1922	Margaret E.	71708	D	1936	Maurice	59370	D	1931
John	38114	D	1924	Margaret Mary	27960	D	1919	May	12399	D	1911
John	45154	D	1926	Margaret Tobin	76077	D	1937	May	53761	D	1929
John	60773	D	1932	Margarite	25160	M	1918	Michael	18250	D	1914
John	71380	D	1936	Maria B.	23622	D	1917	Michael	18951	D	1915
John Francis	18417	D	1915	Maria T.	12399	D	1911	Michael	57739	D	1931
John J.	19290	D	1915	Marian C.	9142	M	1910	Michael	60194	D	1931
John J.	22406	D	1917	Marie	32011	M	1921	Michael	84428	I	1940
John J.	25618	D	1918	Marie	87490	D	1941	Michael	61305	D	1932
John J.	78486	D	1938	Marie S.	47791	D	1927	Michael F.	51681	D	1928
John Joseph	52020	D	1929	Marilyn Theresa	83153	M	1940	Nellie	21604	D	1916
John Joseph	66805	M	1934	Martha	55461	D	1930	Nicholas James	14456	M	1912
John Patrick	51929	M	1929	Martha L.	27379	D	1919	Nora	46383	D	1927
John Patrick	84496	D	1940	Martin	53142	I	1929	Nora Marie	88547	D	1941
John Pius	31627	D	1921	Martin D.	1294	D	1906	Ora Mathewson	40452	D	1924
John Richard	48323	M	1927	Martin J.	80022	D	1938	Patrick	2751	D	1907
Joseph C.	51251	D	1928	Mary	2795	I	1907	Patrick	6729	D	1908
Joseph Thomas	83636	I	1940	Mary	3588	M	1907	Patrick	13883	D	1912
Joseph W.	38859	I	1924	Mary	13679	D	1912	Patrick	19795	D	1915
Josephine	3588	M	1907	Mary	23255	D	1917	Patrick	29757	I	1920
Josephine	35888	D	1923	Mary	31032	D	1921	Patrick	32322	D	1921
Josephine E.	77075	D	1937	Mary	55554	D	1930	Patrick	43790	D	1926
Josephine Frances	61349	D	1932	Mary	60043	D	1931	Patrick	45467	D	1926
Josephine Frances	62348	M	1932	Mary	73002	D	1936	Patrick	61222	D	1932
Julia	7624	M	1909	Mary	63468	D	1933	Patrick Heaney	32758	D	1921
Julia	64081	D	1933	Mary	51559	D	1928	Patrick J.	85510	D	1940
Julia	54226	D	1929	Mary A.	3710	D	1907	Patrick T.	11427	D	1911
Julia Helen	69160	I	1935	Mary A.	12464	D	1911	Paul D.	45853	D	1926
Julia M.	81936	I	1939	Mary A.	32285	D	1921	Peggy	80945	D	1939
Kate	30397	D	1920	Mary A.	40081	D	1924	Philip	30028	D	1920
Katherine	54036	D	1929	Mary Alicia	36336	D	1923	Philip	66805	M	1934
Kathryn	41057	D	1925	Mary Ann	16224	D	1913	Philip C.	66808	D	1934
Lawrence J.	58660	D	1931	Mary Ann	44363	D	1926	Philip Joseph	70579	D	1935
Leo Joseph	47965	D	1927	Mary D.	1295	D	1906	Ray William	62917	M	1932
Leo L.	6731	D	1908	Mary E.	10090	I	1910	Richard	20916	D	1916
Leslie Leven	62917	M	1932	Mary E.	20448	D	1916	Richard	47921	D	1927
Lillian Fitzhenry	71856	D	1936	Mary E.	26349	D	1919	Robert E.	50858	D	1928
Lorenzo Edward	71352	D	1936	Mary E.	38446	D	1924	Rose	28227	I	1919
Louis Russell	61350	D	1932	Mary Eleanor	9591	I	1910	Rose	35617	D	1922
Mae	7109	D	1909	Mary Elizabeth	62348	M	1932	Rose	72527	D	1936
Margaret	8830	D	1909	Mary Ellen	25160	M	1918	Rose A.	73515	D	1936

NAME	NUMBER	TYPE	YEAR	NAME	NUMBER	TYPE	YEAR	NAME	NUMBER	TYPE	YEAR
Sadie	7624	M	1909	Alma	74122	D	1936	George J.	18981	M	1915
Sarah A.	2492	D	1906	Andrew	57299	D	1930	Geroge Harvey	72377	D	1936
Theresia	68358	D	1934	Anna	548	D	1906	Gertrude	30165	I	1920
Thomas	30097	M	1920	Anna	54705	D	1930	Gertrude Etchison	38158	D	1924
Thomas	59746	M	1931	Anna Florence Magdalene	67636	D	1934	Helen Grace	44508	M	1926
Thomas	61047	D	1932	Annie M.	72610	D	1936	Helen Isabel	29488	I	1920
Thomas Francis	70423	D	1935	Arthur Thomas	72018	D	1936	Henry	1329	D	1906
Thomas J.	31960	D	1921	Beatrice Mary	33641	D	1922	Henry	6324	D	1908
Thomas J.	80281	D	1939	Carrie	31605	D	1921	Henry	12612	D	1911
Timothy	10569	D	1910	Catherine	8159	D	1909	Henry	15574	D	1913
Timothy	19425	D	1915	Catherine	11364	D	1911	Hera	44588	M	1926
Virginia	68832	D	1935	Catherine	30177	D	1920	Humphrey	42146	D	1925
Walter J.	20142	M	1915	Catherine	32292	D	1921	Isabel Catherine	7705	M	1909
Walter L.	78980	D	1938	Catherine	32314	D	1921	Isabelle Josephine	59633	D	1931
Warren Harding	62917	M	1932	Catherine	49367	D	1928	J. S., Mrs.	71831	D	1936
William	8440	M	1909	Catherine	60442	D	1931	Jackson Lee	88400	D	1941
William	9316	D	1910	Catherine Gertrude	37152	D	1923	James	28080	D	1919
William	18620	I	1915	Charles R.	87864	D	1941	James	30750	D	1920
William F.	22523	D	1917	Clara	4353	D	1907	James	31926	M	1921
William F.	54471	D	1929	Daniel	58100	D	1931	James Chas.	71940	D	1936
William Francis	66992	D	1934	Daniel Joseph	7705	M	1909	James D.	72942	D	1936
William H.	2109	D	1906	Daniel Joseph	63829	D	1933	Jeannette H.	13253	D	1912
William H.	54631	D	1929	David	3568	D	1907	Jessie	72911	D	1936
William H.	65305	D	1933	Della M.	73245	D	1936	Johanna	106	D	1906
William J.	11571	D	1911	Dennis	24251	D	1918	John	11574	D	1911
William J.	45897	D	1926	Dennis	33001	D	1921	John	23126	D	1917
William J.	88256	D	1941	Dennis P.	62932	D	1932	John Carlton	75645	D	1937
William John	56306	D	1930	E. A. W.	58929	D	1931	John Clyde	31993	D	1921
William Joseph	21374	D	1916	Edson J.	59223	D	1931	John Douglas	12212	M	1911
William K.	75169	D	1937	Edson J.	70862	M	1935	John F.	21979	D	1916
William L., Jr.	62348	M	1932	Edward Francis	59191	I	1931	John F.	54698	D	1930
William P.	35472	D	1922	Edward Francis	84471	D	1940	John J.	79766	D	1938
William Patrick	23982	D	1918	Edward T.	80074	D	1938	John M.	17501	D	1914
William Peter	33995	D	1922	Edward W.	57139	D	1930	John P.	44280	D	1926
William Selby	69346	I	1935	Edwin Francis	41784	M	1925	John T.	37292	D	1923
William T.	66314	D	1934	Edwin Francis	41784	M	1925	Joseph	16358	D	1913
William W.	67181	D	1934	Eliza	6652	D	1908	Joseph	54825	D	1930
Willie	11317	M	1911	Elizabeth	51063	D	1928	Joseph A.	69101	D	1935
MURR				Ella F.	48081	D	1927	Joseph Dayton	11984	D	1911
George W.	17409	I	1914	Ellen	72075	D	1936	Joseph Edward	82428	D	1939
George W.	23252	D	1917	Ellen	44491	D	1926	Joseph F.	38094	D	1924
Joseph	11776	D	1911	Ellen L.	73225	D	1936	Kate	25744	D	1918
MURRAY				Eugene Francis	48055	D	1927	Margaret	10257	M	1910
Ada	59903	D	1931	Florence Ann	88098	D	1941	Margaret	22965	D	1917
Agnes	70861	D	1935	Francis McM.	16181	D	1913	Margaret	45151	D	1926
Alexander F.	74689	D	1937	Francis X.	26612	D	1919	Margaret	58057	D	1931
Alice C.	67409	I	1934	Frank	10257	M	1910	Margaret	76563	D	1937
Alice C.	67622	D	1934	Frank E.	74793	M	1937	Marie Madeline	7705	M	1909
Alice Mabel Cameron	67622	D	1934	George	79240	D	1938	Marjorie Gladys	12212	M	1911

Key: D = death; M = minor; I = incompetent

NAME	NUMBER	TYPE	YEAR
Mary	10249	D	1910
Mary	37335	I	1923
Mary	40940	D	1925
Mary	62541	I	1932
Mary	72756	D	1936
Mary	74428	D	1937
Mary A.	76522	D	1937
Mary Ann	718	D	1906
Mary Cutten	71831	D	1936
Mary E.	85660	D	1940
Mary Ellen	55345	D	1930
Mary L.	69268	D	1935
Maxine Helen	41784	M	1925
Maxine Helen	41784	M	1925
Michael	23610	D	1917
Michael G.	67035	D	1934
Minnie A.	86214	D	1941
Nonna Leona	12212	M	1911
Nora	63552	D	1933
P. H.	55776	D	1930
Patrick	32030	D	1921
Patrick	42390	D	1925
Patrick J.	6796	D	1908
Patrick J.	70121	D	1935
Patrick Joseph	47381	D	1927
Philip	38268	D	1924
Robert	86923	D	1941
Robert Henderson	37064	M	1923
Robert W.	69796	D	1935
Roy Benson	44508	M	1926
S. G.	23908	D	1918
Sumner C.	12744	D	1911
Susan	76398	D	1937
T. Thomas	59509	D	1931
Thomas	10257	M	1910
Thomas	14924	D	1913
Thomas	52128	D	1929
Thomas	59509	D	1931
Thomas	57129	D	1930
Thomas F.	86357	I	1941
Thomas Francis	7705	M	1909
Thomas H.	36694	D	1923
Veronica C. Kennedy	89972	D	1942
Wallace W.	62243	I	1932
Wesley	56948	M	1930
William	65	D	1906
William	30638	D	1920
William	59801	D	1931
William	84781	D	1940

NAME	NUMBER	TYPE	YEAR
William	86147	I	1941
William	86393	D	1941
William F.	17031	D	1914
William H.	68218	I	1934
William J.	4710	D	1907
William K.	71885	I	1936
William Thomas	72018	D	1936
MURREY			
Mary	24835	D	1918
Roy W.	49027	D	1928
MURRIN			
Thomas F.	68846	D	1935
MURRY			
Andrew	60565	D	1931
Sarah E.	7429	D	1909
MURSCHEL			
Albert	74859	D	1937
MURSH			
Abbie R.	39066	D	1924
MURTAGH			
John Anthony	28525	D	1919
Margaret Ruth	39202	M	1924
Margita	39202	M	1924
Michael	34414	D	1922
Ramona Short	39185	D	1924
MURTHA			
Elizabeth	23934	D	1918
Elizabeth	49509	D	1928
James	43152	D	1925
James	57795	D	1931
John	428	D	1906
Joseph M.	80099	I	1938
MURTHIN			
Pher W. W.	45502	D	1926
MURTLE			
Thomas	47411	D	1927
MURTZ			
Edward John	84735	D	1940
MUS			
George	15642	D	1913
MUSANTE			
Angiola	14218	D	1912
Antonio	56859	D	1930
Elvira	81411	D	1939
Francesco	69826	D	1935
Giovanni	6701	D	1908
Giovanni	68646	D	1935

NAME	NUMBER	TYPE	YEAR
Pasquale	72634	D	1936
Pietro	32538	D	1921
Rolando	34728	D	1922
Serafina	58644	D	1931
Victoria	84687	D	1940
Vittoria	84687	D	1940
William	72367	M	1936
MUSANTI			
Giovanni	6842	D	1908
MUSCAT			
Antone	78305	D	1938
Carmelo	25676	D	1918
Joseph C.	87691	D	1941
MUSCH			
Abbie R.	39066	D	1924
Frank	64824	D	1933
Karl F. J.	82293	D	1939
Marta	68269	M	1934
Meta	68269	M	1934
MUSCHOLDT			
Bruno	53701	D	1929
MUSCHOLL			
Bruno	53701	D	1929
MUSCIO			
Theodore H.	33233	M	1922
Virgil A.	33233	M	1922
MUSEN			
Anne	53962	D	1929
MUSER			
Minna	31628	D	1921
Otto	86754	D	1941
MUSETTI			
Eletta	74139	D	1936
MUSGRAVE			
Charles	10065	D	1910
John K.	72866	D	1936
Mary	30963	D	1921
Mary M.	29811	D	1920
Mary M.	78198	D	1938
Timothy	14813	D	1913
MUSICENE			
Gerolamo	33413	D	1922
MUSICK			
Edwin Charles	78157	D	1938
MUSIJA			
Dujo	15642	D	1913
Joe	15642	D	1913

NAME	NUMBER	TYPE	YEAR
MUSIN			
Ephraim H.	48060	D	1927
Ida	82625	D	1939
MUSKAT			
Fred	47612	D	1927
MUSLADIN			
Jimmie Peter	74143	M	1936
Peter	50989	D	1928
MUSOR			
Otto	629	D	1906
MUSSALLEM			
Eva	30969	M	1921
Richard	30969	M	1921
MUSSALLEN			
Rema	63366	D	1933
MUSSBACH			
Erich	23304	D	1917
MUSSEN			
Joseph G.	6212	D	1908
MUSSER			
John Cantrell	3789	D	1907
Medora Cantrell	3707	D	1907
MUSSIEO			
John	2956	D	1907
Michael	2957	M	1907
MUSSIO			
Louis	45081	D	1926
Luigi	61618	D	1932
Michael H.	37439	D	1923
Michael Joseph	89472	D	1942
MUSSO			
Alma LaMere	33112	D	1921
Attilio M.	60429	D	1931
Carlo	69365	D	1935
Charles	69365	D	1935
John, Sr.	70734	D	1935
Vincent Emil	42550	D	1925
MUSTAKAS			
Basilios	51077	D	1928
MUSTARDA			
E.	48376	D	1927
MUSTO			
Clarence E.	46535	D	1927
Clarence E.	46613	M	1927
Florence Adeline	36868	D	1923
Joseph C.	46613	M	1927

NAME	NUMBER	TYPE	YEAR
Margaret	58902	D	1931
Maria	39169	D	1924
Thomas Adam	46613	M	1927
MUSTOVOY			
Rose Morrison	46167	I	1927
MUTANEN			
Alexander	65282	D	1933
Axel	65282	D	1933
MUTCH			
Elija D.	70257	D	1935
William	29803	D	1920
MUTH			
Andreas	11794	D	1911
Jacob	20676	D	1916
MUTIN			
Maria Louisa	87404	D	1941
MUTSCHALL			
Adolf R.	79545	D	1938
MUTTER			
Anna	80612	D	1939
August Albert	15702	M	1913
George Carl	15702	M	1913
MUUS			
Henry	24313	D	1918
MUYLAERT			
Constant	75002	D	1937
John	75002	D	1937
MUZEO			
Luigi	89769	D	1942
MUZINICH			
Joseph W.	67021	D	1934
MUZIO			
Alberto	32038	M	1921
Emelio	32038	M	1921
Emilio	26073	D	1919
Ercale	25927	D	1918
Giacomo	16135	D	1913
Giuseppe	88291	I	1941
Jennie	89339	D	1942
Joseph	88291	I	1941
Luigi	72293	D	1936
Luigi	89457	I	1942
Luigi	89769	D	1942
Mario	32038	M	1921
Paulo	19015	D	1915
MUZZI			
Fabio	47447	I	1927

NAME	NUMBER	TYPE	YEAR
MUZZIO			
Carmela	67998	D	1934
Giaccomo	16135	D	1913
Giovanni	89975	D	1942
MUZZOLETTI			
Pietro	36719	D	1923
MUZZUE			
Ed	89512	D	1942
MUZZY			
Emma L.	27679	D	1919
Hannah Ruth	13899	D	1912
Sara	53156	D	1929
MYELLO			
Orste	46841	I	1927
MYER			
Clara G.	49082	D	1928
Clara Smith	45713	I	1926
Clara Smith	49082	D	1928
Henriette N.	46809	D	1927
Mary	9994	D	1910
O. D.	7833	D	1909
Sidney Bawski	73540	D	1936
Thomas	72019	D	1936
MYERS			
Albert	73904	D	1936
Alvina	53202	D	1929
Andrew Joseph	69835	D	1935
Arthur L.	48390	D	1927
Augusta	43718	D	1926
Barnett	59676	D	1931
Blake D.	65406	D	1933
Caroline M.	75508	D	1937
Charles H.	83471	I	1940
Emily W.	85484	D	1940
Frank V.	47924	D	1927
George W.	72262	D	1936
Harry Brunner	31403	D	1921
Henry	65080	I	1933
Henry	66423	D	1934
Henry Brunner	31403	D	1921
Hyman	46815	D	1927
J. W.	27761	D	1919
James A.	57428	D	1930
Jean B.	50079	M	1928
John	56243	D	1930
Larry	50079	M	1928
Lillian A.	85863	D	1940
Lillian H.	58805	D	1931

NAME	NUMBER	TYPE	YEAR
Lina	54577	D	1929
Louise G.	78823	I	1938
Louise Voorhies	55841	D	1930
Lydia E.	27912	D	1919
Maria	2265	D	1906
Mark C.	44967	D	1926
Martha M.	65348	D	1933
Maurice	73832	D	1936
Pauline	33922	D	1922
Ranie I.	36867	D	1923
Rath	3948	I	1907
Robert A.	35457	D	1922
Rose T.	62364	I	1932
Sarah	20269	D	1916
Seldy Roach	85081	D	1940
Sophie J.	82585	D	1939
Stanley L.	45941	D	1926
William	36417	D	1923
MYERSON			
Sigmund	79500	I	1938
MYGRANT			
Mary Jane	60708	M	1932
MYHR			
Anton Martin	72019	D	1936
MYHRE			
Anton Martin	72019	D	1936
MYLES			
George F.	10655	D	1910
MYLLYMAKI			
George	64154	D	1933
MYLOTT			
Mary Adelaide	52636	D	1929
MYLROIE			
William J.	53387	D	1929
MYRICH			
Merton	89842	D	1942
MYRICK			
Charles M.	40587	D	1924
Edward R.	28876	D	1920
Ella	43891	M	1926
Ellen P.	74854	D	1937
Joseph F.	67631	D	1934
MYSELL			
Lillian C.	67309	D	1934
Metta C.	22602	D	1917
NABARO			
Maria Febronia Jauregui	30721	D	1920

NAME	NUMBER	TYPE	YEAR
NABER			
William H.	37415	D	1923
NABLE			
Ignatius	433	D	1906
NABORS			
Ida R.	64744	I	1933
Miles B.	64745	D	1933
NACE			
Louis	33885	D	1922
Luigi	33885	D	1922
Maria	33884	D	1922
NACHMAN			
Carrie	21004	D	1916
J.	35229	D	1922
NACKE			
Otto	3759	D	1907
NADAL			
Ferdinand	44457	D	1926
NADEAU			
Marie Antoinette	54465	D	1929
NADIN			
Annie Agnes	29492	D	1920
NADLER			
Lena	4521	D	1907
NADRO			
Moritz	28997	D	1920
NAEGELE			
Edward F.	2049	D	1906
NAFTALY			
Abraham	21435	D	1916
NAGAN			
Delphine	48014	I	1927
Delphine A.	50477	D	1928
Marie E.	47889	D	1927
Philemon A.	69341	D	1935
NAGANO			
Ijiro	28284	D	1919
Tsunesuke	88523	D	1941
NAGASAKI			
Fred H.	37699	D	1923
NAGEL			
Alfred R.	84153	D	1940
August	28789	D	1920
Charles Frederick	86321	D	1941
Edna	40208	I	1924
Frida	75298	D	1937

NAME	NUMBER	TYPE	YEAR
Jacob	14826	D	1913
John Jacob	14826	D	1913
Julia C.	78443	D	1938
Katarine	72393	D	1936
Lois	58346	M	1931
Louis	14945	D	1913
Louise	14825	D	1913
M.	58344	D	1931
Marie Francis	69579	D	1935
Merle V.	58344	D	1931
William	67578	D	1934
NAGER			
Anton	5987	D	1908
Ceilia	3564	D	1907
Fidel	19212	D	1915
Helen	88049	D	1941
Johann Marzell	6298	D	1908
John	6298	D	1908
Louise	6305	D	1908
NAGLE			
Arthur D.	56288	D	1930
Charles G.	10801	D	1910
Clara Gertrude	30343	D	1920
Freda	75298	D	1937
Harry Morrison	26571	D	1919
James A.	87303	D	1941
John David	26325	D	1919
Mary	9699	D	1910
Mary Camille	52868	D	1929
Michael R.	49679	D	1928
Richard Hamilton	18733	D	1915
Walter B.	11988	D	1911
NAGLER			
Pauline	32300	D	1921
Pepe	32300	D	1921
Pipi	32300	D	1921
NAGURA			
Hiroshi	60020	D	1931
NAGY			
Alex	33199	D	1922
Elizabeth	64448	D	1933
NAHA			
William Harold	70384	M	1935
NAHAS			
Assad A.	12828	D	1912
Mary L.	81114	D	1939
NAHIGUIAN			
Edward	36511	M	1923

NAME	NUMBER	TYPE	YEAR	NAME	NUMBER	TYPE	YEAR	NAME	NUMBER	TYPE	YEAR
Igalag	36511	M	1923	Ng	79951	D	1938	**NARDINI**			
Yetvard	36511	M	1923	**NAMAKA**				Antonio	68103	D	1934
NAHL				Paul	48336	D	1927	**NARDMAN**			
Constante A.	32985	I	1921	Pawet	48336	D	1927	Leon	40145	D	1924
Paul	82809	D	1939	**NAMARA**				**NARETTO**			
Virgie T.	55100	D	1930	Bridget J.	44150	D	1926	John	68720	D	1935
NAHMAN				**NANCE**				**NARMONT**			
Adolph H.	70409	I	1935	Marha Horn	62801	D	1932	Leo	57914	D	1931
Adolph H.	70630	D	1935	Orval Shaff	36956	M	1923	**NARR**			
Rae C.	58388	D	1931	Wesley Eugene	36956	M	1923	Mathilda	81213	I	1939
NAHRSTADT				**NANCY**				**NARTELSKY**			
Adolph	13064	D	1912	George	87754	D	1941	Isaac	17464	D	1914
NAHRSTET				**NANDAIN**				**NARTON**			
Adolf	17591	D	1914	M.	59347	D	1931	Isabella	44261	M	1926
NAILLEN				**NANI**				Mary	44261	M	1926
Mary A. Vander	28870	I	1920	Virginia	75324	D	1937	Thomas	44261	M	1926
NAIRN				**NANNI**				**NASATO**			
John McKinley	73527	D	1936	Agata	74308	D	1937	Augusta	81544	D	1939
NAISH				D. Max	21845	I	1916	**NASCIMENTO**			
Mary	88149	D	1941	Damian Max	70158	D	1935	Joad F. Do.	4336	D	1907
NAJAC				**NANTZ**				**NASH**			
Jean Camille	54375	M	1929	Eva	39487	D	1924	Bert D.	89447	D	1942
Jeanette Rose	54375	M	1929	**NANZER**				Bridget	28759	D	1920
John	54375	M	1929	Henry	50611	D	1928	Bruce	77919	M	1938
Leopold	54372	D	1929	**NAPHTALY**				Caroline A.	60653	I	1932
Louise	89463	D	1942	Gertrude	20745	M	1916	Effie M.	83773	D	1940
NAKADA				Joseph	10349	D	1910	Elizabeth M.	75214	D	1937
James B.	16149	D	1913	Samuel L.	34790	D	1922	Frederick J.	63141	D	1932
NAKADO				Sarah	25134	D	1918	Harmon F.	41087	I	1925
James B.	16149	D	1913	**NAPOLI**				John B.	54087	I	1929
NAKAHIRO				Carmella	77645	D	1938	Joseph	49764	D	1928
Motomu	57354	M	1930	Ida	52082	M	1929	Joy	77919	M	1938
NAKAMURA				Matteo	43065	D	1925	Rose	81413	D	1939
Kenichi	26770	D	1919	**NAPPI**				Thomas	4440	D	1907
Tetsutaro	70439	D	1935	Saverio	51403	D	1928	William	7269	D	1909
NAKANO				**NARBEBURY**				William J.	21670	D	1916
Fusakichi	67867	D	1934	Francois	81486	D	1939	**NASHMAN**			
Jitsuko	38345	M	1924	Peter	23599	D	1917	Adele	78159	I	1938
NAKE				Pierre	23599	D	1917	Jacob	35229	D	1922
Alexiou H.	24607	D	1918	**NARDI**				**NASO**			
NAKES				Frank Paul	84400	M	1940	Gaetano	43532	D	1926
Alexiou H.	24607	D	1918	Lena	29744	M	1920	**NASON**			
NALOND				Lucille	81022	D	1939	Joseph	9983	D	1910
John Joseph	9313	M	1910	Mary	29744	M	1920	William H.	33070	D	1921
NAM				Mary	60254	M	1931	**NASS**			
Leong See	60198	D	1931	Salvatore	23818	D	1918	Arthur Oscar	60178	D	1931
								David	7945	D	1909

NAME	NUMBER	TYPE	YEAR
NASSANO			
George	25827	D	1918
Gianbattista	25827	D	1918
Giovanni	16033	D	1913
John	16033	D	1913
Luigi	5632	D	1908
William	28355	M	1919
NASSAU			
Samuel Nathan	55566	D	1930
NASSER			
Gertrude Lillian	80141	D	1938
Louise Wier	84093	I	1940
Michael	60833	D	1932
NASSERALLA			
Michael	60833	D	1932
NAST			
Flora	53390	D	1929
Jeannie G.	37218	D	1923
John E.	85590	D	1940
NASTRINI			
Grace	74354	D	1937
Grazia	74354	D	1937
NASTU			
Tham	60207	D	1931
Tom	60207	D	1931
NATALE			
Antonio	55794	I	1930
NATALI			
Pietro	54346	D	1929
NATALINI			
Foresto	24976	M	1918
NATHAN			
Abram Lyman	71407	D	1936
Alfred	62445	D	1932
Annie	53928	D	1929
Bernard I.	39475	D	1924
Bernhard	19563	D	1915
Bertha	24654	D	1918
C. L.	316	D	1906
Charles	2607	D	1907
Charles Garfield	83349	D	1940
Deborah	13126	D	1912
Dorothy	14461	M	1912
Dorothy	42554	I	1925
Dorothy	52870	D	1929
Edward	61716	D	1932
Esther	69055	D	1935

NAME	NUMBER	TYPE	YEAR
Flora	69426	D	1935
Gerson	62716	D	1932
Herman	22055	D	1917
Herman	25207	D	1918
Herman	60880	D	1932
Ida	7785	M	1909
Isaac	45423	D	1926
Jacob	45775	D	1926
Louis	44819	D	1926
Louis D.	31843	D	1921
Lucille Euphrat	23604	M	1917
Lulu	14514	D	1912
Manuel	51100	D	1928
Mary	37606	D	1923
Milton A.	53725	D	1929
Morris	17865	D	1914
Ovadia	60341	I	1931
Pauline	75217	D	1937
Pauline	83963	D	1940
Pete	46568	D	1927
Rachel	45565	D	1926
Rachel	45441	I	1926
Ray	45441	I	1926
Ray	45565	D	1926
Sidney	14461	M	1912
Solomon	909	D	1906
Sophie	26059	D	1919
Suskind	20219	D	1916
NATHANSON			
Judith Ruth	86388	M	1941
NATION			
William S.	58098	D	1931
NATLY			
Victoria	33977	D	1922
NATT			
George	49742	M	1928
Marion	49742	M	1928
Rosalie	49742	M	1928
Theodore M.	49742	M	1928
NAUDAIN			
Harry G.	59347	D	1931
NAUER			
Joseph	28097	D	1919
NAUGHTON			
Anthony A.	74087	D	1936
Charles J.	62627	I	1932
Delia	87050	D	1941
Francis	20113	D	1915

NAME	NUMBER	TYPE	YEAR
Mary E.	16868	D	1914
Patrick	18948	I	1915
Patrick	73460	D	1936
William W.	17000	D	1914
NAUHEIM			
Sophie	57412	D	1930
NAUMAN			
Albert E.	1758	D	1906
Charles	30007	D	1920
Clarence C.	30599	D	1920
Laura	30017	D	1920
NAUMANN			
Agnes Elizabeth	41679	D	1925
E. C.	435	D	1906
Theresa	40415	D	1924
NAUNNAN			
Matilda W.	46634	D	1927
NAUNTON			
Robert H.	4052	D	1907
NAVARLATZ			
Margaret	50729	D	1928
NAVARO			
Clemantina	70268	D	1935
Louis Williams	9657	D	1910
Louisa	20626	D	1916
Raymond	12220	M	1911
Williams	12220	M	1911
NAVARR			
Raymond B.	56949	D	1930
NAVARRA			
Antonio	4104	M	1907
Filippo	4104	M	1907
Giuseppe	4104	M	1907
Salvatore	2811	D	1907
Santo	61199	D	1932
NAVARRET			
Mary	44938	D	1926
Pierre	25377	D	1918
NAVARRI			
Jose Mendiara	56777	D	1930
NAVARRO			
Eligio	47208	D	1927
George	54397	D	1929
Juan	36251	D	1923
William Louis	51599	D	1928
NAVARTH			
Evelyn	47524	M	1927

NAME	NUMBER	TYPE	YEAR	NAME	NUMBER	TYPE	YEAR	NAME	NUMBER	TYPE	YEAR
Michael	68602	I	1934	Mary E.	89317	D	1942	William J.	48906	D	1928
Paul	47524	M	1927	Sophia S.	50847	D	1928	**NEBOUT**			
NAVE				Thomas G.	85388	D	1940	Jean Cazanave	20907	D	1916
G. B.	72576	D	1936	William C.	73602	D	1936	**NECKEL**			
John Batiste	72576	D	1936	William McCrory	56076	D	1930	Adele	11997	D	1911
Michele	67407	D	1934	**NEALAN**				**NEDD**			
William	39959	D	1924	William P.	50237	D	1928	Mabel M.	51536	D	1928
NAVLET				**NEALE**				**NEDDERSEN**			
Eugene Victor	33094	D	1921	Adelaide H.	67554	D	1934	Charles H.	15600	D	1913
NAVONE				Charles A.	18806	D	1915	John H.	79870	I	1938
Angelo	29663	D	1920	James B.	877	D	1906	**NEDDERSON**			
NAVORIAN				**NEALING**				Elizabeth	634	D	1906
Edward Jack	49895	D	1928	Mary	11707	D	1911	**NEDRA**			
John Jack	49895	D	1928	**NEALON**				Ian I. W.	43822	I	1926
NAY				James C.	29134	D	1920	Ian I. W.	82635	D	1939
Gee	21313	D	1916	James Joseph	10458	D	1910	**NEEB**			
NAYBERGER				Matilda	69489	D	1935	William	967	D	1906
Gertrude D.	85200	D	1940	**NEALS**				**NEECE**			
NAYLON				Clara V.	55860	D	1930	Clara May	83042	M	1940
Annie	62468	D	1932	**NEANY**				**NEEDHAM**			
Patrick	62419	D	1932	Pete, Mrs.	89878	D	1942	Danford C.	44755	M	1926
NAYLOR				**NEARY**				Danford F.	44719	D	1926
Charles Elwood	12655	D	1911	Agnes	13927	D	1912	Juanita M.	44755	M	1926
Ellen	48136	D	1927	Agnes A.	69030	D	1935	Madeline	44755	M	1926
Isaac Kensington	44235	D	1926	Annie	7398	D	1909	Margaret Scott	89320	D	1942
Katie E.	29348	D	1920	Charles	20258	M	1916	Michael J.	29152	D	1920
Thomas C.	29349	D	1920	Ellen	69810	D	1935	Mignon M.	44755	M	1926
NAYSON				Emma	9875	D	1910	**NEEFUS**			
George E.	46994	D	1927	George	20258	M	1916	J. Furman	315	D	1906
NAZAR				Geraldine	76734	M	1937	**NEEL**			
Baboo Daniel	33333	D	1922	James	54700	D	1930	Ann	79530	M	1938
NAZARIN				John	55409	D	1930	John Stephenson	78437	M	1938
Antonina	73313	D	1936	John T.	30699	D	1920	Nellie G.	78192	D	1938
NAZZINI				Leonore M.	75502	D	1937	**NEELAND**			
Carlo	44921	M	1926	Mary Agnes	18777	D	1915	Katerine S.	83402	I	1940
NCNALLY				Michael Joseph	89186	D	1942	Katherine S.	85931	D	1940
Margaret	78796	D	1938	N. J., Mrs.	75502	D	1937	**NEELY**			
NEAL				Nicholas	9876	D	1910	David	19950	M	1915
Abbie N.	51937	D	1929	Nicholas E.	40934	D	1925	David Edwin	87155	D	1941
Alice J.	63531	D	1933	Thomas	17944	D	1914	Frank B.	4979	D	1908
Cecile	42036	D	1925	William J.	53597	D	1929	Mary	16864	D	1914
David Nakapaahu	88708	D	1941	**NEASE**				Nellie T.	26822	D	1919
James Craig	39952	D	1924	Julia A.	19101	D	1915	**NEERGAARD**			
James Edward	46666	M	1927	Samuel H.	88063	D	1941	Frederick H.	87174	D	1941
Jane	317	D	1906	**NEATE**				Hannah B.	55234	D	1930
Lizzie	45600	D	1926	John W.	33954	D	1922	William P.	35822	D	1923
Margaret F.	26222	D	1919	William J.	45892	I	1926				

NAME	NUMBER	TYPE	YEAR
NEES			
Wellington H.	41314	I	1925
NEESON			
Daniel	15592	D	1913
Laurenz	7504	D	1909
Nels Petter	4609	D	1907
NEEVES			
India Helen	15172	M	1913
NEFF			
J. H.	7570	D	1909
Mark C.	82186	D	1939
Nancy	21173	D	1916
William H.	22242	D	1917
NEGASAKI			
Fred H.	37699	D	1923
NEGRINHO			
Manuel de Ponte	89564	D	1942
Manuel Ponte	89564	D	1942
NEGRO			
Joseph L.	18329	D	1914
Josephine	18330	M	1914
Marguerite	18330	M	1914
Mario	18330	M	1914
Teresa	18330	M	1914
NEGUS			
Mary	8871	D	1909
NEHAR			
Pearl	31081	D	1921
NEHF			
Frederick L.	42493	D	1925
NEHLS			
Robert F.	29344	D	1920
NEHLSEN			
John	16568	D	1914
NEIBERGER			
Ruby L.	68899	D	1935
NEIDECK			
Isabella	64814	D	1933
NEIDHARDT			
Xavier	47284	I	1927
Xavier	47529	D	1927
NEIDICK			
Frank	20035	D	1915
NEIDLEIN			
Bertha	34715	I	1922

NAME	NUMBER	TYPE	YEAR
NEIL			
Annie Elizabeth	39951	D	1924
Charles	82875	D	1939
Cora E.	28569	D	1920
Daniel	313	D	1906
Michael	10121	D	1910
Paul Francis	59095	M	1931
Robert	86285	D	1941
Robert E.	42995	D	1925
Walter Scott	56486	D	1930
NEILAN			
Alice	51661	D	1928
Joseph	76147	D	1937
Martin	24966	D	1918
Mary	24965	D	1918
Thomas J.	57836	D	1931
NEILL			
Joseph W.	6419	M	1908
Mary L.	6418	M	1908
Sarah Alice	10992	D	1911
William E.	59264	D	1931
NEILS			
John J.	89871	D	1942
NEILSEN			
Andreas Albrecht	53613	D	1929
Annie	15662	D	1913
N. C.	20662	D	1916
Niels J.	24869	D	1918
Wilhelm	36050	D	1923
NEILSON			
Alexander	12894	D	1912
Andreas A.	53613	D	1929
Clarence J.	53479	D	1929
Elizabeth	64142	D	1933
Emil Andrew	32661	D	1921
Hans Christian	20498	D	1916
Isabelle	52738	D	1929
Jessie A. G.	68772	D	1935
Jessie Ann	68772	D	1935
Lauritz	16182	D	1913
Mary Elizabeth	64142	D	1933
Mary Isabelle	52738	D	1929
N. C.	20662	D	1916
Petter	6938	D	1908
NEIMAN			
August	46236	D	1927
Eliza	86253	D	1941
John Richard	59666	D	1931

NAME	NUMBER	TYPE	YEAR
Richard	59666	D	1931
NEIMES			
John	8273	D	1909
NEIMEYER			
Robert L.	80507	D	1939
NEISWANDER			
Christian D.	58799	D	1931
NEKOLA			
Marie	86258	D	1941
NELB			
Fred	41364	D	1925
NELCKE			
Theresa	48525	D	1927
NELLIS			
Babara	54768	D	1930
Bertha	54768	D	1930
Medora	47375	D	1927
NELLMAN			
Edward	30906	D	1920
Peter	5542	D	1908
NELSEN			
Albert	52601	D	1929
Caroline	31634	D	1921
Jacob L.	37653	D	1923
Marte Malene	66523	D	1934
Nels C.	23632	D	1917
Niels	36975	D	1923
Niels Christian	76933	D	1937
Severin Marentius	31473	D	1921
Sven	40951	D	1925
NELSON			
A. L.	66297	D	1934
Adeline M.	39426	D	1924
Adolf F.	82933	D	1939
Agnes	74569	D	1937
Albert	52601	D	1929
Albert W.	37289	D	1923
Alette Sophie	130	D	1906
Alice	32932	I	1921
Alice	45716	D	1926
Alice	46053	M	1926
Allan Owen	44803	M	1926
Andrew	35572	D	1922
Andrew	41457	D	1925
Andrew	61585	D	1932
Anna	38771	M	1924
Anna	66536	D	1934

Key: D = death; M = minor; I = incompetent

NAME	NUMBER	TYPE	YEAR	NAME	NUMBER	TYPE	YEAR	NAME	NUMBER	TYPE	YEAR
Anna Trost	14094	D	1912	Florence E.	20122	D	1915	John	75978	D	1937
Annie	15662	D	1913	Florence O.	20122	D	1915	John	81233	M	1939
Annie S.	84411	D	1940	Frances	29447	D	1920	John	83598	D	1940
Archibald F.	38987	I	1924	Frank	67967	D	1934	John A.	10632	D	1910
Arthur Selby	43191	D	1925	Frank F.	89574	D	1942	John B.	19206	D	1915
August	33159	D	1922	Frank Fernando, Jr.	47806	M	1927	John E.	74057	D	1936
August G.	89665	D	1942	Fred	88355	D	1941	John F.	17363	D	1914
Axel	27892	D	1919	Fred C.	53479	D	1929	John M.	82127	D	1939
Axel Harold	76711	D	1937	Frederick Eugene	1566	D	1906	John Malcom	87390	D	1941
Axel W.	75164	D	1937	Frederick Lawrence	58490	D	1931	John R.	32899	D	1921
Bengt	22654	D	1917	Garti	46894	D	1927	John S.	64644	D	1933
Benjamin P.	61092	D	1932	George	31440	D	1921	Joseph V.	61942	I	1932
Bernice Celeste	20983	M	1916	George	41837	D	1925	Josephina	9929	D	1910
Bertha M.	38241	D	1924	George	41837	D	1925	Josephine	62658	D	1932
Betty	17476	D	1914	George A.	18552	D	1915	Josephine Wilhelmina	67892	D	1934
Carolina	57910	D	1931	George Henry	86752	D	1941	Kathrine R.	81984	D	1939
Carrie M.	51155	D	1928	Gerald	48184	M	1927	Lance Flippin	67852	M	1934
Catherine	55658	D	1930	Grace Deering	47806	M	1927	Laura Charlotte	60236	D	1931
Charles	15002	D	1913	Gustaf Alfred	52542	D	1929	Laurel Ruth	66708	M	1934
Charles	23480	D	1917	Gustav	40086	D	1924	Lena	57910	D	1931
Charles	46894	D	1927	Hannah	59893	I	1931	Leonard	85391	D	1940
Charles	65149	D	1933	Hannah	59938	D	1931	Lillian A.	26217	D	1919
Charles A.	38893	D	1924	Hans Christian	20498	D	1916	Lina A.	39029	D	1924
Charles A.	46614	D	1927	Harriet Emily	30189	D	1920	Lizzie Warren	60795	D	1932
Charles B.	25323	D	1918	Harry C.	25117	D	1918	Lorenz	21100	D	1916
Charles John	59380	D	1931	Hazel Maloy	40450	D	1924	Louis W.	37893	D	1923
Charles O.	33988	D	1922	Helen	46053	M	1926	Louise	9801	D	1910
Charlie E.	10488	D	1910	Helen Maria Stend	72392	I	1936	Louise Pearson	77503	D	1938
Christina	72731	D	1936	Helena	1906	D	1906	Magdalene	40069	D	1924
Christina	43235	D	1925	Helene S.	72574	D	1936	Marforie	61658	M	1932
Claire L.	42707	D	1925	Henning	74949	D	1937	Margaret C.	75936	D	1937
Clara	79161	I	1938	Henry Ernest	74949	D	1937	Maria	34488	D	1922
Cornelius	31374	D	1921	Henry S.	75881	D	1937	Mariette	47695	D	1927
Curtis L.	32829	M	1921	Herbert Arnold	44251	D	1926	Martin	49599	D	1928
David	5970	D	1908	Irene	38771	M	1924	Mary	44118	D	1926
Dorothy May	44803	M	1926	Irene Victoria	45469	M	1926	Mary	57420	M	1930
Edgar Charles	76527	D	1937	Irving	52066	D	1929	Mary E.	34056	D	1922
Edward	41712	D	1925	Isabella H.	58528	D	1931	Matilda	56718	D	1930
Edward	46053	M	1926	Jack	48184	M	1927	Matt	64354	D	1933
Elizabeth	15666	D	1913	Jacob	48286	D	1927	Maurice	32795	D	1921
Elizabeth	51396	D	1928	Jacob N.	37599	D	1923	Mauritz LaVern	45469	M	1926
Elizabeth M.	47084	D	1927	James	28499	D	1919	Minnie D.	70201	M	1935
Ellen	77363	D	1937	James	42062	D	1925	Minnie L.	34698	D	1922
Ellen G.	75021	I	1937	James Arthur	87889	D	1941	Mitchell	80927	D	1939
Elmer I.	72900	D	1936	Johanna	46146	D	1927	N. M.	5990	D	1908
Elwood Robert	48942	M	1928	John	32888	D	1921	Nancy	54111	M	1929
Ephraim	13711	D	1912	John	40719	D	1925	Nels	32016	D	1921
Ethel L.	42380	D	1925	John	61865	D	1932	Nels A.	57620	I	1931
F. C.	24099	D	1918	John	62739	D	1932	Nels J.	24869	D	1918

NAME	NUMBER	TYPE	YEAR	NAME	NUMBER	TYPE	YEAR	NAME	NUMBER	TYPE	YEAR
Nels Oscar	86275	D	1941	**NELSSON**				Stephen Sheridan	7101	M	1909
Nels Sture	59089	D	1931	August	33159	D	1922	**NERSON**			
Nels Sture	85493	D	1940	**NEMECEK**				Edmond	5673	M	1908
Nels T.	78642	D	1938	Aknes	28249	D	1919	Edmond Martin	77684	D	1938
Nelson	38771	M	1924	**NEMECK**				Henriette	5865	D	1908
Nelson J.	21749	D	1916	John A.	7371	D	1909	Marcelle	5673	M	1908
Olaf	63488	D	1933	**NEMELKA**				**NESBETT**			
Oliver	58747	D	1931	Joseph	15885	D	1913	William Warren	80192	D	1938
Olof	4283	D	1907	**NEMENTZ**				**NESBIT**			
Ormond H.	8801	M	1909	John	62289	D	1932	Beulah	34384	D	1922
Oscar Nicholaus	38133	D	1924	**NEMETH**				**NESBITT**			
P. S.	47818	D	1927	Julia	83339	D	1940	Anna Louise	88115	D	1941
Patrick	61066	D	1932	Juliana	83339	D	1940	James R.	49077	D	1928
Paul	75983	D	1937	**NEMETZ**				Margaret H.	49076	D	1928
Pauline	55026	D	1930	John	62289	D	1932	Mary E.	13406	D	1912
Pete	61550	D	1932	**NEMIS**				William Warren	80192	D	1938
Peter	46447	D	1927	Lawrence	82829	M	1939	**NESLE**			
Peter	52488	D	1929	**NEMITZ**				Henry	52067	D	1929
Peter M.	58113	D	1931	John	62289	D	1932	**NESPER**			
Phylis Elwood	20983	M	1916	**NENBERT**				Otto Martin	62132	D	1932
Rene Irene	44501	D	1926	Anna Murphy	34129	D	1922	**NESS**			
Robert Leo	84043	D	1940	**NENE**				Dora Jean	72702	D	1936
Robert Michael	85258	D	1940	Ah	2145	D	1906	Hannah	59893	I	1931
Roberta Miriam	20983	M	1916	**NEOS**				Hannah	59938	D	1931
Rose I.	44501	D	1926	Panagis	12715	D	1911	John	49970	D	1928
Ruth V.	63642	D	1933	**NEPER**				**NESSIER**			
Sadie E.	67435	D	1934	Charles	49815	D	1928	Helen M.	75888	D	1937
Sarah Catherine	77307	D	1937	Charles H.	19631	D	1915	Johan Joseph	74448	D	1937
Sarah E.	61394	D	1932	**NEPPERT**				John J.	74448	D	1937
Sarah Stewart	32165	D	1921	George Philip	69270	D	1935	Lois	39815	D	1924
Sevan	40951	D	1925	Julien Pierre	81075	D	1939	Rosalia	17199	D	1914
Severin Alfred	67966	D	1934	Louise	46017	D	1926	**NESTER**			
Sigurd	6536	D	1908	Louise Clestine	80061	D	1938	Marhias	65876	D	1933
Sofie	31923	D	1921	**NERGER**				Mathias	65876	D	1933
Sophie	43725	D	1926	Hermann	78197	D	1938	**NESTING**			
Soren	40951	D	1925	**NERI**				Sam N.	89909	D	1942
Susan	33612	D	1922	Luigi	77713	D	1938	**NESTOR**			
Svea	38771	M	1924	Virginia	47873	D	1927	Michael M.	17562	D	1914
Theresa	46455	D	1927	**NERLAND**				**NESTORI**			
Thomas A.	67453	I	1934	Edward	33593	D	1922	Adolph	84916	D	1940
Victor M.	46829	I	1927	**NERLICH**				**NESTROY**			
Virginia	57420	M	1930	Edward S.	9763	D	1910	Frank M.	44717	D	1926
Walter A.	32397	D	1921	**NERNEY**				**NETH**			
Walter Leonard	45469	M	1926	Albert Alexis	7101	M	1909	George	47557	D	1927
Wellington H.	41314	I	1925	Hamlin Weldon	7101	M	1909	**NETHERLAND**			
Wilhelmina	59067	D	1931	Hattie V.	28107	D	1919	Annette	50219	D	1928
William R.	42278	D	1925								
Williard N.	32829	M	1921								
Willis L.	24888	D	1918								

NAME	NUMBER	TYPE	YEAR	NAME	NUMBER	TYPE	YEAR	NAME	NUMBER	TYPE	YEAR
NETO				**NEUMANN**				Dora	23503	D	1917
Florence	51368	M	1928	Abraham Lincoln	66205	D	1934	Henry S.	23123	D	1917
Frank M.	53360	D	1929	Adam	11151	D	1911	Jacob	23205	D	1917
NETTER				Agnes Elizabeth	41679	D	1925	Jacob H.	23052	D	1917
Augustus	314	D	1906	Charles William	23189	M	1917	Josephine D.	76571	D	1937
Lehman	46541	D	1927	Claire Alma	67569	M	1934	Mary Anne	25061	M	1918
Lillian	16320	D	1913	Clifton Lloyd	31857	M	1921	**NEUSTAT**			
Marcus J.	16119	D	1913	Elise S. V.	7671	D	1909	Jacob	81000	D	1939
NETTRE				Elizabeth	15237	D	1913	**NEUWIRTH**			
Victoria	63638	D	1933	Elizabeth	15893	I	1913	Emma E.	17285	D	1914
NETZEL				Gustave	43840	D	1926	Henry	48742	D	1927
Anna Christine	37087	D	1923	Hannah	81706	D	1939	William T.	16148	D	1913
NEUBACHER				Henry	22891	D	1917	**NEUWITH**			
Bertha	10687	D	1910	Henry	36850	D	1923	Henry C.	48742	D	1927
NEUBAUER				Katherine	30426	D	1920	**NEVEGOLD**			
Emil	63230	D	1932	Leonard	67563	M	1934	Ella M.	65489	D	1933
Franz Emil	63230	D	1932	Marjorie Erline	67569	M	1934	Emma R.	15713	D	1913
Marie	2004	D	1906	Mervin Aubrey	31856	M	1921	**NEVERMONT**			
Mary E.	8299	I	1909	Olga Christina	59483	M	1931	Elmer J.	84899	D	1940
NEUBERGER				Rosalie	11555	D	1911	**NEVIGOLD**			
Adolph	41930	D	1925	Rudolph	2386	D	1906	William F.	73039	D	1936
Adolph	41930	D	1925	Solomon	30943	D	1921	**NEVILLE**			
Anna Frederike	32021	D	1921	William	69855	D	1935	Bridget	48173	D	1927
NEUBERT				**NEUMEISTER**				Ernest H.	11178	D	1911
Anna Murphy	34129	D	1922	John	36039	D	1923	Frank A.	62354	D	1932
Emily	38704	D	1924	**NEUMERKEL**				Michael J.	29751	D	1920
NEUBURGER				Nellie A.	81819	D	1939	Sarah Ann	11597	D	1911
Gustave	27983	D	1919	**NEUMILLER**				Shirley Louise	84094	M	1940
NEUENBURG				Jacob	24475	D	1918	**NEVILLS**			
John	49669	D	1928	**NEUNABER**				Delia Frances	53421	D	1929
Margaret	49668	D	1928	Walter H.	66848	D	1934	Ray G.	64479	D	1933
NEUENDORFF				**NEUNER**				William Alexander	15504	D	1913
Albert H.	65018	D	1933	George	3094	D	1907	**NEVIN**			
NEUGEBAUER				John	60823	I	1932	Bridget	9869	D	1910
August A.	12303	D	1911	John	61137	D	1932	Caroline Herlitz	81031	D	1939
NEUHAUS				**NEUNERT**				Charles William	23473	D	1917
Hermann	79296	D	1938	Frances	85220	D	1940	George Scott	55824	D	1930
NEUMAN				**NEUROHR**				Henry J.	75477	D	1937
Alexander	27562	I	1919	Henry J.	38190	I	1924	John	7041	D	1909
Carl A.	32570	D	1921	**NEUSTADT**				John B.	72519	D	1936
Fanny	28012	D	1919	Adolph	23157	D	1917	Patrick	43055	D	1925
Henry	10704	D	1910	Francis	68046	D	1934	Thomas	312	D	1906
Israel	3462	D	1907	Henry S.	23123	D	1917	**NEVIT**			
Joseph	48566	D	1927	Jacob	81000	D	1939	Beverley Ann	80933	M	1939
Leopold	2496	D	1906	**NEUSTADTER**				**NEVIUS**			
Margaret	10880	D	1910	Caroline	14416	D	1912	George Forgy	16838	D	1914
				David	36010	D	1923				

NAME	NUMBER	TYPE	YEAR
NEVRAUMONT			
Alphonse J.	52721	D	1929
Joseph	15751	D	1913
Louis	82224	D	1939
NEW			
Theodore	62307	D	1932
NEWA			
Alfredo	50301	I	1928
Glfredo	50301	I	1928
NEWBAUER			
Abraham L.	75746	D	1937
Eugene	57545	D	1930
George S.	30015	D	1920
Helen	19168	M	1915
Helen Louise	32867	M	1921
Henrietta	17967	D	1914
Herman W.	16797	D	1914
Jesse	83365	D	1940
Joseph	3093	D	1907
Julian H., Jr.	19168	M	1915
Julian Herman	61486	D	1932
Lillian	19168	M	1915
Louis	64246	D	1933
Rosa	410	D	1906
William	16319	D	1913
NEWBEGIN			
John J.	28595	D	1920
William VanDillon	59560	I	1931
NEWBELL			
Barbara Jane	87652	M	1941
NEWBERG			
John	49565	D	1928
NEWBERRY			
Carrie Jane	76949	D	1937
James	6706	D	1908
Jane	38906	D	1924
Mary A.	32115	D	1921
Mary E.	87874	D	1941
NEWBERT			
Emelyn J.	46813	D	1927
Emily F.	38704	D	1924
Margaret	33399	D	1922
NEWBERY			
Frederick	32467	D	1921
NEWBEY			
Dean Joseph	72065	M	1936

NAME	NUMBER	TYPE	YEAR
NEWBORN			
Suda K.	36606	D	1923
NEWBURGH			
Adolphus S.	75869	D	1937
NEWBURN			
Suda K.	36606	D	1923
NEWBURY			
Emma W.	28348	D	1919
Frederick E.	18892	D	1915
NEWBY			
Clem	60473	D	1931
NEWCOMB			
Anna	28830	D	1920
G. Bruce	34872	D	1922
Paul	35777	M	1923
Philip H.	75639	D	1937
NEWCOME			
William Ambrose	83575	D	1940
NEWDORFER			
Jennie	28951	D	1920
NEWELL			
Ada Gertrude	83107	D	1940
Allan H.	13762	D	1912
Amanda Memphis	38516	D	1924
Amelia	22085	D	1917
Arthur Debney	85636	D	1940
Daniel	17130	D	1914
David	36281	D	1923
Edward	59767	D	1931
Evelyn Bridget	76990	M	1937
George David	48640	D	1927
George L.	74822	I	1937
Herbert Chase	51076	D	1928
Howard John	20104	D	1915
James	74549	D	1937
James Joseph	76990	M	1937
Mary C.	59263	D	1931
Mary Catherine	76990	M	1937
Michael	9788	D	1910
Michael	60453	D	1931
Ralph Gerard	17050	D	1914
Richard	85669	I	1940
Sabina T.	72570	D	1936
Walter Henry	49109	D	1928
William Henry	15158	I	1913
William Henry	15583	D	1913

NAME	NUMBER	TYPE	YEAR
NEWFIELD			
Theresa	545	D	1906
NEWHALL			
Alice M.	56118	D	1930
Charles K.	69844	D	1935
Edwin W.	19901	D	1915
Elizabeth Slade	64026	D	1933
George Almer, Jr.	25248	M	1918
Georgiana	40679	D	1925
Lyle M.	89882	I	1942
Virginia Whiting	17478	D	1914
Virginia Whiting	46980	D	1927
Walter S.	2625	D	1907
Walter Scott	25248	M	1918
William Mayo	68528	D	1934
NEWHOFF			
Allen Derrick	10091	M	1910
Frederick Edward	78480	D	1938
Sarah L.	50251	D	1928
William Anthony	10091	M	1910
NEWHOUS			
Katherine	40865	D	1925
NEWHOUSE			
Dina	42197	D	1925
Hettie	32860	D	1921
Ida	73403	D	1936
William D.	81727	D	1939
William G.	49396	D	1928
NEWKIRK			
D. J.	3334	D	1907
NEWKURST			
Charles	21708	D	1916
NEWLAND			
Alice J.	60503	D	1931
NEWLANDS			
Edith McAllister	86461	D	1941
James	64516	D	1933
Jane Thompson	82526	M	1939
NEWLIN			
Robert Philip	55974	M	1930
NEWLON			
Frank Blair	35703	D	1923
NEWMAN			
Abraham	18366	D	1915
Abraham George	31185	M	1921
Agnes	3375	D	1907
Alan	75539	M	1937

Key: D = death; M = minor; I = incompetent

NAME	NUMBER	TYPE	YEAR
Alexander	12928	D	1912
Alfred	80168	D	1938
Alice A.	62532	M	1932
Bertha	13576	D	1912
Bertha K.	88773	D	1941
Carrie Heller	68708	D	1935
Charles B.	39574	D	1924
Charles Henry	84930	D	1940
Charles J.	30816	D	1920
Charles N.	84073	D	1940
Clara M.	43771	D	1926
David A.	16038	D	1913
Edward	38631	M	1924
Edward M.	61039	M	1932
Edwin H.	75084	D	1937
Elasinda Belardes	64546	D	1933
Elizabeth A.	76955	D	1937
Ella	55508	D	1930
Ella	77649	D	1938
Ellen	68824	D	1935
Ellen H.	76486	D	1937
Emily A.	64677	D	1933
Fannie	30824	D	1920
Fanny S.	84714	D	1940
George	43409	D	1926
George W.	71011	D	1935
George Washington, Jr.	59651	M	1931
Grace Ruth	9365	M	1910
Hannah	87440	D	1941
Harry H.	37459	I	1923
Helen Louise	75539	M	1937
Henry	10704	D	1910
Henry	22891	D	1917
Irving	30830	D	1920
Irwin	30830	D	1920
Jacob	15034	D	1913
Jacob	40867	D	1925
James T.	76956	D	1937
Jane Ernestine	56922	M	1930
Jessie F.	34274	D	1922
John	78919	M	1938
John M.	34227	D	1922
Joseph	81265	D	1939
Joseph S.	69649	D	1935
Juda	68091	D	1934
Julia	38617	D	1924
June Elizabeth	68021	M	1934
Laurence H.	33164	D	1922
Leopold	49746	D	1928

NAME	NUMBER	TYPE	YEAR
Leslie E.	27808	M	1919
Lucy A.	64546	D	1933
Ludwig Elias	47119	D	1927
Margaret	15035	D	1913
Margaret L.	37001	D	1923
Marguerite E.	27222	D	1919
Marion	2597	M	1907
Max	35500	D	1922
May E.	44970	D	1926
Myrtle	70297	D	1935
Nathan D.	19341	D	1915
Pauline	15654	D	1913
Pauline	53910	D	1929
Peter	75539	M	1937
Philip A.	31093	D	1921
Philip E.	27956	D	1919
Phyllis Emma	68021	M	1934
Ray	49275	D	1928
Robert Carl	56922	M	1930
Robert Carl	70207	M	1935
Robert Edwin	31802	M	1921
Robert O.	37751	D	1923
Rose Lavinburg	34785	D	1922
Ruth Murlin	31802	M	1921
Sally Baxter	85525	D	1940
Sally Sherry	85525	D	1940
Samuel	29561	D	1920
Samuel J.	25223	D	1918
Samuel R.	66884	D	1934
Sarah	56933	D	1930
Sarah Jane	10582	D	1910
Sigmund J.	23080	D	1917
Simon	14262	D	1912
Solomon	34786	D	1922
Sylvan A.	59793	D	1931
Tina	42163	D	1925
Verral	45043	M	1926
Walter J.	81547	M	1939
William	9237	D	1910
William	65731	D	1933
William Abraham	73452	D	1936

NEWMANN

NAME	NUMBER	TYPE	YEAR
H. M.	45271	D	1926
Henry	45271	D	1926

NEWMARK

NAME	NUMBER	TYPE	YEAR
Edna	36561	D	1923
Henry R.	56440	D	1930
Julia M.	82260	D	1939
M. J.	11679	D	1911

NAME	NUMBER	TYPE	YEAR
Sophie	32656	D	1921

NEWNHAM

Margaret	84646	D	1940

NEWPORT

Elizabeth M.	68193	D	1934
Lawrence W.	69560	D	1935

NEWSOM

Alfred C.	14159	D	1912
Elizabeth L.	14158	D	1912
Ernest Pegram	34213	D	1922

NEWSTADT

Jacob	81000	D	1939

NEWSTAT

Jacob	81000	D	1939

NEWSTATE

Jacob	81000	D	1939

NEWSTONE

Effie L.	25641	D	1918

NEWTON

California	17384	D	1914
Elizabeth Gertrude	77380	I	1937
Emily R.	34657	D	1922
Frank J.	55266	D	1930
James Wardell	63540	I	1933
James Wardell	66009	D	1934
James Wardwell	57257	I	1930
John Floyd	26854	D	1919
Lee H.	11650	D	1911
Leray	50854	D	1928
Lillian G.	77380	I	1937
Merlin J.	75852	M	1937
Phillip S.	11190	M	1911
Ralph A.	85034	D	1940
Ruth	76390	I	1937
Suzette C.	11190	M	1911

NEWWALD

Leona R.	78432	D	1938
Lerona	78432	D	1938

NEY

Anne A.	45482	D	1926
Carl	30407	D	1920
Nathan	36404	D	1923
Virginia Catherine	75813	I	1937

NEYLAND

Henry J.	13471	D	1912

NEYLON

Annie	62468	D	1932

NAME	NUMBER	TYPE	YEAR	NAME	NUMBER	TYPE	YEAR	NAME	NUMBER	TYPE	YEAR
Elizabeth M.	88188	D	1941	**NICHOLLS**				Wilfred L.	46074	M	1926
NEYMANN				A. W.	20043	D	1915	William	65167	D	1933
Percy	35761	D	1923	Frank C.	63272	D	1933	William A.	25949	D	1918
NG				**NICHOLS**				William Ford	39372	D	1924
Cheuk	44551	D	1926	Annie	83156	D	1940	William J.	42110	M	1925
Hoo	55736	D	1930	Annie C.	38051	D	1924	William James	21572	M	1916
Kai Chew	63738	M	1933	B. W.	73170	D	1936	**NICHOLSEN**			
Kai Quen	63739	M	1933	Bryant I.	70106	D	1935	Jacob	3920	D	1907
Lun	78244	D	1938	Catherine J.	79110	D	1938	**NICHOLSON**			
Lung Gung	64566	D	1933	Catherine S.	3995	I	1907	Albert Frederick	46868	D	1927
Nam	79951	D	1938	Clara Quintard	75699	D	1937	Angus	46118	D	1926
Ruth	17617	M	1914	Claude	20570	D	1916	Edward J.	26133	D	1919
NGAN				David L.	29634	D	1920	Elizabeth	87403	D	1941
Lillie Dong Suey	83201	M	1940	Dawson	28817	I	1920	Elmer Robert	87734	D	1941
NGIM				Dawson	32173	D	1921	Emma	44023	D	1926
Louie	17522	D	1914	De Albert L.	29629	D	1920	John	26412	D	1919
NIAS				Dorsan	28817	I	1920	Joseph W.	15612	D	1913
Elizabeth	28591	M	1920	Dorsan	32173	D	1921	Katherine H.	52356	D	1929
Gerald J.	28591	M	1920	Edward J.	71165	I	1935	Lizzie	50048	D	1928
Mary	27826	D	1919	Ella May	21572	M	1916	Marie Louise	65256	D	1933
Melville J.	28591	M	1920	Ella R.	17133	D	1914	Mary A.	49933	D	1928
R. H.	17165	D	1914	Eva M.	87630	D	1941	Mary E.	16239	D	1913
NIASON				George	16	D	1906	Phillip D.	86267	D	1941
Raymond J.	33344	I	1922	Gustav	16500	D	1913	Rachel	61388	D	1932
NIBBE				Henry G.	59382	D	1931	William	54025	D	1929
Johanna F.	77761	D	1938	Iota M.	59597	D	1931	William Joseph	71252	D	1935
NIBLOCK				Isabella T.	4565	D	1907	**NICKANDER**			
Gene	45737	D	1926	John Christian	83878	D	1940	Edith	17596	M	1914
Sadie Gene	45737	D	1926	John H.	32362	D	1921	Ferdinand	17597	D	1914
NICE				Joseph Edward	21572	M	1916	Hugo	17596	M	1914
Cephas	10164	D	1910	Josephine P.	20741	D	1916	**NICKEL**			
NICHELL				Katharine	86217	D	1941	Edward R.	69226	D	1935
Blanche	83988	D	1940	Lesley Jean	71095	D	1935	Montana	82371	D	1939
NICHOLAS				Lillian Martina	88896	D	1942	Robert Charles	75909	M	1937
Andrew	381	D	1906	Lyman	4263	D	1907	**NICKELESON**			
Ferdinand P.	69289	D	1935	Lyman, Sr.	4264	D	1907	Margaret C.	80355	D	1939
Ferro	4903	D	1907	Margaret	42182	D	1925	**NICKELL**			
George	16	D	1906	Margaret A.	67282	D	1934	Blanche	83988	D	1940
George	28434	D	1919	Margaret Helen	35243	M	1922	**NICKELS**			
George F.	49044	D	1928	Marjorie Elizabeth	27992	M	1919	Ada Belle	30810	D	1920
James	37483	M	1923	Mary	49150	D	1928	Charles	85836	D	1940
Laurent	43561	D	1926	Mary A.	73792	I	1936	Helen C.	39182	D	1924
Nahum	60602	D	1932	Mary A.	76332	D	1937	Henry	35288	D	1922
NICHOLL				Mary E.	77589	D	1938	Jacob F.	59602	D	1931
John H.	45649	D	1926	Mary J.	41501	D	1925	Lisbeth D.	35745	M	1923
Rose	25243	D	1918	Mary L.	75344	D	1937	Lisbeth D.	55167	D	1930
William Henry	69281	D	1935	Nathan N.	2698	D	1907	**NICKELSBURG**			
				Thomas H.	25254	D	1918	Florence	89189	D	1942
				Walter John	29616	D	1920				

NAME	NUMBER	TYPE	YEAR	NAME	NUMBER	TYPE	YEAR	NAME	NUMBER	TYPE	YEAR
Louis	2367	D	1906	**NICOLACOPOULOS**				Grace F.	19077	D	1915
Moritz	14114	D	1912	Georges D.	44653	D	1926	Helena	14600	D	1912
Siegfried	19498	D	1915	**NICOLAI**				Margaret R.	4790	D	1907
NICKELSEN				Angelo	70029	D	1935	Sussie W.	2638	D	1907
Nickolaus	41090	D	1925	Eugene	39675	D	1924	Wallace C.	82383	D	1939
NICKERSHAM				Frank	80251	D	1939	**NICOLSON**			
Frederick A., Jr.	7846	M	1909	Frederick, Jr.	39675	D	1924	Donald	12619	D	1911
Jane Elizabeth	7846	M	1909	Louisa	2865	D	1907	Priscilla A.	57565	D	1931
NICKERSON				**NICOLAN**				**NICOLUKOPOULOS**			
Charles J.	15399	D	1913	Gregorio	24129	D	1918	Georges D.	44653	D	1926
Ernest Arthur	74585	D	1937	**NICOLAS**				**NICORA**			
Florence K.	75814	D	1937	Alexis	3343	D	1907	Carolina	71761	D	1936
Frank Charles	31266	M	1921	Joseph F.	58751	D	1931	Emilio	8888	D	1909
Sarah	46532	D	1927	Julian	53137	D	1929	Ida	13923	M	1912
Sarah M.	48946	D	1928	Maria	7191	D	1909	Pietro	71762	D	1936
NICKEY				Pierre	46034	D	1926	Romilda	13923	M	1912
John Thomas	58101	D	1931	**NICOLAY**				William	13923	M	1912
NICKLAS				Georg Philipp	6696	D	1908	**NIDEROST**			
Frieda Liess	81287	D	1939	George W.	6696	D	1908	Joseph B.	34483	D	1922
NICKLASSEN				**NICOLE**				**NIDING**			
Wilhelm	30288	D	1920	Charlotte	40495	D	1924	Delia	30618	D	1920
NICKLES				**NICOLES**				**NIDREGGER**			
Andrew	381	D	1906	Charlotte F.	87168	D	1941	Franz	51386	D	1928
Jacob	54150	D	1929	**NICOLET**				**NIEBAUM**			
NICKOLE				Lea	22307	D	1917	Gustave	6367	D	1908
George	59984	D	1931	**NICOLETTE**				Suzanne	72270	D	1936
NICKOLOPOULOS				Antonina	79958	D	1938	**NIEBLA**			
Demitrios	31811	D	1921	Domenico	44563	D	1926	Ignatius A.	433	D	1906
NICKOLS				Joseph	13066	D	1912	**NIEBLING**			
George	59984	D	1931	**NICOLETTI**				Englehart Theodore	35065	D	1922
NICKSON				Rosalia	69839	D	1935	**NIEBOLT**			
Harold	59792	M	1931	**NICOLI**				Ottilie	71724	D	1936
NICLES				Filomena	28651	D	1920	**NIEBORGER**			
James	50538	D	1928	**NICOLINAS**				Auguste	16852	D	1914
NICODEMUS				Tom	10123	D	1910	Heinrich	14255	D	1912
Clio Lucille	49303	D	1928	**NICOLINI**				Otto F.	35908	D	1923
Margaret May	88071	D	1941	Alice	86666	D	1941	**NIEBOUR**			
NICOL				Frank	74118	D	1936	Theodore	58073	D	1931
Amedee	30335	D	1920	John B.	84877	D	1940	**NIEDERMARK**			
Duncan	43849	D	1926	Norma	44291	D	1926	George	36200	D	1923
Henry	46409	D	1927	Vincent M.	44972	D	1926	**NIEDRA**			
Mary	47155	D	1927	Vincenzo	12019	D	1911	Lise	84765	D	1940
William	11570	D	1911	**NICOLINO**				**NIEHLSON**			
William Z.	75103	D	1937	G.	11047	D	1911	Charles	14410	D	1912
NICOLA				**NICOLL**				Mary	15459	D	1913
Chiesa	16384	D	1913	Alexander	83911	D	1940				

NAME	NUMBER	TYPE	YEAR
NIEHOFF			
Violetti J.	84103	D	1940
NIELSEN			
Agnes H.	40871	D	1925
Allan John	12352	M	1911
Andrew	75919	D	1937
Anna Marguerite	13332	M	1912
Anne Margrethe Martha	62921	D	1932
Anne Marie	10790	D	1910
Carl A.	17932	D	1914
Carl K.	51133	D	1928
Carl P.	12544	D	1911
Clarence Holger	86379	D	1941
Edna Anita	12352	M	1911
Elina	14260	D	1912
Frederick H.	12280	D	1911
Frederick H.	36364	D	1923
Frederikke	62230	D	1932
Hans C.	59286	D	1931
Harry	17894	D	1914
John	88524	D	1941
John Christian	63088	D	1932
Lars Peter	26582	D	1919
Lillian Francis	13332	M	1912
Louis	21168	D	1916
Mary	36365	D	1923
Meinert D. K.	88806	D	1941
N. H.	17894	D	1914
N. K.	36975	D	1923
Nels	86220	D	1941
Nels C.	23632	D	1917
Niels	36975	D	1923
Niels Peter	49254	D	1928
Nills C.	23632	D	1917
Nills Mikkelsen	36122	D	1923
Paul Sivert	47818	D	1927
Peter Ludwig	49074	D	1928
Roy Frederick	12352	M	1911
Shirley	53032	M	1929
Sophus A.	53212	D	1929
Soren	82215	D	1939
Theresa	46455	D	1927
Thomas	72957	D	1936
Wilhelm P.	36050	D	1923
NIELSON			
Albert W.	22034	D	1916
Andrew	23925	D	1918
Augusta Emilie	13968	D	1912

NAME	NUMBER	TYPE	YEAR
Frederick Lawrence	58490	D	1931
Isabelle	52738	D	1929
John I.	83766	D	1940
Leonora	20875	D	1916
Mary Isabelle	52738	D	1929
Niels Christian	60841	D	1932
Paul	75983	D	1937
NIEMAN			
Laura	49368	D	1928
Marta	1152	D	1906
NIEMANN			
Henry C.	63502	D	1933
Henry J. F.	59259	D	1931
Marie	9271	M	1910
May	16594	D	1914
NIEMEIER			
Theodore	68231	I	1934
NIEMEYER			
Henry	12662	D	1911
NIENSTADT			
Richard	6956	D	1908
NIERENCE			
Frank	53220	D	1929
NIERI			
Angelo	78364	D	1938
NIESCHALKE			
H. R. G.	4127	D	1907
NIESEN			
Michael Peter	26511	D	1919
NIESS			
Catherine	45580	I	1926
John	30900	D	1920
NIETO			
Antonio	56188	D	1930
Jacob	55366	D	1930
John Jacob	58665	M	1931
John Jacob	82750	D	1939
Mary	88911	D	1942
NIETZEL			
Lina Luise Becker	38762	D	1924
NIETZSCHE			
Emil	79112	D	1938
NIEVES			
Celestina	54039	D	1929
Salestina	54039	D	1929

NAME	NUMBER	TYPE	YEAR
NIEWERTH			
August	37665	D	1923
NIFCAS			
Alexander	41427	M	1925
NIGHTINGALE			
California	56197	M	1930
Ellen	16820	D	1914
John	13251	D	1912
John Joseph	11082	M	1911
John Walton	56198	M	1930
Joseph B.	11159	D	1911
NIGLIS			
Eugene	69095	D	1935
Joseph	21360	D	1916
Josephine	20973	D	1916
NIGO			
Komoto	5994	M	1908
NIGOUL			
Madeleine	21582	D	1916
NIGRO			
Ruffina Maria	59715	D	1931
Vincent	20459	D	1916
NIHIL			
Mary Agnes	61815	D	1932
Peter	61485	D	1932
Peter Cornelius	22959	D	1917
NIHILL			
Cornelius	70920	D	1935
Martin W.	75755	D	1937
NIKANDER			
Einar Daniel	57241	I	1930
Selma	20600	D	1916
NIKIPIDIS			
George	81272	D	1939
NIKITIDAS			
George	81272	D	1939
NIKITIDIS			
George	81272	D	1939
NILAN			
Catherine A.	75778	D	1937
John Joseph	72371	D	1936
NILAND			
J.	12993	D	1912
John	32329	D	1921
Mary A.	64398	D	1933
Mary Teresa	81701	M	1939

NAME	NUMBER	TYPE	YEAR	NAME	NUMBER	TYPE	YEAR	NAME	NUMBER	TYPE	YEAR
Mary Theresa	88441	M	1941	**NIPPER**				Emil C. F.	63980	D	1933
Thomas J.	88439	D	1941	Bertha	3242	M	1907	**NIVEN**			
NILE				Elizabeth C	3242	M	1907	Daniel	9567	D	1910
M. W.	75755	D	1937	Mary A.	49969	D	1928	Elizabeth J.	32405	D	1921
NILES				Rosie M.	3242	M	1907	Thomas Daniel	72257	D	1936
Ketty	6207	I	1908	Rudolph	2225	D	1906	**NIXON**			
Ketty	24292	D	1918	**NIQUET**				Albion Ernest	37537	M	1923
Perley Lewis	36616	D	1923	Charles Frederick	19831	D	1915	Ann Augusta Elizabeth	76122	D	1937
NILLSON				**NISBET**				Bertram E.	31539	D	1921
Mabel Emma	87380	D	1941	Eleanor	8498	D	1909	Caroline A.	31461	D	1921
NILSEN				**NISH**				Carrie	84685	D	1940
Albert	52601	D	1929	Frederick William	87172	D	1941	Elizabeth	76120	D	1937
Henning	74949	D	1937	**NISHIKAWA**				Elizabeth H.	77346	D	1937
Marte Malene	66523	D	1934	Riichi	63800	D	1933	Ellen	30151	D	1920
Rose Ann	4618	D	1907	**NISHIMI**				George	67372	D	1934
Rose Claire	13997	M	1912	Sei	46444	M	1927	George Stuart	32957	D	1921
Severin Marentius	31473	D	1921	Yoshiko	46444	M	1927	Harold Travers	59792	M	1931
Sven	40951	D	1925	**NISPEL**				James, Jr.	28754	M	1920
NILSON				Edward	2586	D	1907	John A.	72770	D	1936
Anna	33224	D	1922	**NISSE**				John E.	83999	D	1940
Axel J.	52744	D	1929	Lorenz	2785	I	1907	Myrtle Eleanor	37537	M	1923
Barbara Jane	50181	M	1928	**NISSEN**				Violet E.	76121	D	1937
Carl August	28822	D	1920	Alfred H.	83035	D	1940	W. J.	1160	D	1906
Caroline	57910	D	1931	Charles F.	78834	D	1938	Wiliam James	37537	M	1923
Charles	23007	D	1917	George	48807	D	1927	William J.	28816	D	1920
Ella Stratton	50488	D	1928	Henry	9062	D	1910	**NIZZOLA**			
Emma	59141	D	1931	Nils Peter	53645	D	1929	Luigi	56048	D	1930
Gerda Kristina	43624	M	1926	Nis Paulsen	24208	D	1918	**NOAD**			
John	52744	D	1929	Paulsen	24208	D	1918	Grace C.	61617	D	1932
John Gottlieb	41837	D	1925	Vollena	46197	D	1927	**NOAH**			
John Gottlieb	41837	D	1925	**NISSUM**				Harriet Teresa	42371	D	1925
Lena	57910	D	1931	Christian W.	86658	D	1941	Jacob A.	6160	D	1908
Margaret	11704	D	1911	James Peter	54001	D	1929	**NOBBS**			
NILSSON				Jens P.	54001	D	1929	Arthur Hyde	47822	M	1927
Amanda	33466	D	1922	**NITSCH**				Virginia Jean	47822	M	1927
Anna	63500	D	1933	Edward	33592	D	1922	**NOBEL**			
Christian	46103	D	1926	Wilhelm Richard	46340	D	1927	Thora A.	63451	D	1933
J. N.	61585	D	1932	**NITSCHE**				**NOBLE**			
Johan	35913	D	1923	Arthur E.	58647	D	1931	A.	8725	D	1909
Nicolaus J.	61585	D	1932	Emil Richard George	79112	D	1938	Chester F.	83431	D	1940
Nils Axel Ferdinand	8889	D	1909	Oswald R.	46122	D	1927	Edith	89903	I	1942
Olaf	63488	D	1933	**NITSCHKE**				Edith L.	72491	I	1936
Olof	30546	D	1920	Adolf	19834	D	1915	Eliza	6765	D	1908
Olof C.	7554	D	1909	Alvina	69485	D	1935	Frederick A., Mrs.	50453	D	1928
Olof C.	7554	D	1909	Alwine	69485	D	1935	Grace	60535	D	1931
Oscar L.	33467	D	1922	**NITZ**				Hamden H.	54726	D	1930
NIMMO				Emil C.	6280	I	1908	J. Shelby	52398	D	1929
James	67562	D	1934					James E.	81294	D	1939

NAME	NUMBER	TYPE	YEAR
John F.	11188	D	1911
Joseph B.	88528	D	1941
Julia C.	52398	D	1929
Leila Crandon	50453	D	1928
Minnie A.	34077	D	1922
Nellie	21175	D	1916
Patrick	30431	D	1920
Peggy	83555	D	1940
Robert Houston	82866	D	1939
Rollin E.	17656	D	1914
William	78332	D	1938
William N.	65328	D	1933
NOBLEA			
Juan Eladio	32902	D	1921
NOBLEA Y ZUBIRIA			
Don Juan Eladio	32902	D	1921
Juan Eladio	32902	D	1921
NOBLITT			
James M.	15173	D	1913
NOBMAN			
Frederick	7631	D	1909
NOCE			
Fred	81918	D	1939
Giovanni	58189	D	1931
Louis	33885	D	1922
NOCELLA			
Ferdinand	56754	D	1930
NOCK			
Alan P.	53043	D	1929
NODEN			
William B.	3823	D	1907
NOE			
Clarence Thomas	78414	D	1938
Frank B. V.	75162	D	1937
Leland E.	66240	D	1934
Shannon Douglas	7117	D	1909
NOEL			
Germaine Nenee Leonide	64310	D	1933
Isaac	10556	D	1910
Myrtle S.	71726	D	1936
Richard C.	16733	D	1914
Thomas	59315	D	1931
NOELL			
Frances	21477	M	1916
NOERR			
J. Geo.	8141	D	1909

NAME	NUMBER	TYPE	YEAR
NOETHEL			
Max	36546	D	1923
NOGAT			
Ernest	30549	D	1920
NOGGLE			
Anna M.	52147	D	1929
NOGUES			
Jean Pierre	12111	D	1911
NOHLING			
Mary	43292	D	1925
NOHS			
Louise F.	60411	D	1931
Louise J.	60411	D	1931
William Frank	67168	D	1934
NOIRE			
W. Drummond	75569	D	1937
NOIRJEAN			
Catherine	44740	D	1926
NOLAN			
Agnes M.	40902	D	1925
Alta	8257	M	1909
Arthur M.	82188	D	1939
Bernard J.	55482	D	1930
Charles	2447	D	1906
Clifford	8257	M	1909
David A.	20256	D	1916
Edmond	55240	D	1930
Edward	24560	D	1918
Edward	79469	D	1938
Edward Stephen	22923	D	1917
Elizabeth	552	D	1906
Elizabeth T.	21487	D	1916
Ellen	88219	D	1941
Ellen M.	4511	D	1907
Hamilton	8257	M	1909
Helen	70692	D	1935
Henrietta	48358	D	1927
Hugh H.	64023	D	1933
James	3368	D	1907
James	30042	D	1920
James C.	40556	D	1924
James E.	79192	D	1938
John	512	D	1906
John	21995	D	1916
John	68673	D	1935
John I.	35432	D	1922
John James	18560	D	1915

NAME	NUMBER	TYPE	YEAR
John K.	10711	D	1910
Katherine L.	4164	D	1907
Leo J.	40759	D	1925
Louise	59405	D	1931
Margaret	31298	D	1921
Margaret	66373	D	1934
Margaret	53733	D	1929
Margaret F.	80428	D	1939
Margaret S.	80428	D	1939
Marian Jane	82494	M	1939
Martin Francis	86233	D	1941
Mary Ann Jane	82494	M	1939
Mary C.	65228	D	1933
Mary Elizabeth	88038	D	1941
Mollie T.	74935	D	1937
Patrick F.	1908	D	1906
Philip	8257	M	1909
Stanley	8257	M	1909
Thomas	17542	D	1914
William H.	8259	D	1909
William H.	21950	D	1916
NOLAND			
Agnes I.	77409	D	1938
Dimmitt	53893	D	1929
H. P.	76293	D	1937
Isabelle	77409	D	1938
Mary E.	75897	D	1937
NOLDEKE			
Sophie	57011	D	1930
T. S. F.	26053	D	1919
NOLI			
Freda	27291	M	1919
Kate	26896	D	1919
Mary	27291	M	1919
Rosa	28743	D	1920
Violet	27291	M	1919
NOLL			
John G.	75086	D	1937
NOLT			
Bessie H.	87316	D	1941
Bessie J.	74876	I	1937
Elizabeth	87316	D	1941
Elizabeth	74876	I	1937
Herman	32912	D	1921
Herman, Mrs.	74876	I	1937
Herman, Mrs.	87316	D	1941
NOLTE			
August F.	1550	D	1906

NAME	NUMBER	TYPE	YEAR	NAME	NUMBER	TYPE	YEAR	NAME	NUMBER	TYPE	YEAR
Clement A.	11234	D	1911	John F.	75124	I	1937	**NORD**			
Sophie	1921	D	1906	John F.	81297	D	1939	Catherine	25865	D	1918
NOLTEMEIER				Kathleen C.	15873	D	1913	Charles G. A.	26099	D	1919
Henry	84873	D	1940	Lawrence E.	11891	D	1911	Olaf	58812	D	1931
NOLTHEL				Louella	14247	I	1912	**NORDELL**			
Max	36546	D	1923	Louella	44804	D	1926	Charles S.	24003	I	1918
NOLTING				Margaret	11139	D	1911	**NORDEN**			
Antonia	8661	D	1909	Margaret	45049	M	1926	Charles	60905	D	1932
William H.	38401	D	1924	Margaret	47111	D	1927	**NORDHAUSEN**			
NOM				Margaret B.	52931	D	1929	Herbert	75430	M	1937
Chin Sir	39969	M	1924	Martin James	52244	D	1929	**NORDIN**			
NONGIER				Mary	2914	D	1907	Andrew	16567	D	1914
Maria	35902	D	1923	Mary	64797	D	1933	Axel	39630	D	1924
NONNENMANN				Mary J.	15104	D	1913	**NORDMAN**			
Albert	26232	D	1919	Michael	5517	D	1908	Adolph	12281	D	1911
Charles	19181	D	1915	Michael	6422	D	1908	Benjamin E.	42918	M	1925
Edward C.	75410	I	1937	Robert	45049	M	1926	Helene L.	42847	D	1925
Gustav	25173	D	1918	Thomas	45049	M	1926	Isabel E.	89693	D	1942
Lucile Alice	10313	M	1910	Thomas	79335	D	1938	Isidor	7450	D	1909
NONNENMENN				**NOONE**				John	27925	D	1919
Anna	33581	D	1922	John	31044	D	1921	Leon	40145	D	1924
NOON				Martin	81234	D	1939	Marie	80537	D	1939
Lee	16527	D	1913	Mary Ann	54400	D	1929	Robert	48519	D	1927
Margaret	18911	D	1915	Michael	33990	I	1922	Victor	26126	D	1919
Mary G.	69979	D	1935	Michael Joseph	44606	I	1926	**NORDSTROM**			
Thomas	66431	D	1934	Patrick C.	72935	D	1936	Axel G.	66878	D	1934
Thomas D.	24236	I	1918	Patrick Joseph	36303	D	1923	Wilhelmina	7328	D	1909
NOONAN				Thomas J.	53145	D	1929	**NORDVALL**			
Agnes L.	83116	D	1940	**NOONEN**				Peter	89450	D	1942
Aimee	87381	D	1941	Caroline A.	54977	I	1930	**NORDWALL**			
Ann	76500	D	1937	Caroline A.	56756	D	1930	Peter	88851	I	1942
Ann Mary	27108	D	1919	**NOONES**				Peter	89450	D	1942
Annie	10682	D	1910	Wilma Emma	23081	M	1917	**NOREEN**			
Annie	77578	D	1938	**NOORDINK**				Henry	75840	D	1937
Catherine	15124	D	1913	John M.	87622	D	1941	Minnie G.	74431	D	1937
Edna L.	50465	D	1928	**NOPANDER**				**NORENBERG**			
Elizabeth	6427	D	1908	Meta	12636	D	1911	Gilbert	46168	D	1927
Elizabeth	29360	D	1920	**NOPPER**				**NORFORD**			
Ellen	33649	D	1922	Albert E.	24591	D	1918	Charles	71436	D	1936
Emma M.	20960	I	1916	Charles	12333	D	1911	**NORGREN**			
Frances	13917	D	1912	**NORBERG**				August	28071	D	1919
Genevive E.	4552	M	1907	Catherine C.	65977	I	1933	**NORGROVE**			
Harry Garfield	86639	D	1941	**NORBY**				James Robert	86798	M	1941
Helen G.	32514	D	1921	Hans Peter	74469	D	1937	Richard Bradley	86798	M	1941
Jane	11223	D	1911	**NORCROSS**				**NORIE**			
Jeremiah	23373	D	1917	Frank G.	16220	D	1913	Luella Drummond	83623	D	1940
John F.	74016	D	1936								

NAME	NUMBER	TYPE	YEAR
NORIEGA			
Frank L.	41271	D	1925
NORIEL			
William	56654	D	1930
NORIN			
Andrew	29277	D	1920
Annie	29867	D	1920
Peter E.	60620	D	1932
NORIO			
Sadaichi	70012	D	1935
Sadaichi	70012	D	1935
NORLOFF			
Einar Louis	87410	D	1941
NORLUND			
Mary	1781	D	1906
NORMAD			
Margrette Amiee	32931	M	1921
NORMAN			
A. E. B. B. N.	51126	D	1928
Amelia Elizabeth	51126	D	1928
Anna M.	38066	D	1924
Arvid Edward	58873	M	1931
Douglas D.	61202	D	1932
Elizabeth	8222	D	1909
Eunice F.	35816	M	1923
Frank G.	17117	D	1914
Frank G.	43712	M	1926
Frank H.	62479	D	1932
Frank S.	39527	D	1924
Fred G.	5547	D	1908
Louise A.	60762	D	1932
Ludwig	32370	D	1921
Mary E.	27032	D	1919
Norma C.	35816	M	1923
Paul C.	74019	D	1936
R. L.	37754	D	1923
Richard	48162	I	1927
Robert E.	37754	D	1923
Zelma S.	43712	M	1926
NORMAND			
Emile Henri	80641	D	1939
James	26210	D	1919
NORMANLY			
James	75657	D	1937
NORRINGTON			
Florence	26721	D	1919
Herbert E.	40892	D	1925

NAME	NUMBER	TYPE	YEAR
NORRIS			
E. J.	27916	D	1919
Ethel	31287	M	1921
Frank	26446	M	1919
Frank, Mrs.	19730	D	1915
George A.	5959	D	1908
Gertrude G.	28187	D	1919
J. H.	74446	D	1937
James	61072	D	1932
Lauren Addison	56171	D	1930
Lena	65100	D	1933
Lucius H.	78773	D	1938
Mary	66971	I	1934
Wilda	31287	M	1921
NORTEMANN			
Martine	67294	D	1934
NORTEN			
Albert Joseph	79483	D	1938
NORTH			
Emeline Morland	30668	D	1920
Eva H.	58821	D	1931
James	73808	D	1936
Mary	37433	D	1923
Nina	11011	D	1911
NORTHAM			
Caroline M.	959	D	1906
NORTHCUTT			
John	68524	D	1934
NORTHEY			
Eileen	76494	D	1937
Linda	87598	D	1941
NORTHINGTON			
Orla	15878	D	1913
NORTHLEY			
Gertrude R.	68244	D	1934
NORTHMORE			
Loveday	3586	D	1907
NORTHON			
Richard L.	61190	M	1932
Robert A.	61190	M	1932
NORTHRUP			
Elmer C.	54218	D	1929
Margaret	27150	D	1919
Rosa	82298	D	1939
NORTON			
Ada	79839	D	1938
Adah Dorris	7374	M	1909

NAME	NUMBER	TYPE	YEAR
Agnes	22440	M	1917
Albert	67544	M	1934
Albert J.	15698	M	1913
Albert J., Mrs.	74180	D	1936
Anne	22440	M	1917
Annie	41429	D	1925
Annie	46313	D	1927
Barbara	22440	M	1917
Bridget	20534	D	1916
Caroline A.	65017	I	1933
Catherine	80085	D	1938
Charles F.	3615	M	1907
David	22550	D	1917
Delia	55762	D	1930
Delia M.	85617	I	1940
Delia W.	87050	D	1941
Edward S.	3615	M	1907
Elsie E.	54031	D	1929
Emma M. M.	71624	D	1936
Ethel Mary	53191	D	1929
Eva F.	49596	D	1928
Evy M.	15698	M	1913
F.	44635	D	1926
Florence A.	33030	D	1921
Florence B.	31680	I	1921
Florence B.	37249	I	1923
Florence B.	86799	D	1941
Francis W.	2026	M	1906
Frederick T.	65181	D	1933
G. N.	19326	D	1915
George	11189	M	1911
George	76109	D	1937
George B.	43141	D	1925
George Flory	56474	D	1930
Gertie	11189	M	1911
Gustaf Adolf	12528	D	1911
H. L.	770	D	1906
Harry Allen	9891	M	1910
Hazel	11189	M	1911
Henry C.	32328	D	1921
Hermine Marie	60361	D	1931
Homer W.	70617	D	1935
Hubert James	74233	D	1936
James	11189	M	1911
James	47845	D	1927
James	53749	D	1929
James Francis	73794	D	1936
James J.	1832	D	1906
Janet S.	3615	M	1907

NAME	NUMBER	TYPE	YEAR	NAME	NUMBER	TYPE	YEAR	NAME	NUMBER	TYPE	YEAR
Jennie	82781	D	1939	Walter W.	54677	D	1930	**NOTTER**			
John	10376	D	1910	William H.	8734	I	1909	Erwin	73436	D	1936
John	21747	D	1916	William J.	27271	D	1919	**NOUGHTON**			
John J.	23543	D	1917	William J.	47223	D	1927	Delia	85617	I	1940
John Joseph	15968	D	1913	William J.	74595	D	1937	**NOUGIER**			
John L.	2165	D	1906	**NORVEL**				Maria	35902	D	1923
John L.	15698	M	1913	Richard	85606	M	1940	Marie	78705	D	1938
John P.	44635	D	1926	**NORVOLD**				**NOUGUE**			
Joseph A.	48234	D	1927	Hans	84237	D	1940	Francois	54336	D	1929
Julia	22440	M	1917	**NORWALK**				Justin	28770	D	1920
Kate Wadsworth	60983	D	1932	Mary M.	29648	D	1920	**NOUGUES**			
Lott Day	86171	D	1941	**NORWALL**				Joseph Marion	44095	D	1926
Mabel	18446	D	1915	Otto Julius	76307	D	1937	**NOUGUIER**			
Malachi	47350	D	1927	**NORWOOD**				Helen C.	85755	M	1940
Malachi	52445	D	1929	Andrew	7795	D	1909	Marie	78705	D	1938
Margaret	1834	D	1906	Isabel W.	48378	D	1927	**NOUIN**			
Margaret	67544	M	1934	Summerfield F.	81728	D	1939	Andrew	29277	D	1920
Margert	19572	D	1915	Tallmadge	70070	D	1935	**NOULIBAS**			
Mary	33944	D	1922	Tallmadge, Jr.	11229	D	1911	Bernard	50066	D	1928
Mary	44261	M	1926	**NORYKO**				**NOUQUE**			
Mary	87050	D	1941	Waclaw	51854	D	1929	Zacharie	75647	D	1937
Mary	85617	I	1940	**NOSANZO**				**NOURRIGAT**			
Mary A.	81876	D	1939	Luigi	30427	D	1920	Eugenie	46473	D	1927
Mary Ann	3247	D	1907	**NOSENZO**				**NOURSE**			
Mary Matilda	62497	D	1932	Luigi	30427	D	1920	Beverly S.	29441	D	1920
May	15698	M	1913	**NOSSEN**				Charlotte Adams	62875	M	1932
Merchelle Harriet	7374	M	1909	Abraham	16525	M	1913	Edith Shepley	62875	M	1932
Michael	33178	D	1922	Amalie	16412	D	1913	Florence L.	57572	D	1931
Murray	3615	M	1907	Joseph	12990	I	1912	James R.	66501	D	1934
Patrick	608	I	1906	Joseph	19120	D	1915	Mary E.	17279	D	1914
Patrick	3637	D	1907	Julius	31072	D	1921	Neysa	74775	M	1937
Patrick	13042	D	1912	Katherine	54271	D	1929	**NOVA**			
Patrick	22440	M	1917	Leslie	16525	M	1913	Louis	27849	D	1919
Patrick	28807	D	1920	**NOST**				**NOVAK**			
Rose Pearson	74180	D	1936	Mary	56872	D	1930	August	81370	D	1939
Samuel	22614	D	1917	**NOTEMAN**				John, Sr.	11245	D	1911
Sara Saxe	7806	D	1909	Alexander	73263	D	1936	Josef	39420	D	1924
Shem N.	42587	D	1925	Felix	3745	M	1907	Mathew	61282	D	1932
Stephen H.	2026	M	1906	**NOTEWARE**				**NOVAKOVICH**			
Thomas	9764	D	1910	Edward W.	17675	D	1914	Josephine	12805	D	1912
Thomas	22440	M	1917	**NOTO**				**NOVANDER**			
Thomas	39972	D	1924	Agostino	34550	D	1922	Anton	45520	D	1926
Thomas	44261	M	1926	**NOTON**				**NOVEK**			
Thomas	44261	M	1926	Eliza A.	86464	D	1941	Joseph	34814	D	1922
Thomas	67544	M	1934	**NOTT**				**NOVELLA**			
Thomas Francis	12985	D	1912	Grace	59503	D	1931	Luigia	6468	D	1908
Thomas J.	15974	D	1913								
Timothy	16735	D	1914								
Tracy R.	3615	M	1907								

NAME	NUMBER	TYPE	YEAR
NOVELLO			
Annie	12980	M	1912
Carlo	62023	D	1932
Carrolina	62946	D	1932
Charlie	12980	M	1912
Concetta	74027	D	1936
Giovanni	66301	D	1934
Josephine	62947	M	1932
Josie	12980	M	1912
Katie	12980	M	1912
Marianna	72186	D	1936
Mary	12980	M	1912
Nathalie	86733	I	1941
Pietro Anthony	12981	D	1912
Pietro Antonio	12981	D	1912
Rosie	12980	M	1912
NOVEMBER			
A. H.	76515	D	1937
Harry A.	76515	D	1937
NOVEMBRI			
Ida	80005	D	1938
NOVESHEN			
George	51156	D	1928
NOVIAKS			
Anthony	59608	D	1931
NOVICH			
Basil	80710	D	1939
NOVIK			
Joseph	34814	D	1922
NOVIKOFF			
Basil	80710	D	1939
George	47489	D	1927
Gregory	47489	D	1927
NOVIKOV			
Vasily	80710	D	1939
NOVIN			
Andrew	29277	D	1920
NOVIOCH			
B. Frank	44569	D	1926
NOVIS			
John	44346	M	1926
Viola	44346	M	1926
NOWAK			
Susanna	53522	D	1929
NOWELL			
Anne Elizabeth	82162	D	1939

NAME	NUMBER	TYPE	YEAR
NOWLAN			
Alfred E.	70989	D	1935
James	40863	D	1925
NOWLIN			
Emma Fellows	30730	D	1920
Thomas W.	29032	D	1920
NOYES			
Catherine C.	66027	D	1934
Charles A.	2184	D	1906
Lauren Addison	56171	D	1930
Mary J.	54455	D	1929
Mollie	86796	D	1941
Sophia	20958	D	1916
William Moody	18229	D	1914
William P.	7114	D	1909
NTAUNIS			
Apostolos Spy	63849	D	1933
NUBER			
William	87400	D	1941
NUBY			
John	69325	I	1935
John	70159	D	1935
NUCKOLLS			
Alfred Marshall	82088	D	1939
Helen	80062	D	1938
Marshall	82088	D	1939
NUFER			
Magnus	17403	D	1914
NUGENT			
Alice F.	34103	D	1922
Anne L.	61159	I	1932
Catherine	18996	D	1915
Edward M.	34148	I	1922
James	15174	D	1913
James	23558	D	1917
James F.	26738	D	1919
James I.	43626	D	1926
Lizzie A.	76102	D	1937
Morgan Thomas	65933	I	1933
Patrick W.	9532	D	1910
Peter	34789	D	1922
Richard	53590	D	1929
Robinson	54741	D	1930
Susan	64399	D	1933
William Edward	34148	I	1922
NUHN			
Arthur E. J.	50499	D	1928

NAME	NUMBER	TYPE	YEAR
Peter Francis	80206	D	1938
NUIZ			
Christina	10076	D	1910
NUMAN			
Beatrice	85707	M	1940
NUMMELIN			
Albert	8622	D	1909
Amanda	13464	D	1912
NUMMER			
Jacob	46760	D	1927
NUNAN			
Aloysius J.	80550	D	1939
Bridget	20522	I	1916
Catherine	6099	D	1908
Delia	20522	I	1916
Delia	60334	D	1931
Ellen	43016	D	1925
Margaret	20271	D	1916
Mary Agnes	43831	D	1926
Matthew	20334	D	1916
Thomas	6098	D	1908
NUNES			
Emily V.	79573	I	1938
Frank	38665	D	1924
Frank Joseph	53528	D	1929
Manuel B.	70414	D	1935
NUNEZ			
Carmen H.	51728	D	1928
Concha	7124	D	1909
Frances	54203	M	1929
George Evaristo	54204	M	1929
Maria	12514	M	1911
Nicolas	77414	D	1938
Ricardo	17643	D	1914
NUNIES			
Alfredo Lisardo	33898	I	1922
NUNN			
Claude	27031	M	1919
Lillian	27031	M	1919
Louise	27031	M	1919
Norman J.	3525	D	1907
William R.	24286	D	1918
NUNSIALE			
Giovanni	43899	D	1926
NURMISTO			
Oiva	86526	D	1941

Name	Number	Type	Year	Name	Number	Type	Year	Name	Number	Type	Year
Nuscheler				**Nybye**				**O'Boy**			
Benedikt	50800	D	1928	Carrie L.	18378	D	1915	Mary	24597	D	1918
Nushida				Lloyd Julius	19268	M	1915	**O'Boyle**			
Manji	64425	D	1933	**Nydecker**				Edward J.	52197	D	1929
Nussbaum				F. L.	60421	D	1931	Patrick	35579	D	1922
Kate Sutro	15529	D	1913	**Nydegger**				**O'Brien**			
Lorenz	48671	D	1927	Robert	3512	D	1907	Adeline	58808	D	1931
Nussenblatt				**Nye**				Agnes Bridget	23170	D	1917
Philip	18648	D	1915	Alexander E. J.	3255	D	1907	Alice M.	9665	M	1910
Nusser				Charles Willis	2556	D	1906	Aloysius P.	53906	D	1929
Bertha	84243	D	1940	Eugene	54775	I	1930	Amelia Cecelia	23524	I	1917
Nutcher				George H.	54775	I	1930	Ann	63033	D	1932
Charles Edwin	15488	M	1913	John W.	3171	D	1907	Anna M.	9664	D	1910
Jessie Esther	13269	D	1912	Marcia	14058	M	1912	Anna T.	76066	D	1937
William Wesley	45427	M	1926	Simeon Nash	59997	D	1931	Annie	19560	D	1915
William Wesley Everard	15488	M	1913	**Nygren**				Annie M.	35013	D	1922
Nuti				Arthur C.	37866	D	1923	Annie M.	62086	D	1932
Guglielmo	86358	D	1941	C. S.	66883	D	1934	Arthur J.	43594	D	1926
Lillian	73887	D	1936	Carl Arthur	37866	D	1923	Bartholomew	58154	D	1931
Zeffero	74730	D	1937	Charles Louis	66738	I	1934	Bessie	78687	D	1938
Nutsen				Charles Louis	66883	D	1934	Bridget	10784	D	1910
Mary A.	38095	D	1924	**Nyhan**				Bridget	23170	D	1917
Nuttall				Dave	28126	M	1919	Bridget	69130	I	1935
Hilda Rosenstock	41739	D	1925	**Nyhen**				Bridget	70256	D	1935
Hilda Rosenstock	41739	D	1925	Jeremiah J.	17755	D	1914	Catharine	61173	D	1932
Irene A.	85061	I	1940	**Nyhuis**				Catherine	1071	D	1906
John	4267	D	1907	Marie Jacqueline	1392	M	1906	Catherine	12419	D	1911
John Robert Kennedy	6008	D	1908	**Nyklicek**				Catherine	38803	D	1924
Nutter				John A.	71116	D	1935	Catherine	75095	D	1937
Frank A.	74210	D	1936	**Nylund**				Catherine	75544	D	1937
Hubbard N.	82997	D	1940	Anna	28976	D	1920	Catherine Easter	65720	D	1933
Nutting				Carl Edward	20030	D	1915	Cora	72449	D	1936
Adele J.	7506	M	1909	Clara	33033	D	1921	Cornelius	2350	D	1906
George Clark	6104	D	1908	**Nyman**				D. J.	20874	D	1916
George L.	7506	M	1909	Bernhard	66969	D	1934	Daniel J.	66054	D	1934
Nelson	7506	M	1909	Dora	66968	D	1934	Daniel W.	33844	D	1922
Stephen E.	73303	D	1936	Julius	10808	D	1910	David	53002	D	1929
William	3895	D	1907	Maria	75992	D	1937	Dennis	30877	M	1920
Nuttman				Sofia	55039	D	1930	Dennis Henry	6328	D	1908
Gertrude C.	83545	D	1940	**Nystrom**				Dennis T.	10418	D	1910
Marie A.	52392	M	1929	Carl	9413	D	1910	Edgar Owen	50965	I	1928
Nutz				Carl Victor	86488	D	1941	Edward	51769	D	1929
Sophia	22636	D	1917	Elizabeth S.	36469	D	1923	Edward J.	24324	D	1918
Ny				Irene C.	38576	M	1924	Edward J.	37912	D	1923
Charles R.	11493	D	1911	John A.	16395	D	1913	Edward N.	81139	D	1939
Julia	72306	D	1936	**O'Berti**				Elizabeth	6376	D	1908
Margaret S.	64024	I	1933	Vincent	45573	D	1926	Elizabeth	18462	D	1915
								Elizabeth	28309	D	1919

NAME	NUMBER	TYPE	YEAR	NAME	NUMBER	TYPE	YEAR	NAME	NUMBER	TYPE	YEAR
Elizabeth	63196	D	1932	John Francis	2846	D	1907	Maria	17259	D	1914
Elizabeth Ann	72300	D	1936	John J.	43222	D	1925	Maria	89626	D	1942
Elizabeth J.	38632	D	1924	John J.	45383	D	1926	Maria A.	4733	D	1907
Ella	28151	D	1919	John Joseph	49370	D	1928	Marie	87525	D	1941
Ella	66435	D	1934	John Joseph	77651	D	1938	Marie Geraldine	39222	M	1924
Ella F.	27049	D	1919	John P.	75092	D	1937	Martin Francis	67395	D	1934
Ellen	12337	D	1911	John Patrick	37542	D	1923	Mary	5585	D	1908
Ellen	20263	D	1916	John Patrick	76935	D	1937	Mary	9098	D	1910
Ellen Josephine	34328	D	1922	John T.	30464	D	1920	Mary	13122	D	1912
Emma	9545	M	1910	John T.	46311	D	1927	Mary	16695	D	1914
Etta	9545	M	1910	John V.	27024	D	1919	Mary	30877	M	1920
Eugene A.	83976	D	1940	Joseph	33442	D	1922	Mary	41469	D	1925
Eugene J.	30877	M	1920	Joseph A.	7072	D	1909	Mary	45630	D	1926
Eva Marianne	52139	M	1929	Joseph H., Capt.	87872	D	1941	Mary	70837	D	1935
Frances Anita	23222	M	1917	Joseph J.	40159	D	1924	Mary	84675	D	1940
Francis	77876	D	1938	Joseph J.	78832	D	1938	Mary A.	13249	D	1912
Francis Cotter	58994	I	1931	Joseph P.	72792	D	1936	Mary Agnes	83971	M	1940
Frank	63197	D	1932	Josephine	13699	D	1912	Mary Ann	43362	D	1926
Frank	87524	D	1941	Julia	28138	D	1919	Mary Betkowski	77398	D	1938
Frank H., Mrs.	87525	D	1941	Julia	61429	D	1932	Mary Elizabeth	16835	D	1914
Frank Henry	55572	D	1930	June Janet	45735	M	1926	Mary Elizabeth	50902	D	1928
Frank M.	62087	D	1932	June Janet	45901	M	1926	Mary Elizabeth	76196	D	1937
Garrett Paul	22849	M	1917	June Jean	54860	M	1930	Mary F.	59717	D	1931
George	28776	D	1920	Katherine	14965	D	1913	Matthew	44456	D	1926
George J.	51092	D	1928	Katherine	36828	D	1923	Matthew S.	61555	D	1932
George Raymond	56289	D	1930	Katherine	60159	D	1931	Maurice	32335	D	1921
Gertrude	33457	D	1922	Katherine M.	44209	D	1926	Maurice	40594	M	1924
Hannah	6374	D	1908	Leonora	89041	D	1942	Maurice Joseph	3667	I	1907
Harry D.	25143	D	1918	Lillian M.	79492	D	1938	Medea T.	51862	D	1929
Helen	39017	D	1924	Loretta Josephine	70506	D	1935	Michael	18526	D	1915
Henry Daniel	25143	D	1918	Lydia Genevieve	82246	D	1939	Michael	20077	I	1915
J. P.	50311	D	1928	Margarer	35133	D	1922	Michael	26682	D	1919
James	15696	D	1913	Margaret	3536	I	1907	Michael	33883	D	1922
James	19895	D	1915	Margaret	4176	D	1907	Michael	41520	D	1925
James H.	45382	D	1926	Margaret	4549	D	1907	Michael	63560	D	1933
James P.	59354	D	1931	Margaret	7409	M	1909	Michael	46796	D	1927
James Patrick	25459	D	1918	Margaret	8852	D	1909	Michael J.	83961	D	1940
James Thomas	59720	D	1931	Margaret	22333	I	1917	Michael Joseph	33442	D	1922
Jane	63319	D	1933	Margaret	23359	D	1917	Michael L.	6377	D	1908
Jennie	63319	D	1933	Margaret	29428	D	1920	Naomi	20207	D	1916
Jeremiah	24638	D	1918	Margaret	31003	D	1921	Nellie	11545	D	1911
John	503	D	1906	Margaret	38892	D	1924	Nellie	24323	D	1918
John	4350	D	1907	Margaret	41191	D	1925	Owen	21636	D	1916
John	23969	D	1918	Margaret	45318	D	1926	Patrick	169	D	1906
John	60751	I	1932	Margaret	76391	D	1937	Patrick	6270	D	1908
John	66486	D	1934	Margaret Coughlin	8423	D	1909	Patrick	11473	D	1911
John	87785	D	1941	Margaret M.	85239	D	1940	Patrick	13192	I	1912
John D.	41025	D	1925	Margaret Mary	21654	M	1916	Patrick	13499	D	1912
John E.	74763	D	1937	Margaret T.	65218	D	1933	Patrick	14830	D	1913

NAME	NUMBER	TYPE	YEAR
Patrick	33170	D	1922
Patrick	47010	D	1927
Patrick	76542	I	1937
Patrick	80113	D	1938
Patrick	84800	D	1940
Patrick C.	38090	D	1924
Patrick T.	67591	D	1934
Peter	9545	M	1910
Philip	19930	D	1915
Richard	12339	D	1911
Rosa A. B.	42301	D	1925
Sepp J.	40159	D	1924
Stella C.	9665	M	1910
T. Joseph	53039	D	1929
T. Philip	86339	D	1941
Terence	53237	D	1929
Thais H.	39030	M	1924
Theresa Anson	88500	D	1941
Thomas	1475	D	1906
Thomas	2006	D	1906
Thomas	5538	D	1908
Thomas	18702	D	1915
Thomas	19785	D	1915
Thomas	89729	D	1942
Thomas D.	8673	D	1909
Thomas J.	45013	D	1926
Thomas J.	47012	D	1927
Thomas J.	70627	D	1935
Timothy	57738	D	1931
Timothy J.	22355	D	1917
Vincent Frank	23290	M	1917
Walter J.	64722	D	1933
Walter J.	66856	D	1934
Wilhelmina Henrietta	69690	D	1935
William	6824	D	1908
William	29384	D	1920
William	31039	D	1921
William C. P.	74746	D	1937
William Henry	56067	D	1930
William M.	42981	D	1925
William P.	21628	D	1916
William S.	10855	D	1910
William Smith	44987	I	1926
William T.	31780	D	1921

O'BRINE

NAME	NUMBER	TYPE	YEAR
Katie	61173	D	1932

O'BRYEN

NAME	NUMBER	TYPE	YEAR
Mollie T.	68087	D	1934

O'BURKE

NAME	NUMBER	TYPE	YEAR
Elizabeth Isabel	83869	D	1940

O'BYRNE

NAME	NUMBER	TYPE	YEAR
Emeline	13957	D	1912
John	18057	D	1914
Victor Kennedy	34590	I	1922

O'CALLAGHAN

NAME	NUMBER	TYPE	YEAR
Daniel S.	56341	D	1930
Dennis	12973	D	1912
Elizabeth	26977	D	1919
George	79359	I	1938
Jeremiah	9008	D	1910
John Bertram	71033	D	1935
John G.	25395	D	1918
Joseph	16776	D	1914
Lou May	61018	D	1932
Margaret	168	D	1906
Mary	37123	D	1923
Mary J.	4971	D	1908
May	61018	D	1932
Michael	54641	D	1930
Thomas M.	46523	D	1927
Timothy	50171	D	1928
Timothy	37122	D	1923

O'CALLAHAN

NAME	NUMBER	TYPE	YEAR
Michael	54641	D	1930

O'CONNELL

NAME	NUMBER	TYPE	YEAR
Agnes	27612	D	1919
Annie	18654	D	1915
Bernadette M.	3632	M	1907
Daniel	562	I	1906
Daniel	25487	D	1918
Daniel	48195	D	1927
Daniel	83121	D	1940
Daniel P.	53031	I	1929
Daniel P.	74734	D	1937
Ellen	7354	D	1909
Ellen	53667	D	1929
Ellen	56775	D	1930
Fred J.	65089	D	1933
George P.	2305	D	1906
Gerald	3632	M	1907
Honora	83450	D	1940
James	57564	D	1931
James	62232	D	1932
Jeremiah	24075	D	1918
John	2844	D	1907
John	17722	D	1914

NAME	NUMBER	TYPE	YEAR
John	76941	D	1937
John A.	37186	I	1923
John A.	57505	D	1930
John Arthur	16620	M	1914
John H.	21563	D	1916
John J.	60063	M	1931
John P.	7278	M	1909
John Wm.	44704	D	1926
Julia	13908	D	1912
Kate	78418	I	1938
Katie	20355	D	1916
Lawrence	27613	D	1919
Lawrence	44907	D	1926
Margaret	58967	D	1931
Margaret A.	24390	D	1918
Maria	15267	I	1913
Maria	15323	D	1913
Marie	27881	D	1919
Mary	2843	D	1907
Mary	88281	D	1941
Mary Corbett	56180	D	1930
Maurice	85644	D	1940
Michael	1824	D	1906
Nan	83450	D	1940
Norah	16595	D	1914
Patrick	4670	D	1907
Patrick	23692	D	1917
Patrick	65352	D	1933
Patrick J.	25577	D	1918
Patrick J.	64087	D	1933
Philip John	58370	D	1931
Raymond	60913	M	1932
Thomas Patrick	71393	D	1936
Thomas Russell	16620	M	1914
Timothy	66565	D	1934
Timothy Francis	19060	D	1915
William	24084	D	1918
William	49847	D	1928
William F.	59126	D	1931
William J.	72318	D	1936
William J., Jr.	31452	M	1921

O'CONNOR

NAME	NUMBER	TYPE	YEAR
Agnes R.	8007	M	1909
Alice F.	4570	D	1907
Alvin	49348	M	1928
Anna J.	80992	D	1939
Annie L.	88210	D	1941
Bessie	87907	D	1941
Blanche	68366	D	1934

NAME	NUMBER	TYPE	YEAR	NAME	NUMBER	TYPE	YEAR	NAME	NUMBER	TYPE	YEAR
Brida M.	75766	D	1937	James J.	34598	I	1922	Mary	61664	D	1932
Bridget	17390	D	1914	James S.	11752	D	1911	Mary	79637	D	1938
Bridget	33703	D	1922	Jeremiah	3728	D	1907	Mary A.	70813	D	1935
Carrie E.	59647	D	1931	Jeremiah	14516	D	1912	Mary E.	79220	D	1938
Catherine	11751	D	1911	Jeremiah J.	31075	D	1921	Mary E.	88211	D	1941
Catherine	75808	D	1937	Jeremiah Joseph	31047	D	1921	Matthew Oliver	68921	M	1935
Charles	48252	D	1927	Joan	48293	M	1927	Maud	67295	D	1934
Charles	83668	D	1940	Joeph G.	8007	M	1909	Maurice T.	75736	I	1937
Charles	86424	D	1941	John	5522	D	1908	Maurice T.	76525	D	1937
Charles A.	49784	D	1928	John	5834	D	1908	Michael	4207	D	1907
Charles J.	36406	D	1923	John	16367	D	1913	Michael	7856	D	1909
Clara E.	62613	D	1932	John	45665	D	1926	Michael	11750	D	1911
Cora	65730	D	1933	John	48293	M	1927	Michael	35119	D	1922
Cornelius	6820	D	1908	John	68509	D	1934	Michael	47400	D	1927
Cornelius	68690	M	1935	John	68690	M	1935	Michael	63625	D	1933
Daisy	65681	D	1933	John	78217	D	1938	Michael John	68921	M	1935
Daniel	5502	D	1908	John C.	67320	D	1934	Michael Joseph	30646	D	1920
Daniel	27935	D	1919	John F.	54413	D	1929	Michael M.	75375	D	1937
Daniel J.	13959	D	1912	John Howard	61544	D	1932	Morris Joseph	84874	D	1940
Daniel T.	82433	D	1939	John Howard	87450	D	1941	Nellie F.	59956	D	1931
Delia	64789	I	1933	John J.	37076	D	1923	Nora	48293	M	1927
E. A.	9618	D	1910	John J.	42616	D	1925	Owen	4994	D	1908
Edward	56404	M	1930	John Joseph	34709	D	1922	Patrick	1598	D	1906
Edward L.	9069	D	1910	Joseph	40754	D	1925	Peter	19749	D	1915
Ella	41738	D	1925	Joseph M.	54975	I	1930	Peter	52804	D	1929
Ella	41738	D	1925	Joseph M.	55179	D	1930	Peter	63379	D	1933
Ellen	57516	D	1930	Joseph S.	55307	D	1930	Peter F.	55786	D	1930
Ellen	76135	D	1937	Julia	39809	D	1924	Redmond	63965	D	1933
Eugene Francis	45272	D	1926	Katherine	44009	D	1926	Richard	42196	D	1925
Francis J.	54533	M	1929	Laura	67254	D	1934	Richard	46208	D	1927
Francis Lauren	54533	M	1929	Lillian C.	56169	D	1930	Richard	45723	I	1926
Frank	16984	M	1914	Lizzie W.	16087	D	1913	Richard C.	25973	D	1918
Georgette	63737	D	1933	Luke	5650	D	1908	Robert	84500	M	1940
Hanora	20404	D	1916	Margaret	6602	D	1908	Ruth	76200	I	1937
Helena F.	61997	D	1932	Margaret	14515	D	1912	Sarah Ann	9093	D	1910
Howard	56984	D	1930	Margaret	15549	D	1913	Shirley	84500	M	1940
Hugh	21128	D	1916	Margaret	58882	I	1931	Sylvester P.	65437	D	1933
Hugh	55283	D	1930	Margaret J.	2167	D	1906	Terence	68083	D	1934
Irene	44792	M	1926	Margaret J.	79746	D	1938	Terence J.	63698	D	1933
Jackie	68690	M	1935	Maria	9765	D	1910	Theresa J.	8131	D	1909
James	14699	D	1913	Martin	26899	D	1919	Thomas	15570	D	1913
James	17792	D	1914	Martin	58083	D	1931	Thomas	39810	D	1924
James	20918	D	1916	Mary	9765	D	1910	Thomas	56404	M	1930
James	46421	D	1927	Mary	13727	D	1912	Thomas	79153	D	1938
James	57094	D	1930	Mary	17619	I	1914	Thomas	84682	I	1940
James	68690	M	1935	Mary	21465	D	1916	Thomas	85298	D	1940
James	77500	D	1938	Mary	42927	D	1925	Thomas E.	38456	I	1924
James	84500	M	1940	Mary	47879	D	1927	Thomas E.	49578	D	1928
James B.	21116	M	1916	Mary	55678	I	1930	Thomas E.	50861	D	1928

NAME	NUMBER	TYPE	YEAR	NAME	NUMBER	TYPE	YEAR	NAME	NUMBER	TYPE	YEAR
Thomas F.	67416	D	1934	Linda	71030	D	1935	John	16436	M	1913
Thomas J.	24121	D	1918	Willard Helen	76854	M	1937	John	23751	D	1917
Thomas J.	24204	D	1918	**O'DOHERTY**				John	67546	D	1934
Thomas M.	28864	D	1920	Edward	45391	D	1926	John Edward	61177	I	1932
Timothy	3668	D	1907	George	64632	D	1933	John T.	32250	D	1921
Timothy	14145	D	1912	Michael	17289	D	1914	John Vincent	27289	D	1919
Timothy	16757	D	1914	**O'DONAGHUE**				Kate	16436	M	1913
Timothy	23572	D	1917	Ellen	85478	D	1940	Katie J.	1026	D	1906
Timothy J.	88055	D	1941	Joseph I.	47369	D	1927	Loretta	55273	M	1930
Virginia	8007	M	1909	**O'DONALD**				Margaret	46329	D	1927
William	9202	D	1910	Mary	46798	D	1927	Marie	8480	D	1909
William	12051	D	1911	**O'DONNELL**				Martin	83603	D	1940
William	53846	D	1929	Abigail	60675	D	1932	Mary	1471	D	1906
William	84608	I	1940	Agnes M.	85825	D	1940	Mary	2426	M	1906
William	44010	D	1926	Aileen	35085	D	1922	Mary	11727	D	1911
William A.	59198	D	1931	Alexander	39569	D	1924	Mary	24542	D	1918
William E.	88209	D	1941	Andrew	15240	D	1913	Mary	25185	I	1918
William J.	82107	D	1939	Andrew	16436	M	1913	Mary	46798	D	1927
William James	61733	D	1932	Ann	5944	D	1908	Mary Anne	16436	M	1913
William M.	47400	D	1927	Annie J.	53835	D	1929	Nancy	24474	M	1918
William Morgan	11455	D	1911	Bert	89062	D	1942	P.	19529	D	1915
O'CURRAN				Bridget	3348	D	1907	Patrick	12338	D	1911
Patience	61978	D	1932	Bridget	4591	D	1907	Patrick	12871	D	1912
Patricia	61978	D	1932	Catherine	59362	D	1931	Patrick	16436	M	1913
O'DAY				Charles C.	13661	D	1912	Patrick	20578	D	1916
Daniel J.	43223	D	1925	Cornelius	59132	D	1931	Patrick Henry	28285	D	1919
Edward	37592	D	1923	Denis	25855	D	1918	Patrick J.	69076	D	1935
Frances Mary	70722	D	1935	Edward	2426	M	1906	Philip	51301	D	1928
John J.	61183	D	1932	Edward	2463	D	1906	Raymond	2426	M	1906
Joseph	8998	D	1910	Edward I.	45740	D	1926	Terrance	41421	D	1925
Mary	21218	D	1916	Elizabeth Lilly	27940	D	1919	Thomas	16436	M	1913
Mary	29013	D	1920	Ellen	14364	D	1912	Thomas	28304	D	1919
Miranda R.	74878	I	1937	Emma M.	18055	M	1914	Thomas J.	53722	D	1929
Patrick	80079	D	1938	Emma R.	50281	D	1928	Virginia	81137	M	1939
Roland	22963	M	1917	Frank	2426	M	1906	William	16436	M	1913
Thomas F.	37860	D	1923	Harry	28285	D	1919	William D.	39583	D	1924
O'DEA				Helen	55273	M	1930	William S.	54985	D	1930
Edward	20647	D	1916	Helena	68792	I	1935	Winifred	84431	D	1940
Edward Aloysius	47574	D	1927	Henry	9604	D	1910	**O'DONOGHUE**			
John A.	517	D	1906	Henry Godfried	51301	D	1928	John	40256	D	1924
Joseph P.	26148	D	1919	James	43187	D	1925	John W.	1559	I	1906
Margaret Helen	80623	D	1939	James	79039	D	1938	John W.	7068	D	1909
Margaret O'Coony	80623	D	1939	James	43229	D	1925	Margaret	14693	D	1913
Martin P.	76824	D	1937	James	45707	D	1926	Margaret	40384	M	1924
Michael	21136	D	1916	James G.	46241	D	1927	Mary C.	35826	D	1923
Sarah	19287	D	1915	Janet Ann	78799	M	1938	**O'DONOVAN**			
O'DELL				Johanna	17710	D	1914	James	17546	D	1914
Charles	52436	D	1929	John	12394	D	1911	William	73041	D	1936

NAME	NUMBER	TYPE	YEAR
O'DOUL			
Eugene Joseph	27261	D	1919
O'DOWD			
Cecilia	60085	D	1931
Daniel J.	56746	D	1930
J.	1085	D	1906
Margaret	21769	D	1916
Sarah	83345	D	1940
O'DRISCOLL			
Cornelius O.	22492	D	1917
Maria	22547	D	1917
Richard	11048	D	1911
O'DUNNING			
James C.	29522	D	1920
O'DWYER			
Thomas, Jr.	35739	D	1923
Thomas, Sr.	39282	D	1924
O'FARRELL			
John J.	778	D	1906
Josephine Alice	85295	M	1940
Margaret	87844	D	1941
Mary A. J.	47097	D	1927
Mary Evelyn	987	M	1906
Patricia Alfreda	85295	M	1940
Thomas	63020	D	1932
William K.	34302	D	1922
O'FLANAGAN			
Daniel John Francis	77462	D	1938
O'GARA			
Annie Mary	70969	D	1935
Edward Francis	15089	M	1913
Eva E.	67203	D	1934
John Joseph	77352	D	1937
O'GORMAN			
Anna	6249	D	1908
Anna M. T.	47410	D	1927
John J.	2007	D	1906
O'GORMAN-MUNKHOUSE			
Alfred Frederich	58331	D	1931
O'GRADY			
Alexander L.	59612	D	1931
Bridget	64213	D	1933
Catherine	47922	D	1927
Jeremiah	59428	D	1931
John	64174	D	1933
John J.	66875	D	1934
Maria	21143	D	1916

NAME	NUMBER	TYPE	YEAR
Michael	47923	D	1927
Michael	40575	I	1924
O'HAGAN			
Edward Francis	42998	M	1925
James	60594	D	1932
Mary J.	12062	D	1911
O'HAIR			
Helen	84035	D	1940
Patrick E.	46930	D	1927
O'HALLORAN			
Bridget	31364	D	1921
Bridget	61169	D	1932
Bridget	65618	D	1933
Frank	4995	D	1908
Honora	23757	D	1917
James O.	14934	D	1913
Maud A.	85468	D	1940
Rose	55062	D	1930
Thomas F.	10828	D	1910
William	25803	D	1918
William Joseph	58401	D	1931
O'HANLEY			
Margaret I.	40480	D	1924
O'HANLON			
Daniel	5893	D	1908
Elizabeth	61452	D	1932
James F.	666	D	1906
Joseph	5894	D	1908
Sarah	8624	D	1909
O'HANNESIAEN			
Kosloff	38172	I	1924
O'HANRAHAN			
Lillian Ella	85921	D	1940
O'HARA			
Alice	80743	D	1939
Barttlett	2842	D	1907
Bridget	6083	D	1908
Edith	3938	M	1907
Ellen	77363	D	1937
Emma	70616	D	1935
Francis	84430	D	1940
Francis J.	79069	D	1938
George W.	57692	D	1931
Gertrude	14746	D	1913
Helen I.	77363	D	1937
Hugh K.	61386	D	1932
James	50984	D	1928
John	43965	D	1926

NAME	NUMBER	TYPE	YEAR
John J.	5598	D	1908
John J.	25612	D	1918
John J.	73152	D	1936
Joseph	43939	I	1926
Joseph	44452	D	1926
Kate	7865	D	1909
Lizzie	68768	D	1935
Louise	45486	D	1926
Louise M.	86734	D	1941
Margaret	58893	D	1931
Mary	13164	D	1912
Mary	82950	D	1939
Michael	80461	D	1939
Olympia	14803	M	1913
Thomas	14803	M	1913
O'HARE			
Annie Regina	11068	M	1911
Eugene	9380	D	1910
George W.	57692	D	1931
Harry M.	53963	D	1929
John	44860	D	1926
Joseph	73	D	1906
Joseph M. F.	330	D	1906
M. H.	53963	D	1929
Margaret	11068	M	1911
Marie	36023	D	1923
Michael	35067	D	1922
Michael	53963	D	1929
Sarah	58263	D	1931
O'HEA			
James	63765	D	1933
O'HEARN			
Daniel Joseph	62570	D	1932
O'HEARNE			
John	26853	D	1919
O'HERN			
James M.	44460	M	1926
Margaret	44461	I	1926
Margaret Helen	44460	M	1926
May Julia	44460	M	1926
O'KANE			
Catherine	4389	D	1907
Edward	40095	D	1924
Francis	10177	D	1910
John	72002	I	1936
John J.	74956	D	1937
Margaret	722	D	1906
Mary	27589	D	1919

NAME	NUMBER	TYPE	YEAR	NAME	NUMBER	TYPE	YEAR	NAME	NUMBER	TYPE	YEAR
Mary E.	11144	D	1911	May F.	72893	D	1936	Nicholas	17938	D	1914
Mary G.	50688	D	1928	Peter Kennefick	52538	D	1929	Theresa	87150	D	1941
Michael	70915	I	1935	**O'KELLY**				Timothy	68653	D	1935
Michael Joseph	78998	D	1938	James	79936	D	1938	William	89736	D	1942
Neil	47033	D	1927	John J.	81687	D	1939	William R.	40294	D	1924
William D.	36639	D	1923	**O'KUDA**				**O'LOONEY**			
O'KEANE				Frank	40464	D	1924	James J.	50437	D	1928
James	7714	D	1909	**O'LAUGHLIN**				Minnie A.	60991	I	1932
O'KEEFE				Della E.	46564	D	1927	Minnie A.	83231	D	1940
Amelia	44646	D	1926	James C.	59203	I	1931	**O'LOUGHLEN**			
Daniel	42665	I	1925	**O'LEARY**				Nellie	63797	D	1933
Daniel	44926	D	1926	Arthur	1897	D	1906	**O'MAHONEY**			
Daniel J.	4574	M	1907	Barry	22298	D	1917	Bridget	41659	D	1925
Daniel J.	21163	D	1916	Betty Lee	63976	M	1933	Florence	50482	D	1928
Denis J.	46301	D	1927	Catherine	85443	D	1940	Margaret	60858	D	1932
Dennis	55061	D	1930	Cornelius	28755	D	1920	**O'MAHONY**			
Edward G.	10277	D	1910	Daniel	9589	D	1910	Jeremiah	23718	D	1917
Elizabeth Agnes	41788	D	1925	Daniel	63461	D	1933	Timothy	56565	D	1930
Elizabeth Agnes	41788	D	1925	Daniel	74227	D	1936	William G.	71821	D	1936
Ellen	36585	D	1923	Daniel	54068	M	1929	**O'MALLEY**			
John	13385	D	1912	Daniel J.	28722	M	1920	Adeline W.	50903	D	1928
John	51622	D	1928	Denis	35180	D	1922	Christopher	23769	D	1917
John E.	4574	M	1907	Denis	45024	D	1926	Edmond	3373	D	1907
John J.	70632	D	1935	Eileen	67796	M	1934	Ellen	39890	D	1924
John R.	7349	D	1909	Elizabeth L.	60896	D	1932	James J.	65889	D	1933
Lawrence	11530	D	1911	Ella	28151	D	1919	Joseph Michael	50607	D	1928
Lawrence	24039	D	1918	Ellen	16693	D	1914	Josephine L.	55468	I	1930
Lizzie L.	59785	D	1931	Ellen	19688	D	1915	Mary	68778	D	1935
Margaret L.	34229	D	1922	Frank, Jr.	78922	M	1938	Owen	35392	D	1922
Martin	8340	D	1909	J.	27885	D	1919	P. H.	23777	D	1917
Mary	1223	D	1906	James	1743	D	1906	Patrick	1525	D	1906
Mary	42664	I	1925	James	13486	D	1912	**O'MARA**			
Mary	46477	D	1927	James	74232	D	1936	Annie	43597	D	1926
Mary	72447	D	1936	James Patrick	39567	D	1924	Denis	10738	D	1910
Melville	23831	M	1918	Jeremiah	4293	D	1907	Sarah Jane	50111	D	1928
Mercedes	44775	D	1926	Jeremiah	24847	D	1918	Terry Jean	70625	M	1935
Michael	34756	D	1922	Jeremiah	27645	D	1919	**O'MARIE**			
Michael	49117	D	1928	Jerome	78922	M	1938	Patrick	77803	D	1938
Patrick John	58418	D	1931	Johanna	8190	D	1909	**O'MEARA**			
Thomas B.	88138	D	1941	Johanna M.	49093	D	1928	D. J.	57295	D	1930
Thomas J.	80522	D	1939	Margaret	51837	D	1929	Daniel J.	17499	D	1914
William	1751	D	1906	Margaret	35413	D	1922	Denis	10738	D	1910
William	4574	M	1907	Margaret	53128	D	1929	Dennis	57295	D	1930
O'KEEFFE				Margaret A.	28722	M	1920	Dennis, Jr.	57297	D	1930
Bridget	81258	D	1939	Margaret Elizabeth	70192	D	1935	John	45214	D	1926
Daniel J. A.	44360	D	1926	Margaret Sweeney	86921	D	1941	John	57160	I	1930
Lawrence	11530	D	1911	Mary	7498	D	1909	Mary	57296	D	1930
Mary J.	87032	D	1941	Mary Jane	65511	D	1933	Mary	77566	D	1938

NAME	NUMBER	TYPE	YEAR	NAME	NUMBER	TYPE	YEAR	NAME	NUMBER	TYPE	YEAR
Richard T.	66920	D	1934	William, Jr.	50640	M	1928	Joseph Charles	18769	D	1915
Timothy	66812	D	1934	Yvonne F.	33537	D	1922	Joseph S.	85779	D	1940
O'MOORE				**O'NEILL**				Katherine	28696	D	1920
Eileen Mitchell	76494	D	1937	Agnes	54472	D	1929	Lavenia C.	58507	D	1931
O'NEAL				Agnes Hilda	31579	D	1921	Maggie	14607	D	1912
Anna	40390	D	1924	Ambrose Woods	56952	M	1930	Margaret A.	42490	D	1925
Edward George	63072	M	1932	Andrew	35118	D	1922	Margaret Mary	85596	M	1940
Margaret H.	55763	D	1930	Annie	30573	D	1920	Maria	45471	D	1926
Mary L.	16644	D	1914	Annie	62609	D	1932	Marjorie Woods	56951	M	1930
O'NEIL				Annie Murphy	24007	D	1918	Martin Milton Joseph	49162	D	1928
Anna	40390	I	1924	Arthur	977	D	1906	Mary	83821	D	1940
Annie Eliza	58717	D	1931	Arthur A.	78950	D	1938	Mary Agnes	84350	D	1940
Arthur Ronald	75927	D	1937	Augusta	11699	D	1911	Mary Jane	77437	D	1938
Bertha	67200	I	1934	Bartholomew	6857	D	1908	Matthew John	15954	D	1913
Cyrus F.	48361	D	1927	Bridget	15991	D	1913	Michael Joseph	55754	D	1930
Edward	85777	D	1940	Bridget	63171	M	1932	Neil, Jr.	70631	D	1935
Edward J.	2488	D	1906	Catherine	67682	D	1934	Nicholas	60521	D	1931
Emeline Amelia	21893	D	1916	Charlotte L.	38351	D	1924	Pat	7151	D	1909
Hannah	54749	D	1930	Daniel	41366	D	1925	Patricia Ann	45237	M	1926
Harry	7539	D	1909	Daniel D.	26825	D	1919	Pauline Welcome	79690	D	1938
Henrietta	31074	D	1921	Daniel John	60289	D	1931	Philip James	85596	M	1940
Isabella	32141	D	1921	Daniel Joseph	78756	D	1938	Raymond L.	17981	M	1914
Jacqueline Ellen	78689	M	1938	Daniel L.	60974	D	1932	Richard M.	73929	I	1936
James	931	D	1906	David John	77730	D	1938	Richard P.	62965	D	1932
Johanna	35588	D	1922	Dorothy	74967	M	1937	Robert P.	8242	D	1909
John	29385	D	1920	Edward	85777	D	1940	Terence	40302	D	1924
John C.	85778	D	1940	Eliza	50721	I	1928	Theorilda C.	9539	D	1910
John T.	86830	D	1941	Eliza A.	21336	D	1916	Thomas	62611	I	1932
Joseph S.	85779	D	1940	Ellen	4588	D	1907	W. J.	49430	I	1928
Leah	28961	D	1920	Ellen	12780	D	1912	Willard Jean	69107	I	1935
Louisa C.	81979	D	1939	Eugene	63171	M	1932	William J.	63023	D	1932
Margaret M.	6169	D	1908	Eugene Thomas	3196	D	1907	William James	82960	D	1939
Margie Lee	78689	M	1938	Felix	75553	D	1937	William Joseph	63466	D	1933
Mary	6125	I	1908	Frank	69767	D	1935	**O'NIELL**			
Mary	7953	D	1909	Genevieve M.	72789	D	1936	William H.	52336	D	1929
Mary	13564	D	1912	George Keys	22691	M	1917	**O'REGAN**			
Mary	16687	D	1914	George Louis	80524	D	1939	Bartholomew	24357	D	1918
Mary	84468	D	1940	George N.	80524	D	1939	Mary A.	21350	D	1916
Mary Agnes	84350	D	1940	James	349	D	1906	Thomas	44509	D	1926
Mary L.	66951	D	1934	James	45732	D	1926	**O'REILLY**			
Mary McDermott	61591	D	1932	Jane	77437	D	1938	Bernard	29130	D	1920
Melville E.	56045	D	1930	John	50980	D	1928	Catherine	6996	D	1908
Peggy	83555	D	1940	John C.	85778	D	1940	Charles	15378	D	1913
Robert Cyrus	33738	M	1922	John F.	61099	D	1932	Cornelius	2270	D	1906
Thomas D.	65653	D	1933	John Francis	61995	I	1932	Elizabeth	2176	D	1906
Thomas F.	23588	D	1917	John H.	85993	D	1941	Henry S.	71817	D	1936
Vincent Arthur	49010	D	1928	John M.	67607	M	1934	James J.	84791	D	1940
William	39026	D	1924	John P.	32194	D	1921	Jane M.	30019	I	1920
				John P., Jr.	77980	D	1938				

NAME	NUMBER	TYPE	YEAR
Jane M.	43154	D	1925
Jeremiah	10761	D	1910
Jermiah	84253	D	1940
John	89093	D	1942
Julia T.	72823	D	1936
Lilly	24923	D	1918
Margaret	31327	D	1921
Mary	49625	D	1928
Nicholas J.	22894	D	1917
Pat	48784	D	1927
Patrick	8990	D	1910
Sarah	3779	D	1907
William	51679	D	1928
William	79740	D	1938
O'RIELLY			
Elvira	29339	M	1920
Joseph F.	58383	D	1931
William	51679	D	1928
William	77608	D	1938
O'RIORDAN			
Daniel	57607	D	1931
Denis W.	57606	D	1931
John	57609	D	1931
Mary	59369	D	1931
Patrick	57608	D	1931
O'ROURKE			
Bridget	1439	D	1906
Catherine	67084	D	1934
Elizabeth	86347	D	1941
James Joseph	23964	M	1918
Jane	70570	D	1935
Joan T.	42668	M	1925
Joanna T.	43284	M	1925
John Edward	23964	M	1918
John F.	23963	D	1918
John Henry Joseph	24670	M	1918
John Joseph	67083	D	1934
Margaret	16973	D	1914
Margaret	54143	D	1929
Mary	7807	D	1909
Mary	16305	D	1913
Mary	35872	D	1923
Mary A.	36452	D	1923
Mary A.	50422	D	1928
Mary E. J.	76503	D	1937
Michael J.	25853	D	1918
Robert A.	42668	M	1925
Robert Anthony	43284	M	1925

NAME	NUMBER	TYPE	YEAR
Rosa	11197	D	1911
Teresa Georgiana	68272	D	1934
Thomas	31772	D	1921
Thomas	57400	D	1930
Thomas F.	60057	D	1931
Thomas Patrick	23964	M	1918
O'RYAN			
Philip	29209	D	1920
O'SHAUGHNESSY			
Catherine Agnes	87122	D	1941
Daniel J.	21564	D	1916
Joseph	66195	D	1934
Margaret E.	49869	D	1928
Margaret.	17179	D	1914
Michael Maurice	68143	D	1934
William	87081	D	1941
O'SHAUNNESSY			
Dorothy	29582	M	1920
John	52901	D	1929
O'SHEA			
Bridget	15329	D	1913
George	72785	M	1936
Helen	23617	D	1917
Henry	16301	D	1913
James	21562	M	1916
James Henry	21490	I	1916
Jeremiah	20217	D	1916
John F.	15140	D	1913
John T.	11375	D	1911
Julia	52722	I	1929
Mary	31410	D	1921
May Virginia	21562	M	1916
Michael	6184	D	1908
Vincent Joseph	60013	D	1931
O'SULLIVAN			
Andrew	8413	D	1909
Bridget	66308	I	1934
Catherine	42782	D	1925
Catherine	43309	D	1926
Cornelius J.	85022	D	1940
Daniel	49265	D	1928
Daniel M.	41129	D	1925
Eugene	66535	D	1934
Eugene P.	76445	D	1937
Fanny	35860	D	1923
Hannah	4081	D	1907
James	84539	D	1940
Jeremiah	4080	D	1907

NAME	NUMBER	TYPE	YEAR
Jeremiah	16640	D	1914
Jeremiah Francis	46232	D	1927
John D.	8032	D	1909
Kathleen Margaret	84729	D	1940
Margaret	76245	D	1937
Michael	65749	D	1933
Michael	88189	I	1941
Nellie	11221	D	1911
Nellie Margaret	51829	D	1929
Patrick	55191	D	1930
Timothy	14001	D	1912
Tom	72471	D	1936
O'TOOLE			
Catherine	7301	D	1909
Catherine T.	7670	D	1909
Festus	79495	D	1938
Henry B.	60456	D	1931
John	33502	D	1922
Joseph P.	48923	D	1928
Louise	65419	D	1933
Mary	23368	D	1917
OAK			
Joe Sing	52996	D	1929
OAKES			
Catherine	47034	D	1927
Emma Armstrong	67947	D	1934
George W.	15975	D	1913
Howard	26541	I	1919
Joseph Lawrence	73676	M	1936
OAKEY			
Frances H.	41755	D	1925
Frances H.	41755	D	1925
OAKLEY			
Alex F.	33650	D	1922
Charles E.	63811	D	1933
Frank D.	67396	D	1934
Jennie	37499	D	1923
Leroy Frank	42039	I	1925
Nan	63259	D	1932
OAKS			
Helen	37213	M	1923
Rosalind	37213	M	1923
OARD			
Ralph	86904	D	1941
OAS			
Henry	56089	D	1930

Key: D = death; M = minor; I = incompetent

NAME	NUMBER	TYPE	YEAR	NAME	NUMBER	TYPE	YEAR	NAME	NUMBER	TYPE	YEAR
OASSER				Joseph	81808	D	1939	OCHOA			
Jack	35871	I	1923	OBERMAIER				Clara	64393	D	1933
OAT				Marea	65537	D	1933	OCHS			
John M.	15070	D	1913	OBERMEYER				Hannah	8791	D	1909
OATES				David	55808	D	1930	Joseph W.	85291	D	1940
Anne	83596	D	1940	Thomas Frederick Adolph	23096	D	1917	OCHSLEIN			
Delia A.	12189	D	1911	Walter	83399	M	1940	Lenard	57828	D	1931
Martin	1753	D	1906	OBERMILLER				OCHSNER			
Martin	28371	I	1919	Raymond Francis	28156	M	1919	Elizabeth	59207	M	1931
Mary	14747	D	1913	OBERSTEG				Washington Henry	47011	D	1927
Mary	41026	D	1925	Ferdinand Im.	53114	D	1929	Winifred J.	59207	M	1931
William J. B.	60756	I	1932	OBERSTELLER				OCKEN			
OATMAN				Oscar A.	72828	D	1936	Charles	33073	M	1921
Charles H.	37502	D	1923	OBERT				Reuben	33073	M	1921
OATS				Anton	7889	D	1909	ODAVICH			
Thomas	38507	D	1924	OBERTELLO				Samuel	14457	D	1912
OBELLO				Eugenio	72099	D	1936	Savo	14457	D	1912
Costanzo	22262	D	1917	OBERTI				ODDONE			
OBENAUER				Serafina	43323	D	1926	Emilio	70408	D	1935
George	12988	D	1912	Tomaso	47448	D	1927	Giulia	53215	D	1929
OBENAUR				Tomassini	47448	D	1927	ODELL			
George	12988	D	1912	Vincent M.	45573	D	1926	Addie M.	62121	D	1932
OBENCHAIN				OBERTO				Helen Willard	76854	M	1937
Emma G.	79800	D	1938	Vincenzo	45573	D	1926	Mary A.	16611	D	1914
Silas	87462	D	1941	OBERTOP				ODELLO			
OBER				Earl H.	29827	D	1920	Ethel	63297	D	1933
John B.	15651	M	1913	F. H.	29827	D	1920	ODENTHAL			
OBERDEENER				OBERTS				Mathilde M.	22767	D	1917
Libba	2436	D	1906	Eva Charlotte	50801	D	1928	ODGEN			
Libba	2686	I	1907	OBIOLS				Ruth	82548	D	1939
OBERFELD				Nelita Estrada	19929	D	1915	ODGERS			
Charles	9191	D	1910	OBITZ				Louise Haste	84741	D	1940
Charles	74702	D	1937	Maxine L.	82240	M	1939	ODLAND			
OBERFELL				Richard D.	82240	M	1939	John O.	47486	D	1927
John W.	47758	D	1927	Yvonne G.	82240	M	1939	ODLUND			
OBERG				OBOY				Alma	41677	D	1925
Axel	67542	D	1934	William H.	58209	D	1931	OEBRICHS			
Kathleen E.	63362	D	1933	OBRADOVICH				Hermann	1748	D	1906
OBERHAUS				Kate	67601	D	1934	OECHSLE			
Julius Joseph	87234	I	1941	OBRAM				Elizabeth	33385	D	1922
Julius Joseph	87582	I	1941	Thomas G.	43035	I	1925	Elizabeth	38471	D	1924
OBERLANDER				Thomas G.	43324	D	1926	Elizabeth Catherine	38471	D	1924
Hermine	87218	D	1941	OBRY				OECHSLIN			
John George	71194	D	1935	Adolph	71513	D	1936	Stephen	14234	D	1912
OBERLE				OBWALD				William	35770	D	1923
John H.	58050	D	1931	Samuel	31204	D	1921				

NAME	NUMBER	TYPE	YEAR	NAME	NUMBER	TYPE	YEAR	NAME	NUMBER	TYPE	YEAR
OEHLER				**OETZEL**				**OHE**			
Elizabeth	19903	D	1915	George William	41257	D	1925	Herman	10218	D	1910
William	78864	D	1938	**OFDENKAMP**				**OHL**			
OEHLERER				Dollie	86767	D	1941	Horace C.	42016	D	1925
Joseph	85992	D	1941	**OFFER**				**OHLAND**			
OEHLERT				Johanna E.	33646	D	1922	Cecilia	36151	D	1923
Frederick	50077	D	1928	**OFFERMANN**				Charles	78766	D	1938
Jennie J.	59461	D	1931	John Frederick	22703	D	1917	John A.	21637	D	1916
OEHLMAN				**OFFI**				**OHLANDER**			
Richard F.	10286	D	1910	Dominico	55411	D	1930	Frans Gunnar Valdemar	31552	M	1921
OEHNE				**OFFT**				**OHLANDT**			
Mary J.	26237	D	1919	Marie	63914	D	1933	Cecilia	36151	D	1923
OEHTERI				**OGAN**				Chester John	28894	M	1920
Henry F.	46063	D	1926	Chester	27167	M	1919	Henry	20078	D	1915
OELLRICH				**OGAWA**				Henry W.	49496	D	1928
Theodor E. H.	25091	D	1918	Chiyo Matsu	35261	D	1922	John C.	1328	D	1906
OELRICHS				Tadakane	1813	D	1906	Matilda G.	28849	D	1920
Hermann	10997	M	1911	**OGDEN**				Nicholas	21594	D	1916
Thersa Alice	46582	D	1927	Adeline B.	74474	I	1937	**OHLERER**			
OERRY				Fred	4577	D	1907	Joseph	86439	D	1941
George	16900	D	1914	Lillian	89927	M	1942	**OHLERICH**			
OERTLI				Olive Belle	76697	D	1937	Amalia	81843	D	1939
Ella Bertha	2798	M	1907	William Albert	88927	D	1942	**OHLEYER**			
Otto Heinrich	2798	M	1907	**OGER**				Helen	67536	M	1934
OESTERMANN				Henri	54255	D	1929	**OHLHOFF**			
Emilie Rosina	77421	D	1938	**OGI**				Alexis	50157	M	1928
Louis	79428	D	1938	Taichi	69062	D	1935	Alice	50157	M	1928
Louis, Mrs.	77421	D	1938	**OGILVIE**				Alice Keeler	49399	D	1928
OESTERREICHER				Clarence H.	36096	D	1923	Lyndall	50157	M	1928
Walter L.	81102	D	1939	Euphenia Katherine	87317	D	1941	Lyndall	51873	D	1929
OESTERRICHER				John	3533	D	1907	Vida	50157	M	1928
Walter	81102	D	1939	**OGLE**				**OHLMAN**			
OESTERRREICHER				Mary Catherine	71304	D	1935	Frank	26526	D	1919
Marie	21131	D	1916	**OGLESBY**				**OHLSEN**			
Mary Emily	21131	D	1916	Ellen	8067	D	1909	Charles William	17101	D	1914
OESTING				**OGNISSANTI**				George	80947	D	1939
Paul	57426	D	1930	Manlio	36352	I	1923	Hans Ludwig	110	D	1906
OESTREICH				**OGNJENOVICH**				**OHLSON**			
John	30444	D	1920	Dan	80413	D	1939	Albert	48152	D	1927
OETTER				**OGULIN**				Alma C.	43460	D	1926
Charles	48899	D	1928	John	40387	I	1924	Charlotta	24350	D	1918
OETTING				John	50183	D	1928	Florine	53331	M	1929
William	60447	D	1931	**OHANNESIAN**				John A.	24351	D	1918
OETTL				Oscar	40766	D	1925	Natalie	53331	M	1929
Arthur C.	66707	D	1934	**OHANNESSIAN**				Otto Julius	67915	D	1934
				Mark	38172	I	1924	**OHLSSEN**			
								Charles E. L.	52037	D	1929

- 184 -

Key: D = death; M = minor; I = incompetent

NAME	NUMBER	TYPE	YEAR
Dorothy Theresa	61213	M	1932
OHLY			
C. H., Mrs.	83786	I	1940
Lillian Theurkauf	83786	I	1940
OHM			
Augusta Louisa	1225	D	1906
Charles L.	6653	D	1908
Emma Bohm	1092	D	1906
Fredrocl A.	4192	D	1907
OHMAN			
Ignatius Joseph	83482	D	1940
OHMEN			
Margaret	16558	D	1914
OHNIMUS			
Grace D.	77310	D	1937
OHNSTEIN			
Louise Helene	9394	D	1910
OIE			
Ah	15420	M	1913
OJEDA			
Jane Isabella	33892	D	1922
OJVALL			
Johan	73219	D	1936
OKAMOTO			
Risabura	83281	D	1940
Riscaburo	83281	D	1940
OKAZAKI			
S.	6372	D	1908
OKERBLAD			
Joseph	4649	D	1907
OKLJEVICH			
Marco I.	88810	D	1941
OKROS			
Andy Lucas	46676	D	1927
Rose	47019	D	1927
OKSA			
Victor	47727	D	1927
OKUM			
Albertina H.	68336	I	1934
OLAFSEN			
Emma	50986	D	1928
OLAFSSON			
Louise H.	58781	D	1931
OLAIJOLA			
Joseph	84995	D	1940

NAME	NUMBER	TYPE	YEAR
OLANDER			
Barbara	74159	M	1936
Carl	74159	M	1936
Harvey J.	74159	M	1936
Helen	74159	M	1936
Matilda L.	19983	D	1915
Oscar	19828	I	1915
Paul James, Jr.	74159	M	1936
Virginia	74159	M	1936
OLARI			
Gioachino	22609	D	1917
OLAWSON			
Jens Julius	73910	D	1936
Leif	77337	D	1937
OLBINSKI			
Ignatius	18107	D	1914
OLCESE			
Andrew	49752	D	1928
Assunta	10085	D	1910
Giuseppe B.	35771	D	1923
Margaret Conklin	48673	D	1927
OLCOTT			
H. W.	64457	D	1933
OLCOVICH			
Hattie	62696	D	1932
Herman	19148	D	1915
Jacob	44784	D	1926
John Andrew	39617	M	1924
Joseph	39572	D	1924
Selig	88177	D	1941
Thomas William	86058	M	1941
OLD			
Ida	80858	D	1939
Mary E.	64752	D	1933
OLDAG			
Katherine	34052	I	1922
OLDAKOWSKI			
Konstanty	72771	I	1936
OLDEIDE			
Peter O.	67003	D	1934
OLDELEHR			
John G.	42165	D	1925
OLDEN			
Benno A.	66650	D	1934
Dorathea	5924	D	1908
OLDENBURG			
Charles, Mrs.	77279	D	1937

NAME	NUMBER	TYPE	YEAR
Emily	77279	D	1937
OLDER			
Thomas William	86058	M	1941
OLDERNESS			
Peter	39803	D	1924
OLDFIELD			
Mary	55785	D	1930
OLDHAM			
Bridget	77530	D	1938
Edward M.	14853	D	1913
OLDIS			
Josephine	13123	D	1912
OLEIS			
Josephine	13123	D	1912
OLENDER			
Samuel	64765	I	1933
OLES			
John Avery	67833	D	1934
Robert W.	64920	D	1933
OLESEN			
Hans Christian	71509	D	1936
Ingvard	44605	D	1926
J. Walter	49356	D	1928
OLESON			
Olaf Martin Verna	79948	I	1938
OLEVERIA			
Julia	31666	D	1921
OLEVIERO			
P.	40717	D	1925
OLHLERT			
Jennie J.	59461	D	1931
OLIN			
Hulda	57756	D	1931
OLINGER			
May B.	79435	D	1938
OLIPHANT			
Joseph A.	79467	M	1938
Joseph F.	52305	D	1929
Mary J.	79410	D	1938
OLITZKY			
Frederick	28154	D	1919
OLIVA			
Annie Elizabeth	86758	D	1941
Camille	1271	D	1906
Carlo	2344	D	1906
Elvira	70603	D	1935

NAME	NUMBER	TYPE	YEAR
Emanuel S.	17913	D	1914
Eugenie Verdelli	45800	M	1926
George J.	17913	D	1914
George J.	19580	M	1915
Joseph	41454	D	1925
Joseph	81965	D	1939
Joseph Peter	52854	D	1929
Leo E.	19580	M	1915
Rosalia T.	19580	M	1915
OLIVEIRA			
Jorge S.	22694	D	1917
Ralph L.	72452	D	1936
Rephene	72452	D	1936
OLIVER			
Betty	67583	D	1934
Cyrus W.	12205	D	1911
Elizabeth	77067	D	1937
Florence Barwick	64690	D	1933
Frank	65947	D	1933
Hester Tyler	66251	D	1934
James Stanley	14224	M	1912
John	41989	D	1925
John	41989	D	1925
Joseph A.	65718	D	1933
Joseph A., Jr.	34889	D	1922
Joseph J., Jr.	77593	D	1938
Margaret G.	26221	D	1919
Marion	52748	D	1929
Melvin O.	70736	D	1935
Muncy C.	62375	I	1932
Roland Danner	80754	M	1939
William Francis	57762	M	1931
OLIVERA			
P.	40717	D	1925
Ralph L.	72452	D	1936
Ralph L.	76128	D	1937
Rephene	72452	D	1936
OLIVERO			
Arturina	41856	M	1925
Arturina	41856	M	1925
Peter	41856	M	1925
Peter	41856	M	1925
Pietro	40717	D	1925
OLIVI			
Arturo	25899	D	1918
OLIVIER			
Francis	17089	D	1914
Jacques	61245	D	1932

NAME	NUMBER	TYPE	YEAR
Jean	76451	D	1937
Paul	76169	D	1937
OLIVIERI			
Carolina	51587	D	1928
Michele	86224	D	1941
Paolo	13866	D	1912
OLIVO			
Domenico	81255	D	1939
OLIVOTTI			
Lino	19153	D	1915
OLLEY			
William R.	84454	D	1940
OLLINO			
Giuseppe	64131	D	1933
OLLIVER			
Perry William	88903	D	1942
OLLRICH			
John Frederick	55183	D	1930
Louise	35445	D	1922
OLMO			
Antonio	15040	D	1913
Bertha G.	77064	D	1937
Caterina	66742	D	1934
Guiseppe	11665	D	1911
Joseph	11665	D	1911
Raymond F.	84659	D	1940
OLMSTAD			
Isabella	27561	D	1919
OLMSTEAD			
Fred L.	87089	D	1941
Freeman E.	13998	D	1912
OLMSTED			
Louise	77873	M	1938
Nancy Wing	88442	M	1941
Ruth	77873	M	1938
OLNEY			
Evelyne Barbara	60956	D	1932
John S.	72660	D	1936
Pierre DeS.	66411	D	1934
OLOFF			
Adele	11997	D	1911
Annie K.	88787	D	1941
OLS			
Johanna	9102	D	1910
OLSAN			
Hans	27478	D	1919

NAME	NUMBER	TYPE	YEAR
OLSEN			
Aage	20569	D	1916
Adolph	48474	D	1927
Albert S.	89904	D	1942
Alek	55020	D	1930
Alfred	77459	D	1938
Alfred Emanuel	52773	D	1929
Alma	47276	D	1927
Anders	84042	D	1940
Andrew	13399	D	1912
Andrew	29110	D	1920
Andrew	84042	D	1940
Andrew Olai	20091	D	1915
Ane Marie	62771	D	1932
Anna K.	71616	I	1936
Anne Mathild	27686	D	1919
Annie Marie	62771	D	1932
Axel	24344	D	1918
Bent O.	2016	D	1906
Berta J.	71103	D	1935
Bertha	19936	D	1915
Bjorn Edward	73009	M	1936
Bridget	4498	D	1907
Carl	30585	D	1920
Carl	42226	D	1925
Carl Axel	87934	D	1941
Carl E.	45635	D	1926
Carl G.	73038	D	1936
Carl Otto	54539	D	1929
Caroline	44099	D	1926
Charles	20526	D	1916
Charles H.	48796	D	1927
Charles V.	28748	D	1920
Chris	56843	D	1930
Christian	69653	D	1935
Daniel Charles	59934	M	1931
Ellen	43595	D	1926
Emelia	16168	D	1913
Emelie	48978	D	1928
Emily	16168	D	1913
Frances G.	64478	D	1933
Franciska G.	63494	D	1933
Gladys	48898	D	1928
Godtskalk	68930	D	1935
Gordon Russell	45050	D	1926
Halvor	55779	D	1930
Hannah	75937	D	1937
Hans	24908	D	1918
Hans	27478	D	1919

NAME	NUMBER	TYPE	YEAR	NAME	NUMBER	TYPE	YEAR	NAME	NUMBER	TYPE	YEAR
Hans T.	32116	D	1921	Peter Daniel	59985	D	1931	Gottfrid Theodore	72351	D	1936
Harvey	11663	D	1911	Peter Matson	82470	D	1939	Hans	27478	D	1919
Helene	29836	D	1920	Ralph	60559	D	1931	Henry A.	61660	D	1932
Hilda	14431	D	1912	Ralph	71289	D	1935	Henry C.	80278	D	1939
Hilma Lovisa	81253	D	1939	Rebecca	35674	D	1923	Hilda C.	74491	D	1937
Holvar	56089	D	1930	Reinert	25491	D	1918	Hilda Maria	25300	D	1918
Jacob	12409	D	1911	Richards Lawrence	65365	D	1933	Hilma Louisa	81253	D	1939
James	12647	D	1911	Rosa	34526	D	1922	Hilma Lovisa	81253	D	1939
James Ralph	11662	M	1911	Ruth	81155	D	1939	Isabel	73859	D	1936
John	1171	D	1906	Sofie Margrethe	63156	M	1932	Iverine T.	40833	D	1925
John	6319	D	1908	Sofie Marguerite	63156	M	1932	Johanes Oskar	63826	D	1933
John	6828	D	1908	Sven	59967	D	1931	John	22822	D	1917
John	7001	D	1909	Sverre K.	69164	D	1935	John	23580	D	1917
John	52822	D	1929	Theodor	54146	D	1929	John	24458	M	1918
John A.	36545	D	1923	Tillie	89359	D	1942	John	35726	D	1923
John Andreas	29825	D	1920	Violet E.	16738	D	1914	John	43086	D	1925
John B.	43291	D	1925	William Bernard	51292	D	1928	John	52822	D	1929
John B.	53634	D	1929	**OLSON**				John	55325	D	1930
Jorjan M	58250	D	1931	Alexander	19921	D	1915	John B.	43291	D	1925
Josephine Agnes	34652	D	1922	Alfred	37268	D	1923	John B.	53634	D	1929
Julius	51220	D	1928	Alice	61963	I	1932	John E.	10486	D	1910
Karen L.	70204	D	1935	Andrew	22792	D	1917	John E.	62687	D	1932
Katie Elise	28380	M	1919	Andrew	58026	D	1931	John S.	41417	D	1925
Knud	2036	D	1906	Andrew	76020	D	1937	Julius	64485	D	1933
Louis	20331	D	1916	Anna Christina	36921	D	1923	Lavinia	54112	D	1929
Louise	41832	D	1925	Anna M.	48873	D	1928	Lloyd Irving	59221	D	1931
Louise	41832	D	1925	Anna Sophia	74636	D	1937	Louise Marie	81417	D	1939
Ludwig	58064	D	1931	Annie B.	74226	I	1936	Manfred Pitter	52547	D	1929
Manfred P.	52547	D	1929	Annie B.	85243	D	1940	Margaret I.	73859	D	1936
Margaret	89914	D	1942	Arvid	50817	D	1928	Mary Elizabeth	72520	D	1936
Marguerite Sofie	63156	M	1932	Axel	24344	D	1918	Nellie	10783	D	1910
Marian Lucile	70650	M	1935	Axel	74011	D	1936	Nels	6116	D	1908
Mary T.	58333	D	1931	Bridget	36276	D	1923	Olaf magnus Werner	55946	D	1930
Matilda	27686	D	1919	Carl A.	55421	D	1930	Olga Christina	8092	M	1909
Mikal	64496	D	1933	Carl Alfred	86352	D	1941	Oliver J.	84582	D	1940
Minnie	77554	D	1938	Catherine	70712	D	1935	Olof	4430	D	1907
Nels	12028	D	1911	Charles M.	51641	D	1928	Oscar	21049	M	1916
Nels	20568	D	1916	Clara	37731	D	1923	Oscar Janrick	20061	D	1915
Nels Norman	79493	M	1938	Delia	44791	D	1926	Oscar William	62059	I	1932
Nestor	60919	D	1932	Edward	59304	D	1931	Peter August	84926	D	1940
O.	4430	D	1907	Elizabeth	73859	D	1936	Rosa Gomez	63934	D	1933
Olaf B.	45056	D	1926	Ellen	72370	D	1936	Sophia	74636	D	1937
Olai	25730	D	1918	Eva Sofia	46390	D	1927	Soren J.	40487	D	1924
Ole	56059	D	1930	Frank	69567	D	1935	Sven M.	15528	D	1913
Olga	25862	D	1918	Frank Olaf	89948	D	1942	Swan	51022	D	1928
Olga	26459	M	1919	Frank T.	61616	D	1932	Telea	89359	D	1942
Oscar B.	16462	D	1913	Fred	65324	D	1933	Tillie	89359	D	1942
Otto	50247	D	1928	Gerda	59704	D	1931	Tillie B.	72626	D	1936
Peter	15515	D	1913	Gottfrid F.	72351	D	1936	Vida E.	64758	D	1933

NAME	NUMBER	TYPE	YEAR
Werner M.	55946	D	1930
OLSSEN			
Augusta W.	27265	D	1919
Jack	22644	D	1917
Nels	47634	D	1927
OLSSON			
Anders Fridolf	84433	D	1940
August	46145	D	1927
Catherine	70712	D	1935
Erhard	21013	D	1916
Frans	69567	D	1935
Fredrich	84433	D	1940
Gustave Otto	82690	D	1939
Ida A. C.	82905	D	1939
Johanes Fred	63826	D	1933
Joseph Orvar	28236	D	1919
Nilla	40206	I	1924
Oscar A.	78639	D	1938
Per	42537	D	1925
OLTMAN			
Lura A.	13543	D	1912
OLWAGE			
Michael F.	57205	I	1930
OLWELL			
Joseph T.	15618	D	1913
OMAN			
Frank Eric	40274	M	1924
George	79560	D	1938
OMARI			
Nobu	69856	M	1935
OMDAL			
John	80361	D	1939
OMEARA			
John D.	45214	D	1926
OMER			
George Perry	17054	D	1914
OMIZZOLA			
Angela	54313	D	1929
OMIZZOLO			
Angela	54313	D	1929
Giacomo	30765	D	1920
OMORI			
Katsumosuke	81837	D	1939
ON			
Alfred Wong	24147	D	1918
Fong	37732	D	1923
Ming	79846	D	1938

NAME	NUMBER	TYPE	YEAR
Mon	79846	D	1938
Ng	20388	D	1916
Wong	24147	D	1918
Wong Lim	47908	D	1927
Woo Wo	44488	D	1926
ONCINA			
Pablo	41360	D	1925
ONE			
Ben Nee	48749	D	1927
ONESTI			
Giuseppe	45070	D	1926
Marie	87232	D	1941
Rasmo	64238	D	1933
ONETO			
Celeste	49664	D	1928
Clorinda	77068	D	1937
Domenico	47644	D	1927
Giuseppe	74593	D	1937
ONGARO			
Eugenia Dall	32005	I	1921
ONGWARSKY			
Catherine E.	30958	M	1921
Ernest L.	30958	M	1921
John J.	30958	M	1921
Michael	30018	D	1920
Michael J.	30958	M	1921
ONISSEMENKO			
Mary Efimanna	54021	D	1929
ONISTO			
Angelo	57954	I	1931
Angelo DiMansueto	57954	I	1931
ONKEN			
Emma M.	19915	D	1915
ONLEY			
Maida C.	75771	D	1937
William F.	39679	D	1924
ONO			
Morinosuke	67297	D	1934
Schuichi	77697	M	1938
ONOPINSKY			
Mary	81880	I	1939
ONORATO			
Anita Dolores	48169	D	1927
Jeanette	67492	M	1934
ONSTOTT			
John Oscar	59022	D	1931

NAME	NUMBER	TYPE	YEAR
ONYON			
Emma J.	88026	D	1941
OOEN			
Sterling H.	65959	D	1933
OOSTERMAN			
Leina	54370	D	1929
OOTHOUT			
William	48001	D	1927
OPENSHAW			
Charles H.	37051	D	1923
Olivia	81314	D	1939
OPET			
Joseph	65599	D	1933
OPETZ			
Henry	88605	D	1941
OPIE			
Kenneth M.	35999	M	1923
OPITZ			
Edna Anna Marie	27621	M	1919
Johanna	57737	D	1931
OPPEL			
John V.	56738	D	1930
OPPENHEIM			
Adolph	1688	D	1906
Adolphe	47492	D	1927
Edna A.	52616	D	1929
Emil W.	70528	D	1935
Emma	36784	D	1923
Helen	39360	M	1924
Helen Louise	23683	M	1917
Hugo Phillip	42019	D	1925
Isabel	26401	D	1919
Jacob S.	1187	D	1906
Lena	11078	D	1911
Milton	76054	D	1937
Morris	39360	M	1924
Mozes	82944	D	1939
Phillip	66720	I	1934
Rafe	89101	D	1942
Rose	13237	D	1912
OPPENHEIMER			
Albert H.	30820	D	1920
Babette Gertrude	42803	M	1925
Babette Gertrude	43436	M	1926
Edgar	19426	D	1915
Emilie	85900	D	1940
Harriet Levy	39983	D	1924

NAME	NUMBER	TYPE	YEAR	NAME	NUMBER	TYPE	YEAR	NAME	NUMBER	TYPE	YEAR
Helene	66367	D	1934	ORDISH				ORMONDE			
Herrmann	19022	D	1915	Joseph D.	5628	D	1908	Jose	25431	D	1918
Isaac	25615	D	1918	Katie D.	8553	D	1909	ORMSBY			
James	52517	D	1929	ORDONIA				Edward Reuben	44728	D	1926
Joan	37659	M	1923	Benito	76233	D	1937	Ella Gorham	63885	D	1933
Julius	79691	D	1938	ORDORIA				Frederick J.	27364	D	1919
Mary	1911	D	1906	Benito	76233	D	1937	ORNAS			
Millie	85900	D	1940	ORDWAY				Alfred	68979	D	1935
Nettie	25120	D	1918	Matilda M.	22847	D	1917	Alfred	68980	M	1935
Rose	79620	I	1938	ORE				George	68980	M	1935
Rose	88105	D	1941	John T., Mrs.	58804	D	1931	ORNDORFF			
Selby C.	86059	D	1941	Maxine	58804	D	1931	Elizabeth M.	20436	D	1916
Simon	55857	D	1930	OREB				Mary E.	27431	D	1919
William	16694	D	1914	Christ	14191	M	1912	ORNER			
Zach	65985	D	1933	ORELLA				Axel W.	87782	D	1941
OPPERMAN				Frank V.	40380	D	1924	ORNSBY			
Clara	53235	D	1929	ORENA				Christopher Thomas	29417	D	1920
Emma	45773	D	1926	Caroline R.	46866	D	1927	ORNSTEIN			
Louis	77214	D	1937	ORENGO				Rose	22481	D	1917
OPPICI				Benjamin A.	55935	D	1930	OROLOFF			
Mary	87870	D	1941	F. M. A.	16323	D	1913	Joseph	46937	D	1927
OPPLIGER				ORERO				OROVICH			
Albert M.	35160	D	1922	Elizabeth	29875	M	1920	John	38783	D	1924
OPPPENHEIM				ORES				ORPHANIDES			
Phillip	69114	D	1935	Skjulda	24840	D	1918	Pyeades J.	9502	D	1910
OPPRECHT				OREZ				ORPHANT			
Julius	48565	D	1927	Domingo	54315	I	1929	James Edward	79195	D	1938
ORAN				ORGAN				ORPIN			
John	61471	D	1932	Mary	11581	D	1911	Ethelwynne F.	34697	D	1922
ORAND				ORLAND				Ethelyn	34697	D	1922
Charles Stephen	74440	D	1937	Charles	12374	D	1911	Francis Watkins	35225	D	1922
ORBELL				ORLANDI				Frank Nathaniel	50845	D	1928
Jane M.	20220	D	1916	Amedeo	38940	D	1924	George W.	87471	D	1941
ORCESE				ORLANDO				ORR			
Assunta	10085	D	1910	Domenico	61129	D	1932	Ada M.	85771	I	1940
ORCHARD				George	76609	D	1937	Annie E.	59103	D	1931
Loretta Oniska	6062	I	1908	ORLICK				Anson E.	85335	D	1940
ORCHID				Wincenty	4029	D	1907	Catherine	73201	D	1936
Sam	57844	D	1931	ORLOFF				Edwin F.	46989	D	1927
ORCHIT				Paul	76033	D	1937	Elizabeth	85381	D	1940
Sam	57844	D	1931	ORMART				Elizabeth H.	64876	D	1933
ORCUTT				Grace	62158	D	1932	James	44451	D	1926
Alice C.	64486	D	1933	Miguel A.	42339	D	1925	Joseph	19899	D	1915
Alice F.	64486	D	1933	ORMOND				Louis H.	27113	D	1919
ORD				Annie	54099	D	1929	Louis H.	27978	D	1919
Edward Otho Cresap	7732	D	1909	Sara	87568	D	1941	Mary A. Carley	81140	D	1939
Mary Mercer Thompson	7731	D	1909					Mary Agnes	81140	D	1939

Key: D = death; M = minor; I = incompetent

NAME	NUMBER	TYPE	YEAR	NAME	NUMBER	TYPE	YEAR	NAME	NUMBER	TYPE	YEAR
Mary Carley	81024	I	1939	John A.	27258	D	1919	Elsie May	14424	D	1912
Mathilda	27119	D	1919	**ORTHOBER**				Grace H.	67884	D	1934
Monroe J.	84279	I	1940	Albert	35974	D	1923	Hollis W.	61731	D	1932
Robert H.	71323	D	1936	Leo	48095	D	1927	James Stuart	64935	D	1933
Winifred	29042	M	1920	**ORTION**				Madeleine	57975	M	1931
ORRETT				Auguste	71443	D	1936	Mary C.	24977	D	1918
Frances	74864	D	1937	**ORTISI**				Mathilde Elizabeth	87526	D	1941
ORRI				Vincenzo	51307	D	1928	Nellie	18449	D	1915
Adele	86163	D	1941	**ORTIZ**				Oakley B.	18202	D	1914
Giacomo	74758	D	1937	Julio, Jr.	84767	M	1940	Orvilla	88600	D	1941
ORRICK				**ORTMANN**				William	9587	D	1910
Emily Johnson	78362	D	1938	John Frederick	14646	D	1912	William Henry	54800	D	1930
ORRILL				**ORTON**				**OSBOURNE**			
Ade	84206	D	1940	Adah Lena	70269	I	1935	George	21555	D	1916
ORSESE				C. K., Mrs.	67908	D	1934	**OSBURN**			
Joseph	71520	D	1936	Collins Knapp	63025	D	1932	Arthur W.	83947	D	1940
ORSI				Forrest Hoy	63836	D	1933	**OSCAR**			
Elisee	20927	D	1916	Joanne	76662	M	1937	George	2901	D	1907
Giusippi	13785	D	1912	Mary Elizabeth House	67908	D	1934	**OSCHE**			
Marie Ryhner	31620	D	1921	Nancy	76662	M	1937	Frances	21512	D	1916
Rosita	88466	M	1941	**ORVIS**				**OSER**			
ORSLAND				Columbus A.	14389	D	1912	Henry A.	86073	D	1941
Oscar Christensen	84603	D	1940	Henry P.	82462	I	1939	Mary	51329	D	1928
ORTEGA				**ORYNSKI**				Rebecca	16683	M	1914
Agustin	62460	D	1932	Florence	89607	D	1942	Rose	88074	D	1941
Antonia	60790	D	1932	Ralph J., Mrs.	89607	D	1942	William	32101	D	1921
Antonio	56584	D	1930	Ralph Joseph	74130	D	1936	**OSGOOD**			
Jacinta	46041	D	1926	**ORZERO**				Charles P.	46735	I	1927
Josefa	62546	D	1932	Matteo	7716	D	1909	Charles P.	54491	D	1929
Maria	21933	D	1916	**OSAWA**				Edwin	71217	M	1935
Natividad	89520	D	1942	Yeizo	51720	D	1928	Eileen	71217	M	1935
ORTELLI				**OSBORN**				Louise M.	48771	D	1927
Mary	32819	D	1921	Anthony	53693	D	1929	**OSHLAND**			
William	25850	D	1918	Corra Mahlon	15147	D	1913	Annie	84559	D	1940
ORTENZI				Ella A.	69820	D	1935	**OSMONT**			
Paul	70965	D	1935	George W.	1787	D	1906	Thomas M.	2244	D	1906
ORTESI				George W.	24433	D	1918	**OSMUN**			
Angelo	70755	D	1935	Jane Elizabeth	42290	D	1925	Annie	49717	D	1928
Domenico	77185	D	1937	Joseph	11268	D	1911	William F. H.	52328	D	1929
Giuseppe	46527	D	1927	Julia	20000	D	1915	Winifred M.	51393	M	1928
Vincenzo	51307	D	1928	Julia	86190	D	1941	**OSMUND**			
ORTET				**OSBORNE**				Harry Theodore	46844	D	1927
Corinne	8107	D	1909	Ada Isabelle	41616	D	1925	**OSNAS**			
ORTH				Allie C. M.	89586	D	1942	Adolph	55819	D	1930
Charles A.	19545	D	1915	Amelia Theresa	20120	I	1915	**OSOSKE**			
Emilie	20531	D	1916	Anthony	53693	D	1929	Isaac	35124	D	1922
Frank	31442	D	1921	David H.	89979	M	1942				

NAME	NUMBER	TYPE	YEAR
OSROWITZ			
David	89495	D	1942
OSSEWAARDE			
James	28613	D	1920
OSSMAN			
Howard Edward	62076	M	1932
Philip	48461	D	1927
OSSMANN			
Gustav Adolph	20897	D	1916
Lena	28589	D	1920
OSSWALD			
Anna M.	66179	D	1934
OST			
Paul J.	83086	D	1940
OSTENDORF			
Bernice	17503	M	1914
OSTER			
George	30434	D	1920
Sophia	64287	D	1933
OSTERBERG			
Christopher H.	60722	D	1932
Julia Catherine	54342	D	1929
OSTERGREN			
Victor	52318	D	1929
OSTERLUND			
Albert	62657	D	1932
OSTERVERE			
Edna	52825	D	1929
OSTHEIMER			
Charles	43505	D	1926
OSTINO			
Maria	51188	D	1928
OSTLUND			
Christine	26439	D	1919
Edward	18897	D	1915
OSTNER			
Louise	11654	D	1911
OSTRANDER			
Eliza W.	27662	D	1919
Elmo, Jr.	81464	M	1939
Frank S.	41378	D	1925
Gilman Marston	41379	M	1925
Marcella	35954	M	1923
Mary Marcella	55030	D	1930
Theda	35954	M	1923

NAME	NUMBER	TYPE	YEAR
OSTRAWSKI			
Catherine C.	67784	D	1934
OSTREICHER			
Julius	26227	D	1919
OSTROFE			
Charles	70574	M	1935
Francis	70574	M	1935
Robert	70574	M	1935
OSTROM			
Charles D. Y., Jr.	60516	M	1931
Daniel Augustus	51417	D	1928
John S.	67839	D	1934
Thomas Ross	60516	M	1931
William A.	83984	D	1940
OSTROSKI			
Amelia	45650	D	1926
Mary	77890	D	1938
OSTROW			
Sam J.	73727	I	1936
OSUNA			
Amelia	31597	M	1921
OSWALD			
Henry W.	22816	D	1917
Jacob	48436	D	1927
John A.	50020	D	1928
Martha	74855	I	1937
Roland A.	72811	I	1936
OSWICK			
Brony	87059	D	1941
OSZDORFF			
Ida Mary	52892	D	1929
William F.	58770	I	1931
William F.	65764	I	1933
William Francis	81637	D	1939
OTA			
Sugi	87367	D	1941
Yujiro	77005	D	1937
OTERO			
Angela	60926	D	1932
OTEY			
Ida C. N.	47485	D	1927
OTIS			
Charles Lowell	41479	D	1925
James	25166	D	1918
James	89596	D	1942
Lucy H.	35390	D	1922
Mary Bours	67058	D	1934

NAME	NUMBER	TYPE	YEAR
Mary Louisa Bours	40674	I	1924
OTT			
Arnold	26137	D	1919
August Louis	81811	D	1939
Charles	58901	D	1931
Christine	14517	I	1912
Emil	60826	D	1932
George	71931	D	1936
Herman A.	39444	D	1924
Johann Arnold	26137	D	1919
Joseph D.	15746	D	1913
Mary Teresa	2744	D	1907
OTTAVIANO			
Secondo	72383	D	1936
OTTEN			
Adelheid	75547	D	1937
Claire	26703	M	1919
Claus	26584	D	1919
Henning P.	63161	D	1932
Jack	26703	M	1919
John	23837	D	1918
John	32214	D	1921
Margaretha	2296	M	1906
OTTENBERG			
Irving	62945	M	1932
OTTENHEIMER			
Milton S.	82271	D	1939
OTTENHIMER			
Arthur William	74125	D	1936
OTTENS			
Mary Ann	68963	I	1935
Mary Ann	69546	D	1935
OTTER			
Mary M.	15837	M	1913
OTTERBACK			
Eline B.	61210	D	1932
OTTERBERG			
Alex Olson	86522	D	1941
OTTIGNON			
John S.	4942	D	1907
OTTINGER			
Adolph	30914	D	1921
Johanna	64149	D	1933
Leila A.	32320	D	1921
OTTINO			
Giovanni	25132	D	1918

NAME	NUMBER	TYPE	YEAR
OTTNAT			
Anna Charlotte	64359	D	1933
Anna Helen	64299	D	1933
Eugene F.	64360	D	1933
OTTO			
Amalia	64175	D	1933
Augusta E. C.	88948	D	1942
Bertha Rose	59849	D	1931
Constance	60109	D	1931
Ellen M.	76324	D	1937
Emil H.	80487	D	1939
Frederick	6768	I	1908
Frederick	31938	D	1921
Henry	8923	D	1909
Hermann	29089	D	1920
Katherine	79598	D	1938
Pauline	12427	D	1911
OTTOBINI			
Luigi	66419	D	1934
OTTOBONI			
Almerina	67173	I	1934
Inez	66325	M	1934
John B.	45903	D	1926
Lorenzo	42014	D	1925
Luigi	66419	D	1934
OTTONELLO			
Bartolomeo	53950	D	1929
Nichola E.	48111	D	1927
OTTOSO			
Pietro	37293	D	1923
OTTS			
Hanna Henrietta	83908	D	1940
William C.	82017	D	1939
William F.	45972	D	1926
William J.	80848	D	1939
OTTSON			
Ann E.	53030	D	1929
George	86437	D	1941
James	11700	D	1911
Reinhold	57360	D	1930
OUDET			
A. J. J.	2899	D	1907
OUELLET			
Berthe	66401	D	1934
Joe	55972	D	1930
OUGHIN			
James P.	83793	D	1940

NAME	NUMBER	TYPE	YEAR
Mary E.	20385	I	1916
Mary E.	69881	D	1935
OULEVEY			
Ernest	2709	D	1907
OULLAHAN			
Alexander Carruthers	88983	D	1942
Audrey Emmington	81264	D	1939
OULTON			
Elizabeth Hoff	35486	D	1922
George	1414	M	1906
OURTH			
Frank	31442	D	1921
OURYANG			
Meroiline	30141	M	1920
Pauline	30141	M	1920
William	30141	M	1920
OUTRAM			
Abraham	61832	D	1932
OUTSEN			
Hans	41756	D	1925
Hans	41756	D	1925
Henry N.	41806	I	1925
Henry N.	41806	I	1925
Henry N.	58983	D	1931
OUTZEN			
Carl Thomas	52775	D	1929
OVALLE			
Soledad	82644	M	1939
OVASEN			
Andrew	45282	D	1926
OVER			
Edwin J.	31294	M	1921
OVERBECK			
Frederick Johann	4690	D	1907
OVEREND			
Alfred E.	16068	D	1913
Elizabeth	16067	D	1913
John A. T.	2633	D	1907
Robert A.	21899	D	1916
OVERFIELD			
Minnie Bieber	44197	D	1926
OVERGAARD			
Soren Knudsen	41876	D	1925
Soren Knudsen	41876	D	1925
OVERHOLTZER			
Margaret Agnes	85108	D	1940

NAME	NUMBER	TYPE	YEAR
OVERLEY			
W. C.	33753	D	1922
OVERMEYER			
Fred	72886	D	1936
OVERMOHLE			
Bernard	51257	D	1928
Paul V.	58120	D	1931
OVERSTREET			
Maggie	57306	D	1930
Maud I.	64652	I	1933
Maud Isabel	75828	D	1937
Maude I.	75622	I	1937
OVERTON			
Charles Parshall	18243	D	1914
Daisybel	20515	M	1916
Robert Hart	78808	D	1938
Susan M.	11551	D	1911
Victor G.	6794	D	1908
OVERWEG			
Garrit A. T.	84552	I	1940
Gerrit Anne Theodow	84649	D	1940
OVESEN			
Andrew	45282	D	1926
OW			
Keong Gar	87076	M	1941
Lou Gar	87076	M	1941
Wing Gar	87076	M	1941
OWEN			
Albert	76454	D	1937
Andrew E.	44338	D	1926
Anna Lewis	77802	D	1938
Arthur C.	56721	D	1930
Eliza M.	49021	D	1928
Eliza Melvin	9174	D	1910
Ellen M.	75598	D	1937
Gladys	62865	D	1932
Henry N.	58166	D	1931
Herman E.	87300	D	1941
Hugh James	22474	D	1917
J. J.	12420	D	1911
Mabel E.	87380	D	1941
Mary Lauretta	17376	D	1914
Melville Griffith	64307	D	1933
Robert L.	77907	M	1938
OWENS			
Bernice Annette	31636	M	1921
Bridget	10572	D	1910

NAME	NUMBER	TYPE	YEAR
Catherine	69016	D	1935
Charles	50420	D	1928
Charles E.	15961	D	1913
Clara Rogers	76256	D	1937
Dora B.	42191	D	1925
Edna	52317	M	1929
Edna	58777	D	1931
Eleanor M	23663	D	1917
Elizabeth	32906	D	1921
Ellen	30918	D	1921
Frances H.	69265	D	1935
Frank	62228	D	1932
Frank A.	81698	D	1939
Frank J.	3330	D	1907
Gertrude	52317	M	1929
Helena	30089	I	1920
Henry M.	31812	D	1921
Hulda	6561	I	1908
Hulda	8143	D	1909
I. B.	71268	D	1935
James	7903	D	1909
James Vincent	51968	D	1929
John	2403	D	1906
John	6562	I	1908
John	18490	M	1915
John E.	17613	M	1914
John E.	22201	D	1917
John G.	14502	D	1912
John T.	36443	D	1923
Lena M.	65554	D	1933
Margarretta	6614	D	1908
Mary	52593	I	1929
Mary	61686	D	1932
Mary Edna	58777	D	1931
Peter	30455	D	1920
Robert Louis	89211	I	1942
William A.	40725	D	1925

OWLES

NAME	NUMBER	TYPE	YEAR
Loretta	69249	D	1935

OWNER

Henry E.	58488	D	1931

OWNSCHILD

Mary Ross	81081	D	1939

OWYANG

Faith Leong	53020	D	1929

OXEN

Philomena	53622	D	1929

OXENDINE

NAME	NUMBER	TYPE	YEAR
George Wesley	62159	D	1932
Orrin H.	79819	D	1938

OXENHAM

Alfred Julian	76798	D	1937
Alice	25097	D	1918
Arthur Howard	85849	M	1940

OXNARD

Alice M.	1464	D	1906
Benjamin A.	49658	D	1928
Bessie B.	15441	D	1913
Henry T.	49955	D	1928
James Guerrero	49871	D	1928
Marie D.	48166	D	1927
Robert	54991	D	1930

OY

Luey Bow	30863	M	1920
Quan	16014	M	1913
Wong Lan	33901	M	1922

OYAKE

Saburo	28417	I	1919

OYEN

Augusta L.	46165	D	1927
Augusta L.	56529	D	1930
Lydia Augusta	46165	D	1927
Lydia Augusta	56529	D	1930

OYHANTCABAL

Pierre	25506	D	1918

OYLER

William H.	61310	I	1932

OYSTER

Nettie T.	43910	I	1926
Nettie T.	68440	D	1934

OZAMIZ

Domingo	27218		1919

OZANNE

Elia	13506	D	1912

OZIEWICZ

Brony	87059	D	1941

OZOR

Wenzel W.	84037	D	1940

PABALA

Frank	76708	D	1937

PABST

Paul	34322	M	1922

PACCIORETTI

NAME	NUMBER	TYPE	YEAR
Antonio	22028	D	1916

PACCULLI

Jim	24205	D	1918

PACE

Charles	37694	D	1923

PACELLA

Angelo	42817	D	1925

PACELLI

Amerigo	89178	D	1942

PACELLO

Angelo	42817	D	1925

PACEY

Frank S.	75982	D	1937

PACHECO

Bessie Corinne	30391	M	1920
Catalina	44370	D	1926
Edith	74084	D	1936
Ethel E.	76197	D	1937
Mary C.	16650	D	1914

PACHTNER

John M.	71925	D	1936

PACI

Amalia DiGiovanni	67894	D	1934
Giovanni	66729	D	1934

PACINI

Dalida	22432	M	1917

PACIULLI

Vincenzo	24205	D	1918

PACK

Lee	22135	D	1917
Mary	46830	D	1927
Walter Alfred	29350	D	1920

PACKARD

Annie I.	79596	D	1938
Eugene Clark	45504	D	1926
William F.	79441	D	1938

PACKER

Elizaeth M. J.	1954	D	1906
James	10237	D	1910

PACKERMAN

Simon	11596	D	1911

PACKSCHER

Anna	35524	D	1922

PACKSHER

Simon	4981	D	1908

NAME	NUMBER	TYPE	YEAR
PACKSON			
Ernest Shear	84265	I	1940
PACROSKE			
E.	79381	D	1938
PACROSKI			
E.	79381	D	1938
PACZOCH			
Louise	61180	D	1932
PADDICK			
Bozo	13196	D	1912
Edward	13196	D	1912
PADDISON			
Mary B.	57887	D	1931
PADDOCK			
Edgar Luzerne	30066	D	1920
Ethelbert S.	35178	D	1922
Frederick B.	70303	D	1935
Jean Ann	78911	M	1938
Lottie I.	74282	D	1936
PADELLA			
Zoila	34387	D	1922
PADFIELD			
Gladys Laurayne	47534	M	1927
PADILLA			
Feliciana E.	69592	D	1935
PAETSCH			
Marie	64016	D	1933
PAETZOLD			
Gustave	23240	D	1917
PAFFLOW			
Charles W.	82964	D	1939
PAGANDER			
Augustus W.	32642	D	1921
PAGANELLI			
Italo	35878	D	1923
PAGANETTI			
John B.	27784	I	1919
PAGANI			
Albini	28143	D	1919
Albino	28143	D	1919
Bartolomeo	62990	D	1932
PAGANINI			
Giambatista	84049	D	1940
Lena	42801	D	1925
Louis Raymond	37668	D	1923
Luigi	61516	D	1932

NAME	NUMBER	TYPE	YEAR
PAGANNUCCI			
Lorraine	68146	M	1934
PAGANO			
Amadeo	7524	M	1909
Amadeo H.	65393	D	1933
Amelia	5630	D	1908
Armida	7524	M	1909
Francesco	46898	D	1927
Giuseppe	5873	D	1908
Giuseppe	18684	M	1915
Giuseppe	25048	D	1918
Rosalia	48002	D	1927
Serafini	13329	D	1912
PAGANONI			
Erminio	69099	D	1935
PAGANUCCI			
Adolfo	16457	D	1913
Carlo	89794	D	1942
Isola	42133	D	1925
Louis J.	68008	D	1934
Paulo Carlo	89794	D	1942
PAGE			
Alwin G.	48288	D	1927
Anna	36128	D	1923
Anne	70620	M	1935
Annie	73256	D	1936
Arthur Edward	40547	D	1924
Arthur H.	56979	D	1930
Atwood Giffen	37916	D	1923
Benjamin	36381	D	1923
Berle B.	61508	D	1932
Bertha	42990	D	1925
Blair Brenton	51038	D	1928
Brett	43039	M	1925
Brett	43147	I	1925
Charles	13114	D	1912
Charles Henry	47971	D	1927
Elmer E.	38092	D	1924
Emelita	70620	M	1935
Frances Howard	57466	D	1930
Frank B.	75989	D	1937
Frederick	1962	D	1906
G. L.	982	D	1906
George Bush	43145	D	1925
George Edward	41251	M	1925
Hamilton	2543	D	1906
Henry Fay	84511	D	1940
James	3284	D	1907

NAME	NUMBER	TYPE	YEAR
James D.	75168	D	1937
Leon M.	52484	D	1929
Louisa	63624	D	1933
Milton Elmer	41251	M	1925
Sally H.	37324	D	1923
Scott	22922	D	1917
Walter J.	11749	D	1911
PAGENDARM			
Clementina	23099	I	1917
Clementina	32861	D	1921
John	23067	D	1917
PAGET			
Alfred G.	48144	D	1927
PAGGI			
Joseph	44674	D	1926
PAGLIETINI			
Giuseppi	33519	D	1922
PAGLINCA			
Felix	26979	D	1919
PAGLITINI			
Giuseppi	33519	D	1922
PAGLIUCA			
Felix	26979	D	1919
PAGOULATOS			
Nickolas	59504	D	1931
PAGUST			
Ernest	39977	D	1924
PAHL			
Henry F.	14471	D	1912
Richard	15021	D	1913
PAHY			
Margaret	87512	D	1941
PAIAZZA			
Maria	51472	D	1928
PAIGE			
Calvin	7783	D	1909
David	9153	D	1910
Edward Denio	51914	D	1929
John	67122	D	1934
Timothy	1042	D	1906
William	27492	D	1919
PAILHAS			
Gustave Pierre	40037	D	1924
PAILHE			
Alfred	57270	M	1930
Anna	55355	D	1930

NAME	NUMBER	TYPE	YEAR
Pierre Rene	57270	M	1930
PAILLASSON			
Louis Z.	88802	D	1941
PAILLASSOU			
Joseph	12340	D	1911
PAILLET			
Joseph Oscar	69665	D	1935
PAILLI			
Marcelin L.	1809	D	1906
PAINE			
Eugenie	65182	D	1933
Naoma R.	18792	M	1915
Naomi	34695	M	1922
PAINTER			
Albert	3219	D	1907
Alice L.	76317	I	1937
Alice L.	81738	D	1939
Caroline A.	8745	I	1909
Edward R.	8823	D	1909
Jean Elizabeth	45537	D	1926
Jerome B.	4651	D	1907
Mary Elizabeth	23745	M	1917
Mary Jane	70212	I	1935
Oscar	3220	D	1907
Walter M.	58824	D	1931
William B.	61863	D	1932
PAIVA			
Jacintho J.	25894	D	1918
PAKY			
Margaret	87512	D	1941
PALACIN			
Eugenie	65168	D	1933
George	77571	M	1938
Gregoire	77329	D	1937
Joseph	83046	D	1940
PALADA			
Gregorio	45861	I	1926
PALADINI			
Achille	32983	D	1921
Catherine	34920	D	1922
PALAGI			
Enrico	79734	D	1938
PALAMOUNTAIN			
Anna	6391	D	1908
F. H., Mrs.	78188	D	1938
Susan Hosken	78188	D	1938

NAME	NUMBER	TYPE	YEAR
PALANDER			
Anna	81261	D	1939
PALANDRI			
Fernando	25817	D	1918
PALANY			
Ermest	60481	D	1931
PALASKY			
Anne	85310	D	1940
PALAZZOTTO			
Madalina	30164	D	1920
Vincenzo	79442	D	1938
PALDAUF			
John	87520	D	1941
PALDI			
J. D.	68475	D	1934
Julia	40975	D	1925
PALDORF			
John	87520	D	1941
PALE			
Jean Bernard	27017	D	1919
Theodora	65320	D	1933
PALEAS			
Andrew	55120	D	1930
PALENCIA			
Librada Avalos	48557	D	1927
PALESI			
Armando	71706	M	1936
Paolo	74441	D	1937
Richard	71706	M	1936
PALEY			
Charles	46263	D	1927
Tobey	55334	D	1930
PALEZZI			
Mary	4156	D	1907
PALICI			
Joseph	85998	D	1941
PALIKAR			
Anton	87884	D	1941
PALIN			
Julien	37942	D	1923
Marie Bonscal	48349	D	1927
PALISI			
Marianna	38638	D	1924
Rose	60160	D	1931
PALLAS			
Andreas	55120	D	1930

NAME	NUMBER	TYPE	YEAR
PALLAVICINI			
Paolo	83967	D	1940
PALLIES			
Marie	68382	D	1934
PALLINI			
Giuseppe	48210	D	1927
Joe	48210	D	1927
PALM			
John	1419	D	1906
Juanita	13446	M	1912
Roy	13446	M	1912
Rudolph H.	8960	D	1910
Wilhelmine	13446	M	1912
PALMA			
Giuseppi	78054	D	1938
PALMBERG			
Anna Z.	71190	D	1935
John A.	55522	D	1930
PALMER			
Aidia S.	81276	D	1939
Andrew Henry	87674	I	1941
Anna Martha	89941	D	1942
Annie	14738	D	1913
Arthur	84554	D	1940
Clarence	42929	M	1925
Edward	82773	D	1939
Edward C.	83028	D	1940
Elizabeth Mildred	68208	I	1934
Emmeline Lord	48042	D	1927
Ernest Henry	65662	D	1933
Fred A.	86963	D	1941
George Dean	38435	I	1924
George H.	83342	D	1940
Harriet Lorraine	66596	M	1934
Harry Clayton	55908	I	1930
Henry H.	26361	D	1919
James G.	32047	I	1921
James G.	34683	D	1922
Jane Alice	80942	M	1939
Jeanie	74033	D	1936
John J.	79278	D	1938
John Saxton	17248	D	1914
Joseph Francis	31254	D	1921
Louise A.	76544	D	1937
Margaret Clarinda	42352	D	1925
Margaret Olarinda	42352	D	1925
Olof P.	23687	D	1917
Patricia Martha	73354	M	1936

Key: D = death; M = minor; I = incompetent

NAME	NUMBER	TYPE	YEAR
Sarah	2494	D	1906
Serene A.	81276	D	1939
Susan C.	59605	D	1931
Thomas	29907	D	1920
Thomas	81833	D	1939
Walter R.	13800	D	1912
Warren I.	65533	M	1933
William Ellsworth	47192	D	1927
William S., Jr.	80547	M	1939
PALMIERI			
Adelina	52344	D	1929
Robert	86670	D	1941
PALMINI			
Milton Joseph	81162	M	1939
Vincent	66845	D	1934
PALMSTEN			
Emma Botilla	44831	I	1926
PALMTAG			
Louise Kathryn	13491	D	1912
PALO			
Osvaldo Riva	15606	D	1913
PALOMBI			
Niccola B.	69036	D	1935
PALOUS			
Ester	46003	D	1926
PALOZZI			
Mary	4156	D	1907
PAMPANA			
Louis O.	62439	I	1932
Luigi O.	62513	D	1932
PAMPELL			
Emma Louise	53942	D	1929
PAMPERIN			
Boline	41619	I	1925
Boline	43919	D	1926
PAMPHILON			
Henry Thomas	88263	D	1941
PAMPINELLA			
Salvador	30980	D	1921
PANAGIOTAROS			
Peter Konstantine	86783	D	1941
PANAGIOTOPOULOS			
Stavros	40306	M	1924
PANAS			
George	9194	D	1910
Thomas M.	86027	I	1941

NAME	NUMBER	TYPE	YEAR
Thomas M.	86203	D	1941
PANATTONI			
Dante	72006	D	1936
PANCHETTI			
Guido	80197	D	1938
PANCOAST			
Clara	76595	D	1937
George G.	76786	D	1937
Helen	10723	D	1910
Mulford L.	19184	D	1915
PANDER			
Fanny	34346	I	1922
PANDES			
S.	30507	D	1920
PANELLA			
Isabel Flora	71117	D	1935
PANELLI			
Rosa	32241	D	1921
Rosa Biagi	27516	D	1919
PANETTA			
Domenico	23648	D	1917
PANGERE			
Joseph	68055	D	1934
PANICACCI			
Paul	62007	M	1932
Serafino	62080	D	1932
PANICO			
Rosaria	89436	D	1942
PANIGADA			
Anna	43011	D	1925
PANINA			
Italo	82340	D	1939
PANIZZARDI			
Hector L.	25129	D	1918
Ludovico Carlo	25968	D	1918
Mary	28788	D	1920
PANLSON			
Dora	34612	D	1922
PANNETIER			
Ellen C.	61688	I	1932
PANNILL			
James R.	54690	D	1930
PANOR			
John	39638	D	1924
PANOS			
Peter K.	86783	D	1941

NAME	NUMBER	TYPE	YEAR
PANTAZY			
Constantine J.	86809	D	1941
PANTOLEON			
Peter	33721	D	1922
PANTOS			
Gatzos	53641	D	1929
PANWILL			
James R.	54690	D	1930
PANZER			
Alfred Maximilian	56199	D	1930
PAO			
John	23107	I	1917
John	61065	D	1932
PAOLETTI			
Leon F.	80344	I	1939
PAOLI			
Katherine Lucy	89554	D	1942
Lucille	89554	D	1942
PAOLINELLI			
Angelina M.	4034	M	1907
Domenico	747	D	1906
Earl	4034	M	1907
Erselia E.	4034	M	1907
Frank A.	4034	M	1907
Humbert V.	4034	M	1907
Irene	4034	M	1907
William L	4034	M	1907
PAOLO			
Bezzone	73175	D	1936
Vento	41500	D	1925
PAONE			
Giovanni	85491	D	1940
Rosa	46153	D	1927
PAPABOGLAU			
George S.	77527	D	1938
PAPADAKIS			
Constantinou Michael	22683	D	1917
PAPADATOS			
Robert	79967	D	1938
PAPADIMITRIOU			
Costa	75838	D	1937
PAPADOPOLOS			
Evaline	85238	D	1940
PAPADOPOULOS			
Eudokia	85238	D	1940
Euthokia	85238	D	1940

NAME	NUMBER	TYPE	YEAR
Evdokia	85238	D	1940
Pashales	51668	D	1928
Peter	51668	D	1928
PAPAGELES			
Peter	32343	D	1921
PAPAGEORGOPULO			
Demetrio	21690	D	1916
Elena De	21706	M	1916
George Demetrio	21691	M	1916
PAPAGIANO			
Joseph	89221	D	1942
PAPAINON			
D.	25489	D	1918
PAPAIOANOU			
Demetreos	25489	D	1918
PAPAJOHN			
Eraine Esther	83016	M	1940
Jane Marie	83016	M	1940
PAPALE			
Angelo	20804	D	1916
Mary	49562	D	1928
PAPAMICHAEL			
Michael Hlia	66244	D	1934
PAPANTONIOU			
Constaninos	13837	D	1912
Spiros	13838	D	1912
PAPAS			
Angilos N.	88304	D	1941
Mike	43682	D	1926
N. D. Z.	80146	D	1938
PAPATHAKIS			
George	73944	M	1936
PAPAZAHURIADES			
N. D.	80146	D	1938
PAPAZOGLAU			
George Stavnou	77527	D	1938
PAPE			
August F.	68182	D	1934
Auguste	22136	D	1917
Carl Heinrich	13298	D	1912
Catharina	16342	D	1913
Friederick L. M.	67595	D	1934
Richard A.	40365	D	1924
PAPENHAUSEN			
Frederick H.	22560	D	1917

NAME	NUMBER	TYPE	YEAR
PAPENHAUSER			
Frederick H.	22560	D	1917
PAPER			
Adolph H. L.	86498	D	1941
PAPESCHI			
Rosa	61986	D	1932
PAPINA			
August P.	44477	I	1926
August P.	84064	D	1940
James	24192	D	1918
James H.	26308	D	1919
Peter	26726	D	1919
Raymond	1715	M	1906
PAPINI			
Armando	50686	M	1928
Italo	50686	M	1928
Silvio	25649	D	1918
PAPONTONION			
Gus	17535	D	1914
PAPPADATOS			
Andreas	37182	D	1923
PAPPADOPOLOUS			
Athanasios Antonion	13656	I	1912
PAPPALARDO			
Louis	50207	I	1928
PAPPANTONE			
Gustavus Emanuel	17535	D	1914
PAPPAPAVEOU			
George John	81414	D	1939
PAPPAS			
Anthony	38111	D	1924
Aristide	58599	M	1931
George	20843	D	1916
George	77527	D	1938
George John	81414	D	1939
Gost	22683	D	1917
James	25489	D	1918
James E.	56280	D	1930
James Nicholson	31811	D	1921
John	67122	D	1934
Louis	58599	M	1931
Maria	58599	M	1931
Nicholas	31228	M	1921
Nicholas	87061	D	1941
Phillip	49945	D	1928
PAPPENFUSS			
Elizabeth	15695	D	1913

NAME	NUMBER	TYPE	YEAR
PAPPENHEIMER			
Julius	38829	I	1924
PAPST			
Penola	48024	D	1927
PAQUETTE			
Fred D.	21019	D	1916
PARA			
August	16267	D	1913
PARACCHINI			
Silvio	27111	D	1919
PARACHINI			
Francisco	64464	D	1933
Madaline	64463	D	1933
PARADIS			
Joseph	71965	I	1936
PARAMIDANI			
Bartolomeo	12686	D	1911
PARANO			
Louis	62764	D	1932
PARASSENTI			
Ettore	33822	I	1922
PARAVAGNA			
Edoardo	18879	I	1915
Edward	76977	D	1937
Giacomo	17468	D	1914
PARAZZO			
Giovanni	1091	D	1906
PARCELS			
Maurice J.	40961	I	1925
PARDALAKES			
Stilianos	30507	D	1920
PARDELLA			
Feruccio	33964	D	1922
PARDES			
S.	30507	D	1920
PARDI			
Annabel Amabilia	67711	M	1934
PARDINI			
Ascanio	87033	D	1941
Carlo	51884	D	1929
Fidalma	39223	I	1924
Giorgia	81458	D	1939
Giuseppe	65668	D	1933
Josephine	52184	D	1929
Leo	87348	I	1941
Lorenzo	31189	D	1921

Key: D = death; M = minor; I = incompetent

NAME	NUMBER	TYPE	YEAR	NAME	NUMBER	TYPE	YEAR	NAME	NUMBER	TYPE	YEAR
Lorenzo	64739	D	1933	Hudson C.	50827	D	1928	Frank L.	67160	D	1934
Lorenzo	87446	D	1941	Isabel	45294	D	1926	Fred	63428	I	1933
PARDY				Jane C.	82755	D	1939	Graham	86192	D	1941
John	8270	D	1909	John	10300	D	1910	Harry	3061	D	1907
William	11036	D	1911	Josephine H.	58380	D	1931	Harry Edwin	43825	D	1926
William S.	63896	D	1933	Mary E.	15476	D	1913	Harry J.	49473	D	1928
PARE				Mary F.	37543	D	1923	Henry	3061	D	1907
Antone Stanislaus	54824	D	1930	Mathilde Emilie	4659	D	1907	Henry L:incoln	49347	D	1928
PAREDES				Robert	71740	D	1936	Horace H.	55077	D	1930
Jesus Maria	6223	D	1908	Robert	71201	I	1935	Howard E.	56456	D	1930
PARENT				William Eli	61499	D	1932	Ida B.	44989	D	1926
Charles E.	49943	D	1928	Woo	20873	D	1916	James S.	74582	D	1937
George William	24780	M	1918	**PARK-O'NEILL**				James Strain	60010	D	1931
William E.	27432	D	1919	Theorilda C.	9539	D	1910	Janet	53838	M	1929
PARENTE				**PARKE**				Janet Agnes	68165	D	1934
Louis	81017	D	1939	Anna May	53579	M	1929	Jean	29216	D	1920
PARENTI				Charles Augustus, Jr.	53579	M	1929	Jeanie	33049	D	1921
Dominico	30289	D	1920	Charles H.	58407	D	1931	John	65552	D	1933
PARFITT				Edward	25344	D	1918	John I.	20765	M	1916
Alfred	40849	D	1925	**PARKER**				John Joseph	75656	D	1937
Frederick Edwin	81503	D	1939	Almira	17759	D	1914	John M. R.	10720	D	1910
PARINI				Alonzo	57195	I	1930	John W.	31947	D	1921
Emanuel	60515	D	1931	Andrew H., Jr.	41692	D	1925	John William	16416	D	1913
PARIS				Angelique	80495	I	1939	Joseph Abbott	54044	D	1929
Alies	22853	D	1917	Anna E.	85027	D	1940	Joseph Maynard	10454	D	1910
J. B.	1499	D	1906	Annie Victoria	47665	M	1927	Kate S.	21514	D	1916
Madeleine	42911	D	1925	B. A.	62456	D	1932	Kingsbury Eastman, Jr.	24760	M	1918
Max	89224	D	1942	Barbara Josephine	37280	D	1923	Lincoln	49347	D	1928
PARISH				Caroline L.	15493	D	1913	Louise M.	43578	D	1926
Isaiah	52225	M	1929	Charles	54895	D	1930	Malverson	54302	M	1929
PARISIEN				Charles E.	37434	M	1923	Marian	80949	D	1939
Ida	82881	D	1939	Clara M.	26006	D	1918	Mary	41356	D	1925
Reinhardt E.	81815	D	1939	David Stout	7923	D	1909	Mary	73855	D	1936
Rene E.	81815	D	1939	Edward A.	10510	D	1910	Mary Ella	81944	M	1939
PARISOTTO				Edward A.	20765	M	1916	Mary Evelyn	65961	D	1933
Luigi	30719	D	1920	Edward Allen	16100	D	1913	Mary F.	25763	D	1918
PARK				Edward C.	57389	D	1930	Mary Rose	84306	M	1940
Allen	65855	D	1933	Edward F.	38554	D	1924	Maynard	7873	D	1909
Catherine E.	17559	D	1914	Edward J.	29980	M	1920	Milton G.	55392	D	1930
Catherine W.	17372	D	1914	Edwin L.	504	D	1906	Ralph D.	51439	D	1928
Charles H.	26790	D	1919	Edwin L.	924	I	1906	Robert	12363	D	1911
Charlotte K.	36132	D	1923	Elinor D.	59845	D	1931	Robert	50358	D	1928
Edwin R.	25776	D	1918	Emma F.	58425	D	1931	Samuel	84227	D	1940
Eva May	58314	M	1931	Esther A. T.	62053	D	1932	Stafford H.	2581	D	1907
Florence L.	58314	M	1931	Evelyn D.	50977	D	1928	Susan	109	D	1906
Frank H.	87088	D	1941	Francis B.	20765	M	1916	Thomas	32563	D	1921
Harold	69858	D	1935	Francis E.	83526	I	1940	Thomas Beede	62880	D	1932
				Frank	57383	D	1930	Thomas D.	85499	D	1940
								Thomas H.	2613	M	1907

        Key: D = death; M = minor; I = incompetent

NAME	NUMBER	TYPE	YEAR
Thomas J.	13173	D	1912
Thomas J.	14973	D	1913
William Boyd	87759	D	1941
William Henry	57807	D	1931
William J.	72133	D	1936
William M., Jr.	29980	M	1920
William Witold	82983	D	1939
Willis D.	23279	D	1917
PARKES			
Ellen	2279	D	1906
R. W.	42463	D	1925
PARKHILL			
Thomas	48663	D	1927
PARKHURST			
John W.	77659	D	1938
PARKINSON			
Bernice D.	20127	M	1915
Edward J.	38790	D	1924
Josephine	61484	D	1932
Marguerite	4341	D	1907
Richard	26847	I	1919
Richard	27244	D	1919
Thomas	14180	D	1912
William	2032	D	1906
PARKISON			
Horace Emerson	54587	D	1929
PARKS			
Anne	33806	M	1922
Catherine	17756	D	1914
Charles E.	3333	D	1907
Lulu Blanch Emerline	70325	D	1935
Mary Pheby	57048	D	1930
Raymond	70667	M	1935
PARLE			
Bridget Mary	58104	I	1931
Charlotte	11861	M	1911
Elisabeth Jane	63252	D	1932
James	24651	D	1918
Jessie	79527	D	1938
PARLIN			
Charles A.	18357	D	1915
PARMA			
Giuseppe	78960	D	1938
Giuseppi	78054	D	1938
Luigi	61278	D	1932
PARMAGIANI			
Ernest	29842	D	1920

NAME	NUMBER	TYPE	YEAR
PARMAGINI			
Ernest	29842	D	1920
PARMELY			
Maud Mary	67067	D	1934
PARMER			
Rebecca L.	49031	D	1928
PARNELL			
John	37445	D	1923
Newton Berryman	46996	D	1927
PARODI			
Adele	4848	D	1907
John	16141	D	1913
Maria	1049	D	1906
PAROLET			
Martin	9434	D	1910
PAROLI			
Pietro	73703	D	1936
PAROLINI			
Mary J.	12891	D	1912
PAROLO			
Andrew	64161	I	1933
PARONI			
Alfred	25525	D	1918
PARONTA			
Fred J.	38953	D	1924
PARONTO			
Fred J.	38953	D	1924
PARPART			
Arthur V.	74537	D	1937
PARQUER			
Jane	55856	D	1930
Mary Claire	20689	M	1916
Sarah J.	55855	D	1930
PARQUETTE			
Juanita M.	65095	I	1933
PARR			
Bertha Bell	52215	D	1929
John D.	27407	D	1919
Lionel Edward	72141	D	1936
Margaret	41861	D	1925
Margaret	41861	D	1925
Rillie	86030	D	1941
Thomas	9789	D	1910
PARRA			
Anna	43059	D	1925
Geronimo P.	32287	D	1921

NAME	NUMBER	TYPE	YEAR
PARRAGA			
Ella	87611	D	1941
PARRATT			
Mary L.	37951	D	1923
PARRELL			
John	88663	D	1941
Patrick J.	812	D	1906
William	55067	M	1930
PARRETT			
Nettie E.	14447	M	1912
PARRISH			
Charles Haraszthy	6078	D	1908
Earle Adelbert	35373	M	1922
Elizabeth Beck	20386	D	1916
Ellis Howard	22121	D	1917
Julia A.	22123	D	1917
Margaret Evelyn	22120	M	1917
Sarah J.	25954	D	1918
PARRNAN			
Jeannette	39010	D	1924
PARROT			
Margherite	82353	D	1939
PARROTHE			
Irene	2672	M	1907
PARROTT			
George E.	67291	D	1934
Joseph	61001	M	1932
Juanita	61001	M	1932
Louis Baldwin	5655	D	1908
Louisa C.	24430	D	1918
Mary Duncan	74551	D	1937
Mary L.	37951	D	1923
PARROTTE			
Margaret T.	380	D	1906
PARRY			
Hannah	78240	D	1938
Harriet	78240	D	1938
Isaac	22641	D	1917
Isaac	63514	D	1933
Julia E.	46998	D	1927
Matilda	22642	D	1917
Minnie	11508	D	1911
Patricia Ann	71158	M	1935
R. W., Mrs.	46998	D	1927
PARSEY			
A. Victor	44521	D	1926
Adalbert V.	44521	D	1926

NAME	NUMBER	TYPE	YEAR	NAME	NUMBER	TYPE	YEAR	NAME	NUMBER	TYPE	YEAR
PARSON				**PARTINICO**				**PASKA**			
Peter	77299	D	1937	Guiseppe	32337	D	1921	Amelia	36029	D	1923
Thomas J.	807	D	1906	**PARTRIDGE**				**PASKO**			
PARSONS				Edward Briggs	37043	D	1923	Miro	78342	D	1938
A. M.	40887	D	1925	Edward Burling	40248	M	1924	**PASKRICH**			
Alfred Cox	54268	D	1929	Emily	79986	I	1938	John Joseph	65308	I	1933
Anna M.	76146	D	1937	Emily M.	82581	D	1939	**PASMORE**			
Austin	76846	D	1937	Frank F.	62889	D	1932	Edgar R.	46647	D	1927
Bertha Brush	70494	D	1935	Harry V.	61554	D	1932	Edith	6486	M	1908
Charles	70161	I	1935	Irene	65059	D	1933	Harriet	6486	M	1908
Christine	39123	D	1924	Jennie S.	42439	D	1925	John	6486	M	1908
David Benton	43759	M	1926	Karl C.	61522	D	1932	John Debayville	35728	D	1923
Edmond W.	71864	I	1936	Louis G.	24767	D	1918	**PASQUALE**			
Edmond William	84145	D	1940	Mary Louise	337	D	1906	Bossi	23263	D	1917
Emma H.	60227	I	1931	Muriel Elizabeth	40248	M	1924	**PASQUALETTI**			
Emma H.	60936	D	1932	Nellie M.	3946	I	1907	Bartolameo	15080	D	1913
Flora A.	85297	D	1940	Nellie M.	10481	D	1910	G. B.	73355	D	1936
George William	84593	D	1940	Peter G.	24766	D	1918	Giambattista	73355	D	1936
Harriet E.	9610	D	1910	Philip Marmaduke	32995	D	1921	Joseph	15081	D	1913
Henry	34505	D	1922	Raymond	10722	M	1910	**PASQUALINI**			
James M.	35187	D	1922	Ruth	10722	M	1910	Ottilie	67809	D	1934
Jane Helyear	15130	D	1913	**PARTSCH**				**PASQUET**			
Jemima	181	D	1906	Charles W.	62004	I	1932	Auguste	33713	D	1922
John Cox	54267	D	1929	**PARYSEK**				**PASQUINE**			
Mary	41539	M	1925	Henry J.	39226	M	1924	Alfonso	4027	D	1907
Oliver S.	55303	D	1930	Vlasta Helen	39226	M	1924	**PASSAGLIA**			
Peter	6295	D	1908	**PASADAS**				Giuseppe	4227	D	1907
Peter	7309	D	1909	J. Zenon	41093	D	1925	**PASSALACQUA**			
Ralph J.	38707	M	1924	**PASCHENKO**				Benedetto	82966	D	1939
Samuel C.	59170	I	1931	John	50023	D	1928	Giuseppe	10212	D	1910
Sarah L.	38568	D	1924	**PASCHINI**				Giuseppe	54093	D	1929
Wallace B. (missing)	87377	D	1941	Celestina	86349	D	1941	Teresa	10974	D	1910
William C.	11869	D	1911	**PASCO**				**PASSAMA**			
PARSSON				Tony	26920	D	1919	Anna	33012	D	1921
Lucinda	48958	D	1928	**PASCOE**				**PASSAUER**			
Peter	77299	D	1937	Florence Carvosso	2168	M	1906	Frank	35653	D	1923
PARTAIN				Harold Edwin Reginald	55479	D	1930	**PASSAVANT**			
Virginia May	59399	M	1931	William C.	83478	I	1940	Henry	14409	D	1912
PARTELLO				**PASERO**				**PASSER**			
Joseph M. T.	67749	D	1934	John	76790	D	1937	Jack	35871	I	1923
PARTENIO				**PASGUALETTI**				**PASSERA**			
Marion	68759	I	1935	Giuseppina	6316	D	1908	Gemma Zolizzi	32926	D	1921
PARTER				**PASHKOVSKY**				**PASSERINO**			
Isabella	41402	D	1925	Tikhon	65394	I	1933	Antonio	59883	D	1931
William G.	61710	D	1932	**PASINI**				**PASSERNAK**			
PARTICELLI				Giacomo	33750	D	1922	Peter	35935	D	1923
Angelo	1310	D	1906	John	74592	D	1937				

NAME	NUMBER	TYPE	YEAR
PASSINISI			
Teresa	66148	D	1934
PASSMAN			
August W.	68384	D	1934
PASSOW			
Henry A. F.	44778	D	1926
PASTEGA			
Florinda	47164	I	1927
Linda	47164	I	1927
PASTEL			
Jack J.	26820	D	1919
PASTENE			
Anthony	35093	D	1922
Daniel	30725	I	1920
Daniel	75031	D	1937
Ernesta	13787	D	1912
Esther	13787	D	1912
John J.	16532	D	1913
PASTERNAK			
Peter	35935	D	1923
PASTON			
George	58562	D	1931
PASTOR			
Nellie Sickler	60129	D	1931
PASTORE			
Luigi	16587	D	1914
PASTORI			
Carlo	38338	D	1924
PASTORINO			
Adelaide	83505	D	1940
Lorenzo	10262	D	1910
Louis	66586	D	1934
Nicola	5740	D	1908
PATANE			
Beatrice Frances	54773	M	1930
PATANIA			
Nungiata	60066	D	1931
PATAU			
Ramon	16931	D	1914
Ramond	16931	D	1914
PATBORSEK			
Anton	39070	I	1924
PATCH			
Ellen	45652	D	1926
PATCHELL			
James M.	73040	D	1936

NAME	NUMBER	TYPE	YEAR
PATCHETT			
Jacob E.	75602	D	1937
Virginia	23919	D	1918
PATCHIN			
Abbie K. Hollister	31502	D	1921
PATEK			
Frederick	80799	D	1939
H., Mrs.	45212	D	1926
Lillie	45212	D	1926
Robert	32504	D	1921
Rosa	4061	D	1907
Sara	73316	D	1936
Tillie	31108	D	1921
PATERSON			
George	33462	D	1922
James	14562	I	1912
James	31324	D	1921
James	49956	D	1928
Letitia Jane	13382	D	1912
William	4021	D	1907
PATIGIAN			
Haig, Jr.	64822	M	1933
Hollis	64823	M	1933
PATINEL			
Edward	33937	D	1922
PATINO			
Mary	7933	M	1909
PATON			
Mary E.	13238	D	1912
Theophilus	24913	D	1918
PATRIARCHE			
Abbie Louise	33604	D	1922
Charles Thomas	35361	D	1922
PATRICIO			
Joseph F.	40831	D	1925
PATRICK			
Albert B.	2965	D	1907
Bernard	43686	I	1926
Charles W.	61680	I	1932
George	82125	D	1939
Harry W.	41194	D	1925
Henry W.	41194	D	1925
Hugh	58200	D	1931
Lena	55944	D	1930
Lena	75041	D	1937
Minna	48061	D	1927
Wellington C.	24302	D	1918

NAME	NUMBER	TYPE	YEAR
PATRICKS			
Bernard A.	44319	D	1926
PATRIDGE			
Harry	44	D	1906
Henry L.	44	D	1906
John J.	61443	D	1932
PATRONI			
Cristina	53557	I	1929
PATRUNO			
Rosa	83853	D	1940
Rose E.	83853	D	1940
PATRY			
Henry J.	12541	I	1911
Joseph	34604	D	1922
PATTEMORE			
Frank T.	57178	I	1930
PATTEN			
Anastacia	6538	D	1908
Anna A.	74633	I	1937
Edmond	1808	D	1906
Henry	52560	D	1929
John	33200	M	1922
Josephine	37386	I	1923
Mary E.	40454	D	1924
Mary M.	7219	D	1909
PATTERSON			
Alexander	30339	M	1920
Alston Stephen	84295	M	1940
Amelia S.	28148	D	1919
Amy Julia	37473	D	1923
Anna Victoria	60541	M	1931
Asel C.	3491	D	1907
Catherine	2571	D	1906
Clyde David	86582	D	1941
Curtis C.	29293	M	1920
Cynthia E.	41803	D	1925
Cynthia E.	41803	D	1925
Cyrus Oerry	84012	D	1940
Daniel James	46102	D	1926
Deborah	18463	D	1915
Edward F.	41221	M	1925
Elizabeth	9285	M	1910
Ellen Henreitta	60541	M	1931
Ellen T.	44027	I	1926
Florine Nadine	58306	D	1931
Geo. W. H.	15299	D	1913
George	26106	M	1919
George A.	11447	D	1911

NAME	NUMBER	TYPE	YEAR
George C.	16288	D	1913
Gloria	67337	M	1934
Grover Smith	84233	D	1940
Harriett	41098	D	1925
Harry K.	8608	D	1909
Helen M.	8142	D	1909
Henry Robert	88910	D	1942
James	14562	I	1912
James	49956	D	1928
James William	9285	M	1910
Jean	58806	I	1931
Jean	60488	D	1931
Jean	41558	D	1925
Jeremiah Joseph	177	D	1906
John George	9285	M	1910
John J.	60685	D	1932
Leland E.	29293	M	1920
Lillian S.	59114	D	1931
Lynn Ernul	11681	D	1911
Mary	82136	D	1939
Mary C.	20870	D	1916
May	9813	D	1910
Olive Belle	49682	M	1928
Robert	5847	D	1908
Robert W.	50424	D	1928
Rose C.	88533	I	1941
Salemma M.	80591	D	1939
Samuel	82782	D	1939
Samuel E.	81319	I	1939
Thomas	87529	D	1941
Walter Calvin	49682	M	1928
William	4642	D	1907
William	6013	D	1908
William John	60541	M	1931

PATTILLO

NAME	NUMBER	TYPE	YEAR
Elmer E.	37331	I	1923

PATTISON

NAME	NUMBER	TYPE	YEAR
George	37229	D	1923
Ida M.	30589	D	1920
Mary A.	76365	D	1937
Mary E.	46491	D	1927
Mary Jane	27428	D	1919
William L.	42217	D	1925

PATTON

NAME	NUMBER	TYPE	YEAR
Cecelia	30448	D	1920
Charles L.	36363	D	1923
Daisy May	66510	D	1934
Eva F.	720	D	1906

NAME	NUMBER	TYPE	YEAR
Florence Jessica	2894	M	1907
Frances	29889	D	1920
James	12885	D	1912
Jessie F.	12675	D	1911
John F.	69774	D	1935
John Herbert	68435	I	1934
Margaret	2894	M	1907
Margaret	13726	M	1912
Marvin Bishop, Jr.	35738	D	1923
Mary S.	42792	I	1925
Maud J.	64209	D	1933
Muriel	2894	M	1907
R. F., Mrs.	66510	D	1934
T. C., Mrs.	720	D	1906
Thomas	7310	D	1909
William Hamilton	81208	D	1939
William Henry	2894	M	1907
William Henry, Jr.	30817	I	1920

PATTOSIEN

NAME	NUMBER	TYPE	YEAR
William J.	37976	D	1923

PATTOSIEUS

NAME	NUMBER	TYPE	YEAR
W. J.	37976	D	1923

PATTYN

NAME	NUMBER	TYPE	YEAR
Bernardine	34929	D	1922

PATUREL

NAME	NUMBER	TYPE	YEAR
Claudius	9845	D	1910
Miriam	30982	D	1921

PAUBA

NAME	NUMBER	TYPE	YEAR
Mary	17119	I	1914
Mary	67148	D	1934

PAUCHER

NAME	NUMBER	TYPE	YEAR
Ralph B.	49860	D	1928

PAUL

NAME	NUMBER	TYPE	YEAR
Almarin B.	8164	D	1909
Almon P.	8094	D	1909
Eben C.	50496	D	1928
George H.	25792	D	1918
Henry	50105	D	1928
Jane A.	52745	D	1929
Jessie	70305	D	1935
Joe	27138	D	1919
John	27138	D	1919
Martha Elizabeth	30499	D	1920

PAULA

NAME	NUMBER	TYPE	YEAR
Francesca	60710	D	1932

PAULER

NAME	NUMBER	TYPE	YEAR
Annie M.	34088	I	1922

PAULEY

NAME	NUMBER	TYPE	YEAR
Harry E.	75291	D	1937

PAULI

NAME	NUMBER	TYPE	YEAR
Arthur J.	77062	I	1937
Hattie	2552	M	1906

PAULIN

NAME	NUMBER	TYPE	YEAR
Harry	89400	M	1942
Julien	37942	D	1923

PAULOS

NAME	NUMBER	TYPE	YEAR
Nick	45993	D	1926

PAULSEN

NAME	NUMBER	TYPE	YEAR
Amandus John Richard	36907	I	1923
Blanca Dohrmann	35177	D	1922
Blanca W.	35177	D	1922
Charles	48021	D	1927
Francesca E.	61922	I	1932
Fred	84867	D	1940
Henry H.	28321	D	1919
Niels	89477	D	1942
Paul C.	65615	D	1933
Peter	57074	D	1930
Sara C.	53088	D	1929
Siegfried Melf	84867	D	1940

PAULSON

NAME	NUMBER	TYPE	YEAR
Charles	24860	D	1918
Dora	34612	D	1922
Elizabeth A.	66881	D	1934
John	85445	D	1940
John Asgar	65430	D	1933
John Asger	65430	D	1933
Matilda	13084	D	1912
Nellie	89197	D	1942
Paul A.	65430	D	1933
Peter	57074	D	1930
Thorleif Bjerke	62882	D	1932

PAULUCCI

NAME	NUMBER	TYPE	YEAR
Dante	57978	D	1931

PAULY

NAME	NUMBER	TYPE	YEAR
Antone	48467	D	1927

PAUNELL

NAME	NUMBER	TYPE	YEAR
Charles N.	38329	D	1924

PAUNER

NAME	NUMBER	TYPE	YEAR
Pascual	67471	D	1934
Pasqual	67471	D	1934

PAURELL

NAME	NUMBER	TYPE	YEAR
Charles N.	38329	D	1924

Key: D = death; M = minor; I = incompetent

NAME	NUMBER	TYPE	YEAR
PAUSE			
Earnest G.	71064	D	1935
George	71064	D	1935
Henry	86753	D	1941
Herman	86753	D	1941
PAUSON			
Barbara H.	41014	D	1925
Charles A.	30243	D	1920
Frank	22087	D	1917
Ida	15675	D	1913
Rose H.	73900	D	1936
PAUWELS			
Theofil	89804	D	1942
PAVANA			
Maria	70370	D	1935
PAVELLAS			
Claire Lucille Harpending	64537	I	1933
Clara Lucille Harpending	64537	I	1933
PAVESICH			
George	84246	D	1940
PAVIA			
Jacintho J.	25894	D	1918
John C.	68106	D	1934
John T.	68106	D	1934
Tancredi Giovanni	68106	D	1934
PAVICH			
Joseph	44519	D	1926
Nick	52501	M	1929
Nick	54064	D	1929
Peter	77149	D	1937
Steve	52501	M	1929
PAVICICH			
Nick	54064	D	1929
PAVLA			
Matt	80309	D	1939
PAVLANSKY			
John	21782	D	1916
PAVLATOS			
Dennis	35720	D	1923
PAVLICH			
Michael	50428	D	1928
PAVLOS			
George	55259	I	1930
George	56541	D	1930
PAVUK			
Adam	85309	D	1940

NAME	NUMBER	TYPE	YEAR
Elizabeth	87607	D	1941
PAWER			
Patrick	55235	I	1930
PAWL			
Matt	80309	D	1939
PAWLICKI			
Casimir Francis	77985	D	1938
Ladislaus	38224	D	1924
PAWLING			
Alonzo	17714	D	1914
PAWLOWSKI			
John	20851	D	1916
John	26828	D	1919
PAXLEITNER			
Margaret	20438	D	1916
PAXON			
Susan I. McDowell	61164	D	1932
PAXTON			
Alexis Rupert	60478	D	1931
Charles Eddy	9924	D	1910
Emmeline Barton	7507	D	1909
Gladys	82670	I	1939
John A.	80594	D	1939
PAYANE			
William H.	26859	D	1919
PAYANT			
James A.	28763	D	1920
John A.	28763	D	1920
Joseph A.	28763	D	1920
PAYLOR			
Alice	21035	D	1916
PAYMILLER			
Christina	39135	D	1924
PAYNE			
Ada Johnson	37011	D	1923
Ada Naomi	37011	D	1923
Adeline	54115	D	1929
Alice A.	74197	D	1936
Alvin Frey	84059	D	1940
Alvin Frey, Jr.	84504	M	1940
Anna May	53367	D	1929
Betsy Barbara	3261	M	1907
Beverley June	84504	M	1940
Cadman	52073	D	1929
Charles Willis	46393	I	1927
Chester L.	69108	I	1935
Dorcas Woodrow	43167	M	1925

NAME	NUMBER	TYPE	YEAR
Dorothy S.	64055	I	1933
Dwight B.	34326	D	1922
Edward F.	26226	D	1919
Emily	33354	D	1922
Erle Vincent	71180	M	1935
George L.	68275	D	1934
George Lingard, Jr.	16098	D	1913
Grace Sabin	62279	D	1932
Harrison Spaulding	71181	M	1935
Hazel Regina	84504	M	1940
Henry	31779	D	1921
Howard E.	44278	I	1926
James Willis	46392	M	1927
John	42561	D	1925
John	67585	D	1934
John Sabin	3261	M	1907
John Southall	85673	D	1940
Joseph J.	27688	D	1919
Josephine	43183	D	1925
Marianne B.	44228	D	1926
May E.	72722	D	1936
Nellie V.	36430	M	1923
Noah	14912	D	1913
Patricia Lois	84504	M	1940
Richard M.	63928	D	1933
Viola C.	66058	M	1934
Warren R.	6257	D	1908
PAYNTER			
Christine	81521	D	1939
Woodman S.	66341	D	1934
PAYOT			
Annie E.	47258	D	1927
Henry	33011	D	1921
PAYSON			
Ella M.	48931	D	1928
PAYTON			
Margaret	70836	D	1935
Stephen D.	62426	D	1932
Thomas H.	49004	D	1928
PAZAURECK			
Franz	25038	D	1918
PAZAUREK			
Franz	25038	D	1918
PEABODY			
Edward	50226	D	1928
Edward William	33859	D	1922
Eugenia D. Hunt	63774	D	1933
Frances Dexter	50456	D	1928

Key: D = death; M = minor; I = incompetent

NAME	NUMBER	TYPE	YEAR	NAME	NUMBER	TYPE	YEAR	NAME	NUMBER	TYPE	YEAR
Thomas	21981	D	1916	Mary Agnes	6657	D	1908	Margaret Ethel	75520	D	1937
PEACE				T. J.	8028	D	1909	Timothy	10709	D	1910
H. H.	57771	D	1931	Thomas J.	58295	D	1931	William J.	14079	M	1912
PEACH				William	61743	D	1932	**PEART**			
Ellen	188	D	1906	William H.	65120	D	1933	Clara H.	42063	D	1925
Ola E.	89143	D	1942	William J., Jr.	63511	M	1933	Lewis	1147	M	1906
PEACHE				**PEARL**				Lewis	9079	D	1910
Alphonso Moncton	16463	M	1913	Alice	5992	D	1908	Lewis N.	9043	D	1910
Dorothy Isabella	16463	M	1913	Arthur M.	66558	M	1934	Sheila Fiske	78742	M	1938
Kathryn Jean	16463	M	1913	Casteel Cleo	67759	D	1934	**PEASE**			
PEACHY				Charles G.	77351	D	1937	Alice	44092	D	1926
A. J.	10068	D	1910	Evelyn B.	66558	M	1934	Charles Julius	22778	D	1917
PEACOCK				Lauren A.	36263	D	1923	Emma S.	838	D	1906
David	29458	D	1920	Marcella	49107	D	1928	Emma Watson	47153	D	1927
Edward	48854	D	1927	Mary E.	66646	I	1934	Frank W.	27424	D	1919
Elizabeth	14484	D	1912	Mary E.	69237	D	1935	Isabelita O.	38769	D	1924
Frederick Henry	39369	M	1924	Max	21528	D	1916	L. M.	57911	D	1931
John	14483	D	1912	Ruth	52416	M	1929	Louise Carpenter	44620	D	1926
Joseph Watson	25494	D	1918	Susan	69294	D	1935	Richard H.	27910	D	1919
Loren	39369	M	1924	**PEARLMAN**				Richard H.	52043	D	1929
Margaret	9862	D	1910	Lester	50206	I	1928	Samuel Wilder	66010	D	1934
Marion	20065	D	1915	Simon M.	22638	D	1917	Vashni H.	14996	D	1913
Matilda F.	19	D	1906	**PEARLSTEIN**				William C.	10226	D	1910
William	18	D	1906	Blanche	72791	D	1936	**PEATH**			
William Hugh	38597	M	1924	Charles Sol.	36225	D	1923	Ernest	16421	D	1913
William P.	44160	D	1926	**PEARLSTONE**				Fritz	53469	D	1929
PEAK				Morton	74705	I	1937	**PEATZOLD**			
Emmet Steadman	74874	D	1937	**PEARSON**				Gustave	23240	D	1917
PEAKE				Albert	88682	D	1941	**PEBODY**			
Bessie M.	24695	D	1918	Anna	72348	D	1936	Thomas	21981	D	1916
Elizabeth Jane	39279	D	1924	Carl F.	27118	D	1919	**PECA**			
William	47306	D	1927	Catherine Louise	44046	D	1926	Angela	75610	D	1937
William A.	34306	D	1922	Charles	60534	D	1931	Luciano	70124	D	1935
PEARCE				Edward K.	75931	D	1937	Richetta	72164	M	1936
Charles H.	45516	D	1926	Henry R.	82802	D	1939	**PECCHENINO**			
Clara E.	56782	D	1930	Henry Richard	76581	I	1937	Mary	83442	D	1940
Clarence Herbert	82953	D	1939	Jacob	43029	D	1925	Rosa	53901	D	1929
Clarence S.	88587	D	1941	James	69264	D	1935	Rosa	53921	D	1929
Earle D'Arcy	88839	D	1942	James Corns	64311	D	1933	**PECCHNINO**			
Fallie T.	39361	D	1924	James John	45508	D	1926	Rose	53901	D	1929
George P.	66849	D	1934	Jennie R.	72424	D	1936	**PECHART**			
George Taft	19320	D	1915	Jessie D.	35516	D	1922	Evelyn Marian	15819	M	1913
Henry R.	45845	I	1926	John	12479	D	1911	Homer	15819	M	1913
John B.	78818	D	1938	John	51322	D	1928	Ruth	15819	M	1913
Laura E.	22211	D	1917	Julia	31169	D	1921	**PECHIN**			
Lottie Louise Kasten	63839	D	1933	Julius	32996	D	1921	Laurence Helen	67821	D	1934
Mary	19191	I	1915	Lucille	70401	D	1935				
Mary	29252	D	1920	Magnus	50749	D	1928				

NAME	NUMBER	TYPE	YEAR
PECHNER			
Carry	1325	D	1906
PECK			
Albert T.	18825	D	1915
Bertha	89087	D	1942
Carl William	60000	D	1931
Charles	60000	D	1931
Charles Imirie	48507	D	1927
Charles Webb	46720	D	1927
Clarence W.	52308	D	1929
David	35867	M	1923
Edward E., Jr.	39136	M	1924
Elsie Jane	60202	M	1931
Eva M.	29069	D	1920
Frank	13280	M	1912
George C.	31956	I	1921
George M.	54244	I	1929
Helen	59972	I	1931
John T.	63857	D	1933
Mary	35598	D	1922
Rebecca Elizabeth	88227	D	1941
Robert H.	89732	D	1942
Ruth	13280	M	1912
Sarah	5503	D	1908
Sophie	35867	M	1923
Stella	47195	D	1927
William Arthur	72837	D	1936
William Ottway, Jr.	57857	D	1931
PECKERMAN			
Joseph L.	8829	D	1909
Simon	11596	D	1911
PECKHAM			
Fannie	74285	D	1937
James Albert	76895	D	1937
Joseph	29780	D	1920
PEDDERSEN			
Martin	74247	D	1936
PEDELIE			
Jean F.	76372	D	1937
PEDEMONTE			
Melvin A.	79854	M	1938
Michele	31549	D	1921
Myrtle	79855	D	1938
PEDERSEN			
Andrew T.	38868	D	1924
Anna M.	56334	D	1930
Annie	84393	D	1940
Carl	44512	D	1926

NAME	NUMBER	TYPE	YEAR
Charles	44512	D	1926
Christ	57073	D	1930
Enock	77668	D	1938
Ervin Jerold	53915	M	1929
Hilda M.	42977	D	1925
Ida	59565	D	1931
Jacob	46986	D	1927
Jens B.	50982	D	1928
John A.	32055	D	1921
John P.	35829	D	1923
Joseph Warren	82758	M	1939
Julia Marie Miller	25154	D	1918
Magnus Christian	56150	D	1930
Marie	49540	M	1928
Mary Elizabeth	43233	D	1925
Mary J.	23315	D	1917
Nicholas M.	44912	D	1926
Niels J.	51267	D	1928
Oscar E.	43115	D	1925
Peter	70607	D	1935
Rachel	76627	D	1937
Violet	57317	D	1930
PEDERSON			
Christian Marius Redsted	88882	D	1942
Ida	59565	D	1931
Jacob	46986	D	1927
John	87904	D	1941
Marie	49540	M	1928
Niels J.	51267	D	1928
Rachel	76627	D	1937
PEDESERT			
Bernard	39062	D	1924
Julian	40858	D	1925
PEDEUBOY			
Jacques	62690	D	1932
PEDEUPE			
Catherine	47829	I	1927
PEDEZERT			
Julian	40858	D	1925
PEDLAR			
Glendora H.	40381	D	1924
PEDLER			
Grace Martha Augusta	2215	D	1906
Louise Ludlow	73982	D	1936
PEDLINA			
Harriette Johanna	81762	D	1939
Harry R.	75369	D	1937
Henry E.	75369	D	1937

NAME	NUMBER	TYPE	YEAR
Henry Reinhardt	75369	D	1937
PEDONE			
Caterina	54460	D	1929
Giuseppe	38562	D	1924
Ignazio	33743	D	1922
Joseph	35840	M	1923
Joseph	38562	D	1924
Lawrence	35840	M	1923
Lena	35840	M	1923
Mary	35840	M	1923
Rosalia	50875	D	1928
Rose Marie	35840	M	1923
PEDONI			
Ignazio	33743	D	1922
PEDRANTI			
E.	72972	D	1936
PEDRAZZINI			
Save J.	1953	D	1906
PEDREIRA			
Alfred	46733	M	1927
Angelo	46733	M	1927
Jacinto	46734	D	1927
PEDRETT			
Mary	83152	D	1940
PEDRICK			
Adelia	46885	D	1927
PEDRINI			
Armando	83268	D	1940
Sisto P.	80786	D	1939
PEDRO			
Annie	18767	D	1915
Emanuel S.	3756	D	1907
Joseph	22799	M	1917
Pete	56577	D	1930
Tony S.	45601	D	1926
PEDROCCHI			
Emil	46233	D	1927
PEDRONE			
Daniel	2018	M	1906
Francesco	2018	M	1906
Fred	2018	M	1906
Katie	2018	M	1906
Maria	2018	M	1906
Pasquale	819	D	1906
PEDRONI			
Abbondio	63619	D	1933
Adolph	14171	D	1912

Key: D = death; M = minor; I = incompetent

NAME	NUMBER	TYPE	YEAR
Erminia	41859	D	1925
Erminia	41859	D	1925
PEDROTTI			
Mary	55384	D	1930
PEDWELL			
Laura Emma	78375	D	1938
PEEBLES			
Anna L.	43337	D	1926
Anna M.	82549	I	1939
Selma	52815	D	1929
PEED			
Elizabeth	52249	D	1929
PEEFF			
Matheo	68592	D	1934
PEEL			
Alfred H.	28287	D	1919
Gladys M.	20589	D	1916
Martin	57213	D	1930
PEEPLES			
Colin McRae	36295	D	1923
PEERS			
Joseph	14777	D	1913
Lois L.	48540	D	1927
Margaret Hatch	73135	D	1936
PEERY			
Caroline Emma	33017	D	1921
Charles S.	48722	I	1927
Harold John	81652	D	1939
PEFFER			
Laura J.	83721	D	1940
Maggie A. Deen	58570	D	1931
Marguerite A.	58570	D	1931
PEGG			
Nina E.	61156	D	1932
PEGNAN			
Elizabeth	85378	D	1940
PEGUILHAM			
Francois	13852	D	1912
PEHKANEN			
Sofia	69686	D	1935
PEHRSON			
Herbert W.	23727	M	1917
Oliver	22988	D	1917
PEHRSSON			
Oscar	70103	D	1935

NAME	NUMBER	TYPE	YEAR
PEIDEL			
Elizabeth	84394	D	1940
PEIN			
George H.	15421	D	1913
Marie Henriette Hermine	49593	D	1928
William	31049	I	1921
PEINI			
Clement C.	83658	D	1940
Evelyn D.	47964	M	1927
PEIRANO			
Andrea	20963	D	1916
Joseph A.	29951	D	1920
PEIRCE			
Joseph Warren	5734	I	1908
PEIRONA			
Giovanni	56616	D	1930
Livio	56974	M	1930
Thomas	56974	M	1930
PEIRSON			
Katherine E.	71962	D	1936
PEIS			
Hedwig Jansen	49639	D	1928
PEISER			
Elizabeth Aneker	38522	M	1924
Israel	13317	D	1912
William Sander	38522	M	1924
PEIXATTO			
Ernest C.	86991	D	1941
PEIXOTTO			
Edgar D.	42070	D	1925
Edgar R.	42179	M	1925
Nina M.	42124	M	1925
Sidney S.	42449	D	1925
PELERIN			
Henri Francoi Eloi	30802	D	1920
PELESSIER			
Fortune, Sr.	89907	D	1942
PELGEN			
Peter	46526	D	1927
PELGIN			
Dorothy	12916	M	1912
James C.	12916	M	1912
PELKES			
John	70868	I	1935
PELL			
Leon	3014	D	1907

NAME	NUMBER	TYPE	YEAR
PELLACANI			
Alberto	32108	D	1921
PELLACCHIA			
Saverio	40376	D	1924
PELLAS			
Carlos F.	53160	D	1929
PELLE			
Alexis Augustus	32161	D	1921
Jules S.	44790	D	1926
PELLEGRINI			
Alfredo	73940	D	1936
Angelo	85747	D	1940
Carmela	81662	D	1939
Domenico	41555	D	1925
Francesca	62046	D	1932
Fred G.	80871	D	1939
Giovanni	80258	D	1939
Giuseppe	50116	D	1928
Paolo	64379	D	1933
Paul	46011	D	1926
PELLEGRINO			
Francesco Gioachino	34787	D	1922
Giogio	82729	D	1939
Maurizio	29984	I	1920
Virginia	47827	D	1927
PELLER			
Annie Elizabeth	21902	D	1916
PELLETIER			
John F.	19877	D	1915
PELLETT			
Clarence E.	82913	D	1939
PELLETTI			
Giovanni	23045	M	1917
PELLICER			
Joseph	87495	D	1941
PELLIN			
P. S.	81190	D	1939
Peter	81190	D	1939
PELLISSIER			
Hippolyte	52983	D	1929
Marie Julie	27772	D	1919
Maurice	12078	D	1911
PELLISSON			
Joseph	12325	D	1911
PELLMANN			
Charles H. F.	73628	D	1936

NAME	NUMBER	TYPE	YEAR
PELLOW			
Richard G.	12738	D	1911
Richard R.	12738	D	1911
Sarah A.	43633	D	1926
PELONIS			
Louis	26788	D	1919
PELS			
Edward M.	39183	M	1924
Lionel M.	39183	M	1924
Marie	32782	D	1921
PELSTER			
William Henry	71481	D	1936
PELTIER			
John H.	43983	D	1926
PELTON			
John Colton	11374	D	1911
Kate E.	23071	D	1917
PELTRET			
Elizabeth C.	8953	I	1910
Elizabeth C.	20654	D	1916
Elizabeth L.	32842	D	1921
PELUSO			
Catherine	48831	I	1927
PELZER			
Anna	59533	M	1931
Stephen	59534	M	1931
PEMALA			
I. O.	39575	D	1924
PEMBERTHY			
Annie	21488	D	1916
PEMBERTON			
James M.	73528	D	1936
PEMBESTON			
Walter B.	51266	I	1928
PEMBROKE			
Annie K.	58194	I	1931
John	86501	D	1941
PEN			
Sue	76461	D	1937
PENBERTHY			
John	14123	D	1912
Mary	83288	D	1940
PENCE			
Clara D.	27542	D	1919
George W.	49385	I	1928
George W.	56078	D	1930

NAME	NUMBER	TYPE	YEAR
Lena J.	87083	D	1941
PENCOVIC			
H.	8355	D	1909
PENDERGAST			
Albert A.	21942	M	1916
Annie Lewis	21638	D	1916
Annie R.	77636	D	1938
Charlotte Elizabeth	26441	M	1919
George E.	69462	D	1935
Harry Matthews	22056	D	1917
Henry Matthews	22056	D	1917
James Francis	6926	M	1908
Jeremiah	5533	D	1908
Margaret	76012	D	1937
Michael	9674	D	1910
Michael	46372	D	1927
PENDERTON			
James M.	73443	D	1936
PENDLEBURY			
Sibyl	32358	D	1921
PENDOLA			
Maria	3323	D	1907
PENE			
Jean Baptiste	52591	D	1929
Jeane	57269	M	1930
John B.	52591	D	1929
Leontine	62644	D	1932
PENEBSKY			
Adolph	24694	M	1918
Frieda	24694	M	1918
Ruth	24694	M	1918
Sarah	22565	D	1917
PENENGER			
R. F.	81765	D	1939
PENEWILL			
Nettie	40112	D	1924
PENFIELD			
Charles O.	79409	D	1938
Fannie W.	31822	D	1921
PENG			
Esther	57308	D	1930
PENGEL			
Elizabeth	33268	D	1922
PENGILLY			
Sarah G.	13255	D	1912
PENICH			
Mark	22299	D	1917

NAME	NUMBER	TYPE	YEAR
PENICK			
Willie Hemphill	76834	I	1937
PENIDO			
Marcel	38719	I	1924
PENIH			
Mark	22299	D	1917
PENINGER			
R. F.	81765	D	1939
PENINOU			
Ernest	59749	M	1931
PENLINGTON			
George	13505	D	1912
PENN			
D. Lewis	77095	D	1937
Daniel L.	77095	D	1937
Elmer	67110	D	1934
Sutia T.	76689	D	1937
Theodore	78582	I	1938
PENNA			
Natalina	61835	D	1932
PENNACHIO			
S.	10705	D	1910
PENNIE			
James Crymes	9598	D	1910
PENNIGTON			
Vera Victoria	15732	M	1913
PENNINGTON			
Andrew R.	72889	D	1936
Hannah	40642	D	1924
Ira S.	53116	D	1929
Martha Ann	50581	D	1928
Mary Jane	49736	D	1928
PENNINO			
Charles	70251	D	1935
PENNY			
Abner	60377	D	1931
Isaac	77904	D	1938
Margaret E.	5565	D	1908
PENNYPACHER			
Elizabeth	60049	I	1931
PENOVICH			
Mari	71174	D	1935
Mike	38820	D	1924
PENOYER			
Chauncey W.	29162	D	1920
Nancy Ellen	50944	M	1928

NAME	NUMBER	TYPE	YEAR
Nancy Elllen	31906	M	1921
PENROD			
Anna	74882	D	1937
PENROSE			
Jesse	41988	D	1925
Jesse	41988	D	1925
Mary Ann	70538	D	1935
PENSA			
Joseph	77280	D	1937
PENSE			
Mamie O.	64074	D	1933
PENTECOST			
Joseph	133	D	1906
PENTLAND			
Edwin Lewis	39422	D	1924
PENZENSTADLER			
Alvena	30338	M	1920
PEOPLES			
Mary Louise	70390	D	1935
Syrine E.	16671	I	1914
Syrine E.	32493	D	1921
PEPE			
Frank Carman	47469	D	1927
Sele	79680	D	1938
PEPIN			
Charles Alfred	67283	D	1934
Esther L.	79542	I	1938
Frank	26609	D	1919
James F.	26609	D	1919
Margaret	13703	D	1912
PEPINO			
Joseph	32143	D	1921
PEPPA			
Nina F.	89328	D	1942
PEPPELL			
William	46277	D	1927
PEPPER			
Alfrd M.	466	D	1906
Frank A.	51597	D	1928
Ilona A.	8785	D	1909
PEPPERT			
Henrietta	49116	D	1928
Marie	69031	I	1935
Rudolph	81439	D	1939
PEPPES			
George F.	19180	D	1915

NAME	NUMBER	TYPE	YEAR
PEPYS			
Helen Forbes	76170	D	1937
PERA			
Letitia	83799	D	1940
Louis	82436	D	1939
Mary	80063	D	1938
Teresa Michelucci	60674	D	1932
PERAGALLO			
Frank	48611	D	1927
Giuseppe	13080	D	1912
Josie	13081	M	1912
Nicholas	13081	M	1912
PERAINO			
Joseph	86735	M	1941
PERALTA			
Lillian L.	78801	D	1938
PERASSO			
Adeline	28412	M	1919
Benedetta T.	27794	D	1919
Eleanor	28411	M	1919
Frank	62520	D	1932
Giovanni	1091	D	1906
Giovanni	77534	D	1938
Herbert	28411	M	1919
Herbert	63634	D	1933
Lorraine	28412	M	1919
Louis	28089	D	1919
Louis	28412	M	1919
Luigi	27393	D	1919
Mario	15206	M	1913
Mario	60883	D	1932
Paolo Mario	60883	D	1932
Remus N.	35354	I	1922
Wesley	62760	M	1932
PERATA			
Anna	21410	D	1916
Bernard	966	D	1906
Emelio	44344	D	1926
Emile	44344	D	1926
Giobatta	74620	D	1937
Louisa Clara	38539	D	1924
Michele	8847	D	1909
PERATI			
Jack	43858	M	1926
PERAZZI			
Giovanni	45007	D	1926
Maria	31218	D	1921

NAME	NUMBER	TYPE	YEAR
PERAZZO			
Angiolina Meda	15098	D	1913
Domenico	46231	D	1927
Frank	62520	D	1932
George	29861	D	1920
George	44851	M	1926
George	48329	D	1927
Giovanni	1091	D	1906
John	36738	D	1923
Louis	16254	D	1913
Luigi	27393	D	1919
Victor	65283	D	1933
Vittorio	65283	D	1933
PERCEVALE			
Carlos	9790	D	1910
PERCEY			
Edward	53056	D	1929
PERCIVAL			
James F.	21130	D	1916
Walter F.	6599	D	1908
PERCIVALE			
Bartolorneo Carlo	79262	D	1938
C.	9790	D	1910
Carlo	79262	D	1938
PERCY			
Anna A.	53353	D	1929
George D.	53423	M	1929
John A.	51065	D	1928
William	4275	D	1907
PEREGRINO			
Filomena C.	37693	L	1923
PEREIRA			
Antonio	9999	D	1910
Domitila	42437	D	1925
Francisco Jose	88952	D	1942
PEREIRAS			
Antonio	22330	D	1917
PERELLI			
Frederico	29429	D	1920
PERERSEN			
Christian	77375	D	1937
PERES			
Fredericke Emilie	138	D	1906
Melchor	9512	D	1910
PERETZ			
Gershon	25554	D	1918

NAME	NUMBER	TYPE	YEAR
PEREYRA			
Domitila	42437	D	1925
PEREZ			
Felipe	35047	D	1922
Gabriella	30511	D	1920
Helen	79723	M	1938
Javier	27741	D	1919
Jesus Rulfo	54398	D	1929
Joaquin	434	D	1906
Justina	66802	D	1934
Lorenzo M.	1443	D	1906
Mary C.	79491	D	1938
Mary Manno	79491	D	1938
Miquel	23537	D	1917
Natalia	46380	D	1927
Sergio	82055	D	1939
PERFETTO			
Fred L.	72862	D	1936
Giovanni	34772	D	1922
PERGER			
Frank	16506	M	1913
Meri	16600	D	1914
PERHACS			
Annie G.	21259	D	1916
Emil M.	6411	D	1908
PERHAM			
Jennie M.	29716	D	1920
PERI			
Louis J.	4742	D	1907
PERIAT			
Harry	32980	M	1921
PERICO			
Victoria	59692	M	1931
PERIER			
Marc	4338	D	1907
PERIERA			
Joao R.	15377	D	1913
PERIGOLD			
May Buttimore	82299	D	1939
PERIN			
Domenico	51525	D	1928
PERINE			
Felix A.	49491	D	1928
Sherman B.	37944	D	1923
PERINI			
Felix A.	49491	D	1928

NAME	NUMBER	TYPE	YEAR
Gottardo	764	D	1906
Gottardo	32738	D	1921
Joseph F.	89500	D	1942
Pietro	28288	D	1919
PERIS			
George	16900	D	1914
PERKES			
A. C. A.	4840	D	1907
PERKILDSEN			
Maren	199	D	1906
PERKINS			
Alice B.	89846	I	1942
Anna I.	71004	I	1935
Anna L.	71004	I	1935
Annie I.	22548	I	1917
Charles	36450	D	1923
Charles B.	34467	D	1922
Eliza J.	7290	D	1909
Ellison C.	85719	I	1940
Emma S. G.	19693	D	1915
Fanny F.	84270	D	1940
Frank J.	89292	D	1942
Gemma Zolizzi	32926	D	1921
Henriette Lucille Johnson	89700	D	1942
James C.	76722	D	1937
Jane L.	32192	D	1921
Jennie Louise	32192	D	1921
Lewis	55300	D	1930
Louise G.	52269	D	1929
Louise T.	52269	D	1929
Mahlon F., Jr.	57368	M	1930
Mary	3720	D	1907
Mirvyn Lee	86858	D	1941
Morgan Lee	82077	M	1939
Raymond P.	86512	D	1941
Samuel	1099	D	1906
Samuel	6624	I	1908
Sophie	72391	D	1936
William F.	41960	D	1925
William F.	41960	D	1925
William Francis	42862	M	1925
Willis T.	8536	D	1909
PERKOCHA			
Antone	49619	D	1928
Martin	57467	D	1930
PERKS			
Augusta Marguerite	29785	D	1920
Hubert Everard	56307	D	1930

NAME	NUMBER	TYPE	YEAR
Hubert Everard	89473	D	1942
PERL			
Helen	86663	D	1941
Herman	46066	I	1926
PERLANDA			
John	3101	D	1907
PERLE			
Johan Frederick	51492	D	1928
PERLENDA			
Jonn	3101	D	1907
PERLET			
Mattie E.	66519	D	1934
PERLEY			
Albion S.	12717	D	1911
Emilie L.	9635	D	1910
Howard Starbird, Jr.	85192	D	1940
Howard Starbird, Jr.	86070	D	1941
PERLMAN			
Henry	70673	D	1935
PERLOW			
Harry	57537	I	1930
PERMAR			
Grace B.	74111	D	1936
Gracie Bell	74111	D	1936
PERMENTO			
Caroline M.	55575	D	1930
PERNAU			
Charles C.	66135	D	1934
Henry Frank	64563	D	1933
PEROSSO			
Luigi	27393	D	1919
PEROTTO			
Enrico	56372	I	1930
PEROZZO			
Luigi	27393	D	1919
PERPOLI			
Placidio	6632	D	1908
PERRAMONT			
Albine	10588	D	1910
PERRAULT			
A. V.	12545	D	1911
Ainslie	17037	M	1914
Edward L.	17037	M	1914
Walter M.	28376	D	1919
PERRAZZO			
Louis	16254	D	1913

NAME	NUMBER	TYPE	YEAR
PERREITER			
John Baptiste	46803	D	1927
PERRET			
Henri	16001	D	1913
Josephine	18356	D	1915
PERREY			
Leon	7584	D	1909
PERRIER			
Andree Helene Leonide	70669	D	1935
Simon John	69085	D	1935
PERRIMAN			
William R.	3874	D	1907
PERRIN			
Arch	24289	D	1918
PERRINE			
Charles C.	85250	D	1940
Francis Joseph	36807	D	1923
PERRONE			
Allan	64421	M	1933
Bartolomeo	74346	D	1937
Emilia Ratto	88583	D	1941
Giobatta	50203	D	1928
Giuseppe	38362	D	1924
Horatio A.	25219	D	1918
Lorenzo	50203	D	1928
Osea	12788	D	1912
Teresa	50202	D	1928
Victor	55439	I	1930
Virgil	63767	D	1933
Virginia	64421	M	1933
PERRSON			
Matilda	13084	D	1912
Stina	64342	D	1933
PERRY			
Alice M.	89201	I	1942
Anna M.	48873	D	1928
Bessie R.	42356	D	1925
C. B.	14874	D	1913
C. O.	19214	D	1915
Carrie	37940	I	1923
Catherine	24936	D	1918
Christine	17676	D	1914
Edward	38019	D	1923
Edward	54822	D	1930
Edward	79594	D	1938
Emile A.	51917	D	1929
Emma Lozier	25913	D	1918

NAME	NUMBER	TYPE	YEAR
Erma E.	28742	M	1920
Eugene Taber	57758	D	1931
Eva E.	67019	D	1934
Francis Berton	47942	M	1927
Frank J.	88952	D	1942
George	16900	D	1914
George Rodgers	49335	D	1928
George W.	37900	D	1923
Helen	62215	D	1932
Helena	2656	D	1907
Henry A.	2783	I	1907
Hermann F.	19703	D	1915
James	9859	D	1910
James Clifford	73728	D	1936
James W.	3465	D	1907
James W.	56109	I	1930
Jessica C.	45479	D	1926
Jessie Louise	47805	M	1927
Johannah	42763	D	1925
John	15377	D	1913
John	41967	D	1925
John	41967	D	1925
John W.	74212	M	1936
John Walter	37618	I	1923
John Walter	87815	D	1941
John, Jr.	3821	D	1907
Josef	17093	D	1914
Josephine	83191	D	1940
Kate	29184	I	1920
Kate A.	47457	D	1927
Kathryn M.	41582	D	1925
Lloyd W.	6593	M	1908
Lydia A.	24526	D	1918
Margaret	56425	D	1930
Martha W.	70474	D	1935
Mary	66165	D	1934
Mary Ann	913	D	1906
Mary C.	7745	D	1909
Mary Josephine	65835	I	1933
Nancy Nash	62012	D	1932
Nellie M.	47167	I	1927
Penelope P.	63262	D	1932
Priscilla	33527	D	1922
Richard Harwood	63823	M	1933
Rosa	27584	D	1919
Sidney Herbert	76724	D	1937
Stephen S.	65491	D	1933
Victor	59300	D	1931
Walter R.	88353	D	1941

NAME	NUMBER	TYPE	YEAR
William H.	25104	D	1918
William S.	6593	M	1908
PERRYMAN			
Jennie E.	84095	D	1940
William Edward	40734	D	1925
PERSCHEID			
Gustave Adolph	45394	D	1926
PERSE			
Joseph Leonard	56437	M	1930
Mary Elizabeth	56436	M	1930
PERSICINI			
Anna	56114	D	1930
Giuseppe	72706	D	1936
PERSON			
Anna	66761	D	1934
Erik G.	6560	D	1908
PERSSON			
Arthur	76803	M	1937
Carol	76802	M	1937
Karolina	86816	D	1941
Lynette	76804	M	1937
Magnus	50749	D	1928
N.	19849	D	1915
Per	11609	D	1911
Sven	76588	D	1937
PERTIGERA			
Giusto	55968	D	1930
PERUZZO			
Liugia	82119	D	1939
PESAK			
Alois	83864	D	1940
Joseph	71349	D	1936
PESANDO			
Ben Faustino	81083	D	1939
Benedetto	81083	D	1939
PESCE			
Antonio	60079	D	1931
PESCHEL			
August	16921	D	1914
PESCIA			
Attilio F.	25637	D	1918
Joseph	3038	D	1907
PESENTI			
Carlo Angelo	17779	D	1914
PESETTI			
Salvatore	40798	D	1925

NAME	NUMBER	TYPE	YEAR	NAME	NUMBER	TYPE	YEAR	NAME	NUMBER	TYPE	YEAR
PESHON				Edward	78213	D	1938	William Samuel	57373	D	1930
Barbara Jean	69880	M	1935	Eliza L.	37762	D	1923	Willy	43268	M	1925
Harry Alfred	69880	M	1935	Grace	30341	D	1920	**PETERSEN**			
PESOLO				Gustave	78298	D	1938	Adolf J.	58141	D	1931
Colletta	20687	D	1916	H. Z.	83112	D	1940	Agnes	77564	I	1938
Giovanni Batista	17484	D	1914	Helen	390	M	1906	Albert F.	8113	M	1909
John B.	17484	D	1914	Henry	18713	M	1915	Amelia L. J.	8554	D	1909
PESONEN				Henry	43303	D	1926	Ane	62343	D	1932
Ulla Sophie	50446	D	1928	Henry	48740	D	1927	Annie	14274	D	1912
PESSEL				Henry C. F.	73110	D	1936	Annie	21817	D	1916
Margaret	82563	D	1939	Henry C. F.	72538	I	1936	Arthur	7131	M	1909
PESSEND				Henry N.	11387	D	1911	Barbara Jane	62433	M	1932
Ernest	72263	M	1936	Henry Raphael	75431	D	1937	Bertha Elizabeth	22070	D	1917
Florence	72263	M	1936	Herman	44489	I	1926	Carl	50939	D	1928
PESTELACCI				Herman	44846	D	1926	Carl F.	40011	D	1924
Tobia A.	64810	D	1933	Herman George Emil	63041	D	1932	Charles Arthur	63270	D	1933
PETELER				Johann Clemens	32822	D	1921	Charles Henry	72534	D	1936
Robert L.	13150	M	1912	Johannes H.	44846	D	1926	Charles R.	70215	D	1935
PETER				John	6232	D	1908	Chris	88673	D	1941
Albert John	14020	D	1912	John	84495	I	1940	Christian	10799	D	1910
Catherine	39098	D	1924	John F. F.	43466	D	1926	Christian (Christ)	4349	D	1907
Ida	74462	D	1937	John M.	76686	D	1937	Christian Adolph	3400	M	1907
Taganetti	26368	D	1919	John Michael	86320	D	1941	Christian E.	57869	D	1931
PETERKA				Joseph M.	40312	D	1924	Christine	47946	D	1927
James	48723	D	1927	Julia Elise	6233	M	1908	Christine	77959	D	1938
PETERKIN				Karl	21174	M	1916	Dora I.	45655	D	1926
John A.	42780	D	1925	Katherine Amelia	61161	D	1932	Dora Todd	45655	D	1926
PETERMAN				Marie	69601	D	1935	Edna Hunter	70913	D	1935
Daniel	17380	D	1914	Marlin	60108	M	1931	Emil	45354	D	1926
PETERS				Mary	4102	D	1907	Eva	57427	I	1930
Adolph Henry	48740	D	1927	Mary	53400	D	1929	Forest Rene	45908	M	1926
Amelia	76714	D	1937	Mary H.	23738	D	1917	Fred	8558	M	1909
Ann Elizabeth	48036	D	1927	Mary Warrin	30683	D	1920	Fred	81952	D	1939
Anna	784	D	1906	McClure	75842	D	1937	Frederick J.	16199	D	1913
Anton	18713	M	1915	Minna	42615	D	1925	Frederick V.	57766	D	1931
Antone T.	56832	D	1930	Nicholas	6314	D	1908	Genevieve	39148	M	1924
Arnold B.	70670	D	1935	Norman Selby	43928	D	1926	Gustavus	16021	D	1913
Arthur Henry	6233	M	1908	Paul	18713	M	1915	Hans	15389	D	1913
August Frederick	6233	M	1908	Peter Henry William	54584	D	1929	Hans	50502	D	1928
Bertha DuBois	49025	D	1928	Raymond Francis	40090	M	1924	Hans L.	69830	D	1935
Carl F.	25318	D	1918	Raymond M.	12001	M	1911	Hans Magnus	51049	D	1928
Carl F. J.	27650	D	1919	Rudolph	18713	M	1915	Hans P.	40767	I	1925
Carlton William	40090	M	1924	Sophia	10779	D	1910	Hans P.	43027	D	1925
Charles B.	74614	D	1937	Victor	18713	M	1915	Hans Peter	20964	D	1916
Charles Bernard	21126	D	1916	Wilhelmine	11540	D	1911	Harry	77532	I	1938
Clay	23186	D	1917	Wilhelmine	42615	D	1925	Harry A.	40311	D	1924
Constance	81887	D	1939	William	16280	D	1913	Henry	8558	M	1909
				William	28616	D	1920	Henry A.	40311	D	1924
				William A.	51549	I	1928	Jacob	56347	D	1930

NAME	NUMBER	TYPE	YEAR	NAME	NUMBER	TYPE	YEAR	NAME	NUMBER	TYPE	YEAR
Jens Peter Emil	85981	D	1941	**PETERSON**				Clara	18732	D	1915
John F.	24662	D	1918	Ada	59565	D	1931	Clara	60433	I	1931
John Frederick	81952	D	1939	Adelaide A.	4109	M	1907	Clara Kern	27946	D	1919
John H.	9766	D	1910	Adeline	34393	D	1922	Clifford Austin	44576	M	1926
John L.	6634	M	1908	Adolf J.	58141	D	1931	David	51319	D	1928
John S.	68080	D	1934	Agnes L.	23385	D	1917	Edgar Carl	30435	M	1920
Jurgen	77323	D	1937	Albert	83943	D	1940	Edward	4429	D	1907
Lars Peter	68906	D	1935	Albert Julius Fabian	57041	D	1930	Edward P.	81796	D	1939
Louis E.	64048	D	1933	Albin	14918	D	1913	Edward Swan	16706	M	1914
Lucille	39148	M	1924	Alfred Cookman	53500	D	1929	Elin A.	24833	D	1918
Margaret Johanna	50190	M	1928	Alfred J.	20533	M	1916	Elizabeth	20932	D	1916
Marian	2307	M	1906	Alice	78178	D	1938	Elizabeth	82288	D	1939
Martin A.	71389	D	1936	Amanda A.	62233	D	1932	Emil	85981	D	1941
Martin Joseph	50190	M	1928	Andrew	25759	D	1918	Emily R.	72236	D	1936
Matilda A.	38818	D	1924	Andrew L.	39799	D	1924	Enewald	15312	D	1913
Max Frederick	73509	D	1936	Andrew Ruedolph	14539	D	1912	Ereka C.	85311	D	1940
Nels	17743	D	1914	Annie	11259	D	1911	Erland L.	79122	D	1938
Niels	85399	D	1940	Arthur S.	6096	D	1908	Eugene Iver	59887	M	1931
Niels Christian	33301	D	1922	Audrey	80402	M	1939	Ferdinand C.	81522	D	1939
Niels F.	5746	D	1908	August	67421	D	1934	Francis Baltzer	67713	D	1934
Niels M.	16898	D	1914	August B.	53886	D	1929	Frank	71164	M	1935
Nielsine Catherine	46984	D	1927	August F.	79586	D	1938	Frank	89395	D	1942
Norma Anita	42118	M	1925	Axel W.	51707	D	1928	Frank D.	24821	D	1918
Olaf L. G.	71837	D	1936	Beatrice Kaerth	11117	M	1911	Frank D.	49921	D	1928
Peter	62680	D	1932	Brienholt	66649	D	1934	Frank M.	61225	D	1932
Peter	67474	D	1934	Burton	61811	M	1932	Fred	81952	D	1939
Peter	80891	D	1939	Carl	21270	D	1916	Frederick A.	36880	D	1923
Peter C.	67473	D	1934	Carl	44512	D	1926	George	11288	D	1911
Peter C.	83293	D	1940	Carl A.	10158	D	1910	George H.	8820	D	1909
Peter Wald	47003	D	1927	Carl August	40203	D	1924	George J.	4109	M	1907
Petrea	67475	D	1934	Carl E.	27171	D	1919	George W.	6584	D	1908
R., Mrs.	57427	I	1930	Caroline Lina	83938	D	1940	Gertrude	59121	D	1931
Rasmus	12387	D	1911	Caroline Meta	47780	D	1927	Gertrude Seaton	82265	D	1939
Raymond B.	19713	M	1915	Catharina	42366	D	1925	Gistaf A.	44042	D	1926
Robert	15026	D	1913	Charles	19774	D	1915	Grata	46031	D	1926
Sheldon Norman	42104	D	1925	Charles	63300	D	1933	Greta	46031	D	1926
Sine D.	38586	D	1924	Charles	81562	D	1939	Gustave	64096	D	1933
Sivert	9124	D	1910	Charles A.	12141	M	1911	Gustave Titus	16105	D	1913
Sophia	74069	D	1936	Charles A.	83717	D	1940	H. W.	18637	D	1915
Theresa Elizabeth	50190	M	1928	Charles Anton	58004	D	1931	Hanna	33329	D	1922
Thomas J.	84006	D	1940	Charles B.	28844	D	1920	Hannah	6045	D	1908
Toldevar	5703	D	1908	Charles F.	76166	D	1937	Hannah	57617	D	1931
Vera A.	31308	D	1921	Charles O.	38333	I	1924	Hans H.	79034	D	1938
W. C.	47003	D	1927	Charles Robert	43556	D	1926	Harold A.	4109	M	1907
Walter	2307	M	1906	Christian	10799	D	1910	Harry A.	67041	D	1934
Walter	8558	M	1909	Christian E.	57948	I	1931	Harry R.	68763	D	1935
Walter H.	26205	D	1919	Christina	47946	D	1927	Helen	21225	D	1916
Wilhelmina D. D.	76931	D	1937	Christine	76017	D	1937	Helen	30435	M	1920
				Christine Marie	12917	D	1912	Herman E.	72324	D	1936

NAME	NUMBER	TYPE	YEAR
Hildur O.	74489	D	1937
Hulda Otilia	29266	D	1920
Ida	59565	D	1931
Ida	66337	D	1934
Ida Mae	70069	D	1935
Irene E.	4109	M	1907
Iris L.	44500	D	1926
J. M.	30411	D	1920
Jakob	4513	D	1907
Jennie	49991	D	1928
Jennie	42966	I	1925
Jennie M.	23120	I	1917
Jens W.	9804	D	1910
John	12991	D	1912
John	31096	D	1921
John	40141	D	1924
John	63334	I	1933
John	69395	D	1935
John A.	22393	D	1917
John A.	85096	D	1940
John Alfred	57135	D	1930
John H.	9766	D	1910
John Olif	75427	M	1937
John Patrick	52856	D	1929
John S.	68080	D	1934
John T.	62632	D	1932
Joseph Honce	77113	D	1937
Julia M.	76809	D	1937
Julia Scott	39957	D	1924
Kate	31624	D	1921
Kate	89834	D	1942
Katherine	25760	D	1918
Katherine Mary	89287	D	1942
Knut Andreas	27937	D	1919
Lawrence	42000	D	1925
Louis	41987	D	1925
Louis	41987	D	1925
Louis H.	24586	I	1918
Louis V.	78939	D	1938
Louisa	32546	D	1921
Mabel P.	20533	M	1916
Margaret	21500	D	1916
Margaret E.	54707	I	1930
Margaret Muller	82676	D	1939
Martha	30435	M	1920
Martha	49598	D	1928
Mary A.	4108	D	1907
Mary Elizabeth	72659	D	1936
Mary Winifred	12141	M	1911

NAME	NUMBER	TYPE	YEAR
Melcher	16961	D	1914
Meta C.	47780	D	1927
Murray	65495	D	1933
Nelda Jean	75427	M	1937
Nels	83775	D	1940
Nettie	32807	D	1921
Nils	49364	D	1928
Olga Josephina	37399	I	1923
Oscar	69615	D	1935
Otto Wedel	27197	M	1919
Patrick	4972	D	1908
Pauline	18803	D	1915
Pauline	56301	D	1930
Peter	11609	D	1911
Peter	58607	D	1931
Peter Fredrick	87620	D	1941
Peter J.	2999	D	1907
Peter S.	20533	M	1916
Reinhold	57402	D	1930
Robert J.	4109	M	1907
Ruth Anita	57656	M	1931
Sarah C.	31516	D	1921
Selma C.	83353	I	1940
Soren B.	2187	D	1906
Swen Peter	58607	D	1931
Theodore	8817	M	1909
Theodore	19617	D	1915
Thomas Andreas	85110	D	1940
Verna A.	4109	M	1907
William H.	51846	D	1929
William O.	54109	D	1929
PETERSSON			
Otto Albin	11608	D	1911
PETIEVICH			
Chris	80470	D	1939
Milevoy	80515	M	1939
PETIT			
Anna E.	18986	D	1915
Edward P.	18987	D	1915
PETITPIERRE			
Genevieve Juliette	43276	I	1925
PETITT			
Harry E.	84761	D	1940
PETKER			
George	51967	D	1929
Gerhard	51967	D	1929
PETRE			
Nelson A.	52221	D	1929

NAME	NUMBER	TYPE	YEAR
PETRI			
Amedeo	43943	D	1926
Clara Louise	50836	D	1928
Raffaello	36829	D	1923
PETRIE			
Alexander H.	19629	D	1915
Elizabeth Lander	48879	I	1928
Elizabeth Lander	49023	D	1928
James R.	42820	D	1925
Jose Alejandro	60704	M	1932
Joseph Alexander	60704	M	1932
Manuela C.	60519	D	1931
PETRINI			
Anna G.	60811	M	1932
Edna	60811	M	1932
PETROCCHI			
Mansueto	25667	D	1918
PETROFF			
Nick	69354	D	1935
PETROMILLI			
Pasquale	69907	D	1935
PETRONE			
Burt	23556	D	1917
Genevieve	23527	D	1917
PETRONI			
Gertrude	64150	D	1933
Guiseppe	64873	D	1933
PETROPOULOS			
Chris K.	87069	D	1941
PETROPULOS			
Gust H.	12533	D	1911
PETROS			
Chris	87069	D	1941
PETROSKER			
E.	79381	D	1938
PETROVICH			
Michael	45592	D	1926
PETRUCCI			
Gabriel	55948	D	1930
James	61925	D	1932
PETRUCELLO			
Raffaela Berlingiere	35212	D	1922
PETRUS			
Catherine	37429	D	1923
PETRUSICH			
John W.	29713	D	1920

NAME	NUMBER	TYPE	YEAR
Martin	62746	D	1932
Mato	62746	D	1932
PETRY			
Frances	78301	D	1938
Harvey Davis	61505	M	1932
William Wentworth	61505	M	1932
PETSAIE			
Andrea	29642	D	1920
PETTEJOHN			
Charles	12495	I	1911
PETTENGILL			
Oscar Woodbury	37957	D	1923
PETTERSEN			
Axel H.	65103	D	1933
Ellen	25871	D	1918
Hazel	27898	M	1919
Mary	24533	D	1918
Melvin	27898	M	1919
Peter	22030	D	1916
PETTERSON			
Bernice	46099	D	1926
Emma C.	30611	D	1920
Ethel	6804	M	1908
Eugene Leslie, Jr.	77447	M	1938
Frank J.	56200	D	1930
Gottfrid	69563	D	1935
Knute Edward	45777	D	1926
Lina	83938	D	1940
Mary B.	46098	D	1926
Nettie	32807	D	1921
Sophia E.	13008	D	1912
Walter	6804	M	1908
William.	5506	D	1908
PETTERSSON			
August L.	80137	I	1938
Erhard	21013	D	1916
John Cornelius	37577	D	1923
PETTEY			
Isadora	75392	D	1937
PETTIGREW			
Belle	8600	D	1909
Elizabeth	40188	D	1924
Nancy	34616	M	1922
Percy B.	7749	D	1909
PETTIJOHN			
Charles	15155	D	1913

NAME	NUMBER	TYPE	YEAR
PETTINELI			
Louis	25733	D	1918
PETTINGER			
Elizabeth	72856	D	1936
PETTINGILL			
Phoebe	69269	D	1935
PETTITT			
Catherine	10056	D	1910
Charles H.	77234	D	1937
Maria C.	33215	D	1922
Susan	3589	D	1907
PETTUS			
Margaret E.	79267	D	1938
PETTYGROVE			
Francis W.	35480	D	1922
PETUS			
Henry R.	75431	D	1937
PETZOLD			
August Carl	43722	D	1926
August, Jr.	14175	D	1912
Henry	3822	D	1907
Herny	6585	D	1908
Paul	10031	M	1910
Sarah Rebecca	55642	D	1930
PEULECKA			
H.	8080	D	1909
PEURALA			
Isaac O.	39575	D	1924
PEW			
Clara Slocomb	66013	D	1934
John W.	55710	D	1930
PEYLOURET			
Emile	57788	I	1931
PEYRE			
August Amedee	8828	D	1909
Jules	71303	D	1935
Marie	58767	D	1931
PEYSER			
Abraham Lincoln	55442	D	1930
Albert	15275	D	1913
Dora	28699	D	1920
Eva	68346	D	1934
Hattie I.	22597	D	1917
PEYTON			
Bernard	907	D	1906

NAME	NUMBER	TYPE	YEAR
PEZOLD			
Elizabeth	4404	D	1907
PEZOLT			
Arthur	38842	M	1924
PEZZI			
Dominic	34939	D	1922
Dominico	32566	I	1921
PEZZOLO			
Gianbatista	17484	D	1914
PFAEFFLE			
Louisa	54126	D	1929
William Robert	34845	D	1922
PFAENDLER			
Albert	8099	D	1909
Anton	70148	D	1935
PFAFF			
Annie E.	992	M	1906
Emilie Louise	24148	D	1918
Frankie	992	M	1906
Louis	4412	D	1907
PFAHLS			
Annie H.	36040	D	1923
PFANDLER			
Antone	70148	D	1935
Louisa	69469	D	1935
PFANKUCHEN			
Ewald	36183	D	1923
PFANN			
Dorothy	25037	M	1918
PFANNER			
Anton	13971	D	1912
PFARR			
Myrtle M.	74545	D	1937
PFARRER			
Alexander R.	47139	D	1927
Johanna F.	60973	D	1932
PFAU			
Arthur	77093	D	1937
Bertha W.	48689	D	1927
Louis J.	54668	D	1930
Paul	87322	D	1941
PFEFFENBERGER			
Ida	82783	D	1939
PFEFFER			
Lena	48625	D	1927

Name	Number	Type	Year
PFEFFERMANN			
Emilie	23470	D	1917
PFEIFENBERGER			
Ida	82783	D	1939
PFEIFER			
George Peter	76612	D	1937
PFEIFFENBERGER			
Ida	82783	D	1939
PFEIFFER			
Anna M.	18629	D	1915
August	22068	D	1917
Carrie A.	35731	D	1923
Charlotte	42700	D	1925
Christine	9115	I	1910
Christine	14715	D	1913
Conrad Henry	22067	D	1917
Elizabeth	76083	D	1937
Fred William Herman	30836	D	1920
Frederick	32025	D	1921
George	409	I	1906
George William	22455	M	1917
Henry	22067	D	1917
Henry	40764	D	1925
Josephine	48644	D	1927
Julia B. Staples	68998	D	1935
Louis A.	67706	D	1934
Marie	89825	D	1942
Otto Henry	55377	D	1930
Paul	68367	D	1934
PFENDER			
Harold	61526	M	1932
PFENNINGER			
Johannes	32535	D	1921
PFFEFER			
Adolph	89120	D	1942
PFINGST			
Edward P.	8538	M	1909
PFISTER			
Martha	79928	D	1938
PFISTERER			
Hans	76432	D	1937
Marie	76431	D	1937
PFITZNER			
John	1428	D	1906
PFLAMBAUM			
Wilhelmina	7172	I	1909

Name	Number	Type	Year
PFLAUMBAUM			
Wilhelmina	7340	D	1909
PFLAUMM			
Eva M.	72649	D	1936
PFLUEGER			
August	67367	D	1934
Louisa	57752	D	1931
PFORR			
Christian	3622	D	1907
John	750	D	1906
PFUND			
Anna Elisabeth	2536	D	1906
Anna Elizabeth	10067	D	1910
C. J.	60177	D	1931
Elizabeth	10067	D	1910
Louise	3149	D	1907
Theodore	42471	D	1925
PHAIR			
Edwin E.	50561	D	1928
Eliza Ann	31669	D	1921
Robert	22280	I	1917
PHALEN			
Duane David	74623	D	1937
PHANKUCHEN			
Ewald	36183	D	1923
PHARES			
Augustus Denison	48167	D	1927
PHARION			
Anna	77507	D	1938
Frederick M.	22217	D	1917
PHARO			
Joel H.	1416	D	1906
PHARR			
Henry	70635	I	1935
PHAYER			
Robert	22280	I	1917
PHAYRE			
Eliza Ann	31669	D	1921
PHELAN			
Albert Edward	23026	D	1917
Alfred Michael	12812	D	1912
Anne	56489	D	1930
Anthony Thomas	42557	D	1925
Caterina	26896	D	1919
Evangeline	75800	I	1937
Gerald F.	82203	D	1939

Name	Number	Type	Year
James	2701	D	1907
James Duval	56401	D	1930
John	50987	D	1928
John Sidney	89682	D	1942
Kate	87359	D	1941
Mary Louise	63566	D	1933
Mary Teresa	87164	I	1941
Mary Teresa	88160	D	1941
Patricia	70977	M	1935
Richard	33782	D	1922
Thomas	45060	D	1926
William John	17840	D	1914
PHELPS			
Agnes	70930	M	1935
Annie C.	66066	I	1934
Asa Hosmer	37853	D	1923
Augustus A.	3467	D	1907
Eliza T.	35302	D	1922
Ethel S.	61170	D	1932
George	84915	D	1940
Hettie Olive	69658	I	1935
Hettie Olive	71162	D	1935
Josephine Hart	80296	D	1939
Louis J.	78109	D	1938
Marion Wills	72055	M	1936
Martha J.	50215	I	1928
Mattie J.	50215	I	1928
Sarah E.	18099	D	1914
William	84794	I	1940
PHEMESTER			
Walter Bernard	1033	D	1906
PHENIX			
Anne Hampton	16576	D	1914
PHERSON			
Oscar Carl	78797	D	1938
PHILAN			
John	8724	D	1909
PHILBON			
Bell	51471	D	1928
Bridget	7313	D	1909
George Gilbert	48197	D	1927
Marie Jessica	11548	M	1911
Martha Jane	78457	D	1938
Mary Elizabeth	9469	D	1910
Mattie	78457	D	1938
Michael	16609	D	1914
Olley Belle Floyd	51471	D	1928
Ollie B.	51471	D	1928

NAME	NUMBER	TYPE	YEAR
PHILBROOK			
Carleton A.	21886	D	1916
Florence E.	25877	D	1918
J. C.	15673	D	1913
Katherine H.	21266	D	1916
PHILIFEX			
Peter	32265	D	1921
PHILIPP			
Hattie	81878	D	1939
PHILIPPET			
Octave	81857	D	1939
PHILIPPI			
Konrad	33327	D	1922
PHILIPPS			
Conrad	6722	D	1908
Katharina	43433	D	1926
PHILIPPSON			
Rebecca	77577	D	1938
PHILIPS			
Caroline Rose	14271	D	1912
Edward	55942	D	1930
PHILLIPPI			
Horatio L.	85498	D	1940
PHILLIPPSON			
Rebecca	77577	D	1938
PHILLIPS			
Adelina F.	60547	D	1931
Adolph	75750	D	1937
Alfred Herbert	72013	D	1936
Alice	82550	D	1939
Alvin E.	55425	D	1930
Anna D.	17677	D	1914
Annie	63364	D	1933
Arvulan	20478	D	1916
Bernard	4099	D	1907
Bertha	6767	D	1908
Bertha	79264	D	1938
Burrus Rucker	54307	D	1929
Carrie	4647	I	1907
Charles M., Jr.	73742	M	1936
Chester J.	36506	D	1923
Christiana A.	26212	D	1919
Dinah	23659	D	1917
Edwin J.	16289	D	1913
Elizabeth Chase	10159	D	1910
Ellsworth A.	55425	D	1930
Eva Harris	80729	D	1939

NAME	NUMBER	TYPE	YEAR
Frances	72919	D	1936
Francisska	72919	D	1936
Frank E.	74110	I	1936
Gage H.	78	I	1906
George	71110	D	1935
Gerald F.	2428	D	1906
Gratten D.	43157	D	1925
Gustav Herman	70437	D	1935
Hannah	63787	D	1933
Harry L.	70544	I	1935
Hattie C.	32323	D	1921
Helene M.	63964	I	1933
Herbert C.	72013	D	1936
Ida J.	72248	D	1936
Ina K.	51975	D	1929
Isador Lincoln	30206	D	1920
Isidor	52234	D	1929
J. N.	13816	D	1912
James Bennett	59868	D	1931
James King	17962	D	1914
James S.	71118	D	1935
Jasper Hosea	72205	D	1936
John	12878	I	1912
John	13214	D	1912
John H.	9141	D	1910
John R.	30932	D	1921
John S.	75307	D	1937
John Sidney	70863	M	1935
Joseph C.	77707	D	1938
Julia	3609	D	1907
Julius	37652	D	1923
Kate	3786	I	1907
Laura J.	68754	D	1935
Lavinia H.	60276	D	1931
Louis H.	35752	D	1923
Margaret Amelia	39435	I	1924
Margaret Amelia	46021	D	1926
Martha Ellen	63164	D	1932
Mary E.	7966	D	1909
Mary E.	11396	D	1911
Milton	52443	D	1929
Nannie J.	83621	D	1940
Nat Bassett	4162	M	1907
Samuel S.	52371	D	1929
Sarah Jane	31395	D	1921
Sarah M.	23589	D	1917
Sidney M.	70818	D	1935
Teague J.	83621	D	1940
Theresa M.	66327	D	1934

NAME	NUMBER	TYPE	YEAR
Violet	61466	D	1932
Walter Carroll	11239	M	1911
William E.	59721	D	1931
William John	62329	D	1932
William Morgan	71547	D	1936
William R.	17074	D	1914
William T.	44348	D	1926
William W.	68974	D	1935
PHILPOT			
Fordyce Victor	31419	M	1921
Mary F.	46032	D	1926
PHILPOTT			
Frederick Thomas	86936	D	1941
Helen Gladys	32458	M	1921
Jane	89020	D	1942
Mary	29573	I	1920
Wiliam Henry	69063	D	1935
PHINNEY			
John B.	22072	D	1917
Louise A.	29955	I	1920
Louise A.	34137	D	1922
PHINNY			
George Keil	30778	M	1920
Thomas Hopewell	30778	M	1920
PHIPPS			
Alice J.	16590	D	1914
Charles James	74771	D	1937
Dorothy	37489	M	1923
Edward	85471	D	1940
James	1029	D	1906
Jessie L.	28370	D	1919
PHISCATOR			
Frank	528	D	1906
Frank	802	M	1906
PHISTER			
Harold	30033	D	1920
Suerre F.	8306	D	1909
PHOEDOVIUS			
Elenor	30622	M	1920
Lena	25242	D	1918
Louise	30622	M	1920
PHOLOPAULOS			
Andrew Ch.	30044	D	1920
PIA			
Carlo	66247	D	1934
PIAMBO			
Joseph	9086	D	1910

NAME	NUMBER	TYPE	YEAR
PIANT			
Frank F.	9535	D	1910
PIAPISA			
Colomba	63905	D	1933
PIASECKI			
Louise M.	47324	D	1927
PIAT			
Baptiste	42483	D	1925
PIATANESI			
Colombo	89883	D	1942
PIATT			
Elizabeth	54795	D	1930
PIATTI			
Emilio	22261	D	1917
Ferdinando	17970	M	1914
Lorenzo	17970	M	1914
Rachele	17970	M	1914
PIAZZA			
Antonio	87647	D	1941
Fillippo	59266	D	1931
Guiseppa G.	55338	D	1930
Guiseppe	45332	D	1926
Josephina	83508	D	1940
Providenza	59265	D	1931
Santa	26861	M	1919
Terris	26861	M	1919
PIAZZONI			
Beatrice	63633	D	1933
Elizabeth	48965	D	1928
PIC			
Alexander	33019	D	1921
Alexis Gastou	33019	D	1921
PICANSO			
Luigia	71627	D	1936
PICARD			
Armand	7095	D	1909
Charles Benoit	87196	D	1941
Edith Strobel	72118	D	1936
Florence	10737	M	1910
Henry	10737	M	1910
Pauline	10737	M	1910
Sarah	50901	D	1928
PICASSO			
Genesio	37294	M	1923
George	43774	M	1926
PICCA			
Battista	69584	D	1935

NAME	NUMBER	TYPE	YEAR
PICCETTI			
Antonio	578	D	1906
PICCINI			
Elaine	75475	M	1937
PICCININI			
Alfredo	26466	D	1919
Battista	40770	D	1925
Catterina	45829	D	1926
PICCONE			
Louis	58117	D	1931
PICCTTI			
Antonio	578	D	1906
PICETTI			
Angelo	22174	D	1917
Giovanni	31016	D	1921
PICHARAS			
John	67267	D	1934
PICHE			
Medor	23105	D	1917
Sallie	62127	D	1932
PICHEAVAS			
John A.	67267	D	1934
PICHEL			
Pietro	30537	D	1920
PICHNOR			
Pete	43165	D	1925
Wilhelm	44499	M	1926
William	44499	M	1926
PICHOIR			
Henry	2208	D	1906
PICILLO			
Palma	22972	D	1917
Raffaele	47125	D	1927
PICK			
Alice	45335	M	1926
Charlotte	45335	M	1926
Minnie T.	26826	D	1919
Regina	44175	D	1926
William	45335	M	1926
William	58245	M	1931
PICKARD			
Ethel	74567	I	1937
Ethel	79977	D	1938
Orson L.	14914	D	1913
PICKEL			
Pietri	30537	D	1920

NAME	NUMBER	TYPE	YEAR
PICKENS			
Mabel I.	50907	D	1928
Nell V.	77747	M	1938
PICKERING			
Edwin	32081	D	1921
John Caldwell	28315	D	1919
Loring	1508	D	1906
Loring, Jr.	40251	M	1924
Marie G.	74891	D	1937
Robert Alexander	40251	M	1924
Rose Anna Crothers	38282	D	1924
PICKETT			
Jesse Cameron	56869	D	1930
Johanna	49330	D	1928
Josephine G.	60055	I	1931
William	60031	D	1931
PICKHARDT			
Martha	29839	I	1920
PICKLES			
Anne Edgar	31129	D	1921
PICKLEY			
William Edward	89673	D	1942
PICO			
Pasqualina	22255	D	1917
PICOLLO			
Angelo G.	64309	D	1933
PICONE			
John A.	64612	D	1933
PICONSO			
Louisa	71627	D	1936
Luigia	71627	D	1936
PIDANCET			
Othilie C.	31302	D	1921
PIDER			
Lawrence D.	88335	M	1941
Lee N.	88335	M	1941
Robert E.	88335	M	1941
PIDGEON			
James	31380	D	1921
Margaret T.	59482	D	1931
PIEDMONT			
Irene	40572	M	1924
PIELHOP			
Alice	18237	M	1914
Frederick	18237	M	1914
Frederick Richard	15910	D	1913

NAME	NUMBER	TYPE	YEAR	NAME	NUMBER	TYPE	YEAR	NAME	NUMBER	TYPE	YEAR
Herbert	18237	M	1914	Loraine R.	58139	D	1931	**PIERSCHKE**			
Minnie	18237	M	1914	Louisa Higginson	58877	D	1931	William Frederick	6739	D	1908
PIEN				Margaret	21814	M	1916	**PIERSON**			
Hans Henry Von	689	D	1906	Maria Louisa	4796	D	1907	Albertus M.	68487	D	1934
PIEPEL				Mary A.	12487	D	1911	Anna R.	18023	D	1914
Emile	27752	D	1919	Mary Boardman	58876	D	1931	Esther	898	D	1906
PIEPENBURG				Mary E.	68253	I	1934	Isaac	28223	D	1919
Mona C.	48377	D	1927	Mary J.	73681	D	1936	Lawrence Haight	25077	D	1918
PIEPER				Maxwell	77179	D	1937	Mabel	77856	D	1938
Alfred	42372	I	1925	Pearl V.	64627	D	1933	Nita	26416	D	1919
Alfred	42988	I	1925	Russell	32621	D	1921	Rachel M.	49351	D	1928
Robert	9052	D	1910	Russell Augustus	38620	D	1924	William	39754	I	1924
PIERALDI				Samuel, Mrs.	84084	D	1940	William Montgomery	32193	M	1921
Frank	87065	M	1941	Sophia Gleason	54015	D	1929	**PIERUCCI**			
PIERANO				Stephen A.	13991	D	1912	Annie	40578	M	1924
Agostino	24910	D	1918	Walter S.	62162	D	1932	Rose	40578	M	1924
PIERARD				William Frank	10544	D	1910	**PIERUCCIONI**			
Victor	7756	D	1909	**PIERCY**				Alibrando	70870	D	1935
PIERATTI				Donald	44220	D	1926	**PIETEO**			
Martha J.	71358	D	1936	Louise C.	83436	D	1940	Pete	56577	D	1930
PIERAZZI				Mary	13818	D	1912	**PIETERS**			
Esther	85681	D	1940	**PIERE**				Isaac	87369	D	1941
Lena	85681	D	1940	Guiseppe	59557	D	1931	**PIETES**			
Pasquina	85681	D	1940	**PIEREN**				Peter	56577	D	1930
PIERCE				David	58435	D	1931	**PIETRONAVE**			
Addie	37719	D	1923	**PIERI**				Alexander	55085	D	1930
Alfred M.	79130	I	1938	Adolfo	37607	D	1923	**PIETRZAK**			
C. E.	19392	D	1915	Guido	41485	I	1925	Kasmer Theodore	88334	D	1941
Caroline Willard	59091	D	1931	Guido	53029	D	1929	**PIETRZYCKI**			
Cecelia	63187	D	1932	Guiseppe	59557	D	1931	Mary	17702	D	1914
Charles W.	75505	D	1937	Narciso	50940	D	1928	**PIETY**			
Dean	58878	D	1931	**PIERINI**				Austin L.	7484	M	1909
Eliza W.	54350	D	1929	Adale	65529	I	1933	Georgia M.	7484	M	1909
Elizabeth	4323	D	1907	Attilio	23119	D	1917	**PIFER**			
Elizabeth J.	15753	D	1913	Jewell Marie	89018	D	1942	Richard	32117	D	1921
Elizabeth Jane	58320	M	1931	Richard F.	86928	D	1941	**PIFFERO**			
Ellen	3931	D	1907	**PIERONI**				Giuseppe	59029	D	1931
Emma J.	54809	D	1930	Antonio	87058	D	1941	**PIGNATARO**			
Frank	13844	D	1912	Gemma	87337	I	1941	Francesco	79139	D	1938
Frank W.	59066	D	1931	**PIEROTTI**				**PIGNAZ**			
Guy	57962	M	1931	Martha J.	71358	D	1936	Antonio	17538	D	1914
Henry	18233	D	1914	**PIERRE**				**PIGOTT**			
Ira	15171	D	1913	Pauline	83985	D	1940	Robert	42901	D	1925
Jacob	4265	D	1907	**PIERRET**				**PIHL**			
Jacob W., Jr.	59092	D	1931	Victorine	38831	I	1924	Alfred Hansen	28287	D	1919
John A.	16598	D	1914	Victorine	39507	D	1924				
Laura A.	72079	D	1936								

Key: D = death; M = minor; I = incompetent

NAME	NUMBER	TYPE	YEAR
PIHLSTROM			
Axel Magnus	71227	D	1935
PIKE			
Alfred Hansen	28287	D	1919
Ann Argo	47934	I	1927
Boaz David	33325	D	1922
C. W.	71924	D	1936
Edwin B.	70259	I	1935
Edwin B., Jr.	61713	M	1932
Erna Claire	61713	M	1932
Eula R.	13111	M	1912
Francis Henry	1605	D	1906
Herman	84139	D	1940
Isa M.	23507	D	1917
Joseph w.	22805	D	1917
Nellie B.	89709	D	1942
William C.	33250	I	1922
PILCHER			
Ella Gertrude	68752	D	1935
Nellie	4964	M	1908
Roy A.	61385	I	1932
William J.	2797	D	1907
Willie	4964	M	1908
PILE			
Lloyd E.	33065	D	1921
PILGER			
Lucy	81655	D	1939
PILHASHY			
Caroline	41071	D	1925
PILILIS			
George Ant.	61808	D	1932
Leon	79485	D	1938
PILKINGTON			
Thomas George	334	D	1906
PILL			
Ada	25096	D	1918
PILLETT			
Clarence C.	82913	D	1939
PILLIS			
George Antonio	61808	D	1932
PILLMAN			
Olga	9923	D	1910
PILLON			
Charles	52533	M	1929
Marie	52533	M	1929
Rose	52533	M	1929

NAME	NUMBER	TYPE	YEAR
PILLSBURY			
Horace Davis	83204	D	1940
PILPEL			
Emile	27752	D	1919
PILSTER			
Elmer F.	32279	M	1921
Theodore H.	4562	D	1907
PILTZ			
Theresa J.	74577	D	1937
PIMENTEL			
Joe J.	69368	D	1935
PINA			
Isabelle Pavon	86981	M	1941
Susan Thomas	47927	D	1927
PINAGLIA			
Giovanni Battista	7986	D	1909
Maria	7987	D	1909
PINCANSCO			
Antone	26920	D	1919
PINCHON			
Frances Lindsey	45525	D	1926
PINCKERT			
Otto H.	70738	D	1935
PINCKNEY			
Thomas C.	5983	D	1908
PINCUS			
Augusta	20474	D	1916
Pauline	57029	D	1930
Sol	84050	D	1940
PINDEL			
Karl	37176	D	1923
PINDER			
Amelia F.	82720	D	1939
Hattie Morgan	75280	D	1937
PINE			
Timothy	57716	D	1931
PINEDA			
Raymon	35046	D	1922
PINELLI			
Angelina	14725	D	1913
PINER			
Henry P.	82883	I	1939
PINET			
Marie	55510	D	1930
PING			
Chuey	39742	M	1924

NAME	NUMBER	TYPE	YEAR
Wong Gock	32400	D	1921
Wong Kwock	32400	D	1921
PINGREY			
Earl	36278	M	1923
Marion	36278	M	1923
PINILLOS			
Artemio	23564	M	1917
Lucy	23564	M	1917
PINKERTON			
Anna	79148	D	1938
James H.	72421	D	1936
John L.	68351	D	1934
PINKHAM			
Adelaide Tillinghast	22690	I	1917
Adelaide Tillinghast	30006	D	1920
Mary E.	28850	D	1920
Walter Edwin	74682	D	1937
PINKNEY			
David	2674	D	1907
Ella	37169	D	1923
PINKUS			
Sigmund H.	71392	D	1936
PINNER			
Eli	79961	D	1938
Emanuel	55045	D	1930
Henry P.	82883	I	1939
PINNICK			
Emmett	10035	M	1910
Etta	10035	M	1910
Evelyn	10035	M	1910
Francis Harry	10035	M	1910
PINNIGER			
Frances	48253	D	1927
William	42342	D	1925
PINNY			
Thomas	2896	D	1907
PINO			
Antonio	40309	D	1924
Pio Dal	88119	D	1941
PINOLI			
Caterina Acquistapace	72746	D	1936
PINON			
Juan	60248	D	1931
PINQUIE			
Marie	64453	D	1933

Key: D = death; M = minor; I = incompetent

NAME	NUMBER	TYPE	YEAR
PINS			
Dagmar de	86271	M	1941
PINSCHOWER			
Marion	23585	D	1917
May	23585	D	1917
PINSKA			
Frank W.	87663	D	1941
PINTHER			
Theodore	24728	D	1918
PINTO			
Marie Vincenza	86024	I	1941
PINZON			
Tomas	32364	D	1921
PIOCH			
Amalia	2121	D	1906
Amelia	85873	I	1940
Frank J.	82597	D	1939
Frank, Mrs.	2121	D	1906
Molly	85873	I	1940
PIOCHE			
J. L. A.	52024	D	1929
PIOLLE			
Catherine	76275	D	1937
PIOMBO			
Giobatta	23285	D	1917
Giovanni Batta	23285	D	1917
Joseph	9086	D	1910
PIOPPO			
Angelo	84215	D	1940
PIOT			
Albert	75246	D	1937
Elisa	83804	D	1940
PIOTROWSKA			
Konstancya	64257	D	1933
PIOTROWSKI			
Edward	64256	M	1933
Lawrence	35519	D	1922
Lorenc	64256	M	1933
Nida	64256	M	1933
PIPER			
Anita	55196	D	1930
Anna	33469	D	1922
Arthur L.	17745	D	1914
Herbert Halsey	1593	M	1906
John	24862	D	1918
John Q.	15494	D	1913

NAME	NUMBER	TYPE	YEAR
Lilly Kate	24460	D	1918
PIPERNI			
Ralph	30587	D	1920
PIPHER			
Emma M.	87521	D	1941
PIPINO			
May Gwin	9321	M	1910
PIPPEY			
Robert N.	14960	D	1913
PIPPONZI			
Adorno	45798	I	1926
PIPPY			
Alice E.	43856	D	1926
George H.	34805	D	1922
PIRAG			
Jacob	83398	D	1940
PIRANI			
Arturo	61415	D	1932
PIRES			
Francisco Ignacio	31645	D	1921
Manuel Vieira	8201	D	1909
PIRMER			
Katherine	22485	D	1917
PIROJA			
Fedele J.	45447	D	1926
PIROZZA			
Eva	14770	D	1913
PISA			
Colomba Pia	63905	D	1933
PISAN			
Antonio Silvestro	48982	D	1928
Guerino	85355	I	1940
PISANI			
Geraldine A.	73305	M	1936
Marie Torrano	40876	D	1925
PISANO			
Giambattista	54499	D	1929
John B.	54499	D	1929
Mary	49450	D	1928
PISAR			
Frances	38926	D	1924
PISCITELLO			
Antonio	79558	D	1938
George	68333	D	1934
PISHON			
Josiah Sturgis	42735	D	1925

NAME	NUMBER	TYPE	YEAR
PISHULIC			
Vladimir	57093	D	1930
PISHULICH			
William	57093	D	1930
PISKE			
Hedwig	7809	D	1909
PISSANO			
Mary	49450	D	1928
PISSENS			
Henry	49690	D	1928
PISSIS			
Albert	17545	D	1914
Emile Manuel	67463	D	1934
Georgia	55940	D	1930
PISTAS			
Laura M.	64955	D	1933
PISTOLESI			
Agnes Cecelia	46428	D	1927
Alice C.	52878	M	1929
Augusta M.	51249	D	1928
Guiseppe	38801	D	1924
Norbert H.	88336	D	1941
PISTONE			
Nicola	74678	D	1937
Severino	78431	D	1938
PITCHER			
Charlotte M.	83600	D	1940
John Henry	66697	D	1934
Mary Ellen	86091	D	1941
PITCHNER			
William	16669	D	1914
PITERSON			
Lina	83938	D	1940
PITKIN			
Charles S.	42861	D	1925
Elizabeth Ann	86800	D	1941
Horace Aldridge	83989	M	1940
Isabel B.	64862	D	1933
Julie M.	88661	D	1941
Peter Brice	83989	M	1940
PITNER			
George W.	45104	D	1926
PITT			
Joseph H.	89234	D	1942
PITTERSON			
Charles John	17221	D	1914

Key: D = death; M = minor; I = incompetent

NAME	NUMBER	TYPE	YEAR
PITTMAN			
Laura C.	67247	D	1934
PITTNER			
Emilie	30606	I	1920
Emilie	30870	I	1920
PITTO			
Gian Lucca	12388	D	1911
Joseph	11626	D	1911
Joseph	19273	D	1915
Kate	23354	D	1917
Theresa	5921	D	1908
PITTORINO			
Anna	52954	D	1929
PITTS			
Frederick W.	39743	D	1924
Mae Purdie	54270	D	1929
William A.	62114	D	1932
PIXLEY			
Frank M.	32059	D	1921
Herbert Ffarington	5608	M	1908
Vera Weller	5608	M	1908
PIXO			
Antonio M.	61106	I	1932
PIZARRO			
Antonio	48044	M	1927
Remilda	48043	M	1927
PIZYBOROWSKI			
Josephine	75833	D	1937
PIZYBUROIOSKI			
Jacob	75832	D	1937
PIZYBURONSKI			
Jacob	75832	D	1937
PIZYBUROWSKI			
Jacobi	75832	D	1937
PIZZELLA			
Raffaelle	86998	D	1941
Ralph	86998	D	1941
PIZZO			
Domenico	7082	M	1909
Lucia	7082	M	1909
Matte	5868	D	1908
Rosy	7082	M	1909
PLACE			
Emma	46689	D	1927
M. B., Mrs.	46689	D	1927
Warren	36510	D	1923

NAME	NUMBER	TYPE	YEAR
PLACIAL			
Amelie Marguerite	21842	D	1916
PLACIDO			
Chris	75207	D	1937
PLACKE			
Fred	22577	I	1917
Fred	51390	I	1928
PLAGEMANN			
Carol Isabella	82309	M	1939
Frederick Gray	82309	M	1939
Frederick P.	82191	D	1939
Henry	6356	D	1908
Jacob Frederick	30913	D	1921
William	8585	D	1909
PLAGGE			
Bernhard	29600	D	1920
Hedwig J. E I.	56967	D	1930
PLAHT			
Carolyn	16473	D	1913
Carrie Coleman	16473	D	1913
PLAMBECK			
Marie O.	17474	D	1914
Maurine	32197	M	1921
Maxine Eleanor	32197	M	1921
PLAMONDON			
James I. M.	58210	D	1931
PLANCICH			
Margaret	66571	D	1934
PLANK			
Clara	29226	D	1920
PLANO			
Michele	43584	D	1926
PLANT			
Grace	511	D	1906
Henry	23059	D	1917
Jessie R.	44785	D	1926
John	37485	D	1923
John W.	39837	D	1924
Lena	20583	D	1916
Lena Harriet	20584	M	1916
Mary Dorcas	20584	M	1916
Noah P.	54341	D	1929
William Peter	20584	M	1916
PLANTE			
Jean	22079	D	1917
Jeanette	46248	M	1927
Joana	46248	M	1927

NAME	NUMBER	TYPE	YEAR
Marie	46449	D	1927
Marie Jane	46248	M	1927
Martha	55539	D	1930
Mary	46237	D	1927
PLANTER			
Henry	23059	D	1917
PLANZ			
Alvina Vellguth	57380	D	1930
Sophie V.	87470	D	1941
Theodore	33322	D	1922
Theodore George Henry	36554	M	1923
PLARINOS			
Denis	39187	D	1924
PLARNIOS			
Nick	11900	D	1911
PLATE			
Matilda A.	17807	D	1914
PLATH			
Ada Margaret	85695	D	1940
Edward H.	3324	D	1907
Fritz	53469	D	1929
Hans	89332	D	1942
Henry	50636	D	1928
John	31990	D	1921
Lucy	52508	I	1929
Minna	29942	D	1920
PLATO			
Freeman F.	34181	D	1922
Joseph F.	54667	D	1930
PLATSHEK			
Mary J.	24031	D	1918
PLATT			
Alfred G.	10745	D	1910
Charles B.	28459	D	1919
Emma F.	72929	D	1936
Ester	37939	D	1923
Horace G.	10353	D	1910
Isabel M.	44984	I	1926
Jean	75566	D	1937
Jennie M.	86821	D	1941
Joseph	19042	D	1915
Malvina	55663	D	1930
Marie Theresa	31643	M	1921
William	82940	M	1939
William P.	44584	D	1926
PLATTS			
Fred Hiram	82448	D	1939

NAME	NUMBER	TYPE	YEAR
PLATZ			
Augusta K.	47078	D	1927
Elizabeth	86927	D	1941
Joseph	71433	D	1936
PLAYER			
Emily Cressey	76218	D	1937
Lionel Paget, Mrs.	76218	D	1937
PLAYFAIR			
Herbert George	56195	D	1930
PLAYTER			
Kathleen A.	51413	D	1928
PLAZA			
Manuel	85583	I	1940
PLEAS			
Elizabeth	54950	D	1930
PLEASANT			
Henry	5531	D	1908
Mary	9982	D	1910
Mary E.	333	D	1906
PLEASANTS			
William E.	3439	D	1907
William Freeland	54957	M	1930
PLECHOT			
Jean	72840	D	1936
PLEDGER			
Nettie V. Clements	88973	D	1942
PLEGAT			
Benoit Auguste	48590	D	1927
PLEMBECK			
Charles Christian Jacob	17469	D	1914
PLENNIS			
Harry H.	33096	D	1921
John	34823	M	1922
Louisa	33095	D	1921
PLESS			
Florence A.	25141	D	1918
Herman August	73838	D	1936
PLEUGSCHAT			
Walter E.	38835	D	1924
PLEVIN			
Ellen	24191	D	1918
Harry	36150	M	1923
James Ralph	64622	D	1933
PLIEFKE			
Carrie	6985	D	1908

NAME	NUMBER	TYPE	YEAR
PLIESHIVCH			
Susanna	53123	I	1929
PLISE			
Washington V.	64513	D	1933
PLOEHM			
Margaret T.	13376	I	1912
PLOTCKE			
Elke	15111	D	1913
PLOTKIN			
Elke	15111	D	1913
Oscar	47123	D	1927
PLOTNER			
Charles Dana	68757	D	1935
Dana	68757	D	1935
Frank O.	32879	D	1921
PLOURD			
Agnes	69797	I	1935
PLOURDE			
Gordon	88308	M	1941
PLOVER			
John	68207	D	1934
PLUGHOFF			
Albert David	56402	D	1930
PLUMBE			
Jean Clark	76560	D	1937
PLUME			
John V.	7931	D	1909
PLUMEL			
J. F.	454	D	1906
PLUMLEY			
Edward	35490	D	1922
PLUMMER			
A. W.	12798	D	1912
Albertine	12103	D	1911
Belle H.	59857	D	1931
Frederick W.	89111	D	1942
Harold Pierson	69499	D	1935
Melville Willis	65034	D	1933
William P.	13055	D	1912
PLUMSTEAD			
Leon	56912	D	1930
PLUMTREE			
Harriet	28790	D	1920
PLUNKETT			
Caroline F.	894	D	1906
James I.	87719	D	1941

NAME	NUMBER	TYPE	YEAR
Joseph	443	D	1906
Joseph M.	62285	D	1932
Josephine	24464	D	1918
Mary R.	1791	D	1906
William T.	56858	D	1930
PLUTT			
Anna	17768	D	1914
PLYMIRE			
Sarah E.	8282	D	1909
Susan E.	80312	D	1939
PO			
Fong	28444	D	1919
Seto Mon	68422	D	1934
Soo Hoo Mon	68422	D	1934
POCHLMAN			
Rosina	14938	D	1913
POCK			
William	51886	I	1929
POCKWITZ			
Louis	37905	D	1923
POCOCK			
Emily Stevanovich	69096	D	1935
PODARAS			
Ernest Efstration	88687	D	1941
PODER			
Juri	67887	D	1934
PODERSKY			
Matilda	46206	D	1927
PODESTA			
Alexander Louis	56886	D	1930
Amy	74235	D	1936
Anastasia	40052	D	1924
Andrea	12794	D	1912
Angela	15095	D	1913
Angelina	15095	D	1913
Antonio	42648	D	1925
Antonio	63724	D	1933
Arturo	17066	M	1914
Assunta	57722	I	1931
Catherine	56947	D	1930
Cecilia	11393	D	1911
Cecilia	63756	D	1933
Eduardo	82726	D	1939
Ellen L.	37141	D	1923
Frank	16141	D	1913
Giacobbe	37605	D	1923
Giambatista	30004	D	1920

NAME	NUMBER	TYPE	YEAR
Gianbatista	30005	D	1920
Giobatta	30004	D	1920
Giobatta	30005	D	1920
Giovanni Battista	56941	D	1930
Giovannini	13489	D	1912
Giuseppe	42750	I	1925
Giuseppe	43499	D	1926
Louisa A.	83896	D	1940
Lucien Robert	73143	D	1936
Lydia A.	86334	D	1941
Rosa	28723	D	1920
Virgil	84251	D	1940
Virginia	54934	D	1930
PODJARSKY			
Louis	51195	D	1928
PODNIGO			
Pietro	12239	D	1911
POE			
Amy	12247	D	1911
Charles Benjamin	82042	I	1939
Genevieve Katherine	48862	M	1927
POECHHACKER			
Henrietta W.	16874	D	1914
POEHLMAN			
Rosina	14938	D	1913
POERSCHKE			
Amelia Barbara Clementi	60222	D	1931
POETSCH			
Ernest	47709	D	1927
Herman	54333	D	1929
POETT			
John Joseph	18604	D	1915
Joseph Henry	2249	D	1906
Julius Edward	17683	D	1914
Sarah	42849	D	1925
POGGETTO			
Raffaello Dal	7940	D	1909
POGGI			
Carlo	81027	D	1939
Emilio Benjamin	89047	M	1942
Gloria S.	89047	M	1942
Martha	89048	D	1942
Robert	64703	D	1933
Silvio	87903	D	1941
William Anthony	89047	M	1942
POGLIANI			
Pierrette	43023	D	1925

NAME	NUMBER	TYPE	YEAR
POGLIANICH			
Annie M.	89157	D	1942
Matthew J., Mrs.	89157	D	1942
POGUE			
Lucy A.	1826	D	1906
POHEIM			
Esther Greenberg	68421	D	1934
Joseph T.	412	D	1906
Katharina Dora	40194	D	1924
POHL			
Albertine	45778	D	1926
Johanna	26363	D	1919
Thelma	71241	D	1935
POHLEY			
Frank G.	49559	D	1928
Lucie W.	49567	D	1928
POHLI			
Austin Ramon	15573	D	1913
Emil	21617	D	1916
POHLMAN			
Charles H.	39646	D	1924
Helen	50255	M	1928
POHLMANN			
Cecelia M.	60197	D	1931
E. H. W.	16377	D	1913
Ethel S.	14336	D	1912
Gustave Frederick	59183	D	1931
Gustave Frederick, Jr.	61488	D	1932
Harry D.	17228	D	1914
Hedwig	31219	D	1921
POHLMEYER			
Minnie Louise	82219	D	1939
POHORILES			
Clara	88440	D	1941
POILO			
Patrick R.	14479	D	1912
POILVE			
Janbatiste	27138	D	1919
Joseph	27138	D	1919
POINDEXTER			
Lucinda	10350	D	1910
POINTET			
Leon J.	49670	D	1928
POINTON			
Arthur M.	36170	D	1923

NAME	NUMBER	TYPE	YEAR
POIRER			
Clemence	35828	D	1923
POIRIER			
Arthur A.	67009	D	1934
Catherine	19431	D	1915
POIRIERA			
Mary Patricia	39931	M	1924
POITRAS			
Herbert D.	48435	D	1927
POKET			
Anna	86433	D	1941
Josephine Mary	68465	D	1934
POKORNY			
Joseph	56326	D	1930
POKRZYWNICKI			
Marie	70385	D	1935
POLACK			
Oscar	24799	I	1918
Samuel	21895	D	1916
POLAK			
Anna A.	39579	D	1924
POLAND			
Harry F.	11586	D	1911
POLANSKA			
Zenaida	65152	D	1933
POLANSKY			
Cyrill	67611	M	1934
POLANT			
Isidor	39407	D	1924
POLAZZOTTO			
Vincenzo	79442	D	1938
POLCHRONOPOULOS			
Nicholas D.	73841	D	1936
POLE			
John	53457	D	1929
Laura V.	30160	D	1920
POLENEC			
Sam	44913	D	1926
POLESTRINI			
Torello	52556	D	1929
POLETAKIS			
Dora	34612	D	1922
POLETTI			
Carla	7337	D	1909
Carlo	7337	D	1909

NAME	NUMBER	TYPE	YEAR	NAME	NUMBER	TYPE	YEAR	NAME	NUMBER	TYPE	YEAR
POLGAR				Torello	52556	D	1929	**POMAKN**			
Mary	73030	I	1936	**POLLEN**				Angelo	16480	D	1913
POLHEMUS				Joseph I.	43366	D	1926	**POMEROY**			
Joanne	62359	M	1932	**POLLEY**				Carter P.	24001	D	1918
John Eric	73696	D	1936	John L.	75350	D	1937	Flora	39252	D	1924
Thomas W.	62359	M	1932	**POLLHAMMER**				Joseph	40118	D	1924
POLI				Alois	67451	D	1934	Mary Flora	39252	D	1924
Dino	34915	M	1922	**POLLIANO**				May S.	89755	D	1942
Francisco	34915	M	1922	Charles	26376	D	1919	Walter M.	47126	D	1927
George	34915	M	1922	**POLLIS**				**POMIER**			
Luigi	34915	M	1922	George W.	76871	D	1937	Alphonsine	1881	I	1906
Massimiliano	9791	D	1910	**POLLITZ**				Jeanne Marie	1880	I	1906
Nello	34915	M	1922	Edward	14068	D	1912	**POMIN**			
POLIDOR				Rosalie	14968	D	1913	William C.	58633	D	1931
Katherine A.	17323	D	1914	**POLLNER**				**POMIROL**			
POLIDORI				William H.	73074	D	1936	Jean Etienne	10127	M	1910
Catherine	17323	D	1914	**POLLOCK**				**POMME**			
POLINSKY				Adelaide M.	11880	D	1911	Anna	76371	D	1937
Max	27528	D	1919	Isabella	72865	D	1936	**POMMER**			
POLIO				James L.	1458	D	1906	August Robert	26739	D	1919
Patrick R.	14479	D	1912	Otis Wheeler	20464	D	1916	Eva	39194	D	1924
POLITAKIS				Robert	13719	M	1912	Josef	47755	D	1927
Stylianos G.	54211	D	1929	Sarah Ann	50055	D	1928	Joseph	53363	D	1929
POLITZ				Violet	13719	M	1912	Rosa	62692	D	1932
Max	61189	I	1932	**POLO**				**POMMEROY**			
POLK				Osvaldo Riva	15606	D	1913	Joseph	40118	D	1924
Armas	71712	D	1936	**POLONSKY**				**POMMIER**			
POLLACCI				Samuel	68573	D	1934	Pierre	26991	D	1919
Letizia	26678	D	1919	**POLONY**				**POMMRENKE**			
POLLACK				Marie	3087	D	1907	Nellie	60669	D	1932
Adele	87682	D	1941	**POLOS**				Nellie	61313	D	1932
Alexander, Mrs.	87682	D	1941	George	25579	D	1918	**POMROY**			
Matthias A.	51868	D	1929	**POLOZZI**				Maria Theresa	67024	D	1934
S. M.	43389	D	1926	Mary	4156	D	1907	Walter M.	47126	D	1927
POLLAK				**POLSON**				**PON**			
Charles	26759	M	1919	Paul	42233	D	1925	Chong	69674	D	1935
Theresa	62015	D	1932	**POLSTLER**				Gracieuse	3150	D	1907
POLLARD				Gustave	11130	D	1911	Jean B.	64317	D	1933
Arthur Whiting	55955	D	1930	**POLTT**				Jean Pierre	46194	D	1927
Earl George	31522	M	1921	Sarah	42849	D	1925	Pauline	8509	D	1909
Laurine	3792	D	1907	**POLY**				**PONAROUSE**			
Samuel A.	2596	D	1907	Isaac	24555	D	1918	Lina	3466	D	1907
Walter S.	31522	M	1921	**POLYMEROPOULOS**				**PONASSO**			
POLLASTRINI				Harry	74845	I	1937	Veronica	42789	D	1925
Lelio	11951	D	1911	Harry	78603	D	1938	**PONCET**			
Thomas	52556	D	1929					Eugenia	79535	D	1938

NAME	NUMBER	TYPE	YEAR
Seraphine	35430	D	1922
PONCINI			
Esther Evelyn	61416	D	1932
PONCINO			
Eugenio	49822	D	1928
POND			
Edward B.	9602	D	1910
Louise F.	61251	D	1932
Marion	9671	D	1910
Sarah C.	31567	D	1921
PONG			
Hoo Sig	35168	M	1922
PONGRACZ			
Hannah	21265	I	1916
Hannah	49962	D	1928
PONS			
Frederic	8181	D	1909
Marie	80080	D	1938
PONSERO			
Giovanni Battista	38819	D	1924
John	36874	I	1923
John	38819	D	1924
PONTACG			
Marie	16850	D	1914
PONTACQ			
Jean	3950	D	1907
Jean	21262	D	1916
John	3950	D	1907
PONTE			
Antonio	31957	M	1921
Claudio	20559	D	1916
Giovanni	31957	M	1921
Maria	32171	D	1921
PONTET			
Emma E.	59457	D	1931
PONTI			
Ernesta	34667	D	1922
Giuseppe	40692	D	1925
Giuseppe	86730	D	1941
PONTONDEARCE			
S.	69272	D	1935
PONTOPPIDAN			
Annie M.	72490	D	1936
PONZIO			
Humbert	31747	I	1921
Humbert	32125	D	1921

NAME	NUMBER	TYPE	YEAR
POO			
Fung Chong	85362	D	1940
Louie Yee	83832	D	1940
POOK			
Justin	89448	I	1942
POOL			
Allen L.	53487	M	1929
Angela	7375	M	1909
Beatrice	7375	M	1909
Harry	7375	M	1909
Jennie R.	11359	D	1911
Joseph R.	4837	D	1907
Margaret	7375	M	1909
Mary	102	D	1906
Raymond	7375	M	1909
POOLE			
Andrew E.	14137	D	1912
Anne E.	15359	D	1913
Bertha	52600	D	1929
Byron Walter	71308	D	1935
Charmain Gerda	81881	M	1939
Charmian Gerda	75270	M	1937
Eugene Dennis	84114	D	1940
George	2640	D	1907
George Thomas	23662	D	1917
John Edward	68004	D	1934
John Edward, Mrs.	86741	D	1941
Marie	86741	D	1941
Mary Elizabeth	48905	D	1928
Robert Lincoln	75270	M	1937
Robert Lincoln	81881	M	1939
Theresa	41854	D	1925
Theresa	41854	D	1925
POOLER			
Chester B.	36637	D	1923
POON			
William	70196	M	1935
POOR			
Whittle	72414	D	1936
POPA			
Alexander	63561	D	1933
POPE			
Agnes	64859	D	1933
Alexander	63561	D	1933
Andrew J.	3679	D	1907
Catherine	60792	D	1932
Charles W.	12689	D	1911

NAME	NUMBER	TYPE	YEAR
Frederick George	76894	D	1937
Grady Haygood	41730	I	1925
Grady Haygood	41730	I	1925
James B.	50457	D	1928
Jessie Frances	79203	D	1938
John	22596	D	1917
John F.	11414	D	1911
John Rudolph	35263	D	1922
John Ryssmer	41609	D	1925
Lillie M.	70347	D	1935
Lizzie	38669	D	1924
Mary A.	20856	D	1916
Melvin	19588	M	1915
Otto A.	64225	D	1933
Reginald Heber	7149	D	1909
Sarah Lee	13903	D	1912
Saxton Temple	45278	D	1926
Thomas	25924	D	1918
Whitney B.	72417	D	1936
William G.	32555	D	1921
Wilson R.	60995	D	1932
POPIEK			
Andrew	56838	D	1930
POPKENS			
Alyne Jacqueline	74274	M	1936
POPKIN			
Harry	42199	D	1925
Sarah Humphreys	63573	D	1933
POPOFF			
Michael Dimitry	66957	D	1934
POPOVIC			
Melko	80540	D	1939
POPOVICH			
Melko	80540	D	1939
Peter J.	21125	I	1916
POPPE			
Elizabeth M.	3852	D	1907
Martha H.	48839	D	1927
POPPENBERG			
Amelia	21447	D	1916
POPPENHAUSEN			
Emil	26477	D	1919
POPPER			
Elfrieda Mathilda	46368	M	1927
Gertrude	33807	D	1922
Leopold	75062	I	1937
Max	17520	D	1914

NAME	NUMBER	TYPE	YEAR
POPPIN			
Elmer	89512	I	1942
POPPLEWELL			
Herbert Cooper	36053	D	1923
POPPOS			
Mikal	43682	D	1926
PORCELLA			
Antonio	61090	D	1932
Attilio	47915	D	1927
John B. F.	54784	D	1930
PORCHER			
John J.	47664	D	1927
Veronica J.	20512	D	1916
PORISCH			
Friedrich Robert	9667	D	1910
PORISKA			
Emanuel	53517	D	1929
POROBICH			
John	16615	D	1914
POROSHIN			
Nikolas V.	67423	D	1934
PORRECA			
Camillo	83693	D	1940
PORT			
Marie Lux S.	10206	M	1910
PORTA			
Amabile	62930	D	1932
Angiolina	55976	D	1930
Edward	77681	D	1938
Emilia	87313	D	1941
Fausto	60948	D	1932
Helen Bassett	27549	D	1919
Ilda	52126	D	1929
Leopold	69017	D	1935
PORTAL			
Laura	82574	D	1939
PORTANA			
Victor	26550	D	1919
PORTE			
Frank	60948	D	1932
Marguerite Larroche	44468	D	1926
PORTER			
Albert James	82255	D	1939
Alexena R.	79787	I	1938
Anne Kennedy	1662	D	1906
Anne Marye	51766	D	1929

NAME	NUMBER	TYPE	YEAR
Beatrice	3490	M	1907
Beverly	31497	M	1921
Carrie A.	9503	D	1910
Chas. N., Mrs.	47485	D	1927
Chester A.	27518	M	1919
Clarke David	12071	M	1911
Edwin C.	12946	M	1912
Edwin James	83469	D	1940
Frances Ann	30154	D	1920
Francis H.	20985	D	1916
Francis H., Mrs.	79787	I	1938
Gertrude	3490	M	1907
Gordon W.	73637	D	1936
Helen	69173	D	1935
Helen	50479	M	1928
Howard M.	59763	D	1931
Ida C. N.	47485	D	1927
Ida C. N.	53545	D	1929
J. B.	33840	D	1922
Jenny	82339	I	1939
Jerome P.	87501	D	1941
Jess	88495	M	1941
Joseph	33840	D	1922
Katherine	21888	D	1916
Kathleen	31488	D	1921
Lucy	52087	D	1929
Mary	21186	M	1916
Mary Barry	27517	D	1919
Mary E.	85660	D	1940
Mary J.	27517	D	1919
Mary Winifred	70549	D	1935
May L.	70994	D	1935
Michael	18183	D	1914
Robert	48327	D	1927
Robert C.	58886	D	1931
Rofena C.	61831	D	1932
Stanley	74177	M	1936
Stella	83370	D	1940
Susan	41141	D	1925
W. N.	42915	D	1925
W. P. S.	24247	D	1918
Wilbur Fisk	34487	D	1922
William	11702	D	1911
William G.	61710	D	1932
William Lent	88495	M	1941
PORTEUS			
William Albert	24432	D	1918
PORTIOLIATTI			
Lionet Michele	80199	D	1938

NAME	NUMBER	TYPE	YEAR
PORTLEY			
James Joseph	11287	D	1911
Mabel Irene	82466	D	1939
PORTO			
Joao Ferreira	17660	D	1914
PORWANCHER			
Florence	8163	M	1909
Gertrude	8163	M	1909
PORZER			
Elizabeth	57455	D	1930
POSENER			
Albert C.	89438	D	1942
Herman	12504	D	1911
POSER			
Emma	76528	D	1937
POSERT			
Frank X.	14205	D	1912
POSKA			
Amelia	36029	D	1923
POSNER			
Edna	68139	D	1934
Hannah	35262	D	1922
Joseph	1969	D	1906
Julius M.	67876	D	1934
Max	42577	D	1925
Philip	53122	D	1929
POSPISIL			
Anna	87893	D	1941
POSSON			
Martha	45856	D	1926
POST			
Ann Eliza	11351	D	1911
Annie	36942	D	1923
Ernest M.	49694	I	1928
Fanny W.	32982	D	1921
Frederick L., Jr.	15264	I	1913
James F.	50991	D	1928
Mattie B.	60223	D	1931
Ralph	14444	I	1912
Ralph	14670	D	1913
Stanley O.	5988	D	1908
William Sylvester	46080	D	1926
POSTAG			
Genevieve	34422	M	1922
Genevieve Gertrude	69145	M	1935
John Nicholas	52413	D	1929

NAME	NUMBER	TYPE	YEAR
POSTEL			
Carl F. A.	65055	D	1933
POSTIGLIONE			
Guiseppe M.	9221	D	1910
POSTLER			
Alma	18659	M	1915
Gustave	18659	M	1915
Herman	18659	M	1915
Otto Ernest	18659	M	1915
Paul	18659	M	1915
POSTREL			
Joseph	86184	D	1941
Monroe A.	86185	M	1941
Morton J.	86185	M	1941
POSWA			
Alice Louisa	17732	D	1914
Hynek	22159	D	1917
POTASZ			
Marceli	66015	D	1934
POTHIG			
Emil	67071	D	1934
POTKIN			
Henry, Sr.	86681	D	1941
POTSMITH			
Charles	13823	D	1912
POTT			
Frederick S.	20930	D	1916
Louise A.	10310	D	1910
POTTER			
Abby	31115	D	1921
Albert R.	31475	D	1921
Annie L.	89258	D	1942
Catherine M.	39867	D	1924
Charles Anson	335	D	1906
Chauncey	50869	D	1928
Clarence Edwin	3923	M	1907
David	22573	M	1917
Edward	8770	M	1909
Edward E.	25182	D	1918
Eliza	336	D	1906
Ella C.	62077	D	1932
Eva G.	27232	D	1919
Florence	8770	M	1909
Frances	51864	M	1929
Frederick W.	40983	D	1925
George F.	39693	D	1924
Gertrude VanWyck	18591	D	1915

NAME	NUMBER	TYPE	YEAR
Helen Hume	3923	M	1907
Ina May	26072	D	1919
Joseph Christopher	6396	D	1908
Leah A.	31711	D	1921
Lucy	19531	M	1915
Luella H.	68916	D	1935
Margaret	26754	D	1919
Mattie	59523	I	1931
Mattie	60150	D	1931
Maude W.	23638	D	1917
May Hume	2767	D	1907
Melissa Amelia	21924	D	1916
Milton Calvert	14969	M	1913
Nellie T.	33091	D	1921
Norman	48813	M	1927
Norman Woolsey	60455	D	1931
Phyllis	22573	M	1917
Robert	48813	M	1927
Samuel	36540	D	1923
Samuel O.	17188	D	1914
Sarah Evans	50018	D	1928
Sheldon E.	22573	M	1917
Susan A.	23064	D	1917
W. George F.	39693	D	1924
Walker S.	27869	D	1919
Walter L.	77058	D	1937
POTTERAT			
William	29887	D	1920
POTTHOFF			
Annie M.	18277	D	1914
POTTIER			
George	75453	D	1937
POTTINGER			
Julia	56672	I	1930
POTTS			
Alexander W.	81045	D	1939
C. W.	47638	D	1927
Eric L	74574	D	1937
Frances A.	67152	D	1934
Frank C.	67971	D	1934
POTVIN			
Henry Sr.	86681	D	1941
POUCHAN			
Germain	82978	D	1939
Louise	77172	D	1937
POUCHER			
Ralph B.	49860	D	1928

NAME	NUMBER	TYPE	YEAR
POUGAL			
Alfred	2461	D	1906
Marie M.	2462	D	1906
POUGETTE			
Martin	56398	D	1930
POULEUR			
Jules B.	2773	D	1907
POULEWE			
Jules B. (missing)	3695	D	1907
POULLAIN			
Robert J.	62548	D	1932
POULOS			
Bill	37235	D	1923
Peter	26173	D	1919
Theodora	37233	M	1923
POULSEN			
Ane Johanne	54704	D	1930
Johanne	54704	D	1930
POULSON			
Ida	82814	D	1939
POULTNEY			
George T.	72790	D	1936
Isabel S.	88800	D	1941
POULY			
Laurence M.	14129	I	1912
Lawrence M	14192	D	1912
Maximilian L.	14129	I	1912
Maximillian L.	14192	D	1912
POUQUETTE			
Peter	86451	D	1941
POURIE			
Gladys Dunne	29165	D	1920
Mary Dunne	29165	D	1920
POURNARAS			
George	71109	D	1935
POURROY			
Victorina Julieta	46379	D	1927
Victorina Zubieta	46379	D	1927
POUS			
Antoine	77199	D	1937
John	18292	D	1914
Marie	80080	D	1938
POUTZ			
Marie Lacanau	72844	D	1936
POUYAL			
Marie M.	2462	D	1906

NAME	NUMBER	TYPE	YEAR
POVER			
James	21709	D	1916
POVEY			
Catherine A.	70400	D	1935
POW			
Tom	53068	D	1929
POWELL			
Abraham	31528	D	1921
Abraham, Jr.	49435	D	1928
Alvira	18539	I	1915
Annie E.	27369	D	1919
Anthony M.	18387	D	1915
Carrie Seineke	75993	D	1937
Christopher Theodore	71523	D	1936
Eda W.	80363	D	1939
Edith W.	80363	D	1939
Edward George	58281	D	1931
Ella May	74572	D	1937
Ellen	41518	D	1925
Emeline M.	15117	D	1913
Evangeline	49696	D	1928
George	73975	D	1936
Henry James	13881	D	1912
Humphrey Brooke	29245	D	1920
Idell	12800	D	1912
James L.	34407	D	1922
John Patrick	67677	I	1934
John Patrick	76509	D	1937
Josephine Victoria	36957	D	1923
Lorena Blanche	34879	D	1922
Louise Dennis	73389	D	1936
Marjorie M.	21717	M	1916
Priscilla Florence	27844	D	1919
Sara R.	51444	D	1928
Sarah Lavinia	53692	D	1929
Sarah Louisa	3896	D	1907
Theodore N.	24332	D	1918
Thomas	1696	I	1906
Welcome N.	86166	D	1941
POWER			
Anne L	77616	D	1938
Bernard	28792	D	1920
Constance	88677	I	1941
David J.	58329	D	1931
Frederick	49080	D	1928
James	8012	D	1909
James D.	9910	D	1910
James E.	58731	D	1931

NAME	NUMBER	TYPE	YEAR
Lillian	73363	D	1936
Lily R.	79314	D	1938
Margaret	14791	D	1913
Mary H.	41596	D	1925
Neal	83519	D	1940
Patrick	74694	D	1937
Patrick	89232	D	1942
Pierce	36938	D	1923
Richard	58947	D	1931
Susan T.	82903	D	1939
Thomas	12808	D	1912
Thomas M.	33406	D	1922
William	14726	D	1913
William	29688	D	1920
William	29707	D	1920
POWERS			
Aaron H.	33732	D	1922
Aaron Hubbard	3684	D	1907
Adessa	21036	D	1916
Agnes	58608	D	1931
Albert Gallatin	30808	M	1920
Annie Theresa	38386	M	1924
Bridget	3066	D	1907
Bridget	38386	M	1924
C. H.	5939	D	1908
Catherine A.	7942	D	1909
Catherine Marie	38386	M	1924
Charles E.	43605	D	1926
Constance	33722	M	1922
Cornelia Chapman	22995	D	1917
Dena Mary	75558	D	1937
E. J.	9378	D	1910
Edward	50404	D	1928
Edward T.	21616	D	1916
Emma F.	30762	I	1920
Emma F.	33361	D	1922
Florence M.	36877	D	1923
Francis	10824	M	1910
Frank E.	85984	I	1941
Frank E.	88242	D	1941
Frank G.	85874	D	1940
Frank H.	30663	D	1920
Frank H.	33722	M	1922
Frank, Jr.	85874	D	1940
George Francis	38386	M	1924
George Herman	16950	D	1914
George J.	38387	I	1924
James	58041	D	1931
James D.	16218	D	1913

NAME	NUMBER	TYPE	YEAR
James T.	47354	I	1927
James T.	52585	D	1929
Jennie Louise	70918	D	1935
Johanna	12688	D	1911
Johanna	28059	D	1919
Johanna	45295	D	1926
Johannah	38386	M	1924
John	17782	M	1914
John	76666	M	1937
John E.	86596	D	1941
John Henry	71492	D	1936
John W.	37427	M	1923
Joseph Anthony	38386	M	1924
Joseph P.	15148	D	1913
Josie	12688	D	1911
Lester	4766	M	1907
Lillian	4766	M	1907
Lulu McKee McKeon	73564	D	1936
Margaret	49187	D	1928
Margaret	75868	I	1937
Margaret	76665	D	1937
Marian H.	30808	M	1920
Mary	6112	D	1908
Mary	41772	D	1925
Mary	41772	D	1925
Mary A.	47096	I	1927
Mary A.	52584	D	1929
Mary A.	83847	D	1940
Mary Adessa	21036	D	1916
Mary Anne	38386	M	1924
Mary E.	58040	D	1931
Michael	8285	D	1909
Michael	21275	D	1916
Michael	36878	D	1923
Michael F.	30072	D	1920
Mike A.	47266	D	1927
P. J.	4114	D	1907
Patrick	59843	D	1931
Peter	33722	M	1922
Pierce	36938	D	1923
Pierce, Jr.	17782	M	1914
Richard	42341	D	1925
Richard	58947	D	1931
Robert G.	35324	D	1922
Ruth	51565	D	1928
Thomas J.	792	M	1906
Thomas J.	39270	D	1924
Timothy T.	24085	I	1918
Timothy T.	32218	D	1921

NAME	NUMBER	TYPE	YEAR
William	10345	I	1910
William	14726	D	1913
POYSELL			
John C.	22032	D	1916
POYSER			
Elizabeth Wiley	66188	D	1934
Thomas	37080	D	1923
POZNANSKI			
Johanna	26954	D	1919
Silvia Pearl	27079	M	1919
William	49809	D	1928
POZZA			
Antonio	81288	D	1939
POZZI			
Silvio	89085	D	1942
POZZODIBORGO			
Antone	15648	D	1913
PRACHT			
Julie	35741	D	1923
PRACY			
Charles Thomas	6563	M	1908
Edna Louise	6563	M	1908
George Wesley	6563	M	1908
Joseph Idell	6563	M	1908
Susie A.	63798	D	1933
PRADA			
Anthony	63556	I	1933
Eduardo	54588	I	1929
Eduardo	60771	D	1932
Pietro	57901	D	1931
PRADELS			
Adolphe	66304	D	1934
PRADO			
Louisa	86594	D	1941
Mary	68159	I	1934
PRAEN			
Elizabeth	17991	D	1914
PRAETZ			
Henry	74206	D	1936
PRAG			
Augusta	8943	D	1910
Caroline	31114	I	1921
Caroline	34809	D	1922
Helen	31356	D	1921
Isabella	29099	D	1920
Mary	69274	D	1935

NAME	NUMBER	TYPE	YEAR
PRAGER			
Nita	8518	M	1909
Raphael	8569	D	1909
Ruth	8517	M	1909
PRAHL			
Macquarie	2837	D	1907
Sarah Antoinette	13302	D	1912
PRAIRO			
Elizabeth	66887	D	1934
PRAKASHANANDA			
Swami	46656	D	1927
PRALLE			
John	15616	D	1913
PRAMENKO			
Theodore	2881	D	1907
PRANKARD			
Francis T.	3513	D	1907
PRASS			
Josephine	65205	I	1933
PRASSO			
Frank	62520	D	1932
Josephine	65205	I	1933
PRAST			
Anders	9500	D	1910
Frederick	43234	D	1925
Hans Jensen	3781	D	1907
PRAT			
Eugene	25616	D	1918
George J.	45433	M	1926
Rose Marie	45433	M	1926
PRATA			
Manuel De Ponte	6621	D	1908
PRATHER			
Charles L.	72517	D	1936
PRATO			
Angela	71166	D	1935
Emanuele	53300	D	1929
PRATT			
Ada B.	56888	D	1930
Albert Edgar	70	D	1906
Alexander	80984	D	1939
Amelia	51624	D	1928
Bessie N.	36723	D	1923
Charlotte	80940	D	1939
Clara F.	62556	I	1932
Clara Frances	68014	D	1934

NAME	NUMBER	TYPE	YEAR
Emily J.	2850	I	1907
Fred J.	63395	D	1933
George E.	51715	D	1928
Georgie Annie	71325	D	1936
Jane A.	23320	D	1917
Jesse	45065	D	1926
John William	89191	D	1942
Josephine Emily	36768	M	1923
Lizzie E.	11146	D	1911
Marion W.	38500	D	1924
Mary Catherine	60662	D	1932
Nora M.	1992	D	1906
Orville C.	459	D	1906
Orville C.	36768	M	1923
Robert	40830	D	1925
Russell Wilson	36768	M	1923
PRATTIS			
George	30592	D	1920
PRAUSE			
August	64104	D	1933
PRAVELL			
Sawyer Elizabeth	73595	D	1936
PRAY			
Lucy Mabel	42519	D	1925
PREBLE			
William H.	2104	D	1906
PRECHT			
Ida	9387	D	1910
PRECHTEL			
Daisy K.	75890	D	1937
George P.	30428	D	1920
PREDDEY			
Betty J.	69451	M	1935
Betty Jean	73732	M	1936
Betty Jean	77444	M	1938
Elsa G.	73731	D	1936
George H.	83200	D	1940
Lucette Mona	73732	M	1936
Margaret	65277	D	1933
Sydney Robert	73732	M	1936
PREDDY			
Betty Jean	76273	M	1937
Luceta Mona	76273	M	1937
Sydney Robert	76273	M	1937
PREECE			
Ellie	49238	I	1928

NAME	NUMBER	TYPE	YEAR
PREEMAN			
Jacob M.	12082	D	1911
PREEPPER			
Arthur	59001	I	1931
PREFONTAINE			
Aner	82959	D	1939
PREGGE			
Henry	19924	D	1915
PREIS			
William	80407	D	1939
PRELOVSKY			
Dimetri	45244	D	1926
PRENDERGAST			
Bridget	38976	D	1924
Clara J.	36635	D	1923
Edward	29555	M	1920
Ella Blanche	73820	D	1936
Ellen Jane	54837	D	1930
James M.	45166	D	1926
James Walshe	48921	D	1928
John	17358	D	1914
John H.	84031	D	1940
Kathrine	34226	M	1922
Nicholas James	29467	D	1920
Nora	64995	D	1933
Norma	34226	M	1922
PRENDLE			
Mary E.	56481	D	1930
PRENGSCHAT			
Walter E.	38835	D	1924
PRENTICE			
Edwin H.	22662	D	1917
F. A.	16271	D	1913
Robert Clarence	19146	M	1915
Zachariah H.	9009	D	1910
PRENTISS			
Margaret G.	5685	M	1908
PRENTKI			
Herman	42808	D	1925
PREOVOLOS			
Peter J.	56055	D	1930
PREPPER			
Arthur	59001	I	1931
PRESBREY			
Mary Elizabeth	28184	D	1919

NAME	NUMBER	TYPE	YEAR
PRESCOTT			
Austin F.	37410	I	1923
Austin F.	88108	D	1941
George W.	1481	D	1906
George W.	19402	D	1915
PRESLER			
Dean Stanley	48564	D	1927
PRESLEY			
George J.	67545	D	1934
Jerry D.	67324	I	1934
PRESS			
Ruby E.	85651	I	1940
Ruby E.	87801	I	1941
PRESSEY			
George W.	24993	D	1918
Meda	38830	D	1924
PRESSMAN			
Dora	81943	D	1939
PRESSMEN			
Samuel	60847	D	1932
PRESSON			
Mary Baker	11648	D	1911
PRESTIDGE			
Phyllis	78153	M	1938
PRESTINONI			
Louis	49984	D	1928
Louis	49829	I	1928
PRESTO			
Giuseppe	87209	D	1941
Joseph	87209	D	1941
PRESTON			
Bertha	84904	D	1940
Betty	37773	M	1923
Charles W.	331	D	1906
Edmund Benj. Geo. Tiel	17975	D	1914
Edward John	59835	D	1931
Elizabeth	48075	D	1927
Frank O.	22073	D	1917
George Harvey	39674	M	1924
Gertrude	7969	M	1909
Gladys Irene	16093	M	1913
Grace	7969	M	1909
John Boulton	58373	D	1931
Joseph B.	37773	M	1923
Joseph Warren. Jr.	85064	D	1940
Lillie	55647	D	1930
Lucy	76913	D	1937

NAME	NUMBER	TYPE	YEAR
Mary	14127	D	1912
Mignon	17700	M	1914
Nina L.	31197	M	1921
O. M.	65941	D	1933
William	51812	D	1929
PRETARI			
Giuseppe	54797	D	1930
PRETI			
Pietro	42173	D	1925
PRETOU			
Jeane	20076	D	1915
Marie	31030	D	1921
PRETRINI			
Alexander	55085	D	1930
PRETTEJOHN			
Charles	12495	I	1911
Charles	15155	D	1913
PREUSS			
Martin	64501	D	1933
PREUX			
Rene Le	1195	D	1906
PREVE			
Lorenzo	25544	D	1918
PREVEZIC			
Luce	19709	D	1915
PREVEZICH			
George	34807	D	1922
PREVOST			
Alexander J.	80125	D	1938
Henry	64419	D	1933
PREWER			
Bertha M.	84524	D	1940
PRIBER			
Emil Clemens	60234	D	1931
PRICE			
Albert J.	69401	D	1935
Anna C.	73081	D	1936
Annie	69876	I	1935
Annie F.	41537	D	1925
Annie J.	51969	I	1929
Archibald Henry	88940	D	1942
Arthur	71649	D	1936
Arthur Benjamin, Jr.	63344	M	1933
Carrie M.	69064	D	1935
Charles G.	24611	D	1918
Clarence Clay	54886	D	1930
Dorothy S.	58060	M	1931

NAME	NUMBER	TYPE	YEAR
Elizabeth H.	58897	D	1931
Ellen	50127	D	1928
Eva L.	87253	D	1941
Eva Wilma	63344	M	1933
Evan J.	22378	D	1917
F. P.	6035	D	1908
Ford Henry	49563	D	1928
Frances Delia	62938	D	1932
George E.	19508	I	1915
George E.	31454	I	1921
George G., Jr.	84285	D	1940
Gertrude R.	68244	D	1934
Harry	51684	D	1928
Henry	44655	D	1926
Henry Bertrand	88077	D	1941
James	41807	D	1925
James	41807	D	1925
James	46838	D	1927
James George	27850	D	1919
Jane D.	71093	D	1935
John B.	16827	D	1914
John T.	37344	D	1923
Josephus A.	58060	M	1931
June	63344	M	1933
Lillian	23608	D	1917
Lily A.	29494	D	1920
Lizzie Louisa	78540	D	1938
Lydia E.	30140	D	1920
Mary	34018	D	1922
Mary B.	32176	D	1921
Mary Eldridge	22858	D	1917
Merton	63271	M	1933
Merton S.	61810	D	1932
Michael	72279	D	1936
Morton J.	63263	D	1932
Myrtle J.	23829	I	1918
Myrtle J.	32544	D	1921
Ralph E.	86930	M	1941
Samuel	85088	D	1940
Susanne	63295	M	1933
Thomas L.	35651	D	1923
Thomas Morgan	33678	D	1922
William	41556	D	1925
William	79875	D	1938
William H., Sr.	74042	D	1936
PRICHARD			
Evan	82062	D	1939
Frances E.	70078	D	1935
Fred A.	70079	D	1935

NAME	NUMBER	TYPE	YEAR
William Anthony	37223	D	1923
PRIDDLE			
Annie Effie	77899	D	1938
PRIDGEON			
Jefferson Frank	86638	D	1941
PRIDHAM			
Annie C.	37509	D	1923
PRIEN			
Johan H. C.	15031	D	1913
Lilian Church	70115	D	1935
PRIESS			
Fred	55434	D	1930
Fritz	55434	D	1930
PRIEST			
Agnes C.	79249	D	1938
Allan A.	60985	D	1932
Catherine	83601	D	1940
Charles Franklin	20602	D	1916
Fay W.	22035	D	1916
Frank J.	73750	D	1936
PRIESTER			
Lyman R.	84071	D	1940
PRIET			
Pierre	1571	D	1906
PRIETO			
Frank	72232	D	1936
PRIETZEL			
Wilhelm	83842	D	1940
PRIEUER			
Albert V.	44449	D	1926
PRIEUR			
Arsene	40234	D	1924
Arthur	19651	D	1915
Caroline	47507	D	1927
Fannie	22338	D	1917
Florence	20832	D	1916
Frank A.	24712	D	1918
PRIGGE			
Henry	19924	D	1915
PRIGMORE			
Jack C.	82120	D	1939
Jay C.	82120	D	1939
PRILL			
Frances Jagielki	32280	D	1921
PRIMET			
Etienne	84083	D	1940

NAME	NUMBER	TYPE	YEAR
Steve	84083	D	1940
PRIMKE			
Auguste L.	40611	I	1924
PRIMROSE			
Ima Jewel	48284	M	1927
Leslie L.	48284	M	1927
Rosella Mae	48284	M	1927
PRINCE			
Albert D.	76982	I	1937
Albert D.	77008	D	1937
Albert Edward	22948	D	1917
Anna	40290	I	1924
Augusta	78820	I	1938
Augusto	79252	D	1938
Catharine	10511	D	1910
Charles A.	50062	I	1928
Charles J.	13587	I	1912
Charles J.	38563	D	1924
Charlotte	40713	D	1925
Daniel	37356	M	1923
David S.	70387	D	1935
Dora	47628	D	1927
Ernest F.	78247	D	1938
Frank R.	1061	M	1906
Frank R.	3692	D	1907
Frank R.	55025	D	1930
Henry	44655	D	1926
Jennie S.	33615	D	1922
Jesus	19671	D	1915
Joseph	60162	D	1931
Joseph P.	27293	D	1919
Lewis M.	53447	D	1929
Lionel D.	89371	D	1942
Louis Jewett	53448	D	1929
Mae E.	56149	D	1930
Mary B.	37340	D	1923
Maud Alice Keet	81089	D	1939
Patricia	37356	M	1923
Paul	37356	M	1923
Ruperto M.	52842	D	1929
PRINCEVALLE			
Angil	35377	D	1922
PRINCIPAL			
Leon, Jr.	51115	M	1928
PRINCIPIANO			
Giulio	81983	I	1939
Julio	81983	I	1939

NAME	NUMBER	TYPE	YEAR
PRINDLE			
George W.	19682	D	1915
PRING			
Ernest	14330	D	1912
PRINGLE			
Agnes	18863	D	1915
Agnes	38550	D	1924
Anita	36244	I	1923
Anita	69632	D	1935
Bella	22625	D	1917
Bella M.	22622	D	1917
Charles Alston	20349	D	1916
Charles E.	63825	D	1933
Chester Thomas	66207	D	1934
Cornelia J.	87675	D	1941
David Waldie	55492	D	1930
Florence	72025	I	1936
James Reid	48004	D	1927
Margaret	1557	D	1906
PRINZ			
Caroline L.	13422	D	1912
PRIOLEY			
Leonie	77817	D	1938
PRIOLO			
Paul	79142	D	1938
Salvatore	18805	D	1915
PRIOR			
Anna L.	85275	D	1940
Helen M.	9148	M	1910
James K.	1243	D	1906
John	46257	I	1927
John L.	14661	D	1912
Katherine	72554	D	1936
Mary	3497	D	1907
Mary	35255	D	1922
Mattie	4782	D	1907
Patrick	24061	D	1918
Toney	69613	D	1935
William H.	83407	D	1940
PRISCO			
Pasquale	39355	I	1924
PRITCHARD			
Frances E.	70078	D	1935
Frederick A.	70079	D	1935
Idona R.	79415	D	1938
Kathryn Fickler	62195	D	1932
Rose Lima	56878	D	1930

NAME	NUMBER	TYPE	YEAR
Samuel H.	52129	D	1929
PRITELLI			
Angelo	3331	D	1907
PROBASCO			
Barbara Sherman	13647	M	1912
George H.	26143	D	1919
PROBST			
Frederick	30947	D	1921
Louise M.	21050	D	1916
Paul August	30947	D	1921
PROCHAZKA			
Frank	1153	D	1906
PROCTER			
Florence M.	32393	D	1921
John	8695	D	1909
Rebecca	29462	D	1920
PROCTOR			
Edward C.	42941	D	1925
Genella	66073	D	1934
Geo. W.	1405	D	1906
Henry J.	78376	D	1938
William Forrest	68063	D	1934
PROEMMEL			
Wilhelmine Johanne	2106	D	1906
PROERES			
Felicite	70940	D	1935
Jacques Emile	62734	D	1932
PROFF			
Hermine F.	11431	D	1911
PROFIT			
James	76485	D	1937
PROFUMO			
Felice	50856	D	1928
Louis J.	25897	D	1918
PROHASKA			
Antoinette	33632	M	1922
Sam	31271	D	1921
PROHN			
Caroline Christine	15295	D	1913
PROKURICA			
Bozo	59008	D	1931
Ivan	58932	M	1931
PROLL			
Conrad	30410	D	1920
Conrad	36903	D	1923
Rudolph L.	51008	D	1928

NAME	NUMBER	TYPE	YEAR
PROMERGOTES			
Stamos	80498	D	1939
PRONGOS			
James	84425	D	1940
PRONZOS			
James	84425	D	1940
PROPFE			
Carl Gustav Theodore	4405	D	1907
Carl Wilhelm	9821	M	1910
Carl Wilhelm	9821	M	1910
Charles	4405	D	1907
Eleanor Jurse	9821	M	1910
Eleanor Jurse	9821	M	1910
PROPPE			
Carl Wilhelm	9821	M	1910
Eleanor Jurse	9821	M	1910
PROPPER			
Adolph	87933	I	1941
Adolph	87999	D	1941
PROPST			
Annie Elizabeth	85721	D	1940
PROSCHOLD			
Henry J.	2059	D	1906
PROSEK			
Edward	6200	D	1908
Emma	57009	D	1930
Eva	50085	D	1928
John	50084	D	1928
Joseph Anton	23277	D	1917
Josephine	43432	D	1926
Marie	56196	D	1930
William	42313	D	1925
PROSOLE			
Richard G.	87074	D	1941
PROSPERI			
Giocomo	57532	I	1930
PROSSER			
Charles M.	3630	M	1907
Edward Grant	69634	D	1935
Mary W.	40407	I	1924
Mary W.	43736	D	1926
Robert H.	50337	D	1928
PROTHEROE			
William H.	955	D	1906
PROTZEL			
Henry S.	53041	M	1929
Jacob	52728	D	1929

NAME	NUMBER	TYPE	YEAR	NAME	NUMBER	TYPE	YEAR	NAME	NUMBER	TYPE	YEAR
PROU				Margaret	65579	D	1933	PUCCI			
Camille	43606	D	1926	Peter	10564	D	1910	Duilio	73103	D	1936
Jean Auguste	123	D	1906	PRUSEIT				Leo Joseph	13672	M	1912
PROUDLEY				Frederick	85953	D	1941	Reno A.	88732	D	1941
Henry W.	86869	D	1941	PRUSSO				Santina	40510	D	1924
PROUSERGUE				Antonio	64734	D	1933	PUCCINELLI			
Leon C.	58483	D	1931	PRUYN				Alberto	77517	M	1938
Louise	52483	D	1929	John Francis	61783	M	1932	Alphonse	77733	D	1938
PROUT				John M.	61782	D	1932	Archimede	19626	D	1915
Annie E.	74958	D	1937	PRUZZO				Archimede	20695	M	1916
PROUTY				Antonio	64734	D	1933	Basilio	30745	D	1920
Fred K.	58783	D	1931	PRYAL				Beatrice	20695	M	1916
PROVENZANO				Andrew	66234	D	1934	Charles	20695	M	1916
Maria	59787	D	1931	George	77654	D	1938	Eleanor Patricia	86891	M	1941
Thomas	88097	D	1941	Georgia	25011	M	1918	Frank	14722	D	1913
PROVIS				Mary Ann	49440	D	1928	Frank	25979	D	1918
Charles Henri	35707	D	1923	PRYDZ				Giuseppe	20697	D	1916
PROVOST				George N.	86964	D	1941	Lorenzo	77623	D	1938
Charlotte E.	74821	D	1937	Helen Emily	53608	M	1929	Louis J.	20695	M	1916
Minnie J.	61935	I	1932	Lawrence Frances	48893	D	1928	Louis Vincent	74390	D	1937
PRUD'HOMME				PRYOR				Norma	20695	M	1916
Delphine Ramona	70666	D	1935	Albert Lawrence	78673	M	1938	Torello	85850	D	1940
John Albert	67782	D	1934	Alfred Edmund	71668	D	1936	Vincenzo	38514	D	1924
Ramona	70666	D	1935	Archibald McKicssack	67231	D	1934	PUCCINI			
PRUDDEN				Augusta May	72639	D	1936	Mabel F.	32	M	1906
Adelia Ann	1432	D	1906	David C.	78471	D	1938	Theresa	32	M	1906
PRUDE				Frank David	35981	M	1923	William	32	M	1906
Emily Laura	77752	D	1938	Gaillard Stoney	35981	M	1923	Wilson	45362	D	1926
Frank, Jr.	77753	D	1938	Irene Tomasek	79105	D	1938	PUCHEU			
PRUDEAUX				Leroy Lipperd	73802	D	1936	Alfred	6889	M	1908
Emily	13752	D	1912	Lorene E.	23057	M	1917	Eugenie	6889	M	1908
PRUDHOMME				Marjorie Louise	78673	M	1938	Jean	6922	D	1908
Francois	16210	D	1913	Theodrick B.	53808	D	1929	Marie	6921	D	1908
PRUETT				PRZYBOROWSKI				Thomas	6889	M	1908
Earle	13448	M	1912	Jacob	75832	D	1937	PUCKHABER			
PRUGH				Josephine	75833	D	1937	David C.	30403	D	1920
Mary Ada	43288	I	1925	PRZYBUROWSKI				Hermann Frederick	63083	D	1932
Torrence	38936	D	1924	Jacob	75832	D	1937	Jacob	82531	D	1939
PRUITT				PRZYSENBEL				Mary E.	12229	D	1911
Elizabeth	61551	D	1932	Alexander	89735	D	1942	Meta	75441	D	1937
Elizabeth	87272	D	1941	PSAILA				William David	43171	D	1925
PRUNTY				Carmela	87639	D	1941	PUE			
Francis Patrick	85219	D	1940	PUBLICOVER				Mary L.	45675	M	1926
John	82590	D	1939	Henrietta	24462	D	1918	Robert A.	45675	M	1926
Kate	2142	D	1906	PUCCETTI				PUENTENER			
Lillian May	85447	D	1940	Alberto	86411	D	1941	Anna	79076	D	1938
								PUGEL			
								Joseph	32936	D	1921

NAME	NUMBER	TYPE	YEAR	NAME	NUMBER	TYPE	YEAR	NAME	NUMBER	TYPE	YEAR
PUGH				Ulysses	83728	I	1940	Mary L.	51181	D	1928
Annie	10676	D	1910	**PULLUM**				**PURINGTON**			
Edwin M.	88388	D	1941	Mary	27993	D	1919	Henrietta Elizabeth	38426	D	1924
Enoch M.	88388	D	1941	**PULOMEROPOULOS**				Jedire M.	21926	D	1916
Francis	15337	M	1913	Harry	74845	I	1937	John M.	21926	D	1916
John	59728	D	1931	Harry	78603	D	1938	**PURLENKY**			
Margaret	63299	D	1933	**PULOMEROPULOS**				Alma Hink	68227	D	1934
Maria	13813	D	1912	Harry	74845	I	1937	Christiana Louise	13577	D	1912
Mary Ada	43288	I	1925	Harry	78603	D	1938	**PURNELL**			
William Henry, Jr.	34221	D	1922	**PULOS**				Alvin J.	74363	D	1937
PUGLIESE				Harry	41725	D	1925	Eva M.	49913	D	1928
Gaetano	47871	D	1927	Harry	41725	D	1925	Frederick	51916	M	1929
Mary	32492	M	1921	**PULS**				Samuel N.	16994	D	1914
Mary B.	32166	D	1921	Armanda	5872	M	1908	Thomas F.	36801	M	1923
Sam	39881	I	1924	**PUMA**				Thomas Frederick	51916	M	1929
PUGLIESI				Michelangelo	72031	D	1936	**PURNER**			
Gaetano	47871	D	1927	**PUNDT**				Henry W.	73249	I	1936
PUHARA				Emil	51870	D	1929	Henry Y.	73249	I	1936
Mitchell J.	57699	D	1931	**PUNNETT**				**PURNHAGEN**			
PUHEK				John M.	89098	D	1942	Anna R.	35318	D	1922
Barbara	52513	D	1929	**PUNTA**				**PURRINGTON**			
Johan	14063	D	1912	Pietro	75875	D	1937	C. W.	21078	D	1916
John	14063	D	1912	**PUNTI**				**PURSCH**			
PUHGUE				Carlo	14245	D	1912	Frank	19052	D	1915
August	26291	D	1919	**PUNZAL**				**PURSEHOUSE**			
PUHR				Marian	75191	M	1937	Richard N.	86558	D	1941
Joseph	53989	I	1929	**PUPPO**				**PURSELL**			
PUIG				Lorenzo	6830	D	1908	Mary E.	74650	D	1937
Frank	25488	D	1918	**PURCELL**				**PURSER**			
PUISSEGUR				James Joseph	69014	D	1935	Edward Thomas	63386	D	1933
Theresa	52134	D	1929	Josephine	47919	D	1927	John	332	D	1906
PUJO				Marie	78452	D	1938	**PURVIS**			
Julien	9038	D	1910	Mary	12583	D	1911	John H.	49975	D	1928
PULASKI				Mary	30437	D	1920	**PUSA**			
Ellen	77902	D	1938	Nora	27175	D	1919	Jacub	58130	D	1931
PULCIFER				Richard	10198	D	1910	**PUTCH**			
Cora M.	77096	D	1937	T. H., Mrs.	47919	D	1927	Philip	74880	D	1937
PULEO				Thomas Henry	49111	D	1928	**PUTHOFF**			
Maria	78865	D	1938	**PURCHASE**				Robert Edmond	88711	M	1941
PULLEN				Violetta H.	47904	D	1927	Thomas Eugene	87145	D	1941
Alfred W.	58056	D	1931	**PURDIE**				**PUTICA**			
Theresa Anna	70014	D	1935	John S.	39650	D	1924	Stevo	33246	D	1922
Theresa Anna	70014	D	1935	**PURDY**				**PUTMAN**			
PULLIAM				Andrew J.	88704	D	1941	Anna	23142	D	1917
Caledonia Clay	44044	M	1926	Frederick A.	65104	D	1933	Franklin W.	21001	D	1916
Harriet Beasley	44044	M	1926	James R.	76845	D	1937				

NAME	NUMBER	TYPE	YEAR
PUTNAM			
Carrie C.	47110	D	1927
Charles	51387	D	1928
Elizabeth W., Sr.	43959	D	1926
Elmer	4142	M	1907
Emily McCoy	84681	D	1940
Fred H.	4803	D	1907
George Choate	57247	M	1930
Helen S.	80224	D	1938
Herbert L.	47308	D	1927
Hildred	3601	M	1907
Howard	4142	M	1907
Ida J.	50285	D	1928
Osgood	26278	D	1919
Robert Harvey	87431	D	1941
Ruth G.	4142	M	1907
William Mason, Jr.	56222	M	1930
PUTTAERT			
Jean Francoi	72336	D	1936
PUTTKAMMER			
Otto	27040	D	1919
PUTTMAN			
Henry	1739	D	1906
PUZINA			
Joseph	50894	D	1928
PUZYBOROWSKI			
Jacob	75832	D	1937
PVADA			
Rafael R.	53281	D	1929
PVOHASKA			
Sam	31271	D	1921
PVORMANN			
John L.	18381	D	1915
PYE			
Alice	16618	I	1914
James	16617	I	1914
John MacGregor	55275	D	1930
PYLE			
Alfred A.	72652	D	1936
Emma C.	49590	D	1928
Ethel Yvonna	29868	M	1920
Grace B.	87873	D	1941
Susan J.	78131	D	1938
William R., Jr.	28260	M	1919
PYNCHON			
Elise K.	66614	D	1934

NAME	NUMBER	TYPE	YEAR
PYNE			
Annabelle	71613	D	1936
Daniel	33564	D	1922
Daniel	45287	M	1926
Gertrude	45287	M	1926
Joseph	45287	M	1926
Margaret E.	31139	D	1921
Mary A.	24370	D	1918
Robert	43859	D	1926
Robert	45287	M	1926
Timothy	57716	D	1931
PYPER			
Henry H.	70516	D	1935
PYROR			
Germaine M.	78743	D	1938
QUACKENBOS			
Mary C.	4612	D	1907
QUACKENBUSH			
Ronald George	29228	M	1920
Thomas M.	10933	D	1910
QUADE			
Helen Bernice	56689	M	1930
QUADRIO			
Mary	88372	D	1941
QUADT			
Emma	76458	D	1937
John	21825	D	1916
QUAGELLI			
Caterina	87284	D	1941
Enrico	56896	D	1930
QUAI			
Kevan Gum	18469	M	1915
QUAID			
Thomas	39300	D	1924
QUAILLE			
Catherine	2740	D	1907
QUALE			
Mary A.	23741	I	1917
Mary A.	23913	D	1918
QUALMAN			
Elizabeth Green	70705	D	1935
Elsie Agnes	19207	M	1915
Florence Mary	19207	M	1915
Frederick H.	845	I	1906
Frederick H.	19089	D	1915

NAME	NUMBER	TYPE	YEAR
QUALTERS			
Patrick	47248	D	1927
Patrick	66640	D	1934
QUAN			
Albert	73775	M	1936
Alberta	73775	M	1936
Betty	73775	M	1936
Chun	73775	M	1936
Ding	73775	M	1936
Dong Hong	83201	M	1940
Dorothy	73775	M	1936
Elsie	73775	M	1936
Harry	73775	M	1936
Hong	36741	D	1923
Jack	37446	M	1923
Jack	73775	M	1936
King	73775	M	1936
Ling	73775	M	1936
Marian	73775	M	1936
May	73775	M	1936
May Yee	60892	D	1932
Me	73775	M	1936
Ming	69508	D	1935
Soon	73775	M	1936
Sun	73775	M	1936
Wing	73775	M	1936
Won	73775	M	1936
Wun Hai	73775	M	1936
Yick	55939	D	1930
QUANDT			
Augusta Marie	86442	D	1941
Frederick	54254	D	1929
Gustav	24445	D	1918
Herbert Louis Theodore	67305	D	1934
Herman	63993	D	1933
QUANG			
Yick	55939	D	1930
QUARE			
Edmund	63080	D	1932
QUARG			
Richard F.	51859	D	1929
QUARLES			
Cromwell B.	57184	I	1930
QUARNSTROM			
Christina	17415	D	1914
QUARRY			
John Albert	50139	D	1928

NAME	NUMBER	TYPE	YEAR
QUARTIER			
Henry	13588	D	1912
QUASC			
Jennie	54107	D	1929
QUASH			
A. C., Mrs.	54107	D	1929
Jennie R.	54107	D	1929
QUAST			
A. C., Mrs.	54107	D	1929
Emma H.	34201	D	1922
Herman Martin	78539	D	1938
Irwin F.	45431	M	1926
Jennie R.	54107	D	1929
QUATI			
Hans	46833	D	1927
QUAY			
John Barton	53702	D	1929
Joseph M.	24218	D	1918
QUAYLE			
Mary A.	58018	D	1931
QUE			
Lee	38425	D	1924
Leung	19121	D	1915
QUEALY			
Buster	43080	M	1925
J. Ambrose	43080	M	1925
Susie Jane	43079	M	1925
QUEEN			
Charles Louis	16455	D	1913
Joseph B.	15473	D	1913
Louis T.	86868	D	1941
Richard Edward	38582	D	1924
QUEENAN			
John	2250	D	1906
Margaret	49226	D	1928
QUEENEN			
Margaret	49226	D	1928
QUEIROLO			
Giovanni	41503	D	1925
Giovanni	79532	D	1938
Giuseppe	83017	I	1940
Giuseppe	83091	D	1940
John	62216	D	1932
Pietro	2693	D	1907
QUELLMALZ			
Babetta	4432	D	1907
Charles	14609	D	1912

NAME	NUMBER	TYPE	YEAR
QUEN			
Ng Kai	63739	M	1933
QUENEL			
Marie	74865	D	1937
QUESADA			
Alice	12492	D	1911
QUEVEDO			
Alfred G.	28832	D	1920
Frances G.	77886	I	1938
Frances G.	78256	D	1938
QUEVILLON			
Azilda	52096	D	1929
QUEYREL			
Ferdinand	16752	D	1914
QUEYROULET			
Marie	14521	I	1912
QUHRE			
Minnie	13045	M	1912
QUI			
Ho	6327	M	1908
Moy	63719	D	1933
QUICK			
Edith Evans	20747	M	1916
J. Earl	23531	D	1917
James R.	19615	D	1915
James R.	20747	M	1916
John W.	12979	D	1912
Margretta Elizabeth	20747	M	1916
Mark W.	45556	D	1926
Mary A. P.	42709	D	1925
Mary Gwynn	20747	M	1916
Susanna P.	72286	D	1936
QUIGLEY			
Anna M.	13163	D	1912
Dennis	53210	D	1929
Doothy Marie	48589	M	1927
Edward	2546	D	1906
George H.	35734	D	1923
Helen Mar	39456	D	1924
James	71449	D	1936
John B.	19332	D	1915
John F.	82345	D	1939
John J.	30368	D	1920
John M.	23344	D	1917
Julia Herzo	54818	D	1930
Lily M.	70778	D	1935
Margaret E.	5565	D	1908

NAME	NUMBER	TYPE	YEAR
Mary Theresa	72967	I	1936
Michael	14974	D	1913
Nellie M.	70778	D	1935
Patrick	14437	D	1912
Patrick J.	38091	D	1924
Raymond H.	47545	I	1927
Thomas	60845	D	1932
Thomas D.	38678	D	1924
QUILICI			
Adolph	52069	I	1929
Alfonse	4887	D	1907
Amedeo O.	84822	I	1940
Anania	4169	D	1907
Inez	6253	M	1908
Ulisse	84440	D	1940
QUILL			
Anthony	20440	D	1916
John	56674	D	1930
Michael	33789	D	1922
QUILLE			
Michael	33789	D	1922
QUILLEN			
Edward J.	82559	D	1939
Ila Marjorie	70372	M	1935
QUILLINAN			
James	7766	D	1909
QUIMBY			
Bertha P.	28780	M	1920
Parchust L.	28780	M	1920
William F.	28780	M	1920
QUIN			
Michael	47429	D	1927
QUINBY			
Albert O.	17733	D	1914
Carmen	22854	D	1917
Carmen	22854	D	1917
Sarah Folger	85973	D	1941
QUINCHE			
Priscilla E.	52866	D	1929
QUINE			
Elizabeth	23357	D	1917
QUINLAN			
Anna Martha	2272	D	1906
Claire Marie	80874	M	1939
Dennis C.	3454	D	1907
Eugenia	82895	D	1939
Frank	89654	D	1942

NAME	NUMBER	TYPE	YEAR	NAME	NUMBER	TYPE	YEAR	NAME	NUMBER	TYPE	YEAR
Gladys	24786	M	1918	Edith Katherine	86046	I	1941	Patrick P.	32739	D	1921
Helen	89237	D	1942	Elizabeth	55350	I	1930	Patrick W.	55365	D	1930
James	11185	M	1911	Elizabeth Pyle	58335	D	1931	Peter	1308	D	1906
James C.	55552	D	1930	Francis A.	68176	D	1934	Peter	6751	D	1908
Jerome	11185	M	1911	Frank J.	73633	D	1936	Peter	19997	D	1915
John	11185	M	1911	Frank Lawrence	40592	D	1924	Peter	20053	D	1915
John	62698	D	1932	Frank Regis	28347	D	1919	Peter F.	68432	D	1934
John Cotter	84707	D	1940	George W.	75809	D	1937	Robert Louis	82404	M	1939
John H.	61864	D	1932	Hattie H.	34480	D	1922	Rose	1568	D	1906
M. M.	19891	D	1915	Hattie H.	85184	D	1940	Sarah	10442	I	1910
Martin	29653	D	1920	Helene G.	29904	D	1920	Teresa Ann	69566	I	1935
Mary Ann	18504	D	1915	Henry	62842	D	1932	Thomas	6933	D	1908
Mary Catherine	34992	D	1922	Herbert Charles	28406	M	1919	Thomas J.	28974	D	1920
Mary L.	65705	D	1933	James	42018	D	1925	Walter	19220	M	1915
Michael	47429	D	1927	James	55447	D	1930	Walter E.	51965	D	1929
Nora	87689	I	1941	James	53635	D	1929	William	77831	D	1938
Patricia Ann	80873	M	1939	John	3461	D	1907	William E.	19711	D	1915
Richard D.	80872	D	1939	John	28694	D	1920	William J.	48202	D	1927
Richard John	80874	M	1939	John	30998	D	1921	William J., Jr.	25202	M	1918
Sarah	9402	D	1910	John	39907	D	1924	William Thomas	57799	D	1931
Thomas J.	6359	D	1908	John	50649	D	1928	Winnie	49961	D	1928
Timothy	36353	D	1923	John	56388	D	1930	**QUINNE**			
Vincent	11185	M	1911	John E.	28512	D	1919	Margaret	8618	D	1909
William	11185	M	1911	John Francis	69782	D	1935	**QUINOLO**			
William	62774	D	1932	John J.	20743	D	1916	Leslie Eldred	38647	D	1924
William	69286	D	1935	Lucy G.	59991	D	1931	**QUINT**			
William S.	18590	D	1915	Margaret	23579	D	1917	Belinda W.	29104	D	1920
QUINLEY				Margaret	41076	D	1925	**QUINTARD**			
Sabina DelCarmen	22854	D	1917	Maria	11067	D	1911	Arthur Judson	27473	D	1919
QUINLIN				Mary	16933	D	1914	Judson Paye	30323	M	1920
Michael	47429	D	1927	Mary	24183	D	1918	**QUINTINELLA**			
William G.	45985	D	1926	Mary	25381	D	1918	Maria	40068	D	1924
QUINLIVAN				Mary	32754	D	1921	**QUINTON**			
Michael	47429	D	1927	Mary	50414	D	1928	Frances	17763	M	1914
QUINN				Mary A.	19063	D	1915	Henry	47433	D	1927
Alice Mary	25202	M	1918	Mary A.	19922	D	1915	Imelda	17763	M	1914
Anna	68550	D	1934	Mary Anna	56992	D	1930	John	6954	D	1908
Annie	83709	D	1940	Mary Cecelia	37196	D	1923	Marcella	17763	M	1914
Annie M.	56992	D	1930	Matilda C.	35600	D	1922	Rose	17763	M	1914
Catherine Elizabeth	36439	D	1923	Michael	11634	I	1911	Walter	17763	M	1914
Catherine L.	69623	D	1935	Michael	33500	D	1922	**QUIRALO**			
Charles	19211	D	1915	Michael	38737	D	1924	John	79532	D	1938
Charles	19220	M	1915	Michael	47429	D	1927	**QUIRK**			
Charles J.	22335	M	1917	Michael Edward	38083	D	1924	Anna May	80458	D	1939
Charles J.	22789	D	1917	Michael H.	3549	D	1907	Catherine	18872	D	1915
Cornelius J.	22287	D	1917	Michael H.	37477	D	1923	Christopher	70144	D	1935
Dorothy	25622	M	1918	Mollie E.	73867	D	1936	Dennis	13178	D	1912
Edith C.	25202	M	1918	Nellie	77943	D	1938	Edward	42913	D	1925
				Patrick	10443	I	1910				

NAME	NUMBER	TYPE	YEAR
Edward William	38577	D	1924
George R.	67279	D	1934
James	12646	D	1911
John J.	9884	D	1910
John Joseph	21169	I	1916
John Joseph	24307	D	1918
Joseph R.	48621	D	1927
Lois Grace	40404	M	1924
Martin P.	49326	D	1928
Nellie	67472	I	1934
Nellie	80477	D	1939
Peter	24732	D	1918
Peter F.	1096	D	1906
Thomas Bernard	56995	D	1930
Viola Ruth	67422	M	1934
William J.	58997	I	1931
William P.	84755	I	1940
QUISLING			
Frank G.	59275	D	1931
Ingeborg	61424	D	1932
QUIVEY			
Robert Willard	23789	M	1917
QUOIA			
Chew Bing	1401	D	1906
QUON			
Hong	36741	D	1923
QUONG			
Chon	61543	D	1932
Choy	61543	D	1932
Gin K.	50975	D	1928
Her	50511	D	1928
Leong Chew	55225	M	1930
Wong	32681	D	1921
Woo Do	77511	D	1938
QURRALO			
Giovanni	79532	D	1938
RAAB			
Anna Hortense	35504	D	1922
Frederick William	14300	D	1912
Hortense Anna	42201	D	1925
RAABE			
John	54699	D	1930
Leon S.	20712	D	1916
RAAEN			
Lawrence J.	63871	I	1933
RAAKA			
Gertrude	86515	D	1941

NAME	NUMBER	TYPE	YEAR
RAAS			
Albert	28	D	1906
Andre	55546	D	1930
Kate	25278	D	1918
RABB			
Henry	79172	M	1938
RABBEN			
Sophia	73339	D	1936
RABBITT			
Louise	83647	D	1940
RABER			
John	61500	D	1932
RABINOWITZ			
Morris	30617	D	1920
RABJOHN			
Ellen	58537	D	1931
RABLIN			
Thomas H.	1182	D	1906
William	36977	D	1923
RABORG			
Cornilia C.	62152	D	1932
Cornilia C.	62152	D	1932
RACHLIN			
Samuel	89644	D	1942
RACIK			
Ferdinand F.	49456	D	1928
Harriette V.	69605	M	1935
Harriette V.	69655	M	1935
Mary	47706	D	1927
Robert H.	69604	M	1935
RACKERBY			
Joseph Henry	28522	D	1919
RACKERLEY			
John	15056	D	1913
RACKLIFFE			
Carl	63940	D	1933
RACLET			
Victorine M.	49855	D	1928
RACOUILLAT			
Albert Numa	11777	D	1911
George A.	71123	D	1935
Ida Mae	74172	D	1936
Mae	74172	D	1936
RADBRUCH			
Herman A.	85871	D	1940

NAME	NUMBER	TYPE	YEAR
RADCLIFF			
Ralph Leon	27080	M	1919
RADCLIFFE			
Gertrude A.	48145	D	1927
Peter E.	49726	D	1928
RADCOVICH			
John F.	55849	M	1930
RADCZEWSKY			
Matilda	58940	D	1931
RADDICH			
Kathryn Margaret	15694	M	1913
Lena	15693	D	1913
RADELFINGER			
Fred Albert	64319	D	1933
Sara Frances	82242	D	1939
RADEMACHER			
Amelia L.	83470	D	1940
Friedrich	33004	D	1921
John H.	88799	D	1941
Sylvester	68006	D	1934
RADEMANN			
Henry Charles	9540	D	1910
RADER			
Christopher J.	4281	D	1907
James Torbit	45916	D	1926
James William	25251	M	1918
Lillian P.	72230	D	1936
Philip Dwight	25251	M	1918
Robert L.	77917	D	1938
RADETICH			
Dane	44536	D	1926
RADFORD			
Francis A.	26064	D	1919
June C.	79225	M	1938
Price	65948	D	1933
Sarah	9402	D	1910
Walter R.	89226	D	1942
RADGES			
Ernest	46663	D	1927
RADGESKY			
Elizabeth	13925	M	1912
Louis D.	2134	D	1906
Marcelle	13926	M	1912
RADICH			
Milton Edward	53643	D	1929

NAME	NUMBER	TYPE	YEAR	NAME	NUMBER	TYPE	YEAR	NAME	NUMBER	TYPE	YEAR
RADIGONDA				**RADRIGUES**				**RAFFAELLO**			
Pasquale	89416	D	1942	Alberto	34368	D	1922	Petri	36829	D	1923
RADIN				**RADSTON**				**RAFFELLO**			
Henry	53246	D	1929	Julius	44963	D	1926	Tony	59253	D	1931
RADINOV				**RADSZWILL**				**RAFFEO**			
Paul	78973	D	1938	William C., Jr.	33798	M	1922	Antonino	59253	D	1931
RADINOVICH				**RADY**				**RAFFERTY**			
Mary Francis	73252	D	1936	Philip	40083	D	1924	Ann	23567	D	1917
RADINSKY				**RAE**				Hugh Edward	43198	D	1925
David	28171	D	1919	Alexander P.	77812	D	1938	John	2826	D	1907
RADIUS				Alice	40225	I	1924	John Henry	76267	M	1937
Walter A.	61461	D	1932	Anna	48739	D	1927	John J.	76264	D	1937
RADKE				Annich	48739	D	1927	Marilyn Frances	76267	M	1937
August Herman	77701	D	1938	Annie Teresa	48739	D	1927	Mary C.	75606	D	1937
Barbara	31988	D	1921	Margery	12273	I	1911	Ogden	33481	D	1922
Delbert W.	81541	D	1939	Patrick H.	3030	D	1907	William	50473	I	1928
Henry Frederich	34154	D	1922	Robert	10835	D	1910	**RAFFETTO**			
Mary T.	44193	D	1926	**RAEDWIN**				Andrea	1285	D	1906
RADLOFF				James W.	1959	D	1906	Angelo Giuseppe	65688	D	1933
Bernard P.	82808	I	1939	**RAEMER**				Angelo J.	65688	D	1933
Bernard Patrick	48125	I	1927	Joe	59306	D	1931	Carlo Emanuele	76869	D	1937
RADNER				**RAETHER**				Willie	3967	M	1907
Moris	58719	D	1931	Harry A.	85522	D	1940	**RAFFO**			
RADNICH				**RAFAEL**				Enrico	56373	D	1930
Stephen A.	71569	I	1936	Clifford	46697	M	1927	Francis John	28528	D	1919
Stephen A.	81587	D	1939	Frank	71435	D	1936	Giovanni	25942	I	1918
RADOJCIC				Ina B.	46470	D	1927	Giovanni	59687	I	1931
Nastasija Dragutinovic	80521	D	1939	Joseph Enos	37299	D	1923	Giuseppe	6974	D	1908
RADONICH				Julius	28721	D	1920	Lena	62324	D	1932
John	40490	D	1924	Manuel E.	28275	D	1919	Lina	62324	D	1932
RADONOVICH				Mary	31870	D	1921	Luigi	7055	D	1909
John N.	54766	D	1930	Polsenia	45273	D	1926	Mary	15289	D	1913
RADOVAN				Russell	46697	M	1927	Raymond	31986	M	1921
Louise Madeline	52683	D	1929	Russell	74426	I	1937	Salvatore	56657	D	1930
RADOVICH				Samuel	54990	D	1930	Victor	31986	M	1921
Eugene S.	3478	M	1907	**RAFAESKY**				Vittorio	43739	D	1926
George Spiro	87694	D	1941	Marie	53953	D	1929	**RAFTERY**			
John L.	50760	D	1928	**RAFAILOVICH**				Catherine	25731	D	1918
Katarina	62181	D	1932	N. M.	7645	D	1909	Thomas J.	70749	I	1935
Lucca	1804	D	1906	**RAFELD**				**RAFTIS**			
Mitchell	81212	D	1939	Henrietta	19970	D	1915	Demos P.	13000	D	1912
Nicholas	45894	D	1926	**RAFF**				Kostantinos P.	12999	D	1912
Nicholas	86219	D	1941	Jose	27189	D	1919	**RAGAN**			
Peter	31554	D	1921	**RAFFA**				Alice Loretta	77465	D	1938
Vivia A.	3478	M	1907	Domenico	52446	D	1929	Denis Francis	21507	D	1916
				Guiseppina	90000	D	1942	Dorothy Duchran	88678	D	1941
				Josephine	90000	D	1942	Jeremiah W.	82748	D	1939

NAME	NUMBER	TYPE	YEAR
Martin	2239	D	1906
Mary L.	20991	I	1916
Rebecca M.	2055	M	1906
Rebecca M.	74399	I	1937
RAGGAS			
Vincenti A.	26465	D	1919
RAGGHIANTI			
Gino	22711	D	1917
RAGGI			
Dora	3102	D	1907
Giacomo	66162	D	1934
James	66162	D	1934
RAGGIO			
Anna	31463	I	1921
Antonio	69433	D	1935
Antonio Luigi	79032	D	1938
Charles	17799	D	1914
Edmund	11338	M	1911
Elvira	11338	M	1911
Gio Battista	7036	D	1909
Inez	31464	M	1921
Luigi	14764	D	1913
Madalena	22048	D	1916
Mary Agnes	56308	D	1930
Rosa	63747	D	1933
Teresa	3415	D	1907
Unieda	11338	M	1911
RAGLAN			
Tom	15182	D	1913
RAGLAND			
Delia	57787	D	1931
Geraldine	57787	D	1931
Lucy C.	62799	D	1932
Rene Chastaine	62446	D	1932
Rufus E.	56611	D	1930
RAGSDALE			
Catherine A.	62365	D	1932
Francis A.	39914	D	1924
RAGUSH			
Andro	30292	M	1920
RAGUSIN			
Marco	21960	D	1916
RAHAM			
Emma Christine	53356	D	1929
Lewie P.	26195	D	1919
RAHE			
John Joseph	18624	D	1915

NAME	NUMBER	TYPE	YEAR
RAHLVES			
Anna	64348	D	1933
August D.	36700	D	1923
RAHM			
Oscar	46818	D	1927
RAHMER			
Mary G.	66538	D	1934
RAHN			
Nathan C.	69156	D	1935
RAHSSKOPFF			
Carl	32804	D	1921
RAHT			
August	22092	D	1917
RAHWYLER			
Charles Gotfried	16859	D	1914
RAIBLE			
Godfrey	8698	D	1909
Gottfried	8698	D	1909
RAICEVICH			
Antoinette	7744	D	1909
Lydia	3041	M	1907
Maria	3041	M	1907
Peter	3041	M	1907
Rudolph	3041	M	1907
Spiro, Jr.	3041	M	1907
RAIL			
Lucretia E.	44141	D	1926
RAILEY			
Oliver R.	69944	D	1935
RAILLIE			
Catharine	16577	D	1914
RAILTON			
Edward W.	884	D	1906
Helen H.	35951	D	1923
RAILY			
Margaret	2821	D	1907
RAIMONDI			
Salvatore	69818	D	1935
Vincenzo	65440	D	1933
RAIMONDO			
Giovanni	29985	I	1920
RAINBOW			
Marshall Dean	79554	D	1938
RAINER			
Camille	74727	D	1937

NAME	NUMBER	TYPE	YEAR
RAINES			
William Kent	40136	M	1924
RAINEY			
Ella C.	8358	D	1909
Mary A.	9637	D	1910
William Austin	76779	D	1937
William Sibet	3243	D	1907
RAINFORD			
Alma Dolores	55562	M	1930
Mary	55765	D	1930
RAINIER			
Camille	74727	D	1937
RAINIERI			
Francesco	68117	I	1934
RAININEN			
Daaved	38150	D	1924
RAINOW			
Lucinda T.	18375	D	1915
RAINS			
Cora Jane	51729	D	1928
Fred	40324	D	1924
Mary E.	69959	D	1935
RAINSBURY			
John	41786	D	1925
John	41786	D	1925
Miller Anker	63974	D	1933
RAINSFORD			
Edmond	48365	D	1927
Maurice Joseph	84054	D	1940
Patrick J.	69962	D	1935
RAINWATER			
Geroge E.	59282	I	1931
RAISCH			
Emma Valentine	87837	D	1941
Gottfried	29262	D	1920
Laura	74538	D	1937
RAISS			
Carl	81827	D	1939
RAKICH			
Rose	30021	D	1920
RAKOFSKY			
Helena	40817	D	1925
RALMER			
Joe	59306	D	1931
RALPH			
Frank	69493	D	1935

NAME	NUMBER	TYPE	YEAR
James Thomas	27425	D	1919
John I.	74326	D	1937
Rutherford B.	62523	D	1932
William Thomas	29368	D	1920
RALSTON			
Henry R.	17512	D	1914
Margaret	27451	M	1919
Maud Amilie	89881	D	1942
William C.	27930	D	1919
William C.	39455	D	1924
RAMACIOTTI			
Richard	64804	D	1933
RAMAGANA			
Clara	71130	D	1935
RAMARI			
Selina	45523	D	1926
Selinda	45523	D	1926
RAMAZZINA			
Giacomo	60247	D	1931
Luisa	29622	D	1920
RAMBAUD			
Clemence	16889	D	1914
Joseph	39263	D	1924
RAMBERG			
Charles	69367	D	1935
Gustaf S.	13445	D	1912
RAMBKE			
David F.	31372	D	1921
RAMBO			
Edward B.	1364	D	1906
RAMDOHR			
Elizabeth Jane	12723	D	1911
RAMEL			
Juan	58324	D	1931
RAMELLA			
Joseph	62582	D	1932
RAMELLI			
Alessio	68886	D	1935
David	86560	D	1941
Marie A.	72160	D	1936
Philip	68886	D	1935
RAMETTA			
Sam	39993	D	1924
RAMEY			
Noble Ralph	74619	D	1937
Ralph Noble	74619	D	1937

NAME	NUMBER	TYPE	YEAR
RAMIRES			
Margarito M.	70294	D	1935
RAMIREZ			
Jose	67893	D	1934
Lillian Marie	63529	M	1933
RAMISON			
Rosanna	445	D	1906
RAMLOT			
Emile	1118	D	1906
RAMM			
Elizabeth Anne	84929	M	1940
Ida K.	28464	D	1919
Johanna	14272	D	1912
Johanne M.	38082	D	1924
Matilda	21539	D	1916
RAMMEL			
Ferdinand	20546	I	1916
RAMON			
Anselmo	7372	D	1909
George	25465	D	1918
RAMONDA			
Giuseppe	72666	D	1936
RAMONDO			
Giovanni	13981	D	1912
RAMOS			
Joseph C.	71336	D	1936
Manuel	48823	D	1927
RAMPONE			
Filippo	69250	D	1935
RAMSAUER			
Albert	80239	D	1939
RAMSAY			
Martha Estelle	7823	D	1909
RAMSDELL			
Drucilla C.	5927	D	1908
Fred W.	14287	D	1912
Harry Vinton	30579	D	1920
RAMSDEN			
Thomas	11541	D	1911
Thomas	27829	D	1919
RAMSELIUS			
Adoldp	33263	D	1922
RAMSELL			
Charlotte J.	30972	D	1921
RAMSEY			
Edith	84066	D	1940

NAME	NUMBER	TYPE	YEAR
Frank	88157	D	1941
Helen Jane	36490	D	1923
Mamie	72180	D	1936
RAMSFORD			
Edward	31581	D	1921
RAMSPOTT			
Anna	78790	D	1938
Joseph	57595	D	1931
RAMUSSEN			
Anton	65659	D	1933
RANCATORE			
Felice	40440	D	1924
Marie	51472	D	1928
RANCKE			
Adolph Emanuel	23471	D	1917
Hermann M.	25707	D	1918
RAND			
Willis E.	55910	D	1930
RANDALL			
Abbie L.	6755	D	1908
Billy	71222	M	1935
Charles A.	89641	M	1942
Frank S.	47690	D	1927
Frederick Howard	80675	D	1939
Harold B.	69914	I	1935
Horatio C.	27501	D	1919
Horatio C.	30174	M	1920
John B.	30294	D	1920
Laurence George	5706	M	1908
Lawrence George	5706	M	1908
Louise	71222	M	1935
Mary Elizabeth	59349	D	1931
Merriam Adell	75425	D	1937
Richard W.	48523	M	1927
Robert	83713	M	1940
William C.	37032	D	1923
William Edgar	5706	M	1908
William H.	60967	D	1932
RANDANICH			
Mitchell	81212	D	1939
RANDELL			
Gertrude Kellogg	46047	D	1926
Hannah	16700	I	1914
Jacob	41202	D	1925
Joseph	41202	D	1925
Julia G.	46047	D	1926
Julia Kellogg	46047	D	1926

Key: D = death; M = minor; I = incompetent

NAME	NUMBER	TYPE	YEAR
Leo Frederick	41172	M	1925
Margaret J.	17149	D	1914
William W.	45952	D	1926
RANDHAHN			
A. N.	65578	D	1933
H.	65578	D	1933
Henry	6052	D	1908
Richard	76339	D	1937
RANDIG			
Herman K.	53109	D	1929
Hermann C.	53109	D	1929
Hulda	51546	D	1928
RANDO			
Silvestro	49765	D	1928
RANDOL			
James Butterworth	342	D	1906
RANDOLPH			
B. W.	74662	D	1937
Beacher	74662	D	1937
Beatrix	64728	D	1933
Edgar	77994	M	1938
Frank H.	3252	D	1907
Georgie Anna	60888	D	1932
Hiram	26811	D	1919
John W.	45622	D	1926
Mary McIntire	76199	I	1937
Wallace H.	74664	M	1937
RANDOW			
Henry	34763	D	1922
Karl H.	34763	D	1922
RANEY			
Phoebe	63821	I	1933
RANFT			
Henry Andrew	57598	D	1931
RANIERI			
Enrico	78041	I	1938
RANISIO			
Antoine	31486	D	1921
RANKEN			
Augustus	28140	M	1919
Augustus J.	26601	D	1919
Bridget	23050	D	1917
Geraldine	28140	M	1919
Minnie E.	36051	I	1923
William	28140	M	1919
RANKIN			
Beverly	43461	M	1926

NAME	NUMBER	TYPE	YEAR
Birdie	30729	D	1920
Clara B.	23440	D	1917
Cora Isabella	18376	D	1915
Ellen P.	52257	D	1929
Elsie M.	43615	D	1926
Fred D., Mrs.	42788	D	1925
Gertrude L.	25726	D	1918
Joseph James	74287	D	1937
Lillie Louisa	42788	D	1925
Lilliian W.	42788	D	1925
Louise	26637	D	1919
Louise	42788	D	1925
Phebe	46882	D	1927
Richard F.	43461	M	1926
Robert	85265	D	1940
Sarah	18583	D	1915
RANNIE			
Alexander	49072	D	1928
RANNON			
George	25465	D	1918
RANSFORD			
Edmond	48365	D	1927
John	38900	D	1924
RANSKE			
Bell	68309	D	1934
Jutta Bell	68309	D	1934
RANSOHOFF			
Joan	86808	D	1941
Leopold	23812	D	1918
Rosalie	21874	D	1916
RANSOM			
Allan	32695	D	1921
Caroline White	38674	D	1924
Ethel Pearl	56600	I	1930
Ethel Pearl	60800	D	1932
Lily L.	63899	D	1933
Mary Aurelia	68991	D	1935
Tom W.	38129	D	1924
RANSON			
Thomas E.	57536	I	1930
RANZONI			
Louisa	19882	D	1915
RANZULO			
Martin	25390	D	1918
RAPALEE			
Mary I.	89312	D	1942

NAME	NUMBER	TYPE	YEAR
RAPER			
Alfred P.	74843	D	1937
Nellie E.	81369	D	1939
Nellie Hollaren	81369	D	1939
RAPETANOS			
Chris	14254	D	1912
RAPHAEL			
Benjamin B.	80805	D	1939
Bertha	78836	D	1938
Bertha Braham	19144	D	1915
Edward J.	1778	M	1906
Elisha Ernest	44393	I	1926
Hannah	55175	D	1930
Harry Irving	20562	M	1916
Henrietta	19970	D	1915
Isaac	1920	D	1906
Louise	2784	D	1907
Myer	47419	D	1927
Nat	22866	D	1917
Nathan	37478	D	1923
Norman L.	80015	M	1938
Robert	11486	D	1911
Samuel	54990	D	1930
Sarah	72200	D	1936
RAPHELD			
Jacob L.	35215	D	1922
RAPKEN			
Elizabeth B.	61311	D	1932
Joshua D.	70433	D	1935
Moses A.	43435	D	1926
Ruth Elizabeth	25453	M	1918
RAPOSA			
Louis	48954	D	1928
RAPOZO			
Alfred	72874	M	1936
George	72874	M	1936
RAPP			
Caroline	51094	D	1928
Frank	49632	D	1928
George	17583	D	1914
Helena	54503	D	1929
Johanna	33260	D	1922
John	6598	D	1908
June	54503	D	1929
Louis	3154	D	1907
Wilhelmina	73234	D	1936

Key: D = death; M = minor; I = incompetent

NAME	NUMBER	TYPE	YEAR	NAME	NUMBER	TYPE	YEAR	NAME	NUMBER	TYPE	YEAR
RAPPE				Arthur	84605	D	1940	**RATCLIFFE**			
Mary L.	12153	D	1911	Carl	26248	D	1919	Winifred	11893	D	1911
RAPPLE				Catherine	34298	I	1922	**RATERMANN**			
John W.	21054	D	1916	Christian	33044	D	1921	Michael K.	12858	D	1912
RAPS				Christian	79996	D	1938	**RATHBONE**			
Rose	78758	D	1938	Dorathea	13979	D	1912	Anna F.	17839	D	1914
RAPSO				Elmer Andrew	67930	D	1934	Augusta	6700	M	1908
Paul	16937	D	1914	Gertrude B.	55929	D	1930	Jared L.	8787	D	1909
RARIFT				Gertrude Doris	61101	M	1932	Maria Alejandra	16474	D	1913
Henry Andrew	57598	D	1931	Henry A.	48514	D	1927	**RATHBUN**			
RARIG				Ida	65435	D	1933	Harry C.	20785	D	1916
A. K.	42355	D	1925	Jens	11927	D	1911	Robert Packer	49958	D	1928
RASCH				Jens P.	9251	D	1910	**RATHGIESER**			
Carle E.	18593	D	1915	John	1864	D	1906	Eugenia	67207	D	1934
RASCHE				Lucille	79422	I	1938	**RATHJE**			
Gus	43832	D	1926	Mariane C.	14944	D	1913	Albertina	77413	D	1938
RASCHEN				Matilda	21757	I	1916	August	22926	D	1917
Eloisa F.	48569	D	1927	Peter	33565	D	1922	**RATHJEN**			
Lueder	31805	D	1921	Peter	58596	I	1931	Frieda	79484	D	1938
Margarethe	29683	D	1920	Petrea	8722	I	1909	**RATHJENS**			
Sueder	31805	D	1921	Rasmus	68054	D	1934	Peter F.	49834	D	1928
RASCHKE				Rasmus	69054	D	1935	**RATHMANN**			
Gus	43832	D	1926	Robert John	61101	M	1932	Peter J.	53426	D	1929
Herman W. L.	51074	D	1928	Rosalie Marie Sophie	89116	D	1942	**RATHY**			
RASEHORN				William	45006	D	1926	Stephen	48522	D	1927
Harry David	33487	D	1922	William A.	68895	D	1935	**RATIGAN**			
Karen	33935	D	1922	**RASO**				Edward	12167	D	1911
RASHALL				Atilius	59917	I	1931	Kate	51583	D	1928
Morris H.	69711	D	1935	Frank	33596	D	1922	Mary	28740	D	1920
RASHATNECOFF				**RASOR**				Mary	78946	D	1938
Johar M.	76343	D	1937	David Walter	34655	D	1922	William Christy	28739	D	1920
RASHTON				**RASORE**				**RATLIFF**			
Charles S.	66597	M	1934	Louis S.	58604	D	1931	Alice	26599	D	1919
RASK				**RASPILLER**				Bessie Brown	28834	I	1920
Emilda	32181	M	1921	Marie Louise	44859	D	1926	**RATNER**			
James	32181	M	1921	**RASSETTO**				Bertha	82893	D	1939
RASKIN				Bartolomeo	63387	D	1933	Hyman M.	69528	D	1935
Virginia	86374	D	1941	**RAST**				**RATONDA**			
Virginia	87146	D	1941	Marie	12864	D	1912	Nicola	24599	I	1918
RASMUSEN				**RASTEDT**				**RATOWSKY**			
Rasmus	68054	D	1934	Gustav	22225	D	1917	Julia	25442	I	1918
RASMUSON				**RASTLER**				**RATSCHAT**			
Andrew	25715	D	1918	Mariana	84453	M	1940	Julius	44539	D	1926
RASMUSSEN				**RASUMOFF**				**RATSHAT**			
Alice	56265	M	1930	Paul	60212	D	1931	Julius	44539	D	1926
Arthur	38604	D	1924	**RATALJ**							
				Mieka	38487	M	1924				

NAME	NUMBER	TYPE	YEAR
RATTARO			
Gioseppina	85508	D	1940
RATTENBURY			
Lavinia L.	34053	D	1922
RATTI			
Mary	57562	M	1931
RATTIGAN			
Mary	78946	D	1938
RATTO			
Antone	13909	D	1912
Antonio	13909	D	1912
Bernardina	48915	D	1928
Carlotta	15851	M	1913
David	1400	M	1906
Domenico	19517	D	1915
Eugene	27638	M	1919
Federico	35254	D	1922
Florence	27638	M	1919
Francesco	40106	D	1924
G. B.	79049	D	1938
George W.	52461	D	1929
Giambatista	79049	D	1938
Giovanni B.	60182	D	1931
Ida	1400	M	1906
John	1400	M	1906
John	30971	D	1921
Joseph	15851	M	1913
Laura B.	81199	D	1939
May A.	52999	D	1929
Minnie M.	36037	D	1923
Nicola	20872	D	1916
O. M.	21639	D	1916
Otto	27637	D	1919
Palmira	1400	M	1906
Rose	15851	M	1913
Rosie T.	84850	D	1940
Stefano	15851	M	1913
Stefano	32365	D	1921
RATYE			
Angelo	68500	D	1934
RATZER			
Ella Marie	36071	M	1923
Elsa Gerda	36071	M	1923
Ernst Gottlob	36071	M	1923
Ewald Reinhard	36071	M	1923
Hilmar Friedrich	36071	M	1923
Johann Martin	36071	M	1923
Kurt	36071	M	1923

NAME	NUMBER	TYPE	YEAR
Oscar F.	34402	D	1922
Paul Otto	36071	M	1923
Werner Karl	36071	M	1923
RAU			
Benjamin F.	83511	D	1940
John F.	45960	D	1926
Sophie	18545	D	1915
Stephen S.	47090	D	1927
RAUBINGER			
Louise	35388	D	1922
RAUCCI			
Frances	39059	M	1924
RAUCH			
Jacob	18092	D	1914
John Henry	1420	D	1906
Pauline	42119	D	1925
Sohie	21889	D	1916
RAUCHFUSS			
Otto	25311	D	1918
RAUEN			
Rudolph P.	89291	D	1942
RAUER			
J. J.	87276	D	1941
RAUH			
Annie	26516	D	1919
RAUHAUT			
Pauline	70202	D	1935
RAUHUT			
Cecil	69467	D	1935
Christiane	12188	D	1911
RAULET			
Charles Marie	2540	D	1906
Rosalie	40762	D	1925
RAUM			
George	34904	D	1922
RAURO			
Thomas	52521	D	1929
RAUSCH			
Elisabeth	32710	I	1921
Elisabeth	88999	D	1942
John	3248	D	1907
Pauline	42119	D	1925
Paulita	42119	D	1925
Sohie	21889	D	1916
RAUSCHER			
Ferdinand	66104	D	1934

NAME	NUMBER	TYPE	YEAR
RAUSCHKOLB			
Anna	12561	D	1911
Friedrick	7218	I	1909
RAUSCHKOLD			
Friedrich	717	D	1906
RAUSH			
Paula	42119	D	1925
RAVA			
Celestino	83239	I	1940
RAVANI			
Guiseppina	56012	D	1930
Henry J.	84348	D	1940
Josephine	56012	D	1930
Maria Josepina	56012	D	1930
Richard Eustace	9422	D	1910
Sebastian	36663	D	1923
RAVANNI			
Maria	834	D	1906
RAVANO			
Louis	82939	D	1939
RAVASCHIO			
Domenich Francesco	88752	D	1941
RAVAZZA			
Antonio	44624	I	1926
RAVELEY			
Z. W.	74842	D	1937
RAVELLA			
Clotilda	72384	D	1936
Filomena	73236	D	1936
Giovanni	42658	D	1925
Luis	82854	I	1939
RAVEN			
Catherine	27276	D	1919
Ermiania	79381	D	1938
RAVENS			
Agnes L.	83116	D	1940
Henry William	73268	D	1936
RAVENTOS			
Helen	18296	D	1914
Lida Helen	18296	D	1914
RAVERA			
Giovanni	81009	D	1939
Therese	81008	D	1939
RAVERLEY			
Samuel W.	74842	D	1937

NAME	NUMBER	TYPE	YEAR
RAVEZZANI			
Emil Joseph	80735	D	1939
Emilio	19874	D	1915
RAVICIOTTI			
Henriette	5507	M	1908
Marie	76805	D	1937
Pauline	5507	M	1908
Victor	3897	D	1907
RAVINALE			
Francesco	67702	D	1934
RAVN			
Ermiania	79381	D	1938
Hans	56797	D	1930
RAVO			
Giacomo	85278	D	1940
RAWDON			
Mary Ellen	85336	D	1940
RAWE			
Cecelia	12802	D	1912
Otto	20576	D	1916
RAWLANDS			
Mary Martin	68990	D	1935
RAWLES			
Jacob B.	27575	D	1919
RAWLINGS			
Ella	76010	D	1937
Lola M.	59124	M	1931
RAWLINS			
Rebecca A.	27480	D	1919
RAWLINSON			
Elizabeth	31815	D	1921
RAWSON			
Edwin Leo	76646	D	1937
RAY			
Alvin	36537	M	1923
Barbara	65834	D	1933
Charles	36537	M	1923
Edgar P.	51397	D	1928
Fred W.	20671	D	1916
Grace Evelyn	22785	D	1917
Helen	79845	D	1938
Hubert Carlisle	65452	D	1933
James A.	37441	D	1923
John	16559	M	1914
John	36537	M	1923
John M., Mrs.	65834	D	1933
Julia E.	69978	I	1935

NAME	NUMBER	TYPE	YEAR
Madalina	8840	M	1909
Margaret	561	D	1906
Margaret	36537	M	1923
Margaret E.	16529	D	1913
Marie	73607	D	1936
Mary Ellen	84614	D	1940
Paul F.	88551	D	1941
Robert G.	32113	D	1921
Scott A.	47106	D	1927
Susie	59133	I	1931
Virginia	16559	M	1914
William	36537	M	1923
William E. A.	37682	D	1923
William S.	18831	D	1915
William Wesley	47774	I	1927
RAYCHESTER			
George Ira	1027	D	1906
Rose	30985	D	1921
RAYCROFT			
Thomas H.	47593	D	1927
RAYER			
Edward C.	54476	D	1929
RAYHILL			
Margaret	36664	D	1923
William	34739	D	1922
RAYMER			
Delphina Ellen	40171	M	1924
Donald Floyd	40171	M	1924
Lillian Claudine	29407	M	1920
Ronald Lloyd	40171	M	1924
RAYMOND			
Albert	35068	D	1922
Alexander	81600	I	1939
Alexander	88699	D	1941
Aubrey L.	43491	M	1926
Charles M.	43103	D	1925
Charles M., Jr.	43491	M	1926
Dana M.	43491	M	1926
Donald P.	79613	D	1938
Eleanor	51037	M	1928
Elizabeth B.	63148	D	1932
Florence M.	43491	M	1926
Frances B.	2551	D	1906
Frank C.	15113	D	1913
George	42338	D	1925
George A.	28965	D	1920
Gertrude	51037	M	1928
Harriet	51611	D	1928

NAME	NUMBER	TYPE	YEAR
Jack Joe	48758	M	1927
Jane	30249	D	1920
Jennie	74169	I	1936
Jennie	74735	D	1937
John Patterson	77974	D	1938
Lee B.	11090	D	1911
Lee Burgess	24263	M	1918
Olga	43416	D	1926
Peter	79613	D	1938
Ralph	34769	D	1922
Robert M.	43491	M	1926
Thomas	30601	D	1920
William B., Jr.	57670	M	1931
William Henry Vining	12824	D	1912
RAYMOURE			
Gertrude	82028	D	1939
RAYNAUD			
Charles F.	55364	D	1930
Mary Theresa	52507	D	1929
RAYNER			
Lillian	24459	M	1918
Maggie	11624	I	1911
Sarah J.	10087	D	1910
William	57508	D	1930
RAYNES			
Mary Louise Koppitz	3715	D	1907
RAYNIER			
August L.	48259	D	1927
RAYNOR			
Henry	10057	D	1910
William	57508	D	1930
RAYSON			
Harriet	82974	D	1939
RAZEE			
George B.	57159	I	1930
RAZILLARD			
Gustave	40264	D	1924
RAZOVICH			
Vincent	78601	D	1938
Visko	78601	D	1938
RAZZANTI			
Catherine	18398	D	1915
RAZZAUTI			
Catherine	18398	D	1915
RAZZI			
Faustino	45543	D	1926

NAME	NUMBER	TYPE	YEAR
RAZZO			
Christopher	5914	D	1908
RE			
Leonardo	76387	D	1937
Luigi	52041	D	1929
Stefano	31796	D	1921
REA			
Alta Helen	34224	M	1922
Emma May	32554	D	1921
Harry Hamlin	37846	D	1923
Robert Lee	34224	M	1922
Walter Carl	34224	M	1922
READ			
E. B.	30336	D	1920
Emily J.	76079	D	1937
Ernest C.	60827	D	1932
Fred W.	24900	D	1918
George	59730	D	1931
George N.	64121	I	1933
Henry Lawrence	10234	D	1910
Jack	84395	D	1940
John Mack	53897	D	1929
Kate B.	77122	D	1937
Richard Lee	84823	M	1940
Tillie I.	46030	D	1926
Walter Edward	42374	D	1925
William P.	55485	D	1930
READE			
Frederick Eustace	59468	D	1931
James	6423	D	1908
Lucile Whitney	21738	D	1916
READER			
Alfred C.	53834	D	1929
READING			
Emma	79807	D	1938
Ernest Edgar	61482	D	1932
Ethel	63133	D	1932
READY			
Helen Alice	28819	M	1920
Herbert V.	9249	D	1910
Sarah Ann	22314	D	1917
REAGAN			
Edward	58834	M	1931
Gertrude	58834	M	1931
James P.	81594	D	1939
Jane E.	3824	D	1907
Kate	88403	D	1941

NAME	NUMBER	TYPE	YEAR
Ruby Pearl	24601	M	1918
Ruth Miller	78719	D	1938
Thomas	44482	D	1926
Thomas	58834	M	1931
REAL			
Manuel	23664	I	1917
REALE			
Antonio Lorenzo	64910	D	1933
REALI			
Adelina	37928	D	1923
Giuseppe	52552	D	1929
REALINI			
Humbert U.	52612	D	1929
REANEY			
William	37815	D	1923
REARDAN			
Catherine	55427	D	1930
REARDEN			
Ada F.	356	D	1906
Dennis	4856	D	1907
REARDON			
Aileen J.	62873	D	1932
Anna J.	37407	D	1923
Catherine F.	73250	D	1936
Dorothy	64420	M	1933
Ellen	50346	D	1928
Jeremiah	7574	D	1909
Johanna G.	12307	D	1911
John	13021	D	1912
John M.	55525	D	1930
Josephine	24464	D	1918
Luke	45607	D	1926
Mary	15585	D	1913
Maurice	53025	I	1929
Maurice A.	57648	D	1931
Nellie	41579	I	1925
Nellie	83646	D	1940
Nora	7575	D	1909
Patrick	4119	D	1907
Stephen	45607	D	1926
Susan	36027	I	1923
Thomas	45836	D	1926
REASONER			
Geo. E.	46680	M	1927
John S.	46680	M	1927
REASONS			
Jane Elizabeth	45495	D	1926

NAME	NUMBER	TYPE	YEAR
Thomas Day	60230	D	1931
REAVEY			
James	35586	D	1922
Jane	33274	D	1922
REAY			
Christiana G.	40996	D	1925
Christiana Gunn	15023	I	1913
Joseph W.	12250	D	1911
Wallace Roper	42438	D	1925
REBBERG			
Frank	46115	D	1926
REBER			
George J.	51985	D	1929
Josephine	31891	D	1921
Katherine	79919	M	1938
REBHAN			
George	40455	D	1924
REBHOLTZ			
Mary	30173	D	1920
Roman S.	26431	D	1919
REBHOLZ			
Aloysius J.	69018	D	1935
REBIERE			
Baptistine	84745	D	1940
REBIZZO			
Angelo	39301	D	1924
Mose	89905	D	1942
Rosa	39302	D	1924
Vittorio	30059	D	1920
REBMANN			
Charles William	83101	D	1940
REBOLINI			
Giovanni	27456	D	1919
REBOLLEDO			
Rene	83094	M	1940
REBORI			
Vincent A.	83228	D	1940
REBOTTARO			
Louis	59540	D	1931
REBSTOCK			
Anna Maria	24660	D	1918
Josephine	60245	D	1931
Mary	11410	I	1911
RECCHIA			
Giuseppe	60242	D	1931

Key: D = death; M = minor; I = incompetent

NAME	NUMBER	TYPE	YEAR
RECHTER			
Maria	18010	D	1914
Maria	18110	D	1914
Marie	18110	D	1914
RECK			
George W.	10786	M	1910
H. C.	68570	D	1934
Hannorah	14623	D	1912
RECKE			
Gerhard F.	24141	D	1918
RECKENBEIL			
Katharina	21337	D	1916
RECKER			
Charles	56973	D	1930
RECKEWELL			
Christoph	8281	D	1909
RECTOR			
B. F.	3358	D	1907
Elmer C.	47643	D	1927
Emogene Morse	20070	D	1915
John E.	41125	D	1925
Marion F.	30420	I	1920
REDAHAN			
Bernard Charles	37632	D	1923
REDDALL			
Mary	74290	I	1937
Mary	85285	D	1940
REDDELL			
Robert A.	53984	D	1929
REDDIN			
Mary A.	72478	D	1936
REDDING			
Albert Putnam	40919	D	1925
Allen Calvin	50661	D	1928
Charlotte	28038	D	1919
Elizabeth E.	73488	D	1936
Frederick Grant	35207	D	1922
George Herbert	10250	D	1910
Libbie E.	73488	D	1936
M.	28038	D	1919
May I.	8861	D	1909
Ruth	8824	M	1909
William	1818	D	1906
REDDINGTON			
Katherine	44258	D	1926
REDDISH			
Effie W.	11248	D	1911

NAME	NUMBER	TYPE	YEAR
Fielding L.	4410	D	1907
REDDY			
Carolyn S.	3098	D	1907
Catherine M.	19648	D	1915
Charles Francis	56448	D	1930
Ellen	39927	I	1924
Ellen	45141	D	1926
Emily M.	2617	D	1907
Frank	38608	D	1924
Henry Giles	46877	D	1927
Patrick	1279	D	1906
REDEAU			
Charles Harry	72003	D	1936
REDECKER			
August	21935	D	1916
REDFIELD			
Edna Marie	3947	M	1907
Hannah Ida	2531	D	1906
REDFORD			
Mary Agnes	624	D	1906
REDINGER			
Julien	69276	I	1935
Louise	51845	D	1929
Michael	81686	D	1939
REDINGTON			
Ada L.	52833	D	1929
Catherine Agnes	77524	D	1938
J. P.	79987	D	1938
Margaret V.	83926	D	1940
William Pearson	26168	D	1919
REDKAY			
George W.	5710	M	1908
Lillia M.	5710	M	1908
Mary Lorean	5710	M	1908
Samuel L.	6256	D	1908
REDLICK			
Fannie G.	39284	D	1924
Henry	70219	D	1935
Joseph	71457	D	1936
Ludwig	8015	D	1909
REDMAN			
Anna Chalmers	57847	D	1931
Eliza Maria	14219	D	1912
Lander Augustine	56490	D	1930
REDMOND			
Amelia J.	60639	D	1932
Andrew	22896	D	1917

NAME	NUMBER	TYPE	YEAR
Daniel J.	14252	D	1912
Esther	1546	D	1906
Ezekiel	52457	D	1929
Francis C.	23156	M	1917
George Joseph	23722	D	1917
Henrietta	10971	D	1910
James J.	35330	D	1922
Joseph	23155	D	1917
Julia Josephine	18285	D	1914
Martha L.	51108	D	1928
Mary A.	65670	D	1933
Matthew	7503	D	1909
Robert	18595	D	1915
Rose	26348	D	1919
REDMONDE			
Michael	4680	D	1907
REDNALL			
Mary	47700	D	1927
REDPATH			
James Charles	30104	D	1920
William	43428	D	1926
REDSTED			
Christian Marius	88882	D	1942
REDSTONE			
Lillian	34468	D	1922
William	7831	D	1909
REDY			
Christiana G.	40996	D	1925
REED			
Alfred Ernest	25591	D	1918
Annie M.	73150	D	1936
Bert	87714	I	1941
Carmel	16498	D	1913
Charles	20280	D	1916
Charles H.	34768	D	1922
Charles R.	69734	D	1935
Charles W.	18139	D	1914
Christopher C.	17771	D	1914
Clarence Clifford	29172	M	1920
Dianne	79945	M	1938
Dolores	79943	M	1938
Donald	79943	M	1938
Donna Marie	67237	M	1934
Edgar C.	37256	D	1923
Ellen T.	51638	D	1928
Emma A.	20229	D	1916
Frank William	10977	D	1910
Fred A.	46243	D	1927

NAME	NUMBER	TYPE	YEAR	NAME	NUMBER	TYPE	YEAR	NAME	NUMBER	TYPE	YEAR
Gay E.	41167	I	1925	**REEF**				**REGAHL**			
George A.	85859	D	1940	Catherine C.	12357	D	1911	Johanne	75196	D	1937
George M.	84821	D	1940	Joseph S.	34947	D	1922	**REGALIA**			
George W.	21822	D	1916	**REEHER**				Mario	78970	I	1938
Georgia Alice	65156	D	1933	Reba	80377	M	1939	Mary	87832	D	1941
Grafton T.	3854	M	1907	**REEL**				**REGAN**			
Harold William	29172	M	1920	James Arthur	46327	D	1927	Anna M.	56155	D	1930
Harriette E.	85966	I	1941	Nellie	83384	D	1940	Annie M.	9573	D	1910
Harriette Ellen	87105	D	1941	**REENG**				Burnett L.	65263	D	1933
Harry	34626	D	1922	Daniel J.	76731	D	1937	Catherine	67804	D	1934
Helen Blanch Maroney	57727	I	1931	Joseph D.	88386	D	1941	Cornelius T.	15542	M	1913
Helen Blanche Maroney	70550	D	1935	**REES**				Daniel	1361	D	1906
Helen Louise	77791	D	1938	David	35684	D	1923	Daniel	61535	D	1932
Henry	2449	D	1906	David R.	15524	D	1913	Daniel J.	75153	D	1937
Henry Washburn	36792	D	1923	Frederick G.	61818	D	1932	Edward F.	2683	M	1907
Howard N.	25919	M	1918	John	26281	D	1919	Elizabeth A.	1853	D	1906
Jackson Charles	67237	M	1934	Louise	4307	M	1907	Elizabeth Virginia	63322	D	1933
James H.	15566	D	1913	Lydia	87256	D	1941	Ellery C.	89423	D	1942
Jane	23058	D	1917	May	41732	D	1925	Eugene B.	64151	D	1933
Janet	79944	M	1938	May	41732	D	1925	Florence M.	25646	D	1918
Jean Mary	62618	D	1932	Thomas	13618	D	1912	George E.	15542	M	1913
Joseph C.	59002	I	1931	William J.	67903	D	1934	James	58840	D	1931
Joshua	80433	D	1939	William M.	49386	D	1928	James A.	62743	I	1932
Julia A.	45816	D	1926	**REESE**				James Joseph	60543	D	1931
Katrine Van	1216	D	1906	Amelia	50504	D	1928	Jeremiah	11797	D	1911
Lena L.	26028	D	1918	Emilie B.	41224	D	1925	John	41572	D	1925
Lillian	30369	D	1920	Henry	38532	D	1924	John	55557	D	1930
Margaret Dorothy	73266	D	1936	Johan Christian Heinrich	38532	D	1924	John A.	57012	D	1930
Mary Ella	24407	D	1918	Maybelle	37568	D	1923	Joseph D.	4223	D	1907
Maurice	59002	I	1931	**REEVE**				Josephine M.	15542	M	1913
Ruth E.	16454	I	1913	Charles Taylor	49086	D	1928	Julia	26633	D	1919
Sophie	81144	I	1939	Minnie A.	80275	D	1939	Julia	89756	D	1942
Thelma	79944	M	1938	**REEVES**				Lincoln B.	65263	D	1933
Thomas C.	3139	D	1907	Alfred Vernon	88724	D	1941	Margaret A.	81188	D	1939
Walter	45262	D	1926	Anna	76598	D	1937	Martin	2239	D	1906
Walter D.	61469	D	1932	Blanche	59684	I	1931	Mary	84401	D	1940
William H.	63852	D	1933	C. O.	19675	D	1915	Mary A.	1104	D	1906
William Roland	30370	M	1920	Edward L.	32203	D	1921	Mary A.	47085	D	1927
REEDE				Evie L.	51874	I	1929	Mary Ann	74293	D	1937
Mary Matilda Catherine	63292	D	1933	James	53097	D	1929	Mary W.	69236	D	1935
Maurice	59002	I	1931	John Diven	69121	M	1935	Michael	19064	D	1915
REEDY				Louise J.	65928	D	1933	Michael	22363	D	1917
Albert S.	85050	D	1940	Mabel D.	89605	D	1942	Patrick	65596	D	1933
Elizabeth G.	26118	D	1919	Margaret	60646	D	1932	Patrick J.	85897	D	1940
John Francis	66437	D	1934	Theresa F.	55276	D	1930	Raymond T.	15542	M	1913
Mary A.	35660	D	1923	Thomas	2753	D	1907	Rebecca N.	74399	I	1937
Michael	10902	D	1910	W. J.	463	D	1906	Stephen J.	56841	D	1930
				William Cunningham	68633	D	1935	Thomas	50629	D	1928

NAME	NUMBER	TYPE	YEAR
Timothy	22363	D	1917
Timothy	28648	D	1920
Virginia	63322	D	1933
REGENSBURGER			
Alfred E.	50708	D	1928
Arthur T.	17196	D	1914
Blanche	86612	I	1941
Cathie	2383	D	1906
Emma	85412	D	1940
Fannie	13845	D	1912
Louis	54885	D	1930
Martin	40189	D	1924
Melville M.	781	D	1906
Theresa	42909	D	1925
REGGAN			
Patrick	85897	D	1940
REGINATO			
Frank	88046	D	1941
REGIS			
Alfred Emile	84193	D	1940
Antonio	34919	D	1922
Lucien	63960	D	1933
REGLEY			
Charles	20042	D	1915
Joseph	17757	D	1914
REGLI			
Edward	59352	D	1931
Joanna	64181	D	1933
John J.	42651	D	1925
Joseph	17757	D	1914
Joseph	64183	D	1933
Joseph Francis	66074	D	1934
Josephine	67802	D	1934
William	64182	D	1933
REGLIN			
August J.	52283	D	1929
REGNART			
Carl W.	30853	D	1920
REGNIER			
Armand J.	66899	D	1934
Paul B.	30311	D	1920
Vernon G.	43061	D	1925
REH			
Catherine Ann	7862	D	1909
Fridrich August	7860	D	1909
REHAGE			
Pauline A. E.	44957	D	1926

NAME	NUMBER	TYPE	YEAR
REHFELD			
Elias	17961	I	1914
REHFISCH			
Caroline Adeline	10580	M	1910
Farnham Morse	80481	M	1939
John Morse	10580	M	1910
John Morse	70565	D	1935
John Morse	80481	M	1939
Lina	81404	D	1939
Morris	8058	D	1909
REHHE			
John	84676	D	1940
REHKER			
Louise	51725	D	1928
REHLMEYER			
August G.	58890	D	1931
REHM			
Kresenzia	32114	D	1921
REHMKE			
Henry J. O.	29098	D	1920
REHMSTEDT			
William Henry	77348	D	1937
REHN			
Adelheide	6630	D	1908
Charles.	15231	D	1913
Rose Louise	53490	D	1929
REHQUATE			
William	66459	D	1934
REHWOLDT			
G.	42892	D	1925
Heinrich Gustaf	42892	D	1925
REIBEL			
Joseph	28802	D	1920
REIBMAN			
Ida	88002	D	1941
REICH			
Amalie	67190	D	1934
Frederick W.	39898	D	1924
Gustave	53890	D	1929
Ida	73729	D	1936
Leopold	32480	D	1921
Margaretha	4954	D	1907
Victor	62830	D	1932
REICHARDT			
Katharina	10332	D	1910

NAME	NUMBER	TYPE	YEAR
REICHE			
Louis	28000	D	1919
REICHEL			
Georg Walter	62068	D	1932
John Martin	81033	D	1939
Karl Rudolf	56543	D	1930
Rudolf	56543	D	1930
Walter	62068	D	1932
Walter	62265	D	1932
REICHELT			
Alfred B.	84852	D	1940
Ernest D.	19164	D	1915
Fred H.	33343	I	1922
REICHENBACH			
Alice	643	D	1906
Charles	33379	D	1922
Edwin Lincoln	34031	D	1922
Oscar I.	54324	D	1929
REICHENBERG			
Bella	87885	D	1941
Fannie	58290	D	1931
REICHERT			
Anna	65099	D	1933
Edward	44946	I	1926
Edward	45000	D	1926
Flora	31670	I	1921
Flora	31750	D	1921
Ida K.	13962	D	1912
Isabella	82199	D	1939
Louise	60611	D	1932
Theodore	10102	D	1910
REICHERTS			
Louis	60611	D	1932
REICHHOLD			
Charles	32481	D	1921
John	71809	D	1936
REICHLIN			
Carolina	68167	D	1934
Eva	41716	D	1925
Joseph, Mrs.	41716	D	1925
Xavier Paul	69894	D	1935
REICHLING			
Caspar	52453	D	1929
Catherine Bulger	75419	I	1937
Oscar H.	34828	D	1922
REICHMAN			
John M.	25788	D	1918

NAME	NUMBER	TYPE	YEAR	NAME	NUMBER	TYPE	YEAR	NAME	NUMBER	TYPE	YEAR
REICHMANBERG				Mary E.	69039	I	1935	Edna M.	81244	D	1939
John	42097	D	1925	Mary E.	69805	D	1935	Harry H.	19655	D	1915
William John	42097	D	1925	Robert Allan	43631	D	1926	REILINGER			
REICHMANN				Robert James	64628	D	1933	Clara	7086	D	1909
Bertha Rosine	60269	D	1931	Sophie A.	6153	D	1908	Samuel	14164	D	1912
Gustav Heinrich	2221	D	1906	Thomas Harold	68112	M	1934	REILL			
Rosa	6604	D	1908	Walter B.	6757	D	1908	Mary	15114	D	1913
REICHMUTH				William E.	6756	D	1908	REILLEY			
Margaret	56061	M	1930	William E.	7625	D	1909	Charles	44556	D	1926
Mary V.	53977	D	1929	William Joseph	62039	D	1932	Fannie	18479	D	1915
REICHOLD				REIDEL				George Cannon	67437	D	1934
John	71809	D	1936	Max	52368	D	1929	John J.	41267	D	1925
REICHOVA				REIDFORD				Stephen	83857	D	1940
Ida	73729	D	1936	Clark R.	41331	D	1925	REILLY			
REICHOW				REIDMAN				Adelaide E. R.	14418	D	1912
Paul	57019	D	1930	George	4821	D	1907	Agnes S.	5800	D	1908
REICHSTETTER				REIDNER				Alice	11124	M	1911
William	79503	D	1938	Charles T.	31997	D	1921	Annie	44178	D	1926
REID				REIDY				Arabella	59283	D	1931
Alice	43677	D	1926	Audray	73970	M	1936	Bridget	35402	D	1922
Anderson, Mrs.	37870	D	1923	Daniel	87540	D	1941	Bridget	54693	D	1930
Anna Odlin	74988	D	1937	Dennis	85259	D	1940	Catherine	21898	D	1916
Catherine	76412	D	1937	Edward	73627	D	1936	Catherine	81328	D	1939
Catherine (widow)	9374	I	1910	Jeremiah	23519	D	1917	Cora G.	76670	D	1937
Charles	39836	D	1924	John	35883	D	1923	Cornelius	2270	D	1906
Cordelia	36343	I	1923	Joseph C.	89029	D	1942	Cornelius J.	36204	I	1923
Edmond B.	3000	D	1907	Mary Dodge	5845	I	1908	Daniel O.	17500	D	1914
Edward	89579	M	1942	Mary Louise	86677	M	1941	Delia M.	60711	D	1932
Edward F.	7490	D	1909	William	46205	D	1927	Edward T.	60684	M	1932
Elizabeth Weir	9553	D	1910	William Anthony	27323	D	1919	Edward Thomas	68249	D	1934
Eva Charlotte	84122	D	1940	REIEL				Elizabeth	46483	D	1927
Fred W.	86559	D	1941	Daisy	87850	D	1941	Ellen	35924	D	1923
Genevieve	37870	D	1923	REIF				Ellen	85332	D	1940
George	58923	I	1931	Elizabeth A.	86877	D	1941	Elva	69496	D	1935
Henry	54771	D	1930	Meyer	23959	D	1918	Florence	22895	M	1917
Henry H.	14241	D	1912	REIFF				Frank J.	34839	D	1922
Hugh	35450	I	1922	Lena	41827	D	1925	George	63269	D	1933
Hugo	173	D	1906	Lena	41827	D	1925	George	86082	D	1941
Isabelle Knox	82965	D	1939	Line	41827	D	1925	Imelda	4945	M	1907
James Atkinson, Jr.	23728	M	1917	Line	41827	D	1925	Isabella J.	45927	D	1926
James D.	88626	D	1941	REIGER				James	5804	D	1908
Jane W.	49951	M	1928	Conrad	10562	I	1910	James	22895	M	1917
John	34699	D	1922	REIGHLEY				James W.	67837	D	1934
John J.	89266	D	1942	James B.	10820	D	1910	Jeremiah G.	66358	D	1934
Jule McDonald	51216	D	1928	Mary R.	34186	D	1922	Johanna	15762	D	1913
Margaret E.	19133	D	1915	REIGLE				John	11124	M	1911
Marigladys	71079	M	1935	Edna M.	67891	I	1934	John	35569	D	1922
Martha	36343	I	1923					John	45715	D	1926

NAME	NUMBER	TYPE	YEAR
John	79756	D	1938
John J.	41267	D	1925
John J.	47434	D	1927
John J.	74943	D	1937
John W.	37945	D	1923
Joseph F.	55343	D	1930
Julia	786	D	1906
Julia T.	72823	D	1936
Lawrence	84764	D	1940
Lillian B.	24923	D	1918
Loretta	4945	M	1907
Lucy V.	73599	D	1936
Mae Beck	68403	D	1934
Margaret	6197	D	1908
Mary	2759	D	1907
Mary	9198	I	1910
Mary	9212	D	1910
Mary	11568	D	1911
Mary	11600	D	1911
Mary E.	49128	D	1928
Mary F.	38476	D	1924
Mary Hansan	38476	D	1924
Michael	26709	I	1919
Michael	80127	D	1938
Michael F.	37633	D	1923
Michael J.	44222	D	1926
Nicholas J.	22894	D	1917
Patrick	17802	D	1914
Patrick	19296	D	1915
Patrick	45553	D	1926
Patrick J.	33213	D	1922
Peter	51311	D	1928
Robert M.	83609	D	1940
Susan	2527	D	1906
Theresa M.	43005	D	1925
Thomas	29646	D	1920
Thomas B.	64047	D	1933
William Patrick	73942	I	1936
William Patrick	87357	D	1941
REILY			
Johanna	5805	D	1908
John J., Jr.	59159	D	1931
Margaret	2821	D	1907
REIMANN			
Alexander	73129	D	1936
August	71263	D	1935
Edith A.	66159	D	1934
Herman	17217	D	1914

NAME	NUMBER	TYPE	YEAR
REIMER			
Ellen	46273	D	1927
Josephine M.	88479	D	1941
Laura Margaret	46201	M	1927
Leopold C.	88478	D	1941
Nettie	46273	D	1927
REIMERS			
Adolf	29589	D	1920
Adolph	29248	I	1920
Catharina	21698	D	1916
Claus	20649	D	1916
Henny	62622	D	1932
Herman	71656	I	1936
John	16638	D	1914
John P.	29309	D	1920
Louis	30144	D	1920
REIN			
Hilda	75962	D	1937
Leah	53888	D	1929
REINA			
Frank	70885	I	1935
Giuseppe	84672	D	1940
REINAUDO			
Anna	83637	D	1940
Antonio	80013	D	1938
REINECKE			
Alfred W.	80587	D	1939
Harold Andrew Peter	17252	M	1914
Mabelle	17252	M	1914
Marie Anna	17209	D	1914
REINECKER			
Robert Firmin	54328	D	1929
REINER			
Fred	8702	D	1909
Margaretha S.	67307	I	1934
Margaretha S.	78248	D	1938
REINERS			
Antone	29019	D	1920
REINERT			
John J.	72777	D	1936
REINFELD			
Charles J.	70638	D	1935
James William	58773	D	1931
REINGOLD			
Rose	56494	I	1930
REINHARD			
Anna	39108	D	1924

NAME	NUMBER	TYPE	YEAR
Emerentia	82843	D	1939
Emma	82843	D	1939
Franz	4091	D	1907
John D. J.	44789	D	1926
Sebastian E.	10320	D	1910
REINHARDT			
Annie	61369	D	1932
Conrad	63487	D	1933
D. H.	20553	D	1916
Edward	13761	M	1912
Edward W.	12531	D	1911
Franz	4091	D	1907
George	13761	M	1912
Hannah L.	13761	M	1912
Henry	13761	M	1912
Johanna L.	9459	D	1910
Louis Frederick	12532	D	1911
Louisa	16493	D	1913
REINHART			
Amson	41684	D	1925
Conrad	16164	I	1913
Conrad	63487	D	1933
Franz	4091	D	1907
Jacob	52659	D	1929
Joseph	2608	D	1907
Mary	3688	D	1907
Rosalie	72040	D	1936
Simon	20100	D	1915
Simon	77726	D	1938
REINHERTZ			
Isaac	36940	D	1923
Lotta	77290	D	1937
Max I.	53810	D	1929
REINHOLD			
Bruno R.	40275	D	1924
Erich Paul	83547	D	1940
Ernest P.	83547	D	1940
Jacob	32549	D	1921
Pauline	24090	D	1918
REINILA			
August	24705	D	1918
REININGER			
Eugene	49861	D	1928
Robert Joseph	26909	M	1919
REINISCH			
Benjamin	60435	D	1931
REINIUS			
Hazel May	11630	M	1911

NAME	NUMBER	TYPE	YEAR
REINKE			
Bertha	8114	D	1909
REINKEMEYER			
Katherine M.	88315	D	1941
REINKMEYER			
Frederick H.	88316	D	1941
REINSTADLER			
Vitus	89408	D	1942
REINSTEIN			
Arthur Henry	67767	D	1934
Jacob B.	11563	D	1911
Lizzie	88240	D	1941
Maurice	73064	D	1936
Sara	87104	D	1941
REIPRICH			
Bernard G.	78171	D	1938
REIS			
Clara May	47670	D	1927
Ellen W.	39846	D	1924
Fannie L.	8552	D	1909
Ferdinand	647	D	1906
Gustav	11862	M	1911
John	11862	M	1911
John	18868	M	1915
John O'Neal	1349	D	1906
Julius	84448	I	1940
Julius	84662	D	1940
Julius C.	1004	D	1906
Rose	66560	D	1934
REISCHMAN			
Jack W.	34004	M	1922
REISEN			
Hilda Caroline	80512	D	1939
Peter Christian	50937	D	1928
REISENBERG			
Frederick M.	73211	D	1936
REISER			
Katherine	13674	D	1912
Katherine E.	52035	D	1929
REISFELT			
Abraham	68729	D	1935
REISHMAN			
John M.	25788	D	1918
REISINGER			
John	26997	D	1919

NAME	NUMBER	TYPE	YEAR
REISLER			
Kathleen	70047	M	1935
REISS			
Jeanette	36819	D	1923
Max B.	31040	D	1921
Salomon	2003	D	1906
REITENPRAC			
F. G.	49601	D	1928
REITER			
Antonia	19511	I	1915
Aurelia	52294	D	1929
Berthe	47481	D	1927
Charles Edward	66087	D	1934
James Edward	49099	D	1928
Josephine M.	22649	D	1917
May J.	22649	D	1917
REITH			
Alexander H.	75629	D	1937
Annie	69210	D	1935
Charles Edwin	69242	D	1935
Matilda	69210	D	1935
Sophia	38932	D	1924
REITZ			
Mary E.	33278	D	1922
Sophia	15997	D	1913
REJSENHOFF			
Edward	83055	D	1940
REKOW			
Fred W.	81995	D	1939
RELEI			
Enrico	37383	D	1923
RELES			
Peter	27292	D	1919
RELIHAN			
Thomas	75530	D	1937
RELYEA			
Ellsworth West	18999	M	1915
REMANDAS			
Peter	61738	D	1932
REMARC			
Jas. M.	88363	D	1941
REMBOLD			
Gustav A.	22813	D	1917
REMENSPERGER			
Ulrich	30374	D	1920
Ulrich Frederick	56939	D	1930

NAME	NUMBER	TYPE	YEAR
Veronika	49472	D	1928
REMER			
Martha	25335	D	1918
REMHARK			
Charles	33400	D	1922
REMILLARD			
Cordule	66331	D	1934
REMINGTON			
Hal M.	72015	D	1936
REMMEL			
Ferdinand	26190	D	1919
REMMELT			
Anton	70967	D	1935
REMNAP			
Frederick C.	33627	D	1922
REMSCHEL			
Emil L.	49153	D	1928
Emil Ludwig Heinrich	49469	D	1928
REMUSAT			
Joseph	34725	D	1922
REMY			
Mary Ann	42575	D	1925
RENALDI			
Goffrado	6109	D	1908
RENARD			
Charles	16849	D	1914
Ernestine	1663	D	1906
Louise	18901	M	1915
Louise Marie	41086	D	1925
Roland	18901	M	1915
RENCINEL			
Celestin	33521	D	1922
RENCUREL			
Celestin	33521	D	1922
RENDSBURG			
Fanny	10886	D	1910
RENE			
Adelaide Ernestine	13003	D	1912
Adrien	10635	D	1910
Henry	10631	D	1910
Jean Hilaire Henry	10631	D	1910
Marie Adele H. Adrien	13002	D	1912
Martin	21140	D	1916
RENEAR			
Daniel Novak	87354	M	1941

NAME	NUMBER	TYPE	YEAR	NAME	NUMBER	TYPE	YEAR	NAME	NUMBER	TYPE	YEAR
RENEAU				RENNY				RESING			
Humphrey S.	88765	D	1941	J. W.	17953	D	1914	George Leo	48892	D	1928
Humphrey S.	89160	D	1942	RENO				William J.	41686	D	1925
RENEBOME				Joe	67263	D	1934	RESLER			
Robert H.	79235	D	1938	Manuel	17904	D	1914	Adolf Rudolf	81576	D	1939
RENFORT				RENSHAW				Leonard	54134	D	1929
Augusta	79486	D	1938	Edwin Thomas	15813	I	1913	RESLEURE			
RENFREW				Edwin Thomas	21150	D	1916	Jacques Francois	82105	D	1939
Lila Olivia	54498	M	1929	RENTON				RESNICK			
RENFROW				Henry Herbert	30180	D	1920	Abraham	68975	D	1935
Mae	88550	D	1941	Jack	33283	D	1922	Hyman	88428	D	1941
Mary	88550	D	1941	James R.	2929	D	1907	RESSEGHINI			
RENGLI				Violet Carolina	33974	M	1922	Rosa	19898	D	1915
Anton	61631	D	1932	RENTSCHLER				RESSEGUIE			
RENISH				Eva M.	66667	D	1934	Frank Judkins	75426	D	1937
Jeanne S.	83530	D	1940	Frederick W.	27576	D	1919	RESSMANN			
RENN				John G.	7606	D	1909	Carl E. T.	81968	D	1939
Frederick W.	27450	I	1919	RENWANZ				Charles E. T.	81968	D	1939
Frederick W.	44300	D	1926	Annie	57982	D	1931	RESTANI			
William	27450	I	1919	RENWICK				Giovanni	71766	D	1936
William	44300	D	1926	Catherine F.	82030	D	1939	Giovanni	71906	D	1936
RENNA				Ellen	29310	D	1920	Giuseppe	52378	D	1929
Vincent A.	1157	D	1906	James A.	71204	D	1935	RESTE			
RENNER				Myron H.	39430	D	1924	George	12865	I	1912
Berthe	77230	D	1937	RENZ				George	14243	D	1912
Frederick Joseph	68277	I	1934	Edna E.	76393	D	1937	RESTIVO			
Katherine	54488	D	1929	Frederick	72555	I	1936	America	71648	D	1936
Louis	12115	D	1911	Herman Gustavus	79266	D	1938	Giovanni	19638	D	1915
RENNERT				REO				RESTOVICH			
Julia	18698	D	1915	Jose	30495	D	1920	Ida May	64260	D	1933
RENNIE				REOM				RETA			
Alberta Caroline	22981	M	1917	Emily	64295	D	1933	Candido Fernandez	39707	D	1924
Alfred Edward	13985	D	1912	REPETTO				RETEUNA			
Alfred Ronald	22981	M	1917	Lodovico	71888	D	1936	Celestino	75413	D	1937
James	41794	D	1925	Louis	54760	D	1930	RETFISCH			
James	41794	D	1925	Ludovico	71888	D	1936	Paul	3755	D	1907
James	41840	M	1925	William	71504	D	1936	RETHERS			
James	41840	M	1925	REPPEN				Harry	86292	D	1941
Mary Eunicia	26479	D	1919	Adolph	20635	D	1916	Theodore C.	40458	D	1924
RENNILSON				REPSOLD				RETHMEYER			
Margaret Cecelia	62742	D	1932	Amandus	13523	D	1912	Betty Marie	55314	M	1930
RENNINGER				Herbert A.	14950	D	1913	RETHWILM			
Annabelle	48953	M	1928	RESENDEZ				Anna Maria	64499	D	1933
RENNISON				Juan	81229	D	1939	Anna Marie	64999	D	1933
Rosanna	445	D	1906	Leobardo	63485	D	1933	RETHY			
								George	33024	D	1921

NAME	NUMBER	TYPE	YEAR	NAME	NUMBER	TYPE	YEAR	NAME	NUMBER	TYPE	YEAR
RETTAGLIATA				Annie	15502	I	1913	Margaret	561	D	1906
Charles	15857	M	1913	Edward Francis	15503	M	1913	Marie	63411	D	1933
Paolo	88664	D	1941	REVEL				Samuel	11154	D	1911
Sylvia	15857	M	1913	Felix Victor	44849	D	1926	REYBERG			
RETTE				Marius	45116	D	1926	Charles	49835	D	1928
May J.	22649	D	1917	REVELES				REYBURN			
RETTENMAYER				Joseph	16905	D	1914	Edward A.	67224	D	1934
J. A.	75044	D	1937	REVELLO				Margaret E.	42932	D	1925
RETTER				Peter	46589	D	1927	McGrady Bruce	80652	D	1939
Ada	33061	D	1921	Teresa	13135	D	1912	REYES			
Benjamin F.	73601	D	1936	REVER				Celia	73114	M	1936
RETTIG				Max	35694	D	1923	Samuel Clow	85628	D	1940
Anna Francisca Ida	67266	D	1934	REVERA				William	73114	M	1936
Jacob	23100	M	1917	John	81009	D	1939	REYMAN			
RETTTBERG				REVERISCO				Julia	65268	D	1933
Edward	20710	M	1916	Barney	74706	D	1937	Marcus	13058	D	1912
Joseph	20710	M	1916	Vincent R.	70899	D	1935	REYMOND			
May	20710	M	1916	REVERISKO				August B.	78554	D	1938
Robert Conrad	20710	M	1916	Baldo	74706	D	1937	G. A.	19031	D	1915
RETZKE				REVERMAISE				Joseph A. R.	19031	D	1915
Marie	11165	D	1911	Otilia	65372	D	1933	Martin	20542	D	1916
Richard	11469	I	1911	REVERMAN				REYNANDO			
Richard	12829	D	1912	Otillia	65372	D	1933	Umberto	47680	D	1927
REUBEN				REVETT				REYNARD			
Adelia	89559	D	1942	Benjamin Stanley	47527	D	1927	Julius	62534	D	1932
Millie	37161	D	1923	REVEYRON				REYNAUD			
Moses	76746	D	1937	John Bapliste	59011	D	1931	Jules	15602	D	1913
REUBOLD				REVIHYAK				REYNELL			
Albert F.	70519	D	1935	Verona	64539	D	1933	Wm. J.	30701	D	1920
REUCK				REVILYOCK				REYNOLDS			
Jack M.	79091	I	1938	Verona	64539	D	1933	Alexander W.	17088	D	1914
REUFFERT				REVITCH				Alice Raycraft	1070	I	1906
Fritz	13367	D	1912	Mayer	35694	D	1923	Alice Raycraft	3658	D	1907
REUHLE				REW				Anne	33996	D	1922
May L.	37600	D	1923	Horatio G.	49821	D	1928	Annie	35644	D	1923
REUSCHE				REX				Ansel Faren	66002	D	1934
August	27405	D	1919	George T.	66193	D	1934	Anthony	15957	D	1913
Marie	50897	D	1928	REY				Arthur	56651	D	1930
REUSS				Candido Gay	81296	D	1939	Benjamin K.	62954	D	1932
Herman	60430	D	1931	Catherine	44111	D	1926	Blanche M.	8772	M	1909
REUTER				Emile	19918	I	1915	Bridget	5928	D	1908
Inez Rose	79124	M	1938	Emilo	54831	D	1930	Charles	56416	D	1930
REUTERSHAN				Emily	25678	D	1918	Charles	62552	D	1932
Max	84866	D	1940	George W.	44321	D	1926	Claire J.	70466	M	1935
REVALEON				Jean Baptiste	52520	D	1929	Clara Maude	66795	D	1934
Albert L.	15503	M	1913	Leon Louis	47242	D	1927	David L.	28806	D	1920
								Edith A.	66159	D	1934

NAME	NUMBER	TYPE	YEAR
Edward B.	44430	M	1926
Elizabeth	35584	D	1922
Elizabeth.	25284	D	1918
Ellen	47222	D	1927
Frank William	45338	D	1926
Franklin D.	6769	M	1908
George T.	1530	D	1906
Harriet L.	10505	D	1910
J. A.	77191	D	1937
James	2887	D	1907
James	42539	D	1925
John	86676	M	1941
John	77191	D	1937
John A.	56618	M	1930
John Aloysius	73522	M	1936
Louise Irene	80227	D	1938
Martin J.	79369	D	1938
Mary	927	D	1906
Mary	38799	D	1924
Mary Ann	6813	D	1908
Mary Vivian	6769	M	1908
Ora	82409	D	1939
Patrick	31524	D	1921
Sophie E.	73629	D	1937
Suthena	2639	D	1907
William H.	14970	D	1913
William King	6769	M	1908
RHEAUME			
Cleo	67759	D	1934
RHEE			
Reuben	53051	D	1929
RHEEL			
Frank	34668	D	1922
RHEIN			
Philippine	24784	D	1918
RHEINHOLD			
Knuth	46079	D	1926
RHEINSTEIN			
Alexander	18745	D	1915
RHEINSTROM			
Harry A.	10659	I	1910
RHINE			
Adeline Blanche	85572	D	1940
Charles	34261	D	1922
Dina	85398	D	1940
Ellis	34907	D	1922

NAME	NUMBER	TYPE	YEAR
RHOADES			
Charles D.	20782	D	1916
Marvin D.	54979	D	1930
RHOADS			
Albert Washington	82481	M	1939
Alma W.	53826	D	1929
Emily T. Connolly	81574	I	1939
Frank Palmer	80523	D	1939
Frederic Hemingway	56042	D	1930
Joanna	55005	D	1930
Mina G.	86350	D	1941
RHODE			
August	42152	D	1925
RHODES			
Anita	48350	M	1927
Charles Durell	20782	D	1916
Daisy	83018	D	1940
Daniel William	72755	D	1936
Emma J.	69847	D	1935
Frances	48350	M	1927
Margaret McE.	49575	D	1928
Marvin D.	54945	M	1930
Marvin D.	54979	D	1930
Mary Isabel	87126	D	1941
Sadie D.	29579	D	1920
Stanley	89058	D	1942
Thomas	21380	D	1916
Wesley	2905	D	1907
Wilbur	48350	M	1927
William H.	50026	I	1928
William H.	58318	D	1931
RHOMBERG			
John	74251	D	1936
RHONE			
Florence O.	80173	D	1938
RHYNE			
Veron	84743	D	1940
RHYS			
Kate	57834	D	1931
RIALDINI			
Michael	30554	D	1920
RIANDA			
Victor	71739	D	1936
RIBBY			
James	7666	D	1909
Mary	4132	D	1907

NAME	NUMBER	TYPE	YEAR
RIBEIRO			
John B.	79340	D	1938
RIBERA			
Anna	55748	D	1930
RIBERO			
Giacomo	51764	D	1929
Jack	51764	D	1929
Meiglia	67669	I	1934
Miglia	67669	I	1934
RIBIERO			
Joao Angelo	40879	D	1925
RIBOLINI			
Aristide	75519	D	1937
RIBONI			
Enrico	25373	D	1918
Henry	25373	D	1918
Rinaldo	28283	D	1919
RICCARDI			
Abelle	32179	D	1921
RICCI			
Alice	64927	D	1933
Dorcas Jane Powers	55792	D	1930
Giovanni Lepoldo	84432	D	1940
Jane Dorcas Powers	55792	D	1930
John Leopold	84432	D	1940
Lawrence	80950	M	1939
Louise	84349	M	1940
Mario	80950	M	1939
Zeffiro	61553	D	1932
RICCIARDI			
Avelle	32179	D	1921
RICCO			
Angelina	87306	D	1941
RICCOMI			
Angelo	39316	D	1924
Celestina	56998	M	1930
Emilia	56998	M	1930
Emilia	70922	D	1935
RICE			
Anna Belle Wilson	52438	D	1929
Anna Maria	72326	D	1936
Caroline E.	12267	D	1911
Catherine	24787	D	1918
DeWitt C.	19099	D	1915
Eva Corinne	77805	D	1938
Eva Louise	11088	D	1911
Felix	50994	D	1928

NAME	NUMBER	TYPE	YEAR
Francis A.	16696	D	1914
Frank J.	16753	M	1914
Henry D.	69804	D	1935
Jennie	46	M	1906
John A.	25893	D	1918
John S.	49817	D	1928
John W., Jr.	87324	M	1941
Josephine E.	32993	D	1921
Julia W.	75380	D	1937
Manuel A.	77561	D	1938
Margaret	22057	D	1917
Maria	18598	D	1915
Marion S.	78274	D	1938
Mary Elizabeth	58109	D	1931
Mary Julia	70142	M	1935
Nora	62129	D	1932
Octavia Matilda	69680	D	1935
Patrick	2921	D	1907
Patrick	30547	D	1920
Peter	23578	D	1917
Peter Christian	43131	D	1925
Richard J.	1412	D	1906
Robert L.	41982	D	1925
Robert L.	41982	D	1925
Sarah	46	M	1906
Sarah	19584	D	1915
William Steains	79055	D	1938

RICETTA

NAME	NUMBER	TYPE	YEAR
Lui	88507	D	1941

RICH

NAME	NUMBER	TYPE	YEAR
Alfred J.	67570	D	1934
Alfred Joseph, Jr.	8866	M	1909
Arthur Milton	59757	D	1931
Bella	87885	D	1941
Bernard	13664	D	1912
Claire Gloria	43393	M	1926
David	36788	D	1923
Dunning	64099	M	1933
Dunning	39200	M	1924
Elizabeth Viola	64099	M	1933
Elizabeth Viola	39200	M	1924
Geary	51273	D	1928
Henry	15976	D	1913
Joseph	60242	D	1931
Lawrence B.	54009	D	1929
Lee B.	45434	D	1926
Lenora A.	24364	I	1918
Lenora A.	63935	D	1933
Louis	41778	D	1925

NAME	NUMBER	TYPE	YEAR
Louis	41778	D	1925
Maria	88937	D	1942
Minerva	37947	D	1923
Norma	53299	I	1929
Obadiah	41560	D	1925
Paul C.	29046	D	1920
Samuel Herman	50324	D	1928
Seville	74856	D	1937
Sophie	82086	D	1939
Thomas E.	59896	D	1931
Virginia	52387	M	1929

RICHARD

NAME	NUMBER	TYPE	YEAR
Dorothy	86316	M	1941
Eleanor Barbara	83187	M	1940
Eleanor Barbara Watson	83187	M	1940
Ellen	4201	D	1907
Emma	76492	D	1937
George	7473	D	1909
George	86315	D	1941
Helen	4201	D	1907
John E.	86316	M	1941
Kathleen	86316	M	1941
Martin Alexander	38157	D	1924
Nellie	3994	D	1907
Rosemary B.	69599	M	1935

RICHARDES

NAME	NUMBER	TYPE	YEAR
Olive Sarah	55975	D	1930

RICHARDS

NAME	NUMBER	TYPE	YEAR
Albert	12393	D	1911
Ann M.	29322	D	1920
Caroline Martha	17467	I	1914
Caroline Martha	27084	D	1919
Catherine	55460	D	1930
Catherine Hazlet	88153	D	1941
Charles E.	75448	D	1937
Charles M.	15718	D	1913
Charles Wesley, Jr.	22152	D	1917
Coy L.	43647	I	1926
Darrell S.	84825	M	1940
David	65252	D	1933
David M.	1619	D	1906
David M.	41368	D	1925
Edwin L.	86049	D	1941
Eleanor W.	53824	D	1929
Emily Clayton	17870	D	1914
Emma	76492	D	1937
Emma	88154	D	1941
Felix	47621	D	1927

NAME	NUMBER	TYPE	YEAR
Frank	19938	D	1915
Fred	31275	D	1921
Fronia L.	63752	D	1933
George F.	49459	D	1928
George H.	82040	I	1939
Hannah D. R.	82118	D	1939
harry DeCourcy	69902	D	1935
Ida M.	51970	D	1929
Isabella	73474	D	1936
J. H.	39779	D	1924
J. H., Mrs.	73364	D	1936
James	15432	D	1913
James J.	18248	D	1914
John F.	2708	D	1907
John Francis	19938	D	1915
Joseph I.	30600	I	1920
Josephine	75181	D	1937
Julia Luella	73364	D	1936
Leoline M.	67298	D	1934
Lorenzo H.	22413	D	1917
Louis George	11089	D	1911
Margaret	88152	D	1941
Margaret Alta	82566	D	1939
Mariana Christina	73893	D	1936
Marie	32153	M	1921
Mary	88155	D	1941
Mary A.	28116	D	1919
Mary E.	37578	D	1923
Mary Louise	35123	D	1922
Norma	43232	M	1925
Owen J.	9014	D	1910
Richard	58171	D	1931
Sarah Elizabeth	35803	D	1923
Stephen H.	72816	D	1936
Theo, Mrs.	55460	D	1930
Thomas	20544	D	1916
William Alfred	21851	D	1916
William Alfred	42933	D	1925
William T.	80634	D	1939

RICHARDSON

NAME	NUMBER	TYPE	YEAR
Addie Mary	63728	D	1933
Albert Orson	79682	D	1938
Allen W.	86165	D	1941
Benjamin Franklin	39488	D	1924
Bettie Erikson	74221	D	1936
Charles	34099	I	1922
Charles	41248	D	1925
Charles	67157	D	1934
Charles F.	84640	D	1940

NAME	NUMBER	TYPE	YEAR	NAME	NUMBER	TYPE	YEAR	NAME	NUMBER	TYPE	YEAR
Charles Spaulding	5813	M	1908	William J.	58368	D	1931	Marie Julia	83429	D	1940
Clotilda R.	1415	D	1906	William J.	74064	D	1936	Mary Elizabeth	51211	D	1928
Dagmar	24524	D	1918	**RICHARDSPM**				Oscar Fred	53686	D	1929
Dorothy Catherine	59049	M	1931	Harry D.	37491	D	1923	William	8185	D	1909
Edward N.	82328	D	1939	Henry D.	37491	D	1923	**RICK**			
Elizabeth	81275	M	1939	**RICHARME**				Albert B.	61650	D	1932
Emma	45545	I	1926	Ernest	16794	D	1914	Bernard	13664	D	1912
Ernest James	37503	D	1923	**RICHARTZ**				Elizabeth	49108	D	1928
Erskine	6471	D	1908	Gertrude	28018	D	1919	John G.	3113	D	1907
Eugene T.	73980	D	1936	**RICHBERGER**				Robert	26522	D	1919
Frances Cary	4115	M	1907	Anna	35014	D	1922	**RICKABAUGH**			
Francis Allen	72543	D	1936	Frederick	44416	M	1926	Lovell	56765	D	1930
Fred C.	84640	D	1940	**RICHCREEK**				**RICKARD**			
George F. J.	34497	D	1922	Paul	52912	M	1929	Alma A.	74122	D	1936
George Forrest	54318	D	1929	**RICHER**				Alma D.	74122	D	1936
George H., Jr.	38978	D	1924	Joseph	79256	D	1938	Irene Penrose	63682	D	1933
George Henry	82899	D	1939	**RICHERT**				Katherine B.	68025	D	1934
George Henry, Jr.	24922	M	1918	George	7473	D	1909	Kenneth C.	77021	D	1937
Harold	4539	M	1907	**RICHET**				Martha S.	58469	D	1931
Harold McElroy	17924	M	1914	August Bernard	1501	D	1906	Mary	24408	D	1918
Hattie A.	59987	D	1931	Bernard	7427	M	1909	**RICKARDS**			
Hersie	65784	D	1933	**RICHFORD**				Carlton	70129	D	1935
John Francis	39168	M	1924	Thomas H.	45341	D	1926	**RICKE**			
John William	43896	D	1926	**RICHICHI**				Augusta	45746	D	1926
John William	80065	D	1938	Giuseppina	79757	D	1938	Charles W.	45736	D	1926
Joseph	30333	I	1920	**RICHLEY**				Henry	42441	D	1925
Josephine	58014	D	1931	Eugene Frank	55337	D	1930	**RICKELTON**			
Lancelot	71426	D	1936	**RICHMOND**				John	1191	D	1906
Lillian G.	75550	D	1937	Arabella M.	10165	D	1910	**RICKER**			
Lora Jane	78505	D	1938	Charles	79141	D	1938	Arthur M.	62809	D	1932
Louise	4376	D	1907	Frank L.	36178	D	1923	Emma Marie	34811	I	1922
Louise M.	42106	D	1925	George C.	42938	D	1925	**RICKERD**			
Mary	51371	D	1928	Mary H.	588	I	1906	Mary	24408	D	1918
Mary Curtis	60172	D	1931	Nellie M.	87692	D	1941	**RICKERLY**			
Mary R.	29257	D	1920	**RICHMONDS**				W.	6835	D	1908
Rachael B.	3152	D	1907	Mary E.	9937	D	1910	**RICKEY**			
Robert	15499	D	1913	**RICHON**				Charles W.	21545	D	1916
Russ R.	57706	D	1931	Harry	76950	D	1937	Jeanette	21560	M	1916
Samuel	25528	D	1918	**RICHTER**				**RICKMAN**			
Sarah J.	10058	D	1910	Charles Alfred	71024	I	1935	Frederick	1858	D	1906
Smith P.	16170	D	1913	Clemens Max	72573	D	1936	**RICKON**			
Suzanne Wainwright	50844	D	1928	Emma Louise	77004	D	1937	Billy Boy	35042	M	1922
Theresa	82061	D	1939	George J.	35478	D	1922	Fred M.	35042	M	1922
Victoria Grace	16171	D	1913	Gertrude	52838	D	1929	Frederic J. H.	18007	D	1914
W. D.	18565	D	1915	John	9215	D	1910	Harry	76950	D	1937
William	8708	D	1909	John	40456	D	1924	Henrietta	25838	D	1918
William	43218	D	1925					Henrietta	26111	D	1919
William Ernest	53001	D	1929								
William Graham, Jr.	5813	M	1908								

Key: D = death; M = minor; I = incompetent

NAME	NUMBER	TYPE	YEAR
Richard D.	35042	M	1922
RICO			
Bernice A.	7390	M	1909
Clarice L.	7390	M	1909
Corlos N.	7390	M	1909
Ernestine L.	7390	M	1909
James F.	7390	M	1909
Joseph S.	7390	M	1909
Juanita	7390	M	1909
Norice L.	7390	M	1909
Rudolph R.	7390	M	1909
RICORD			
Mattie Ellen	81020	D	1939
RIDDELL			
Benjamin	71691	D	1936
Charles	88610	D	1941
Edward J.	47925	I	1927
Edwin Belmont	10255	M	1910
Edwin Belmont, Jr.	55848	M	1930
Frances E.	31212	D	1921
George H.	10402	D	1910
Hannah	25298	I	1918
Hannah	30422	D	1920
Lee Ernest	55848	M	1930
Leslie L.	10255	M	1910
Lucille Wickware	10255	M	1910
Lulu C.	50142	I	1928
Robert McAlpine	55848	M	1930
Wilbur J.	10255	M	1910
RIDDLE			
H. J.	71784	D	1936
Haden E.	71784	D	1936
Joseph Ross	64931	M	1933
Percy S.	29649	D	1920
Ruth O.	82539	D	1939
Ruth Trimbur	82539	D	1939
RIDDOCK			
Grace B.	61206	D	1932
RIDELLA			
Antonio	25468	D	1918
RIDEOUT			
Edward	42257	D	1925
James R.	1877	D	1906
Mabelle Helene	47009	D	1927
Phebe M.	61778	D	1932
RIDER			
Ada Elinor	13604	I	1912
Fannie M.	22697	D	1917

NAME	NUMBER	TYPE	YEAR
Frances Almira	28328	D	1919
Fred C.	87686	D	1941
John B.	25327	D	1918
Samuel P.	74951	D	1937
RIDGE			
Helen Catherine	24830	M	1918
Margaret	4743	D	1907
RIDGEWAY			
Katharine	81010	D	1939
Mary E.	89165	D	1942
RIDGWAY			
Charles Wesley	29375	D	1920
Clara M.	71711	D	1936
Lawrence V. B.	26394	D	1919
Marion R.	78896	D	1938
Ralph	57951	I	1931
RIDLER			
William	21288	D	1916
RIDLEY			
A. E. Brooke	28337	D	1919
Eva E.	49451	D	1928
Laura	73368	D	1936
Robert Morsley, Jr.	65722	M	1933
RIDLINGTON			
Pauline C.	29863	D	1920
Thomas	341	D	1906
RIDOLFI			
Charles	47445	D	1927
RIDOUT			
Thomas	11874	D	1911
RIEBE			
Amelia Louisa Sophia	20314	D	1916
RIECH			
Otto	21318	D	1916
RIECHERS			
Gretchen	85751	D	1940
Louis F.	53925	D	1929
Selma Matilda	52815	D	1929
RIECK			
Emma	55022	I	1930
Emma Marie	34811	I	1922
Frank J.	16753	M	1914
John H.	81269	D	1939
Tillie	44163	D	1926
RIED			
Thomas	2013	D	1906

NAME	NUMBER	TYPE	YEAR
RIEDEL			
Anna Elizabetha	67598	D	1934
Annie	61479	D	1932
Auguste	40611	I	1924
Christiane Friderike	61479	D	1932
Conrad	57880	D	1931
George	43750	D	1926
Gustave	42239	D	1925
Helena Johanson	17406	I	1914
Helena Johanson	27780	D	1919
Hermann	10215	D	1910
Mathilde Agnes	21852	D	1916
Richard	18642	D	1915
Wilhelmina	43630	D	1926
RIEDELL			
William	26174	D	1919
RIEDINGER			
Elizabeth R.	29595	D	1920
George L.	27982	M	1919
Helena	27981	D	1919
RIEDMANN			
Anne Marie Josephine	28825	D	1920
RIEDY			
Charles C.	77164	D	1937
Jane	79603	M	1938
Mary	79603	M	1938
Michael	10902	D	1910
Robert	79603	M	1938
RIEFFEL			
Emily J.	62283	D	1932
Eugene Henry	61285	D	1932
RIEGE			
August	65447	D	1933
RIEGELHAUPT			
Philip	27	D	1906
RIEGELHUTH			
Charles	80036	D	1938
Conrad	2764	D	1907
Frank John	79429	D	1938
RIEGGER			
Anna	65057	D	1933
Julie	653	D	1906
RIEGLING			
Henry	46160	D	1927
Joseph	38905	I	1924
Joseph	41515	D	1925

Key: D = death; M = minor; I = incompetent

NAME	NUMBER	TYPE	YEAR
RIEHA			
Jennie	40839	D	1925
Johanna Jassman	40839	D	1925
RIEHE			
Luella H.	68916	D	1935
RIEHL			
Luella H.	68916	D	1935
Richard	61496	D	1932
RIELLY			
Charles P.	713	M	1906
Francis D.	713	M	1906
Margaret D.	713	M	1906
Patrick	17802	D	1914
RIELY			
Daniel	25542	D	1918
RIEMER			
Clara E.	32367	D	1921
Herbert R.	84328	D	1940
Julius A.	84029	D	1940
Rudolph	22076	D	1917
RIEN			
Leah	53888	D	1929
RIENECKER			
Ethel Louise Babcock	34704	D	1922
Hulda Marie Sophia	61243	D	1932
RIEP			
E. August	61822	D	1932
RIEPEN			
Anna Maria Amelia	26931	D	1919
Leonie A.	84652	D	1940
RIEPENHAUSEN			
Carl	70465	D	1935
RIEPER			
Jacob	6482	D	1908
RIERSON			
John	13951	D	1912
RIES			
Julius	84662	D	1940
RIESE			
David	26142	D	1919
David, Mrs.	61848	D	1932
Paul Ernest	33	M	1906
Theresa	61848	D	1932
RIESENER			
Auguste	78417	D	1938

NAME	NUMBER	TYPE	YEAR
RIESER			
John Woodward	68551	M	1934
Katherine E.	52035	D	1929
Robert Edwin	68551	M	1934
RIESINGER			
Margaretha	6049	D	1908
RIESS			
Louis	10814	D	1910
William	89440	D	1942
RIETZE			
Margarethe	67857	D	1934
RIETZKE			
Mary E.	23411	D	1917
RIFE			
Rose A.	50574	D	1928
RIFFE			
Frederick C.	73958	D	1936
RIGAL			
Henri	37452	I	1923
Isidore	69664	D	1935
Marie Theron	36859	D	1923
RIGANTI			
Lorenzo	52701	D	1929
RIGDON			
Eva Burns	71687	D	1936
Rufus Lee	71688	D	1936
RIGEN			
Sadie	35755	D	1923
RIGG			
George A.	45027	D	1926
RIGGER			
William	74249	D	1936
RIGGIO			
Rosario	12935	D	1912
RIGGS			
Orval R.	74759	D	1937
RIGHETTI			
Elsie	57778	D	1931
Giuseppe	51103	D	1928
Perseo	49232	D	1928
Selide	70945	D	1935
RIGHTER			
Frederick McEwen	24957	M	1918
RIGNEY			
Edward	79272	D	1938
Hannah B.	68523	D	1934

NAME	NUMBER	TYPE	YEAR
John Edward	83182	D	1940
Patrick J.	38376	I	1924
RIGUZZI			
Joseph	32742	D	1921
RIIS			
Jacob	17723	D	1914
RILEE			
Anna A.	41568	D	1925
RILEY			
Alvina T.	13092	M	1912
Ann	9555	D	1910
Ann	18108	D	1914
Ann F.	745	I	1906
Ann Foley	1057	D	1906
Bernice K.	13092	M	1912
Catherine	12795	D	1912
Catherine	18976	D	1915
Catherine	29120	D	1920
Catherine C.	25374	D	1918
Catherine S.	5672	D	1908
Cornelius	14163	D	1912
Daniel	18038	D	1914
Daniel	25542	D	1918
David	28056	D	1919
David B.	88804	I	1941
Earll T.	76628	D	1937
Edward	47295	I	1927
Edward	57612	D	1931
Edward G.	13092	M	1912
Elizabeth	20892	I	1916
Elizabeth	21219	I	1916
Ella	30773	I	1920
Ella	32094	I	1921
Ellen	30773	I	1920
Ellen Marie	9294	M	1910
Emma F.	82285	D	1939
Francis J.	80988	D	1939
Francis William	53919	D	1929
Friend	46239	D	1927
George E.	77317	D	1937
Grace C.	75864	D	1937
Harry C.	75166	D	1937
Henry William	1583	I	1906
Hugh J.	13872	D	1912
Jack	47434	D	1927
James	51698	M	1928
James L.	13092	M	1912
James Wheeler	38120	D	1924

NAME	NUMBER	TYPE	YEAR
Jennie M.	37209	D	1923
Johanna	15762	D	1913
John	15942	D	1913
John	16277	D	1913
John	62187	D	1932
John	63234	D	1932
John D.	73321	D	1936
John Francis	33038	D	1921
John Francis	76059	D	1937
John Henry	49828	D	1928
John Layton	42979	M	1925
John P.	37611	M	1923
Joseph P.	45055	D	1926
Layton	42979	M	1925
Margaret	6197	D	1908
Marie	24593	D	1918
Mary	7733	D	1909
Mary	9198	I	1910
Mary	9212	D	1910
Mary	63918	D	1933
Mary	66235	D	1934
Mary Jane	41978	D	1925
Mary Jane	41978	D	1925
May	31675	I	1921
Michael M.	29465	D	1920
Nanette C.	12104	D	1911
Patrick	96	D	1906
Peter T.	14378	D	1912
Phillip J.	26319	D	1919
Rebecca	19767	D	1915
Reginald Oakes	33195	M	1922
Silas	70240	D	1935
Thomas	36087	D	1923
Thomas	80418	D	1939
Thomas F.	16999	D	1914
Thomas F.	37611	M	1923
Thomas J.	63810	I	1933
Thomas J.	67081	D	1934
Thomas Orville	66841	D	1934
Venice	28955	D	1920
William	659	D	1906
William	4946	D	1907
William F.	58132	D	1931
William J.	14045	M	1912
William J.	14073	D	1912
William K.	13092	M	1912
William V.	71634	D	1936
RILL			
Billy	29284	D	1920

NAME	NUMBER	TYPE	YEAR
Isidor	29284	D	1920
RILLEY			
Patrick O.	3526	D	1907
RILYE			
Catherine	18976	D	1915
RIMASSA			
Rosa	45904	D	1926
RIMELL			
Ellen	4394	I	1907
RIMLINGER			
Catherine	36017	D	1923
RIMMER			
Eber Lincoln Crook	56432	D	1930
Lincoln	56432	D	1930
Minnie C.	53266	D	1929
RINALDI			
Alberto	47680	D	1927
RINALDO			
Cecelia L.	52568	D	1929
David	55138	D	1930
Hyman	61655	D	1932
Isidore George	75360	D	1937
Joseph	54234	D	1929
Milani	50586	D	1928
RINANDO			
Theresa	73455	D	1936
RINAUDI			
Alberto	47680	D	1927
RINAUDO			
Antonio	80013	D	1938
Assunta	58081	D	1931
Giuseppe	56676	D	1930
Teresa	73455	D	1936
RINCKEL			
David Wesley	81578	D	1939
Marcella E.	64428	D	1933
RINDGE			
Elyse C.	48538	D	1927
Joseph A.	338	D	1906
RINEHART			
George	48614	M	1927
Marguerite	48409	D	1927
Marguerite	48614	M	1927
RINELLA			
Teresa	63134	D	1932

NAME	NUMBER	TYPE	YEAR
RINES			
Gertrude M.	80886	D	1939
RING			
Charles	573	D	1906
Charlotte M.	67854	D	1934
Edward Barron	7512	D	1909
Edward F.	81797	D	1939
Edward G.	74692	D	1937
Edward Thomas B.	26760	M	1919
Gerald J.	81826	D	1939
John	61501	D	1932
Katherine	89539	D	1942
Lottie B.	58564	D	1931
Mary	26984	D	1919
Timothy	18315	D	1914
Toring	60649	I	1932
William	9576	D	1910
William N.	53313	D	1929
RINGBERG			
Charles J.	23962	D	1918
RINGE			
Gustav	59723	D	1931
RINGEN			
George W.	67196	D	1934
John C.	34260	D	1922
Katherine Helena	85279	D	1940
Peter A.	65583	D	1933
RINGGOLD			
Nancy	52192	M	1929
RINGHAM			
Loretta E.	81593	D	1939
RINGHOLM			
Olaf M.	78934	D	1938
RINGLER			
John August	56020	D	1930
RINGOLE			
Aaron	74862	D	1937
RINGOT			
Joseph Henry	44088	D	1926
RINGROSE			
Mary E.	61639	D	1932
Rhody	24158	D	1918
Rhody	24160	D	1918
RINGSMITH			
Jack	84011	M	1940
RINGWOOD			
Thomas	21089	D	1916

NAME	NUMBER	TYPE	YEAR
RINK			
Louis	12697	D	1911
RINKER			
William H.	29593	D	1920
RINNE			
Harry	89686	D	1942
RINTA			
Victor	77403	D	1938
RIOARDAN			
Michael	14059	D	1912
RIOLO			
Joseph M.	38619	D	1924
Victor	45128	M	1926
Vito P.	43664	D	1926
RIORDAN			
Annie Elizabeth	87039	D	1941
Annie M.	62204	D	1932
Bridget	11210	D	1911
Catherine	55427	D	1930
Daniel	14987	D	1913
Daniel	18270	D	1914
Daniel F.	16433	D	1913
Daniel Joseph	33554	D	1922
Delia A.	12189	D	1911
Elizabeth Agnes	32464	D	1921
Elizabeth Caroline	49104	M	1928
Ellen	67776	D	1934
Gertrude	14984	M	1913
Grace	38805	D	1924
Grace Margaret	49104	M	1928
Hannah	29149	D	1920
Hannah Imelda	33048	M	1921
Helen Marie	49104	M	1928
James	33048	M	1921
Johanna	27092	D	1919
John	86957	D	1941
John D.	69677	D	1935
John H.	13395	D	1912
Joseph	71473	D	1936
Kate	60665	I	1932
Kate	81890	D	1939
Margaret	28649	D	1920
Mary	185	D	1906
Mary	37936	D	1923
Mary C.	84419	D	1940
Mary Frances	19810	D	1915
Mathew	9641	D	1910
Maurice F.	89188	I	1942

NAME	NUMBER	TYPE	YEAR
Maurice F.	89372	D	1942
Michael	14059	D	1912
Michael	51694	D	1928
Michael	68049	D	1934
Patrick	4119	D	1907
Patrick M.	44649	D	1926
Patrick W.	86951	D	1941
Patrick William	18425	D	1915
Richard R.	29128	D	1920
Rose A.	51910	D	1929
Stephen W.	76938	D	1937
Teresa M.	88362	D	1941
Thomas	7248	D	1909
Thomas Daniel	1873	D	1906
Thomas F.	73312	D	1936
William F.	62292	I	1932
William F.	64072	D	1933
RIORDEN			
Denis Matthew	50599	D	1928
Dennis	4856	D	1907
RIORDENS			
Dennis	4856	D	1907
RIOS			
Frances	28379	D	1919
Thomas	32368	D	1921
Valentin Lopez	35944	D	1923
RIOTTE			
Mary C. Poster	29729	D	1920
RIOUX			
Cypren	38941	D	1924
RIPLEY			
Almena Pelouze	6832	D	1908
Catherine	14833	D	1913
Charles Avery	84109	D	1940
Charles J.	22223	D	1917
Penina E.	22702	D	1917
William James	66874	D	1934
RIPODAS			
Maria	33779	D	1922
RIPPE			
A. M. Dorothie	42620	D	1925
Elizabeth H.	18847	D	1915
Elsbeth	61584	D	1932
Elsie	61584	D	1932
Emmet	18821	M	1915
Gladys Vaughan	86186	D	1941
Henry H.	16759	D	1914
John D.	9082	D	1910

NAME	NUMBER	TYPE	YEAR
John H.	79470	D	1938
RIPPLE			
Pauline	61981	D	1932
RIPPON			
Ann	4286	D	1907
Francis Carl	79693	M	1938
Jean	80294	I	1939
Margaret	74044	D	1936
William	18244	D	1914
RIPPSTEIN			
Hermann	6947	M	1908
Rosa	6947	M	1908
RISCH			
Wilhelmina	47366	D	1927
RISCHMULLER			
Marie	61651	D	1932
RISDON			
Sarah J.	44176	I	1926
Sarah Jane	44743	D	1926
RISE			
Mary E.	26051	D	1919
RISHTON			
Henry	25101	I	1918
Henry	25287	D	1918
RISI			
Herman	15786	D	1913
Mary	50145	D	1928
RISING			
Mary H.	16063	D	1913
RISIO			
Giuseppe	57285	D	1930
RISLEY			
Sarah M.	31309	I	1921
RISPAUD			
Eugenie	32651	D	1921
RISPIN			
Annette A.	87924	D	1941
Henry A., Mrs.	87924	D	1941
RISSER			
Frank	88972	D	1942
RISSMAN			
Alma	28414	D	1919
RISSMANN			
Lois M.	80463	M	1939
Louise W.	31877	D	1921
Violet	80463	M	1939

Key: D = death; M = minor; I = incompetent

NAME	NUMBER	TYPE	YEAR	NAME	NUMBER	TYPE	YEAR	NAME	NUMBER	TYPE	YEAR
RISSO				**RITSCHY**				**RITZENTHALER**			
Caterina	80161	D	1938	Valentine	18516	I	1915	Birdie E.	68443	D	1934
Catherine	85323	D	1940	**RITTER**				**RITZMANN**			
Elena	41649	M	1925	Albert	18754	D	1915	Max	82268	D	1939
Francesco	27636	D	1919	Anna	8228	D	1909	**RIVADENEYRA**			
Frank	60866	D	1932	Arthur	85623	D	1940	Alfredo	65551	D	1933
Giuseppe	15137	D	1913	Arthur, Mrs.	83607	D	1940	**RIVARA**			
Giuseppe	47182	D	1927	Carl	43854	D	1926	Adele	4848	D	1907
Giuseppe	85503	D	1940	Clara M.	55540	D	1930	Luigi	18941	I	1915
Gustav	11429	D	1911	Edith	83691	D	1940	Ruby	58495	M	1931
Joseph J.	75266	D	1937	Edith L.	88036	D	1941	Ventorino	15086	D	1913
Maria	61051	D	1932	Edward	39100	D	1924	Victorina	15086	D	1913
Pietro	57326	D	1930	Elizabeth	75945	D	1937	**RIVARD**			
RIST				Henry	68290	I	1934	Ethel	44304	D	1926
Frederick	70668	D	1935	Herman Heinrick	13277	D	1912	May E.	44304	D	1926
Friederika	14679	D	1913	John Francis	79716	I	1938	**RIVAS**			
RISTOW				Joseph	17477	D	1914	Auguste	24931	D	1918
Emma D.	15971	I	1913	Joseph	18952	D	1915	Felix	75957	D	1937
John	2404	D	1906	Josephine Augusta	81243	D	1939	Manuel	80653	D	1939
RITCHI				Josephine Louise	85904	D	1940	**RIVE**			
Fred	58470	D	1931	Louis Eugene	5837	D	1908	Jules	47605	D	1927
RITCHIE				Mary Ann	87658	M	1941	**RIVELLA**			
Augusta	42747	D	1925	Mary Margaret	83607	D	1940	Secondo	55491	D	1930
Daniel Sinclair	3027	D	1907	William	76131	D	1937	Secondo	57493	M	1930
Daniel St. Claire	3027	D	1907	**RITTIGSTEIN**				**RIVENBURGH**			
David	42195	D	1925	Ella M.	64821	D	1933	Bertram G., Jr.	40816	M	1925
Dorothy J.	8492	M	1909	**RITTLER**				**RIVERA**			
Edwin Frank	8492	M	1909	Ada	17515	D	1914	Alfred	8298	M	1909
George W.	59244	D	1931	Emil	24693	D	1918	Crescencia Williams	24055	D	1918
Harry R.	18294	D	1914	Lina	81753	D	1939	Dewey, Jr.	74224	M	1936
James	23927	D	1918	**RITTORE**				Victoriano	61144	M	1932
Kathryn	2741	D	1907	Henry A.	46699	D	1927	William C.	37637	D	1923
Mary	77429	D	1938	Marianna	19532	D	1915	**RIVERS**			
Mary A.	31874	D	1921	**RITTTHALER**				Charlotte E.	10993	D	1911
Sophia	84173	D	1940	Rueben	59217	I	1931	Edward George Charles	81868	D	1939
RITCHLEY				**RITZ**				Katherine A.	15831	D	1913
Eugene Frank	55337	D	1930	Adelma P.	34036	M	1922	Lewis Lester	12304	D	1911
RITER				Arthur G.	30962	D	1921	Lily	10993	D	1911
Philip J.	83266	D	1940	Roy A.	33002	D	1921	Sarah E.	8758	D	1909
Rosa M.	57218	D	1930	Thomas	76230	D	1937	Wilhelmina	67393	D	1934
RITH				**RITZENBAIN**				**RIVERSMITH**			
Amanda	59931	D	1931	Kathe	46952	M	1927	Everard S.	88064	D	1941
RITHMOELLER				Kurt	46952	M	1927	**RIVES**			
John C.	76897	D	1937	**RITZENHAIN**				Minnie A.	23686	D	1917
RITSCHER				Albert W.	44498	D	1926	**RIVEST**			
Haakon	26391	D	1919	Kathe	46952	M	1927	John Leon	40414	D	1924
				Kurt	46952	M	1927	John Leon	40482	D	1924

Key: D = death; M = minor; I = incompetent

NAME	NUMBER	TYPE	YEAR	NAME	NUMBER	TYPE	YEAR	NAME	NUMBER	TYPE	YEAR
RIVIECCIO				John	28707	D	1920	Annie L.	34410	D	1922
Giovanni	86296	D	1941	John H.	49897	D	1928	George J.	52274	D	1929
RIVIERE				John T.	41340	I	1925	Irvin	58017	D	1931
Auguste	80618	D	1939	John T.	48534	D	1927	John S.	1377	D	1906
RIVOIR				John Tobias	68121	D	1934	Louise Marie Tollefsen	7403	M	1909
Alexander	8881	D	1909	Joseph	49622	D	1928	Margaret C.	23808	D	1917
RIVOLO				Margaret	84386	D	1940	Patricia Ann	71158	M	1935
Antonio	707	D	1906	Maria Louise	8027	D	1909	Patricia Ann	71158	M	1935
RIX				Mary T.	83663	D	1940	Sidney H.	30517	M	1920
Agnesta C.	31151	D	1921	Michael	16432	D	1913	Thomas Hinckley, Jr.	19819	M	1915
Agneta C.	31151	D	1921	Michael	44595	D	1926	William	79963	D	1938
Anna	76305	D	1937	Patrick	35075	D	1922	William Bradford	19819	M	1915
Lorimer	81468	D	1939	Thomas	27904	D	1919	**ROBBITT**			
Mabel S.	58374	M	1931	Thomas	38318	D	1924	Robert Edward	84780	D	1940
RIXFORD				Thomas F.	8370	D	1909	**ROBCKE**			
Emmet	77495	D	1938	**ROACHE**				Charles Frederick	693	D	1906
Gulian Pickering	57087	D	1930	Anmarie Blanche	54174	D	1929	**ROBEL**			
RIXON				Annmarie	54174	D	1929	Andrew	72266	D	1936
Albert	52824	D	1929	Elizabeth	82648	I	1939	**ROBERSON**			
RIZZA				Kate	28543	I	1919	C. H.	16814	D	1914
Frank	63070	D	1932	Margaret Edith	54174	D	1929	Maria Ygnacia	82003	D	1939
Rosa	45787	D	1926	Margaretedith	54174	M	1929	**ROBERT**			
Salador Frank	63070	D	1932	Valton Granger	53986	D	1929	Johan	20537	D	1916
RIZZIO				William Dowd	54174	D	1929	John	15236	D	1913
Edith	26169	D	1919	**ROATH**				John	61704	D	1932
Maria	73695	D	1936	Louise M.	35469	D	1922	Joseph	18716	D	1915
RIZZO				M. Louise	35469	D	1922	Julia Perdrizat	77742	D	1938
Alfred	27347	M	1919	Warrington D.	23555	D	1917	Suzanne	39922	D	1924
Andrew	27823	D	1919	**ROBATTA**				**ROBERTE**			
Bernice	27347	M	1919	Angela	53466	D	1929	Antonio	80624	D	1939
Gio Batto	86174	D	1941	**ROBATTO**				**ROBERTS**			
Lena	77315	D	1937	Angela	53466	D	1929	Ada E.	45346	D	1926
Milton	27347	M	1919	**ROBB**				Adam	58721	D	1931
Salvatore	49299	D	1928	James	64454	D	1933	Adda Estelle	71655	D	1936
Tommaso	22569	D	1917	James	65220	D	1933	Addie	75140	D	1937
Tonaso	22569	D	1917	Jean	29903	M	1920	Adelbert E.	82778	D	1939
Walter	27347	M	1919	Margaret	66381	D	1934	Ann	24451	D	1918
RIZZOLI				Margaret M.	11599	I	1911	Anna H.	70628	I	1935
John B.	40314	D	1924	**ROBBELL**				Anna M.	41740	D	1925
RIZZUTO				Walter O.	48423	I	1927	Anna M.	41740	D	1925
Giovanni	17895	D	1914	Walter O.	50340	D	1928	Anthony J.	75676	D	1937
ROACH				**ROBBEN**				Bridget	41750	D	1925
David L.	2304	D	1906	William B.	87819	D	1941	Bridget	41750	D	1925
Hannah	6336	D	1908	**ROBBIE**				Charles	69734	D	1935
James	28580	D	1920	Mary L.	74566	D	1937	Cora	70827	D	1935
James F.	40001	D	1924	**ROBBINS**				Cora D.	42021	D	1925
Jane	80981	D	1939	Annie J.	34410	D	1922	Daniel H.	53612	D	1929
								David	13913	D	1912

NAME	NUMBER	TYPE	YEAR	NAME	NUMBER	TYPE	YEAR	NAME	NUMBER	TYPE	YEAR
David	16990	D	1914	Mary	21796	I	1916	Harriette S.	52464	D	1929
Duncan Ingraham	41588	M	1925	Mary	38016	D	1923	Helen Rix	66712	D	1934
E. Neville	50966	D	1928	Mary A.	8997	D	1910	Hugh R.	7516	D	1909
Edward J.	41591	D	1925	Mary Ann E.	8082	D	1909	James L.	46936	D	1927
Edward M.	67671	D	1934	Mary D.	70894	D	1935	Jane	81568	D	1939
Edward M.	73369	D	1936	Mary Elizabeth	9040	D	1910	John	39208	D	1924
Edward W.	28800	D	1920	Maude	20321	D	1916	John H.	56439	D	1930
Edwards A.	53869	D	1929	Morris E.	3001	D	1907	John Milne	27055	D	1919
Elmer E.	69555	D	1935	Nellie	21994	I	1916	John Milne	30366	M	1920
Emilie L.	79204	D	1938	Ollie	10181	M	1910	John P.	21052	D	1916
Ernst	10181	M	1910	Peter L.	63367	D	1933	John Robert	30185	D	1920
Evalyn	85718	D	1940	Phoebe E.	13466	D	1912	Joshua H.	64609	D	1933
Francis J.	72894	D	1936	Raymond	47415	M	1927	Kathleen	37589	D	1923
Frederick Alfonso	10683	D	1910	Rhodena C.	47168	D	1927	Lucy A.	41496	D	1925
Frederick T.	52957	D	1929	Richard M.	11463	D	1911	Marion	11274	D	1911
George H.	77234	D	1937	Robert	47415	M	1927	Mary D.	2207	D	1906
George Henry	65013	D	1933	Roger	47415	M	1927	Mary D.	39845	D	1924
George Phillips	41588	M	1925	Roy	11191	M	1911	Mary Louise	36074	M	1923
Grace E.	78284	D	1938	Suzanne	39922	D	1924	Maud Ann	86473	D	1941
Grace Edith	73221	I	1936	Theodore	47415	M	1927	May F.	54739	D	1930
Griff	53248	D	1929	Thomas	41990	D	1925	Melford H.	32049	D	1921
Harold William	39639	D	1924	Thomas F.	73032	I	1936	Minnie Hooker	32873	D	1921
Harry Hillman	56037	D	1930	Thomas H.	35570	D	1922	Mirren	11274	D	1911
Hattie	46479	D	1927	Thomas Z.	39295	D	1924	Nellie	42841	D	1925
Henry	83906	D	1940	Velda Ann	46312	M	1927	Quintilla	79078	D	1938
Henry Elliott	13467	D	1912	Victor T.	39991	D	1924	Robert Mortimer, Sr.	76349	D	1937
Hugh D.	21750	D	1916	W. H.	11346	D	1911	Rose	84121	D	1940
Ida	77320	I	1937	William	31299	D	1921	Stanley	76154	M	1937
James	68423	D	1934	William	76303	D	1937	Theodore	30237	D	1920
James E.	75794	D	1937	William A.	35218	D	1922	Theodore, Mrs.	37589	D	1923
Jane	15827	D	1913	William Andrew, Jr.	56300	M	1930	Walter Taylor	49425	M	1928
Jessie Louise	43111	D	1925	William C.	51217	D	1928	William	18354	D	1915
John	6642	D	1908	William D.	61714	D	1932	William	66031	D	1934
John	39895	D	1924	William Frederick	39950	D	1924	William R.	88714	D	1941
John	64404	D	1933	William Henry	32876	D	1921	**ROBESON**			
John H.	29033	D	1920	William L.	1844	D	1906	James Logan	30766	M	1920
Joseph W.	84249	D	1940	William Rees	33659	D	1922	**ROBICHAU**			
Julia A.	21516	D	1916	Winifred Claire	56300	M	1930	Matthausen Celestine	75198	D	1937
Julius	75399	I	1937	**ROBERTSON**				**ROBIN**			
Leonard William Bellows	9439	M	1910	A. J.	86274	D	1941	Jean Andrew	8521	D	1909
Lewis Howard	46761	D	1927	Alexander Marshall	18044	M	1914	John	8521	D	1909
Louise	50523	D	1928	Augusta C.	60080	D	1931	Mary	78210	D	1938
Margaret	51691	D	1928	Bancroft Edwards	36074	M	1923	**ROBINET**			
Margaret	84247	I	1940	Cecelia M.	26289	D	1919	Henry	43598	D	1926
Margaret A.	85165	D	1940	Dudley Pirie	22739	M	1917	Margretta Milner	15058	D	1913
Margaret A.	87703	D	1941	Edward William	17310	M	1914	Sophie M.	70402	D	1935
Margaret W.	82301	D	1939	Elizabeth Jane	81568	D	1939	**ROBINETT**			
Mary	4721	D	1907	George A., Sr.	84550	D	1940	Thomas W.	74001	D	1936
Mary	11409	I	1911	George W.	77620	D	1938				

NAME	NUMBER	TYPE	YEAR	NAME	NUMBER	TYPE	YEAR	NAME	NUMBER	TYPE	YEAR
ROBINS				Frank Belton	2550	D	1906	Margaret B.	67175	D	1934
Mary	78210	D	1938	Frank C.	28144	D	1919	Maria M.	41012	D	1925
ROBINSON				Fred E.	51062	D	1928	Mary Crittenden	18983	D	1915
Al	43296	D	1926	Geneva Elizabeth	15712	D	1913	Michael J.	31602	D	1921
Alberta Chess	83141	D	1940	Genevieve Agnes	53899	M	1929	Nannie	38794	D	1924
Allen	44187	D	1926	George	9792	D	1910	Nannie Minge	81090	D	1939
Allen Macdermot	8112	M	1909	George	11023	I	1911	Oscar Maynard	77327	D	1937
Ambrose E.	59176	M	1931	George F.	63170	D	1932	Rabbi Bernard	60959	D	1932
Anita L.	73083	M	1936	George Henry	9548	D	1910	Reuben	45031	D	1926
Anna Amelia	81820	D	1939	George Marland	83703	D	1940	Reuben G.	81018	D	1939
Arthur	43296	D	1926	George W.	68943	D	1935	Robert	45031	D	1926
Augustus W.	7198	D	1909	Georgia E.	69854	D	1935	Robin Maria	54008	D	1929
Austin Elliott	66184	D	1934	Gerald E.	47237	D	1927	Ruth A.	36131	I	1923
Bernard	60959	D	1932	Harry C.	82914	D	1939	Ruth B.	87040	D	1941
Bernice	8069	M	1909	Helen	83791	D	1940	Sarah F.	30364	I	1920
Bertha C.	79739	D	1938	Henrietta	64127	D	1933	Sarah Frances	35791	D	1923
Bessie	8112	M	1909	Henry	6432	D	1908	Sarah J.	10036	I	1910
Betty	87483	D	1941	Henry Clay	8112	M	1909	Sarah J.	43754	D	1926
Bridget	3952	D	1907	Henry E.	9947	D	1910	Theodore G. C.	47669	D	1927
Bridget	27500	D	1919	Isaac	70765	D	1935	Thomas B.	41601	D	1925
C. P.	21856	D	1916	Isabelle	76940	D	1937	Thomas W.	37408	D	1923
Caroline A.	4050	D	1907	Isadore	70765	D	1935	William	44341	D	1926
Carrie D.	62107	D	1932	J.	34172	D	1922	William Burnell	63621	M	1933
Carrie S.	12083	D	1911	J. H., Mrs.	76940	D	1937	William C.	49015	D	1928
Charles H.	1274	D	1906	James Chester	26538	D	1919	William E.	51755	D	1929
Charles Joseph	37501	D	1923	James M.	24211	D	1918	William H.	34205	D	1922
Charlotte	8112	M	1909	James W.	47134	D	1927	Willis G.	29005	D	1920
Clara Belle	50450	I	1928	Jane Foster Byrd	79687	D	1938	ROBISON			
Crittenden	12886	D	1912	Jay H.	31851	D	1921	Bernice	8069	M	1909
David	3480	D	1907	Jennie Curtis	89613	I	1942	Charles	8069	M	1909
David Cunningham	8112	M	1909	Jessie A.	87236	D	1941	Dwight DeWitt	57331	M	1930
David William	21244	D	1916	John	8712	D	1909	Jane S.	958	D	1906
Derry Thurman	29804	D	1920	John	28773	D	1920	John S.	85532	D	1940
Dollie	86767	D	1941	John C.	20620	D	1916	ROBITSCHER			
Doris Elizabeth	27792	D	1919	John S.	85532	D	1940	Lisie	12266	D	1911
Edward Gordon	67158	D	1934	Jonas	22141	D	1917	Samuel	12458	I	1911
Edward John	78360	M	1938	Joseph	11255	D	1911	Samuel	15670	D	1913
Edward Johnstone	8112	M	1909	Joseph	23246	D	1917	ROBKY			
Edward Mott	8876	D	1909	Joseph	70084	D	1935	Violet	85928	D	1940
Edwin B.	74573	D	1937	Joseph Henry	30484	D	1920	ROBL			
Elizabeth	57060	D	1930	Joseph R.	75245	D	1937	Catherine A.	19230	M	1915
Elizabeth Jane	27793	M	1919	Josephine	54732	D	1930	Catherine E.	16688	D	1914
Elizabeth May	57028	D	1930	Kathleen	66370	D	1934	Frank W.	19379	D	1915
Ella F.	78855	D	1938	Liston C.	19003	D	1915	James A.	14866	M	1913
Ella R.	72216	D	1936	Louise M.	49904	D	1928	Margaret	1444	D	1906
Emma B.	31977	D	1921	Luella Cross	79933	D	1938	Margaret	8493	D	1909
Emma E.	49046	D	1928	Lulu Cross	79933	D	1938	Margaret E.	14865	M	1913
Esther	8112	M	1909	Mae L.	57327	D	1930				
Eugenia F.	22519	D	1917	Margaret A.	9327	D	1910				

NAME	NUMBER	TYPE	YEAR
ROBLEDO			
Charlotte Gashweiler	71450	I	1936
Charlotte L.	71450	I	1936
Joseph J.	30265	D	1920
ROBLES			
Ralph	10360	M	1910
ROBLING			
Richard Paul	89870	M	1942
ROBOHM			
Cord	10002	D	1910
Sophie	68286	D	1934
ROBRECHT			
August	30050	D	1920
ROBSON			
Agnes Gray	38289	D	1924
Allen M.	39413	D	1924
Hannah	4916	D	1907
Susan B.	89333	I	1942
ROBUSCIOTTI			
Carlo	25563	D	1918
ROBUSON			
Caroline	21781	D	1916
George R.	23880	D	1918
Sophie	42102	D	1925
ROBY			
Carol Jean	86567	M	1941
Gordon	86567	M	1941
ROCCA			
Assunta	77309	D	1937
Francesco	87664	D	1941
Frank	33136	D	1922
Giacomo	37862	D	1923
Joseph	76514	D	1937
Joseph Mathieu	42221	D	1925
Josephine	81409	D	1939
Maria	105	D	1906
Maria	28195	D	1919
Mary	52109	D	1929
Raymond	48498	M	1927
Rosa	42479	D	1925
Victor	46134	D	1927
ROCCAFORTE			
Domenico	74375	D	1937
ROCCATAGLIATA			
Frank	33136	D	1922
Kate	69056	D	1935

NAME	NUMBER	TYPE	YEAR
ROCCHIA			
Michele	46045	D	1926
Mickele	46045	D	1926
Theresa	78521	D	1938
ROCCO			
Bossetto	68696	D	1935
Cereghino	51254	D	1928
Josephine F.	81409	D	1939
Rossetto	68696	D	1935
Stagnaro	26047	D	1919
ROCCOS			
George N.	62219	D	1932
ROCHA			
Andres	32987	D	1921
John Monica	70388	D	1935
Maria	105	D	1906
ROCHAT			
Ernest A.	21372	D	1916
ROCHE			
Annie J.	5563	D	1908
Bessie	41264	D	1925
Claire	4936	M	1907
Dorothy	4936	M	1907
Dorothy	10614	M	1910
Ella Agnes	25926	D	1918
Fred Walter	55328	D	1930
George W.	28577	D	1920
Gertie	60676	D	1932
Gertruce Latey	75540	D	1937
Gertrude V.	27021	M	1919
Hanoria	38739	D	1924
Herbert W.	42804	D	1925
Jack	73207	M	1936
James	14808	M	1913
James H.	79523	D	1938
John	14808	M	1913
John	17454	D	1914
John H.	13753	D	1912
Lawrence	14808	M	1913
Leo J.	68342	D	1934
Leonard	8539	D	1909
Lilly M.	42985	I	1925
Lilly M.	67605	D	1934
Margaret	14778	D	1913
Mary	3262	D	1907
Mary	14808	M	1913
Mary	23111	D	1917
Mary Elizabeth Frances	4652	I	1907

NAME	NUMBER	TYPE	YEAR
Mary Elizabeth Frances	63479	D	1933
Mary F.	47368	D	1927
Mary Katherine	10279	D	1910
Myrtle R.	56268	D	1930
Roland M.	40699	D	1925
Thomas B.	1081	D	1906
Thomas F.	29213	D	1920
Virgil T.	27263	M	1919
Walter E.	12947	D	1912
William	58201	D	1931
William D.	7306	D	1909
ROCHESTER			
Haydon	31413	D	1921
ROCHETTA			
Louis	88507	D	1941
ROCHFORD			
James Riley	27724	D	1919
ROCHFORT			
Joseph N.	20752	D	1916
ROCHON			
Esther	19004	D	1915
ROCK			
Amelia C.	69288	D	1935
Annie	1676	D	1906
Bridget	34641	D	1922
Charles	37322	M	1923
Edward R.	17098	D	1914
James J.	16919	D	1914
John P.	23715	D	1917
Joseph F.	12092	D	1911
Margaret Louise	9899	M	1910
Mary	35836	D	1923
Mary R.	5793	D	1908
Mary R.	70783	D	1935
Michael J.	57485	D	1930
Rose E.	53965	D	1929
Theodore Henry	2522	M	1906
William	51886	I	1929
ROCKER			
Christina F.	45080	D	1926
ROCKFORD			
Janet E.	53459	D	1929
ROCKHILL			
Amanda	12692	I	1911
ROCKMAN			
Emily	19131	I	1915
Emily	24807	D	1918

NAME	NUMBER	TYPE	YEAR
ROCKO			
William	73128	D	1936
ROCKS			
Emily Ann	18394	D	1915
William	57535	I	1930
ROCKSTROH			
Frederick E.	57967	D	1931
ROCKWELL			
Phoebe Clark	64125	D	1933
Virginia	33770	D	1922
ROCKWITZ			
Gottlieb W.	4557	D	1907
Maria	4558	D	1907
ROCKWOOD			
Louise	57745	D	1931
ROCQUIN			
Constant	44730	D	1926
RODDA			
Christina	74067	D	1936
Edith E.	21510	D	1916
RODDEN			
Cornelius	44670	D	1926
Patrick	76394	D	1937
William Patrick	79224	D	1938
RODDIE			
J. Millar	25483	D	1918
RODDS			
Christina	74067	D	1936
RODDY			
Catherine W.	33198	M	1922
Francis J.	36631	D	1923
James J., Mrs.	53776	D	1929
James P.	33198	M	1922
John J.	33198	M	1922
Mary E.	33198	M	1922
Mary M.	53776	D	1929
Patrick J.	31743	D	1921
Robert Dunn	57882	D	1931
RODE			
Charles	4074	D	1907
Christian B.	3962	D	1907
Mary	34095	D	1922
RODEFELD			
Friedrich	18384	I	1915
Wilhelmina	18325	D	1914

NAME	NUMBER	TYPE	YEAR
RODEFFER			
Newman R.	55988	D	1930
RODEFORD			
Thomas	5932	D	1908
RODEN			
Gustav F.	30462	D	1920
Jane A.	89980	I	1942
Marie	14521	I	1912
Sue	9382	D	1910
William H.	67963	D	1934
RODENBACK			
Gerhard	32576	D	1921
RODENBERG			
Carrie	17537	I	1914
RODERICK			
Jeanne	26744	D	1919
Joseph	47317	I	1927
Julia Ethel	47636	D	1927
RODESTROM			
Bengt A.	74979	D	1937
RODEWALD			
Charles H.	3956	D	1907
RODEWOLDT			
Christian H. W.	46038	D	1926
RODEY			
Helen Johanna	85945	M	1940
Helen Johanna	86259	M	1941
Marie Nekola	86258	D	1941
RODGER			
William	26793	D	1919
RODGERS			
Alice	46869	D	1927
Amy Dorothy	2863	M	1907
Ann Jane	42254	D	1925
Anna T.	60881	D	1932
Arthur	339	D	1906
Augustus F.	6928	D	1908
Ellen Cunningham	69443	D	1935
Esther F.	39336	D	1924
Frederick John	42538	D	1925
George D.	78236	D	1938
Henry R.	57388	D	1930
James L.	22462	D	1917
James Stanford	53858	D	1929
John	46456	D	1927
John Mills	62826	I	1932
John Mills	63038	D	1932

NAME	NUMBER	TYPE	YEAR
Mary	15082	D	1913
Mary	72976	D	1936
Mary C. E.	55732	D	1930
Mary J.	55659	D	1930
Mary Louise	53014	D	1929
Michael	15850	D	1913
Sarah A.	20461	D	1916
Teresa Elizabeth	25608	D	1918
Terrence	41187	D	1925
W. A.	79021	D	1938
Wilhelmina	79021	D	1938
William H.	14065	D	1912
RODIACK			
Joseph	59140	D	1931
RODICK			
Eleanora	37697	D	1923
Walker	15164	D	1913
RODIGOU			
John	65693	D	1933
RODIGUEZ			
Mary Louise	53014	D	1929
RODIN			
Anton	70499	D	1935
Mary	87459	D	1941
Matia	78551	I	1938
Matia	87459	D	1941
Matilda	87459	D	1941
RODIS			
James George	45991	D	1926
RODMAN			
Frank L.	65628	D	1933
John B.	8364	D	1909
RODNEY			
F. A.	29752	D	1920
George Brydges	48156	D	1927
Harry Cromwell	88703	D	1941
James D.	51337	D	1928
John Joseph	52927	D	1929
John Joseph	52985	M	1929
Mary	30204	D	1920
Thomas Edward	52985	M	1929
RODOLPH			
Erwin G.	70301	D	1935
RODONI			
Anselmo	84702	D	1940
Sam A.	84702	D	1940
Samuel L.	77758	I	1938

NAME	NUMBER	TYPE	YEAR
RODOPOULOS			
Demitrios George	45991	D	1926
RODOPULOS			
Nicholas	28915	D	1920
RODOSY			
Emma R.	39807	I	1924
RODOTA			
Rachela	84795	D	1940
RODRIGO			
Arlene Sylvia	88786	M	1941
Bonafacio Peter	88786	M	1941
RODRIGUE			
Winifred M.	58111	D	1931
RODRIGUES			
Joseph C.	41758	I	1925
Joseph C.	41758	I	1925
Mary	47608	D	1927
Raymond Joseph	41780	M	1925
Raymond Joseph	41780	M	1925
RODRIGUEZ			
A. A.	44232	D	1926
Albert	48188	M	1927
Albert	34368	D	1922
B. A.	44232	D	1926
Christ	78753	M	1938
Ella	84070	D	1940
Fred	29009	D	1920
Fred Philip	49627	D	1928
George	78753	M	1938
Jose	66375	D	1934
Jose Fernandez	71153	D	1935
Juana Tovar	85426	M	1940
Lorita	79351	D	1938
Maria	77384	D	1937
Numa	50792	I	1928
Ofilia Tovar	85426	M	1940
Pura	78860	I	1938
Rafael	48188	M	1927
Rafael	63661	D	1933
Rafaela	78753	M	1938
Simona	48188	M	1927
Thomas	72680	D	1936
RODRIQUEZ			
Alfred	21865	D	1916
Antonio	10180	D	1910
Belinda	35654	D	1923
Carmelita	33689	M	1922

NAME	NUMBER	TYPE	YEAR
Eda	75620	D	1937
Fermamdo	29009	D	1920
Gloria	62261	D	1932
Jose	80752	D	1939
Joseph T.	43148	D	1925
Josephina Maria	74875	M	1937
Juan	30631	D	1920
Manuel	52780	D	1929
Mary	82513	D	1939
Numa	50792	I	1928
Tulio	35819	M	1923
ROE			
Anna	74882	D	1937
George E.	58661	D	1931
George H.	10597	D	1910
John J.	25733	D	1918
Max	54927	D	1930
Patrick H.	3030	D	1907
Thomas E.	52611	D	1929
William	23193	D	1917
ROEBER			
Albert A.	88100	D	1941
ROEBLING			
Genevieve	55216	M	1930
Robert	55216	M	1930
ROECKNER			
Mary A.	17314	D	1914
William	15915	D	1913
ROEDER			
Nell	46837	D	1927
William F.	83117	D	1940
ROEDIGER			
Ernestine	26728	D	1919
ROEDING			
Ethel Allis	20740	D	1916
Gertrude Thompson	68996	D	1935
ROEFER			
Henry A.	19484	D	1915
ROEGNO			
Ginbatista	37201	D	1923
ROEHE			
Irma S.	65919	D	1933
ROEMER			
Adolph P.	62766	D	1932
Edwin W.	42958	D	1925
Oscar, Sr.	65438	D	1933
Philip	78294	D	1938

NAME	NUMBER	TYPE	YEAR
ROESCH			
Augusta	18451	D	1915
Friedrich	58629	D	1931
Louis	21058	D	1916
ROESCHEISE			
Louis	28334	D	1919
ROESCHISE			
Loui	28334	D	1919
ROESE			
Charlotte Julia	12598	M	1911
ROESLER			
Eleanor	54020	D	1929
Ellen A.	54020	D	1929
ROESMAN			
Thomas Jefferson	64274	D	1933
ROESSEL			
Louisa	20714	D	1916
Louise	13934	I	1912
ROESSING			
Richard	3058	D	1907
ROESSLE			
John	41559	D	1925
Julia F.	52688	D	1929
ROESTI			
Paul G.	20270	D	1916
ROETHE			
Edward J.	65755	D	1933
ROETHLISBERGER			
Katherine	57236	I	1930
Ray Herbert	50666	M	1928
ROETTGER			
Fred	70990	D	1935
ROFF			
Harry L.	31148	D	1921
ROGALLE			
Jeanne	6204	D	1908
ROGAN			
George	51751	D	1929
Isabelle	89313	D	1942
ROGAWAY			
Roderick M.	68610	D	1934
Roderick M.	68686	M	1935
ROGE			
Louis	28472	D	1919
ROGENFELD			
John	77779	D	1938

NAME	NUMBER	TYPE	YEAR
ROGENFELDT			
John	77779	D	1938
ROGER			
Dorothy	53816	M	1929
Gabrielle	53816	M	1929
Joseph	53816	M	1929
Leon H.	43451	D	1926
Loretto	53816	M	1929
Margaret	48497	D	1927
Paul	53816	M	1929
ROGERS			
Agnes Eleanor	20367	M	1916
Alletta Cre	16370	M	1913
Anga A.	68566	I	1934
Anna	765	D	1906
Augusta M.	75312	I	1937
Augusta M.	80851	D	1939
Bethel	50711	M	1928
Charles	24277	D	1918
Charles H.	25867	D	1918
Charles Henry	20439	D	1916
Charles Oliver	20673	M	1916
Charles P.	61758	D	1932
Clara Walbridge	23291	D	1917
Claude F.	36817	I	1923
Claude F.	47802	D	1927
Delia	19418	D	1915
Dennis	84813	D	1940
Dolores	71040	M	1935
Dorothy	10858	M	1910
Earl W.	19429	M	1915
Earlene Alberta	4146	M	1907
Edward	28969	M	1920
Edward	58429	D	1931
Edward	34594	D	1922
Edward F.	19388	D	1915
Edward J.	19429	M	1915
Eli Philip	63844	D	1933
Elizabeth Rutherford	39456	D	1924
Ellen Eliza	71765	D	1936
Emily L.	1486	D	1906
Florence I.	64852	D	1933
Glen Spencer	85237	D	1940
Glenn H.	20673	M	1916
Harry	5759	D	1908
Herbert M.	26529	D	1919
Herbert O.	3186	D	1907
Herman	50711	M	1928

NAME	NUMBER	TYPE	YEAR
Herman M.	20225	D	1916
James	15994	D	1913
James A.	76400	D	1937
Jennie	17644	D	1914
Jennie E.	31595	D	1921
Jesse Wakeman	68671	D	1935
Jessie J.	36413	D	1923
John	77855	D	1938
John A.	45978	D	1926
John M.	58768	D	1931
John Olwin	25560	D	1918
John W.	56261	D	1930
John W.	88377	D	1941
Joseph	48468	D	1927
Josephine	2940	D	1907
Josephine	3925	I	1907
Josiah B.	68951	D	1935
Katherine C.	60121	D	1931
Lorena	19429	M	1915
Louse Mitchell	30737	D	1920
Lucy Marie	87509	D	1941
Lydia Amelia	72810	D	1936
Malcolm A.	41886	M	1925
Malcolm A.	41886	M	1925
Marguerita V.	36346	D	1923
Maria	3776	D	1907
Mary	19429	M	1915
Mary A.	17798	D	1914
Mary E.	81491	D	1939
Mary Josephine	20367	M	1916
Melvin G.	36414	M	1923
Milton N.	12754	D	1911
Nathan	41844	D	1925
Nathan	41844	D	1925
Nelson J.	14208	D	1912
Phillipa H. A.	8746	I	1909
Samuel	41886	M	1925
Samuel	41886	M	1925
Samuel	47508	D	1927
Samuel L.	85752	D	1940
Samuel Lucius	20673	M	1916
Sanford H.	67120	D	1934
Virginia May	50711	M	1928
W. H.	14065	D	1912
W. H., Mrs.	1486	D	1906
Walter Dean	48317	I	1927
Walter Dean	54124	D	1929
ROGERSON			
Bernard	8854	M	1909

NAME	NUMBER	TYPE	YEAR
Cecilia	8854	M	1909
John Bernard	64681	D	1933
John J.	45638	D	1926
Mary	8854	M	1909
ROGET			
Henriette	59771	D	1931
ROGG			
Lena	33475	D	1922
ROGGERMANN			
Charles C.	22288	D	1917
ROGGERO			
Marianna	56838	D	1930
ROGGIO			
John C.	62113	D	1932
ROGMANN			
Johann H. R.	55789	D	1930
ROGOFF			
Julia	42758	D	1925
ROGOWSKI			
John	3980	D	1907
ROHATCH			
Francis Thomas	63261	M	1932
Helen Mildred	63261	M	1932
ROHATSCH			
John F.	77450	D	1938
ROHDE			
Carl Arthur	84724	D	1940
Claudina	400	M	1906
Lina M.	31525	D	1921
Magretha	13268	D	1912
Otto H.	36223	I	1923
Otto John	62741	D	1932
William Henry	32536	I	1921
ROHE			
Meta	12937	D	1912
ROHL			
Herman August	50075	D	1928
ROHLER			
August	21622	D	1916
ROHLFFS			
Auguste Marie	88936	D	1942
Edward	56686	D	1930
Mary	17762	D	1914
ROHLWINK			
Erika	8816	M	1909
Hans	8816	M	1909

NAME	NUMBER	TYPE	YEAR
Heinz Ludwig	8816	M	1909
Kurt	8816	M	1909
Lieschen	8816	M	1909
Rita	8816	M	1909
ROHM			
Harry C.	51523	I	1928
Harry C.	85814	D	1940
ROHNER			
Ethel Francis	52299	D	1929
ROHR			
Eppa	65309	D	1933
Jane	35489	M	1922
ROHRBACH			
Henry G.	58272	D	1931
Louisa	4393	I	1907
Moritz	63331	D	1933
Wilhelmini	68914	D	1935
ROHRBACHER			
Phillip	25784	M	1918
ROHRBORN			
Anna	38198	D	1924
ROHRER			
Catherine E.	83132	D	1940
Ignaz	14949	D	1913
Joseph	3044	D	1907
Minna	34021	D	1922
ROHRICHT			
Ferdinand	38084	D	1924
ROHRS			
John H.	18569	D	1915
ROHWEBER			
Gustav	40873	D	1925
ROIG			
Medea T.	51862	D	1929
ROITENSTEIN			
Annie	40709	D	1925
Clara	40709	D	1925
Frances	40709	D	1925
Julius M.	40709	D	1925
Maeyer	40709	D	1925
ROJAS			
Andreas	78839	D	1938
ROJCES			
Andres	78839	D	1938
ROJO			
Mary	76323	I	1937

NAME	NUMBER	TYPE	YEAR
ROJOLS			
Andres	78839	D	1938
ROJSZ			
A. John	39528	I	1924
John	39528	I	1924
ROKKA			
Adam	37421	D	1923
ROLAND			
Les M.	85591	D	1940
Louis I.	81609	D	1939
Oscar Jacob	54673	D	1930
ROLANDELLI			
Antonio	74171	D	1936
Eugenio	88713	D	1941
ROLANDI			
Frederick Sereno	67385	D	1934
ROLANDO			
Elizabeth Simpson	32149	D	1921
Maria	72406	D	1936
Pietro P. R. G.	66079	D	1934
ROLANDONE			
Lorenzo	65251	D	1933
ROLESON			
Edward James	82811	M	1939
Ralph Fletcher	82811	M	1939
ROLFE			
Helena	40235	D	1924
ROLFER			
Henry A.	19484	D	1915
ROLFF			
Charles	50830	D	1928
Frank	47013	I	1927
Hans W.	58989	D	1931
Mary Ann	71086	D	1935
ROLFI			
Giuseppe	61798	D	1932
Joseph	61798	D	1932
ROLKER			
Edward S	39134	D	1924
ROLKIN			
Edward	86425	D	1941
ROLLA			
Maria	78542	D	1938
Quinto	77655	D	1938
ROLLER			
Carolina	39184	D	1924

NAME	NUMBER	TYPE	YEAR
Charles A.	85365	D	1940
Emma D.	14087	I	1912
Emma D.	14251	D	1912
Josephine E.	14781	D	1913
Susan E.	16922	I	1914
ROLLERI			
Alfred	46973	M	1927
Nat	46962	D	1927
ROLLINS			
Alice F.	42268	I	1925
Alice F.	43304	D	1926
Annie	66208	I	1934
Dollie C.	30122	D	1920
Magaret A.	70167	D	1935
Margaret A.	66208	I	1934
Mary Patricia	67504	M	1934
ROLLINSON			
Albert W.	44756	M	1926
Earle G.	44756	M	1926
ROLLMAN			
Ella	75252	D	1937
ROLOFF			
Herbert	46715	D	1927
ROLPH			
George Morrison	62203	D	1932
Gertrude	26451	M	1919
Henry Renton	48275	M	1927
James	24656	D	1918
James, Jr.	67290	D	1934
Katherine Jane	48275	M	1927
Mary	27789	D	1919
ROLS			
Louis	8182	D	1909
ROLTHE			
Edward J.	65755	D	1933
ROLTON			
Herbert	46715	D	1927
ROM			
Theresa	61302	D	1932
ROMA			
Rafael	83946	D	1940
ROMAGNA			
Giacomo	38167	D	1924
James	38167	D	1924
ROMAGNANI			
Guido	70221	D	1935

NAME	NUMBER	TYPE	YEAR	NAME	NUMBER	TYPE	YEAR	NAME	NUMBER	TYPE	YEAR
ROMAGNOLO				**ROME**				**ROMMINGER**			
Frederick	63597	D	1933	Paul	33110	I	1921	Anna	51149	D	1928
Richard David	78245	M	1938	Paul	33545	I	1922	**ROMOSER**			
ROMAINE				**ROMEO**				Henry	16565	D	1914
Anna Ayres	67459	D	1934	Albert	74931	M	1937	**RONALD**			
Benjamin	61703	D	1932	Antonio	74632	D	1937	Frank, Mrs.	85928	D	1940
Isabella M.	51601	D	1928	Dominic	74931	M	1937	**RONALDES**			
John Clare	49008	D	1928	Katherine	53683	D	1929	Camille	55704	D	1930
Mabel Freeman	73985	D	1936	Mary	74931	M	1937	**RONAN**			
ROMAN				**ROMER**				Annabelle	71678	D	1936
Augusta	64965	D	1933	J. Gordon Lo.	32697	I	1921	Joseph H.	8371	M	1909
Mary A.	7866	D	1909	John L.	22989	D	1917	Joseph H.	8459	D	1909
Priscilla	69714	D	1935	Magdalena	15855	D	1913	Mary	50469	D	1928
Simon	37204	D	1923	Otto Bismarck	11479	D	1911	Mary	54854	D	1930
ROMANDER				**ROMERI**				Thomas Peter	28680	D	1920
Margaret	65024	D	1933	Peter Paul	77070	D	1937	**RONAYNE**			
ROMANI				**ROMERO**				John	43345	D	1926
Domenico	41897	D	1925	Alice	36547	D	1923	**RONCALLO**			
Domenico	41897	D	1925	Ampara Ramirez	27280	D	1919	Martino	72340	D	1936
Frank	69292	D	1935	Blanche Josephine	87514	D	1941	**RONCELLI**			
Lena Camoriani	44139	D	1926	Juan	79841	D	1938	Frank	171	D	1906
Vincent	88743	D	1941	Pedro	73666	I	1936	**RONCHI**			
ROMANO				Pedro	75856	D	1937	Benedetto	80403	D	1939
Angelo R.	56621	D	1930	Reinaldo	77492	D	1938	Eileen Sybil	84968	D	1940
Feliciano	8964	D	1910	**ROMESTANT**				S. Eileen	84968	D	1940
Joseph	46611	M	1927	Salomon	15475	D	1913	**RONCHIN**			
Mollie	13634	D	1912	**ROMEY**				Catherine	40737	D	1925
Tiziano	60093	D	1931	Angelo Joseph	74026	D	1936	**RONCONI**			
Vincent	60842	I	1932	Maud Evelyh Critchfield	61792	D	1932	Antonio	28818	D	1920
ROMANS				**ROMICK**				Appolonia	85996	D	1941
Elnathan	89362	D	1942	Ephriam M.	70092	D	1935	Polonia	85996	D	1941
Nathan	89362	D	1942	**ROMIGUIERE**				**RONCOVIERI**			
ROMARIE				Berthe	27229	D	1919	Alfred	64412	D	1933
Francisco	26919	D	1919	Justin Fulein	78694	D	1938	Alfred Donald	67127	M	1934
ROMARIS				**ROMIGUIERE'**				Audrey	67127	M	1934
Francis	26919	D	1919	Justin	78694	D	1938	Betty Jane	67127	M	1934
Nicolas Frederic Francois	32943	D	1921	**ROMINGER**				**RONDEAU**			
ROMAY				Ana	51149	D	1928	Louis A.	14734	D	1913
Gloria	72153	M	1936	**ROMIQUIERE**				Rosella	25277	D	1918
Louis	62485	D	1932	Justin	78694	D	1938	**RONDELLE**			
Mary Alice	72154	M	1936	**ROMITI**				Russell Eugene	84016	M	1940
ROMAYNE				Ceasar	55000	D	1930	**RONDINOTTI**			
Harmony	67756	M	1934	**ROMMEL**				Maria	13198	D	1912
ROMBERGE				August	62475	I	1932	**RONDO**			
Arthur	38751	M	1924	Carl	4566	D	1907	Phillip J.	82110	D	1939
Valberg Alena	38751	M	1924	Henry	51621	D	1928				
				Regina	60404	D	1931				

NAME	NUMBER	TYPE	YEAR
RONDONI			
Clara	71499	I	1936
RONEBERG			
Ella	40200	D	1924
William	47533	D	1927
RONEY			
Annie	8869	D	1909
Edmund Burke	56309	I	1930
Frederick S	64968	D	1933
Joseph A.	83074	D	1940
Lucy	50529	I	1928
Nina Carol	64723	M	1933
RONNER			
Joseph Antone	57228	D	1930
RONNIGER			
Anna Emilie	42926	D	1925
Otto William	55803	M	1930
Paul Curt	55803	M	1930
ROOCKS			
Fred H.	87760	D	1941
ROOD			
Agnes V.	62389	D	1932
Elizabeth B.	15836	M	1913
Elizabeth E.	23042	D	1917
Elizabeth N.	23042	D	1917
Frank H.	65225	D	1933
Hugh R.	13792	D	1912
Lee Seaton	37868	M	1923
ROOHT			
Gustaf Hjalmer	81694	D	1939
ROOKE			
James W.	58486	D	1931
ROOKES			
John A.	58949	D	1931
ROOKS			
Emily Ann	18394	D	1915
John Alexander	58949	D	1931
ROOME			
Albert E.	17397	D	1914
Mabel T.	78870	D	1938
ROOMERS			
Emeline	21988	D	1916
ROONEY			
Albert	76806	D	1937
Annie	8869	D	1909
Bee I.	75743	D	1937
Bridget I.	75743	D	1937

NAME	NUMBER	TYPE	YEAR
Caroline Amelia	22442	D	1917
Charles Hugh	28852	D	1920
Ellen Martha	55357	D	1930
Gilbert Peter	48837	D	1927
Harriett V.	56215	D	1930
Harry T.	34499	D	1922
Helen M.	59791	I	1931
Henry Thomas	34499	D	1922
Hugh	28014	D	1919
James F.	63104	D	1932
James J.	38292	D	1924
John	12628	D	1911
John Joseph	85704	D	1940
Joseph	22699	D	1917
Joseph Stanislaus	53553	I	1929
Margaret M.	67907	D	1934
Margaret T.	30983	D	1921
Mary	2273	D	1906
Mary	81494	I	1939
Nora	71954	D	1936
Owen F.	7411	D	1909
Peter M.	23920	D	1918
Thomas	55356	D	1930
Thomas J.	22699	D	1917
ROOP			
Frank P.	29477	D	1920
ROORK			
James L.	67789	I	1934
ROOS			
Achille	51107	D	1928
Adolph	26506	D	1919
Anders G.	18553	D	1915
Andrew G.	18553	D	1915
Carl	56808	D	1930
Eliza	32494	D	1921
Jacques	71680	D	1936
Moses	26506	D	1919
Moyse	26506	D	1919
ROOSA			
George	48977	D	1928
ROOT			
Abdon Hidalgo	80366	D	1939
Aileen Lilian	25574	M	1918
Charlotte	81330	I	1939
Corydon B.	48972	D	1928
Daniel Edwin	84219	D	1940
Dorothy Elizabeth	7365	M	1909
Drucius V.	12501	I	1911

NAME	NUMBER	TYPE	YEAR
E. J., Mrs.	74722	D	1937
Ebbon	80366	D	1939
Elliott M.	20109	D	1915
Frederick S.	47787	D	1927
George A.	13822	D	1912
Harold E.	76856	D	1937
Hattie A.	74722	D	1937
James Ralph	44658	M	1926
John M.	67679	D	1934
John W.	11293	D	1911
Rebecca A.	18474	D	1915
Ruby Mae	44658	M	1926
Seth B.	27100	D	1919
ROOTH			
Benjamin Stephenson	34581	M	1922
George Anthony	38152	D	1924
ROOTSTEIN			
Paul	49041	D	1928
ROPCKE			
Mary	37534	D	1923
ROPER			
Belinda	18533	D	1915
John	37748	M	1923
Joseph	33746	D	1922
Nora Martha	52202	D	1929
Thomas	85780	D	1940
William	39932	D	1924
ROPPOLO			
Ellena	51756	D	1929
ROQUET			
Amelia	71869	L	1936
RORABACK			
James L.	59758	D	1931
RORIFT			
Henry Andrew	57598	D	1931
ROS			
John Savant	31262	I	1921
ROSA			
Alberta	37075	D	1923
Belle A.	18404	D	1915
Charles J.	35109	M	1922
Francis	34015	M	1922
Giovanni	46881	D	1927
Manoel Peter	32346	D	1921
Vilma	74617	D	1937
Walter Joseph	78393	D	1938
Walter Paul	78244	D	1938

NAME	NUMBER	TYPE	YEAR	NAME	NUMBER	TYPE	YEAR	NAME	NUMBER	TYPE	YEAR
William P.	34015	M	1922	Robert Lee	71734	D	1936	Frank L., Jr.	61445	M	1932
ROSAIA				Robert Lee, Jr.	48135	M	1927	**ROSENBACH**			
Adolph Martin	85025	D	1940	Samuel M.	44828	D	1926	Adele	76672	I	1937
Beatrice	66914	D	1934	Tillie	69700	D	1935	Leonie	28273	D	1919
Caterina	31755	D	1921	Willard C.	47476	I	1927	Max, Mrs.	85949	D	1941
Pietro	78433	D	1938	William Henry	24938	D	1918	Nettie Appleton	85949	D	1941
William	70854	D	1935	William T.	26513	D	1919	Rosalie	24124	M	1918
ROSALES				**ROSEBERRY**				**ROSENBAUM**			
Francisca Terrasaz	62506	D	1932	Eleanor E.	75265	D	1937	Albert M.	48518	D	1927
ROSALLES				Ellen I.	4913	D	1907	Bena	22655	D	1917
Dianne	77012	M	1937	**ROSEDALE**				Bertha	28027	I	1919
ROSBURG				Elizabeth	27921	I	1919	Bertha	28639	D	1920
Ella	35278	I	1922	Helga	27921	I	1919	Charles W.	22757	D	1917
ROSCELLI				**ROSEK**				Charles W., Jr.	22758	M	1917
Domenico	88671	D	1941	Katherine V.	14965	D	1913	Elsa	4624	M	1907
Giovanni	18162	D	1914	Minna Alyce	21831	D	1916	Hattie	57616	D	1931
Lorenzo	88671	D	1941	**ROSEKIND**				Herbert I.	28621	M	1920
ROSDAHL				Morris	52414	D	1929	Herman A.	35637	D	1923
John	26591	D	1919	**ROSEKRANS**				Irene	28621	M	1920
ROSE				Chester Wilson	86815	D	1941	Isaac S.	11708	D	1911
Alexander	62441	D	1932	Josephine	3678	D	1907	Izetta	20003	M	1915
Bertram	48742	D	1927	**ROSELER**				Johanna	27643	D	1919
David	33762	D	1922	George W.	56916	D	1930	Julia	86085	D	1941
Elbert A.	76495	M	1937	**ROSELLA**				Mervin F.	22758	M	1917
Ella	48089	D	1927	George	40903	D	1925	Nettie	78275	D	1938
Emma Lewis	87448	D	1941	**ROSELLE**				Sigmund D.	4036	D	1907
Frances Marion	54776	M	1930	Louise	13934	I	1912	**ROSENBERG**			
Frank	74760	D	1937	**ROSELLINI**				Aaron Benjamin	59084	D	1931
Fred Wiley	45477	D	1926	Augustino	76872	D	1937	Abraham	54361	D	1929
Freeman Edgar	55227	M	1930	Joseph J.	87908	D	1941	Adolph	36487	D	1923
George	17730	D	1914	Victor	54622	D	1929	Arthur M.	52940	D	1929
Henry	69247	D	1935	**ROSEMON**				Benjamin	79580	D	1938
Hulda P.	24428	D	1918	Peter	43873	D	1926	Bernard	32201	D	1921
Isabell	23276	D	1917	**ROSEMONT**				Bernard	79580	D	1938
J.	1378	D	1906	August Leslie	85087	D	1940	Beth T.	85856	D	1940
Johanna	18269	D	1914	Eugene	42993	M	1925	Charles	80178	D	1938
John	14599	D	1912	**ROSEN**				Clara	12135	D	1911
John J.	75564	M	1937	Adolph	72481	D	1936	David	68150	D	1934
John Joseph	18344	D	1915	Arthur J. A. O. A.	57235	D	1930	Dora	26980	D	1919
Jonas	41410	D	1925	Bernhardt	50805	D	1928	Dora	67340	D	1934
Lewis S., Jr.	75563	D	1937	Chaie Rasch	488	D	1906	Ella	71455	D	1936
Lina	79979	D	1938	Merton	54434	M	1929	Esther	22912	D	1917
Louis Albert	21580	D	1916	Morris	51262	I	1928	Eva	10796	D	1910
Louis Simon	11385	D	1911	Samuel	71618	D	1936	Fannie	36747	D	1923
Marguerite	54776	M	1930	Sonia Stella	70181	D	1935	Frank	54304	D	1929
Mary	72256	D	1936	**ROSENAU**				Fred	63867	M	1933
Melville S.	68252	I	1934	Frank L.	58683	D	1931	Goetz	23756	D	1917
Ralph W.	16692	D	1914					Grace	78732	D	1938

NAME	NUMBER	TYPE	YEAR	NAME	NUMBER	TYPE	YEAR	NAME	NUMBER	TYPE	YEAR
Hannah	2353	D	1906	Henry	47051	D	1927	Louis	21285	D	1916
Harry Louis	39347	D	1924	Herman	47142	D	1927	Minnie Wise	80336	D	1939
Hattie	48086	D	1927	Jennie	83500	D	1940	Sarah	11614	D	1911
Hattie	87223	D	1941	Joseph	14991	D	1913	**ROSENFELDT**			
Herman	31652	D	1921	Maximo	73116	D	1936	Herman	83380	D	1940
Hyman	36535	M	1923	Sophie	84304	D	1940	**ROSENFIELD**			
I., Mrs.	87223	D	1941	**ROSENBOHM**				Anna J.	72064	D	1936
Isidor	36770	D	1923	George H.	12036	D	1911	William Woodward	42571	D	1925
Jacob	72757	D	1936	John H.	5619	D	1908	**ROSENGARDEN**			
Jennie	48577	D	1927	**ROSENBOOM**				Henrietta	40222	D	1924
Jennie	67417	D	1934	Harold Eugene	61577	M	1932	**ROSENGRAVE**			
Joseph	35918	D	1923	Raymond Edward	61577	M	1932	Bartholomew	10333	D	1910
Joseph H.	83163	D	1940	**ROSENBRACK**				**ROSENGREEN**			
Joseph L.	33699	D	1922	William Henry	84573	D	1940	James Peter	88195	D	1941
Kate	9832	D	1910	**ROSENCRANTZ**				**ROSENHEIM**			
Lena	28514	D	1919	Gustavus	86774	D	1941	Aaron	6803	D	1908
Leon	14320	M	1912	Helen	23661	M	1917	Samuel	31920	D	1921
Louise Alice	33661	M	1922	Julius	13827	D	1912	**ROSENKIND**			
Marcus	54989	D	1930	N.	22634	D	1917	Morris	52414	D	1929
Martha	61297	D	1932	Rosalind	23661	M	1917	**ROSENLUND**			
Maurice	18843	D	1915	Samuel	39356	D	1924	Gustaf T.	11523	D	1911
Max L.	59052	D	1931	**ROSENDAHL**				Louise F.	86769	D	1941
Morris	77860	D	1938	Mary	78483	I	1938	**ROSENSHINE**			
Myron	75283	M	1937	Ossian	81822	D	1939	Adolph	40825	D	1925
Natalie	41047	D	1925	**ROSENDORF**				Elizabeth	60424	D	1931
Nathan	52107	D	1929	Oscar	89889	D	1942	Morris W.	46334	D	1927
Rose	23334	D	1917	Samuel	60546	I	1931	**ROSENSTEIN**			
Theresa	32682	D	1921	Samuel	62998	D	1932	Harry	52558	D	1929
ROSENBERGER				**ROSENDORN**				Lina	30315	D	1920
Edward J.	61795	D	1932	Elsia	45305	M	1926	Louise Marie	61602	M	1932
Johanna	61760	D	1932	Elsie	45305	M	1926	Morris	33522	D	1922
ROSENBLAD				Emillie	45305	M	1926	**ROSENSTIEN**			
John Edward	58760	D	1931	Natalie	45305	M	1926	Fritz	28775	D	1920
ROSENBLATT				Solomon	22132	D	1917	**ROSENSTIRN**			
Albert	17844	D	1914	**ROSENER**				Julius	44195	D	1926
Caroline F.	48337	D	1927	Beatrice S.	79327	D	1938	Julius Talbot	26824	M	1919
Carrie Frauenthal	48337	D	1927	Esther	20965	D	1916	Sylvia J.	26824	M	1919
Diana	68355	M	1934	Fannie	16979	D	1914	**ROSENSTOCK**			
Esther	68356	M	1934	H.	5989	D	1908	Isidore	48820	D	1927
Henry	28130	D	1919	Morris	34793	D	1922	Sarah	52639	D	1929
Irving Stern	76887	D	1937	**ROSENFELD**				**ROSENTHAL**			
Marcus	35401	D	1922	Abraham	9522	D	1910	Abraham	36551	D	1923
Rose	47209	D	1927	Herman	5707	D	1908	Abraham S.	80777	D	1939
ROSENBLUM				Jeanne Martha Frances	34640	M	1922	Amelia	88606	D	1941
Bena	22655	D	1917	Jeannne Martha	58414	M	1931	Ben	44518	D	1926
F. E.	38211	D	1924	John	1624	D	1906	Cerf	65420	D	1933
Harry	47142	D	1927	June	58414	M	1931	Charles M.	18724	D	1915
Helen	40817	D	1925								

Key: D = death; M = minor; I = incompetent

NAME	NUMBER	TYPE	YEAR	NAME	NUMBER	TYPE	YEAR	NAME	NUMBER	TYPE	YEAR
Daniel	86781	I	1941	**ROSEVEAR**				Donald	3002	D	1907
David	55282	D	1930	Margaret	74336	M	1937	Dorothea Meta	76637	D	1937
Earl V.	2269	M	1906	**ROSEWALD**				Eliza Jane	43950	D	1926
Esther	82212	D	1939	Julie	1175	D	1906	Elizabeth A.	40732	D	1925
Eugenie	59302	D	1931	**ROSHIN**				Ethel	1290	D	1906
Fannie	84345	D	1940	Harry	59526	D	1931	Francis Stuart	39676	D	1924
Florence	6387	M	1908	**ROSICH**				Frank	2444	D	1906
Florence	12450	M	1911	Nicholas C.	32066	D	1921	Fred E.	78847	D	1938
Hannah	46621	D	1927	**ROSIE**				Fred S.	69961	D	1935
Hubert S.	45703	D	1926	John	72537	D	1936	George	14880	D	1913
Isaac L.	78545	D	1938	Walter	20641	D	1916	George H.	69863	D	1935
Jeanette Ruth	2813	M	1907	**ROSIER**				George W.	47854	D	1927
Jennie	46621	D	1927	Lucie	62841	D	1932	H.	31210	D	1921
Jennie	48661	D	1927	**ROSIN**				Hannah	27224	D	1919
Joseph	31724	D	1921	Carl	13138	D	1912	Henry Y.	1474	D	1906
Leo	6387	M	1908	**ROSINA**				Hugh F.	895	D	1906
Leo	12450	M	1911	Clemente	42232	D	1925	Ida L.	36199	D	1923
Liebchen	3529	D	1907	**ROSINTHAL**				Irene	70923	D	1935
Louis	89740	D	1942	Bertha	48622	D	1927	James	6293	D	1908
Lucia	89437	D	1942	**ROSKE**				James	71907	D	1936
Madeline	6387	M	1908	John Wright	29715	M	1920	James Scobie, Mrs.	56726	D	1930
Madeline	12450	M	1911	**ROSLAND**				Jemima S.	56726	D	1930
Maurice	21464	D	1916	Oscar Paulsen	64742	D	1933	John	508	D	1906
Maurice	44116	D	1926	**ROSNER**				John	11093	D	1911
Max	51515	D	1928	Anna	13201	D	1912	John	34333	D	1922
Max	68314	D	1934	Edmund Maurice	21776	D	1916	John	45152	D	1926
Millie	57874	D	1931	Hannah	13201	D	1912	John N.	43343	D	1926
Minnie S.	19920	D	1915	Simon	1262	D	1906	Laura A. Wilder	64147	I	1933
Moses S.	16727	D	1914	**ROSS**				Lilly M.	48368	D	1927
Nathan	41382	D	1925	Adam	18609	D	1915	Lydia	72388	D	1936
Oscar	89913	I	1942	Adolphe	7022	D	1909	Malcolm A.	72027	D	1936
Rachel	44312	D	1926	Agnes M.	83694	D	1940	Margaret	42595	D	1925
Ray	44312	D	1926	Alexander	9971	D	1910	Martha	29027	D	1920
Samuel T.	66830	D	1934	Alexander	20089	M	1915	Martin F.	67794	D	1934
Sigmund	78272	D	1938	Barton Gilbert	50389	D	1928	Mary	34654	D	1922
Sol	77631	D	1938	Benjamin	37602	D	1923	Mary J.	68393	D	1934
Sophie C.	49743	I	1928	Bernard	4407	M	1907	Mary Louise	54935	M	1930
Vera	23460	D	1917	Bertha	87659	D	1941	Maurice J.	82164	D	1939
Vera M.	2269	M	1906	Carl	56808	D	1930	Permelia E.	64318	D	1933
Wilhelmina	3314	D	1907	Carroll Howard	50004	D	1928	Ronald Lloyd	78892	M	1938
ROSENWINKEL				Catherine	20693	D	1916	Sadie	54792	D	1930
Elsie	36894	I	1923	Catherine	71589	D	1936	Sarah B.	32118	D	1921
Henry	44848	D	1926	Charles Carney	49334	D	1928	Selina	13131	D	1912
ROSENZWEIG				Charles L.	5817	D	1908	Thomas	55670	D	1930
Isidor	1378	D	1906	Charles William	89675	D	1942	Thomas Patterson	37149	I	1923
Janet	26149	D	1919	Cheristie H.	27224	D	1919	William	20243	D	1916
ROSETTE				Daniel D.	3522	D	1907	William	55078	D	1930
Camillia A.	83921	I	1940					William	74075	D	1936
								William	81082	D	1939

NAME	NUMBER	TYPE	YEAR
William Andrew	79498	D	1938
William Edward	16667	D	1914
William Glyndyr	33174	D	1922
William J.	18685	D	1915
William P.	14585	D	1912
William P.	79236	D	1938
Willis Edwin	54935	M	1930
Ross-Wilder			
Laura A.	67529	D	1934
Rosseau			
Fannie	64290	D	1933
Rosselat			
Louis	9767	D	1910
Rosselet			
Louis	9767	D	1910
Rosselli			
Carmelina	75492	D	1937
Charles	87800	I	1941
Charles	89563	D	1942
G. B.	79978	D	1938
Giovani	79978	D	1938
Rosser			
Benjamin	82935	D	1939
William G.	33174	D	1922
Rosseter			
John Henry	72427	D	1936
Rossetti			
Cesare	42719	D	1925
Vincenzo	36837	D	1923
Rosshirt			
Grace	77231	D	1937
Rossi			
A. L.	34780	D	1922
Alfredo	34780	D	1922
Alfredo	52229	D	1929
Alfredo	77996	D	1938
Amelie A.	22514	D	1917
Andrea	29484	I	1920
Angelo	16779	D	1914
Angelo	36562	D	1923
Anthony O.	85427	D	1940
Antonio	11228	D	1911
Antonio	60466	D	1931
Antonio	64938	D	1933
Antonio	81891	I	1939
Antonio	82818	D	1939
Aurelia	1935	M	1906

NAME	NUMBER	TYPE	YEAR
Bartolomeo	23181	D	1917
Blanche M.	15531	D	1913
Carlo	29914	M	1920
Carlo David	63497	D	1933
Catherina	71937	D	1936
Clotilde	86032	D	1941
David	63497	D	1933
David	57330	D	1930
Domenico G.	1589	D	1906
Domenico P.	3641	D	1907
Enrico	6664	M	1908
Francesco	2941	D	1907
Frank	89588	D	1942
Gianbatista	1589	D	1906
Giovanni	55359	D	1930
Giovanni	80222	D	1938
Giovanni	63927	D	1933
Giuseppe	27260	D	1919
Giuseppi	1930	D	1906
Giusseppe	3130	D	1907
John	30873	D	1920
John F.	63617	D	1933
Louis A.	73496	D	1936
Luciano Fortunato	84408	I	1940
Luigi	32747	D	1921
Margherita	87976	D	1941
Maria	68380	D	1934
Maria Albina Clara	73953	D	1936
Marita	4072	M	1907
Marita	8008	M	1909
Mary	41846	D	1925
Mary	41846	D	1925
Pacifico	25582	D	1918
Peter H.	88464	D	1941
Pietro	33364	I	1922
Pietro	75018	D	1937
Pietro Carlo	12372	D	1911
Stephen J.	15371	D	1913
Theodore M.	87977	D	1941
Umberto	6664	M	1908
Vincenzo	7618	D	1909
Wm. J.	23981	D	1918
Rossie			
David	57330	D	1930
Rossier			
Charlew W. Pope	17475	M	1914
Lotta P.	83397	D	1940
Mary	17475	M	1914

NAME	NUMBER	TYPE	YEAR
Rossini			
Alberto	14860	D	1913
Peter	14860	D	1913
Victor	59589	D	1931
Rossiter			
Gertrude L.	46704	D	1927
James	1536	D	1906
Rosskothen			
Ferdinand	37890	D	1923
Rossman			
Peter	69377	D	1935
Rosso			
Filippo	81864	D	1939
John	24395	D	1918
Louis Thomas	77400	M	1938
Rossovich			
Maria	56827	D	1930
Rossum			
Margaret	54779	D	1930
RossWilder			
Laura A.	64147	I	1933
Rost			
Maria	12864	D	1912
Sophie	80895	D	1939
Rostkowski			
Frank	78039	D	1938
Rostovich			
Mitchell	37096	D	1923
Rota			
Camillo George	44073	D	1926
Katherine	31537	D	1921
Peter	21529	D	1916
Rotando			
Frances	68449	D	1934
Rotberg			
Jacob	55702	I	1930
Rotbert			
Louis	66468	D	1934
Rote			
Mary Jane	9708	D	1910
Rotenkolber			
George	6542	D	1908
Rotger			
Adele C.	77900	D	1938
Roth			
Anna Sandahl	82416	D	1939

Key: D = death; M = minor; I = incompetent

NAME	NUMBER	TYPE	YEAR	NAME	NUMBER	TYPE	YEAR	NAME	NUMBER	TYPE	YEAR
Arnold Edward	50597	D	1928	**ROTHENBERG**				**ROTROSKY**			
Arthur	29121	D	1920	Eva	67835	D	1934	Anna	85594	D	1940
Bertha	36451	D	1923	F. M., Mrs.	38544	D	1924	**ROTTANZI**			
Bertha	44976	D	1926	John	35435	D	1922	Eliza	13095	D	1912
Catherine	5607	D	1908	Louis	55127	D	1930	Tullio A.	11110	D	1911
Christina	54762	D	1930	Mendle	12519	D	1911	**ROTTGERS**			
Daniel	50159	D	1928	Mindell	54534	M	1929	Lambert J.	45936	D	1926
Edward Joseph	2194	D	1906	Walter	54534	M	1929	**ROTTIGNEN**			
Emma D.	34166	D	1922	**ROTHENBERGER**				John Johnson	32469	D	1921
Frances	64805	D	1933	Thomas K.	64487	D	1933	**ROUDEZ**			
Frank	88082	D	1941	**ROTHENSTEIN**				Jean	45240	M	1926
Fred	26569	M	1919	Lillian	34468	D	1922	**ROUECHE**			
Gottfried	32547	D	1921	Rose	70422	D	1935	Armand Louis	51287	D	1928
Henry	46710	D	1927	Samuel	84645	D	1940	**ROUENTINI**			
Henry	81612	D	1939	**ROTHERMEL**				Anibale	69483	D	1935
Henry John	30793	D	1920	Mary Patton	27341	D	1919	**ROUGH**			
Henry William	86760	D	1941	**ROTHGANGER**				John M.	13510	I	1912
James Richard	46711	M	1927	Gladys	14054	M	1912	Margaret	13509	I	1912
Jeanette	46410	D	1927	**ROTHGEBER**				**ROUGIER**			
Johanna	33418	M	1922	John H.	4431	D	1907	Pierre Emmanuel	64624	D	1933
John	17605	D	1914	**ROTHI**				**ROUILLON**			
John	32547	D	1921	Robert C.	18851	D	1915	Alphonsine	61121	D	1932
John Francis	87239	D	1941	**ROTHKOPF**				**ROULEAU**			
John Henry	33418	M	1922	A. P.	35592	D	1922	Augusta	88596	D	1941
John Michael	46711	M	1927	**ROTHMAN**				Francis A.	7333	D	1909
Martin A.	57835	D	1931	Lottie	85342	D	1940	**ROULLET**			
Max	70186	D	1935	**ROTHSCHILD**				Emile Edouard	3138	M	1907
Otto	26794	D	1919	Abraham	74461	D	1937	Etienne Frederic	23151	D	1917
Paul G.	57206	I	1930	Charles	72833	D	1936	Henry Guy	3138	M	1907
Solomon	23669	D	1917	Charlotte	11428	D	1911	**ROULLIER**			
Stanley John	62775	M	1932	Fanny	38353	D	1924	Albert	57920	D	1931
William Henry	62775	M	1932	Frederick	11930	D	1911	Blanche Eugenie Louise	64304	D	1933
William Herman	25966	D	1918	Hugo	6166	D	1908	Christian Jean Marie	46784	D	1927
ROTHBACH				Joseph	71357	D	1936	Gerald M.	68327	D	1934
Benjamin	69333	D	1935	Joseph A.	58287	D	1931	Henri	46784	D	1927
ROTHBLUM				Max	68305	D	1934	**ROUMAS**			
Emanuel	16005	D	1913	Rose	18781	D	1915	Jeanne	25808	D	1918
ROTHCHILD				Sigfried	72467	D	1936	**ROUNDEY**			
Adelaide E.	19925	D	1915	**ROTHSPRACK**				Catherine A.	37820	D	1923
Adelaide M.	19925	D	1915	John Henry	63533	I	1933	Charles E.	59495	D	1931
Anne Falk	55750	D	1930	**ROTHWELL**				John L.	15512	D	1913
Herbert Lionel	70634	D	1935	John Percy	43087	D	1925	**ROUNDS**			
Johanna	56204	D	1930	**ROTKOVITZ**				Anna K.	40045	D	1924
Joseph	41164	D	1925	Sol	78967	D	1938	**ROUNTREE**			
Joseph M.	30385	D	1920	**ROTOS**				Caroline H.	53823	D	1929
Morris	39033	D	1924	Nick	28915	D	1920				
Samuel	57102	D	1930								
Walter	77245	D	1937								

NAME	NUMBER	TYPE	YEAR
ROUQUETTE			
Jean P.	703	D	1906
Philippe	13549	D	1912
Philippe	68175	D	1934
Valerie	704	D	1906
ROURKE			
Allan P.	73440	D	1936
Charles S.	31813	D	1921
John	11992	D	1911
Julia	63549	D	1933
Mary Ciscelia	46454	D	1927
Michael	17453	D	1914
ROUSETT			
Jerome A. B.	22583	D	1917
ROUSH			
Nathan B.	29068	D	1920
Paula Matinez	42119	D	1925
Pauline	42119	D	1925
ROUSSEAU			
Charles Marion	25787	D	1918
Lovell C.	82747	I	1939
Mildred T.	77883	D	1938
ROUSSIN			
Ernest L.	33135	D	1922
ROUSSY			
Gaston E.	78634	D	1938
Jeanne Marie Louise	42107	D	1925
Marie	42107	D	1925
ROUX			
Julius	61803	D	1932
Maria	58371	D	1931
ROUZER			
Mary Ada	69326	D	1935
ROUZO			
Edward J.	29182	D	1920
ROVAI			
Francesco Pietro	52635	D	1929
ROVEGLIA			
Marcella	56576	I	1930
ROVEGNO			
Anthony L.	75522	D	1937
Domenico	29243	D	1920
Giovanni Battista	37201	D	1923
Jack	84443	D	1940
James	84443	D	1940
Maria	29028	D	1920
Pietro	13457	D	1912

NAME	NUMBER	TYPE	YEAR
Rosa M.	45552	D	1926
ROVELLA			
Joe	60419	I	1931
ROVELLI			
Augusto Caesar	88942	D	1942
ROVENTINI			
Alfredo	83734	D	1940
Gustavo	74641	D	1937
ROVER			
Martha	45274	D	1926
ROVERA			
Alfonso	84756	D	1940
ROVERE			
Amelia	89988	D	1942
ROWAN			
Anna Maria	71316	M	1935
Celia	2394	M	1906
Elizabeth	73004	D	1936
Ethel	2394	M	1906
James M.	4457	D	1907
James P.	59611	D	1931
John P.	2394	M	1906
Maggie H.	45963	D	1926
Maria	18036	D	1914
Patrick J.	2393	D	1906
Theresa	3514	D	1907
Thomas J.	35656	D	1923
ROWDEN			
Catherine M.	30530	D	1920
ROWE			
Alice	40225	I	1924
Ann	343	D	1906
Bessie	87956	D	1941
Bridget	60364	D	1931
Celestine Cornelia	35245	D	1922
Charles B.	7888	D	1909
Clemence Agnes	54349	D	1929
Edwin Rembert	64880	M	1933
Ernest G.	88318	D	1941
Ethel	70947	D	1935
Ethel P.	10196	M	1910
Frances	89418	D	1942
Frank	25226	D	1918
Frederick William	74229	D	1936
George	5564	D	1908
Howard A.	53200	D	1929
James T.	85774	D	1940

NAME	NUMBER	TYPE	YEAR
John F.	41439	D	1925
Julia	17893	D	1914
Lyons	68124	D	1934
Margaret	67655	D	1934
Maud	86362	D	1941
Maude M.	22025	D	1916
Nettie O.	52118	D	1929
Orphe	52118	D	1929
Phyllis Dorothy	62005	M	1932
Robert Albert	67603	D	1934
Thomas S., Mrs.	86362	D	1941
William B.	7568	D	1909
ROWELL			
Cyrus K.	1359	D	1906
George F.	38662	D	1924
Joseph	24733	D	1918
ROWER			
Amandus E.	27363	D	1919
Wilhelmina A.	52179	D	1929
ROWLAND			
James Joseph	13343	D	1912
Jeannette	39010	D	1924
Louis D.	83475	D	1940
Mary E.	27763	D	1919
Ottilia	33468	D	1922
Sarah	6041	D	1908
William	25890	D	1918
ROWLANDS			
Selina	1984	D	1906
ROWLEY			
Forrest S.	71813	D	1936
Mary Eleanor	29389	D	1920
Thomas	40630	D	1924
ROWND			
Albert I.	19732	M	1915
Anna V.	19732	M	1915
Charles W.	19732	M	1915
Harold R.	19732	M	1915
Harry J.	15245	D	1913
ROWSON			
John	20982	D	1916
ROXAS			
Felix	33342	I	1922
ROY			
Albert R.	27809	D	1919
Arthur	33237	D	1922
Constance	20779	D	1916

NAME	NUMBER	TYPE	YEAR
Herman	1211	D	1906
Louis	13330	D	1912
Margaret Jane	82682	D	1939
N. E.	35807	D	1923
Reginald A.	57186	I	1930
Samuel	15931	D	1913
ROYAL			
Arthur F.	44190	I	1926
William	30565	D	1920
ROYCE			
Charles H.	7594	D	1909
ROYCROFT			
Albert	32298	D	1921
ROYER			
Frederick	54276	D	1929
ROYLANCE			
Joseph	37878	D	1923
ROYLE			
Frederick J. P.	39467	D	1924
ROYSTER			
George Parke	73682	D	1936
ROYSTON			
Clarence Edgar	10477	M	1910
Howard Lester	10477	M	1910
ROZANSKI			
Ijnacy	30800	D	1920
ROZVODA			
Josef	44840	D	1926
ROZZANI			
Matilda	47712	D	1927
RPBBINS			
Pauline	6150	I	1908
RUA			
Edward	1537	D	1906
RUANE			
James	41678	D	1925
Patrick	77909	D	1938
RUANO			
Emeterio Segundo	31640	D	1921
RUBEL			
Emma B.	74635	D	1937
RUBELL			
William T.	40430	D	1924
RUBEN			
Jane	45613	I	1926
Jane	47036	D	1927

NAME	NUMBER	TYPE	YEAR
RUBENS			
Lee	52941	D	1929
Lillie L.	53026	I	1929
Lillie L.	87210	D	1941
Lipman	52941	D	1929
Mildred G.	83320	I	1940
RUBENSOHN			
Reuben	45031	D	1926
RUBENSTEIN			
Albert	11418	D	1911
Annie	85650	D	1940
Martin	57155	I	1930
RUBERT			
Nettie A.	30074	D	1920
RUBIA			
Mamie	46660	M	1927
RUBIN			
Florence	12643	M	1911
Jewell	80642	D	1939
Lizzie Cohen	81793	D	1939
Morris	64212	D	1933
Pauline Lasserman	79290	D	1938
Ruth Henrietta	14284	M	1912
Sarah	12642	D	1911
RUBINI			
Edward	82756	D	1939
RUBINO			
Giuseppe	16756	D	1914
James L.	80196	D	1938
Maria	89007	D	1942
RUBKE			
Diedrich	42590	D	1925
Elizabeth	51409	D	1928
RUBLE			
Diedrich	42590	D	1925
RUBY			
Abram	44213	D	1926
John T.	61834	D	1932
RUCKER			
Annie Bliss	67277	D	1934
Gertrude A.	48145	D	1927
James T.	48649	D	1927
William H.	51352	D	1928
RUCKSTELL			
John R.	73014	D	1936
RUCOVIC			
Bozo	46091	D	1926

NAME	NUMBER	TYPE	YEAR
RUDD			
Bertram H.	43193	D	1925
Sedolph	57231	D	1930
William	52006	D	1929
William P.	25151	D	1918
RUDDELL			
Constance	8512	M	1909
RUDDEN			
Annie M.	70522	D	1935
RUDDICK			
Julia	85289	D	1940
William J.	82853	D	1939
RUDDOCK			
Andrew Jackson	46281	D	1927
Delia	12566	D	1911
Eugene Barnett	61295	D	1932
James	3557	D	1907
RUDDON			
Howard	31443	D	1921
RUDDY			
Bernard	1964	D	1906
Ellen	1947	D	1906
William	83250	D	1940
RUDE			
Ruamie	45118	M	1926
RUDEBECK			
Bothilde	35820	D	1923
Rasmus J.	39503	D	1924
RUDEE			
Cecilia	75605	D	1937
David	75764	D	1937
Elliot	72542	M	1936
Isaac	30562	D	1920
Joseph	72608	D	1936
Milton	72542	M	1936
Rebecca	78338	D	1938
Vera	75974	D	1937
RUDGE			
Ina E.	47913	D	1927
RUDGEAR			
Andrew	29694	D	1920
William A.	53911	I	1929
William A.	80668	D	1939
RUDINGER			
John F. B.	11113	D	1911
RUDLSIN			
Frank H.	58792	D	1931

NAME	NUMBER	TYPE	YEAR
RUDOLF			
Adolf	36586	D	1923
Elizabeth Jane	51250	I	1928
RUDOLPH			
Adolph	36586	D	1923
Arthur	44274	D	1926
Charles Ray	51073	D	1928
Isaac	80396	D	1939
Jacob	11653	I	1911
Jacob	20990	D	1916
Otto	4720	D	1907
Theresa	50837	D	1928
RUDOLPHUS			
Harry	49777	D	1928
RUDY			
Amelia	69474	D	1935
B. M.	87942	D	1941
Pauline Spiro	76836	D	1937
Samuel	69473	D	1935
RUEB			
Fred, Jr.	80220	D	1938
RUECHERT			
Minna	74280	I	1936
Minnie	74502	D	1937
RUECKERT			
John	13139	D	1912
RUEDEIN			
Clement	33524	D	1922
RUEDIN			
Augusta D. Kiene	48079	D	1927
Clement Adolph	33524	D	1922
RUEF			
Abraham	71983	D	1936
Catherine C.	12357	D	1911
RUEGER			
Emil, Jr.	74756	I	1937
Emil, Jr.	74889	D	1937
John Alfred	21820	D	1916
RUEGG			
Gallus	39939	D	1924
John Paul	37081	D	1923
RUEHLE			
May	85006	D	1940
RUEN			
John B.	27926	D	1919

NAME	NUMBER	TYPE	YEAR
RUEPP			
Simon, Jr.	71822	D	1936
RUESCHE			
Marie	50897	D	1928
RUESS			
William	52331	D	1929
RUETER			
Frederick	85986	D	1941
RUETHER			
Auguste	25647	D	1918
Elma Ruth	23869	D	1918
RUF			
Annie F.	9824	I	1910
RUFENER			
Louis E.	40215	D	1924
RUFF			
Anna	82425	I	1939
Anna Whedelsted	82528	D	1939
Benjamin	87615	I	1941
Lawrence	48681	D	1927
RUFFELO			
Julian	22008	D	1916
RUFFIEUX			
Louis	12194	D	1911
Marcel A. L.	78468	D	1938
RUFFIN			
David T.	51236	D	1928
RUFFINO			
Fortuna	28186	D	1919
Francisca	3942	D	1907
Serafino	9277	D	1910
RUFFNER			
Henrietta Monteith	76090	I	1937
RUFNER			
Jacob	25857	D	1918
Joseph W.	73301	D	1936
RUGAARD			
Louis	61252	D	1932
RUGGERA			
Maria	13156	D	1912
RUGGERI			
Lazzaro	52206	D	1929
RUGGERIO			
Costanza	31844	D	1921
RUGGIERO			
Battista	60884	D	1932

NAME	NUMBER	TYPE	YEAR
Fedele	25013	D	1918
Francesco	34970	D	1922
Pasquale	50976	D	1928
Rosaria	69323	I	1935
RUGGLES			
A. B.	15798	D	1913
Edward Francis	83144	D	1940
Frank E.	69738	D	1935
Howard Edwin	83034	D	1940
John E.	854	D	1906
Josephine L.	29249	D	1920
Martha J.	32479	D	1921
Mary	57824	D	1931
RUHE			
Berthold	82029	D	1939
RUHL			
Christian	74870	D	1937
Emily P.	74783	D	1937
George A.	66511	D	1934
Otto	66511	D	1934
RUHLAND			
Caroline	21449	D	1916
Marie Lucile	60490	M	1931
Robert Joseph	60490	M	1931
RUHSER			
Friedrich	71641	D	1936
Martha	51426	D	1928
RUIZ			
Alvaro	50657	D	1928
Anna H.	60952	D	1932
Antonia Nieves	66858	D	1934
Antonio Nieves	66858	D	1934
Juan	63714	D	1933
Juan	66859	D	1934
Julio	35672	D	1923
Lydia	71889	I	1936
Manuel	64102	D	1933
Ramon	66859	D	1934
Robert Rubin	63946	D	1933
RULAND			
Caroline Shindler	23166	D	1917
Janet B.	23167	M	1917
RULDIN			
Augusta D. Kiene	48079	D	1927
RULE			
Cassandra D.	86860	D	1941

NAME	NUMBER	TYPE	YEAR
RULER			
Sidney Clifford	31073	I	1921
RULEY			
Archer E.	58965	D	1931
RULF			
Louise	18368	D	1915
Meyer	18350	D	1915
RULISON			
Alpha	6772	M	1908
Benjamin Joseph	60406	D	1931
Winifred C.	6772	M	1908
RULLE			
Bertha	71991	D	1936
RULOFSON			
Alfred Carrie	50691	D	1928
Alfred Currie	50691	D	1928
James M.	43987	D	1926
RULOPON			
Mary Jane	17622	D	1914
RUMBOLD			
Bessie	72744	D	1936
RUMEL			
George	24050	D	1918
RUMMELSBURG			
Charles	35666	D	1923
Eva	46123	I	1927
Selig	84598	D	1940
RUMSEY			
Elizabeth	14652	D	1912
Emma Forsyth	41069	D	1925
Samuel Lewis	10800	D	1910
RUMWELL			
Arnold	21432	M	1916
Reginald	21432	M	1916
RUNCALLO			
Maria	47198	D	1927
Martino	72340	D	1936
RUNDE			
Fred H.	19820	D	1915
RUNDLE			
Ashie L.	2497	M	1906
Corney	2497	M	1906
Ethel	2497	M	1906
George G.	2490	D	1906
Raymond Edison	76369	M	1937
Richard T.	2497	M	1906

NAME	NUMBER	TYPE	YEAR
RUNEMANN			
Evelyn Frances	21627	M	1916
RUNGE			
Alfred Carl	25700	D	1918
Belle Constance	65408	D	1933
Constance I.	65274	I	1933
Constance I.	65408	D	1933
Frederick William	3232	D	1907
Friedrich	15807	D	1913
Friedrika	18361	D	1915
Johan	19919	D	1915
Theodore Otto	60857	D	1932
RUNICKER			
Ethel L.	34704	D	1922
RUNKEL			
Charles J.	62595	D	1932
RUNKLE			
Lucia Gilbert	36321	D	1923
RUNLAS			
Edmond L.	7546	D	1909
Edward L.	7546	D	1909
RUNSALA			
Edward	59879	D	1931
RUNYON			
Elizabeth D.	87342	D	1941
Stanley Tilden	7832	M	1909
RUOFF			
Anna Marie	69769	D	1935
Emma	22510	D	1917
RUPKE			
Arthur F.	70473	M	1935
Leopold	32864	I	1921
Leopold	35258	I	1922
Leopold	78968	D	1938
RUPP			
George	33433	D	1922
RUPPA			
John	6681	D	1908
RUPPEL			
Adam	71255	D	1935
Charles	9109	D	1910
Christiean Friderich	16583	D	1914
Mabel G.	19173	M	1915
RUPPERT			
Annie	10947	D	1910

NAME	NUMBER	TYPE	YEAR
RUPRECHT			
Celia	41922	D	1925
Celia	41922	D	1925
RUS			
Johanna	80398	D	1939
RUSAC			
Alice G.	14908	M	1913
RUSCELLI			
John	18162	D	1914
RUSCH			
Adeline H.	20573	D	1916
Catherine	15450	D	1913
John W.	2033	D	1906
Lena	20573	D	1916
Raymono W.	16786	M	1914
RUSCHE			
Marie	50897	D	1928
RUSCONI			
Joan	75222	M	1937
John B.	41058	D	1925
Nancy	75222	M	1937
Virginia	86089	D	1941
RUSER			
Frederick J.	3213	I	1907
Frederick J.	26110	D	1919
RUSH			
Adeline	20573	D	1916
Deborah H.	69037	D	1935
Elizabeth	26350	D	1919
Flora Elizabeth	70355	D	1935
Mary	42589	D	1925
Patrick	2236	D	1906
Patrick J.	19951	D	1915
RUSHER			
Joseph W.	76167	D	1937
RUSHING			
Grace	75893	D	1937
William	82732	I	1939
RUSHTON			
Alfred	12908	D	1912
Charles A.	66691	D	1934
RUSIKA			
Marie	55047	D	1930
RUSK			
William Gee	67972	D	1934

NAME	NUMBER	TYPE	YEAR
RUSKE			
Albert	87805	D	1941
Gustav A.	82713	D	1939
RUSLOFF			
John	6286	D	1908
RUSS			
Albet Herman	1511	D	1906
Anne L.	78794	D	1938
Anton	88926	D	1942
Gustav A.	83331	D	1940
Henry B.	2015	D	1906
Inyo A.	25683	D	1918
Inyo Atherton	1617	M	1906
Katherine Marie	84778	M	1940
Linda Blanche	1616	M	1906
Lottie Edith	34373	D	1922
Mitzi	84778	M	1940
Robert R.	68024	D	1934
Ruth	56928	M	1930
RUSSELL			
Agnes Esther	83206	I	1940
Albert	27817	M	1919
Alexander	29711	D	1920
Alexander McLaren	21445	D	1916
Andrew B.	39485	D	1924
Annie	483	M	1906
Anthony Philip	61886	D	1932
Caroline	58207	D	1931
Charles	48032	I	1927
Charles	48314	D	1927
Charles Byron	7775	D	1909
Charles Lewis	77891	I	1938
Clara	70004	D	1935
Clara	70004	D	1935
Coleridge	48032	I	1927
Coleridge	48314	D	1927
David	56871	D	1930
Dominga Atherton	27800	M	1919
Earl A.	19536	M	1915
Earle Brewster	71348	D	1936
Edwin L.	34031	D	1922
Eleanor Swift	68948	D	1935
Ella G.	57561	D	1931
Elmer E.	62400	I	1932
Emma	58563	D	1931
Emma F.	10638	D	1910
Francis Edward	1072	M	1906
Francis Edward	2721	M	1907

NAME	NUMBER	TYPE	YEAR
Frederick Hamilton	43641	M	1926
George	16411	I	1913
George Washington	68135	I	1934
George Washington	68807	D	1935
Gordon	45050	D	1926
Harriet B.	52987	D	1929
Harriet B.	53534	D	1929
Harriet S.	19499	D	1915
Harry A.	18666	D	1915
Harry M.	45114	D	1926
Hattie Bateman	53534	D	1929
Henry Judson	74681	D	1937
Henry Lyman	7275	M	1909
Hilliard	27242	D	1919
Hulda S.	27816	D	1919
Ida Evelyn	23355	D	1917
Iona E.	18320	D	1914
J. B.	24242	D	1918
Jane	23055	D	1917
Jessie	81147	D	1939
John	1072	M	1906
John	2721	M	1907
John A.	19535	M	1915
John H.	37669	D	1923
John Leonard	69359	D	1935
John W.	62356	D	1932
Joseph J.	70177	D	1935
Lillian F.	76319	I	1937
Lyman	4664	M	1907
Martin	89771	D	1942
Mary	25969	D	1918
Mary A.	59425	D	1931
Mary C.	85422	D	1940
Mary Elizabeth	63360	D	1933
Mary Ellen	4567	D	1907
Mary Ellen	17589	D	1914
May S.	45902	D	1926
Mitchell, Jr.	27817	M	1919
Nora	33409	D	1922
Oliver	75623	D	1937
Oscar Arden, Jr.	43642	M	1926
P. H., Mrs.	19499	D	1915
Philip	36676	M	1923
Richard James	20226	M	1916
Robert	48032	I	1927
Robert	48314	D	1927
Samuel G.	38200	D	1924
Stephen D.	23463	D	1917
Tracy George	64691	D	1933

NAME	NUMBER	TYPE	YEAR
William	2196	D	1906
William	31639	D	1921
William S.	26998	D	1919
RUSSELMANN			
Hermann	33320	D	1922
RUSSI			
Frank John	50842	D	1928
Marian	69218	M	1935
Rosa	64086	D	1933
William	49013	D	1928
Wm. J.	23981	D	1918
RUSSMAN			
Florence	70228	D	1935
RUSSO			
Basilio	56220	D	1930
Rosa	64086	D	1933
Salvatore	61459	D	1932
RUST			
Abraham	55116	D	1930
Ada Morris	22289	D	1917
Cecil I.	83590	D	1940
Chauncey G.	59592	D	1931
George	25852	D	1918
Mattie Ellen	49477	I	1928
RUSTICA			
Giovanni	77829	D	1938
Maria	38462	D	1924
RUSTICH			
Giuseppe	3060	D	1907
RUSTICI			
Angelo	66950	D	1934
Annunziata	47886	D	1927
Maria	38462	D	1924
RUSTON			
Donald A.	66597	M	1934
RUTAN			
Joan	45113	M	1926
RUTENBERG			
Johann Herman	340	D	1906
RUTER			
Marcus	48776	D	1927
RUTH			
Delbert Miles	81384	D	1939
John McPherson	46227	D	1927
Ralph Peter	15633	M	1913
RUTHE			
Charles E.	48221	D	1927

NAME	NUMBER	TYPE	YEAR	NAME	NUMBER	TYPE	YEAR	NAME	NUMBER	TYPE	YEAR
Emma A.	47549	D	1927	Alice Gertrude	85791	D	1940	George	51234	D	1928
Pearl Mignon	89296	I	1942	Alice J.	34035	M	1922	Gladys	13077	M	1912
RUTHERFORD				Annette E.	55610	I	1930	Hannah	6374	D	1908
Barbara	76229	M	1937	Arthur W.	48764	D	1927	Henry P.	70247	D	1935
David	39441	D	1924	Belle	66566	D	1934	Homer C.	49602	I	1928
Helen Mar	39456	D	1924	Bernard C.	6786	D	1908	Homer C.	56463	D	1930
Hugh	39261	I	1924	Catherine	3357	D	1907	Isabelle	89866	D	1942
Joseph	40198	D	1924	Catherine	15445	D	1913	James	36945	D	1923
Mary Ann	40694	D	1925	Catherine	68978	D	1935	James	69425	D	1935
Ruth	44361	M	1926	Catherine	54836	D	1930	James	88436	D	1941
Thomas	36013	D	1923	Catherine J.	46641	D	1927	James A.	35110	D	1922
William	13856	D	1912	Cecilia	83312	D	1940	James C.	61511	D	1932
RUTHRAUFF				Charles Anthony	72593	D	1936	James J.	72887	D	1936
Sadie Louise	42402	D	1925	Charles P.	26524	D	1919	Jane	14638	D	1912
RUTLAND				Constance	10275	M	1910	Jeannette Loretta	11820	M	1911
Jack	53478	I	1929	Daniel	6140	D	1908	John	5848	D	1908
RUTLEDGE				Daniel	13067	D	1912	John	10751	D	1910
David Thompson	53498	D	1929	Daniel A.	64617	D	1933	John	13958	D	1912
John D.	65242	D	1933	Dorothy	13077	M	1912	John	19451	D	1915
Sarah Jane	64807	D	1933	Dorothy M.	72710	D	1936	John	58815	D	1931
Walter Palmer	53171	D	1929	Dorothy Winifred	80792	M	1939	John	62494	D	1932
RUTTEN				Edmond	39577	D	1924	John	76328	D	1937
John C.	29735	D	1920	Edmund Thomas	49033	D	1928	John	86223	D	1941
RUTTER				Edward	39577	D	1924	John Ambrose	69170	D	1935
Cloud D.	30303	M	1920	Edward S.	16551	D	1913	John C.	55136	D	1930
Cloudsley D.	30303	M	1920	Elise B.	82579	M	1939	John F.	46791	D	1927
Effie McIllniach	34841	D	1922	Elizabeth	56233	D	1930	John Francis	54815	D	1930
Frederick John	9698	M	1910	Elizabeth Josephine	61241	D	1932	John H.	39995	D	1924
RUTTMANN				Elizabeth Russell	64390	D	1933	John J.	12431	D	1911
John George	12228	D	1911	Elizabeth T.	65565	D	1933	John J.	15935	D	1913
RUTY				Ellen	7016	D	1909	John J.	16769	D	1914
Annie Marie	40299	D	1924	Ellen	11058	D	1911	John J.	81741	D	1939
RUWICH				Ellen	29695	D	1920	John L.	33809	M	1922
Alexander	34868	D	1922	Ellen	50236	D	1928	John R.	51595	D	1928
RUZICKA				Ellen Elizabeth	49126	D	1928	John S.	26203	D	1919
Frank	86549	D	1941	Ellen M.	2938	D	1907	John T.	6407	D	1908
RUZICKE				Emeline S.	14752	D	1913	John T.	33330	D	1922
Maria	55047	D	1930	Emmons Blackburn	27520	D	1919	John T.	41312	D	1925
RYALL				Esther	71121	D	1935	John W.	27311	D	1919
James B.	36820	D	1923	Eustace John	76328	D	1937	Jonathan	22154	D	1917
RYAN				Florence Henrietta	69197	D	1935	Joseph	23329	I	1917
Agnes	86054	D	1941	Frances	50309	D	1928	Joseph	57121	D	1930
Agnes D.	10275	M	1910	Frances	42775	I	1925	Kate	31362	D	1921
Alexander	2816	M	1907	Frank	65604	D	1933	Katharine	9560	D	1910
Alexander S.	66864	D	1934	Frank J.	77065	D	1937	Lawrence	71851	D	1936
Alice	22272	M	1917	Frank M., Mrs.	64390	D	1933	Leda	61241	D	1932
Alice Gertrude	10202	D	1910	Frank P.	45626	I	1926	Lillian J.	57753	D	1931
				Frank P.	52934	D	1929	Lillian W.	88321	M	1941
				Genevieve K.	31177	D	1921	Lizzie M.	16045	D	1913

NAME	NUMBER	TYPE	YEAR	NAME	NUMBER	TYPE	YEAR	NAME	NUMBER	TYPE	YEAR
Lloyd	13077	M	1912	Nora A.	32156	D	1921	**RYBITZKI**			
Lois	27028	M	1919	Patrick	182	D	1906	Arthur C.	18502	D	1915
Loretta Isabel	81460	D	1939	Patrick	20188	D	1915	**RYCHOLD**			
Louis X.	55979	D	1930	Patrick	45942	D	1926	Thomas	6999	D	1908
Luke	45607	D	1926	Patrick	47867	D	1927	**RYCKMAN**			
Madge	53292	D	1929	Patrick E.	34603	D	1922	G. W.	4257	D	1907
Margaret	3332	D	1907	Patrick J.	16188	D	1913	**RYDELL**			
Margaret	4713	D	1907	Patrick J.	66869	I	1934	Annie	46353	D	1927
Margaret	11809	D	1911	Patrick J.	85246	D	1940	John August	69261	D	1935
Margaret	14859	D	1913	Philip F.	73603	D	1936	Justine	74712	D	1937
Margaret	15937	D	1913	Raymond W.	87567	D	1941	**RYDEN**			
Margaret	26092	D	1919	Richard J.	19494	D	1915	Carl O.	69901	D	1935
Margaret	32484	D	1921	Robert H.	71112	D	1935	**RYDER**			
Margaret	36016	D	1923	Robert H., III	82579	M	1939	Adner E.	84837	D	1940
Margaret	36821	D	1923	Robert X.	71112	D	1935	Annie L.	57513	D	1930
Margaret	48683	D	1927	Rose Clare	82952	D	1939	Carrie E.	21711	D	1916
Margaret	56485	I	1930	Sheila Marie	88514	M	1941	Charles H.	57393	D	1930
Margaret T.	27655	D	1919	Sheila Marie	88516	M	1941	Elizabeth H.	15398	D	1913
Maria Teresa	77582	D	1938	T. Frank	81740	D	1939	Frances Agnes	88951	D	1942
Martin	45386	D	1926	Thomas	9156	D	1910	Grace A.	42460	D	1925
Martinez Wilber	13110	M	1912	Thomas	61373	D	1932	Henry	4255	D	1907
Mary	11686	D	1911	Thomas E.	3198	D	1907	James M.	56007	D	1930
Mary	29232	D	1920	Thomas Francis	28703	M	1920	Lawrence Lewis	32238	M	1921
Mary	47408	D	1927	Thomas J.	84962	D	1940	Nellie Margaret	52295	D	1929
Mary	56043	D	1930	Thomas Joseph	72930	D	1936	Raymond Thomas	67564	D	1934
Mary	56485	I	1930	Thomas Michael	88515	M	1941	Robert Royal	39997	D	1924
Mary	67201	I	1934	Timothy H.	4423	I	1907	**RYDMAN**			
Mary	87254	D	1941	Timothy J.	47021	D	1927	Axel	53895	D	1929
Mary	89001	D	1942	Veronica	37203	M	1923	**RYER**			
Mary A.	41682	D	1925	Walter James	69963	D	1935	Blanche Fletcher	80429	D	1939
Mary Alice	63611	D	1933	Wilhelm	27028	M	1919	**RYERSON**			
Mary E.	13620	D	1912	William	8276	D	1909	George	63093	I	1932
Mary E.	40906	D	1925	William	33360	D	1922	George Martin	81779	D	1939
Mary Elizabeth	38056	D	1924	William	40771	D	1925	Isaac	27664	I	1919
Mary Eugenia	88515	M	1941	William	44277	D	1926	Jennie	27899	I	1919
Mary Grace	50274	D	1928	William	45607	D	1926	Jennie	31873	D	1921
Mary J.	35910	D	1923	William	50544	D	1928	**RYFFKOGEL**			
Mary Josephine	62953	D	1932	William	63202	D	1932	Henry Anthon Lewis	67316	D	1934
Mary Louise	35094	D	1922	William E., Jr.	9205	M	1910	**RYFKOGEL**			
Matthew	7989	D	1909	William J.	13633	D	1912	Blanche	89937	D	1942
Michael	749	D	1906	William J.	89854	D	1942	**RYGERSBERG**			
Michael	7678	D	1909	William S.	48998	D	1928	Joseph	54261	D	1929
Michael	10184	D	1910	William T.	10574	D	1910	**RYKEN**			
Michael	20648	D	1916	**RYANHART**				William Paul	23424	D	1917
Michael	33628	D	1922	Hanora	23361	D	1917	**RYKEN-JONES**			
Michael C.	35750	D	1923	**RYBERG**				Josephine M.	80941	D	1939
Michael J.	15936	D	1913	Earnest	50606	M	1928				
Michael Joseph Emmet	28703	M	1920	Petra	50605	D	1928				
Neil	62967	D	1932	Raymond	50606	M	1928				

Key: D = death; M = minor; I = incompetent

NAME	NUMBER	TYPE	YEAR
RYLAND			
Mary Agnes	85857	D	1940
RYLANDER			
George William	68619	D	1934
John	39522	D	1924
RYLES			
James Hayward	8148	D	1909
RYLEY			
Samuel Paul	60755	D	1932
RYNNING			
Olivius	55251	D	1930
SAADALLAH			
George	11652	D	1911
Mary	10989	D	1911
SAALBURG			
George H.	57863	D	1931
Samuel W.	11401	D	1911
SAALFIELD			
Leopold A.	489	D	1906
Raye G.	39844	D	1924
SAARI			
Oskar	29930	D	1920
SAARIMEN			
Oskar	29930	D	1920
SAARINAN			
Selma Louisa	69552	D	1935
SAARINEN			
A.	57258	D	1930
Oskar	29930	D	1920
Selma Louisa	69552	D	1935
SAARM			
August Oscar	46142	D	1927
SAASTAMOINE			
Anna F.	70222	D	1935
SABA			
Essie	50345	D	1928
Osma	50345	D	1928
SABAK			
Mary	72948	I	1936
SABATINO			
Adele L.	34020	M	1922
Antonio	14228	D	1912
Cono	791	D	1906
Saveria	71811	D	1936
SABATO			
Anna P.	52954	D	1929

NAME	NUMBER	TYPE	YEAR
Antonio	37486	D	1923
Gloria	55675	M	1930
SABBADINI			
Antonio Ulisse Clito	27933	M	1919
Martino	26785	D	1919
SABBATO			
Antonio	37486	D	1923
SABELLA			
Accursia	81377	D	1939
Francisco	75297	D	1937
SABER			
Asma	50345	D	1928
Asner	50345	D	1928
SABIA			
Saletta	30438	D	1920
SABIN			
John Ira	766	D	1906
Joseph F.	83020	D	1940
Laura Leona	72244	D	1936
Lester B.	73173	D	1936
Mary Ellen	83019	D	1940
Patricia Willifer	77246	M	1937
SABINE			
John Henry	51835	D	1929
Joseph F.	83020	D	1940
Mary Ellen	83019	D	1940
SABINI			
Carmel	88850	D	1942
Giuseppe	79384	D	1938
John	38395	D	1924
SABLICISH			
Archillis G.	18922	D	1915
SABLICK			
Archillis G.	18922	D	1915
SABLIER			
Louis Henri Casimir	18447	D	1915
SABURA			
Odaka	28417	I	1919
SACAZE			
Joseph	36899	D	1923
SACCA			
Nunzio	48485	D	1927
SACCO			
Nunzio	48485	D	1927
SACCONE			
Vivian	33010	D	1921

NAME	NUMBER	TYPE	YEAR
SACCUZZO			
Giovanna	55422	D	1930
SACHAU			
Elinor	67649	M	1934
William D.	67649	M	1934
William Otto	67588	D	1934
SACHE			
John	31589	I	1921
SACHENRODER			
Rheinhard Wilhelm	46484	D	1927
SACHER			
Caroline	72962	D	1936
SACHERER			
Edna F.	7514	M	1909
Elmer F.	7514	M	1909
SACHS			
Amson	56968	D	1930
Arnson	13944	I	1912
Bertha	39157	D	1924
Carrie Hart	11554	D	1911
Clara	17150	D	1914
David	30279	D	1920
David M.	28391	D	1919
Edgar D.	67015	D	1934
Fannie H.	9463	D	1910
Flora	63069	D	1932
Gerald	71956	D	1936
Harrold	10162	M	1910
Hattie	41947	D	1925
Hattie	41947	D	1925
Henry Newell	9352	M	1910
Isaac	4483	D	1907
John	31589	I	1921
Lippmann	13663	D	1912
Louis	2729	D	1907
Mary	58678	D	1931
Samuel	716	D	1906
Samuel L.	2688	D	1907
Sanford	58729	D	1931
Walter Thomas	6306	D	1908
SACHSENMEIER			
Katherina	75433	D	1937
SACK			
Bernhard	46918	D	1927
George Ludwig	35342	D	1922
Simon	45744	D	1926

NAME	NUMBER	TYPE	YEAR	NAME	NUMBER	TYPE	YEAR	NAME	NUMBER	TYPE	YEAR
SACKETT				SAFIER				SAHRE			
Mary E.	17336	D	1914	Benjamin	46503	M	1927	William	69007	D	1935
Nancy	29044	D	1920	Frederick	46503	M	1927	SAIAS			
SACKMANN				Friedrich	46503	M	1927	Ramon	39623	I	1924
Henry	15227	D	1913	SAFLIDES				SAID			
SACKS				Harry A.	64488	D	1933	Mary	33407	I	1922
Bennie	20429	M	1916	SAFTIG				SAILLY			
Carl V.	2498	M	1906	Katherine G.	66396	I	1934	Edgar P.	12146	D	1911
Ida	20429	M	1916	SAGAR				SAILOR			
SACKWITZ				Edward F.	38286	D	1924	George	41468	M	1925
George F.	28940	D	1920	SAGARIA				SAINAGHI			
SACRE				Peter	22669	D	1917	Christopher	75127	D	1937
Harry August	55674	D	1930	Pietro	22669	D	1917	SAINSOT			
SADANAGA				Virginia	28297	D	1919	Anna	1894	D	1906
Nobuske	28157	D	1919	SAGAUD				Bertha	62683	I	1932
SADLEIR				Jean	48511	D	1927	Myrtle M.	34067	I	1922
T. Otway	4845	D	1907	SAGE				SAINTLEZIN			
SADLER				Harvey E.	22350	D	1917	Jean	38270	D	1924
Delia J.	73397	D	1936	Louise M.	44565	D	1926	SAITO			
Edna	25210	M	1918	Orlando G.	25161	D	1918	Katsugoro	66356	D	1934
Hermann	5833	D	1908	Sidney A.	8581	D	1909	SAKAI			
Mary	19385	D	1915	SAGEHORN				Ayako	35973	M	1923
Nettie	72565	I	1936	Charles H.	14618	D	1912	George Massami	35973	M	1923
Nettie W.	80798	D	1939	Mary	14907	I	1913	SAKELLARIS			
Wilhilmiena	3487	D	1907	SAGER				Gost	8314	D	1909
William	3486	D	1907	Evelyn	39386	M	1924	SAKODA			
SADLIS				SAHATI				Umeyo	11598	M	1911
Ellis	62528	D	1932	Michael N.	57105	D	1930	SAKOTA			
SAEHLMANN				SAHIYABU				Milos	45910	D	1926
Henry	62346	D	1932	Umeyo	18256	D	1914	SAKOVICH			
SAELTZER				SAHL				Vladimir J.	60651	D	1932
Jennie C.	83061	D	1940	Andrew	85917	D	1940	SALA			
SAETTEM				Martin William	42809	D	1925	Ethel S.	55569	M	1930
Leiv O.	55766	D	1930	SAHLE				John	41669	D	1925
SAFCHIK				Mary	12315	M	1911	Martha Diane	80906	M	1939
Samuel	83447	D	1940	SAHLEIN				Theresa L.	80114	I	1938
SAFFAS				Belle M.	83887	D	1940	SALABERT			
Constantine Z.	75446	D	1937	Henry	35301	D	1922	Louis	38029	D	1923
SAFFORD				SAHLENDER				SALACONE			
A. P. K.	363	D	1906	Grover	25500	D	1918	Maria	86721	D	1941
Anna J.	73095	D	1936	SAHORES				Mariano	22473	D	1917
Maria Cooper	32604	D	1921	Pierre	54066	D	1929	SALANAVE			
May K.	32604	D	1921	SAHRBACHER				Jean	45374	D	1926
Pansy A. J.	73095	D	1936	Charles F.	26090	D	1919	Marianne	65885	D	1933
SAFIDES				SAHRBACKER				Marie	65885	D	1933
Harry A.	64488	D	1933	Henry John	77887	D	1938				

NAME	NUMBER	TYPE	YEAR
SALAS			
Antonia	60790	D	1932
SALAZAR			
Arthur G.	70450	D	1935
Francisco	56332	D	1930
Miguell Monaz	44832	I	1926
SALBACH			
Mary	25881	D	1918
SALBADO			
Vicente	65963	D	1933
SALBERG			
Helen Nellie Haas	73066	D	1936
Nellie Haas	73066	D	1936
SALCH			
George C.	40281	D	1924
SALCICCIO			
Settimo	88837	D	1942
SALDUBEHERE			
Gratien	44732	I	1926
SALDUNBEHERE			
Domingo	1312	D	1906
SALEEBY			
Anna	70020	M	1935
Anna	70020	M	1935
Samuel	25818	D	1918
Sara	70020	M	1935
Sara	70020	M	1935
SALEM			
Helen	53243	D	1929
SALEMI			
Maria	77336	D	1937
SALEMINO			
John	19160	D	1915
SALENEEK			
August Martin	83213	D	1940
SALER			
Maria	68377	D	1934
SALES			
Abe	36108	D	1923
Aguilino	30685	M	1920
Bentura	30685	M	1920
Hugo S.	28145	D	1919
Richard Thomas	38272	M	1924
Ursula	30685	M	1920
SALET			
Frank	47581	D	1927

NAME	NUMBER	TYPE	YEAR
Victorine	68114	D	1934
SALETZKE			
John A.	63443	D	1933
SALFIELD			
Carl D.	52758	D	1929
Elizabeth Alma	69851	D	1935
Libby A.	69851	D	1935
SALHINGER			
Samuel	66156	D	1934
SALIEBY			
Anna	70020	M	1935
Sara	70020	M	1935
SALIN			
August	55072	D	1930
Peter	53287	D	1929
SALINA			
Archangelo	27736	D	1919
Paul	27736	D	1919
SALINAS			
Luis	43969	D	1926
SALINE			
Clara	83391	D	1940
SALINERO			
Juan	82667	D	1939
SALING			
Alta May	36427	D	1923
SALINGER			
Cecilia	344	D	1906
Samuel	66156	D	1934
SALIOW			
Victor	6445	D	1908
SALISBURY			
Alphonso	14594	D	1912
Chester Laverne	48322	D	1927
Elizabeth Elliott	61464	D	1932
Kate C.	8451	D	1909
Monroe	3749	D	1907
Sidney J.	4284	D	1907
Thomas	43905	I	1926
Willie A.	17713	D	1914
SALL			
Ida Josephine	74527	D	1937
SALLAY			
Moosa	2825	D	1907
SALLIER			
Reinhold Edward	82536	D	1939

NAME	NUMBER	TYPE	YEAR
SALLINGER			
Ella	229	D	1906
SALLMAN			
Adolph	85026	D	1940
SALLUSTIO			
Domicilio	33647	D	1922
SALM			
W. M.	71524	D	1936
William	71524	D	1936
SALMAN			
Mary C.	4612	D	1907
SALMAS			
Margaret	79931	I	1938
SALMI			
Martin H.	38689	D	1924
SALMON			
Ann	40220	D	1924
Carrie W.	51540	D	1928
Federick	57309	D	1930
George W.	34005	D	1922
John James	86463	D	1941
Mary	48367	D	1927
Michael	75493	D	1937
Minnie	18762	I	1915
Minnie	39339	D	1924
Peter	8612	D	1909
Thomas	86689	D	1941
SALMOND			
Mary Ellen	70699	D	1935
SALO			
John	56924	D	1930
Oscar	72181	I	1936
Oscar	79706	I	1938
Toivo O.	72181	D	1936
Toivo O.	79706	I	1938
SALOMAN			
Max	58092	D	1931
Rose	27988	I	1919
SALOMON			
Bertha	34692	D	1922
Caroline	47540	D	1927
Carrie	47540	D	1927
Eleanor B.	66913	D	1934
Eleanor Chase	66913	D	1934
Evelyn Louise	76823	M	1937
Jacob	52077	D	1929
Marie Eppie	40757	D	1925

NAME	NUMBER	TYPE	YEAR
Maurice	76608	D	1937
Maurice, Jr.	76823	M	1937
Moses	16345	D	1913
Newman	7974	D	1909
SALOMONE			
Costanzo	25659	D	1918
SALOSHIN			
Martha	82938	D	1939
SALOSKI			
Martin	26643	D	1919
SALSBURY			
Henry A.	82739	I	1939
SALSCHEIDER			
Florence Lucy	55561	D	1930
Lucy	55561	D	1930
SALSIG			
Anna E.	78488	D	1938
SALSMAN			
Isaac	78425	D	1938
SALT			
Susan	83593	D	1940
SALTER			
Bernice	16711	M	1914
Gertrude F.	38553	D	1924
J. Wesley, Jr.	16711	M	1914
John Wesley	31405	D	1921
John Wm.	14832	D	1913
Josephine Frances	69143	D	1935
Kate B.	22384	D	1917
William	75094	D	1937
Woodley G.	34420	D	1922
SALTS			
James A.	28720	D	1920
SALTURAS			
Basilios S.	30172	D	1920
SALTZMAN			
Mary	37779	D	1923
Samuel L.	89037	D	1942
SALUSSOLIA			
Severino	59813	D	1931
SALVADOR			
Segunda Alaman	82580	D	1939
SALVAGNI			
Achile	6362	D	1908
SALVAR			
Frank	2809	D	1907

NAME	NUMBER	TYPE	YEAR
SALVAREZZA			
Antonio	13776	D	1912
SALVATO			
Giuseppe	49394	D	1928
Vincingo	65963	D	1933
SALVATOR			
Joseph	18663	D	1915
SALVATORE			
Accusio	47199	D	1927
Pesetti	40798	D	1925
SALVEININI			
Jennie	25171	M	1918
SALVI			
Bartolomeo	31320	D	1921
Giovanni	44528	D	1926
SALVO			
Lillian	85765	M	1940
SALVONI			
Milania	25801	D	1918
SALVOTTI			
Ilda	52126	D	1929
SALZ			
Edward	48196	D	1927
Jacob	8945	D	1910
Joseph W.	60340	D	1931
Joseph Warren	60767	M	1932
Matilda K.	39525	D	1924
SALZBACHER			
Matilda	6448	D	1908
SALZCHEIDER			
Florence L.	75294	D	1937
Lucy	75294	D	1937
SALZMAN			
Evelyn	55419	D	1930
SALZSCHEIDER			
Albert J.	55513	D	1930
SAM			
Don Julio Yon	87396	D	1941
Ng	16652	D	1914
Wong	45809	D	1926
SAMADUROFF			
Matthew	67957	D	1934
Matvey	67957	D	1934
SAMARJIAN			
E. H.	63067	D	1932
Edward	63067	D	1932

NAME	NUMBER	TYPE	YEAR
SAMBADO			
Domenico	72728	D	1936
SAMBERTRANT			
Ellen	7339	D	1909
SAMBUCK			
Catterina	61825	D	1932
SAMEDO			
Amelia	24999	D	1918
SAMEK			
Josephine	33368	M	1922
Tony	33144	D	1922
SAMISH			
Carolyn	74804	M	1937
SAMM			
Rosalie	14531	D	1912
SAMMANN			
Charles	80593	D	1939
SAMMI			
Betty	28397	D	1919
John H.	48301	D	1927
SAMMON			
Patrick J.	67268	D	1934
SAMPLE			
Mary J.	41317	D	1925
Robert A.	5639	D	1908
SAMPSON			
Bettie	80720	I	1939
Edward	77392	D	1937
Helen L.	47993	I	1927
Helen L.	49446	D	1928
William Ashford	85574	I	1940
SAMS			
Abram L.	77680	D	1938
SAMSEL			
Claude Lionel	32363	M	1921
SAMSON			
Camilla	82198	D	1939
Ernest	89916	D	1942
Frank	78721	M	1938
George Leon	86956	D	1941
Hilda	23737	D	1917
John, Jr.	78721	M	1938
Lucie	37450	D	1923
O. L., Mrs.	37450	D	1923
Pauline Blanche	63606	D	1933
Rudolph Walter	59488	M	1931

NAME	NUMBER	TYPE	YEAR	NAME	NUMBER	TYPE	YEAR	NAME	NUMBER	TYPE	YEAR
Rudolph, Mrs.	82198	D	1939	Matilda	48857	D	1927	Encarnacion Ruis	21933	D	1916
SAMTER				Nathan	52250	D	1929	Helen	42976	I	1925
Hannah	10223	D	1910	Rachel	41653	D	1925	Jose	27690	M	1919
Leonhard	53539	D	1929	Raquel	41653	D	1925	Jose	43530	D	1926
Louis	5755	D	1908	Ronald Lloyd	78892	M	1938	Josephine Uzeta	81390	D	1939
SAMUD				Sarah	50115	D	1928	Juan Perez	53837	D	1929
Anna M.	68222	I	1934	William C.	67609	D	1934	Manuel Ruiz	64102	D	1933
Elizabeth	17920	D	1914	**SAMUELSON**				Marie	65873	D	1933
SAMUEL				Albin M.	89553	D	1942	Maud	53980	D	1929
Byron J.	59861	D	1931	Edwin	10428	D	1910	Philip	57487	D	1930
Byron J., Jr.	60716	M	1932	Lillian Amelia	88617	M	1941	Ramon	51109	I	1928
Gertrude	88796	D	1941	**SAMULS**				**SAND**			
Harris	33886	D	1922	Bertha	41003	I	1925	Joseph C.	63365	D	1933
Henry	57392	D	1930	**SAN**				Joseph E.	3389	D	1907
Jennie	22549	D	1917	Lee Bo	10578	D	1910	Paul S.	40211	M	1924
Lena	64768	I	1933	**SANBERG**				William	24391	D	1918
Mortimer A.	67626	D	1934	Carl J.	71459	D	1936	**SANDAHL**			
Moses	32967	D	1921	Charles J.	71459	D	1936	Anna	82416	D	1939
Paul	56146	D	1930	**SANBORN**				August Christian	80552	D	1939
Phoebe	40410	D	1924	Alice Cary	88652	D	1941	Charles Ludwig	85794	D	1940
Wavle A.	69821	D	1935	Annie M.	41915	D	1925	Chris	80552	D	1939
William	49686	D	1928	Annie M.	41915	D	1925	**SANDAI**			
SAMUELS				Arthur B.	11443	D	1911	Catherina	17964	D	1914
Adolph	1951	D	1906	Charles J.	75947	D	1937	**SANDAKIS**			
Annie	81676	D	1939	Charlotte E.	27256	D	1919	Emanuel S.	87344	D	1941
Benjamin	69687	D	1935	Edward Kenneth	18128	M	1914	**SANDAY**			
Bertha	35564	I	1922	Fred G.	19679	D	1915	Catherina	17964	D	1914
Bertha	41003	I	1925	Hamilton	14404	D	1912	Milo	58970	D	1931
Charles	85360	I	1940	Harriet E.	2758	D	1907	Miro	58634	D	1931
Charles	85408	D	1940	Helen A.	33430	D	1922	Miro	58970	D	1931
Charles Carl	44029	D	1926	Horace Herbert	47238	D	1927	Pera	50218	D	1928
David	4126	D	1907	Luther	84947	D	1940	**SANDBERG**			
David L.	45411	M	1926	Sheffield S.	2155	D	1906	Anna F.	57117	D	1930
Dixie C.	71231	D	1935	Walter Henry	65072	I	1933	Jergen	29933	D	1920
Edwin	66282	D	1934	Walter Henry	79283	D	1938	**SANDBURG**			
Frances Jane	58672	M	1931	William B.	31239	D	1921	Charles	37971	D	1923
Frank	82137	D	1939	William H.	45456	D	1926	**SANDEEN**			
Gerson	22420	D	1917	**SANCHES**				William	72707	D	1936
Harris	78624	D	1938	R. P.	48842	D	1927	**SANDELL**			
Jacob	62167	D	1932	Randolph P.	48897	D	1928	Carl Victor	41102	M	1925
Jacob L.	35514	I	1922	**SANCHEZ**				Ebba Viola	41102	M	1925
John Arthur	78077	D	1938	Abraham	85338	D	1940	John August	14193	I	1912
Kenneth	48157	M	1927	Alberto Sanchobal	83285	D	1940	Rudolph T.	41102	M	1925
Lena	23731	D	1917	Ana	72927	D	1936	Selma	71022	D	1935
Lena	52251	D	1929	Angel Jorge	35995	D	1923	**SANDEN**			
Leon	82495	D	1939	Antonio	27690	M	1919	Louis F.	87932	D	1941
Manuel A.	78382	D	1938	Antonio	72218	M	1936				
Margaret	45411	M	1926	Audrey Jean	72218	M	1936				

Key: D = death; M = minor; I = incompetent

NAME	NUMBER	TYPE	YEAR	NAME	NUMBER	TYPE	YEAR	NAME	NUMBER	TYPE	YEAR
SANDER				**SANDERSON**				William H.	67253	D	1934
Frank	56697	D	1930	Barbara	89757	M	1942	**SANDQUIST**			
H. F.	18575	D	1915	Effie M.	78006	D	1938	Alice S.	24701	D	1918
Katherina	48721	D	1927	Geraldine	67912	M	1934	Andrew Persson	55925	D	1930
Sally	33896	D	1922	Gorham D.	66652	D	1934	**SANDRETTO**			
Sylvan	33896	D	1922	James L.	11262	D	1911	Antonio	80335	D	1939
SANDERFELD				John	31650	D	1921	**SANDROCK**			
John	82467	D	1939	John James	80077	D	1938	Frederick Wilhelm	73240	D	1936
SANDERS				Marguerite Dalton	85757	D	1940	Susan	23008	D	1917
Alice Maude	79420	D	1938	Mildred Emma	30076	M	1920	**SANDS**			
Caterina	17964	D	1914	Nellie	11261	D	1911	Bessie B.	83425	D	1940
Celestine	67705	D	1934	Sophie	63008	D	1932	Charles	63371	D	1933
Claude James	59478	D	1931	William Webster	19400	D	1915	**SANDSTONE**			
David Henry	32403	D	1921	**SANDFORD**				Charles	33149	D	1922
E.	26877	D	1919	Clara Josephine	47639	D	1927	**SANDSTROM**			
Elmer Lloyd	36429	M	1923	Elliot	22673	D	1917	Alfred J.	74098	D	1936
Frank	36966	M	1923	Joseph Head	18258	D	1914	Alma C.	86142	D	1941
Fred	13469	D	1912	**SANDINO**				Anton	62817	D	1932
Gertrude H.	73883	D	1936	Leonardo	25296	D	1918	Emil August	48114	D	1927
Hulda C.	10999	D	1911	**SANDIQUE**				John Edward	82541	D	1939
Jane	24596	D	1918	Teodula	59522	D	1931	William	56327	D	1930
Joan Marie	64112	M	1933	**SANDLEBEN**				**SANDWALL**			
John A.	12406	D	1911	Gesche Adelheid	10838	I	1910	Joseph Harris	83224	D	1940
June	36966	M	1923	**SANDLER**				**SANDY**			
Margaret McGregor	9493	D	1910	Bertha	8563	D	1909	Frank E.	32929	I	1921
Marie	72473	D	1936	**SANDMAN**				**SANFELIZ**			
Marion Manona	78167	D	1938	Solomon	51238	D	1928	Bernardine	60014	D	1931
Martin	3638	D	1907	**SANDMANN**				Justo	3450	D	1907
Michael	54168	D	1929	Anna	75664	D	1937	Justo Lorenzo	8930	D	1909
Patricia Ann	64112	M	1933	George	78964	D	1938	**SANFILIPPO**			
Pauline	7859	D	1909	**SANDMARK**				Andrea	11925	D	1911
Peter G.	51678	D	1928	Augusta	84909	D	1940	Antonio	12201	D	1911
Rachel	26832	D	1919	Charlotte	84909	D	1940	Carmela Gampisa	44390	D	1926
Rebecca	76807	D	1937	**SANDOBAL**				Salvatore	25843	D	1918
Samuel F.	10438	I	1910	Antonio	83285	D	1940	**SANFORD**			
Samuel F.	14222	D	1912	**SANDOE**				Agnes	85135	D	1940
William Peters	85371	D	1940	James	45307	D	1926	Charles W.	59246	D	1931
William MacGregor	71474	D	1936	**SANDONI**				Clara	66312	D	1934
William P.	12408	M	1911	Riccardo	48756	D	1927	Clifford Thornton	55932	D	1930
William Richard	86062	D	1941	**SANDOVAL**				James Milton	55354	D	1930
Wolf	12211	D	1911	Antonio	75922	D	1937	Josephine L.	21138	D	1916
SANDERSEN				Bernard	15883	D	1913	Mary Jones	43553	D	1926
Isabel	78759	D	1938	Bernard	15883	D	1913	Nichol Edward, Jr.	80545	M	1939
Walter W.	68885	M	1935	**SANDOW**				Roy L.	65115	D	1933
SANDERSFELD				Emil Schulze	56247	D	1930	Tony	59000	I	1931
Gabrielle	26691	M	1919	George A.	8123	D	1909	William L.	27801	I	1919
George Charles	74740	D	1937	James	45307	D	1926				

NAME	NUMBER	TYPE	YEAR
SANFRANSKY			
Andrey	46389	D	1927
SANFT			
Harry Jack	66278	D	1934
SANG			
Hung	932	D	1906
Lee Yee	86789	D	1941
Wong Yan	40924	M	1925
Yee	50439	D	1928
SANGALLI			
Luigi	89849	D	1942
Maria	79552	D	1938
SANGER			
Elizabeth B.	30483	D	1920
Leo	1066	D	1906
Milton Hall	15728	D	1913
SANGSTER			
Josephine Pearl	53312	M	1929
SANGUINETTI			
Annie	55161	D	1930
Clara D.	25536	D	1918
Eugene	47909	D	1927
George B.	84015	D	1940
Giambatista	84015	D	1940
Giuseppe	55346	D	1930
Louisa	62392	D	1932
Maria	50791	D	1928
SANJURJO			
Arsenio	79375	D	1938
SANJURJO Y DESGUAL			
Arsenio	79375	D	1938
SANKER			
Marion G.	6902	D	1908
SANMARTIN			
Manuel Llama	79104	D	1938
SANNA			
Grazia	39640	D	1924
SANNER			
Pauline A.	70706	D	1935
SANOFF			
Celia Adler	89297	D	1942
SANPEDRO			
Manuel	33259	D	1922
SANQUINET			
Marie Albina Virginie	34576	D	1922
SANS			
Brigitte	69260	D	1935
Peter S.	69414	D	1935
SANSOME			
Frances Isabelle	67484	M	1934
SANT			
Giuseppe	23597	D	1917
Joseph	23597	D	1917
SANTAANA			
Agapito C.	41713	D	1925
SANTACRUZ			
Amparo Carmen L deG.	10440	D	1910
Dominica	59413	D	1931
SANTAL			
Jesus	28785	D	1920
SANTALLASSI			
Mary	88872	I	1942
SANTANIELLO			
Francisco	60206	D	1931
SANTEL			
Rudolph	27485	M	1919
SANTERRE			
Marie	39252	D	1924
SANTIBANEZ			
Raymonde	84832	D	1940
SANTICH			
George M.	11524	D	1911
Mate	55594	D	1930
SANTIF			
Cecilia Ellen	70267	D	1935
SANTILLANA			
Anastacia	45001	D	1926
Joseph	50510	D	1928
SANTINA			
Belle Grace Della	81956	D	1939
Melvin Della	87797	M	1941
Pietro Della	26399	D	1919
Robert Della	87797	M	1941
Theresa Della	19547	D	1915
Vera Della	87797	M	1941
SANTINI			
Adelaide	75861	I	1937
Giuseppe	51461	D	1928
SANTO			
Abbruzzo	20060	D	1915
Antonio	51832	D	1929
Giordano	66854	D	1934
SANTONI			
Goffredo	67942	D	1934
Natalina	35715	D	1923
SANTORO			
Dante	65607	M	1933
Domenico	63889	D	1933
SANTOS			
Emma	25281	D	1918
Joe	34794	D	1922
John	12241	I	1911
John	12585	D	1911
Manuel J.	54981	D	1930
Peter E.	26877	D	1919
Teresa Garcia	86029	D	1941
Tony	51832	D	1929
SANTRUCK			
Frank J.	63851	I	1933
SANTRY			
Julia	40508	I	1924
Julia	51084	D	1928
Michael	6620	D	1908
SANTSCHI			
Eugene	84423	D	1940
SANTUCCI			
Giuseppe	84107	D	1940
Luci	39395	I	1924
Pietro	37676	I	1923
SANWALD			
Otto	35418	D	1922
SANZ			
Antonio F. Fontaine	53874	D	1929
Domingo	53851	D	1929
Ignacio	51976	M	1929
Jean	74013	M	1936
Micheline	74013	M	1936
SAPER			
Antonio	44298	D	1926
Pearl	63568	D	1933
Petronilla	63568	D	1933
SAPHIR			
Walter L.	12696	M	1911
Walter L.	32307	I	1921
SAPIN			
Charles George	74048	D	1936
SAPOULIN			
Pierre C.	52598	D	1929

NAME	NUMBER	TYPE	YEAR
SAPPEI			
Caterina	34495	D	1922
SARA			
Asma	50345	D	1928
SARABIA			
Ignacia	27536	D	1919
SARABIN			
Ygnacia	27536	D	1919
SARACENO			
Concetta	64584	D	1933
SARAFIAN			
Nazareth	79067	D	1938
SARAGA			
Mateo	63578	I	1933
SARAIVA			
F. C.	7418	D	1909
SARANTIDIS			
Sarantis	42776	D	1925
SARANTITIS			
Elaine	73037	D	1936
Helen	73037	D	1936
SARAT			
Theophile	946	D	1906
SARCANDER			
Catherine V.	11275	D	1911
SARCHET			
Charles	83432	D	1940
SARDI			
Gaetano	30236	D	1920
SARDINHA			
Manuel Gonzales	89737	D	1942
SARES			
Emanuel S.	87344	D	1941
SARGANIS			
Antonio	47472	M	1927
Constance	47472	M	1927
Crisso	40476	D	1924
Stamatios	47472	M	1927
SARGEANT			
Sidney B.	89974	D	1942
Winthrop W.	54630	D	1929
SARGENT			
A. A.	4941	D	1907
Aaron M.	14637	M	1912
Abe L.	8337	D	1909
Albert A.	2435	M	1906

NAME	NUMBER	TYPE	YEAR
Alice G.	52860	D	1929
Betty E.	85131	I	1940
Betty E.	85340	D	1940
Bradley E.	89824	D	1942
Catherine B.	46139	D	1927
Charles	76008	D	1937
Charles H.	43617	I	1926
Cyrus R.	41288	D	1925
Edward M.	14637	M	1912
Ellen C.	12166	D	1911
Frank A.	33425	D	1922
George Clark	56287	D	1930
Helen M.	14637	M	1912
Jefferita Davista	4250	D	1907
John	43134	D	1925
Kate W.	62795	D	1932
Katherine	2435	M	1906
Minnie Gilbert	40082	D	1924
Ruth W.	2435	M	1906
William	50848	D	1928
SARGENTELLI			
Albo	46713	M	1927
Domenico	46581	D	1927
Raffraella	46713	M	1927
SARGENTINI			
Guisseppe	34580	D	1922
SARIBALIS			
Apostolos	79099	D	1938
SARINEN			
A.	57258	D	1930
SARINI			
Frank	46602	D	1927
SARKIS			
Wehan	63067	D	1932
SARLANDT			
Alexander	80368	D	1939
C. R.	76643	D	1937
SARLE			
Erminie B.	17180	D	1914
SARLET			
Julia R.	16060	D	1913
SARLIS			
John A.	79096	D	1938
SARMENT			
Rose	12125	D	1911
SARMENTO			
Donald Hill	69035	M	1935

NAME	NUMBER	TYPE	YEAR
Joao Pereira	10502	D	1910
SARNO			
Ferdinando	83043	D	1940
SARNSEN			
Murl J.	79674	M	1938
SAROLEA			
Carolina	29140	D	1920
SARONI			
Alfred B.	88163	M	1941
Amalia	8683	D	1909
Belle	59102	D	1931
Louis, Mrs.	59102	D	1931
SARRABEITIA			
Eustouio Agustin Eizaga	3433	D	1907
SARRAGOSSA			
Albert	46976	M	1927
Evelyn	46976	M	1927
SARRAILLE			
Adolph James	85744	D	1940
Michael Joseph	85686	D	1940
Pierre Francois	37238	D	1923
SARRALES			
Sindolfo	77436	D	1938
SARRANO			
Dolores	44406	D	1926
SARRAZIN			
Alphonse	86908	D	1941
SARRE			
George N.	51443	D	1928
SARRET			
Joseph E.	27878	D	1919
Pierre	76817	D	1937
SARSFIELD			
John Henry	74840	D	1937
Kate	36962	D	1923
SARSO			
Ignazio	69641	D	1935
SARTHOU			
Eugene P.	84058	D	1940
Martha	81100	D	1939
Octavie	19943	D	1915
SARTHOW			
Marie Jeanne	36319	D	1923
SARTINI			
Raymond	68236	D	1934

NAME	NUMBER	TYPE	YEAR
SARTO			
Ettore	63192	D	1932
SARTOR			
Louis W.	51509	D	1928
SARTORELLO			
Ettore	63192	D	1932
SARTORI			
Emilio	21059	D	1916
Guiseppe	88892	D	1942
SARTORIO			
Charles	41276	D	1925
Magno Charles	41276	D	1925
SARTORIUS			
Helen	10299	D	1910
SARUBBI			
Francesco	74607	D	1937
Frank	49266	D	1928
George	49267	M	1928
Peter	49267	M	1928
Rosanna	49267	M	1928
SARVANELLO			
Carlo	29741	D	1920
SARVER			
Rachel	11503	D	1911
SASCHE			
John	31589	I	1921
SASCO			
John	54133	I	1929
SASEA			
John	54133	I	1929
SASIA			
John	54133	I	1929
SASLAVSKY			
Alexander	39886	D	1924
SASO			
Antonio	54484	D	1929
SASS			
Catherine	31366	D	1921
Charles	81509	D	1939
Frieda C.	35142	M	1922
Henry	28329	D	1919
Henry Paul	35142	M	1922
Isbelle A.	35142	M	1922
Peter	73275	D	1936
SASSELLI			
Desolina	65174	D	1933

NAME	NUMBER	TYPE	YEAR
Louis	63079	D	1932
Patricia	70206	M	1935
SASSER			
Henry Thomas	59279	D	1931
SASSIDES			
Harry	64488	D	1933
SASSO			
Frances M.	58675	D	1931
Gaetano	87570	D	1941
SASSUS			
Jacques	9523	D	1910
SATARAIN			
Angela	8955	M	1910
Qeresa	8955	M	1910
SATARIANO			
Giuseppe	43391	D	1926
Joseph	31279	D	1921
Maria	86811	D	1941
SATARINO			
Giuseppe	43391	D	1926
SATHER			
John Wm.	14832	D	1913
SATO			
M.	25640	D	1918
Natsuo	67560	D	1934
SATTELKAU			
Paul	67986	D	1934
SATTER			
Antonio	25420	D	1918
SATTERWHITE			
Minnie S.	75233	D	1937
SATTI			
John	47940	M	1927
SATTLER			
Aurelya Helen	87115	D	1941
Emilie	6086	D	1908
William	50995	D	1928
William Nicholas	39715	D	1924
SATTUI			
Apostina	71036	D	1935
Mario Angelo	36736	D	1923
Vittorio Georgio	36735	M	1923
SAUBLE			
Jonas	78315	D	1938
SAUCEDO			
J. A., Mrs.	19302	D	1915

NAME	NUMBER	TYPE	YEAR
SAUDERS			
Harriett	75456	M	1937
SAUER			
Adam	78143	D	1938
Clemens	4038	M	1907
Ellen	18358	D	1915
Fitus	55416	I	1930
Fred	55416	I	1930
Fredericka	78142	D	1938
George	16890	D	1914
George Frederick	73153	D	1936
Gertrude	4038	M	1907
Henry Lewis	17417	D	1914
Hermann	15492	D	1913
Johannes Conrad	55304	I	1930
Patricia Anne	81063	M	1939
Paul	39729	D	1924
SAUL			
Adeline Klemeyer	85518	D	1940
Anna M.	65039	D	1933
Arthur W.	41802	D	1925
Arthur W.	41802	D	1925
Frances Teresa	74372	D	1937
John T.	17243	D	1914
Margaret E.	16131	D	1913
Mary	33407	I	1922
Mary	35753	D	1923
Mary C.	8797	D	1909
Rosina	9322	D	1910
SAULOVICH			
George	53086	D	1929
Nikolas	71604	D	1936
SAUMER			
Henri	48031	D	1927
SAUNDERS			
Albert E.	64592	D	1933
Anna Elizabeth	45462	D	1926
Clara Ann	86778	D	1941
E.	26877	D	1919
Elizabeth	38058	D	1924
Harriet	6837	D	1908
Harry M.	54848	D	1930
I. F., Mrs.	35421	D	1922
J. J.	28952	D	1920
James	65255	M	1933
Jennie	45932	D	1926
John D.	50330	D	1928
Thomas Francis	77539	D	1938

NAME	NUMBER	TYPE	YEAR
SAUR			
Charles L.	65795	D	1933
SAURAT			
Margaret	41762	D	1925
Margaret	41762	D	1925
Vincent	57932	D	1931
SAURET			
Constant	66107	D	1934
Margaret	41762	D	1925
Margaret	41762	D	1925
Vincent	57932	D	1931
Vincent John	66108	M	1934
SAUSEVA			
Francisco	73438	D	1936
SAUTER			
Edward	85204	D	1940
Edward J.	87143	I	1941
Frank Ignaz	9088	D	1910
Herman	69731	D	1935
John M.	34189	D	1922
SAUTTER			
Nellie	65893	D	1933
SAUVE			
Caroline	7040	I	1909
Claire	12112	D	1911
Henrietta	12102	M	1911
SAUVEE			
Edith M.	86934	D	1941
SAVAGE			
Ann Augusta	6862	D	1908
Chester A.	56837	D	1930
Edward H.	67829	I	1934
Elizabeth J.	18371	D	1915
Fanny	82919	D	1939
Florence Toy	23433	D	1917
Francis	16534	D	1913
George H.	18187	D	1914
John	41168	I	1925
John A.	9768	D	1910
John J.	87669	D	1941
Lilian M.	87077	I	1941
Lincoln E.	40128	D	1924
M. J.	79884	I	1938
M. J.	86665	D	1941
Margaret	85632	M	1940
Marian W.	79649	I	1938
Mary A.	74164	D	1936

NAME	NUMBER	TYPE	YEAR
Mortimer	70763	D	1935
Natalie	41879	M	1925
Natalie	41879	M	1925
Patrick H.	8494	D	1909
Peter R.	50089	D	1928
Virginia	85632	M	1940
William A.	61413	D	1932
SAVANELLA			
Angela	36172	D	1923
Carlo	29741	D	1920
SAVANELLO			
Angela	36172	D	1923
Carlo	29741	D	1920
SAVANNAH			
Ben	44279	D	1926
Esther Rose	19654	D	1915
SAVARESE			
Antonio	38011	D	1923
SAVARY			
Clement	57639	D	1931
Emma	24517	I	1918
Madeleine	58305	D	1931
SAVAS			
Christos	87412	D	1941
Euthernia	87488	M	1941
SAVELLI			
Giocondo	30184	D	1920
SAVENBLAD			
Carl H.	26229	D	1919
Charles	26229	D	1919
SAVENIUS			
Robert	85139	D	1940
SAVERCOOL			
Edward M.	70704	D	1935
SAVERIO			
Curina	30295	D	1920
SAVERY			
George Walter	2084	M	1906
Maud Elizabeth	2084	M	1906
SAVICH			
Stephen	50445	D	1928
SAVILLE			
Eula Elizabeth	73679	M	1936
Frances	58976	I	1931
Frances	71138	D	1935
Sylvia M.	42974	D	1925

NAME	NUMBER	TYPE	YEAR
SAVIN			
Nathan	63059	D	1932
SAVIO			
Charles	32653	I	1921
Victor	14763	D	1913
Vittorio	14763	D	1913
SAVORY			
George, Mrs.	87389	D	1941
Helen Ellessifaen	87389	D	1941
SAWDON			
J. W.	41131	D	1925
Jack	41131	D	1925
William J.	41131	D	1925
SAWER			
Elizabeth A.	23619	D	1917
SAWERS			
Charles Gordon	4469	D	1907
SAWERY			
John J.	87159	D	1941
SAWIN			
James C.	44942	D	1926
SAWTELLE			
Benjamin Niles	68627	M	1934
Elizabeth S.	2068	D	1906
Jennie	38463	D	1924
William H.	68727	D	1935
SAWYER			
Abbie H.	34085	D	1922
B. O.	44078	D	1926
Belle A.	22726	D	1917
Edward E.	24823	D	1918
Elizabeth	73595	D	1936
Gabrielle	50558	M	1928
George	36881	D	1923
George Washington	29491	D	1920
Harold Edmund	2373	M	1906
Jennie C.	15638	D	1913
Lavinia T.	15162	D	1913
Lewis E.	37307	D	1923
Loy Elliott	2373	M	1906
Lucy Haight	25953	D	1918
Marie L.	52174	D	1929
Marion Marguerite	2373	M	1906
Mary A.	20315	I	1916
Mary A.	20417	D	1916
Mary B.	4092	D	1907
Robert J.	54034	D	1929

Key: D = death; M = minor; I = incompetent

NAME	NUMBER	TYPE	YEAR	NAME	NUMBER	TYPE	YEAR	NAME	NUMBER	TYPE	YEAR
Samuel T.	23980	D	1918	William	74482	D	1937	Thomas, Fr.	65083	M	1933
Sarah Elizabeth	73595	D	1936	**SAYNER**				**SCALA**			
Thomas	1973	D	1906	Alfred	89225	D	1942	Ettore	47000	D	1927
William F.	25239	D	1918	**SAYRE**				**SCALES**			
William Peter	45784	D	1926	Betty Lee	56343	M	1930	Amanda M.	1484	D	1906
SAX				**SAYWELL**				Edith Frances	79453	D	1938
Morris	13741	D	1912	Fannie	89786	I	1942	**SCALIONE**			
SAXE				**SBARBORO**				Antonio	65445	D	1933
Arthur Griggs	86050	D	1941	Andrea	36111	D	1923	Charles Caesar	34174	I	1922
Elizabeth	13734	D	1912	Augustine J.	87792	D	1941	Charles Caesar	36946	D	1923
Frances A.	47353	D	1927	Rosa	50045	D	1928	**SCALISE**			
Harry Asa	70529	D	1935	**SBARRA**				Pietro	81502	D	1939
Homer P.	33376	D	1922	John	80780	D	1939	**SCALLY**			
Leonard	81550	M	1939	**SBRAGIA**				John H.	59905	D	1931
Mary A.	41868	D	1925	Amedea	87084	D	1941	**SCALMANINI**			
Mary A.	41868	D	1925	Angelo	33541	D	1922	Antonio Benjamin	61270	D	1932
SAXENMEIER				Maria	33540	D	1922	Costante	50942	D	1928
Katherina	75433	D	1937	**SCACCABAROZZI**				Edwin	85271	I	1940
SAXON				Gaspare	67824	D	1934	Enrico	60155	D	1931
Henry	58984	D	1931	**SCACIGA**				Enrico Henry	13336	D	1912
SAXTON				Domenico	63720	D	1933	Tullio	20835	D	1916
Alan Joseph	79200	D	1938	Sam	71276	D	1935	**SCAMELL**			
Alexander Charles	50191	D	1928	Serafino	71276	D	1935	Vera Agnes	19307	D	1915
Judson Hiram	84512	D	1940	Tomaso	63720	D	1933	**SCAMMAN**			
Roy	17030	M	1914	**SCADDEN**				Francesca B.	57685	D	1931
SAXTORPH				Jane Ann	26801	D	1919	Henry	563	D	1906
Eleonora Camilla	19155	D	1915	**SCAFANI**				**SCAMMON**			
SAYAL				Anna Marie	73733	D	1936	Anna	15219	D	1913
Madeleine Bonito	73891	D	1936	Antonio	63710	D	1933	Elizabeth	36563	D	1923
Madeleine Leontine	73891	D	1936	Giuseppa	40565	D	1924	Justin	25739	D	1918
SAYER				**SCAFFANI**				Meltiah L.	12687	D	1911
Ada L.	37055	M	1923	Giuseppa	40565	D	1924	**SCANDRETT**			
Agnes E.	54992	D	1930	Pasquale	30742	D	1920	Alfred J.	44936	D	1926
SAYERS				**SCAFIDI**				Richard	13333	D	1912
Charles Arthur	58230	I	1931	Angelina Mary	66433	D	1934	Sarah	26153	D	1919
Mary	88556	D	1941	Domenico	8214	D	1909	**SCANLAN**			
Percy	47330	D	1927	Gaetano	3876	D	1907	Dominic Charles	57459	D	1930
Thomas	66893	D	1934	Grazzia	60664	D	1932	Dominic S.	57460	D	1930
SAYLES				Kathleen Angelina	69299	M	1935	George Joseph	24159	D	1918
Carrie A.	59243	D	1931	**SCAFINE**				Hannah	74997	D	1937
Frank Arthur	33064	D	1921	Antonia	79259	D	1938	James H.	76825	D	1937
Marjorie	85609	D	1940	**SCAFIRE**				Marian	56550	M	1930
SAYLOR				Joseph	47213	D	1927	Roger Joseph	9298	D	1910
David R.	86417	D	1941	**SCAHILL**				Ruth	56549	M	1930
Genevieve K. M.	73487	D	1936	Barbara	65083	M	1933	William H.	54734	D	1930
Norman M., Jr.	69570	M	1935	Lolita	67686	D	1934	**SCANLIN**			
Warrie D.	73405	D	1936					Annie	10138	I	1910

NAME	NUMBER	TYPE	YEAR
Annie Agnes	10957	D	1910
SCANLON			
Anna M.	51304	D	1928
Catherine	27897	D	1919
Cornelius	53146	D	1929
Daniel B.	74421	D	1937
Hannah	74997	D	1937
James	53718	D	1929
James Joseph	56009	D	1930
Johanna J.	39832	D	1924
Martin	56867	M	1930
Martin J.	82019	D	1939
Mary A.	56438	D	1930
Nellie	64336	D	1933
Patrick	916	D	1906
Peter	85989	D	1941
Thomas	21597	D	1916
Thomas	49340	D	1928
Timothy F.	6557	D	1908
William H.	54734	D	1930
SCANNELL			
Annie	34621	D	1922
Margaret	31187	D	1921
William	16863	D	1914
SCAPARONE			
Elisa	53739	M	1929
Mirra	53739	M	1929
SCARBOROUGH			
Floris	53174	D	1929
SCARCERIOUX			
Adolph C.	46181	D	1927
SCARDIGLI			
Fred	40846	M	1925
Leo	40846	M	1925
Nathan	40846	M	1925
Roy	40846	M	1925
SCARLETT			
Frank C.	25734	D	1918
SCARLOCK			
William D.	36301	D	1923
SCARPERI			
Vincent	52183	D	1929
SCARPONA			
Domenica	23631	D	1917
SCARPULLA			
Onofrio	50771	D	1928

NAME	NUMBER	TYPE	YEAR
SCARRITT			
Bertha L.	82145	I	1939
Bertha Lenore	82315	D	1939
Grace E.	89491	D	1942
SCASE			
Walter John V.	52760	D	1929
SCATCHERD			
Hugh Crofton	67513	D	1934
SCATENA			
Aristide Guglielmo	74575	D	1937
Fiovo	3355	D	1907
Fortunato	36929	D	1923
Francesco	84344	D	1940
Frank M.	26502	D	1919
Hazel	54449	D	1929
Lorenzo	56554	D	1930
Martin	75784	D	1937
Rosa Barsotti	40700	D	1925
Virginia	30389	D	1920
SCAVOGLIO			
Salvatore	60686	D	1932
Savatore	60686	D	1932
SCCHANACK			
Lena	71104	D	1935
SCECCHITANO			
Nunziata	53982	D	1929
SCERESINI			
Francesco	24131	D	1918
SCERI			
Virginia	85948	D	1941
SCERRA			
Filomena	33460	D	1922
SCERRI			
David	51338	D	1928
Virginia	85948	D	1941
SCHAAB			
George	85052	D	1940
SCHAACK			
Lena	71104	D	1935
SCHAADT			
Agnes	4279	D	1907
Ethel	1918	M	1906
John	4280	D	1907
Russell M.	59847	D	1931
SCHAAF			
Mary	83944	D	1940

NAME	NUMBER	TYPE	YEAR
SCHAAR			
Adolph	19987	D	1915
SCHABAT			
Emile	40517	D	1924
Fannie	53966	D	1929
SCHABERT			
Josephine	83981	D	1940
SCHABIAGUE			
Thomas	70988	D	1935
SCHACH			
Charles	7604	M	1909
SCHACHT			
Henry	31406	D	1921
Robert C.	12742	D	1911
SCHACHTER			
Jack	28482	D	1919
SCHAD			
Ronald	3727	M	1907
SCHADE			
Christine	31174	D	1921
Ferdinand C.	61510	D	1932
Fred	45804	D	1926
Ida G.	30113	D	1920
Oswald	48211	D	1927
SCHADLER			
Fred	51422	D	1928
SCHAEDLER			
Ferdinand	51422	D	1928
SCHAEFER			
Anna F.	88351	D	1941
August	62858	D	1932
Carrie	49438	D	1928
Charles Julius	88865	D	1942
Clarence	48398	D	1927
Frederick	50790	D	1928
Frederick	60235	D	1931
John	38955	I	1924
John	39244	D	1924
John	50455	D	1928
John E. D.	22675	D	1917
John Joseph	12578	I	1911
Joseph	34332	D	1922
Leo Stierlin	8132	D	1909
Louis	60524	D	1931
Ludwig Anderas	60525	D	1931
Margaret	88197	I	1941
Mary E. F.	16499	I	1913

Key: D = death; M = minor; I = incompetent

NAME	NUMBER	TYPE	YEAR
Mary E. F.	37698	D	1923
Peter	30679	D	1920
Phyllis	46151	D	1927
Rudolph	13484	D	1912
Stephen J.	51545	I	1928
Walter C.	86314	D	1941
William	51866	D	1929
William	84297	D	1940
William B.	86250	D	1941
William B., III	86251	M	1941
William T.	83753	D	1940
SCHAEFERTAENS			
Amalie	66926	D	1934
SCHAEFFER			
Alfred	86853	D	1941
Benjamin	42679	I	1925
SCHAER			
Lydia L.	83873	D	1940
SCHAERLIN			
Elizabeth	40191	D	1924
SCHAERTZER			
Henry C.	15842	D	1913
Irma Dorothy	16024	M	1913
SCHAEZLEIN			
Maretta	71065	D	1935
SCHAFER			
Anna R.	61613	D	1932
Augustus F.	44389	D	1926
Catherine J.	80655	I	1939
Friedricke	40582	D	1924
George	13640	D	1912
George	28005	D	1919
Harry F.	49727	I	1928
Heinrich Friedrich Wilhelm	25664	D	1918
Henry F. W.	25664	D	1918
John	65405	D	1933
Katharina	47811	D	1927
Margaret Bell	60570	I	1931
Sophie W.	39520	D	1924
SCHAFERTONS			
Amalie	66926	D	1934
SCHAFFER			
Adena Lee	61030	M	1932
Catherine	89347	I	1942
Walter R. W.	14998	M	1913
SCHAFFLER			
Anselm M.	51576	D	1928

NAME	NUMBER	TYPE	YEAR
SCHAFFNER			
Fredericka M. E.	50146	D	1928
Jennie	15410	D	1913
SCHAFFT			
Robert Charles	86206	D	1941
SCHAFMEISTER			
Henry	64605	D	1933
SCHAFRO			
Emile	40437	D	1924
SCHAFROTH			
Emile	40437	D	1924
SCHAICH			
Christian Jacob	76463	D	1937
SCHAINMAN			
Paul	79452	D	1938
SCHAKE			
Alfred P.	39297	I	1924
SCHALCK			
Johann F.	57672	D	1931
SCHALICH			
Thomas	18147	D	1914
SCHALK			
Johann Friedrich	57672	D	1931
SCHALL			
Anna F.	84044	D	1940
George H.	29987	D	1920
Walter Henry	18630	D	1915
SCHALLE			
Carl Albert	84326	D	1940
SCHALLER			
Alfred	46960	D	1927
SCHALLICH			
Sophia	35575	D	1922
SCHALLINGER			
Carl	79524	D	1938
SCHALLOCK			
Emil	82059	D	1939
SCHAMOWITZ			
Isaac	52771	D	1929
SCHANEMAN			
Frank	68311	I	1934
SCHANFELE			
Mary L.	46758	D	1927
SCHANZ			
Francis Herbert	62134	M	1932

NAME	NUMBER	TYPE	YEAR
SCHANZER			
Margaret	10235	D	1910
SCHAPER			
Rudolph O. C.	53355	M	1929
SCHAPIRO			
Bernbard	56861	D	1930
SCHARBACH			
Florence May	47739	D	1927
SCHARETG			
Ann G.	77301	D	1937
Francis M.	15417	D	1913
May Frances	15417	D	1913
Walter	61291	D	1932
Walter C.	78852	M	1938
SCHARFF			
Louis F.	73142	D	1936
Rosa	75575	D	1937
SCHARKE			
Agnes Carlton	57589	D	1931
SCHARLACH			
Gustav J.	28632	D	1920
SCHARLANDT			
C. R.	76643	D	1937
SCHARLIN			
Abraham	82584	D	1939
Josephine L.	26455	D	1919
SCHARM			
Paul W.	79918	D	1938
SCHARTAN			
Benjamin	404	D	1906
Bernhard	404	D	1906
SCHARTAU			
Benjamin	404	D	1906
Bernhard	404	D	1906
SCHARTON			
Paulina	32231	D	1921
SCHARY			
Fannie	48381	D	1927
Hattie	21355	D	1916
Julius	10081	D	1910
Sarah Fannie	48381	D	1927
SCHASTEY			
G. A., Jr.	62915	D	1932
George A.	52519	I	1929
George A.	62915	D	1932

NAME	NUMBER	TYPE	YEAR
SCHAUB			
Francis H.	36564	M	1923
John	1505	D	1906
Mary	52435	D	1929
Rose Mary	27558	D	1919
Victoria	33562	D	1922
SCHAUBEL			
Etta S.	67999	D	1934
Henrietta	67999	D	1934
Marie	53317	D	1929
SCHAUBELL			
Mamie	52986	I	1929
SCHAUBLE			
Emil	56796	D	1930
SCHAUER			
Agnes Judd	71050	D	1935
Agnes M.	71050	D	1935
Annie E.	59103	D	1931
SCHAUFEL			
Anna	40916	D	1925
Ludwig	13941	D	1912
SCHAUMLEFFEL			
Millie D.	68153	D	1934
SCHAYER			
Fannie	37571	D	1923
SCHEARER			
Mae	51659	D	1928
SCHEEL			
Harry A.	24714	D	1918
John H.	33841	D	1922
SCHEELE			
Fritz	54429	D	1929
Heinrich	20505	D	1916
SCHEELINE			
Henriette	28553	D	1919
Louise B.	84538	D	1940
Sol E., Mrs.	84538	D	1940
Solomon E.	65831	D	1933
SCHEER			
Edwin B.	56293	I	1930
Eliza	21333	D	1916
Mabel E.	89708	D	1942
Samuel	64165	D	1933
SCHEFFAUER			
Fiona Francisca	50155	M	1928
Therese	40726	D	1925

NAME	NUMBER	TYPE	YEAR
SCHEFFERLING			
Jane Hill	63675	D	1933
SCHEFLER			
Selma	59945	D	1931
SCHEFSKY			
Esther	67457	D	1934
Harry	67458	D	1934
SCHEGGIA			
Elmo	10928	M	1910
Evelyn	10928	M	1910
SCHEHR			
John D.	645	D	1906
SCHEIB			
Annie	45789	D	1926
Elizabeth	36294	D	1923
SCHEIBE			
Bernard	8912	D	1909
Erwin A.	47816	D	1927
SCHEIBLI			
Jakob	9496	D	1910
James	9496	D	1910
Rudolf	26620	D	1919
SCHEIDEMANN			
John	8172	D	1909
SCHEIDMANN			
Theresa M.	45057	I	1926
Theresa M.	57544	D	1930
SCHEIER			
Gabriel	23073	D	1917
Johan Friedrich	23132	D	1917
SCHEIFLER			
Augusta	11306	M	1911
Frank	11306	M	1911
Frank J.	64462	M	1933
SCHEIHING			
Jacob William	52586	D	1929
John	52586	D	1929
SCHEINER			
George	17879	D	1914
SCHELE			
Katharina	5852	D	1908
SCHELEY			
William Theodore	3236	D	1907
SCHELL			
George W.	4026	D	1907
James	49410	D	1928

NAME	NUMBER	TYPE	YEAR
Samuel	49487	D	1928
SCHELLER			
Ceda	85970	D	1941
Victor A.	79465	D	1938
Victor A., Mrs.	85970	D	1941
SCHELLING			
Charles J.	26096	D	1919
Wilhelm	87405	D	1941
SCHELLPEPER			
Conrad August	25629	D	1918
Edward Conrad	35285	M	1922
Elfreda	35285	M	1922
Theresa Louisa	18527	D	1915
SCHEMBRI			
Mabel Sloan	85513	D	1940
Vincent	80595	D	1939
SCHEMEL			
Charles	8124	D	1909
SCHEMIT			
Marie B.	359	D	1906
SCHENCH			
Mary Simons	57482	D	1930
SCHENCK			
Caroline A.	6783	D	1908
Elmer	47837	D	1927
Harry E.	47837	D	1927
Lina	71104	D	1935
Lina	71104	D	1935
SCHENER			
Annie Elizabeth	43993	D	1926
SCHENK			
Carolina	74915	D	1937
Eugenie	88490	D	1941
Hubert	84986	I	1940
Hubert	85337	D	1940
William A.	19851	D	1915
William Adam	19852	M	1915
SCHENKBERG			
Adolph E.	82576	D	1939
Annie	82575	D	1939
SCHENKEL			
Charles J.	36687	D	1923
Elizabeth M.	31942	D	1921
SCHENN			
Martha A.	9810	I	1910
SCHENNE			
Rudolf	48469	D	1927

NAME	NUMBER	TYPE	YEAR
SCHENONE			
Carlo	65162	D	1933
Charles	65162	D	1933
SCHENZ			
Eduard	60803	D	1932
Mary	61112	D	1932
SCHEPER			
Andrew	5806	D	1908
Arthur	25822	M	1918
Gertrude	25822	M	1918
Louis	25822	M	1918
Ludwig	5807	D	1908
Slophia M. D.	16912	D	1914
SCHEPHARDT			
Max	38328	D	1924
SCHEPPLER			
Emma Bertha	50589	D	1928
Laura M.	47320	D	1927
Mamie Laura M.	47320	D	1927
Pauline	73349	D	1936
William H.	64583	D	1933
William W.	49997	D	1928
SCHEPTE			
Henry	50540	D	1928
SCHERER			
Fannie	66103	D	1934
George	30129	D	1920
Josefa	86390	D	1941
Katherine Mary	44061	M	1926
Maggie	27628	D	1919
Mary A.	71175	D	1935
SCHERF			
Anna	50899	M	1928
Annie	88437	D	1941
Annie	48310	D	1927
Julia	50899	M	1928
SCHERINI			
Giuseppi	36863	D	1923
SCHERMERHORN			
Eugenia Burns	40999	D	1925
SCHERNIKOW			
Ernest	65979	D	1933
SCHERNING			
Emma	74596	D	1937
SCHERNSTEIN			
Fannie	79650	D	1938
Fannie Hackenschmidt	65898	D	1933

NAME	NUMBER	TYPE	YEAR
SCHERR			
Carl F.	10111	D	1910
Charles F.	10111	D	1910
Ferdinand A.	55128	D	1930
Helen A.	39113	D	1924
SCHERRER			
Lauren	17318	D	1914
SCHERSCHEL			
Henrietta Maria	31028	M	1921
SCHERZER			
A. J.	896	I	1906
Guillermo Arrazola	9187	D	1910
Rachael	993	M	1906
Teresa	993	M	1906
William Arrazola	9187	D	1910
SCHETTE			
Louis	23414	D	1917
SCHETTEL			
Louis	23414	D	1917
SCHETTER			
Rose	63474	D	1933
SCHETZEL			
Kate F.	81592	I	1939
Katherine F.	83440	D	1940
SCHEUBER			
August	75589	D	1937
SCHEUCH			
Ferdinand	544	M	1906
Lillie	544	M	1906
Marie	543	D	1906
SCHEUER			
Annie Elizabeth	43993	D	1926
E. B. Richard	34783	D	1922
J. J.	64245	D	1933
John	64245	D	1933
SCHEUFELE			
Charles	83164	D	1940
SCHEUNEMAN			
Anna	72226	D	1936
SCHEUNERT			
Hugo	69993	D	1935
SCHEURER			
William	56359	M	1930
SCHEURINGER			
Gottlob	6797	D	1908

NAME	NUMBER	TYPE	YEAR
SCHEVERS			
Arnold J.	55982	D	1930
SCHEWE			
Carl E.	29214	D	1920
SCHEY			
Isaac S.	34815	D	1922
John	24379	D	1918
SCHEYER			
Jane	55818	M	1930
Joan	55818	M	1930
Max	63815	D	1933
Regina	76596	D	1937
Sallusch	76597	D	1937
SCHIAFFINO			
Armanda	21455	D	1916
Camillo	75097	D	1937
SCHIAVI			
Luigi	890	D	1906
Nicholas	68431	D	1934
SCHIAVONE			
Edna Patricia	59765	D	1931
SCHIBI			
John B.	26669	D	1919
Walter L.	60045	I	1931
SCHIBUSCH			
Annie Hart	82595	D	1939
Frank C.	87515	D	1941
SCHICK			
Frank F.	12614	D	1911
SCHIEB			
Emma	57767	D	1931
SCHIEBE			
George L., Mrs.	83608	D	1940
Josephine Marie	83608	D	1940
SCHIEBEL			
Margaret	55714	D	1930
SCHIEFER			
Herman J.	78872	D	1938
SCHIEFFER			
Catherine	22205	D	1917
SCHIELDS			
Frederick	85492	D	1940
Frederick Henry	85492	D	1940
Mary Elizabeth	85494	M	1940
SCHIEMPF			
Margaretha	27787	D	1919

NAME	NUMBER	TYPE	YEAR	NAME	NUMBER	TYPE	YEAR	NAME	NUMBER	TYPE	YEAR
SCHIERLOH				**SCHILTER**				**SCHIVO**			
Friedrich	42630	D	1925	Karl	87660	D	1941	Catherine	45392	D	1926
SCHIFF				**SCHIMMELPFENNIG**				Emma	48948	D	1928
Benno L.	59908	D	1931	George W.	46681	D	1927	Peter Paul	86731	D	1941
Edward	73177	D	1936	**SCHIMPF**				**SCHJETMAN**			
Edwin R.	73177	D	1936	Clara	1603	I	1906	Mario	49300	M	1928
Henrietta	21726	D	1916	Margaretha	27787	D	1919	**SCHJODT**			
Jacob B.	17742	D	1914	**SCHIMPFERMAN**				Gustav M.	46095	D	1926
Rebecca	32986	D	1921	Pauline	27183	D	1919	**SCHLABERG**			
SCHIFFERLI				**SCHIMPFF**				Frank	16396	D	1913
John	51655	D	1928	John	31707	D	1921	**SCHLACK**			
SCHILDKRET				**SCHINDLER**				Elizabeth	77211	I	1937
Elias	85244	D	1940	Adam C.	66453	D	1934	**SCHLAGAL**			
SCHILDT				G.	51053	D	1928	Mary	63668	D	1933
Fred	84967	D	1940	John	51053	D	1928	**SCHLAICH**			
SCHILING				Margaret J.	68820	D	1935	Madeleine	19378	D	1915
John Walter	56649	D	1930	**SCHINICK**				Magdalena	19378	D	1915
SCHILLER				Nellie	89821	D	1942	**SCHLAUDEDKER**			
Bertha E.	75633	D	1937	**SCHINKEL**				Matthew	4496	D	1907
David M.	84906	D	1940	Alice E. B.	2845	M	1907	**SCHLEEMANN**			
Dorothy Vivian	21739	M	1916	Elsie D.	2845	M	1907	John	17115	D	1914
Frederick V.	58125	D	1931	Herny	48767	D	1927	Mathilde M.	59542	D	1931
Leonard	11509	D	1911	Hinny	48767	D	1927	**SCHLEGEL**			
Mamie	54676	D	1930	Ida C.	57446	D	1930	Anton	41488	D	1925
Margaret Jean	85592	M	1940	Otto	2831	D	1907	Constantin	38117	D	1924
Marie Louise	85592	M	1940	Susan	73061	D	1936	Edward Joseph	25783	D	1918
Max	31310	D	1921	Susie May	73061	D	1936	Fred	5883	D	1908
Yette	17510	D	1914	Theresa	66024	D	1934	Izora D.	61492	D	1932
SCHILLIGER				**SCHIPPER**				Katherine	21761	D	1916
Louis	82981	D	1939	John Carl August	18342	D	1915	Markus	78945	D	1938
SCHILLING				**SCHIPPERT**				William L.	18925	D	1915
Anna M.	16077	D	1913	Kunigunde (nee Kettler)	17886	D	1914	**SCHLEICHER**			
Anna Margaretha	2735	D	1907	**SCHIRMEIER**				A. F.	59593	D	1931
Claus	42337	D	1925	Fritz	2418	D	1906	William	34444	D	1922
Ernest Herman	89350	D	1942	**SCHIRMER**				**SCHLEIER**			
Frank	48781	D	1927	Adelaide	23302	D	1917	Elisabeth	49925	D	1928
George W.	75415	D	1937	Arthur	19034	D	1915	John G.	44314	D	1926
Gustav Henry	28232	D	1919	Joan Louise	81899	M	1939	**SCHLEIGER**			
John E.	2959	D	1907	Louise	62840	D	1932	William	34444	D	1922
Louis	44578	D	1926	William	81617	D	1939	**SCHLEIMER**			
Marie A.	75414	D	1937	**SCHIVELY**				Georgia Dell	33983	D	1922
Pauline	68425	D	1934	Dora Hammar	81267	M	1939	**SCHLEMMER**			
SCHILLINGS				**SCHIVERIN**				Margaret Bassett	87371	D	1941
Marie	40401	M	1924	Lotta Bean	87922	D	1941	**SCHLENKER**			
Marion	40401	M	1924	**SCHIVERN**				Auguste	11095	D	1911
Mary	40401	M	1924	Rychard C.	86795	D	1941	B.	11095	D	1911
Peter	40400	D	1924								

NAME	NUMBER	TYPE	YEAR
Matt	89389	D	1942
SCHLESINGER			
Bert	52609	D	1929
Bertha	89484	D	1942
Charles	56025	D	1930
Charles	74777	D	1937
David Jerome	67708	D	1934
Henrietta	69538	I	1935
Henry	24895	D	1918
Julius M.	55715	D	1930
Lily	49412	D	1928
Louis	3040	D	1907
Merwyn J.	4765	M	1907
Nancy Lee	79668	M	1938
Samuel	15626	D	1913
Sette	24314	D	1918
Sydney	67438	D	1934
Wallea	60863	M	1932
SCHLESSELMANN			
Caroline M.	13411	D	1912
Walter F.	38170	D	1924
SCHLESSINGER			
Anna M.	37897	D	1923
Charles	89044	D	1942
Mabel B.	40703	D	1925
Sidney	67438	D	1934
SCHLETT			
Emil	38346	D	1924
SCHLEYER			
B.	25234	D	1918
SCHLICHTER			
Gustav Adolph	70458	D	1935
SCHLICHTING			
August W.	44783	D	1926
August W., Mrs.	55589	D	1930
Henrietta	55589	D	1930
Henrietta	55590	M	1930
SCHLICHTMANN			
Albertine	88186	D	1941
Henry	28858	D	1920
SCHLICKER			
Frederick	16987	D	1914
SCHLIKENRIEDER			
Armella	31767	D	1921
SCHLINGHEYDE			
Carl E.	51529	D	1928

NAME	NUMBER	TYPE	YEAR
SCHLINK			
Celestine Elizabeth	31323	D	1921
Leonard James	44105	I	1926
Leonard James	51938	D	1929
SCHLINKE			
Ottilie Louisa Marie Laura	13778	D	1912
SCHLITTER			
Alexander	31886	D	1921
SCHLOH			
Anna C.	33936	D	1922
Bernhard A.	81824	D	1939
Dolores	54511	D	1929
SCHLOKE			
Harry	53651	D	1929
SCHLOSS			
Benjamin	16335	D	1913
Benjamin	44219	D	1926
Elizabeth	67594	D	1934
Florence F.	84229	D	1940
Frederika Florence	84229	D	1940
Philippe	18776	D	1915
Simon	70615	D	1935
Solomon	17367	D	1914
SCHLOSSBERG			
Jacob	76912	D	1937
SCHLOSSER			
Jacob	18802	D	1915
Matthew	32196	D	1921
SCHLOTER			
Eugene	72531	D	1936
SCHLOTT			
Ernest Frederick	84686	D	1940
Frederick Ernst Hermann	21276	D	1916
SCHLOTTERBECK			
George	86329	D	1941
SCHLOTTNER			
Wilhelm	65851	D	1933
SCHLUCHTERER			
Philipp	15358	D	1913
SCHLUETER			
Edgar W.	60725	D	1932
Edward W.	6452	D	1908
Harry William	61962	I	1932
Henry	28668	D	1920
SCHLUND			
Fidel	22494	D	1917

NAME	NUMBER	TYPE	YEAR
SCHLUNDT			
A. Christian	53037	D	1929
August Otto H.	72312	D	1936
SCHLUTER			
William	7026	D	1909
SCHLUTTER			
F. W.	19272	I	1915
F. W.	19905	D	1915
SCHMADEL			
Elisa	7076	D	1909
SCHMAELZGER			
Jennie	37115	D	1923
SCHMAH			
Hans	83740	D	1940
John	83740	D	1940
SCHMALING			
Charles	43579	D	1926
SCHMALZ			
Louise E.	62173	D	1932
William	33435	D	1922
SCHMAUS			
Franz	8018	D	1909
John E.	9282	D	1910
SCHMECKPEPER			
Rieke	35234	D	1922
SCHMEDES			
Emma H.	87939	D	1941
Hermann Frederich	22950	D	1917
SCHMEDING			
Carl	86497	D	1941
SCHMEISS			
Carl E.	13225	D	1912
SCHMELDING			
Emil	66092	D	1934
SCHMELZER			
Bertha	33729	M	1922
Lorenz	33729	M	1922
SCHMENKEL			
Robert W. T.	19972	D	1915
SCHMERL			
Maida C.	75771	D	1937
Maida Ella	75771	D	1937
SCHMETZER			
Joseph	14302	D	1912
SCHMID			
August	15888	D	1913

NAME	NUMBER	TYPE	YEAR	NAME	NUMBER	TYPE	YEAR	NAME	NUMBER	TYPE	YEAR
Frank	52007	D	1929	Emilia	13880	D	1912	Junius	52074	D	1929
John	81533	D	1939	Emilie M. M.	39696	D	1924	Karl C.	35292	D	1922
John J.	4380	D	1907	Ernest	33966	D	1922	Lena	1795	D	1906
Maria	44372	D	1926	Ernst August	32806	D	1921	Lena Margaret	52570	D	1929
Marie	73199	I	1936	Ferdinand	60143	D	1931	Leonard	23560	D	1917
Otto Geo.	24858	D	1918	Florence	13797	D	1912	Lillian R.	52992	I	1929
William	60960	D	1932	Frances	51793	D	1929	Lizzie Dondero	60666	D	1932
SCHMIDLI				Frank	19647	D	1915	Lizzie M.	32567	D	1921
Florence I.	36283	D	1923	Frank A.	41151	D	1925	Louis	67426	D	1934
SCHMIDT				Franz T.	86599	D	1941	Louis	75685	I	1937
A. H. R.	42412	D	1925	Fred J.	44329	D	1926	Louis Carl	37795	D	1923
Albert	37389	D	1923	Fred J., Jr.	53113	D	1929	Louise	27856	D	1919
Albert	84185	D	1940	Freda	88598	I	1941	Lydia K.	26819	D	1919
Albert D.	39870	D	1924	Frieda	27281	M	1919	M. A.	37297	D	1923
Albert, Jr.	84420	M	1940	Friederike	88769	I	1941	Margaretha	38218	D	1924
Ali	6331	D	1908	Friederike	89576	D	1942	Marie	27773	D	1919
Anna	22712	D	1917	Fritz	27281	M	1919	Marie Caroline	82073	M	1939
Anna	57310	M	1930	Fritz	58095	M	1931	Martin P.	85611	I	1940
Anna Maria	1423	D	1906	George	51773	D	1929	Martin P.	86144	D	1941
Annie	65673	D	1933	George	75680	D	1937	Mary	25653	D	1918
Annie E.	58636	D	1931	George Henry	83936	D	1940	Mary E.	11601	D	1911
Annie L.	87361	I	1941	Gottlieb	57005	D	1930	Mary Helen	13454	D	1912
Antone	1578	D	1906	Gustav A.	56431	D	1930	Mathilda Elizabeth	30992	D	1921
Arthur Frederick	76277	D	1937	Gustave F.	25068	D	1918	Mathilde	76905	D	1937
August	32806	D	1921	H. D. W.	19553	D	1915	Maud	29074	D	1920
August W.	81252	I	1939	H. H.	77405	D	1938	Max	72567	D	1936
Barbara Nellie	50876	D	1928	H. H.	83211	D	1940	Max John	38772	D	1924
Barbetta	36690	D	1923	Hans	12854	D	1912	Olive Hunt	2804	D	1907
Bernhard August	81094	D	1939	Hans	77265	D	1937	Oliver S.	88270	D	1941
Bertha M.	25568	D	1918	Hans B.	7665	D	1909	Oscar	1425	D	1906
Carl	38684	I	1924	Hedwig Reck	26745	D	1919	Otto	29976	D	1920
Catherina M.	66673	D	1934	Henry	34255	D	1922	Otto Francis	82073	M	1939
Charles	7937	D	1909	Henry	75713	D	1937	Pauline	56393	D	1930
Charlotte	61858	D	1932	Henry V.	28652	M	1920	Peter	26472	D	1919
Conrad	52441	D	1929	Herbert A.	55190	D	1930	Peter	29671	D	1920
Conrad	52946	D	1929	Herman J. W.	39996	D	1924	Peter	86111	D	1941
Cornelia A. L.	32252	D	1921	Hermie	35931	D	1923	Petrine Jacobine	84022	D	1940
E. A.	32952	D	1921	Irma	21606	M	1916	Phyllis Rita	82073	M	1939
Edward	76692	D	1937	J. Lillian Hohwiesner	84923	D	1940	Robert Lauren	86412	D	1941
Edward B.	1054	D	1906	J. W. E.	54459	D	1929	Rudolph William	83472	D	1940
Edward Nicholas	63094	D	1932	Jack H.	31733	D	1921	Seli B.	40006	I	1924
Edwin Val	89265	D	1942	Jacob	81438	D	1939	Shirley W.	43787	M	1926
Edwina A.	11417	M	1911	John	12854	D	1912	Sophie	89393	D	1942
Eleonore	69770	D	1935	John	13117	D	1912	Soren	37545	D	1923
Elinor Carlson	77795	D	1938	John	57310	M	1930	Stefan	28550	D	1919
Elizabeth A.	60666	D	1932	John C.	51865	D	1929	Valentine	29367	D	1920
Elnore	68065	M	1934	John Carl	72951	M	1936	Victor	25366	D	1918
Elsie M.	32567	D	1921	John H.	29971	D	1920	W. H.	7103	D	1909
Emil	50562	D	1928	Josephine	49990	D	1928	Wilhelmina A.	34340	D	1922

NAME	NUMBER	TYPE	YEAR
William	23339	D	1917
William	77009	D	1937
William F.	83115	D	1940
William Friedrich Christian	81737	D	1939
William Henry	84637	D	1940
SCHMIEDECKE			
Frederick W.	71802	D	1936
SCHMIEDELL			
Fronie W.	24636	D	1918
SCHMIEDER			
Ewald J.	50353	I	1928
Jean B.	83689	D	1940
SCHMIERER			
Chas. J.	17072	D	1914
Gottlieb	6093	D	1908
John G.	13435	D	1912
Minnie J.	9541	D	1910
SCHMIT			
Marie A.	89758	D	1942
Theresa	52951	D	1929
SCHMITH			
Bertha	38071	I	1924
George	14723	D	1913
SCHMITT			
Ada L.	34145	D	1922
Aina Emily	6521	M	1908
Alfred	3003	D	1907
Amelia Elizabeth	52058	D	1929
Anna	85860	D	1940
Bertha F.	68215	I	1934
Bertha F.	69133	D	1935
Blaise L.	97	D	1906
Carl	11457	D	1911
Carol Marie	78049	M	1938
Charles	11457	D	1911
Charles A.	865	D	1906
Charles E.	40840	D	1925
Charles G.	20863	D	1916
Eugene A.	2968	D	1907
F.	52703	D	1929
Frederick	15674	D	1913
Frederick E.	44607	D	1926
George	13283	D	1912
George J.	67077	D	1934
Grace Rose	33083	D	1921
Henry C.	68787	D	1935
Jacob	9769	D	1910
Jacob M.	18786	D	1915

NAME	NUMBER	TYPE	YEAR
Jessie E.	8662	D	1909
John J.	62070	D	1932
Joseph	2283	D	1906
Joseph L.	17976	D	1914
Joseph William	81421	D	1939
Josephine B.	22518	M	1917
Leonard	23560	D	1917
Minnie	27656	D	1919
Pauline	513	D	1906
Peter	4711	D	1907
W. W.	193	D	1906
SCHMITZ			
Albert	60871	D	1932
Catherine E.	56976	D	1930
Charlotte	12551	D	1911
Eugene E.	52212	D	1929
Franz Xavier	10935	D	1910
John Peter	1022	D	1906
Karoline	10367	D	1910
Peter	60878	D	1932
William	18898	D	1915
William A.	83412	I	1940
William H.	83412	I	1940
William L.	24182	D	1918
SCHMITZER			
Ferdinand H.	17427	D	1914
SCHMOECKEL			
Mina Theresa	75886	D	1937
SCHMOLL			
Adam	26743	D	1919
Emile	29173	D	1920
Emile (Dr.)	22942	I	1917
Nellie	65329	I	1933
SCHMOLLE			
Helen M.	44693	D	1926
Martha	28211	I	1919
SCHMUCK			
Herman G.	52191	M	1929
SCHMUCKERT			
Anita A. M.	997	M	1906
Hermione R. A.	997	M	1906
Lillian E.	997	M	1906
SCHMUHL			
William	89935	D	1942
SCHMULOWITZ			
Solomon	47055	D	1927

NAME	NUMBER	TYPE	YEAR
SCHNAITTACHER			
Sylvain	43704	D	1926
SCHNAKENBERG			
John C.	64978	D	1933
SCHNALLE			
Mary A.	43710	D	1926
Richard A.	69525	D	1935
SCHNAPP			
Adam	21775	D	1916
Morris	29732	D	1920
SCHNAUFER			
William, Jr.	60501	D	1931
SCHNEBLY			
Frederick D.	59165	D	1931
SCHNECK			
Celia	81911	I	1939
Celia	88006	D	1941
Joseph	19867	D	1915
Louis	76117	D	1937
SCHNEE			
Gustave	70496	D	1935
Marcus	14280	D	1912
SCHNEEGASS			
Bertha	89217	D	1942
Fred	52194	D	1929
SCHNEIDE			
Florentine	3225	D	1907
SCHNEIDER			
Albrecht Friedrich Philipp	45843	D	1926
Anna F.	84044	D	1940
Anna.	11718	D	1911
Annette Lila	51377	M	1928
Annie	50672	D	1928
Anton	50180	D	1928
Arlie	44180	I	1926
August	52444	D	1929
August	49963	D	1928
Bertha Maria	48072	D	1927
Carl	11292	M	1911
Carl	31182	D	1921
Charles G.	3606	D	1907
Charlotte	34109	D	1922
Clara	11864	D	1911
Conrad Rudolf	18438	D	1915
Edith J.	51376	I	1928
Edith Taylor	42174	D	1925
Edward W.	37212	D	1923

Key: D = death; M = minor; I = incompetent

Name	Number	Type	Year	Name	Number	Type	Year	Name	Number	Type	Year
Elise	54421	D	1929	William A.	67596	D	1934	**Schobert**			
Emilie F.	50263	D	1928	William G.	83871	D	1940	George	17076	D	1914
Emma M.	78282	D	1938	**Schnell**				**Schocken**			
Ernest G.	30106	D	1920	Edna	7213	M	1909	Clara	65914	D	1933
Ernestine	30094	D	1920	**Schnellbacher**				Lillie	82982	D	1939
Fred	6590	D	1908	Anna	53636	D	1929	Solomon	61796	D	1932
Frederick Walter	11292	M	1911	**Schneller**				**Schocken-Feibusch**			
George	48805	D	1927	Frank	57912	D	1931	Mignon	69840	D	1935
George E.	40332	D	1924	**Schnier**				**Schockway**			
George H.	88394	D	1941	Matilda	27798	D	1919	Victor	77698	D	1938
George W. E.	57875	D	1931	**Schnipper**				**Schoeder**			
Henry	81927	D	1939	Hans H. R.	19931	D	1915	Margaretha	41583	D	1925
Isaac	25815	D	1918	Hilma	45193	D	1926	**Schoefield**			
Jacob	48181	I	1927	**Schnitz**				Ira V.	42829	D	1925
John	24308	D	1918	J. H.	18470	D	1915	**Schoemaker**			
John	51900	D	1929	**Schnitzer**				Delia J.	79929	D	1938
John	54501	D	1929	Albert	45343	D	1926	John D.	89569	D	1942
John C.	64401	D	1933	Frank	29556	D	1920	**Schoemann**			
John F.	88914	D	1942	Gertrude	35369	M	1922	Max	75731	D	1937
John N.	13091	D	1912	Gertrude	43949	D	1926	Robert	89760	D	1942
John, Jr.	65138	D	1933	**Schnoder**				**Schoen**			
Joseph W.	8671	D	1909	Sadie	68986	D	1935	Elizabeth	21439	D	1916
Klara	11864	D	1911	**Schnoeberg**				Frances H.	69265	D	1935
Konrad	52764	D	1929	Frank	51295	D	1928	Frances Owens	69265	D	1935
Kusiel	24317	D	1918	**Schnoor**				John Joseph	21280	D	1916
Leon	19154	D	1915	John	47846	M	1927	**Schoenberg**			
Lizzie	79762	D	1938	Robert	74591	D	1937	Louis	44920	D	1926
Louis	9420	D	1910	**Schnuriger**				Milton Henry	86818	D	1941
Louis	67757	I	1934	Joseph	24696	D	1918	Pauline	71647	D	1936
Louis	71365	D	1936	**Schnurman**				Sarah	47200	D	1927
Louis	50671	D	1928	Audrey L.	89633	M	1942	**Schoenberger**			
Manuel	55399	M	1930	**Schnurr**				Adolph	25073	D	1918
Marie	38837	D	1924	Philipp	28098	D	1919	**Schoenblein**			
Marie C.	62295	D	1932	**Schnutenhaus**				Marie E.	68841	D	1935
Martin	18804	D	1915	Edmund	25457	D	1918	**Schoendaller**			
Mary	56696	I	1930	Lizzie	37598	D	1923	Alvin Jacob	88122	D	1941
Mary	59446	D	1931	Ottilie	80617	D	1939	**Schoene**			
Mathilda	26930	D	1919	Richard	44365	I	1926	Harriet	17198	D	1914
N., Mrs.	44180	I	1926	Richard	55472	I	1930	**Schoenegg**			
Otto A.	45145	M	1926	Richard	57927	D	1931	Anton August	82390	D	1939
Pauline	69516	D	1935	**Schnuternhaus**				**Schoeneman**			
Rollo C.	45145	M	1926	Margaretha	19507	D	1915	Robert	88738	I	1941
Roy	69215	M	1935	**Schober**				Robert, Mrs.	88737	D	1941
Seymour Nathan	85236	D	1940	Fred E.	75309	D	1937	Rose	88737	D	1941
Tobie	50739	D	1928	Henry J.	32736	D	1921	**Schoenenberger**			
W. H.	8892	D	1909	John	18782	D	1915	Marie Christine	83336	I	1940
Wilhelm G.	9344	D	1910								
William	30781	D	1920								
William	49614	D	1928								

NAME	NUMBER	TYPE	YEAR
SCHOENFELD			
Adaline	27799	D	1919
Berman	88150	D	1941
Bertha	23862	I	1918
Bertha	30317	D	1920
Carl	63138	D	1932
David Charles	10589	D	1910
David M.	26720	D	1919
Eva	37049	D	1923
Fanny	21341	D	1916
Gertrude	11875	D	1911
Hattie	79318	D	1938
Henry N.	42830	D	1925
Jacob	35757	D	1923
Jonas	16039	D	1913
Joseph	62966	D	1932
Julius	62955	D	1932
L. E., Mrs.	79318	D	1938
Maurice David	84437	I	1940
Pauline	22716	D	1917
Selma	67744	D	1934
SCHOENFELDER			
Henrietta Berger	47641	D	1927
SCHOENFISCH			
Mary	61038	D	1932
SCHOENHALS			
Catherine B.	42984	M	1925
Margaret E.	42984	M	1925
SCHOENHOLZ			
Sigmund	4400	D	1907
SCHOENIG			
Richard	59109	M	1931
SCHOENIGER			
Louis E.	42026	D	1925
SCHOENITZER			
Emil	76963	D	1937
SCHOENSTEIN			
Felix Frindolin	72190	D	1936
Ferdinand B.	54783	D	1930
Franziska	57322	D	1930
Magdalena	59281	D	1931
SCHOENWASSER			
Bertha	8700	D	1909
SCHOEPLEIN			
Nikolas	20075	D	1915
SCHOEPPE			
Gustav M.	55213	D	1930

NAME	NUMBER	TYPE	YEAR
SCHOERLIN			
Elizabeth	40191	D	1924
SCHOETTLER			
Julius	20810	D	1916
SCHOFIELD			
Agnes	52276	D	1929
Belle L.	65737	D	1933
Jacob	554	I	1906
Louvica Belle	65737	D	1933
Mary	68323	D	1934
Mary	78405	D	1938
Miles E.	64653	D	1933
Robert Mills	53	D	1906
Thomas J.	86134	D	1941
W. B.	1842	D	1906
William F.	87330	D	1941
SCHOHAN			
Herman	63102	D	1932
Sarah	54804	D	1930
SCHOKNECHT			
Emma	1543	D	1906
SCHOLES			
Sarah Elizabeth	62448	D	1932
SCHOLFIELD			
Ira V.	42829	D	1925
Walter H.	25486	D	1918
SCHOLL			
Albert L.	39088	D	1924
SCHOLLE			
Frederica	81231	D	1939
Gustave	78853	D	1938
Jacob	28212	D	1919
Lillie	29396	D	1920
William	28213	D	1919
SCHOLLER			
Louis	73948	D	1936
SCHOLTENBRANDT			
Maria F.	86487	D	1941
SCHOLTES			
Bernhard	79821	D	1938
SCHOLTZ			
Edward A.	81342	I	1939
Theodor Peter	38144	D	1924
SCHOLTZHAUER			
John	68448	D	1934

NAME	NUMBER	TYPE	YEAR
SCHOLZ			
August J.	61354	D	1932
Carl Joseph	71249	D	1935
Caroline	46737	D	1927
Caroline	62785	D	1932
Frank B.	84847	D	1940
Pauline	71250	D	1935
Robert	22379	D	1917
Robert	35641	D	1923
Theodor Peter	38144	D	1924
SCHOMAKER			
Andrew	17364	D	1914
Charles C.	31837	D	1921
Drewes	17364	D	1914
Gerd	23485	D	1917
Joseph T.	71279	D	1935
SCHOMALSER			
Theodore	57475	D	1930
SCHOMBERG			
Nellie F.	77574	I	1938
Nellie F.	78115	D	1938
SCHOMER			
George	70753	D	1935
SCHONBECK			
Ethel	2603	M	1907
SCHONFELD			
Anne M.	65246	D	1933
Annie Sabina	14913	D	1913
SCHONHOFF			
Benjamin	86272	D	1941
SCHONIG			
Franz Jacob	58343	D	1931
Helene	41743	D	1925
Helene	41743	D	1925
SCHONING			
Anna C.	64445	D	1933
SCHONT			
Alice J.	24943	I	1918
Alice J.	43811	D	1926
Marie A.	9521	M	1910
SCHONTHALER			
Johann	80972	I	1939
Johann Frederick	88443	D	1941
SCHONWASSER			
Jennie	75871	D	1937
SCHOOF			
Martin	27731	D	1919

Key: D = death; M = minor; I = incompetent

NAME	NUMBER	TYPE	YEAR
SCHOOLER			
Nellie E.	73377	D	1936
William Henry	70454	D	1935
SCHOPPEL			
Thomas A.	15011	D	1913
SCHOPPLEIN			
George	77139	D	1937
SCHOPPLIEN			
John	44683	D	1926
SCHORCHT			
Christian Frederick	74453	D	1937
SCHORD			
Louis G.	10949	D	1910
Milford H.	63039	D	1932
SCHORNSTHEIMER			
Henry	49823	D	1928
SCHORR			
Robert	29320	D	1920
SCHOSS			
Arthur	37818	D	1923
SCHOTT			
Herman	51778	D	1929
Louis	45010	D	1926
William	75023	D	1937
SCHOTTLER			
Isabelle F.	88072	D	1941
Julius	20810	D	1916
SCHOU			
Jack	61897	D	1932
Maye Eleanor	78662	D	1938
Nora	56201	D	1930
SCHOUTEN			
Walter George	50608	D	1928
SCHOW			
Alyce	36522	M	1923
Jack	61897	D	1932
Lester	42572	M	1925
Marie	36521	D	1923
Nina	36521	D	1923
SCHRADER			
Jennie	86322	D	1941
Otto	80273	D	1939
SCHRAEDER			
Otto	82624	I	1939
SCHRAFT			
Bertha	50410	D	1928

NAME	NUMBER	TYPE	YEAR
Eleonore L.	82039	I	1939
SCHRAM			
Allan	33357	M	1922
Hugo F.	33081	D	1921
John	39080	D	1924
Martin	75536	I	1937
Martin	82775	D	1939
Minnie	36851	D	1923
Richard	33357	M	1922
SCHRAMM			
Andrew	26436	D	1919
Charles F.	37036	D	1923
Eleanor S.	36287	D	1923
Elizabeth Fredricka	37290	I	1923
Frederick	9709	D	1910
Willy H. K.	83830	D	1940
SCHRANZ			
Clara	78170	D	1938
SCHRAUBSTADTER			
Ernst O.	29844	D	1920
Helen Elizabeth	55708	M	1930
SCHRAY			
George	618	D	1906
SCHRECKENBERG			
Rebecca	19767	D	1915
SCHREIBER			
Amalia	46616	D	1927
Amalie	38910	I	1924
Amelia	38910	I	1924
Anton H.	29974	D	1920
Cornelia	5754	D	1908
Dorothea	21840	D	1916
Emil R.	59630	I	1931
Grace Coleman	86297	D	1941
Herman	66379	D	1934
John	84165	D	1940
John Carl	77248	D	1937
Joseph, Mrs.	10476	D	1910
Louis	62472	D	1932
Milton Bernard	59272	I	1931
Richard	53532	D	1929
William Martin August	21408	D	1916
SCHREIER			
Anna	32849	I	1921
Anna	32908	D	1921
August	26320	D	1919
Fred	57569	D	1931

NAME	NUMBER	TYPE	YEAR
SCHREINER			
Clayton Stafford	81633	I	1939
Harriette J.	81762	D	1939
Paul	70950	D	1935
Sophie	5864	D	1908
SCHREK			
Saretta Grace	70203	I	1935
SCHREPFER			
Casper	41818	D	1925
Casper	41818	D	1925
SCHREPGER			
Frederick	62991	D	1932
SCHREPPER			
Caspar	10189	D	1910
SCHREYER			
M.	17527	D	1914
SCHRICK			
Antone Joseph	72636	I	1936
Antonia	15977	D	1913
Elmer	15202	M	1913
Frederick	36297	M	1923
Joseph	15202	M	1913
Joseph E.	88731	D	1941
Rudolph	15202	M	1913
SCHRIER			
Andrew	6839	D	1908
SCHRODER			
Catherine A.	72273	D	1936
Elevin	13197	M	1912
Elwin	19724	M	1915
George	43546	D	1926
Harry	66773	D	1934
Henry A.	76046	D	1937
Howard	13197	M	1912
John C. C.	7921	D	1909
John F.	20073	D	1915
John Frederick	19423	D	1915
Louise	57831	D	1931
Mary	10549	D	1910
Mary Ann	12161	D	1911
Matilda	88900	D	1942
Nellie	77445	D	1938
Otto	82624	I	1939
Otto	84124	D	1940
Sophie	16545	D	1913
SCHRODT			
Mary L.	32670	I	1921

NAME	NUMBER	TYPE	YEAR	NAME	NUMBER	TYPE	YEAR	NAME	NUMBER	TYPE	YEAR
Mary L.	70592	D	1935	**SCHROTH**				**SCHUDMACK**			
SCHROEDE				Charles A., Jr.	35466	M	1922	Daniel	52031	D	1929
Ralph Lloyd	89921	D	1942	Charles F.	35467	M	1922	Lena M.	73423	D	1936
SCHROEDER				Dorothy L.	35466	M	1922	**SCHUEKER**			
Albertine	38225	D	1924	Freda M.	57276	I	1930	Thomas	81477	D	1939
Caroline	41074	D	1925	John R.	35467	M	1922	**SCHUELER**			
Claus	1196	D	1906	John Robert	54077	M	1929	Erich	55731	M	1930
Edward George	44553	D	1926	M. Alice	31974	D	1921	Hans	55731	M	1930
Elizabeth Anna	89061	D	1942	**SCHRUL**				**SCHUEMANN**			
Elizabeth M.	40339	D	1924	Charles	18199	D	1914	Frederick W. J.	6852	M	1908
Eugenie Hawes	59744	D	1931	**SCHUBACH**				**SCHUENEMANN**			
Francis C.	57384	D	1930	Albert	86856	D	1941	Louise A.	10310	D	1910
Friedrich William	22105	D	1917	**SCHUBENER**				**SCHUENEMANN-POTT**			
Henry	6920	D	1908	Cecelia	80727	I	1939	Louise A.	10310	D	1910
Henry	47570	D	1927	**SCHUBERT**				**SCHUETT**			
Henry K.	43368	D	1926	Albert E.	29766	D	1920	Marie C.	77652	D	1938
Jodocus	3509	D	1907	Christian Wilhelm	71601	D	1936	**SCHUETTE**			
John	61540	D	1932	Edwin G.	59323	I	1931	Marie E.	7092	D	1909
John A.	11413	D	1911	Elsa	3164	I	1907	**SCHUETTEN**			
John B.	59547	D	1931	Georgina D.	86023	D	1941	Jacob	7119	D	1909
John H.	25589	D	1918	Grace	3165	M	1907	**SCHUETZ**			
Lillian L.	10464	M	1910	Harry Charles	82227	D	1939	Annie	31365	D	1921
Lillian W.	60719	D	1932	Herman	24472	D	1918	Friedrich W.	25305	D	1918
Margaretha	41583	D	1925	Herman	82784	D	1939	**SCHUG**			
Maria	5688	D	1908	Hugo G.	57084	D	1930	Henry G.	81832	I	1939
Marie	34446	D	1922	Minette	3165	M	1907	Henry G.	81992	D	1939
Meta	62923	D	1932	Ruth	3165	M	1907	Joseph	32716	D	1921
Milton H. R.	84372	D	1940	Virginia Catherine	75813	I	1937	Theresa	43976	D	1926
Otto	39486	I	1924	Willy	71601	D	1936	**SCHUHL**			
Otto	84124	D	1940	Witold	82983	D	1939	Sylvan	15927	D	1913
Paul August Heinrich	40423	D	1924	**SCHUCHERT**				**SCHULDT**			
R. G.	423	D	1906	Phillip	33902	D	1922	Bessie	60304	I	1931
Robert Albert Edward	83083	D	1940	**SCHUCK**				Catherine	75762	D	1937
Rose	25482	D	1918	Arthur F.	43676	D	1926	William	26834	D	1919
Wilhelmina C.	68000	D	1934	Beverly Jane	50138	M	1928	**SCHULER**			
Wilhelmine C.	10464	M	1910	Mary J.	16404	D	1913	Albert	79915	D	1938
William	9793	D	1910	Thomas L.	13896	D	1912	Charles	9943	D	1910
William G.	31034	D	1921	**SCHUCKERT**				Elizabeth	65446	D	1933
SCHROFF				Georgia	70487	M	1935	George	16538	D	1913
Minnie	50447	D	1928	**SCHUCKL**				Jacob	28039	D	1919
SCHROFFEL				Alice	56863	D	1930	Joseph A.	65882	M	1933
Bella	58406	D	1931	Max	76681	D	1937	Josephine	55650	D	1930
SCHROLL				**SCHUDEL**				Marie Marc	86675	D	1941
Catherine E.	83132	D	1940	Ernst	73286	D	1936	William	6779	D	1908
SCHROOT				John	24358	D	1918	William A.	75738	M	1937
Albert	71949	D	1936	**SCHUDELL**							
SCHROTER				Louise	43301	D	1926				
Ann	43297	D	1926								

NAME	NUMBER	TYPE	YEAR
SCHULHOFER			
Edwin	16816	M	1914
SCHULKE			
Emily	77123	D	1937
Jerry	74175	M	1936
SCHULKEN			
Frederick D.	47298	D	1927
Frederick J.	47298	D	1927
Margaret	84320	D	1940
SCHULLER			
John	75447	D	1937
SCHULT			
Herman M.	33548	D	1922
SCHULTE			
Fannie	88783	D	1941
Frank	65627	D	1933
Franz	65627	D	1933
Gustavus	85588	I	1940
Helene Auguste Elsie	36464	D	1923
John C.	34399	D	1922
John G. W.	3144	D	1907
Wilhelm Heinrich Gerhard	32700	D	1921
William Henry	32700	D	1921
SCHULTHEIS			
Agnes J.	59966	D	1931
Edward A.	82306	M	1939
Henry R.	12164	M	1911
J. George	2376	D	1906
SCHULTHERS			
Roland	57162	I	1930
SCHULTZ			
Adolph	85603	D	1940
Adolph John	75574	I	1937
Albert F. W.	20444	D	1916
Amelia L.	83371	I	1940
Aner	21792	D	1916
Catherine	75762	D	1937
Charles R.	15677	D	1913
Clara	41227	D	1925
Clara	55050	D	1930
Clara L.	61643	D	1932
Edward L.	32487	M	1921
Ferdinand	8864	D	1909
Florence F.	24792	D	1918
Friedrich W.	25305	D	1918
George Amandus	1086	D	1906
George T.	53507	D	1929

NAME	NUMBER	TYPE	YEAR
Henry E.	733	D	1906
Herman	79308	D	1938
Herman M.	33548	D	1922
Hermann M.	27105	I	1919
Jane Dolores	54527	M	1929
Johanna	61015	D	1932
John	31378	D	1921
John	52290	D	1929
Katherine	39274	M	1924
L. J., Mrs.	43200	D	1925
Linneaus A.	79308	D	1938
Louis	6234	D	1908
Louis	8701	D	1909
Magdalena	15287	I	1913
Marcella M.	16349	D	1913
Martin	66980	D	1934
Mary Margaret	89796	D	1942
Mildred	83371	I	1940
Paul Oswald	43169	D	1925
Rasmus Christoffer	89525	D	1942
William	23696	I	1917
William	39274	M	1924
William August	27123	D	1919
William J.	70231	D	1935
SCHULTZE			
Carrie	34346	I	1922
Chester Lloyd	8169	M	1909
Ervin	14034	I	1912
Ferdinand	8527	I	1909
Heinrich	54683	D	1930
Lawrence Gene	79911	M	1938
Rudolph W.	6943	D	1908
William Fredrick	77734	D	1938
SCHULZ			
Albert P. G.	37629	D	1923
Alfred	80097	D	1938
Alfred H.	83230	D	1940
Alvine Emily	2918	D	1907
Anna	80096	D	1938
Anna M.	20969	D	1916
Anna Marie	46832	D	1927
Auguste	46801	D	1927
Charles	72848	D	1936
Christian	64476	D	1933
Christian Friedrich	80571	D	1939
Diana	69430	M	1935
Elise	43632	D	1926
Ernst G. A.	36991	D	1923
Fredrick F.	85459	D	1940

NAME	NUMBER	TYPE	YEAR
Fridrich Johann	63951	D	1933
Frieda	26694	D	1919
Friedricka	35609	D	1922
Henry	62078	D	1932
Herman	19738	I	1915
Jerusha V.	80269	D	1939
Johanna	61015	D	1932
Johanna	52948	D	1929
Julius	39294	D	1924
Louise	43200	D	1925
Ludwig	69547	D	1935
Marcella M.	16349	D	1913
Marie	87414	I	1941
Mary	8916	D	1909
Paul	40634	D	1924
Paul	88790	D	1941
Ruth Geraldine	66398	M	1934
SCHULZE			
Charles F.	20898	D	1916
Daisy L.	25725	D	1918
Edith Janice	55711	M	1930
Etta Hortense	5617	D	1908
Gustav Carl	73853	D	1936
Hattie	79520	I	1938
Helen Lorraine	55711	M	1930
Johan	51662	D	1928
Johann Julius	88217	D	1941
SCHULZESANDOW			
Emil	56247	D	1930
SCHUM			
Max	64757	D	1933
SCHUMACHER			
Agnes E.	87358	I	1941
Anna	2295	M	1906
Antone W.	88573	D	1941
Catharina	1433	D	1906
Elizabeth	4625	D	1907
Emil	48150	D	1927
Emma Mary	57750	D	1931
Ernst A.	10622	D	1910
Eva Marie	64449	D	1933
Frederick A.	44638	D	1926
Herman A.	50610	D	1928
Hinrich Diedrich	20825	D	1916
John	73320	D	1936
Julia L.	79905	D	1938
Katharena	60734	D	1932
Martha	85327	I	1940

NAME	NUMBER	TYPE	YEAR	NAME	NUMBER	TYPE	YEAR	NAME	NUMBER	TYPE	YEAR
Wilhelmina B.	86505	D	1941	Frederick P.	45197	D	1926	Bella	57452	D	1930
William H.	86130	D	1941	Johanna F. M.	9230	D	1910	Louis	8039	D	1909
SCHUMAN				Justine	67394	D	1934	Louis A.	70241	D	1935
Emilio G.	26809	D	1919	Lewis P.	30626	I	1920	Ludwig	12948	D	1912
Fanny R.	68823	D	1935	Lewis P.	31865	D	1921	Rose	81875	D	1939
SCHUMANN				Marie	24477	I	1918	Sarah	88998	D	1942
Paul G. C.	9945	D	1910	**SCHUSZLER**				Sigmund	22527	D	1917
SCHUMASKY				Wilhelmina	9071	D	1910	**SCHWABE**			
Aaron	84280	D	1940	**SCHUT**				Jennie	51795	D	1929
SCHUMM				Henry	78844	I	1938	**SCHWAERIG**			
Fred	25449	D	1918	**SCHUTT**				Oswald	20435	D	1916
SCHUNHOFF				Henry	12491	D	1911	**SCHWAGERL**			
Burchard Henry	43463	D	1926	Peter	9563	D	1910	Alois	60026	D	1931
Charlotte M.	42967	D	1925	**SCHUTTE**				**SCHWAIN**			
SCHUNTER				John	66537	D	1934	Charles R.	68711	D	1935
Adolph F.	50945	D	1928	**SCHUTTEN**				Kate Couch	83095	D	1940
Meta	25034	D	1918	Rebecka C.	33120	D	1921	Kate V.	83095	D	1940
SCHUPFER				**SCHUTTLER**				**SCHWALBE**			
Mathias	40278	D	1924	Robert W.	81382	D	1939	Sarah	89274	D	1942
SCHUPP				**SCHUTZ**				**SCHWALL**			
Joseph A.	40187	D	1924	Henry Ernest	63416	D	1933	Margaret Theresa	62705	D	1932
Joseph S.	40187	D	1924	Jacob	79678	D	1938	William Francis	56257	D	1930
SCHUPPERT				**SCHUTZE**				**SCHWALLIE**			
Adam	2509	D	1906	Frederick J.	55597	D	1930	William A.	64380	D	1933
Adam L.	16870	D	1914	**SCHUURR**				**SCHWALM**			
Agnes F.	11958	M	1911	Philipp	28098	D	1919	Carl	54740	D	1930
Magdalena	2510	D	1906	**SCHUYLER**				John G.	4904	D	1907
SCHURHOLZ				Emeline N.	2769	D	1907	Katherine	69166	D	1935
Agnes	21463	D	1916	Everett	45121	D	1926	**SCHWAMON**			
SCHURMAN				Frank	25089	D	1918	Matthaus	12298	D	1911
Robert	86387	D	1941	William B.	30548	D	1920	**SCHWARETG**			
SCHURR				**SCHVEGEL**				Julia	29598	I	1920
Philipp	28098	D	1919	John S.	56016	D	1930	**SCHWARIG**			
SCHUSSLER				**SCHWAB**				Oswald	20435	D	1916
Alice C.	68857	D	1935	Edith M.	35097	D	1922	**SCHWARTING**			
C. Henry	3311	D	1907	Emma	26185	M	1919	John Henry	17295	D	1914
Frederick J.	58116	D	1931	Fred J.	84746	D	1940	Michael A.	78320	D	1938
Hermann F.	27202	D	1919	Fritz	26185	M	1919	**SCHWARTZ**			
Israil	37567	D	1923	Henrietta	75723	D	1937	Adleheid	66255	D	1934
John	37567	D	1923	Markus	20245	D	1916	Adolph	44821	D	1926
Louise A.	66011	D	1934	Mary	45559	D	1926	Adolph	86351	D	1941
Maximillian	13474	D	1912	Max	20245	D	1916	Alexander	27980	D	1919
Michael	12477	D	1911	Regina	38418	D	1924	Annie	50642	D	1928
SCHUSTER				Rudolph	38958	D	1924	August	42564	D	1925
Anna	57055	D	1930	William Gottlieb	20456	D	1916	Bernard	14279	D	1912
Ella	28436	D	1919	**SCHWABACHER**				Bertha	32284	D	1921
Frank J.	55817	D	1930	Abraham	8520	D	1909	Carrie	18030	D	1914

NAME	NUMBER	TYPE	YEAR	NAME	NUMBER	TYPE	YEAR	NAME	NUMBER	TYPE	YEAR
Charles E.	60912	I	1932	Sarah	30703	D	1920	**SCHWARZSCHILD**			
Clara	87584	D	1941	Solomon	27845	D	1919	Ferdinand Jacob	14100	D	1912
Daniel	29038	M	1920	Sophia	13868	D	1912	Morris	44992	I	1926
Dorothy	5995	M	1908	Walter Leonard	65468	M	1933	**SCHWATKA**			
Edith	56632	M	1930	Walter R.	85737	D	1940	Anna Leland	52339	D	1929
Ernest	40741	D	1925	**SCHWARZ**				**SCHWEBS**			
Esther	43650	M	1926	Anna H.	27859	D	1919	Louisa	353	D	1906
Esther	71923	D	1936	Anna M.	71267	D	1935	**SCHWEDER**			
Fabian	30704	D	1920	August	42564	D	1925	Paul	2952	D	1907
Fabian	43217	D	1925	August Paul	63894	D	1933	**SCHWEDT**			
Flora	8316	D	1909	Bernhard Sigmund	45966	D	1926	August	6026	D	1908
Gustav	33447	D	1922	Charles	73598	D	1936	**SCHWEEN**			
Gustav Sutro	19826	M	1915	Charles Frederick	42870	M	1925	Augusta	22955	D	1917
Harold J.	53751	D	1929	Emma Feisel	49302	D	1928	Diedrich	22345	D	1917
Harry	84329	D	1940	Frank R.	58219	D	1931	Dora	63510	D	1933
Henrietta E.	26275	D	1919	George Frederick	85247	D	1940	Frieda	25105	M	1918
Henrietta G.	75057	D	1937	Gustav	89567	D	1942	Harold	25105	M	1918
Hildred	29038	M	1920	Gustav Carl Frederick	37680	D	1923	Henry	86958	D	1941
Howard	29039	M	1920	Helen M.	65436	D	1933	Richard	25105	M	1918
Isidor	1259	D	1906	Helen Virginia	42871	M	1925	Walter	25105	M	1918
Isidor	40395	D	1924	Henrietta	4607	D	1907	**SCHWEGMAN**			
Jacob	23796	D	1917	Henry	2893	D	1907	Catherine A.	38966	D	1924
Jacob	31477	D	1921	Henry Lawrence	42872	M	1925	Catherine J.	38966	D	1924
Joseph	63207	D	1932	Hermann	80572	D	1939	**SCHWEIGERT**			
Julie J.	41455	D	1925	Julia	20372	D	1916	Ernst	24322	D	1918
Leonard	79115	D	1938	Minnie W.	37804	D	1923	Joseph	9771	D	1910
Louis	10232	D	1910	Morris	38623	D	1924	**SCHWEISS**			
Mathilda	65751	D	1933	Otto J.	917	D	1906	Richard	12116	D	1911
Max Joel	61467	I	1932	Rudolph C.	6724	D	1908	**SCHWEITZER**			
Meyer	3387	D	1907	William Charles	7288	D	1909	Anna Katherine	86281	D	1941
Minnie	51548	D	1928	**SCHWARZBACH**				Bernhard	8006	D	1909
Morris	28781	D	1920	Helmut	80719	M	1939	Elise	17245	D	1914
Morris	80531	D	1939	Helmut	84863	M	1940	Jacob	40064	D	1924
Muriel	29039	M	1920	**SCHWARZBAUM**				John J.	49	I	1906
Myer	3387	D	1907	Ray	72280	D	1936	Joseph	3620	D	1907
Nettie	1461	D	1906	**SCHWARZCHILD**				Joseph	42350	D	1925
Paul A.	63894	D	1933	Amalia	10228	D	1910	Joseph L.	44248	M	1926
Pauline	61981	D	1932	**SCHWARZE**				Lawrence W.	24000	D	1918
Pearl	29038	M	1920	Frederocl J.	56595	D	1930	Maurice	31961	D	1921
Philip	7826	D	1909	**SCHWARZENBEK**				Mollie	71311	D	1935
Ramona Harriet	29964	D	1920	Hermine	76673	D	1937	Rebecca	18397	D	1915
Rosa	25376	D	1918	**SCHWARZENBERG**				Sam	80158	D	1938
Rose Gertrude	11331	M	1911	John	9770	D	1910	Samuel	39408	D	1924
Rose Y.	63628	D	1933	**SCHWARZMANN**				Simon	80158	D	1938
Rudolph	69303	D	1935	Christina	20719	D	1916	William F.	17989	D	1914
Salvador	27531	D	1919	Dorothea	74638	D	1937	**SCHWEIZER**			
Samuel	19768	D	1915	Gustav	76311	D	1937	David C.	47270	D	1927
Samuel	85754	D	1940								
Samuel C.	88223	I	1941								

NAME	NUMBER	TYPE	YEAR
Fritz	25113	D	1918
John J.	1517	D	1906
Joseph F.	38271	D	1924
Julius P.	52572	D	1929
Mildred W.	58958	D	1931
Sophie Litzberg	32921	D	1921
SCHWELLAR			
Ellen M.	78007	D	1938
SCHWELLER			
Ellen M.	78007	D	1938
SCHWELLINGER			
Louise	21365	D	1916
Rose	60568	I	1931
SCHWENDER			
Charistian A.	46331	D	1927
L. D.	95	D	1906
SCHWENKE			
John	2033	D	1906
SCHWEOGER			
Charles	47799	D	1927
SCHWER			
August	55963	D	1930
SCHWERDT			
Katharina Wilhelmina	6467	D	1908
Louis P.	62686	D	1932
Philip	41367	D	1925
SCHWERDTMANN			
Henry	24914	D	1918
Hinrich	24914	D	1918
SCHWERIN			
Adolph	26957	D	1919
Emma Montgomery	44517	D	1926
Gustave	83649	D	1940
Henry	40249	D	1924
Lytton	3725	M	1907
Richard de C.	86795	D	1941
SCHWERS			
Lawrence	37817	D	1923
SCHWIEGER			
Henry A.	59921	I	1931
SCHWINDELAUF			
Matilda	74570	D	1937
SCHWINDT			
Adolf	57125	D	1930
SCHWINN			
Adolph	89	D	1906
Emily	2347	D	1906
SCHWITTER			
John	41328	D	1925
SCHWITZER			
Lizzie C.	39074	D	1924
SCHWOEBEL			
Margaretha	26354	D	1919
SCHWORMSTEDE			
Carl	20846	D	1916
Diedrich	16336	D	1913
John	37836	D	1923
SCHWORMSTEDTE			
Diedrich	16336	D	1913
SCHY			
Frank	51026	M	1928
Marguerite	51026	M	1928
SCIAPITI			
Therodore	81239	D	1939
SCIARINI			
Paul	25696	M	1918
Paul P.	25620	D	1918
SCIARONI			
Achille	84814	D	1940
Caterina	73069	D	1936
James Anthony	27913	D	1919
SCIARRA			
Irene	45561	D	1926
SCIASCIA			
Gaetano	39905	I	1924
SCICLUNA			
Carmena	63342	D	1933
SCILLITOE			
Asher	58436	D	1931
SCIOCCHETTI			
Luisa	25947	D	1918
SCIUME			
Michele	33772	D	1922
SCIUTTO			
Andrea	37884	D	1923
SCJRAU			
George	618	D	1906
SCLAFFANI			
Pasquale	30742	D	1920
SCLAVOS			
John	70843	D	1935
SCOBIE			
Annie Elizabeth	55252	D	1930
James	30099	D	1920
John Joseph	39378	D	1924
SCOBLE			
Laura	23924	D	1918
William	23989	M	1918
SCOFIELD			
Frank K.	31035	D	1921
Grace M.	36052	D	1923
Margaret	54523	M	1929
Mary	73930	I	1936
Norman E.	84311	D	1940
SCOGIN			
Dick	82050	D	1939
Elmer D.	82050	D	1939
SCOLA			
Rocco	33326	D	1922
SCOLARI			
Pasquale	55358	D	1930
SCOLES			
Mary A.	33752	D	1922
SCOLEY			
Helen	39911	D	1924
SCOLIO			
Fannie	31321	D	1921
SCOLLIN			
Hannah T.	43782	D	1926
Joseph C.	63693	D	1933
SCOMA			
Giuseppe	78083	D	1938
SCOORTIS			
Michael Elias Papamichael	66244	D	1934
Michael Hlia	66244	D	1934
SCORE			
Henry H.	89449	D	1942
SCOTCHBURN			
Alice A.	21687	D	1916
SCOTT			
Ada M.	9265	I	1910
Agnes	82902	D	1939
Albert W.	6909	D	1908
Alice Compton	82459	D	1939
Allen E.	24764	D	1918
Andrew C.	30115	D	1920
Angelia	57	D	1906

Key: D = death; M = minor; I = incompetent

NAME	NUMBER	TYPE	YEAR	NAME	NUMBER	TYPE	YEAR	NAME	NUMBER	TYPE	YEAR
Anna L.	65369	D	1933	James	9799	D	1910	Thomas J.	41525	I	1925
Annie	28316	D	1919	James Harold	56501	M	1930	Thomas W.	27114	D	1919
Annie	86917	D	1941	James Keyes	26387	D	1919	Trinidad R.	59094	D	1931
Annie B.	35271	D	1922	James Nimmo	49797	M	1928	Vera P.	17905	D	1914
Annie R. E.	81615	D	1939	James S.	65270	D	1933	Walker D.	15161	D	1913
Archibald	46509	D	1927	James W.	61879	D	1932	Walter	77598	I	1938
Arthur	76388	D	1937	Jennie M.	33104	D	1921	Walter A.	30652	D	1920
Arthur W.	61519	D	1932	Jerome B.	75258	D	1937	William	53322	M	1929
Blanche	76820	I	1937	John	15210	D	1913	William H., Jr.	84664	M	1940
Catharine V. C.	49982	D	1928	John	84635	D	1940	William Huddlestone	43764	D	1926
Catherine	14223	D	1912	John Alison	43101	D	1925	William O.	26659	D	1919
Catherine Mary Burns	63991	D	1933	John Charles	83382	D	1940	William Patrick	84742	D	1940
Charles Gordon	68815	D	1935	John E.	32449	D	1921	William Vincent	56501	M	1930
Charles H.	58864	D	1931	John H.	9772	D	1910	**SCOTTO**			
Clarence Sydney	56571	D	1930	John J.	9906	D	1910	Giuseppe	29106	D	1920
Constantine Dena	53321	D	1929	John V.	11083	D	1911	Joseph	29106	D	1920
Ebenezer	57816	D	1931	John V., Mrs.	39534	D	1924	Nicolo	78589	D	1938
Edith Mabel	33991	M	1922	John W.	78276	D	1938	**SCOUFOS**			
Elise Therese	6208	I	1908	Joseph J.	76435	D	1937	Gus	75082	D	1937
Eliza Margaret	51823	D	1929	Kate	14909	D	1913	**SCOULER**			
Elizabeth	15550	D	1913	Kate	39534	D	1924	Benjamin	62038	D	1932
Ellen	79358	I	1938	Laura Hord	48975	D	1928	James	7871	D	1909
Elmon	32495	D	1921	Lela C.	82894	D	1939	Jennie Ralston	64498	D	1933
Emily Justus	47495	D	1927	Lillian T.	8275	D	1909	Lydia A.	1028	D	1906
Eva	86399	D	1941	Margaret	1793	D	1906	**SCOUPHOPOULOS**			
Fern R.	11324	M	1911	Margaret	4735	I	1907	Constantine	75082	D	1937
Florence	55471	I	1930	Maria A.	36935	D	1923	**SCOUTETIN**			
Florence	56054	D	1930	Mary	64543	D	1933	Emile Joseph	76937	D	1937
Frank	75982	D	1937	Mary A.	89850	D	1942	**SCOVEL**			
Frank I.	35454	D	1922	Mary Agnes	2619	D	1907	Alma Lang	88742	D	1941
Frank Steven	28900	D	1920	Mary E.	13662	I	1912	Dean	56966	D	1930
Frank W.	14677	D	1913	Mary E.	18899	D	1915	Merrill Dean	56966	D	1930
Fred A.	18689	D	1915	Mary Eastwood	24849	D	1918	**SCOVERN**			
George	23855	D	1918	Mathilde Marie	76434	D	1937	Clara Lee	45937	D	1926
George	26941	D	1919	Minnie	51712	D	1928	Harry Glanville	44671	D	1926
George Mitchell	81565	D	1939	Mollie	51712	D	1928	Stanley G.	58124	D	1931
George W.	35139	D	1922	Nellie Burrell	16388	D	1913	**SCOVILLE**			
Hattie B.	48547	D	1927	Oliver C.	45170	D	1926	Nellie L.	56294	D	1930
Hazel	14569	M	1912	Oliver L.	25050	D	1918	**SCOW**			
Helen A.	62470	D	1932	Patrick	1564	D	1906	William C.	24255	D	1918
Helen B.	28352	D	1919	Ramona	14569	M	1912	**SCRAMAGLIA**			
Henry J.	71861	D	1936	Ramona	41472	I	1925	Emilio	86344	D	1941
Henry William	63799	D	1933	Ray C.	79710	I	1938	Guido	32119	D	1921
Herbert Marvin	82235	D	1939	Rofena C.	61831	D	1932	**SCREEN**			
Horace V.	78128	I	1938	Samuel F.	24488	I	1918	James B.	82666	D	1939
Horace V.	79528	D	1938	Samuel F.	31513	D	1921	**SCRIBANTE**			
Irving M.	3545	D	1907	Samuel Stanley	64646	D	1933	Quinto	69852	D	1935
Isabelle McKee	65993	M	1933	Shailer M., Jr.	6970	D	1908				
Jacob	4203	I	1907	Thelma	53322	M	1929				

NAME	NUMBER	TYPE	YEAR
SCRIBNER			
Elsie M.	6524	D	1908
Harold	8406	M	1909
Othello	46453	D	1927
Theodore Edward	8407	M	1909
SCRINE			
Eliza	63153	D	1932
SCRIPKO			
Nicholas Alexander	57140	D	1930
SCRIVANI			
Angelo	72319	D	1936
Antonio	83030	D	1940
SCRIVEN			
Thomas J.	6991	D	1908
SCRIVENER			
Leopold Hesse	8580	D	1909
Thomas Stephen	85107	D	1940
SCRIVNER			
John James	33078	D	1921
SCRUTCHFIEL			
Madge	15550	D	1913
SCRUTTON			
Lindsay	83948	D	1940
SCUDDER			
Nellie A.	85059	D	1940
William F.	69515	D	1935
SCUDERO			
Cecilia	68360	D	1934
SCULATI			
Carlo	36046	D	1923
SCULLEN			
Mary A.	74153	D	1936
SCULLIN			
Daniel	4403	D	1907
SCULLION			
Patrick	66872	D	1934
SCULLY			
Anne K.	55772	D	1930
Annie	59152	M	1931
Charles Peter	19984	M	1915
Edgar P.	12146	D	1911
Edward	19984	M	1915
Elizabeth Winifred	83749	D	1940
Frank M.	78494	D	1938
Jeremiah	13345	D	1912
John Edward	62584	D	1932

NAME	NUMBER	TYPE	YEAR
John Edward	68843	D	1935
John F.	9433	D	1910
M., Mrs.	72238	D	1936
Margaret Ellen	75831	D	1937
Mary A.	57924	D	1931
Mary Geraldine	31972	D	1921
Mary Lee	72238	D	1936
Nellie A.	19984	M	1915
Patrick J.	35727	D	1923
Ralph, Mrs.	72238	D	1936
Rose M.	19984	M	1915
Thomas M.	13223	D	1912
SCULNICK			
Sylvia	29982	D	1920
Sylvia	49219	M	1928
SCURATI			
Carlo	36046	D	1923
SCURLOCK			
William D.	36301	D	1923
SEABERG			
Charles William	63397	D	1933
SEABRIGHT			
Mary	10777	M	1910
SEABURG			
John William	87537	D	1941
SEAFORTH			
Antone	27732	D	1919
SEAGER			
Albert L.	14921	D	1913
Claude Russel	28396	D	1919
Harold L.	59499	D	1931
Henry	9959	D	1910
SEAGRAVE			
Russell Curtis	88398	M	1941
SEAL			
Alfred H.	84798	D	1940
SEALE			
Ethel Alice	74133	D	1936
Fannie	49673	D	1928
Henry W., Mrs.	51105	D	1928
Jessie D.	51105	D	1928
SEALY			
Charles Bennett	40032	D	1924
Nellie F.	61745	D	1932
SEAMAN			
Genevieve	55812	D	1930
George B.	27081	D	1919

NAME	NUMBER	TYPE	YEAR
George W.	46977	D	1927
Margaret	37179	D	1923
Mary	30378	D	1920
Murvin Bernhart	82122	D	1939
Samuel S.	16186	D	1913
SEAMEN			
Erika	52657	D	1929
SEARBY			
Alice Elizabeth	49779	D	1928
Eliza Maria	3812	D	1907
Ellen	88784	D	1941
William Martin	8615	D	1909
SEARCY			
Allen Gilbert	67577	D	1934
Allen Gilbert	67604	M	1934
Robert N.	67604	M	1934
SEAREY			
Anastasia	34591	I	1922
Miles T.	18223	M	1914
Thomas M.	18207	D	1914
SEARFOSS			
John W.	79316	M	1938
SEARIGHT			
Beath P.	32427	D	1921
SEARLE			
Robert R.	3833	D	1907
SEARLES			
Catherine Canovan	88190	D	1941
Rachael	988	D	1906
SEARLS			
Frank H.	78821	D	1938
Helen Pond	87859	D	1941
Jean Perry	61902	M	1932
Marion	61902	M	1932
Niles Isham	61902	M	1932
SEARS			
Eleanor I.	81007	I	1939
Eleanor I.	85118	D	1940
Ellen	31732	D	1921
Eunice	50223	D	1928
Jennie G.	71562	D	1936
Lucian M.	37947	D	1923
Thomas J.	88125	D	1941
SEASON			
Valentine	9170	D	1910
SEATON			
Annie E.	15715	D	1913

Key: D = death; M = minor; I = incompetent

NAME	NUMBER	TYPE	YEAR	NAME	NUMBER	TYPE	YEAR	NAME	NUMBER	TYPE	YEAR
Lee	37868	M	1923	**SEBRING**				**SEEBECK**			
Thomas Lee	37868	M	1923	May	70456	D	1935	Herman M.	70133	D	1935
SEATTERY				**SEBUSKIE**				Margareta	40911	D	1925
John Henry	2776	D	1907	Lewis	60809	I	1932	**SEEBER**			
SEAVAN				**SECCO**				Tennie	81157	I	1939
Annie E.	18209	I	1914	Joseph	73882	D	1936	Tinnie	81157	I	1939
SEAVER				**SECHINI**				Tinnie	82410	D	1939
Dan W.	8231	D	1909	Joseph P.	83054	D	1940	**SEEBURGER**			
SEAVEY				Rosa	68378	D	1934	Harmen J.	6271	D	1908
Florence	85357	D	1940	**SECHRIST**				**SEEBURT**			
Soloman	19569	D	1915	Adele Moulty	13453	D	1912	Emma Augusta	34107	D	1922
SEAWELL				Henrietta W.	88306	D	1941	Emma B.	34107	D	1922
James Mary	23481	D	1917	**SECONDO**				**SEEGELKEN**			
Washington	6986	D	1908	Arnabaldi	14849	D	1913	Elizabeth J.	12923	D	1912
Washington	46604	D	1927	Florence	77809	D	1938	John	26577	I	1919
William M.	23584	D	1917	**SECOR**				John	46766	D	1927
SEBALD				James F., Jr.	59766	D	1931	Oliver Edwin	15428	M	1913
George	37197	I	1923	Joan E.	62212	D	1932	Roy Clemens	15428	M	1913
Gesine	51436	D	1928	William B.	34813	D	1922	**SEEGER**			
SEBANO				**SECREST**				Maria	18399	D	1915
Frank Joe	55202	M	1930	George H.	34354	D	1922	Sarah Alice	10992	D	1911
SEBASTIAN				**SECRIST**				Sophie	81883	D	1939
Johann Z.	13307	D	1912	C. M.	38102	D	1924	**SEEHUBER**			
John Z.	13307	D	1912	**SEDGEWICK**				Grace	69245	D	1935
Leo J.	42731	M	1925	William A.	30598	D	1920	**SEEK**			
Mary P.	79860	D	1938	**SEDGLEY**				Charles F.	8471	D	1909
Philyspine	88018	D	1941	Harry T.	35507	D	1922	**SEEKAMP**			
Thomas	63662	D	1933	Rillie	35135	D	1922	Caroline	75238	D	1937
SEBASTIANI				Rillie A.	39209	D	1924	Ernest	75237	D	1937
Giuseppe	63995	D	1933	**SEDGWICK**				George	75239	D	1937
Joseph	63995	D	1933	James	4788	D	1907	**SEELEY**			
SEBASTIANO				**SEDLAS**				Catherine	30383	I	1920
Marchi	23999	I	1918	Joseph	44830	D	1926	Emily	24056	I	1918
SEBBELOV				**SEDLEY**				Emily	28821	D	1920
Golla Marguerite	75210	M	1937	Harry	33230	D	1922	Emma	28821	D	1920
SEBELLE				**SEDWICK**				Helen Mar	29728	D	1920
Leslie	22604	M	1917	Robert S.	72548	D	1936	Joseph	73053	D	1936
Samuel T.	19040	D	1915	**SEE**				Joseph Benton	50579	D	1928
William T., Jr.	18141	I	1914	Go	12727	D	1911	Katherine Redding	75138	D	1937
William T., Sr.	20628	D	1916	Leong Tom	58195	D	1931	Thomas	40491	D	1924
SEBERG				**SEEBA**				**SEELIG**			
Gustaf	84931	D	1940	Elizabeth Henrietta	63075	D	1932	Fannie	40199	D	1924
Mary Josephine	72024	M	1936	Nan	56519	D	1930	Henrika	18076	D	1914
SEBREE				**SEEBAK**				**SEELIGSOHN**			
John	86915	D	1941	Margareta	40911	D	1925	Estelle	1825	D	1906
								Selig Max	68865	D	1935

Key: D = death; M = minor; I = incompetent

NAME	NUMBER	TYPE	YEAR
SEELOS			
Jacob M.	81580	D	1939
SEELY			
Corabel	63555	D	1933
Lewis W.	5501	D	1908
Lizzie H.	55887	D	1930
Mack J.	55886	D	1930
SEEM			
Wong Yoke	40478	M	1924
SEEMAN			
Fridrick	87862	D	1941
SEEMANN			
Charles L.	45752	D	1926
Marie	50286	D	1928
Robert H.	77435	D	1938
SEERY			
Bridget	11502	D	1911
Sarah	48535	D	1927
Thomas	18049	D	1914
SEETH			
Della	7648	D	1909
SEEVOLD			
Max	61656	D	1932
SEFER			
Rudolph	54046	D	1929
SEFEROVICH			
Steve	39804	D	1924
SEFFER			
Rudolph	54046	D	1929
SEFL			
Albert	67115	M	1934
SEFRIN			
Amalia Marjory	42222	D	1925
SEGAL			
Abraham Harry	62659	D	1932
Myrtle	83359	D	1940
SEGALAS			
Marie	85331	D	1940
SEGALE			
Carlo	77934	D	1938
Louisa	35664	D	1923
Luigi	34600	D	1922
Luigia	35664	D	1923
SEGALES			
Marie	85331	D	1940

NAME	NUMBER	TYPE	YEAR
SEGALI			
John	58739	D	1931
SEGALL			
Abraham	62659	D	1932
Moritz	53302	D	1929
Rebeca	45750	D	1926
SEGAR			
Henry	9959	D	1910
SEGARINI			
Angela	9515	I	1910
Angela	10691	D	1910
Angiola	9515	I	1910
Angiola	10691	D	1910
Giovanni	77013	D	1937
Martino	19733	D	1915
SEGELBAUM			
Othnel C.	45457	D	1926
SEGELKE			
William F.	2675	D	1907
SEGELKEN			
Anna	64551	D	1933
Harry H.	63099	D	1932
Herman D.	31411	D	1921
SEGER			
Henry	9959	D	1910
Lillian	10717	I	1910
SEGGAS			
Nick	67319	D	1934
SEGGERSON			
John	351	D	1906
SEGHIERI			
Dante	28409	D	1919
SEGOVIA			
Romigio G.	44034	D	1926
SEGRUE			
Barbara	53021	M	1929
Emmett J.	53021	M	1929
Emmett P.	52324	D	1929
Patrick J.	52324	D	1929
SEGUR			
Howard Bradbury	29562	D	1920
SEGURSON			
Ellen	5937	D	1908
SEHABIAGUE			
Marie	12581	M	1911
Michel	35560	D	1922

NAME	NUMBER	TYPE	YEAR
Thomas	70988	D	1935
SEHL			
John Joseph	12382	D	1911
SEHRING			
Edward W.	65545	D	1933
SEIB			
Carry W.	47229	D	1927
Charles	16691	M	1914
Martin	16691	M	1914
Michael Joachim	13478	D	1912
Robert J.	77456	I	1938
Wilhelmine K.	47229	D	1927
SEIBEL			
Cecelia Marguerite	71736	M	1936
Herbert E.	44359	D	1926
Philip Henry	82826	D	1939
SEIBERLICH			
Edward H.	8530	D	1909
Nellie A.	34406	D	1922
SEIBERT			
Caroline	75381	D	1937
Emma Louise	43413	D	1926
George	72353	D	1936
George	80291	D	1939
Gustav	45847	D	1926
Jacob Miller	35287	D	1922
Julia J.	61379	D	1932
Louise M.	43413	D	1926
SEIBURT			
Emma B.	34107	D	1922
SEICHEPINE			
Catherine	21345	D	1916
SEID			
Eva	83096	D	1940
Lena	45642	D	1926
Marilyn	78098	M	1938
Morris	72288	D	1936
Pak Sing	62916	D	1939
SEIDAT			
Johanna	32130	D	1921
SEIDEL			
Bertha Piesker	60902	D	1932
F. E.	6428	D	1908
SEIDKIN			
Abram	33610	D	1922
SEIFER			
Jacob	63324	D	1933

Key: D = death; M = minor; I = incompetent

NAME	NUMBER	TYPE	YEAR	NAME	NUMBER	TYPE	YEAR	NAME	NUMBER	TYPE	YEAR
SEIFERD				**SEIP**				Herbert K.	62587	D	1932
Richard	87	D	1906	Alfred	25313	D	1918	Janet Angela	44185	M	1926
SEIFERT				**SEIPEL**				Joseph V.	13967	D	1912
Anna J.	65643	D	1933	Alice May	58042	I	1931	L.	47735	D	1927
Charles Albert	85007	D	1940	Charles T., Jr.	41491	M	1925	Miriam	81505	M	1939
Emma	47176	D	1927	Katharina	52329	D	1929	Vera Blanche	75857	D	1937
Franz E.	61624	D	1932	Katherine	23188	D	1917	Walter James, Jr.	44185	M	1926
Marie H.	59154	D	1931	Maria Johanna	13372	D	1912	**SELCHOW**			
SEIFRIED				Minnie	38142	D	1924	Catherine	51637	D	1928
Grace D.	4993	D	1908	Raymond	41491	M	1925	**SELECMAN**			
SEIGEL				**SEIR**				Joseph S.	45196	I	1926
Anna	80966	D	1939	Alois	46645	D	1927	**SELENERI**			
Clara	45946	D	1926	**SEISE**				Giovanna	69149	D	1935
Maurice L.	56001	D	1930	George	46981	I	1927	**SELFRIDGE**			
SEIGER				**SEITNATER**				E. A.	34874	D	1922
Ansell Woolworth	22256	M	1917	Dudley L.	57980	M	1931	Lydia Gordon	47963	D	1927
Charles H.	87125	D	1941	Margaret L.	58142	D	1931	Minnie L.	40507	D	1924
Dorothy Woolworth	32069	D	1921	**SEITZ**				**SELHEIMER**			
Herman C.	40065	D	1924	August	84226	D	1940	Marie E.	89107	D	1942
SEIKAVIZZA				Carl L.	71005	D	1935	**SELHORN**			
Christobal	12067	D	1911	Catherina Brigetta	78929	D	1938	Laura Lage	55246	D	1930
SEIKE				Hulda	46478	D	1927	**SELIG**			
John F.	17978	D	1914	Marie A.	55761	D	1930	Alvin C.	70812	D	1935
SEILER				Mary E.	21470	D	1916	Daisy E.	32801	D	1921
A. Victor	64089	D	1933	Peter A.	77035	D	1937	David	84585	D	1940
Adolph	17973	D	1914	Sarah	60075	D	1931	Fredericka	70531	D	1935
Albert	12550	D	1911	Wilhelm DeSt.Paul	52963	D	1929	Jack	30567	D	1920
Cassie	49490	D	1928	**SEKARA**				Jacob	30567	D	1920
Ferdinand	73247	D	1936	John M.	56957	D	1930	Julius	71195	D	1935
H.	10856	D	1910	Laura C.	78008	D	1938	Kossuth	68172	D	1934
Paul	18071	I	1914	**SEKELY**				Leonard	86136	D	1941
Paul	18102	D	1914	Julia	64643	D	1933	Matilda	82821	I	1939
SEIMES				Martin	51288	D	1928	Maurice C.	62057	D	1932
Hulda	60409	I	1931	**SELAH**				Samuel S.	82805	D	1939
SEIMONS				Boris	39166	D	1924	Sophie	10336	D	1910
Joseph	41674	D	1925	**SELANDER**				Sylvan	65923	D	1933
SEINEKE				Andrew	41984	D	1925	**SELIGMAN**			
Frank W.	33372	M	1922	Andrew	41984	D	1925	Alfred L.	15909	D	1913
Mary L.	33372	M	1922	**SELBY**				Annie	83271	D	1940
William	33372	M	1922	Annie A.	19561	D	1915	Evelyn L.	80836	D	1939
SEINES				Clara Elise	84545	D	1940	**SELIGSBERG**			
Hulda	60409	I	1931	Doris	81505	M	1939	Regine	37165	D	1923
SEINTURIER				Dorothy May	44185	M	1926	**SELINGER**			
Jean	64573	D	1933	Dorothy May	79254	D	1938	Alexander Morris	54016	D	1929
John	64573	D	1933	Elise	84545	D	1940	Elizabeth	62950	D	1932
Pauline	67974	I	1934	Hazel A.	43325	D	1926	Michael	18949	D	1915
Pauline	89984	D	1942	Henrietta I.	22258	D	1917				

NAME	NUMBER	TYPE	YEAR
SELK			
Edna Karla	89831	D	1942
James, Mrs.	89167	D	1942
Mary	89167	D	1942
Wilhelmina H.	71752	D	1936
SELL			
Alva O.	43923	D	1926
Edward Newell	60307	D	1931
Paula	63591	I	1933
SELLECK			
Hugh H.	75994	D	1937
Jacob D.	65666	D	1933
Jennie A.	62126	I	1932
Ruth	28393	D	1919
SELLENEIT			
Henry L.	73587	D	1936
SELLER			
Doris	49971	D	1928
Estelle	78917	D	1938
Frederick H.	26220	D	1919
Samuel	27919	D	1919
Sanford E.	30319	D	1920
SELLERS			
Elizabeth Esther	82288	D	1939
Millard F.	29684	D	1920
Orrin Pickens	20786	D	1916
Wm. G.	20368	D	1916
SELLICK			
Albert W.	41307	D	1925
Jennie A.	62126	I	1932
SELLIER			
Olivia	53916	D	1929
SELLING			
Henriette	24496	M	1918
Margaret	77239	I	1937
Nathalie	56864	D	1930
Samuel E.	37806	D	1923
Simon Herman	23813	D	1918
SELLMAN			
Caroline	13377	D	1912
Francis Walden	30406	M	1920
Mary Alice Walden	30404	D	1920
SELLO			
Giovanni	17933	D	1914
SELLON			
Edward	80438	D	1939

NAME	NUMBER	TYPE	YEAR
SELMI			
Joseph	88187	D	1941
SELSBACH			
Carl Petter	56772	D	1930
SELVITELLA			
Mary	70067	D	1935
SELWAY			
William F.	57185	I	1930
SELWOOD			
Frank	26858	D	1919
Thomas Frank	26858	D	1919
SELZ			
Frank	52847	D	1929
SEMBERTRANT			
Ellen	7339	D	1909
Frank	7611	M	1909
Frank	71125	D	1935
John James	7611	M	1909
Rose Christina	71124	I	1935
Rose Christina Mary	7611	M	1909
SEMENZA			
Anton	79090	D	1938
Antonio	10119	D	1910
Antonio	11281	D	1911
Giovanni	42187	D	1925
John	42187	D	1925
John J.	88245	D	1941
SEMERAU			
Comma	25306	D	1918
William	35661	D	1923
SEMERIA			
Francesco	68920	D	1935
Henry	76246	D	1937
SEMESIA			
Maria	80290	I	1939
SEMINARIO			
Joseph Y.	60768	M	1932
Yda	69949	D	1935
SEMM			
Jasefina	61547	D	1932
SEMMEL			
Eduard	20181	D	1915
Helene	24365	D	1918
SEMMELHAACK			
Magdalena	77709	D	1938
Marie A.	44975	D	1926

NAME	NUMBER	TYPE	YEAR
SEMMELMAN			
Ellis	44571	M	1926
Rubin	44571	M	1926
Saul	44571	M	1926
SEMON			
Maud	54546	M	1929
Pauline	84881	D	1940
SEMORILE			
Charlotte Agnes	40929	D	1925
John B.	26049	D	1919
SEMPLE			
Agnes C.	61441	I	1932
Agnes Clements	61518	D	1932
Charles	53756	D	1929
Hewson C.	53074	I	1929
SEMSEN			
Charles S.	60311	D	1931
Gusta M.	63713	D	1933
SEN			
Gee	74025	D	1936
Ken	41067	D	1925
Lem	73918	D	1936
SENATORE			
Angelo	44747	D	1926
SENBERG			
George Christian	48748	D	1927
SENDER			
Emil	6912	D	1908
SENEPH			
Ernest William Jr.	89991	M	1942
SENGER			
Henry	78617	D	1938
SENGLER			
Martin	49755	D	1928
SENGSTACKEN			
Charles H.	7890	M	1909
Clara C.	7890	M	1909
SENN			
Edith Wiles	79010	D	1938
SENNA			
Esther Drucilla	43210	M	1925
SENNATI			
Giacomo	62422	I	1932
SENNER			
Mary E.	46524	D	1927
Wiliam F.	70938	I	1935

NAME	NUMBER	TYPE	YEAR
SENSENSCHMIDT			
Richard	75882	D	1937
SENTER			
Edward	6692	D	1908
Katherine G.	77880	D	1938
Nellie (nee Egan)	3043	D	1907
SENTIBANEZ			
Raymonde	84832	D	1940
SEPPEL			
Johannes	53389	D	1929
John	53389	D	1929
SEPPICH			
Alma Hermana	85659	D	1940
Arthur William	10274	M	1910
SEPPINEN			
Alfred	40258	D	1924
SEPULVEDA			
Edward G.	70253	M	1935
Robert N.	70253	M	1935
SEPUT			
Cvitko	60692	D	1932
Czitko	60692	D	1932
Nick	60692	D	1932
SERAFINO			
Angelo	56588	D	1930
Virginio	11148	D	1911
SERAMIN			
Frederick Andrew	71825	I	1936
SERATO			
Pietro Gioachino	27753	D	1919
SERCOMBE			
Louise	81136	D	1939
SERE			
Lucile	20566	M	1916
SERENS			
Daniel F.	17424	D	1914
Lena	40078	D	1924
SEREX			
Mary Ellen	73981	D	1936
SEREY			
William Henry	60060	D	1931
SERFINI			
Angelo	56588	D	1930
SERGEANT			
Katherine	3849	M	1907

NAME	NUMBER	TYPE	YEAR
SERGESON			
Harvey L.	43361	D	1926
SERIAN			
Ulrich	42035	D	1925
SERIN			
Charles A.	10199	D	1910
SERKLAND			
Hans M.	50943	D	1928
SERLIJA			
Vlaho	22692	D	1917
SERMANS			
Jeanette Marie	40531	M	1924
SERMATTEI			
Peter	78700	D	1938
SERNA			
E. J.	71918	I	1936
Edward J.	89132	D	1942
SERNACK			
Henry August	87375	M	1941
SERNIO			
Antonio	41383	D	1925
SERPA			
Anthony F.	37144	D	1923
Roxene	41210	D	1925
SERPAS			
Mary J.	20666	D	1916
SERRANO			
Dolores	44406	D	1926
Emily	38983	M	1924
Francis Joseph	71605	M	1936
John	83563	D	1940
SERRANTI			
Domenica Herbana	60200	D	1931
SERRAS			
Rose Anna	44166	D	1926
SERRATTO			
Luigi	34409	D	1922
SERRES			
Jean Pierre	14412	D	1912
Jeanpierre	14412	D	1912
Rose Anna	44166	D	1926
SERRETTO			
Lucie	67538	D	1934
SERROTT			
Thomas Edward	61659	D	1932

NAME	NUMBER	TYPE	YEAR
SERSEN			
Marie	48501	I	1927
SERTORELLI			
Giuseppe	19021	D	1915
SERVAS			
John	16403	D	1913
SERVEAU			
Charles Eugene	58493	D	1931
Muriel	51857	M	1929
SERVEL			
Marie Rose	7376	M	1909
SERVENTI			
Angela	56492	D	1930
Attilio	45730	D	1926
SERVIDIS			
Alfonso	44005	D	1926
SERVIERES			
Joseph	77460	D	1938
SERVIS			
Rhyllis M.	837	D	1906
SERVISS			
Paulina	32231	D	1921
Thomas Wilson	36981	D	1923
SESNON			
Mary Porter	54805	D	1930
William T.	53326	D	1929
SESSER			
Arthur F.	48351	M	1927
SESSIONS			
Lyle J.	69358	D	1935
SESSLER			
Max	17960	D	1914
SESSOMS			
Edmund	73611	I	1936
Edward	73611	I	1936
Edwin	73611	I	1936
SESTIAA			
Peter	12305	D	1911
SETARO			
Antonio	16917	D	1914
Eugene	72323	M	1936
SETENCICH			
Spaso L.	68224	D	1934
SETHMANN			
Catherina	61693	D	1932
Henry, Mrs.	61693	D	1932

NAME	NUMBER	TYPE	YEAR
SETKOSKIE			
John	73493	D	1936
SETLIFF			
Mary Alice	30052	D	1920
William Thomas	36014	D	1923
SETO			
Mon Po	68422	D	1934
SETRIGHT			
John	3506	I	1907
SETTEGAST			
Julius	44696	D	1926
SETTERLIND			
Nels	10364	D	1910
SETTLE			
Dora J.	65326	D	1933
SETZER			
Albert	31547	D	1921
SEUBERT			
Pauline G.	65658	D	1933
SEVENING			
Christiane	17701	D	1914
Roy	17822	M	1914
SEVERANCE			
Frederick Vernon	76911	D	1937
Zella Gertrude	9454	M	1910
SEVERIN			
Sophie C.	89670	D	1942
SEVERINI			
Augusto	27074	D	1919
SEVERINO			
William	9886	D	1910
SEVERNS			
Bartholemew Erle	14845	D	1913
SEVETT			
Arthur S.	44189	D	1926
SEVIER			
Lois Ann	44281	D	1926
SEVILLA			
Robert Victor	55423	M	1930
Rose	76080	D	1937
SEVINT			
Fred	37100	D	1923
SEWALL			
Oscar T.	19729	D	1915

NAME	NUMBER	TYPE	YEAR
SEWALT			
Sophie	48542	D	1927
SEWARD			
Sally E.	43439	D	1926
Sarah E.	43439	D	1926
SEWELL			
Alice Lee	79440	D	1938
Emma L.	24598	D	1918
Joseph T.	32217	D	1921
Robert Lee	44490	M	1926
SEWELOH			
Theodor Louis	53561	D	1929
SEWISS			
Thomas Wilson	36981	D	1923
SEXON			
Charles	42711	D	1925
Della	42712	D	1925
SEXTON			
Augusta	8943	D	1910
Benedict D.	39314	I	1924
Denis	46917	D	1927
Hazel Rodenbeck Bond	25829	D	1918
James	14119	D	1912
James	49409	D	1928
Mary	4435	D	1907
Mry Ellen	14957	M	1913
Rose	47423	D	1927
Sarah Frances	89582	D	1942
Thomas	13451	D	1912
Timothy	39631	D	1924
W. A.	37966	D	1923
William	21286	D	1916
SEYBOLD			
John	35746	D	1923
Vernie May	8630	M	1909
Violet Alberta	8630	M	1909
Virgil LaFayette	8630	M	1909
SEYDEN			
Gustave	16393	D	1913
John H. J.	12553	D	1911
SEYMAND			
John	27188	D	1919
SEYMOUR			
Addison	87910	I	1941
Albert	57490	D	1930
Annie I.	53181	D	1929
Beatrice Ryder	89681	D	1942

NAME	NUMBER	TYPE	YEAR
Catherine	70173	D	1935
Helena	4921	D	1907
James	4754	D	1907
Jennie	41614	D	1925
John F.	27581	D	1919
John S.	57491	D	1930
Martha A.	71483	D	1936
Simon H.	1398	D	1906
Susan C.	1101	D	1906
SEYNED			
Joseph	22663	D	1917
SFERLAZZO			
Charles	25769	D	1918
SFORZINA			
Agostino	19935	D	1915
August	19935	D	1915
SHABLOVSKI			
William J.	39632	D	1924
SHABLOVSKY			
Bill	39632	D	1924
SHACKELFORD			
Barton Warren	72510	M	1936
SHACKEY			
James B.	78356	D	1938
SHACKLETON			
Christiana	14177	D	1912
SHAD			
Anna C.	32725	I	1921
SHADDICK			
Edward Pratt	60462	D	1931
SHADE			
Elizabeth G.	70646	D	1935
SHADELL			
Dorothy E.	68301	D	1934
SHADER			
Eleanor	32689	D	1921
Laura I.	25167	D	1918
SHAEN			
Jacob	44345	D	1926
Joseph	4240	D	1907
Lillie	76607	D	1937
Sarah	4568	D	1907
SHAFER			
Ben	82987	D	1939
Cory Frederick	78328	D	1938
Devilla M.	49246	D	1928

Name	Number	Type	Year	Name	Number	Type	Year	Name	Number	Type	Year
James M.	42886	D	1925	James L.	87517	D	1941	Catherine Winnefred	64452	M	1933
John M.	42886	D	1925	John	4314	M	1907	Cherie	71664	D	1936
Mary Poggi	34375	D	1922	John W.	75200	D	1937	Daniel Joseph	87858	D	1941
William D.	24982	D	1918	Martin	4313	M	1907	Frances	89458	M	1942
SHAFFER				Mary	19822	D	1915	Gene	52131	D	1929
Emma	24657	D	1918	Mary	69576	D	1935	James P.	37623	D	1923
Roda M.	31854	D	1921	Michael	84715	D	1940	John	89458	M	1942
Rose	43022	I	1925	Stella M.	4661	D	1907	John J.	63516	D	1933
SHAHAN				William E.	70438	D	1935	John R.	89593	D	1942
John Joseph	18461	D	1915	**SHANE**				Joseph P.	22029	D	1916
Peter	81160	D	1939	Albina Lucinda	17425	D	1914	Katherine Burke	78693	D	1938
Thomas J.	50761	D	1928	Catherine	63129	D	1932	Majorie	29547	M	1920
SHAHINIAN				Eleanor	36120	D	1923	Malcolm J.	83325	D	1940
G. Coutken	3005	D	1907	Eva	33599	D	1922	Margaret A.	81733	D	1939
Kasbar	80479	D	1939	Harry	63543	D	1933	Marie	7723	M	1909
SHAIN				John	17164	D	1914	Mary Ann	6918	D	1908
Alter	30112	D	1920	Sarah L.	30417	D	1920	Mary Grace	87583	D	1941
SHAINWALD				**SHANEDLING**				Maurice	79708	D	1938
Barbara	38038	M	1924	Jessie	78876	D	1938	Michael	6881	D	1908
Dick	72398	M	1936	Joshua	52932	D	1929	Michael Thomas	64429	D	1933
Herman	19744	D	1915	Lewis	78875	D	1938	Molly	83795	D	1940
Mathilde M.	5929	D	1908	**SHANK**				Nellie	67512	D	1934
Ruth	38038	M	1924	Abram	85211	D	1940	Percy	7723	M	1909
SHAKESPEARE				Elias	2876	D	1907	Peter	10623	D	1910
William	81041	D	1939	Elias	3775	D	1907	Robert	77961	D	1938
SHAKLES				**SHANKEY**				Sadie	32851	D	1921
Andra	61275	D	1932	Sarah	7297	D	1909	Sarah Jane	32851	D	1921
Andrew	61275	D	1932	**SHANKLIN**				Sharrron	71664	D	1936
SHAKLIS				Georgia	65603	D	1933	Simon	66902	D	1934
Andra	61275	D	1932	**SHANKS**				W. E.	34741	D	1922
SHAKOTT				Alvin R.	78812	I	1938	Walter John	71971	D	1936
Mike	45910	D	1926	David W.	85174	D	1940	William W.	20493	D	1916
SHALLENMILLER				Frederick Hastings	64992	D	1933	**SHANTON**			
Mary	3004	D	1907	Mary Ann	13481	D	1912	Trimble	57179	I	1930
SHALLOCK				**SHANLEY**				**SHAPERO**			
Hermina	88391	D	1941	Elizabeth	89251	D	1942	Aaron	1606	D	1906
SHAMA				**SHANLY**				Sam W.	35581	D	1922
A.	38598	I	1924	Ruth Lester	70609	D	1935	Shapro	1606	D	1906
Ezra	19720	I	1915	**SHANNON**				**SHAPIRA**			
SHAMP				Ada	71664	D	1936	Jennie	21425	M	1916
Thomas B.	73797	D	1936	Annie	17925	D	1914	**SHAPIRER**			
SHANABARGER				Annie Louise	81532	D	1939	Leo	75845	D	1937
George Roy	81350	M	1939	Annie Louise	84532	D	1939	**SHAPIRO**			
SHANAHAN				Bridget	453	D	1906	Abe	44114	D	1926
Edward	71220	D	1935	Bridget	23202	D	1917	Anna	73710	D	1936
Elizabeth	80763	D	1939	Carol Ann	89458	M	1942	Baruch	4989	D	1908
				Catherine	45292	D	1926	Daniel	56030	M	1930
								Iris Inger Nebeling	69695	M	1935

NAME	NUMBER	TYPE	YEAR
Jacob	8749	D	1909
Louis	43902	D	1926
Lozarus	17523	D	1914
Samuel Peter	80728	D	1939
SHAPLEY			
Elizabeth M.	79258	D	1938
SHAPRO			
Aaron	1606	D	1906
Abaham L.	76974	D	1937
Alvin Louis	77089	M	1937
Sarah	6138	D	1908
SHAPTER			
Emma S.	36762	D	1923
William I.	43446	D	1926
SHARBACH			
Christine	23640	D	1917
SHARBACKER			
Henry J.	77887	D	1938
SHARKEY			
Agnes	38326	D	1924
Alice	4218	M	1907
Alice T.	38693	D	1924
Bernard C.	9495	D	1910
Charles	37888	D	1923
Charles E.	9495	D	1910
Edward	2334	D	1906
Elizabeth	4218	M	1907
George	77485	D	1938
James J.	88683	D	1941
James W.	52151	D	1929
John	4088	D	1907
John	4218	M	1907
Lucy	4218	M	1907
Margaret	4218	M	1907
Mary	71356	D	1936
Mary C.	83980	D	1940
Sarah Agnes	38326	D	1924
Thomas J.	4818	D	1907
SHARMAN			
Hugh M.	21787	M	1916
SHARON			
Alexander D., Mrs.	71472	D	1936
Charlotte Annie	71472	D	1936
Frederick William	19405	D	1915
James Henry	48552	I	1927
John J.	87282	D	1941
May C.	84450	D	1940
William	11031	D	1911

NAME	NUMBER	TYPE	YEAR
SHARP			
Alexander	3569	D	1907
Andrew	84455	D	1940
Arthur M.	67025	D	1934
Caroline	10803	D	1910
Daniel Asher	86401	M	1941
Eliza M.	5569	D	1908
Elizabeth G.	85924	D	1940
Elizabeth M.	78166	D	1938
Ellen Jane	64836	D	1933
Fred	87825	D	1941
George F.	8020	D	1909
George L.	69216	D	1935
Harry	33821	I	1922
Honora	52	D	1906
James B.	86121	D	1941
John Daniel	88895	D	1942
Joseph C.	86401	M	1941
Margaret	71313	D	1935
Mattie Pauline	54890	D	1930
Max	45608	D	1926
Raymer	53935	I	1929
Raymer	65799	D	1933
Solomon A.	68994	D	1935
Sydney Filmer	78423	D	1938
William Richard	79482	D	1938
SHARPE			
Frank	14005	D	1912
Herbert H.	68940	D	1935
John Henry	30677	D	1920
SHARPLESS			
Edward R.	30510	D	1920
SHARPONSKI			
Henry	46389	D	1927
SHARRATT			
Frank Gray	60627	D	1932
SHARROCKS			
Gertrude E.	13702	M	1912
SHARTS			
A. J.	51796	D	1929
SHARTZER			
Roy Newton	18317	D	1914
SHATMAN			
Edward	23458	D	1917
SHATTUCK			
Ann	5582	D	1908
L. Lenora	71807	D	1936

NAME	NUMBER	TYPE	YEAR
Marilla	35153	D	1922
Martha M.	39121	D	1924
Paul W.	74095	D	1936
Phebe J.	17758	D	1914
SHAUGHNESSY			
Alice	2518	M	1906
Anne	16626	D	1914
Coleman	82681	D	1939
Effie G.	43485	D	1926
Ella	2518	M	1906
Ella	2518	M	1906
Patrick H.	42935	D	1925
Patrick J.	16724	D	1914
William	2518	M	1906
William A.	44812	D	1926
SHAUNESSY			
Johanna	5724	D	1908
SHAW			
A. A.	38332	D	1924
Alexander	5996	D	1908
Alice Harriman	20403	D	1916
Anna	82548	D	1939
Antoinette	22551	D	1917
Arthur Guy	68770	D	1935
Bena Eyford	56892	D	1930
Benjamin F.	80166	D	1938
Bernard T.	76417	D	1937
Blanche E.	41320	D	1925
Bridget A.	1901	D	1906
C. Everett	53863	D	1929
Chales E.	53863	D	1929
Charles Everett	89738	D	1942
Charles H.	65862	D	1933
Charlotte M.	82820	D	1939
Christopher	3199	D	1907
Clarence	26922	D	1919
Clyde B.	43518	D	1926
Cynthia M.	67047	D	1934
Eleanor May	20514	M	1916
Eliza J.	50137	D	1928
Elizabeth	793	D	1906
Elizabeth A.	24082	D	1918
Emma L.	84105	D	1940
Emmerson N.	31966	D	1921
Eugenie Louise	71199	D	1935
Frances Tyler	65501	D	1933
Frank E.	39671	D	1924
G. A.	13487	D	1912

Key: D = death; M = minor; I = incompetent

NAME	NUMBER	TYPE	YEAR
Gardiner Howland	50719	D	1928
George T.	790	D	1906
George W.	18167	D	1914
Guillermo	24441	D	1918
Helen Elizabeth	20514	M	1916
Henry	3187	D	1907
James	56755	D	1930
James Samuel	26395	D	1919
Joanne Lee	89375	M	1942
John B.	48110	D	1927
John Eyford	52662	D	1929
John M. A.	2922	D	1907
John Mitchell	89376	I	1942
John Mitchell, Jr.	89375	M	1942
John W.	20310	M	1916
Johnsie	87881	D	1941
Kate	59807	D	1931
L. E., Mrs.	50137	D	1928
Laura E.	79822	I	1938
Lawrence King	38706	M	1924
Lena L.	48451	D	1927
Lionel	75188	I	1937
Lionel	77688	D	1938
Louise E.	71199	D	1935
Lyle	77688	D	1938
Lynne	89375	M	1942
Madeleine A.	45835	I	1926
Madeleine A.	64155	I	1933
Mary F.	79156	D	1938
Peter J.	14684	D	1913
Ruth	82548	D	1939
Thomas	40743	D	1925
Thomas VanDyke Tyler	65614	M	1933
Wallace Burton	42584	D	1925
Will	24441	D	1918
William A.	35415	D	1922
William J. J.	19017	D	1915
William Thomas	4077	D	1907

SHAWBUT

NAME	NUMBER	TYPE	YEAR
Frederick	16920	D	1914

SHAWL

NAME	NUMBER	TYPE	YEAR
Charles	79056	D	1938
Philip	46940	D	1927

SHAWLER

NAME	NUMBER	TYPE	YEAR
William M.	21966	D	1916

SHAY

NAME	NUMBER	TYPE	YEAR
Edwin Joseph	8168	M	1909
Frank Willis	14433	D	1912
James	32505	D	1921
John	77236	D	1937
Katherine	35730	D	1923
Marie Carmel	8168	M	1909
Mildred Ann	44056	M	1926

SHAYLOR

NAME	NUMBER	TYPE	YEAR
Justin D.	63378	D	1933
William	12535	D	1911

SHE

NAME	NUMBER	TYPE	YEAR
Lin	17593	D	1914

SHEA

NAME	NUMBER	TYPE	YEAR
Ambrose M.	13185	M	1912
Anita	662	M	1906
Anna C.	68985	D	1935
Annie	27966	D	1919
Charles A.	89106	D	1942
Charles P.	67874	D	1934
Christina M.	13185	M	1912
Christopher A.	15926	D	1913
Daniel	1926	D	1906
Daniel	8053	I	1909
Daniel	9120	D	1910
Daniel	85317	D	1940
Dennis	50878	M	1928
Dennis F.	86309	D	1941
Donald L.	89346	M	1942
Eden E.	13185	M	1912
Edward	18119	D	1914
Elizabeth	10591	D	1910
Eva L.	70866	D	1935
Gertrude Dorothy	73885	D	1936
Helen Kathleen	7947	M	1909
Hugh L.	7947	M	1909
Irene	87262	D	1941
James	6605	D	1908
James	23798	D	1917
James Patrick	38657	I	1924
James W.	66576	D	1934
Johannah	17550	D	1914
John	662	M	1906
John	4812	D	1907
John C.	22047	D	1916
John Francis	85358	D	1940
John J.	57113	D	1930
John Joseph	12620	D	1911
John Joseph	33850	D	1922
John William	81192	D	1939
Joseph T.	68202	D	1934

NAME	NUMBER	TYPE	YEAR
Joseph W.	66960	D	1934
Julia Gertrude	55517	D	1930
Katherine G.	14235	D	1912
Kathleen Costello	73725	D	1936
Kathleen Maria	71644	M	1936
Maggie K.	6826	D	1908
Margaret	48786	D	1927
Margaret	62926	M	1932
Marguerite F.	13185	M	1912
Mary	71644	M	1936
Mary A.	83277	D	1940
Michael	3674	D	1907
Michael	6184	D	1908
Michael	68147	D	1934
Michael	80897	D	1939
Nora	78848	I	1938
Patrick	27233	D	1919
Timothy Edward	84623	D	1940
W. J.	44355	D	1926
Wellin	13185	M	1912
William	59781	I	1931
William D.	59341	D	1931
William E.	43909	D	1926

SHEAHAN

NAME	NUMBER	TYPE	YEAR
Alma Marie Hoar	86541	I	1941
Frank I.	59953	D	1931
John E.	53825	D	1929
Ruth Dorman	1724	D	1906
Thomas	5850	D	1908
Thomas M.	87886	D	1941

SHEALY

NAME	NUMBER	TYPE	YEAR
Patrick Terrance	71335	M	1936

SHEAN

NAME	NUMBER	TYPE	YEAR
Barbara	23260	M	1917
James E.	14349	D	1912
John Joseph	18461	D	1915

SHEAR

NAME	NUMBER	TYPE	YEAR
David	11490	D	1911
Theodore F.	45181	D	1926

SHEARER

NAME	NUMBER	TYPE	YEAR
Bertha	70640	D	1935
George B.	8922	D	1909
Mary H.	76972	D	1937

SHEARN

NAME	NUMBER	TYPE	YEAR
John E.	84972	D	1940
Robert E.	87535	M	1941

SHEBLE

NAME	NUMBER	TYPE	YEAR
Charles Joseph	88299	D	1941

NAME	NUMBER	TYPE	YEAR	NAME	NUMBER	TYPE	YEAR	NAME	NUMBER	TYPE	YEAR
Sadie	88298	D	1941	Frances Josephine	9225	M	1910	Minnie	62291	D	1932
SHEDDEN				Frank J.	78513	I	1938	Robert V.	58794	D	1931
William	37390	D	1923	George A.	29010	D	1920	Rose H.	73900	D	1936
SHEE				Henry Edward	67495	D	1934	**SHEELE**			
Chin Lim	41681	D	1925	Henry Edward	68122	D	1934	Alvina Marie	77740	D	1938
Chin Lum	41681	D	1925	James William	31013	D	1921	**SHEEN**			
Fong	81428	I	1939	Jeremiah G.	38970	D	1924	Catherine	39428	D	1924
Fong	81751	D	1939	Johanna	364	D	1906	Henry	59829	D	1931
Jew	14964	D	1913	Johanna	37242	D	1923	Jennie Augusta	57972	D	1931
Jung	39006	D	1924	Johanna	82688	D	1939	Lee	49344	D	1928
Lee	54972	D	1930	John	2604	D	1907	**SHEERIN**			
Leong	81751	D	1939	John	4877	D	1907	Agnes M.	47264	D	1927
Leong Tom	58195	D	1931	John	21647	D	1916	David W.	63547	I	1933
Lum	73804	D	1936	John	69184	I	1935	David W.	64158	D	1933
Soo Hoo	81428	I	1939	John C.	9414	D	1910	Frank L.	47263	D	1927
Tom	58195	D	1931	John D.	47852	D	1927	Jeanne Theresa	65797	M	1933
Wong	39006	D	1924	John F.	84410	D	1940	Jeanne Theresa	73568	M	1936
Wong ho	47629	D	1927	John Joseph	70816	D	1935	John Joseph	49065	D	1928
Wong Yee	82780	D	1939	John T.	3376	D	1907	Theresa	47948	D	1927
SHEEDON				Joseph	12105	D	1911	**SHEESLEY**			
Mary L.	5657	D	1908	Kate T.	6213	D	1908	James Joseph	51367	I	1928
SHEEDY				Kathleen Elizabeth	36937	M	1923	**SHEETS**			
Jeremiah	44410	D	1926	Lawrence V.	10934	M	1910	Oliver H. P.	2452	D	1906
SHEEHAN				Margaret	37807	M	1923	Tina	36774	I	1923
Aileen Lillian	36937	M	1923	Marguerite G.	22750	D	1917	**SHEFTEL**			
Alice Logan	9225	M	1910	Mary	11689	D	1911	Joseph	20789	D	1916
Annabelle	72227	D	1936	Mary	16869	D	1914	Marcus	64284	D	1933
Anne	47121	D	1927	Mary	34609	D	1922	**SHEIBLEY**			
Bridget	8380	D	1909	Mary Adelaide	33432	D	1922	Charles F.	1487	D	1906
Catherine	55097	D	1930	Mary E.	14214	I	1912	Emma E.	4600	D	1907
Catherine S.	81406	D	1939	Mary Elizabeth	75107	D	1937	**SHEIDEMAN**			
Catherine W.	64544	D	1933	Michael	67219	D	1934	Bahr	15220	D	1913
Daniel	347	D	1906	Patrick	2604	D	1907	**SHEILS**			
Daniel	17421	D	1914	Paul	42454	D	1925	John	57409	D	1930
Daniel Edward	76814	D	1937	Peter	18484	D	1915	**SHELBY**			
Daniel J.	47072	M	1927	Philip J.	87331	D	1941	Edward T.	87891	D	1941
Daniel J.	54355	D	1929	Ruth Frances	30639	M	1920	James	77379	D	1937
Daniel J.	88997	D	1942	Thomas	5850	D	1908	**SHELDON**			
David D.	67770	D	1934	Timothy J.	60106	D	1931	Agnes M.	37234	D	1923
Delia	8380	D	1909	William Francis	22978	M	1917	Blaine Watson	59250	D	1931
Denis	82341	D	1939	**SHEEHY**				Cora B.	50297	D	1928
Denis J.	8549	D	1909	Augustine Louis	15232	D	1913	Edward Harmon	3828	D	1907
Denis Joseph	31585	D	1921	Charles Parnell	59130	D	1931	Edwin R.	71976	D	1936
Edgar Maurice	79626	D	1938	Elizabeth	42365	D	1925	Frank P.	86794	D	1941
Edward P.	73343	D	1936	Eugene V.	33396	D	1922	Frederick N.	71006	D	1935
Elizabeth	8548	D	1909	Hannah	39924	D	1924	George B.	68126	D	1934
Ellen	18586	D	1915	Katherine Frances	77541	D	1938	George M.	16714	D	1914
Ellen	43414	D	1926	Leo Joseph	55361	D	1930				
				Mary A.	86911	D	1941				

NAME	NUMBER	TYPE	YEAR	NAME	NUMBER	TYPE	YEAR	NAME	NUMBER	TYPE	YEAR
Isaac	43706	D	1926	**SHENK**				**SHEPPENS**			
Jeremiah	362	D	1906	Edith Campbell	16596	D	1914	Ellen	13638	M	1912
John	86178	D	1941	**SHEONG**				John Morrison	13638	M	1912
Lela	27709	M	1919	Yee	72298	D	1936	**SHEPSTON**			
Mary L.	3675	I	1907	**SHEPARD**				Catherine M.	639	D	1906
Miamna	11983	D	1911	Amanda M.	4662	D	1907	William J.	2671	D	1907
Nellie A.	69153	I	1935	Bert	9427	D	1910	**SHERBECK**			
Richardson	27709	M	1919	Mary E.	29742	D	1920	George	26420	D	1919
Walter D.	40540	D	1924	Patrick H.	63352	D	1933	**SHERBERG**			
SHELFORD				William M.	66502	D	1934	Amelia	7549	D	1909
Charles V.	35447	D	1922	**SHEPHARD**				**SHERBURN**			
SHELLARD				Alfred	27865	D	1919	James O.	67582	D	1934
Helen C.	65558	D	1933	Bert	9427	D	1910	**SHERBURNE**			
SHELLEY				Charles T. L.	86914	D	1941	John P.	11118	D	1911
Ann	72137	M	1936	Columbus C.	41896	D	1925	**SHERDIAN**			
Luke	45607	D	1926	Columbus C.	41896	D	1925	Mary	27931	D	1919
Thomas S.	65254	D	1933	Mary	22730	D	1917	Thomas Michael	62362	D	1932
Zenith Eugene	36901	I	1923	Minnie M.	57098	D	1930	**SHERER**			
SHELLGRAIN				Robert C.	25060	D	1918	Catherine	25736	D	1918
Charles F.	73456	D	1936	Virgil I.	59594	D	1931	William A.	26769	D	1919
SHELLMAN				**SHEPHERD**				**SHERID**			
Gustave	58386	I	1931	Donald A.	82147	M	1939	Hermie William	63608	I	1933
SHELLNET				Emma B.	15306	D	1913	**SHERIDAN**			
Tumey Lee	34452	I	1922	Grace	33459	M	1922	Bernard Domonic	86482	D	1941
SHELLY				Jeannette W.	40293	D	1924	Christopher	46728	D	1927
Frank B.	67641	D	1934	Jessie M.	55911	D	1930	Daniel Merritt	35696	D	1923
Robert	80219	D	1938	Julia	64917	D	1933	Elizabeth	48244	I	1927
SHELOW				June	44340	M	1926	Elizabeth	49042	D	1928
John L.	78086	D	1938	Marie	44340	M	1926	Elizabeth A.	20925	D	1916
SHELTON				Richard Lefel	48162	I	1927	Elizabeth B.	82907	D	1939
Emily F.	87264	D	1941	Roberta	78750	M	1938	Frederick R.	17611	D	1914
George B.	68126	D	1934	Ruth	85266	D	1940	George A.	56445	D	1930
John W.	59491	D	1931	**SHEPLEY**				Harry	40939	D	1925
Leigh Roland	49739	D	1928	George B.	2629	D	1907	Henrietta G.	3850	D	1907
William Frank, III	54720	M	1930	**SHEPMAN**				John	8743	D	1909
SHEMANSKI				Amelia M.	85227	D	1940	John J.	45631	D	1926
Etta	72022	D	1936	W. E.	3750	D	1907	John P.	77395	D	1937
Harris	57128	D	1930	William J.	75577	D	1937	Joseph Patrick	70848	D	1935
Isadore	75402	D	1937	**SHEPPARD**				Julia F.	59150	D	1931
SHEMANSKY				Ann	3704	D	1907	Mary	27931	D	1919
Isadore	75402	D	1937	Calvin	4866	M	1907	Mary Ann	10139	D	1910
SHEN				George	4866	M	1907	Owen	31992	D	1921
Lee	49344	D	1928	Harry J.	67076	D	1934	Peter	4215	D	1907
SHENDA				Rose	36636	D	1923	Thomas	10140	D	1910
Dora F.	64372	D	1933	Samuel	20490	D	1916	Thomas F.	40214	D	1924
SHENEFIELD				William J.	80160	D	1938	Thomas Michael	62362	D	1932
Margaret E.	65005	D	1933					William A.	20289	D	1916

Key: D = death; M = minor; I = incompetent

NAME	NUMBER	TYPE	YEAR
William Thomas	72794	D	1936
SHERIDEN			
Phillip	59567	D	1931
SHERITT			
Ruby Ethel	63782	D	1933
SHERLOCK			
William S.	60451	D	1931
SHERMAN			
A. J.	46042	I	1926
Adam J.	49863	D	1928
Agnes	36226	D	1923
Agnes C.	40413	D	1924
Albert Wilcox	83991	D	1940
Alvina P.	58732	D	1931
Anna M.	31763	D	1921
Annie C.	44055	D	1926
Annie R.	42451	D	1925
Becky	60021	D	1931
Bernard A.	22297	M	1917
Charles Hoyt	15644	D	1913
Charles Seymour	12095	D	1911
Clifford W.	55487	D	1930
Edward E.	38121	D	1924
Ethan Henry	45300	D	1926
Flora M.	68818	D	1935
Frank	82324	D	1939
Frank A.	87685	I	1941
Frank H.	42748	M	1925
Frank P.	37311	D	1923
Harry	53250	D	1929
Henry J.	24276	D	1918
Jacob S.	85603	D	1940
Joseph	52289	D	1929
Julius	85603	D	1940
Katie	35619	D	1922
Leander S.	44170	D	1926
Lewis	80794	D	1939
Lillie A.	14367	D	1912
Peter D.	32039	D	1921
Philip F.	22296	D	1917
Philys	26888	M	1919
Raymond H.	28536	D	1919
Sara	78903	D	1938
Sarah	58674	D	1931
Sarah C.	47349	I	1927
Sarah C.	48049	D	1927
Theodore L.	33957	D	1922
William Francis	40010	M	1924

NAME	NUMBER	TYPE	YEAR
SHERR			
Charles A.	20556	D	1916
SHERRATT			
James Conlin	78727	D	1938
SHERRY			
Arthur P.	82911	D	1939
David	51338	D	1928
Franz F.	88635	D	1941
Joseph	81752	M	1939
Margaret E.	32291	D	1921
Mary	72729	D	1936
SHERWOOD			
Alice M.	84546	D	1940
Eliza N.	13692	D	1912
Fredrika C.	34449	D	1922
Harry	67446	D	1934
Leonore Mary	45399	M	1926
Martha E.	30674	D	1920
Martin L.	44429	D	1926
Minnie	15585	D	1913
Rhoda J.	28264	D	1919
Robert L.	2655	D	1907
W. R.	22751	I	1917
William Robert	24851	D	1918
SHETTERLEY			
John Leslie Monroe	20227	D	1916
SHEUERMAN			
Hannah	80115	D	1938
J., Mrs.	80115	D	1938
SHEVLIN			
Catherine	41695	I	1925
Rose J.	34942	D	1922
SHEW			
Annie K.	55301	D	1930
Lee	49344	D	1928
Sing	82762	D	1939
SHEWAN			
James	49766	D	1928
Jessica A.	71532	D	1936
Patricia C.	71092	M	1935
SHEWBRIDGE			
Andrew	12173	D	1911
Bridget	10932	D	1910
Margaret	38252	D	1924
Peter	38878	D	1924
SHEWMAKER			
Grayce E.	79060	D	1938

NAME	NUMBER	TYPE	YEAR
SHEY			
Iney	34815	D	1922
SHIBATAI			
Hilokite	46901	D	1927
SHIBELEY			
Frank P.	42960	D	1925
Sarah K.	41045	D	1925
SHIBODAI			
Hilokite	46901	D	1927
SHIELDS			
A. M., II	49662	M	1928
Alexander M.	49424	D	1928
Alexander McMillen	49662	M	1928
Alvin W.	73345	I	1936
Alvin W.	75667	D	1937
Anna M.	77106	D	1937
Annie	44424	D	1926
Barbara	49662	M	1928
Cecile C.	23006	D	1917
Christina	45581	D	1926
Clara Margaret	36383	M	1923
Elizabeth	10059	D	1910
Everett E.	39382	D	1924
Frances	70606	D	1935
Francis	70606	D	1935
Garrison C.	3550	M	1907
Garrison F.	36428	D	1923
Grace	67976	D	1934
John W.	20460	D	1916
Josephine	82181	D	1939
Laura C.	3550	M	1907
Louisa	70260	D	1935
Lydia M.	18063	D	1914
Mary A.	60542	D	1931
Mary Convery	70606	D	1935
Thomas	42057	D	1925
Thomas Joseph	47336	D	1927
Violette	84103	D	1940
Walter J.	13590	D	1912
William Stephens	59646	D	1931
SHIELS			
Belle Elizabeth Lynham	15630	M	1913
Charles H.	47120	D	1927
J. Wilson	54652	D	1930
John	57409	D	1930
Suzanne	57221	M	1930
SHIERS			
Della Gordon	55614	D	1930

Key: D = death; M = minor; I = incompetent

NAME	NUMBER	TYPE	YEAR
SHILLABER			
Joseph S.	59981	D	1931
SHILLINGS			
Peter	40400	D	1924
SHIMADA			
Kazuo	73251	M	1936
SHIMAN			
Abraham	73655	D	1936
Eva Sarah	54301	D	1929
Joseph	78235	D	1938
Ruby	46152	M	1927
Solomon D.	41068	D	1925
SHIMEK			
Alma	35281	M	1922
Emil E.	35280	D	1922
Frank	35281	M	1922
SHIMINSKY			
Max.	54249	D	1929
SHIMIZU			
Harukichi	61117	D	1932
SHIMMONS			
Charles	7590	D	1909
SHIMMONZ			
Charles	7590	D	1909
SHIMONOWSKY			
Betti	51069	D	1928
SHIMOSE			
Mutsu	14285	M	1912
SHINDLER			
Harry C.	46141	D	1927
SHINE			
Annie L.	5738	D	1908
Cahterine	45949	D	1926
Daniel J.	45420	D	1926
James	59965	D	1931
John T.	81629	D	1939
Nicholas	2063	D	1906
Raymond	6748	M	1908
William P.	61955	D	1932
SHINEBERGER			
John	93	D	1906
SHING			
Gee Ack	79701	D	1938
Quan Yuen	25150	D	1918
SHINGLEBERGER			
Nellie Morse	76766	D	1937

NAME	NUMBER	TYPE	YEAR
Suzanne Niebaum	84648	D	1940
SHINGU			
Kiyoko	30135	M	1920
Sumiye	30135	M	1920
SHINICK			
John H. L.	34679	D	1922
SHINKWIN			
Joyce	84862	M	1940
SHINN			
Lavern	46040	I	1926
Lavern	48991	D	1928
SHIPLEY			
G. H., Mrs.	41098	D	1925
George Jerome	77485	D	1938
John H.	30845	D	1920
Mattie Irene	67506	D	1934
William Alexander	64436	D	1933
SHIPMAN			
Charles H.	71372	D	1936
Helen M.	48947	I	1928
Helen M.	58551	I	1931
Ida Frances	85679	D	1940
Oliver T.	89502	I	1942
Rebecca A.	38467	D	1924
SHIPPEY			
Charles E.	61439	D	1932
SHIREK			
Adolph	16840	D	1914
Dorothea	31594	D	1921
Gertrude M.	79578	D	1938
Herbert M.	82430	D	1939
SHIRINGTON			
Fanny	75532	D	1937
Fanny Thompson	75532	D	1937
Francis	75532	D	1937
SHIRKIE			
Caroline G.	28772	D	1920
SHIRLEY			
Ann R.	7321	D	1909
John	11207	D	1911
John W.	19872	D	1915
Sebastian C.	32421	D	1921
SHIRPSER			
Ernst G.	75670	D	1937
Max	13101	D	1912
SHIVELY			
Emily Josephine	80831	I	1939

NAME	NUMBER	TYPE	YEAR
Emily Josephine	80893	D	1939
Laura D.	53760	D	1929
SHIVETZER			
Jacob	4753	D	1907
SHIVNER			
David	88974	M	1942
SHKEL			
Iron	29129	D	1920
SHKONDIN			
Peter	44861	D	1926
SHLOSS			
Rosa	47809	D	1927
SHNIDER			
T.	50739	D	1928
SHOCKLEY			
Laura M.	84484	D	1940
SHODRY			
Anna	58971	D	1931
SHOEMAKER			
Alvin	81088	D	1939
Jack N.	76575	D	1937
John E.	41120	D	1925
William Rawle	78649	D	1938
SHOEMANN			
Otto Ernst August	28445	D	1919
SHOENBERG			
Sigmund	1862	D	1906
SHOJI			
Yoshiji	53258	D	1929
SHOLTE			
Carl F.	63784	D	1933
SHOLTZ			
Helen J.	86129	D	1941
SHOMO			
John Andrew	71405	D	1936
SHONE			
Law	73151	D	1936
Low	73151	D	1936
SHOOK			
Emanuel L.	54154	I	1929
Emanuel Lewis	77402	D	1938
Margaret	77505	D	1938
SHOOR			
Pearl	26945	D	1919
SHOOTMAN			
Ina Gertrude	26568	M	1919

NAME	NUMBER	TYPE	YEAR
Sue Ella	26568	M	1919
Thomas Winfield	26568	M	1919
SHOOTS			
Sallie	21621	D	1916
SHOPERA			
Louis	47112	D	1927
SHOPHOFEN			
Arthur	50782	D	1928
SHOR			
Bennie	26460	M	1919
Fannie	26460	M	1919
SHORB			
Donald McNeal	64503	D	1933
J. Campbell, Mrs.	54695	D	1930
Mae Ellen	54695	D	1930
Thomas	20088	D	1915
Yorba Adelaide	19830	M	1915
SHORE			
Mary Elizabeth	15569	D	1913
SHORER			
Clara	32388	D	1921
SHORES			
Merle	88019	D	1941
Merle M.	85654	D	1940
SHORKLEY			
Syrna Burdick	14386	M	1912
SHORT			
Arthur	24495	M	1918
Carrie Mabel	2851	M	1907
Carrie Mabel	24495	M	1918
Edward	16232	M	1913
Edward N.	69756	D	1935
Edward P.	16263	D	1913
Eleanor	60185	D	1931
Emma K.	35241	D	1922
Ethel S.	89652	D	1942
H. G.	12987	D	1912
Hannah Mary	59834	D	1931
Ida Elizabeth	59396	D	1931
Iva Elizabeth	24495	M	1918
J. Eleanor	60185	D	1931
James	34239	D	1922
James	57468	I	1930
James Blake	7167	D	1909
Joseph H.	16232	M	1913
Julia B.	19137	D	1915
M. E.	13984	D	1912

NAME	NUMBER	TYPE	YEAR
Margaret	37857	D	1923
Norma E.	33933	D	1922
Norman Truesdell	2851	M	1907
Norman Truesdell	24495	M	1918
Peter	24346	D	1918
Sarah A.	19417	D	1915
William	58400	D	1931
William B.	43592	D	1926
SHORTEN			
Benjamin	35946	M	1923
Catherine	39643	D	1924
Catherine	35946	M	1923
Eileen	35946	M	1923
George	36248	D	1923
George W.	30062	D	1920
SHORTLIDGE			
Beatrice Lillian	86115	D	1941
SHORTT			
Nellie M.	29692	I	1920
SHOSBERG			
Rose	72241	D	1936
SHOSTER			
Lowis	57272	D	1930
SHOTWELL			
Minnie P.	41374	D	1925
SHOUDY			
Kenneth Dexter	34445	M	1922
SHOUP			
Betsy Claire	27306	M	1919
SHOVLIN			
Edward	30838	D	1920
Mary	37442	D	1923
SHOW			
Martin S.	51687	D	1928
SHRADER			
Andrew Warren	41991	D	1925
Jackson L.	25558	D	1918
SHRAGGE			
Meyer F.	83492	D	1940
SHRAMEK			
Louisa	7157	D	1909
SHREVE			
Jennie W.	62887	D	1932
SHRIER			
Augusta	85762	I	1940

NAME	NUMBER	TYPE	YEAR
SHRIMPLIN			
Louis	38670	I	1924
SHROYIER			
Eliza	30709	D	1920
SHRYNE			
Margaret	63424	I	1933
SHUBERT			
Anna M.	77885	D	1938
SHUCK			
Betty	63169	I	1932
Betty M.	66871	D	1934
Gin Wing	70958	D	1935
Luther M.	25713	D	1918
SHUCKING			
Theodore Emil	68092	D	1934
SHUENGGREN			
Adolph	29061	D	1920
SHUFELT			
Lizzie C.	3429	D	1907
William J.	12817	D	1912
SHUGRUE			
Maggie	52840	I	1929
SHUHAN			
John J.	73088	D	1936
SHULER			
Davis W.	83072	D	1940
SHULMAN			
Hyman	78886	D	1938
Samuel	76028	D	1937
SHULTES			
Frances	81368	D	1939
SHULZ			
Anna	80096	D	1938
SHUMAN			
Caroline V.	62122	D	1932
Percy L.	61777	D	1932
Perseus L.	61777	D	1932
SHUNK			
Jacob	53176	D	1929
SHURART			
Jesse H.	2041	D	1906
SHURIGAN			
John	45990	I	1926
SHUTES			
Hattie E.	67045	D	1934

NAME	NUMBER	TYPE	YEAR
SHUTEY			
George	48772	D	1927
SHUTEZ			
George	48772	D	1927
SHUTTEN			
Henry L.	19122	D	1915
SHUTTLEWORTH			
Charles A.	26302	D	1919
SHUTTS			
Carl	81772	D	1939
SHUTZ			
William F.	84418	D	1940
SIAUS			
Manda	77828	D	1938
SIBERI			
Don	84621	D	1940
SIBLEY			
Henry Clay	22812	D	1917
Levi B.	83714	D	1940
William R.	87632	D	1941
SICA			
Guiseppe	53453	D	1929
SICCO			
Annie	48803	D	1927
John Joseph	78030	D	1938
SICHEL			
Cecilia	16744	D	1914
Charles Philip	14705	D	1913
Max	4873	D	1907
Philip	8209	D	1909
SICHLAW			
Carl E.	34160	D	1922
Juliana	35376	D	1922
SICKELS			
George L.	39139	D	1924
Jacob Henry	29239	D	1920
SICKLER			
Sarah Jane	16750	D	1914
SICKOS			
Annie Irene	68972	D	1935
SICOCAN			
George	41610	D	1925
SICOTTE			
Arthur	23993	M	1918
Irving	23993	M	1918
Margaret	13025	D	1912

NAME	NUMBER	TYPE	YEAR
Margaret	60332	D	1931
Peter Irving	23993	M	1918
Rita	60332	D	1931
Thomas Arthur	23993	M	1918
SIDARI			
Felice	15577	M	1913
SIDEL			
Charles Philip	14705	D	1913
SIDENER			
Clarence B.	6382	I	1908
Hilary M.	6003	M	1908
SIDJINOFF			
Steve	13477	D	1912
SIDLOWSKI			
Lottie C.	33891	D	1922
Manuel	32293	D	1921
SIDOROFF			
Alex John	66901	D	1934
SIEBE			
Christiane	34934	D	1922
Frederick C.	15332	D	1913
John D.	16147	D	1913
John F.	10508	D	1910
SIEBECKER			
Annie M.	71738	D	1936
Dolores	56186	M	1930
Louis	6640	D	1908
SIEBENHAUER			
Levy	6859	D	1908
Mathilde	80845	D	1939
Sally	23415	D	1917
SIEBER			
Alfred	60997	I	1932
Alfred	62141	D	1932
Clara A.	75722	D	1937
Henry Frederick	32245	D	1921
Julia F.	65832	D	1933
SIEBERT			
Frank William	84076	D	1940
Louisa A.	84075	D	1940
Mathilda	16492	I	1913
William F.	84076	D	1940
William J.	68546	D	1934
SIEBOLD			
Carrrie E.	10658	M	1910
SIEBRECHT			
Gustav	59950	D	1931

NAME	NUMBER	TYPE	YEAR
Lucille Amelia	75955	D	1937
SIEDEL			
William	21875	D	1916
SIEDENBERG			
Henry Joseph	72337	D	1936
SIEFKE			
Elise	29154	D	1920
Ferdinand	18979	D	1915
SIEG			
Wilmer	60932	D	1932
SIEGEL			
Channah	80966	D	1939
Evelyn	41729	M	1925
Evelyn	41729	M	1925
Harold	32863	M	1921
Hortense	49323	D	1928
Martin	18627	D	1915
Maurice L.	56001	D	1930
Meyer L.	32724	D	1921
Morris	4023	D	1907
Oscar	55845	D	1930
Oscar	56144	D	1930
Rachel Lena	54765	D	1930
SIEGELE			
Adele K.	11845	M	1911
Henry	59431	D	1931
Minnie	10323	D	1910
SIEGERT			
Mary	74304	D	1937
SIEGFRIED			
Alfred H.	20639	D	1916
SIEGLE			
Dora	61565	D	1932
SIEGLER			
Jacob	60636	D	1932
SIEGRIST			
Annie	7046	D	1909
SIEK			
Herman F.	51457	D	1928
SIEKAVIZZA			
Christobal	12067	D	1911
SIELAFF			
Albert	37409	D	1923
SIELOFF			
Albert	37409	D	1923

NAME	NUMBER	TYPE	YEAR	NAME	NUMBER	TYPE	YEAR	NAME	NUMBER	TYPE	YEAR
SIEMENS				**SIEVERT**				**SILAGI**			
Albert Garnett	76119	D	1937	Andrew J.	12523	M	1911	Emma	56123	D	1930
SIEMER				Frieda C.	12523	M	1911	John	87906	D	1941
Marie A.	83534	D	1940	Julius	9909	D	1910	Robert E.	56124	M	1930
SIEMERS				**SIEWERT**				Sara F.	56124	M	1930
Christina Maria	31203	D	1921	Willard William	58108	M	1931	**SILBEISTEIN**			
Johann Diedrich	38097	D	1924	William S.	58037	D	1931	Yettle	55401	D	1930
Maria	31203	D	1921	**SIGEL**				**SILBERBERG**			
SIEMON				Anna	80966	D	1939	Max	25128	D	1918
Charlotte E.	3427	M	1907	**SIGG**				**SILBERMAN**			
Willie J.	3427	M	1907	Emil	24240	D	1918	John	73654	D	1936
SIEMS				**SIGGINS**				Joseph Albert	73654	D	1936
Harry P.	26543	D	1919	Alice	18308	D	1914	**SILBERMANN**			
SIENES				Nicholas	14946	D	1913	Israel	28718	D	1920
Caesario	78082	D	1938	**SIGGS**				**SILBERSTEIN**			
SIEPEN				Minnie	68102	D	1934	Alfred S.	10965	I	1910
John	25405	D	1918	**SIGISMUND**				Alfred S.	42866	D	1925
SIER				William	11000	D	1911	Bernice Irene	49132	M	1928
Philip	20936	M	1916	**SIGLER**				Charles M.	10965	I	1910
SIERCK				Bertha Laura	83979	D	1940	Charles M.	16911	D	1914
Frederick	54623	D	1929	**SIGNA**				Frances Sonia	49132	M	1928
Henry J.	11181	D	1911	Antoinette	52646	D	1929	Harold	49132	M	1928
Rudolph A.	83134	D	1940	**SIGNER**				Ira	49132	M	1928
Sophie	56154	D	1930	Chester William	48601	M	1927	Irwin	49132	M	1928
SIEREVELD				John Robert	87843	M	1941	Jacob	21530	D	1916
Mary O'Brien	82851	D	1939	**SIGNORELLO**				Julius C.	48402	D	1927
SIERK				Providenzia	68941	D	1935	Miriam	49132	M	1928
William	79202	D	1938	**SIGNORETTI**				Morris	47711	D	1927
SIERLING				Bartholomew	7049	D	1909	Sophia	47769	D	1927
Wilda	24928	D	1918	**SIGNORI**				Vera Sonia	49132	M	1928
SIEROTY				Alex	67738	I	1934	**SILBERZAHN**			
Arthur	22732	M	1917	**SIGNORRELLO**				Philippine	20481	D	1916
Ella F.	20978	D	1916	Francisco	11126	D	1911	**SILCOTT**			
Henry	67623	D	1934	**SIGOND**				Emma A.	53242	D	1929
Stuart Elmer	70643	M	1935	Paul G.	34155	D	1922	Thornton	50933	D	1928
SIESBUTTEL				**SIGRIST**				**SILCOX**			
Minnie	46658	D	1927	Mary	32100	D	1921	A. F.	19853	D	1915
SIESEVELD				**SIGUERE**				Frances	19818	M	1915
Mary O'Brien	82851	D	1939	Frances Adeline	29810	D	1920	Frances	20463	D	1916
SIEU				**SIGWART**				**SILENERI**			
Henrietta	21587	M	1916	Florence Henrietta	42881	M	1925	Giovanna	69149	D	1935
SIEVERS				Henriette J.	61892	D	1932	**SILGER**			
Carl August Magnus	38180	D	1924	Joseph Anton	75267	D	1937	Homer J.	84140	I	1940
John H.	10394	D	1910	Joseph Frederick, Jr.	42881	M	1925	**SILHAM**			
John W.	75816	D	1937	**SIKORA**				Edward	47511	D	1927
Marie	48165	D	1927	Charles	35410	D	1922	**SILINERE**			
								Giovanna	69149	D	1935

NAME	NUMBER	TYPE	YEAR
SILJAC			
Joseph	80788	D	1939
SILK			
Andrew	8227	D	1909
Edward C.	29773	M	1920
Howard F	29773	M	1920
James W.	11565	D	1911
James, Mrs.	89167	D	1942
Malachy F.	27583	D	1919
Mary	89167	D	1942
Mary Isabelle	69873	D	1935
Michael J.	61194	D	1932
SILL			
Lena H.	63111	D	1932
SILLAMEKE			
Erik	67101	D	1934
SILLEMAN			
Emma Emelia	30429	D	1920
Miriam Emma	30961	M	1921
SILLER			
John Lenhart	53954	D	1929
Mary M.	83682	D	1940
SILLERSTROM			
Erik	43102	D	1925
SILLESEN			
Godske	17845	D	1914
SILLIFANT			
Stanley Herbert	80560	D	1939
SILLINERI			
Lena E.	89214	D	1942
Stella	76519	D	1937
SILLS			
Annie T.	2218	D	1906
William G.	28106	D	1919
SILVA			
Adelina	24438	D	1918
Ana Eleto	55688	D	1930
Angie F.	58948	D	1931
Anna Carolinda	49341	D	1928
Anthony	78004	D	1938
Bernard J.	80212	M	1938
Caroline	53268	D	1929
Cornelia B.	43961	D	1926
Drusilla I.	82337	D	1939
Elsie Louise	82336	D	1939
Frank M.	40877	D	1925
Frank, Jr.	56234	M	1930

NAME	NUMBER	TYPE	YEAR
Frank, Jr.	79885	M	1938
George	6502	M	1908
Gregory	53709	D	1929
Jeronimo P.	50893	D	1928
Joaquin B.	67238	D	1934
Joaquin John	67238	D	1934
Joe S.	86204	D	1941
John	56221	D	1930
John	74583	D	1937
John J.	44523	D	1926
John J.	70559	D	1935
John L.	51950	D	1929
John M.	36411	D	1923
John S.	56221	D	1930
Joseph	85705	I	1940
Joseph	41083	I	1925
Joseph D.	47424	D	1927
Joseph E.	84355	D	1940
Julia E.	70708	I	1935
Manuel	6621	D	1908
Manuel B.	74313	D	1937
Mary	59856	M	1931
Merle	43778	M	1926
Millet	23486	I	1917
Paul	77345	M	1937
Roberta	77345	M	1937
Vernon	56234	M	1930
Vernon	79885	M	1938
SILVARER			
Thomas A.	56468	I	1930
SILVEIRA			
M. A.	47149	M	1927
SILVER			
Abraham	15448	D	1913
Doris	44035	M	1926
F.	64968	D	1933
Frank D.	40213	D	1924
Heiman	49884	D	1928
Henry	81927	D	1939
Jeanette	31719	M	1921
Joseph	71595	D	1936
Joseph H.	34287	D	1922
Joseph M.	54466	D	1929
Lillian	31719	M	1921
Max	85729	D	1940
Miriam	54340	D	1929
Theodore	83299	D	1940

NAME	NUMBER	TYPE	YEAR
SILVERBERG			
Bernhard	52154	I	1929
Irvin	42357	D	1925
Isaac	29444	D	1920
Jeannette	23895	D	1918
Joseph	24259	D	1918
Joseph S.	38613	D	1924
Louis	18920	D	1915
Simon	1032	D	1906
Yetta	17276	D	1914
SILVERBLATT			
Samuel	53213	D	1929
SILVERFIELD			
Mindell	72483	D	1936
Saul	56132	D	1930
SILVERIA			
Joseph Mathias	1087	D	1906
Manuel Gularte	84758	D	1940
SILVERMAN			
Esther	39012	D	1924
Frieda D.	18396	D	1915
Gisela	48413	D	1927
Henry	85630	D	1940
Jacob	35536	D	1922
Joseph	23135	D	1917
Louis	62008	D	1932
Lysbeth	80633	D	1939
Moritz	64553	D	1933
SILVERMANN			
Hannah	11212	D	1911
SILVERRA			
John	5884	D	1908
SILVERSTEIN			
Bertha	52180	D	1929
Dora	33986	D	1922
Jacob	12309	D	1911
Malie	50143	D	1928
Mollie	50143	D	1928
Morris	77274	D	1937
SILVERSTONE			
Louis	33262	D	1922
Tillie	65646	D	1933
SILVERTHORN			
Martha H.	32512	D	1921
William Henry	3192	D	1907
SILVESTER			
Henry	24425	D	1918

NAME	NUMBER	TYPE	YEAR	NAME	NUMBER	TYPE	YEAR	NAME	NUMBER	TYPE	YEAR
Leander	4832	D	1907	Morris	3134	D	1907	James H.	3353	D	1907
SILVESTRE				Nathan	7778	M	1909	John P.	38495	D	1924
Michel J.	32086	D	1921	Peter	3121	M	1907	John Thomas	8171	D	1909
SILVESTRI				Rose	24151	I	1918	Joseph Leonard	56437	M	1930
Antonio	35092	D	1922	**SIMKINS**				Juan O.	55857	D	1930
Francesco	1140	D	1906	Clifford Elwood J.	80118	D	1938	Levi W.	15215	D	1913
Giovanni	55914	D	1930	Florence L.	6190	M	1908	Louise	22388	D	1917
Giuseppe	47399	D	1927	**SIMMEN**				Lucy H.	34474	D	1922
SILVESTRO				Alexander	25547	D	1918	Lula H.	22388	D	1917
Joseph	78495	D	1938	John	64434	D	1933	Martha Ann	88003	D	1941
SILVEY				Leo F.	46949	D	1927	Mary Elizabeth	56436	M	1930
John M.	36411	D	1923	Maria	1077	D	1906	Mattie A.	88003	D	1941
John Meredith	87046	D	1941	Samuel	59447	D	1931	Nell B.	74990	D	1937
Mary E.	31816	D	1921	**SIMMIE**				Nell Church	74990	D	1937
SILVIA				James Andrew	1452	D	1906	Phebe L.	37988	D	1923
John	5884	D	1908	Lenore Emma	59445	D	1931	Philip	11528	D	1911
Michael	77720	D	1938	**SIMMIN**				Samuel Darrow	53061	D	1929
SILVIERA				Samuel	59447	D	1931	Samuel W.	45913	D	1926
John Thomas	86161	D	1941	**SIMMINS**				Thomas Francis	42279	D	1925
SIM(M)EN				Leonard A.	56715	D	1930	William Marvin	84752	D	1940
Anton	1974	D	1906	**SIMMON**				**SIMOLJAN**			
SIMASON				Gustav	40550	D	1924	August	25562	D	1918
Martin	86078	D	1941	Karl A.	75507	D	1937	**SIMON**			
SIMCICH				**SIMMONDS**				Abram	31529	D	1921
Jennie	65721	D	1933	Edwin	66958	M	1934	Albert Bernd	79995	D	1938
SIME				Ella	66958	M	1934	Alexander	4771	D	1907
Arthur P.	9398	M	1910	Elmore	66958	M	1934	Alfred	6117	D	1908
Arthur P.	20447	I	1916	Richard E.	37852	D	1923	Alfred	49478	D	1928
Enid M.	47005	D	1927	Sarah E.	37851	D	1923	Bettie Blanch	26897	D	1919
Harry C.	3928	D	1907	Thomas	66958	M	1934	Charles D.	27775	D	1919
SIMENS				William	66958	M	1934	Charles J.	65278	D	1933
Ole L.	34010	D	1922	**SIMMONS**				Charles R.	65279	M	1933
SIMI				Alonzo R.	11885	D	1911	Constance A.	73716	M	1936
Aladino	16124	D	1913	Benjamin F.	38721	D	1924	Esther	63884	M	1933
Albert	6450	D	1908	Charles Alonzo	59033	D	1931	Fannie	36196	M	1923
Angelo	56352	D	1930	Elizabeth Catherine	13369	I	1912	Fanny	10318	D	1910
Arturo	85094	D	1940	Elizabeth K.	52148	I	1929	Hattie	34089	D	1922
Attilio	74726	D	1937	Elizabeth K.	55756	D	1930	Henriette	18807	D	1915
Carolina	53071	D	1929	Ella	23935	D	1918	Henriette	65478	D	1933
Cesira	52741	D	1929	Elmer Ernest	62032	D	1932	Henry	439	D	1906
Oreste	51585	D	1928	Hannah J.	48907	D	1928	Isidore	14891	D	1913
Pietro	3476	D	1907	Harry	52152	D	1929	Jennie	31363	D	1921
Robert A.	87430	M	1941	Hattie	40272	D	1924	Jessie	74888	D	1937
Victoria A.	26244	D	1919	Haydn M.	83405	D	1940	Joan	69889	D	1935
Walter Peter	5986	M	1908	Henry	73163	D	1936	John J.	34702	D	1922
SIMINOFF				Herbert O.	10043	D	1910	Joseph	65031	I	1933
Emma	81070	D	1939	Hugh	71865	D	1936	Jules A.	9939	D	1910
				Jack	55857	D	1930	Kaufmann	60495	D	1931
								Lena	6625	D	1908

Key: D = death; M = minor; I = incompetent

NAME	NUMBER	TYPE	YEAR	NAME	NUMBER	TYPE	YEAR	NAME	NUMBER	TYPE	YEAR
Lucien	24306	D	1918	Ben	60231	I	1931	Emilie	21331	M	1916
Margaret M.	40310	D	1924	Carrie	46295	D	1927	Francis Jane	15778	D	1913
Marie Rose	70107	D	1935	Clark	3109	D	1907	George S.	39221	D	1924
Mary	49660	D	1928	Edward William	87258	D	1941	Harriett	16429	M	1913
May	14888	D	1913	Fred Baldwin	60808	M	1932	Harry W.	19660	D	1915
Meta	14888	D	1913	H. A.	27824	D	1919	Henry H.	30987	D	1921
Meyer	3210	D	1907	Isadore S.	54830	D	1930	James	17100	D	1914
Narcisse	3977	D	1907	Lena	35103	D	1922	James Arthur	21331	M	1916
Narcisso	348	D	1906	Mary Ashmead	4073	D	1907	Jennie G.	39096	D	1924
Paul	14823	D	1913	Ole L.	34010	D	1922	Jessie G.	21331	M	1916
Sally	42280	D	1925	Theodore Cornelius	83642	D	1940	John Laidlaw	40965	D	1925
Salome	88405	D	1941	**SIMONSEN**				Joseph W.	74386	D	1937
Samuel M.	26259	D	1919	Chresten	28047	D	1919	Josiah Adams	71947	D	1936
Sarah	81078	D	1939	Elisabeth	7025	D	1909	Katie	53209	D	1929
Scott S.	17215	D	1914	Fanny Martina	71138	D	1935	Malin	52259	D	1929
Sigfried	41888	D	1925	**SIMONTACCHI**				Margaret	21331	M	1916
Sigfried	41888	D	1925	Ambrogio	63932	D	1933	Margaret	30859	D	1920
Sigmund	82789	D	1939	Giuseppe	14147	D	1912	Mary Ann	203	D	1906
Silas	25416	D	1918	**SIMONTON**				Mary E.	57925	D	1931
Simon	25039	D	1918	Adelaide F.	73348	I	1936	Mary Grace	7054	M	1909
Sylvain L.	4772	M	1907	Fred W.	20680	D	1916	Nellie	21331	M	1916
Theresa	76026	D	1937	Marie	23627	D	1917	Nettie M.	63744	D	1933
Thomas	41581	D	1925	**SIMOSSI**				Ray Daniel	73465	D	1936
Velma R.	73715	D	1936	Clelia	53726	D	1929	Robert D.	58536	D	1931
SIMONART				**SIMPERS**				Robert G.	13199	D	1912
Frank Eugene	12694	D	1911	George James	83599	D	1940	Sarah	17481	D	1914
Maria	68871	D	1935	**SIMPKINS**				Sarah	20759	D	1916
Maria	66627	I	1934	Charles H.	3558	D	1907	Sophie S.	8449	D	1909
SIMONDS				Donald	84688	M	1940	Thomas C.	32722	D	1921
Lizzie C.	9835	D	1910	Doris Mae	84688	M	1940	Thomas J.	62079	D	1932
Mary L.	43503	D	1926	Harry Ritchie	67167	D	1934	Vern S.	15823	M	1913
Samuel E.	15744	D	1913	John Leroy	84688	M	1940	William	34028	D	1922
Walter M.	9578	D	1910	Kate R.	12136	D	1911	William F. L.	24868	D	1918
SIMONELLI				**SIMPSON**				William H.	25795	D	1918
Giovanni	9773	D	1910	Albert	37824	I	1923	William J.	81973	D	1939
SIMONETTA				Albert	39256	D	1924	Wm. A.	36549	D	1923
Joseph	6923	D	1908	Alice P.	78178	D	1938	**SIMPTON**			
SIMONI				Anna M. J.	84626	D	1940	Elizabeth	8633	D	1909
Carmen	52268	D	1929	Arthur Carl	960	M	1906	**SIMRAK**			
Frank	52124	M	1929	Asa M.	18480	D	1915	Anna	46140	D	1927
SIMONINI				Benjamin Franklin	47992	D	1927	Mitchell Stanley	23642	D	1917
Adele	75791	D	1937	Bert L.	50530	D	1928	Slovinke	46140	D	1927
Antoinetta	49711	D	1928	Bertram Benjamin	77148	D	1937	**SIMS**			
Ferdinando	83738	D	1940	Carl James	82389	D	1939	Charles	34762	D	1922
SIMONITTI				Caroline	472	D	1906	Elizabeth M.	86568	D	1941
Cesira	55189	D	1930	Charles J.	60036	D	1931	Jack William	43883	M	1926
SIMONS				Diedrich	3185	D	1907	James Coker	28548	D	1919
Anna Doretta	14392	D	1912	Dorothy	52823	I	1929	James Nathan	78203	D	1938

NAME	NUMBER	TYPE	YEAR
John R.	67861	D	1934
Josiah	37150	D	1923
Laura J.	28697	D	1920
Mary A.	36098	D	1923
SIMUNOVICH			
Gregri	39053	M	1924
Jack	39053	M	1924
SINAN			
Orivon	53472	D	1929
SINCLAIR			
Albert George	63471	D	1933
Alice	68134	D	1934
Arthur Pyne	74302	D	1937
Atholl	85811	M	1940
Catherine E.	31809	D	1921
Cenoira	56753	I	1930
Cenovia	58617	D	1931
David Lister	86759	D	1941
Florence L.	46187	D	1927
James Henry	62486	D	1932
John William	3472	I	1907
John William	7596	D	1909
Kate C.	31728	D	1921
Lawrence R.	69883	D	1935
Lou	46593	D	1927
Nellie	27827	D	1919
Sadie	78560	D	1938
W. J.	15517	D	1913
SINDEL			
Jacob	23331	D	1917
John Jacob	23331	D	1917
SINECK			
Marie	72260	D	1936
SING			
Ah	82762	D	1939
Chan	75046	D	1937
Chin	75046	D	1937
Ching	17593	D	1914
Cum	45957	D	1926
Gee	74007	D	1936
Gee Chung	74007	D	1936
Gee Fook	36290	D	1923
Hoo Too	74006	D	1936
Joe	49612	D	1928
Jow Kim	45957	D	1926
Lee	75046	D	1937
Lee Him	45679	D	1926
Leong	31622	D	1921

NAME	NUMBER	TYPE	YEAR
Leong Yick	7759	D	1909
Low Gam	59303	D	1931
Ng Quong	26913	D	1919
Quan Yong	25150	D	1918
Seid Pak	82916	D	1939
Shew	82762	D	1939
Wong	16556	D	1914
Wong	42244	D	1925
Wong	79208	D	1938
Wong Suey	17883	D	1914
SINGDAHL			
Severin N.	84317	D	1940
SINGER			
Charles, Jr.	89504	D	1942
Clara A.	64711	D	1933
Dora	13425	D	1912
Edward	47080	I	1927
Joseph	61093	D	1932
Julius	25540	D	1918
Kate	42332	I	1925
Max	66397	D	1934
Minnie	6873	D	1908
Richard L.	65829	D	1933
William C.	22775	D	1917
William Menzies	45204	D	1926
Wm., Jr.	15190	D	1913
SINGH			
Anokh	12884	D	1912
Baba	26127	D	1919
Banta	26156	D	1919
Buddon	26127	D	1919
Canyon	21271	D	1916
Gurdit	33492	D	1922
K. B. Marain	60571	I	1931
Narian	60571	I	1931
Odam	65853	D	1933
SINGINSON			
Gerald	78319	D	1938
SINGLETON			
Alice	46439	D	1927
Daniel	23066	I	1917
Josephine M.	70123	D	1935
SINGLEY			
Carrie	54850	D	1930
Frank B.	32342	D	1921
George	54851	D	1930
George William	13443	D	1912
Lucy A.	27866	D	1919

NAME	NUMBER	TYPE	YEAR
SINK			
William D.	56036	M	1930
William F.	56036	M	1930
SINKO			
Joe	75206	D	1937
SINKOVEITZ			
Joseph	75206	D	1937
SINNER			
Richard T. F.	365	D	1906
William	56346	D	1930
SINNOTT			
Anna	89105	D	1942
Ellen	60890	D	1932
Ellen F.	27164	D	1919
Ellen M.	4529	I	1907
SINON			
William J.	3887	D	1907
SINSHEIMER			
Bernard	50068	D	1928
Fannie	62002	D	1932
Henry	62623	D	1932
Nettie K.	44700	D	1926
Samuel Charles	54145	D	1929
SINTON			
Henry	46188	M	1927
Robert	46188	M	1927
Stanley H.	46188	M	1927
SIPARY			
Daniel	18744	M	1915
Mary	18743	M	1915
Reinhold	2023	D	1906
SIPE			
Thomas Ellsworth	41159	D	1925
SIPPEL			
Ellen	29695	D	1920
John	63788	D	1933
John T.	29412	D	1920
SIPPLE			
Henry	74966	D	1937
SIPRELLE			
Chester D.	45997	I	1926
Chester Danil	82867	D	1939
SIRAGUSA			
Frances	49544	D	1928
SIRI			
Antioco	49197	D	1928

NAME	NUMBER	TYPE	YEAR	NAME	NUMBER	TYPE	YEAR	NAME	NUMBER	TYPE	YEAR
B., Mrs.	65262	D	1933	SIVERTSEN				Margaret	32619	D	1921
Catherina	65262	D	1933	Adolph	69154	D	1935	SKALA			
Frank	45215	I	1926	SIVERTSON				Matija	22286	D	1917
Maria	84922	D	1940	Adolf	69154	D	1935	SKALD			
Marina	84922	D	1940	SIVETT				Theodora	89066	D	1942
Sebastiano	48539	D	1927	Arthur S.	44189	D	1926	SKANG			
SIRRINE				SIVORI				Nicolai	85901	D	1940
Emmeline	3279	D	1907	Angelo	76948	I	1937	SKANV			
SIRVIO				Angelo	77184	D	1937	Mary	34632	D	1922
Anna Wolpuri	89390	D	1942	Pietro	83301	D	1940	SKAUG			
SISCAN				SIYAKOVICH				Nicolay Martin	85901	D	1940
Mathilde	39248	D	1924	Risto	41395	D	1925	SKAUV			
SISENVINE				SJAGREN				Mary	34632	D	1922
Caroline	48613	D	1927	Charles J. C. P.	39789	D	1924	SKAVLAN			
Irving Charles	58220	M	1931	SJOBERG				Harold	30394	D	1920
Mary	75570	D	1937	Axel Fredrik	80628	D	1939	SKEEHAN			
Moses	18333	D	1914	Carl Wilhelm	63397	D	1933	John	4877	D	1907
SISK				Johnnes	87537	D	1941	John	8263	D	1909
Cathrine	34665	D	1922	SJOGREN				SKEEL			
John	46963	I	1927	Carl Jacob	29190	D	1920	Robert A.	49142	D	1928
William M.	77953	I	1938	Oscar L. A.	66277	D	1934	SKEGGS			
SISKROU				SJOLANDER				Florence F.	56981	D	1930
Clara Ann	6070	D	1908	Carl T.	49683	D	1928	SKEHAN			
SISSMAN				Charles	49683	D	1928	Henry	9213	D	1910
Max	88525	D	1941	SJOLUND				Mary	10437	D	1910
SISSON				Emma	9875	D	1910	SKELLENGER			
Bridget A.	10263	D	1910	Emma A.	10161	D	1910	Margaret McCabe	20979	D	1916
Clair C.	66544	I	1934	SJOSTEDT				SKELLEY			
Cyrus T.	82364	D	1939	Carl Eugene	34090	M	1922	Catharine	3095	D	1907
Frank H.	35709	D	1923	Frey A. R.	31871	D	1921	SKELLY			
Joseph H.	30297	D	1920	George	34090	M	1922	Amelis Denniston	7491	D	1909
Maria C.	66302	D	1934	Hildegard Loyisa	34090	M	1922	Augustine M.	88058	D	1941
SITKOSKIE				Robert Ake	34090	M	1922	Bartholomew Jerome	20692	M	1916
John	73493	D	1936	SJOSTROM				Catharine	3095	D	1907
SITRIN				Theodore E.	79754	D	1938	Edward D.	72712	D	1936
Helen Silvia	84398	M	1940	SKADBERG				Edward Denniston	7626	M	1909
SITTON				Pauline	17020	D	1914	Edward J.	72910	D	1936
Naomi Belle Frame	60240	D	1931	SKAE				Gregory John	20692	M	1916
SIVELL				Alice	4905	D	1907	Gregory V.	1965	D	1906
Albert J.	29958	D	1920	SKAHAN				Helen Virginia	33109	M	1921
SIVEMIUS				Lawrence A.	78279	I	1938	James Denniston	84142	D	1940
Eva	50789	D	1928	SKAIFE				Jerome C.	56630	D	1930
SIVEN				Alfred	24489	D	1918	Juan Fay	3191	D	1907
Eva	50789	D	1928	Frances Mary	27633	D	1919	Margaret	54101	D	1929
SIVERS				SKAINE				Margaret A.	20316	D	1916
John H.	31236	I	1921	Margaret	17752	I	1914	Patricia Rose	33109	M	1921
								William John	69155	D	1935

NAME	NUMBER	TYPE	YEAR
SKELTON			
Ennion Woods	40728	D	1925
SKERNAN			
Lillie B.	39642	D	1924
SKERRETT			
Catherine	15385	D	1913
Daniel	7965	D	1909
Ellen	18710	D	1915
SKEWES-COX			
Joan	68568	M	1934
SKIFF			
Jane E.	49597	D	1928
SKIFIC			
John	13695	D	1912
SKILLEN			
Albert Ernest	62727	D	1932
SKILLERUP			
Aksel	79902	D	1938
Axel	79902	D	1938
SKILLICORN			
John	3665	D	1907
Walter H.	73340	D	1936
SKILLING			
James	66963	D	1934
Samuel Kerr	62808	D	1932
SKILLMAN			
Oliver Ernest	53188	I	1929
Oliver Ernest	57718	D	1931
SKINKLE			
Henriette H.	89639	D	1942
SKINNER			
Andrew Francis St.	13314	D	1912
David E.	49151	D	1928
Eugene N.	74473	D	1937
Francis	17999	D	1914
Francis St. Duthus	13314	D	1912
Freda M.	48300	D	1927
Gunnar Evert	83544	D	1940
Ida	17224	D	1914
John H.	56134	D	1930
John P.	82614	I	1939
Lemont W.	34819	D	1922
Lintine McCreery	71890	D	1936
Lucy Evans	31178	D	1921
Norah	10441	D	1910
Robert Henry	73899	M	1936
Rose M.	14787	D	1913

NAME	NUMBER	TYPE	YEAR
Sarah E.	354	D	1906
Sidney Lawrence	78548	D	1938
Stella	58763	D	1931
Thelma	14942	M	1913
William H.	22975	D	1917
SKIPPER			
John J.	44122	D	1926
SKIPPICH			
J.	13695	D	1912
SKIRK			
Antoinette	72356	D	1936
SKIRVIN			
Harvey L.	69628	D	1935
SKLAR			
Andrew	53050	D	1929
SKLAREK			
Edward	54862	D	1930
SKLAVOS			
George	55305	D	1930
SKOGLAND			
Hazel	24899	D	1918
SKOLD			
Charles A.	56615	D	1930
SKOLL			
Louis	71785	D	1936
SKOOTSKY			
Harold	29093	M	1920
Israel	29092	D	1920
Theodore	50881	D	1928
SKORKO			
Michael	33304	D	1922
SKREPNEK			
Nick	58995	D	1931
SKREPNICK			
Nicholas	58995	D	1931
SKRYPNGK			
Nick	58995	D	1931
SKUJA			
Mathilde	57431	D	1930
SKYRME			
William	42536	D	1925
SLACK			
Charles Allen	51312	D	1928
Cora C.	66268	I	1934
Cora C.	66509	D	1934
Coreen C.	66268	I	1934

NAME	NUMBER	TYPE	YEAR
Coreen C.	66509	D	1934
Enoch	44814	D	1926
Gladys E.	64363	D	1933
Henry Berry	50468	D	1928
Katherine W.	79337	D	1938
Marjorie	64363	D	1933
SLADE			
Elizabeth Finnell	70551	M	1935
Russell Clark	70453	D	1935
SLAGHT			
Archer J.	48667	D	1927
Edwin R.	37271	D	1923
SLAGLE			
William C.	45821	D	1926
SLANO			
John	20815	D	1916
SLARIGHT			
Beath P.	32427	D	1921
SLASSON			
M. Ella	50725	D	1928
SLATER			
Charles H.	32126	D	1921
Clara M.	67550	D	1934
Elizabeth	11284	D	1911
John	72374	D	1936
Mary	14327	D	1912
Susanna B.	71893	I	1936
Susanna B.	74802	D	1937
SLATTERY			
Annie	60632	D	1932
Annie	43227	I	1925
Annie C.	15940	D	1913
Charles Deane	18515	M	1915
Grace Margaret	18515	M	1915
Jerry	43226	D	1925
John	35941	D	1923
Kate	28673	D	1920
Maurice Daniel	21438	D	1916
Michael F.	10679	D	1910
Patrick	31386	D	1921
Ronald	41176	I	1925
Ronald Francis	43550	D	1926
Rosie M.	37108	D	1923
Sophie	77689	I	1938
William J.	18515	M	1915
SLAVAN			
Annie E.	18209	I	1914

NAME	NUMBER	TYPE	YEAR
Annie E.	19781	D	1915
Mary H.	30187	D	1920
SLAVEN			
Georgie R.	54379	D	1929
SLAVICH			
John	33535	I	1922
Mary	68159	I	1934
Therese	50283	D	1928
SLAVIENSKI			
Paul	65052	D	1933
Teofila	88294	D	1941
SLAVIERO			
Pietro	73561	I	1936
SLAVIN			
John W.	114	D	1906
Mary	16737	D	1914
SLAYTON			
Edmund E.	26741	D	1919
Edward	74905	D	1937
Edwin	74905	D	1937
George A.	82817	D	1939
Samuel	38204	D	1924
SLEDGE			
Daisy	76591	D	1937
Jean	86892	M	1941
SLEIGHT			
Harold	58645	M	1931
SLEMMONS			
Fred L.	89955	D	1942
SLESSINGER			
Lewis	30580	D	1920
SLETCHER			
John A.	83005	D	1940
SLEVIN			
Constantine Dena	53321	D	1929
Daniel Aloysius	62428	D	1932
James M.	70139	M	1935
Thelma	53322	M	1929
Thomas Pierce	83915	D	1940
SLEWING			
Vere T.	47892	I	1927
SLICKMAN			
Barbara	69742	M	1935
SLIKERMAN			
Heyman	85223	D	1940
Hyman	85223	D	1940

NAME	NUMBER	TYPE	YEAR
SLIMMON			
Ellen	17531	D	1914
Robert	17530	D	1914
SLINKEY			
Lilian	76879	D	1937
SLITH			
Learner B.	8748	D	1909
SLOAN			
Anna Kingston	66583	D	1934
Anna Mary	66583	D	1934
Burt W.	81650	D	1939
Clarence Barstow	10667	D	1910
David Henry	87133	D	1941
Eva B.	44761	D	1926
Hannah Beatrice	84856	D	1940
Harry	71296	D	1935
James Joseph	66704	D	1934
Mabel Elenora	85513	D	1940
Mary	66583	D	1934
Ruth C.	87167	D	1941
Theresa	56019	I	1930
SLOANE			
Charles Robert	70332	D	1935
James	26113	D	1919
John J.	46096	D	1926
Sarah	28947	D	1920
SLOAT			
Ada B.	72322	I	1936
Ada B.	73324	D	1936
Charles B., Mrs.	72322	I	1936
SLOBOHM			
Berniece	66499	D	1934
SLOCUM			
Charles B.	41726	D	1925
Charles B.	41726	D	1925
Emily W.	66782	D	1934
SLOMAN			
Ernest Eugene	47272	M	1927
Francis Donnell	35412	M	1922
Frank H.	36641	D	1923
SLONAKER			
Laurence B.	30416	I	1920
SLOSS			
Joseph	80484	D	1939
Leon	29609	D	1920
Levi	27687	D	1919
Louis	64021	D	1933

NAME	NUMBER	TYPE	YEAR
Mary W.	27620	D	1919
Sarah	29989	D	1920
SLOTTER			
Harry	46429	I	1927
SLOUGH			
Max R.	72124	D	1936
SLOWENIS			
Frank	33341	I	1922
SLOWINSKI			
Frank	33341	I	1922
SLUTZKER			
Al	80308	D	1939
SLVIN			
William	53322	M	1929
SLYE			
Eveline L. Harrison	78295	D	1938
Joseph	77618	D	1938
SLYTER			
Annie J.	87429	I	1941
Hiram Emmett	64400	D	1933
Sol	50108	I	1928
SMALE			
Anna E.	6075	D	1908
Annie M.	75362	D	1937
William J.	16477	D	1913
SMALL			
Allen	15386	D	1913
Annie E.	20262	D	1916
Frances	6674	D	1908
George	53408	D	1929
George K.	34853	D	1922
Hugh	78674	D	1938
Isabella Duquid	83631	D	1940
James M.	350	D	1906
Julia Helen	24369	D	1918
Julia J.	88603	D	1941
Katherine	20224	D	1916
Maria M.	1494	D	1906
Perry	67315	D	1934
William Alexander	6277	I	1908
William, Mrs.	26628	D	1919
Zephy	26628	D	1919
SMALLEY			
Fay Richard	81904	D	1939
SMALLMAN			
Catherine	346	D	1906

NAME	NUMBER	TYPE	YEAR
SMALLS			
Edgar H.	66299	D	1934
SMARR			
Hazel	41232	D	1925
SMART			
Annie Lee	11811	D	1911
George C.	19050	D	1915
George Stanley	19246	M	1915
Grace Margaret	19246	M	1915
Jane	17705	D	1914
Laura G.	27444	D	1919
Margaret Evelyn	19068	M	1915
Richard Palmer	26334	M	1919
William	63204	D	1932
SMAZAL			
George	71514	D	1936
SMEDBERG			
Fannie M.	56921	D	1930
W. R.	12253	D	1911
SMEDLEY			
Emily	32079	D	1921
SMEETH			
Fannie	58291	D	1931
SMEITH			
Thomas	23172	D	1917
SMELLIE			
Bridget Mary	88733	D	1941
SMELTING			
Max	88402	D	1941
SMERDEL			
John P.	22570	D	1917
SMIETANA			
Chaim	87091	D	1941
SMILEY			
Edith Hurst	84961	D	1940
Frank T.	87528	D	1941
SMIRCICH			
Anthony J.	86319	D	1941
SMIRLE			
Eliza Jane	69986	D	1935
Robert J.	34926	D	1922
Winifred	69986	D	1935
SMIRNOFF			
Alexander	56082	D	1930
SMISTAD			
Ole G.	23647	D	1917

NAME	NUMBER	TYPE	YEAR
SMISTH			
Ella Roberta Wilson	1775	D	1906
SMITH			
A.	37389	D	1923
A. Blanche	72994	D	1936
A. Thomas H.	56453	D	1930
Aaron J.	63351	D	1933
Abina	64801	D	1933
Ada B.	56888	D	1930
Ada Belle	4137	M	1907
Adam	45695	D	1926
Addison A.	59714	D	1931
Adele	8411	D	1909
Agnes	44447	D	1926
Agnes	76289	I	1937
Agnes F.	65629	D	1933
Agnes Kelly	70851	D	1935
Aidney Henry	16612	D	1914
Albert C.	29029	D	1920
Albert M.	24291	D	1918
Albert W.	76691	D	1937
Albina	64801	D	1933
Alex	28899	D	1920
Alexander	18203	D	1914
Alexander D.	3123	D	1907
Alexander F.	73550	D	1936
Alexander T. H.	56453	D	1930
Alfred	26938	M	1919
Alfred Atherton, Sr.	51664	D	1928
Alfred Cookman	84734	D	1940
Alfred Edward	80978	D	1939
Alfred Lewis	87867	D	1941
Alice	40628	D	1924
Alice B.	56893	D	1930
Alice E.	53394	D	1929
Alice Hamilton	8102	D	1909
Alice M.	31582	D	1921
Alma K.	55655	D	1930
Amy	12247	D	1911
Amy Bessey	89036	D	1942
Andrew	9405	D	1910
Andrew	9586	D	1910
Andrew F.	82741	D	1939
Andrew H.	62429	I	1932
Andrew H.	75450	D	1937
Angeline Lorion	80843	D	1939
Anita Evelyn	20828	D	1916
Anita Page	66456	D	1934
Ann	10610	D	1910

NAME	NUMBER	TYPE	YEAR
Anna	12530	D	1911
Anna	51024	D	1928
Anna C.	44503	D	1926
Anna E.	47403	D	1927
Anna Evelyn	21113	M	1916
Annie	8619	D	1909
Annie	10719	D	1910
Annie	74466	D	1937
Annie Kelly	39919	D	1924
Annie M.	66619	D	1934
Annie Winter	67500	D	1934
Anthony	2190	D	1906
Antonette	25645	M	1918
Arthur Augustus	53000	D	1929
Arthur Henry	47602	M	1927
Arthur L.	45122	D	1926
Arthur O.	54866	D	1930
Augusta W.	54185	D	1929
Augustine A.	46719	I	1927
Augustine A.	56143	D	1930
Augustine A.	42261	I	1925
Austin W.	17131	D	1914
Barbara A.	4970	D	1908
Barbara Howland	54194	M	1929
Barbetta	36690	D	1923
Barclay	33827	D	1922
Benitia	21161	D	1916
Benjamin F.	83559	D	1940
Benjamin O.	59828	D	1931
Benjamin P.	54505	D	1929
Bertha	23047	D	1917
Bertha	41602	M	1925
Bertha	38071	I	1924
Bessie B.	43192	D	1925
Bessie M.	16298	M	1913
Betty	36751	M	1923
Blanche Dewey	36567	D	1923
Boys Jenkin Chambre	17084	D	1914
Bridget Agnes	15216	D	1913
Bridget Dyson	85077	D	1940
Bridget L.	68160	D	1934
Bridget Mary	85077	D	1940
Bryon K.	84310	D	1940
Burtis W.	25147	M	1918
Butler	1369	D	1906
Byron O.	69400	M	1935
Calvin M.	45599	D	1926
Caroline L.	88330	D	1941
Carrie E. Fabian	23534	D	1917

NAME	NUMBER	TYPE	YEAR	NAME	NUMBER	TYPE	YEAR	NAME	NUMBER	TYPE	YEAR
Carrie E. L.	23474	D	1917	Daniel J.	7960	D	1909	Ellen Jane	57000	D	1930
Carrie Lester	24632	D	1918	David Albert	57214	D	1930	Ellen Jane	57243	M	1930
Carrie M.	60110	D	1931	David H.	62511	D	1932	Emery Tritle	56073	D	1930
Catherine	6924	D	1908	David J.	7620	D	1909	Emily	25645	M	1918
Catherine	26938	M	1919	Della	48811	D	1927	Emily I.	73308	D	1936
Catherine	55684	D	1930	Donald L.	85048	M	1940	Emma	37998	D	1923
Catherine	63653	D	1933	Donzella Jewell	89826	D	1942	Emma	59007	D	1931
Catherine	65582	M	1933	Doreen Yale	65381	M	1933	Emma A.	2140	D	1906
Catherine	63748	D	1933	Dorothy	39827	I	1924	Emma A.	35107	D	1922
Catherine E.	41875	D	1925	Douglas B.	58725	D	1931	Emma Ann	84934	D	1940
Catherine E.	41875	D	1925	Driesbach	2113	D	1906	Emma Louise	43071	D	1925
Cecil E.	65916	D	1933	Dunois E.	66061	D	1934	Emma M.	58888	D	1931
Celia A.	6469	D	1908	E. J.	47902	D	1927	Emma M. L.	3047	D	1907
Charles	11725	D	1911	E. R.	49122	D	1928	Emmet	72580	D	1936
Charles	86714	D	1941	Eben J.	60077	D	1931	Enos	72308	D	1936
Charles	45615	D	1926	Edith A.	78928	D	1938	Estella	31692	D	1921
Charles A.	61227	D	1932	Edith H.	27060	D	1919	Estelle Meyer	75500	D	1937
Charles A., Jr.	19152	D	1915	Edith H.	34380	D	1922	Esther	47823	D	1927
Charles Arthur	17663	D	1914	Edith Hazel	86591	D	1941	Esther L.	89223	D	1942
Charles D.	40739	D	1925	Edith M.	76040	D	1937	Eugene	1907	M	1906
Charles E.	46004	D	1926	Edith M.	85526	D	1940	Eva M.	87630	D	1941
Charles E.	58456	D	1931	Edith Mary	85735	D	1940	Evangeline C.	84531	D	1940
Charles H.	45695	D	1926	Edmund Oliver	74427	M	1937	Evangeline Tadd	69920	I	1935
Charles I.	43791	D	1926	Edward	6127	D	1908	Evelyn Hale	4137	M	1907
Charles Joseph	18663	D	1915	Edward Lawrence	68493	D	1934	Evelyn Smith	12520	M	1911
Charles Raymond	8925	M	1909	Edward Luke	85792	D	1940	Fannie	64135	I	1933
Charlotte Anne	83419	D	1940	Edward M.	27439	D	1919	Fannie Hyman	64832	D	1933
Charlotte Louise	52121	D	1929	Edward Nicholas	63094	D	1932	Felix T., Jr.	82825	M	1939
Chas.	76504	D	1937	Edwin Bruce	49525	D	1928	Florence	26938	M	1919
Chas. M.	39219	D	1924	Edwin T.	12986	D	1912	Florence A.	3768	M	1907
Chester C.	14878	M	1913	Edwin Victor	21255	D	1916	Florence Christina	66199	M	1934
Chester S.	13809	I	1912	Eleanor	48586	D	1927	Florence Edith	40600	M	1924
Chester S.	14475	D	1912	Elina	13938	M	1912	Frances Anna	58944	D	1931
Christian W.	38981	D	1924	Eline Maria	15724	M	1913	Francis	54127	I	1929
Christine	45841	D	1926	Eline Maria	28998	D	1920	Francis	54153	D	1929
Clara E.	75485	D	1937	Eliza	9045	D	1910	Francis Earl	81573	D	1939
Clarence George	34424	I	1922	Eliza A.	45802	D	1926	Frank	52848	D	1929
Clarence M.	41150	D	1925	Eliza Kezia	27944	D	1919	Frank	80757	D	1939
Claudia	54194	M	1929	Eliza M.	681	D	1906	Frank	80881	D	1939
Clinton M.	84982	D	1940	Elizabeth	8738	D	1909	Frank	89334	D	1942
Clyde E.	60799	I	1932	Elizabeth	10110	I	1910	Frank	48093	D	1927
Constance Grace	66199	M	1934	Elizabeth	10265	D	1910	Frank A.	61417	D	1932
Cookman H.	84734	D	1940	Elizabeth E.	2264	D	1906	Frank A.	77619	D	1938
Cora B.	32826	D	1921	Elizabeth E.	55079	D	1930	Frank Edward	88766	D	1941
Cora B.	50961	D	1928	Elizabeth Jane	2649	D	1907	Frank Ellison	76550	D	1937
Cora Butterworth	50786	M	1928	Ella A.	58891	I	1931	Frank F.	52703	D	1929
Cornelia A.	77920	I	1938	Ella A.	77667	D	1938	Frank H.	53936	D	1929
Cornelia J.	357	D	1906	Ella Augusta	36673	D	1923	Frank J.	21110	D	1916
Daniel	15811	D	1913	Ellen Brooke	77117	D	1937	Frank M.	88137	I	1941

NAME	NUMBER	TYPE	YEAR	NAME	NUMBER	TYPE	YEAR	NAME	NUMBER	TYPE	YEAR
Frank R.	69158	D	1935	Harriett J.	49307	D	1928	Isabel M.	37369	D	1923
Frank W.	21329	D	1916	Harry	13938	M	1912	Isabella	48372	D	1927
Frank, Mrs.	83828	D	1940	Harry	86613	D	1941	Isabelle	67729	D	1934
Fred Freeman, Mrs.	67676	I	1934	Harry	83208	M	1940	Isadora N.	27786	D	1919
Frederica	36932	D	1923	Harry D.	49239	D	1928	Isidore J.	30350	D	1920
Frederick	15674	D	1913	Harry G.	17540	D	1914	J. D.	2480	I	1906
Frederick	41602	M	1925	Harry G.	33458	D	1922	J. D.	87291	D	1941
Frederick	81561	D	1939	Harry L.	33230	D	1922	J. G.	49635	I	1928
Frederick D.	13181	D	1912	Harry W.	23985	D	1918	Jack	50980	D	1928
Frederick H. B.	42129	D	1925	Hattie Augusta	66829	D	1934	Jack R.	59869	D	1931
Frieda J.	14887	D	1913	Helen Atherton	82892	D	1939	Jackie Michael	84231	M	1940
G. W., Mrs.	16239	D	1913	Helen Charlotte	31933	M	1921	Jacob R.	59869	D	1931
Genella	66073	D	1934	Helen R.	57553	I	1930	James	7798	D	1909
Genevieve Edith	72779	D	1936	Helen R.	66897	I	1934	James	19672	D	1915
George	24319	D	1918	Henrietta L.	36691	D	1923	James	22454	D	1917
George	37352	D	1923	Henry	3940	D	1907	James	37387	I	1923
George A.	23174	D	1917	Henry	24412	D	1918	James	37469	D	1923
George A.	24959	M	1918	Henry	25645	M	1918	James	37926	D	1923
George Dent	59751	D	1931	Henry	28899	D	1920	James	41694	D	1925
George F.	4184	D	1907	Henry A.	38855	D	1924	James A.	10429	D	1910
George Henry	49485	D	1928	Henry Clay	46851	D	1927	James A.	26969	D	1919
George Henry	79852	D	1938	Henry E.	73111	D	1936	James A.	85656	D	1940
George J.	6164	D	1908	Henry Marcius	19850	D	1915	James Albert	65299	D	1933
George J.	44611	D	1926	Henry Mortimer	67643	D	1934	James C.	7600	D	1909
George John Rogers	26708	D	1919	Henry P.	17347	D	1914	James D.	49327	D	1928
George Law	11482	D	1911	Henry R.	4165	D	1907	James E.	23900	D	1918
George Lee	68838	D	1935	Herbert C.	60741	D	1932	James F.	50969	D	1928
George Norbert	8925	M	1909	Herbert McKenzie	24647	M	1918	James Francis	82888	D	1939
George S.	1759	D	1906	Herbert Ronald	82393	D	1939	James H.	68508	D	1934
George S.	13735	D	1912	Herman	9653	D	1910	James Harry	78482	D	1938
George Waterman	50005	D	1928	Heyman	72220	D	1936	James Henry	72359	D	1936
Geraldine	84231	M	1940	Hilda E.	65093	D	1933	James J.	18893	D	1915
Gerrit	47374	D	1927	Hiram C.	57034	D	1930	James J., Mrs.	64260	D	1933
Gertrude	25146	D	1918	Hjoe	45607	D	1926	James Joseph	36119	D	1923
Gertrude E.	66513	D	1934	Holland	12994	D	1912	James L.	62588	I	1932
Gladys L.	76340	D	1937	Homer L.	70184	D	1935	James W.	78728	D	1938
Glenn Edward	14986	M	1913	Horace J.	87044	M	1941	Jane	65642	D	1933
Grace Z.	70289	D	1935	Horace J.	87073	D	1941	Jane H.	16250	D	1913
Grant C.	60638	D	1932	Howard A.	63132	D	1932	Jane Leach	53614	D	1929
Gregor John	34636	D	1922	Howard William	54956	M	1930	Janette Lillian	31933	M	1921
Gussie	604	M	1906	Howland	54194	M	1929	Jennie	1621	D	1906
H. A.	644	D	1906	Hugh A.	25607	D	1918	Jennie	41921	D	1925
H. Stephenson	63301	D	1933	Ida F.	58837	D	1931	Jennie	41921	D	1925
Hamilton	9349	D	1910	Ida J.	8875	I	1909	Jennie	55854	D	1930
Hannah M.	62517	D	1932	Ida K.	64260	D	1933	Jennie	81378	D	1939
Hans	88868	D	1942	Ida M.	18191	D	1914	Jennie S.	7701	D	1909
Harold E.	27194	I	1919	Ida Mae	64260	D	1933	Jens	47344	D	1927
Harold Everett	47602	M	1927	Ira Perry	45177	D	1926	Jessie	24189	D	1918
Harriet Jane	8194	D	1909	Irving C.	1902	D	1906	Jessie	24297	D	1918

NAME	NUMBER	TYPE	YEAR	NAME	NUMBER	TYPE	YEAR	NAME	NUMBER	TYPE	YEAR
Jessie	29641	D	1920	Julia A.	62067	D	1932	Manley Norman	66199	M	1934
Jessie	47701	D	1927	Julia M.	3474	M	1907	Maregaret	89803	I	1942
Jessie	64944	D	1933	Julia Peabody	3063	D	1907	Margaret	1907	M	1906
Jessie	82392	D	1939	Julia Rodolph	88871	D	1942	Margaret	9404	D	1910
Jessie M.	59299	D	1931	Julia Weber	56258	D	1930	Margaret	16748	D	1914
Joe	45607	D	1926	Julie	20212	D	1916	Margaret	18213	D	1914
John	1907	M	1906	Julie	37998	D	1923	Margaret	26779	D	1919
John	32452	D	1921	Julius Paul, Mrs.	78017	D	1938	Margaret	50025	D	1928
John	34317	D	1922	Kate	86988	D	1941	Margaret	77744	D	1938
John	58436	D	1931	Kate Baillie	63505	D	1933	Margaret	77914	D	1938
John A.	28349	M	1919	Kate Dorsey	62910	D	1932	Margaret	39079	D	1924
John Alfred	32928	I	1921	Katherine	11506	D	1911	Margaret A.	7150	D	1909
John C.	54113	M	1929	Katherine	29021	D	1920	Margaret A.	63709	D	1933
John C.	65500	I	1933	Katherine	76782	D	1937	Margaret Allen	71757	D	1936
John C.	75037	D	1937	Katherine Helena	85279	D	1940	Margaret E.	44682	D	1926
John Clinton	47602	M	1927	Kathleen	80835	M	1939	Margaret Spaulding	26902	D	1919
John Edward	66149	D	1934	Kathryn	42670	D	1925	Margaret T.	52063	D	1929
John F.	26606	D	1919	Kathryn E.	2309	M	1906	Marguerite	25645	M	1918
John Henley	4701	D	1907	Katie M.	82153	D	1939	Maria A.	44253	D	1926
John Irvine	76465	D	1937	Kenneth J.	55243	M	1930	Maria L.	936	D	1906
John J.	4380	D	1907	Larz A.	70819	I	1935	Maria Louise	155	D	1906
John J.	9533	D	1910	Lawrence Hall	82825	M	1939	Marie	21457	D	1916
John J.	15482	D	1913	Lawrence J.	30941	D	1921	Marie	26938	M	1919
John Jacob	76842	D	1937	Leonard A.	43877	D	1926	Marie	54598	D	1929
John Joseph	65944	D	1933	Levi	56586	D	1930	Marie A.	88579	D	1941
John Joseph	79357	D	1938	Lewis, Mrs.	11802	D	1911	Marilyn Jean	53443	D	1929
John Lloyd	3474	M	1907	Lillian S.	81998	D	1939	Marjorie E.	25147	M	1918
John M.	36369	D	1923	Lillian T.	79541	D	1938	Martha	83828	D	1940
John P.	81981	D	1939	Lorraine	15241	M	1913	Martha Jane	36379	D	1923
John S.	9974	D	1910	Lottie	15108	D	1913	Martha L.	82616	D	1939
John S.	46258	D	1927	Lottie I.	59389	D	1931	Martha Marie	61228	M	1932
John W.	7353	D	1909	Louis	13273	D	1912	Martin	79458	D	1938
John W.	60899	D	1932	Louis	37795	D	1923	Martin Jackson	47717	M	1927
John W.	78512	D	1938	Louis	43094	I	1925	Mary	3178	D	1907
Jordan	83208	M	1940	Louis A.	3508	D	1907	Mary	3584	D	1907
Joseph	13667	D	1912	Louis C.	79726	D	1938	Mary	11198	D	1911
Joseph	78695	D	1938	Louis M.	83969	D	1940	Mary	19264	D	1915
Joseph	84677	D	1940	Louis Wardlaw, Jr.	35633	M	1922	Mary	24342	D	1918
Joseph C.	7302	D	1909	Louisa C.	38461	I	1924	Mary	37558	D	1923
Joseph L.	18578	M	1915	Louise C.	40485	D	1924	Mary	46259	D	1927
Joseph Malachi	76271	D	1937	Louise E.	49209	M	1928	Mary	72667	D	1936
Joseph P.	2309	M	1906	Louise E.	55623	D	1930	Mary	82950	D	1939
Joseph R.	57181	I	1930	Lucetta H.	22000	I	1916	Mary A.	19805	D	1915
Joseph S.	77551	I	1938	Lucile Morris	35624	D	1922	Mary A.	25098	D	1918
Josephine	2828	D	1907	Luella M. H.	44207	I	1926	Mary A.	88446	D	1941
Josephine	40972	D	1925	Lura R.	7827	D	1909	Mary C.	3617	D	1907
Josephine A. H.	66288	D	1934	Mabel	1907	M	1906	Mary C.	24295	I	1918
Josephine Augusta	66288	D	1934	Madison	66568	D	1934	Mary Curryer	24887	D	1918
Josephine H.	73386	D	1936	Maisie Eleanore	88657	D	1941	Mary E.	158	D	1906

Key: D = death; M = minor; I = incompetent

NAME	NUMBER	TYPE	YEAR	NAME	NUMBER	TYPE	YEAR	NAME	NUMBER	TYPE	YEAR
Mary E.	11922	D	1911	Nora	61969	D	1932	Russell Burdette	57156	I	1930
Mary E.	16239	D	1913	Normal William	13763	D	1912	Russell E.	49208	M	1928
Mary E.	24076	D	1918	Norton P	14878	M	1913	Ruth	76200	I	1937
Mary E.	25257	D	1918	Ole	51180	D	1928	Ruth Elizabeth	9253	M	1910
Mary F.	46019	D	1926	Olive	48709	D	1927	Sadie Ann	47674	D	1927
Mary Fairchild	79614	D	1938	Oliver	35998	D	1923	Sallie J.	11651	D	1911
Mary Frances	88494	D	1941	Oliver B.	25895	D	1918	Samuel	31009	D	1921
Mary Guinness	58294	D	1931	Oscar T.	51573	D	1928	Samuel Harris	58286	D	1931
Mary H.	65542	D	1933	Owen Edward	36529	D	1923	Samuel Harrison	6678	D	1908
Mary J.	20131	D	1915	Patricia Wymore	46731	M	1927	Samuel W.	55595	D	1930
Mary Jane	11459	D	1911	Patrick	51189	D	1928	Sara Adeline	47717	M	1927
Mary Jane	38402	D	1924	Paul H.	81860	I	1939	Sara Barker	78017	D	1938
Mary L.	56208	D	1930	Paul R.	86380	D	1941	Sarah	5503	D	1908
Mary Louise	66403	D	1934	Pauline	44650	M	1926	Sarah	27646	D	1919
Mary Lucinda	48779	D	1927	Pearl	88430	D	1941	Sarah J.	11651	D	1911
Mary P.	79860	D	1938	Percy L.	69282	D	1935	Sarah P.	36224	D	1923
Mary Pierce	7971	D	1909	Percy W.	14331	M	1912	Schuyler C.	15184	D	1913
Mary T.	53008	D	1929	Perina R.	65750	D	1933	Seth	57170	I	1930
Matilda	11152	D	1911	Peter	10954	D	1910	Shella	25645	M	1918
Matilda L.	24177	D	1918	Peter	86111	D	1941	Sidney H.	74255	D	1936
Matilda R.	78254	D	1938	Peter A.	63004	D	1932	Sidney Henry	16612	D	1914
Matthew Francis	26882	D	1919	Peter J.	28695	D	1920	Sidney Herbert	89074	D	1942
Mattie Estelle	53644	D	1929	Peter J.	68161	D	1934	Sidney Mason	4237	D	1907
Mattie Estelle	53880	D	1929	Peter J.	89806	D	1942	Sidney V.	42614	D	1925
Maud	53980	D	1929	Philip	81422	D	1939	Sidney V., Jr.	50786	M	1928
Maud J.	64209	D	1933	Phillippa	11802	D	1911	Soren B.	14943	D	1913
Maud M.	67676	I	1934	Pit	45521	D	1926	Stanley Kenneth	84174	M	1940
May	83885	D	1940	Rachael	53076	D	1929	Stella K.	39235	D	1924
May Irene	40765	D	1925	Randolph Wilson	2133	M	1906	Stephen Lawrence	27939	D	1919
May W.	67945	D	1934	Raymond	3474	M	1907	Stuart F.	83805	D	1940
Michael	20205	D	1916	Reba Athey	64572	M	1933	Teresa	11437	D	1911
Michael	36627	D	1923	Reginald Knight	75462	D	1937	Terrance	6317	D	1908
Michael	82920	D	1939	Reinholdt	49355	D	1928	Theodore H.	81661	D	1939
Michael L.	32988	D	1921	Richard Jerome	35648	D	1923	Thirza	7794	D	1909
Michael William	66440	D	1934	Rita M.	66380	M	1934	Thomas	21370	D	1916
Mildred	21896	M	1916	Robert	2507	D	1906	Thomas	33594	D	1922
Mildred L.	16298	M	1913	Robert E.	59403	D	1931	Thomas	33834	D	1922
Morrison Struart	46731	M	1927	Robert Edgar	71451	D	1936	Thomas A.	63303	D	1933
Murray	57070	D	1930	Robert Menzo	58705	I	1931	Thomas A.	66961	D	1934
Nathan Sutton	82825	M	1939	Robert Neil	84483	D	1940	Thomas B.	68539	D	1934
Nellie	54506	D	1929	Robert P.	39170	D	1924	Thomas Chester	55511	D	1930
Nellie E.	59220	D	1931	Robert W.	33591	D	1922	Thomas D.	9281	D	1910
Nellie E.	86881	I	1941	Roberta Genevieve	2133	M	1906	Thomas F.	76210	D	1937
Nellie Elizabeth	84958	D	1940	Rose	20132	D	1915	Thomas G.	69098	D	1935
Nels Elmer	66142	D	1934	Rose	49313	D	1928	Thomas H.	21109	D	1916
Nelson Chrissie	73478	M	1936	Rose C.	17470	D	1914	Thomas J.	70651	D	1935
Nicholas	4827	D	1907	Rosie F.	16557	D	1914	Thomas John	14871	D	1913
Nicholas F.	67788	D	1934	Ross W.	31890	D	1921	Thomas Lewis	29189	D	1920
Nicholas, Mrs.	82153	D	1939	Ruby	13938	M	1912	Thomas N.	9280	D	1910

Key: D = death; M = minor; I = incompetent

NAME	NUMBER	TYPE	YEAR	NAME	NUMBER	TYPE	YEAR	NAME	NUMBER	TYPE	YEAR
Thomas W.	49207	M	1928	SMITHA				SMYTHE			
Thomas Walter	42568	I	1925	Charles H.	65116	D	1933	Herman	87091	D	1941
Thomas Walter	45425	D	1926	SMITHER				Mary S.	18789	D	1915
Vinnie B.	84827	D	1940	Joseph	5832	D	1908	Thomas H.	9938	D	1910
Virginia A.	14524	D	1912	Lawrence H.	42154	I	1925	William M.	67016	D	1934
Virginia Evans	23533	D	1917	SMITHSON				SNAIDER			
W. A. C.	6866	D	1908	David E.	78326	D	1938	Mary B.	88080	D	1941
Walter Edward	61557	D	1932	James	55323	D	1930	SNAITH			
Walter Henry	33657	M	1922	SMITT				Rose A.	82335	D	1939
Walter Howard	47602	M	1927	Augusta W.	44133	I	1926	SNALE			
Walter V.	30563	D	1920	Frederick E.	47977	D	1927	William	16477	D	1913
Wellington Treat	73290	D	1936	SMITTON				SNAPP			
Wilhelm	51978	D	1929	Frederic Harrison	57623	D	1931	Frank P.	17171	D	1914
Wilhelmina A.	34340	D	1922	SMOLENSKY				SNEAD			
William	8711	D	1909	Elsie	37574	M	1923	Francis A. V.	20353	D	1916
William	19806	I	1915	Theodore	37574	M	1923	Michael	20352	D	1916
William	30293	D	1920	SMOLJAN				SNEDAKER			
William	73248	D	1936	August	25562	D	1918	Lena M.	79088	D	1938
William A.	39205	D	1924	Maria	36620	D	1923	William H.	69588	D	1935
William Aloysius	65449	D	1933	SMULCKY				SNEDDON			
William Barclay	33827	D	1922	Max	39349	D	1924	Charles	19001	I	1915
William C.	29469	D	1920	SMULSKY				SNEE			
William C.	85048	M	1940	Max	39349	D	1924	Catherine	81170	D	1939
William Carlton	28573	D	1920	SMYLEY				Michael	32140	D	1921
William E.	57453	D	1930	Kate S.	75442	D	1937	SNEERINGER			
William E.	62425	D	1932	SMYRLIS				William F.	16059	D	1913
William Edward	83341	D	1940	Athanasios	15356	D	1913	SNEIDER			
William F.	31916	D	1921	SMYTH				Anna E.	11369	D	1911
William H.	3499	D	1907	Alice A.	1796	D	1906	Emma	78625	D	1938
William H.	18755	D	1915	Bridget	30013	D	1920	George C.	24250	D	1918
William H.	40028	I	1924	Edna Pluma	26604	D	1919	SNELL			
William H.	52712	D	1929	Elizabeth	26186	D	1919	Clara May	78150	I	1938
William H.	60915	D	1932	Elizabeth Arabella	74222	D	1936	Clarence Richard	78151	M	1938
William H.	61361	I	1932	George P.	7913	D	1909	Edward L.	55038	D	1930
William H.	68855	D	1935	Horace	26182	D	1919	Edwin Herbert	69307	D	1935
William J.	17203	D	1914	John	34317	D	1922	John Arthur	59411	D	1931
William J.	55607	D	1930	Joseph S.	29746	D	1920	SNELLGROVE			
William J. L.	63453	M	1933	Margaret J.	27696	D	1919	Charles Royal, Sr.	77870	D	1938
William Jacob	65155	D	1933	Mary A.	14052	D	1912	SNELLMAN			
William James	49623	D	1928	Mary G.	36235	D	1923	Eelo	42383	D	1925
William P.	82321	D	1939	Mary H.	18389	D	1915	SNIDER			
William Preston	43963	D	1926	Maysie	36235	D	1923	Charles E.	77124	D	1937
William Richard	67069	D	1934	Michael	18336	D	1914	John C.	52381	I	1929
Willma T.	57596	D	1931	Thomas H.	9938	D	1910	SNIPES			
Wilson Teetors	27545	D	1919	Thomas J.	15709	I	1913	James E.	18854	D	1915
Winfield R.	64726	I	1933	Thomas J.	27124	D	1919				
Wm. A., Mrs.	66829	D	1934	William J.	10219	D	1910				
Wm. Henry	83568	I	1940								

NAME	NUMBER	TYPE	YEAR
SNODGRASS			
Beatrice Ruth	27635	D	1919
SNOEK			
Adelheid	15328	I	1913
Samuel	69337	D	1935
Simon Israel	69337	D	1935
SNOLK			
Adelheid	15328	I	1913
SNOOK			
Caroline A.	72211	D	1936
Charles W.	3809	D	1907
Frederick W.	74493	D	1937
George A.	3659	D	1907
Kara R.	65553	D	1933
Kathryn Haderie	60855	D	1932
Samuel	69337	D	1935
Simon Israel	69337	D	1935
William Sayer	13617	D	1912
SNOW			
Asa C.	52175	D	1929
Charles L.	33308	I	1922
Emanuel	71097	D	1935
Hedley John	75370	I	1937
Jane Rae	39541	M	1924
Parker Bearse	52057	M	1929
Robert	74591	D	1937
Sam	51561	D	1928
Sarah	35556	D	1922
Theresa J.	74577	D	1937
SNOWBALL			
Alexander Leon	10763	D	1910
Leon	10763	D	1910
SNOWDEN			
George A.	16496	D	1913
James H.	19116	D	1915
SNOWGRASS			
Florence Ellis	64941	I	1933
Jennie M.	429	D	1906
Jennie M.	2541	I	1906
John Gray	25445	D	1918
Perlie Louise	8243	M	1909
Sarah Louise	10248	D	1910
SNOWMAN			
Oscar	76331	D	1937
SNYDER			
Alice M.	53740	D	1929
Anna Beachy	71552	D	1936

NAME	NUMBER	TYPE	YEAR
Catherine A.	43512	D	1926
Clara	52034	D	1929
Frank	25412	D	1918
George	18641	D	1915
Harry S.	69943	D	1935
Harry, Jr.	71467	M	1936
Harvey G.	40435	D	1924
Joe H.	46255	D	1927
Joseph	46255	D	1927
Laura	28105	D	1919
Louis W.	18424	D	1915
Louise J.	35968	D	1923
Martin	2931	D	1907
Mathias B.	22449	D	1917
Peter	88492	D	1941
Thomas	79571	I	1938
Thomas L.	54138	D	1929
William H.	9460	D	1910
William M	41785	I	1925
William M	41785	I	1925
William Martinez	77339	D	1937
SO			
Chan	40285	M	1924
SOARES			
John B.	63048	D	1932
Thereza J.	70176	D	1935
SOBBE			
John M.	77989	D	1938
SOBEK			
Olive Merle	31402	M	1921
SOBEL			
Joseph Leonard	56712	M	1930
Nathan	54637	D	1930
Pearl	56712	M	1930
SOBERANES			
Constantino	82159	D	1939
SOBEY			
Esther	44734	D	1926
Frank John	61301	I	1932
Fred	69625	D	1935
SOBIESKI			
Effie	2022	D	1906
SOBOSLAY			
Elisa	50689	D	1928
Elizabeth	62198	D	1932
Julius	55593	D	1930

NAME	NUMBER	TYPE	YEAR
SOBRIO			
John A.	640	D	1906
SOCIC			
Louis A.	153	D	1906
SOCKOLOV			
Rose	38136	D	1924
SODEN			
Henry	15468	D	1913
SODER			
Emanuel	35130	D	1922
SODERBERG			
Alfred E.	34574	M	1922
Carrie	35800	D	1923
Edna	34573	D	1922
Emil W.	34574	M	1922
Oscar	53009	D	1929
Victor	36718	D	1923
SODERGREN			
Laura	36454	D	1923
SODERLIND			
Peter	10862	D	1910
SODERLUND			
Edwin	49279	D	1928
John Edwin	49279	D	1928
Olof Svenssen	31559	D	1921
SODHUNTER			
Christina Maria	44052	D	1926
SODINI			
Paul	39421	D	1924
SOEFER			
Belle	47215	M	1927
Herman	47215	M	1927
Jennie	47215	M	1927
Rebecca	47216	I	1927
SOEHLMANN			
Henry	62346	D	1932
SOENKE			
William Claud	167	D	1906
SOETJE			
George	35781	D	1923
Henry	13104	D	1912
SOFFAS			
Nicolaos	17830	D	1914
SOFKA			
Caroline	52920	D	1929

NAME	NUMBER	TYPE	YEAR	NAME	NUMBER	TYPE	YEAR	NAME	NUMBER	TYPE	YEAR
SOGNARO				Natale	53291	D	1929	**SOLIN**			
Vincenzo	21481	D	1916	P. Rosa	41108	D	1925	Frank B.	87868	D	1941
SOHER				Pietro	34774	D	1922	**SOLINSKY**			
Gus A.	75887	D	1937	Rose	17269	D	1914	Frank J.	61940	D	1932
SOHL				Rose	41108	D	1925	William H.	45623	I	1926
Axel L.	4633	D	1907	Salvatore	29565	I	1920	**SOLIS**			
William N.	48871	D	1928	Stefano	2817	D	1907	Lorenzo	52707	I	1929
SOHLKE				Stefano	61855	D	1932	**SOLLMAN**			
Anna	32051	D	1921	**SOLBERG**				Anna P.	32296	D	1921
Franziska	24315	D	1918	Jenny	88060	I	1941	**SOLMINA**			
G. B.	49397	D	1928	**SOLD**				John	19160	D	1915
Gustave	49397	D	1928	Ida Minna	2774	M	1907	**SOLMINO**			
SOHRIAKOFF				Marie Phillipina	3329	D	1907	John	19160	D	1915
Alex	89404	D	1942	Marie Phillipina	3329	D	1907	**SOLMUS**			
SOKOLOFF				Max Gustave	2774	M	1907	Mary	79931	I	1938
Nadia	84186	I	1940	William	44244	D	1926	**SOLOMAN**			
SOLA				**SOLDANELS**				Rose	89315	D	1942
Torger	58443	D	1931	John	44527	D	1926	Seare H.	12165	M	1911
SOLACHE				**SOLDANO**				Sidney L.	12165	M	1911
Frederick	68003	D	1934	Accusio	47199	D	1927	**SOLOMON**			
SOLAGHIAN				**SOLDATI**				Aaron	13281	D	1912
Thomas	84510	D	1940	Giuseppe	47331	D	1927	Adolph	8268	D	1909
SOLARI				**SOLDATOFF**				Augusta	22253	D	1917
Alberto	14814	D	1913	Basily George	58260	D	1931	Baruch	22130	D	1917
Angela	58646	D	1931	Vasily George	58260	D	1931	H. I.	75825	D	1937
Angelina	2258	D	1906	**SOLDIVANI**				Isaac R.	46744	I	1927
Annie	36571	I	1923	Penna	41415	M	1925	Isadore Isaac R.	46744	I	1927
Annie	39451	D	1924	Perina	41415	M	1925	Israel	3183	D	1907
Bittorio	21876	D	1916	**SOLDT**				Jane	76308	D	1937
Camille M.	23488	D	1917	William	44244	D	1926	Jennie	76308	D	1937
Carlo	15571	D	1913	**SOLE**				John F.	74406	D	1937
Charles	15571	D	1913	Femme	46016	I	1926	Leah	46451	D	1927
Domenico	47174	D	1927	Juan	41406	D	1925	Lenore Forgan	87972	D	1941
Elisa	30083	D	1920	**SOLEMINA**				Leo	52880	D	1929
Emilio	89585	D	1942	John	19160	D	1915	Louis Albert	22131	M	1917
G. B.	3097	D	1907	**SOLEN**				Mary	29340	D	1920
Giusepina	66030	D	1934	Ellen	22284	D	1917	Max	85832	D	1940
Giusippe Vittorio	21876	D	1916	**SOLER**				Morris	26116	D	1919
Guilia	79809	D	1938	Maria	68377	D	1934	Naomi V.	57340	D	1930
Ida B.	26091	D	1919	**SOLESKI**				Raymond Henry	70230	I	1935
Joseph	21876	D	1916	Jenny	41728	D	1925	Rose	16365	D	1913
Joseph	35204	D	1922	Jenny	41728	D	1925	Rose	27988	I	1919
Joseph L.	60963	D	1932	Johanna	41728	D	1925	Rose	89315	D	1942
Louis	36572	M	1923	Johanna	41728	D	1925	Samuel	11672	D	1911
Louis	50244	D	1928	**SOLIMANO**				Samuel	69459	D	1935
Luigi	25509	D	1918	Caterina Giusepina	37759	M	1923	Sarah	49917	D	1928
Luigi	45725	D	1926					Savel	54137	D	1929

Key: *D = death; M = minor; I = incompetent*

NAME	NUMBER	TYPE	YEAR	NAME	NUMBER	TYPE	YEAR	NAME	NUMBER	TYPE	YEAR
Selena Belle	1374	D	1906	Walter William	25689	M	1918	SONDEREGGER			
Sophie L.	35488	D	1922	SOMMARIVA				Gottlieb	17668	D	1914
Sophy	62526	D	1932	Carlo	74508	D	1937	SONDERUP			
Victor	57020	D	1930	SOMMER				Joachim B.	27932	I	1919
SOLORZANO				Arthur Henry	13902	M	1912	Joachim B.	28245	D	1919
Federico	77022	D	1937	C.	26419	D	1919	Maria	56917	D	1930
SOLOVIEFF				Flora	52001	D	1929	SONDHEIM			
Aaron M.	83997	D	1940	Katherine	74719	M	1937	Eugene, Mrs.	48320	D	1927
SOLOVINE				Marie	30924	D	1921	Gretta B.	48320	D	1927
Milo	40620	D	1924	Max	24275	D	1918	Ida	32057	D	1921
Saul	40649	M	1924	Max	72750	D	1936	Nathan M.	32733	I	1921
SOLOZANO				Robert	39775	D	1924	SONDHEIMER			
Carlos	72378	D	1936	Rose	83797	D	1940	Henrietta Weil	57638	D	1931
SOLTJE				Sigmund	53168	D	1929	Moses	30217	D	1920
George	35781	D	1923	SOMMERLAD				Sol	64921	D	1933
SOLUAGO				Sophia	574	D	1906	SONGEY			
Edward D.	82476	D	1939	SOMMERS				William	30826	I	1920
SOLUM				Alexander	26249	D	1919	William	32103	D	1921
Magnus	86688	D	1941	John F.	34940	D	1922	SONNE			
SOLVIN				Nellie B.	61407	D	1932	Charles F.	15559	D	1913
Charles G.	58946	D	1931	Samuel	71767	D	1936	Frederick	35492	M	1922
Emil R.	44249	D	1926	SOMMERVIILLE				Herman Theodor	69671	D	1935
SOMARUGA				Hugh	70132	D	1935	John H.	68988	D	1935
Mary	85881	D	1940	SOMMO				SONNEBORN			
SOMARUGO				Ernesto	85560	D	1940	Evelyn	37856	M	1923
Mary	85881	D	1940	SOMMOR				Jewell	37856	M	1923
SOMDAHL				Katherine	74719	M	1937	Jewell	43871	D	1926
Peter	80371	M	1939	SOMMORUGA				SONNENBERG			
SOMEKH				Mary	85881	D	1940	Bertha A.	89983	D	1942
Eddie Maurice	58581	D	1931	SOMORUGO				Louis B.	11328	D	1911
SOMERS				Mary	85881	D	1940	SONNENSCHEIN			
Burbank Hooper	47066	D	1927	SOMTUM				Elsa	61952	D	1932
Eliza F.	24709	D	1918	Johane C.	52817	D	1929	Irwin Sanford	58713	M	1931
Ellen H.	45405	D	1926	SON				Samuel	65895	D	1933
Harvey C.	2926	D	1907	Adolph A.	13961	D	1912	SONNENTAG			
James R.	38600	I	1924	Albert A.	2595	D	1907	Edward	60376	I	1931
James R.	68702	I	1935	SONAHEIM				SONNERICHEIN			
James R.	74788	D	1937	Eugene	53599	D	1929	Jacob	60136	D	1931
John	78600	D	1938	SONBURG				SONNICHSEN			
Kate B.	18971	D	1915	A. F.	18086	D	1914	James N.	11395	D	1911
William J.	12278	D	1911	SONDAY				SONNINGSON			
SOMERVILLE				Catherina	17964	D	1914	Sonke	13476	D	1912
Alfred Henry	25689	M	1918	Miro	58634	D	1931	SONNTAG			
Isabella	87892	D	1941	Miro	58970	D	1931	Charles Pringle	34729	D	1922
Julia Faith	25689	M	1918	Pera	50218	D	1928	Charlotte	50009	D	1928
Mary Jane Campbell	57237	D	1930					Elizabeth P.	18564	D	1915
Polly Dirks	25419	D	1918					Ella B.	74637	D	1937

NAME	NUMBER	TYPE	YEAR	NAME	NUMBER	TYPE	YEAR	NAME	NUMBER	TYPE	YEAR
Henry P.	6556	D	1908	Elizabeth	77565	D	1938	**SORENZON**			
Isabella Reis	19986	D	1915	Luigia Oneto	81922	D	1939	Jens	64475	I	1933
Julian	20885	D	1916	Maria	69787	D	1935	**SORG**			
Lincoln	53310	D	1929	**SORBE**				Dorothea	17254	D	1914
Winthrop Dent	29066	M	1920	Elsie	27253	D	1919	**SORGENFREY**			
SONTUM				**SORBER**				Ellen L.	56051	I	1930
Johane C.	52817	D	1929	Julia Leahy	51528	D	1928	**SORGENFRLY**			
SOO				**SORBI**				Florence C.	50870	D	1928
Gee Kee	79701	D	1938	Dusolina	73952	D	1936	**SORGENSALY**			
Hoo Mon Po	68422	D	1934	**SORBIER**				Florence C.	50870	D	1928
Hoo Shee	81428	I	1939	Louise A.	54450	D	1929	**SORIA**			
Lee	67628	D	1934	**SORDANO**				Louis	82436	D	1939
Wong	28036	D	1919	Accusio	47199	D	1927	**SORITELLI**			
SOOMAN				**SOREFF**				Giovanni	56694	I	1930
Edward Robert	57997	D	1931	John F.	29081	D	1920	**SORLIE**			
SOOMANN				**SORENSEN**				Fredrick	35448	D	1922
Johann J. T.	31959	D	1921	Alwine	76168	M	1937	**SORLINI**			
John H.	85618	D	1940	Annie Christina	28026	D	1919	Prospero	27955	D	1919
John J. T.	31959	D	1921	Bent C.	82705	D	1939	**SORNBORGER**			
SOON				Carl	17917	D	1914	George	1370	D	1906
Chin Bing	85584	D	1940	Charles M.	78522	D	1938	**SORNIN**			
Woo	79701	D	1938	Emma Mathilde Eleonora	86542	D	1941	Noemie	67680	D	1934
SOOREFF				Frederick	11914	D	1911	**SOROLA**			
John F.	29081	I	1920	George	79406	D	1938	Axel F.	56469	D	1930
SOOT				Gladys	77250	D	1937	**SORRACCO**			
Leing	49776	D	1928	Herbert G.	75140	D	1937	Angelo F.	41292	D	1925
SOOY				John	64475	I	1933	Daniel	68964	D	1935
Charles H., Mrs.	75702	D	1937	John B.	26764	D	1919	**SORRENTINO**			
Leonore Evelyn	75702	D	1937	Lars	48927	D	1928	Madeleine	53795	D	1929
Leonore Wear	75702	D	1937	Louisa	13651	D	1912	**SORRITELLI**			
SOPER				Marie	85276	D	1940	Giovanni	56694	I	1930
Katherine Lang	50378	D	1928	Marius	66863	D	1934	**SORTVIT**			
Mary E.	705	D	1906	Martine L.	85276	D	1940	Ole	6001	D	1908
SOPHEY				Rasmus	83863	D	1940	**SORTWELL**			
Abraham	24097	D	1918	Sibyl	12639	M	1911	Alvin F.	10561	D	1910
Margaret	24262	D	1918	Soren P.	57653	D	1931	**SORVO**			
SOPHIA				Soren Peter	54441	D	1929	Maria Karolina	87588	D	1941
Abdalla M.	50088	D	1928	Soren Peter	65887	D	1933	**SOSEENE**			
SOPOTINES				Stanley	59383	D	1931	William John	15183	D	1913
N. S.	13969	D	1912	Walter	27510	M	1919	**SOSIN**			
SORACCO				**SORENSON**				Morris	80854	D	1939
A.	80246	D	1939	Aksel	41751	D	1925	Vasili Ivan	15183	D	1913
Ambrogio	80246	D	1939	Aksel	41751	D	1925	William John	15183	D	1913
Cesare	16966	D	1914	Jens	64521	D	1933	**SOSNOWSKI**			
Daneul	68964	D	1935	John	64521	D	1933	Marie	43236	D	1925
Daniel	68964	D	1935	Katie	36259	D	1923				
Daniele	68964	D	1935	Soren	63369	I	1933				

NAME	NUMBER	TYPE	YEAR
SOSSO			
Henry Joseph	58643	D	1931
J. Emma Henley	19471	D	1915
Teresa	33047	D	1921
SOTELLO			
Theodore	74223	I	1936
SOTO			
Frank	62278	I	1932
Frank J.	45598	I	1926
R. M. F.	52564	D	1929
SOTO-HALL			
Susan	89182	M	1942
SOTTOVIA			
Pietro	33305	I	1922
SOUARN			
Bernard	78670	D	1938
SOUBIES			
Josephine	53155	D	1929
Josephine	52136	I	1929
SOUBIROU			
Jean Baptiste	19159	D	1915
SOUC			
Leonore A.	84981	D	1940
Louis A.	153	D	1906
SOUD			
Herman	24130	D	1918
SOUKOIAN			
George	82399	D	1939
SOULE			
Abbie L.	19814	D	1915
Beach C.	42659	D	1925
Dorcas Maria	16317	D	1913
Milan	50904	D	1928
Samuel P.	20097	D	1915
Susan Maria	11542	D	1911
William Fulton	38813	D	1924
SOUMER			
Henri	47283	D	1927
Henri	48031	D	1927
SOURIAU			
Desire	6519	D	1908
SOUSA			
Emery Charles	83010	D	1940
Frank	25873	D	1918
Freda	74767	D	1937

NAME	NUMBER	TYPE	YEAR
SOUTHARD			
Albert Burley	89366	D	1942
Frank R.	21101	D	1916
SOUTHER			
Anna	83183	D	1940
Frank B.	44825	I	1926
SOUTHERLAND			
Evelyn	49651	D	1928
SOUTHERN			
Anne A.	32457	D	1921
Cathrine	4022	D	1907
Thomas R.	39746	D	1924
SOUTHWORTH			
John	46569	D	1927
May Elizabeth	71836	D	1936
SOUVA			
Charles K.	72690	D	1936
SOUZA			
Frank	75358	D	1937
John J.	355	D	1906
Maxine	28644	M	1920
SOW			
Gong Hong	89493	D	1942
SOWARD			
Florence E.	42527	D	1925
SOWER			
Louisa	50147	D	1928
SOWICK			
Helmar	30990	D	1921
SOY			
Sun T.	18860	M	1915
SPACE			
Samuel	23455	D	1917
SPACHER			
Edward E.	80638	I	1939
Ida C.	10919	D	1910
Peter J.	17977	D	1914
SPADE			
John	63337	D	1933
SPADER			
Barbara Jane	33026	M	1921
Charles Toms	61564	D	1932
SPADERO			
Giralamo	35081	D	1922
SPAETH			
Bertha	33236	D	1922

NAME	NUMBER	TYPE	YEAR
SPAETTI			
Frederick	6279	I	1908
SPAFFORD			
W. B.	78112	D	1938
SPAGNA			
Jean	81056	M	1939
SPAHN			
William Rudolf	52769	D	1929
SPAHR			
Bertie L.	84793	I	1940
SPAICH			
Lena	39318	D	1924
SPAIGHT			
Catherine	10755	I	1910
Patrick	24554	D	1918
SPAIN			
Caroline	89360	D	1942
J. H., Mrs.	89360	D	1942
Ruth	70337	D	1935
SPALASSO			
Umberto	34502	D	1922
SPALATRINI			
Louisa	22466	D	1917
SPALDING			
Dora Minerva	31025	D	1921
Leonard H.	53947	M	1929
Louis	35721	D	1923
Mary Polhemus	57559	D	1931
Robert B.	83123	I	1940
Robert F.	53947	M	1929
Vera Elizabeth	12978	M	1912
Virginia	53947	M	1929
SPALETTA			
Pio	48656	D	1927
Pius	48656	D	1927
SPAMER			
Elise Wilhelmine	53883	D	1929
Herbert A.	56354	D	1930
Justus Augustus	1860	D	1906
SPANDAU			
Matilda L.	76439	D	1937
SPANDRIO			
Giovanni	68722	D	1935
SPANEY			
Alice Elizabeth	40286	M	1924
August	79946	D	1938

Key: D = death; M = minor; I = incompetent

NAME	NUMBER	TYPE	YEAR	NAME	NUMBER	TYPE	YEAR	NAME	NUMBER	TYPE	YEAR
Johanna	22371	I	1917	Michael M.	70714	D	1935	**SPEAR**			
Johanna	84100	D	1940	Thomas J.	15768	D	1913	Anna B.	16561	I	1914
Paul L.	40438	D	1924	Volney Leroy	81675	D	1939	Anna B.	16736	D	1914
Pauline Anita	40286	M	1924	William	43044	D	1925	Frederick P.	41256	D	1925
SPANGENBERG				**SPARRE**				James Alexander	13970	D	1912
Louise C.	53206	D	1929	Grefue C.	26468	D	1919	Jean B.	50161	M	1928
Wilhelm	38627	D	1924	**SPARROW**				John C.	50161	M	1928
William	38627	D	1924	Elizabeth	63548	D	1933	Julia Scott	39957	D	1924
SPANGLE				Joseph	45826	D	1926	Mary Anne	50161	M	1928
Earl Leigh	9473	M	1910	**SPATAFORD**				Mary E.	30536	D	1920
SPANGLER				Myrtle M.	67801	I	1934	Phoebe C.	32172	D	1921
Ira Herman	71412	I	1936	**SPATES**				Robert F.	50161	M	1928
Ira Herman	74647	D	1937	Dewey	5830	M	1908	Robert Francis	8043	D	1909
Mary	71413	I	1936	Neta	5830	M	1908	Samuel J.	42282	D	1925
SPANLY				**SPATH**				Sarah	11808	D	1911
Paul L.	40438	D	1924	Mamie R.	78594	D	1938	William John	11772	D	1911
SPANNAGEL				Michael	25778	D	1918	**SPEAREL**			
Johanna	62406	D	1932	**SPATHIS**				Emma C.	70179	I	1935
SPANO				Edward William	42965	M	1925	**SPEARMAN**			
Angela	85136	I	1940	M., Mrs.	42548	D	1925	Andrew Deeves	20327	D	1916
SPANOS				Susan M.	42548	D	1925	William M.	994	D	1906
Dimitrios G.	84766	D	1940	**SPATZ**				**SPEARS**			
Georgios Emmanuel	69159	D	1935	Elizabeth	5971	D	1908	Lulu	13767	D	1912
James	33335	I	1922	**SPAULDING**				Mabel G.	82703	D	1939
James Geary	84766	D	1940	Calista	65079	D	1933	Nellie	15188	M	1913
SPANOVER				Collin M.	28206	D	1919	**SPECHT**			
John	82906	D	1939	Emma L.	10124	D	1910	Charles	15794	D	1913
SPANTON				Frederick D.	6268	D	1908	Charles	30293	D	1920
Dorothy Curle	30026	M	1920	George C.	21008	D	1916	R. V.	80903	D	1939
Harley Melville	30026	M	1920	John Ralph	26002	M	1918	Reinhold F.	80903	D	1939
Robert Bruce	30026	M	1920	Leland John	8394	M	1909	**SPECK**			
William	26324	D	1919	Lyle E.	64153	D	1933	Alfred	6029	M	1908
William Delbert	30026	M	1920	Mae M.	64763	D	1933	Charles	59216	I	1931
SPAR				Margaret S.	26902	D	1919	Frank	28051	D	1919
William	55746	D	1930	Marion Stuart	12631	D	1911	Joseph	74729	I	1937
SPARAVALO				Mary D. N.	64763	D	1933	Lillian	69772	D	1935
William	55746	D	1930	Nell Grier	89768	D	1942	Louis	44608	D	1926
William	55814	D	1930	Olive G.	74801	D	1937	Sarah A.	25907	D	1918
SPARGO				Susan	20049	D	1915	**SPECKMAN**			
John	46931	D	1927	Walter I.	42806	D	1925	Adolph	18072	M	1914
John C.	54103	D	1929	**SPAVEN**				Bessie	64388	D	1933
SPARK				Adam	61374	D	1932	F. F.	17334	D	1914
John H.	81862	D	1939	**SPAWR**				John Edward	33464	M	1922
SPARKS				Edward E.	35106	D	1922	**SPECKTER**			
Charles Edward	29591	D	1920	**SPEAKMAN**				Sophie C.	88935	D	1942
Edward Bray	47606	D	1927	Hayes P.	53889	D	1929	**SPEDDY**			
Mary	18683	D	1915					Eva	12809	D	1912

NAME	NUMBER	TYPE	YEAR
SPEDIACCI			
Beatrice	68556	D	1934
Federico	79526	D	1938
Pellegrino	57661	D	1931
Silvio	57661	D	1931
Steve	57661	D	1931
SPEED			
Agnes	50355	D	1928
SPEER			
Jaqueline	76226	M	1937
Neal	76226	M	1937
Neil	76192	M	1937
Olney	18355	D	1915
SPEETZEN			
William F.	57637	D	1931
SPEGEL			
Abraham	23163	D	1917
Fannie	23843	M	1918
Ida	23826	M	1918
SPEIER			
Bertha	21440	D	1916
Godel	83366	D	1940
Hannah	27474	D	1919
Henry	24100	I	1918
Isaac	30764	D	1920
SPEIGHT			
John C.	22417	D	1917
SPEIR			
Frank H.	30676	M	1920
SPEIRS			
Harrison	66639	D	1934
SPEIZER			
Abraham	80530	D	1939
SPELLMAN			
Anna	40626	D	1924
George H.	30223	D	1920
Kate	26060	D	1919
Katie	38408	D	1924
Michael	38397	D	1924
Walter E.	9188	M	1910
SPELMACHER			
Andrew G.	34513	D	1922
SPELMAN			
Mary W.	28183	D	1919
SPELT			
Albert William	48848	D	1927
George Simmons	48382	D	1927

NAME	NUMBER	TYPE	YEAR
SPELTS			
Edwin Wayne	56305	D	1930
SPENCE			
Catherine	6162	D	1908
Charles P.	69897	I	1935
John	36318	D	1923
Laura	38431	D	1924
Mary T.	38465	D	1924
SPENCER			
A. J.	61167	D	1932
Arthur	75927	D	1937
Arthur Edward	67109	D	1934
Arthur R.	43423	D	1926
Avery J.	4841	M	1907
Carnot Rozzle	28568	D	1920
Catharine Esten	38895	D	1924
Edgar H.	30916	D	1921
Edward	53998	M	1929
Esther A. M.	76162	I	1937
Eugene W.	21578	D	1916
Florence	62777	D	1932
Florence Harr	23816	D	1918
Forrest Eugene	29723	D	1920
Francesca	22667	M	1917
George Herbert	4841	M	1907
George W.	5662	D	1908
Harry J.	68060	D	1934
Ida	44514	D	1926
J. W.	8325	D	1909
James Marshall	69352	D	1935
John	29737	D	1920
John C.	21707	D	1916
John D.	5745	D	1908
Leneca	85879	D	1940
Martha Louise	31500	D	1921
Mary	18033	D	1914
Mary E.	49050	I	1928
Moira M.	5744	D	1908
Ralph Herbert, Jr.	77267	M	1937
Richard	40097	I	1924
Richard	42157	D	1925
Thomas W. C.	34991	D	1922
Warren Pierce	39461	D	1924
William C.	51809	D	1929
SPENGEMANN			
Emma Lottie	37221	D	1923
SPENGLER			
George Edward	85117	D	1940

NAME	NUMBER	TYPE	YEAR
Lena	29848	D	1920
S. H.	45618	D	1926
SPERBECK			
Frank	34553	D	1922
Sarah Green	52656	D	1929
SPERBER			
John	75045	D	1937
SPERISEN			
John F.	58338	D	1931
Mary	56129	I	1930
SPERISENI			
John F.	58338	D	1931
SPERKA			
Marjorie G.	70901	M	1935
SPERLICH			
Fridrich	7080	D	1909
SPERLING			
Frank	28719	D	1920
Morris	345	D	1906
SPEROU			
Dimitrios	81657	M	1939
Evagelos D.	81641	D	1939
George	81657	M	1939
SPERRING			
Hannah	24054	D	1918
John	46537	D	1927
SPERRY			
Ann Whitney	44048	D	1926
Caroline E.	1035	D	1906
Emily Rose	33251	M	1922
Georgea Mary	24762	D	1918
Horace B.	84974	D	1940
Lucy C.	74780	D	1937
Mary A.	27255	D	1919
Mary Simpson	31642	D	1921
Myrtle M.	41414	D	1925
SPETZ			
Harry	37232	D	1923
Henry	37232	D	1923
SPEYER			
Charlotte	57447	D	1930
Louis	48814	D	1927
Rose	35846	D	1923
Walter	6622	D	1908
SPEZ			
Andro	55917	D	1930

NAME	NUMBER	TYPE	YEAR
SPICER			
John	62501	D	1932
SPICHIGER			
Anna	68736	D	1935
Maria	68737	D	1935
SPIECIGER			
Marie	2754	D	1907
SPIEGEL			
Albert W.	50417	M	1928
Chrisian W.	86622	D	1941
Edward L.	68967	D	1935
Hamlin M.	70685	D	1935
Louis	16893	D	1914
Mary	63813	D	1933
Maud M.	36726	D	1923
Sarah	29177	D	1920
William	68785	D	1935
SPIEGLER			
Fanny	68854	D	1935
SPIEKER			
Jane	55311	M	1930
Suzanne	55313	M	1930
Warren Edward	55312	M	1930
Warrren	51489	D	1928
SPIELMAN			
Haim	67697	D	1934
Hyman	67697	D	1934
SPIER			
Donald P.	61712	M	1932
SPIERING			
Emil H.	61746	D	1932
SPIERO			
Caesar N.	9568	D	1910
SPIERS			
Elizabeth	74709	D	1937
James	88884	D	1942
Kate E.	43045	D	1925
Katharine E.	77212	D	1937
Katharine S.	77212	D	1937
William Gladstone	88156	D	1941
SPIESS			
Maria F.	86487	D	1941
SPILIOTIS			
John A.	66334	D	1934
SPILLANE			
Daniel	45686	M	1926
John	438	D	1906

NAME	NUMBER	TYPE	YEAR
Lawrence	75241	D	1937
Margaret	42031	D	1925
Maurice J.	74779	M	1937
SPILLER			
Joseph Aloysius	36504	D	1923
Richard W.	52814	D	1929
Rose Ellen	45698	D	1926
SPILLMAN			
August	71305	D	1935
Cleo Bessie	64176	D	1933
Hyman	67697	D	1934
Mignon Laura	68747	D	1935
SPINDLER			
Dorothea	63090	D	1932
Gustav	53704	D	1929
Nellie	26959	I	1919
Ottmar Ferdinand	55341	D	1930
SPINETTA			
Evelyn	82529	M	1939
Inez	82529	M	1939
SPINETTI			
Flavio P.	7404	M	1909
J. A.	9596	D	1910
SPINETTO			
Giovanni	26131	D	1919
SPINGOLA			
Antonio	43057	D	1925
Domenica	70066	D	1935
Francesco	46714	D	1927
Francisco	53462	D	1929
Maria Domenica	70066	D	1935
Maria Michela	82770	D	1939
Marie G.	87883	D	1941
Pasquale	47022	D	1927
Rachael	86277	D	1941
Vincenzo	35538	D	1922
SPINI			
Giovanni	17720	D	1914
SPINK			
Clarence E.	7669	D	1909
Elizabeth Viola	62722	D	1932
James Edward	11099	D	1911
Samuel Phillip	85428	D	1940
SPINKS			
Jasper	70440	D	1935
SPINNER			
Charles Frederick	12518	D	1911

NAME	NUMBER	TYPE	YEAR
SPINNEY			
Arthur W. E.	55846	D	1930
Charles S.	23788	I	1917
Edith Virginia	28909	M	1920
Fanny M.	86153	D	1941
Sarah Elizabeth	1914	D	1906
SPINOSA			
Louis	42334	M	1925
Maria	71932	D	1936
Pietro	71933	D	1936
SPINOY			
Francis	14291	D	1912
SPIRO			
Ruth	63188	D	1932
SPIROW			
Antonio D.	70799	D	1935
SPITZ			
Abraham	21048	D	1916
Bertha	33453	D	1922
Hannah	29853	D	1920
Henry	82446	D	1939
Jacob	19945	D	1915
SPIVOCK			
Sophie	66790	D	1934
SPLAINE			
Francis J.	65996	D	1933
Nellie Langdon	89832	D	1942
Robert E.	57817	D	1931
William Francis	31258	D	1921
William Francis	31446	M	1921
SPLANE			
Mary E.	33688	D	1922
Thomas	10193	D	1910
SPLETT			
August Ludwig	82082	D	1939
SPLIVALO			
C. R.	16315	D	1913
Elizabeth	77995	D	1938
Horace	88689	I	1941
SPOERER			
Herbert C.	84694	D	1940
SPOFFORD			
Aurelia J.	11132	D	1911
Bryan W.	84771	D	1940
James Wallace	32230	I	1921
Wallace Bartlett	77656	I	1938
Wallace Bartlett	78112	D	1938

NAME	NUMBER	TYPE	YEAR
SPOHN			
Alfred F.	21040	D	1916
John	82370	D	1939
Joseph H.	51212	D	1928
Katherie A.	19581	D	1915
Mary	20771	D	1916
SPONAGEL			
Johannes	16660	D	1914
SPONAGLE			
Carlos Edward	17576	M	1914
Milton	17576	M	1914
SPONOGLE			
F. M.	22374	D	1917
SPOONCER			
Frederick H.	62009	D	1932
SPOONE			
Richard	47398	D	1927
SPOONER			
Edmund Lewis	37617	I	1923
Francis Xavier	42467	D	1925
Mary Louisa	22182	D	1917
Nora	6940	D	1908
Richard	47398	D	1927
SPOONES			
Sarah M.	19194	D	1915
SPOOR			
John Walter	9580	D	1910
Scott	63472	D	1933
SPOTARNO			
Gaston P., Jr.	38789	M	1924
SPOTORNO			
Gaston Pierre	37332	D	1923
Wilhelmina	30275	D	1920
SPOTTISWOOD			
John	20902	D	1916
Leslie	38296	M	1924
Paul L.	38296	M	1924
Philip	21624	I	1916
Ruth	38296	M	1924
Sophia	25704	D	1918
SPOTTS			
Albert Tunstall	7312	D	1909
SPRAGUE			
Fanny Louise	3596	D	1907
Idabel W.	80564	I	1939
Jane M.	7819	D	1909
John F.	13047	D	1912

NAME	NUMBER	TYPE	YEAR
Lorenzo D.	39505	D	1924
Magaret J.	59623	D	1931
Margaret J.	62490	D	1932
Nellie F.	85983	D	1941
Phineas	83027	D	1940
Richard H.	80548	D	1939
Robina G.	55435	D	1930
SPRATT			
Robert	40830	D	1925
SPRECKELS			
Adolph B.	39652	D	1924
Adolph Bernard	32391	M	1921
Adolph Frederick	39654	M	1924
Alma Emma	39720	M	1924
Anna C.	9224	D	1910
Claus	6977	D	1908
Dorothy Constance	39653	M	1924
Emma	39998	D	1924
Geraldine	49139	M	1928
Henry	3827	D	1907
John D., III	32391	M	1921
Marie Huntington	32391	M	1921
Oroville D.	67515	D	1934
SPRECKLES			
John D., Jr.	32366	D	1921
SPREEN			
Carl Frederick August	71105	D	1935
Frederick	71105	D	1935
George	80518	D	1939
William	44423	D	1926
SPRENG			
Gottfried	25409	D	1918
Julia	65358	D	1933
Louis G.	66541	D	1934
SPRENGER			
Elizabeth	14570	D	1912
Ida M.	70636	D	1935
SPRENKEL			
Ivan E.	63224	I	1932
SPRIGG			
Marguerita	88633	I	1941
SPRIGGS			
Joseph D.	65748	M	1933
Lem Walter	36015	D	1923
Roosevelt	72869	I	1936
SPRING			
George	28413	I	1919

NAME	NUMBER	TYPE	YEAR
Howard B.	40956	I	1925
Howard B.	84136	I	1940
John H.	41830	D	1925
John H.	41830	D	1925
John R.	458	D	1906
Robert Sparhawk	20175	I	1915
SPRINGER			
Abraham C.	66880	D	1934
Anna	61448	D	1932
Charles Richard	75193	M	1937
Francis Herbert	75192	M	1937
Hugh E.	76876	D	1937
Jack	84379	D	1940
Joe Milton	79831	D	1938
Mae	76754	D	1937
Melva A.	84893	D	1940
Paul Eugene, Jr., Mrs.	84893	D	1940
Stella B.	11264	D	1911
Susie E.	21450	D	1916
Theodore	734	D	1906
William A.	70512	I	1935
William H.	78502	D	1938
SPRINGETT			
Annie F.	42377	D	1925
Donald	73856	M	1936
Thomas W.	72981	D	1936
SPRINGFIELD			
Margaret Quinn	29977	D	1920
SPRINGSTEEN			
Laura Ann	61371	M	1932
Zella	61218	L	1932
SPROLES			
Ella	18268	D	1914
SPROUL			
Carl H.	75242	D	1937
Theodore W.	81677	I	1939
SPROULE			
George W.	23730	D	1917
Lily	81756	I	1939
William	68828	D	1935
SPRUANCE			
John	6990	D	1908
Lizzie A.	22872	D	1917
SPRUNG			
Hiram	9477	D	1910
Mary A.	9478	D	1910
Milton	10662	M	1910

NAME	NUMBER	TYPE	YEAR	NAME	NUMBER	TYPE	YEAR	NAME	NUMBER	TYPE	YEAR
Ray	10662	M	1910	**St.Amant**				James J.	85080	D	1940
Walter W.	38061	D	1924	Mary	40475	D	1924	Maurice	65416	D	1933
Spunn				**St.Clair**				Michael J.	51738	D	1929
Isidor	12218	D	1911	Edward	80514	D	1939	Nan	89577	D	1942
Reuben	12219	M	1911	Jean	59002	I	1931	Nellie J.	27703	D	1919
Spurck				Madeline M.	50278	D	1928	Patrick A.	21117	D	1916
Ed C.	27326	D	1919	Margaret	45989	I	1926	Thomas	10369	D	1910
Spurgeon				Walton Douglas	72229	D	1936	Timothy J.	80132	D	1938
Clarence E.	31708	D	1921	**St.George**				**Stacker**			
Spurlock				Margaret	38404	D	1924	Joseph	67533	D	1934
William A.	16907	D	1914	Richard	51025	M	1928	**Stackhouse**			
Spurr				**St.Germain**				Park Henry	85053	D	1940
John P.	47098	D	1927	Theophile Adelaide De	5890	D	1908	**Stackpole**			
Spurrier				**St.John**				Edward C.	15761	D	1913
William W.	37533	D	1923	Adelia	39410	D	1924	**Stackpoole**			
Spuur				Chauncey M.	23565	D	1917	John M.	71992	D	1936
Mary Bergitte	46116	D	1926	Eva	89245	D	1942	**Stacy**			
Spyker				Richard Austin	17736	D	1914	Annie Cook	33781	D	1922
Bruce T.	77617	D	1938	Robert Lester	82669	D	1939	Henry Lee	55905	D	1930
Squaglia				**St.Lupery**				**Stad**			
Angelina	85260	D	1940	Alfred	26101	D	1919	Lilly A.	61601	D	1932
Squier				**St.Lykakis**				**Stadden**			
Patience	12933	D	1912	George	11160	D	1911	Richard M.	78450	D	1938
Squire				**St.Martin**				**Stademan**			
Dorothy J.	75950	D	1937	Jean	55798	D	1930	Herman F.	30264	D	1920
James Arthur	39516	D	1924	**St.Mary**				**Stademann**			
Squires				Peter	10521	D	1910	Corinne A.	58185	D	1931
Jessie	34998	D	1922	**St.Onge**				**Stadman**			
Victoria	9561	D	1910	Lullus	7818	D	1909	Petronilla	78598	D	1938
William D., Sr.	76736	D	1937	**St.Supery**				**Stadthous**			
William Dunning	76736	D	1937	Alfred	26101	D	1919	August	32978	I	1921
Srahn				Elizabeth	1012	D	1906	**Stadtmuller**			
Gustaf Frid	28403	D	1919	**Staacke**				Ellen Smith	88915	D	1942
Sresovich				Barbara	25933	D	1918	**Stadtner**			
Byron L.	8044	M	1909	George	361	D	1906	David	48941	M	1928
Carrie	2440	D	1906	George	3254	D	1907	Edith	48941	M	1928
Clarisse R.	14151	M	1912	**Stabens**				**Staedler**			
John Dolphin	80694	D	1939	Joseph	58115	D	1931	Lena B.	52984	D	1929
John N.	24708	D	1918	**Stacey**				**Staeglich**			
Mary Caroline	2440	D	1906	Herbert D.	85325	D	1940	Frederick J.	63081	D	1932
Sroufe				Malcolm	62867	M	1932	**Staehli**			
John	1164	D	1906	**Stack**				Casper	1522	I	1906
Zelda A.	8224	D	1909	Dennis	30715	D	1920	**Staemmler**			
Sschultze				Edmond	31520	D	1921	Hugo Alfred	79293	D	1938
Ferdinand	3503	M	1907	Garrett G.	18362	D	1915	Jennie Louisa	63925	D	1933
				Helena	10991	D	1911				

NAME	NUMBER	TYPE	YEAR
STAENGEL			
Amelia	42677	D	1925
STAFF			
Edward	68877	D	1935
John	76835	D	1937
Louise	89678	D	1942
STAFFORD			
A. P. K.	363	D	1906
Charles Emil	2746	M	1907
Cornelia M.	13169	D	1912
Harriet Bendire	2746	M	1907
Harry Falk	50758	M	1928
Harry I.	78092	D	1938
Harry I., Jr.	78089	M	1938
James N.	62578	D	1932
Keithly I.	78089	M	1938
L. H., Mrs.	37163	D	1923
Leona H.	36953	I	1923
Lillian E.	51349	D	1928
Margaret	15053	M	1913
Margaret E.	73659	D	1936
Maria Helena	55222	D	1930
Martha E.	66706	D	1934
Mary R.	2019	D	1906
Olga Falk	32129	D	1921
Roland	49986	D	1928
Timothy W.	8769	D	1909
William	66590	I	1934
William C.	87290	D	1941
William J.	67088	D	1934
STAGE			
Agnes	57252	D	1930
STAGEL			
Joseph	47535	D	1927
STAGG			
James S.	89945	D	1942
STAGI			
Lawrence	20010	I	1915
STAGNARO			
Agostino	52699	D	1929
Antonietta	882	M	1906
Antonio	49713	D	1928
Assunta	78013	D	1938
Bartolomeo	40570	D	1924
Clorinda	70605	D	1935
Domenica	73525	D	1936
Giovanni	1038	D	1906
Giovanni	45264	D	1926

NAME	NUMBER	TYPE	YEAR
Louis	75460	D	1937
Louis J.	78249	D	1938
Maddalena	79378	D	1938
Pietro	21418	D	1916
Rocco	26047	D	1919
Rocco	31014	D	1921
STAHL			
Adele	78635	D	1938
Barbara M.	89597	M	1942
Bille Vern	85376	M	1940
Catherine E.	20792	D	1916
Charlotte I.	46528	D	1927
Fremont George	62417	D	1932
H. C. F.	21298	D	1916
Jasper	8197	D	1909
Joan Patricia	89597	M	1942
John A.	89597	M	1942
John Christopher Hans	87651	D	1941
Louis	55403	D	1930
Margaretha	41905	D	1925
Margaretha	41905	D	1925
Veronica	23775	I	1917
STAHLBERG			
Gistave	42392	D	1925
STAHLECKER			
Jacob	918	I	1906
Jacob	1744	D	1906
STAHLER			
Horace	36045	D	1923
STAHLGREN			
Karl A.	49306	D	1928
STAHLMANN			
Fred	14478	D	1912
STAHMER			
Herman F.	76561	D	1937
Wayne Herman	76663	M	1937
STAHR			
Margaret	672	D	1906
STAIB			
Annie D.	74211	D	1936
Conrad	17070	D	1914
Frank Conrad	78948	D	1938
George	77463	D	1938
Georgina A. M.	63306	D	1933
STAIGER			
Frederick	43396	D	1926
Thelma L.	49024	M	1928

NAME	NUMBER	TYPE	YEAR
STAIR			
Maude Cheffers	69310	I	1935
STAKE			
Denis Herman	62925	D	1932
STALDER			
Albert Joseph	67982	M	1934
Joseph	2132	D	1906
Mary C.	22944	D	1917
Pauline	16944	D	1914
Pauline Eleanore	67982	M	1934
Roy Frederick	25240	M	1918
STALEY			
Annie	54462	D	1929
George W.	40977	I	1925
John W.	32082	D	1921
William A.	83073	D	1940
STALKER			
Hulda D.	75344	D	1937
J. C.	75344	D	1937
STALLARD			
Thomas F.	41425	I	1925
Thomas F.	67432	D	1934
W. M. G.	368	D	1906
STALLMAN			
Bertha Agusta	38106	D	1924
Charles C.	18046	D	1914
Frank Oscar	76924	D	1937
Nettie C.	66283	D	1934
STAMANT			
Anson William	57581	M	1931
Loretta	57477	M	1930
William	57581	M	1931
STAMATELOS			
Demitrios J.	79345	D	1938
Stavroula	62630	D	1932
STAMATES			
Harry	53679	D	1929
STAMATOPULOS			
Peter	16713	D	1914
STAMBLER			
Celia	680	D	1906
Louis	1699	D	1906
STAMEN			
Nicola	53747	D	1929
STAMENOVICH			
Nicola	53747	D	1929

NAME	NUMBER	TYPE	YEAR
STAMEY			
Henry Tom	57173	I	1930
STAMM			
Celia	66131	I	1934
Christian W.	6259	D	1908
STAMMER			
Augusta W. H.	55254	D	1930
Carl	87766	D	1941
Max August	72647	D	1936
STAMOGIANIS			
Xenofon	47300	D	1927
Zenofon	47300	D	1927
STAMOPOLIS			
Ioannides	54211	D	1929
STAMOS			
George K.	7226	D	1909
Peter	16713	D	1914
STAMP			
Frederick	26494	D	1919
STAMPER			
George Washington	33636	D	1922
Lena	46685	D	1927
Marks J.	58138	D	1931
Sarah	37258	D	1923
STANBERG			
Alexander Borden	86376	D	1941
STANBERY			
Alexander Borden	86376	D	1941
STANBOURG			
Pontus	59416	D	1931
STANBURG			
A. P.	44754	D	1926
Albert	44754	D	1926
STANBURY			
Martha Virginia	74953	D	1937
Virginia	74953	D	1937
STANCIL			
Benjamin Franklin	46955	D	1927
STANDART			
William Henry	45284	D	1926
STANDERSON			
Ellen Fenwick	18212	D	1914
STANDIFEID			
Ellis D.	55999	M	1930
June L.	55999	M	1930

NAME	NUMBER	TYPE	YEAR
STANDIGNGER			
Elsie	34395	M	1922
STANDINGER			
Elsie	34395	M	1922
STANDISH			
Beatrice	63904	M	1933
Clarence	38186	M	1924
George G.	45380	D	1926
Katherine C.	79556	D	1938
Margaret Little	66175	D	1934
Martha	1538	D	1906
STANDOW			
Emil	43384	D	1926
STANDRIDGE			
Vera Tina	46957	M	1927
STANDSTROM			
Gus	38718	I	1924
STANEK			
James F.	82871	D	1939
STANFER			
J. A.	19771	D	1915
STANFIELD			
Dorothy	79707	D	1938
Newell F.	50369	M	1928
STANFORD			
Agnes	33667	D	1922
Albert	45857	D	1926
Annie A.	39027	D	1924
Belle May	28638	D	1920
Bridget	33667	D	1922
Jasper	77137	D	1937
Joseph	47888	D	1927
Leland	31526	D	1921
Mary	9390	D	1910
Myron E.	804	D	1906
Thomas N.	72682	D	1936
STANG			
David	81892	M	1939
Emma R.	3271	D	1907
STANGE			
Amelia	17361	D	1914
Carl	61411	D	1932
Emilie	17361	D	1914
Gerard	40497	I	1924
Henriette	23102	D	1917
STANGER			
Martin	28054	M	1919

NAME	NUMBER	TYPE	YEAR
STANGHELLINI			
Annie	27769	M	1919
Tommaso	25900	D	1918
STANICH			
Matilda	72345	I	1936
Obren	36331	D	1923
STANILAND			
Jane	43833	D	1926
STANKE			
Emma	28837	D	1920
Florian	41900	D	1925
Florian	41900	D	1925
Hugo	35073	D	1922
STANLE			
Frederick H.	19235	D	1915
Louisa Jennie	38774	D	1924
STANLEY			
Addie M.	83625	D	1940
Alice E.	9510	D	1910
Benjamin B.	29043	I	1920
Charles T.	55211	D	1930
Claude	42723	M	1925
Cornelia Baldwin	3390	D	1907
Dana V.	57182	I	1930
Fanny L.	43779	D	1926
Frank	60558	I	1931
Frederick H.	419	D	1906
George A.	74053	D	1936
George William	30408	M	1920
Gladys Inez	30408	M	1920
Harry M.	72768	D	1936
Helen Clinton	68740	M	1935
Ida May	18563	D	1915
Jane	46387	D	1927
John F.	46708	D	1927
Leonard Milton	59180	D	1931
Mary	13460	D	1912
Mary Ann	6875	D	1908
Millie	37993	D	1923
Milton Dudley	32543	D	1921
Minnie Ellen	69758	D	1935
Miriam Luella	56895	D	1930
Owen G.	43821	M	1926
Patrick	9440	D	1910
Randolph L.	43821	M	1926
Richard Joseph	88615	M	1941
T. W., Mrs.	69758	D	1935
Thelma	68705	M	1935

Key: D = death; M = minor; I = incompetent

NAME	NUMBER	TYPE	YEAR	NAME	NUMBER	TYPE	YEAR	NAME	NUMBER	TYPE	YEAR
Violet W.	63426	D	1933	**STANWORTH**				August P.	29299	D	1920
William H.	57334	D	1930	Maude Walker	49105	D	1928	Bertha	38035	D	1924
STANNARD				**STANYAN**				Calvin P.	68670	I	1935
Maria	32150	D	1921	Charles Hendee	72922	D	1936	Charles J.	74219	I	1936
STANOVICH				**STAPELFELDT**				David	72523	I	1936
Martin P.	89698	D	1942	William	13015	D	1912	Edwin P.	55074	D	1930
STANQUIST				**STAPFER**				Ellen W.	8105	D	1909
Edward	83217	D	1940	Emily Barbara	48864	D	1927	Emil T.	79379	I	1938
STANS				**STAPLEFORD**				Fred B.	45771	I	1926
John J.	26322	D	1919	Grace	40800	M	1925	Grace	1396	M	1906
STANSBURY				**STAPLES**				Jane	673	D	1906
Delphine	2057	D	1906	Ellen E.	21609	D	1916	John	28280	D	1919
Ralph Byron	49860	D	1928	Mary	12128	M	1911	Lillian M.	65775	D	1933
STANSFIELD				**STAPLETON**				Mabel Amelia	1396	M	1906
H. A.	5764	D	1908	Ann	13807	D	1912	Rosa	63801	D	1933
Joseph E.	59055	D	1931	Bridget	41750	D	1925	Rose	47136	D	1927
STANTON				Bridget	41750	D	1925	Rose	86127	I	1941
A. W.	23930	I	1918	Catherine	24008	D	1918	Sarah Frazee	67404	D	1934
Amy W.	87683	D	1941	Edward	32976	D	1921	Susie	58836	D	1931
Bella	24890	D	1918	Joseph W.	36974	D	1923	William Garfield	42185	D	1925
Bridget	35535	I	1922	Louella Noonan	14247	I	1912	**STARKE**			
Charles Egbert	64974	D	1933	Mildred I.	84833	D	1940	Friedrich	30296	D	1920
David James	76582	D	1937	Percy W.	60274	D	1931	Marie A.	60944	D	1932
Dora Josephine	34718	D	1922	Phillis	73058	D	1936	Thomas J.	47409	D	1927
Edward J.	15426	I	1913	William	4842	D	1907	William Waldemar	37041	D	1923
Edwin Kenneth	76496	D	1937	William	58718	D	1931	**STARKEY**			
Elizabeth	60081	D	1931	William J.	38436	I	1924	Mattie E.	39496	D	1924
Ellen F.	1275	D	1906	**STAPP**				**STARKS**			
Francis Cyril	31485	M	1921	Agnes May	13016	D	1912	Frank L.	81889	D	1939
Francis E.	27336	I	1919	Neil Robson	88811	D	1941	Harold Z.	24994	M	1918
Francis Joseph	29086	D	1920	**STAPPENBECK**				**STARKWEATHER**			
Isador J., Mrs.	34718	D	1922	Charles	66221	D	1934	Gertrude	54091	D	1929
John J.	45178	I	1926	Letitia	15212	D	1913	**STARLESE**			
Joseph	76750	D	1937	**STAR**				Lorenzo	61690	D	1932
Lewis Edgar	88779	D	1941	Max	61566	D	1932	**STARLING**			
Maria L.	7879	D	1909	**STARBIRD**				Andrew J.	51384	D	1928
Mary A.	38795	D	1924	Maria J.	16857	D	1914	**STAROWEISKY**			
Mathias	75748	D	1937	**STARC**				Josephine	44386	D	1926
Patrick	12252	D	1911	Katarina	80351	I	1939	**STARR**			
Patrick	36182	D	1923	**STARCKE**				A.	66396	I	1934
Peter	56513	D	1930	Agnes	55497	I	1930	Barney	17941	D	1914
Ralph Raymond	34769	D	1922	Agnes	73489	D	1936	George William	83223	D	1940
T. J.	62586	D	1932	**STARK**				Lawrence	75318	M	1937
Thomas	6762	D	1908	Alameda	52786	D	1929	Lydia A.	24397	D	1918
Thomas	26742	D	1919	Albert Henry	27907	I	1919	Marie	75318	M	1937
Thomas James	16092	D	1913	Anna	40899	D	1925	Mary A.	17205	D	1914
Walter B.	22191	D	1917	Annie	51731	D	1928	Owen L.	75317	M	1937
William	60977	M	1932					Sidney L. M.	21340	D	1916

NAME	NUMBER	TYPE	YEAR
Walter A., Jr.	65219	D	1933
William	80333	D	1939
STARRETT			
Ada A.	50863	D	1928
Bertha Rock	86056	D	1941
David James	38596	D	1924
Lizzie	60443	I	1931
Mary Amelia	25172	D	1918
STARRING			
Fred	79418	D	1938
STARRS			
James I.	66629	D	1934
STARTI			
Mary	87818	D	1941
STASCHEN			
Bernice	63345	M	1933
Fred G.	62668	D	1932
Shirley A.	63346	M	1933
STASHUK			
Boris	47855	M	1927
Eugene	47855	M	1927
Michael	47855	M	1927
Michael E.	46436	D	1927
Tamara	47855	M	1927
Vasily	54873	D	1930
STASULAT			
Anthony	54820	D	1930
Anton	54820	D	1930
STATHAKIS			
Harry	45848	D	1926
STATHAM			
William Matthew	60584	D	1932
STATHIS			
Lulu Curlett	76096	D	1937
STAUB			
Frank	89746	D	1942
STAUCH			
Mary	9579	D	1910
STAUDACHER			
Helen M.	53988	M	1929
STAUDE			
Elisabeth	6964	D	1908
STAUDIGNGER			
Frank	42660	D	1925
STAUDINGER			
Frank	42660	D	1925

NAME	NUMBER	TYPE	YEAR
STAUF			
Emil Heinrich Alexander	20845	D	1916
STAUFFER			
Eva C.	65708	D	1933
John	83660	D	1940
STAUNTON			
Joseph	76750	D	1937
STAVDAL			
Peter Martinus	39727	D	1924
STAVER			
William Marion	17914	M	1914
STAVRAU			
Emmanuel A.	77759	D	1938
STAYER			
John	35769	D	1923
STAYNER			
Laura	80611	D	1939
STAYTON			
Bertha W.	24227	D	1918
STCLAIR			
Lizzie	13929	D	1912
STDENIS			
Jules	8207	D	1909
STEAD			
Amelia	31507	D	1921
Annie Constance	52793	D	1929
STEAHLE			
Eva	23060	D	1917
STEAKLESON			
Ellen O. H.	16495	D	1913
STEALEY			
Emma V.	87837	D	1941
Mary L.	50097	D	1928
Nellie	60283	D	1931
STEALY			
Mary L.	50097	D	1928
STEARNS			
Bridget	77	D	1906
Frederic A.	82382	D	1939
George W.	85573	D	1940
Gustavis C.	26423	D	1919
Samuel Elliott	52012	M	1929
Victor J.	39353	D	1924
William A.	49431	D	1928
STEARRETT			
David James	38596	D	1924

NAME	NUMBER	TYPE	YEAR
STEBBING			
William H.	80761	D	1939
STEBBINS			
Anna E.	10423	D	1910
Cara E.	64854	D	1933
Florence S.	50664	D	1928
Lillian A.	77602	D	1938
STEBBONS			
Edith Large	66362	D	1934
STEBER			
Anna F.	29425	D	1920
Victoria	57115	D	1930
STECHELE			
Anton	41337	D	1925
STECHER			
George	59978	I	1931
STECKENREITER			
Eugenie C.	44911	D	1926
STECKER			
Mary Elizabeth	2157	D	1906
STECKLER			
Lois Anna	25999	M	1918
Louis Charles	25632	D	1918
STECKNER			
Eugenie C.	44911	D	1926
STEDMAN			
Charles	1999	D	1906
Emily	32830	D	1921
Warren B., Mrs.	32830	D	1921
STEED			
Bella Jean	50959	M	1928
STEEL			
George	86	D	1906
Sarah H.	89412	D	1942
STEELE			
Anna Marie	33005	M	1921
Catherine A.	7461	M	1909
Charles	76751	D	1937
Della	62452	D	1932
Frederick	11657	D	1911
Geary H.	7461	M	1909
George	82921	D	1939
Henry A.	45326	D	1926
James A.	82679	D	1939
James G.	16892	D	1914
John	83067	D	1940
Joseph	28196	D	1919

NAME	NUMBER	TYPE	YEAR	NAME	NUMBER	TYPE	YEAR	NAME	NUMBER	TYPE	YEAR
Lucy	73670	D	1936	John	55285	D	1930	**STEIL**			
Mabel	35499	I	1922	Margaret Rosalie	71420	M	1936	Adelaide E.	20400	I	1916
Mabel	53796	D	1929	Mina Mary	66695	M	1934	Adelaide E.	36669	D	1923
Mary J.	59604	D	1931	**STEFFENS**				Ellen	39277	D	1924
Omer E.	57524	I	1930	Agnes L.	65214	M	1933	Frank W.	64233	D	1933
Renssalaer E.	70537	D	1935	Andrew	29993	D	1920	Henry	20174	D	1915
Robert E.	52181	D	1929	Helen E.	65214	M	1933	Peter	50520	D	1928
Robert W.	78965	D	1938	Henry A.	27972	D	1919	**STEIMKE**			
Sophronia W.	5647	D	1908	Henry C.	65383	D	1933	Diedrich J.	29738	D	1920
Thomas John	8946	D	1910	Hermann	2282	D	1906	**STEIMLE**			
William C.	62085	D	1932	John R.	83743	D	1940	Herman F.	64976	D	1933
William J.	31070	D	1921	Raymond J.	65214	M	1933	**STEIN**			
STEEN				**STEFFERUD**				A.	8544	D	1909
Carl Heinrich	33858	D	1922	Florentine L.	77573	D	1938	Abraham	58810	D	1931
Jacob	42741	D	1925	**STEFFES**				Abraham C.	69020	D	1935
STEENSON				Douglas	62834	M	1932	Albert	23602	M	1917
William Herbert	79303	D	1938	Edith May	75898	D	1937	Anna	50770	D	1928
STEEP				William F.	56953	D	1930	Bertha	59658	D	1931
William	4131	M	1907	**STEFFIN**				Betty	59658	D	1931
STEERS				Joseph A.	31225	I	1921	Betty	63842	M	1933
Edward E.	44467	D	1926	**STEGE**				Carl J.	61977	D	1932
Ida M.	30023	D	1920	John	29254	D	1920	Charles	23609	D	1917
Keene Oliver	62527	D	1932	Kate B.	19678	D	1915	Charles J.	44380	D	1926
Mary C.	64520	D	1933	**STEGEMAN**				Christopher H.	3865	M	1907
STEESE				Galen Earnest	41346	M	1925	Ellen	54738	I	1930
Mary Frances	40551	D	1924	Julia	62540	I	1932	Frederick J.	1244	I	1906
STEFANELLI				Julia	65736	D	1933	Frederick J.	45194	I	1926
Vivian Sylvia	65819	D	1933	**STEGEMEIER**				Frederick Jacob	56026	D	1930
STEFANI				Heinrich	16895	D	1914	Frederick L.	52019	D	1929
Mike	86396	D	1941	**STEGER**				Fredericka	3593	D	1907
STEFANINI				Constantin	72760	D	1936	Gashie	23046	D	1917
Emilio	87205	D	1941	Jane	68637	D	1935	Gerson	23046	D	1917
Lucia	74644	D	1937	Jeanette G.	68637	D	1935	Harold	23602	M	1917
Lucy	74644	D	1937	**STEGMAN**				Henry L.	46149	D	1927
STEFANO				Heta C.	63757	D	1933	Jacob Henry	31057	D	1921
Cuneo	32174	D	1921	**STEHLIN**				Jessie Cowan	71253	D	1935
STEFFAN				Emma M.	13324	D	1912	Jessie E.	71253	D	1935
Jacob Frederick	38488	D	1924	**STEIGER**				Louis	63251	D	1932
Mathilda	21406	D	1916	Bertha	62117	D	1932	Magdalena	40349	D	1924
STEFFANI				George J.	89532	D	1942	Marie Emily	8296	D	1909
Paulina	1604	D	1906	Jack	24871	M	1918	Morris	77033	D	1937
STEFFEN				Ludwig	87211	D	1941	Rachel	27525	D	1919
Carl Edmund	87225	I	1941	Russell	55373	D	1930	Raphael I.	52178	D	1929
Claus Heinrich	57935	D	1931	William Russell	57049	M	1930	Regina T.	40350	M	1924
Ernest	64465	I	1933	**STEIGLEMAN**				Samuel	2474	D	1906
Ernest	64707	I	1933	Sarah Louise	10311	D	1910	Sarah	44381	D	1926
Frank Hubert	76063	D	1937					Simon D.	16034	D	1913
								William A.	9118	D	1910

NAME	NUMBER	TYPE	YEAR
William S.	37937	D	1923
STEINACHER			
Helen	83396	D	1940
Josef	62559	D	1932
Victoria	61967	D	1932
STEINAU			
Arthur B.	30332	D	1920
STEINBACH			
William	65217	D	1933
STEINBACK			
Edward	45442	M	1926
STEINBAUER			
Charles Frederick	30928	D	1921
STEINBAUGH			
D. A.	58464	I	1931
D. A.	59339	D	1931
STEINBECK			
Georgie	58820	I	1931
STEINBERG			
Abraham	85373	D	1940
Albert, Mrs.	74042	D	1936
Annie	40172	D	1924
August	64514	D	1933
Ethel Rebecca	48303	M	1927
Helen	89696	D	1942
Jules	57274	M	1930
Marcus	80004	D	1938
Marcus Max	48303	M	1927
Myer	47364	D	1927
Rose	64210	D	1933
Sadie	74041	D	1936
Samuel	48303	M	1927
Sigmund	42875	D	1925
Solomon	74744	D	1937
STEINBERGER			
Adolph	47703	D	1927
Irving Wilmot	51883	M	1929
Julius	21999	D	1916
Mary L.	53432	D	1929
Nathan	49444	D	1928
Pilar	4030	I	1907
Sophie	18907	D	1915
William Edward	83604	D	1940
STEINBRING			
Albert, Jr.	38008	M	1923
STEINDLER			
Henry	31311	D	1921

NAME	NUMBER	TYPE	YEAR
Isaac	77471	D	1938
STEINEGGER			
Lawrence Henry	37523	I	1923
STEINER			
Albert	8560	D	1909
Alfred Emil	84463	D	1940
Anna M.	54003	D	1929
Bertha Alice	81758	D	1939
Cathareno	51657	D	1928
Charles William	56104	D	1930
Christian David	2537	D	1906
Dora	65584	I	1933
Dora	78353	D	1938
Esther	15588	D	1913
Henry	58761	D	1931
Joan Rae	85761	M	1940
John	55992	M	1930
Joseph	1841	D	1906
Joseph	51658	D	1928
Joseph S.	64828	D	1933
Mabel	57664	D	1931
Martin	6349	D	1908
Martin	8543	M	1909
Patricia	55992	M	1930
Paul	28623	M	1920
Pauline	86615	D	1941
Robert David	28623	M	1920
Rose	1568	D	1906
Rose E.	49529	D	1928
Sarah	2868	D	1907
Theodore	86158	D	1941
STEINFELS			
Charles	38455	D	1924
STEINFORT			
Katie	36793	D	1923
STEINGEN			
Helen	84811	D	1940
STEINHARDT			
Hienrich	37700	D	1923
Max	41863	D	1925
Max	41863	D	1925
STEINHART			
Amy S.	61506	D	1932
Emanuel	60390	D	1931
Harold	1648	M	1906
Ignatz	22797	D	1917
Louise	51943	D	1929
Nathaniel	1648	M	1906

NAME	NUMBER	TYPE	YEAR
Sigmund	9868	D	1910
Theodore	1648	M	1906
Theresa	1648	M	1906
William	35379	D	1922
STEINHOFF			
Elise	9015	D	1910
STEINKAMP			
John L.	29268	D	1920
William	54721	M	1930
STEINMAN			
B. U.	16954	D	1914
Herman	13105	D	1912
Irving L.	33543	D	1922
Martin J.	82058	D	1939
Mojsze Icek	82058	D	1939
Olga	80921	D	1939
Rebecca	73986	D	1936
STEINMANN			
Julie	653	D	1906
Rosa	49243	D	1928
STEINMETZ			
Charles Hencken	88780	D	1941
Mamie	1497	D	1906
Matthias	3893	D	1907
STEINMEYER			
Emma	70179	I	1935
Emma	80277	D	1939
STEINWEG			
Charles G.	6699	D	1908
Emma J. Nutt	72539	D	1936
Emma Maria	72539	D	1936
STELKER			
Hasting	28612	D	1920
Xavier	32407	D	1921
STELLA			
Clara Ramagana	71130	D	1935
Elvie	73351	M	1936
George	73351	M	1936
Henry	73351	M	1936
Italo	73351	M	1936
Rose Ruth	73351	M	1936
Vincenzo	58035	D	1931
STELLING			
August William	54438	D	1929
Charles	21373	D	1916
Charles F.	50421	D	1928
Christine M.	49361	D	1928

NAME	NUMBER	TYPE	YEAR	NAME	NUMBER	TYPE	YEAR	NAME	NUMBER	TYPE	YEAR
Claus	11285	D	1911	**STENINGER**				Viola I.	12657	M	1911
Claus	21373	D	1916	Patsy Ruth	67406	M	1934	William	10175	D	1910
Dora Margaretha	6957	M	1908	**STENSON**				William F.	81362	D	1939
Frederick Henry	2659	M	1907	Addie Mary Cooper	30354	D	1920	**STEPHENSON**			
Henry	1650	D	1906	Ellen	39990	D	1924	Blanche	79570	D	1938
Henry	24444	D	1918	Ellen M.	66735	D	1934	Dean	41458	I	1925
Henry	39476	D	1924	Margaret M.	86180	D	1941	Dorothy	51991	M	1929
Henry Peter	2659	M	1907	**STENTIFORD**				George	34242	D	1922
Herbert William	13188	M	1912	Arthur C.	72796	D	1936	Howard Elton	34559	M	1922
John	6957	M	1908	George E.	72767	D	1936	Juanita Adele	27468	M	1919
John D.	47023	I	1927	**STENZEL**				Lucy C.	51935	D	1929
Louise Sophie	77775	D	1938	Catherine	67040	D	1934	Robert Paul	20920	M	1916
Margaret	9542	D	1910	**STEPANENKO**				Thomas L.	31699	D	1921
Mary Alice	81365	D	1939	Irene	59735	I	1931	Thomas L.	39151	D	1924
Mildred Chrissie	13187	M	1912	Vera	59736	M	1931	Viola	27468	M	1919
STELLJES				**STEPF**				William M.	24063	D	1918
Henrietta	22545	D	1917	Louis	44339	D	1926	**STEPHON**			
Henry	19475	D	1915	**STEPHANBLOME**				Ellen	76306	D	1937
STELTER				William	88770	D	1941	**STEPPACHER**			
William	47453	D	1927	**STEPHANI**				Maier	9631	D	1910
STELZNER				Mary F.	25763	D	1918	**STERCHI**			
Louise	62112	D	1932	**STEPHEN**				John	60544	D	1931
STEMBERG				Carl	59040	D	1931	**STERETT**			
Samuel	61711	D	1932	Charles	59040	D	1931	Mary C.	84571	D	1940
STEN				Eliza	19300	D	1915	**STERGIOS**			
Erik R.	43662	D	1926	**STEPHENS**				Maurice	69302	M	1935
STENBERG				Abbie E.	12657	M	1911	**STERIA**			
John	62465	D	1932	Bartlett	9694	M	1910	Caterina	89717	D	1942
Karolina	54219	D	1929	Emily Maud	35622	D	1922	**STERLING**			
STENBORG				Georgiana Harlow	23106	D	1917	Edward T.	11131	D	1911
John	62465	D	1932	Gertie G.	12657	M	1911	George	32128	D	1921
STENCEL				Green Alexander	47494	D	1927	George	45882	D	1926
Frances	83060	D	1940	Harlan Page	49419	D	1928	Maria	22373	D	1917
STENDEBACH				Henry O.	12657	M	1911	**STERN**			
Susan B.	65288	D	1933	Jessie M.	39920	D	1924	Abraham	13012	D	1912
STENDER				Mary Frances	34944	D	1922	Annie	75078	D	1937
Frank Arthur	83515	D	1940	Mary Jane	59073	M	1931	Caroline Kalisher	51265	D	1928
Jean	74327	D	1937	Mary McCullough	79333	D	1938	Carrie	81806	D	1939
John	74327	D	1937	Mary S.	72868	I	1936	Charles Nussbaum	81349	D	1939
Kate	83291	D	1940	Mathilde M.	66651	D	1934	Clara Madeline	47294	D	1927
STENGELE				Maude O.	35622	D	1922	Edythe T.	76471	D	1937
Mary	35972	D	1923	Melissa A.	79207	D	1938	Emanuel Lionel	59301	D	1931
STENGER				Michael	64066	D	1933	Florence	66941	D	1934
Anna	51252	D	1928	Nettie P.	12656	I	1911	Hattie	59332	D	1931
Bertha	7638	D	1909	Robert A.	12657	M	1911	Henry	17241	D	1914
STENGL				Thomas B.	47815	D	1927	Ida	43415	D	1926
Josephine	43432	D	1926	Thomas John	60784	D	1932	Jacob	20921	D	1916

NAME	NUMBER	TYPE	YEAR
Jacob	47798	D	1927
Jacob	52168	D	1929
Jacob W.	41667	D	1925
Jeanette	22985	D	1917
John	11607	M	1911
John David	13322	M	1912
Joseph	13102	D	1912
Josua	14920	D	1913
Juanita	11607	M	1911
Louis	7864	D	1909
Martin	9544	D	1910
Martin, Mrs.	9543	D	1910
Mathilde	83777	D	1940
Max	22869	D	1917
Moses	34583	D	1922
Moses Leopold	11133	D	1911
Nora Glover	88597	D	1941
Philip	52803	D	1929
Rosa	49338	D	1928
Rose	15207	D	1913
Selina	352	D	1906
Sidney	19735	D	1915
Sigmund	38851	D	1924
Sigmund	49914	D	1928
Theresa	9543	D	1910
Thomas L.	82037	M	1939
STERNAU			
Herman	68268	D	1934
STERNBERG			
Arthur W.	21228	D	1916
David	1468	D	1906
Davis	1468	D	1906
Francis	79188	D	1938
Jacob	17441	D	1914
STERNFELD			
Moritz	7609	D	1909
Morris	7609	D	1909
STERNHEIM			
Benjamin F.	83929	D	1940
STERNITZKY			
Richard F.	25931	D	1918
Robert R.	65164	D	1933
STERNS			
Arthur W.	21228	D	1916
STERNSHER			
Max	38650	D	1924
Meyer	38650	D	1924

NAME	NUMBER	TYPE	YEAR
STETECSKA			
Mari	71174	D	1935
STETSON			
Helen	89835	M	1942
James B.	8338	D	1909
Lelia I.	51198	D	1928
Mildred	9795	D	1910
Robert T. S.	34972	D	1922
Will C.	84036	D	1940
STETTHEIMER			
Barbara	25063	M	1918
Forence Jean	25063	M	1918
Henrietta B.	9317	D	1910
Jeanne	25063	M	1918
STETTIN			
Hermann	21119	D	1916
Minna	48054	D	1927
STETTINER			
Walter M.	61755	D	1932
STEUCK			
Hugo Ewald	22728	D	1917
STEUDNER			
Fritz	20197	D	1915
STEUR			
Jacques Barthelemess	74826	D	1937
STEVELER			
Annie R.	65318	D	1933
STEVEN			
A. D.	25126	D	1918
William Henry	48297	D	1927
STEVENS			
A. K.	13671	D	1912
Alexander H.	51980	D	1929
Alexander Hamilton	67652	D	1934
August	26189	D	1919
Augustus K.	12944	I	1912
Billy	38052	M	1924
Burt S.	62757	D	1932
Calvin Blaine	77538	D	1938
Caroline E.	4118	D	1907
Cassie	62645	D	1932
Cora May	89801	D	1942
D. E.	51612	D	1928
Eleanor	44264	D	1926
Eliza A.	35551	D	1922
Ella	64984	D	1933
Eva M.	24971	D	1918

NAME	NUMBER	TYPE	YEAR
Everett L.	71581	I	1936
Everett L.	73284	D	1936
George J.	11910	D	1911
Gertrude M.	54794	D	1930
H. H.	8684	D	1909
Harry	34539	I	1922
Helen Fuller	88148	D	1941
Helena J. W.	35551	D	1922
Henry R.	87771	D	1941
Irene Eleanor	44264	D	1926
James H.	33643	D	1922
Jim	62675	M	1932
John	31332	I	1921
John	32998	D	1921
John Edward	88824	D	1942
John Harrington	86977	D	1941
Kathryne Harrington	18487	D	1915
Laura M.	69969	D	1935
Martha A.	62600	M	1932
Mary	83021	I	1940
Mary E.	49346	D	1928
Mary Ellen	85927	D	1940
Mary Frances	34944	D	1922
Mary J.	59670	D	1931
Minnie	26766	D	1919
Minnie	61341	D	1932
Nellie A.	59295	D	1931
Richard Paine	69386	D	1935
Samuel B.	71269	D	1935
Samuel Morton	37527	D	1923
Sarah W.	71424	D	1936
Teresa M.	3673	D	1907
Thomas Aubin	72536	D	1936
Vena Elizabeth	87810	D	1941
Virginia	38052	M	1924
Will	62600	M	1932
William	62970	D	1932
William Henry	65828	D	1933
Willis Albert	60139	D	1931
STEVENSEON			
John J.	1229	D	1906
STEVENSON			
Alfred J.	26646	D	1919
Alfred J.	62674	D	1932
Annie I.	14453	D	1912
Bridget	84703	I	1940
Cecelia McFadden	17881	D	1914
Charles	41038	D	1925
Charles C.	88081	D	1941

NAME	NUMBER	TYPE	YEAR	NAME	NUMBER	TYPE	YEAR	NAME	NUMBER	TYPE	YEAR
Denzil R.	55002	I	1930	Charles	26673	D	1919	McCants	27126	D	1919
Ellen C. Strong	56181	D	1930	Charles	70619	D	1935	Norma	75277	M	1937
Evans William	74433	M	1937	Charles A.	42944	D	1925	Olive S.	22554	D	1917
Frank M.	34846	D	1922	Charles E.	27018	D	1919	Richard A.	35171	I	1922
Frederick DeWitt	35627	D	1922	Charles Lockwood	27195	M	1919	Robert John	85172	D	1940
Gertrude L.	25598	D	1918	Christina A.	30224	D	1920	Rose	32960	D	1921
H. Ernest	56945	D	1930	Clara J.	52897	D	1929	Ruve Margaret	16982	D	1914
Holland Newton	12344	D	1911	Clara J.	53654	D	1929	Stewart D.	47436	D	1927
Horatio E.	56945	D	1930	David E.	65568	D	1933	Thomas	17620	D	1914
Josephine	76193	I	1937	Dell	9659	D	1910	Thomas	44697	D	1926
Mary	51441	D	1928	Easter Belle	26927	D	1919	William B.	68774	D	1935
Mary Jane	74434	M	1937	Elizabeth Catherine	87984	D	1941	William H.	54840	D	1930
Mildred	9795	D	1910	Emma M.	85781	D	1940	William James	9680	D	1910
Mildred	25020	D	1918	Ethel M.	72678	D	1936	William S.	64676	D	1933
Rebina Longwill	27618	D	1919	Eugene A.	65368	D	1933	**STIAVETTI**			
Robert	16970	D	1914	Frank L.	30593	D	1920	Angelo	87082	D	1941
Sophie E.	43277	D	1925	George	65096	D	1933	Marta	52379	D	1929
Sydney Bernice	36412	M	1923	George E.	79238	D	1938	**STIAVIETTI**			
Thomas	27078	D	1919	George R.	55059	D	1930	Marta	52379	D	1929
Thomas	75223	D	1937	Gertruce E.	38938	M	1924	**STICH**			
Ward A.	76988	D	1937	Granville E.	83289	D	1940	Anna	84152	D	1940
William G.	27447	D	1919	Granville Q.	61647	D	1932	Benjamin Mitchell	35387	D	1922
STEVENTON				Granville, Jr.	67176	I	1934	Rosalie	63523	D	1933
Job	84502	D	1940	Harvey Jonson	65560	D	1933	Zorka	75853	D	1937
STEVER				Herbert Calloway	48356	D	1927	**STICHEL**			
Carl W.	59875	D	1931	Ida H.	84717	D	1940	Charles	37768	D	1923
Carl William	45	M	1906	James	9680	D	1910	**STICHTENOTH**			
Robert F.	34851	D	1922	James	16839	D	1914	Albert	9073	D	1910
STEVERNS				James W.	35420	D	1922	**STICHTERNATH**			
Sarah	1387	D	1906	Jennie	61914	I	1932	Adam Franz Wilhelm	21279	D	1916
STEVES				Jennie I.	66150	D	1934	**STICKEL**			
Gertrude	88832	D	1942	Jessie	15477	D	1913	John Lincoln	39673	D	1924
Oliver H.	77072	D	1937	Jessie	20290	D	1916	**STICKLESON**			
STEVING				Jessie Margaret	75625	D	1937	Charles	32408	D	1921
Geraldine	83244	M	1940	John	25835	D	1918	Ellen O. H.	16495	D	1913
STEVINSON				John Newton	22971	D	1917	**STICKNEY**			
Louisa Jane	63595	D	1933	John Newton	27214	M	1919	Benjamin W.	35980	D	1923
STEWARD				Lelia Elizabeth	69318	D	1935	Oscar	76810	D	1937
Lorenzo Sawyer	68644	D	1935	Lionel H.	4855	D	1907	**STIEBEL**			
Lucy A.	7820	D	1909	Lucinda Ellen	61944	D	1932	Henry Gordon	72721	D	1936
Rosa J.	37269	D	1923	Margaret	20677	D	1916	**STIEFEL**			
STEWART				Margaret	71975	D	1936	Gottlob	16227	D	1913
Adam, Jr.	72773	D	1936	Margaret Louisa	7160	D	1909	Helen	1014	M	1906
Albert L.	86985	D	1941	Mary	48172	D	1927	Helen	1015	D	1906
Alexander Murray	35558	D	1922	Mary A.	6031	D	1908	John Veit	72983	D	1936
Alice A.	65813	D	1933	Mary F.	37440	D	1923	Lillian Francis	27512	D	1919
Barbara	44077	M	1926	Mary J.	29988	D	1920	Louis	23536	D	1917
Catharine	10819	D	1910	Mary R.	73212	D	1936				
				Matthew C.	64140	D	1933				

Name	Number	Type	Year
Mildred Lucille	29476	M	1920
Pauline	1014	M	1906
Pauline	1015	D	1906
STIEGLITZ			
George E.	52973	D	1929
Helene Dingeon	6229	D	1908
Henry	57965	D	1931
STIEPCICH			
Michel J.	75504	D	1937
STIER			
Anton	441	D	1906
STIERLE			
Herman	23915	D	1918
STIERLEN			
George	34758	D	1922
STIERS			
Barbara Margaret	55790	D	1930
STIGLIE			
Joseph	71659	I	1936
STIH			
Anna	84152	D	1940
STIHL			
Susanna	23871	D	1918
STILE			
Vivienne M.	81006	D	1939
STILES			
Jot E.	86801	D	1941
STILIADES			
Maria K.	64870	D	1933
STILL			
Alden P.	18542	D	1915
Charles W.	47218	D	1927
Edward Marsdon	19944	D	1915
G.	49601	D	1928
Louise Emily	51690	D	1928
Mary E.	75344	D	1937
STILLER			
Reinhold C.	4823	D	1907
Wenzel	29672	D	1920
STILLINOVIC			
Ivan	9864	D	1910
STILLMAN			
Stanley	68154	D	1934
STILLWELL			
William	14822	D	1913

Name	Number	Type	Year
STILSON			
W. A.	8309	D	1909
STILWELL			
Arthur N.	80342	D	1939
STILWILL			
Arthur N.	80342	D	1939
STIMMEL			
Agnes	11029	D	1911
James Louis	23791	M	1917
Joseph	2112	M	1906
Lillie Pauline	23792	M	1917
Pauline	23791	M	1917
Racie	23791	M	1917
Sophie	23791	M	1917
STIMSON			
Ezra T.	39196	D	1924
Margaret	59481	D	1931
Sheldon H.	81537	D	1939
STINCEN			
Alice Margaretta	45722	D	1926
Emma E. C.	3616	D	1907
STINE			
George	49709	D	1928
Hanna May	55558	D	1930
Oliver C.	23940	D	1918
STINER			
Leota	6846	M	1908
STINSON			
Andrew Flood	7844	D	1909
Basil	33286	M	1922
Donald	48762	M	1927
Douglas	48762	M	1927
Guy L. M.	53493	D	1929
J. Coplin	24	D	1906
Jean	48762	M	1927
Kenneth	48762	M	1927
Louisa	2002	D	1906
STIOVETTI			
Marta	52379	D	1929
STIPICEVIC			
Bozo	30373	D	1920
STIPICHEVICH			
Bozo	30373	D	1920
STIPPEKOHL			
Carl	15472	D	1913
Ida M.	87220	D	1941

Name	Number	Type	Year
STIPPEL			
Lottie	3177	M	1907
STIREWALT			
Jane	21703	D	1916
Rebecca	21703	D	1916
STIRLING			
Mary A.	16158	D	1913
Mattie G.	79895	D	1938
STIRRAT			
Robert	47906	D	1927
STITH			
Learner B.	8748	D	1909
STITT			
Robert	5878	D	1908
STITZ			
Johanna	49738	D	1928
William J.	52660	D	1929
STIVENS			
Charles P.	39788	D	1924
STIVER			
A. G.	50840	D	1928
STJOHN			
Chauncey M.	23565	D	1917
STLYKAKIS			
George	11160	D	1911
STMARY			
Peter	10521	D	1910
STOBENER			
Delia	12682	D	1911
John W.	17614	D	1914
Raymond Edgar	13597	M	1912
STOCK			
Clara	55071	D	1930
Edward H.	32680	D	1921
Henriette Marie	34300	D	1922
John E.	23028	D	1917
John VanMaren	67823	M	1934
Leo I.	69784	D	1935
Lester H.	67232	D	1934
Lester Howard Francis	67823	M	1934
Louis	40976	I	1925
Louis	47048	D	1927
Louise	87613	D	1941
Marguerite R.	4272	D	1907
Mary	74809	D	1937
Otto	44432	D	1926
Paul H.	86313	D	1941

Name	Number	Type	Year
STOCKAN			
Camilla	63116	D	1932
Peter	63117	M	1932
Rachael	63117	M	1932
William	63117	M	1932
STOCKELBYE			
Peter. M.	16734	D	1914
STOCKER			
Eli James	56239	D	1930
Henry F.	54670	D	1930
James	56239	D	1930
Joseph	21903	D	1916
Joseph	67533	D	1934
STOCKIG			
Edward	84673	D	1940
STOCKIGT			
Edward	84673	D	1940
STOCKING			
Frank Lines	19555	D	1915
STOCKMAN			
D. M.	4590	D	1907
J. M.	4590	D	1907
Ralph	45229	D	1926
STOCKMON			
Ralph	45229	D	1926
STOCKREITER			
Alfred	39970	D	1924
STOCKSTROM			
Carl	2099	D	1906
Ono	6033	D	1908
STOCKTON			
Jane F.	66820	D	1934
Josephine D.	72001	D	1936
Max Riebenack	66793	D	1934
N. S.	30458	D	1920
Robert	59218	I	1931
STOCKVIS			
Emma	21221	D	1916
Emma	21307	I	1916
STOCKWELL			
Bettie C.	1358	D	1906
Bettie C.	1490	M	1906
Betty Green	85564	D	1940
STOCKWITZ			
Emma	34543	D	1922

Name	Number	Type	Year
STODDARD			
Agnes Pease	64972	D	1933
Cora Maria	25224	M	1918
Cyrenuis Horace	51663	D	1928
Eugene Warren	82052	D	1939
Johannah N.	89600	D	1942
Margaret	65778	D	1933
Mary Elizabeth	68179	D	1934
Nannie	24891	D	1918
Russell Wilburn	45439	I	1926
STODDART			
Archibald C.	10359	D	1910
STOELZLE			
Henriette Elisa	18445	D	1915
STOETERS			
Fred	68848	D	1935
Fritz	68848	D	1935
STOETZER			
George	66542	D	1934
STOFEN			
Peter Nicholas	11002	D	1911
STOFF			
Gerald A.	21281	M	1916
Lucile R.	21281	M	1916
STOFFEL			
Margith	54374	D	1929
STOFFER			
August W.	83552	I	1940
STOG			
Samuel B.	31777	D	1921
STOHLMANN			
Henrietta	84839	D	1940
STOHR			
Frank	8589	I	1909
Frank	34588	D	1922
STOJEBA			
Frank	86328	I	1941
Frank	87341	D	1941
STOKES			
Henry	46178	D	1927
Johanna J.	8844	D	1909
John A.	64062	D	1933
Josephine	82647	D	1939
Mark J.	76543	D	1937
Mary Elizabeth	76851	D	1937
Maude Granger	82623	D	1939

Name	Number	Type	Year
STOKKEBY			
Christian L.	33133	D	1922
STOKKEBYE			
Peter M.	16734	D	1914
STOLBERG			
Maria	21892	D	1916
STOLL			
Alice Summerfield	13799	D	1912
Carl	19393	D	1915
Charles	19393	D	1915
Charlie	78786	D	1938
Elizabeth	72157	D	1936
Margaret	75058	D	1937
Nathaniel	85842	D	1940
Susie M.	65791	D	1933
Walter	49613	D	1928
STOLLE			
Charles H.	68534	D	1934
Grace Aissa	66809	M	1934
Herbert R. G.	79753	D	1938
R. G.	79753	D	1938
Rosa Gomez	63934	D	1933
Wendell Fagrelius	88075	M	1941
STOLLENWERK			
Arthur E.	47763	I	1927
STOLOWITZ			
Sophie	71229	D	1935
STOLTE			
George August	25504	D	1918
Stanley George	25505	M	1918
STOLTENBERG			
Andrew V.	33157	D	1922
STOLTZ			
Charles M.	68178	D	1934
Charlotte M.	42326	D	1925
Joseph L.	48909	D	1928
STOLZ			
August	80327	D	1939
Belmont Henry	22268	M	1917
Dorothy Edna	22268	M	1917
Emanuel M.	88836	D	1942
Frederick L.	52377	D	1929
Kathleen	72849	M	1936
Peter J.	77432	D	1938
Rose B.	54684	D	1930
Ruby	46488	D	1927
Yvonne	72849	M	1936

NAME	NUMBER	TYPE	YEAR
STOLZENBURG			
Albert	66028	D	1934
STOLZENWALD			
Caroline	31588	D	1921
Fred	88368	D	1941
STOME			
Ellen L.	2090	D	1906
STONE			
Abbott	21663	I	1916
Abraham L.	59175	D	1931
Andrew L.	48163	D	1927
B. W.	81437	D	1939
Barbara	23260	M	1917
Belle	72892	D	1936
Benjamin Lester	48729	D	1927
Berneice	16418	M	1913
Bertody Wilder	81437	D	1939
Carl William	44906	M	1926
Charles B.	23260	M	1917
Clarence Percy	54807	D	1930
David	23260	M	1917
Dora Catherine	16279	D	1913
Dorothy	55930	M	1930
E. A.	66008	D	1934
E. B.	73499	D	1936
Edward Henry	69181	D	1935
Edwin W.	81760	D	1939
Eleanor	55930	M	1930
Elizabeth Lowell	32541	M	1921
Elizabeth McC.	80169	D	1938
Elizabeth Poore	80169	D	1938
Elsina C.	25380	D	1918
Emma Lillian	55380	D	1930
Erik Reinhold	43662	D	1926
Florence	23260	M	1917
Florence N.	23701	D	1917
Florence W.	65350	D	1933
Frank F.	41398	D	1925
Frank H.	42376	D	1925
Frank M.	7322	D	1909
Frederick P.	15452	D	1913
George Willard	18610	D	1915
Gordon Heath	47351	M	1927
Hannah	47567	D	1927
Hattie Grace	67387	D	1934
James	31283	D	1921
Jennie F.	54632	D	1929
John	23260	M	1917

NAME	NUMBER	TYPE	YEAR
John Leonard	35970	D	1923
Joseph Earl	66575	D	1934
Kate	50652	D	1928
Kate Rosalie	21272	D	1916
Leon D.	18793	I	1915
Leonard Holmes	74324	D	1937
Leta Fay	11896	M	1911
Lillian	23260	M	1917
Louilla	1708	D	1906
Louisa V.	4379	D	1907
Louise Josephine	18550	M	1915
Marcus	9341	D	1910
Maria Louise	16978	D	1914
Maria Wheeler	29833	D	1920
Marion	76023	D	1937
Mark L.	82696	D	1939
Mary Gardiner	7540	D	1909
Peter V.	13381	D	1912
Raymond A.	84068	D	1940
Reinhold	53861	D	1929
Sarah M.	61372	D	1932
Silas	80904	I	1939
Sophie G.	49775	D	1928
Stephen A. Douglas	78816	D	1938
Theresa	57095	D	1930
Thomas	50653	D	1928
Wilhelmina Havemeyer	57488	D	1930
William	44888	D	1926
STONEBACK			
Hazel L.	89751	D	1942
William	83792	D	1940
STONEBERGER			
Mabel R.	69817	D	1935
STONEHAM			
George	40098	I	1924
STONER			
Kate M.	2979	D	1907
Randell C.	2255	D	1906
William P.	986	D	1906
STONEY			
Emmie Sharratt	64117	D	1933
Gaillard	49505	D	1928
George M.	7918	D	1909
George N.	7918	D	1909
Georgiana	51157	D	1928
STONKUS			
Anna R.	34076	M	1922
Eva D.	34076	M	1922

NAME	NUMBER	TYPE	YEAR
Ignatius J.	34076	M	1922
Julia	34076	M	1922
Maggie K.	34076	M	1922
STONUM			
John	78708	M	1938
Joseph	78708	M	1938
Kevin	78708	M	1938
Margaret M.	78707	D	1938
Walter	78708	M	1938
STOPELLI			
Ettore L.	34615	D	1922
Louis	34615	D	1922
STOPSKI			
Abraham	8756	D	1909
STORE			
Evelyn	75064	M	1937
Marjorie	75064	M	1937
Robert	75064	M	1937
STOREBY			
Alfred Melvin	69761	D	1935
STOREIDE			
Arthur	69968	M	1935
Harry	69968	M	1935
STOREK			
Fred	69045	M	1935
STORER			
Agnes Winifred	85387	D	1940
Edward W.	46266	D	1927
Margaret VanNest	75194	I	1937
STOREY			
Isaac Holgate	22745	D	1917
Nellie T.	54871	D	1930
STORIE			
Edgar	11010	D	1911
STORLESE			
Nicola	20134	D	1915
STORM			
Elsie	43845	M	1926
Herman	35031	D	1922
Hilda	87960	D	1941
Israel	28738	D	1920
John Herman	52211	M	1929
Martin William	52211	M	1929
Matt	2229	D	1906
Naomi	24209	D	1918
Victor	43427	D	1926

NAME	NUMBER	TYPE	YEAR
STORMFIELD			
Oscar	22429	D	1917
STORMS			
Nelson Joseph	42120	D	1925
STORRS			
Adelbert L.	64367	D	1933
Catherine J.	59719	D	1931
John Henry	47482	M	1927
STORRY			
John	27357	D	1919
STORTI			
Costanza	46450	D	1927
Edward	55326	D	1930
STORVIK			
Paul I.	79873	D	1938
STORY			
David G.	58614	D	1931
Sophie	85535	D	1940
STOTHARD			
Thompson	11513	D	1911
STOTT			
Joseph Hood	52167	D	1929
STOTTS			
Walter M.	62258	I	1932
STOTZ			
Abraham	7244	D	1909
STOUT			
Alice	69179	D	1935
Forrest Eldred	74707	D	1937
Maria	85431	D	1940
Milton Worthington	74708	D	1937
Shirley Eugene	84801	D	1940
William	63912	D	1933
STOUTENBOROUGH			
Charles	4540	I	1907
Charles H.	803	D	1906
STOUTENBURGH			
Augusta K.	45965	D	1926
STOVEL			
H. Roy	63766	D	1933
STOVER			
Christopher	48273	D	1927
Edmund	19435	D	1915
Frank Caleb	58690	D	1931
Linville Newton	75701	D	1937
Louis Edmund	19435	D	1915

NAME	NUMBER	TYPE	YEAR
Mary Gray	61813	D	1932
Voyle V.	64970	D	1933
STOVESAND			
Elizabeth M.	31388	D	1921
STOW			
Ann Eliza	4937	D	1907
Joseph W.	7100	D	1909
Vanderlynn	27644	D	1919
STOWE			
Fannie R.	41111	D	1925
STOWELL			
Fred W.	13573	D	1912
John Matson	71312	D	1935
Marion Lucille	34115	M	1922
Sonia	81248	M	1939
STOWERS			
Ernest A.	63003	I	1932
STOY			
Samuel B.	31777	D	1921
STRACH			
Harold B.	66860	I	1934
Harold B.	67281	D	1934
STRACHAN			
George McEwen	32918	D	1921
Gertrude B.	30584	D	1920
Janet	6951	D	1908
Walter James	69500	D	1935
STRACK			
Frank W.	21279	D	1916
John George	11475	D	1911
STRADLING			
LaFayette F.	10533	D	1910
STRAESSLER			
Jacob	42855	D	1925
STRAHAN			
Mary	17910	D	1914
STRAHLE			
Anna H.	84242	D	1940
Jacob J.	12601	D	1911
Mary Ann	71692	D	1936
Paul C.	86603	D	1941
STRAHLMANN			
Henry	69423	D	1935
STRAIN			
Charles	53596	D	1929
William W.	19694	D	1915

NAME	NUMBER	TYPE	YEAR
STRAKA			
Steve	39586	D	1924
STRAKON			
John A.	14867	D	1913
STRAND			
Clara	84149	D	1940
Conrad F.	3903	D	1907
Jeanette	63610	I	1933
John A.	7388	D	1909
Olava Jacobsen	54373	D	1929
Oscar	35419	D	1922
Pauline	81415	D	1939
Susan T.	7387	D	1909
William F.	66774	D	1934
William J.	7389	D	1909
STRANDBERG			
Edea S.	16658	D	1914
Mary Frances	64105	D	1933
STRANDELL			
Carl Victor	15342	D	1913
Charles V.	15342	D	1913
STRANDGAVELOU			
Salvas K.	25573	D	1918
STRANDGREN			
Emil	21134	D	1916
STRANDLUND			
Richard	20922	D	1916
STRANG			
Christina	77968	D	1938
STRANGE			
Ada Rea	64914	D	1933
Elizabeth	831	D	1906
Herman P.	47987	D	1927
STRANGFELD			
Joseph F.	75091	D	1937
STRANGREN			
Emil	21134	D	1916
STRANZULA			
Domenico	54801	D	1930
Rosa	89528	D	1942
STRASDEN			
Hans	70298	D	1935
STRASDIN			
August W.	24052	D	1918
Hans	70298	D	1935

Key: D = death; M = minor; I = incompetent

NAME	NUMBER	TYPE	YEAR
STRASHILL			
Fritz	74504	D	1937
STRASSBURGER			
Betty Ann	88860	M	1942
Fay	88860	M	1942
Isaac	88558	D	1941
Julia	57663	D	1931
Sigmund	5941	D	1908
Virginia	28521	D	1919
STRASSEMEIER			
Henry	61750	D	1932
STRASSER			
Francis X.	76755	D	1937
STRASSMAN			
Ben M.	67955	D	1934
STRASSNER			
Lue	37341	D	1923
STRATA			
Maria	52273	D	1929
STRATH			
William O., Jr.	34788	M	1922
STRATHER			
Abraham	19013	D	1915
Susan T.	63492	D	1933
STRATHMANN			
John	13312	M	1912
STRATIDAKIS			
Constantine	58931	I	1931
STRATOS			
C.	58931	I	1931
STRATTA			
Antonio	74040	D	1936
Maria	52273	D	1929
STRATTON			
Amanda G.	25484	D	1918
Charles Jacob	38392	D	1924
Clara Jane	82006	D	1939
Emerson Oliver	42466	D	1925
Jean	73988	M	1936
Nellie R.	41878	D	1925
Nellie R.	41878	D	1925
Rosa I.	81671	D	1939
Rose Amanda Hervey	17234	D	1914
Sara E.	7166	D	1909
STRATUS			
C.	58931	I	1931

NAME	NUMBER	TYPE	YEAR
Gust	58931	I	1931
STRAUB			
Elizabeth	12007	D	1911
Ernest	88136	I	1941
Frank Joseph	87335	D	1941
John	68304	D	1934
Marie	16000	D	1913
Nicholas	28016	D	1919
Nicholas	57903	D	1931
STRAUBE			
Elizabeth	8017	I	1909
STRAUCH			
John O.	964	I	1906
John O.	2423	D	1906
Waldermar G.	54816	D	1930
STRAUS			
Adele	1827	D	1906
August Lazare	73931	I	1936
August Lazare	75790	D	1937
Augusta	15540	D	1913
Henrietta	88971	D	1942
Joseph D.	83761	D	1940
Louis	79636	D	1938
Sally	71273	I	1935
Sylvan	89271	D	1942
STRAUSBACH			
Anna	82548	D	1939
David Ambrose	49312	D	1928
STRAUSE			
Emilie	64291	D	1933
Jeffrey	30084	M	1920
Josephine	30086	M	1920
Lehman	52597	D	1929
Shirley	30085	M	1920
STRAUSER			
Joseph M.	22769	D	1917
STRAUSS			
Anna	66191	D	1934
Arthur B.	48331	D	1927
Babette	25876	M	1918
Bernard	10797	D	1910
Dorothy S.	9122	M	1910
Edgar L.	43108	D	1925
Edgard	18704	D	1915
Edward	76180	D	1937
Emanuel S.	34530	D	1922
Emma B.	60854	D	1932
F. M.	24476	D	1918

NAME	NUMBER	TYPE	YEAR
Gloria	64198	M	1933
Hugo	74807	D	1937
Irene	82043	D	1939
Joseph B.	78572	D	1938
Joseph M.	25875	D	1918
Kaufman	21515	D	1916
Martha W.	3997	M	1907
Max	76358	D	1937
Michael	76769	D	1937
Moses	13241	D	1912
Nelly	78475	D	1938
Rosa B.	29422	I	1920
Rosa B.	38919	D	1924
Samuel	3834	D	1907
Samuelita J.	18729	I	1915
Sarah	42865	D	1925
Simon	8627	D	1909
STRAVAPODIS			
Charles	29393	D	1920
Henry	29393	D	1920
STRAWBRIDGE			
Chester Wright	43599	D	1926
Wilbur S.	86712	D	1941
STRAZULLO			
Rosa	89528	D	1942
STRAZZALINO			
Giuseppe	28996	D	1920
STRAZZULLA			
Domenico	54801	D	1930
STRAZZULLO			
Domenico	54801	D	1930
STRAZZULO			
Domenico	54801	D	1930
Rosa	89528	D	1942
STREAM			
Augusta	42747	D	1925
STREATHER			
Sarah	76214	D	1937
STREBLOW			
Jessie	57018	D	1930
STRECKER			
Adolph	49557	D	1928
Johanna	17699	D	1914
STREEBY			
Hannah M.	88346	D	1941
STREET			
Alice	48705	D	1927

NAME	NUMBER	TYPE	YEAR
Charles E., III	48896	M	1928
Charles Thomas	81635	D	1939
Francis L.	40883	I	1925
George	64811	D	1933
George	62047	I	1932
Katherine G.	41881	D	1925
Katherine G.	41881	D	1925
Nancy	48896	M	1928
Sarah A.	31739	D	1921
Sarah A.	31828	D	1921
STREETER			
Martin Josiah	49158	D	1928
STREETT			
Edwin John	47546	M	1927
STREHL			
Alice	16811	M	1914
Alice	16811	M	1914
Charles	15742	D	1913
Charles	80172	D	1938
Mary	15741	I	1913
Mary	63672	D	1933
Mary	79346	D	1938
STREI			
Edwin	4296	M	1907
George	4296	M	1907
Grace	4296	M	1907
John Herman	1407	D	1906
Lorraine A.	62253	M	1932
Thomas J.	62253	M	1932
Violet	4296	M	1907
STREICHER			
Emma	60261	D	1931
Sophia	72224	D	1936
STREIFING			
Elise	43656	D	1926
Katharine Marguerita	43656	D	1926
STREIT			
Anna	12568	D	1911
Peter	46692	D	1927
STRELER			
Edward	23877	D	1918
STRELITZ			
Esther	49260	I	1928
Jacob	12235	D	1911
Robert	41959	M	1925
Robert	41959	M	1925

NAME	NUMBER	TYPE	YEAR
STRELOW			
Bertha E.	87366	D	1941
STRENG			
Regina	15175	D	1913
STRESEMAN			
William H.	71789	D	1936
William S.	71789	D	1936
STRETTON			
Louise M.	84038	I	1940
Louise M.	85941	D	1940
Louise Wakefield	85941	D	1940
STREUBER			
Emil	58322	D	1931
STREULI			
Emil, Jr.	19038	D	1915
Walter	68071	D	1934
STRIBOLT			
Ejnar	47895	D	1927
STRICHER			
Sophia	72224	D	1936
STRICKER			
Christian	62811	D	1932
John D.	19244	D	1915
STRICKERT			
Paul	12868	D	1912
STRICKLAND			
Agostine deH.	15676	D	1913
Charles F.	87834	I	1941
Charles O.	60923	D	1932
Hugh B.	69313	D	1935
Marie	74099	D	1936
STRICKLER			
Benka Earl	65789	M	1933
John Robert Dunlop	65788	M	1933
STRIDE			
George Spencer	3327	D	1907
STRIDING			
William	23893	D	1918
STRIKER			
Arthur	65171	D	1933
STRINGER			
Claire Katherine	18471	M	1915
Evelyn G.	41065	M	1925
Helen Elizabeth	18471	M	1915
Johanna	5724	D	1908
William	18218	D	1914

NAME	NUMBER	TYPE	YEAR
William Arthur	62703	D	1932
STRINGFELLOW			
Clarence L.	82710	D	1939
STRIPPEL			
Mildred	3177	M	1907
STRITCH			
Charles	54293	D	1929
STRITTMATTER			
Joseph	18728	D	1915
STRITZINGER			
Jacob	68746	D	1935
STROBECK			
Godfrey Leonard	75121	D	1937
STROBEL			
Edith Rose	72118	D	1936
Frederick George	7800	D	1909
Harry	83479	I	1940
Jacob Frederick	6761	D	1908
Katharina	24190	D	1918
STROH			
Adam L.	67978	D	1934
Anton George	80050	D	1938
Elizabeth	385	D	1906
Frederick T.	35436	D	1922
George A.	38521	D	1924
George Noyes	65006	D	1933
STROHL			
Louis	63749	D	1933
STROHM			
P. A.	77046	D	1937
STROHMAIER			
Christian Robert	82326	M	1939
STROHMEIER			
Edward J.	77588	D	1938
Joseph	1882	D	1906
Louis	40964	D	1925
William August	31621	D	1921
STROHSAHL			
Alvina F.	70498	D	1935
STROLL			
Rudolph	47926	D	1927
STROM			
Carl August	15702	D	1906
Charles	54877	D	1930
Charles	86031	D	1941
Claus	79513	D	1938

NAME	NUMBER	TYPE	YEAR
Freda	49844	D	1928
Lola	33652	M	1922
Madeline	33652	M	1922
Rudolph	33652	M	1922
STROMBORG			
Claus Victor	65807	D	1933
STROME			
Anthony	65710	D	1933
STROMINGER			
Curtis	59933	D	1931
STRONG			
Adeline Birdsall	16830	D	1914
Alonzo	1737	D	1906
Chester Percival	46270	I	1927
Edward B., Jr.	66470	D	1934
Elizabeth V.	59636	D	1931
George J.	4040	D	1907
Leslie T.	39585	D	1924
Nellie E.	30533	D	1920
Robert William	63536	D	1933
Rose Agnes	63537	D	1933
Theodore P.	44215	D	1926
STROTHER			
Elizabeth	15374	D	1913
Josephine B.	14220	D	1912
Julia A.	27062	D	1919
STROUD			
Amelia	25694	I	1918
Amelia	41715	D	1925
Eugene R.	29025	D	1920
Harriett S.	46035	D	1926
John R.	25389	D	1918
Mamie E.	24509	D	1918
STROUSE			
Mark	34816	D	1922
STROUT			
Elsie Parker	89021	D	1942
STROUTMAN			
Fred	89272	D	1942
STROW			
Mary J.	60370	D	1931
STROZYNSKI			
Boleslaus	55390	D	1930
STRUB			
Isidore W.	14796	D	1913
Rebecca L.	83190	D	1940

NAME	NUMBER	TYPE	YEAR
STRUBEL			
Elizabeth	12953	I	1912
Elizabeth	47598	D	1927
George	7083	D	1909
Martin Thorsen	47718	M	1927
Thelma Thorsen	47718	M	1927
Valentine, Jr.	7083	D	1909
STRUEFING			
Katharine Marguerite	58212	D	1931
STRUER			
Rose	89050	D	1942
STRUFING			
Elise	43656	D	1926
STRUGNELL			
Fay	52561	M	1929
Janet	52561	M	1929
STRUIDER			
M. J.	3706	D	1907
STRULFING			
Elise	43656	D	1926
Katharine Marguerita	43656	D	1926
STRUNK			
Barbara Helen	80049	M	1938
Ervin	32779	M	1921
Harold	32779	M	1921
Rudolph Alfred	80049	M	1938
STRUVE			
Hans	61909	D	1932
STRUVEN			
Christine Louise	37848	D	1923
John Theodore	29442	D	1920
STRYBING			
Helene	46097	D	1926
STRYCKER			
Charles	79853	I	1938
Walter Pierce	63061	D	1932
STRYE			
Albert	88943	D	1942
STRYKER			
Martha B.	926	M	1906
Wallace E.	926	M	1906
STUART			
Della	62452	D	1932
Ella	78201	D	1938
Ida	25797	D	1918
J. C. G.	6662	D	1908

NAME	NUMBER	TYPE	YEAR
James F.	14421	D	1912
James Fargus	18655	D	1915
Joseph	78199	D	1938
Lenora	21287	D	1916
Mary	3842	D	1907
Mittie R.	60423	D	1931
Pauline	79064	D	1938
R. B.	49101	D	1928
Sarah Ellen	49802	D	1928
Thomas	78200	D	1938
William A.	1084	D	1906
William J.	3841	D	1907
William T.	68203	D	1934
STUBBLEFIELD			
Sarita	67581	D	1934
Sarita	65464	I	1933
STUBBS			
Bessie D.	66604	D	1934
STUBEN			
Emma	75538	D	1937
STUBENRAUCH			
Emma	75538	D	1937
STUBO			
K. C.	4171	D	1907
STUCKERT			
Christina	772	I	1906
Christina	12398	D	1911
STUDD			
Gertrude	88875	I	1942
STUDENER			
Fritz	20197	L	1915
STUDINGER			
Edna	34512	D	1922
Emma	17485	D	1914
George	28153	M	1919
George W.	20844	D	1916
STUDLEY			
Abbie Amanda	29496	D	1920
George W.	2029	D	1906
Warren	14070	D	1912
STUEVEN			
Anna Louise	78631	M	1938
Henry Claus George	78631	M	1938
STUHLMACHER			
Catherine M.	8212	D	1909
William M.	8213	D	1909

NAME	NUMBER	TYPE	YEAR
STUHR			
August	29335	D	1920
Mabelle	57403	M	1930
Mary Jane	14692	D	1913
Raymond A.	22431	D	1917
Robert	57403	M	1930
Wallace	57403	M	1930
Wallace E.	40164	D	1924
STUHT			
Adolphina Maria Karoline	30036	D	1920
Wilhelm Johann Moritz	30037	D	1920
William	30036	D	1920
STULL			
Aurora A.	83676	D	1940
STULZ			
Joseph A.	15899	D	1913
William G.	3975	D	1907
STUMKE			
Gotlieb H.	22445	D	1917
Henry	74781	D	1937
STUMM			
Ernest C.	70888	D	1935
STUMP			
Margaret	54240	D	1929
STUMPF			
Annie R.	50476	D	1928
Frank S.	76030	I	1937
John, Jr.	40341	I	1924
John, Jr.	40486	D	1924
STUMPFF			
Frank F.	76030	I	1937
STUMPT			
John Mark	53264	M	1929
STURART			
William	970	D	1906
STURDIVANT			
Lulie M.	12882	D	1912
May F.	73078	D	1936
STURGE			
Annie Eugenie	24582	D	1918
STURGEON			
Constance	14881	M	1913
STURIZA			
George	3570	M	1907
Henry	3570	M	1907
Marco	3570	M	1907

NAME	NUMBER	TYPE	YEAR
Nicholas	11026	D	1911
Vincenza	60154	D	1931
STURKE			
Anna	30469	D	1920
STURLA			
G. B.	13420	D	1912
John	67413	D	1934
John B.	82695	D	1939
Louis	14812	D	1913
STURLESI			
Lorenzo	61690	D	1932
STURM			
Adele Marie Osborne	72605	D	1936
Adele Osborne	72605	D	1936
Anna M. M.	13910	D	1912
Charles	68908	D	1935
Herman	83855	D	1940
Teresa	55665	D	1930
STURMTHAL			
Benjamin	21682	D	1916
STURTEVANT			
Emma E.	35927	D	1923
James Forse	72048	D	1936
Mary E.	31017	D	1921
Ruth	12200	D	1911
STURTS			
Carl Frederick Amos	89192	D	1942
Charles	89192	D	1942
STUSSER			
Sam	57329	D	1930
STUTH			
Adolphina	30036	D	1920
STUTZMAN			
Herny Shafer	45263	D	1926
STYCHE			
George Frederick	48826	D	1927
Lucinda	39662	D	1924
STYLES			
Catherine	7452	D	1909
George	17260	D	1914
Robert	86293	D	1941
SUACCI			
Americo	56000	D	1930
SUAMI			
John	71437	D	1936

NAME	NUMBER	TYPE	YEAR
SUAVE			
Claire	12112	D	1911
SUBOTICH			
Nada	70483	M	1935
SUBRA			
Gedeo	85813	D	1940
Joseph Gideon	85813	D	1940
SUBTROPICO			
Angelo	63962	D	1933
SUCHORSYNSKA			
Frances	31086	D	1921
SUCHORZYNSKA			
Frances	31086	D	1921
SUCKAW			
Charles, Jr.	70936	D	1935
SUCKOW			
Charles W.	70936	D	1935
Charles, Jr.	70936	D	1935
George Ludwig	8535	D	1909
Margaret Elizabeth	45231	D	1926
SUCTCH			
Rudolph	30337	D	1920
SUDA			
Okuji	20788	D	1916
SUDALL			
Joseph	11940	D	1911
Mary L. Harper	70592	D	1935
Mary Lillian Harper	70592	D	1935
SUDAR			
Maksim	29909	D	1920
SUDBRACK			
Albert	12760	D	1911
SUDDARTH			
Daniel W.	10633	D	1910
SUDDEN			
Catherine	35948	D	1923
Catherine G.	16431	M	1913
Charles E.	13983	D	1912
Edwin R.	16430	M	1913
Robert	6456	D	1908
SUDEN			
Otto Tum	33571	D	1922
SUDHEIMER			
Geroge A.	62349	M	1932
Mabel O.	62350	D	1932

Name	Number	Type	Year	Name	Number	Type	Year	Name	Number	Type	Year
Sudin				Madeline	33498	M	1922	Agnes Ann	17127	M	1914
Anna	29514	I	1920	Mary	37526	D	1923	Alfred F.	75568	D	1937
M.	24763	D	1918	Timothy	33129	D	1922	Alice	41852	M	1925
Sue				**Suhling**				Alice	41852	M	1925
Wong Hip	45164	D	1926	Cecelia	20051	M	1915	Alice M.	33863	M	1922
Yin	35732	D	1923	Lloyd	20051	M	1915	Andrew	66550	M	1934
Suelflohn				Mary	19726	D	1915	Angela	78628	D	1938
Benjamin F.	44433	D	1926	**Suhnel**				Anna M.	44793	D	1926
Suen				Paul	79768	D	1938	Annie	9858	M	1910
Lee Yow	78164	D	1938	**Suhr**				Annie	88715	D	1941
Suennen				Anna	20062	D	1915	Annie	42854	D	1925
George William	77502	M	1938	Elise	75757	D	1937	Annie	58021	D	1931
Johanna Elizabeth	77502	M	1938	Ferdinand	74924	D	1937	Annie F.	785	D	1906
Leo, Jr.	77502	M	1938	Fred	10611	D	1910	Annie M.	30688	D	1920
Patricia	77502	M	1938	George L.	65569	D	1933	Anthony	6388	M	1908
Suess				Gertrude A.	24260	M	1918	Anthony	8674	M	1909
Ignatz	71556	D	1936	Hermann F.	31541	D	1921	Bartholomew	36167	D	1923
Suey				Marie J.	66391	D	1934	Bessie	6022	M	1908
Yin	35732	D	1923	**Sui**				Betty	82238	M	1939
Suezbacher				Frances	72140	D	1936	Bridget	24170	D	1918
Frederick	29079	D	1920	**Suich**				Bridget	83189	D	1940
Suffa				Mary	9266	D	1910	Bridget	80870	D	1939
William G.	52287	I	1929	**Suicher**				Bridget D.	85538	D	1940
Suffel				Elvira	84683	D	1940	Bridget Ellen	16621	D	1914
Joseph E.	88846	I	1942	**Suisman**				Catherine	29726	D	1920
Suffner				John A.	44071	D	1926	Catherine	31045	D	1921
Theresa	56592	D	1930	**Suit**				Catherine	57051	D	1930
Sugarman				Stephen Daniel	36044	D	1923	Catherine Eileen	61912	M	1932
Bessie	20816	M	1916	**Suize**				Catherine F.	23550	D	1917
Isaac	19954	D	1915	Philippe	51629	D	1928	Catherine F.	33370	D	1922
Mary	20816	M	1916	**Sujak**				Cecelia M.	62749	I	1932
Michael	33531	D	1922	Chris	41395	D	1925	Charles	87340	I	1941
Michel	33531	D	1922	**Sujo**				Charles A.	50609	D	1928
Mollie	20816	M	1916	Chon	56900	D	1930	Charles Edward	88171	D	1941
Pauline S.	88946	D	1942	**Sukovitzen**				Claire Cecelia	73174	M	1936
Rosie	20816	M	1916	Ivan	51828	D	1929	Cornelius	22477	D	1917
Stanley	46542	M	1927	**Sullenberger**				Cornelius	34572	D	1922
Zelda	33707	M	1922	Harry V.	12905	D	1912	Dan	66548	M	1934
Suggett				**Sullivan**				Danial Patrick	68519	I	1934
Louise Steffens	22595	D	1917	Abbie	6022	M	1908	Daniel	16623	D	1914
Sugiyama				Abbie	89841	D	1942	Daniel	17508	D	1914
Hiroshi	34821	M	1922	Abby	1151	I	1906	Daniel	23298	D	1917
Sugrue				Abby	4383	D	1907	Daniel	28010	D	1919
Gertrude	33498	M	1922	Adelaide	55719	I	1930	Daniel	41129	D	1925
Katherine	56075	I	1930	Adelaide	56706	D	1930	Daniel	58275	D	1931
Katherine	87454	I	1941	Agnes	30967	D	1921	Daniel E.	22403	D	1917
				Agnes	70748	D	1935	Daniel J.	1554	D	1906
								Daniel J.	16878	D	1914
								Daniel J.	59372	D	1931

NAME	NUMBER	TYPE	YEAR	NAME	NUMBER	TYPE	YEAR	NAME	NUMBER	TYPE	YEAR
Daniel J.	66929	D	1934	Frank F.	80606	D	1939	John D.	11142	D	1911
Daniel P.	85833	D	1940	George	67128	D	1934	John Daniel	50557	D	1928
Daniel, Mrs.	64951	D	1933	George A.	15369	D	1913	John Dennis	57839	D	1931
David	82238	M	1939	George E.	69252	D	1935	John E., Mrs.	80238	D	1939
Delia	360	D	1906	Geraldine F.	61912	M	1932	John F.	66441	D	1934
Delia	66414	D	1934	Gertrude J.	74050	D	1936	John Francis	28808	D	1920
Denis	57658	D	1931	Hannah	6566	D	1908	John H.	30482	D	1920
Dennis	536	D	1906	Hannah	34377	D	1922	John H.	39553	D	1924
Dennis	4748	D	1907	Hannah	36701	I	1923	John J.	8267	D	1909
Dennis	20757	D	1916	Hannah Fitzpatrick	41997	D	1925	John J.	18836	D	1915
Dennis J.	42111	D	1925	Hannah M.	16721	D	1914	John J.	28631	D	1920
Dennis J.	50768	D	1928	Hanora	10374	D	1910	John J.	57321	D	1930
Dennis J.	68859	D	1935	Helen B.	33290	D	1922	John J.	59631	D	1931
Dennis J.	78651	D	1938	Helen M.	26445	D	1919	John J.	81975	D	1939
Dennis T.	5856	D	1908	Henriette T.	52618	D	1929	John J.	87988	D	1941
Dolores	68020	M	1934	J. F.	999	D	1906	John Joseph	49964	D	1928
Edna M.	33863	M	1922	James	59961	D	1931	John L.	30041	D	1920
Edward	9858	M	1910	James H.	20882	D	1916	John L.	35990	D	1923
Edward J.	11870	D	1911	James J.	17144	D	1914	John Lawrence	10939	D	1910
Edward Joseph	64926	D	1933	James P.	73412	I	1936	John M.	52363	D	1929
Edward T.	42621	M	1925	Jane	58020	D	1931	John M.	65858	D	1933
Elizabeth	6060	D	1908	Jennie	41112	D	1925	John P.	16624	D	1914
Elizabeth Caroline	55878	D	1930	Jeremaih J.	26758	D	1919	John P.	67827	D	1934
Elizabeth Gertrude	80238	D	1939	Jeremiah	9794	D	1910	John S.	75471	D	1937
Ellen	642	D	1906	Jeremiah	16625	D	1914	John Stephen	22727	D	1917
Ellen	18029	D	1914	Jeremiah	34886	D	1922	John T.	84497	D	1940
Ellen	31347	D	1921	Jeremiah	36707	D	1923	John V.	48985	D	1928
Ellen A.	55526	D	1930	Jeremiah D.	72466	D	1936	John V., Jr.	17127	M	1914
Ellen M.	45648	D	1926	Jeremiah F.	49133	D	1928	John W.	80358	D	1939
Emma Gertrude	88101	I	1941	Jeremiah F.	61911	D	1932	Joseph	1741	D	1906
Emmet	1612	M	1906	Jeremiah F.	64946	D	1933	Joseph	6388	M	1908
Esther	45878	D	1926	Jeremiah W.	28359	D	1919	Joseph	8674	M	1909
Eugene	74328	D	1937	Jeremiah William	47018	D	1927	Joseph	49574	D	1928
Eugene D.	26383	D	1919	Jerry	32790	D	1921	Joseph	64054	D	1933
Florence	41833	D	1925	Jerry M.	20340	D	1916	Joseph	66263	D	1934
Florence	41833	D	1925	Johanna	1555	D	1906	Joseph A.	73171	D	1936
Florence J.	12848	D	1912	Johanna	22576	D	1917	Joseph B.	35842	I	1923
Frances A.	75990	D	1937	Johanna E.	71597	I	1936	Josephine	78412	D	1938
Francis Benedict	43302	D	1926	Johannah	15352	D	1913	Josephine H.	83841	D	1940
Francis Fontenoy	41648	I	1925	John	4378	D	1907	Joyce	82238	M	1939
Francis Fontenoy	57324	D	1930	John	11013	D	1911	Julia	5781	D	1908
Francis J.	41648	I	1925	John	41675	D	1925	Julia	13447	D	1912
Francis J.	57324	D	1930	John	66552	M	1934	Julia	76139	D	1937
Francis J.	78630	D	1938	John	85830	D	1940	Julia F.	49336	D	1928
Francisco St. John	57324	D	1930	John A.	70113	D	1935	Julia Patricia	38437	M	1924
Frank	6022	M	1908	John A.	83265	I	1940	Kate	28679	D	1920
Frank	6388	M	1908	John C.	83363	D	1940	Kate	70834	D	1935
Frank	8674	M	1909	John D.	5581	D	1908	Kate	77167	D	1937
Frank C.	75952	D	1937	John D.	9208	D	1910	Kathryn	22888	D	1917

NAME	NUMBER	TYPE	YEAR	NAME	NUMBER	TYPE	YEAR	NAME	NUMBER	TYPE	YEAR
Leah	55862	D	1930	Michael	26224	D	1919	Rose	9507	D	1910
Leo F.	33863	M	1922	Michael	28278	I	1919	Rose Bartels	11968	D	1911
Letitia McPhail	55862	D	1930	Michael	73501	D	1936	Russell Alger	69816	D	1935
Lillian E.	26335	D	1919	Michael Dennis	48788	D	1927	Russell Alger	70444	D	1935
Lucinda A.	78629	D	1938	Michael John	61289	D	1932	Sarah A.	60650	D	1932
Maisie	88657	D	1941	Michael Joseph	40613	D	1924	Sarah M.	14962	D	1913
Margaret	37713	D	1923	Michael Joseph	82662	D	1939	Sister Mary Euphrasia	30967	D	1921
Margaret	38844	D	1924	Michael P.	2630	D	1907	Stephen	66551	M	1934
Margaret	41282	D	1925	Michael S.	12381	D	1911	Thomas	1391	M	1906
Margaret	63329	D	1933	Mildred	44530	D	1926	Thomas	38683	D	1924
Margaret	75486	D	1937	Murt	82521	I	1939	Thomas B.	34978	D	1922
Margaret C.	46847	D	1927	Nelle A.	76420	D	1937	Thomas D.	6193	I	1908
Margaret J. V.	10355	D	1910	Nellie	6910	D	1908	Thomas D.	28165	D	1919
Margaret M.	71493	D	1936	Nellie A.	14342	D	1912	Thomas F.	26944	D	1919
Margaret Mary	27960	D	1919	Nellie F.	19606	D	1915	Thomas F.	41099	D	1925
Margaret Mary	29720	M	1920	Noel	33926	M	1922	Thomas Francis	39606	D	1924
Margaret T.	38060	D	1924	Nonie M.	13808	D	1912	Thomas H.	60947	D	1932
Marguerite	1612	M	1906	Nora	57861	D	1931	Thomas J.	54642	D	1930
Maria	84878	D	1940	Nora	81332	D	1939	Thomas Joseph	41490	D	1925
Mark Cornelius	45906	D	1926	Nora	84650	D	1940	Thomas P.	74123	D	1936
Mary	3863	D	1907	Nora A.	17181	D	1914	Timothy	6421	D	1908
Mary	13575	D	1912	Nora Casey	77972	D	1938	Timothy	7996	D	1909
Mary	29510	D	1920	Nora G.	15351	D	1913	Timothy	9733	D	1910
Mary	34658	D	1922	Nora Gertrude	77972	D	1938	Timothy	17770	D	1914
Mary	42621	M	1925	Nora H.	17127	M	1914	Timothy	19228	D	1915
Mary	47020	D	1927	Nora S.	78411	D	1938	Timothy	70091	D	1935
Mary	54643	I	1930	Oliver	63209	D	1932	Timothy C.	33863	M	1922
Mary	74376	D	1937	Patricia Margaret	52527	M	1929	Timothy E.	83051	D	1940
Mary	85954	D	1941	Patrick	10064	D	1910	Timothy J.	35833	D	1923
Mary	43334	D	1926	Patrick	22508	D	1917	Timothy J.	53969	I	1929
Mary A.	1727	D	1906	Patrick	37337	D	1923	Timothy J.	85543	D	1940
Mary A.	8266	D	1909	Patrick	38784	D	1924	Timothy Joseph	54548	D	1929
Mary A.	61845	D	1932	Patrick	45881	D	1926	Virginia	46781	D	1927
Mary A.	78628	D	1938	Patrick Andy	55703	D	1930	William	6388	M	1908
Mary Ann Canty	38440	D	1924	Patrick Andy	66549	M	1934	William	8674	M	1909
Mary E.	6680	D	1908	Patrick F.	65344	D	1933	William	61426	D	1932
Mary E.	33277	D	1922	Patrick H.	50843	D	1928	William B.	12086	I	1911
Mary E.	64951	D	1933	Patrick J.	43282	D	1925	William H.	44003	D	1926
Mary Ellen	64408	I	1933	Patrick J.	86652	D	1941	William I.	66803	D	1934
Mary Ellen	67745	D	1934	Patrick John	38437	M	1924	William J.	84168	D	1940
Mary F. C.	11775	I	1911	Patrick Joseph, Jr.	77109	D	1937	William Joseph	36488	M	1923
Mary Jane	58020	D	1931	Patrick M.	9290	D	1910	William Joseph	69606	D	1935
Mary Josephine	63562	D	1933	Paulena A.	45535	D	1926	William P.	2202	D	1906
Mary M.	15274	D	1913	Peter	7905	D	1909	William T.	16622	D	1914
Mary T.	86230	D	1941	Peter Francis	42752	D	1925	William V.	40412	M	1924
Matilda	82223	D	1939	Ralph T.	58952	D	1931	Winifred J.	49961	D	1928
Matthew I.	76260	D	1937	Richard	17127	M	1914	**SULLUSTE**			
Matthew P.	33863	M	1922	Richard	31421	D	1921	Frank	73084	D	1936
Michael	6911	D	1908	Rosanna	23297	D	1917				

Key: D = death; M = minor; I = incompetent

NAME	NUMBER	TYPE	YEAR
SULON			
Eva M.	43547	D	1926
SULSBERG			
Emma	77244	D	1937
SULTAN			
Walter D.	41376	D	1925
SULZBACHER			
Frederick	29079	D	1920
SULZBERGER			
William	57323	D	1930
SUMISKI			
Leah	55023	D	1930
SUMMERFIELD			
Herman	42241	D	1925
Joseph	17774	I	1914
Lesser	34825	D	1922
SUMMERFORD			
Hally Edward	57207	I	1930
SUMMERHAYES			
Alice Louise	5985	M	1908
Annie L.	3414	D	1907
Helen Mar	5985	M	1908
SUMMERS			
Amos W.	53994	D	1929
C. M.	26463	D	1919
Charles A.	26419	D	1919
Doris Olive	70116	M	1935
Elizabeth E.	51047	D	1928
Gerald	27120	M	1919
Harry C.	46126	D	1927
Jack Merlin	74341	M	1937
Rosie A.	64831	D	1933
Rufus Arelious Adron	22870	D	1917
SUMMERVILLE			
Alexander	38968	D	1924
Joseph	65741	D	1933
Lizzie	67220	D	1934
Matilda	4794	D	1907
Robert	65740	D	1933
Thomas	8196	D	1909
Thomas	65739	D	1933
SUMMY			
John	13793	D	1912
SUMNER			
Frank W.	18051	D	1914
Heralda Ruth	62148	M	1932
Heralda Tyng	62147	D	1932

NAME	NUMBER	TYPE	YEAR
Richard D.	42549	D	1925
Samuel B.	11714	D	1911
SUMSKI			
Helen Rosenthal	79505	D	1938
Levi	56874	D	1930
Levy	56874	D	1930
SUN			
Chew Koon	41067	D	1925
Dea Gong	21462	M	1916
Gee	74025	D	1936
Ho	82923	D	1939
Wong Sui	40924	M	1925
SUNDBERG			
August H.	6410	D	1908
Gustavia W.	62643	D	1932
Jennie	14827	D	1913
Mildred E.	82582	D	1939
SUNDBLAD			
Suzanne	39922	D	1924
SUNDELIN			
Henning R.	64003	I	1933
Henning R.	68217	D	1934
Matilda	50723	D	1928
SUNDELL			
Ethel C.	67959	D	1934
SUNDERER			
August L.	21675	D	1916
SUNDERHAUS			
G. H. O., Mrs.	12311	D	1911
SUNDGREN			
Carl	63139	D	1932
SUNDSTROM			
Bror F.	20470	D	1916
John Paul	20391	D	1916
SUNG			
Law Gum	70585	M	1935
SUNMAN			
Julia Ada	60386	D	1931
SUNSERI			
Franco	8038	D	1909
Lena	51147	M	1928
Luciano	44787	D	1926
Mariana	24484	D	1918
Nerzia	30067	M	1920
Nicola	78255	D	1938
Nina	30067	M	1920
Paulina	26274	D	1919

NAME	NUMBER	TYPE	YEAR
Salvatore	30067	M	1920
Samuel	36025	D	1923
SUOMINEN			
Hjalmar A.	57960	D	1931
SUPF			
George	19865	D	1915
SURDYKA			
Joseph	82941	M	1939
Ronald	82941	M	1939
SURGES			
Emma Viola	67386	D	1934
SURIA			
Louis	82436	D	1939
SURIAN			
Francesco	39448	M	1924
Luigia	39448	M	1924
SURPRENANT			
Lena	29279	D	1920
SUSA			
Konstantin Paul	77006	D	1937
SUSANI			
Giovanni	32757	D	1921
SUSANY			
Giovanni	32757	D	1921
SUSDALEVA			
Natalia	80762	D	1939
SUSLOWITZ			
Harry	81841	D	1939
SUSMAN			
Leland	61233	M	1932
Leo H.	51734	D	1929
Louis	8634	D	1909
Marjory	61233	M	1932
Mildred	27305	D	1919
SUSOEFF			
John	44090	M	1926
SUSOLFF			
John	44090	M	1926
SUSSKIND			
Henry E.	28622	M	1920
Joanne	87281	M	1941
Rosa	75423	D	1937
Sylvan H.	33241	D	1922
SUSSMAN			
Leo I.	44765	D	1926
Paul	37960	I	1923

NAME	NUMBER	TYPE	YEAR
Paul	38181	D	1924
Samuel	12160	D	1911
SUTCLIFFE			
Marie Abeille	30809	D	1920
SUTER			
Barbara	23643	D	1917
Daniel	15603	D	1913
Frank	85647	D	1940
SUTERS			
Mary Elizabeth	44284	M	1926
Mary Elizabeth	71981	D	1936
SUTHERLAND			
Alexander J.	46199	D	1927
Alexander Taylor	59724	D	1931
Augusta A.	63462	D	1933
Carlisle	25135	M	1918
George	18352	D	1915
George R.	32282	D	1921
Grace F.	70264	D	1935
Hannah	29410	D	1920
Hannah I.	25993	D	1918
Jemima M.	67111	D	1934
Lena T.	88608	D	1941
Mark Layton	14529	D	1912
Mary	34122	D	1922
Mary Theresa	47378	I	1927
Minnie A.	75263	D	1937
William	56844	D	1930
SUTHERLUND			
Ellen Pauline	36882	D	1923
SUTKAMP			
Anna C.	86926	D	1941
August	54086	D	1929
Clara	46437	D	1927
SUTLIFF			
Henry	1053	D	1906
SUTRO			
Adolph	51	D	1906
Adolph Newton	13585	M	1912
Adolphine Charlotte	13585	M	1912
Albert	6818	D	1908
Charles W.	72350	D	1936
Edgar D.	79861	M	1938
Edgar Douglas	33837	M	1922
Edgar E.	33725	D	1922
Florentine S.	89680	D	1942
Marian	30430	D	1920
Marian Jane	33837	M	1922

NAME	NUMBER	TYPE	YEAR
Marie B.	21334	I	1916
Marie B.	66715	I	1934
Oscar	69926	D	1935
Rose Victoria	33837	M	1922
Therese	52303	D	1929
SUTTER			
Alphonse	48386	D	1927
Christene H.	82958	D	1939
Eugene L.	57289	D	1930
Gabriel	16140	D	1913
George	64265	D	1933
Ida Elizabeth	59396	D	1931
John Albert	41880	D	1925
John Albert	41880	D	1925
John N.	75109	D	1937
Juan	87603	D	1941
Nicolasa	34847	D	1922
Oswald	63864	D	1933
Theresia	33904	D	1922
Walter Samuel	78769	D	1938
SUTTON			
Agnes	89426	D	1942
Alberta	5829	M	1908
Allen M.	20293	D	1916
Anna Fidelia	5829	M	1908
Anna Maria	51135	D	1928
Byron	47463	D	1927
Frank L.	52875	I	1929
George E.	74609	D	1937
Helen B.	77836	I	1938
Helen Borone	85232	D	1940
James	46223	I	1927
Joseph	59702	D	1931
Lee J.	51225	D	1928
Lillian J.	80436	D	1939
Marie Louise	80043	M	1938
Martha	19023	D	1915
Mary	51135	D	1928
Samuel W.	51158	D	1928
Walter	59197	D	1931
SUVANTO			
Selma	69552	D	1935
Wilho	25878	D	1918
SUYDAM			
Charles H.	89685	D	1942
SUZANNE			
Joseph	62003	I	1932

NAME	NUMBER	TYPE	YEAR
SUZDALEVA			
Natalia	80762	D	1939
SUZUKAWA			
Harry C.	7405	M	1909
Harry M.	24679	D	1918
SUZUKI			
Naoye	48251	M	1927
Nobuko	48251	M	1927
SVABEK			
Jan	63390	D	1933
John	63390	D	1933
Juan	63390	D	1933
Veronica	64695	D	1933
SVAHN			
Gustaf Frid	28403	D	1919
SVAINAZ			
Antonio S.	22927	D	1917
SVANE			
Christian	48728	D	1927
Jorgen C.	48728	D	1927
SVANGREN			
Adolf	29061	D	1920
SVANSON			
Gustava	38509	D	1924
Oscar L.	80480	D	1939
Peter	32646	D	1921
SVAVEK			
John	63390	D	1933
SVEC			
Charles	75951	I	1937
Frank	30182	D	1920
SVENDSEN			
Dagmar A.	38509	D	1924
Ferdinand	67670	D	1934
Gustafa	38509	D	1924
Mallie C.	66046	D	1934
SVENDSON			
Ole	56059	D	1930
SVENSON			
Frank W.	11929	D	1911
Gus	88421	D	1941
Gustava	38509	D	1924
Morten Sigfrid	49935	D	1928
Peter	67343	D	1934
Sven	79840	D	1938

Key: D = death; M = minor; I = incompetent

NAME	NUMBER	TYPE	YEAR
SVENSSON			
George Gustav	73169	D	1936
Peter	67343	D	1934
SVETICH			
Christina	72905	D	1936
SVETINA			
Lucia	86484	D	1941
SVITARK			
Jacob	5519	D	1908
SVITAVSKY			
Richard	44212	D	1926
SWABACKER			
Louis	47836	D	1927
SWADLEY			
W. W.	53620	D	1929
SWAGER			
Carolyn Dorothy	80437	M	1939
SWAIN			
Caroline Furber	39777	D	1924
Charles R.	25844	D	1918
D. Dwight Moulton	73869	D	1936
Hadinen	47278	D	1927
Isaac	5967	D	1908
John	77515	D	1938
Julius Curtis	66922	D	1934
Mary H.	37468	D	1923
Minerva N.	74672	D	1937
Minnie	69629	D	1935
Nellie Phipps	62750	D	1932
Richard	38861	D	1924
Sarah S.	885	D	1906
Susan W.	5551	D	1908
SWAINE			
Charles	3797	D	1907
SWALES			
Edward B.	42586	D	1925
Henrietta Jane	43728	D	1926
Thomas E. J.	32483	D	1921
SWALL			
Carrie	27178	D	1919
Peter	5661	D	1908
SWALLOW			
Verne D.	22319	D	1917
SWALVE			
Hermann	724	D	1906

NAME	NUMBER	TYPE	YEAR
SWAN			
Anna	56989	M	1930
Benjamin Ralph	23960	D	1918
Edward E.	78588	D	1938
Eva C.	10513	D	1910
Frederick W.	2732	D	1907
George	67487	I	1934
Gerald	84658	M	1940
Henry G.	18100	D	1914
Katherine Hope	27569	D	1919
Katherine M.	27568	D	1919
Laura	73368	D	1936
Martha A.	17411	D	1914
Roberta B.	52810	M	1929
Roberta V.	52810	M	1929
William	28791	I	1920
SWANBERG			
Anton	73059	D	1936
Julie A.	68594	D	1934
SWANEY			
Adelia S.	1052	D	1906
Ella	61807	D	1932
SWANGGREN			
Adolph	29061	D	1920
SWANK			
John Louis	72980	D	1936
SWANN			
John C.	77581	D	1938
SWANNACK			
Daniel	22192	D	1917
Sarah M.	29636	D	1920
SWANSEN			
A. B.	76143	D	1937
Annie	22837	D	1917
Daniel	23802	D	1917
SWANSON			
A. M.	42562	D	1925
Albert Daniel	24014	M	1918
Alexander G.	57759	D	1931
Alfred	22139	D	1917
Amy B.	36808	D	1923
Andrew	10149	D	1910
Andrew	44676	D	1926
Anna Sophia	16513	D	1913
Anton B.	76143	D	1937
August	9734	D	1910
Carl	84737	D	1940

NAME	NUMBER	TYPE	YEAR
Carl Gustaf	23851	D	1918
Charles August	13172	D	1912
Charles J.	33595	D	1922
Charles John	55560	M	1930
Daniel G.	23802	D	1917
Elvira	24014	M	1918
Emma	46880	D	1927
Esther	11141	M	1911
Frank W.	11929	D	1911
Fred	21771	D	1916
Fritz Fritlyof	62500	D	1932
Gustaf	24347	D	1918
Gustaf A.	52223	D	1929
Gustav	84220	D	1940
Henry G.	88746	D	1941
Ida C.	25140	D	1918
John	46235	D	1927
Joseph Clarence	87229	D	1941
Louise	64999	D	1933
Madge E.	86187	I	1941
Margaret A.	52708	D	1929
Martin	37423	D	1923
Maybelle	70394	M	1935
Morten Sigfrid	49935	D	1928
Noah	74056	D	1936
Ole W.	68872	D	1935
Oscar	59698	D	1931
Oscar L.	80480	D	1939
Sigfrid	49935	D	1928
Sven B.	77906	D	1938
Swan	45435	D	1926
Swan	60599	D	1932
Vandla	24093	D	1918
William	48241	D	1927
SWANSTROM			
Charles Robert	4563	D	1907
SWANTON			
Agnes E.	77913	D	1938
Bernard Hutchinson	63959	D	1933
Bert	63959	D	1933
Ellen M.	88576	D	1941
Hazel V.	82872	D	1939
Nellie	87523	I	1941
Nellie	88576	D	1941
SWARSTAD			
Harry M.	43096	I	1925
SWART			
Bodel Marie	19520	D	1915

NAME	NUMBER	TYPE	YEAR	NAME	NUMBER	TYPE	YEAR	NAME	NUMBER	TYPE	YEAR
Marie	19520	D	1915	George E.	15784	D	1913	**SWEENY**			
William Preston	55574	D	1930	George Enright	38611	M	1924	Edward	14024	D	1912
SWARTLEY				George Enright	54653	M	1930	Mary Shumate	86348	D	1941
Mary E.	26124	D	1919	George Joseph	54636	D	1930	Natailia Estrada	73706	D	1936
William	23348	D	1917	Hannah	46670	D	1927	**SWEET**			
SWARTS				Harry	22689	I	1917	Ada C.	51060	D	1928
Beckie	68794	D	1935	Hugh John	50057	D	1928	Annie E.	39814	D	1924
SWARTZ				Isabel	9482	M	1910	Elna B.	73497	I	1936
Charles L.	76830	D	1937	J. P.	45491	D	1926	George W.	33999	D	1922
Henry B.	88193	D	1941	James	12929	D	1912	Isaac	70602	D	1935
Irving	79068	D	1938	James E.	29265	D	1920	**SWEETMAN**			
Leslie C.	46643	I	1927	James Lawrence	67030	D	1934	Annie J. M.	80562	D	1939
SWARTZBURG				James P.	88562	D	1941	George Alexander	76268	D	1937
Dorothy	89602	D	1942	John	33446	D	1922	James Francis	44797	M	1926
SWASEY				John	55187	D	1930	Joseph	55040	D	1930
Amanda A.	51700	D	1928	John J.	6539	I	1908	Mary	89444	D	1942
Gustavus A.	1119	D	1906	John J.	7980	D	1909	Walter	25192	D	1918
Gustavus A.	1322	I	1906	John J.	54188	D	1929	**SWEETSER**			
SWAYNE				John M.	82195	D	1939	Algernon W., Jr.	85682	M	1940
Junior Melville	40604	M	1924	Joseph G.	43788	D	1926	Algernon Warren, III	85682	M	1940
SWEENEY				Joseph H.	12032	M	1911	Carrie M.	46650	D	1927
Aemon V.	9482	M	1910	Joseph J.	62913	I	1932	John E.	4235	D	1907
Alice	537	D	1906	Josiah	49365	D	1928	Leon O.	41032	D	1925
Alice V.	16466	M	1913	Kate	10893	I	1910	Stephen	4236	D	1907
Anita	9482	M	1910	Kate	27632	D	1919	**SWEGEL**			
Annie M.	79322	D	1938	Katherine M.	67027	D	1934	Marko	68270	D	1934
Anthony	668	D	1906	Leonard Grant	38611	M	1924	**SWEGGEN**			
Bridget	26433	D	1919	Leonard Grant	54653	M	1930	Ole Rasmussen	56349	D	1930
Catherine Letitia	20182	D	1915	Marie Isabel	30125	M	1920	**SWEIGERT**			
Chandler P.	3447	D	1907	Mary A.	15725	D	1913	Mary	25400	D	1918
Clara J.	21257	D	1916	Mary A.	26295	D	1919	**SWEITZER**			
Conrelius	17929	D	1914	Mary Leinad	49322	D	1928	James Harrison	84472	D	1940
Cornelius	85637	D	1940	Mary Louisa	79521	D	1938	Mollie	71311	D	1935
Daniel	33868	D	1922	Mary T.	12032	M	1911	**SWENDSEN**			
Daniel	41253	D	1925	Minnie	6144	D	1908	Carl Oluf	71486	M	1936
Daniel	85637	D	1940	Patrick	24070	D	1918	Catherine Christine	71486	M	1936
Delia	26433	D	1919	Patrick C.	10892	D	1910	Georgia Grace	71486	M	1936
Della	50626	I	1928	Rose A.	12032	M	1911	John Robert	71486	M	1936
Denis	57610	D	1931	Sarah	44031	D	1926	Mary Joanne	71486	M	1936
Edward	32186	D	1921	T. M.	828	D	1906	**SWENSEN**			
Edward	48802	D	1927	Thomas	65186	D	1933	John J.	74994	D	1937
Edward	51358	D	1928	Thomas F.	52886	D	1929	Peter	56962	D	1930
Eugene	15218	D	1913	Thomasine	50812	M	1928	**SWENSON**			
Eugene	68522	D	1934	Timothy	12089	D	1911	George G.	73169	D	1936
Eugene B.	9482	M	1910	Timothy Dayton	33747	D	1922	Henry	78243	D	1938
Francis D.	30125	M	1920	Virginia M.	56788	M	1930	Johanna	58133	D	1931
Frank D.	9482	M	1910	William	57555	D	1931	John A.	26838	I	1919
George	58775	D	1931	William B.	9482	M	1910				
				William B.	25597	D	1918				

NAME	NUMBER	TYPE	YEAR	NAME	NUMBER	TYPE	YEAR	NAME	NUMBER	TYPE	YEAR
John A.	28013	D	1919	Mary F.	3161	D	1907	Z. E. Reidel	80012	D	1938
Ole W.	68872	D	1935	Thelma Dean	87787	M	1941	**SWORI**			
Peter	66479	I	1934	William Francis	87787	M	1941	Angelo	76948	I	1937
Peter	67343	D	1934	**SWIGERT**				**SWYTISCHER**			
Sigrid G.	47552	D	1927	Charles Frederick	70285	D	1935	Aurelia	25826	D	1918
Sophia	58311	D	1931	**SWIGGETT**				**SYCE**			
Theodore E.	66197	D	1934	Levin VanCleave	52729	D	1929	A.	27571	D	1919
SWENSSON				**SWIM**				Mary Agnes	27571	D	1919
Cassaline	62645	D	1932	Lena	40560	I	1924	**SYDEKUM**			
Edith J.	69754	I	1935	Mary Elizabeth	11073	I	1911	Ernest	26159	D	1919
SWENY				**SWINDELLS**				**SYDEL**			
George W.	60776	D	1932	Archie K.	53177	D	1929	Herman	47515	D	1927
SWERGER				**SWINERTON**				**SYDELMAN**			
Frederick Albert	76468	D	1937	Jane	36612	M	1923	Herman	47515	D	1927
SWETICH				William Arthur	36612	M	1923	**SYDNOR**			
Christina	72905	D	1936	**SWINEY**				Eppa W.	32428	D	1921
SWETNAM				Linda P.	47093	D	1927	**SYKES**			
Bryan	89581	I	1942	**SWINK**				Jane A.	100	D	1906
SWETT				Riley W.	82254	D	1939	Mary Jane	58068	D	1931
Abbie L.	36887	D	1923	**SWINNERTON**				Thomas R.	48572	D	1927
Florence E.	58216	D	1931	Delia Laura	1977	I	1906	**SYLVA**			
Frederick C.	58541	D	1931	Delia Laura	6429	D	1908	Antone	37068	D	1923
Hannah L.	75734	D	1937	**SWINNEY**				Henry G.	45108	D	1926
Harriett N.	3884	D	1907	John Chesley	84176	D	1940	Margaret J.	39593	D	1924
Harry Emmons	42487	D	1925	Joseph G.	43788	D	1926	**SYLVESTER**			
Helen Marion	19756	D	1915	Thomas C.	23548	D	1917	Charles A.	60667	D	1932
Hurbert C.	42897	M	1925	**SWINT**				Charles B.	12175	I	1911
Joseph D.	688	D	1906	Fred	37100	D	1923	Claus	50486	D	1928
Leo E.	42897	M	1925	**SWITTON**				Daniel A.	31861	D	1921
Sarah F.	1848	D	1906	Max	51650	D	1928	Daniel Milton	32148	M	1921
Thomas J.	42897	M	1925	**SWITZER**				Ellen F.	27164	D	1919
Tomasa	1102	D	1906	Edward	4441	M	1907	Frank	51762	D	1929
SWEZEY				Frederick	4441	M	1907	Frederick H.	25497	D	1918
Helen M.	48340	D	1927	Herbert Cunningham	78022	D	1938	George I.	14233	I	1912
SWEZY				John H.	37819	D	1923	George I.	15176	D	1913
Anna L.	67177	D	1934	Leopold	47668	D	1927	Helene	41329	D	1925
SWIFT				**SWOFFORD**				Henry	15623	D	1913
Alice Mae	87787	M	1941	Wilford T.	54585	I	1929	Jennie K.	51146	D	1928
Bartholomew	31600	D	1921	**SWORD**				Johanne Juliane	50487	D	1928
Charles H.	20776	D	1916	Charles W.	39544	I	1924	Maria	11283	D	1911
Charles J.	77540	D	1938	George	53148	D	1929	Mary F.	60979	D	1932
Eugene Leo	62502	D	1932	**SWORDS**				Sybil E.	29705	M	1920
Florence	65840	D	1933	Birdie Belle	80012	D	1938	William	89947	D	1942
George Raymond	2186	M	1906	Budd	80012	D	1938	**SYLVESTRE**			
Henry C.	53706	D	1929	J. W., Mrs.	80012	D	1938	Frank	51762	D	1929
John	59137	D	1931	Raymond	80012	D	1938	Louie	16763	M	1914
John	85288	D	1940								

Name	Number	Type	Year
SYLVESTRI			
Baptiste	48153	M	1927
Clarence	60309	M	1931
Eda	48153	M	1927
Francesco	1140	D	1906
Frank	51762	D	1929
Joseph	78495	D	1938
SYLVESTRO			
Joseph	78495	D	1938
SYLVIA			
Millet	23486	I	1917
SYME			
Elias R.	17670	D	1914
John F.	77848	D	1938
SYMINGTON			
Robert B.	26165	D	1919
SYMON			
Adele	71588	D	1936
Anna E.	80111	D	1938
Charles M.	78895	D	1938
George	48754	D	1927
George, Mrs.	80111	D	1938
Grace	9075	D	1910
James Armit	71347	D	1936
James C.	42737	D	1925
Marcella Grace	71814	M	1936
Mary Adele	71588	D	1936
SYMONDS			
Hannah M.	24921	D	1918
SYMONS			
Aaron	75361	D	1937
Hattie R.	80544	D	1939
Mary Anne	15153	D	1913
William S.	70270	D	1935
SYNAN			
Emmanuel	75805	D	1937
James E.	45555	D	1926
SYNOTT			
Mary	28667	D	1920
SYSAGHT			
Cletus G.	15740	M	1913
SYVERSEN			
Ole	49751	I	1928
Ole	51501	D	1928
SYZ			
Harvey William	10384	D	1910

Name	Number	Type	Year
SZABO			
Jakob	45768	D	1926
SZAFCSUR			
Irma	12984	D	1912
SZAKALL			
Margaret P.	87512	D	1941
SZALATESKY			
Verona	64539	D	1933
SZALAY			
John	40301	D	1924
SZANIK			
Ella	32785	D	1921
Emilie	49308	D	1928
Samuel	68189	D	1934
SZATHMARY			
Threase	61542	D	1932
SZATMARY			
Anna Sabo	52160	D	1929
Marian	56791	M	1930
Thomas	56790	M	1930
Thompson	56790	M	1930
SZEGHY			
Kalman	51840	D	1929
SZEMANSKI			
Stefan	62331	D	1932
SZERMATA			
Michael	38337	I	1924
Michael	52784	D	1929
SZEROCZYNSKI			
John	27066	D	1919
SZIGMANDI			
Frances	53818	D	1929
Francis	53818	D	1929
SZIGMANDY			
Francis	53818	D	1929
SZIICS			
Stephan	78291	D	1938
SZILAGYI			
John	87906	D	1941
SZYMANSKI			
Victoria	43982	D	1926
TAAFFE			
Bridget	15480	D	1913
Edward Joseph	81872	D	1939
Elizabeth	8313	D	1909
Elizabeth	66306	D	1934

Name	Number	Type	Year
John Joseph, Jr.	73213	M	1936
Lydia	66306	D	1934
Marilyn	73213	M	1936
Randal Dunne	5842	M	1908
TABARINI			
Giovanni	16964	D	1914
Joseph	26706	M	1919
Teresa	26704	D	1919
TABER			
Celina	41389	D	1925
Charles W.	18664	D	1915
Hilda	62333	D	1932
Ruby E.	85651	I	1940
Ruby Elizabeth	87801	I	1941
TABOADA			
Pilar	52751	M	1929
TABOAS			
Frank C.	89299	D	1942
TABOR			
Fannie R.	23211	D	1917
Julius	68521	D	1934
William James	23821	D	1918
TABRETT			
Henry Charles	22960	D	1917
TACCHINI			
Teresa	9554	D	1910
TACCHINO			
Michael	37504	D	1923
Teresa	9554	D	1910
TACK			
Gee	79701	D	1938
TACKABERRY			
Selma H. F.	17270	D	1914
TACKABURY			
George K.	30994	D	1921
TADD			
Emma	69465	D	1935
Mary	69466	D	1935
TADDEUCCI			
Joseph	46367	D	1927
Martino	24974	D	1918
TADICH			
Antoinette	63977	D	1933
TAENNLER			
Casper	37790	D	1923

NAME	NUMBER	TYPE	YEAR
TAFFE			
James L.	34613	D	1922
TAFFINDER			
Geoffe	29301	D	1920
William Geoffe	29301	D	1920
TAFT			
Anna	17004	D	1914
Harry Cheney	89531	D	1942
Myrtle	82998	D	1940
TAGANETTI			
Peter	26368	D	1919
TAGGART			
Helen	17082	D	1914
Jessie Victoria	62131	M	1932
Mary Ellen	17082	D	1914
William Henry	51682	D	1928
TAGGS			
Myron Oliver	54149	D	1929
TAGNOTTI			
Serafino	47319	D	1927
TAHANEY			
Annie	19578	D	1915
James	55740	D	1930
TAHE			
Catherine	11450	D	1911
TAHNBACH			
Helene	25727	D	1918
TAIARIOL			
Fioravante	78644	D	1938
TAIT			
Amelia M.	4675	D	1907
Dudley	24197	D	1918
Dudley, Jr.	4230	M	1907
Errol A.	3770	M	1907
Frances	7493	D	1909
Frederick Dudley	24197	D	1918
Georgie Chapin	3412	M	1907
James Boiston	74562	D	1937
John D., Jr.	69350	M	1935
Laura A.	28105	D	1919
Mary Ann	36208	D	1923
Millie Rice	9065	D	1910
Millie S. J.	9065	D	1910
Oenone	23124	M	1917
Phyllis Marion	69350	M	1935
William D.	13354	D	1912

NAME	NUMBER	TYPE	YEAR
TAITMEYER			
Martha	88568	D	1941
TAKAHASHI			
George F.	22329	D	1917
TAKEI			
Yuri	39375	D	1924
TALAMANTES			
Robert	86547	D	1941
TALBOT			
Abigail Ann	48753	D	1927
Alice Campbell	12846	D	1912
Andrew B., Jr.	79221	M	1938
Andrew Burton	9597	M	1910
Andrew Burton	77674	D	1938
Annie Douglass	19786	D	1915
Charles F. A.	59325	D	1931
Ellen A.	14500	I	1912
Elodie	87251	I	1941
Hazel Mary	49231	I	1928
Helen Sophia	12429	M	1911
Herbert Arthur	19197	D	1915
Hurbert	5947	D	1908
Irene J.	89599	D	1942
James Arnold	73736	D	1936
John E.	10283	D	1910
Lorna	79221	M	1938
Simeon Bailey	32907	D	1921
Sophia Gleason	11487	D	1911
Thomas H.	40298	D	1924
Walter J.	13018	D	1912
TALBOTT			
Fred K.	50327	I	1928
Homer I.	41262	D	1925
TALCOTT			
James C.	64615	D	1933
Louis	6671	D	1908
TALIAFERRO			
Janice Jean	53949	M	1929
TALLANT			
Eliza S.	29080	I	1920
Eliza S.	43181	D	1925
Elsie	88143	D	1941
Elsie	54451	I	1929
Frederick W.	10086	D	1910
Helen Landers	63394	D	1933
John Drury	7644	D	1909

NAME	NUMBER	TYPE	YEAR
TALLAS			
Paul	64531	D	1933
TALLENT			
Thomas Aloysius	48121	D	1927
TALLMADGE			
Adaline	33945	D	1922
Charles E.	69622	D	1935
TALLMAN			
Stephen	30693	D	1920
TALLON			
Kate Walsh	23014	D	1917
TALPFER			
Louise	59510	D	1931
TALUA			
Neva C.	89108	D	1942
Olivette C.	89108	D	1942
Olivette C.	89108	D	1942
TAMAGNI			
Achille	39634	D	1924
TAMASKOVICH			
Joseph	35146	I	1922
TAMBELLINI			
Joseph	48734	I	1927
Leonardo	45527	D	1926
Marie	48735	I	1927
TAMBOURY			
Irving P.	87763	D	1941
TAMIETTI			
James	36187	D	1923
TAMKE			
William D.	47997	D	1927
TAMKIN			
Sophia	27920	D	1919
TAMLANDER			
Emil	66819	D	1934
TAMM			
Ernest T.	22880	D	1917
Henry C.	55971	D	1930
Johann	50013	I	1928
TAMMEYER			
George J.	38284	D	1924
TAMMLER			
Eugen M. A.	72044	D	1936
Wilhelmina	16897	I	1914
Wilhelmina	18340	D	1915

NAME	NUMBER	TYPE	YEAR
TAMONY			
Cornelius P.	53603	M	1929
Ella M.	66517	D	1934
John	12606	D	1911
John	73026	D	1936
Mary	88202	D	1941
Michael J.	20513	D	1916
Peter	24144	D	1918
Peter P.	5875	D	1908
TAMOSELLO			
V.	42671	D	1925
TAMPA			
Maria	71932	D	1936
TAMPCKE			
Maria	88035	D	1941
TAMS			
Sampson	14668	D	1913
TAMURA			
Sumiko	73618	M	1936
TAN			
Manuel Liu	80795	D	1939
Yee	63091	D	1932
TANAKA			
Akira	19752	M	1915
Geigiro	38031	D	1923
Jeigiro	38031	D	1923
Yeijiro	38031	D	1923
TANARELLI			
Ulisse	50036	D	1928
TANCELLI			
Paolo	28381	D	1919
TANFORAN			
Jennie	12055	D	1911
Toribio	19509	D	1915
TANG			
Leo	80795	D	1939
TANGER			
Jeanette	85419	M	1940
TANGERDING			
Josepha J.	70441	D	1935
TANGHETTI			
John	77143	D	1937
TANGNEY			
Maria J.	84878	D	1940
TANIERE			
Eugene	13340	D	1912

NAME	NUMBER	TYPE	YEAR
Leontine	29507	D	1920
TANIGUCHI			
Tokichi	52787	D	1929
TANIWAKI			
Michio	75627	M	1937
TANKE			
John	739	D	1906
TANNEBAUM			
B.	1646	D	1906
TANNEN			
Harry	84579	D	1940
TANNER			
Carl	12430	D	1911
Charles	12430	D	1911
Edward Adolph	27250	M	1919
Emmett	37317	D	1923
Jessie Ruth	23612	M	1917
John Baptist	27250	M	1919
Leroy Hill	29274	D	1920
Mary B.	58349	I	1931
Mary E.	969	M	1906
Mary Helena	23785	D	1917
Walter William	24613	D	1918
TANNEY			
Lewis L.	82839	D	1939
TANNLER			
C.	37790	D	1923
Henry	10706	D	1910
TANSEY			
Michael	72696	D	1936
TANSMAN			
Anna Mary	41502	D	1925
Catherina	38591	D	1924
TANSSIG			
Rudolph J.	33350	D	1922
TANSZKY			
Edmund	32215	D	1921
TANTARDINI			
Melchiorre	24960	I	1918
TANZI			
Henry R.	30424	D	1920
TAORMINA			
Kenneth	63021	M	1932
Sam	62052	D	1932
TAPLIN			
George	88691	D	1941

NAME	NUMBER	TYPE	YEAR
TAPORCO			
Arlene Sylvia	88786	M	1941
Bonafacio Peter	88786	M	1941
TAPP			
George	37236	D	1923
Mary A. R.	24857	D	1918
TAPPARO			
Carlo	71626	D	1936
TAPPER			
Abraham	35088	D	1922
Eva	34484	D	1922
Helen	37302	M	1923
Horace	37302	M	1923
Norman	37302	M	1923
Rudolph	31696	D	1921
Sophie Emilie	47401	D	1927
TARA			
Germana	59110	D	1931
TARABOCHIA			
Germana	59110	D	1931
TARALSDOTTER			
Tina	69984	D	1935
TARAN			
Erna Braun	76061	D	1937
Erna H.	76061	D	1937
TARANTA			
Maria Louisa	50785	D	1928
TARANTINO			
Giovannina	85122	D	1940
Grazia	39640	D	1924
Josephine	68952	D	1935
Pietro	8546	D	1909
Salvatore Vincingo	52794	D	1929
TARANTO			
Domenico	26881	D	1919
Maria	8359	M	1909
Maria Louisa	50785	D	1928
Marianna	59520	D	1931
Rosalia	8359	M	1909
TARAVELLIER			
Louis	43781	D	1926
TARBIT			
James	84356	D	1940
TARBOX			
Benjamin Laidley	51356	D	1928

NAME	NUMBER	TYPE	YEAR
TARDELLI			
Agostina	62900	D	1932
Amerigo	84406	D	1940
Cherubino	35630	D	1922
Edward	58530	I	1931
Giorgio	13254	M	1912
Guido	74052	D	1936
Raffaello	9056	D	1910
TARDIF(F)			
William	4797	D	1907
TARICCO			
Giuseppe	44751	D	1926
TARIEL			
Nelson H.	81865	D	1939
TARISKA			
Jessie	42212	D	1925
TARISKY			
Jessie	42212	D	1925
TARLETON			
Augusta	9996	M	1910
Elizabeth	9996	M	1910
Eva	9996	M	1910
Frank	9996	M	1910
TAROT			
Rosalie	36813	D	1923
TARPEY			
E., Mrs.	81871	D	1939
Emma B.	81871	D	1939
TARPY			
Ellinor	18834	M	1915
Violet Elizabeth	18834	M	1915
TARR			
Calista Booth	28936	D	1920
S. H.	6805	D	1908
TARRANO			
Vincenzo	23294	D	1917
TARRANT			
Marie Rosalie	19269	D	1915
Roy P.	62221	D	1932
TARRELL			
William Patrick	18486	M	1915
TARROU			
Baptiste	61126	D	1932
Emilie	52733	D	1929
Francois Baptiste	61126	D	1932

NAME	NUMBER	TYPE	YEAR
TARTINI			
Isaac G.	29178	D	1920
TARVER			
Joe	39406	M	1924
TASH			
Marcus	32508	D	1921
TASHJIAN			
Kirkos	39766	I	1924
TASSARA			
Nicolo	48111	D	1927
TASSELL			
Clara Julina	23824	D	1918
Henrietta G.	46302	D	1927
Henrietta Moule	46302	D	1927
TASSETT			
Dorothy Helen	77569	M	1938
Henry L.	16809	D	1914
Joanne Frances	77569	M	1938
TASSI			
Jennie V.	75333	D	1937
TASTSIS			
Kiriacos	70782	D	1935
TATARO			
Angelo	86699	D	1941
TATE			
Catherine	11450	D	1911
Eudora	45898	I	1926
TATEHARA			
Hiroko	85066	M	1940
Kimiko	85066	M	1940
Kiyosho	85066	M	1940
TATEM			
Allen	5909	D	1908
TATRO			
Anthony B.	82121	D	1939
TATROE			
William F.	52478	D	1929
TATSUDA			
Masaichi	28661	I	1920
T.	28661	I	1920
TATTENHAM			
Rosina	43215	D	1925
TATTERSALL			
James Louis, III	47834	M	1927
Josephine Tyman	38081	D	1924

NAME	NUMBER	TYPE	YEAR
TATUM			
Archie Brownlaw	46148	D	1927
Charles Robbins	57057	D	1930
Claiborne Randolph	23029	M	1917
Mary	47901	M	1927
Minna P.	1886	D	1906
Randolph	4428	M	1907
TAUBERT			
Arthur	33340	I	1922
TAUBLES			
C. M.	46320	D	1927
Caroline	46320	D	1927
TAUCHUS			
Benjamin	61662	D	1932
TAUER			
Henry A.	72275	D	1936
Letitia	71794	D	1936
TAUFENBACH			
Kathryn	67078	D	1934
TAUGHER			
Aurore	81221	D	1939
John	38698	D	1924
Louis L.	63147	D	1932
TAULBEE			
Clarence F.	58445	I	1931
TAULIS			
Joseph	68648	D	1935
TAUSSIG			
Annette	81434	D	1939
Edward	11726	D	1911
Emma A.	11129	D	1911
Emma M.	11129	D	1911
Hugh A.	86706	M	1941
Hugo A.	13483	D	1912
Josephine I.	23860	D	1918
Laureen	86706	M	1941
Laurence R.	83434	D	1940
Pauline	19100	D	1915
Rosa G.	45189	D	1926
Rudolph J.	33350	D	1922
Samuel	71843	D	1936
TAVEIRA			
Antonio B.	41017	D	1925
TAVELLI			
Lou	30419	D	1920
TAVERNER			
Louisa Yarnold	36775	D	1923

NAME	NUMBER	TYPE	YEAR	NAME	NUMBER	TYPE	YEAR	NAME	NUMBER	TYPE	YEAR
TAVERNIER				Clara	43636	D	1926	James King	25328	D	1918
Clara Belle	50450	I	1928	Clara M.	21051	D	1916	Jeannette Gilmour	73495	M	1936
TAVIS				Clarence Westel	86793	M	1941	Jennie	7757	M	1909
Heinrich Friedrich	67098	D	1934	Clinton J.	40663	M	1924	John Charles	20431	D	1916
TAW				D. E.	6677	D	1908	John Charles	68473	I	1934
Wong Hang	32784	D	1921	David	14090	D	1912	John G.	61084	D	1932
Wong Hong	32784	D	1921	Duane P.	26223	D	1919	John George	35176	D	1922
TAY				Edith A.	60450	D	1931	John H.	12951	D	1912
Charles Fox	33873	D	1922	Edna	69449	D	1935	John James	11091	D	1911
He	44349	D	1926	Edward F.	59652	D	1931	John M.	58087	D	1931
Hoy	44349	D	1926	Edward Robeson	37016	D	1923	John Patrick	4530	D	1907
TAYFOROS				Edward S.	52046	D	1929	John Spotswood	78869	D	1938
Helen L.	50756	I	1928	Elijah A.	6186	D	1908	John T.	26250	D	1919
Helen L.	51347	D	1928	Elisa V.	56422	D	1930	Joseph M.	19487	D	1915
Helena	51347	D	1928	Eliza	24366	D	1918	Josephine	16368	D	1913
TAYLER				Elizabeth	21224	I	1916	Josephine M.	28827	D	1920
Joseph	32603	D	1921	Elizabeth	21437	D	1916	Kate E.	69449	D	1935
William Henry	55160	D	1930	Elizabeth	27157	D	1919	Katherine	88057	D	1941
TAYLOE				Elizabeth (Bee)	4406	D	1907	Katherine Mayer Howard	81921	D	1939
Willie	75851	D	1937	Elizabeth A.	60647	D	1932	Kathryn	60560	D	1931
TAYLOR				Emma	42746	M	1925	Laura M.	14230	D	1912
Adaline Fildes	71439	D	1936	Everett B.	73704	D	1936	Leon A.	45884	D	1926
Agnes C.	36165	D	1923	Finis Edward	70960	D	1935	Lilla	56205	D	1930
Agnes S.	598	M	1906	Forrester	4643	M	1907	Linda	69403	D	1935
Agnes Stanford	2411	D	1906	Francis Norton, Jr.	82477	D	1939	Louise	66176	D	1934
Albert	42746	M	1925	George Edwin	73121	D	1936	Lucretia Estelle Watson	15394	D	1913
Albert Miles	42612	D	1925	George W.	53040	D	1929	Lydia	88740	D	1941
Albert S.	61201	D	1932	George Wray	15835	D	1913	Manuel Francis	56548	D	1930
Alberta	42746	M	1925	Georgia M.	56355	D	1930	Martha E.	75154	D	1937
Alenia	6847	M	1908	Gus E.	89608	D	1942	Mary	45899	D	1926
Amy H.	69023	D	1935	Hannah M.	75652	D	1937	Mary A.	32275	D	1921
Ann Alexander	81991	D	1939	Harriot k.	31596	D	1921	Mary D.	14091	D	1912
Annie S.	4770	D	1907	Harry B.	68545	D	1934	Mary F.	26520	D	1919
Arthur	13691	I	1912	Henry Benedict	52881	D	1929	Maude A.	82641	D	1939
Arthur	21803	I	1916	Henry D.	21155	I	1916	Maxine	55668	M	1930
Bacon S.	63594	M	1933	Henry D.	21217	D	1916	Michael C.	21537	D	1916
Bessie Davis	35796	D	1923	Henry Huntly	12060	D	1911	Morley	45756	M	1926
Bessie Kittle	56876	I	1930	Henry Huntly	75345	D	1937	Nettie B.	81447	D	1939
Bessie Kittle	58236	D	1931	Honorah Corbett	52923	D	1929	Obadiah Thomas	82045	D	1939
Byron I.	3835	D	1907	Hugh W.	13915	M	1912	Oscar Nettleton	7876	D	1909
Charles E.	51600	D	1928	Isaac N.	34890	D	1922	Patrica J.	88268	D	1941
Charles Edward	67028	D	1934	J. D.	71	D	1906	Paul	42746	M	1925
Charles Francis	76002	D	1937	J. E.	1867	D	1906	Petrina G.	88268	D	1941
Charles J.	32818	I	1921	J. Felton	68260	D	1934	Raymond W.	50033	D	1928
Charles J.	75079	D	1937	J. I.	63594	M	1933	Robert Beverly	85228	D	1940
Charles L.	4685	D	1907	James	1798	D	1906	Robert L.	5721	D	1908
Charles L.	5784	D	1908	James	88473	D	1941	Robert W.	32667	D	1921
Charles L.	73827	D	1936	James Archibald	67977	D	1934	Rose	64203	D	1933
				James D.	8842	D	1909	Ruth S.	29615	D	1920

NAME	NUMBER	TYPE	YEAR
Sara T.	8779	I	1909
Sumner J.	24846	D	1918
Thomas	53929	M	1929
Thomas C.	49432	D	1928
Thomas Francis	56211	D	1930
Thomas G.	54722	D	1930
W. R.	1513	D	1906
Walter E.	70954	I	1935
William	72201	D	1936
William Arthur	70857	D	1935
William H.	4083	D	1907
William H.	55160	D	1930
William I.	34607	I	1922
William I.	34985	I	1922
William I.	37978	D	1923
William Robert	69676	D	1935
William Rodgers	80048	D	1938
Willie	75851	D	1937
TAYRAC			
Ernest	9143	D	1910
TEACHOUT			
Henry	11451	D	1911
TEANEY			
Rose	2419	D	1906
TEARE			
Charles	5858	D	1908
TEARLE			
Josephine Park	58380	D	1931
TEASLAND			
Frederick A.	48594	D	1927
TEASS			
Helen McKeag	32461	D	1921
Melba	28295	M	1919
TEBBETS			
Josephine	85663	D	1940
TEBBETTS			
George P.	7234	D	1909
TEBBUTT			
John Edward	41768	D	1925
John Edward	41768	D	1925
TEDALDI			
Joe	40023	D	1924
TEDEKIOS			
Stazsos	11539	D	1911
TEDTSEN			
Marie	65585	M	1933
Mary C. G.	28600	D	1920

NAME	NUMBER	TYPE	YEAR
TEECHER			
Charles G.	63587	D	1933
TEED			
Elmo Arthur	46900	D	1927
TEEHAN			
Jeremiah E.	67819	D	1934
TEELING			
James J.	57704	I	1931
James J.	79747	D	1938
Joseph W.	73097	D	1936
TEES			
Harry K.	28147	D	1919
TEESDALE			
Sara J.	35266	D	1922
TEESE			
Hannah	3999	D	1907
Lewis	13609	D	1912
TEGELER			
Frieda	72850	D	1936
William	45401	D	1926
TEGGART			
Bernard	35020	D	1922
James	52671	I	1929
James	55537	D	1930
TEHAN			
Ellen	18029	D	1914
TEHANEY			
Annie	57346	D	1930
TEICHERT			
Gladys L.	39495	M	1924
TEICHNER			
Theresa	22542	I	1917
TEIGELER			
Henry R.	65071	D	1933
Lewis H.	65190	M	1933
William H.	84908	D	1940
William Henry	367	D	1906
TEIJEIRO			
Amador	43353	M	1926
Antonio	43353	M	1926
Domingo	43353	M	1926
Manuel	43353	M	1926
TEISSEIRE			
Benjamin	48675	D	1927
TEITELBAUM			
Jacob	51947	D	1929

NAME	NUMBER	TYPE	YEAR
TEITZ			
Sarah	60075	D	1931
TELFER			
Frank	36656	I	1923
TELFORD			
William Heugh	69330	D	1935
TELLEEN			
Charles A.	23118	D	1917
TELLEFSEN			
Arthur E.	83935	D	1940
T. E. Arthur, Sr.	83935	D	1940
TELLER			
Frances	62872	D	1932
Francis	62872	D	1932
TELLERIA			
Balbino	73157	D	1936
Lorenzo	26167	D	1919
TELLIFSEN			
Tellif	77480	D	1938
TEMAHOWICH			
Olga	15303	D	1913
TEMASNEY			
Bertha M.	25568	D	1918
TEMKOW			
Michael	85971	D	1941
TEMPLE			
Albert	55131	D	1930
Isabella	8731	D	1909
James Howard	34836	D	1922
Thomas Niblo	47204	D	1927
TEMPLEMAN			
Florence E.	83064	I	1940
Gertrude Slater	84199	D	1940
TEMPLETON			
Mary Agnes	85857	D	1940
William A.	50354	D	1928
TEMPONE			
Maria	72443	D	1936
Vincenzo	37465	D	1923
TEMPS			
Ernest	31718	D	1921
Gustave C.	64887	D	1933
TENCE			
Aline	4261	D	1907
Alma M.	4261	D	1907

NAME	NUMBER	TYPE	YEAR	NAME	NUMBER	TYPE	YEAR	NAME	NUMBER	TYPE	YEAR
TENCH				TERBUSH				TERRELL			
William Mundle	30857	D	1920	George F.	52085	D	1929	Alice M.	31908	D	1921
TENG				TERESA				George W.	33720	D	1922
Charles	19911	D	1915	Bertone Maria	40176	D	1924	Theresa	66145	D	1934
TENGBORG				TERESI				TERRET			
Edward	35743	D	1923	Bertha J. C.	9263	D	1910	Francois	15657	D	1913
John Edward	35743	D	1923	Johanna Christiana	9263	D	1910	TERRILL			
TENNANT				TERESINA				Annie Hamilton	27303	D	1919
Agnes	31678	M	1921	Viola	30082	D	1920	Annie Marian	87497	I	1941
Agnes	33602	M	1922	TERHEYDEN				Annie Marian	87550	D	1941
Edward	31678	M	1921	Ann Albers	84627	D	1940	G. M., Mrs.	87550	D	1941
Edward	33602	M	1922	Frank J.	54156	D	1929	George S.	32676	M	1921
Frank	31678	M	1921	Frank, Mrs.	84627	D	1940	John G.	43237	D	1925
Franklin	33602	M	1922	Theresia Elizabeth	67786	D	1934	Teresa B.	66145	D	1934
John	31678	M	1921	TERHUNE				William H.	32676	M	1921
John	33602	M	1922	Lewis	76576	I	1937	TERRRILL			
John H.	11822	D	1911	Louis Phillip	80303	D	1939	Charles C.	2156	D	1906
John H.	31677	D	1921	TERNABEN				TERRY			
Mary A.	30586	D	1920	Gustav	79764	D	1938	Alfred N.	73120	D	1936
TENNENT				Hermine	87851	D	1941	Caroline	65999	D	1933
Mary A.	30586	D	1920	Karl	81723	D	1939	Detly Earl	74463	D	1937
TENNEY				TERNAHEN				Florence May	25786	D	1918
Charles	42785	D	1925	Albertine	45778	D	1926	Frank K.	72344	D	1936
Frank D.	24578	D	1918	TERNES				George C.	23896	D	1918
Mary Jane	2094	M	1906	Frank Bernard	23104	M	1917	Geraldine H.	83218	D	1940
May B.	44225	D	1926	TERNULLO				John Chase	86389	D	1941
TENNIEN				Domenico J.	52966	I	1929	Joseph E.	75935	D	1937
Frank J.	58097	D	1931	Domenico J.	67048	I	1934	Joseph T.	32775	D	1921
TENNLER				TERRAGNO				Leonard	77489	D	1938
C.	37790	D	1923	Carmelina	73567	D	1936	Regina M.	54252	D	1929
TENNYSON				Marcello	82100	D	1939	Sarah	14642	D	1912
Howard Allen	65518	D	1933	Valente E.	31235	D	1921	Susan	43571	D	1926
Theodor	74154	D	1936	Valentino	31235	D	1921	Thaddeus Wesley	81558	D	1939
TENORIO				TERRANOVA				Walter F.	83610	D	1940
Jose	47243	D	1927	Antonio	38864	D	1924	William	71695	M	1936
TENSFELDT				Giovanna	86026	D	1941	William Stanley	52717	D	1929
Hans F.	31825	D	1921	Giuseppa	70613	D	1935	TERSCHINEN			
TENTEN				Giuseppe	21937	D	1916	Gerhard F.	33997	D	1922
Peter	67373	D	1934	Giuseppe	72412	D	1936	TERWILLEGER			
TEPPA				Joanna	86026	D	1941	Nellie	48851	D	1927
Carlo	52961	D	1929	Stefano	89255	D	1942	TERWILLIGER			
TEPSICH				TERRASAZ				Arthur Ray	76932	D	1937
Nikola	34278	D	1922	Francisca	62506	D	1932	TERZI			
TERAMO				TERRAZAS				Guiseppe	56183	D	1930
Pasquale	36985	D	1923	Francisca	62506	D	1932	TERZIAN			
								Michran Hovanes	77399	D	1938

NAME	NUMBER	TYPE	YEAR
TESCH			
Augustus	7451	M	1909
Gustav	7451	M	1909
Walter	7451	M	1909
TESCHER			
Joseph	50517	D	1928
Pauline	58595	D	1931
TESCHNER			
Herman	57999	D	1931
TESKE			
Minna	86475	D	1941
TESMER			
Henry A.	35495	D	1922
TESSIEN			
Marie G.	49332	D	1928
TESSIER			
Annie	20548	D	1916
Mary Eva	89891	D	1942
William	50582	D	1928
TESSLER			
Marian	46073	I	1926
TESSMER			
Robert	34370	D	1922
TESTA			
Giacomo	29763	D	1920
Mary	50145	D	1928
TESTINO			
Antonio	66109	D	1934
Giacomo	75973	I	1937
TETLEY			
Emily D.	76770	D	1937
Thomas Wilkinson	8682	D	1909
William L.	48215	D	1927
TETREAU			
Louis E.	53871	D	1929
TETZER			
Elizabeth	58027	D	1931
Frederick	41623	D	1925
TETZLAFF			
Paul	66189	I	1934
TEUBNER			
Rosalie A.	75970	D	1937
TEUCHER			
Emily Louise	62962	D	1932
TEULIER			
Pierre	59480	D	1931

NAME	NUMBER	TYPE	YEAR
TEVEBAUGH			
Jacques L.	56659	D	1930
TEVIS			
Lloyd Pacheco	57414	M	1930
Mabel P.	36320	D	1923
Richard Lee	57414	M	1930
Susan G.	19202	D	1915
TEVLIN			
James F.	38227	D	1924
Mary	49094	D	1928
TEWELES			
Josephine	5777	I	1908
TEWKSBURY			
Emily S.	10280	D	1910
THACKER			
Audrey Annette	26700	M	1919
Irwin William	26699	D	1919
Milton	49546	D	1928
THACKRAY			
George William	62286	D	1932
THAIN			
Alexander	22800	D	1917
James W.	22873	M	1917
THAL			
Alfred	26396	M	1919
Arthur Philip	19674	D	1915
Doris	26396	M	1919
Elese	8278	I	1909
Emily	24903	D	1918
F. M.	27734	D	1919
Fred	25685	D	1918
THALHEIM			
Leo	59054	D	1931
THAM			
Frank A. E.	55880	D	1930
Mary E.	45098	D	1926
THAMES			
Billie Ramsay	52756	M	1929
O. Laupsa	82659	D	1939
THANACOS			
M.	9444	D	1910
THANASOCOSTAS			
George K.	7226	D	1909
THANE			
Agnes	8592	M	1909
Bartlett Lee	48618	D	1927

NAME	NUMBER	TYPE	YEAR
Joseph M. B.	8592	M	1909
THANNHAUSER			
Louisa	12895	D	1912
THARP			
Ira A.	54911	D	1930
THATCHER			
Arthur T.	80216	D	1938
Coney Robert	61574	D	1932
George	29201	D	1920
George P.	26403	D	1919
THAU			
Dorathea	47314	D	1927
THAUWALD			
Augusta	84087	I	1940
THAXON			
Bedford	82605	D	1939
Belford	82605	D	1939
THAXTER			
Jonas W.	7323	D	1909
THAYER			
Charles C.	32369	D	1921
Clara G.	83009	D	1940
Clarence Allen	50563	D	1928
Frank S.	48414	D	1927
Gettie A.	17283	D	1914
Kate	3475	D	1907
M.	35623	D	1922
Mae Clemantyne	32444	D	1921
Marie L.	43247	D	1925
N. D.	4408	D	1907
Sarah	18770	I	1915
Sarah	23689	D	1917
Silas E. C.	990	D	1906
Virginia	35623	D	1922
THEAS			
Maria Luisa	3245	D	1907
THEBAUD			
Joseph	44352	D	1926
Ricardo	19917	I	1915
THEBERATH			
Erminie T.	8735	M	1909
THEDE			
Sidney A.	36001	M	1923
THEDEU			
John C.	45046	D	1926
THEDY			
Julia	16585	D	1914

NAME	NUMBER	TYPE	YEAR
Margaret	6744	M	1908
THEEN			
Gerjet	142	D	1906
THEIL			
Emile	28314	D	1919
Francois	7256	D	1909
THEILEN			
Henry	15894	D	1913
Henry E., Jr.	25609	I	1918
Ludwig A.	25521	D	1918
THEINER			
Minna	76932	D	1937
THEISEN			
Adolphine	22407	D	1917
Caroline Bell	23451	M	1917
Charles	23451	M	1917
Johanna Adolphine	22407	D	1917
John Rex	23451	M	1917
May Adele	23451	M	1917
Miriam Rose	61410	D	1932
Vivian	23451	M	1917
THEISS			
Katherine Seymour	63526	D	1933
THELEN			
Otto Joseph	14487	D	1912
THELLER			
Annie H.	20241	D	1916
Olive Elizabeth	62879	D	1932
THEMPER			
Jack	20485	D	1916
THEODORE			
Theodore	82554	I	1939
THEODORELOS			
John D.	42045	D	1925
Nikolaos G.	7481	D	1909
THEODOROPOLOS			
Theodore	82554	I	1939
THEODOSIOU			
John	69887	D	1935
THEODOSIU			
Pantages	69887	D	1935
THEOHARIS			
George	42403	D	1925
THEORIN			
Justine	64342	D	1933

NAME	NUMBER	TYPE	YEAR
THERIOT			
Florence	35759	D	1923
THERKOF			
Gustav Henry	49137	D	1928
THERNSDROM			
Henrik	57413	D	1930
THERNSTROM			
Charles H.	27730	D	1919
Hannah	47462	D	1927
Johan Henrik	57413	D	1930
THESING			
Mary	50778	D	1928
THEUERKANF			
August H.	49137	D	1928
THEWES			
Heinrich Friedrich	67098	D	1934
THEWS			
Julius	1510	M	1906
THIAS			
Adele	28103	D	1919
Carl H.	35396	D	1922
THIBAULT			
C. S.	38201	D	1924
THIBEAULT			
Cleophas	35763	I	1923
THIBODEAU			
Elaine	79403	M	1938
THIEBAUD			
Delphine	12836	D	1912
THIEBAUT			
H. H.	76538	D	1937
Hippolyte H.	38073	D	1924
THIEBEN			
Tillie	83524	D	1940
THIEBOUT			
Hippolyte H.	38073	D	1924
THIEDEMANN			
William F.	10509	M	1910
William Joost	58972	D	1931
THIEL			
Auguste	4039	D	1907
THIELE			
Charlotte Frances	13449	M	1912
George, Sr.	61635	D	1932
THIELEMANS			
Theresa	89383	D	1942

NAME	NUMBER	TYPE	YEAR
THIELER			
Henry J.	10685	D	1910
THIEMANN			
Edward Robert	86771	D	1941
THIEN			
Caspar	22219	M	1917
Fred C.	69069	D	1935
Frieda	22219	M	1917
Helene	22219	M	1917
Maria	22219	M	1917
THIERBACH			
Charles F.	58270	D	1931
Emma	47572	D	1927
George W.	11619	M	1911
Louis M.	4069	D	1907
THIERIOT			
Albert	20841	D	1916
Charles DeYoung	29508	M	1920
Ferdinand Melly	31562	M	1921
Fredinand	29424	D	1920
Yvonne	29508	M	1920
THIERMAN			
Bertha	53304	D	1929
THIERRY			
Virginie	64599	D	1933
THIES			
Betty L.	60928	D	1932
Hugo F.	70160	D	1935
John Henry Frederick	29341	D	1920
THIESSEN			
George	30376	D	1920
Lillian	17160	M	1914
Robert	17160	M	1914
THIFT			
Joseph P.	46355	D	1927
THILL			
Auguste	4039	D	1907
THIME			
Louis	36798	D	1923
THING			
Charlie	19911	D	1915
THINGLER			
Jeanette	10060	D	1910
THIRD			
William	8680	D	1909

NAME	NUMBER	TYPE	YEAR
THIRKETTLE			
T. J.	13511	D	1912
THIRON			
Henry L.	17292	D	1914
Henry Lardi	1399	D	1906
THIRWELL			
William Richard	62420	D	1932
THODAS			
John	8561	D	1909
Vasiliki	8626	M	1909
THODE			
Bertha M.	73586	I	1936
Charles Julius	36692	D	1923
Frederick George	72653	D	1936
Henning	79407	D	1938
Henrietta	67001	D	1934
Johanna M. M. S.	30016	D	1920
John	6992	D	1908
Loretta	73594	D	1936
Olga	40479	I	1924
THODT			
Frederika M.	84628	I	1940
THOENGER			
Edna	30691	M	1920
Esther	30691	M	1920
THOENGES			
Arthur W.	30002	D	1920
William	29619	D	1920
THOERNER			
Fred, Jr.	39734	M	1924
Lois	81463	M	1939
Louis	69371	D	1935
Louis T.	39734	M	1924
Louise	39734	M	1924
Rosemary	39734	M	1924
THOGERSEN			
Serina	77340	D	1937
THOLIX			
Anders	10414	D	1910
Andrew	10414	D	1910
THOLKE			
Diedrich	60759	D	1932
H. D.	60759	D	1932
Marie S.	75708	D	1937
THOM			
Edmund	65293	D	1933

NAME	NUMBER	TYPE	YEAR
THOM-WOHRDEN			
John Henry	40878	D	1925
THOMA			
John George	56281	D	1930
THOMANN			
Harry	18635	D	1915
THOMANS			
Mary E.	60380	D	1931
THOMAS			
Agnes Gertrude	63892	D	1933
Albert W.	74594	D	1937
Alice	39116	M	1924
Allan Bertrand	49586	M	1928
Angelo B.	52903	D	1929
Anna Catherine	75111	D	1937
Anna L.	87954	D	1941
Anna M. J.	84626	D	1940
Annie	30159	D	1920
Armin	41293	D	1925
Arthur Denny	40209	D	1924
Arthur Edward	71674	M	1936
Arthur H.	35112	I	1922
Arthur M.	15779	D	1913
Audrey	80809	M	1939
Auguste	65377	D	1933
Belle R.	82236	D	1939
Bertha A.	67321	D	1934
Bertram A.	54030	D	1929
Bertrand M.	46517	D	1927
Catherifne	1239	D	1906
Charles	11298	D	1911
Charles C.	88238	D	1941
Charles P.	29046	D	1920
Charles Walter	54846	M	1930
Clementina M.	68035	D	1934
Clifton B.	41009	I	1925
Cora Belle	65730	D	1933
Cyril Anthony	41386	M	1925
David R.	7867	D	1909
Donald	79446	M	1938
Donald K.	40747	M	1925
Dora Elizabeth	34386	D	1922
Earl J.	81930	I	1939
Edgar C.	8762	D	1909
Edward W.	8638	D	1909
Eleanore Grace	66719	M	1934
Elizabeth	80763	D	1939
Elizabeth A.	75760	D	1937

NAME	NUMBER	TYPE	YEAR
Ellen	11907	D	1911
Ellen	57110	D	1930
Emile Lucien, Jr.	66719	M	1934
Emily Newell	51495	D	1928
Emma	65175	D	1933
Emma Doris	84855	D	1940
Ernestine H.	52120	D	1929
Evan	10774	D	1910
Everard C.	31863	D	1921
F. A.	79712	L	1938
Fernand	16913	D	1914
Francis James	54846	M	1930
Frank	34215	D	1922
Frederick Fernando	86169	D	1941
George	15896	D	1913
George	70492	D	1935
George H.	89096	D	1942
George M.	53624	D	1929
George P.	78745	D	1938
George W.	67272	D	1934
Grace Shields	67976	D	1934
Grace Williams	58978	D	1931
Gustave F.	86108	D	1941
H. B., Mrs.	88374	D	1941
Hasford P.	63978	D	1933
Henry	80809	M	1939
Hugh	13274	D	1912
Ida Mae	36426	M	1923
Ila Mae	66730	D	1934
Isabella E.	7560	D	1909
J. Elizabeth	57066	D	1930
James	33339	I	1922
James	57892	I	1931
James	43442	D	1926
James L.	84842	D	1940
James Madison	19106	D	1915
Jennie	34740	D	1922
Jennie	84606	D	1940
John	38924	D	1924
John Cedric	15105	M	1913
John, Jr.	39149	M	1924
Joseph	7900	D	1909
Joseph B.	63750	D	1933
Joseph Henry	67768	D	1934
Joseph Leo	56562	D	1930
Josephine Anna	88620	D	1941
Larry	77271	D	1937
Lavinia	31598	D	1921
Lawrence H.	84373	D	1940

NAME	NUMBER	TYPE	YEAR
Lillian E.	84895	D	1940
Louis	13275	D	1912
Louis William	1976	D	1906
Louise Lovie	9347	M	1910
Lucy	1068	I	1906
Lucy	12403	D	1911
Lyle C.	75903	D	1937
Margaret E.	38288	D	1924
Marie Alice Drouaillet	3147	D	1907
Marie Clemintina	64069	I	1933
Mary	39116	M	1924
Mary C.	89683	D	1942
Mary Eva	75690	D	1937
Mary H.	43478	D	1926
Mary J.	88374	D	1941
Mary McNamara	84841	D	1940
Mary Sarah	67104	D	1934
Miranda May	15105	M	1913
Myrtle	70297	D	1935
N.	41990	D	1925
Nataniel Fisher	10837	D	1910
Nathaniel Fisher	15105	M	1913
Nora M.	51925	D	1929
Percy	88908	D	1942
Perry Silas	36205	I	1923
Philip Matson	58227	D	1931
Ralph	6220	D	1908
Rebecca	80809	M	1939
Richard	75296	D	1937
Robert	69038	M	1935
Robert H.	78842	D	1938
Robert Lester	71674	M	1936
Rosanna	66374	D	1934
Ruth Ellen	45103	D	1926
Ruth Powers	45103	D	1926
Samuel	54502	D	1929
Samuel G.	69356	D	1935
Sarah	28676	D	1920
Sarah Jane	28601	D	1920
Selwin Edward	41386	M	1925
Susan	47927	D	1927
Theresa	46819	D	1927
Verlin C.	65027	D	1933
Vincent	4506	M	1907
W. H.	3941	D	1907
William	25275	D	1918
William	34253	D	1922
William	73770	D	1936
William A.	20980	D	1916

NAME	NUMBER	TYPE	YEAR
William A.	28117	D	1919
William E.	71411	I	1936
Willis E.	87148	D	1941
Winifred	34701	D	1922
Zero L., Sr.	14728	D	1913
THOMASON			
Edwin Oscar	11269	D	1911
Edwin R.	11028	D	1911
Jeannette	10573	D	1910
THOMASSIN			
Ernest Paul	72896	D	1936
THOMEY			
E.	89368	D	1942
THOMMEN			
Jacob	33917	D	1922
THOMNPSON			
James	89289	D	1942
THOMPSON			
Adeline	45107	M	1926
Adrienne	79724	D	1938
Agnes	14467	D	1912
Albert Rees	36185	D	1923
Alexander	38912	D	1924
Allen	65082	M	1933
Almira	8312	D	1909
Amanda Christina	20066	D	1915
Amelia	2191	D	1906
Andrew M.	86409	I	1941
Anna	76740	D	1937
Annie	36121	D	1923
Arthur	29221	D	1920
Bertha	24171	I	1918
Bertha	27307	D	1919
Beverly	85437	M	1940
California	16408	D	1913
Carl Tuttle	76921	D	1937
Cathenka L.	66353	D	1934
Cecil	45238	M	1926
Chadwick	64904	D	1933
Charles	88672	D	1941
Charles L.	58047	D	1931
Charles W.	21074	D	1916
Charles W.	57188	I	1930
Christis	82452	D	1939
Christopher	33448	D	1922
Clara Gertrude	75459	D	1937
Clarence Julian	12075	M	1911
Clemonce	36485	I	1923

NAME	NUMBER	TYPE	YEAR
Cornelia A.	13547	D	1912
Daniel	3438	D	1907
Daniel	38330	D	1924
Delilah	32288	D	1921
Dorethea	7460	D	1909
Elizabeth	11106	D	1911
Ellen	12227	D	1911
Ellen Etta	59789	D	1931
Ellen L.	20277	D	1916
Ellen M.	29272	D	1920
Emanuel	84293	D	1940
Ernest Paul	72896	D	1936
Ezra W.	43176	I	1925
F. H.	31615	D	1921
Felisa Guerra	39416	D	1924
Frank	18532	M	1915
Frank W.	24095	D	1918
Fred	49398	D	1928
Frederick H.	30316	D	1920
G. Howard	16177	D	1913
G. W.	53431	D	1929
George	37823	D	1923
George	53431	D	1929
George	75496	D	1937
George Alan	9310	M	1910
George B.	83499	D	1940
George Robert	62035	M	1932
Godtfred	49398	D	1928
Hans	31674	D	1921
Harold George	22568	M	1917
Harold George	38498	D	1924
Harriet	6246	D	1908
Harriet	6935	M	1908
Harriet Jean	35762	M	1923
Harry Jay	66850	D	1934
Hattie	56357	D	1930
Helen G.	86662	D	1941
Helen M.	5733	D	1908
Henry	45107	M	1926
Ida	178	D	1906
Ida C.	76249	D	1937
Jack	85437	M	1940
Jack Murray	87156	M	1941
James A.	54246	M	1929
James E.	27220	D	1919
James E.	38948	D	1924
James E.	45257	D	1926
James Malcolm	20123	D	1915
James Merideth	19253	D	1915

Key: *D = death; M = minor; I = incompetent*

NAME	NUMBER	TYPE	YEAR	NAME	NUMBER	TYPE	YEAR	NAME	NUMBER	TYPE	YEAR
James P.	47348	D	1927	Ralph	49328	M	1928	William G.	55660	D	1930
James S.	58710	M	1931	Rebecca	23495	D	1917	William H.	3597	D	1907
Jane A.	6355	D	1908	Richard P.	37330	D	1923	William Neely	7326	D	1909
Jesse Hale	7144	D	1909	Robert C.	86843	D	1941	William Percival	18081	D	1914
Johanne M.	45481	D	1926	Robert Edwin	48363	D	1927	Winfield S.	34537	I	1922
John	4728	D	1907	Robert Morris	64057	D	1933	**THOMS**			
John	32102	D	1921	Robert P.	35762	M	1923	Benjamin H.	80818	D	1939
John D.	36840	D	1923	Roy	2818	M	1907	Franklin B.	40043	D	1924
John Emanuel	45107	M	1926	Rufus W.	9668	D	1910	**THOMSEN**			
John Jamison	46109	D	1926	Russell G.	83767	D	1940	Antonie E.	26487	D	1919
John P.	18084	D	1914	Ruth L.	63688	M	1933	Christian Frederick	10370	D	1910
John William	52762	I	1929	Sally Jean	85283	M	1940	Elizabeth	13049	D	1912
John William	57688	D	1931	Sam, Mrs.	16236	D	1913	Friedericha	66237	D	1934
Joseph Alden	24449	M	1918	Samuel Francis	66098	D	1934	Friedericke	66237	D	1934
Joseph L.	28308	D	1919	Sarah Gardiner	66122	D	1934	Georgen	59434	D	1931
Juanita L.	29838	M	1920	Sarah Hobart	74303	D	1937	Jens Johannes	4728	D	1907
Julia	26342	D	1919	Sophia	86468	I	1941	Jurgen Odefey	46506	D	1927
Julia C.	52545	D	1929	Stanley	65082	M	1933	Magnus A.	57898	D	1931
Katherine F.	59878	D	1931	Sylvester	8010	D	1909	T.	19848	D	1915
Kathleen M.	24666	D	1918	T. D.	31146	D	1921	Theresa C.	71159	D	1935
Laura C.	29193	D	1920	Terry Trent	67130	M	1934	**THOMSON**			
Leander	59006	D	1931	Thelma	45238	M	1926	Agnes Elizabeth Gladys	14551	M	1912
Lottie L.	56972	D	1930	Thelma	64829	I	1933	Alison	35460	M	1922
Louise Frances Folk	85073	D	1940	Thomas	82771	D	1939	Annie M.	21729	D	1916
M. Hulit	56316	D	1930	Thomas	71500	D	1936	Barbara	41924	D	1925
Mace DeSacia	39001	D	1924	Thomas F. A.	89508	D	1942	Barbara	41924	D	1925
Majorie	40808	M	1925	Thomas Hansen	52070	D	1929	Carl Rohlffs	7724	M	1909
Mamie	74237	I	1936	Thomas J.	39082	D	1924	Cornelia Knecht	50674	D	1928
Margaret	15795	D	1913	Thomas W.	44909	D	1926	Douglas H.	6398	D	1908
Margaret H.	79216	D	1938	Thomas William	45107	M	1926	Edward James	55777	D	1930
Margaret M.	78740	D	1938	Thornton	13121	D	1912	Elizabeth	30823	M	1920
Margaret Shanahan	78740	D	1938	Thornton	59877	D	1931	George	27740	D	1919
Marie	61317	D	1932	Thorwald O.	59786	D	1931	James	25584	D	1918
Marion Sallertee	2455	D	1906	U. E.	20242	D	1916	John McEwen	71682	D	1936
Marjorie Janice	87156	M	1941	Verna Louise	38832	D	1924	Lucy Emeline	69521	D	1935
Martha W.	20483	D	1916	Walter	44260	I	1926	Marie Edna	14551	M	1912
Mary A.	71322	I	1936	Walter Adolph	49328	M	1928	Mary	13747	D	1912
Mary Agnes	55147	D	1930	Walter E.	62820	D	1932	Neil Sinclair	3656	D	1907
Mary Ann	29315	D	1920	Walter G.	83529	D	1940	Robert	40514	D	1924
Mary Townley	15143	D	1913	Walter J.	38720	M	1924	Robert	51357	D	1928
Mary W.	67985	D	1934	Walter James	38963	D	1924	Samuel Edwin	449	D	1906
Melvin	85437	M	1940	Walter S.	24623	D	1918	Strother	30823	M	1920
Nellie	46920	D	1927	Wesley	32731	I	1921	Thelma	68734	D	1935
Nellie F.	16236	D	1913	William	15180	D	1913	Thomas	7647	D	1909
Nelson Walter	72156	M	1936	William	46506	D	1927	Thomas F. A.	89508	D	1942
Octavia M.	38720	M	1924	William Edward	81418	D	1939	Thomas W.	84589	I	1940
Otto	79362	D	1938	William Ezra	43176	I	1925	William	79969	D	1938
P.	9735	D	1910	William F.	42219	D	1925	William Crabb	10915	D	1910
Paul S.	75674	I	1937	William F.	45222	D	1926				

Key: D = death; M = minor; I = incompetent

NAME	NUMBER	TYPE	YEAR
William Edward	81418	D	1939
THOMWOHRDEN			
Elizabeth Barbara	42907	D	1925
Elizabeth Barbara	43112	D	1925
THON			
Margaret	6016	D	1908
THONE			
Lula	84421	D	1940
THONHOLT			
Anna M.	52300	D	1929
THORBJORNSEN			
Tobias	85214	D	1940
THORBURN			
Euphemia	50352	D	1928
THORELL			
Axel S.	36442	D	1923
THOREN			
Aurora R.	87301	D	1941
THORESON			
Annie	32482	D	1921
THORGENSEN			
Marie	64603	D	1933
THORGERSEN			
Marie	64603	D	1933
THORMAHLEN			
Gerdt	38517	M	1924
Peter H.	36441	D	1923
Peter W.	36441	D	1923
Wilhelm	38517	M	1924
THORMEIER			
Anna Marie	44388	D	1926
Carl Gustaf	45356	D	1926
Gustav Charles	41549	D	1925
THORN			
Frances	50038	D	1928
Joseph S., Sr.	32271	D	1921
S. F.	26590	D	1919
William Wilner	47956	D	1927
THORNAGLE			
Alice E.	80669	D	1939
THORNBERG			
A. F.	78211	D	1938
Bertha	73701	D	1936
John	46114	D	1926
THORNBOROUGH			
Ellen Smith	56189	I	1930

NAME	NUMBER	TYPE	YEAR
THORNBURG			
Charles G.	62293	I	1932
Samuel M.	62308	D	1932
THORNBURGH			
Florence Ella	81745	D	1939
THORNDAHL			
Peter Christian	65735	D	1933
THORNE			
Clara J.	800	D	1906
Edwin P.	25225	D	1918
Jesse Douglass Seale	20168	M	1915
Julian	57344	D	1930
Lawrence	17534	D	1914
Leonard C.	84085	I	1940
Margaret C.	19823	D	1915
Margaret Hannon	19823	D	1915
Marjorie Vivien	44727	M	1926
Mathilde E.	31076	D	1921
Paula	82988	D	1939
Sarah	4166	D	1907
Thomas Lester	89782	D	1942
Walter S.	15403	D	1913
THORNER			
Theodore	38457	D	1924
THORNHILL			
Jane	29493	M	1920
THORNLEY			
Ida Sresovich	83574	D	1940
John Dolphin	80694	D	1939
William H.	60764	D	1932
THORNTON			
Alice T.	80923	D	1939
Alvin William	61268	I	1932
Cornelia H.	20140	D	1915
Edward J.	39973	I	1924
Elizabeth F.	32071	D	1921
Ellen F.	28289	D	1919
George W.	65450	D	1933
Harry Innes	1919	D	1906
Helen Turner	42041	M	1925
James	23376	D	1917
James D.	685	D	1906
John	42041	M	1925
John Edwin	80408	D	1939
John W.	24485	D	1918
Julia	9003	D	1910
Kate Amelia	2080	D	1906
Margaret Ritter	42041	M	1925

NAME	NUMBER	TYPE	YEAR
Michael	24207	D	1918
Michael	38182	D	1924
Nellie F.	28289	D	1919
Nora	70343	D	1935
Patrick E.	12803	D	1912
Rose I.	47803	D	1927
Sarah Francis	683	D	1906
Thomas	60530	D	1931
William I.	7088	D	1909
THORP			
Adelaide Gillett	61168	M	1932
Anna	66396	I	1934
Elbridge	68781	D	1935
Mary Zihn	79659	D	1938
Norman W.	66985	D	1934
Robert Williamson	11863	D	1911
Sandra Lee	80906	M	1939
THORPE			
Charles D.	47318	D	1927
J. E. Mason	52614	D	1929
John Thomas	65325	D	1933
Katherina	70209	D	1935
Leonard	33509	D	1922
Marie A.	82034	D	1939
Sophie	53158	D	1929
THORROLD			
Eliza	70090	D	1935
THORSEN			
Charles	57069	D	1930
Maline	51391	D	1928
Martin	47718	M	1927
Thelma	47718	M	1927
Theodore	56384	I	1930
THORSON			
Bjorne	78331	D	1938
THORSTEINSSON			
Sigurdur	25922	D	1918
THORSTEN			
Anna	50752	D	1928
Conrad	28134	D	1919
THORSTON			
Anna	50752	D	1928
THORT			
Frederika M.	84628	I	1940
THORTON			
John T.	66454	D	1934

NAME	NUMBER	TYPE	YEAR	NAME	NUMBER	TYPE	YEAR	NAME	NUMBER	TYPE	YEAR
THORWICK				THUNBERG				TIBBETTS			
Martha G.	32887	D	1921	Charles A.	65509	D	1933	Frederick Horace	79136	D	1938
THORWICK-DI				Edna Virginia	37357	M	1923	John F.	7782	D	1909
Martha G.	32887	D	1921	Gustaf Emil	35442	D	1922	Mary J.	23315	D	1917
THORWICKDIGIANNINI				Hilda Catherine	72253	I	1936	TIBBITTS			
Martha G.	32887	D	1921	Pearl Marie	37357	M	1923	George W.	7847	D	1909
THOUSTRUP				THURAU				Howard Clinton	77442	D	1938
Anna	52326	D	1929	Paul	83531	D	1940	Minnie L.	45149	D	1926
THRALL				THURBER				Robert	46297	I	1927
Frederick Verner	26846	M	1919	Howard Michael	81247	D	1939	TIBBS			
THRASHER				John W.	11823	D	1911	Henry William	40760	D	1925
Carroll	11519	D	1911	THURESON				Julia	81789	D	1939
THRELKELD				Carl W.	3127	D	1907	TIBURZIO			
James B.	86859	D	1941	THURM				Benvenuto	14848	D	1913
THROCKMORTON				Abraham	57994	D	1931	TICE			
Fred T.	61395	D	1932	THURMAN				Mary E.	8640	D	1909
Susanna M.	23853	D	1918	John William	50795	D	1928	TICHENOR			
THRONSEN				Stephen A.	85595	D	1940	Elleanor L.	36298	D	1923
Hernry	84235	D	1940	THURNREITER				Theresa B.	73178	D	1936
THRONSON				Anna	51252	D	1928	TICHNER			
Sylvester	37952	M	1923	Anna	51252	D	1928	Gusta	20549	D	1916
THRONTON				THURSBACHER				Mary	14106	D	1912
John	12635	D	1911	Julia	60258	D	1931	TICKNER			
THROWELL				THURSTON				Mary A.	18321	D	1914
Stephen	16410	D	1913	Adela	88830	I	1942	TICKNOR			
THRUSTON				Charles F.	848	D	1906	Cecilia	49774	M	1928
Charles Mynns	89465	D	1942	Clotilde	33672	D	1922	TICKONOFF			
THUESEN				Dora M.	27961	D	1919	Nickolas	71223	D	1935
Emma Emilie	25716	D	1918	Ernest	14401	D	1912	TIDERMAN			
Katherine Sophia	20538	D	1916	Eugene L.	89278	D	1942	Gustaf Adolf	89575	D	1942
Peter	17804	D	1914	George Edgar	52267	D	1929	TIEDEMANN			
THULANDER				George W.	8110	D	1909	Adeline	21786	D	1916
Carl A.	64058	D	1933	Harry	29156	D	1920	Adolph	82687	D	1939
THULIN				Julia Adelaide	32787	D	1921	Charles	76337	D	1937
Melissa	33405	D	1922	Norman V.	73650	D	1936	Ervin Adolph	10604	D	1910
THULSEN				THURY				Martin	76158	D	1937
Emma Emilie	25716	D	1918	John	69416	D	1935	Meta	36855	D	1923
Peter	17804	D	1914	THWAITES				TIEMAN			
THUM				Joseph	42843	D	1925	Henry F. W.	89386	D	1942
Charles William	30769	M	1920	THYARKS				William	89386	D	1942
Milton Franklin	30769	M	1920	Helene M. D.	21987	D	1916	TIEMANN			
THUMAS				THYES				Frieda	79168	D	1938
Frank	77420	I	1938	Adrian J.	8463	D	1909	TIEMROTH			
THUMLER				Ernest P.	8464	D	1909	Herman K.	14130	D	1912
Charles W.	75583	D	1937	TIBBALS				TIENCKEN			
				Clarence P.	38944	D	1924	Hermann	63000	D	1932

NAME	NUMBER	TYPE	YEAR	NAME	NUMBER	TYPE	YEAR	NAME	NUMBER	TYPE	YEAR
TIERNAN				Margaret	12453	I	1911	**TILDEN**			
Ada	29090	D	1920	Marjory	42044	D	1925	B. S.	60422	D	1931
Alice	63237	I	1932	Martin	13530	D	1912	Calvin Voorman	3813	M	1907
Alice	69837	D	1935	Martin J.	67962	D	1934	Charles L.	7472	D	1909
Bridget	9278	D	1910	Mary	60791	D	1932	Frank Neely	10294	D	1910
Evelyn L.	6131	M	1908	Mary F.	88898	I	1942	Heber C.	520	D	1906
Frank	62888	M	1932	Matthew	16675	M	1914	Heber Voorman	3813	M	1907
Frank C.	6131	M	1908	Patrick	32326	D	1921	Thomas H.	366	D	1906
Jane	12215	D	1911	Thomas	3224	D	1907	**TILDSLEY**			
Lawrence	74529	D	1937	Thomas J.	89942	D	1942	Lucille	30474	D	1920
Mabel Stevenson	30229	D	1920	**TIERRIAN**				**TILFORD**			
Madeline	66737	D	1934	John W.	57541	D	1930	Frank	3007	D	1907
Margaret Ann	77296	I	1937	**TIETGEN**				**TILGHMAN**			
Mary	6131	M	1908	Henry	58153	D	1931	Henry Ashe	4780	D	1907
Mary	7850	I	1909	**TIETJEN**				**TILGNER**			
Mary Jane	62888	M	1932	Anna C.	8658	D	1909	Henry	72989	D	1936
May Rose	47957	D	1927	Annie	68362	D	1934	**TILHOW**			
Michael	963	D	1906	Berndt H.	48763	D	1927	Eugene	35774	D	1923
Michael J.	6131	M	1908	Beta	9338	D	1910	**TILING**			
Patrick H.	9209	D	1910	Diederich W.	19906	D	1915	Anne	89485	D	1942
Richard L.	48775	M	1927	Elizabeth	40152	D	1924	**TILL**			
Richard L.	87042	D	1941	Harold	59632	D	1931	Maude E.	84641	D	1940
Sarah J.	6131	M	1908	John H.	68790	D	1935	Ottilie C.	79940	D	1938
Thomas	75527	M	1937	Sophie	23695	D	1917	**TILLANDER**			
Thomas J.	6131	M	1908	William M. J.	83340	D	1940	Pete	54967	I	1930
Virginia	48775	M	1927	William M. J., Mrs.	68362	D	1934	Peter	55125	D	1930
Virginia	88234	M	1941	**TIETZ**				**TILLAUX**			
TIERNER				Alexander	30529	D	1920	Paul	3009	D	1907
Hugh	1805	D	1906	Carl J.	32446	M	1921	**TILLEY**			
TIERNEY				Charles	43093	D	1925	Bridget	46330	D	1927
Agnes	67932	D	1934	Charlotte	36403	D	1923	Christopher	50266	D	1928
Agnes	69534	D	1935	James G.	17831	D	1914	Edwin	88375	D	1941
Annie	10271	D	1910	Wilhelm A.	32446	M	1921	Harriet G.	76357	D	1937
Annie J.	37456	D	1923	**TIFFANY**				**TILLIE**			
Catherine Agnes	67932	D	1934	George Curtis	76223	D	1937	Alexander	66791	D	1934
Catherine Agnes	69534	D	1935	**TIGER**				Alexander, Jr.	21382	D	1916
Edwin W.	40054	I	1924	Sarah	36341	D	1923	**TILLING**			
Ellen	4681	D	1907	**TIGHE**				Sidney	89745	D	1942
Ellen	60739	D	1932	Annie	2895	D	1907	**TILLINGHAST**			
Ellen J.	35219	D	1922	James Charles	81499	D	1939	Ella P.	9489	D	1910
James	8004	D	1909	M. F.	34098	D	1922	Eva	40017	D	1924
James F.	30454	I	1920	Mae Evelyn	73872	D	1936	**TILLMAN**			
James F.	30973	D	1921	Mary	73872	D	1936	Annie	86061	D	1941
John	52472	D	1929	Michael John	85835	D	1940	Chrestina	32164	D	1921
John L.	4982	D	1908	Thomas J.	4302	D	1907	Clarence F.	10553	D	1910
Joseph James	62673	D	1932	Thomson Henry	47250	D	1927	Elsie	7893	M	1909
Julia Ann	9915	D	1910	**TIKOTZKY**							
Lawrence A.	64378	D	1933	Abraham	52888	D	1929				

NAME	NUMBER	TYPE	YEAR	NAME	NUMBER	TYPE	YEAR	NAME	NUMBER	TYPE	YEAR
Harry J.	58565	I	1931	**TIMM**				Nancy	14492	D	1912
Henry	75847	D	1937	Franziska	15821	D	1913	**TINGMAN**			
John E.	21905	D	1916	Hinrick	54297	D	1929	Hattie A.	58498	D	1931
John Henry	69971	D	1935	Mathilda	63140	D	1932	**TINKER**			
Lena K.	73836	D	1936	Theodore H.	88820	D	1942	Jay	83069	D	1940
Mary Ellen	32325	I	1921	Wilhelm Henry	54297	D	1929	**TINKHAM**			
Tilton E.	85804	D	1940	**TIMMERMAN**				Mary T.	9119	D	1910
Walter F.	68022	D	1934	Bertha Josephine	53059	D	1929	**TINKLER**			
TILLMANN				Marie	69048	D	1935	Catherine	46212	I	1927
Agnes	3216	M	1907	**TIMMERMANN**				Catherine	46855	D	1927
Emma Maria	35722	D	1923	Anna Margaret	65678	D	1933	**TINNEY**			
Frederick	3216	M	1907	Henry W.	9976	D	1910	Robert R.	59044	M	1931
Frederick	5816	D	1908	**TIMMINS**				**TINSLEY**			
Helena	1906	D	1906	John H.	6114	D	1908	Maria F.	52970	I	1929
TILLMANNSHAFER				**TIMMONS**				Mayme Duffy	80744	D	1939
Pauline	61749	D	1932	Anna C.	85985	D	1941	Wilma Marguerite	27587	M	1919
TILLMANNSHOEFER				Katherine A.	77308	D	1937	**TIPP**			
Pauline	61749	D	1932	Thomas F.	17685	I	1914	Frank	77826	D	1938
TILLMANNSHOFER				**TIMNEY**				**TIPPETT**			
Pauline	61749	D	1932	Ellen J.	39254	I	1924	Adrene P.	39008	M	1924
TILLMANNSHOFFER				Ellen J.	47441	D	1927	John Charles	47158	D	1927
Pauline	61749	D	1932	Ellen May	47441	D	1927	Sidney James	28439	D	1919
TILLOTSON				**TIMONEY**				**TIRADANI**			
John W.	52419	D	1929	Joseph Patrick	72395	D	1936	Dante	76335	D	1937
Robert S.	54412	D	1929	**TIMONIERI**				**TIRET**			
William S.	35520	D	1922	Teresa	66148	D	1934	Jean E.	51556	D	1928
TILLSON				**TIMOSSI**				John	51557	D	1928
Alice	43826	M	1926	Antonio	88214	D	1941	**TIRRELL**			
Anna O.	70380	D	1935	Biovanni	59741	D	1931	Anna M.	3978	D	1907
Carolyn	43826	M	1926	Fred	43138	I	1925	Mary Alice	16989	D	1914
Elizabeth	43826	M	1926	Fred	72738	D	1936	Prince H.	7381	D	1909
Irene	43826	M	1926	Luigi	84458	D	1940	**TISCH**			
William	43826	M	1926	**TIMPI**				Emil	50392	D	1928
TILLY				Theobald	59682	D	1931	**TISCONIO**			
Bernard	1925	D	1906	**TIN**				Giovanni	28072	D	1919
Bernard	43623	D	1926	Yee	42498	D	1925	**TISCORNIA**			
TILMAN				**TINCELEN**				Amelia	16607	M	1914
Eddie, Mrs.	85788	D	1940	Margaret	7565	D	1909	Angelo	14941	D	1913
Hansine	85788	D	1940	**TINDOC**				Cesare	1516	D	1906
TILTON				Gregorio R.	62246	D	1932	Eugene	16607	M	1914
Charles Stephen	5881	D	1908	**TINGBERG**				Geronim	2451	D	1906
Chloe T.	3065	D	1907	Daisy A.	64579	D	1933	Giacomo	3581	M	1907
Margaret	86234	D	1941	Daisy Davis	64579	D	1933	Giovanni	28072	D	1919
Robert Fletcher	72950	D	1936	**TINGLEY**				Maria	73182	D	1936
William H.	6752	D	1908	Lucrata Atwood	70155	D	1935	Mary	3581	M	1907
TIMLIN				Margaret M.	14491	D	1912	Raolo	3581	M	1907
Thomas	13756	M	1912					Raymond	73183	D	1936

NAME	NUMBER	TYPE	YEAR
Rocco	16607	M	1914
TISDALE			
Lieuella	57067	D	1930
TISNERAT			
Jean	8516	D	1909
TISSOT			
Albert J.	68788	D	1935
TISTEL			
Mathaes B.	77755	D	1938
Mathias	77755	D	1938
TITCHWORTH			
J. C.	43566	D	1926
TITCOMB			
Harry Stanley	24163	D	1918
TITLOW			
Emma I.	67365	D	1934
John Oliver	72623	D	1936
TITT			
Mary A.	48223	D	1927
TITTEL			
Christian A.	730	I	1906
Christian A.	5692	D	1908
Elizabeth	63548	D	1933
TITTLE			
Horatio Seymour	63384	D	1933
TITUS			
Albert J.	674	M	1906
Albert S.	63789	D	1933
Henry C.	674	M	1906
John	136	D	1906
Josephine V.	1296	D	1906
Thomas	52380	D	1929
TJARKS			
Tjark Remers	67755	D	1934
TLG			
Eliza	57292	D	1930
TLUMAC			
Frank	77420	I	1938
TO			
Harry Sz	82160	M	1939
TOBALSKI			
Victoria	77277	D	1937
TOBBENBASKE			
Margaret	37453	D	1923
TOBBENORKE			
Margaret	37453	D	1923

NAME	NUMBER	TYPE	YEAR
TOBELMAN			
Margaret Ann Tittel	18054	I	1914
Margaret Ann Tittel	34912	D	1922
TOBENER			
Georgiana	18151	D	1914
Hartman Henry	88654	D	1941
Mary J.	48951	D	1928
TOBEY			
William H. H.	1994	D	1906
Winifred	68932	I	1935
Winnifred	69498	D	1935
TOBIAS			
Arline	47292	M	1927
Elliott B.	81945	D	1939
Hazel	6802	M	1908
Nathan J.	43405	D	1926
Samuel L.	30571	D	1920
TOBIN			
Agnes	80830	D	1939
Alice	66305	D	1934
Ann	16629	D	1914
Arthur	80171	D	1938
Catherine	4079	I	1907
Catherine Helena	23726	M	1917
Celia E.	61081	I	1932
Clement	30087	D	1920
David J.	72168	D	1936
Helen	23726	M	1917
Honore	14799	D	1913
James	2972	D	1907
James	42563	D	1925
James J.	57748	D	1931
James P.	24579	D	1918
James Whitney	57782	M	1931
James Whitney	60090	M	1931
John P.	52658	D	1929
John R.	3244	D	1907
Joseph	53684	M	1929
Joseph P.	77201	D	1937
Joseph S.	24043	D	1918
Juana Sophia	66753	D	1934
Lilian A.	30892	D	1920
Margaret E.	44154	D	1926
Mary A.	27791	D	1919
Mary A.	89672	D	1942
Mary B.	11483	D	1911
Mary E.	16697	D	1914
Mary E.	59806	D	1931

NAME	NUMBER	TYPE	YEAR
Mary I.	81695	D	1939
Michael A.	63120	D	1932
Michael E.	67154	D	1934
Michael Edward	64101	I	1933
Myles E.	48228	M	1927
Patrick J.	1982	I	1906
Patrick J.	19445	D	1915
Peter Arthur	80171	D	1938
Philip	2122	D	1906
Richard	89671	D	1942
Robert	82079	D	1939
Robert J.	1772	D	1906
Rose E.	64189	D	1933
Sarah Jane	68064	D	1934
Thomas	88	D	1906
Thomas L.	55641	D	1930
William J.	48228	M	1927
William M.	36371	M	1923
Wm.	57109	D	1930
TOBLY			
Alida S.	76065	D	1937
TOBNER			
Mary J.	48951	D	1928
TOBONI			
James	73629	M	1936
John	73629	M	1936
TOBRINER			
Ida Louise	9940	D	1910
Isaac	34284	D	1922
TOBSEN			
Amalie	78187	D	1938
Thomas	58689	D	1931
TOCCHINI			
Steve	30116	D	1920
TOCK			
Katrina	27472	D	1919
TOD			
James	11572	D	1911
TODD			
Clara Louise Holly	67715	D	1934
David R.	12053	D	1911
Eliza	16122	D	1913
Elizabeth	16122	D	1913
Ella I.	80534	D	1939
H. L., Mrs.	88252	D	1941
Henry L.	77749	D	1938
Holly	67715	D	1934

NAME	NUMBER	TYPE	YEAR	NAME	NUMBER	TYPE	YEAR	NAME	NUMBER	TYPE	YEAR
James D.	41403	D	1925	Freda M.	77286	D	1937	**TOLAND**			
John E.	2280	D	1906	Hans J.	83050	D	1940	Daniel	31655	D	1921
Mary A.	88252	D	1941	Myrtle W.	83580	D	1940	Edward J.	42596	D	1925
Mary E.	47796	D	1927	Neils B.	20880	D	1916	Margaret	51449	D	1928
Norman G.	71989	D	1936	Nelson B.	20880	D	1916	**TOLARI**			
Robert	74972	D	1937	**TOGNAZZI**				Mario	32168	D	1921
Robert Manson	60945	M	1932	Frances E.	34104	D	1922	**TOLCHARD**			
Rollin Q.	74770	M	1937	**TOGNAZZINI**				Henry A.	24978	D	1918
Samuel	43328	D	1926	Ellid	16189	M	1913	Ruth Marion	28635	M	1920
Stedman F.	70282	D	1935	Lionel	16189	M	1913	William F.	67541	D	1934
Thomas P.	8666	D	1909	Milo D.	53682	D	1929	**TOLENTINO**			
Walter Archie	74770	M	1937	**TOGNETTI**				Acacio	31245	I	1921
TODDARD				Natale	48513	D	1927	Isabelle	40429	D	1924
Irene J.	89599	I	1942	**TOGNI**				**TOLFORD**			
TODHUNTER				Lorenzo	34968	D	1922	Caroline C.	58284	D	1931
Charles Louis	87037	D	1941	**TOGNOLI**				**TOLGIEN**			
Charles Martin	87096	M	1941	Stefano	52272	D	1929	Henry J.	58628	D	1931
Christina Maria	44052	D	1926	**TOGNOTTI**				**TOLHURST**			
TODMAN				Edwin J.	53807	M	1929	Helen Edwina	26061	M	1919
Moses Herrington	76156	D	1937	Ernestine	53806	I	1929	**TOLLE**			
TODT				Giovanni	64252	D	1933	Minnie J.	43467	D	1926
John	20180	D	1915	Guglielmo	75278	D	1937	**TOLLEFSEN**			
John W.	18549	I	1915	Joseph A.	77605	D	1938	Ragnvald E.	19369	D	1915
Pearl M.	59417	D	1931	Lillie	13346	M	1912	**TOLLEFSON**			
TODTER				Maria	77592	D	1938	Lewis	79519	D	1938
Catherine	10527	D	1910	Marie E.	79097	I	1938	**TOLLET**			
Peter	12703	D	1911	Mary	53806	I	1929	Alphonse	17465	D	1914
TOEDTER				Onesto	8303	D	1909	**TOLLEY**			
Catharina	10527	D	1910	**TOHER**				Cora E.	71665	D	1936
Peter	12703	D	1911	Susan	23956	D	1918	Frank J.	74339	D	1937
TOEPFER				**TOICH**				**TOLMAN**			
Frank, Jr.	34252	D	1922	Katie	75979	D	1937	Eddy, Mrs.	67952	I	1934
TOFANELLI				Morris	10570	M	1910	Eddy, Mrs.	85788	D	1940
Francesco	60372	D	1931	Morris	78996	M	1938	Eliza M.	3409	D	1907
Giorgina	72097	D	1936	Unborn child	10570	M	1910	Hansine	67952	I	1934
Giovanni	29298	D	1920	**TOJETTI**				Hansine	85788	D	1940
Maria	52141	I	1929	Beatrice M.	23953	D	1918	**TOLNI**			
TOFFEL				Katherine	66057	D	1934	Bernardino	3761	D	1907
Frederick	4190	D	1907	Margaret	27588	D	1919	**TOLONY**			
TOFFINDER				**TOKER**				Madeleine	21582	D	1916
Geoffe	29301	D	1920	John	7023	D	1909	**TOLOS**			
William Geoffe	29301	D	1920	**TOKLAS**				H. L.	74418	D	1937
TOFFY				C. Fred	76639	D	1937	Harry	74418	D	1937
Aleck	16480	D	1913	Clarence Ferdinand	76639	D	1937	**TOLOSKI**			
TOFT				Ferdinand	40193	D	1924	Charles E.	79549	D	1938
Christian P.	13368	D	1912	Laura A.	23360	D	1917				
Erma Emily	69442	M	1935								

NAME	NUMBER	TYPE	YEAR
TOLPFER			
Frank, Jr.	34252	D	1922
TOLSTONAGE			
Erma C.	30205	M	1920
Herschall M.	30205	M	1920
TOLTON			
William Russell	49977	M	1928
TOM			
Pow	53068	D	1929
Quong Wah	53467	M	1929
Too	64709	D	1933
TOMAGHELLI			
Giovanni	53720	D	1929
TOMAN			
Eliza A.	42858	D	1925
TOMANOVICH			
Drage	46574	D	1927
Thomas V.	20682	D	1916
TOMASCOVICH			
Steve J.	43534	D	1926
TOMASEK			
Irene	79105	D	1938
TOMASELLO			
Giuseppe	82603	D	1939
Vincent	42671	D	1925
TOMASEVIC			
Ignjo	67752	D	1934
TOMASEVICH			
I. J.	67752	D	1934
Ignjo	67752	D	1934
John	67752	D	1934
TOMASINI			
Filiberto	36866	I	1923
Henry R.	12005	D	1911
TOMASKOVICH			
Steve J.	43534	D	1926
TOMASSINI			
Filiberto	37563	D	1923
TOMASSONE			
Remigio	41727	D	1925
Remigio	41727	D	1925
TOMASZEWSKI			
John	21453	D	1916
Ludwig	53625	D	1929
TOMAVICH			
Martin M.	25425	D	1918

NAME	NUMBER	TYPE	YEAR
TOMAZELLO			
Vincent	42671	D	1925
TOMB			
Henry William	17650	M	1914
TOMBLINSON			
Bruce W.	54231	D	1929
TOMBOLESI			
Frieda Gertrude	74857	D	1937
Sigismondo	69001	D	1935
Sigmond	69001	D	1935
TOMEI			
Alfred	50323	M	1928
Edoardo	45514	D	1926
Massimo	76866	D	1937
May	50554	D	1928
TOMINSKI			
Ida	6491	D	1908
Theodore	74279	I	1936
TOMIYAMA			
Fuji	70421	D	1935
TOMKE			
Edward	86897	D	1941
TOMKINS			
Florence B.	64508	D	1933
Harriet Virginia	89014	I	1942
Harriet Virginia	89290	D	1942
Henry John	80931	I	1939
Henry John	87319	D	1941
Margaret N.	56537	D	1930
TOMLIN			
Benjamin L.	85076	D	1940
C. W.	88968	D	1942
Elizabeth Jane	14458	D	1912
TOMLINSON			
Bruce W.	54231	D	1929
Georgia G.	24929	D	1918
Richard C.	48062	M	1927
Richard Frank	75218	D	1937
W. E.	51736	D	1929
TOMOKIYO			
Tayo	11476	M	1911
TOMOLA			
Andrea	48010	D	1927
Natale	84653	D	1940
TOMPKINS			
Clarence Joseph	6682	M	1908
Jessie Lois	69280	D	1935

NAME	NUMBER	TYPE	YEAR
Jessie P.	69280	D	1935
Mary Gertrude	6682	M	1908
Merritt	89867	D	1942
Sarah	7164	D	1909
Sina M.	31795	D	1921
William A.	58477	D	1931
TOMPKINSON			
George William	79311	D	1938
Joseph	1001	D	1906
Katherine	14411	D	1912
TOMPSON			
Sarah Hobart	74303	D	1937
TOMS			
Emma Clara	31102	D	1921
TOMSKY			
Samuel C.	64242	D	1933
TOMSON			
Charles B.	78302	D	1938
TONAKIS			
Christ	40610	D	1924
TONALA			
Angelo	25030	D	1918
TONARELLI			
Ulisse	50036	D	1928
TONASELLI			
Ulisse	50036	D	1928
TONDER			
Hans	17166	D	1914
TONELLA			
Camillo	89568	D	1942
TONELLO			
Luigi	25508	D	1918
TONER			
Edward Hugh	51759	D	1929
Ellen	8670	I	1909
Hugh	73404	I	1936
Hugh	73476	D	1936
J. M.	76843	D	1937
Rolland P.	12684	D	1911
William J.	34771	D	1922
William J.	53731	D	1929
TONESA			
Giuseppe	8021	D	1909
TONESI			
Giuseppe	8021	D	1909

NAME	NUMBER	TYPE	YEAR
TONETT			
John	17526	D	1914
TONG			
Chew Wah	79476	M	1938
Chin Chuk	36188	D	1923
Fong Kim	40389	M	1924
Lillie	19909	M	1915
TONGE			
Frederick	45093	D	1926
TONINI			
Antonietta	53913	D	1929
TONIOLO			
Victor	44263	I	1926
TONJES			
Martin	40071	D	1924
TONKIN			
Adelaide B.	51500	I	1928
Fred	55827	D	1930
Rebecca C.	68733	D	1935
Ruth C.	68733	D	1935
Walter C.	87681	D	1941
TONKON			
Esther	83053	D	1940
TONKS			
Percy	60648	I	1932
TONN			
Adolph	47775	D	1927
Dorothy	3702	M	1907
TONNA			
Carmela	84492	D	1940
Giuseppe	84493	D	1940
M. Assunta	80703	D	1939
TONNELLI			
Assunta Maria N. Arata	39054	D	1924
Maria	39054	D	1924
TONNER			
Amanda	42566	D	1925
TONNESON			
Hans M.	35613	D	1922
Otto Theodore	35780	D	1923
TONNIES			
Dora M.	54172	D	1929
TONNINGS			
Lucille	60271	D	1931
TONNINGSEN			
Elizabeth	1854	D	1906

NAME	NUMBER	TYPE	YEAR
John	65875	D	1933
Pauline E.	71575	D	1936
TONNISSON			
S.	18465	D	1915
TONOLA			
Angelo	25030	D	1918
TONS			
John F.	56907	D	1930
TONZI			
George	14292	M	1912
TOO			
Edward Tom	64598	D	1933
Sing Hoo	74006	D	1936
Tom	64709	D	1933
TOOGOOD			
William H. A.	18736	D	1915
TOOHEY			
Cornelius	64033	D	1933
Frank Edward	33797	I	1922
Inez Vincent	43649	D	1926
Martin	10864	D	1910
William H.	80135	I	1938
Ynez Vincent	43649	D	1926
TOOHIG			
Catherine	65212	D	1933
TOOHY			
Inez Vincent	43649	D	1926
Ynez Vincent	43649	D	1926
TOOLIS			
John	83875	D	1940
TOOMBS			
Maude S.	78363	D	1938
Roy Abbott	40664	D	1924
TOOMEY			
Annie	30841	D	1920
Daniel J.	30842	D	1920
Henry C. J.	63318	D	1933
Hugh	81775	D	1939
Jessie	42172	D	1925
John	45258	I	1926
Matthew J.	3008	D	1907
Richard J.	45258	I	1926
Thomas B.	43411	M	1926
TOPALOVICH			
Dreka	15919	D	1913
TOPANELLI			
Giorgina	3310	I	1907

NAME	NUMBER	TYPE	YEAR
TOPINI			
Caterina	60355	D	1931
Helen	81308	D	1939
Peter	32660	D	1921
TOPLITIZ			
Melville S.	31778	D	1921
TOPLITZ			
Fabian	9658	D	1910
Minnie	48986	D	1928
Monroe F.	73700	D	1936
TOPORKE			
Frances	26696	M	1919
TOPPER			
Clara J.	14183	D	1912
TOPPING			
Harriet Elizabeth	36453	D	1923
TORAL			
Giovanni	13062	D	1912
TORANTO			
Joseph	28162	D	1919
TORASSA			
John L.	36093	D	1923
TORBECK			
John	68521	D	1934
TORBERT			
Mary Pennock	52010	I	1929
TORCHIANA			
Henry Albert VanCoenen	83653	D	1940
TORELLI			
Carrie	81525	D	1939
TORESON			
James	62179	D	1932
TORGERSEN			
George	35126	D	1922
Marie	42095	D	1925
TORGERSON			
Henry	52905	D	1929
TORIGGINO			
Gian Battista	20817	M	1916
Ignatius	20817	M	1916
Rinaldo	20817	M	1916
TORIK			
Marion	72380	D	1936
TORJESEN			
Christian	21589	D	1916

NAME	NUMBER	TYPE	YEAR
TORMEY			
Agnes M.	57662	I	1931
Agnes M.	62450	D	1932
Christine	8065	D	1909
Frank	2598	D	1907
Louise A.	39204	D	1924
Marjorie Ellen	60864	M	1932
Mary E.	60506	D	1931
Robert Sheehy	52544	M	1929
TORNACE			
Giuseppe	8021	D	1909
TORNAY			
Marian	79344	M	1938
TORNBERG			
Carl A.	84446	D	1940
TORNEY			
Edward J., Jr.	76479	M	1937
Jeanette	76479	M	1937
Mary D.	84966	D	1940
Robert	76479	M	1937
TORNICH			
Annie	50796	D	1928
Frank T.	53183	D	1929
TORNQUIST			
Adolph R.	70877	D	1935
TORO			
Delfina D.	43828	D	1926
TOROK			
Alexander	65421	D	1933
Sandor	65421	D	1933
TORONCZYK			
Davis	71760	D	1936
TORPEY			
James J.	41075	D	1925
Thomas J.	57929	D	1931
William Harold	84501	D	1940
TORPINO			
Giambattista	61787	D	1932
John	61787	D	1932
TORRANCE			
Jennie	72884	D	1936
TORRANNO			
Prospero	25789	D	1918
TORRANO			
James Vincent	23294	D	1917
Marie	40876	D	1925

NAME	NUMBER	TYPE	YEAR
Nicola	81665	D	1939
TORRE			
Agostino	10408	D	1910
Albert E.	75087	D	1937
Angelina	54541	D	1929
Angelina C.	57437	D	1930
Antonio	1552	D	1906
Batista G.	18761	D	1915
Charles F.	50196	D	1928
Charles S.	50227	D	1928
David	47797	D	1927
Emilio	46350	D	1927
Frank B.	30650	D	1920
G. B.	57963	D	1931
Giambastista	22976	D	1917
Giambattista	57963	D	1931
Giovanni	70475	I	1935
Giovanni	73778	D	1936
Giovanni	44625	D	1926
Giovanni Batista	30650	D	1920
Giovanni Battista	22976	D	1917
Giuseppe	57238	D	1930
Giuseppe	80058	D	1938
Guiseppe	9577	D	1910
John	57371	M	1930
Joseph	9577	D	1910
Joseph	57238	D	1930
Luigi	83659	D	1940
Mary	77562	D	1938
Modesto Gilbert	75503	D	1937
Ottavius J.	79643	D	1938
TORRES			
Lucy	41274	I	1925
Lucy J.	55749	D	1930
TORRESEN			
Anna	32482	D	1921
Annie	32482	D	1921
TORRESSEN			
Anna	32482	D	1921
TORREY			
Edwin Allan	81441	D	1939
George W.	39861	D	1924
TORRIGGINO			
Felice	19059	D	1915
TORRITO			
Lily	67790	I	1934
TORSCHI			
Pietro	54166	D	1929

NAME	NUMBER	TYPE	YEAR
TORSEN			
M. T.	29749	D	1920
Theodore	29749	D	1920
TORTI			
Maria	57471	D	1930
TORTORICE			
Vincent	89424	D	1942
TORTORICI			
Mariano	21399	D	1916
TORTOROLO			
Geronima	27461	M	1919
Giovanni	27461	M	1919
Girolomo	25772	D	1918
Nicolo	27461	M	1919
TOSCANINI			
Giuseppe	57387	D	1930
Maria	51954	D	1929
TOSCHI			
Angelo	69169	D	1935
Rizzieri	42065	D	1925
TOSCO			
Agostino	26323	I	1919
Agostino	27086	D	1919
TOSHEY			
Frank Edward	33797	I	1922
TOSI			
Alberto	7052	M	1909
Dilsolina	7052	M	1909
Georgi	7052	M	1909
Hazel	7052	M	1909
Vincent	53691	M	1929
TOSICH			
Andrew C.	76115	D	1937
TOSO			
Giovanni Battista	38779	D	1924
Maria	81545	D	1939
Rosa	84232	D	1940
Samuel	14432	D	1912
Simone	14432	D	1912
TOSTADO			
Rosa	86303	D	1941
TOSTE			
Joe Paim	32240	I	1921
TOTARO			
Angelo	86699	D	1941

NAME	NUMBER	TYPE	YEAR	NAME	NUMBER	TYPE	YEAR	NAME	NUMBER	TYPE	YEAR
TOTHEROH				TOWATA				May Gertrude	78940	M	1938
William H.	10269	D	1910	Noe	11477	M	1911	Phoebe	49182	M	1928
TOTONI				TOWE				TOY			
Angelos Christo	70644	D	1935	James	23322	D	1917	Cheung	84591	M	1940
TOTTEN				Robert	86201	M	1941	Daniel	1112	D	1906
Joseph C.	75614	D	1937	TOWER				Dong	45659	D	1926
Mary A.	15496	D	1913	James	8012	D	1909	Fook Young	39629	M	1924
TOTTENHAM				TOWERS				George Daniel	31067	D	1921
Georgiana Emily	22027	D	1916	John	45168	D	1926	Lillie B.	34234	D	1922
TOUCAR				TOWEY				Lillie Preston	55647	D	1930
Ida L.	29048	D	1920	James Roddy	71839	M	1936	TOYE			
TOUDY				TOWLE				William O.	81619	D	1939
Julius C.	22451	D	1917	Augusta	6656	D	1908	TOYETTI			
TOULOUSE				Frances Augusta	42038	D	1925	Emilia Musto	31078	D	1921
Jean Baptiste	82182	D	1939	George W.	17353	D	1914	TOZER			
Jules	74398	D	1937	John Henry	13611	M	1912	Henry C.	60321	D	1931
TOURAN				John Henry	26539	M	1919	Llewellyn	5589	D	1908
Jean B.	66680	D	1934	Lizzie B.	23199	D	1917	Rosa H.	36285	D	1923
TOURNOUR				William W.	59678	D	1931	TOZI			
Angelo	89659	D	1942	TOWLES				Matsuya	1697	M	1906
TOURNY				Thomas Ramsden	12970	M	1912	TRABER			
George	64049	D	1933	TOWNE				August	6092	D	1908
TOURON				Alice N.	80971	D	1939	TRABUCCO			
Jean Baptiste	66680	D	1934	Arthur G.	55453	D	1930	Ann	87549	D	1941
TOUSSAINT				Edward B.	72183	M	1936	TRACEY			
Frank Joseph	81997	D	1939	Harriet	7135	D	1909	Helen	77710	I	1938
TOUSSAU				Marie Foster	49628	M	1928	John	59293	D	1931
Simon	40320	D	1924	Percy Edgar	87722	D	1941	John	71317	D	1935
TOUSSIN				Roger E., Jr.	72183	M	1936	Mary Agnes	15320	D	1913
Carrie S.	31055	D	1921	TOWNER				TRACHSEL			
TOUVINEN				Charles W.	57594	D	1931	Gotlieb	53165	D	1929
John A.	48405	D	1927	TOWNES				TRACISCO			
TOUZEL				George Edmund	75943	D	1937	Richard	81214	M	1939
Frank	57476	D	1930	TOWNLEY				TRACY			
TOVANI				Jean A.	40632	D	1924	Ann Jane	42254	D	1925
Lawrence	71145	D	1935	Mignon	37402	M	1923	Annie	4456	I	1907
Libera	62106	D	1932	TOWNS				Annie	6174	D	1908
Lorenzo	71145	D	1935	Euphemia	65303	D	1933	Annie	15324	D	1913
TOVARAZ				Frank Carlton	48154	D	1927	Augusta F.	27013	D	1919
Martin	88776	D	1941	George	24836	D	1918	Bernard	20839	M	1916
Mary	54338	D	1929	John B.	953	M	1906	Catherine	12224	D	1911
TOVERUD				William C.	9621	D	1910	Catherine	20840	D	1916
Hanna	49343	D	1928	TOWNSEND				Cecelia	20839	M	1916
TOW				Annie L.	78941	D	1938	George	20839	M	1916
Leong En	31622	D	1921	Arthur Charles	78940	M	1938	Helen	20839	M	1916
				John	45298	D	1926	James	60689	D	1932
				Katherine	39843	D	1924	Jane	13079	D	1912

NAME	NUMBER	TYPE	YEAR
Joseph	54058	I	1929
Joseph	57711	I	1931
Joseph L.	51863	D	1929
Margaret	42675	D	1925
Mary	7961	D	1909
Mary A.	88014	D	1941
Mary C.	42535	D	1925
Mary Jane	83227	D	1940
Norman T.	80824	D	1939
Richard Donald	69808	M	1935
Sarah Elizabeth	52896	D	1929
Susan Corbell	58865	D	1931
Theodore F.	70914	D	1935
Thomas	10811	D	1910
Thomas A.	77777	D	1938
Thomas E.	20244	D	1916
Tom	42618	D	1925
William Augustus	89558	D	1942
TRADER			
Glenn D.	40050	I	1924
TRAENESS			
Peter	16659	D	1914
TRAFANO			
Battista	73773	D	1936
TRAFFE			
Jenevieve	44241	D	1926
TRAGER			
Morris	17077	D	1914
TRAIL			
Andrew Thompson	89170	D	1942
TRAINER			
Patrick	6079	D	1908
William H.	68538	D	1934
TRAINESS			
Peter	16659	D	1914
TRAINOR			
Charles E.	56826	D	1930
Charles F.	75281	D	1937
Frank J.	55778	D	1930
Joseph H.	56845	D	1930
Katherine B.	77641	D	1938
Kathryn L.	77641	D	1938
Thomas J.	37833	D	1923
TRAMBLEY			
Herbert P.	81791	D	1939
TRANERSO			
Luisa	59230	D	1931

NAME	NUMBER	TYPE	YEAR
TRANFIELD			
Georgiana	31973	D	1921
Rose	55985	D	1930
TRANGER			
Samuel C.	38163	D	1924
TRANLSEN			
Jochim Friedrick	36630	D	1923
TRANQUILLO			
Laloli	88599	D	1941
TRANT			
Katie	32124	D	1921
Maggie	75301	D	1937
Patrick J.	6961	D	1908
TRAPANI			
John	87762	D	1941
Luigi	44021	D	1926
TRAPP			
Elizabeth	86717	D	1941
Ferdinand C.	22143	D	1917
John G.	62268	D	1932
Madelina	22434	D	1917
Mary Ann	69510	D	1935
Meta M.	81203	D	1939
Sophie	83808	D	1940
Walter Joseph	58494	D	1931
TRAPY			
Lucie A.	31371	D	1921
TRASH			
Joseph	27781	D	1919
TRASK			
Adele P.	20630	D	1916
Emily Frances	58459	D	1931
Gardner G.	43777	D	1926
Helen C.	46157	D	1927
Martha	11033	D	1911
Sampson	30004	D	1920
TRATHEN			
Richard	45751	D	1926
TRAUGER			
Samuel C.	38163	D	1924
TRAULSEN			
Jochim Friedrich	36630	D	1923
TRAUNG			
Charles F.	83354	D	1940
Ella	44749	D	1926
Eva Belle	88196	D	1941

NAME	NUMBER	TYPE	YEAR
TRAUT			
Josephine H.	65506	D	1933
TRAUTMANN			
Bertha	75204	D	1937
TRAUTNER			
Charles	43448	D	1926
Gustave Adolph	60024	D	1931
Theodore Adolph F. C.	19323	D	1915
TRAUTSCH			
Selma C.	52898	D	1929
TRAUTVETTER			
Otto	16282	D	1913
TRAVAGLINI			
Carolina	51587	D	1928
Giacomo	26312	D	1919
TRAVAS			
Michael T.	26029	D	1918
TRAVELL			
J. B., Mrs.	73595	D	1936
TRAVERS			
Carolita G.	34291	D	1922
George	8783	D	1909
Peter	3251	D	1907
Richard	9362	D	1910
TRAVERSA			
Filippo	76944	I	1937
TRAVERSARO			
Angela	19554	D	1915
Giovanni	1963	D	1906
Giovanni	25588	D	1918
Ignacio	84456	D	1940
Stefano	59576	D	1931
TRAVERSO			
Annetta	61318	D	1932
Francesco	42258	D	1925
Giovanni	35026	D	1922
Giuseppe	31222	D	1921
Innocenzo Luigi	43040	D	1925
Luisa	77376	D	1937
Madalena	50436	D	1928
Michele	18287	D	1914
Raimondo Roy	89643	M	1942
TRAVESO			
Michele	18287	D	1914
TRAVI			
Mary	65645	D	1933
Pietro	17142	D	1914

NAME	NUMBER	TYPE	YEAR
TRAVIS			
Clara P.	23838	D	1918
Ellen	68442	D	1934
George A.	46130	D	1927
George W.	86628	D	1941
Julia A.	30	D	1906
Kathleen A.	63521	D	1933
Lulen Robert	73124	D	1936
William C.	78026	D	1938
TRAWNEY			
Gustav John	50082	D	1928
TRAY			
John W.	66042	D	1934
TRAYNOR			
John	79312	D	1938
John J.	46108	D	1926
TREACY			
Edmund	12396	D	1911
Ellen M.	49652	D	1928
Francis Joseph	35501	M	1922
Harold	18104	M	1914
Irma	18104	M	1914
James J.	19285	D	1915
John	38207	D	1924
John	59293	D	1931
John J.	53931	D	1929
John Patrick	35501	M	1922
John T.	71317	D	1935
Nora Patricia	66007	D	1934
Thomas	17387	D	1914
Thomas J.	84548	D	1940
Ursula Mary	35501	M	1922
TREADWELL			
Alfred B.	17187	D	1914
Eric L.	34882	I	1922
Francis Joseph	35213	I	1922
Inez Genevieve	4554	M	1907
James Parker	1238	D	1906
Kathryn C.	53325	D	1929
Mabel	45344	D	1926
Maud Marie	11233	D	1911
TREANKLE			
Edith	64649	I	1933
TREANOR			
J. P.	54071	D	1929
TREAT			
Celia J.	86989	I	1941

NAME	NUMBER	TYPE	YEAR
Emma	8867	D	1909
Helen Sarah	79102	D	1938
Hugh P.	86141	D	1941
Isabel	76142	D	1937
W. W.	1483	D	1906
TREBELL			
John	6281	D	1908
Mary	33254	D	1922
Thomas	80362	D	1939
William	50703	D	1928
TREBITSCH			
Leopold	21916	D	1916
TRECY			
Ann Jane	42254	D	1925
Ann Jeane	42254	D	1925
TREFEIL			
Hippolyte	88451	D	1941
TREFTS			
Edward C.	14178	D	1912
Ruth Evelyn	1221	M	1906
TREFZ			
Anna M.	63399	D	1933
Lena	29848	D	1920
TREGANOWEN			
William H.	61817	D	1932
TREGASKIS			
Martin B.	78785	D	1938
TREGEAR			
James	62168	D	1932
TREGENZA			
Clara	34285	D	1922
Joseph Daniel	59043	D	1931
TREGIDGO			
D. A.	60105	D	1931
TREICH			
Peter	71338	D	1936
TREICHEL			
Harold L.	18715	D	1915
TREK			
Lena	29848	D	1920
TRELEASE			
Jessie	82234	D	1939
TREMAIN			
George Shirley	87034	D	1941
TREMAYNE			
William	44890	D	1926

NAME	NUMBER	TYPE	YEAR
TREMONT			
Marion Kingdon	56758	M	1930
TREMONTI			
Giulio	22026	D	1916
TRENEAR			
Richard Henry	53196	D	1929
TRENGOVE			
Arthur Earle	83541	D	1940
Mary	59858	D	1931
Samuel J.	60670	D	1932
TRENKNER			
Walter	28571	D	1920
TRENOR			
Pauline	13279	I	1912
Thomas Francis	37769	D	1923
TRENT			
George A.	82932	D	1939
TRENTO			
Dominico	59031	D	1931
Maria	72357	D	1936
TRENTT			
Cecilia	71860	D	1936
TRESANGUE			
Anselme	47130	D	1927
Harold	47255	M	1927
Lucile	47255	M	1927
Tillie	47129	D	1927
TRESARRIEN			
Jean Baptiste	41533	D	1925
TRESCH			
Joseph	27697	D	1919
Josephine	37420	D	1923
TRESCONY			
Katie M.	58362	D	1931
TRESPAILLE			
Marian	87601	D	1941
Victor	66026	D	1934
TRESSLER			
George	49543	D	1928
TRETHEWAY			
Thomas	54110	D	1929
TRETTEN			
Emil Leon	48962	D	1928
Minerva Mary	60241	D	1931
TREUGE			
Ella	43318	D	1926

Key: D = death; M = minor; I = incompetent

NAME	NUMBER	TYPE	YEAR	NAME	NUMBER	TYPE	YEAR	NAME	NUMBER	TYPE	YEAR
TREUTLEIN				TRIEBER				TRIMMEL			
Peter	74381	D	1937	Beverley	83957	I	1940	John	36720	D	1923
TREVARTHA				Edythe	83958	M	1940	TRINCA			
Oliver	35170	D	1922	TRIEDEL				Vincenzo	25515	D	1918
TREVETHICK				Henry	55316	I	1930	TRINCHERIO			
Edward Champlain	49810	D	1928	TRIEKILIS				Adelio	67065	M	1934
TREVIA				George	15640	D	1913	TRINCHERO			
Domenico	37778	D	1923	TRIENBACH				Dora	67066	D	1934
TREVILLIAN				Max Otto	59262	D	1931	Henry	67065	M	1934
Mary Elizabeth	43994	D	1926	TRIEST				James	67065	M	1934
Thomas	8863	D	1909	Bertha	17220	D	1914	TRINCHITELLA			
TREVISAN				Dorothy	48911	M	1928	John	66847	D	1934
Rosa	47128	D	1927	Jane	74472	M	1937	TRINETT			
TREVOR				Martin	21206	D	1916	Dodrothy Anne	73991	M	1936
W. H. G.	63593	D	1933	TRIFIRO				TRINGALI			
TREVORROW				Giuseppe	44781	D	1926	Annie	78751	M	1938
James Edward	80529	D	1939	TRIFOCOICH				TRINKEL			
TREWREN				George	63055	D	1932	William	37350	D	1923
Joseph Francis	83093	D	1940	TRIGG				TRINKLER			
TREWRICK				Theresa Alice	1875	M	1906	Carl	2964	D	1907
R. L.	9663	D	1910	William Leo	1875	M	1906	TRINKO			
TREZISE				TRIGGEY				Sergei A.	86533	D	1941
John Samuel	40607	D	1924	Joseph Fielding	17265	D	1914	TRIPIDI			
Philip H.	35879	D	1923	TRIGGS				Luigi	62207	D	1932
Samuel	40607	D	1924	James	25462	D	1918	TRIPLETT			
TRIBUKAIT				TRIGUERIS				Emma	83811	D	1940
Frank	78040	D	1938	Ellen A.	58654	D	1931	TRIPP			
John Ferdinand	84570	M	1940	TRIGUEROS				Albert	68434	D	1934
TRICE				Emelia	61654	M	1932	Beatrice G.	77851	D	1938
Gussie	87101	I	1941	Fernando	61654	M	1932	Edwin B.	80148	D	1938
TRICHILO				Victor	61654	M	1932	Helen S.	9360	D	1910
Tommaso A.	45764	D	1926	TRILARRY				Katie	59603	D	1931
TRICK				Gracieuse	3150	D	1907	Mary	32991	D	1921
Laura J.	38672	D	1924	TRILLEY				Minnie	69209	I	1935
TRICKLER				Joseph	11357	D	1911	Wilson	36739	M	1923
Ellenor G.	40377	D	1924	TRIMBLE				TRIQUNATITA			
Harry B.	78234	D	1938	Grace Georgia Clara	20105	D	1915	Swami	18625	D	1915
Henry B.	78234	D	1938	James F.	54235	D	1929	TRIVETT			
Joseph Charles	51825	D	1929	James J.	55735	D	1930	Dodrothy Anne	73991	M	1936
TRICOU				Lucy	89753	D	1942	TRIZISE			
Marguerite B.	35164	D	1922	Lulu M.	19495	D	1915	Lillie May	88625	D	1941
TRIEBEL				William James	75576	D	1937	TROBOCK			
Augusta	89176	D	1942	TRIMBUR				Bartholomew N.	23561	D	1917
Auguste	6799	I	1908	John Mathieu	77499	M	1938	Madeline B.	12230	M	1911
William	2287	M	1906	Ruth O.	82539	D	1939	TROEDSON			
				Sylvester M.	77499	M	1938	Emanuel	84293	D	1940

NAME	NUMBER	TYPE	YEAR
TROGLER			
George F.	4317	D	1907
TROLAN			
Peter	5514	D	1908
TROLL			
Mary E.	51058	D	1928
TROLLE			
Holger Marcus	87876	D	1941
TROLLER			
Herman	57151	D	1930
Joseph	14469	M	1912
Maria	9842	D	1910
TROLLIET			
Charles H.	70600	D	1935
TROLLMANN			
Ignatz	61016	D	1932
Wencel	58030	D	1931
Wenczel	58030	D	1931
TROLSEN			
Nels	66589	D	1934
TROLTSCH			
Franz Oskar	53198	D	1929
TROMBETTA			
Giuseppe	48570	D	1927
TROMBOTTI			
Pasquale	86290	I	1941
TROMPETER			
Oscar H.	44994	D	1926
TRONCY			
Mary	27438	M	1919
Noel	64067	D	1933
TROOST			
Nora	68042	D	1934
TROPPMAN			
Chas. M.	27995	D	1919
TROSETH			
Arthemise Marie	15084	D	1913
George Adolph	15085	M	1913
TROST			
Louis Henry	56767	D	1930
Marie	53161	D	1929
Marie Ann	88591	D	1941
Mildred M.	56910	M	1930
William	43056	D	1925
TROSTMAN			
Otto J.	58759	D	1931

NAME	NUMBER	TYPE	YEAR
TROTH			
Laura E.	75344	D	1937
TROTTER			
Betty Emelia	41158	M	1925
Mary Barbara	41158	M	1925
Phyllis	41158	M	1925
Roy S.	29082	D	1920
William	88795	D	1941
TROUBAT			
Catherine	67470	D	1934
TROUILH			
Anna	17002	D	1914
TROUILLET			
Caroline Elise	8234	M	1909
Jules	7721	D	1909
TROUIN			
Theodore L.	54535	D	1929
TROUTH			
Frances O.	85269	D	1940
TROUTT			
Ferdinand	15739	D	1913
TROWBRIDGE			
Archie	29794	D	1920
Eliza Jane	24421	D	1918
Georgia Shaw	63764	D	1933
Henry Otis	44707	D	1926
Mary E.	54939	D	1930
Mayte Cole	54939	D	1930
TROWELL			
W. H.	12186	D	1911
TROXEL			
John	35668	D	1923
TROXELL			
Elmer	20475	D	1916
TROY			
Cahterine Eustace	6360	D	1908
Elizabeth	6639	D	1908
John W.	41834	D	1925
John W.	41834	D	1925
John W.	66042	D	1934
Margaret	17580	I	1914
Margaret	32619	D	1921
Martin J.	73864	D	1936
Martin, Jr.	76097	D	1937
Patrick	18995	D	1915
Thomas F.	57719	D	1931

NAME	NUMBER	TYPE	YEAR
TROYE			
John	19143	D	1915
TROYER			
Roderic Arthur	50631	D	1928
TRUAX			
Isaac Leads	48296	D	1927
TRUCKENBRODT			
Anton	29991	D	1920
Johanna D.	77692	D	1938
TRUCO			
Marguerite	58651	D	1931
TRUDAUNG			
Karl	65714	D	1933
TRUDEAU			
Elisa Niding	26331	D	1919
TRUDELL			
Elenor E.	35049	M	1922
TRUDO			
Edward	12134	D	1911
TRUDRUNG			
John	49474	M	1928
John J.	31931	D	1921
Karl	65714	D	1933
TRUEB			
Henry	60911	D	1932
TRUESDALE			
Wilton W.	89969	D	1942
TRUESDELL			
Amelia Woodward	14672	D	1913
TRUETT			
Anna Elizabeth	8628	D	1909
Bertram B.	80724	D	1939
Carroll W.	61667	D	1932
Daisy D.	10887	I	1910
Miers F.	3160	D	1907
TRUEWORTHY			
Alonzo Thomas, Jr.	76204	D	1937
TRUITT			
Harvey	39644	D	1924
Ruth Sues	70337	D	1935
TRULL			
Catherine	24505	D	1918
TRUMAN			
Alexander Bryan	2900	D	1907
Asa A.	9736	D	1910
Asa H.	9736	D	1910

NAME	NUMBER	TYPE	YEAR
Catherine J.	62169	D	1932
Paulina J.	68971	D	1935
TRUMBETTA			
Giuseppe	48570	D	1927
TRUMPOWER			
Joseph H.	83317	D	1940
TRUNK			
Frank Jacob	74896	D	1937
TRUSWELL			
T. F.	73490	D	1936
Thomas Francis	61721	I	1932
TRUTTMAN			
Joseph	83435	D	1940
TRYON			
A. E., Mrs.	73593	D	1936
Addie I.	73593	D	1936
Edward Francis	6887	D	1908
Eleanor Madonna	6541	M	1908
Ephraim H.	32383	D	1921
Sherman Merrill	45724	M	1926
Susan Elizabeth	15652	D	1913
Victor Hammond	45724	M	1926
TSAGRASULE			
Theod.	31902	D	1921
TSAI			
Lu Tse	85097	D	1940
TSAN			
Lau Sing	59432	D	1931
TSANG			
Benjamin	48749	D	1927
TSCHARNER			
Gaudenz	41983	D	1925
Gaudenz	41983	D	1925
Robert	83554	D	1940
TSCHEINEN			
Annie	9228	M	1910
Caroline	7543	D	1909
John	9228	M	1910
TSCHIRCH			
Caroline	53853	D	1929
William	7190	D	1909
TSCHIRKY			
Bernhard	38607	D	1924
TSCHRICH			
Carolina	53853	D	1929

NAME	NUMBER	TYPE	YEAR
TSCHURR			
Michael A.	448	D	1906
TSE			
Tsai Lu	85097	D	1940
TSIKITAS			
Rallis	43123	D	1925
TSIKOOREO			
George T.	16	D	1906
TSING			
George Earl	51615	M	1928
Jensine	51613	D	1928
TSIOLAS			
Nick	75434	D	1937
TSOULIAS			
Nicholaos P.	75434	D	1937
TSOUTSOUVAS			
Guadalupe P.	67218	D	1934
Nicholaus Louis	25621	D	1918
TSOUVAN			
Nicholas	4143	D	1907
TSUKANE			
Tom K.	61224	D	1932
TSUTSOS			
Tom	72252	D	1936
TSUYUGUCHI			
Shigeyuki	19161	D	1915
TTOM			
Shee	58195	D	1931
TUBB			
Constance Emma Sirea	19265	M	1915
Dorothy Evelyn	19265	M	1915
Edith Rose Mae	19265	M	1915
Etta Evelyn	18833	D	1915
Farrel Henry	19265	M	1915
Georgia Marie	19265	M	1915
Lawrence Alfred Martin	19265	M	1915
Martha Colton	19265	M	1915
William Henry	27096	D	1919
TUBBS			
Alfred S.	69347	D	1935
Austin Chapin	5648	D	1908
Austin Tallant	36382	D	1923
Edward	81514	D	1939
Elizabeth Chapin	21446	D	1916
Gertrude D.	86343	D	1941
Jennie Filkins	78209	D	1938

NAME	NUMBER	TYPE	YEAR
Leslie C.	81963	D	1939
Orinda E.	40151	D	1924
Richard W.	60401	D	1931
Tallant	13877	M	1912
William Bray	20145	D	1915
TUBBY			
Walter George	45710	D	1926
TUBEIRENQ			
Jean Desire	88825	D	1942
TUBERIENQ			
Anna	34231	D	1922
TUBERIENZ			
Anna	34231	D	1922
TUCCORI			
Clementina	84526	D	1940
Pietro	88301	D	1941
Rena	88696	M	1941
Renato	88696	M	1941
TUCH			
Samuel	33690	D	1922
TUCHOLASKI			
Alexander	32647	D	1921
TUCHOLSKI			
Albert	29799	D	1920
Alexander	29799	D	1920
Alexander	32647	D	1921
TUCHOLSKY			
Ida	69946	D	1935
Johanna	8286	D	1909
TUCK			
Gertrude L.	21511	D	1916
Harry Emanuel	66121	D	1934
Harry Robert	22193	D	1917
Helen Elizabeth	29100	M	1920
Helen Elizabeth	81487	D	1939
Thomas Jared	29312	D	1920
TUCKER			
Albert N.	53311	D	1929
Anna Laura	30157	D	1920
Antoinette	17439	M	1914
Benjamin G.	55124	D	1930
C. P.	15554	D	1913
Clinton	29917	I	1920
Edwin Warren	49085	D	1928
Emma	39822	I	1924
George	6088	D	1908
George C.	36642	D	1923

NAME	NUMBER	TYPE	YEAR
George F.	34897	I	1922
George Joseph	87444	D	1941
Harry	5951	D	1908
Herbert James	49354	D	1928
Hugh Mercer	20484	M	1916
Ione Brownell	64118	D	1933
Irving Waits	60579	D	1932
John	26117	D	1919
Julia Ann	11697	D	1911
Julia Ann A.	526	D	1906
Leona	26490	M	1919
Louisa Jane	56716	D	1930
Mabel Lucile	17623	D	1914
Mary	1553	D	1906
Minnie	47660	D	1927
Shepard Stanley	17439	M	1914
Sophia S.	21868	D	1916
Thaddeus Charles	72407	D	1936
William John	35742	D	1923
TUCKETT			
Lois G.	39584	D	1924
Louie G.	39584	D	1924
TUCKEY			
Matilda R.	44873	D	1926
TUDHOPE			
George	3006	D	1907
TUDZINSK			
Steve	9646	D	1910
TUFFT			
Jane Crawford	19411	D	1915
TUFO			
Madeline	41593	M	1925
Paolo	44753	D	1926
TUFOASON			
Bengta	15656	D	1913
Ola	15655	D	1913
TUFT			
William	18773	D	1915
TUFTS			
James	69452	D	1935
TUGENDLIEB			
Mary	33067	D	1921
TUGGLE			
Philip	3825	D	1907
Phillip	9948	D	1910
TUHTE			
Catherine	5695	D	1908

NAME	NUMBER	TYPE	YEAR
TUILE			
Patrick	4847	D	1907
TUIMBLE			
Mary A.	79243	D	1938
TUITE			
Annie M.	8068	I	1909
James	22162	D	1917
James Mitchell	68246	D	1934
TULL			
Thomas W.	61232	D	1932
TULLBERG			
Carl O.	58642	D	1931
TULLIHAM			
Honoria A.	85287	D	1940
TULLIHAN			
Honora A.	84651	I	1940
Honoria A.	85287	D	1940
TULLOCH			
Minnie	16406	D	1913
TULLOCK			
J. E.	41319	D	1925
TULLY			
Charles F.	51029	D	1928
Ellen	2151	D	1906
James	11134	I	1911
James W.	20563	D	1916
Julia Gertrude	55517	D	1930
Michael Francis	83746	D	1940
Patrick	3703	D	1907
Robert	84077	M	1940
Thomas	84077	M	1940
Thomas J.	84759	I	1940
Wilford H., Jr.	51839	M	1929
Wilford Hamilton	45206	D	1926
William	37556	D	1923
William F.	84239	I	1940
TUMELTY			
Margaret	14693	D	1913
TUMSUDEN			
Hedwig	19625	D	1915
TUNG			
Chan	73574	I	1936
TUNGATE			
George S.	11732	M	1911
TUNGENLIEB			
Mary	33067	D	1921

NAME	NUMBER	TYPE	YEAR
TUNIS			
Josephine Mary	62537	D	1932
TUNISON			
Effie Frances	54178	D	1929
TUNNELL			
Robert	41718	D	1925
TUOHEY			
James W.	37345	D	1923
TUOHY			
Mary A.	58597	D	1931
TUOMEY			
Michael	7182	D	1909
TUPANJIAN			
John	25513	D	1918
TUPPER			
Andy	37737	M	1923
Sam	53997	D	1929
TUPPETT			
Adrene P.	39008	M	1924
TUPPITZ			
Conrad	36125	D	1923
TUQUAT			
Jean	66311	D	1934
TURBITT			
William Alexander	21570	D	1916
TURCO			
Flamininio	76904	I	1937
Flaminio	77568	D	1938
Salvatore	82509	D	1939
TUREN			
John Frederick	85554	D	1940
TURILL			
Madison Hollister	3998	D	1907
TURK			
Alexander	65421	D	1933
Charlotte W.	27535	I	1919
Charlotte W.	33906	D	1922
Frank James	85740	D	1940
Sandor	65421	D	1933
TURKE			
Theresa	40342	I	1924
TURLEY			
Catherine	26269	D	1919
Patrick	21133	D	1916
TURNBLAD			
Charles A.	70594	D	1935

Key: D = death; M = minor; I = incompetent

NAME	NUMBER	TYPE	YEAR	NAME	NUMBER	TYPE	YEAR	NAME	NUMBER	TYPE	YEAR
TURNBULL				Mary E.	50527	D	1928	Isabella	23397	D	1917
Albert C.	66896	D	1934	Mary E.	54250	D	1929	TURRI			
TURNER				Mary Elizabeth	23247	D	1917	Caterina	47147	D	1930
Abbie H.	16094	D	1913	Mary Jane	11459	D	1911	TURRILL			
Alfred H.	58199	D	1931	Nellie Eugenia	80205	D	1938	Charles B.	47254	D	1927
Allison H.	80635	D	1939	Reuben B.	80847	D	1939	TURRITTEN			
Amelia	44894	D	1926	Robert	26507	M	1919	Lillian B.	84130	I	1940
Anna J.	32170	D	1921	Robert	86090	D	1941	TURRITTIN			
Annie	36175	D	1923	Robert L.	26885	D	1919	Lillian B.	84189	D	1940
Archie	50497	D	1928	Shannon Cecil	75725	D	1937	TURTON			
Arthur Cephas	3298	I	1907	Stephen A.	63786	D	1933	A. C.	39744	D	1924
Charles A.	19128	D	1915	Ted	32390	D	1921	TURTURECI			
Charles B.	22150	D	1917	Thomas	88992	D	1942	Joseph	20351	M	1916
Dale Aldridge	78910	M	1938	Thomas Argo	62474	M	1932	Milton	20351	M	1916
Doris	62062	M	1932	Thomas N.	26241	D	1919	Vincent	20351	M	1916
Elizabeth	33454	I	1922	Virginia	32106	M	1921	TUSARRIEU			
Elizabeth Howard	38460	D	1924	Walter	37077	M	1923	Jean Baptiste	41533	D	1925
Ella	57793	D	1931	Wilhelmina	53401	D	1929	TUSKA			
Florian	32107	M	1921	William	70554	D	1935	Valencia R.	45288	D	1926
Frances	65549	D	1933	William	55014	D	1930	TUSTIN			
Francis Hutton	87134	D	1941	William Maxwell	85083	D	1940	Mary A.	13658	I	1912
Frank Warren	41245	D	1925	TURNEY				Mary Ann	24542	D	1918
Fred H.	58199	D	1931	Delmar	11094	M	1911	TUTHILL			
George A.	55412	D	1930	Martin	13530	D	1912	William G.	83410	I	1940
George Frederick	61427	D	1932	Ross	11094	M	1911	William G.	89621	D	1942
George L.	2954	D	1907	Sayles A.	11094	M	1911	TUTT			
Grace G. Hart	50058	D	1928	TURNIC				Magdalene	89420	D	1942
Horatio N.	817	D	1906	Nicholas	32180	D	1921	TUTTLE			
James F.	25575	D	1918	TURNICH				Anna M.	4581	D	1907
James T.	32106	M	1921	Nicholas	32180	D	1921	Augusta Findersen	58816	D	1931
James W.	53855	D	1929	Nikola	32180	D	1921	B. F.	4580	D	1907
Janie	60349	D	1931	Peter	25440	D	1918	Benjamin B.	32966	D	1921
John	30748	D	1920	TURNQUIST				Eliza G.	72687	I	1936
John C.	13889	D	1912	Thelma	86402	M	1941	Ellen T.	69300	D	1935
John H.	10214	D	1910	TURNROSS				George Reid	8646	D	1909
Julia Jean	57776	M	1931	Alf	54417	D	1929	Harriette Evelyn	49221	D	1928
Kate	25112	D	1918	TURON				Jessie Hill	89088	D	1942
Katherine	65883	D	1933	Antoine	55518	D	1930	Joseph	26625	D	1919
Leslie F. B.	23146	D	1917	TUROUNET				Mary B.	4505	D	1907
Louis H.	40426	D	1924	Jean	69235	D	1935	Rollin Asa	47544	D	1927
Louise Anna	74739	I	1937	Joanes	69235	D	1935	TUTTY			
Louise Anna	75320	D	1937	John	69235	D	1935	Michael John	65548	D	1933
Margaret	26507	M	1919	TURPAN				TUUAX			
Margaret	33454	I	1922	John	25513	D	1918	Stephen A.	5908	D	1908
Margaret M.	32105	M	1921	TURPIN				TVEITMOE			
Marjorie Holden	86449	D	1941	Francis C.	79464	D	1938	Randi A.	49433	D	1928
Martha Jane	65608	D	1933	Frederick Light	17667	D	1914				
Martin Henry	40885	D	1925								
Mary	72946	D	1936								

Key: D = death; M = minor; I = incompetent

NAME	NUMBER	TYPE	YEAR
TWAMLEY			
William R.	64211	D	1933
TWAY			
George Schuster	13074	M	1912
Joan Florence	44075	M	1926
John H., Jr.	13074	M	1912
TWEDT			
Agnes Margaret	73049	M	1936
Helen O.	73049	M	1936
Margaret A.	73049	M	1936
Otilia Helen	73049	M	1936
TWEED			
John Olson	22478	D	1917
TWEEDALE			
Fannie C.	1734	D	1906
TWEEDIE			
Charlotte Jane	69353	D	1935
Emma Harriet Fletcher	49833	D	1928
R. H., Mrs.	49833	D	1928
TWEEDY			
Mary A.	57342	D	1930
TWEITMANN			
Maria	5948	D	1908
Nicolaus	15830	D	1913
TWELLMAN			
Barbara	53494	M	1929
Louise	53494	M	1929
TWIGG			
Daniel A.	13087	D	1912
Elizabeth J.	25501	D	1918
George C.	26855	I	1919
George T.	26855	I	1919
TWISELTON			
Rose Ellen	45698	D	1926
TWIST			
Joseph Franklin	11252	D	1911
TWITCHELL			
Milton Sidney	80033	D	1938
TWITCHETT			
Jenny Carolina	81281	D	1939
TWITSCHEL			
Milton Sidney	80033	D	1938
TWOHEY			
Johanna	12003	D	1911
John J.	13414	D	1912

NAME	NUMBER	TYPE	YEAR
TWOHIG			
Hannah	57288	D	1930
Johanna	57288	D	1930
Joseph I.	49123	D	1928
Mary Ellen	27830	D	1919
TWOHY			
James C.	7265	D	1909
John D.	56585	D	1930
John R.	64650	M	1933
John R.	65650	M	1933
Mary Lucy	64650	M	1933
May Lucy	65650	M	1933
Patricia	64650	M	1933
Patricia	65650	M	1933
Robert	64650	M	1933
Robert	65650	M	1933
Robert Edmund	27408	D	1919
TWOMEY			
Daniel	8204	D	1909
Daniel	27172	D	1919
Daniel P.	89997	D	1942
Ellen	59173	D	1931
Emmanuel A. Julia	23549	D	1917
James	20557	D	1916
John	57657	D	1931
John J.	51071	D	1928
John M.	49811	I	1928
Mary V.	15195	D	1913
Matthew	48263	D	1927
Michael	57660	D	1931
Patrick	57659	D	1931
R. J.	45258	I	1926
TWOMY			
Dominick L.	73546	D	1936
TWONEY			
Daniel J.	89997	D	1942
TWYFORD			
Alfred	9351	I	1910
Alfred	10911	D	1910
John J.	81717	I	1939
John J.	82051	D	1939
Kate	64217	D	1933
William	64505	D	1933
William J.	5741	D	1908
TWYMAN			
Gertrude	41377	D	1925
TYCKSEN			
Clara Schmidt	29906	D	1920

NAME	NUMBER	TYPE	YEAR
TYE			
Ko Ah	81107	D	1939
Lee Yut	54972	D	1930
Sarah F.	21060	D	1916
TYFORAS			
Helen L.	51347	D	1928
TYING			
Heralda Tyng	62147	D	1932
TYLER			
Allegra	27573	M	1919
Annie Louise	21216	D	1916
Blanche B.	80245	I	1939
Blanche B.	86378	D	1941
Charles E.	18056	D	1914
Christie	86377	D	1941
E. B.	27153	D	1919
Ella H.	69074	D	1935
Everett A.	19839	M	1915
Fannie Louise	24687	D	1918
Frances K.	65501	D	1933
Frances T.	73380	D	1936
Frank H.	50755	D	1928
Henry L.	460	D	1906
John	47322	D	1927
John F.	81372	D	1939
John G.	50787	D	1928
Katherine	70045	D	1935
Llewellyn Joseph	62011	D	1932
Madeline	27573	M	1919
Richard H.	53670	D	1929
Ruth Delia	24368	M	1918
Sybil H.	59796	D	1931
Thomas VanDyke	65614	M	1933
Viola	75449	D	1937
W. W., Jr.	17876	D	1914
TYLLESEN			
John	87170	D	1941
TYM			
Hester I.	82824	D	1939
Sarah Elizabeth	87913	D	1941
TYNAN			
John	37046	M	1923
Joseph J.	64588	D	1933
Josephine Maria	36081	D	1923
Lucile	37046	M	1923
Margaret Jane	31213	D	1921
Thomas	66052	D	1934

NAME	NUMBER	TYPE	YEAR
TYNDALL			
Frances Adelaide	19689	I	1915
Frances Adlade	27797	D	1919
George Edward	27611	M	1919
James F.	77983	D	1938
James T.	63398	I	1933
John E.	68373	D	1934
Katharina Alberta	27611	M	1919
Mary T.	66164	D	1934
Nettie	60986	D	1932
TYNE			
Jacob	29017	D	1920
TYNG			
Gong	23472	D	1917
TYRA			
Curtin C.	59517	D	1931
TYRRELL			
Edward B.	48499	I	1927
Frederick J.	36141	D	1923
John G.	17812	D	1914
Joseph R.	41631	D	1925
Roy	41631	D	1925
Sherwood	10586	M	1910
Vernor	67637	M	1934
Walter J.	81582	D	1939
TYSCHEN			
Clara Schmidt	29906	D	1920
TYSON			
Carlotta Carson	61856	D	1932
George H.	50360	D	1928
John J.	37869	D	1923
Joseph	44239	D	1926
TZINTI			
Paulo P.	26366	D	1919
TZOUKLARIS			
Dimitrios	88184	D	1941
James	88184	D	1941
UAMANE			
Tatsuichi	40075	D	1924
UBALDI			
Giovanni	33769	D	1922
UBHAUS			
John H.	16766	D	1914
Margaret E.	22347	D	1917
UBHEFF			
Charles L.	49941	D	1928

NAME	NUMBER	TYPE	YEAR
UBHOFF			
Charles L.	49941	D	1928
Charles William	82067	D	1939
UBIGAU			
Theodore	38977	D	1924
UBIGAW			
Caroline C.	34351	D	1922
UBOJCICH			
Olga	42458	D	1925
UDER			
John	76034	D	1937
UEBEL			
Charles	18913	D	1915
UEBELACKER			
Anton	26268	D	1919
UEBLER			
Elfrieda M.	55256	D	1930
UEBNER			
Adolph	79456	D	1938
Frederick	83049	D	1940
UFEN			
Reinhard Janson	30256	D	1920
UGHETTO			
Caterina	34495	D	1922
UGLOW			
Arthur	29872	D	1920
Dorothy Virginia	29872	D	1920
UGOLINI			
Edgardo	43046	M	1925
Vera	43046	M	1925
UGOLNIKOFF			
John	65962	D	1933
Mihailmovich	65962	D	1933
UHART			
Sylvestre	40636	D	1924
UHL			
Rena	59745	D	1931
UHLENBERG			
Peter Hansen	37391	D	1923
UHLER			
Camille	65494	D	1933
UHLIG			
Carl	27196	D	1919
Robert	40431	D	1924
UHLMAN			
John	25964	D	1918

NAME	NUMBER	TYPE	YEAR
UHODA			
Sime	23085	D	1917
UHR			
Johann Bernard	25351	D	1918
UHREN			
Betty	58336	D	1931
John Gustav	76104	D	1937
UHRICH			
Wilhelmine	31370	D	1921
UHTE			
Minnie	79144	D	1938
UIBIGAN			
Caroline C.	34351	D	1922
UIBIGAU			
Caroline C.	34351	D	1922
Theodore	38977	D	1924
UJCIC			
Albert A.	66280	M	1934
UJIHARA			
Kameki	20787	D	1916
UL-KHOURI			
Mishell	80722	D	1939
ULBRICH			
Bruno Ernst	53359	D	1929
Bruno Ernst	53703	D	1929
ULDALL			
John	37367	D	1923
ULEX			
Richard	17058	D	1914
ULFELDER			
Cecelia	49296	D	1928
Lester	76794	D	1937
ULIOI			
Pio	61068	D	1932
ULIVI			
Angelo	25119	D	1918
Pete	61068	D	1932
ULLERY			
Octavia	15169	D	1913
ULLMAN			
Daniel	32882	D	1921
ULLOA			
Aida	17880	M	1914
Eva	17880	M	1914
ULLRICH			
Henry	49101	D	1928

Name	Number	Type	Year
Roy	52177	D	1929
Ulm			
Adam	11887	D	1911
Cecelia	11585	D	1911
Zirzila	11585	D	1911
Ulman			
Alfred J.	4245	D	1907
Ida G.	52969	D	1929
Ida S.	52969	D	1929
Victor R.	55500	D	1930
Ulmer			
Caroline	20967	D	1916
Moses	13402	D	1912
William S.	29391	D	1920
Ulps			
Alfred	34766	D	1922
Ulrey			
Charles M.	13132	D	1912
Ulrich			
Alice Natalie	81894	D	1939
Gladys	40943	M	1925
John Alvin	41173	D	1925
John Alvin, Mrs.	81894	D	1939
Linus	40943	M	1925
Marian	40943	M	1925
Roy	52177	D	1929
Ulsemer			
Helena	80055	D	1938
Louis	81388	D	1939
Ultmann			
Therese	73156	D	1936
Umbach			
Adele M.	79001	D	1938
Christian Ludwig	6791	D	1908
Emily K.	30975	D	1921
Emily Mary	30975	D	1921
Umbsen			
G. Helen	12358	D	1911
Gustave H.	30977	D	1921
Ida K.	66206	D	1934
Philippine	17178	D	1914
Umeura			
Seiichi	51602	D	1928
Umland			
Hattie	73444	D	1936
Marie K.	6462	D	1908

Name	Number	Type	Year
Umlauf			
Herman	75273	D	1937
Umstot			
Anna	66663	D	1934
Anna M.	57804	I	1931
Nathanael	70412	M	1935
Russell M.	70252	D	1935
Undelstvedt			
Bernhard Sorensen	39649	D	1924
Underhill			
George L.	5969	D	1908
George Shelah	54746	D	1930
Henry B.	27950	D	1919
James T.	80346	I	1939
Victor S.	65753	D	1933
Underwood			
Catherine Elizabeth	2932	D	1907
George H.	28777	D	1920
Henry W. Y.	22943	M	1917
John Crittenden	63396	D	1933
Louis C.	22943	M	1917
Marie Elinor	22943	M	1917
Mattie A.	70420	D	1935
Nellie Gertrude	23032	D	1917
Vernon M. S.	22943	M	1917
William	40099	D	1924
Unfrid			
Michael	42308	D	1925
Michail	42308	D	1925
Unfried			
Michael	42308	D	1925
Peter	54521	D	1929
Ungano			
Harry C.	71238	D	1935
Ungar			
Emma	81070	D	1939
Ungaretti			
Pasquale	25667	D	1918
Unger			
Adolph	14582	D	1912
Fritz	36922	D	1923
Hannah	8195	D	1909
Harry H.	63875	D	1933
Mary Ann Elizabeth	27760	D	1919
Matthew	87457	D	1941
Milton Edwin	88094	D	1941
Peter	22194	M	1917

Name	Number	Type	Year
Roy	52561	M	1929
Uniack			
Mary	24268	D	1918
Union			
Helen	65984	M	1933
Unna			
Henry	3547	D	1907
Jacob	61857	D	1932
Unsinn			
Maria	43766	D	1926
Unsworth			
Annie R.	68096	D	1934
Ruth LeClare	33578	D	1922
Unti			
Arturo	40561	D	1924
Enrico	3317	D	1907
Unwin			
Edward	2335	D	1906
Updike			
Dorothy	22964	M	1917
Margaret	22964	M	1917
Upham			
Carl Crosby	82361	D	1939
James Lincoln	22639	D	1917
Walter S.	74043	D	1936
Uphoff			
Lawrence	23577	M	1917
Upman			
Josephine Marie	83953	D	1940
Upright			
Carrie	83930	D	1940
Morris	61401	D	1932
Upson			
Miller H.	33075	M	1921
Upton			
Edward P.	66777	D	1934
William B.	21424	D	1916
Urbach			
Pauline	32231	D	1921
Urbais			
Catherine	20807	D	1916
Louis	41685	D	1925
Rudolph	43081	D	1925
Urban			
Emile C.	68285	D	1934
Helen Elizabeth	40567	M	1924

NAME	NUMBER	TYPE	YEAR
Johanna	50141	D	1928
Julius	35481	D	1922
Nicholas	33338	I	1922
URBANI			
Pasquale	30602	D	1920
URBANUS			
Leo M.	2136	D	1906
Michael S.	1677	D	1906
UREN			
Herbert	48158	D	1927
Maria Tressa	29840	D	1920
Mary Bowie	70526	D	1935
Peder Olsen	17012	D	1914
Thomas Penberthy	18070	D	1914
William S.	67593	D	1934
URI			
Isaac	15288	D	1913
Joseph	77385	D	1937
Moses	71721	D	1936
Sol C.	76658	D	1937
Sophie	19142	D	1915
URIBE			
Matea	68445	D	1934
URICK			
Oscar Richard	78992	D	1938
URIDGE			
Mildred	65926	D	1933
URNER			
Milton E.	22626	D	1917
URQUHART			
Mary	71331	D	1936
URRY			
Alfred	36104	D	1923
URTASUN			
Anselmo	24757	I	1918
URY			
Selma	88542	D	1941
USAMI			
Yasu	85397	D	1940
USCHMANN			
Colleen	89112	M	1942
Frank T.	84047	D	1940
USEDOM			
Anna	53559	D	1929
USEHOLD			
George J.	81583	D	1939

NAME	NUMBER	TYPE	YEAR
USEVICH			
Annie	25502	D	1918
USHER			
Rosamond E.	77071	D	1937
W. A., Mrs.	77071	D	1937
USINGER			
Roy M.	59249	I	1931
USREY			
Henry	44996	D	1926
USSAT			
Julius K.	15955	D	1913
USSELMANN			
Johann Herbert	60266	M	1931
USSHER			
Alexander Penrice	48108	D	1927
Eva	85528	D	1940
USTENOVICH			
Steve	27532	I	1919
USTINOWIZ			
Steffan	27532	I	1919
UTECHT			
Carl H. J.	29490	D	1920
Charles H. J.	29490	D	1920
UTLEY			
Harvey B.	70213	D	1935
UTMAN			
Irene A.	73793	M	1936
James E.	73793	M	1936
UTOFT			
Niels	89326	D	1942
UTZ			
George	61025	I	1932
UYEDA			
Sugi	87367	D	1941
UYEMURA			
J.	56145	D	1930
UYENO			
M.	59986	D	1931
UYTTEBROCK			
Hortense	13855	D	1912
UZETA			
Joseph Eugene	32401	D	1921
UZZARDI			
Vincenza	61615	D	1932

NAME	NUMBER	TYPE	YEAR
UZZARDO			
Vincenza	61615	D	1932
UZZOVICH			
Giovanni	12199	D	1911
VACARRO			
Victor A.	60577	D	1931
VACCARI			
Evelyn Ellen	16426	M	1913
Mamie	16627	D	1914
Vincenzo	3599	D	1907
VACCARO			
Rosa	44686	D	1926
Victor A.	60577	D	1931
VACCHETTA			
Domenico	82665	D	1939
VACHE			
Henry S.	60126	D	1931
VACKE			
Henry K.	63195	D	1932
VACKETTA			
D.	82665	D	1939
VACLOV			
Peterka	48723	D	1927
VAGENAS			
Peter	30940	D	1921
VAIL			
A. H., Mrs.	28296	D	1919
Edith Rising	55488	D	1930
Frank A.	38301	D	1924
George Stroud	17322	D	1914
Harriet Williams	28296	D	1919
Margaret Parker	50174	D	1928
VAIO			
Alessandro	73754	D	1936
VAIR			
Roger R.	63212	I	1932
Roger R.	76452	D	1937
VAISSIERE			
Marie	68396	D	1934
Theophile	50316	D	1928
VALCALDA			
Robert A.	87747	D	1941
VALDALA			
Vito	21483	D	1916
VALDE			
Apolonio	34884	I	1922

NAME	NUMBER	TYPE	YEAR
VALDESPINO			
Henry C.	81512	D	1939
VALDEZ			
Silberio Martesio	88750	D	1941
VALDORA			
Guiseppe	28626	D	1920
VALE			
Laura I.	4760	D	1907
VALEN			
Martin	87790	D	1941
VALENCIA			
Andrew	84750	I	1940
Linda	69403	D	1935
VALENCOURT			
Pauline	50132	D	1928
VALENTE			
Andrea	3796	M	1907
Cipriano	32374	D	1921
Domenico	45011	D	1926
Filippo	84708	D	1940
Gotardo	77488	D	1938
Luigi J.	859	D	1906
Maria	34019	D	1922
Norman	3796	M	1907
Romilda	3796	M	1907
Virgil A.	45748	D	1926
VALENTI			
Charles	55769	D	1930
VALENTIN			
Louis Auguste	72998	D	1936
Margaret	45712	D	1926
VALENTINE			
Alexander	83381	D	1940
Andrew W.	3844	D	1907
Clarence A.	15281	D	1913
Dora	67464	D	1934
Doreen J.	67464	D	1934
Edward J.	17866	D	1914
Emilie	36999	D	1923
Hannah	89308	I	1942
Jennie A.	21200	I	1916
Jennie A.	21644	D	1916
John	21160	D	1916
Josephine	62055	M	1932
Louisa F.	30500	D	1920
Margaret Martin	52615	D	1929
Maria Christina	50195	M	1928

NAME	NUMBER	TYPE	YEAR
Matilda	75581	D	1937
Richard	14368	D	1912
Susan	4798	D	1907
Thomas B.	6994	D	1908
William L.	15315	D	1913
VALENTINI			
Giovanni	76035	D	1937
VALENTINO			
Carmita	49854	D	1928
Lena	23500	D	1917
Paolini	23500	D	1917
VALENTO			
Alice B.	80203	D	1938
VALEON			
Leon	89468	D	1942
VALERGA			
Domenico	33960	D	1922
Giacomo	16967	D	1914
VALERIE			
Elise	58129	D	1931
Elsie	58129	D	1931
VALERIO			
Luigi	47352	D	1927
VALEU			
Martin	87790	D	1941
VALLADAO			
Dorris	73614	M	1936
Joe F.	36086	D	1923
VALLANCE			
Clara Julia	60458	D	1931
VALLARINO			
Davide	45612	D	1926
Domenico	76254	D	1937
VALLE			
Annie Monte	67830	D	1934
Antonio	54597	D	1929
Giovanni	25651	D	1918
Giuseppe	4635	D	1907
Mary	5656	M	1908
Mary	69053	D	1935
Monte	57582	D	1931
Nicoletta	4636	D	1907
Pasqualina	41812	D	1925
Pasqualina	41812	D	1925
Stephen O.	45162	I	1926
VALLEJO			
Frank	13359	D	1912

NAME	NUMBER	TYPE	YEAR
Martha B.	24641	D	1918
Napoleon Primo	37990	D	1923
VALLELY			
Allie E.	40548	D	1924
Peter J.	83495	D	1940
VALLERGA			
Pietro	11108	D	1911
VALLERINO			
Giovanni	83503	D	1940
VALLEY			
Elizabeth	29875	M	1920
VALLEYS			
Leo Harry	89468	D	1942
VALLI			
Emilio	59617	D	1931
VALLIER			
John	15924	D	1913
VALLINS			
Agnes Newton	73167	D	1936
Evelyn J.	67211	D	1934
VALLON			
Fanny	83276	D	1940
VALLOS			
Demetrios G.	62533	I	1932
James	62533	I	1932
VALLOT			
Henry Howard	86143	D	1941
VALMAS			
John L.	69549	I	1935
VALOIS			
Robert L.	71922	M	1936
VALSANGIACOMO			
Arnold	9113	M	1910
Louis	9113	M	1910
Mary	9112	D	1910
May A.	9113	M	1910
VAMDENBERGH			
Julia	40174	D	1924
VAMELIUS			
Harold	44572	D	1926
VAMENOS			
Jim	80697	D	1939
VAN			
Alice	16785	D	1914
William A.	15983	D	1913

Key: D = death; M = minor; I = incompetent

NAME	NUMBER	TYPE	YEAR
VAN WINKLE			
Isabella	9244	D	1910
Peter W.	1288	D	1906
VAN WYCK			
Henry L.	23712	D	1917
VANACKER			
Francis	40595	D	1924
VANALSTINE			
Willard P.	27083	D	1919
VANAMRINGE			
Jennie Elizabeth	12047	D	1911
VANARSDALE			
William W.	7667	D	1909
VANASEK			
Rose	69328	D	1935
VANAUKEN			
Leve	12522	D	1911
VANBAALEN			
Joseph D.	16273	D	1913
VANBAAREN			
Albert	44145	D	1926
VANBARGER			
George	14407	M	1912
VANBENTHUSEN			
Ella L.	70737	I	1935
Ella L.	74120	D	1936
VANBERGAN			
Edward A.	9324	D	1910
George H.	1278	D	1906
VANBERGEN			
Carl Theodore	4116	D	1907
Edgar Tourny	50383	M	1928
Harriet Gloria	50383	M	1928
Harry	34971	D	1922
Henry	59566	D	1931
John	1429	D	1906
John W.	22015	D	1916
Nicolaus	3055	D	1907
Rebecca	27855	D	1919
Walter F. L.	4485	D	1907
William C. N.	4055	D	1907
VANBEUSECHEM			
Eleanor	76987	D	1937
VANBRUNT			
Charles	40708	D	1925
John E.	76838	D	1937

NAME	NUMBER	TYPE	YEAR
VANBUREN			
Herminia	13684	D	1912
Luke	24284	M	1918
VANBUSKIRK			
David	55877	I	1930
Guy B.	53583	D	1929
Isabelle Keefe	47672	D	1927
VANCAMPEN			
John E.	9259	D	1910
VANCE			
Edward	37128	D	1923
Ira LeRoy	11116	M	1911
James Edward	37128	D	1923
James Edward	38193	M	1924
John	76044	D	1937
Otis G.	70942	D	1935
Patrick Wilson	40576	I	1924
Robert A.	17456	D	1914
William J.	56766	D	1930
VANCISE			
Mary	67519	D	1934
VANCRAEYNEST			
Victor J.	28760	D	1920
VANDAALEN			
Edward Francis	12119	D	1911
VANDALEN			
John Adolf Cornelis	77557	D	1938
VANDALL			
Murray F.	34081	D	1922
VANDECASTEELE			
Joseph A.	48094	D	1927
VANDELL			
Myrtle	80110	D	1938
VANDEMARK			
George F.	16872	D	1914
Nellie	54509	D	1929
Tena, Mrs.	19442	D	1915
VANDENBERG			
Alfred John	51414	M	1928
Marie	52929	I	1929
Marie Janey	51414	M	1928
VANDENBERGH			
Bridget	74913	I	1937
Caspard L.	5595	M	1908
Julia	35845	I	1923
Julie	29234	D	1920

NAME	NUMBER	TYPE	YEAR
VANDENBURG			
Grace Wilson	82458	D	1939
VANDENBURGH			
John	40253	D	1924
VANDENHENDE			
Petrus	7207	D	1909
VANDERBOEGH			
Abraham	82556	D	1939
VANDERBORGH			
Abraham	82556	D	1939
VANDERCASTEELE			
Mattie	78893	I	1938
VANDERCASTULE			
Mattie	84223	D	1940
VANDERHOOF			
Virtress Lawrence	33093	M	1921
VANDERHURST			
Albert Sidney	89000	D	1942
VANDERKAMP			
Lucie	70701	D	1935
VANDERLINDE			
Peter W.	54332	D	1929
VANDERLINDEN			
Omer G.	64729	D	1933
VANDERLIP			
Annie Adeline	86777	D	1941
F. D.	49177	D	1928
Frederick Douglas	38526	D	1924
John J.	6973	D	1908
VANDERMEHDEN			
Wilhelmine	21678	D	1916
VANDERSHALK			
Caroline	87472	D	1941
VANDERSLICE			
William K.	6882	D	1908
VANDERVEER			
Bastiaan	54383	D	1929
VANDERVOORT			
Nora	57837	D	1931
VANDERWALKER			
John H.	33126	D	1921
Thelma E.	33127	M	1921
VANDERZEE			
Diena	74392	D	1937

NAME	NUMBER	TYPE	YEAR	NAME	NUMBER	TYPE	YEAR	NAME	NUMBER	TYPE	YEAR
VanderZweip				William	86649	D	1941	**VanHees**			
Ariel	996	M	1906	**VanDyne**				Elizabeth	65349	D	1933
Easter	996	M	1906	Annie	78979	D	1938	Hendrik Cornelis	39831	D	1924
Emanuel	996	M	1906	Catherine Young	29586	D	1920	Thomas	68254	M	1934
Emanuel	996	M	1906	Frances	72621	D	1936	**VanHerick**			
James	996	M	1906	**VanEd**				Herman	71318	D	1935
Lena	996	M	1906	Gerrit	76044	D	1937	**VanHeuvel**			
Mabel	996	M	1906	Jan	76044	D	1937	Gertrude	64150	D	1933
Marie	996	M	1906	**VanEdsinga**				**VanHorn**			
Maud	996	M	1906	James Albert	55060	D	1930	George H.	88225	D	1941
VanDeuser				**VanEl**				Leanore	25189	M	1918
Mary E.	20250	D	1916	Hattie Holt Kemp	42704	D	1925	Martin Francis	88527	D	1941
Vandever				**VanEmon**				Ross H.	28737	D	1920
Belle H.	85267	D	1940	Burton C.	89216	M	1942	**VanIderstine**			
VanDeWater				Virginia	60514	D	1931	Edna	18153	D	1914
Herman	26263	D	1919	**VanEps**				Henrike	13507	D	1912
Mary Ann	17032	D	1914	Ellen	70191	D	1935	**VanIerland**			
Vandor				L. T., Mrs.	70191	D	1935	Leonard	12661	M	1911
Agnes	9242	D	1910	Louis	77776	D	1938	Leonard Henry	83860	I	1940
VanDoren				**VanErkelens**				**VanJones**			
Amanda D.	22236	D	1917	Victoria A.	55132	D	1930	Rachel H.	85023	D	1940
Charles E.	45084	D	1926	**VanErp**				**VanJwoll**			
VanDrake				Dirk	64900	D	1933	Garrett	12027	D	1911
Theresa	58221	D	1931	Mary	64901	D	1933	**VanKirk**			
VanDries				**VanEtten**				Mary E.	87478	D	1941
Theodarine	86386	D	1941	Jessie M.	11295	M	1911	**VanLaak**			
Vandruff				Margaret	11205	D	1911	Lambert, Jr.	23035	D	1917
Emily L.	75535	D	1937	Roy Lee	35355	M	1922	**VanLandingham**			
VanDusen				V. C.	5516	D	1908	Ida	77576	D	1938
Elizabeth A.	30862	D	1920	**VanEvera**				**VanLoree**			
VanDussen				John H.	54264	D	1929	Sarah	63827	D	1933
George	12782	D	1912	**VanFleet**				**VanLuven**			
VanDuyn				Allen T.	77678	D	1938	Hermon	22190	D	1917
Annie	78979	D	1938	Lizzie C.	77321	D	1937	**VanMeter**			
VanDuzer				William C.	37358	D	1923	Barbara Clare	89902	M	1942
Ellen G.	34579	D	1922	**VanGelder**				Betty May	89902	M	1942
Emma L.	7612	D	1909	David G.	69298	D	1935	Clare B.	87944	D	1941
Oliver	2129	D	1906	Eleanor	87233	D	1941	Gerald	89902	M	1942
VanDyck				Onsa	33489	D	1922	Joan Grace	89902	M	1942
Margaret Grimm	62241	D	1932	**VanGlahn**				Miles Edwin	7812	D	1909
VanDyk				David H.	58247	D	1931	Roberta Clare	89902	M	1942
Anne	72005	D	1936	John H.	21210	D	1916	**VanMoos**			
Yohanna	72005	D	1936	**Vangness**				Theresa	31495	M	1921
VanDyke				Andrew	26851	D	1919	Theresa	50885	D	1928
Bernard	49680	D	1928	**VanHeerick**				Theresa	51057	M	1928
Margaret Grimm	62241	D	1932	Herman	71318	D	1935				

NAME	NUMBER	TYPE	YEAR	NAME	NUMBER	TYPE	YEAR	NAME	NUMBER	TYPE	YEAR
VanMourik				VanOrden				VanStraaten			
Lottie	25601	D	1918	Lincoln	53249	D	1929	Celia	78395	D	1938
VanNne				VanOrder				VanStuddiford			
Josephine T.	56652	D	1930	Helen	10276	M	1910	Laura Cecilia	29193	D	1920
VanNeil				VanOsten				VanSyckel			
Bernice	23319	M	1917	Thomas D.	65970	D	1933	Annette S.	77042	D	1937
VanNes				VanOverbeck				VanTassel			
Dirk Balthaser	1968	D	1906	Harold H. C.	11389	I	1911	John	30196	D	1920
VanNess				VanPelt				Marie	2328	D	1906
Garrett	7614	D	1909	Alice	76604	D	1937	VanTilburg			
T. C.	43120	D	1925	F. Tiffany	83424	I	1940	Henry F.	80716	D	1939
VanNest				Frank Eugene	83420	D	1940	VanTrees			
Ettie M.	69123	D	1935	Henry M.	57966	D	1931	Frank S.	18230	D	1914
VanNneste				John	36698	D	1923	VanVales			
Felix	89301	D	1942	VanPett				Mary Josephine	27145	D	1919
Vanni				Alice Maria	3594	D	1907	Mitchell D.	46922	D	1927
Emanuele	59999	D	1931	VanPienbroek				VanValkenburgh			
Giulia	70887	D	1935	Gerard	69343	D	1935	William Whitney	85569	D	1940
John Andrew	35987	D	1923	VanPoppel				VanVliet			
Kathleen	37654	D	1923	Emil	32565	I	1921	Martha	68013	D	1934
VanNiel				VanPragg				Maurice	48248	D	1927
Joseph A.	22504	D	1917	Charles J.	26510	I	1919	VanVolkenburgh			
Matilda	22893	D	1917	VanProoyen				Chrissie	10826	D	1910
VanNoorden				Elizabeth	42603	D	1925	VanVoorhis			
Harry	60943	D	1932	VanReed				Henry W.	32024	D	1921
Theodore	15568	D	1913	Katrine	1216	D	1906	VanVorst			
VanNorden				VanRegemortel				Caroline R.	89584	D	1942
Fay Jackson	51923	D	1929	Henriette	4149	D	1907	Lillian	89852	I	1942
Rowena Fay	51923	D	1929	VanRonkel				VanWart			
Vannoy				Samuel	36268	D	1923	Abram J.	2276	D	1906
Jasper N.	4802	D	1907	VanSanten				VanWermer			
Jasper N.	6269	M	1908	Frank	72619	D	1936	Essie M.	36628	D	1923
Vannucchi				VanSchoiack				VanWie			
Bernardo	4377	D	1907	Charlotte	69051	D	1935	Arie	20659	D	1916
Vannucci				VanScoyk				Emma	23539	D	1917
Alfred	70226	D	1935	Dorothy	35102	M	1922	VanWinkle			
Casimiro	55978	D	1930	Lloyd	35102	M	1922	Emma F.	59273	I	1931
Frank	70226	D	1935	VanSicklen				Emma F.	59407	D	1931
Lawrence Victor	58267	M	1931	Frederick W.	66615	D	1934	Jane	57271	D	1930
Louis	23583	D	1917	VanSloun				Lawrence E.	2871	D	1907
Raffaelle	89838	D	1942	Frank J.	79367	D	1938	VanWolbeck			
Raffaello Luigi	63783	D	1933	Frank R.	79367	D	1938	Cristina S.	87604	D	1941
Vittorio	19957	D	1915	Leonore M.	49533	D	1928	VanWyck			
Vannuti				VanSlyck				Lawrence Hamilton	72382	D	1936
Felix	89301	D	1942	Bertram Randall	4535	M	1907	Sidney M., Jr.	60059	D	1931
				George G.	4366	D	1907				

NAME	NUMBER	TYPE	YEAR	NAME	NUMBER	TYPE	YEAR	NAME	NUMBER	TYPE	YEAR
VanZandt				**Varner**				**Vasques**			
Clara	59516	M	1931	Eleanor M.	67832	D	1934	Caroline	58700	D	1931
Cordelia	73176	D	1936	**Varney**				Carrie	56675	I	1930
VanZant				Ada Eliza	9081	D	1910	Epifanio	52573	D	1929
Ernest	53034	D	1929	Agnes E.	39550	D	1924	**Vasquez**			
John H.	85576	D	1940	Anna Elmira	65650	D	1933	Jesus	70249	D	1935
Vara				Caista Roberts	56709	D	1930	Maud	18775	D	1915
Cosuelo	67735	M	1934	Charles	17549	D	1914	Raymond	34118	D	1922
Enedina	67735	M	1934	Ella Isabel	48964	D	1928	**Vassallo**			
Varadian				Frank H.	20380	D	1916	Cetta	24506	M	1918
Mehran	58650	D	1931	Frank M.	1016	I	1906	Eugenio	22796	D	1917
Varalli				Kit Roberts	56710	D	1930	Salvatore	24506	M	1918
Giuseppe	75341	D	1937	Lena	56526	I	1930	**Vassar**			
Varcoe				Nathan Roberts	58688	M	1931	Verona	54549	M	1929
John J.	26042	D	1919	Waldo J.	43332	D	1926	**Vassault**			
Vardas				Walter	56525	D	1930	Katherine	84151	D	1940
George	58618	D	1931	**Varnhagen**				Lawrence S.	6354	D	1908
Varella				Meier	87078	I	1941	Theodora E.	1887	D	1906
David	79479	M	1938	Seamon	34106	D	1922	**Vasseur**			
Frances	79479	M	1938	Simon	34106	D	1922	Clemence Viot	10450	D	1910
John	79479	M	1938	**Varni**				**Vastag**			
Martin	79206	M	1938	Elizabeth	84078	D	1940	Elizabeth	46347	D	1927
Martin	79412	D	1938	Lorraine	85959	M	1941	**Vathe**			
Victoria	79479	M	1938	Maria	22311	D	1917	Thomas	44995	D	1926
Varellas				Raymond	85959	M	1941	Tom	44995	D	1926
Anthony	79250	M	1938	Tomaso	84052	D	1940	**Vathne**			
Maguerite P.	36699	D	1923	**Varnum**				Torger	44995	D	1926
Peter N.	76428	D	1937	Walter S.	59665	D	1931	**Vattuone**			
Peter Nicholas, Jr.	78840	M	1938	**Varonick**				Giovanni Batista	62859	D	1932
Reno P.	78840	M	1938	Efram G.	34538	I	1922	**Vatuone**			
Varello				**Varsi**				Domenico	31265	D	1921
Alexander	77165	D	1937	Eugenia	68062	D	1934	Emanuele	3405	D	1907
Varelopoulos				Giovanni	46834	D	1927	Emanuele	23262	D	1917
Stelianos D.	30308	D	1920	**Vasconi**				Norma	36105	M	1923
Varga				Pio	55707	D	1930	Paul	36105	M	1923
Stephen	19586	D	1915	**Vashell**				**Vaugelatos**			
Vargas				Nellie S.	37922	D	1923	Chris	82787	D	1939
Anna A.	59832	D	1931	**Vasicek**				**Vaugh**			
Clara	64393	D	1933	John	82693	D	1939	Mildred McAlister	86945	D	1941
Frank	49051	D	1928	**Vaski**				**Vaughan**			
Vargha				Marija	82976	D	1939	Annie	77043	D	1937
Emery E.	37814	D	1923	**Vason**				Daniel Francis	43652	D	1926
Varley				Ida F.	35421	D	1922	Ellen	51758	D	1929
Ella	74753	D	1937	**Vasone**				Frank H.	54184	D	1929
Varnam				Ernest	35708	D	1923	Fred W.	42192	D	1925
W. S.	68223	D	1934	Ida	35421	D	1922	James	72953	I	1936
								James	74300	D	1937

NAME	NUMBER	TYPE	YEAR
Mary Ogden	87614	D	1941
Reuben G.	35360	D	1922
Rudolph Benjamin Francis	86124	I	1941
Sarah	54162	D	1929
VAUGHN			
Bernard	30263	M	1920
Edward H.	35960	D	1923
Mary Jane	30263	M	1920
Nellie	89561	D	1942
Thomas	60393	D	1931
VAURS			
Jules	64564	I	1933
Jules	64760	D	1933
VAVATSIKOZ			
Lotirios	12679	D	1911
VAWTER			
Benjamin S.	65997	D	1933
Henry Francis	58920	D	1931
VAYSSADE			
Joseph	19523	D	1915
VAYSSIE			
Marie	78648	D	1938
VEALE			
Almer F.	15906	D	1913
VEASEY			
Daniel	41642	D	1925
VEATCH			
Hazel A.	49642	D	1928
Hazel R.	49642	D	1928
VECCHIA			
Joe	12783	D	1912
VECCHIONE			
Leonard	63031	M	1932
VECKI			
Herbert	57977	M	1931
Marion, Jr.	57977	M	1931
Minnie Anita	33490	D	1922
VEDEL			
Amos	24427	D	1918
VEEDER			
Barney H.	32874	D	1921
Harmon	49942	D	1928
VEEN			
August C.	2978	M	1907
August C.	37933	D	1923
Elizabeth F. F.	2978	M	1907

NAME	NUMBER	TYPE	YEAR
Frank J.	11377	D	1911
VEGA			
Esther	52796	M	1929
Frank	52955	D	1929
Vincent Frank	52796	M	1929
VEGHTE			
John H.	50109	D	1928
VEGNAU			
Frank	47175	I	1927
VEGNUTI			
Roberto	76806	D	1937
VEHLBEHR			
William	53194	D	1929
VEIGA			
Joe	28551	D	1919
VEIGEL			
Henry	41902	M	1925
Henry	41902	M	1925
Louise	41902	M	1925
Louise	41902	M	1925
VEIL			
Ernest G.	67726	D	1934
VEILLER			
Leon	16294	D	1913
VEINZIATO			
Frank	57382	D	1930
VEIRS			
Ray Bellamy	72185	D	1936
VEIT			
Anton	42837	D	1925
Ernest G.	67726	D	1934
Irma	27400	D	1919
Martha Nancy	88104	D	1941
VEITCH			
Thomas E.	85743	D	1940
VELADO			
Joan Alfonso	52115	D	1929
VELAND			
Alexander	56434	D	1930
VELARD			
Alexander, Jr.	56434	D	1930
Evelyn	21627	M	1916
VELASCO			
Josefina	17874	D	1914
VELDON			
Thomas Patrick	85824	D	1940

NAME	NUMBER	TYPE	YEAR
VELISSARATOS			
Constantine D.	20996	M	1916
Dimitrios E.	17125	D	1914
Eustace	21517	D	1916
George D.	20995	M	1916
Nicholas D.	20997	M	1916
VELJKOVICH			
Acim	6409	D	1908
VELKUEKIOCOSKA			
Mary Botwick	58176	D	1931
VELLA			
Antonia	38098	D	1924
Mary A.	42176	I	1925
Teresa	62166	D	1932
VELLGUTH			
William Frederick	40763	D	1925
VELLIS			
Diamond	84211	D	1940
VELLNER			
Gerald	39749	I	1924
VELLOCINO			
Lucas	85084	D	1940
VELLONE			
Carmela	75417	D	1937
Concettina	75228	M	1937
VELLUDO			
Joaquin A.	56023	D	1930
Joaquin Alves	55884	D	1930
VELOS			
Peter	40076	D	1924
VELOSO			
Jennie	88630	I	1941
VELPS			
William Charles	33092	D	1921
William R.	75836	D	1937
VELVET			
Joaquin	73411	M	1936
Joseph	73411	M	1936
Mary	73411	M	1936
VEMMER			
Catharine	369	D	1906
VENABLE			
Charles W. H.	26621	D	1919
VENAGLIA			
Clorinda	70739	D	1935

NAME	NUMBER	TYPE	YEAR
VENCELAU			
Nora	68042	D	1934
VENDIGLIO			
Guiseppi	9907	D	1910
VENDT			
Albert, Jr.	3904	D	1907
VENEGAS			
Roberto	79849	M	1938
VENETUCCI			
Anthony	64410	D	1933
VENEZIA			
Frances Veronica	79664	D	1938
Gaetano	53662	D	1929
Guido	33480	M	1922
VENIKOFF			
Tamara	81334	M	1939
VENKER			
Charles Henry	69283	D	1935
VENN			
Ina Lucie	29830	D	1920
VENSANO			
Alexander	28061	D	1919
Kittie C.	37217	D	1923
VENTINI			
Taleti	38034	D	1924
VENTNER			
Elise L.	86422	D	1941
VENTO			
Paolo	41500	D	1925
Peter	82414	D	1939
VENTON			
Arscott Crawford	6760	M	1908
VENTRE			
Stefano	86197	D	1941
VENTURA			
George S.	53445	D	1929
John	39759	I	1924
Lorenzo	89956	D	1942
Tommaso	39304	D	1924
VENTURI			
Giovanni	44990	D	1926
Lorenzo	83776	D	1940
Pia Simi	56267	D	1930
Pietro	40894	D	1925
Pilade	25312	D	1918
Sabatina	46238	D	1927

NAME	NUMBER	TYPE	YEAR
Sebastiano	85058	D	1940
Talete	37999	D	1923
Tatehe	16202	I	1913
Vincenzo	29782	D	1920
VENTURINI			
Jennie	87726	I	1941
VENTURINO			
Antonio	67927	I	1934
Antonio	81071	D	1939
Antonio	81351	D	1939
VERBARG			
Adele Dressler	85394	D	1940
VERBER			
Thelma	61523	D	1932
VERCELLI			
Antoni	22947	D	1917
Joseph	35688	M	1923
Mario	35688	M	1923
VERCEVICH			
Adam L.	34899	D	1922
Ella D.	37958	D	1923
Mae	87031	D	1941
May	37959	M	1923
VERCOVITZ			
Frank	19647	D	1915
VERDENHALVEN			
John	85155	D	1940
VERDIER			
Armandine	44391	D	1926
Ellen G.	51191	D	1928
Louis Gaston	19241	D	1915
Paul	33076	D	1921
VERDINI			
Antonio	67501	D	1934
VERDON			
Mary J.	84963	D	1940
VERDUCCI			
Antone	54401	D	1929
VERDUGO			
Michael J.	50601	D	1928
VERDUZCO			
Francisco	40422	D	1924
Miquel E.	22938	D	1917
VERDUZZO			
Refugia	19297	D	1915

NAME	NUMBER	TYPE	YEAR
VERELLI			
Antoni	22947	D	1917
VERGA			
Barbara	89776	M	1942
Charleeen	89776	M	1942
John	89776	M	1942
VERGARI			
Frank	83942	D	1940
VERGATIS			
James	42455	D	1925
VERGES			
Jean Pierre	13621	D	1912
John P.	13621	D	1912
VERGEZ			
Adolph	76578	D	1937
Caroline	32269	D	1921
Celeste Marti	60324	D	1931
Marie	69951	D	1935
VERGOME			
Coye C.	36579	D	1923
VERGOWE			
Coye Clinton	36579	D	1923
VERHAGEN			
Albertus	87163	D	1941
Pauline	38569	D	1924
VERHELLEN			
Ellen C.	29125	D	1920
VERHOEVEN			
Theodore	15311	D	1913
VERINES			
Aimee	78472	D	1938
VERKAAIK			
Jacoba	29317	I	1920
VERLEGER			
Frederick	46591	D	1927
Mary Elizabeth	81566	D	1939
VERME			
Agostino	12725	D	1911
VERMEHR			
Edith Conner	37304	D	1923
VERMEIL			
Jean Louis	21980	D	1916
VERMEULEN			
Maria Cornelia	75020	D	1937
VERNAZZA			
Andrea	79395	D	1938

Key: D = death; M = minor; I = incompetent

Name	Number	Type	Year	Name	Number	Type	Year	Name	Number	Type	Year
Benedetto	72739	D	1936	**Vesquez**				**Viarques**			
Verne				Marcus Leo	34508	M	1922	Dominque	23806	D	1917
Cesar	53079	D	1929	**Vessey**				**Vibert**			
Verner				Henry	13995	D	1912	Maria Albertine	9021	D	1910
Joseph H.	57551	D	1930	**Vessoni**				Walter Cyril	87605	D	1941
Vernon				Rafaello	13100	D	1912	**Vicini**			
Eva Margaret Knight	50431	M	1928	**Vestal**				Stephen P.	41893	D	1925
Frank	4216	D	1907	Logan	21614	D	1916	Stephen P.	41893	D	1925
Howard	84188	D	1940	**Vester**				**Vicino**			
Louami	63255	D	1932	John H.	27720	D	1919	Giovanni	52125	D	1929
Louamini	63255	D	1932	**Vestey**				**Vickers**			
Thomas	63255	D	1932	Elizabeth Alker	43317	D	1926	Elmo	82213	D	1939
Vernor				**Veto**				**Vickerson**			
Mary E.	68526	M	1934	Ingoglia	85734	D	1940	Charles S.	53609	M	1929
Vero				**Vetrornile**				**Vickovich**			
Clara	17190	D	1914	Gaetano	79330	D	1938	Peter Bozo	89222	D	1942
Veroni				**Vetter**				**Victkovich**			
Berthe	77230	D	1937	Anna	84481	D	1940	Ivan	66713	D	1934
Hattie	36615	D	1923	Annie	52254	D	1929	**Victors**			
Veronica				Frederick J.	19477	D	1915	Ernst Albrecht	86828	D	1941
Ponasso	42789	D	1925	Harry H.	61947	D	1932	**Victory**			
Verran				William A.	29371	D	1920	Alice	20178	D	1915
Alfred	39560	D	1924	**Vetterlein**				**Vidaillac**			
Vers				Frank	3939	M	1907	Philomene	51452	D	1928
Rosa	43974	D	1926	Joseph	13286	D	1912	**Vidaillet**			
Versace				Morris	8804	D	1909	Etienne	14666	D	1913
Antonio	88367	D	1941	**Veuve**				**Vidak**			
Versalovich				H. H.	5616	D	1908	Cecilia	24243	D	1918
Rose	61150	D	1932	**Vevoda**				**Vidal**			
Vincent P.	15782	D	1913	Robert B.	77893	M	1938	Gonzalo	31127	D	1921
Verschoyle				**Veyhle**				Michael	44675	D	1926
Benjamin J.	65360	D	1933	Theodore	79232	I	1938	Rodolfo	39571	M	1924
Versterren				**Vezin**				**Vidaner**			
Alphonse	23753	D	1917	Karl A.	15006	D	1913	Alivina	46419	D	1927
Vert				**Vezina**				**Vidania**			
Lillie Florence	50214	D	1928	Alvina A.	61888	D	1932	Matea	68289	I	1934
Verzanni				**Viacava**				Matea	68445	D	1934
Angelina	57557	M	1931	Richard	70211	I	1935	**Videau**			
Isabel	57557	M	1931	**Vialatte**				Francine	3382	D	1907
Lucy	57557	M	1931	Etienne	78672	D	1938	Francoise	3382	D	1907
Mildred	57557	M	1931	**Viale**				**Viderton**			
Verzello				George	45767	D	1926	Victor	23076	D	1917
Virginia	58979	D	1931	**Viant**				**Vides**			
Vesper				Rose T.	62364	I	1932	Trinidad	36702	D	1923
Edythe	63973	D	1933	**Viargues**				**Vidmar**			
				Dominque	23806	D	1917	Jackob	27268	I	1919

NAME	NUMBER	TYPE	YEAR
Jacob	35438	D	1922
Jacob	55043	I	1930
John	57280	D	1930
Kristina	72905	D	1936
Martin	58188	D	1931
Mary	66732	I	1934
Matthew	41975	D	1925
Matthew	41975	D	1925
Matthew	43521	M	1926
VIDMORE			
Martin	58188	D	1931
VIDOJEVICH			
Kate	41339	D	1925
VIDONE			
Alfredo	35853	I	1923
VIDOVICH			
Anna	3843	M	1907
Charles	3843	M	1907
Kate	41339	D	1925
Katherine	75040	D	1937
Katie	24328	D	1918
Peter	3843	M	1907
Peter	30238	D	1920
Peter	86935	D	1941
VIDOVITCH			
Peter	30238	D	1920
VIDY			
Dora	19866	I	1915
VIEHOEFER			
Arthur	46452	D	1927
VIEILLE			
Elizabeth	68138	D	1934
Mary Twohig	27830	D	1919
VIEIRA			
Antonio Xavier	48395	D	1927
Joaquin	69297	D	1935
John	31351	D	1921
VIELHABER			
Carrie	20418	D	1916
VIENA			
Manuel	36622	D	1923
VIER			
Bastiaan Vander	54383	D	1929
VIERA			
Adelaide	14911	M	1913
Frank	14911	M	1913
Rose	14911	M	1913

NAME	NUMBER	TYPE	YEAR
VIERECKT			
Conrad	12442	D	1911
Edythe A.	67785	D	1934
Emilie	70016	D	1935
Emilie	70016	D	1935
William C.	53162	D	1929
VIERHUS			
Frank	8100	M	1909
Philip Arthur	8101	M	1909
William Robert	5794	D	1908
VIERIA			
Elizabeth	49808	D	1928
VIERRA			
Joseph O.	73257	D	1936
VIETHEER			
Mary Jennie	68873	D	1935
VIG			
George P.	81004	M	1939
VIGANEGO			
Adelaide	49180	D	1928
Giacomo	24655	D	1918
Giambattista	85613	D	1940
Giobatto	85613	D	1940
James	24655	D	1918
Louis J.	62001	D	1932
VIGDEL			
George	57885	D	1931
VIGE			
Betty	37220	D	1923
VIGFUSSON			
Robert H.	71658	I	1936
VIGIL			
Laura	81371	D	1939
VIGLIENZONE			
Luigi	28946	D	1920
VIGLIETTI			
Andrea	78517	D	1938
Andrew G.	78517	D	1938
Andrew J.	78517	D	1938
VIGLIONE			
Giuseppe	69090	D	1935
VIGNA			
Caterina	60774	D	1932
John	48576	D	1927
VIGNAU			
Francois	47175	I	1927

NAME	NUMBER	TYPE	YEAR
Joseph	45637	D	1926
VIGNE			
Victoire Joubert	446	D	1906
VIGNEAU			
Laurent	39724	D	1924
VIGNOLA			
Pietro	71134	D	1935
VIGNOLI			
Carlo	69585	D	1935
VIGNOLO			
Luigi	79658	D	1938
Pietro	71134	D	1935
VIGNON			
Paul	39172	D	1924
VIGUERA			
Josefa	26684	D	1919
VIJANELO			
Made	3176	D	1907
VILAS			
Helen M.	12289	D	1911
VILELLE			
Germaine	69134	D	1935
VILLA			
Francisco Jose	59378	M	1931
Gaetano	61154	D	1932
Giovanni	64115	D	1933
John	64115	D	1933
Lucy	77030	D	1937
Pietro	43189	D	1925
Thomas	61154	D	1932
VILLACIS			
Francisco	26942	D	1919
VILLAIN			
Jean B.	4306	D	1907
John	4306	D	1907
VILLANUEVA			
Domingo Oroz	54315	I	1929
Francisco	60454	I	1931
VILLEGAS			
Andrea	11246	D	1911
VILLEGIA			
Agathe L.	43170	D	1925
Leopold Joseph Michel	32073	D	1921
VILLEMEUR			
Emmanuelle	15861	D	1913

NAME	NUMBER	TYPE	YEAR	NAME	NUMBER	TYPE	YEAR	NAME	NUMBER	TYPE	YEAR
VILLIERS				**V**INEL				**V**IRGIL			
Grace E.	17440	M	1914	Victor	53941	D	1929	Laura	81371	D	1939
VILLMER				**V**INER				**V**IRIGIGUERRO			
Anna Maria	38810	D	1924	James William	71114	D	1935	Vingenso	46371	D	1927
VILLOTA				Susanna	87925	D	1941	**V**IRTUE			
Juan Ruiz Y.	63714	D	1933	**V**INEZ				Charles E.	29644	D	1920
VINAY				George	83538	D	1940	**V**ISALLI			
Alice	89443	D	1942	**V**INGLICH				Anthony S. M.	40777	D	1925
VINAZZA				Jim	25233	D	1918	**V**ISCIDO			
Alberto	55080	D	1930	**V**INSON				Marallino	31614	I	1921
VINCE				John William	67888	D	1934	**V**ISELOPOULOS			
Edward	37127	D	1923	**V**INTER				Delia	78849	I	1938
VINCENOT				Fred Bowskill	54847	D	1930	**V**ISER			
Elizabeth	478	D	1906	**V**INZENT				Albert Anton	58903	D	1931
Louise	16324	D	1913	Caroline A.	27725	D	1919	**V**ISHER			
VINCENT				Edward Graham	19111	D	1915	Harriet M.	34945	D	1922
A.	68669	D	1935	**V**IOHL				**V**ISSER			
Albert	7487	D	1909	Charles Carl	60606	D	1932	John P.	14892	I	1913
Anne	58919	I	1931	Ida	52962	D	1929	**V**ISTICA			
E. M.	54339	D	1929	**V**IOLA				Edward	10805	D	1910
Elizabeth	54017	D	1929	Teresina	30082	D	1920	**V**ISTICER			
George	24856	D	1918	Victor	22994	I	1917	Edward	10805	D	1910
George L.	64046	D	1933	Victor	24252	D	1918	**V**ITALE			
Guillame	7487	D	1909	**V**IOLETTI				Sam	71904	D	1936
Henry Collier	52237	D	1929	Celeste	24644	D	1918	**V**ITALINI			
Henry P.	12974	D	1912	**V**IORA				Carlo H.	44301	D	1926
John	39682	D	1924	Aldo Fumagalli	69012	D	1935	**V**ITALJICH			
John R. A.	41626	D	1925	**V**IORATO				Peter J.	79116	D	1938
Lizzie Maie	76252	D	1937	Joseph T.	79899	D	1938	**V**ITALONI			
Lydia	72984	D	1936	**V**IOSCA				Alfred	39568	D	1924
Roger Blair	81109	M	1939	James	11501	D	1911	**V**ITELLI			
Stanley Robert	81043	D	1939	Rosita	82098	I	1939	Elvira	53101	I	1929
Virginia	20808	D	1916	Santiago	11501	D	1911	Elvira	63656	D	1933
Virginia	42706	M	1925	**V**IOT				Stanislao	6147	D	1908
Walter Ladd	81993	D	1939	Eugene Parfait	2293	D	1906	**V**ITERI			
William A.	77827	D	1938	Franciose	10449	D	1910	Adolfo Dellrioste y	18980	D	1915
William Henry	42397	D	1925	Hyacinthe	10463	D	1910	**V**ITO			
VINCENZO				Marie Franciose	10449	D	1910	Ingonlie	85734	D	1940
Piano	21848	D	1916	Stanislaus Hyacinthe	10463	D	1910	**V**ITS			
Trinca Rampelini	25515	D	1918	**V**IQUERA				Jacob	16248	D	1913
VINCKE				Josefa	26684	D	1919	**V**ITSOS			
Prosper	33691	I	1922	**V**IRASSI				Kalomera	81801	D	1939
Prosper	35251	D	1922	Domenico	15956	D	1913	Kalomira A.	81801	D	1939
VIND				**V**IRDEN				**V**ITTI			
Marie Therese	48486	D	1927	Charles Edgar	61494	D	1932	Antonio	81891	I	1939
VINE											
Margaret Holland	33784	D	1922								

Key: D = death; M = minor; I = incompetent

Name	Number	Type	Year
Antonio	82818	D	1939
VITTORINO			
Galeazzi	58593	D	1931
VITTORIO			
Grasso	45414	D	1926
VIVALDO			
Antonio	52998	D	1929
VIVELL			
Katherine L.	58172	D	1931
VIVIAN			
Eliza	44822	D	1926
Ida May	27648	D	1919
VIVODA			
John K.	25455	D	1918
VIVONE			
Raffaele	61640	I	1932
Ralph	61640	I	1932
VIVONI			
Raffaele	61640	I	1932
Ralph	61640	I	1932
VIXON			
Robert H.	71658	I	1936
VIZINA			
J. M.	3500	D	1907
VIZZARD			
Joseph B.	48524	D	1927
Mary I.	63127	D	1932
VLAHISLAVICH			
Therese	50283	D	1928
VLAHOS			
Anastaseos I.	53131	D	1929
VLASAN			
Mildred McAlister	86945	D	1941
VLASIC			
Philip	71803	D	1936
VLASICH			
Filip	71803	D	1936
VLASS			
Anna	75843	D	1937
VLAUTIN			
Maude J.	35658	D	1923
VOARINO			
Ernesto	41898	D	1925
Ernesto	41898	D	1925
VOCKE			
Frederick Grover	35209	D	1922

Name	Number	Type	Year
Wilhelmina	7205	D	1909
VODDEN			
Mary E.	36022	D	1923
Thomas	80474	D	1939
VODERER			
Karl	64162	D	1933
VODOPIA			
Mark	19344	D	1915
VOEGTLIN			
Charles	15978	D	1913
VOELKER			
Christina M.	43305	D	1926
Helen	49630	D	1928
VOELPEL			
August	72863	D	1936
VOG			
Anna	28384	D	1919
VOGEL			
Arvona F.	68284	M	1934
August	60164	D	1931
Caroline	41074	D	1925
Edward	8422	D	1909
Hans Bruno	7263	D	1909
Henry	32848	D	1921
Henry	67774	D	1934
Herman	2565	D	1906
Joseph Marcel	68118	D	1934
Mary	32155	D	1921
Minnie C.	68284	M	1934
Minnie G.	38602	D	1924
Philip	649	D	1906
Rudolph	30942	I	1921
Solomon John	88284	D	1941
William Arthur	88763	D	1941
VOGELMANN			
Adolph	46812	D	1927
VOGELSANG			
Alexander T.	56822	D	1930
Fraces J.	82284	D	1939
William H.	34194	D	1922
VOGELSDORFF			
Rosa	4426	D	1907
VOGLER			
Andreas	57614	D	1931
Anna	41396	D	1925
Catherine	75754	D	1937
Sigmond	37148	D	1923

Name	Number	Type	Year
Sigmund	35844	I	1923
VOGT			
Augusta Marie	88936	D	1942
Henry Frank	86222	D	1941
Karl	71535	I	1936
Karl	79745	D	1938
Mary Margaret	30367	D	1920
Theodore	83550	D	1940
VOGTMANN			
Jack A.	42774	M	1925
VOGULKIN			
Margaret F.	46827	D	1927
VOIGHT			
Catherine A.	84161	D	1940
Christian Heinrich	13456	D	1912
Clara	70852	D	1935
VOIGT			
Bernhard	42509	D	1925
Eda	80354	I	1939
Frank	56980	D	1930
Frederick	9125	D	1910
Fredric W.	57916	D	1931
George Sophus	16390	D	1913
Margaret Cecelia	80313	D	1939
VOISINE			
Octave	47382	D	1927
VOJE			
Julius C.	24753	D	1918
VOJKOVICH			
Vincent	49952	D	1928
VOLCAN			
Carmella	52231	I	1929
Carmella	71397	I	1936
VOLGER			
Charles O.	68257	D	1934
VOLGUARDS			
Lillie Sophia Sulsberg	10782	D	1910
VOLK			
Alois	1009	D	1906
Helen Josue	85041	D	1940
VOLKAMUTH			
Marie	39247	D	1924
VOLKEL			
Carl August	12369	D	1911
VOLKER			
Helen	49630	D	1928

Key: D = death; M = minor; I = incompetent

NAME	NUMBER	TYPE	YEAR
Henry	10362	D	1910
VOLKERTS			
Geide I.	76712	D	1937
VOLKMAN			
Alfred A.	40408	D	1924
Charles M.	29943	D	1920
Eda H.	89929	D	1942
Erwin H.	43358	D	1926
Pauline	42135	D	1925
VOLKMANN			
Agnes	87897	D	1941
Alwine	80060	D	1938
Daniel G., Jr.	66388	M	1934
Louisa M.	62357	D	1932
Ottilia	74051	D	1936
Ottilia Irma	65011	I	1933
Virginia	66387	M	1934
VOLL			
Alfred	25354	D	1918
Minnie	25811	D	1918
Willaim H.	51167	D	1928
VOLLENWEIDER			
Theodor	39500	D	1924
VOLLER			
Alfred	73915	D	1936
V. A. T.	73915	D	1936
VOLLERS			
Claus	55388	D	1930
VOLLMAR			
Benjamin E.	20774	D	1916
VOLLMER			
Anna Maria	38810	D	1924
August	57819	D	1931
Berthe L.	67497	D	1934
Gerogiana	46471	I	1927
Johann	62877	D	1932
John	62877	D	1932
John A.	42725	D	1925
VOLLRATH			
John H.	49787	D	1928
VOLLUM			
Cora G.	76670	D	1937
VOLMER			
Rudolph	56225	D	1930
VOLOS			
Andrew M.	59995	I	1931
Andrew M.	77041	I	1937

NAME	NUMBER	TYPE	YEAR
Andrew M.	85797	I	1940
VOLOSING			
Cora May	89801	D	1942
VOLPATTI			
G. D.	53429	D	1929
Giacinto	53429	D	1929
Maria	31551	D	1921
VOLPE			
Carlo	85674	D	1940
Joseph A.	61425	D	1932
VOLPIN			
Abraham M.	77797	D	1938
VOLQUARDSEN			
Valerie M.	62624	D	1932
VOLTZENLUGAL			
Jules	56047	D	1930
VOLTZENLUGEL			
Julius	56047	D	1930
VOLZ			
Ernest G.	56344	D	1930
Freda	64808	D	1933
George Frederick	20637	D	1916
Mary E.	29103	I	1920
VONACH			
Emma P.	58313	D	1931
VONAHN			
William	21693	I	1916
William	25183	D	1918
VONARNOLD			
Gabrielle	60142	D	1931
VONBARGEN			
Alfred	10026	D	1910
VONBARGER			
George	14407	M	1912
VONBELOW			
Bogislav	37688	D	1923
VONBERGAN			
Johann J.	1429	D	1906
VONBERGEN			
Henry	59566	D	1931
VONBORSTEL			
Charles	12373	D	1911
Theodore	7630	D	1909
VONBORSTOL			
Louisa	6344	D	1908

NAME	NUMBER	TYPE	YEAR
VONBREMAN			
Herman	36156	D	1923
VONCLEVE			
Hartwig	20254	D	1916
VONDAKLERN			
Marie	58007	D	1931
VONDEMANDOWSKI			
Armandus	17207	D	1914
VONDERHELLEN			
George B.	79611	D	1938
VONDERLIETH			
Dorette C. R.	18940	D	1915
VONDERMEHDEN			
Jacob Louis	3305	D	1907
Mary A.	18282	D	1914
VONDERNIENBURG			
Anna Rebecca	64357	D	1933
William A.	75961	D	1937
VONDERVOLK			
William	69494	D	1935
VONDITTEN			
Erwin Hartwig	43161	D	1925
Helen Auguste Hartwig	40108	D	1924
Henrietta Helena	40108	D	1924
Hermann Wilhelm	43161	D	1925
VONDOHREN			
Peter Hinrich	19252	D	1915
VONENDE			
Grace May	49488	D	1928
Helen	23351	M	1917
VONFRANK			
Elfreda Clara	7475	D	1909
Vazel	7753	M	1909
VONGALL			
Lucia	9450	D	1910
VONGERZABEK			
Ella P.	39483	D	1924
VONGLAHN			
John	6997	D	1908
VONGOODAT			
Herman Fear	33700	M	1922
VONGOSLIGA			
John	2706	D	1907
VONHAGEN			
Edna Katharine	6199	M	1908
Henry Edward	30974	D	1921

NAME	NUMBER	TYPE	YEAR
VonHavasy			
George Albini	55853	D	1930
VonHofen			
Madelene	63330	D	1933
VonHoffmann			
Charles August	22808	D	1917
VonHusen			
Frederick L.	37374	D	1923
VonJacobowski			
Otto	79876	D	1938
Otto	79876	D	1938
VonJakubowski			
Otto	79876	D	1938
VonJohannsen			
Walter Edler	4167	D	1907
VonKauffmann			
Jeanne Marie	75873	D	1937
VonKoll			
Gladys Katherine	82974	D	1939
VonKrakau			
James Henry William	53660	D	1929
W. Esters	53660	D	1929
VonLeicht			
Eugenie	41817	D	1925
Eugenie	41817	D	1925
VonLengerke			
Emma	74096	D	1936
VonLinden			
Belle Mordaunt	63236	D	1932
Isabel	63236	D	1932
VonLoesecke			
Adella C.	4697	M	1907
VonLubbke			
Johann	67727	D	1934
VonMandelsloh			
Alfred Conrad	63763	I	1933
Alfred Conrad	68037	D	1934
VonMandelslon			
Alfred Conrad	68037	D	1934
VonMatzen			
Emma	37487	D	1923
VonMitrowitsch			
Eva	15038	D	1913
VonMoas			
Edward T.	32188	D	1921

NAME	NUMBER	TYPE	YEAR
VonMoos			
Edward T.	32188	D	1921
Theresa	50885	D	1928
Theresa	51057	M	1928
VonNiel			
James Joseph	63408	D	1933
VonNorman			
Charles	47960	M	1927
VonOesen			
Irma Minna	7511	M	1909
VonOlsen			
Irma Minna	7511	M	1909
VonOsten			
Alva M.	71819	I	1936
VonOverbeck			
Harold, Jr.	69523	D	1935
VonParpart			
Arthur	73582	I	1936
Arthur	74537	D	1937
VonPelt			
Becci M.	50051	D	1928
Bessie M.	50051	D	1928
VonPien			
Hans Henry	689	D	1906
VonPiotrowska			
Konstancya	64257	D	1933
VonPoehl			
Frank Frederick Rider	61240	D	1932
VonRabenau			
Arwed	66832	D	1934
VonRhein			
Frank L.	31571	D	1921
VonRigalGrunland			
Roberta Louise	34273	D	1922
VonRitter			
Frederick	62640	D	1932
Mary June	56069	M	1930
VonRoehl			
Carolina	50925	D	1928
Vonron			
Leslie Grant	55550	M	1930
VonRonkel			
Samuel	36268	D	1923
VonRonn			
Westley Grant	55550	M	1930

NAME	NUMBER	TYPE	YEAR
VonRonne			
Rose Helen	53789	D	1929
VonRotsmann			
Clarence Adolph Paul	80920	D	1939
VonRubens			
Rudolph	43510	D	1926
VonSalzen			
Henriette	32216	D	1921
VonSchmidt			
Middleton A.	82627	I	1939
VonSchroeder			
Mary Ellen	46857	D	1927
VonSeiberlich			
Edward H.	8530	D	1909
VonSoosten			
Alice	41598	M	1925
Charles	41598	M	1925
Frederick	76444	D	1937
Grace	41598	M	1925
Louis	25415	D	1918
Margaretha	58173	D	1931
VonStaden			
George	25682	D	1918
Jurgen	25682	D	1918
Maria	4049	D	1907
VonTassell			
Leland Richbourg	81227	D	1939
VonTillow			
Frances Alma	39399	D	1924
John	80198	D	1938
William Thomas	80198	D	1938
VonVorst			
Carrie	89397	I	1942
VonVoss			
Amalia	14536	D	1912
William	56903	D	1930
VonWartburg			
August	72492	D	1936
VonWefelsburg			
Aloha Barack	41839	M	1925
Aloha Barack	41839	M	1925
VonWerthern			
Constance	37929	D	1923
VonWhitcomb			
Louise Palmyre	32601	D	1921

NAME	NUMBER	TYPE	YEAR
VonWye			
Agnes	13439	D	1912
Alois	44103	D	1926
VonWyl			
Alois	44103	D	1926
Voorhamme			
Francis	5588	D	1908
Francoise	5588	D	1908
Voorheis			
Edward G.	41664	D	1925
Voorhies			
Albina Durand	58072	D	1931
Voorman			
Annie Laura	36033	D	1923
Henry	2824	D	1907
Henry A.	25055	D	1918
Ida V.	29210	I	1920
Mary	1938	I	1906
Mary	41584	D	1925
Voorsanger			
Abraham W.	57291	D	1930
Elkan C.	5828	M	1908
Elsie	21728	D	1916
Eva	34473	D	1922
Jacob	5801	D	1908
Voorter			
George	82848	D	1939
Gerardus	82848	D	1939
Vooys			
Maria	17256	D	1914
Vorbe			
Auguste F.	46941	D	1927
Vorce			
Mary F.	69240	D	1935
Vordick			
William J.	82483	D	1939
Vorlander			
Doris	13099	D	1912
Vorrath			
Carl C.	1384	D	1906
Christiane	21613	D	1916
Elizabeth	19585	D	1915
Sophie Louise	5843	D	1908
Vorroth			
Max D.	9571	D	1910

NAME	NUMBER	TYPE	YEAR
Vorsanger			
George Edward	40982	M	1925
Vorst			
Lillian Van	89852	I	1942
Vorwerk			
Leo	3647	M	1907
William	3647	M	1907
Vosberg			
Majorie	50485	D	1928
Margaret Majorie	50485	D	1928
Vosburgh			
Emily Jane	22715	D	1917
Voshell			
Frank	39197	I	1924
Nellie S.	37922	D	1923
Voss			
Anna	47756	M	1927
August	47157	M	1927
August J.	29632	D	1920
Charles F.	25476	D	1918
Charles F.	79211	D	1938
Clemens	40942	D	1925
Clemens	47157	M	1927
Florence F.	20781	D	1916
Hattie Mallack	80304	D	1939
John	47157	M	1927
Mana	67334	D	1934
Maria	47756	M	1927
Mary	67334	D	1934
Pauline	77311	D	1937
Rudolph F.	34601	D	1922
Tony	47157	M	1927
Wiebke	28375	D	1919
Vosti			
Annette May	74794	M	1937
Anthony A.	74794	M	1937
Anthony A.	83644	M	1940
Anthony August	89414	D	1942
Maria	79339	D	1938
S. R.	29076	D	1920
Serafino	29076	D	1920
Stefano (Stephen)	4641	D	1907
Votaw			
Lydia H.	71178	D	1935
Vowles			
Johanna H.	6569	D	1908

NAME	NUMBER	TYPE	YEAR
Voy			
Annie K.	51078	D	1928
Edward Lathrop	74984	D	1937
Voyages			
Nick	44715	D	1926
Vozga			
Wenzel	61961	I	1932
Vozgo			
Wenzel	61961	I	1932
Vragnisan			
Augusta	62090	D	1932
Vragnizan			
Augusta	62090	D	1932
Vincenza	50282	D	1928
Vrahoritis			
Paraskevoula George	70128	D	1935
Vranjos			
Frank	40155	D	1924
John	78697	D	1938
Vrzich			
Rade	18121	D	1914
Vucanovich			
Christopher L.	9248	D	1910
Vucasovich			
Louis	22910	D	1917
Vuccovich			
Louise	59872	I	1931
Vujnovich			
Silvo	31914	I	1921
Vujovich			
Elena	57822	I	1931
Elinor	57822	I	1931
Ellen	57822	I	1931
Vukovich			
Aneta	75469	I	1937
Chris	28917	D	1920
Crsto	28917	D	1920
Donald	86368	M	1941
Milan	86368	M	1941
Roy	86368	M	1941
Spiro	55741	I	1930
Violet	86368	M	1941
Vuletic			
John	53205	D	1929
Jovo	53205	D	1929

NAME	NUMBER	TYPE	YEAR
VULETICH			
John	53205	D	1929
Jovo	53205	D	1929
VULICEVICH			
Eleanor M.	10222	I	1910
Eleanor M.	24742	D	1918
VULTAGGIO			
Vito	39769	I	1924
VUNDER			
William	35249	I	1922
VUSCOVICH			
Louise	59872	I	1931
VYACHEFLAVOV			
Alexander M.	78400	D	1938
WAAGE			
Delia T.	34024	D	1922
WACHOLDER			
Benjamin	50059	D	1928
Rose	46112	D	1926
WACHS			
Sallie Fischel	64619	D	1933
WACHTER			
Addie M.	89095	D	1942
Charles F.	79823	D	1938
John	4901	D	1907
WACHTERHAUSES			
John F.	8705	D	1909
WACHTERSHEUSER			
Conrad	14533	M	1912
Elisabetha	14533	M	1912
Franz	14533	M	1912
Friedrich	14533	M	1912
Hermann	14533	M	1912
Kathrina	14533	M	1912
Wilhelm	14533	M	1912
WACK			
John	67589	D	1934
Margaret	14028	D	1912
WACKENREUDER			
Ernest	2830	D	1907
Vitus	11187	D	1911
WACKER			
Annie	37103	D	1923
Isabelle Eunice	71502	D	1936
WACKNITZ			
Margaritha	34462	D	1922

NAME	NUMBER	TYPE	YEAR
WACLOWSKI			
Frank J.	35934	D	1923
WADDELL			
George Martin	10130	D	1910
William	8620	D	1909
WADDILL			
George Martin	10130	D	1910
WADE			
Anna	63368	D	1933
Blanche	79084	I	1938
Blanche	87923	D	1941
Charles Malcolm	86833	D	1941
Edward E.	87310	D	1941
George W.	68364	D	1934
James	21767	D	1916
James Henry	71873	D	1936
Jane B.	67816	D	1934
Jane R.	67816	D	1934
John Holmes	8193	D	1909
Lucy M.	78712	D	1938
Madeline Clara	77422	D	1938
Nellie Mae	63679	D	1933
Robert L.	9196	D	1910
William M.	55912	I	1930
William Meier	58786	D	1931
William N.	67811	D	1934
WADEN			
Eilert	10764	D	1910
WADHAM			
Edward L.	11381	D	1911
Elizabeth S. T.	32837	I	1921
Elizabeth Sarah Taunton	37047	D	1923
WADLEIGH			
William Millard	77958	D	1938
WADMAN			
John O'Riley Webster	38173	D	1924
WADSWIRTH			
Joseph	88521	D	1941
WADSWORTH			
Charles Henry	15094	D	1913
R. M.	73580	D	1936
WAEGNER			
Phillip J.	46563	D	1927
WAERNER			
Mary A.	70684	D	1935
WAFER			
Estella F.	18299	I	1914

NAME	NUMBER	TYPE	YEAR
Sarah A.	56879	D	1930
Thomas	7841	D	1909
WAFFORD			
Henry	14999	D	1913
WAFLER			
Emma	87314	D	1941
WAFTALY			
Sarah Tobah	27372	D	1919
WAGEN			
Louise	15039	D	1913
Wilhelmine Louise	15039	D	1913
WAGENER			
Francis Emil	35172	I	1922
Rose A.	78278	D	1938
Wilhelm	42891	D	1925
William	42891	D	1925
WAGENKNECHT			
Hugo	84210	D	1940
WAGENR			
Marion	1580	D	1906
WAGER			
Anna	28851	I	1920
Anna	43054	D	1925
WAGGERHAUSER			
Fred	19837	D	1915
Fritz	19837	D	1915
WAGGOMAN			
Adolphus Stokes	70691	D	1935
WAGGONER			
H. G.	84208	I	1940
Hamilton George	85549	D	1940
Logan Jacob	49747	D	1928
Melvin A.	70750	D	1935
WAGNER			
Adam	11104	D	1911
Adam	14801	D	1913
Agnes B.	58472	D	1931
Alexander	66204	D	1934
Andrew Olsen	26851	D	1919
Anna	74191	D	1936
Anna M.	48254	D	1927
Annie Edwards	59189	D	1931
Carl	80629	D	1939
Carla H.	86466	D	1941
Chas. A.	55524	D	1930
Edna Annie	51711	M	1928
Elsie	88369	D	1941

NAME	NUMBER	TYPE	YEAR
Emilie	6850	D	1908
Emilie E.	65078	D	1933
Emma R.	25026	D	1918
Francis J.	58354	D	1931
Franz Robert	151	D	1906
Frederick	79269	D	1938
Frederick Andrew	82439	D	1939
Gerald J.	67198	D	1934
Harr	87729	D	1941
Harry C.	34236	D	1922
Helen Ann	56609	D	1930
Helena	35817	D	1923
Henry	18832	D	1915
Henry A.	63097	I	1932
Henry A.	68825	D	1935
Henry Francis	8784	M	1909
Henry Francis	48404	D	1927
Henry J.	42250	D	1925
Henry Lewis	74310	D	1937
Ida	31975	D	1921
Jacob	10878	D	1910
James	40474	D	1924
John	12584	D	1911
John M.	52385	D	1929
Joseph	43562	D	1926
Joseph Edward Christian	20523	D	1916
Julius K.	73233	D	1936
Kathryn Keith	51564	D	1928
Katie A.	65974	I	1933
Katie A.	68812	D	1935
Katie Sophie	28501	D	1919
Laura Rose	35531	D	1922
Lawrence Talcott	86971	D	1941
Lillian A.	53286	D	1929
Louis	28677	D	1920
Ludwig	7967	D	1909
Margaret	46299	D	1927
Margaret	58497	M	1931
Marguerite	88370	D	1941
Mary	25292	I	1918
Mary	30029	D	1920
Mary Almene Eaton	28449	I	1919
Mary Frances	54555	D	1929
Patricia Gladys	51711	M	1928
Rebecca M.	1438	D	1906
Richard	65297	D	1933
William	10813	D	1910
William	70533	D	1935
William A.	73722	D	1936

NAME	NUMBER	TYPE	YEAR
William E.	52676	D	1929
William Henry Busch	50271	M	1928
WAGONER			
Eva J.	63037	D	1932
Grace A.	41422	D	1925
WAGSTAFF			
Albert Alfred	83137	D	1940
Charlotte	52372	D	1929
Denman Sully	72039	D	1936
Ella A.	35157	D	1922
Margaret B.	87286	D	1941
Thomas H.	34345	I	1922
Thomas H.	35405	D	1922
WAH			
Gee Leen	40062	M	1924
Hom Kwong	53467	M	1929
Lee Gin	50413	D	1928
Lee Yin	50413	D	1928
Leong	82097	D	1939
Lew Fay	83322	M	1940
Ming Chang	54879	D	1930
Tom Quong	53467	M	1929
Wan	81084	D	1939
Wong Kock	33901	M	1922
Woo	26796	D	1919
Yee Sok	42498	D	1925
Yung	49339	D	1928
WAHINGTON			
Louis	52235	I	1929
WAHL			
Emily	25391	D	1918
Frederick Drewes	19166	M	1915
Katherine	42715	D	1925
Katie	65758	D	1933
Ray M.	89065	D	1942
Robert F.	74397	D	1937
Robert G.	64871	D	1933
Ton King	74436	M	1937
WAHLBERG			
John	20497	D	1916
Paul Frank John	72569	D	1936
Ruth Amelia	72945	M	1936
WAHLER			
A. W.	1335	D	1906
WAHLGREEN			
Albert	89886	D	1942
Beulah H.	69454	D	1935
George Albert	89886	D	1942

NAME	NUMBER	TYPE	YEAR
Gustave A.	89886	D	1942
Oscar E.	85230	D	1940
WAHLGREN			
Bessie	8896	D	1909
Emma	59579	D	1931
Gust	53587	D	1929
Rose Theresa Cecelia	85017	D	1940
Rosimere	85231	D	1940
WAHLHEIM			
George P.	48568	D	1927
Jeanne Adele	51043	M	1928
Ottmar	29994	D	1920
WAHLQUIST			
William H.	5818	D	1908
WAHLRAF			
Gertrude	28018	D	1919
WAHLSTROM			
Axel	9967	D	1910
WAHNIG			
Hermann	22245	D	1917
WAHREN			
John	77187	D	1937
WAI			
Ag Sing	25238	D	1918
Woo Ting	25080	M	1918
WAIBEL			
Carlotta Marian	26947	I	1919
WAIDELICH			
Christian	52204	I	1929
WAINWRIGHT			
Annetta M.	25244	D	1918
Elizabeth F.	47014	D	1927
Harry S.	40460	M	1924
James	13709	D	1912
WAISMAN			
Matilda J.	19182	D	1915
WAISSMAN			
Idal	86766	D	1941
WAITE			
Barbara Ann	71031	M	1935
Doris	24516	M	1918
Fannie Rollins	79190	I	1938
Madeleine Elizabeth	71031	M	1935
Marjorie Janet	71031	M	1935
Robert	72934	D	1936

Name	Number	Type	Year
WAITES			
Beatrice G.	77173	D	1937
Ila B.	32762	M	1921
Ila B.	80814	D	1939
Melville G., Jr.	32762	M	1921
WAITMAN			
June Elizabeth	61491	M	1932
WAIWAIOLE			
David P.	25564	D	1918
WAIZMAN			
Fredericka	34217	D	1922
Max	19597	D	1915
Olga	60297	I	1931
Olga	74610	D	1937
WAKARUK			
John	57952	I	1931
John	67197	D	1934
WAKEFIELD			
Charles Henry	75335	D	1937
Elizabeth M.	64714	D	1933
Florence Mary	55844	D	1930
Franklin W.	72438	D	1936
Jean	76118	I	1937
Mary E.	47840	D	1927
WAKELEY			
Mattie Martha	9506	D	1910
WAKEMAN			
Ernest H.	39345	D	1924
WAKERLEY			
Clara E.	56986	D	1930
Robert M.	47950	D	1927
William A.	10115	D	1910
WAKROOM			
Charles	42819	D	1925
WAKU			
Sophia	83994	D	1940
WAL			
Julia M.	1694	D	1906
WALBERG			
Andrew	14711	D	1913
WALBRIDGE			
E. L.	77131	I	1937
Margaret	39590	D	1924
WALCOM			
George Washington	53870	D	1929
Ida Frances	67245	D	1934

Name	Number	Type	Year
Ida Francis	67245	D	1934
William	37025	D	1923
WALCOTT			
Agnes P.	6993	D	1908
Ashley V. R.	62442	M	1932
Earle Ashley	57644	D	1931
Francis John	62442	M	1932
Mary E.	77097	D	1937
WALCRAK			
Stanislaus	2148	D	1906
WALD			
Charles T.	54725	D	1930
Nellie O.	37506	I	1923
Philip A.	74214	D	1936
William	63189	I	1932
WALDAU			
Christian	51992	D	1929
WALDECH			
Amy W.	37625	D	1923
WALDECK			
Alice	38649	M	1924
Amy W.	37625	D	1923
Dolores Ann	89344	M	1942
Herman	59096	D	1931
Hugo	39363	D	1924
Minnie	21309	I	1916
WALDENMEIER			
August	78097	D	1938
WALDHAUSER			
Jules	79366	D	1938
Julius	79366	D	1938
WALDMAN			
Amalie	77343	I	1937
Amalie	81300	D	1939
August	55582	D	1930
Bertha	3687	D	1907
Lena S.	22367	D	1917
WALDNER			
Ferdinand	30550	D	1920
WALDO			
Ellen	69503	D	1935
Ralph E.	71415	I	1936
Ralph E.	71529	D	1936
WALDOMAR			
Ramon H.	31660	D	1921
WALDORF			
Janet Mary	82054	D	1939

Name	Number	Type	Year
WALDOW			
Bertha J.	85138	D	1940
WALDRICH			
Filomena	66063	D	1934
WALDRON			
Edward	2937	M	1907
Joseph F.	12745	D	1911
William B.	56461	D	1930
William Wesley	2937	M	1907
WALDVOGEL			
Elizabeth	56273	D	1930
Moritz	52018	D	1929
WALE			
Genoa	57315	D	1930
Margaret	9737	D	1910
WALES			
Albert Vincent	51232	D	1928
Geo. B.	11218	D	1911
George F.	79261	D	1938
James Henry	39141	D	1924
WALFENDEN			
Andrew	21620	D	1916
WALFORD			
William E.	35818	D	1923
WALHAUS			
Fanny	39158	D	1924
Ricka	39159	D	1924
WALK			
Charles	22113	D	1917
Leon	22114	M	1917
Mayer	22412	D	1917
Sophie	22114	M	1917
WALKENSHAW			
Crystal	86788	M	1941
Donald	86788	M	1941
Doris	86788	M	1941
Lois	86788	M	1941
WALKER			
Agnes	61926	D	1932
Amy	18190	D	1914
Anna Honora	11211	D	1911
Annie	81536	D	1939
Annie Alice	53480	D	1929
Athern L.	76203	D	1937
Axson E.	4305	D	1907
Barbara M.	69973	D	1935
Belle	15413	D	1913

NAME	NUMBER	TYPE	YEAR	NAME	NUMBER	TYPE	YEAR	NAME	NUMBER	TYPE	YEAR
Caroline	85127	D	1940	Mary	73698	D	1936	Mary	48494	D	1927
Charles A.	79341	D	1938	Mary Ann	56655	D	1930	Mary A.	864	D	1906
Charles P.	18937	D	1915	Mary S.	3067	D	1907	Mary A.	81403	D	1939
Clare Agnes	12793	M	1912	Miriam Earsla	51959	M	1929	Michael	82035	D	1939
Claudia L. Waller	83210	I	1940	Mitchcell Porter	72906	D	1936	Patrick	2593	D	1907
Cloyce H.	78334	D	1938	Owen J.	64988	D	1933	Patrick	17814	D	1914
David J.	14304	D	1912	Robert A.	3888	D	1907	Patrick	81184	I	1939
Edgar C.	83307	D	1940	Samuel	41304	D	1925	Regina	20325	D	1916
Edmund Waddell	88498	D	1941	Samuel T.	66970	I	1934	Robert	30568	D	1920
Elizabeth E.	13900	D	1912	Susan Ann	35982	D	1923	William L.	88001	D	1941
Forrest Eugene	38445	M	1924	Thomas	31434	D	1921	William W., Jr.	73639	I	1936
Frances	39000	D	1924	Warren C.	58605	M	1931	**WALLACE**			
Frederick R.	67761	D	1934	Wesley	80057	M	1938	Albert	26598	D	1919
George R.	43172	D	1925	Will T.	54464	D	1929	Amelia	24999	D	1918
Grace Marie	77061	D	1937	William	20489	D	1916	Andrew	3846	D	1907
Grant	86246	D	1941	William C.	23941	D	1918	Annie Louise	81909	D	1939
Harry	13834	D	1912	William Hiram	29734	D	1920	Arthur O.	45822	I	1926
Harry	39970	D	1924	William K.	81729	D	1939	Arthur O.	45880	I	1926
Harry	51676	D	1928	**WALKINGTON**				August	84396	D	1940
Henry C.	35718	D	1923	John H.	19284	D	1915	Blanche Maud	22471	D	1917
Hermine Kolhler	83539	D	1940	Ray	32765	D	1921	Bridget J.	11675	D	1911
Hugh	66740	D	1934	**WALKMEISTER**				Corinne	82184	D	1939
Irene M.	74186	D	1936	George C.	26810	D	1919	Daniel W.	85183	D	1940
Irma	76651	M	1937	**WALKNER**				Ebenezer G.	7277	D	1909
Jacob L.	56855	I	1930	Leopold	86672	D	1941	Edith	72505	I	1936
James G.	18369	D	1915	**WALKUP**				Edward B.	64629	D	1933
James G.	48489	D	1927	Elizabeth	31263	D	1921	Edwin	7415	D	1909
James Gordon	61572	M	1932	Ward B.	51399	D	1928	Elizabeth	22180	D	1917
Jane	1413	D	1906	**WALL**				Ellen O. Hendy	87221	D	1941
Jane A.	17600	D	1914	Alice	16799	D	1914	Erma	88358	D	1941
Jane Aedlaide	72453	D	1936	Alice M. M.	18295	D	1914	Fred	89357	D	1942
Jane Elizabeth	37091	M	1923	Anna T.	23758	D	1917	George E.	45033	D	1926
Jesse A.	38340	I	1924	Clara S.	66710	D	1934	Gladys	89238	M	1942
Jesse A.	60214	D	1931	Daniel	8431	D	1909	Harry Augustus	32545	D	1921
Jessie E.	50714	D	1928	Delia	1261	D	1906	Harry P.	41194	D	1925
John	36816	I	1923	Elizabeth	46799	D	1927	Henry Edward	14590	M	1912
John	59122	D	1931	Eugene R.	56066	D	1930	Hiram J.	47753	D	1927
John C.	3398	D	1907	George Samuel	75967	D	1937	James H.	22181	D	1917
Joseph F.	18798	D	1915	Herman	65284	D	1933	James Margraves	22181	D	1917
Josephine A.	75075	D	1937	James	8430	D	1909	James P.	28898	D	1920
Josephine E.	49960	I	1928	James H.	35459	D	1922	James W.	5998	D	1908
Josephine Elizabeth	84422	D	1940	John J.	4908	D	1907	Jane	9902	D	1910
Katherine Mitchler	73954	D	1936	John J.	25635	D	1918	Jeannette H.	9874	D	1910
Katherine P.	73997	D	1936	Joseph P.	25029	D	1918	Jeannie	70052	I	1935
Lillian	43668	D	1926	Laura	39893	I	1924	Jeannie	70086	D	1935
Lottie M	89789	D	1942	Margaret	9737	D	1910	John	54322	D	1929
Maggie R.	7059	D	1909	Margaret	11604	D	1911	John E.	83964	D	1940
Margaret Jane	13024	D	1912	Martin J.	12029	D	1911	John J.	7896	D	1909
Mary	30051	D	1920					John Perret	83088	D	1940

NAME	NUMBER	TYPE	YEAR
John W.	53501	D	1929
John W.	66253	I	1934
Josephine	32537	D	1921
Kate	16083	D	1913
Kathryn B.	56466	D	1930
Leonora Kerr	88877	D	1942
Lillian Sheridan	28592	D	1920
Lloyd	14374	M	1912
Mabel H.	81982	I	1939
Margaret	16471	D	1913
Margaret	28480	D	1919
Martha E.	54872	M	1930
Mary A.	82626	D	1939
Mary B.	14347	D	1912
Mary Frances	67301	D	1934
Mary S.	67301	D	1934
Matilda Agnes	37512	D	1923
May	72662	D	1936
Michael	2727	D	1907
Ora Ayleene	36426	M	1923
Patrick Joseph	57720	D	1931
Richard	6945	D	1908
Richard R.	53918	D	1929
Robert	32420	D	1921
Robert	89238	M	1942
Robert	39081	D	1924
Robert H.	58677	M	1931
Robert, Jr.	44325	D	1926
Romietta J. B.	8461	I	1909
Romietta J. B.	11398	D	1911
Ruth Blanche	14374	M	1912
Ryland B.	12108	D	1911
Ryland Burnett, Mrs.	81909	D	1939
Sally Alfreda	73877	D	1936
Samuel	78838	D	1938
Sarah	10882	D	1910
Scott H.	86213	D	1941
Staley L.	25423	D	1918
Susan	28588	I	1920
Thomas	29788	D	1920
Thomas A.	12331	D	1911
Timothy J.	16082	D	1913
Walter Lynn	85137	D	1940
William	11312	I	1911
William	11411	D	1911
William	32715	D	1921
William	44015	D	1926
William A.	65684	D	1933
William J.	65684	D	1933

NAME	NUMBER	TYPE	YEAR
William M.	40329	D	1924
William T.	8307	D	1909
WALLACH			
Emilio	20613	D	1916
Georgia Crim	67134	I	1934
Marshall Brown	23749	D	1917
Mary Cannon	43179	D	1925
Minnie	13353	D	1912
WALLDEN			
Henning E.	49455	I	1928
WALLDORF			
Harold	80334	D	1939
Ida W.	23509	D	1917
Mary	25512	D	1918
WALLEEB			
Albert	83259	D	1940
WALLEN			
Clarence Howard	59528	D	1931
George	72400	D	1936
Ida Sophia	82493	D	1939
Jean	84587	M	1940
Robert	84587	M	1940
WALLENROD			
George	39539	D	1924
Mamie	60044	D	1931
WALLENSTEIN			
Bernhard	7104	I	1909
H. M.	50556	D	1928
Helena	54006	D	1929
Morris	48122	D	1927
WALLER			
Bert	75891	D	1937
Christain	542	D	1906
Julian L.	82730	D	1939
William A.	4170	D	1907
WALLERSTEIN			
Bertha Cohen	60145	D	1931
Carol Cohen	62123	M	1932
Jerome	62123	M	1932
Selma Shirley	62123	M	1932
Shirley	62123	M	1932
WALLERT			
Jennie	48738	D	1927
WALLEY			
Emil Englebert	77663	D	1938
WALLFISCH			
Herman	63641	D	1933

NAME	NUMBER	TYPE	YEAR
WALLGREN			
Mae L.	44826	I	1926
WALLHEIM			
Ida	69440	I	1935
WALLIN			
Emma	73394	D	1936
Ernst Gustaf Edward	84222	D	1940
Mary Sophie	33635	D	1922
Ransom Harris	83587	D	1940
WALLING			
George Allen	38655	D	1924
WALLIS			
Albert E.	69663	D	1935
Edward Bennett	48766	M	1927
Katherine	86504	D	1941
M. C.	39394	D	1924
Ralph W.	79655	I	1938
Virginia	48766	M	1927
WALLOCHA			
Paul	86472	D	1941
WALLOP			
Kasper	52361	D	1929
WALLOPE			
Albert	83259	D	1940
WALLQUIST			
Hannah K.	89185	D	1942
WALLRIDGE			
Margaret	39590	D	1924
WALLS			
Annie Louisa	78805	D	1938
WALLSTEAD			
Clarence Elmer	37691	M	1923
WALLSTEIN			
Arthur Earl	7236	M	1909
Mildred Eleonora	7236	M	1909
Ole	5594	D	1908
WALLTER			
Samuel	43801	D	1926
WALLY			
Bertha	60902	D	1932
WALMER			
Eli	67368	D	1934
WALMI			
Eli	67368	D	1934
WALMSLEY			
William Wallace	26627	D	1919

NAME	NUMBER	TYPE	YEAR	NAME	NUMBER	TYPE	YEAR	NAME	NUMBER	TYPE	YEAR
William Wallace	45952	D	1926	Jno.	10718	D	1910	Mary Agnes	66618	D	1934
WALMU				Johanna	5805	D	1908	Mary Agnes	77643	D	1938
Eli	67368	D	1934	Johanna	7692	D	1909	Mary Alice	51626	D	1928
WALPERT				John	17109	D	1914	Mary Anne	14838	D	1913
Frederick	84252	D	1940	John	31188	D	1921	Mary Margaret Teresa	85759	D	1940
WALROSE				John	46992	D	1927	Matthew J.	86746	D	1941
Helen E.	65830	D	1933	John	65815	D	1933	Melvin Harrison	3801	M	1907
WALSH				John E.	41466	D	1925	Michael	1123	D	1906
Albert M.	86493	D	1941	John F.	10718	D	1910	Michael	31216	D	1921
Alice Josephine	43380	D	1926	John Francis	10518	I	1910	Michael	47402	I	1927
Ambrose	23084	D	1917	John Francis	10651	I	1910	Michael	47939	D	1927
Amelia	24282	D	1918	John Francis	65480	D	1933	Michael J.	85643	D	1940
Annie Marie	21367	D	1916	John J.	2292	D	1906	Mildred Lorraine	50866	M	1928
Bartholomew J.	69728	D	1935	John J.	2364	D	1906	Morgan A.	83834	D	1940
Bernard N.	51628	D	1928	John J.	10798	D	1910	Myles A.	52415	I	1929
Carmelita	60736	D	1932	John J.	78070	I	1938	Myles Anthony	54041	D	1929
Catherine	48869	D	1928	John Joseph	61087	M	1932	Nora	16332	D	1913
Catherine Florence	55947	D	1930	John K.	1031	D	1906	Nora	88408	D	1941
Catherine L.	70937	D	1935	John O'Hara	39801	D	1924	Patrick	4150	D	1907
Charlotte	87918	D	1941	John Richard	20159	D	1915	Patrick	12726	D	1911
Clara	77216	D	1937	Joseph	34584	D	1922	Patrick	31303	M	1921
Coleman	37920	D	1923	Joseph J.	10798	D	1910	Patrick	33513	D	1922
Daniel F.	65227	D	1933	Joseph S.	41804	I	1925	Patrick	61420	D	1932
David V.	11208	D	1911	Joseph S.	41804	I	1925	Patrick	63273	D	1933
Edward J.	50865	D	1928	Julia M.	67112	D	1934	Patrick	82592	D	1939
Edward Paul	85345	D	1940	Julio A.	21819	D	1916	Patrick J.	5715	D	1908
Edward T.	9642	I	1910	Kate	23014	D	1917	Patrick Joseph	61266	M	1932
Ellen	40354	D	1924	Katherine	50700	I	1928	Peter	7158	I	1909
Ellen Maria	75759	D	1937	Katherine Loretta	17994	D	1914	Peter	14680	D	1913
Ellen Mary	76418	D	1937	Lawrence	31121	D	1921	Peter Joseph	80375	D	1939
Elsie E.	56191	D	1930	Lawrence F.	57254	D	1930	Philomene	85982	I	1941
Eugene Sherwood	40261	D	1924	Lawrence M.	25347	D	1918	Philomene	88474	D	1941
Florance P.	11911	D	1911	Lillian Regina	3801	M	1907	Robert	60095	I	1931
Frances C.	80718	D	1939	Loretta	51020	M	1928	Robert T.	39052	D	1924
George	51020	M	1928	Margaret	4311	D	1907	Rosey	11734	D	1911
Hannah	31996	D	1921	Margaret	82021	D	1939	Stephen	61287	D	1932
Hannah	55936	D	1930	Margaret	88493	D	1941	Thelma	51020	M	1928
Irene C.	78084	D	1938	Margaret Isabelle	73217	D	1936	Thomas	4996	D	1908
James	7861	D	1909	Margaret M.	1659	D	1906	Thomas	9397	D	1910
James	11980	D	1911	Maria	14161	D	1912	Thomas	75584	D	1937
James	58353	D	1931	Maria A.	51260	D	1928	Thomas E.	12366	M	1911
James E.	61529	D	1932	Maria B.	44515	D	1926	Thomas J.	28207	D	1919
James Patrick	66259	D	1934	Marie Inez	77643	D	1938	Ursula	36392	M	1923
James, Mrs.	88408	D	1941	Mary	16013	D	1913	Walter F.	70715	D	1935
Jane	700	D	1906	Mary	18566	D	1915	Wiliam F.	78071	D	1938
Jane C.	69866	D	1935	Mary	31303	M	1921	William	36392	M	1923
Jerome	33525	D	1922	Mary	59772	D	1931	William	45607	D	1926
Jerome M.	34349	D	1922	Mary	86819	D	1941	William	47568	D	1927
				Mary A.	29475	D	1920	William	83857	D	1940

Key: D = death; M = minor; I = incompetent

NAME	NUMBER	TYPE	YEAR
William G.	9935	I	1910
William H.	88986	D	1942
William J.	12024	D	1911
William J.	50862	D	1928
William J.	67418	D	1934
William John	24563	M	1918
William P.	34963	D	1922
WALSHE			
Martin	62206	D	1932
Richard J.	11628	D	1911
WALSJ			
Sarah J.	50551	D	1928
WALSTER			
Kathleen Maud	53780	M	1929
William	49985	D	1928
WALT			
Milo	47246	D	1927
WALTER			
Alfred	63685	D	1933
Alice H.	25781	D	1918
Carol	70379	M	1935
Caroline	69046	D	1935
Clara	20701	D	1916
Edgar	77947	D	1938
Edward	78725	D	1938
Elise	66911	I	1934
Emanuel	1996	D	1906
Ethel	49329	M	1928
Hannah	48935	D	1928
Harvey W.	35147	D	1922
Henry Franklin	39424	D	1924
Isaac N.	42860	D	1925
Jacob	42404	D	1925
John I.	55233	D	1930
Juliana	81473	I	1939
Juliana	83348	D	1940
Kittie E.	42545	D	1925
Krischjohn	78725	D	1938
L. M.	28333	D	1919
Laura L.	62186	D	1932
Lizzie	2048	D	1906
Margaret Hannah	49329	M	1928
Mary	66842	D	1934
Mary E.	11065	D	1911
Mildred	25064	M	1918
Nellie	16486	D	1913
Otto	53458	D	1929
Pauline Jacobs	80739	D	1939

NAME	NUMBER	TYPE	YEAR
Pearl S.	16485	D	1913
Philip	38000	D	1923
Philip Carl	87063	D	1941
Rosalie	25064	M	1918
Rose	79462	I	1938
Rudolph C.	81474	D	1939
Sanford F.	54121	D	1929
Wilhelm	24826	D	1918
William	30093	D	1920
William Charles	38357	M	1924
WALTERS			
Albert	45015	D	1926
Alexander	50645	D	1928
Annie B.	16167	D	1913
August	55232	D	1930
Charles P.	44025	D	1926
Edward	78725	D	1938
Fred	8525	D	1909
Harry	87750	D	1941
Helen	70856	D	1935
Henry L.	78148	D	1938
Irene	58813	D	1931
John B.	10904	D	1910
John B.	11072	M	1911
Joseph	32872	D	1921
Laura Belle	56290	D	1930
Louis N.	28224	D	1919
Mildred	48431	M	1927
Nancy Ellen	72042	D	1936
Samuel	56883	D	1930
St. D. Gynlais	62931	D	1932
Thomas P.	11072	M	1911
William	30093	D	1920
William Wirt	28225	D	1919
WALTERSTEIN			
Albert	6036	D	1908
Ella	8890	M	1909
Frank	8890	M	1909
WALTHER			
Frank, Mrs.	7193	D	1909
Marie	66602	D	1934
Mary	7193	D	1909
Philip	38000	D	1923
William H.	79436	D	1938
WALTHERS			
Ellen	55755	D	1930
Frances Elizabeth	51805	D	1929
Melissa C.	85915	D	1940

NAME	NUMBER	TYPE	YEAR
Theresa	24703	D	1918
WALTHOUR			
Annie A.	32769	D	1921
John F.	32679	I	1921
John Franklin	40529	D	1924
WALTON			
A. G.	1150	D	1906
Andrew Victor	87621	D	1941
Annie C.	88295	D	1941
Augustus	9518	D	1910
Benjamin G.	17170	D	1914
Carlos	2288	M	1906
Carrie E.	3899	D	1907
Carroll J.	47801	D	1927
Charles H.	3011	D	1907
Donald J.	8037	M	1909
Earl Lee	67548	M	1934
Elias H.	9550	D	1910
Elizabeth M.	7610	D	1909
Emma	54666	D	1930
Eugene Warren	67548	M	1934
Francis W. B.	33016	D	1921
George H.	33715	D	1922
Gladdis	2288	M	1906
Hensrietta	37784	D	1923
James A.	55250	D	1930
James P.	9375	D	1910
Jeannette Henrieta	37784	D	1923
Jerry	52500	D	1929
John	7396	D	1909
John Ryerson	1506	D	1906
Josephine M.	57749	D	1931
Lottie	49959	D	1928
Mattie	77536	D	1938
Merced	2288	M	1906
N. B.	12567	D	1911
Thomas H. O.	17272	D	1914
WALTS			
Lucius Eugene	78553	M	1938
WALTZ			
Zacharias	89885	M	1942
WAN			
Wah	81084	D	1939
Woo Ng	44488	D	1926
WAND			
Jacob	69666	D	1935
Joseph	58709	D	1931
Louise	32223	D	1921

NAME	NUMBER	TYPE	YEAR	NAME	NUMBER	TYPE	YEAR	NAME	NUMBER	TYPE	YEAR
Philip M.	53437	D	1929	Althea Juanita	65638	M	1933	John C.	23898	D	1918
Samuel	1207	D	1906	Ann	7736	D	1909	John J.	60152	D	1931
WANDERER				Ann E.	16774	D	1914	John W.	55051	D	1930
Frank Anton	89853	D	1942	Annie	26258	D	1919	Josephine	8992	D	1910
WANDKA				Annie	59169	D	1931	Josephine	58613	D	1931
Adlinda W.	40131	D	1924	Annie M.	77794	D	1938	Julia	8013	D	1909
WANDS				Annie Schooley	56737	D	1930	Julia E.	36812	D	1923
Amelia E.	13694	D	1912	Augustus W.	62653	I	1932	Kathryne Belle	81603	D	1939
Delia	9693	D	1910	Beatrice M.	29001	D	1920	L. T.	375	D	1906
Minnie K.	45811	D	1926	Catherine	2908	D	1907	Lillian M.	71301	I	1935
Samuel A.	32934	D	1921	Catherine	23850	I	1918	Lucile	57895	I	1931
Winfield Scott	84383	D	1940	Catherine	23904	D	1918	Lucille L.	77716	D	1938
WANEK				Catherine	46495	I	1927	Lucy R.	57116	D	1930
Christy James	79847	D	1938	Charles	37887	D	1923	Mae Evelyn	60469	M	1931
WANG				Charles E.	8500	D	1909	Malachy L.	78541	D	1938
Julius	30605	D	1920	Charles H.	60469	M	1931	Margaret R.	27875	D	1919
WANGENHEIM				Charles Henry	17907	D	1914	Maria Ygnacia	28256	D	1919
Emil S.	82993	D	1939	Charles Herbert	21951	D	1916	Martha	81302	D	1939
Fanny	25007	D	1918	Charlotte Mary	6097	I	1908	Martin	46186	D	1927
Henry	29758	D	1920	Clyde M.	80766	D	1939	Mary	12270	D	1911
Rose B.	29843	D	1920	Dorothy	13643	M	1912	Mary	17491	D	1914
Solomon	25799	D	1918	Edward	11452	D	1911	Mary C.	70471	D	1935
WANIOREK				Edward F.	8014	D	1909	Mary L.	74012	D	1936
Milczyslaw	72094	D	1936	Eliza	39490	D	1924	Mary M.	34937	D	1922
WANNENMACHER				Elizabeth Josephine	68613	D	1934	Mary Randall	51162	D	1928
Robert	37252	D	1923	Ernest E.	37894	D	1923	Matthew	9345	D	1910
WANNER				Florence N.	28516	D	1919	Matthew J.	15116	D	1913
Carl Rudolph	11828	D	1911	Forrest S.	13565	D	1912	Matthew J.	35189	D	1922
WANSHOP				Francis A.	27623	M	1919	Michael	71786	D	1936
William	46988	D	1927	Francis Jesse	52452	D	1929	Michael J.	11740	D	1911
WANSKY				Frank H.	19858	D	1915	Nancy Beale	72409	M	1936
Mary Cleophas	56411	D	1930	Fred	18997	D	1915	Norma	74930	D	1937
WANZER				George Morton	88047	D	1941	Patrick	22850	D	1917
Lucy Maria Field	56825	I	1930	George Ryland	23879	D	1918	Patrick J.	67946	D	1934
Lucy Maria Field	56977	D	1930	George Ryland	55838	M	1930	Patrick J.	70059	D	1935
WAR				Harriett B.	77163	D	1937	Reuel Sylvester	13566	M	1912
Adaline	4507	D	1907	Harry J.	27623	M	1919	Robert	33955	D	1922
WARA				Herbert Merritt	45731	D	1926	Robert W.	21808	D	1916
Edna May	77687	I	1938	I. F., Mrs.	57895	I	1931	Rosa	30633	D	1920
William	85965	D	1941	James	55548	D	1930	Rosine Thavonat	13017	I	1912
WARBURTON				James Creighton	57876	D	1931	Saida	79349	I	1938
Jeremiah	78901	D	1938	James Francis	85845	D	1940	Saida	84354	D	1940
WARBY				James H.	52582	D	1929	Sarah	82496	D	1939
Frank	62957	D	1932	James J.	5536	D	1908	Thomas	12271	D	1911
WARD				James J.	86948	D	1941	Thomas	54410	D	1929
Ada C. Friend	26040	D	1919	James W.	81771	D	1939	Thomas G.	54404	D	1929
				Jean	13643	M	1912	Thomas G.	58612	D	1931
				Jessie Matheson	80781	D	1939	Thomas Gratton	29132	M	1920
				John	17581	D	1914	Thomas P.	2137	D	1906

NAME	NUMBER	TYPE	YEAR
Thomas S.	54288	D	1929
Wilfrid Kay	19692	I	1915
William	27043	D	1919
William H.	1838	D	1906
William J.	43197	D	1925
William R.	85100	D	1940
WARDEN			
Albin	83226	D	1940
Carlos	1637	D	1906
Clinton E.	39622	D	1924
Frank	5540	D	1908
William J.	74244	D	1936
WARDLAW			
James Joseph	70618	D	1935
Robert	31010	I	1921
WARDMAN			
Delia	28312	D	1919
Elizabeth	67733	D	1934
George Francis	40598	D	1924
Hazel	49377	D	1928
Peter	9692	D	1910
WARDWELL			
Anna Oaks	76614	D	1937
Franklin Robert	76784	M	1937
Josephine A.	22418	D	1917
Louise Watts	1215	D	1906
WARE			
Adina Gertrude	60186	I	1931
Adina Gertrude	61406	D	1932
Artemus L.	48307	D	1927
Danwel Houston	59333	M	1931
E. F.	25190	D	1918
Everett	60246	M	1931
Frank E.	15254	D	1913
Howell Horne	86684	D	1941
John H.	4646	D	1907
Lillian G.	68507	D	1934
Mary C.	87368	D	1941
Samuel	60246	M	1931
William H.	45250	D	1926
William H., Jr.	87970	I	1941
WARFIELD			
Henry	87245	D	1941
Luta E.	9063	D	1910
Righard Henry	1098	D	1906
WARFORD			
Geraldine C.	32709	M	1921

NAME	NUMBER	TYPE	YEAR
WARING			
Clarence A.	25583	D	1918
Marjorie	58814	D	1931
WARLNOUGH			
Mary Ann	42368	D	1925
WARMAN			
Robert A.	85319	D	1940
WARMBOLD			
Augustus Henry	52871	D	1929
Bernhard F.	68927	D	1935
WARMBRUN			
Alexander	1723	D	1906
WARMHOLZ			
Chas.	14769	D	1913
WARMING			
Martin L.	3075	D	1907
WARMOTH			
Emma B.	77699	I	1938
WARNCKE			
Franicsca	35362	M	1922
WARNE			
Fred L.	49428	D	1928
May Thorpe	71058	I	1935
WARNECKE			
August Henry	9140	D	1910
Charles Henry	50900	D	1928
Edward J.	40962	D	1925
Henry	50900	D	1928
Henry, Jr.	20756	D	1916
WARNEKE			
Christian	4188	D	1907
Christy	80609	D	1939
WARNER			
Alexander	27223	D	1919
Alfred	59733	D	1931
Armand Camille	83696	D	1940
Caroline L.	23341	D	1917
Carrie	23341	D	1917
Catherine	60442	D	1931
Charles A.	10061	D	1910
Charles Edward	87542	D	1941
Charles H.	41107	D	1925
Edwin Romaine	27818	D	1919
Foronda Bestor	54190	D	1929
Frank	19350	D	1915
Hazel	53562	D	1929
Hazile L.	53562	D	1929

NAME	NUMBER	TYPE	YEAR
Honora	35782	D	1923
John	9985	D	1910
Joseph H.	41612	I	1925
Joseph H.	41971	D	1925
Joseph H.	41971	D	1925
Julie Ny	79073	I	1938
Julie Ny	79424	D	1938
Lorraine Elizabeth	72968	M	1936
Lucie D.	46384	D	1927
Margaret	73485	D	1936
Minnie Bell	81048	D	1939
Murray	30731	D	1920
Nellie	88183	D	1941
Peter A.	61956	D	1932
Ray L.	70193	I	1935
William J. B.	60511	D	1931
William James	69050	D	1935
WARNES			
Margaret Pleasance	73485	D	1936
Pleasance	73485	D	1936
WARNHOLZ			
Henry	65302	D	1933
WARNIE			
Margaret	73485	D	1936
WARNKE			
Ferdinand H. M.	61116	D	1932
Fred M.	61116	D	1932
Frederick William	79151	D	1938
WARNKEE			
Christine	41792	D	1925
Christine	41792	D	1925
WARNOCK			
Flora S.	80588	D	1939
James	11327	D	1911
James	29058	D	1920
Mary	3871	D	1907
Philip Armstrong	55528	D	1930
WARNYGORA			
Edward	82735	M	1939
Mary	82930	D	1939
Walter	82736	M	1939
WARRELL			
Mae K.	39243	D	1924
WARREN			
Albert T.	161	D	1906
Anna C.	73133	I	1936
Arthur	12563	D	1911

NAME	NUMBER	TYPE	YEAR	NAME	NUMBER	TYPE	YEAR	NAME	NUMBER	TYPE	YEAR
Bell G.	41569	D	1925	**WARSHFSKY**				N. A.	19298	D	1915
Bernie	27691	M	1919	Joseph	39966	D	1924	Olive Maria	19082	D	1915
Bessie	15510	D	1913	**WARSHOFSKY**				Olive Marie	15107	I	1913
Charles C.	25889	D	1918	Joseph	39966	D	1924	**WASHINGTON**			
Charles M.	89331	I	1942	**WARSZAWSKI**				Alexander	63264	D	1932
Charlotte M.	637	D	1906	Raychel	11421	D	1911	John Thorton	52355	D	1929
Christina J.	57777	D	1931	Raychel	12510	D	1911	Matilda	11838	D	1911
Estelle S.	57845	M	1931	**WARTBURG**				**WASHY**			
Francis Wreden	56345	M	1930	August	72492	D	1936	C. A., Mrs.	54890	D	1930
Frank E.	24110	D	1918	Elmer E.	72684	M	1936	**WASILLEFF**			
Frank E.	88643	D	1941	**WARTENBERG**				Gregory	66300	D	1934
Frank W.	54615	D	1929	Henry M.	77964	D	1938	**WASKY**			
Frederick	29899	D	1920	**WARTENSLEBEN**				Mary	82976	D	1939
Helen	27691	M	1919	David	20975	D	1916	**WASON**			
Henry B.	61124	M	1932	**WARTENWEILER**				Edward P.	39101	D	1924
Jane C.	33625	D	1922	Aelia	51797	D	1929	**WASS**			
Jessie	18077	D	1914	Alfred	15625	D	1913	Isabella	71056	D	1935
Joel Frank	17235	M	1914	**WARWICK**				**WASSEL**			
Lizzie	3290	M	1907	Rosana	36963	D	1923	Josephine	43815	D	1926
Margaret	3290	M	1907	Thomas D.	19279	I	1915	**WASSERLEBEN**			
Margaret Ellen	88159	D	1941	Thomas David	36526	D	1923	Carl F.	64881	D	1933
Martha J.	4948	D	1907	**WARY**				**WASSERMAN**			
Mary	82930	D	1939	Emily	36717	D	1923	Edwin Adams	23103	D	1917
Mary A.	73669	D	1936	**WASCERWITZ**				Genevieve	17163	D	1914
Mary J.	25069	D	1918	Mae B.	51568	D	1928	Joseph Moses	41100	I	1925
Mary L.	10498	D	1910	Morris H.	32763	D	1921	Silla	39551	D	1924
Michael	86586	D	1941	**WASCHLE**				Solomon	3272	D	1907
Nellie	88212	D	1941	Gottfried	10167	D	1910	Solomon	50426	D	1928
Oscar	15278	D	1913	**WASER**				Sophia Frances	61480	D	1932
Robert L.	15083	M	1913	Michael	76001	D	1937	Victor Hugo	17006	D	1914
Roberta R.	85234	D	1940	**WASERMAN**				**WASSERMANN**			
Rose I.	77087	D	1937	Cila	39551	D	1924	Ludwig	88888	D	1942
Thomas	3289	M	1907	**WASH**				**WASSILKO**			
Thomas M.	53912	D	1929	Gertrude	14198	D	1912	Stefan	43932	D	1926
Wilhelmina A.	78676	D	1938	**WASHAUER**				**WASSMER**			
William Baker	47989	D	1927	Harry	41117	D	1925	Nicholas	27666	D	1919
William Dressler	23451	M	1917	Jacob	41116	D	1925	**WATANABE**			
William True	87901	D	1941	**WASHBURN**				Gisaku	43032	I	1925
Winnie	78676	D	1938	Alice M.	54186	D	1929	Gisaku	43279	D	1925
WARRENDER				Charles H.	49665	D	1928	**WATERBURY**			
Robert	78741	D	1938	George Benjamin	62598	D	1932	Charlotte	73360	D	1936
WARRINGTON				Gertrude E.	64394	D	1933	Elizabeth Seymour	32311	D	1921
Joseph	190	D	1906	Josiah Harrison	81919	D	1939	Mary E.	55169	D	1930
Samuel W.	69657	D	1935	Leonard	10575	D	1910	Maud M.	11233	D	1911
WARSHAWSKY				Lettie C.	40723	D	1925	Murl Clifford	81552	D	1939
Minnie	59195	D	1931	Martin L.	11589	D	1911				
Philip	42242	D	1925								

Key: D = death; M = minor; I = incompetent

NAME	NUMBER	TYPE	YEAR
WATERHOUSE			
Clarence Perry	57507	D	1930
Edson Peter	28728	M	1920
Edson Willey Alden	26534	D	1919
Elliott J.	40439	I	1924
Gladys Amelia	28728	M	1920
Henry	57480	D	1930
J. Elliott	40439	I	1924
Katherine	6800	D	1908
WATERMAN			
Alice B.	64576	M	1933
Amy Schussler	69702	D	1935
Anna	19614	D	1915
Anna E.	83616	D	1940
Earl E.	801	D	1906
Emil M.	29627	D	1920
Evelyn K.	76975	D	1937
Ferdinand	25732	D	1918
George	30488	D	1920
Glen S.	64576	M	1933
Helene F.	38423	M	1924
Herman	29696	D	1920
Jesse H.	79198	D	1938
Jesse S.	38423	M	1924
Lawrence J.	47138	D	1927
WATERS			
Amy	45484	D	1926
Ann Cecelia	85619	D	1940
Annie Helen	12855	D	1912
Billie	32761	M	1921
Catherine	24135	D	1918
Eugenia Mercedes	32761	M	1921
Florence B.	40812	D	1925
George	63882	I	1933
George	80793	D	1939
James F.	87072	D	1941
Jane Young	64879	D	1933
John Charles	42823	I	1925
Joseph	35700	D	1923
Kate	18291	D	1914
Mary E.	88179	D	1941
Richard	4564	D	1907
Richard James	57576	D	1931
Rose Teresa	55457	D	1930
Sarah A.	70238	D	1935
Soloman	28731	D	1920
Thomas	15555	D	1913
William	30471	D	1920

NAME	NUMBER	TYPE	YEAR
William	39708	D	1924
William Francis	71996	D	1936
William W.	45952	D	1926
WATHEN			
Florence Anna	84527	D	1940
Joseph Theodore	36158	D	1923
WATKIND			
Clarence J.	4384	M	1907
WATKINS			
Alice Mary	77750	D	1938
Anita B.	67751	D	1934
Arthur	35224	D	1922
Ernest L.	63060	D	1932
Frank H.	23214	D	1917
Fred	76414	I	1937
Ida	23213	I	1917
James Thomas	66432	D	1934
John W.	4705	M	1907
Lottie J.	30398	D	1920
Matison A.	46543	D	1927
Rose	81235	D	1939
Vine A.	3892	D	1907
WATKINSON			
Henrietta Pierce	30075	D	1920
WATLEAU			
Joseph Marie	15707	D	1913
WATROUS			
Charles L.	31553	D	1921
Frank H.	30627	I	1920
WATSON			
Ada R.	69795	I	1935
Ada Rhoda	73892	D	1936
Albert J.	40367	D	1924
Ambrose A.	46724	D	1927
Ann	78044	D	1938
Annie Mann	82259	D	1939
Arthur B.	47843	D	1927
Ben C.	31574	D	1921
Benjamin F.	61178	D	1932
Charles	31953	D	1921
Charles R.	45161	D	1926
Charles W.	11833	D	1911
Charlotte	73811	D	1936
Daniel M.	32406	D	1921
Dr.	49601	D	1928
Ed	45160	D	1926
Ed.	47752	I	1927
Edward	47999	D	1927

NAME	NUMBER	TYPE	YEAR
Elizabeth C.	76136	I	1937
Elizabeth C.	78453	D	1938
Ella V.	84826	I	1940
Ella V.	88592	D	1941
Emma Claudine	39998	D	1924
Emma L.	41272	D	1925
Fannie	31321	D	1921
Frances	4300	D	1907
Frank E.	50882	D	1928
Frank G.	77521	D	1938
George T.	89874	D	1942
Henry	1373	D	1906
Irwin S.	45889	D	1926
Jack	68340	D	1934
James Andrew	72733	D	1936
James J.	39736	D	1924
James R.	16674	I	1914
James R.	16910	D	1914
James S.	50614	D	1928
Jerome W.	54296	D	1929
Johanne Marie	27986	D	1919
Joseph	39736	D	1924
Joseph A.	33681	D	1922
Joseph Oliver	18964	D	1915
Lauretta E.	76821	D	1937
Loretta May	76821	D	1937
Margaret Wickham	67102	D	1934
Martha A.	54694	D	1930
Mary	15589	D	1913
Mary	58728	D	1931
Mary A.	34999	D	1922
Mary E.	87808	I	1941
Mary G.	36502	D	1923
Mary J.	3808	D	1907
Mary Pease	66446	D	1934
Orean Wesley	56773	D	1930
Peter W.	5667	D	1908
Rennie	50826	D	1928
Robert Ellis	41006	I	1925
Rosalie	78465	I	1938
Sally	71219	D	1935
Sarah Ann	86481	D	1941
Thomas	15928	D	1913
Thomas	19889	D	1915
Thomas Douglas	57841	M	1931
W. W.	68389	I	1934
William	10888	D	1910
William C.	66186	D	1934
William W.	26921	D	1919

Key: D = death; M = minor; I = incompetent

NAME	NUMBER	TYPE	YEAR
William Walter	81222	D	1939
WATT			
Alexander	23952	D	1918
Alexander Linn Woodrow	30460	D	1920
Andrew	27651	D	1919
Arthur	28761	D	1920
Barbara	31000	D	1921
Charles Oliver	71482	I	1936
David	51784	I	1929
Despina	15870	D	1913
Elizabeth Dewey	49674	D	1928
George K.	64730	D	1933
Hattie Patterson	3493	D	1907
Jennie Tyler	13186	D	1912
Jessie	41453	I	1925
Jessie P.	43143	D	1925
Jessie S.	80580	I	1939
Jessie S.	82689	D	1939
John Stewart	56705	D	1930
Margaret H.	82718	D	1939
Nellie	17359	D	1914
Robert Frederick	73994	M	1936
Robert.	4067	D	1907
Rolla	44545	D	1926
WATTERLOT			
Louis	4922	D	1907
WATTERS			
Alexander	50645	D	1928
Alexander	50645	D	1928
Alf J.	30222	D	1920
James Arthur	39781	D	1924
WATTS			
Amelia M.	38833	M	1924
Eliza Mills	14718	D	1913
George	55644	D	1930
George W.	30200	D	1920
Ida C. F.	38015	D	1923
Jeremiah	22160	D	1917
John	55178	D	1930
Joseph	37772	D	1923
Joseph A.	65809	D	1933
Lydia J.	38833	M	1924
Margaret E.	62974	I	1932
Mary E.	17821	D	1914
Mary Frances	9559	I	1910
Mary S.	35920	D	1923
Rosamond	37788	I	1923
Ruth	85351	D	1940

NAME	NUMBER	TYPE	YEAR
Stanford E.	24802	D	1918
William	69900	D	1935
William John	41753	D	1925
William John	41753	D	1925
WATTSON			
Belle	85208	D	1940
George A.	51197	D	1928
George Amsa	87616	D	1941
Margaret	84864	D	1940
Margaret E.	28597	D	1920
Mary I.	85208	D	1940
WATTUNEN			
John H.	80885	D	1939
WAUGH			
Harry Frankword Gordon	9816	D	1910
James	78916	D	1938
Samuel J.	56786	D	1930
WAUNER			
Aurelia S.	6648	D	1908
Sophie Aurelia	6648	D	1908
WAXMAN			
Louis	71967	D	1936
Sara	50325	D	1928
WAXON			
Tony	59923	I	1931
WAXSTOCK			
Annie	81278	D	1939
Daisy Ellen	76726	D	1937
WAY			
Beatrice K.	83950	I	1940
Beatrice Kate	85947	D	1941
WAYBRANDT			
Sarah	28300	D	1919
WAYBRANT			
John A.	47303	D	1927
WAYBUR			
Julian Rehn	42760	D	1925
WAYMARK			
Thomas	42188	D	1925
WAYNE			
Mary Louise	6559	D	1908
Stanley P.	75986	D	1937
WAZPECHA			
Agnes Carlton	57589	D	1931
WEALE			
Absolom Harry	51984	D	1929

NAME	NUMBER	TYPE	YEAR
Emily	55331	D	1930
WEAN			
Charles Raymond	48302	M	1927
Raymond J.	46282	D	1927
WEAR			
Catherine Richards	55460	D	1930
John	13579	D	1912
Thomas	20672	D	1916
WEART			
John Allan	36133	I	1923
WEATHERILL			
Carrie H.	83441	D	1940
WEATHERLY			
Lewis Gatty	73945	D	1936
Louis G.	73945	D	1936
Mary Cornelia	46668	I	1927
Mary Cornelia	46756	D	1927
WEATHERS			
D. H.	75451	D	1937
David	75451	D	1937
Ella T.	89434	D	1942
WEATHERWAX			
Harry	56028	D	1930
William H. H.	56028	D	1930
WEAVER			
Ada H.	89985	D	1942
Alonzo Jason	88412	D	1941
Alton Roy	89341	D	1942
Annie A.	47705	D	1927
Benson C.	43158	D	1925
Charlie Hayes	71287	D	1935
Dwight Smith	10074	D	1910
Elizabeth A.	12079	D	1911
Ella E.	52357	D	1929
Florence M.	41534	D	1925
Frederick A.	41166	D	1925
George E.	78379	D	1938
Hammond S.	56291	D	1930
Harry	3790	D	1907
I. O.	75662	D	1937
J. M.	2082	D	1906
Nicholas	2599	D	1907
Violet	13159	D	1912
Virginia	41013	M	1925
WEBB			
Angustias Abrego	39432	D	1924
C. C.	10517	D	1910

Key: D = death; M = minor; I = incompetent

NAME	NUMBER	TYPE	YEAR
Edith P.	77213	D	1937
Eli	15565	D	1913
Ellen M.	67776	D	1934
Eloise A.	43888	D	1926
Florence F.	38135	D	1924
George H.	76599	D	1937
John A.	78091	M	1938
Joseph	18505	D	1915
Julia R.	68430	D	1934
Martha Michele	72011	D	1936
May L.	70994	D	1935
Peter	25921	D	1918
Phebe Marsh	24498	D	1918
Robert L.	36972	D	1923
Robert, Jr.	38904	M	1924
Thomas F.	67579	D	1934
William	38778	D	1924
William C.	72705	D	1936
William H.	36339	I	1923
WEBBER			
Antone	12347	D	1911
Charlotte G.	58468	D	1931
Harry William	30595	M	1920
Jane T.	68107	I	1934
L. Ross	6958	M	1908
Marie	28001	D	1919
Mary	16099	M	1913
Mary E.	11396	D	1911
Nora	4623	D	1907
Pearl C.	83624	D	1940
Sophia Jane	13693	D	1912
William	14485	D	1912
William M.	41492	D	1925
William P.	62415	D	1932
WEBER			
Adolph C.	393	D	1906
Albert	27486	D	1919
Alfred L.	75013	D	1937
Andreas	18324	D	1914
Anna Maria	1423	D	1906
Barbara	7548	D	1909
Bridget	7548	D	1909
Bruce Arthur	36996	M	1923
Carl F.	26949	D	1919
Cecelia	32204	M	1921
Christian Bernard	30901	D	1920
Edward	73521	D	1936
Emil J.	55907	D	1930
Emilie Marie Herman	68085	D	1934

NAME	NUMBER	TYPE	YEAR
Ernest	87235	D	1941
Ernest Carl	80924	D	1939
Ethel	73636	D	1936
Frances Mary	89959	I	1942
Frank	21229	D	1916
Frank W.	3697	D	1907
Fred	13438	D	1912
Frederick J. M.	66815	D	1934
George	58232	I	1931
George J.	53343	D	1929
Grace Nannette	36995	M	1923
Harry	25559	D	1918
Harry R.	53224	D	1929
Hattie O.	30630	D	1920
Henry	1599	D	1906
Henry Christian	30902	M	1920
Jacob	43991	D	1926
John D.	34097	I	1922
John D.	43673	I	1926
John Diedrich	54609	D	1929
John William	82928	D	1939
Karolina	39818	D	1924
Katie	58285	D	1931
Katie B.	89957	D	1942
Lorenz Valentin	42523	D	1925
Louise	20374	D	1916
M. Jeannette	85346	D	1940
Max	18988	D	1915
Meta	54251	D	1929
Michel	45602	D	1926
Oscar T.	20629	D	1916
Peter	43908	D	1926
Philip	76003	D	1937
Rudolph	69497	D	1935
Wilhelmina	78499	D	1938
William	18177	D	1914
William	37349	D	1923
William Henry	7634	D	1909
William M.	41492	D	1925
WEBERG			
Emma	21629	D	1916
WEBORG			
Emma	21629	D	1916
WEBSTER			
Ada Mary	73471	D	1936
Anna C.	87323	D	1941
Benjamin Franklin	4943	D	1907
Charles C.	23390	D	1917

NAME	NUMBER	TYPE	YEAR
Christine Luhrs	87793	D	1941
Claude D.	30054	I	1920
Daniel	63461	D	1933
Fanny Eliza	48065	D	1927
Gladys	88514	D	1941
Grace Hilborn	82712	D	1939
James S.	67140	D	1934
James Scott, Jr.	41605	M	1925
John W.	42949	D	1925
Kate B.	56514	D	1930
Lillias	66326	D	1934
Louis Alfred	80899	D	1939
Luella Gillespie	4724	D	1907
Mary Patricia Kirkpatrick	47591	D	1927
Mary T.	8508	D	1909
Millie H.	726	D	1906
Minnie Louise	58657	D	1931
Percy E.	65674	D	1933
Richard P.	7246	D	1909
Ruth Mae	41605	M	1925
Sarah H.	25010	D	1918
Walter B.	26857	D	1919
William	975	D	1906
William W.	48670	D	1927
WECK			
Carl Gustav	74082	D	1936
Frank Albert	58298	D	1931
Franz	49253	D	1928
WECKERLE			
Thomas Rudolph	87080	D	1941
WECKERTSHEIMER			
Frederick	9588	D	1910
WEDDLE			
Alice	36854	M	1923
WEDEKIND			
Edwin Hutter	36598	D	1923
Fred	18276	I	1914
Marcellous	62223	D	1932
Marcellus	61188	I	1932
WEDEL			
Carl	51741	D	1929
Charles	51741	D	1929
Charles John	25169	D	1918
Gustave	1117	D	1906
Maria Louisa	47430	D	1927
Petersen	8884	D	1909
Wilhelmina	8884	D	1909

Key: D = death; M = minor; I = incompetent

NAME	NUMBER	TYPE	YEAR
WEDEMEYER			
Anna M.	17769	D	1914
Frances C.	62020	D	1932
Georgie	72568	D	1936
Ida	72568	D	1936
William Andrew	2206	M	1906
WEDER			
Marie	86807	D	1941
WEDINA			
Frank	40382	D	1924
WEDLE			
Francis L.	62381	I	1932
WEDLL			
Francis L.	62381	I	1932
WEDSTED			
Christian	54973	D	1930
Laura	54974	D	1930
WEED			
Alice	12415	D	1911
Anna	46192	I	1927
Edward	23353	D	1917
Ida B.	54128	D	1929
James Merritt	35765	D	1923
Minnie G.	74020	I	1936
Minnie G.	76882	D	1937
Samuel R.	24547	D	1918
WEEDEN			
Ida S.	84670	D	1940
Jack B.	68939	I	1935
Jane L.	87067	D	1941
WEEK			
M. Lena	38758	D	1924
Martha Lena	38758	D	1924
WEEKS			
Annie F.	9392	D	1910
Beatrice W.	58855	D	1931
Blanche Tisdale	7214	D	1909
Charles E. S.	72599	D	1936
Charles Peter	49689	D	1928
Clyde	88255	D	1941
David F.	79970	D	1938
Edward	68099	D	1934
James R.	25260	D	1918
John Francis	68132	D	1934
Nellie M.	24664	D	1918
Ora Crawford	41737	D	1925
Ora Crawford	41737	D	1925

NAME	NUMBER	TYPE	YEAR
Sadie R.	88401	D	1941
Samuel	89311	D	1942
WEFELSBURG			
Alexancer B.	47219	D	1927
WEGENER			
August	18440	D	1915
Catherine	31328	D	1921
Gesine	71515	D	1936
Henry	39668	D	1924
Louisa A.	45755	D	1926
William B.	8699	D	1909
WEGER			
Robert	70556	D	1935
WEGG			
Walter George	52143	D	1929
WEGH			
Julia	52770	D	1929
WEGLEIN			
Isaac	40997	D	1925
WEGMANN			
Louise	7143	D	1909
WEGNER			
Carl	36149	D	1923
Emma Marie	60428	D	1931
Louise M.	19123	D	1915
WEGSCHEIDER			
Jean James	22317	M	1917
WEHE			
Dorothy	25625	M	1918
Gertrude	25626	D	1918
Mervyn	25625	M	1918
Mervyn	25627	D	1918
William	25625	M	1918
WEHER			
Dorothy	27344	M	1919
WEHILE			
Herman	88128	D	1941
WEHLAN			
Eva	65915	I	1933
WEHLAU			
Eva	65915	I	1933
WEHLE			
Augusta	34363	D	1922
Benedict	31453	D	1921
Isaac	200	D	1906
Johann	83941	D	1940

NAME	NUMBER	TYPE	YEAR
Martin	53881	D	1929
WEHLIN			
Arnold	81721	D	1939
WEHMEYER			
August	48950	D	1928
WEHNENBERG			
Christ	73388	D	1936
WEHR			
Dora	26004	D	1918
Henry John	23284	D	1917
WEHRENBERG			
Christ	73388	D	1936
WEHRLE			
Catherine	60323	D	1931
WEHRLEY			
Marguerite M.	20887	D	1916
Peter	20889	D	1916
WEHRLI			
Emma	35953	D	1923
Samuel	37738	D	1923
WEHSER			
Gisela	73819	D	1936
Johanna H.	37917	D	1923
WEIBERT			
John	57611	D	1931
WEICHERT			
Marie	70385	D	1935
WEICHT			
Lewis	51779	D	1929
WEIDELING			
Henry	48026	D	1927
Mary	50475	I	1928
WEIDEMANN			
Jacob	11935	D	1911
WEIDEMEIR			
Otto	9796	D	1910
WEIDEN			
Josef	31765	D	1921
WEIDENBACH			
Frederick	54865	D	1929
WEIDENHEIMER			
Charles	87204	D	1941
WEIDENREICH			
Michael	32191	D	1921
WEIDENTHAL			
Samuel H.	21506	D	1916

NAME	NUMBER	TYPE	YEAR	NAME	NUMBER	TYPE	YEAR	NAME	NUMBER	TYPE	YEAR
WEIDMAN				Leopold	5809	D	1908	Esther	70031	D	1935
George Elias	48856	D	1927	Leopold	32319	D	1921	Isadore	86139	D	1941
WEIDMANN				Martin John	18031	M	1914	Isidor G.	30386	D	1920
Jacob	11935	D	1911	Mary Elizabeth	18031	M	1914	John A.	83040	D	1940
WEIDNER				Meyer	34337	D	1922	Joseph	87806	D	1941
Carl J.	89503	D	1942	Moritz	50514	D	1928	Julia	59814	D	1931
Karl	84212	D	1940	Nettie L.	60326	D	1931	Louis	44119	D	1926
Viola Lee	76960	M	1937	Samuel	34270	D	1922	Marjorie	74333	M	1937
WEIGEL				Victor	86838	D	1941	Morris	34347	D	1922
Esther	1268	M	1906	William	34372	D	1922	Morris	43026	I	1925
John	1051	D	1906	William M.	11494	D	1911	Morris	78263	D	1938
Lillian	1268	M	1906	**WEILBYE**				Sam	45807	D	1926
Mabel	1268	M	1906	Bodel Christine	85113	D	1940	Samuel	36993	I	1923
Martha	1268	M	1906	**WEILER**				**WEINBERGER**			
Pearl	1268	M	1906	Annie	80214	D	1938	Francis	62636	M	1932
WEIGHT				F. G.	65454	D	1933	Jacques	58364	M	1931
William McM.	942	D	1906	Guy	48847	D	1927	Leah	62636	M	1932
WEIHE				John	14553	D	1912	Nathan	30290	D	1920
C. August	18319	D	1914	**WEILERSTEIN**				Ray	72086	D	1936
WEIHMANN				Rose	75537	I	1937	**WEINER**			
Catherine	9067	D	1910	**WEILHEIMER**				Chane	80966	D	1939
Charles	23356	D	1917	Fannie	82989	D	1939	Max	43404	D	1926
Elbert J.	31090	M	1921	Julius	38113	D	1924	**WEINGARTEN**			
John	31768	D	1921	**WEILL**				Milton	73018	D	1936
Joseph	26362	D	1919	Armand	19294	D	1915	**WEINHAUER**			
Margaretha	26354	D	1919	Bertha	10671	D	1910	Marie F.	41052	D	1925
WEIHS				Charles L.	11430	D	1911	Marie J.	41052	D	1925
Joseph	16380	D	1913	Hattie Bruman	77038	D	1937	**WEINIGER**			
WEIKERT				Jules	48282	D	1927	Gustav	28978	D	1920
George J.	67968	D	1934	Leopold	21766	D	1916	**WEINLANDER**			
WEIL				Raphael	30801	D	1920	Lena	20706	D	1916
A. W.	58532	D	1931	Rebecca Kaiser	39275	D	1924	Sarah	42787	D	1925
Benjamin	70088	D	1935	Sylvain	5963	M	1908	**WEINMAN**			
Bernard J.	48883	M	1928	Sylvain	6809	D	1908	Annie	48693	D	1927
Elizabeth Ann	18031	M	1914	Virginia	75885	D	1937	**WEINMANN**			
Eugene Herman	32509	D	1921	Will R.	11557	M	1911	Friedrich	88520	D	1941
Eva G.	35992	D	1923	**WEIMAN**				Robert Ruben	58417	D	1931
Fannie B.	36548	D	1923	George Fred	64962	D	1933	**WEINOEHL**			
Florence G.	62238	D	1932	**WEIMER**				Anna	4585	M	1907
Helena	11664	D	1911	Fannie	32429	D	1921	Dora	4585	M	1907
Henrietta	35997	M	1923	**WEIN**				Dora	6301	D	1908
Henry	64199	D	1933	Jack	23899	M	1918	Frederick	4585	M	1907
Ida	14319	D	1912	Josephine	50822	M	1928	Frederick W.	19504	D	1915
Isabelle	32746	M	1921	**WEINBERG**				**WEINRED**			
John Perez	18234	D	1914	Agnes	55378	D	1930	Joe	82294	D	1939
Julius Cecil	30724	D	1920	Bernhard	33139	D	1922	**WEINRIB**			
Lauretta N.	46758	D	1927	Charles	28733	D	1920	Max	82294	D	1939

Key: D = death; M = minor; I = incompetent

NAME	NUMBER	TYPE	YEAR
WEINRICH			
Emma	45545	I	1926
WEINSCHENK			
Julius	76626	D	1937
WEINSHENK			
Johanna	25245	D	1918
Rose	72832	D	1936
WEINSTEIN			
Arthur L.	57262	M	1930
Helen	14125	M	1912
Jerome	14125	M	1912
Leopold	12592	D	1911
Meredythe	57262	M	1930
Morris	17795	D	1914
Morris	57203	I	1930
Samuel	79877	D	1938
Sara	76240	I	1937
WEINSTOCK			
Anna	66236	D	1934
Charles	65124	D	1933
Harris	34891	D	1922
WEINVEB			
Max	82294	D	1939
WEINZIERE			
Joseph	79137	D	1938
WEINZIERL			
Joseph	79137	D	1938
Sofie	49331	D	1928
WEIR			
Burnell S.	37871	M	1923
Eleanor W.	29566	M	1920
F. T.	37871	M	1923
George Cavan	39177	D	1924
John	63	D	1906
John	55604	D	1930
Lulu E.	54436	D	1929
Mary	85918	D	1940
Mary	34877	D	1922
Mary	35270	D	1922
Ray	34232	I	1922
Ray	44538	I	1926
W. F. P.	37871	M	1923
William	39909	D	1924
William B.	79730	D	1938
William Boyd, Jr.	29566	M	1920
William T.	54581	D	1929
Winnifred	1903	I	1906

NAME	NUMBER	TYPE	YEAR
WEIRICH			
Gustav	18678	D	1915
WEIS			
Curt H.	89321	D	1942
Elizabeth	2484	I	1906
Elizabeth	7768	D	1909
WEISCHEDEL			
Ernest	56164	I	1930
WEISE			
Butilda	73957	D	1936
Fritz	39875	D	1924
Gustav Adolph	38442	D	1924
Margaret	1895	D	1906
WEISENBORN			
Emilie	1224	D	1906
WEISENHORN			
Franz	64114	D	1933
WEISER			
Alex	86452	D	1941
Laura	89119	D	1942
Rosalie	82103	D	1939
WEISGERBER			
Margaret J.	3794	D	1907
Maud	78826	I	1938
WEISHEIMER			
Charles	41973	D	1925
Charles	41973	D	1925
Frances	35950	D	1923
Frederick Joseph	35725	D	1923
Laura Josephine	37484	I	1923
Laura Josephine	39863	D	1924
WEISHOLZ			
Abraham	53572	D	1929
WEISMANN			
George	3701	D	1907
Marie O.	17428	D	1914
WEISS			
Agnes	49830	D	1928
Amalia	38752	D	1924
Claude G.	36715	I	1923
Daisy	30415	D	1920
Edward M.	66698	D	1934
Estella	14689	I	1913
Frank J.	26280	D	1919
Gustave	28373	D	1919
Helena Catherine	49852	M	1928
Herman	55383	D	1930

NAME	NUMBER	TYPE	YEAR
Jacob	3085	D	1907
Jacob	15392	D	1913
John	18496	D	1915
Joseph	16380	D	1913
Joseph	56891	D	1930
Lazar	22376	D	1917
Leon	57858	D	1931
Lilly	79290	D	1938
Marie	62952	D	1932
Mark	39482	D	1924
Martha Gosliner	80535	D	1939
Mathilda	62146	D	1932
Max	68127	D	1934
Moritz B.	22911	D	1917
Morris B.	22911	D	1917
Nellie	49588	M	1928
Nettie	45203	D	1926
Philip	47859	D	1927
Rebecca	15292	D	1913
Richard R.	19078	D	1915
Richard R.	22572	M	1917
Robert Aloysius	49852	M	1928
WEISSBARTH			
Louise	60550	D	1931
WEISSBAUM			
Flora	28527	D	1919
WEISSBEIN			
Joseph	19240	D	1915
WEISSENBACH			
Nicholas	22215	D	1917
WEISSER			
James	63901	I	1933
WEISSHAAR			
Carl A.	69718	D	1935
Charles A.	69718	D	1935
WEISSMAN			
P. H.	70062	D	1935
Philip	70062	D	1935
WEISSMUELLER			
Charles Frederick	67378	D	1934
WEITNAUER			
Bini	45030	D	1926
Emil	33972	D	1922
WELBY			
Catherine	30997	D	1921
WELCH			
Albert	59004	D	1931

NAME	NUMBER	TYPE	YEAR	NAME	NUMBER	TYPE	YEAR	NAME	NUMBER	TYPE	YEAR
Alice Frances	49350	D	1928	John J.	66212	D	1934	Sophie B.	37561	D	1923
Alvadore	59004	D	1931	John R.	76386	D	1937	William	18252	D	1914
Andrew	8084	D	1909	John W.	13106	D	1912	**WELFARE**			
Anna	30501	D	1920	John W.	82602	D	1939	Elmer E.	38933	D	1924
Annie	38496	D	1924	Joseph Warren	72658	D	1936	**WELFITT**			
Archibald	34525	D	1922	Julia	59012	D	1931	Mary	85927	D	1940
Benjamin	8704	D	1909	Katie	9739	D	1910	**WELIN**			
Berthe L.	33589	D	1922	Leila A.	68915	D	1935	Albert Fabian	56203	D	1930
Blanche	16290	M	1913	Leila Mann	68915	D	1935	**WELISCH**			
Bridget	4699	D	1907	Lullus	7818	D	1909	Armand L.	72873	D	1936
Catherine	33417	D	1922	Margaret	10040	D	1910	Herman	22787	D	1917
Catherine W.	55044	D	1930	Marian	36660	D	1923	**WELJHOWICH**			
Charles	58862	D	1931	Mary A.	20118	D	1915	Mim	6408	D	1908
Charles	68119	D	1934	Mary Ann	36660	D	1923	**WELKAR**			
Charles W.	10028	D	1910	Mary H.	60816	D	1932	Gladys	2153	D	1906
Cornelius	56693	D	1930	Mary Jane	71554	D	1936	**WELKE**			
Edward C.	50308	D	1928	Mary T.	51695	D	1928	Louise	3149	D	1907
Elizabeth Boobar	81046	D	1939	Masry Ann Goddard	70185	D	1935	**WELKER**			
Elizabeth H.	81046	D	1939	Merrit	16290	M	1913	Alice Burris	21671	D	1916
Ellen L.	11703	D	1911	Michael	2590	D	1907	Caroline	64581	D	1933
Elmer	34961	M	1922	Michael	9901	D	1910	Carrie K.	64581	D	1933
Francis Joseph	85565	I	1940	Michael F.	19832	D	1915	**WELKUS**			
Garrett	50683	I	1928	Michael J.	19832	D	1915	Joachin Marcus	77806	D	1938
Garrett	51132	D	1928	Richard	11057	D	1911	**WELLBURG**			
George	16290	M	1913	Roberyt Mallones	71567	D	1936	Roberta Clare	89902	M	1942
George Bergez	65002	D	1933	Russell Warren	58365	M	1931	**WELLDE**			
George E.	70280	D	1935	Sarah	27301	D	1919	Gertrude Josephine	85446	M	1940
George F.	26254	D	1919	Susan	19914	D	1915	**WELLER**			
George W.	14441	D	1912	Thomas	4996	D	1908	Barnett J.	25711	D	1918
George W.	70280	D	1935	William	69537	D	1935	Bettie McMullin	86294	D	1941
Glofira M.	87769	I	1941	William F.	30171	D	1920	Charles L., Mrs.	86294	D	1941
Grace A.	41422	D	1925	William J.	933	D	1906	Eline Elizabeth	25955	M	1918
harriet L.	21142	D	1916	**WELCHER**				John C.	65160	D	1933
Harriett Jane	15621	D	1913	Elmer	54709	M	1930	**WELLESLEY**			
Henrietta J.	57811	D	1931	**WELCOME**				Blanche E.	20800	D	1916
Henry Cyril	63217	D	1932	Mary	46441	D	1927	**WELLGE**			
Henry Howard	3335	D	1907	Richard	14927	D	1913	Henry Max	39828	D	1924
Herbert W.	50256	D	1928	**WELD**				**WELLHOUSE**			
Herman L.	44724	D	1926	Charles W.	89249	D	1942	Belle L.	87950	D	1941
Irene C.	11573	M	1911	**WELDEN**				**WELLINGTON**			
Isabella A.	39025	I	1924	Frances E.	49634	D	1928	Anna R.	19424	D	1915
Isabella A.	81835	D	1939	Ida S.	73457	D	1936	Florence M.	74429	D	1937
James	2271	D	1906	**WELDIN**				Mary F.	3456	D	1907
James	15987	D	1913	Joseph H.	37119	D	1923	Mary Winifred	55826	D	1930
James F.	55274	D	1930	**WELDON**				**WELLMAN**			
James W.	71080	D	1935	Agnes Catherine	75694	I	1937	Jule W.	75975	D	1937
John	54651	D	1930	Frances E.	49634	D	1928				
John	70137	D	1935	Harry E.	44332	I	1926				
John Edward	30334	D	1920								

NAME	NUMBER	TYPE	YEAR	NAME	NUMBER	TYPE	YEAR	NAME	NUMBER	TYPE	YEAR
Norma	53894	M	1929	**WELSCH**				**WELTER**			
WELLOR				Kathryn Clare	53325	D	1929	Josephine	55662	D	1930
Annie E.	30250	D	1920	**WELSER**				**WELTI**			
WELLS				Ivy Kate	63702	D	1933	John G.	49561	D	1928
Alice E.	26057	D	1919	Ivy L.	63702	D	1933	**WELTY**			
Arthur	18364	D	1915	**WELSH**				Lizzie E.	34865	D	1922
Arthur Francis	13444	M	1912	Alfred Henry	20971	M	1916	Rufus W.	48904	D	1928
Arthur Francis	25362	D	1918	Alice	21115	M	1916	**WELZ**			
Asa R.	937	D	1906	Alice	84787	D	1940	George	59920	D	1931
Bulkeley	59098	D	1931	Anna	30501	D	1920	George G.	59184	D	1931
Carlyle	13444	M	1912	Barbara Jean	80820	M	1939	**WEMPE**			
Charles H.	16069	D	1913	Betty June	80820	M	1939	Catherine Elizabeth	26953	M	1919
Charlotte Marie	15856	M	1913	Charles J.	45406	D	1926	Henry L.	5609	D	1908
Clayton	16022	D	1913	Daniel	21115	M	1916	Marie	32531	D	1921
Douglas	1424	D	1906	Daniel William	21730	D	1916	Marie Josephine	26953	M	1919
Edith Chittenden	11810	D	1911	Edward F.	37782	D	1923	William	72313	D	1936
Edna	54907	I	1930	Ellen	43589	D	1926	William C.	26961	D	1919
George	85561	D	1940	Emilia M.	41284	D	1925	**WEMPLE**			
George Frederick	13444	M	1912	Georgia E.	28804	M	1920	E. L.	2745	D	1907
George Griffis	34177	M	1922	Grace Mary	50461	M	1928	Kathryn L.	54962	D	1930
George R.	18846	D	1915	Howard A.	83233	D	1940	**WENBAN**			
Henry J.	24737	D	1918	Jack Horner	80820	M	1939	Caroline S.	23863	D	1918
Ida May	63484	D	1933	James	74557	D	1937	**WENCK**			
James R.	85688	D	1940	James Crawford	41448	D	1925	Paul	68758	D	1935
Jerome Balder	37466	D	1923	Johanna	5805	D	1908	**WENDE**			
jOhn Arthur	34177	M	1922	John	17109	D	1914	Anna	73258	D	1936
Joseph	12469	D	1911	John	60877	D	1932	Simon F. T.	50580	D	1928
Leathe M.	23017	I	1917	John C.	52917	D	1929	**WENDEL**			
Lizzie C.	9594	D	1910	John Felix	63795	D	1933	Georg	53253	D	1929
Louis A.	10007	D	1910	John H.	25791	D	1918	John	17257	D	1914
Louisa A.	6492	I	1908	Kate	23014	D	1917	**WENDELL**			
Marion	524	D	1906	Katie	9739	D	1910	Lulu	88772	M	1941
Mary Elinor	54955	M	1930	Marjorie E.	83373	D	1940	**WENDER**			
Matilda M.	52145	D	1929	Martin	33744	D	1922	Joseph	29686	D	1920
Mattie Abigal	14493	D	1912	Mary Anne	14838	D	1913	**WENDLE**			
Paul	2069	D	1906	Mary Cecile	74923	M	1937	Michael	12608	D	1911
Percy L.	3367	D	1907	Mattie Edith	77007	D	1937	**WENDLING**			
Refugia	19297	D	1915	Michael	35825	D	1923	George X.	40950	D	1925
Richard Vernon	15856	M	1913	Michael	63753	D	1933	Inez Amanda	70175	D	1935
Robert	3010	D	1907	Minnie	21731	D	1916	**WENDT**			
Robert Julius	80539	D	1939	P. W.	10504	D	1910	Augusta W.	56119	D	1930
Rollin	17268	D	1914	Patricia Josephine	74923	M	1937	Fritz	24279	D	1918
Rosemary	28351	M	1919	Thomas J.	28804	M	1920	**WENDTE**			
Thomsa Cooper	50627	D	1928	Thomas J., Jr.	27065	D	1919	Clifford E.	78056	D	1938
William H.	50543	I	1928	Veronica Maria	74923	M	1937	**WENE**			
William H.	64846	D	1933	William	21115	M	1916	Abraham J.	62401	I	1932
William P.	40257	D	1924	William P.	34963	D	1922				

Key: D = death; M = minor; I = incompetent

NAME	NUMBER	TYPE	YEAR
Abraham J.	65613	D	1933
WENES			
Aline Bertin	47116	D	1927
WENGER			
Bertin A.	64934	D	1933
Emma E.	49782	D	1928
Emma Mehl	49782	D	1928
Frank J.	51646	D	1928
Gladys	62649	M	1932
Leland	62649	M	1932
Phillip	62684	D	1932
WENIGER			
Peter John	6027	D	1908
WENISCH			
William Henry	86857	D	1941
WENISTEIN			
William	64331	D	1933
WENK			
Mary May	28177	D	1919
WENMAN			
Byrd Wilson, Jr.	22588	M	1917
WENNER			
George W.	32703	D	1921
WENNERBLAD			
Axelina E.	70647	D	1935
Einar G.	64996	D	1933
WENNERLUND			
Victor Vitales	35416	D	1922
WENSCHEL			
Theodore	63979	D	1933
WENSTEFELD			
George	36075	D	1923
WENTWORTH			
Ernest N.	2973	D	1907
George K.	21961	D	1916
J. P. H.	23907	D	1918
Maria M.	31592	D	1921
Myra A.	85599	D	1940
WENTZ			
Henry	45450	D	1926
Winfield Scott	37325	D	1923
WENTZEL			
Ernest	63793	I	1933
John	7562	D	1909
Sadie	60400	D	1931

NAME	NUMBER	TYPE	YEAR
WENZ			
Rosina K.	78783	I	1938
WENZEL			
Emilie	44413	D	1926
Emilie M.	45984	D	1926
G. G. A.	11995	D	1911
George Leonhard	427	D	1906
Katherina	45134	D	1926
Lucie	79593	D	1938
Mary	35116	D	1922
Olga	17360	D	1914
Paul	82036	D	1939
Robert G.	38798	M	1924
WENZELL			
William Theodore	15912	D	1913
WEPPENER			
Adelheid Sophie	45100	D	1926
Sophie Adelheid	45100	D	1926
Theodore C.	64208	I	1933
WERDEN			
Helena	41241	D	1925
WERFORD			
Frank	28082	D	1919
WERLIN			
Annie A.	58966	D	1931
George W.	16192	D	1913
WERLING			
Peter	15941	I	1913
WERMOUTH			
Carrie	51540	D	1928
WERNE			
Herman	58758	D	1931
Regina	27090	M	1919
WERNER			
Alva	30645	M	1920
Carl O. E.	52242	D	1929
Charles A.	69202	D	1935
Charles E. P.	61794	D	1932
Charles M.	34051	D	1922
Christian	75310	D	1937
Christian H.	7136	D	1909
Edward N.	51939	D	1929
Edwin N.	51939	D	1929
Elmere	30645	M	1920
Elwine	8657	M	1909
Gabriel A.	51222	D	1928
George	13768	D	1912

NAME	NUMBER	TYPE	YEAR
George	47882	D	1927
George A.	27901	D	1919
Gesina	2290	D	1906
Gustave Louis E.	15704	D	1913
Hanora	10309	D	1910
Harold John	61704	D	1932
Harry S.	17680	D	1914
Louis	45742	D	1926
Mathilda	80557	D	1939
Matilda	79386	D	1938
Morton	61704	D	1932
Paul	86472	D	1941
Philip	9740	D	1910
Ray	43344	D	1926
Rhea	43344	D	1926
Richard	61704	D	1932
Robert Morton	61704	D	1932
WERNICKE			
Gladys E.	58180	D	1931
WERNSTROM			
Ernest Robert	77628	D	1938
WERRY			
Mary	54923	D	1930
WERT			
Catherine	76351	D	1937
Harriet	21543	D	1916
WERTH			
Gertrude	37948	D	1923
WERTHEIM			
Ann	81548	M	1939
Frederick Edwin	81548	M	1939
Mary K.	81798	D	1939
Morris	62959	D	1932
Nate	76907	D	1937
WERTHEIMER			
Banjamin J.	57314	D	1930
Clifford Lewis	48237	M	1927
Jacob	26426	D	1919
Kaufman	20343	D	1916
Leopold J.	39864	D	1924
Mark H.	59460	D	1931
Rachel R.	31786	D	1921
Ray	31786	D	1921
Sarah	45285	D	1926
WERTHMAN			
Claire	17038	M	1914

NAME	NUMBER	TYPE	YEAR
WERTHNER			
Louisa	41688	D	1925
WERTSCH			
Louisa	68200	D	1934
William	56810	D	1930
WERTZ			
Alice	48920	D	1928
Joseph	27777	D	1919
Kate M.	8691	D	1909
Lorraine	49390	M	1928
Margaret	49390	M	1928
Robert H.	37088	D	1923
WERY			
Pon Wing	4900	D	1907
WERZ			
Joseph Christian	69636	D	1935
WESCH			
Emil	7069	M	1909
Henry	7069	M	1909
Meta	89195	D	1942
Meta J.	6023	D	1908
WESCOTT			
Bernadayna	60336	M	1931
WESENDUNK			
Andrew A.	49185	D	1928
Arnold A.	49185	D	1928
Mary J.	40591	D	1924
WESLEY			
John	30851	D	1920
Karoline R.	47577	D	1927
Mary	67107	D	1934
WESMAN			
M. J., Mrs.	19182	D	1915
WESNER			
Severine Julia	78207	D	1938
WESSBERG			
John E.	83477	I	1940
WESSEL			
Christine M.	41891	D	1925
Christine M.	41891	D	1925
Maria Eliesabeth	62544	D	1932
WESSELHOFT			
H.	11280	D	1911
Martin H.	11280	D	1911
WESSELL			
Margaret T.	53337	D	1929

NAME	NUMBER	TYPE	YEAR
WESSELLS			
Archena T. E.	13318	M	1912
WESSELS			
Frances	70081	D	1935
WESSELY			
Joseph R.	63498	D	1933
Mary A.	63499	D	1933
WESSLING			
Augustus E.	59053	D	1931
Margaret	39540	D	1924
WESSMAN			
Emily L.	75535	D	1937
WESSON			
Edward	13718	D	1912
WEST			
Abbie R.	9741	D	1910
Annie A.	75211	D	1937
Appleton Burr	20729	D	1916
Audrey Marilyn	73057	M	1936
Beatrice	86740	D	1941
Caroline Amelia	11424	M	1911
Charles P.	64440	D	1933
Claude, Mrs.	85912	D	1940
Cora E.	85313	D	1940
David	62263	D	1932
Della M.	85912	D	1940
Eliza Lander	16415	D	1913
Ernest Hope	85125	D	1940
Eugene F.	32044	D	1921
F. W.	80352	D	1939
Frank	31607	D	1921
Frank J.	80734	D	1939
Fred	80352	D	1939
Fred A.	57801	D	1931
Grace	18168	D	1914
Hannah Jane	51059	D	1928
Harry J.	80742	D	1939
Henry	501	D	1906
Henry P. P.	42500	D	1925
Ida M.	18882	D	1915
James B.	78866	D	1938
James J.	66841	D	1934
Jeanette C.	48638	D	1927
John	12362	D	1911
John C.	57894	D	1931
John Wendell	41115	I	1925
Lucia C.	45806	D	1926
Mary Elizabeth	36277	M	1923

NAME	NUMBER	TYPE	YEAR
Mary Elizabeth	77394	D	1937
Mary J. Stevens	30707	D	1920
Petronella	68168	D	1934
Samuel G.	24680	D	1918
Samuel M.	8363	D	1909
Sarah	15119	D	1913
Thelma Claire	43808	M	1926
Thomas	53477	D	1929
Thomas Jefferson	79829	D	1938
William Allen	25414	D	1918
WESTBERG			
Salomon	19782	D	1915
WESTBY			
August	65943	D	1933
WESTCOTT			
Emma Arena Melissa	75357	D	1937
Philip Noyes	44768	D	1926
Thomas F.	75631	D	1937
WESTDAHL			
Ferdinand	28169	D	1919
Olaf Peter Ferdinand	28169	D	1919
WESTDORP			
Edgar	13682	D	1912
Edward G.	6570	D	1908
WESTELNIK			
Israel	62620	D	1932
WESTER			
Josephine R.	82248	D	1939
WESTERBERG			
Anna	61358	I	1932
Anna C.	34979	I	1922
Mathilda Elizabeth	30658	I	1920
Mathilda Elizabeth	32971	D	1921
WESTERFELD			
Carl	72694	D	1936
H. William	16259	D	1913
Herman	11445	D	1911
WESTERLAND			
Dolores Lillian	69559	M	1935
WESTERLUND			
Albert	52130	D	1929
Amanda J.	49947	D	1928
WESTERMAN			
Gloria Rodrizuez	62261	D	1932
Loth, Jr.	71799	M	1936
WESTFALL			
Janet G.	64459	D	1933

NAME	NUMBER	TYPE	YEAR	NAME	NUMBER	TYPE	YEAR	NAME	NUMBER	TYPE	YEAR
Janet Marjorie Gilchrist	64459	D	1933	**WESTPHAL**				**WETTERAU**			
Jessie Siddall	28377	D	1919	Charles	68767	D	1935	George	53218	D	1929
WESTFELDT				Claus Friederich	2387	D	1906	**WETTERQUIST**			
Gerhard	43542	D	1926	Elvira	5508	M	1908	Annie	18647	D	1915
WESTGATE				Emma	74435	D	1937	**WETTIG**			
M. Halford	54963	D	1930	Eva R.	50017	D	1928	Anna	75147	D	1937
Mark A.	54964	D	1930	Florence A.	49277	D	1928	August F.	75761	D	1937
WESTHAUS				Frederick	44147	M	1926	Ernest A.	63377	D	1933
Anna W.	33815	D	1922	Harry T.	6335	D	1908	**WETTSTEIN**			
WESTHOFF				Henry T.	6335	D	1908	Fred	21297	M	1916
Louise C.	48520	I	1927	Henry W.	43838	D	1926	**WETZ**			
Louise C.	62133	D	1932	Joseph	25252	D	1918	Margaret	46029	D	1926
WESTLAKE				Joseph L.	83782	D	1940	**WETZEL**			
Bromby S.	32552	M	1921	Lucile	44147	M	1926	Joseph	89805	D	1942
Florissa	33085	D	1921	Margaret	19815	D	1915	Louise H.	68472	D	1934
Grace M.	32552	M	1921	Margaret F.	59046	D	1931	Winifred	76304	D	1937
J. S.	32551	D	1921	Mary	78871	I	1938	**WEULE**			
May Frances	60147	D	1931	Minna	52867	D	1929	Emma	65398	D	1933
Norman Elmer	54544	D	1929	Rudolph	5508	M	1908	Louis	48668	D	1927
WESTLUND				Rudolph	59725	D	1931	Minna	79858	D	1938
Albert	52130	D	1929	Samuel W.	50170	I	1928	**WEUSTEFELD**			
Edith Dorothea Cecelia	22175	M	1917	Sanford William	62614	M	1932	George	36075	D	1923
Edwin Arne	22175	M	1917	**WESTREM**				**WEUSTER**			
Karl William Henry	22175	M	1917	John	52625	D	1929	Anna	72718	D	1936
Walfred Constantine	22175	M	1917	**WESTRING**				**WEWETZER**			
William	32706	M	1921	August	23453	D	1917	August	58671	D	1931
WESTMAN				Charles Angus	20302	D	1916	**WEXEL**			
Andrew	88254	D	1941	**WESTRUP**				Joseph	41666	D	1925
Barbara Ann	86518	M	1941	Oline	22906	D	1917	**WEY**			
Dorothy Jean	86518	M	1941	**WESTWATER**				Julius	78899	D	1938
Godfred	17229	D	1914	Eunice E.	72459	D	1936	**WEYANT**			
Lewis	44596	D	1926	**WESTWICK**				Isabelle A.	50763	D	1928
Walter Donald	64981	M	1933	Joseph Brown	49641	D	1928	**WEYBURN**			
Walter W., Jr.	64981	M	1933	**WETHERED**				Emily H. E.	87468	D	1941
WESTON				Wiliam L.	72716	D	1936	Thomas	46435	I	1927
Agnes Hunt	72908	D	1936	**WETJEN**				Thomas	47475	D	1927
Agnes N.	72908	D	1936	Cord H.	26452	D	1919	**WEYDEMANN**			
Camilla I.	56223	D	1930	Henry	15922	I	1913	Henry	7951	D	1909
Erma	56429	D	1930	Henry	28579	D	1920	**WEYER**			
George Herbert	85497	D	1940	Liese	14959	D	1913	Frank Earle	89815	M	1942
John A.	64983	D	1933	**WETMORE**				**WEYERMAN**			
Marie Antoinette	59192	M	1931	Clarence Jesse	72499	D	1936	A. E.	42328	D	1925
Virginia Nena	30768	D	1920	Mary	47839	D	1927	Elizabeth	88697	D	1941
WESTOVER				Mary A.	56530	D	1930	**WEYGANT**			
Delbert L.	82628	D	1939	Olive W.	82963	D	1939	Mary E.	5838	D	1908
John Wallace	10955	D	1910	William Brown	43929	D	1926				

NAME	NUMBER	TYPE	YEAR
WEYL			
George O.	69234	I	1935
Jonas	26587	D	1919
Louis Charles	82904	D	1939
WEYMANN			
Clyde Lester	61946	D	1932
WEYRATHER			
Nettie	37458	D	1923
Thewald Ferdinand	10315	D	1910
WHALEN			
Annie	617	D	1906
Ellen	36509	D	1923
Gilland	60861	I	1932
Horace J.	44705	D	1926
James	15200	D	1913
James H.	44705	D	1926
Joan K.	84528	M	1940
Judith Ann	84528	M	1940
Mary	15818	D	1913
Mary C. Bentley	31561	D	1921
Sarah	9917	D	1910
Thomas H.	21494	D	1916
William	41135	D	1925
William	60861	I	1932
WHALEY			
Alice Jean	81436	M	1939
Daniel C.	59082	D	1931
Earl	22091	M	1917
Elinor C.	43688	D	1926
George Phillip, Jr.	81436	M	1939
Helen Marjorie	81436	M	1939
Ida	25262	D	1918
Kathleen	53132	D	1929
Phillip	81436	M	1939
William Francis	71840	D	1936
WHALL			
Emanuel Arthur	87482	D	1941
Emmanuel Arthur	87321	I	1941
Sarah A.	88530	I	1941
WHALLEY			
Arthur Hale	29062	D	1920
WHAN			
William Weir	36144	D	1923
WHARTON			
Sophia	34456	D	1922
Sophie	34220	I	1922
Violet E.	79606	D	1938
WHATLEY			
Fanny	7707	D	1909
WHEAR			
Elizabeth	21391	I	1916
WHEARTY			
Thomas A.	2704	D	1907
WHEAT			
Kenneth M.	89509	D	1942
WHEATE			
Justus M.	64950	D	1933
WHEATLEY			
Cora	54027	D	1929
Edward Thomas	80215	D	1938
Logan W.	35899	D	1923
Lottie Elizabeth	13892	D	1912
Mildred Lesley	82879	D	1939
T. E.	80215	D	1938
William	35936	D	1923
William F., Mrs.	82879	D	1939
WHEATON			
Dora	17308	D	1914
Edward	27893	D	1919
H. B.	75271	D	1937
Ida	84203	D	1940
John Milton	42307	D	1925
Jose	54568	D	1929
Joseph	40909	I	1925
Joseph	54568	D	1929
Milton Alverd	11156	D	1911
Roxanna Libby	35141	D	1922
William Henry	72305	D	1936
WHEDELSTED			
Anna	82425	I	1939
Anna	82528	D	1939
WHEELAN			
Fairfax Henry	18855	D	1915
Peter	9269	D	1910
WHEELAND			
James	9272	D	1910
Margaret J.	4673	D	1907
Samuel	580	D	1906
WHEELER			
Adeline	2278	D	1906
Alfred A.	49999	D	1928
Alfred Potwin	43419	M	1926
Ann Rebecca Lamb	63064	D	1932
Arthur E.	24629	D	1918
Beryl Labell	79380	D	1938
Budd	30582	M	1920
Carol L.	70172	M	1935
Catherine	22848	I	1917
Catherine C.	6987	D	1908
Catherine J.	42223	I	1925
Charles Melvin	88174	I	1941
Charles Stetson	36647	D	1923
Charles Stutson	72243	D	1936
Clayton Eugene	70339	D	1935
Cordelia Charlotte	49305	D	1928
Daniel A.	1754	D	1906
Dorothy L.	87413	D	1941
Ernest S.	78446	D	1938
Florence M.	89028	D	1942
Forrest E.	61498	I	1932
Frances America	56770	D	1930
Frank Aloysius	83403	D	1940
Gertrude	976	M	1906
Harold	17362	M	1914
Harold	78182	D	1938
Harry F.	40648	D	1924
Hiram C.	38279	D	1924
Ida E.	50423	D	1928
Ira M.	11792	D	1911
J. Hugh	70275	D	1935
Jean	30582	M	1920
Jean Louise	43419	M	1926
Jennie	88361	D	1941
Judson	3024	D	1907
Julia Carolina	19136	M	1915
Lily K.	19399	D	1915
Lorenzo G.	11522	D	1911
Margaret Y.	46043	I	1926
Margaret Young	53023	D	1929
Marion P.	1755	D	1906
Mary R.	83247	I	1940
Miller H.	55135	D	1930
Olive Anne	62153	D	1932
Peter Lansing	70785	D	1935
Phillip Francis	19136	M	1915
Sara G.	21099	D	1916
William Joseph	63177	D	1932
WHEELLER			
Harriet	57691	D	1931
WHELAN			
Agnes	4282	D	1907
Agnes	7169	D	1909
Annie	21913	D	1916

Key: D = death; M = minor; I = incompetent

NAME	NUMBER	TYPE	YEAR	NAME	NUMBER	TYPE	YEAR	NAME	NUMBER	TYPE	YEAR
Catherine	7448	D	1909	**WHIPPLE**				Anna E.	19939	D	1915
Christopher	41573	D	1925	Ellen	9001	D	1910	Anna M.	66086	D	1934
Edward	82275	M	1939	Grace H.	52404	D	1929	Annie	3881	D	1907
Ellen	4930	D	1907	**WHITAKER**				Arthur	49369	M	1928
Hanora	39131	D	1924	B. June	72197	M	1936	Bertha	55306	D	1930
James A.	33098	D	1921	Buton D.	58074	D	1931	Bertha L.	71577	I	1936
John	39792	D	1924	Fannie Jane	37643	D	1923	Beryl Umitot	75081	D	1937
John A.	14167	D	1912	George E.	58697	D	1931	Bridget	4068	D	1907
John G.	38701	D	1924	J. A., Jr.	70679	D	1935	C. C.	76920	D	1937
John J.	85486	D	1940	J. Atwood	70679	D	1935	Catherine	12695	D	1911
Lena	38321	D	1924	June	72197	M	1936	Catherine	48261	I	1927
Mary	14031	D	1912	Lena T.	17080	D	1914	Catherine Helen	79114	D	1938
Mary J.	25974	D	1918	Margaret	51112	D	1928	Catherine M.	68821	D	1935
Mary J.	67753	D	1934	May	84536	D	1940	Cecil M.	81781	D	1939
Maude M.	46743	D	1927	Roscoe J.	86235	D	1941	Charels R.	81202	D	1939
Michael	13157	D	1912	Washington Stanley	17081	M	1914	Charles	72463	M	1936
Patrick	28811	D	1920	**WHITBY**				Charles Aubrey	70061	I	1935
Patrick F.	19577	D	1915	Clara	39150	D	1924	Charles E.	43119	D	1925
Patrick Henry	64192	D	1933	**WHITCHER**				Charles Gustave	1515	D	1906
Patrick M.	22433	D	1917	Mary Louisa	71530	D	1936	Charles Harold	39132	D	1924
Peter J.	38105	D	1924	**WHITCOMB**				Charles T.	67917	D	1934
Susan	33443	D	1922	A. C.	50794	D	1928	Daniel J.	84509	D	1940
Thomas	29690	D	1920	Adolphe	19046	D	1915	Dave, Mrs.	28565	I	1920
WHELDEN				Alonzo	12669	D	1911	Dave, Mrs.	34083	D	1922
Alexander Whelden	16327	D	1913	Bonner	62447	D	1932	David A.	30732	D	1920
Edward F.	78889	D	1938	Elbridge	15156	D	1913	Delia M.	1023	D	1906
WHELIHAN				Elbridge	35632	D	1922	Donald L.	81866	D	1939
John H.	4178	D	1907	Emeline M. North	30668	D	1920	Douglas	36101	D	1923
WHELIN				George F.	11342	D	1911	Edie L.	82779	D	1939
Annie Elizabeth	62218	D	1932	Harry	36528	I	1923	Edna B.	8929	D	1909
WHELTON				Harry S.	42989	I	1925	Edwin D., Jr.	66746	D	1934
Honora	17195	D	1914	Lelia A.	40337	D	1924	Eleanor Lee	77171	L	1937
Michael J.	45082	D	1926	Louis Sawyer	12404	D	1911	Electa L.	14176	D	1912
WHETSTON				Louise Adolphine France	19367	M	1915	Eliza	8977	D	1910
Vernon Glenn	59701	D	1931	Lydia Louise Ida	16300	M	1913	Eliza	26008	D	1918
WHETTON				Sybell H.	12668	D	1911	Elizabeth	6785	D	1908
Honora	6087	I	1908	**WHITE**				Elizabeth Edson	24820	M	1918
WHICHER				A. L.	12718	D	1911	Ellen	64377	D	1933
Isabelle C.	17506	D	1914	Adeline F.	25553	D	1918	Ellen M.	75696	D	1937
John	86810	D	1941	Adeline V.	22935	I	1917	Emma	27739	D	1919
WHILDIN				Adeline V.	25553	D	1918	Ethel	60658	I	1932
David	71592	D	1936	Al	80308	D	1939	Frances C.	22939	D	1917
WHIMS				Alice	51039	M	1928	Frances J.	28253	D	1919
Hiram	51928	D	1929	Allen	72463	M	1936	Frances T.	81087	D	1939
Walter Hiram	51928	D	1929	Amelia	28565	I	1920	Francis I.	24258	D	1918
WHIPPEY				Amelia	34083	D	1922	Francis Timothy	8834	D	1909
George Frederic	5520	D	1908	Amy A.	59574	D	1931	Frank	19156	D	1915
				Ann	1623	I	1906	Frank	25541	D	1918
								Frank	27873	D	1919

NAME	NUMBER	TYPE	YEAR	NAME	NUMBER	TYPE	YEAR	NAME	NUMBER	TYPE	YEAR
Frank	65340	D	1933	John J.	75474	D	1937	Raymond Monroe	86600	D	1941
Frank Irvin	23012	D	1917	John Roseboom	67322	D	1934	Rebecca Agnes	85079	D	1940
Frank Irwin	23012	D	1917	John W.	53295	D	1929	Richard M.	493	D	1906
Frank M.	4087	D	1907	John Worden	46538	D	1927	Robert	1447	D	1906
Frederick	85672	D	1940	Joseph T.	14673	D	1913	Robert	28478	D	1919
Genevieve	53294	D	1929	Julia Anna	8175	D	1909	Robert D.	86181	D	1941
George	17909	D	1914	Lambert W.	51090	D	1928	Robert H.	8583	D	1909
George	57744	D	1931	Laura Lyon	20396	D	1916	Robert John	30092	D	1920
George G.	44347	D	1926	Lawrence	15100	M	1913	Robert Keane	72664	D	1936
George J.	15622	D	1913	Lillian B.	69617	D	1935	Rollin W.	29706	D	1920
George M.	32053	D	1921	Lillie N.	46136	D	1927	Rose	66091	D	1934
George W.	64124	D	1933	Lorenzo Abbott	88373	D	1941	Ruth	20348	D	1916
George William	67330	D	1934	Lorranine Margaret	57586	M	1931	Ruth L.	6178	M	1908
Georgia Annie	10386	D	1910	Lovell	9172	D	1910	S. A., Mrs.	77171	D	1937
Georgina Frances	57586	M	1931	Lulu A.	58842	I	1931	Sadie A.	74524	D	1937
Hallie E.	61351	D	1932	Margaret	54899	D	1930	Sally Ann	82776	M	1939
Harold F.	27788	I	1919	Maria Y.	6178	M	1908	Sam	47781	D	1927
Harriet	81731	D	1939	Marjorie	47177	M	1927	Samuel Allen	76647	D	1937
Harriet Burt	4175	D	1907	Mary	5704	D	1908	Samuel Shreve	74947	M	1937
Harry J.	67055	D	1934	Mary	25142	D	1918	Sarah F.	65567	D	1933
Helen	79114	D	1938	Mary	68141	D	1934	Scott Cedric, Jr.	75765	D	1937
Helen F.	77854	D	1938	Mary A.	218	I	1906	Selina Levy	80864	D	1939
Henry	33066	D	1921	Mary A.	27421	D	1919	Stela	58676	D	1931
Henry Austin	81218	D	1939	Mary Ann	4553	D	1907	Stella	58367	D	1931
Horace Granville	2618	D	1907	Mary Berg	64735	D	1933	Thomas	66984	D	1934
India W.	65810	D	1933	Mary E.	22134	D	1917	Thomas Joseph	57949	I	1931
Irene Tina	78795	I	1938	Mary E.	25687	D	1918	Thomas Joseph	68196	D	1934
Irene Tina	78878	D	1938	Mary F.	45130	D	1926	Timothy	11787	D	1911
Isabelle Kathryn	78881	I	1938	Mary Jane	17237	D	1914	W. J. H.	6158	D	1908
James	22115	D	1917	Mary Jane Clair	54500	D	1929	W. W.	13347	D	1912
James	72808	D	1936	Mary Jane Clare	35066	M	1922	Walter	68142	D	1934
James Clarence	3423	D	1907	Mary Margaret	45270	M	1926	Warren Joseph	53465	M	1929
James F.	15812	I	1913	Matilda Louise	83918	D	1940	Warren W.	85132	I	1940
James F.	18415	D	1915	May A.	63805	D	1933	Wiliam P.	67234	I	1934
James J.	28634	D	1920	Michae Cecil	81781	D	1939	William	22941	D	1917
James P.	35451	D	1922	Milton	79162	D	1938	William	32109	D	1921
James Raymond	44074	M	1926	Minnie	72463	M	1936	William	83417	D	1940
James T.	35063	D	1922	Morris S.	52894	D	1929	William A.	49353	D	1928
James W.	65105	D	1933	Nellie Stevens	73484	D	1936	William H.	23909	D	1918
Jane	35066	M	1922	Norma A.	75773	D	1937	William Lee	82473	D	1939
Jane Clair	54500	D	1929	Orin Elmer	13508	D	1912	William Raymond	23083	M	1917
Jane Graham	12804	D	1912	Patrick	41246	D	1925	Winifred E.	21634	D	1916
Jean Lytton	49667	M	1928	Patrick	41889	D	1925	**WHITED**			
Joan Claire	75440	M	1937	Patrick	41889	D	1925	Jean S.	58222	D	1931
John	65849	D	1933	Patrick A.	82885	D	1939	Jerry H.	15995	D	1913
John	88609	D	1941	Patrick G.	84307	D	1940	Mary Elizabeth	85598	D	1940
John	35533	D	1922	Patrick J.	11270	D	1911	Sarah J.	58222	D	1931
John D.	57726	D	1931	Paul	71630	D	1936	**WHITEFORD**			
John Henry	88794	D	1941	Peter	67005	D	1934	Hugh	89631	D	1942

NAME	NUMBER	TYPE	YEAR
WHITEHEAD			
Adelaide M.	41953	D	1925
Adelaide M.	41953	D	1925
Charles	53411	D	1929
Daniel	6854	M	1908
Daniel	61953	I	1932
Frances S.	69629	D	1935
Helen	6854	M	1908
James	57108	D	1930
Margery	20867	M	1916
WHITEHILL			
William	44255	D	1926
WHITELEY			
Frank A.	70830	I	1935
WHITELL			
Anna L.	59292	I	1931
WHITELY			
Ellen M.	31161	D	1921
James	8562	D	1909
WHITEMAN			
James	5998	D	1908
William Field	73093	D	1936
WHITENER			
William Riordan	61990	M	1932
WHITESIDE			
Harry H.	76313	D	1937
James Huggins	22370	D	1917
John A.	8424	D	1909
Josephine Frances	89129	D	1942
Mary E.	37079	D	1923
Robert B.	60900	D	1932
William L.	25153	D	1918
WHITESIDES			
Robert B.	60900	D	1932
WHITFIELD			
E. W.	34369	D	1922
George Frederick	34369	D	1922
Henry	81462	D	1939
WHITFORD			
Harry C.	9179	M	1910
Lena Irene	9179	M	1910
WHITGOB			
J.	39348	D	1924
John	37113	D	1923
WHITING			
Caroline M.	1145	I	1906
Caroline M.	1388	D	1906

NAME	NUMBER	TYPE	YEAR
Charles F.	58867	D	1931
Eva H.	19055	D	1915
Fernando T.	13924	D	1912
Henry C.	2907	D	1907
Margaret Pollock	62714	D	1932
Nora	28111	D	1919
Robert E.	58867	D	1931
Susan H.	51120	D	1928
WHITLEIS			
Ethel M.	73978	I	1936
WHITLEY			
Harry T.	64361	D	1933
Jeanette M.	59525	D	1931
William P.	46665	D	1927
WHITLOCK			
Edgar	33818	D	1922
Mary Frances	79037	M	1938
WHITLOW			
Edith C.	41322	D	1925
Theodore I.	41128	D	1925
WHITMAN			
Albert	23522	D	1917
Elizabeth	20655	D	1916
K. Miriam	43007	M	1925
Laura Margaret	24377	M	1918
Michael	8339	D	1909
Patricia A.	43007	M	1925
Phebe Beeson	37231	D	1923
W. F.	2039	D	1906
WHITMER			
Cora May Stevens	89801	D	1942
WHITMIRE			
Jacob R.	89373	D	1942
WHITMORE			
Creighton P.	49507	I	1928
Edna M.	60489	I	1931
Fannie Grover	13864	D	1912
Hirschel Ona	2873	M	1907
Margaret	36217	D	1923
Martin V.	16855	D	1914
Mary Edna	45850	I	1926
Sarah	2662	D	1907
William Davie	37638	M	1923
WHITNEY			
Charles C.	35735	D	1923
Clara Josephine	49721	D	1928
Dora C.	4672	I	1907

NAME	NUMBER	TYPE	YEAR
Edwin W.	63503	I	1933
Elbert E.	31490	D	1921
F. L., Mrs.	49721	D	1928
Frances W.	70180	M	1935
Francis L.	14354	D	1912
Harriet Angel	60392	M	1931
J. J., Mrs.	14472	D	1912
James	2567	D	1906
James G.	70180	M	1935
James Lyman	69278	D	1935
James Palache	53418	D	1929
James, Jr.	15552	D	1913
Joel Parker	15074	D	1913
John B.	11846	D	1911
John Parker	37564	M	1923
John Vernon	36782	M	1923
Julia	7201	D	1909
Louis Parker	18143	M	1914
Lucy	71705	D	1936
Lucy Ann	44522	D	1926
Maria	14472	D	1912
Narisse	78194	D	1938
Narisse Crittenden	15731	I	1913
Narrissa C.	3891	D	1907
Patrick	21083	D	1916
Pearl Landers	73928	D	1936
Peter D.	70180	M	1935
Thomas Carpenter	37564	M	1923
Thomas H.	7258	D	1909
Vincent Parrott	18143	M	1914
WHITSEL			
Minnie E.	59284	D	1931
WHITSETT			
Frank	10760	D	1910
Nancy E. Canty	22648	D	1917
WHITSON			
John Witherspoon, Jr.	69662	M	1935
WHITTAKER			
J. E., Mrs.	84536	D	1940
John	37042	D	1923
May	84536	D	1940
William	30012	D	1920
WHITTELL			
Alexander P.	77580	D	1938
Anna L.	60023	D	1931
George	33833	D	1922
WHITTEMORE			
Hazel M.	75115	D	1937

Name	Number	Type	Year	Name	Number	Type	Year	Name	Number	Type	Year
Henry Clay	24875	D	1918	**WHORISKEY**				**WICKE**			
Louise	85691	I	1940	Mary B.	4344	D	1907	Carl Edward	85739	D	1940
Marion	12288	M	1911	**WHYRE**				Ernst August Richard	9969	D	1910
WHITTEN				Hilda	12140	M	1911	Meta	1177	D	1906
Carlton Francis	41764	D	1925	Irene	12140	M	1911	**WICKENHOEFER**			
Carlton Francis	41764	D	1925	Selma	12140	M	1911	Clara F.	80563	D	1939
James	21486	D	1916	**WHYTE**				Harry	80702	D	1939
Marietta	25670	D	1918	Edward Harris	68429	D	1934	Jacob	69879	D	1935
WHITTIER				Freda M.	88249	D	1941	**WICKER**			
Alicia Gloria	49290	M	1928	James A.	15934	D	1913	Herman E.	16169	I	1913
Carrie H.	61382	D	1932	John P.	1980	D	1906	Herman E.	20510	D	1916
Charles P.	59162	D	1931	Luella E.	70737	I	1935	**WICKERSHAM**			
Emma Frances	14745	D	1913	Luella E.	74120	D	1936	Annie E.	1440	D	1906
Gloria	49290	M	1928	Malcolm C.	27509	D	1919	Frederick Augustus	11060	M	1911
Vernon S.	53765	I	1929	Mary Jane	36106	D	1923	Mary Brooke	66603	M	1934
W. Frank	22226	D	1917	**WIANDER**				William Henry	39251	D	1924
William F.	22226	D	1917	Emil	62124	D	1932	**WICKERT**			
William F.	61021	I	1932	**WIATROWSKI**				August George	202	D	1906
William F.	61120	M	1932	Carl	83960	D	1940	Emilie M.	57640	D	1931
William F.	61215	D	1932	Charles A.	83960	D	1940	Heinrich	65355	D	1933
William R.	31342	D	1921	Karol Charles	83960	D	1940	Henry	65355	D	1933
WHITTLE				**WIBERG**				Rose	77427	D	1938
A. M.	76748	I	1937	A. E. E.	71510	D	1936	**WICKES**			
Annie	20735	D	1916	Axel E.	71510	D	1936	Ethel May	83557	D	1940
Frances Mary	63268	D	1933	**WICHMAN**				George W.	38257	D	1924
James V.	15726	D	1913	Hermann	66554	I	1934	Kate Harvey	39041	D	1924
Mary A.	20735	D	1916	Ida B.	80965	D	1939	**WICKET**			
WHITTOCK				**WICHMANN**				Frederick	76507	D	1937
Charlotte	23372	D	1917	Carl	25283	D	1918	**WICKHAM**			
William Henry	21127	D	1916	Charles	25283	D	1918	Ella W.	74497	I	1937
WHITTY				Elizabeth A.	14795	D	1913	Ella W.	75036	D	1937
James	77790	D	1938	Hermann	67087	D	1934	John	42507	D	1925
WHITWELL				Katherine	60120	D	1931	**WICKLUND**			
William S.	376	D	1906	Paul	48101	D	1927	Adelia	6458	M	1908
WHO				**WICHROWSKI**				Eric	61128	I	1932
Yee Sok	42498	D	1925	Raymond A.	5904	M	1908	Nees W.	6458	M	1908
WHOLEY				Thaddeus	29584	I	1920	Sanford	6458	M	1908
John Carlos	38033	D	1924	Thaddeus	51566	D	1928	Sydney	6458	M	1908
WHOLLEY				**WICK**				Verner	6458	M	1908
Agnes	74498	D	1937	Anton	79793	D	1938	Walter	6458	M	1908
WHOLTMANN				Henriette Abadie	62366	D	1932	**WICKMAN**			
Oscar William	59429	D	1931	John N.	42721	D	1925	Carl Ove	54853	D	1930
WHORFF				Knute Andreas	87423	D	1941	Constantine	7718	D	1909
Albert D., Mrs.	20592	D	1916	Mary A.	10266	D	1910	Emily A.	10698	D	1910
Matilda	20592	D	1916	**WICKBOM**				Henrietta Dutton	60557	D	1931
William Ryder	61799	D	1932	Rose E.	89917	D	1942	James Frederick	9927	D	1910

NAME	NUMBER	TYPE	YEAR
WICKS			
Edith Hope	78462	D	1938
May E.	55725	D	1930
Minnie	78518	D	1938
Oscar	72782	D	1936
Theodore	24156	D	1918
WICKSTEED			
Pauline	84017	I	1940
Pauline	85051	D	1940
WICKSTROM			
William	63755	D	1933
WICKWARE			
George C.	5774	D	1908
WICOX			
Julia J.	73082	D	1936
WIDBER			
Eugenie	82596	D	1939
WIDDECKE			
Henry	7920	D	1909
WIDDER			
Margaret	48338	D	1927
Meta	48338	D	1927
WIDDOP			
James	16745	D	1914
WIDEGGER			
Anthony	75697	D	1937
Anton	75697	D	1937
Josef	78260	D	1938
WIDEMAN			
Eliza	16020	D	1913
WIDER			
F. K.	11282	D	1911
Leslie Edwin	54865	M	1930
Olive Bernice	52386	M	1929
WIDERSTROM			
Allfrieda	40797	D	1925
Frieda	40797	D	1925
John	57918	D	1931
WIDGERY			
Albert E.	70807	D	1935
WIDHOLM			
Florence V.	84808	D	1940
WIDING			
Maria	53352	D	1929
WIDMAN			
Herman G.	8894	D	1909

NAME	NUMBER	TYPE	YEAR
Louis	62648	D	1932
WIDMAR			
Annie	13730	D	1912
Jacob	35438	D	1922
Jakob	78611	D	1938
WIEBE			
John	83937	D	1940
WIEBOLDT			
Marianne	67280	D	1934
Mary A.	67280	D	1934
WIECHERS			
A. J.	28084	D	1919
Anthony Joseph	47029	M	1927
Eileen	47030	M	1927
Lawrence	47031	M	1927
WIECHERT			
Alice M.	16908	D	1914
WIEDEMANN			
Louis	22483	D	1917
WIEDER			
Mary Elizabeth	28859	D	1920
May	28859	D	1920
WIEDERKEHR			
Frances	75706	D	1937
WIEDIWICH			
Katie	24328	D	1918
WIEDMANN			
Emmy	85745	D	1940
WIEGAND			
Gustave W.	62245	D	1932
WIEGEL			
John	1051	D	1906
WIEGER			
William	52465	D	1929
William	77973	D	1938
WIEGMANN			
E. M., Mrs.	83525	D	1940
Florence	83525	D	1940
Fredrick	54838	D	1930
Henry F.	10891	D	1910
WIEGNER			
Anne C.	30090	D	1920
WIEHE			
Rochus	74138	D	1936
WIEKING			
Heinrich	3274	I	1907

NAME	NUMBER	TYPE	YEAR
WIEL			
Alfred Louis	45352	D	1926
Elsie Hecht	75997	D	1937
Harry I.	89252	D	1942
Henrietta Hecht	36242	D	1923
Irvin J.	75996	D	1937
Jacob	32442	D	1921
WIELAND			
Albert G.	5663	D	1908
Alfred F.	50365	D	1928
Annie M.	47076	D	1927
Charlotte Marie	81003	D	1939
George	14979	D	1913
Helen R.	59334	D	1931
Herman E.	4656	M	1907
John	3743	D	1907
John P.	4656	M	1907
Mina	62768	D	1932
Stella M.	62270	D	1932
WIELKE			
Fred	30917	D	1921
WIEMARTH			
Ora C.	24873	D	1918
WIEMEYER			
Frank H.	35831	D	1923
WIENEKE			
Anna Lola	49506	M	1928
Fred	49506	M	1928
Frederick	88054	D	1941
Robert	49506	M	1928
Robert	72720	D	1936
Roy	49506	M	1928
WIENER			
Adolph	13257	D	1912
Bernard	3790	D	1907
Edward	141	D	1906
Elizabeth B.	86183	D	1941
Frances	41529	M	1925
Henry	61433	D	1932
Jacob	43868	D	1926
Maxine	45337	M	1926
Minnie	66128	D	1934
Sydney L.	18551	D	1915
WIENERS			
Bernard	17010	D	1914
WIENHOLZ			
Arthur	45566	M	1926

Key: D = death; M = minor; I = incompetent

Name	Number	Type	Year
Arthur N.	44652	M	1926
Paul J.	44651	M	1926
Paul J.	45567	M	1926
Wieniawski			
Jules E.	64560	D	1933
Wienrank			
Christoph	71854	D	1936
Elizabetha	50199	D	1928
Wierzchoslawski			
Frank	35934	D	1923
Wiese			
Jacob	57854	D	1931
John	40120	D	1924
Lillian H.	68587	D	1934
Wiesenhutter			
Sarah	24146	D	1918
Wiesenthal			
Otto F.	78078	D	1938
Wieshert			
Franz	13996	D	1912
Wiesner			
Philippine Sophie	69381	D	1935
Philippine Sophie	81106	D	1939
Wiess			
Stella	35548	I	1922
Wiest			
Regina Barr	66257	D	1934
Wiester			
William H.	14640	D	1912
Wietanen			
Waino Wilho	38942	I	1924
Wigan			
Maxine Dolores	89687	M	1942
Wigand			
August W.	51520	D	1928
Wiget			
Barbara	87635	D	1941
Wigger			
Sophie	80895	D	1939
Wiggin			
Cynthia A.	19661	I	1915
Harmon Parker	68310	D	1934
Harry	68310	D	1934
Helena	65774	D	1933
Wiggins			
Caroline F.	41957	D	1925

Name	Number	Type	Year
Caroline F.	41957	D	1925
Jessie May	78671	D	1938
Katherine	30175	D	1920
Margaretta Thomas	8777	D	1909
Walter	77825	D	1938
Wigholm			
John A.	65901	D	1933
Wight			
Frank J.	69267	D	1935
Wightman			
Celesta Augusta	28150	I	1919
Mary A.	15000	D	1913
Wigington			
Charles Robert	49618	M	1928
Wigley			
Edwin	73826	D	1936
Edwin	87480	D	1941
Wigney			
Agnes	671	D	1906
Benjamin A.	83181	D	1940
Wihill			
Bridget	27396	D	1919
Wihndsor			
Josephine	43968	D	1926
Wihs			
George William	66139	M	1934
Wik			
Oscar C.	87173	D	1941
Wikander			
Verna May	77416	M	1938
Wike			
John H.	3708	D	1907
Wiklund			
Frank	53370	D	1929
Wikstrom			
Hulda Adelia	56383	I	1930
Wilber			
Cassie Whelan	12025	D	1911
Celia E.	48052	I	1927
DeLong C.	32297	D	1921
Mattie A.	86872	I	1941
Wilbert			
Mary A.	18570	D	1915
Wilbur			
Celia	20240	I	1916
Charles E.	38006	D	1923

Name	Number	Type	Year
Edith M.	83891	D	1940
George A.	20255	D	1916
I. R.	30594	D	1920
Leonard Fisk	89068	D	1942
Olive D.	89402	D	1942
Oscar E.	88066	D	1941
Wilchynski			
Jon	18541	D	1915
Wilcox			
Albert Spencer	29941	D	1920
Amelia	10625	D	1910
Betsey I.	67514	D	1934
Charles G.	26256	D	1919
Edward Nelson	42315	D	1925
Emma E.	63260	D	1932
Gloria Edna	34042	M	1922
Glover B.	33941	D	1922
J. Agnes	4148	D	1907
Jessie R.	49255	I	1928
John E.	46469	D	1927
Katie	35646	D	1923
Lois	37187	M	1923
Lydia A.	37243	D	1923
Matilda Louise	38047	D	1924
Meredith H.	74697	M	1937
Walter E.	61378	D	1932
Willard C.	9336	D	1910
Wilcoxen			
Andrew Jackson	33229	D	1922
Wilcoxon			
Floride	42240	D	1925
Wild			
Arthur	33751	D	1922
John	40499	D	1924
Otto J.	31818	D	1921
Sarah	35577	D	1922
Wildberg			
Howard S.	21421	D	1916
Wildberger			
George	27007	D	1919
Wilde			
Arthur G.	44316	D	1926
Arthur Henry	51672	D	1928
Charles Noel	63103	D	1932
Ella	81673	D	1939
Forrest B.	87936	M	1941
Lina	31106	D	1921

NAME	NUMBER	TYPE	YEAR
WILDENSTEIN			
Gertrude	40366	M	1924
Gertrude	51581	M	1928
James	40366	M	1924
James	51581	M	1928
Mary	40366	M	1924
Mary	51581	M	1928
WILDER			
Charles J.	8573	D	1909
Charles N.	33877	D	1922
Isabel C.	57931	D	1931
James A.	11801	M	1911
James J.	8258	D	1909
Laura A. Ross	64147	I	1933
Laura A. Ross	67529	D	1934
Margaret A.	44580	D	1926
Martha	11801	M	1911
Samuel Gardner, Jr.	32594	I	1921
Vera	11801	M	1911
Vera Frances	65341	D	1933
William T.	11801	M	1911
WILDERMUTH			
William	48335	D	1927
WILDERSON			
Harry L.	64817	I	1933
WILDES			
Ed	9491	D	1910
Margaret	49325	D	1928
WILDGANS			
Jeanne	74215	D	1936
WILDHABER			
Robert	26789	D	1919
WILDHAVER			
Robert	26789	D	1919
WILDT			
Valentine	6237	D	1908
WILEN			
Oskar E.	16843	M	1914
WILEY			
Anna	16781	D	1914
Carrie	38409	D	1924
J. W.	11877	D	1911
James Hogle	14839	D	1913
Mary E.	89336	D	1942
Sarah A.	53214	D	1929
William	30991	D	1921
William D.	44886	D	1926

NAME	NUMBER	TYPE	YEAR
William Herbert	63975	D	1933
WILFERT			
Christoph	55342	D	1930
WILFORD			
Albert	20002	D	1915
Charlotta C.	11209	D	1911
WILFSON			
May Teresa	18909	D	1915
WILHART			
John	66882	I	1934
WILHELM			
Elsie M.	75788	D	1937
Ludavica	33597	D	1922
Marjorie Pauline	75672	M	1937
Thomas	35300	D	1922
Thomas	41998	I	1925
Thomas	50992	D	1928
Walter A.	58825	D	1931
Xavier	34355	I	1922
Xavier	34398	D	1922
WILHELMINE			
Clara	37510	D	1923
Mary	37510	D	1923
WILHELMSON			
Oscar M.	53078	D	1929
WILHOIT			
Jasper T.	78306	D	1938
WILHOYTE			
John P.	4875	D	1907
WILIAM			
Charles Henry	59484	D	1931
WILK			
Dina	56413	D	1930
WILKE			
Adeline	89460	D	1942
Adolph	57082	D	1930
Beatrice S.	41050	D	1925
Carl E. M.	6675	D	1908
Charles D.	87053	D	1941
Diana	56413	D	1930
WILKENS			
Heinrich	34804	D	1922
Jacob A.	47201	D	1927
Johanna E.	71597	I	1936
Johanna E.	74320	D	1937
Thusnelda	48957	D	1928

NAME	NUMBER	TYPE	YEAR
WILKERSON			
Erastus N.	41042	D	1925
Harry Leroy	83879	D	1940
Marie E.	41225	M	1925
Phyllis Jeanne	83149	M	1940
WILKES			
Max	54399	D	1929
William M.	81012	I	1939
WILKIE			
Andrew	52526	D	1929
Andrew H.	75319	D	1937
Catherine	61223	D	1932
Edwin L.	55193	D	1930
Esther	16142	D	1913
Isabelle	81128	D	1939
WILKING			
Mary Victoria	75001	D	1937
WILKINS			
Annie LeGay	61634	D	1932
Elizabeth	89251	D	1942
Frank	81002	D	1939
Frederick J.	13690	D	1912
Henry H.	49528	M	1928
Isabella S.	23335	D	1917
James E.	54026	D	1929
James M.	46763	D	1927
John D.	19673	D	1915
John G.	1584	D	1906
Kenneth Warren	79692	M	1938
Orvin H.	3853	D	1907
Sarah	45119	D	1926
Thusnelda	48957	D	1928
WILKINSON			
Alfred	79109	D	1938
Annie W.	13334	I	1912
Eli J.	40861	D	1925
Eli James	34831	I	1922
Elizabeth G.	30248	D	1920
Emma B.	77979	D	1938
Emma Forbes	55881	D	1930
Ethel Asenaph	21090	D	1916
Ettie Gertrude	84558	D	1940
Frank Irving	72296	D	1936
George R.	24456	D	1918
Gilbert L.	76618	D	1937
Hannah M.	57454	D	1930
James	30210	D	1920
Jane A.	30770	D	1920

NAME	NUMBER	TYPE	YEAR	NAME	NUMBER	TYPE	YEAR	NAME	NUMBER	TYPE	YEAR
Jennie R.	44879	D	1926	Edward	42315	D	1925	Alice McKeone	33388	D	1922
John S.	17509	D	1914	John F.	9838	M	1910	Amos M.	52839	D	1929
Mary F.	88404	D	1941	**WILLCUTT**				Anita	67132	D	1934
Mary Frances	88213	I	1941	George Beal	59848	D	1931	Ann	39377	D	1924
Mathilda	61563	D	1932	**WILLDE**				Anna E.	16023	D	1913
Thomas H.	56805	D	1930	Cerita	40930	D	1925	Arthur H.	85701	D	1940
William	11920	D	1911	Charles	78101	D	1938	Arthur Henry	78952	D	1938
William J.	54487	D	1929	Dorothy	76448	M	1937	Arthur Lambert	37400	D	1923
WILL				Henry	12294	D	1911	Augusta	79486	D	1938
Annie M.	24352	D	1918	John Henry	12294	D	1911	Barbara	76472	M	1937
Frederick A.	14459	D	1912	Magdalena Johanna	31106	D	1921	Beatrice Steele	20265	M	1916
Julius	29512	D	1920	Margaret Young	69998	D	1935	Benjamin F.	48717	D	1927
Lottie	27748	I	1919	**WILLEBRAND**				Bert	33719	D	1922
William Frederick	77377	D	1937	Carmen	56598	D	1930	Bethania Dunbar	13195	D	1912
WILLAMS				**WILLEMANN**				Bruce Prior	88123	M	1941
Rebecca E.	36374	D	1923	Katharina	49405	D	1928	C. F.	13391	D	1912
WILLAND				**WILLEMS**				C. T.	13391	D	1912
Augusta	28092	D	1919	Emelie	73938	D	1936	Calvin L.	54483	D	1929
Emil J.	55258	D	1930	Pearl	88430	D	1941	Catherine	74340	D	1937
WILLARD				Petrus	66946	D	1934	Catherine	86164	I	1941
Alfred J.	23013	I	1917	**WILLER**				Catherine C.	62027	D	1932
Charles W.	35530	D	1922	Godfrey	84668	D	1940	Charles	11014	D	1911
Clara	73760	D	1936	**WILLETT**				Charles H.	32824	D	1921
Elisa May	86962	D	1941	John Joseph	77396	D	1937	Charles H.	52926	I	1929
Emma S.	72077	D	1936	Walter Marinus	84001	D	1940	Charles Henry	59514	D	1931
Harvey	89133	D	1942	**WILLEVER**				Chauncey B.	64137	D	1933
Jessie L.	22054	D	1917	Mark M.	81611	D	1939	Chester L.	36249	D	1923
Joseph A.	40137	D	1924	**WILLEY**				Chris	55395	D	1930
Joseph M.	70364	D	1935	Charles Walter	1989	D	1906	Clara L.	54380	I	1929
Julia Reid	23068	D	1917	Frank Roy	74532	D	1937	Clara L.	71060	D	1935
Mary T.	77430	D	1938	Mary E.	89336	D	1942	Clark Marshall	37400	D	1923
Maurice	73138	D	1936	**WILLFANG**				Daniel R.	60221	D	1931
WILLARTS				Anna Augusta	84736	D	1940	David Irving	88123	M	1941
F. P., Mrs.	79975	D	1938	Anna C.	84736	D	1940	Della	17073	I	1914
Margot	79975	D	1938	Christian	85610	D	1940	Dide M.	27198	D	1919
WILLATS				**WILLGEROTH**				Dolores Adel	29535	M	1920
Daniel	13152	D	1912	Emil	89043	D	1942	Dora F.	35943	I	1923
WILLATZ				**WILLI**				Dora F.	46276	D	1927
Harold P.	16346	M	1913	Edward Frederick	61100	D	1932	Dr.	49601	D	1928
WILLBACH				**WILLIAMS**				Earl	48503	D	1927
Sarah	80229	D	1938	Abram Pease	12395	D	1911	Edgar D.	21650	D	1916
WILLBERG				Adeline	52480	M	1929	Edith	72505	I	1936
Elizabeth Ellen	12152	I	1911	Agnes	42321	I	1925	Edward	24115	D	1918
WILLCOT				Agnes	78982	D	1938	Edward	41617	D	1925
E. B.	34381	D	1922	Albert G.	79166	D	1938	Edward Cook	2150	D	1906
WILLCOX				Alexander F.	23574	D	1917	Edward J.	13628	D	1912
E. B.	34381	D	1922	Alfonso R.	53449	D	1929	Edward John	41445	D	1925
								Edward Maxwell	82270	D	1939
								Eleanor	76472	M	1937

Key: D = death; M = minor; I = incompetent

NAME	NUMBER	TYPE	YEAR	NAME	NUMBER	TYPE	YEAR	NAME	NUMBER	TYPE	YEAR
Elisha	43190	D	1925	Grace Young	31171	D	1921	Leontine M.	55787	D	1930
Eliza J.	12674	D	1911	Gus	82096	D	1939	Lucy A.	2517	D	1906
Elizabeth	76472	M	1937	Hannah	76134	D	1937	Lynne	79274	M	1938
Elizabeth	77389	D	1937	Hannah Maher	3815	D	1907	Mansfield W.	50388	M	1928
Elizabeth Stark	43477	D	1926	Hannibal	2944	D	1907	Marcella	53827	D	1929
Ella C.	66445	D	1934	Harold Clyde	66699	D	1934	Mareth	58896	D	1931
Ellen Mary	17704	D	1914	Heloise R.	13297	I	1912	Margaret	13826	D	1912
Ellis	89578	D	1942	Heloise Ruppine	18255	D	1914	Margaret	44293	D	1926
Emily	65857	D	1933	Herman	30053	D	1920	Margaret Kruege	72134	D	1936
Emma L.	28756	D	1920	Honora J.	67420	D	1934	Marie Genevieve	22088	M	1917
Emma Morehead	45647	I	1926	Howard Smith	71101	D	1935	Marius S.	59320	D	1931
Ernest G.	44028	D	1926	Ivor	40498	D	1924	Mary	6149	D	1908
Esek Hartshorn	41635	D	1925	James L.	33065	D	1921	Mary	7901	D	1909
Esek Hartshorne	38384	I	1924	James Marshall	85179	D	1940	Mary	15624	D	1913
Esther	52480	M	1929	James Merton	33801	M	1922	Mary	87640	D	1941
Eugene Albert	89906	D	1942	Jasper	80937	D	1939	Mary A.	67674	D	1934
Eulis K.	49661	I	1928	Jennie Teresa	39305	D	1924	Mary Ann	17034	M	1914
Evan	1305	D	1906	Jenny	66748	D	1934	Mary Ann	30819	D	1920
Everette M.	78884	D	1938	Johanna M. C.	30700	D	1920	Mary B.	5527	D	1908
F. C., Mrs.	79486	D	1938	John	4800	D	1907	Mary B.	6057	D	1908
Felix Albert	59583	D	1931	John	6906	D	1908	Mary Catherine Salisbury	55730	M	1930
Flora B.	74407	D	1937	John	7509	D	1909	Mary E.	46060	D	1926
Florence Abigal	16955	D	1914	John	23564	M	1917	Mary G.	60226	D	1931
Florence D.	33123	D	1921	John	28888	D	1920	Mary M. Caseres	27385	D	1919
Florence Estelle	81412	D	1939	John	46570	D	1927	Mattie A.	81073	D	1939
Forest C.	26644	D	1919	John	74981	D	1937	Maud S.	53980	D	1929
Frances S.	12741	D	1911	John B.	22511	D	1917	Mercy C.	67980	D	1934
Francis Churchill, Jr.	34178	M	1922	John C.	33737	D	1922	Mervine F.	8893	M	1909
Frank	11485	M	1911	John Edward	44629	D	1926	Millie E.	62693	D	1932
Frank	26702	D	1919	John Francis	89300	D	1942	Minnie A.	67674	D	1934
Frank	87275	D	1941	John H.	14101	D	1912	Nellie	67164	D	1934
Fred W.	26875	D	1919	John H.	87653	D	1941	Nicholas	26865	D	1919
Fred W.	69446	D	1935	John Marshall	29386	I	1920	Norma Cecelia	22088	M	1917
Fremont J.	8893	M	1909	John Sebastian	36727	D	1923	Olive L.	49316	D	1928
Genevieve	76472	M	1937	John T.	53604	D	1929	Owen	50855	D	1928
George	11485	M	1911	John W.	20704	D	1916	Owen P.	2372	D	1906
George	13513	D	1912	Joseph	16856	D	1914	Peter	39405	D	1924
George	22559	D	1917	Joseph	76280	D	1937	Peter	76281	D	1937
George	29727	D	1920	Joseph C.	21076	D	1916	Peticolas G.	83579	D	1940
George	77485	D	1938	Joseph W.	63304	D	1933	Phyllis Eleanor	33801	M	1922
George A.	22172	D	1917	Josephine Mary	76536	D	1937	R. Neil, Mrs.	72134	D	1936
George A.	43655	D	1926	Josiah C.	37984	D	1923	R. T. R.	5583	D	1908
George D.	30505	D	1920	Julia	75269	D	1937	Raymond Melvin	72766	D	1936
George E.	30505	D	1920	Julia	70796	I	1935	Rena W.	15001	D	1913
George E.	70378	D	1935	Julia Annie	7924	D	1909	Richard	13070	D	1912
George W.	27169	D	1919	Julia Madeline	22088	M	1917	Richard S.	36987	D	1923
Gertrude	11485	M	1911	Justin Lowell	79274	M	1938	Robert	43565	D	1926
Gertrude E.	86188	D	1941	Katherine	52811	D	1929	Robert Adrain	23395	D	1917
Grace	76472	M	1937	Kathleen	66370	D	1934	Robert B.	52652	D	1929

Key: D = death; M = minor; I = incompetent

NAME	NUMBER	TYPE	YEAR	NAME	NUMBER	TYPE	YEAR	NAME	NUMBER	TYPE	YEAR
Robert George	21120	D	1916	Annie	63363	D	1933	**WILLIGROD**			
Robert Henry	10818	D	1910	C. Y.	17556	D	1914	Julius	2349	D	1906
Robert N.	5895	D	1908	Carroll B.	24926	M	1918	**WILLIMAN**			
Rose	43796	I	1926	Charles	34765	D	1922	Jacob	66721	D	1934
Roy	33719	D	1922	Charles S.	11579	D	1911	**WILLIS**			
Sarah E.	48417	D	1927	Chester	61975	D	1932	Ambrose Madison	10750	D	1910
Sidney	34212	D	1922	Daisy	46326	I	1927	Emmeline	5898	M	1908
Simon	24995	D	1918	Eleanor D.	53681	M	1929	Frank A.	1000	D	1906
Susan Gertrude	82033	I	1939	Elizabeth	69391	D	1935	Frank Gloucester	1218	M	1906
Thomas	46890	D	1927	Ella R.	56063	D	1930	Hugh J.	84300	D	1940
Thomas A.	40590	D	1924	Emma	31633	D	1921	India Scott	18145	D	1914
Thomas H.	19928	D	1915	Ethel L.	19448	D	1915	J. P. Mary	59475	D	1931
Thomas Hansford	20264	M	1916	Ethelinda	19448	D	1915	Jennie	9742	D	1910
Thomas Hopkins	37038	D	1923	Frank H.	73577	D	1936	Marmaduke	6868	D	1908
Thomas Jeffreys	18714	D	1915	Fred L.	74589	D	1937	William A.	66889	D	1934
Thomas M.	83296	D	1940	Frederick	74589	D	1937	William Walter	41298	D	1925
Thomas Robert	83305	M	1940	George	10182	D	1910	**WILLISON**			
Thomas S.	55210	D	1930	George	45348	D	1926	Cornelius	79451	D	1938
Thomas T.	57157	I	1930	Herbert J.	77781	D	1938	**WILLITS**			
Townsend S.	38854	D	1924	James	56097	D	1930	Charles Davis	71160	D	1935
Violet Grace	81913	D	1939	James G.	52887	D	1929	Lola Oakley	64337	D	1933
Virgil	40105	D	1924	James H.	73830	D	1936	**WILLLIAMSON**			
Virginia	47376	M	1927	James Robert	84115	D	1940	John	21748	D	1916
Virginia G.	40029	D	1924	John D.	24926	M	1918	**WILLMAN**			
Walter	45018	M	1926	John Henry	8233	D	1909	August	34988	D	1922
Webster	76363	D	1937	John M.	61432	D	1932	William	89795	D	1942
William	45018	M	1926	Juline M.	58348	D	1931	**WILLMORE**			
William	45400	D	1926	Louisa Belle	73420	D	1936	William	13898	D	1912
William	68735	D	1935	Lucy G.	67873	D	1934	**WILLMSEN**			
William A.	17034	M	1914	Martin Arthur	23867	D	1918	William	68735	D	1935
William A.	18422	D	1915	Mary E.	80987	D	1939	**WILLNER**			
William A.	40101	D	1924	Mary L.	23513	D	1917	Adolf	88688	D	1941
William A.	74817	D	1937	Otto	31369	D	1921	Clara W.	40360	I	1924
William B.	6230	D	1908	Rachel P.	54448	I	1929	**WILLOH**			
William E.	65866	D	1933	Richard	81572	D	1939	August B.	9037	D	1910
William Edward	39255	D	1924	Rufus W.	76508	D	1937	**WILLRACHER**			
William Edward	54590	D	1929	Samuel	21096	D	1916	Henry	34953	D	1922
William F.	45133	D	1926	William	36861	D	1923	**WILLRADER**			
William George	62037	D	1932	William	68735	D	1935	Myrtle W.	86414	D	1941
William Harrison	27498	D	1919	William E.	64222	D	1933	**WILLS**			
William Henry	29329	D	1920	**WILLIAR**				Adrainne	5557	M	1908
William L.	2414	D	1906	Harry Riemen	80289	D	1939	Alice	44153	D	1926
William L.	10557	D	1910	**WILLIG**				Anna	51670	D	1928
William W.	17184	D	1914	John	36076	I	1923	Annie	20337	D	1916
Winfield Scott	32136	I	1921	John	51243	D	1928	Consuelo	5557	M	1908
Winfield Scott	36609	D	1923	John	53371	D	1929	Ellen Irene	5557	M	1908
WILLIAMSON				Joseph	58352	D	1931	Emilie	71211	I	1935
Aninai	63363	D	1933	Louis	87693	D	1941				
Annia Annia	63363	D	1933								

NAME	NUMBER	TYPE	YEAR	NAME	NUMBER	TYPE	YEAR	NAME	NUMBER	TYPE	YEAR
Emilie	71359	D	1936	Alexander William	78095	D	1938	Early	81154	M	1939
John	59241	D	1931	Alice	17800	D	1914	Edgar M.	76776	D	1937
Kate	15037	D	1913	Alice C.	73198	D	1936	Edward	10338	D	1910
Mariana Alley	42895	D	1925	Alice P.	52309	I	1929	Edward George	77940	D	1938
Walter	18662	M	1915	Almeda S.	1549	D	1906	Edwin V.	23425	D	1917
William	5557	M	1908	Amanda	2247	D	1906	Eliza T.	61827	D	1932
Wyman L.	86438	D	1941	Andrew	8390	D	1909	Elizabeth	11952	D	1911
WILLSON				Andrew	12376	D	1911	Elizabeth	88084	I	1941
Charlotte L.	4503	I	1907	Ann B.	572	D	1906	Elizabeth G.	47454	D	1927
Charlotte L.	12877	D	1912	Ann R.	12341	D	1911	Elizabeth M.	6965	D	1908
Harry Charles	88510	D	1941	Anna	70023	D	1935	Elliott M.	48652	D	1927
Herbert Charles	23670	I	1917	Anna May	84590	D	1940	Elvira Mathelda	25241	D	1918
Phoebe A.	20022	D	1915	Annie	14305	D	1912	Emma Finley	54540	D	1929
WILLWEBER				Annie Easton	42359	D	1925	Erie J.	55551	D	1930
Henry	34953	D	1922	Annie L.	83905	D	1940	Ernest Robert	33730	D	1922
WILMANS				Antoinette	73322	I	1936	Erwin M.	17819	D	1914
J. M.	29828	D	1920	Arthur Alling	69848	D	1935	Ethel May	21932	M	1916
WILMES				Arthur Carroll	22755	M	1917	Everett W.	83379	D	1940
Clara L.	78341	D	1938	B. F.	43062	D	1925	F. B.	43062	D	1925
Henry John	25856	D	1918	Benno	36501	D	1923	Florence	53285	D	1929
Rafael Katherine	79634	D	1938	Bernard James	58571	D	1931	Frances J.	17638	D	1914
Ray	79634	D	1938	Bessie	54582	D	1929	Frances Livingston	19730	D	1915
WILMETH				Bessie M.	73974	D	1936	Frances Rose	14858	M	1913
Toutant B.	39463	M	1924	Caroline A.	38086	D	1924	Francis P.	19799	M	1915
WILMOT				Carroll A.	35835	D	1923	Frank	63567	D	1933
George C.	31250	D	1921	Catherine	20196	D	1915	Frank	75163	D	1937
WILMOTH				Charles	7345	D	1909	Frank	74241	D	1936
Robert	77929	D	1938	Charles	74978	D	1937	Frank F.	61364	D	1932
WILNAR				Charles E.	21652	D	1916	Frank P.	19622	D	1915
Morris S.	26527	D	1919	Charles Edward	49757	D	1928	Fred A.	25658	D	1918
WILSEN				Charles H.	23001	D	1917	Fred B.	65836	D	1933
Carl	29823	D	1920	Charles Harry	54671	D	1930	Frederick	28529	D	1919
Charles	29823	D	1920	Charles Jasper, Jr.	88248	D	1941	Frederick A.	68944	D	1935
WILSHIRE				Charles M.	30516	D	1920	Frederick G.	19813	D	1915
William B.	27056	D	1919	Charles Peter	43182	D	1925	Frederick Miles	22601	D	1917
William B.	39960	D	1924	Charles T.	29457	D	1920	George E.	19232	D	1915
WILSLOW				Charles William	84806	D	1940	George E.	44823	D	1926
Maria C.	46225	D	1927	Christine N.	36949	D	1923	George Edward	67658	D	1934
Thomas	47539	D	1927	Clara E.	35479	I	1922	George F.	63567	D	1933
WILSON				Daisy Crothers	81131	D	1939	George Hazelton	46686	D	1927
Adeline S.	75260	I	1937	Daniel	64173	D	1933	George L.	18645	D	1915
Agnes D.	857	D	1906	Daniel Lynch	19522	M	1915	Georgiana Raye	56027	M	1930
Alacia A.	21932	M	1916	David	3253	D	1907	Hannah	17345	D	1914
Albert	87991	D	1941	David	58798	D	1931	Harriet	13362	D	1912
Albert J.	52548	D	1929	Dean	73010	I	1936	Harriet B.	38986	D	1924
Albert Wing	67535	I	1934	Diana Gordon	78014	D	1938	Harry	10874	M	1910
Albert Wing	67624	D	1934	Dorothy Evelyn	13562	M	1912	Harry	31515	D	1921
				E. H.	55767	D	1930	Harry W.	68116	D	1934
				Earl Douglas	33046	M	1921	Helen	41408	D	1925

NAME	NUMBER	TYPE	YEAR	NAME	NUMBER	TYPE	YEAR	NAME	NUMBER	TYPE	YEAR
Henrietta K.	13561	D	1912	John Vincent	21481	D	1916	May Teresa	18657	D	1915
Henry Church	18307	D	1914	John W.	63684	D	1933	May Teresa	18909	D	1915
Henry Harrison	43746	I	1926	John W.	64559	D	1933	Morgan B.	55937	D	1930
Henry J.	64494	D	1933	John Wallace	18975	D	1915	Morris	35494	D	1922
Homer	85091	D	1940	John, Mrs.	32394	D	1921	Nellie F.	82015	D	1939
Horace Bertram	60249	D	1931	Jose Theodore	71414	M	1936	Nellie P.	86410	D	1941
Howard E.	60190	D	1931	Joseph A.	21263	D	1916	Nona H.	54136	D	1929
Ida J.	22377	D	1917	Joseph N.	4185	D	1907	Orrin Allen	21493	D	1916
Ignacia	857	D	1906	Joseph P.	6691	D	1908	Oscar	40579	D	1924
Irving Melville	75717	D	1937	Joseph Wybert Palmer	20636	D	1916	Oscar	49749	D	1928
James	21709	D	1916	Josephine	89487	I	1942	Oscar	81914	D	1939
James A.	16831	D	1914	Josephine K.	40727	D	1925	Otto	14703	I	1913
James B.	54228	D	1929	Julia	56617	I	1930	Otto	72121	D	1936
James Carroll	44236	D	1926	Julia Agnes	77134	D	1937	R. C., Mrs.	29395	D	1920
James E.	77657	D	1938	Laura Kellogg	58963	D	1931	Ralph D.	58811	D	1931
James G.	19716	D	1915	Leonore Louise	74731	M	1937	Richard	11730	D	1911
James J.	18522	D	1915	Leroy G.	76682	D	1937	Richard B.	61049	I	1932
James K.	86306	D	1941	Lillian J.	45964	M	1926	Richard Leroy	33046	M	1921
James N.	73781	D	1936	Lloyd Arthur	9705	D	1910	Robert	62562	D	1932
James Robert	26951	D	1919	Louise	81907	I	1939	Robert A.	17087	D	1914
James William	55031	D	1930	Lulu M.	44128	D	1926	Robert A.	52730	I	1929
Jane	67793	D	1934	Mabel	14857	M	1913	Robert C.	33299	D	1922
Jay Crittenden	12900	D	1912	Mabel	19522	M	1915	Robert Henry	26103	D	1919
Jennie A.	26677	D	1919	Mack Henry	39394	D	1924	Robert J.	89614	D	1942
Jeremiah Judson	24169	D	1918	Malvin L.	4094	D	1907	Robert L.	75941	D	1937
Jessey Caroline	47285	D	1927	Marcella M.	9662	I	1910	Robert W. T.	19972	D	1915
Jessie Lenore	51463	D	1928	Marcella M.	12236	D	1911	Rose	32394	D	1921
John	10339	D	1910	Margaret	22817	I	1917	Roselin	5622	M	1908
John	33321	D	1922	Margaret	39311	D	1924	Ruby	82016	D	1939
John	42924	D	1925	Margaret	40880	D	1925	Russel J.	386	D	1906
John	49436	D	1928	Margaret	59451	D	1931	Russell G.	8048	M	1909
John	64204	M	1933	Margaret T.	48690	D	1927	Samuel J.	14434	D	1912
John	71607	D	1936	Maria C.	29736	D	1920	Samuel John	73451	D	1936
John A.	59663	D	1931	Marion Ramon	67597	D	1934	Samuel Mountford	75651	D	1937
John A.	87273	D	1941	Martha	29395	D	1920	Sara A.	45852	D	1926
John Archibald	47301	D	1927	Mary	30803	D	1920	Sara M.	1678	D	1906
John C.	19412	D	1915	Mary	71612	D	1936	Sara T.	58504	D	1931
John C.	19436	M	1915	Mary	73165	D	1936	Sarah W.	62453	D	1932
John C.	43971	D	1926	Mary A.	20891	D	1916	Shirley Ellen	74731	M	1937
John H.	3666	D	1907	Mary A.	54582	D	1929	Sidney	82091	D	1939
John H.	87569	D	1941	Mary A.	64110	D	1933	Sidney Vernon	74010	D	1936
John Jacob	56834	D	1930	Mary Agnes	69225	D	1935	Sophia E.	10411	D	1910
John Joseph	2396	D	1906	Mary E.	7567	D	1909	Stephen	80905	I	1939
John Pendleton	73101	D	1936	Mary Ellen	15939	D	1913	Stokely	19799	M	1915
John Ralph	82316	D	1939	Mason Kissling	6386	D	1908	Thomas	1470	D	1906
John Scott	25611	D	1918	Mattie Lindley	50720	D	1928	Thomas	9169	D	1910
John Stewart	57081	D	1930	Maud	33586	D	1922	Thomas	21474	D	1916
John T.	39468	D	1924	Maude Ashley	70586	D	1935	Thomas Cluff	19522	M	1915
John Thomas	12392	D	1911	May	74797	D	1937	Thomas H.	57708	D	1931

NAME	NUMBER	TYPE	YEAR	NAME	NUMBER	TYPE	YEAR	NAME	NUMBER	TYPE	YEAR
Thomas Riley	81171	D	1939	**WIMMER**				**WINDING**			
Thomas S.	33145	D	1922	Catherine	68992	D	1935	Gerhard J. F.	6894	D	1908
Ulysis Grant	36031	D	1923	George Washington	41059	D	1925	**WINDLEY**			
Unknown H.	4	D	1906	**WIMPERLY**				Michael	12608	D	1911
Vernon	57166	I	1930	Laura Martha	46576	D	1927	**WINDMAN**			
Virginia Pendleton	70448	D	1935	**WINANT**				Freddie W.	10253	D	1910
Walter	4754	D	1907	Edward	43013	D	1925	**WINDMILLER**			
Warren S.	19799	M	1915	Jennie	53543	D	1929	Amelia	82332	D	1939
Wilhelmina	76638	D	1937	**WINANTS**				Henry	66	D	1906
William	30365	D	1920	Newell	15509	D	1913	Maurice	37116	D	1923
William	48217	D	1927	**WINASSO**				**WINDMULLER**			
William	49181	D	1928	Francesco	46474	D	1927	Jacob	8551	D	1909
William	85578	D	1940	**WINCAPAW**				**WINDROW**			
William A.	67410	D	1934	Leland Stephen	87035	D	1941	Elizabeth	6384	D	1908
William Arthur	10665	D	1910	**WINCH**				**WINDSOR**			
William E.	35964	D	1923	Frederick C.	8056	D	1909	Annie	45789	D	1926
William F.	12693	D	1911	Myrtle Olive	87888	D	1941	Josephine	43968	D	1926
William F.	14334	D	1912	Rose Campbell	822	D	1906	**WINDT**			
William Harbison	37799	D	1923	**WINCHESTER**				Albert	66020	D	1934
William M.	7358	D	1909	Curtis M.	8022	D	1909	Anna Elise	27712	D	1919
William M.	61781	I	1932	Ezra H.	372	D	1906	Bertha	46219	D	1927
William M.	62115	D	1932	Robert	14060	D	1912	Henry	81720	D	1939
William Sydney	69526	D	1935	**WINCKEL**				Henry C.	27622	D	1919
William W.	61421	D	1932	August Hans	70966	D	1935	Henry, Jr.	48048	D	1927
Wilma Leigh	33872	M	1922	**WINCKLER**				Morris	23799	D	1917
WILT				William F.	65197	D	1933	**WINER**			
Ella B.	1569	D	1906	**WIND**				Solomon	70258	D	1935
May	27714	D	1919	Anne P. H.	2321	D	1906	**WINEROTH**			
WILTEN				Christian Wilson	8957	D	1910	Audrey	58516	M	1931
Aline	58858	M	1931	Emma	47002	D	1927	Harry	58516	M	1931
WILTON				**WINDAMAN**				Isaac	49644	D	1928
Bessie L.	27484	D	1919	Wendell O.	51648	D	1928	Lucille	58516	M	1931
Catherine	34161	D	1922	**WINDBLAD**				**WINES**			
Marie Benedicta	53103	D	1929	F. R.	62344	D	1932	Nicholas C.	12014	D	1911
Mary	53103	D	1929	**WINDEL**				**WINFREY**			
WILTS				Henri F.	3395	D	1907	William H.	69092	D	1935
F. H.	16180	I	1913	**WINDELER**				**WING**			
WILTZ				Anna H.	87749	D	1941	Chillingworth C.	25058	D	1918
Peter Ferdinand	51418	D	1928	George	88011	D	1941	Chung	26010	D	1918
WILY				William F.	68875	D	1935	Fong	26056	D	1919
Ellen	10471	I	1910	**WINDFELDT**				Hing	81751	D	1939
Ellen	10767	D	1910	George Peterson	56014	D	1930	Lee	10578	D	1910
WILZINSKI				**WINDHAM**				Lee	72430	M	1936
Jennie	44661	D	1926	M. Dedrick	52013	D	1929	Lee Moon	34477	M	1922
William	58609	D	1931	**WINDHAUS**				Leon	34706	D	1922
WIMBUSH				Bernard	9092	D	1910	Leong	81293	D	1939
James	13654	D	1912					Lew Fay	83322	M	1940

NAME	NUMBER	TYPE	YEAR
Lum			
Ow Gar	38666	D	1924
Tom	87076	M	1941
Wong	30557	D	1920
Wong Det	87702	D	1941
	28486	D	1919
WINGATE			
John D.	11962	D	1911
WINGER			
Martin R.	34712	I	1922
Martin R.	40158	D	1924
WINGERTER			
Emma M.	22809	D	1917
Herman	22810	D	1917
WINK			
John S.	44429	D	1926
WINKELMAN			
Paul D.	76517	D	1937
Robert E.	62488	M	1932
Stillman J.	64335	D	1933
WINKELMANN			
Johann Christoph	67608	D	1934
WINKLE			
Peter W. Van	1288	D	1906
WINKLER			
Anna	74560	D	1937
Caroline	25258	D	1918
Charles	53631	D	1929
Freda Alice	36815	M	1923
Henry E.	17585	D	1914
Julia	54893	D	1930
Minnie	35341	D	1922
WINKLEY			
Walter W.	25402	D	1918
WINN			
Alma H.	45662	D	1926
Charlotte Chapin	63683	D	1933
Dora J.	12248	M	1911
Frederick Lorne	37024	D	1923
Margaret E.	45167	I	1926
Margaret E.	58487	D	1931
Minnie R.	60849	D	1932
William H.	12756	D	1911
WINNEBERG			
Fred	19777	D	1915
WINNETT			
Margaret Anna	73454	D	1936

NAME	NUMBER	TYPE	YEAR
WINNIE			
M.	39502	I	1924
WINSELL			
Ella C.	83310	I	1940
WINSHIP			
Kate Dillon	30574	D	1920
Mamie	44204	D	1926
WINSLOW			
Anna Marie Louise	8740	M	1909
Charles F.	3365	D	1907
Edwin L.	73092	D	1936
Joseph	2329	D	1906
Josephine Barbat	55440	D	1930
Josephine E.	55440	D	1930
Norah	11257	I	1911
Ruth Louise	8739	M	1909
Sallie F.	85973	D	1941
Sarah F.	85973	D	1941
Sarah Stetson	81584	D	1939
Sophia H.	27315	D	1919
Thomas Howard	37950	D	1923
WINSOR			
Augustus W.	373	D	1906
Ella A.	4453	D	1907
WINSTANLEY			
Ann Augusta	76122	D	1937
Elizabeth Augusta	76122	D	1937
WINSTEDT			
Charles Elof	46412	D	1927
Emma	66570	D	1934
Emma	65934	I	1933
WINTER			
Anna Margaret	38679	D	1924
Anne	6453	I	1908
Annie	43697	D	1926
Elise	55458	D	1930
Emily	84875	D	1940
Emma	20681	D	1916
Eugene V.	86429	D	1941
Francis Hall	28458	M	1919
Frank W.	27228	D	1919
Helen Ruth	88053	M	1941
Henry	371	D	1906
Henry F.	47731	D	1927
James W.	9627	D	1910
Jessie P.	88052	D	1941
John F.	24355	D	1918
John M	88244	D	1941

NAME	NUMBER	TYPE	YEAR
Josephine E.	2243	I	1906
Kenneth Henry	28458	M	1919
Lewis R.	10871	D	1910
Melissa	6745	D	1908
Michael	63198	D	1932
Minnie C.	38235	D	1924
Patrick D.	15142	D	1913
Richard	24073	D	1918
Susanna Elizabeth	15752	D	1913
Thomas P.	76346	D	1937
William	8954	D	1910
William	25067	D	1918
WINTERBERG			
Adolf	18670	M	1915
Anna	18670	M	1915
Fritz	18670	M	1915
Waltrad	65407	D	1933
WINTERBOTTOM			
Orlando	7853	D	1909
WINTERBURN			
George H.	11560	D	1911
Harriet	45827	D	1926
Joseph	28752	D	1920
Josephine	24249	D	1918
Louise Eugenia	80926	D	1939
Susana L. E.	28950	D	1920
Wilbur Irving	30760	M	1920
WINTERHALTER			
Ferdinand	80181	D	1938
Wilhelm Karl	52630	D	1929
WINTERS			
Amelia	36372	D	1923
Catherine I.	51429	D	1928
Eugene H.	51062	D	1928
Fred	54504	D	1929
Frederick	9814	D	1910
Helen K.	51429	D	1928
John	47642	D	1927
John	60580	D	1932
Marie Louise	2768	D	1907
Mary	18337	D	1915
Michael	19262	D	1915
Reginald E.	31695	D	1921
WINTERSTEIN			
Tillie M.	74396	D	1937
WINTHER			
Arthur T.	87993	D	1941
Axel O.	55351	D	1930

Name	Number	Type	Year
Martin	42688	D	1925
Viggo C.	7760	D	1909
WINTHROP			
Catherine	42331	D	1925
Mary	68104	D	1934
WINTITZER			
Eugene F.	41587	D	1925
WINTON			
Ulyses Nathaniel	84730	I	1940
Wm. Wilkins	60180	D	1931
WIPF			
John	30952	D	1921
WIPFLI			
Paula Lee	84728	M	1940
WIREN			
Amanda W.	69544	D	1935
Gustav A.	26328	D	1919
John	58749	D	1931
WIROTH			
Edmond	86650	D	1941
WIRSCH			
Cecelia	20790	D	1916
WIRSCHNLEIT			
Emma	87743	D	1941
WIRSCHULEIT			
Edward	45451	D	1926
Emma	87743	D	1941
WIRTANEN			
Waino Wilho	38942	I	1924
WIRTH			
Leo Lucien	70815	D	1935
WIRTNER			
John J.	70410	D	1935
Joseph Asher	32422	D	1921
WIRTZ			
Carrie B.	13707	D	1912
Louis	101	I	1906
WIRUM			
Ella	72781	D	1936
WISE			
Alice Swain	40917	D	1925
Betty Lou	59705	M	1931
Charles Emile	68640	D	1935
Clara Hannah	77289	D	1937
Elizabeth J.	72498	D	1936
Emily M.	75183	D	1937

Name	Number	Type	Year
Francis Joseph	40835	D	1925
Fred W.	72162	D	1936
George	22616	D	1917
Gladys Lowell	84586	I	1940
Harry E.	16904	D	1914
Jacob	10084	D	1910
John Alfred	76383	D	1937
John Henry	31690	D	1921
John W.	80502	D	1939
Joseph C.	55544	D	1930
Margaret	1895	D	1906
Milton G.	60822	D	1932
Otto Irving	26359	D	1919
Rachael S.	8719	D	1909
Rauhl	43723	D	1926
Rose	85016	D	1940
Roy Spencer	31244	M	1921
Tully R.	19447	D	1915
Wallace A.	17132	D	1914
William Francis	48463	D	1927
William Francis	71000	D	1935
WISEMAN			
Jacob	74267	D	1936
John Tipton	37310	D	1923
Thomas	12316	D	1911
WISHEROP			
Frances	33836	I	1922
WISHMAN			
Henry	16175	D	1913
Julia Ann	18353	I	1915
Julia Ann	18546	D	1915
WISKOTSCHILL			
Charles Edward	54767	M	1930
WISMAR			
Jens Loren	4524	D	1907
WISMER			
Herman	71345	D	1936
WISNER			
Anna	36804	D	1923
Josie	31641	I	1921
Josie	40021	D	1924
WISPLEAR			
Jane	18524	D	1915
WISSEL			
Bertha	20754	D	1916
Christine Margaretha	41891	D	1925
Christine Margaretha	41891	D	1925

Name	Number	Type	Year
WISSELINCK			
Amelia	71671	D	1936
WISSELL			
Albert F.	21558	D	1916
WISSIG			
Elizabeth	19150	D	1915
Henry	32884	D	1921
WISSING			
Frederick W.	51134	D	1928
Henry A.	23787	D	1917
Irene L.	27415	D	1919
WISSMAN			
Anna R.	51744	D	1929
Frederick Lewis	46068	D	1926
WISWELL			
Edward Smith	22254	D	1917
WITASUN			
Anselmo	24757	I	1918
WITBECK			
Ray C.	79233	D	1938
WITCHEN			
Henry	18857	D	1915
WITCHER			
Frances E. C.	59690	D	1931
WITHAM			
Charles H.	21033	I	1916
Charles H.	21039	D	1916
Frederick H. M.	22969	D	1917
Heber W.	38422	D	1924
WITHERBY			
Charles S.	60064	D	1931
WITHERS			
David C.	34646	D	1922
George L.	378	D	1906
Mary Adeline	54861	I	1930
William K.	58859	D	1931
WITHEY			
James	43454	D	1926
WITHROW			
Eva	50451	D	1928
Evelyn Almond	50451	D	1928
Katharine H.	36311	D	1923
Katherine H.	58838	D	1931
WITKOWSKI			
Feliks	13052	D	1912

NAME	NUMBER	TYPE	YEAR	NAME	NUMBER	TYPE	YEAR	NAME	NUMBER	TYPE	YEAR
WITLE				WITTLAND				WOBIG			
Paul S.	30834	D	1920	Gertrude Emilie	36153	D	1923	Anna Louise Emilie	72276	D	1936
WITMER				WITTMAN				WOCKER			
Gottlieb	3048	D	1907	John	12624	D	1911	Hermine	32259	M	1921
Gottlieb	83124	D	1940	WITTMANN				Isabel	13078	D	1912
Gus	83124	D	1940	Carolina	32688	D	1921	WODRICH			
WITOVETSKI				Cecile	38390	D	1924	Charles J.	77490	D	1938
Abraham	33583	D	1922	John	12574	M	1911	Herman	23706	D	1917
WITOWITSKI				Joseph	12574	M	1911	WOEBCKE			
Abraham	33583	D	1922	Jules	25642	D	1918	John H.	42937	D	1925
WITT				Mary A.	12574	M	1911	WOEGER			
Adolf	36240	D	1923	WITTNER				Friedrich	12386	D	1911
Al. G.	56493	D	1930	Jacob	8156	D	1909	WOEHLER			
Elise	60563	D	1931	WITTROCK				William	44093	D	1926
George F.	25123	D	1918	Adolph H. C.	47379	D	1927	WOELFEL			
George Harold	60282	M	1931	Edwin A.	41239	D	1925	John	13400	D	1912
Gertrude M.	67934	D	1934	WITTS				WOELL			
Gustave A.	56493	D	1930	Charlotte	27785	D	1919	Elizabeth	46799	D	1927
Harold John	60282	M	1931	William	10426	D	1910	WOENER			
Jochim	38313	D	1924	WITTY				William	7919	M	1909
Julius	19373	D	1915	Caroline E.	88029	D	1941	WOENNE			
Nathalie	24863	D	1918	WITWER				Emil	7230	D	1909
Otto J.	36269	M	1923	Walter E.	81126	D	1939	WOERNER			
Theodore	48949	D	1928	WITZ				David	861	D	1906
WITTE				Anna	79979	D	1938	Dorothy Ann	54050	M	1929
Adele M.	29755	D	1920	WITZEL				Eleanor Margaret	54050	M	1929
Henry	32076	D	1921	Anna W. A.	64784	D	1933	Elizabeth Jane	54050	M	1929
Paul	30834	D	1920	Gustav	27886	I	1919	Frederick W.	53770	D	1929
WITTEN				WITZEMANN				Henry Francis	73402	D	1936
Eleanor Bernice	24964	M	1918	Christiana H. S.	78347	D	1938	Loretta	55155	D	1930
WITTENBERG				Henry William	4180	D	1907	Louis P.	74535	D	1937
Charles	16114	D	1913	WLY				WOERZ			
WITTENBERGER				Alois	81700	M	1939	Shirley May	88616	M	1941
Herman	7291	D	1909	Monika	81700	M	1939	WOESSNER			
Nace	67730	D	1934	WO				Martin L.	59048	D	1931
Theodore	85760	D	1940	Yee	86273	D	1941	WOEST			
WITTENMYER				Yee Na	89822	D	1942	Laura Frances	4696	M	1907
Clara K.	35134	D	1922	Yee Sok	42498	D	1925	WOGE			
WITTER				Yee Tai	82085	D	1939	Henriette	10378	D	1910
Eva L.	46059	D	1926	Yu Wee	79951	D	1938	WOHEDEN			
WITTICH				WOBBER				Henry A. Thom	57588	D	1931
Theophilus Keffer	20107	D	1915	Emma W.	44057	D	1926	WOHLANDER			
WITTIG				Harold B.	66601	I	1934	Ellen	44874	D	1926
Gebhard	34027	D	1922	Maria Henrietta	27340	D	1919	Ursula E.	3816	M	1907
Joseph	42857	D	1925	Rose Elvira	40973	D	1925	WOHLER			
WITTING								Ana M.	14217	D	1912
Ferdinand A.	25863	D	1918								

NAME	NUMBER	TYPE	YEAR
Dalton	84658	M	1940
Emma Louisa	1780	M	1906
Martha Elizabeth	11546	D	1911
WOHLERS			
Henry	56681	D	1930
Hinrich	56680	D	1930
WOHLFRAM			
John Henry	87278	D	1941
WOHLFROM			
A. W.	64276	D	1933
Anthony Francis	64276	D	1933
WOHLKEN			
Allrich	46158	D	1927
Madeline A.	89722	D	1942
WOHLMUTH			
Leo	29880	I	1920
WOHLSDORS			
Lou Marie	77897	D	1938
WOHLSEN			
William H.	37247	D	1923
WOHLSTEIN			
Annie M.	11656	D	1911
WOHLTMANN			
Emma	5532	D	1908
Maria	78069	D	1938
William	67252	D	1934
Willie	40173	D	1924
WOHN			
Wendel	16117	D	1913
WOHRDEN			
Adeline Thom	2673	D	1907
Barbara Elizabeth Thom	43112	D	1925
Elizabeth Barbara	42907	D	1925
John H. Thom	40878	D	1925
WOITA			
Albert T.	63504	D	1933
WOJCIECHOWSKI			
Anna	28851	I	1920
Anna	43054	D	1925
WOKER			
George	1760	D	1906
WOLBERT			
Henry	75436	D	1937
WOLD			
Julia	24172	D	1918

NAME	NUMBER	TYPE	YEAR
WOLDEN			
Russell Lewis	80767	D	1939
WOLDENBERG			
Fred	15365	M	1913
WOLDERICH			
Filomena	66063	D	1934
WOLDRICH			
Filomena	66063	D	1934
WOLF			
Adelia	86725	D	1941
Adeline	35925	D	1923
Amelia	2614	D	1907
Annabel Rose	40362	M	1924
Carl A.	79644	D	1938
Charles G., Jr.	69219	D	1935
Charles Robert	70741	M	1935
Chester James	42285	M	1925
Clyde John	84604	D	1940
David	27201	D	1919
E. Myron	25680	D	1918
Edward	6459	D	1908
Edward	40254	D	1924
Eleanor L.	77171	D	1937
Elias	12774	D	1911
Eliza	1040	D	1906
Emma	62558	D	1932
Fannie	86480	D	1941
Fannie B.	61538	I	1932
Fannie B.	62704	D	1932
Fred	25796	I	1918
Fritz, Mrs.	57345	D	1930
Genevieve G.	35626	D	1922
Helena	15309	D	1913
Hermine B.	57345	D	1930
Hyman	86209	D	1941
Hyman	86479	D	1941
Isaac	34648	D	1922
Isabella	6944	D	1908
Jack	37303	D	1923
Jacob W.	64675	D	1933
Joseph	73494	D	1936
Joseph H.	44564	D	1926
Joseph J.	40361	M	1924
Julia K.	11830	D	1911
Julius	50906	D	1928
Julius L.	37859	D	1923
L. M.	36576	I	1923
Lena	63392	D	1933

NAME	NUMBER	TYPE	YEAR
Leon	59501	D	1931
Lester M.	40363	I	1924
Lorraine Ardyth	42285	M	1925
Max	54764	D	1930
Minna	48492	D	1927
Morris	11966	D	1911
Myron	25680	D	1918
Philip	9250	D	1910
Rebecca	64528	D	1933
Richard	70840	D	1935
Rosalia	10984	D	1910
Rosie	82253	D	1939
Rudolph	1806	M	1906
Simon	14647	D	1912
Sophia A.	17155	D	1914
Walter	22992	D	1917
Walter J.	59667	D	1931
Walther	52788	D	1929
Wilhelm Young	21207	D	1916
William	13124	D	1912
William Young	21207	D	1916
WOLFE			
Bertha L.	64866	D	1933
Della	86030	D	1941
Edward	84718	D	1940
Ellen Louise	57556	D	1931
Gloria W.	81172	M	1939
Jack	75557	M	1937
Leonora	62763	D	1932
Nellie	21994	I	1916
R. L., Mrs.	54503	D	1929
Samuel	35773	D	1923
Sarah	30570	D	1920
Sidney	79350	D	1938
WOLFEN			
Mary	30450	D	1920
WOLFENDEN			
Andrew	21620	D	1916
WOLFENDER			
Martin	15596	D	1913
WOLFER			
Carl	75858	M	1937
WOLFF			
Aaron	23594	D	1917
Adolf E. E.	57842	D	1931
Albert	26176	D	1919
Anna D.	12625	D	1911
Benjamin J.	38253	D	1924

Key: D = death; M = minor; I = incompetent

NAME	NUMBER	TYPE	YEAR	NAME	NUMBER	TYPE	YEAR	NAME	NUMBER	TYPE	YEAR
Bernard	8439	D	1909	**WOLFSTEIN**				**WOLLNER**			
Bernhard	64694	D	1933	Errol P.	26109	D	1919	Jacob	3861	D	1907
Betsey	4342	D	1907	**WOLFUT**				William C.	57668	M	1931
Carrie	60345	I	1931	Carl	73035	D	1936	William Christian	57833	D	1931
Charlotte Victoria	59234	D	1931	**WOLHETER**				**WOLLPERT**			
Cornelius F.	15692	D	1913	Elizabeth Jane	50851	M	1928	Alfred	20221	D	1916
D. B.	377	D	1906	Jeanne Harriett	50851	M	1928	**WOLLWEBER**			
Edna	74204	D	1936	**WOLHLER**				Emily M.	13646	D	1912
Edward M.	75295	D	1937	William	44093	D	1926	G. A.	68520	D	1934
Ella J.	88919	D	1942	**WOLKI**				Margaret M.	76707	D	1937
Elma	22804	D	1917	Frank	33220	D	1922	**WOLMER**			
Frank W.	82226	D	1939	Franz	33220	D	1922	Max	71936	D	1936
George	5942	D	1908	Fred	33220	D	1922	**WOLONGIEWRICZ**			
George Walter	9354	M	1910	Fritz	33220	D	1922	Michael	12118	D	1911
Harris	3988	D	1907	**WOLL**				**WOLPMAN**			
Harry N.	80347	D	1939	Anna L.	34738	D	1922	Amalia	27908	D	1919
Helen Marie	23586	M	1917	Charles	31546	D	1921	Mollie	27908	D	1919
Henry	43844	D	1926	Charles J.	45930	D	1926	**WOLPMANN**			
Henry Norbert	9354	M	1910	Eliza	46799	D	1927	Bernhard	1661	D	1906
Herman	48339	I	1927	**WOLLAB**				**WOLTER**			
Hugo A.	74820	D	1937	Albert	83259	D	1940	Herman	63458	I	1933
Illinois	11123	I	1911	**WOLLAK**				**WOLTERS**			
Isaac	67029	D	1934	Eugene	76100	D	1937	Carl	46133	D	1927
Johanna	45473	D	1926	**WOLLBERG**				Catherine	7419	I	1909
Johanna	75654	D	1937	A. S., Mrs.	84600	D	1940	Catherine M.	69438	D	1935
Matilda	8071	D	1909	Claudina	84600	D	1940	Francis M.	17786	M	1914
Rosa	32447	D	1921	**WOLLEB**				Henry	12098	D	1911
Theodore	25024	D	1918	Albert	83259	D	1940	Henry J.	4298	D	1907
William	23805	D	1917	Casper	52376	D	1929	Herman R.	27148	I	1919
William	63957	D	1933	**WOLLENBERG**				John Bernard	36873	D	1923
WOLFFE				Dorothea	76893	M	1937	John Julius	25256	M	1918
George E.	3370	D	1907	Gertrude A.	27390	D	1919	Louis A., Jr.	17786	M	1914
WOLFGRAM				I. E.	75025	I	1937	Marie	32035	D	1921
August	79760	D	1938	Isidor	75346	D	1937	Sylvester E.	77316	D	1937
WOLFORD				Isidore	75025	I	1937	William	17786	M	1914
Rose	61041	I	1932	J. Roger	29743	M	1920	Wm. E.	719	D	1906
WOLFROM				J. Roger	49930	M	1928	**WOLTMANN**			
Adam	17803	D	1914	Jacob	76891	D	1937	Gacha Adelheid Schulze	61384	D	1932
George E.	82046	D	1939	Julia	32925	D	1921	**WON**			
WOLFSDORF				Millie	86036	I	1941	Dow Mon	38285	D	1924
Elsie May	14424	D	1912	Ralph J.	29802	D	1920	Jack Ho	79100	D	1938
WOLFSKILL				Rose	76892	I	1937	Lee	38285	D	1924
Margaret	22347	D	1917	**WOLLESEN**				Yum	38767	M	1924
WOLFSOHN				Magdalena	44871	D	1926	**WONDERLICH**			
Eva	70374	D	1935	**WOLLFEL**				Walter S.	72646	I	1936
Rachel M.	18603	D	1915	John	13400	D	1912	**WONG**			
WOLFSON								Chew	71894	D	1936
Ferdinand	84903	D	1940								

Key: D = death; M = minor; I = incompetent

NAME	NUMBER	TYPE	YEAR	NAME	NUMBER	TYPE	YEAR	NAME	NUMBER	TYPE	YEAR
Choon Wah	79834	M	1938	Tin Hee, Mrs.	54972	D	1930	Catherine C.	53164	D	1929
Choon Wah	80387	D	1939	Tin Hi	45476	D	1926	Charles H.	16877	D	1914
Chu Dun	79208	D	1938	Tun Kan	46610	M	1927	Clayton G.	45389	D	1926
Chun Chack	73273	D	1936	W. D.	28486	D	1919	Delia J. F.	16871	D	1914
Chung	85008	I	1940	Wah	33901	M	1922	Dora	7561	D	1909
Doris	40478	M	1924	William	15075	M	1913	E. K.	12667	D	1911
Foo	33901	M	1922	William	78890	D	1938	E. Melvin	15434	D	1913
Foo	41858	D	1925	Willy	36517	M	1923	Edna Rose	64302	M	1933
Foo	41858	D	1925	Worley	15075	M	1913	Edward	2443	D	1906
Foo, Mrs.	82780	D	1939	Y. Y.	20183	D	1915	Edward	89516	D	1942
Gee	88536	M	1941	Yan Sang	40924	M	1925	Eliza A.	16708	D	1914
Gee Chong	36290	D	1923	Yee Shee	82780	D	1939	Elizabeth	58335	D	1931
Gee You	55502	D	1930	Yep Yuen	78890	D	1938	Emily Jane	13533	D	1912
Gladys	46366	D	1927	Ying	33901	M	1922	Floyd H.	25289	D	1918
Goot	33901	M	1922	Ying	60330	D	1931	Francis C.	31994	D	1921
Haim	84033	D	1940	Yoke Seem	40478	M	1924	Frank F.	27504	D	1919
Henry	15075	M	1913	Yow	78851	D	1938	Frank Pixley	89973	I	1942
Herschel	87921	M	1941	**WONZOD**				Frederick	47245	D	1927
Hip Sue	45164	D	1926	John F.	49719	D	1928	Frederick D.	31484	D	1921
Ho Shee	47629	D	1927	**WOO**				Frederick Edwin	36769	D	1923
Hong Lon	42244	D	1925	Chow	16518	D	1913	Fremont	74496	D	1937
Hung	42115	M	1925	Do Quong	77511	D	1938	George A.	65238	D	1933
Jennie	15075	M	1913	Lee	89155	D	1942	George Arthur	10834	M	1910
Jin	33901	M	1922	Ng	26956	D	1919	George C.	51119	D	1928
Kow	33302	D	1922	Ng Wan	44488	D	1926	George G.	33897	D	1922
Lily	36517	M	1923	Soon	79701	D	1938	Gertrude H.	71386	D	1936
Lim On	47908	D	1927	Sue Chai	39180	M	1924	Gertrude S.	71386	D	1936
Lin Fong	43369	D	1926	Wai Young	89056	D	1942	Grant Ulysses	48352	I	1927
Lun	79999	D	1938	Wo On	44488	D	1926	Hamilton G.	7065	M	1909
Mabel	41051	D	1925	You	44534	D	1926	Hamilton Holton	15033	D	1913
Me Heung	42114	M	1925	**WOOD**				Harry A.	82200	D	1939
Mei Ho	41051	D	1925	Abbie Rose	51227	I	1928	Helen L.	62706	D	1932
Mi Jaun	61785	D	1932	Abbie Rose	78010	D	1938	Henry	23367	D	1917
Min Ying	79999	D	1938	Ada M.	75924	D	1937	Horace Bertram	49060	D	1928
Oie Yoke	48416	M	1927	Alice G.	65067	D	1933	Irving W.	36116	D	1923
Oy	33901	M	1922	Andrew	40515	D	1924	James Cleveland	59513	D	1931
Oye Oye	17617	M	1914	Andrew Younger	67425	D	1934	Johanna	43555	D	1926
Polly	79834	M	1938	Anna Elisabeth	81132	D	1939	John Arthur	43772	D	1926
Polly	80387	D	1939	Anna M.	61948	D	1932	John Wortham	9168	D	1910
Rose	56256	M	1930	Annie	26900	D	1919	Josephine	55737	I	1930
Sam	45809	D	1926	Arnold L.	58091	M	1931	Josephine	55869	D	1930
She Dow	59754	D	1931	Arthur	56814	D	1930	Kate G.	53907	D	1929
Shee	39006	D	1924	B.	9797	D	1910	Laura Etta	83360	D	1940
Sing	42244	D	1925	Benjamin	7299	D	1909	Lester H.	27974	M	1919
Sing	79208	D	1938	Benjamin	8873	D	1909	Lester H.	31940	D	1921
Sui Sun	40924	M	1925	Bryon C.	43978	D	1926	Lewis	54198	D	1929
Tim	51642	D	1928	Caroline Langton	36322	D	1923	Louis	33561	D	1922
Tin Hee	45476	D	1926	Carrara R.	72644	D	1936	Maggie E.	68330	D	1934
Tin Hee	45476	D	1926					Margaret	27051	D	1919

Key: D = death; M = minor; I = incompetent

NAME	NUMBER	TYPE	YEAR
Margaret Cary	55509	M	1930
Marian	19490	M	1915
Mary A.	77084	D	1937
Mary Baldwin	60873	D	1932
Mary Baldwin	59691	I	1931
Mary C.	18114	D	1914
Mary E.	29416	D	1920
Mary J.	2833	D	1907
Mary Wilhelmena	60151	M	1931
Meyer	66717	D	1934
Nancy Annette	42364	D	1925
Norman K.	58091	M	1931
Norman W.	56725	D	1930
Olga Jungbluth	82183	D	1939
Paul	54567	D	1929
Ralph W.	1560	D	1906
Roldo Mortimer	48366	D	1927
S. Viola	32501	D	1921
Sallie	65588	D	1933
Samuel A.	80825	D	1939
Sarah L.	65588	D	1933
Selden C.	60867	D	1932
Thomas	72479	D	1936
Thomas E.	23434	D	1917
Wilfred Sterling	85506	D	1940
William D.	76696	D	1937
William F.	61948	D	1932
William Gavin	17653	D	1914
William M.	39713	D	1924
William Richard	10831	D	1910
William Thomas	2820	D	1907
WOODALL			
Annie	62466	D	1932
John Thomas	51401	D	1928
Mary Anne	69669	D	1935
WOODARD			
Arthur V.	10417	D	1910
Belle R.	82236	D	1939
Julia E.	70005	I	1935
Julia E.	70005	I	1935
Silas	4209	D	1907
Sylvina L.	39146	D	1924
WOODBURN			
D. M.	2719	D	1907
WOODBURY			
Frances S.	70893	D	1935
George E.	9410	D	1910
Isaac Allen	14882	D	1913

NAME	NUMBER	TYPE	YEAR
John James	87755	D	1941
W. D.	39735	D	1924
WOODEN			
Eli	9744	D	1910
WOODFIELD			
Annie Maria	10592	D	1910
Ruby A.	36952	D	1923
Walter Lincoln	45397	D	1926
WOODHEAD			
Peter	74360	D	1937
WOODHOUSE			
Bert E.	22090	D	1917
Gertrude A.	370	D	1906
J. J.	2324	D	1906
WOODHULL			
Melvina E.	40907	D	1925
WOODLAND			
Evelyn	28368	M	1919
Evelyn E.	19551	M	1915
WOODLING			
Vera	24958	M	1918
WOODMAN			
E. D.	22505	D	1917
Ella Jane	6972	I	1908
Esther Serafia	43387	D	1926
Harrison G.	6105	D	1908
WOODROW			
Margaret	75209	I	1937
Oscar F.	78218	D	1938
WOODRUFF			
Anne Bryce	86289	D	1941
Charles William	24267	M	1918
David William	50407	D	1928
Edith	32382	D	1921
Ellen M.	44282	D	1926
J. J., Mrs.	32382	D	1921
Lora A.	14930	D	1913
Louise Virginia	89918	D	1942
Minnie J.	57316	D	1930
WOODS			
Ann Eliza	1241	D	1906
Anna May	73667	D	1936
Anne Eliza	39437	D	1924
Annie	14547	D	1912
B.	9797	D	1910
Charles	21504	D	1916
Charles	54620	D	1929

NAME	NUMBER	TYPE	YEAR
Charles M.	42002	D	1925
Edith C.	10918	D	1910
Edmund Leyland	84973	D	1940
Elizabeth	51746	D	1929
Ellen	21673	D	1916
Enos	41250	D	1925
F. W.	47245	D	1927
Frank H.	3229	D	1907
Frank Meek	69571	D	1935
Frank Westly	85738	D	1940
Frederick Nickerson	10652	D	1910
Harry Frank	67748	D	1934
Helen	72269	D	1936
Henry	34567	D	1922
James	83840	D	1940
Joseph	4481	D	1907
Joseph	56687	D	1930
Joseph K.	71528	I	1936
Joseph Lougheed	39605	I	1924
Joseph Lougheed	41551	I	1925
Josephine G.	20419	D	1916
Kitty	76967	D	1937
Lambert L.	28319	D	1919
Lenore M.	72269	D	1936
Louisa	7770	D	1909
Louisa Castro	58096	D	1931
Louise Barr	61503	D	1932
Martha	68695	D	1935
Mary E.	7525	D	1909
Mary Jane	21872	D	1916
May Belle	85481	D	1940
Minnie E.	82109	D	1939
Morrell	75314	D	1937
Owen	9743	D	1910
Patrick	21674	D	1916
Retta Thompson	87775	D	1941
Robert J.	38238	D	1924
S. D., Mrs.	14547	D	1912
Samuel D.	20376	D	1916
Samuel Moseley	9384	D	1910
Thomas	19855	I	1915
Thomas	20204	D	1916
Thomas J.	85049	D	1940
Vincent	2665	D	1907
Walter H.	22875	D	1917
William, Mrs.	76967	D	1937
WOODSEN			
Lottie E.	59909	D	1931

Key: D = death; M = minor; I = incompetent

NAME	NUMBER	TYPE	YEAR	NAME	NUMBER	TYPE	YEAR	NAME	NUMBER	TYPE	YEAR
WOODSIDE				WOODYARD				WORD			
Alexander	31738	D	1921	A. C.	27672	D	1919	James	30525	M	1920
Alexander F.	25613	D	1918	WOOLARD				WORDEN			
Alonzo Colby	70007	D	1935	William T.	37794	D	1923	Charles E.	86920	D	1941
Alonzo Colby	70007	D	1935	WOOLDRDGE				Clinton E.	39622	D	1924
Isabella	75226	D	1937	Doris	34295	D	1922	Ralph W.	10447	M	1910
WOODSON				WOOLDRIDGE				William H.	84248	D	1940
Betty	77054	M	1937	Mable H.	43097	D	1925	WORES			
Frances Thorn	50038	D	1928	WOOLER				Gertrude	68446	D	1934
Fred	74080	D	1936	William	14489	D	1912	Joseph	432	D	1906
WOODTHORPE				WOOLEY				Theodore	82303	D	1939
James M.	23494	D	1917	John Cyrus	12222	D	1911	WORK			
WOODWARD				William P.	59976	I	1931	George A.	84441	D	1940
Anne Spain	35540	D	1922	WOOLF				WORKMAN			
Davis A.	62327	D	1932	Rachael	64030	D	1933	Charles H.	34101	D	1922
Dorothy	10530	M	1910	WOOLLEY				Henry I.	34510	D	1922
Frank	10530	M	1910	Albert W.	31797	D	1921	WORLD			
Frederick William	36239	D	1923	Barbara Roberta	44895	M	1926	John Washington	15400	D	1913
George Holmes	78994	D	1938	Eldon Wirt	44895	M	1926	WORLEY			
Harry	65215	D	1933	Eusebia	16723	D	1914	Dean B.	46727	D	1927
Jessie R.	48170	D	1927	Kenneth Eugene	44895	M	1926	Dorothy	48780	M	1927
Lizzie Loucks O'Keefe	59785	D	1931	WOOLNOUGH				Lou Bush	78003	D	1938
Louisa	10530	M	1910	Mary Ann	42368	D	1925	Raymond	48780	M	1927
Mary A.	2182	D	1906	Walter	42037	D	1925	WORMALD			
Melinda	1395	D	1906	WOOLRICH				Henry	66472	D	1934
Robert B.	10666	D	1910	George L.	63343	D	1933	WORMELL			
Robert S.	70276	D	1935	WOOLSEY				Ernest E.	78544	D	1938
Sarah Alice	43018	D	1925	Charlotte A.	47024	I	1927	Kate E.	80813	I	1939
Thomas P.	35539	D	1922	Elizabeth	84110	D	1940	Katherine E.	82385	D	1939
W. E.	49188	D	1928	Florence E.	87456	D	1941	WORMSER			
Walter M., Sr.	53607	D	1929	Henry	60476	D	1931	Blanche	38828	D	1924
WOODWORTH				Margaret S.	68960	D	1935	Ella K.	62163	D	1932
Annie	38903	D	1924	Mark Hopkins	57889	D	1931	Gustav	31331	D	1921
Edward L.	12277	D	1911	Olive	25546	D	1918	Helene	60993	I	1932
Evelyn Lydia	4792	M	1907	William J.	63470	D	1933	Julius	31119	D	1921
Frederick A.	26498	D	1919	WOOLVERTON				Louis	11481	D	1911
George L.	72997	D	1936	Albert T.	33210	I	1922	Pauline A.	36142	D	1923
Harvey Elijah	23885	D	1918	WOOLWORTH				W.	13130	D	1912
Helen F.	82868	D	1939	Helen Irene	1460	D	1906	WORMUTH			
John	41704	D	1925	WOOSTER				Martin E.	17727	D	1914
Newton	59642	D	1931	Arthur R.	60088	D	1931	WORN			
Ruth G.	75747	D	1937	Fletcher L.	40986	D	1925	Annie Giblin	73089	D	1936
William McMichael	14014	D	1912	William	50596	D	1928	WORNALL			
WOODY				WORCESTER				Sophie E.	38438	D	1924
Charles Sumner	41866	D	1925	Joseph	15914	D	1913	WORNER			
Charles Sumner	41866	D	1925					Elizabeth McGeary	6159	D	1908
Mary Ann	57890	M	1931					John	6375	M	1908

NAME	NUMBER	TYPE	YEAR
WORNES			
Lucinda S.	62608	D	1932
WORRALL			
Sarah	6635	D	1908
WORRELL			
Alice Estelle	15803	M	1913
Lucia	20379	D	1916
WORSCH			
Beatrice A.	54835	D	1930
WORSDORFER			
John	66668	D	1934
WORSINICK			
Charles William	46673	D	1927
WORST			
John	7941	D	1909
WORSTER			
Emma L.	20222	D	1916
WORT			
Henry	14036	D	1912
WORTH			
Charles A.	37388	D	1923
Clifford Lewis	48237	M	1927
Florence E.	75395	D	1937
Henry Charles	79368	D	1938
L. E.	75344	D	1937
Mary A.	19875	D	1915
Mary L.	63333	I	1933
Mary L.	78408	D	1938
Minnie I.	77482	D	1938
Obed	2320	D	1906
WORTHAM			
Fern	85123	M	1940
WORTHEN			
Burt L.	25136	D	1918
WORTHINGTON			
Daisy J.	28002	D	1919
Dee	46540	D	1927
Ella	56764	D	1930
Herbert	13708	D	1912
Musa	16536	D	1913
WORTMAN			
David B.	57036	D	1930
WORTSMITH			
Hannah	1354	D	1906
J. J.	9738	D	1910

NAME	NUMBER	TYPE	YEAR
WRALDSEN			
Ole L.	7126	D	1909
WRAY			
Dan Ernest Henry	27676	D	1919
Enily	36717	D	1923
Samuel	10603	D	1910
WRBA			
Alice	6714	M	1908
Joseph	1011	D	1906
Joseph	6714	M	1908
Joseph	23128	D	1917
Olga	6714	M	1908
WREDE			
August	72726	D	1936
Augusta	25158	D	1918
Augusta	86407	D	1941
Henry	76789	D	1937
Julius G.	51890	D	1929
WREDEN			
Elizabeth	23538	D	1917
Emma M.	65922	D	1933
Henry M.	50406	D	1928
Wilhelmina A.	78676	D	1938
WREM			
Victor E. A.	13355	D	1912
WREN			
Bartholomew I.	60783	D	1932
Catherine	15331	D	1913
Catherine M.	58575	D	1931
Daniel J.	65874	D	1933
Edward J.	37850	D	1923
Herbert	48158	D	1927
Lawrence	11277	D	1911
Victor E. A.	13355	D	1912
William John	47553	D	1927
WRENN			
Harriet D.	32274	D	1921
WRIG			
Ferdinand	36215	D	1923
WRIGHT			
Adeline	81312	M	1939
Agnes	711	D	1906
Alexina M.	35150	D	1922
Alfred Charles	29198	M	1920
Alfred Charles	30695	M	1920
Alfred Charles	54024	M	1929
Alfred William	79466	D	1938

NAME	NUMBER	TYPE	YEAR
Alice Beatty	10528	D	1910
Alice M.	56524	D	1930
Alice P.	72192	I	1936
Almeda D.	42099	D	1925
Andrew J.	54772	D	1930
Angie L.	40953	D	1925
Anna	59164	I	1931
Anna	72120	I	1936
Anna	74104	D	1936
Annie	42155	D	1925
Annie E.	54051	D	1929
Arminda	77857	D	1938
Arthur L.	63605	D	1933
Benjamin C.	33375	D	1922
Bertha Mildred	27076	D	1919
Bertram E.	25406	D	1918
Carlos Antonio	4640	M	1907
Carlos Antonio	77082	D	1937
Caroline V.	9949	I	1910
Caroline V.	12434	D	1911
Charles W.	52193	D	1929
Chester F.	12410	D	1911
Clara M.	17995	D	1914
Correnah Wilson	67899	D	1934
Cyrus S.	16296	D	1913
Edmund A.	72632	D	1936
Edna Vina	50350	D	1928
Edward Clark	39908	D	1924
Edward J.	43255	I	1925
Edward J.	70174	D	1935
Eileen Gladys	30381	M	1920
Ellen	11446	D	1911
Elvirda	22328	D	1917
Emmet Rector	78856	M	1938
Ernest Crocker	89953	I	1942
Gaberilla	81976	M	1939
George J.	20424	D	1916
George M.	4640	M	1907
George S.	1348	D	1906
Gordon	55465	D	1930
Grace Gilmer	68676	D	1935
Guy	89210	M	1942
Harold S.	55966	D	1930
Harry F.	45503	D	1926
Helen A.	22806	D	1917
Helen B.	50536	D	1928
Helen Louise	65724	D	1933
Henry	21103	D	1916
Henry A.	88438	D	1941

Name	Number	Type	Year	Name	Number	Type	Year	Name	Number	Type	Year
Hiram French	66291	D	1934	Robert J.	10863	D	1910	John C.	5618	D	1908
Howard A.	63806	D	1933	Rose	56950	D	1930	Wilhelm	19201	D	1915
Isabella H.	76906	D	1937	Sadie	8441	D	1909	William	19201	D	1915
Jack	81312	M	1939	Selden Stuart	11378	M	1911	**Wuelfken**			
James	69656	D	1935	Selden Stuart	72655	D	1936	Anna	11812	D	1911
James F.	15812	I	1913	Timothy J.	68368	D	1934	Raymond	11963	M	1911
James F.	18415	D	1915	Verna	89210	M	1942	**Wuersching**			
James Montgomery	4829	D	1907	Vinnia	50350	D	1928	John Berthold	30475	D	1920
Jessie Orene	24353	M	1918	Walter K.	48517	D	1927	John Leonard	56442	M	1930
Jessie S.	18991	I	1915	William	47726	D	1927	**Wuest**			
Joanna Maynard	31293	D	1921	William Beatty	11378	M	1911	Eberhard Paul Gerhard	87422	D	1941
John	19697	D	1915	William H.	18705	D	1915	**Wuestefeld**			
John A.	16338	D	1913	William J.	39800	D	1924	Conrad	35917	D	1923
John H.	29105	D	1920	William Stewart	81935	D	1939	Gussie	80683	D	1939
John H.	30518	M	1920	Wm.	8486	D	1909	Herman	74558	D	1937
John M.	28882	D	1920	**Wrightson**				Johann	70964	D	1935
John P.	62848	I	1932	Harold	81039	D	1939	**Wuesterfeld**			
John T.	13928	D	1912	**Wrigley**				Sarah Theresa	75930	D	1937
John T.	52017	D	1929	Effie Nash	83773	D	1940	**Wuger**			
John T., Jr.	4640	M	1907	**Wrin**				Edward	58582	D	1931
Joseph	30078	D	1920	Fidelis	21880	M	1916	**Wuhrmann**			
Joseph	79450	D	1938	James	21476	D	1916	Henry A.	80419	D	1939
Julia	29468	D	1920	Mary Ellen	23347	D	1917	**Wujnovich**			
June	33869	M	1922	Sarah W.	485	D	1906	Silvo	31914	I	1921
Leslie	33869	M	1922	Thomas	1579	D	1906	**Wulbern**			
Lillian Marian	73079	D	1936	William	486	M	1906	John	1667	D	1906
Louie	87162	D	1941	William	21880	M	1916	**Wulbers**			
Louise	9476	D	1910	**Wrinkle**				Herman	46871	D	1927
Lucius L.	24811	D	1918	Herbert Lawrence	3384	D	1907	Louise	46430	D	1927
Lydia M.	18063	D	1914	**Wrinn**				**Wulf**			
M. J.	1592	I	1906	Elizabeth Jane	17255	M	1914	Henry C.	50083	D	1928
Manuel	44317	D	1926	Ellen	18837	D	1915	**Wulff**			
Margaret	50737	D	1928	Michael	2862	D	1907	Anna Eva	18606	D	1915
Martin J.	8806	D	1909	Rose	17255	M	1914	Anna Marie	78058	M	1938
Mary	52103	D	1929	**Wristen**				Anna T.	68418	D	1934
Mary Elizabeth Gentle	21392	M	1916	Cameo	77942	M	1938	Catherine M	21017	D	1916
Mary Graham	28655	D	1920	James Francis	85293	M	1940	Franklin	85451	D	1940
Mercedes M.	1640	D	1906	Levi E.	68322	D	1934	Hans	1043	D	1906
Michael D.	12196	D	1911	William Arthur	85293	M	1940	Jurgen Hinrich	54938	D	1930
Millie Langley	74054	D	1936	**Wrixon**				Mae	88550	D	1941
Minnie	46658	D	1927	John	72461	D	1936	Meta M.	63812	D	1933
Nathaniel Bill	11231	D	1911	**Wu**				Sine	20369	D	1916
Olivia Galbraith	55815	D	1930	Robert Wilson	41637	M	1925	**Wulzen**			
Ora Lee	24353	M	1918	**Wucherer**				Anna	35357	D	1922
Paula Rae	81976	M	1939	Adria	80791	M	1939	Anne M.	22563	D	1917
Percy Arthur	67286	D	1934	Cristof C.	3758	D	1907	Hannah E.	72936	D	1936
R. Percy	172	D	1906	Johannes	5618	D	1908				
Robert Creighton	70943	D	1935								
Robert Earnshaw	172	D	1906								

NAME	NUMBER	TYPE	YEAR
WUN			
Ah Kin	64566	D	1933
Benjamin	48749	D	1927
WUNCHE			
Anna	19299	D	1915
WUNDER			
Adam D.	63963	D	1933
Conrad	53187	D	1929
Emma	20883	D	1916
Henry	86252	D	1941
John C.	51699	D	1928
William	35249	I	1922
WUNDERLICH			
Charles	54123	D	1929
Emma Maria	84555	D	1940
Hannah	35542	I	1922
Hannah	44885	D	1926
Otto	27883	D	1919
WUNSCH			
J. Edmund	59899	M	1931
Minna	28645	D	1920
WUNSCHER			
Christian Caroline Marie	9822	D	1910
WUNSHEL			
Theodore	63979	D	1933
WUOLLE			
Onni A.	41507	D	1925
WUOTILLA			
Eframi	49102	D	1928
Exeami	49102	D	1928
WUPSON			
May	33074	D	1921
WURDINGER			
Anton	33967	D	1922
WURKHEIM			
Paula	13987	D	1912
Sylvan	65950	D	1933
WURLITZER			
Eugene F.	41587	D	1925
WURM			
Charles A.	74964	D	1937
Charles M.	74964	D	1937
Theodore A.	71458	D	1936
WURMBACH			
Albert O.	64625	I	1933

NAME	NUMBER	TYPE	YEAR
WURSTER			
Doris	64403	M	1933
Jean	64403	M	1933
WURTZ			
Maria Eva	1674	D	1906
WUSTERFELD			
Barbara	87130	M	1941
Eugene Richard	87130	M	1941
Helen Jean	87130	M	1941
WUSTERHAUSEN			
Cecilia	58114	D	1931
WUTH			
Charm Ivy	47968	D	1927
WUTHRICH			
Edward	3193	M	1907
William R.	3193	M	1907
WY			
Joyce	80256	M	1939
Lowe How	80253	D	1939
Wendall	80256	M	1939
WYANT			
Linda May	36611	M	1923
Mark	39695	D	1924
WYATT			
Allen Ray	62236	D	1932
Claude W.	89006	D	1942
Harriett	18631	D	1915
John P.	45497	D	1926
Mary E.	80475	D	1939
Thomas	1528	D	1906
William Andrew	26756	D	1919
WYCHE			
Marietta	28532	M	1919
Thomas J.	38032	D	1924
WYER			
Mary	9994	D	1910
WYLER			
Josephine Elizabeth	74188	D	1936
WYLIE			
Alfred	86840	D	1941
Anna	78066	D	1938
Anna Belle	81092	D	1939
Anna Heal	374	D	1906
Caroline	52834	D	1929
Edward Harry	70744	M	1935
Elmer E.	86330	D	1941
Henry	23690	M	1917

NAME	NUMBER	TYPE	YEAR
Joseph Hatfield	30876	D	1920
Robert E.	57149	D	1930
WYLLIE			
John	38570	D	1924
Margaret	4868	D	1907
Robert	58685	D	1931
WYMAN			
Caroline E.	1649	D	1906
Frank	49441	D	1928
James G.	76553	D	1937
Walter H.	7089	M	1909
WYMORE			
William W.	79131	D	1938
WYNDHAM			
Alward	9220	I	1910
WYNEKEN			
L. E.	12890	I	1912
Leopold Ernest	16245	D	1913
WYNN			
Catherine J.	28687	D	1920
Elizabeth	6282	D	1908
Grover	39271	D	1924
Mary Elizabeth	49714	D	1928
Mathew	12314	D	1911
WYNNE			
Abbie	57418	D	1930
Arthur W.	6750	M	1908
Clarence	18932	M	1915
Dorothy Fayette	73531	D	1936
Eliza	15424	I	1913
Eliza	15481	I	1913
Elizabeth A.	67020	I	1934
Elizabeth A.	74195	D	1936
Ellen	1343	D	1906
Faye Dorothy	73531	D	1936
Henry M.	6750	M	1908
John J.	18932	M	1915
Lorraine	18932	M	1915
Martin	18932	M	1915
Mary A.	11372	D	1911
WYNTER-SMITH			
Annie	67500	D	1934
WYRICH			
Caroline	42950	D	1925
WYRICK			
William H.	18170	D	1914

NAME	NUMBER	TYPE	YEAR	NAME	NUMBER	TYPE	YEAR	NAME	NUMBER	TYPE	YEAR
WYSS				**YAMAZAKI**				**YAUNKE**			
Joseph A.	67278	D	1934	Flora Michiko	33113	M	1921	Louise	82357	D	1939
XAVIER				William Toshi	33113	M	1921	**YAYTSKY**			
Manuel Machado	70999	D	1935	**YAN**				Michael Tichon	78891	D	1938
XENOS				How Yem Yan	64566	D	1933	**YAZIJIAN**			
James	25417	D	1918	Jue Yick	47252	D	1927	C. H.	45067	D	1926
XEPOLEAS				Tam	2398	M	1906	Casbar H.	45067	D	1926
Belle	83684	D	1940	**YANES**				Caspar	45067	D	1926
XERRI				Rachel	41653	D	1925	Caspar, Jr.	45069	M	1926
David	51338	D	1928	Raquel	41653	D	1925	Robert Warren	45069	M	1926
XYPOLIAS				**YANG**				**YBARRA**			
Vasile	83684	D	1940	Helen	63113	M	1932	Estella	88432	I	1941
Vasilike	83684	D	1940	Lillian	63113	M	1932	**YBERT**			
Vasiliki	83684	D	1940	Moses	63113	M	1932	Jean	6896	D	1908
YABLONSKY				**YANKEY**				**yDeLASTRA**			
John	19347	D	1915	Michael	33510	D	1922	Francisco	4620	D	1907
YABLOWSKI				**YANO**				**YDEN**			
Meyer	1172	D	1906	Hiroshi	73242	D	1936	John	62221	D	1932
YACHN				**YARBROUGH**				**YEAGER**			
Charles	53167	D	1929	Berthol	24081	I	1918	Joe D.	69553	D	1935
YAEGER				**YARD**				**YEARING**			
Frederick W.	79856	D	1938	Henry Herbert	18097	D	1914	James Thomas	82686	D	1939
YAEST				**YARL**				Lucia Alice	63017	D	1932
Mary	15149	D	1913	Floyd	37610	M	1923	Lucille Annette	64688	M	1933
YAGER				**YARNALL**				**YEATES**			
Christian	75096	D	1937	David H.	38365	D	1924	Aida	75327	D	1937
Eyvend	2252	D	1906	**YARROW**				**YEATMAN**			
William W.	77859	D	1938	Alice Enright	88981	D	1942	Elizabeth	81812	I	1939
YAKE				**YASHIMA**				**YEATON**			
Ah	34062	D	1922	Tei	3752	M	1907	Oliver R.	71772	D	1936
Lee	34062	D	1922	**YATES**				**YEE**			
YAKUBOVSKY				Amelia	36272	D	1923	Alfred DeVoe	60893	D	1932
Vadin	64845	M	1933	Charles M.	7454	D	1909	Ben Hong	73194	D	1936
YALE				Edwin F.	85256	I	1940	Benjamin D.	60894	D	1932
Charles Gegory	44039	D	1926	Eugene A., Mrs.	36272	D	1923	Chung	46027	D	1926
YALE-SMITH				Eugene Adolph	57120	D	1930	Ella	67480	M	1934
Doreen	65381	M	1933	Eula	89879	D	1942	Emily	39032	M	1924
YAM				Florence	2358	D	1906	Fanny	87911	M	1941
How Yem Yan	64566	D	1933	Julia J.	37789	D	1923	Francis	34309	M	1922
YAMAGUCHI				Lillie T.	12317	D	1911	Hong	67480	M	1934
Shohei	85272	D	1940	Luther L.	67741	D	1934	Jae	72299	D	1936
YAMANE				Mary	16251	D	1913	Jessie	67480	M	1934
Tatsuichi	40075	D	1924	Mary Elisabeth Fish	85255	I	1940	Jue	87571	D	1941
YAMASAKI				Thomas	27296	D	1919	Kum Jon	82780	D	1939
Senkichi	51451	D	1928	**YAU**				Lan Lai	39383	D	1924
				Hoo Yuet	47850	M	1927	Leonard	82765	M	1939
				Low Men	69230	D	1935	Leung Kie	57761	D	1931

NAME	NUMBER	TYPE	YEAR	NAME	NUMBER	TYPE	YEAR	NAME	NUMBER	TYPE	YEAR
Li Chow	50975	D	1928	**YERINGTON**				**YITTNER**			
Lung Kie	57761	D	1931	Clara V.	66200	D	1934	Louis	67960	D	1934
May	60892	D	1932	H. M.	11320	D	1911	**YLINEN**			
May	67480	M	1934	**YERKES**				Sigrid	78575	D	1938
Sang	50439	D	1928	Thomas M.	63577	D	1933	**YLITA**			
Sheong	72298	D	1936	**YERKICH**				Jacob	26338	D	1919
Sok Wah	42498	D	1925	Samuel	75371	D	1937	**YLITER**			
Sok Who	42498	D	1925	**YERTAN**				Jacob	26338	D	1919
Sok Wo	42498	D	1925	Ora Mary	89638	D	1942	**YOCUM**			
Tai Wo	82085	D	1939	**YERZYKOWICZ**				Anita May	39320	M	1924
Tan	63091	D	1932	Francis	69875	D	1935	Virginia May	39320	M	1924
Tin	42498	D	1925	**YETT**				**YODER**			
Yen	74025	D	1936	Rebecca	71798	D	1936	Holly F.	65726	D	1933
Yen Gong	80279	D	1939	**YETTA**				Louis M.	41296	D	1925
Yeung Ah	24878	M	1918	Henry	63988	D	1933	**YOELL**			
YELICH				**YEW**				Abraham E.	64585	D	1933
Samuel R.	49722	D	1928	Cheong Lung	54151	D	1929	J. A.	56	D	1906
YELIN				**YICK**				Lawrence	12417	M	1911
Otto	17543	D	1914	Quan	55939	D	1930	**YOEST**			
YELLAND				Quang	55939	D	1930	Elsie	61916	M	1932
Walter Borden	24817	M	1918	**YIM**				John	61916	M	1932
YELLITZ				Arthur	39531	M	1924	**YOKE**			
Henry	12348	D	1911	Dorothy	39531	M	1924	Chan Ho	7045	M	1909
YELMINI				Ham Bing	43308	M	1926	Szto	21586	M	1916
Clemente	15966	D	1913	Henry Wong	69183	D	1935	Wong	30689	D	1920
YELTON				Lawrence Harold	84535	M	1940	Wong Ah	2720	M	1907
Billy F.	67485	M	1934	Lincoln	39531	M	1924	Wong Oie	48416	M	1927
YEMANS				Louie	17522	D	1914	**YOKELA**			
Bina Frances	17091	D	1914	Luella	39531	M	1924	John	24168	D	1918
Herbert W.	28912	D	1920	Pearl	39531	M	1924	**YOLDI**			
YEN				William Henry	69183	D	1935	Juan	29291	D	1920
Chin	36188	D	1923	Wong	69183	D	1935	**YON**			
Louie	42845	M	1925	**YIN**				Julio	87396	D	1941
Yee	74025	D	1936	Sue	35732	D	1923	**YONDERS**			
YENIS				Suey	35732	D	1923	Lizzie	19903	D	1915
Mary	26025	D	1918	**YING**				**YONG**			
YEO				Huie Guey	14754	D	1913	Caroline	83627	M	1940
Catherine	34096	D	1922	Kum	21585	M	1916	**YONKE**			
YEP				Lee	21844	M	1916	Marcus	34391	D	1922
Charlie Chin	39037	D	1924	Lee Won	59774	D	1931	Mary	72278	D	1936
Chin	39037	D	1924	Lum Que	18507	M	1915	**YOONG**			
Jue	48629	D	1927	Tom Sun	14635	M	1912	Moy	51099	D	1928
YERBY				Wong	33901	M	1922	**YORE**			
Frank B.	47863	D	1927	Wong	60330	D	1931	Matthias	1115	I	1906
YERGEY				Wong Ming	79999	D	1938	**YORISH**			
George B.	68691	D	1935	**YIP**				Frank	60840	D	1932
				Lui	29311	D	1920				

NAME	NUMBER	TYPE	YEAR
YORK			
Charles Barron	21097	D	1916
Emma Isabella	81709	D	1939
Henry James	67391	D	1934
Isabella	81709	D	1939
May	86839	D	1941
YORKE			
Peter C.	41477	D	1925
YOSHIDA			
Kikuya	52334	D	1929
Shukichi	41901	D	1925
Shukichi	41901	D	1925
Sukichi	41901	D	1925
Sukichi	41901	D	1925
YOSHIMI			
Keichi	41199	D	1925
YOSHIMOTO			
Jenmitsu	25201	D	1918
YOSHINO			
Cecil	52487	D	1929
YOSHIOKA			
Matsusuke	25248	D	1918
Matsusuke	28248	D	1919
YOST			
Edgar F.	23958	M	1918
Emily J.	73630	D	1936
Emma	73630	D	1936
Florence Agnes	50585	I	1928
Florence Agnes	55478	D	1930
Helen Katherine	16281	M	1913
Henry	62387	D	1932
Henry D.	13424	D	1912
John Dixon	45919	D	1926
Josephine Virginia	89893	D	1942
Margaret C.	36099	D	1923
Marian	16281	M	1913
Michael	21805	D	1916
Raymond Edwin	54998	M	1930
YOT			
Toy	37601	I	1923
YOU			
Chew	20865	D	1916
Chieng Do	73273	D	1936
Lee	88216	D	1941
Low Men	69230	D	1935
Mok Joey	8491	D	1909
Suen	78164	D	1938

NAME	NUMBER	TYPE	YEAR
Woo	44534	D	1926
Yuan	55553	D	1930
YOUDALL			
Leonard F.	65978	D	1933
YOUMAN			
Burt Cain	59213	D	1931
YOUNCE			
Virginia	71219	D	1935
YOUNG			
Adele	82969	D	1939
Adele	64271	I	1933
Agnes	59988	D	1931
Ah	73807	D	1936
Albert E.	77704	D	1938
Alexander	108	D	1906
Alexander J.	59884	D	1931
Amelia	24706	M	1918
Andrew S.	43043	M	1925
Anna	21196	I	1916
Anna Bolting	29862	D	1920
Anna M.	12707	D	1911
Annie	13060	D	1912
Arthur A.	75733	D	1937
Arthur Lawrie	34197	D	1922
Arthur S.	42511	D	1925
Arthur S.	83008	D	1940
Aubrey C.	60350	D	1931
Barbara Frances	62735	M	1932
Bernice M.	43043	M	1925
Bessie	63062	D	1932
C. Y.	56405	D	1930
Carrie Ogier	27567	D	1919
Catherine	63748	D	1933
Charles	2911	M	1907
Charles	26830	D	1919
Charles Austin	41929	D	1925
Charles Austin	41929	D	1925
Charlie H.	82923	D	1939
Charlie O.	89056	D	1942
Clara K.	67919	M	1934
Clara Kimball	36713	M	1923
Daniel E.	24304	M	1918
David	24706	M	1918
David Henry	71608	D	1936
Dora	52454	D	1929
E. W.	2644	D	1907
Earl	43246	I	1925
Edward	43085	M	1925

NAME	NUMBER	TYPE	YEAR
Edward Livingstone	27858	D	1919
Edwin Curtis	58334	D	1931
Elizabeth	12739	D	1911
Elizabeth	43085	M	1925
Elizabeth	54385	D	1929
Ella florence	49848	D	1928
Ella R.	34350	D	1922
Ethel	24706	M	1918
Etta	44256	D	1926
Etta L.	65473	D	1933
Eugenie	77545	D	1938
Frances E. A.	57050	D	1930
Francis	43085	M	1925
Francis G.	25121	M	1918
Francis J.	88287	D	1941
Frank	70648	D	1935
Frank E.	4491	D	1907
Frederick Jacob	80918	D	1939
Frederick O.	61717	D	1932
George	46431	M	1927
George M.	13891	D	1912
George W.	16782	I	1914
Georgia Elizabeth	88220	D	1941
Gertrude I.	71571	D	1936
H. G., Mrs.	64271	I	1933
Haldimand P.	66974	D	1934
Harry G.	82970	I	1939
Harry R.	60574	D	1931
Hazel F.	56236	D	1930
Helen Maud	52726	D	1929
Henry Eugene	36662	D	1923
Henry F.	58626	D	1931
Henry Hinchley	25297	D	1918
Henry R.	24304	M	1918
Hong	82923	D	1939
Isabelle	43085	M	1925
J. B.	27881	D	1919
Jacob	80918	D	1939
James	33911	D	1922
James S.	43043	M	1925
Jean Marie	43085	M	1925
Jean Marie	76513	M	1937
John	18146	D	1914
John E.	59009	D	1931
John Edward	68359	D	1934
John G.	22168	D	1917
John J.	20565	D	1916
John J.	24304	M	1918
John P.	14242	D	1912

NAME	NUMBER	TYPE	YEAR	NAME	NUMBER	TYPE	YEAR	NAME	NUMBER	TYPE	YEAR
John P.	31850	D	1921	Rosena C.	41906	D	1925	**YOW**			
John Russell	87339	D	1941	Samuel	75565	D	1937	Choy	47452	D	1927
John S.	26036	D	1918	Samuel W.	6296	D	1908	Irene Arkana	37438	M	1923
John VanCott	60074	M	1931	Smith P.	39367	D	1924	Leong	19492	D	1915
John Victor	78817	D	1938	Sy	56405	D	1930	Rufus H.	37437	I	1923
John W.	27299	D	1919	Theresa	12914	D	1912	Rufus H.	86905	D	1941
Jong	30790	D	1920	Thomas	25805	D	1918	Virginia Marie	37438	M	1923
Joseph	16479	D	1913	Thomas	31317	D	1921	Wong Get	12975	D	1912
Joseph	24793	D	1918	Thomas Francis	79932	D	1938	**YOWELL**			
Joseph Clifford	78051	D	1938	Thomas M.	4749	D	1907	Ernest	25675	D	1918
Kate	6262	D	1908	Tom Ah	30523	M	1920	**YPARRAGUIRRE**			
Kue	47629	D	1927	Toy Fook	39629	M	1924	Juan Francisco	36686	D	1923
Leland	75793	M	1937	Valerie	45096	M	1926	Pablo	8648	D	1909
Lewis Harman	79801	D	1938	Virginia	71219	D	1935	**YTURRIAGA**			
Linnie L.	46549	D	1927	Virginia R.	22680	M	1917	Ruth	73813	M	1936
Louis D.	24304	M	1918	Walter	11001	D	1911	**YU**			
Louis H.	24303	D	1918	Walter	23140	M	1917	Wee Wo	79951	D	1938
Louis Irving	36925	D	1923	Warren	59117	M	1931	**YUAN**			
Louis Michael	58797	D	1931	Wilhelmina C.	86530	D	1941	Lee	49339	D	1928
Louise	82357	D	1939	William Eben	53857	D	1929	You	55553	D	1930
Lum	54100	D	1929	William Harrison, Jr.	66794	D	1934	**YUE**			
Lyman Foster	74899	D	1937	William J.	56405	D	1930	Lee	64672	D	1933
Madeline	24304	M	1918	William J.	72594	D	1936	**YUEN**			
Mae P.	68629	D	1934	William L.	3734	D	1907	Dear Tung	79846	D	1938
Margaret Rachael	55214	D	1930	William W.	1489	D	1906	Leong Shee	59269	D	1931
Margaret T.	76844	D	1937	William W., Mrs.	49848	D	1928	Leung Kam	16064	M	1913
Maria	18785	D	1915	Willie	89779	D	1942	Louie	52059	D	1929
Maria H.	56719	D	1930	Yetta	75793	M	1937	Wong	86116	D	1941
Marion G.	49237	D	1928	**YOUNGER**				Wong Yep	78890	D	1938
Marjory M.	74088	D	1936	Alexander James	2835	D	1907	**YUHRE**			
Martha R.	12706	D	1911	**YOUNGHANS**				Minnie	13045	M	1912
Mary A.	82396	I	1939	Marie	23094	D	1917	**YUILL**			
Mary A.	89595	I	1942	**YOUNGMAN**				Peter Nelson	31697	D	1921
Mary Ann	88426	D	1941	Maria J.	40815	D	1925	**YUK**			
Mary Elizabeth	62735	M	1932	**YOUNGREN**				Wong Ah	6175	M	1908
Mary Elizabeth	72315	D	1936	Gustafvia	15166	D	1913	**YULE**			
Mary Paulina	69324	D	1935	John O.	81249	D	1939	Andrew	24674	D	1918
Maud	52726	D	1929	**YOUNGS**				Charlotte E.	79421	D	1938
May Pearl	85579	D	1940	William	13147	D	1912	**YULICH**			
Melville	73401	I	1936	**YOUNT**				Annie	13653	D	1912
Michael	46069	D	1926	Jesse Morton	72093	D	1936	**YUM**			
Milton	75793	M	1937	John Burnette	77341	D	1937	Dora	78804	M	1938
Orville	59928	I	1931	**YOVANOVITCH**				Lee	50351	D	1928
Peter	49957	D	1928	Slobedan S.	61468	D	1932	Violet	24311	M	1918
Robert A.	53262	D	1929	**YOVER**				Won	38767	M	1924
Robert D.	67640	I	1934	Thomas	64489	I	1933				
Robert W.	56379	I	1930								
Robert W.	56665	D	1930								
Rosena C.	41906	D	1925								

NAME	NUMBER	TYPE	YEAR
YUMIYA			
Taketora	63287	D	1933
YUNG			
Magdalena	38782	D	1924
Wah	49339	D	1928
Wong Kwong	87224	D	1941
Wong Yuen	20183	D	1915
YUNKER			
Carl Frederick	43106	D	1925
Lizzie	19903	D	1915
Louise F.	82144	D	1939
Walter R.	59359	D	1931
YUON			
Wong Wing	87702	D	1941
YUP			
On	87951	I	1941
On	88180	D	1941
YURETICH			
Peter	44962	D	1926
YZEIR			
Muharem	71044	D	1935
ZABALA			
Adelberto J., Jr.	67779	M	1934
Honore F.	67779	M	1934
Juan L.	67779	M	1934
Satero	23541	D	1917
ZABALDANO			
Alexander	15607	D	1913
ZABALURTANA			
Antonio	23000	D	1917
ZABALZA			
Juan	67950	D	1934
ZABEL			
Clementine	37841	D	1923
Johan Diedrich	24774	D	1918
John D.	24774	D	1918
ZABELLA			
Benjamin Victor	67633	D	1934
Frances	76484	D	1937
ZABRISKIE			
Asa	47296	D	1927
Sabriz Asa	47296	D	1927
ZACHARIAH			
Abraham Nicholas	86462	D	1941
Kalil Nicholas	41195	D	1925

NAME	NUMBER	TYPE	YEAR
ZACHARIAS			
Charles Henry	14716	D	1913
Estelle	42243	D	1925
Fred H.	31608	D	1921
Hazel	41476	I	1925
Theresa	12245	D	1911
ZACHARONSKY			
Abram	55137	D	1930
Sadie	37908	D	1923
Samuel	86626	D	1941
ZACHAU			
Eugene A.	55588	D	1930
ZACHIRALIS			
Dimadis	31209	D	1921
ZACHORECK			
Elizabetha	11991	D	1911
ZACHRISSON			
Carl Uddo	34367	M	1922
ZACK			
Simon	45744	D	1926
ZACZMARSKI			
Joseph	50555	D	1928
ZADIG			
Alfred H.	43262	M	1925
Bertha	28706	D	1920
Herman	47699	D	1927
ZADORKIN			
Gasty	61322	D	1932
ZAFEIROPOULOS			
Nikolaos	45993	D	1926
ZAFFARONI			
Laura	86729	M	1941
ZAHAREIDES			
N. D. P.	80146	D	1938
ZAHARIA			
John	45974	M	1926
ZAHN			
Charles O.	80310	D	1939
Charles W.	13356	D	1912
Lena	31700	D	1921
William Otto	36998	D	1923
ZAHRINGER			
William	12139	D	1911
ZAIBEK			
Assad	61294	M	1932
Charles	61294	M	1932

NAME	NUMBER	TYPE	YEAR
Isabel	61294	M	1932
Ruth Rose	61294	M	1932
ZALA			
Otto	25364	D	1918
ZALBERT			
Louis	14314	I	1912
Louis	57928	D	1931
ZALENKA			
Susie	22301	D	1917
ZALES			
Pasko	30847	D	1920
ZALKIND			
Joseph	81399	D	1939
ZALLES			
Josephine Huljev	31751	M	1921
Pasco	30847	D	1920
ZALTER			
Pasko	30847	D	1920
ZAMB			
Anthony J.	80052	D	1938
ZAMBELICH			
Ralph M.	41943	D	1925
Ralph M.	41943	D	1925
ZAMBELLI			
Louisa	83818	D	1940
Walter S.	73000	D	1936
ZAMBONI			
John	40074	D	1924
ZAMMIT			
Anthony	79796	L	1938
Peter Paul	40585	D	1924
ZAMMITT			
John J.	3862	D	1907
ZAMORA			
Macario	45797	I	1926
ZAMORANSDEMADRID			
Feliza	54469	D	1929
ZANARDI			
Ernesto	51388	D	1928
Louis	61537	D	1932
ZANCA			
Domenico	22867	D	1917
ZANDER			
Dorothy Thelma	27991	M	1919
Helen Virginia	27991	M	1919
Lucile Marian	27991	M	1919

NAME	NUMBER	TYPE	YEAR	NAME	NUMBER	TYPE	YEAR	NAME	NUMBER	TYPE	YEAR
ZANE				**Z**ATKIN				**Z**EBU			
Elizabeth	71876	D	1936	Sam	42491	D	1925	James J.	81920	D	1939
ZANETTI				**Z**AUN				**Z**ECH			
John	31459	D	1921	Henry	51336	D	1928	Vera A.	69823	D	1935
ZANETTIN				Henry, Jr.	81198	D	1939	**Z**ECHER			
Liugi	12866	D	1912	**Z**AVADA				Ernestine	31141	D	1921
ZANGRILLO				Vincent	48239	D	1927	Frederick William	27279	D	1919
Civita	22356	I	1917	**Z**AVAGNO				Louise M.	30509	D	1920
Civita	42579	D	1925	Lena E.	89214	D	1942	**Z**ECHLIN			
Fred	70015	D	1935	**Z**AVATARRI				Otto	52132	D	1929
Fred	70015	D	1935	Antonio	55532	D	1930	**Z**ECKENDORF			
ZANIN				**Z**AVATORI				Jeanne	76577	D	1937
James	77529	D	1938	Antonio	55532	D	1930	**Z**EDERMAN			
ZANINI				**Z**AVODNEK				Ferdinand	12056	D	1911
Celso	48304	I	1927	J.	39596	D	1924	**Z**EFF			
ZANKERT				**Z**AVOYIANIS				Lena	28502	D	1919
Ellen	80692	I	1939	Irene	89667	M	1942	**Z**EH			
Nellie	59050	I	1931	**Z**AYCHUK				Anna P.	29439	I	1920
ZANONE				Alexander M.	40207	I	1924	**Z**EHENDER			
Andrew	61179	D	1932	**Z**AZAN				Magdalena	17328	D	1914
ZANT				George	85225	D	1940	**Z**EHFUSS			
Thomas E.	69190	D	1935	**Z**AZZETTI				Frederick William	80133	D	1938
ZANZI				Dorina	62220	I	1932	Hrederick William	1585	D	1906
Maria	83148	D	1940	Luisa	67747	D	1934	**Z**EHNDER			
Pietro	86574	D	1941	Thomas	57731	D	1931	Alphonse	66816	D	1934
ZAPATA				**Z**AZZI				Ben	42382	D	1925
Louis, Jr.	75735	M	1937	Louise	68647	D	1935	Daniel	53316	D	1929
ZAPPETTINI				Paul	60092	D	1931	Dora	24338	D	1918
John	18075	D	1914	Theresa	42473	D	1925	**Z**EIGLER			
Maria	73130	D	1936	**Z**EBEC				Wilbur G.	35905	D	1923
ZARA				James J.	81920	D	1939	**Z**EILE			
Ciriaco	46629	D	1927	**Z**EBER				Carl D.	9145	D	1910
ZARAGOZA				James J.	81920	D	1939	Carl Ulrich	4247	M	1907
Teodoro	78711	D	1938	**Z**EBIC				Frederick	9189	D	1910
ZARELLA				James J.	81920	D	1939	Frederick Adolph	4246	M	1907
Anthony	56634	D	1930	**Z**EBJIEFF				Frederick W.	10872	D	1910
ZAREMSKI				James J.	81920	D	1939	Henrietta	22322	D	1917
Paul	87166	D	1941	**Z**EBO				John	69104	D	1935
Teresa	71919	D	1936	David	46938	M	1927	John, Jr.	79604	M	1938
ZARONI				David	47077	D	1927	Marie	939	D	1906
Pietro	26484	D	1919	Davide	47077	D	1927	Marion	2088	M	1906
ZARUBA				**Z**EBRACKI				Marion	73873	D	1936
Vaclav	61460	D	1932	Arthur Stanislaus Egues	7393	D	1909	Marjorie	79604	M	1938
ZASNIKOFF				Witold Stanislaw Antoni	52491	D	1929	Robert	2365	D	1906
Wolf Bear Zelikoff	80417	D	1939	**Z**EBREB				Ruth	2089	M	1906
				Frank	60050	I	1931	Sophie Smith	2228	D	1906

NAME	NUMBER	TYPE	YEAR
ZEILIN			
Winfield Scott	787	D	1906
ZEIMER			
Hannah Kahn	81897	D	1939
ZEINER			
Wendelin	116	D	1906
ZEIPH			
Sal	42722	D	1925
ZEIS			
Auguste	8462	D	1909
ZEISING			
Emeline H.	10994	D	1911
Frank M.	21319	D	1916
ZEISLER			
Louis	29924	D	1920
ZEISS			
Conrad	26330	D	1919
Katharine	52537	D	1929
Louis	17625	D	1914
ZEITER			
Antone	50320	D	1928
ZEKIND			
Juliet	22163	D	1917
ZELENKA			
Marie L.	22301	D	1917
Susie	22301	D	1917
ZELGIRS			
Felix	88680	D	1941
ZELICH			
Dorothy	59257	M	1931
Evelyn	75232	D	1937
ZELINSKY			
Barbara	78692	M	1938
Celia	64830	I	1933
Celia	85570	D	1940
David	64937	D	1933
Edward Galland	78692	M	1938
Herbert E.	43042	I	1925
Raphael	81470	D	1939
ZELL			
Paul	19704	D	1915
ZELLENSKY			
Bernard L.	70237	D	1935
ZELLER			
Albert	30520	D	1920
Caroline	33712	D	1922

NAME	NUMBER	TYPE	YEAR
Elizabeth	47032	D	1927
Marian	71148	M	1935
Michael	28415	D	1919
William	25364	D	1918
ZELLERBACH			
Anthony	12444	D	1911
Antonette Theresa	34980	M	1922
Arthur	75017	D	1937
Etta T.	24140	D	1918
Isadore	87721	D	1941
Jacob C.	29237	D	1920
Sarah Lillian	34980	M	1922
Stephen Anthony	88162	M	1941
Theresa	33207	D	1922
ZELLERS			
Edward E., Mrs.	26286	D	1919
Erna O.	26286	D	1919
ZELNER			
Jessie Margaret	49948	I	1928
ZELTSPERGER			
Markus	87411	D	1941
ZEMAN			
Mary	64347	D	1933
ZEMANEK			
Pauline	71606	I	1936
ZEMANN			
Mabel C.	76573	D	1937
ZEMANSKY			
Julia	154	D	1906
Philip	47996	M	1927
Sol	89662	D	1942
ZEMON			
Harry	73562	D	1936
ZENKER			
Marie T.	69667	D	1935
Robert	70806	D	1935
ZENOVICH			
Olga	59190	D	1931
Sam	76831	D	1937
ZENSEN			
Fred, Jr.	25428	D	1918
ZENTACOLI			
Giovanni	29131	D	1920
ZENTNER			
Josie	53983	D	1929

NAME	NUMBER	TYPE	YEAR
ZENTOCCOLI			
Maria	22311	D	1917
ZEPF			
John Philip, Jr.	19149	D	1915
ZERBE			
Charles F.	68478	I	1934
ZERBO			
Vincenza	77786	D	1938
ZERCHA			
Asunta	56166	D	1930
ZERGA			
Asunta	56166	D	1930
John	76425	D	1937
Joseph	30643	D	1920
Rose	28743	D	1920
Serafina	45277	D	1926
ZERICH			
Simeone	12384	D	1911
ZERMANI			
Giovanni	84286	D	1940
ZERTANNA			
Matilde	43538	D	1926
Roy	13754	D	1912
ZERVAS			
John	16403	D	1913
Peter	49470	D	1928
ZETT			
August L.	16540	D	1913
Frederick	6615	D	1908
Mary A.	15368	D	1913
ZETTEL			
Kathryn	46024	D	1926
ZETTL			
John	62463	D	1932
ZGANTSAKIS			
Demetrius John	89660	D	1942
ZHAND			
Mary	5876	D	1908
ZIBIRIA			
Juan Eladio Noblea	32902	D	1921
ZICCARELLI			
Francesco	15349	D	1913
ZICKEL			
Birdie	62580	D	1932
John	20942	D	1916
John W.	54793	D	1930

Key: D = death; M = minor; I = incompetent

NAME	NUMBER	TYPE	YEAR
ZICOVICH			
Anton	16028	D	1913
ZIDELL			
Abraham	32659	D	1921
ZIDO			
Theodore	31396	I	1921
ZIEBELL			
Albert	57650	D	1931
ZIEFLE			
Phillip John	33973	D	1922
ZIEGELMAYR			
William W.	22304	D	1917
ZIEGENENFUSS			
John Henry William	23496	D	1917
ZIEGENFUSS			
Winifred C.	18391	D	1915
ZIEGLER			
Alphonse	57522	D	1930
Charles L.	26151	D	1919
F. H.	43031	D	1925
James Edwin	77032	D	1937
Rayden James	71067	D	1935
ZIEGLMAYR			
Ferdinand	15049	D	1913
William W.	22304	D	1917
ZIELLENBACH			
Joseph	50000	D	1928
ZIEMANN			
Wilhelmine	68320	D	1934
ZIER			
Leiser	26478	D	1919
Louis	84970	D	1940
ZIFFERINO			
Lafranchi	73297	D	1936
ZIFFERO			
Lafranchi	73297	D	1936
ZIGANTO			
Anna	38703	D	1924
ZILIANI			
Carlo	590	I	1906
ZILIOTTO			
Giovanni	22824	I	1917
Giovanni	26160	D	1919
ZILKE			
Edward J. A.	49786	D	1928
Mary	62202	D	1932

NAME	NUMBER	TYPE	YEAR
ZILLER			
Ida	77369	D	1937
ZILLMER			
John Gottlieb	401	D	1906
ZILS			
Peter Joseph	51276	D	1928
ZIMANSKY			
Curt Ferdinand	62524	D	1932
ZIMELLI			
Lulu	41037	I	1925
Lulu	41056	D	1925
Maurice J.	40937	D	1925
ZIMET			
David H.	87231	D	1941
Eleanor B.	86098	M	1941
Emanuel	35114	D	1922
Goldie	17060	D	1914
ZIMMER			
Bertha	33292	D	1922
Christopher	53694	D	1929
John	32583	D	1921
Mary A.	76617	D	1937
Mary E.	76617	D	1937
Nicholas	57008	D	1930
ZIMMERLIN			
Jules A.	64515	D	1933
ZIMMERMAN			
August	54205	I	1929
Caroline Magdalena	31519	D	1921
Della	79006	D	1938
Ernest Edward	33280	D	1922
Frank	11303	D	1911
Frank C.	12361	D	1911
Franz	11303	D	1911
George L.	39999	I	1924
Gustav	47500	D	1927
Hannah	47144	M	1927
Herman F.	87579	D	1941
Jane Elise	83510	M	1940
John B.	86876	D	1941
Katherine A.	74831	D	1937
Leonhard	43500	D	1926
Margaret	2580	D	1907
Margaret	33332	I	1922
Margaret J.	33673	D	1922
Matthew	13755	D	1912
Max R.	57760	D	1931

NAME	NUMBER	TYPE	YEAR
Nettie	47144	M	1927
Oscar R.	62856	D	1932
Thomas J.	79585	D	1938
Vera Flora	74137	D	1936
Warren A.	53069	M	1929
ZIMMERMANN			
Anna M.	65678	D	1933
August	7338	D	1909
August H.	43620	D	1926
Edward	44343	D	1926
Luisa R.	79159	D	1938
Mary L.	7445	D	1909
Philipp	56653	D	1930
Reinhardt	79947	I	1938
Reinhardt	80268	D	1939
Robert	7292	D	1909
Wilma Fleisch	22010	M	1916
ZINCKE			
William	14238	D	1912
ZINDAL			
Caspar	25777	D	1918
ZINI			
Venceslas	49439	D	1928
Vincent	49439	D	1928
ZININI			
Maria	40530	D	1924
ZINK			
George Joseph	75418	D	1937
ZINKAND			
Babette	63406	D	1933
Charles A.	16328	D	1913
Charlotte Adelina	31469	M	1921
Clarence Allen	31469	M	1921
ZINKE			
Carl	7791	D	1909
ZINN			
Fritz Siegfried	88359	D	1941
Henry John	16265	D	1913
Walter C.	50819	D	1928
ZINNAMAN			
Abraham	3349	D	1907
ZINNANMON			
Abraham	3349	D	1907
ZINNEN			
Kate	30120	D	1920
ZINSLI			
Josephine	22889	D	1917

NAME	NUMBER	TYPE	YEAR	NAME	NUMBER	TYPE	YEAR	NAME	NUMBER	TYPE	YEAR
ZIPF				**ZOBEL**				**ZONTANOS**			
Albert F.	73709	D	1936	Jerome F.	40345	M	1924	George D.	40998	I	1925
Albert Fairfield	44891	M	1926	Ludwig	2703	D	1907	**ZOPALOS**			
Charlotte Carolyn	44891	M	1926	Maybelle	37228	D	1923	Anthy	64095	M	1933
John Philip	78094	D	1938	Rose	43497	D	1926	**ZOPOLOS**			
Marie Theodora	36680	D	1923	**ZOBERBIER**				Anthy	64095	M	1933
ZIPFEL				Emma K.	62411	D	1932	**ZOPPETTI**			
Camilla H.	74786	D	1937	Frances	30558	D	1920	Giacomo	74684	D	1937
ZIPP				**ZOBLER**				**ZOPPI**			
Frank	60173	D	1931	Harry	83622	D	1940	Madelina Ferrari Maritata	5513	D	1908
John V.	58602	D	1931	**ZOBRIST**				**ZORADI**			
Saidee	30477	D	1920	Herman Henry	61058	D	1932	Dan	41021	D	1925
ZIPPAR				**ZOERB**				Demiro	41021	D	1925
James	50043	D	1928	Gladys C.	53714	M	1929	**ZORATTI**			
ZIRBES				William Joseph	53714	M	1929	John	81849	D	1939
Henry	4627	D	1907	**ZOGRAFOU**				**ZORICH**			
ZIRKER				Demetriou John	23316	D	1917	Simeone	12384	D	1911
Henry	58973	D	1931	**ZOGRAPHOD**				**ZRVIEG**			
Morris	57680	D	1931	James	23316	D	1917	Julie	37419	D	1923
ZIRN				**ZOHARIADIS**				**ZUARDO**			
Frank Xavier	37106	I	1923	Nickolaos D.	80146	D	1938	Vincenzo	86137	D	1941
ZIRNGIBL				**ZOHN**				**ZUBER**			
Alois	40669	D	1924	Charles O.	80310	D	1939	Charles M.	38573	I	1924
ZISKA				**ZOHNER**				**ZUBERBUHLER**			
Dora	33759	D	1922	John E.	48679	D	1927	Albert J.	80149	D	1938
ZITA				Louesa	58181	D	1931	**ZUBIETA**			
Giuseppe	75060	D	1937	**ZOLEZI**				Victorina	46379	D	1927
Maria	80185	D	1938	Louis B.	62227	D	1932	**ZUBLER**			
Prospero	44898	D	1926	**ZOLEZZI**				Frederick L.	37569	D	1923
ZITNIK				Angelo	51813	M	1929	**ZUCCA**			
Marie	79985	D	1938	Caterina	41390	D	1925	Camillo	32648	M	1921
ZITO				Giovanni	51499	D	1928	Ferruccio	32648	M	1921
Giuseppe	75060	D	1937	Marco	51813	M	1929	George C.	32648	M	1921
Maria	80185	D	1938	Maria Helen	51813	M	1929	Lawrence	32648	M	1921
Prospero	44898	D	1926	**ZOLLER**				Steve	30588	D	1920
ZITTING				Charles	8321	D	1909	Valeria	32648	M	1921
Eva	67488	M	1934	Karl Gottlieb	8321	D	1909	Virginia	64471	D	1933
ZITTL				Leo	34463	D	1922	**ZUCHELLI**			
John	62463	D	1932	Monika	34708	D	1922	Angelo	39979	D	1924
ZIVIAN				**ZOLLIKOPER**				Edna	48199	M	1927
Dorothy Estelle	77066	M	1937	Antonio C.	8639	D	1909	**ZUCK**			
ZLOBINSKY				**ZOLLINGER**				Amelia Clara	14297	I	1912
Dora	47628	D	1927	Francis H.	84378	I	1940	**ZUCKER**			
ZMMERMAN				**ZONTANAS**				Esther	59755	I	1931
Edward	22391	D	1917	George D.	40998	I	1925	Margheiete	82353	D	1939
								Maurice	82348	D	1939

Key: *D = death; M = minor; I = incompetent*

NAME	NUMBER	TYPE	YEAR	NAME	NUMBER	TYPE	YEAR	NAME	NUMBER	TYPE	YEAR
ZUCKERMAN				Dorothea Mary	56299	D	1930	**Z**WILLINGER			
Isaac	19954	D	1915	**Z**URINI				Isadore	59358	D	1931
Isidore	39213	D	1924	Caesar	34152	D	1922	**Z**WOLSKI			
Jennie S.	53104	D	1929	Ceasar	34152	D	1922	Francis Andrew	36683	M	1923
Max W.	5976	D	1908	**Z**URN				**Z**YSKIND			
Oscar R.	47548	D	1927	Charles	65675	D	1933	Barney	72592	D	1936
Richard O.	47548	D	1927	Johann Carl	65675	D	1933				
ZUEFLE				**Z**URNSTEIN							
George	89820	D	1942	Benhart	52252	D	1929				
ZUERN				**Z**USSMAN							
Fred	57770	D	1931	Samuel	68957	D	1935				
ZUFFI				**Z**UST							
Cesare	47337	D	1927	Matthias	24825	D	1918				
ZUGAR				**Z**VORSKY							
John	80250	D	1939	Alex	46057	D	1926				
Martin	32626	D	1921	**Z**WANZIGER							
ZUGAS				Ernest	46747	D	1927				
Olga	31494	M	1921	Karl	44961	D	1926				
ZUIHARA				**Z**WEIFEL							
Nikichi	18303	D	1914	Ellen	14414	D	1912				
ZUKERMAN				John H.	80671	D	1939				
Jennie S.	53104	D	1929	**Z**WERIN							
ZULBERTI				Eva	63445	D	1933				
Julia R.	54802	I	1930	Joel	61720	D	1932				
ZULLO				**Z**WEYBRUCK							
Salvatore	13696	D	1912	Edith	48791	D	1927				
Salvatore	77792	D	1938	**Z**WICK							
ZUMWALT				Anton	10025	D	1910				
Jean Adlaide	54842	M	1930	Arthur	24806	M	1918				
Nora Mae	50295	M	1928	Gladys	24806	M	1918				
ZUNDORF				Lizzie	45986	D	1926				
Johann	9712	D	1910	Mary Anna	66900	D	1934				
ZUNDORP				Rudolph	24806	M	1918				
Johann	9712	D	1910	Rudolph	26317	D	1919				
ZUNICH				Walter	24806	M	1918				
George	21314	D	1916	**Z**WICKER							
ZUNINO				Katherine	79226	D	1938				
Andrea	49827	D	1928	**Z**WIDER							
Carolina	30661	D	1920	Abraham	31420	I	1921				
Gerald	83825	M	1940	**Z**WIEG							
Guiseppe Giovanni	72277	D	1936	Claire Luise	61346	M	1932				
Joseph John	72277	D	1936	Dorothea A.	60927	D	1932				
ZURFLUH				Walter Claus	61346	M	1932				
Ambrose	17806	D	1914	**Z**WIERLEIN							
Anna	15714	D	1913	Sophie	63848	D	1933				
Dorothea Mary	55533	I	1930	William	58569	I	1931				

   Key: D = death; M = minor; I = incompetent

Publications from the California Genealogical Society and Library

To order publications from the California Genealogical Society and Library visit the society's website at
CaliforniaAncestors.org.

San Francisco Probates 1906-1942: Register of Actions, Volumes 1-2, is an index, for the first time in print, to the 179 Registers of Action for Probate cases, each containing 500 pages, dating from the 1906 earthquake and fire through March 27, 1942. Included are 108,998 names representing over 85,500 probates and guardianship proceedings. Vernon A. Deubler, comp., pub. 2010, softbound, 8 1/2 x 11 format, 487 pp. (vol. I), 480 pp.(vol. II). ISBN 978-0-9785694-7-1 (vol. I, A-K); ISBN 978-0-9785694-8-8 (vol. II, L-M); LOC 2010926283.

San Francisco Deaths 1865-1905: Abstracts from Surviving Civil Records, Volumes 1-4, is an index, unsurpassed for accuracy and completeness, to over 96,000 civil records known to have survived the 1906 earthquake and fire. Barbara Close and Vernon A. Deubler, comp., pub. 2010, softbound, 8 1/2 x 11 format. ISBN 978-0-9785694-1-9 (vol. I, A-D); ISBN 978-0-9785694-2-6 (vol. II, E-K); ISBN 978-0-9785694-3-3 (vol. III, L-P); ISBN 978-0-9785694-4-0 (vol. IV, Q-Z); LOC 2009940489.

Raking the Ashes is a "must have" for researching San Francisco ancestors, providing invaluable guidance on which records were lost in the 1906 San Francisco earthquake and fire, which records survived, and where to find the surviving records. Nancy Peterson, pub. 2006, softbound, 8 1/2 x 11" format, 222 pp. ISBN 978-0-9672409-8-5; LOC 2006920734.

A Most Dreadful Earthquake, based on the previously unpublished correspondence of a young San Francisco woman describing the aftermath of the 1906 San Francisco earthquake and fire, graphically describes the sights of the city and gives details of everyday life in the chaos of those first days. Dorothy Fowler, Pub. 2006, Softbound, 5 1/2 x 8 1/4" format, 174pp. ISBN 978-0-9672409-7-8; LOC 2005935823.

San Francisco, California: Columbarium Records 1847-1980 is an index listing nearly 6,000 names found in previously unpublished records of San Francisco's Odd Fellows Columbarium. Vernon A. Deubler, comp., pub. 2003, softbound, 8 1/2 x 11 format, 130 pp. ISBN 978-0-9672409-4-7; LOC 2003112862.

San Francisco, California: I.O.O.F. Crematory Records is an index to approximately 10,000 previously unpublished cremation records of the Independent Order of Odd Fellows, dating primarily from 1895 to 1911. Records providing each person's birthplace, date of death and age, place and cause of death, and indication of obituaries are available. Barbara Ross Close, comp., pub. 2001, softbound, 8 1/2 x 11" format, 413 pp. ISBN 978-0-9672409-2-3; LOC 2001093990.

California Surname Index: Biographies From Selected Histories provides an integrated index to more than 18,000 biographical sketches of early Californians named in 42 historical works on the shelves of the California Genealogical Society's George R. Dorman Collection. Barbara Ross Close, comp., pub. 2000, hard-bound, 8 1/2 x 11" format, 325 pp. ISBN 978-0-9672409-1-6; LOC 9976177.

San Francisco Probate Index 1880-1906: A Partial Reconstruction contains more than 10,000 names in pre-1906 San Francisco records, compiled and indexed, from a variety of sources. Kathleen C. Beals, comp., pub. 1996, softbound, 8 1/2 x 11" format, 239 pp. ISBN 978-0-9672409-9-2; LOC 97179094.

Index to San Francisco Marriage Returns 1850-1858 presents a compilation of some of San Francisco's earliest marriage returns, indexed alphabetically and chronologically. Kathleen C. Beals, comp., pub. 1992, softbound, 8 1/2 x 11" format, 109 pp. ISBN 978-0-9785694-0-2; LOC 97179098.

> Please do not remove this page from the book! Make a photocopy for your use. Thank you.

Order Form for a Copy of the Register of Actions for a Probate

To order a copy of the original Register of Actions, you may use the Lookups feature on the society's website, CaliforniaAncestors.org.

If you prefer to place your order by regular mail, please make a copy of this form and fill in the blanks, or write a letter and be sure to provide the surname, given name, and probate number. The current fee at publication is $10 per probate number. These rates will be honored through 2012 on orders using a copy of this form. For fees after 2012, please check the society's website under Lookups or call 510- 663-1358. Please send your request(s), with a *check or money order payable to the California Genealogical Society, to:

California Genealogical Society
2201 Broadway, LL2
Oakland, CA 94612-3031

*Request from outside the United States: Please order using our online system and PayPal at CaliforniaAncestors.org. Otherwise you will need to provide a foreign draft in U.S. dollars payable on a financial institution in the United States.

Records Requested

	Surname	Given Name	Probate No.	Type	Year	Fee
1.	_____	_____	_____	____	_____	$_____.____
2.	_____	_____	_____	____	_____	$_____.____
3.	_____	_____	_____	____	_____	$_____.____

Total payment $_____.____

Contact Information

_____
Your Name

_____
Telephone

_____
Address Line 1

_____
Email Address (optional)

_____
Address Line 2

_____
City/State/Zip

www.ingramcontent.com/pod-product-compliance
Lightning Source LLC
Chambersburg PA
CBHW081425270326
41932CB00019B/3105